PSYCHOLOGY

AN INTRODUCTION

PSYCHOLOGY
AN INTRODUCTION

PAUL MUSSEN
MARK R. ROSENZWEIG

University of California, Berkeley

ELLIOT ARONSON
University of Texas
DAVID ELKIND
University of Rochester
SEYMOUR FESHBACH
University of California, Los Angeles
P. JAMES GEIWITZ
University of California, Santa Barbara
STEPHEN E. GLICKMAN
University of California, Berkeley
BENNET B. MURDOCK, JR.
University of Toronto
MICHAEL WERTHEIMER
University of Colorado

D. C. HEATH AND COMPANY
Lexington, Massachusetts Toronto London

The cover of this book was designed by Milton Zolotow. Photographs for the section openings, for Figure 11 of the perception color section, and for illustrations elsewhere in the text, as credited, were taken by Ted Polumbaum. Joshua Clark prepared the biological drawings in Section Eight, and Wayne Emery the biological drawings in the last color section. Robert and Marilyn Dustin prepared the artwork and photographed Figure 9 for the perception color section, as well as designing and coordinating the printing of all the color sections. The text was set in 10 on 12 point Caledonia by Book Graphics, Inc. Kingsport Press printed and bound the book, and the Oxford paper was supplied by Ris-John Carter Paper Company.

Published simultaneously in Canada.

Printed in the United States of America.

International Standard Book Number: 0-669-61382-7

Library of Congress Catalog Card Number: 72-2761

PREFACE FOR STUDENTS AND INSTRUCTORS

Most students in an introductory psychology course expect to study facts and theories related to their own lives and to critical social issues. Instructors and textbook writers want to respond to the students' needs and interests and also to reach three additional goals: (1) to present a well-rounded account of the most significant concepts and findings of contemporary psychology; (2) to give students a basic understanding of how psychologists go about studying behavior—how they conduct research and evaluate their findings; and (3) to provide a firm foundation for students who will take other courses in psychology or who would like to study further on their own. Our attempt to reach these goals has led us to plan and write a book that differs in significant respects from others in the field.

What are the special features of this introductory psychology textbook? How does it differ from other introductory textbooks of psychology? One difference is that each of the eight main sections of the book was written by an expert in a basic area of psychology. The expert is best qualified to select, from the vast information in his own area, the subject matter that is most significant, most relevant for understanding personal and social problems, most essential in preparing students for further study in this speciality. Together, the sections of the book present a broad overview of the field of psychology, spanning the range from complex human social interaction to species-specific animal behavior. Psychology is defined operationally in terms of the problems with which specialists in psychology are concerned and their methods of working on these problems. The objective scientific approach to psychological problems is stressed, but the contributions of the humanities and philosophy to our understanding of these problems are acknowledged. The field of psychology is viewed as an active changing one; many age-old problems are unsolved and many new problems are being formulated. The focus of the book is on how psychologists are trying to solve these problems through research.

To keep the book from being a series of isolated unrelated treatises and to achieve integration within the text, the authors collaborated from the very start, meeting together in several sessions, and they continued to exchange ideas, outlines, and drafts. Together they made judgments about what materials should be included and emphasized, and they decided on the order of presentation of topics. A psychologist-writer, P. James Geiwitz, worked with the authors throughout the project, integrating contributions from the individual authors, editing to achieve some consistency of style and presentation, and moving materials from one section to another to improve the presentation.

The order of presentation of the areas in this book is the reverse of the usual one. We begin with those specialties within psychology that are closest to the students' own experiences and interests and are thus intrinsically meaningful to him—the areas of social psychology, personality, and development. These sections introduce some of the major problems of psychology but they require very little technical or specialized background. They help develop interest in the later more technical sections, those that deal with the areas of learning, perception, biological, and comparative psychology.

The design of the book has been carefully thought out to make it highly readable. The type is large and many headings are used to make the topics clear. When new terms are introduced, they are defined simply and the definitions are clarified by examples. An extensive glossary is given at the end of the book; words included in the glossary are indicated in the text by the use of boldface type. Numerous photographs and drawings illustrate points where words would be inadequate. Color is employed to emphasize headings and to clarify figures. Each chapter contains a number of Spotlights, special short sections that highlight particular points or give examples of research or clinical observations to illustrate topics discussed in the text. There are many cross references in the text, and a detailed index is provided. General sources are given at the end of each section; complete bibliographic data for the many specific studies cited are given in the back matter to help the reader follow up on subjects of interest.

In planning the introductory psychology course, the instructor must consider the needs, interests, and abilities of his students as well as the time available for the course. Some instructors may wish to omit parts of the book or present topics in a different order. The book can be used flexibly; there are many possible alternative arrangements. Here we present three such possibilities, one for a course with a personal-social emphasis, one for a course with an experimental-biological emphasis, and one for a broadly based, but shorter, general course. These are only three of many possible combinations and/or orders. Some instructors may prefer an entirely different order of chapters or sections.

The authors gratefully acknowledge the help of many people in the preparation of this book: our fellow psychologists on whose research we have drawn; our colleagues who made construc-

Section	*Personal-Social Emphasis*	*Experimental-Biological Emphasis*	*Shorter General Course*
		Chapters	
Introduction	1	1	1
	2	2	2
Social	3	3	3
	4	4	4
	5	5	
	6		6
	7		
Personality	8	8	8
	9		9
	10	10	10
	11		11
Developmental	12	12	12
	13	13	13
	14		14
Cognitive and Educational	15	15	15
	16	16	16
Learning and Memory		18	18
		19	
Perception		20	
		21	21
	22	22	22
Biological		23	23
		24	
	25	25	25
Comparative		27	
	28	28	28

tive suggestions on the manuscript; our students in a variety of courses who have responded to successive versions of the ideas in this text; Betty Ann Tyson, production editor, who clarified the text at many points and integrated words and illustrations; Judy Arisman, designer, who created the format of the book and coordinated all the graphic elements; the secretaries, particularly Vivien March and Rosemary Hendrick, who worked on the many manuscripts involved.

ABOUT THE AUTHORS

Paul Mussen
Director, Institute of Human Development, University of California, Berkeley
The author of Section Four, Developmental Psychology, specializes in research on socialization and personality development. He is co-author of *Child Development and Personality* (Harper & Row); author of *The Psychological Development of the Child* (Prentice-Hall); editor of *Carmichael's Manual of Child Psychology* (Wiley) and of *Annual Review of Psychology*.

Mark R. Rosenzweig
University of California, Berkeley
The author of Section Eight, Biological Psychology, is active in research on brain functions in behavior. He is a member of the Executive Committee, International Union of Psychological Science and an editor of *Annual Review of Psychology.*

P. James Geiwitz
University of California, Santa Barbara
The general editor is a professional writer, particularly in the area of personality. He is author of *Non-Freudian Theories of Personality* (Brooks-Cole).

Elliot Aronson
University of Texas
The author of Section Two, Social Psychology, is active in research on interpersonal attraction and winner of the American Association for the Advancement of Science prize in social psychology (1970). He is author of *The Social Animal* (Viking) and co-editor of *Handbook of Social Psychology* (Addison-Wesley).

David Elkind
University of Rochester
The author of Section Five, Cognitive and Educational Psychology, does research in cognitive development; he spent a year studying with Piaget at the University of Geneva. He is author of *Children and Adolescents* (Oxford), co-author of *Child Development: A Core Approach* (Wiley), and co-editor of *Studies in Cognitive Development* (Oxford).

Seymour Feshbach
Director of Fernald School at University of California, Los Angeles
The author of Section Three, Personality, is active in research on violence and aggression. He is author of *Television and Aggression* (Jossey-Bass).

Stephen E. Glickman
University of California, Berkeley

The author of Section Nine, Comparative Psychology, does research on behavior of animals in the laboratory, in zoos, and in natural settings. He has studied animals of many species, including anteaters, hawks, gerbils, skunks, opossums, lions, and owls.

Bennet B. Murdock, Jr.
University of Toronto

The author of Section Six, Learning and Memory, has contributed many studies of human learning and memory; he now concentrates his research on human short-term memory.

Michael Wertheimer
University of Colorado, Boulder

The author of Section Seven, Perception, has done much research in perception. He is author of *A Brief History of Psychology* (Holt, Rinehart and Winston) and coauthor of *Psychology: A Brief Introduction* (Scott, Foresman). During 1970–71 he served as the American Psychological Association's Acting Administrative Officer for Educational Affairs.

CONTENTS

COLOR SECTIONS

SECTION ONE

PSYCHOLOGY: THE STUDY OF BEHAVIOR

By Paul Mussen, Mark R. Rosenzweig, & P. James Geiwitz

1

The Science of Psychology

What is psychology?
How do psychologists study aggression?
What are the varieties of psychologists?
What's the difference between basic and applied psychology?
What are the special features of this text?

Psychology is a rapidly evolving field with increasing impacts on life. This text is an innovative attempt to present some of the main findings and methods of psychology, and this chapter opens the gates. You will find here an overview of the book and some preparatory discussions to help you understand and enjoy later chapters.

What is psychology?

The continual growth of psychology as a scientific discipline makes it hard to define. Originally, about a century ago, **psychology** was defined as "the study of the mind"—the normal, adult, European, human mind. Each of these limiting adjectives was eventually discarded—psychologists began to investigate abnormal as well as normal individuals, children as well as adults, people of other cultures as well as Europeans, and animals as well as human beings. Even the noun was changed from "mind" to "behavior." The study of the individual was supplemented by studies of groups and societies.

The expansion and redefinition of psychology continues today. Most current texts define psychology as "the scientific study of behavior" and view psychologists as students and investigators of behavior. Perhaps such definitions are sufficient if not entirely

Psychologists at work in diverse settings.
(L. to R.: B. Le Boeuf; Van Bucher, Photo Researchers; Charles Gatewood; Richard Fauman)

satisfying. What psychologists actually *do* as students and investigators of behavior, however, is the substance of the definition. This chapter, this section, and this book all represent amplifications of the fundamental definition; they depict in increasing detail the vast range of psychologists' activities and the results of these activities.

There are many different kinds of psychologists, each with specialized interests. There are social psychologists and personality psychologists, clinical psychologists, developmental psychologists, cognitive psychologists, learning psychologists, perception psychologists, biological psychologists, and comparative (or animal) psychologists. Some psychologists devote themselves primarily to research and teaching; others seek to *apply* findings and methods to social and psychological problems such as mental illness, tensions between groups, or education of the disadvantaged. Psychologists can be found at work in a variety of settings including colleges and universities, hospitals and clinics, elementary and secondary schools, and governmental and industrial laboratories and offices. Many also serve the public in private practice. Somewhere in all these goings-on lies an adequate definition of psychology.

Let us begin to add substance to this abstract definition of psychology with a look at *different* psychologists at work investigating a *common* behavioral topic, aggression.

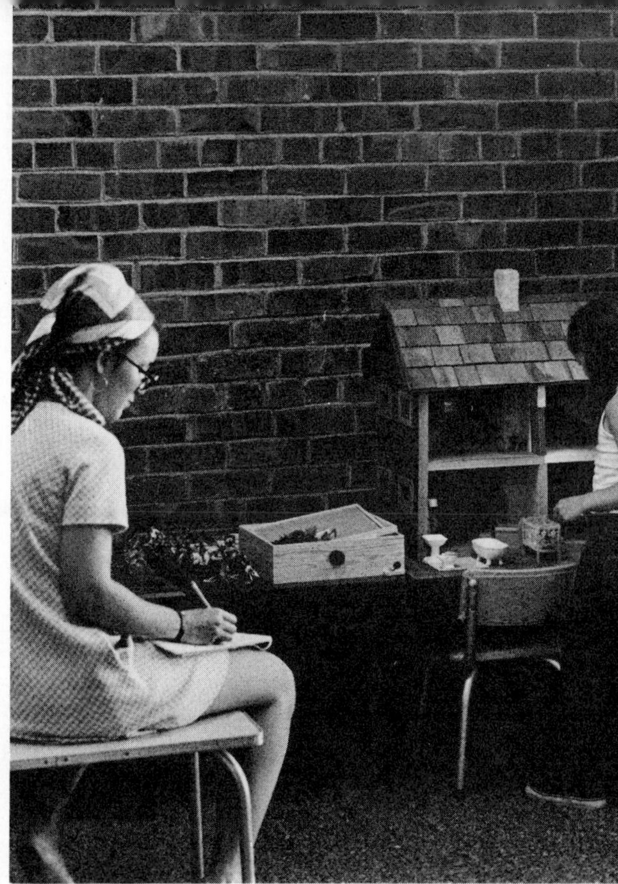

How do psychologists study aggression?

"Study" usually begins with a question or problem. What questions would you ask a psychologist about aggressive behavior? Perhaps the first would be, "What causes aggression?" The first response of any psychologist would not be an answer; it would be an attempt to rephrase the question, changing it into a form capable of being answered by objective and systematic observations.

For example, he would ask you to "define your terms." What do you mean by "causes"? If you mean you want to know what external, environmental, or internal events (within the body) invariably precede violent or aggressive behavior, psychology has little to offer; very few (if any) strictly cause-effect relationships have been established through psychological research. But if you are interested in factors that are consistently—though not invariably—associated with aggressive behavior, then the psychologist can offer quite a bit. "What are the factors related to aggression?" The question is improving.

But what exactly do you mean by **aggression?** Perhaps you might answer, "Intentionally inflicting pain or injury on another person." This is a reasonable definition of aggression, one not uncommonly used by psychologists. But it elicits a further question:

What do you mean by "intentional"? How would you answer that? "I mean that harm or injury is inflicted in such a way that the aggressor shows clearly that he wants to hurt the other person; he threatens, prepares himself to inflict injury, he is clearly angry, and every action indicates his deliberate intention to hurt the other person." You are specifying the observations that you consider indicative of intentionality, much as courts allow certain observations to be used as evidence of premeditation (as in "premeditated murder")—factual evidence of anger and of planning and preparatory behavior. Your question to the psychologist is much improved; you are now asking about factors related to certain observable behaviors and events that are commonly taken to mean aggression. Now you've asked a question he can answer.

The sources of aggressive behavior are studied by many kinds of psychologists.
(P. 8: Ken Heyman; p. 9: Bert Hardy, Black Star)

This is not to say there are not subtle overtones, uncertainties, and annoying complexities still remaining. For example, Freud demonstrated that an aggressor's intentions may not be *clearly* evident—he may not even be consciously aware of them himself—and sometimes they must be unearthed by careful, lengthy, and subtle analysis. This is another way of saying that there may be aggression that is unconsciously motivated, apparent "accidents," such as pushing or tripping someone, that may not be accidents at all. Many obviously intentional injuries are not generally considered aggression—shooting deer or slaughtering hogs, just to cite two illustrations. These complexities in the definition of aggression should not be discounted. There are, however, many kinds of behavior that almost all of us would agree are obvious examples of aggression—

assault, homicide, insult, quarreling. We can focus on these as we look for answers to our revised question about the factors related to aggression.

The first part of our answer can be drawn from a disgraceful American social-historical phenomenon, a blatant, tragic example of man's inhumanity to man. During the last part of the nineteenth century, and continuing into the early part of the present one, there were a substantial number of lynchings, usually of blacks, in the southern part of the United States. In a typical case of lynching, mobs of angry whites would storm a jail in which a black man accused of some crime (often with very little or no evidence) was being held. The mob would capture the prisoner, drag him out of the jail, torture and lynch him.

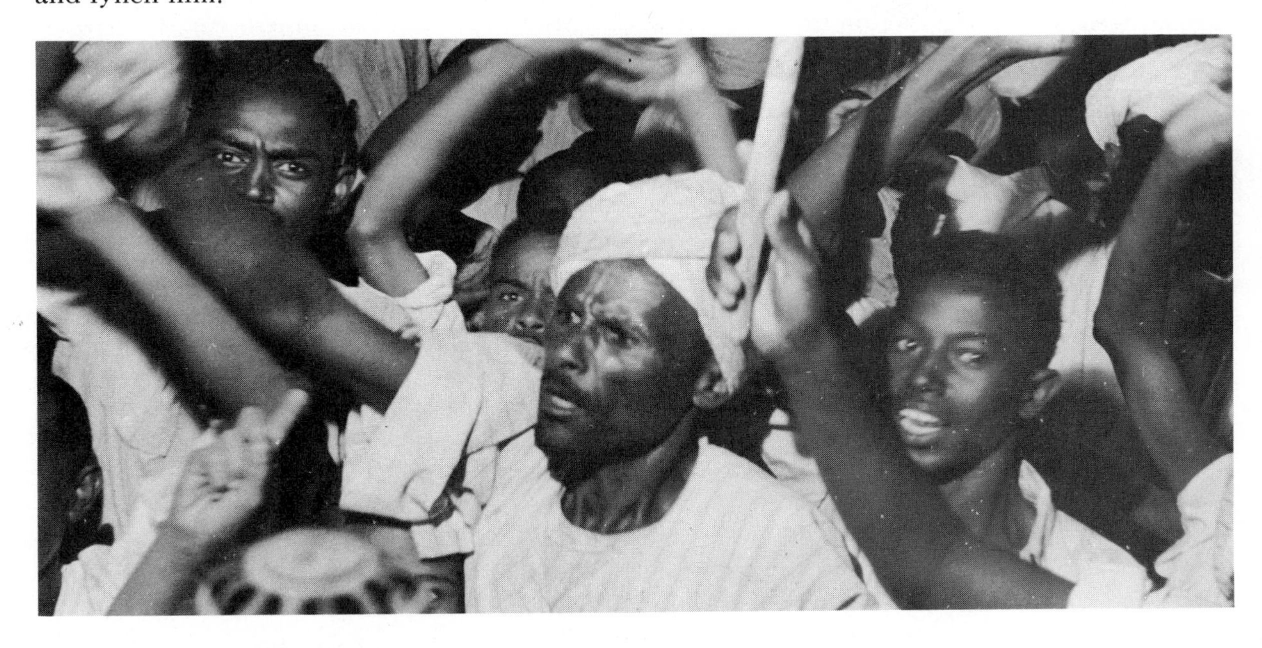

Two psychologists examined the relationship between economic conditions and the number of lynchings in the South in the years between 1882 and 1930. They discovered that when the price of cotton was low, the number of lynchings was high; when the price of cotton was high, the number of lynchings was low (Hovland & Sears, 1940).[1] So here is one factor related to aggression—the economic situation.

How should we interpret this relationship? In that era, when cotton was the South's major economic product, low cotton prices meant hard times for Southern farmers and businessmen, resulting in deprivation and frustration. The psychologists were in-

[1]References are given at the back of the book.

vestigating the **hypothesis** that frustration leads to aggression; they used an economic index (price of cotton) as a crude estimate of economic frustration, and the number of lynchings as an observable indication of aggression. They predicted that as the price of cotton dropped, the number of lynchings would increase. Their prediction was supported by the records.

There are two additional features of this study worth mentioning. The psychologists' hypothesis also stated that if frustrated, people will tend to attack the *source* of frustration. But what is the source of economic frustration, whom do you attack? Brokers on the commodity exchange? God, for producing a surplus of cotton? "The economic system"? Such targets are unavailable, too powerful, or too nebulous. In such situations, people will *displace* their aggression from the "real" targets to specific "convenient" targets that are available and weak. In the situation we have been discussing, the aggression was displaced to helpless blacks. Poor blacks were obviously not the source of frustration but they were convenient targets —and relatively safe targets in that societal structure. So racial **prejudice** was involved.

What are the varieties of psychologists?

The answers to our question about aggression which we extracted from the example above lie within the province of the *social psychologist*. As specialists within the field of psychology, social psychologists focus their research on how aspects of behavior such as aggression, affection, or political affiliation are affected by social structure, socioeconomic status, and interpersonal relationships.

Of course social psychologists are not the only specialists in psychology who are concerned with the origins and development of aggressive behavior. We will briefly describe the perspectives and research interests of several different kinds of psychologists who are also concerned with this kind of behavior. At the same time, you will learn something about psychologists' vast range of activities and interests, as well as the special areas that constitute the field of psychology.

The *personality psychologist* focuses on factors "within" the individual that affect his behavior and personal characteristics. He is interested in finding the conditions that account for the striking individual differences among people. For example, people differ in aggressive tendencies partly because of innate genetic factors and partly because of their own personalities and unique histories.

The *clinical psychologist* applies the findings of the personality psychologist in treating patients and in alleviating emo-

SPOTLIGHT 1-1

Psychologists Study Love and Affection

Although we have used aggression as an example of a type of behavior studied by many different kinds of psychologists, this should not be taken to mean that psychologists do not also study affectionate behavior. You will see examples of studies on the warmer affectionate emotions at several places in this book. Chapter 7 in the section on social psychology is entitled, "Attraction: Who Likes Whom and Why." In the section on personality, you will find also material on love and affection. Comparative psychologists and other students of animal behavior are investigating affection as one of the cohesive forces that help to hold groups together in many species. These studies include both laboratory studies of peer-group affection and parent-child affection among monkeys and observations of affectionate behavior among primates living naturally in wild conditions. Fortunately, affection develops earlier in the life of the individual than does aggression, as Harlow (1972) has emphasized. It is this which makes social life possible – and enjoyable.

(Alan Mercer)

(Russ Kinne, Photo Researchers)

tional problems. Suppose a young man comes to see a clinical psychologist because he is having a great deal of trouble adjusting to college or to a job. He is constantly rebellious and hostile toward everyone he sees as having power over him—teachers, bosses, and policemen.

In this case, the clinical psychologist might explore his client's early relationships with his parents, especially with his father. The assumption is that our parents are the first authority figures we encounter, and our basic responses to authority are learned in our interactions with them. Perhaps the patient has intense, pent-up frustrations, generated in those early years but only now finding release, resulting in aggressive behavior toward authority—or "father"—figures.

The *developmental psychologist* is also interested in childhood experiences and their effects on later behavior, but he studies them directly by observing children. An illustrative investigation dealt with the children's tendencies to *imitate* the aggressive behavior of adults. In the experiment, one group of nursery-school children, the **experimental group,** observed an adult punching, kicking, throwing, and hammering a large plastic doll (a "punching-bag" toy). Later these children were given an opportunity to play with this toy and to do anything they felt like doing with it. Most of them punched, kicked, tossed, or hammered the doll, just as the adult "model" had done. A second group of children, the **control group,** was also permitted to play with the toy, but these children had not previously witnessed the aggressive behavior of the adult. They exhibited much less aggression than the children in the experimental group who had witnessed an adult behaving aggressively toward the toy (Bandura, Ross, & Ross, 1963). (It is important to note that it was necessary to have a control group for comparison purposes. Without this group, we would have no way of knowing whether the aggressive behavior of children in the experimental group was more, the same, or even less than what we could expect without the antecedent conditions.) Clearly, then, imitation can be an important factor in aggression. At least with children the observation of another person acting aggressively results in *more* aggression later, more aggression, that is, than one finds with children without such prior experience.

The *biological psychologist* is a specialist in the physiological, neural, and endocrinal roots of behavior. When he studies aggression, his focus is on such factors as the brain structures and hormones involved in violent behavior. In one experiment a lynx—one of the most savage members of the cat family—had a very small portion of its brain removed, a section called the "amygdala." After the operation, the previously vicious lynx behaved like a kitten; it played with small animals it would have killed before, and it could be fed by hand (Schreiner & Kling, 1956).

A savage animal can be tamed by removing a small region of the brain.
(Leonard Lee Rue III, National Audubon Society)

Such experiments are of great importance in understanding the biological roots of aggression. Knowledge of the relationships between brain and aggressive behavior has already been used in the treatment of people who become pathologically violent due to slight brain injuries or tumors. Fortunately, many of these people can now lead normal lives if they use certain "calming" drugs.

The *comparative psychologist*, as his name implies, compares the forms, sources, and functions of different kinds of behaviors in various species of animals. The study of many species affords a broad perspective on behavior, and it sharpens the problems of defining aggression. Violent behavior arising when animals compete (for dominance, territory, food, or mates) is unquestionably classified as aggressive. Defensive behavior against a predator or an intruder is often classified as aggressive, too, although it often involves different patterns of activity. Predatory behavior, as when a cat stalks a bird, involves still different patterns of behavior, and many comparative psychologists do not classify this as aggression, just as we excluded human activities such as hunting or slaughtering animals for food.

A representative study of competitive aggression was made by observing northern elephant seals on their home grounds, an island near Santa Cruz, California. Soon after they arrive on the island early in December each year, the elephant seal bulls begin fighting and threatening one another. Unlike fur seals who fight only to defend their "territory," the elephant seal bulls fight to determine who is stronger and more dominant. The most dominant bulls do most of the copulating after the elephant seal cows arrive late in December

Male elephant seals fighting to claim breeding territory. (Courtesy B. Le Boeuf)

and thus father most of the pups born the following year (Le Boeuf, 1971).

The aggression of the elephant seal is a complex behavior pattern largely controlled by inborn, instinctive, or "wired-in" biological systems, although experience (learning) can modify such patterns to some extent. From an evolutionary point of view, there is a significant advantage to the species if the strongest and healthiest bulls are those who reproduce, for this helps assure the survival and adaptation of the species. Establishing the dominance hierarchy by fighting reduces the need for active battle once the cows arrive; once the hierarchy is established a threatening gesture from a dominant bull is usually sufficient to drive away a competitor, leaving the dominant one to copulate with the cow.

We have used aggression as a behavioral topic that interests psychologists in a number of specialties, to describe briefly some of the range and diversity of approaches in psychology. There are other specialties that we have not yet defined simply because researchers in these areas do not ordinarily investigate phenomena like aggression directly. This is not to imply that their work is irrelevant for the study of this kind of behavior for, as we shall see, their research may make important indirect contributions to our understanding of aggression.

Cognitive Psychology

"Cognitive" is a broad, general term that refers to the acquisition, processing, and utilization of knowledge. In his research, the *cognitive psychologist* deals with intelligence (and its measurement), thinking, reasoning, concept formation, problem solving, and creativity. Language development is also a topic of concern, since our ability to communicate is intricately related to our ability to reason and to our intellectual superiority over other animals.

Learning Psychology

How does a person profit from experience? This is the question a *learning psychologist* seeks to answer. The concept of association is fundamental. In learning, associations are formed where they did not exist before, associations between a stimulus (e.g., "green light") and a response (e.g., "go"), between an activity (studying) and a reward (a good grade), or between one idea and another (apples and oranges are both fruits). The learning psychologist studies the nature and determinants of associations, as well as memory (the retention of associations) and forgetting (the loss of associations).

Learning is a process of interest to all psychologists because so much of behavior is learned. Theories and findings in learning psychology therefore have a marked influence on the work in other specialties. To cite a simple example, learning psychologists have demonstrated that when a subject's response is followed by a reward—when it is reinforced, in technical terms—the organism is likely to repeat that response the next time he encounters the same situation or stimulus. Thus, if a rat receives a pellet of food (a reward or reinforcement) when he turns left, rather than right, at a choice point in a maze, he is more likely to turn left the next time he is at this point.

Psychologists in other areas—for example, personality and social psychologists—attempt to use this kind of finding in understanding problems in their own domains. Thus, the social

The rat demonstrates learning as he makes his way through the maze to the food reward.
(Robert J. Smith, Black Star)

psychologist looks for social rewards or reinforcements (high status, high income) that strengthen certain kinds of social behavior, for example, striving for achievement. The developmental psychologist considers the rewards a parent can offer (milk or food, attention, approval, love and affection) in training a child.

While *established* principles are being used in other fields, the learning psychologist is going deeper and deeper, trying to understand even more fundamental processes. When more precise research yields results replicated many times and is broad enough to generate new integrative principles, new explanations of the learning process begin to diffuse into other areas of psychology.

Perception Psychology

Perception is the process by which information acquired through the sensory receptors—eyes, ears, nose, skin—is transformed into a **percept**—loosely, what we *think* we see, hear, smell, taste, or touch. Perception is a creative process that involves much more than simple transformation of stimulus energy by the sensory receptors. We see with eyes that have a "hole" in them (a blind spot) and which "jiggle" constantly; if the perception were a true reproduction—rather than the active, constructive process it is—we would "see" only foggy objects with large gray patches. Somehow a collection of stimuli is changed into a meaningful and organized percept – a "table" or "good old Joe." What processes bridge objects or events in the environment and our perception of them? This is the question the *perception psychologist* tries to answer.

What's the difference between basic and applied psychology?

In describing psychological activities or psychologists, it is useful to make a distinction between *basic* and *applied* science, although this is somewhat artificial. The basic aspects of a science are its fundamental facts and principles, and therefore research (discovering) and teaching (disseminating) are considered basic activities. The fields we have already discussed—social psychology, personality, perception, and so forth—are generally called the basic fields. "Applied" refers to the use of these facts and principles to accomplish some practical goal such as educating a child or helping an individual adjust more effectively to his environment.

The distinction is somewhat arbitrary for a number of reasons. A clinical psychologist who diagnoses and treats adjustment difficulties—an applied activity—may in the process gather a number of "case histories" that can be used in a scientific investigation of factors related to mental disorder—a basic activity. And what is "basic" to one psychologist may be "applied" in the view of another;

a study of learning in the classroom, for example, may uncover principles of learning that seem basic to the school psychologist, but not to the learning psychologist, who works with much more precise

SPOTLIGHT 1-2

Psychology Around the World

In this book, we are emphasizing psychology in the English-speaking countries—chiefly the United States, Canada, Great Britain, and Australia—because our text is intended primarily for use in these countries. American psychologists account for well over half of the world's total population of psychologists. But it certainly would be inaccurate to think that psychology does not flourish elsewhere as well. All advanced nations and many of the developing countries have large numbers of psychologists engaged in teaching, research, and application. An international congress is held every three years to encourage direct communication among psychologists of different nations, and many psychological journals and books are read around the world.

Illustrated here is the XXth International Congress of Psychology in Tokyo, 1972. Previous recent International Congresses of Psychology were held in London (1969), Moscow (1966), Washington (1963), and Bonn (1960).

第20回　国際心理学会議

Professor Moriji Sagara, President of the Japanese Psychological Association, welcomes participants from 53 countries to the XXth International Congress of Psychology in Tokyo, 1972.

measures, and considers this study to be an applied one. But if we do not push it too far, our distinction can be useful.

Roughly half of all American psychologists are involved in basic activities, mainly teaching and research. These activities are carried on primarily in the colleges and universities, and, to a lesser extent, in laboratories supported by governmental or private agencies. The psychologists found in these settings and engaged in such work produce most of the fundamental knowledge you will encounter in this textbook. You have already been introduced to the main specialties of basic psychology. Each of these will be taken up in a major section of the text.

Applied Psychology

We have said little about the other half of the picture of American psychology—actually a little more than half—psychologists engaged in applied activities. These psychologists use the basic facts, principles, and methods to solve personal and social problems, and it is this "problem orientation" that most clearly distinguishes their activities from the fundamental activities of discovery. These psychologists are located where they can help others: in private or government hospitals or clinics, in schools, in industry, or in private practice. Not infrequently they engage in applied research, studying ways in which basic knowledge can best be applied to help solve important problems.

Clinical Psychology

The two primary activities of the clinical psychologist are diagnosis and treatment of emotional problems. These may be as specific as a "reading deficiency" or as general as "neurosis." By using information from tests, interviews, and observations, the clinical psychologist attempts to diagnose the exact nature of a patient's difficulty. These personal data must be arranged and integrated, and this is generally done in accordance with some personality theory developed by personality psychologists. In other words, how the psychologist "feels" about the patient's difficulties, and how he interprets them, depends to some extent on his theory of how personality as a whole is organized. The method of treatment used in attempting to eliminate or reduce the difficulty also depends largely on the theory of personality that the clinician holds. For example, some therapists would attempt to alleviate a phobia (an extreme, irrational fear) by conditioning techniques, while others would employ psychotherapeutic methods involving intensive interviews to find the underlying causes of the phobia (see pp. 262, 259).

We should distinguish between a *clinical psychologist* and a *psychiatrist*. The clinical psychologist has an academic degree (Ph.D.) rather than a medical one (M.D.), and he has more extensive training in psychology. A psychiatrist can prescribe drugs whereas a clinical psychologist cannot; the psychologist treats difficulties by "talking them out" or by using scientifically based principles of behavior modification. Quite often, especially in hospitals, the clinical psychologist and psychiatrist work as a team; the psychiatrist knows more about the body and bodily functions and the psychologist more about psychological processes and the diagnosis of personality difficulties through personality tests and questionnaires.

Another type of practitioner frequently mentioned is the **psychoanalyst.** His title comes from a particular theory of personality he employs—psychoanalysis, the theory of Freud (but of course modified on the basis of more recent studies). Usually the psychoanalyst has an M.D. also.

Counseling Psychology

Not everyone who seeks help from a psychologist has a severe emotional disorder. Many people have relatively minor or temporary difficulties or important decisions to make that can be aided by counseling in the relevant principles and facts of psychology. "Should I pursue a career in law?" "Why do I do poorly on exams when I know the material?" Problems in work, study, love, and life in general can often be helped with a little sophisticated psychological guidance. Clinical psychologists can counsel and guide as well as treat more serious disorders. The *guidance counselor*, however, focuses on these "normal" problems. He usually works in a counseling center at a school, college, university, or industrial plant, advising those who have some major decisions to make.

The *industrial psychologist* counsels industry. He may be called upon to help to ease conflict in labor-management negotiations or to advise on the psychological—as contrasted with technological—aspects of a major company decision such as installing automated equipment, modifying work schedules, or moving the plant to a new location. The *personnel psychologist* is an expert in placing people in the right jobs, integrating the "job requirements" of the company and the "job qualifications" of the applicant. In his work, he makes use of interviews, questionnaires, and specialized tests of aptitude and ability. The *management psychologist* focuses on the human factors involved in executive decisions—he may interview prospective executives or he may suggest more effective administrative procedures.

Educational Psychology

The school system has an obvious need for applied psychologists. It is often in the elementary school that serious emotional problems are first observed outside the family, and many schools retain clinical psychologists to deal with these problems. Counseling psychologists treat less serious problems and give advice on careers, study methods, and other aspects of education. The *school psychologist* serves in a variety of ways, bringing psychological knowledge to bear on school problems. He works with students, teachers, and administrators, and his tasks may include counseling, administering and interpreting aptitude and achievement tests, or evaluating teaching programs. The *educational psychologist* is a specialist on teaching and learning and is often engaged in developing or testing out new teaching techniques. Many educational psychologists are found in colleges and universities teaching prospective teachers or school psychologists, i.e., presenting to them the psychological theories and facts related to the educational process, including principles of testing.

Other Applied Activities

The psychologist is an expert in behavior and for this reason his knowledge is of use to a wide variety of people, groups, and organizations. We have already discussed some of the more common examples, but there are many more (less easily categorized). Some psychologists work as animal trainers, for example, and an "applied" comparative psychologist might work for a zoo. *Engineering psychologists* are concerned with the interaction between man and machines, investigating the human factors in the operation of mechanical equipment. The placement of the switch or knob in an airplane or on a computer may be an important issue; it should not be placed in such a position that it confuses the operator or puts unnecessary stress on his physical capacities.

Psychological principles are used in practical situations by applied psychologists. (Wide World Photos)

Knowledge gained through psychological research is used in developing testing procedures.
(Van Bucher, Photo Researchers)

Many psychologists work for the state or federal government in an effort to apply psychological principles to institute humane welfare or penal systems. Many others work in the advertising business, investigating why people buy—or don't buy—certain products or trying to influence the public's response to these products. *Social psychologists* may draw upon their technical knowledge of attitude testing in conducting public-opinion polls on the popularity of political candidates or on reactions to social issues. Or they may apply the principles of persuasion and attitude change in campaigning for a political candidate or influencing people to give up smoking or to change their attitudes about minority groups.

The picture of American psychology presented in this chapter has been verbal and generally descriptive. A more precise, statistical picture is given in Spotlight 1-3. Our principal intention has been to give you a sense of what psychology is, what it means, and who the psychologists are. Psychology consists of a wide variety of approaches and activities and, in the next chapter, we will consider the ways psychologists study behavior. No matter what the setting, the topic, or the general approach, all psychologists abide by the canons of objective scientific investigation and interpretation. Before taking up questions of scientific investigation, let us consider briefly some special features of this text.

SPOTLIGHT 1-3
A Statistical Picture of American Psychology

In 1968 there was a voluntary registration of psychologists by the National Register of Scientific and Technological Manpower. Overall there are approximately 35,000 people now identified in this country as "psychologists" and from their responses to questionnaires the following picture emerges (Cates, 1970).

1. Designations of specialties show clinical psychology as the most common (29%). "Experimental," which includes specialties in learning, perception, biological, and comparative psychology, accounts for 10%, and "Social" — social psychology, personality, developmental, and so forth — accounts for 11%. Other subfields include Counseling-Guidance (10%), Educational (10%), School (9%), and Industrial or Personnel (7%). Obviously there is some overlap between categories; a clinical psychologist could, for example, designate his specialty as "clinical," "personality," or even "educational" or "industrial," depending on where he works and what he does — and, no doubt, on how he would prefer to see himself.

2. Almost half (44%) list their principal employer as a college or university, a medical school, or a junior college.

3. "Work activities" also show an overlap, but 37% cite "teaching and/or research," 21% "clinical or counseling practice," and 10% "testing." A surprising 19% list "management or administration"; this category includes those who supervise programs of research, those who supervise programs of clinical treatment (as in hospitals), and a number of other activities — running CBS, for example (Dr. Frank Stanton), or Common Cause (Dr. John Gardner).

4. Of the total, about 25% are women.

5. Two thirds have the doctor of philosophy degree (Ph.D.); one third have the master's degree; less than 1% have their bachelor's or no college degree.

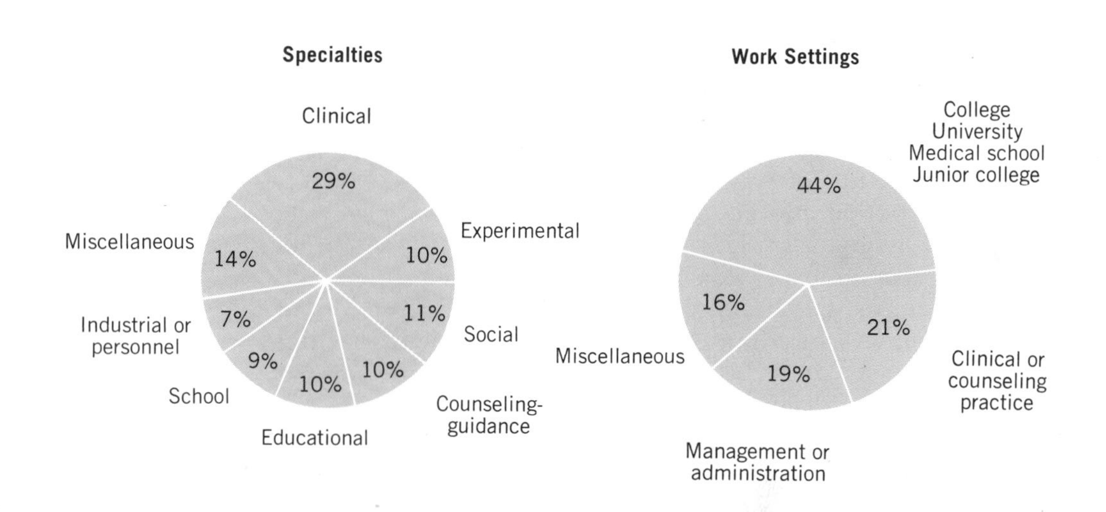

What are the special features of this text?

This textbook is an innovative introduction to psychology in several respects. Two features are unusual and deserve some comment: the order of the chapters and number of authors. The order of chapters is the reverse of that found in most introductory textbooks. Each of the eight major sections that follow this introduction is devoted to one of the basic areas of psychology and was written by an expert in the area; the typical book has a single author or two or three.

Introductory psychology books usually begin with the specialties most closely related to the natural sciences, such as biological psychology, perception, and learning, and then proceed to the social science areas—personality and social psychology. There is a "building-block" assumption underlying this ordering, an assumption that you need to know how the eye functions before you can study perception and you have to know how simple associations are formed before you can understand learning in complex social situations.

We have reversed this order and begin with social psychology, proceeding to the more biological areas later in the text. We believe that presenting the social science areas earlier is preferable for two reasons. First, these areas require little in the way of specialized or technical background. The issues discussed are immediately recognizable and intrinsically interesting from the reader's own experience, though many of the findings go far beyond common sense or general knowledge. Second, the first sections help to develop an interest in the later, more technical chapters. As you read the sections on social psychology, personality, and development you will find frequent references to *learned* behavior. Such references make clear the importance of understanding the nature of learning processes more fully and more deeply. The later section on learning, therefore, is more interesting because it is more meaningful. In contrast to a "building-block" assumption, we have based our order on a "desire-to-dig-deeper" assumption, with the earlier sections providing both motivation and some background for the later sections.

The second unusual feature of this book is the number of authors. The expert is in the best position to know which facts and principles in his specialty are the most important, both for increasing your understanding of the area and for preparing you for further study. Any introductory survey can do no more than present some of the major findings and major trends; this means selection is necessary, and recognized authorities can select most knowledgeably.

Even though there are many authors, the book does not consist of a number of isolated treatises with little or no relationship to each other. The authors have worked on this project as a group effort, continually exchanging ideas, outlines, and drafts, and they have collaborated together closely to integrate the text in terms of content, style, and level of presentation.

This is not to say that each section will read like all the others, as if a single author had written the book. On the contrary, many aspects of individual style have been deliberately retained, for the style of writing in a field communicates a great deal about the work in that area. As we mentioned earlier, the social psychologist and the personality psychologist know that the reader has had some personal experiences related to the topics of their field, so some terms are readily comprehended and do not need special definitions; examples are more easily found and understood. The clear, crisp, precise style of the later, more basic sections, with more technical, special definitions of terms, and more attention to detail, tells us much about the concerns of those fields. For example, it is easier to discuss research on prejudice than to describe the functions of a brain region such as the amygdala—and that fact is reflected in writing styles. Do not think, however, that it is easier to *do* research on prejudice or that the scientific requirements of proper investigation are less strict in social psychology than in biological psychology.

All in all, we have done our best in a group effort to give you a sensible introduction to the science of psychology, presenting the major facts and principles, the classic experiments along with exciting new discoveries, some answers to old questions, and even some new questions generated by old answers. We feel that psychology is an exciting field, still a young science, full of arguments and controversies, with a subject matter—behavior—that is important to the individual, to groups, to nations, and to the world. We hope you will agree.

SUMMARY

The field of psychology is continually expanding and undergoing redefinition. To give substance to the definition—"Psychology is the scientific study of behavior"—we show what psychologists *do;* each section of the book depicts the range of the psychologists' activities and the results of these activities.

Different kinds of psychologists contribute to our understanding of socially significant behavior, and this was illustrated by showing how different psychological specialists investigate the problems of aggression. Thus, the social psychologist studies the influences of social structure, socioeconomic status, and interpersonal relationships on social responses, including aggression, while the personality psychologist concentrates on individual differences in personal characteristics and their consequences. The developmental psychologist focuses his attention on childhood experiences and their later effects, studying these directly by observing children. The biological psychologist contributes to the understanding of the neural and hormonal roots of social behavior. By comparing the forms, sources, and functions of different kinds of responses of various species of animals, the comparative psychologist provides us with a broad perspective on social phenomena.

In perception, stimuli from the outside world are transformed into meaningful and organized percepts; the perception psychologist is concerned with the processes underlying these transformations. The learning psychologist attempts to answer the fundamental question of how we remember and profit from experience. Intelligence, thinking, reasoning, and creativity are the major topics to which cognitive psychologists devote their efforts.

A useful but admittedly arbitrary distinction may be drawn between *basic* and *applied* psychology. The discovery of fundamental facts and principles is considered "basic." Applied psychologists use these facts and principles to accomplish practical goals, such as educating children or helping people to adjust more effectively. Among the best-known applied specialists are clinical psychologists, who diagnose and treat emotional disturbances, and industrial psychologists who counsel industry and help place people in the right jobs.

Eight major basic areas of psychology are presented in the eight following sections. Each section was written by an expert in that field and the order of presentation goes from the more social and personal areas to the more technical and biological aspects of psychology.

2

How Do Psychologists Study Behavior?

How does a psychologist apply the scientific method?
How does statistics give meaning to findings?
But what does psychology mean to me?
Where do we begin our study of psychology?

The problems of human beings, their behavior, and their relationships to one another are inherently interesting. Almost everyone—the bartender, the banker, the beautician—feels that he is an expert in these matters and has his own "theories" or at least opinions and beliefs: "War is inevitable because aggression is an innate characteristic of men." "Blacks are less intelligent than whites and most of them cannot benefit from the usual educational and training programs." "Youth is rebellious and nonconforming because of early parental permissiveness and spoiling." "The use of drugs weakens the mind."

If pressed, the layman can cite evidence for his beliefs. "Drugs weaken the mind because, well, look at the hippies!" But this evidence is based on casual, unsystematic, and often biased observations. Events are likely to be perceived selectively and interpreted in ways consistent with preconceived opinions and beliefs.

How does a psychologist apply the scientific method?

The psychologist is also interested in these significant social and personal questions, although he often rephrases them carefully so that they can be answered objectively and reliably. As a scientist, the psychologist goes far beyond the layman in formulating theories about these problems and in investigating them.

The scientist formulates a **hypothesis** (informed guess or idea) about the problem he is investigating. Generally this hypothesis involves tentative explanations of relationships between characteristics, conditions, or events (variables); for example, between permissive child-rearing and adolescent rebelliousness, or between a stimulating environment in early life and later intelligence. Some hypotheses reflect current or popular beliefs; other hypotheses are founded on preliminary observations or pilot research; others are creative, new ways of thinking about behavior. These last often lead to the most important advances.

A coherent, integrated set of interrelated hypotheses is called a **theory.** A good theory is useful in summarizing, bringing together, integrating, and explaining different kinds of data. Einstein's theory of relativity encompassed explanations for two kinds of phenomena that had previously seemed unrelated: gravitation and electromagnetic forces. Analogously, Freud's psychoanalytic theory brought together several psychological phenomena that had previously seemed unrelated: dreams, slips of the tongue, humor, and personality disorders.

But a good theory does more than integrate; it is an additional source of suggestions and hypotheses for further research. With a good theory we can make predictions that can be tested scientifically. In this sense, hypotheses or theories *guide* research. The scientist's hypothesis points to the next steps he must take in his research.

Unlike the layman, the scientist systematically tests his hypotheses and theories to determine whether or not they are valid. He does not rely on opinion but he looks for facts based on the data he collects. He accepts or rejects his hypothesis on the basis of systematic empirical evidence derived from careful and objective observation. Quantitative, precise measurements are used wherever possible. Experiments are conducted and observations made very carefully, so that they can be repeated, and thus verified, by other psychologists.

Hypotheses must be stated in testable form. This means the broad general problems often have to be restated and formulated so that they are capable of scientific solution. Thus the question "Does frustration increase aggression?" is too broad and must be rephrased in more precise terms so that everyone knows exactly what is meant. This is accomplished by means of *operational definitions:* each term in the hypothesis is defined objectively as an observable response or a measurement. Thus in the investigation of the relationship between "frustration" and "aggression," frustration could be defined operationally as preventing someone from doing something he wants to do—for example, preventing young children from playing with attractive toys. Aggression could be defined in terms of overt responses such as hitting or arguing.

Note how the question has changed. It now reads, in operational terms, "Does preventing young children from playing with attractive toys increase the number of hitting or arguing responses?" This question can be answered by careful observation.

Once he has defined his terms operationally, the researcher can proceed with his investigation. The preferred method of research in many areas of psychology, as in most scientific fields, is the laboratory experiment. We will therefore take this up first and will later consider objective, nonexperimental research methods.

Experimental Method

The experimental method has two distinctive characteristics. First, the experimenter manipulates something—called the **independent variable**—creating, changing, or controlling it. Second, he systematically observes or measures the effects of his manipulation on some other behavior or condition—the **dependent variable.** For example, to investigate the hypothesis that "frustration leads to aggression," the experimenter could manipulate the independent variable, frustration, by showing some children attractive toys and refusing to allow them to play with them. He could then determine whether this frustration produced increases in aggression, the dependent variable, as measured by the number of aggressive acts the children commit. Of course, the investigator would not be cruel; after the experiment was completed he would allow the children to play with the attractive toys so there would be no lasting frustration.

Experimental and Control Groups

Recall, also, the experiment on children's imitation of aggression cited in Chapter 1 (p. 12). The investigator wanted to determine whether children's observations of models behaving aggressively toward a large doll stimulated their own aggressive behavior. He started with a large number of nursery-school children and assigned each one, at random, to either the experimental or control group. The experimental group was given the experimental treatment—the opportunity to observe aggressive models—while the control group did not get this treatment (see Figure 2-1).

Random assignment of children to groups is a procedure something like putting all the names in a hat, mixing them thoroughly, and then drawing blindly an equal number for each group or subgroup. This means essentially that *no* characteristic of the subject is used to determine which group a child will join. So when a large group is subdivided at random into subgroups, we assume that these subgroups are essentially equal in all respects—in all characteristics that might affect aggressive behavior such as sex, health, intelligence, excitability, and neurotic trends, and even in nonessential characteristics such as proportion of people with red hair or blue eyes.

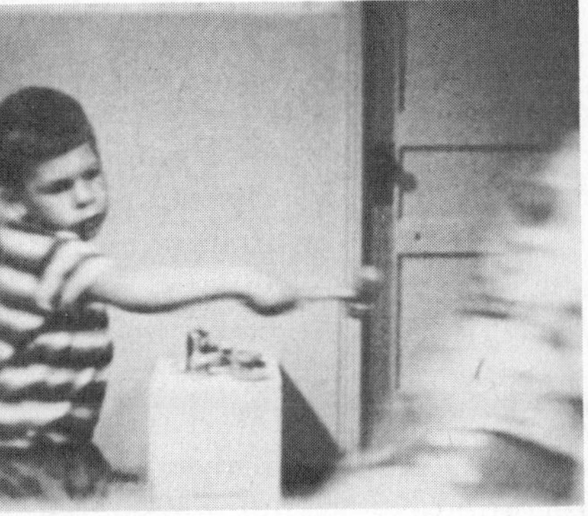

Children imitating an aggressive model they have observed.
(Courtesy A. Bandura)

If children are assigned randomly to the groups, the two groups are alike at the beginning of the experiment. *Then* the independent variable is applied; one group is treated differently from the other. Any difference between them *after* the experiment must be due to the effect of the independent variable—in this case, exposure to aggressive models—since there was originally no other difference between the groups. In our example, the dependent

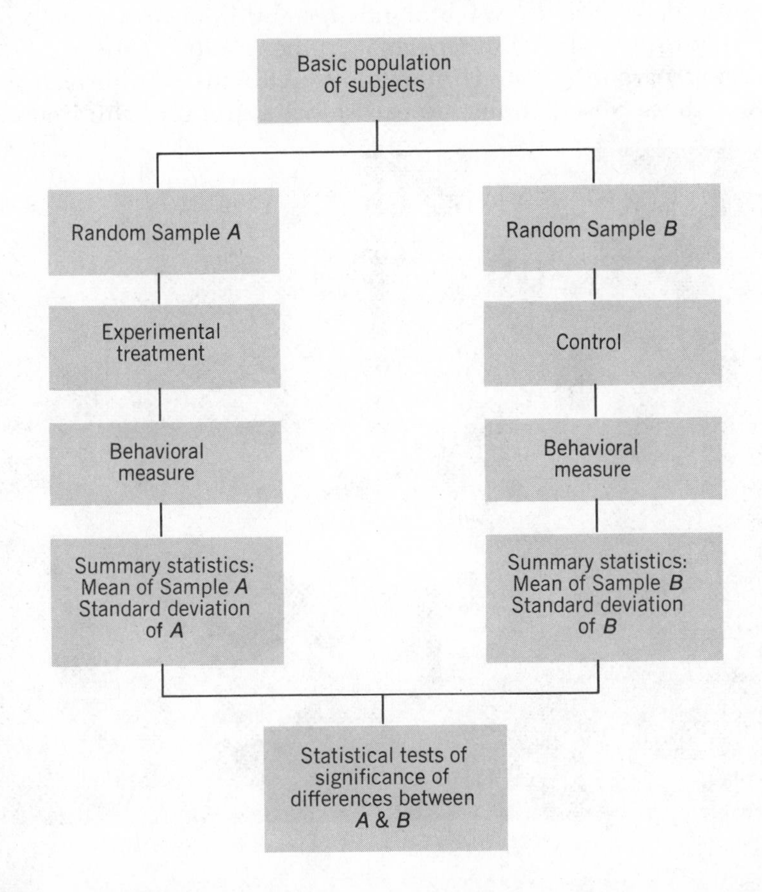

FIGURE 2-1
OUTLINE OF STEPS IN AN EXPERIMENT

variable was the amount of aggression expressed toward a doll and the children who observed the aggressive model were more aggressive than those who had not. We can conclude that this difference was the result of watching the models because the groups differed from each other *only* in one way, their exposure to aggressive models.

The unique and critical advantage of the experiment is that it makes possible the precise evaluation of changes in dependent variables. The logic of the experiment is simple and straightforward. Groups are matched at the outset; the subjects in one group are given an experimental intervention but those in the other do not receive this treatment. A response measure, the dependent variable, is then recorded. Any differences between the experimental and control groups must be attributable to the experimental intervention.

Systematic Observation and Nature's Experiments

Many problems of human behavior cannot be investigated by experimental methods. Consider the hypothesis that permissive child-rearing (allowing children a great deal of freedom) produces rebelliousness against authority. Permissiveness would be considered the independent variable; the child's tendency to rebel would be the dependent one. Obviously a researcher cannot control or manipulate parents' ways of raising children simply for experimental purposes. But he can go into the "field," people's homes, observing parents' natural interactions with their children. On the basis of these observations, he can select a group of children raised

A psychologist observes family interaction in the home.
(Richard Fauman)

permissively and a group raised nonpermissively. Permissiveness might be defined operationally in terms of such variables as strictness or laxity of rules of the home and children's role in making their own, and family, decisions. The amount of rebellion in the permissively and nonpermissively reared groups would then be compared. Rebelliousness could be measured operationally by teachers' ratings of children's rebelliousness in the classroom, as revealed by their willingness to comply with rules and instructions. If the permissively reared children actually manifest more rebelliousness than those raised by nonpermissive parents, the hypothesis is supported—permissiveness is in fact related to rebellion against authority. The study cannot be considered an experiment in the usual sense, since the experimenter did not intervene in any way; he did not actively manipulate the independent variable, permissiveness. Essentially the hypothesis was tested by observing naturally occurring events and determining relationships between these—in essence, by observing an "experiment" in which nature manipulated the independent variable.

It must be recognized, however, that the relationship between permissiveness and rebellion has not been demonstrated as clearly or directly as the relationship between exposure to aggressive models and aggression in the experiment cited earlier. There is still a possibility that other factors not specifically investigated also influenced the rebelliousness of the permissively reared children. For example, these children may come from homes in which there is considerable friction between parents and as a consequence, lax discipline. If this were the case, the children's rebelliousness might be, at least in part, a reaction to tensions in the family rather than a product of permissiveness in the home. In short, a factor associated with permissiveness, rather than permissiveness itself, may account for the differences between the two groups. In a laboratory experiment, on the other hand, we can be certain that the differences between the experimental and control groups result from the experimenter's manipulation, because all other factors are rigorously controlled.

How does statistics give meaning to findings?

Making observations or conducting experiments usually produces quantitative data—for example, the *numbers* of aggressive acts in a specified situation, or *scores* on a test of reasoning, or *ratings* of conformity, or *measures* of parental permissiveness. Psychologists regularly use statistical methods to put their raw data into manageable form, to measure relations within the data, and to interpret the results.

Almost all of the findings and conclusions in this book depend upon the use of statistical concepts and methods, although we will not usually present the results in statistical form. In some cases we will want to present results rather precisely and therefore will employ such terms as "mean," "median," "standard deviation," "coefficient of correlation," or "statistical significance." Because the use of statistics is so pervasive and so basic, we will consider some of the most important concepts briefly here. Our purpose at this point is only to give you some comprehension of these concepts, not computational skills. A brief presentation of statistical formulas and computational methods appears in an appendix.

Describing Data

Suppose that you want to describe the performance of a group of people in some test or experiment or to determine where a particular individual stands in relation to the rest of the group. The measure in question could be the number of aggressive responses children made in an experimental situation, estimates of intelligence, or scores on a test of creativity. Each person in the group is observed or tested and gets a score. But it is hard to tell much about the group or about any person just by examining the list of scores. For example, consider the intelligence test scores for 100 people given in Table 2-1. If you are interested in a particular individual, for example the one whose score is circled, and want to know where he stands in the group, you need to have a way of describing the whole set of data, or the **distribution** of scores.

TABLE 2-1
SCORES OF 100 SUBJECTS ON AN INTELLIGENCE TEST

72	91	139	78	99	79	100	84	100	124
128	88	92	85	109	96	90	93	75	98
84	95	81	119	102	123	100	92	82	69
81	106	95	97	88	89	110	132	(111)	116
101	101	96	102	97	127	108	112	107	107
113	137	104	120	61	105	98	80	121	100
103	93	83	94	87	99	109	100	120	106
94	105	87	114	103	87	115	110	98	113
101	108	104	80	95	107	97	102	112	118
86	91	76	117	99	104	92	102	77	99

Determine the Distribution

The first step in describing the distribution is to arrange the scores in order from the lowest to highest and to see how many people made each score. This has been done in Figure 2-2 which shows the number of people making each score (the **frequency**). Each dot stands for one person. Now you can easily see that the lowest score in the group is 61, the highest is 139, and that most of the scores cluster around 100. Five people scored 100; 4 received

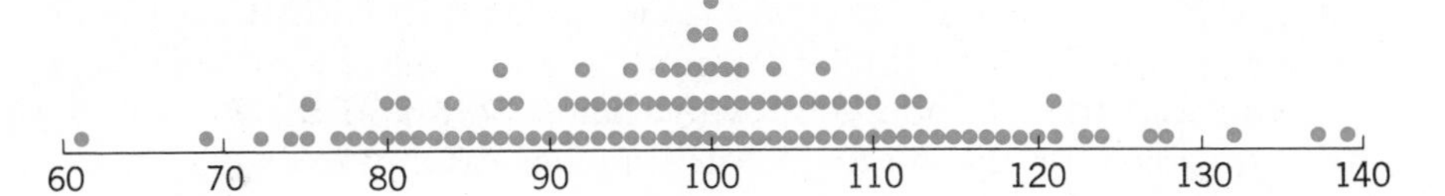

FIGURE 2-2 DISTRIBUTION OF I.Q. SCORES FROM LOWEST TO HIGHEST FROM SAMPLE OF TABLE 1

the score of 99, 3 scored 101, and 4 are at 102. In order to describe the distribution of scores more adequately, we need some measure of the average of the group or central tendency. And we also need a measure of how much the scores vary around the center, a measure of variability. This kind of measure tells us whether the scores are closely clustered around the average or are dispersed and spread out over a wide range.

Two frequently used measures of central tendency are the median and the arithmetic mean, both of which can be called an "average." The **median** is the point that divides the group into equal halves—the upper and lower halves of the distribution. To get the median, you arrange the scores in order from the lowest to the highest, then you find the middle score. Thus, if there are 5 scores, the third is the median; if there are 100 cases, you take a value halfway between the 50th and 51st. To get the arithmetic average or **mean,** you find the sum of all the scores and then divide by the number of cases. In the example of Table 2-1, the median and the mean are both 100. This is the mean I.Q. of a representative sample of the population; the mean I.Q. of a group of college students would of course be higher. Using the mean as a reference point, we can now say that the circled score is 11 points above the mean.

The mean and median tend to be similar when the scores are distributed symmetrically around the center, but they may differ widely in other types of distributions. For example, take the following set of numbers: 1, 1, 2, 2, 3, 4, 50. The median is 2 while the mean is 9. A few extreme scores in a distribution affect the mean but not the median. In this example, the median would still be 2 if the largest number had been 50, 5, or 5,000, but the mean would be changed considerably. The mean family income in the United States is much higher than the median because the mean is influenced by a few very high incomes. But the median more accurately reflects the fact that most people have low or moderate incomes. The mean is the more frequently used measure of central tendency because it is based on more information, that is, each and every score plays an equal role in its determination.

Find the Standard Deviation

We cannot adequately describe a distribution just by giving the average; we also need a measure of **variability.** For example, we need to know whether a score 11 points above the mean puts the individual who makes that score very high, or only moderately high, within the total distribution. The range from the lowest to the highest score gives a rough measure of variability. A better measure is the average deviation of all scores from the mean; to get this, you find the difference between each score and the mean, and then you find the arithmetic average of these differences. The most commonly used measure of variability of scores is the **standard deviation,** a statistic based on squaring the deviations from the mean.

The primary advantage of the standard deviation is that it describes with great precision the distribution of scores in a normal curve. The frequency distribution of Figure 2-2 was somewhat irregular because it was based on a relatively small number of cases drawn randomly from a large population. If a large number of people —say, thousands—were sampled, the overall distribution of I.Q. scores would become more regular and would approach the bell-shaped curve shown in Figure 2-3. This is called a **normal curve.**

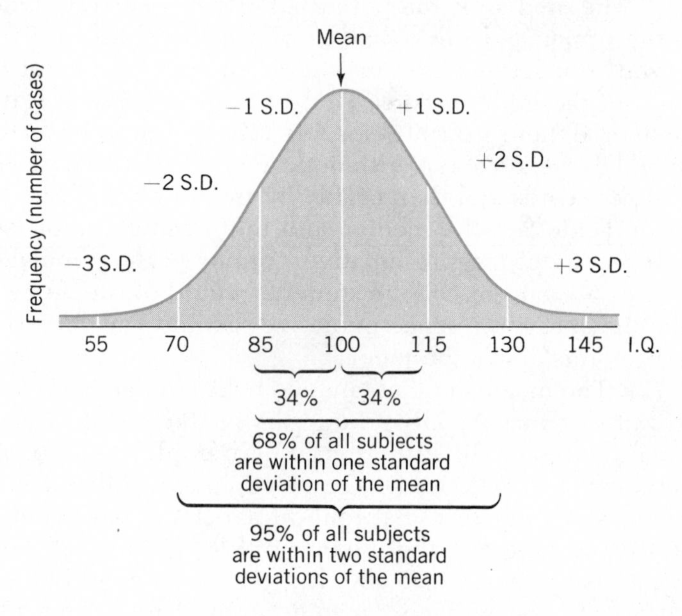

**FIGURE 2-3
THE NORMAL CURVE DISTRIBUTION OF I.Q. SCORES**

The distribution of I.Q. scores in a large sample approximates closely the bell shape of a normal curve. Here the mean is 100 and the standard deviation (S.D.) is 15.

As is clear from Figure 2-3, in a normal distribution the score with the highest frequency is the mean; that is, more people get the mean score than any other. The farther a score is from the mean, the lower the frequency of that score. In a normal distribution, 68 percent of all scores are within one standard deviation (S.D.) of the mean, 34 percent above and 34 percent below the mean. And 95 percent are within two S.D. of the mean. Figure 2-3 represents the distribution of intelligence (I.Q.) scores in the general population; the mean is 100 and the standard deviation is 15 points. An I.Q. score of 130, therefore, is two S.D. above the mean; a score above 130 occurs only about 25 times in 1,000 people drawn from the general population.

Opinion surveys require representative samples of subjects.
(Charles Gatewood)

We can now describe the set of I.Q. scores of Table 2-1 with only two numbers—the mean (99.8 in this case) and the standard deviation (14.9 in this case). These two statistics also help us to locate the individual's standing in the group. For example, the circled score of 111 is now seen to be 11 points, or not quite one standard deviation, above the mean. It is better than 77 percent of the others—in the top quarter of the distribution.

Sampling

When we test a hypothesis, we usually work with a limited number of subjects but we hope to generalize the results to a much larger group. For example, we might use twenty or thirty nursery-school children in an experiment and phrase our conclusion in terms of what nursery-school children in general are likely to do. The small group used in the experiment is called a **sample,** hopefully a representative sample from the total population—in this case, all nursery-school children.

Adequate sampling requires the application of precise and mathematical rules, as you know if you follow public-opinion polls. The opinions of a thousand individuals, chosen in such a way that they are representative of the larger population, give us a fairly accurate estimate of an entire nation's TV preferences or political beliefs. But results based on biased sampling can be very misleading. If you asked only your friends what they thought of marijuana, you might incorrectly assume that that sample was representative of the thoughts of a nation. But your friends are probably a restricted group in several ways – they come from a certain geographical area, and they are above average in education and intelligence. In principle, nonbiased samples from the population which you hope to understand must be selected *randomly*, so that any member of the total population has an equal chance of being selected.

Even if a sample is not biased, it may give misleading conclusions if the number of subjects is too small. Imagine asking three people what their favorite TV shows were and basing next year's schedule on their answers; even if they were randomly selected, their answers would not be likely to reflect the judgments of millions of TV watchers.

Let us return to our sample of 100 I.Q. scores in Table 2-1. We discovered that the mean and standard deviation of the "total population" were 99.8 and 14.9 respectively. Suppose we randomly sample 10 scores from that group; since there are 100 scores, we can form 10 such "subsets" of 10 scores each. The means and standard deviations of 10 subsets drawn this way are given in Table 2-2. Most of the means and standard deviations of the samples are fairly close to the total population values, but none hits them "right on the nose." This demonstration illustrates that sampling provides "estimates" and that these estimates are subject to error.

TABLE 2-2
I.Q. SCORES IN TEN RANDOM SAMPLES OF TEN SUBJECTS EACH

Sample	A	B	C	D	E	F	G	H	I	J
Mean	96.3	101.5	95.7	100.6	94.0	101.6	101.9	100.7	100.3	105.0
S.D.	16.5	14.3	17.8	16.3	13.3	15.2	8.2	15.1	17.1	15.4

The larger the sample in relation to the total population, the less the sampling error, of course. While we have been using these terms—"estimates," "error"—in a rather casual fashion, statisticians can give us precise measures of the probable error in any estimate based on a small sample if they know the size of the sample. This brings us to our last statistical question: When does a difference make a difference?

Deciding When a Difference Makes a Difference

In Table 2-2, we have ten independent estimates of the mean of the total group, most of which are close to, but none match exactly, the true value (99.8). Suppose we performed an experiment using two Groups, *X* and *Y*. We injected subjects in Group *X* with a chemical we felt might "increase intelligence," but we gave the subjects in Group *Y* no special treatment. After the experiment, we test the intelligence of subjects in both groups and find that the mean for Group *X* is 101.9 while the mean for the untreated Group *Y* is 97.3, a difference of 4.6 points. Can we confidently assume the chemical was effective? Or is this difference one that could have occurred even if the treatment had no real effect? That is, could it be caused by sampling errors resulting from the use of relatively small samples?

These questions can be given a probable answer by statistics that determine the **significance** of a difference. As used statistically, significant means trustworthy, or likely to be replicated. That is, if the same experiment were repeated with two new groups, the results would be similar: the two groups would probably differ in the same way, although not necessarily in the same exact amount. In short, a statistically significant difference is one that is likely to be reproducible or replicable.

There are very few experiments in psychology that yield *no* measured differences between groups, so we almost always use statistics to tell us if our obtained difference is significant or not. In the case above, the statistics would of course show the differences between Group *X* and Group *Y* were *not* significant. If we took two new samples, say Groups *K* and *L*, and repeated the experiment, we might find the treated group (*K*) scoring 100.5 and the untreated subjects (*L*) averaging 103.1, and our grand hopes for an "intelligence-enhancing" chemical would be dashed.

In general, statistical tests of significance compare the obtained difference to differences that might occur due to sampling errors. If a very large number of subjects is used and the measuring techniques are very precise, these variations will be relatively small and a quite small difference can be significant. On the other hand, if the sample is small and the measures crude and imprecise, a very large difference can be nonsignificant. The degree of "trustworthiness" in a difference is typically assigned a **probability** (p) that indicates the likelihood that one could get a difference of this magnitude *if* the treatment had no real effect, given the sampling error in the particular situation. A probability of less than .05 ($p < .05$) indicates that a difference this large would have occurred by chance less than five times in a hundred; such a difference is considered significant. A probability of "less than once in 100 cases" ($p < .01$) indicates an even more trustworthy result.

Relating Measures to Each Other

Often we want to know how closely two sets of measures are related to each other. For example, how closely are the I.Q. scores of children related to those of their parents? Table 2-3 presents some representative data for 63 families, with one parent and one child taken from each family. Looking over the figures, you get the impression that if the parent has a relatively high score, so does the child; low parental scores tend to be associated with low children's scores. But the relationship is not perfect, some parents with relatively high scores have children with relatively low scores. We can get a better idea of the relationship if we plot the scores in what is called a **scatterplot**, as shown in Figure 2-4. Here each parent-child pair is

TABLE 2-3
I.Q. SCORES OF 63 REAL PARENT-CHILD PAIRS

Parent	Child	Parent	Child	Parent	Child	Parent	Child
136	131	117	113	112	96	114	105
98	125	92	107	116	95	112	109
114	126	94	106	118	99	124	106
113	129	93	100	120	98	121	108
102	122	96	108	83	91	83	100
111	121	103	104	94	90	87	104
115	123	105	100	95	92	89	101
127	124	108	103	104	94	121	91
93	116	107	111	107	93	83	85
97	119	114	102	118	94	88	89
118	117	132	118	107	78	86	86
126	118	80	95	76	82	120	88
127	119	84	99	99	84	124	87
125	117	79	99	87	80	107	81
129	115	76	97	63	67	102	79
112	111	104	98	107	107		

represented by one point on the graph. To place the point, you find the parent's score on the horizontal axis, and then go over to the position of the child's score on the vertical axis. The first pair in the table—parent, 136, child, 131—is represented by a black point with dashed lines showing the two scores on the axes. The **coefficient of correlation**—generally referred to simply as the correlation—is the statistic used to quantify the relationship between two variables—for example, between parents' and childrens' I.Q. scores, between measures of frustration and measures of aggression, between intelligence and creativity. The correlation shows the extent to which paired measures vary together and correlation values range from 0 (no relationship) to 1.00 (perfect relationship); the higher the coefficient, the stronger the relationship. Suppose, for example, the paired measures are public school grades and college grades. If the correlation is high, the person who stands high relative to his public school group is also likely to get good grades in college.

The correlation (abbreviated r in statistical work) in Figure 2-4 is 0.52 ($r = .52$). In psychological research, a correlation of .50 or more is considered relatively strong; correlations between .30 and .50 are moderate; those below .30 are considered low. Correlations can be positive (+, or often no sign is shown) or negative (always indicated by −). A positive correlation indicates that if the score on one variable is high, the other is also likely to be high; for example, if the parent's I.Q. is high, the child's is also likely to be high. A negative correlation indicates that if the score on one variable is high, the other is likely to be low; for example, the *higher* the

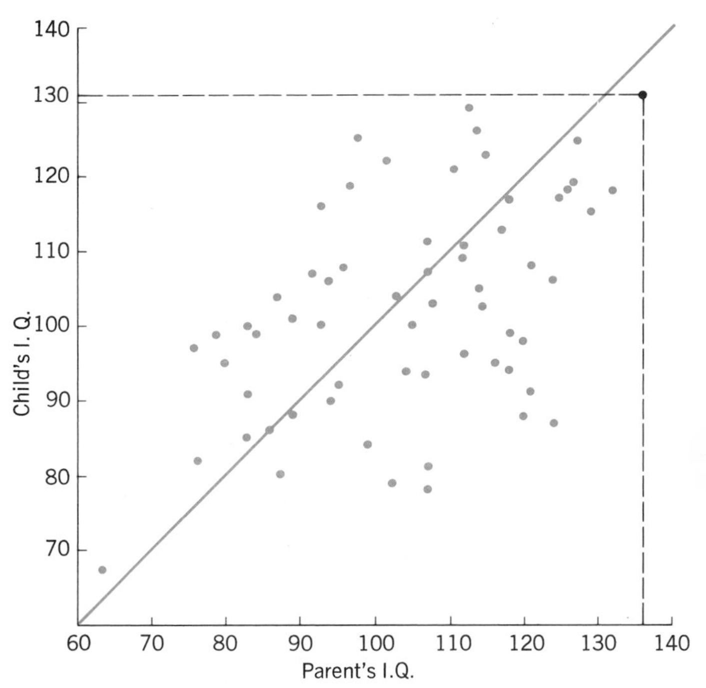

FIGURE 2-4 SCATTERPLOT SHOWING RELATIONSHIP BETWEEN CHILD'S AND PARENT'S I.Q.'S

This scatterplot is constructed from the data given in Table 2-3 to show the relationship between the I.Q. scores of parents and their children. The point for parent 136–child 131 is shown in black to illustrate how points are plotted on the graph.

individual's intelligence, the *less* often he will yield to group pressures to conform in experimental situations.

A perfect correlation (+1.00 or −1.00) would have all the points in the scatterplot falling on a straight diagonal line; there is perfect correspondence in relative standing in the two measures; if a subject scores third (or thirteenth) from the top in one variable, he also stands third (or thirteenth) from the top in the other. A scatterplot for +1.00 is shown in Figure 2-5. The more the points deviate from such a straight line, the lower is the correlation.

Figure 2-6 shows two scatterplots for I.Q. data. Figure 2-6A is based on scores of parents and scores of their adopted children; one can barely detect a relationship, and the correlation is only .18. The closest possible hereditary relationship occurs between identical twins; these are twins formed from a single egg cell. Even if they are raised apart from infancy, such twins usually resemble each other closely in intelligence and many other characteristics. A scatterplot for I.Q. scores of identical twins raised apart is given in Figure 2-6B; the correlation is .82. The size of this correlation, which is very high, and the fact that I.Q. correlations are higher the closer the hereditary relationship, suggest that there is a strong genetic factor in intelligence.

One of the primary uses of a correlation is to predict the standing on one variable if you know the standing on the other. For example, if you know the I.Q. score of a person, you can predict the I.Q. of his identical twin with high accuracy, you can predict the I.Q. of his biological child with reasonable accuracy, but you can do little

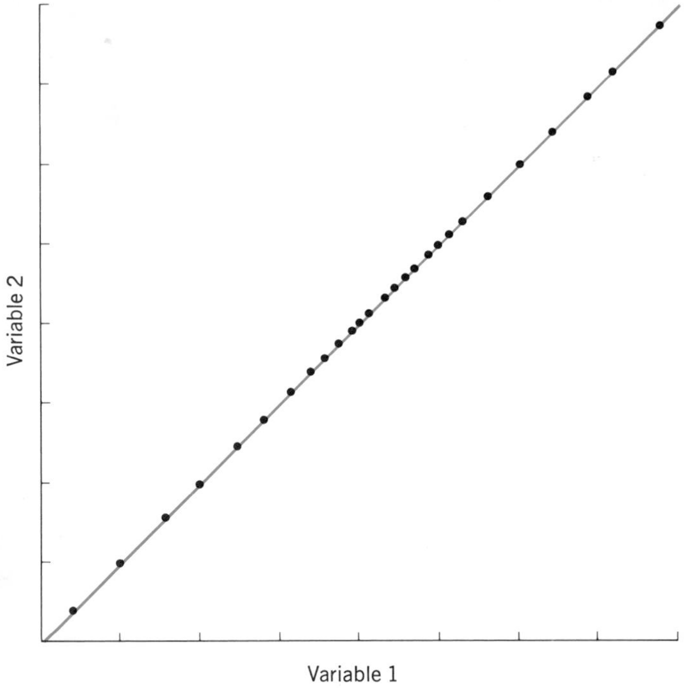

Variable 2

Variable 1

FIGURE 2-5
SCATTERPLOT SHOWING +1.00 CORRELATION
With a correlation of +1.00 there is perfect predictability of the relationship of scores on one measure to scores on the other.

more than guess the I.Q. of his adopted child. College admission boards use high school grades as a major factor in selecting applicants because it has been demonstrated that there is a clear correlation between public school and college grades; those who earn relatively high grades in public school are likely to get good grades in college.

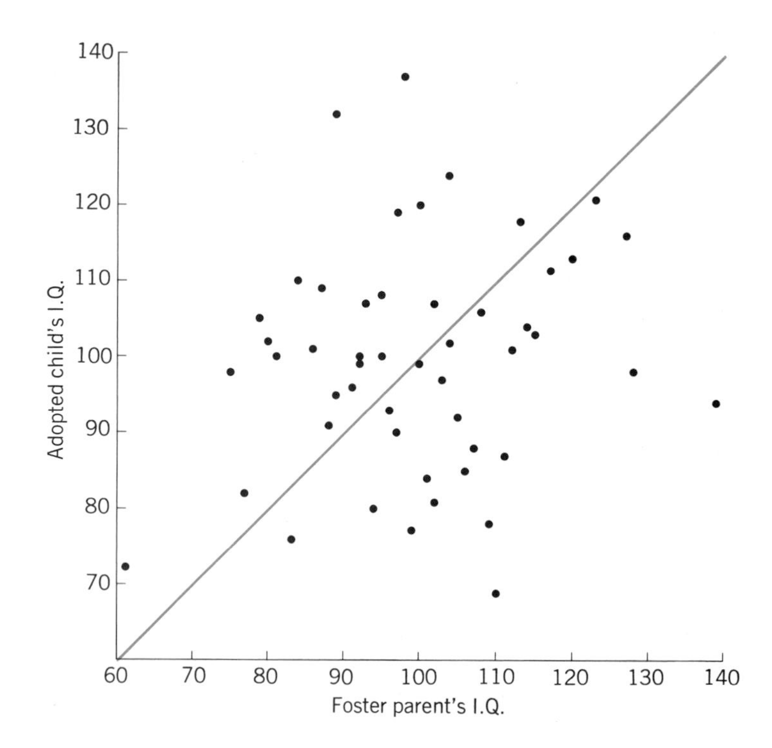

FIGURE 2-6A
SCATTERPLOT SHOWING RELATIONSHIPS BETWEEN I.Q.'S OF FOSTER PARENTS AND THEIR ADOPTED CHILDREN

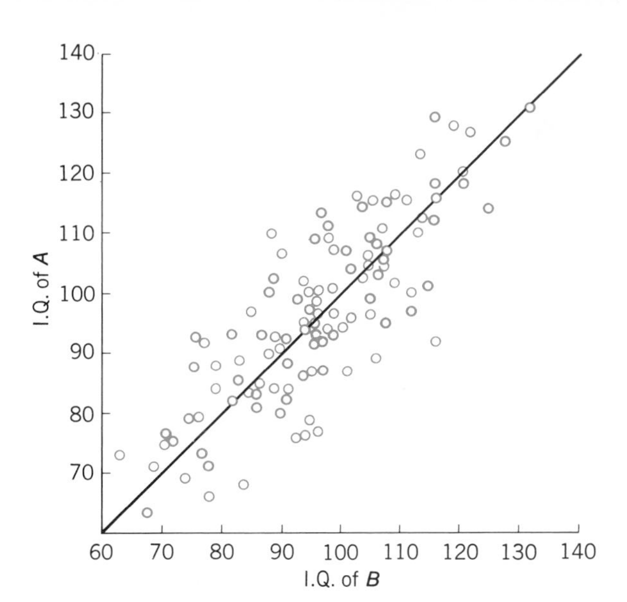

FIGURE 2-6B SCATTERPLOT SHOWING CORRELATION BETWEEN I.Q.'S OF 122 SETS OF CO-TWINS (A AND B ASSIGNED AT RANDOM)

A prediction based on such a correlation is not infallible, but it is much better than a guess.

But what does psychology mean to me?

Are there genuine psychological laws or invariable relationships between psychological variables? Can the findings from experiments be applied to practical, real-life situations? People are so different and variable—their reactions are so complex and influenced by such a multiplicity of factors—that it sometimes seems as if real scientific understanding of human behavior is impossible. Old sayings like "One man's meat is another man's poison" and "There's no accounting for tastes" emphasize the difficulties of making generalizations about human behavior.

On the other hand, there are clearly some regularities in behavior and we rely on these regularities in our everyday lives. For example, in the United States we expect that everyone will drive on the right side of the road, while in Great Britain we expect everyone will drive on the left. We drive in accordance with these regularities, operating with well-learned habits; furthermore, we assume that everyone in our culture has learned these same habits.

Improving Prediction of Behavior

While some aspects of behavior are generally predictable, it is difficult to generalize because individual exceptions occur. In a way psychology may be compared with meteorology. While meteorologists have learned a great deal about the physical processes that cause variations in the weather, prediction is far from perfect. It would be wonderful to be able to predict exactly when the weather will be favorable for launching a satellite, for landing astronauts, for harvesting crops, for picnicking. The fact that meteorologists make mistakes does not make us doubt that it is worthwhile to try to predict the weather.

Progress in psychological research to date justifies similar hopes for better prediction in the future. But we must be very cautious in the application and generalization of psychological research findings. Certainly each human is, to some extent, unique. Each person is in some ways like all other people, in some ways like some other people, and in some ways like no other person. Adding the perspective of comparative psychology, we can state that in some ways the human is like all mammals, while in other ways humans are like no other animal.

Some principles or laws of psychology seem to hold in broad spheres; other principles hold only in narrow spheres. For example, the muscular and neural development of all mammals, including humans, progresses from the head downward, that is, the organs of the upper part of the body are mature before those in the lower part. But if we look at other parts of the animal kingdom we find that there are exceptions to this order of progression. The chick, for example, stands on its legs before it can use its wings, which are its forelimbs. The Russian biopsychologist P. Anokhin formulated the broad principle of **systemogenesis**, which maintains that bodily and behavioral systems develop in the order required by the type of life that a given species lives. The chick must be able to peck grain as soon as it hatches, so it must be able to walk and to perceive bits of food or it will not survive.

It is important to recognize that the principles of psychology are generally based on a limited number of observations and on a limited range of subjects; children, rats, and college sophomores are popular subject populations. A conclusion derived from observations in a highly specialized situation, such as a laboratory, or a particular sample, such as nursery-school children, may prove on later testing to have rather broad applicability. On the other hand, it may not; the conclusion may be valid only for this particular situation or for the specific population studied. The important caution is this: conclusions from such studies can be generalized *only* after they have been tested more widely. If the investigator is studying learning processes in rats, he cannot be sure that the principles he derives apply to humans unless he tests them with humans. In the same way, we cannot be sure, without further testing, whether a program of instruction that helps students of average intelligence will also benefit mentally retarded children or geniuses.

We must also be careful about generalizing from one experimental situation to other kinds of situations. In the illustration given earlier, exposure to aggressive models produced increased aggression among children—in this specific laboratory situation. Does this mean that seeing violent TV shows leads to more aggressive behavior? We cannot be sure without more direct tests, since this situation—TV viewing—is different in many respects from the laboratory. In fact, more direct tests have been made, and they indicate that a number of additional factors must be considered, so that we cannot make simple and direct generalizations (see personality section, p. 204).

In brief, we must be very cautious in generalizing psychological findings, particularly in applying them to subjects or situations that are quite different from the original ones—for example, generalizing from rats to humans or from a laboratory situation to the schoolroom. The reader should consider the applications of each experimental finding with the same healthy skepticism that a scientist displays. Generalizations to different situations or populations should be regarded merely as hypotheses or educated guesses; the validity of generalizations cannot be assumed. Each hypothesis must be tested by systematic study.

The rat learns to press the lever to get a food reward. By studying conditioning in a rat, we can learn much about the behavior of other animals and humans.
(Courtesy Pfizer Inc.)

Applying Ethical Standards

As psychology has grown in scope and effectiveness, increasing numbers of psychologists have become concerned with using their scientific knowledge to promote human welfare. Many achieve that goal directly in their professional activities: clinical psychologists strive to relieve anxiety and enhance personal adjustment; counseling psychologists seek to help people make rational decisions that will be in their best interests; educational psychologists are pleased if their work and advice facilitate effective learning and greater creativity among school children.

The desire to promote human welfare can sometimes place a psychologist on the horns of an ethical dilemma. Suppose he discovers something that could potentially benefit mankind—a technique to reduce prejudice or intergroup tension, for example—

but this technique could be misused to the detriment of mankind—for example, to control votes or political behavior. Should the psychologist communicate this finding that could benefit millions, but, if misused, could have harmful or immoral results? What are the actions appropriate to the "moral" scientist as a knowledgeable citizen? And what role should professional associations such as the American Psychological Association play? Should they actively lobby in Congress for sound and humane governmental programs?

Volumes could be written on the relationships among psychology, society, and ethics. Only two prominent issues will be mentioned here: the treatment of research subjects and the researcher's ethical responsibilities for the use of his findings.

Treatment of Research Subjects

In order to discover something of value the psychologist must do research. He must use subjects and the rights of these subjects must be respected. It is for this reason that certain experiments which are potentially of great social value will never be performed. No ethical psychologist would investigate the sources of mental illness by subjecting babies to cruel and harsh treatment or by depriving them of psychological care and attention. Such experiments are unthinkable, however great their potential benefit to others might be.

Unfortunately, ethical decisions are rarely so clear-cut. Should the psychologist do experiments involving mental or physical stress or the use of drugs? Should the subjects be asked to reveal information that is embarrassing or possibly incriminating? These are not easy questions to answer. Psychologists generally agree that the researcher is, first and foremost, responsible for the welfare of his subjects. He must take all necessary steps to guarantee their privacy, and he is ethically bound to protect any confidences he receives.

Whenever possible, the investigator should inform his subjects of the general nature of the experiment, including any possible discomforts, before asking for voluntary consent to participate in the study. In the case of children, the informed consent of parents is obtained. In the case of animals, committees dedicated to humane treatment of animals are consulted.

It may sometimes be necessary to deceive subjects about the true purpose of an experiment or to give them only limited information. For example, you could not test reactions to surprising information if you forewarned the subjects that they would be surprised. In making a decision about the use of deception in research, the psychologist must carefully balance the welfare of the subjects with the potential benefits of the study. Most subjects are willing to be deceived a bit or to undergo minor discomforts if the results of the study are of real value. After the experiment is completed, the psychologist explains in detail the nature of the deception and the reasons for it, answers any questions, and discusses the research issues at length. The investigator must also be careful to relieve any stress created by the study, and he should give the subject some understanding of his role in the collection of data and of the potential benefit of the study to others.

The Scientist's Responsibility for the Use of Research Findings

Most scientific discoveries are, by themselves, ethically neutral. While they might be used to benefit many, often they could be used in immoral ways as well. There was a time when scientists believed that their sole responsibility was to "search for the truth"; they considered the use of scientific findings to be beyond the scope of science and of their responsibility. But most scientists today do not share this view. In a technological age such as ours, the scientist is often the only one with enough information and understanding to evaluate the consequences of using the findings of his research. If improper use is contemplated, it is the moral scientist who can best prescribe effective countermeasures.

Facing the Ethical Dilemmas

Two concrete incidents will indicate the nature of the ethical dilemmas faced by psychological researchers. These are two accounts of actual happenings taken from a report of the American Psychological Association (1971).

One investigator describes a study involving behavioral measures of the effect of chemical substances and notes that among the uses intended for the substances was the lowering of the will to resist and fight during war and riots. While he hesitated to become involved, he pointed out that the chemical substances were to be substituted for more lethal weapons. He wondered, nevertheless, whether the substances might not be used in military and police actions to which he would be opposed. (APA Monitor, *1971, p. 28*)

What should he have done? If he discovered that a chemical affects the "will to resist," how should that discovery be made public? If you were the scientist, would you publish at all?

A psychologist contributed to a pool of survey research data the data from his study of determinants of opinion on key social and political issues. Among his variables were religious and ethnic affiliation. Later he discovered that another investigator was using his data . . . [to advise] a candidate for political office who hoped to use the results to guide his political campaign. The psychologist in question believed the election of this candidate would be a serious blow to the welfare of the people whom the candidate would govern. . . . Should he do everything possible to withdraw his data or should he take the position that to conduct the proposed analysis . . . , however much he disliked it, is the right of the other investigator? (APA Monitor, *1971, p. 28*)

How would you answer these ethical questions?

Where do we begin our study of psychology?

The eight basic areas of psychology discussed in this book are all interrelated, so that studying any one would be easier if you already knew something about the others. For example, social behavior and personality characteristics are, to a great extent, learned. It would therefore be helpful to know something about how learning occurs before you study social psychology or personality. Learning, in turn, depends on the consequences of behavior—how it is "reinforced." But what reinforces the behavior of a person in the learning situation depends in part upon social factors and in part upon the personality of the learner. So each topic or area circles back on others.

Five Key Concepts

But we have to start somewhere, so let us briefly consider five basic concepts that are important in many sections of the text. These will give you some background for studying the following sections, and they are useful as bridges, relating the sections to each other. Each of these concepts will become richer and more meaningful as it is used in various contexts throughout the book.

Feedback

The first concept, **feedback,** will be used in both a restricted and a broad sense. A person or animal is constantly active, even during sleep, as we will see. He continually monitors and adjusts his activity in accordance with his intentions and with changing circumstances. In the restricted sense, feedback means "the return of part of the output of a system to the input for purposes of regulation and control." For example, when you reach to pick up a pencil, you use the visual information from your hand (input) to reduce steadily the distance between your hand and the pencil (output) (see Figure 2-7). There is also internal feedback, entirely within the body; this

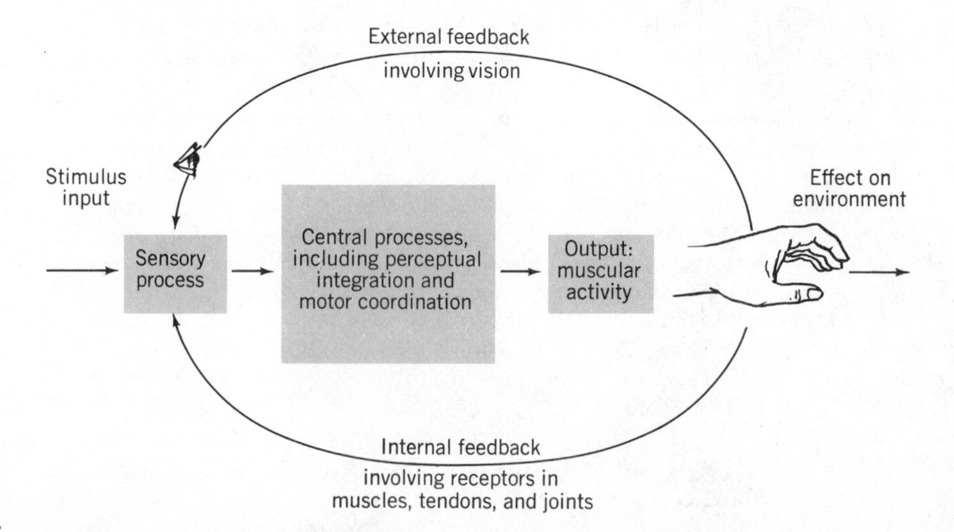

FIGURE 2-7
FEEDBACK INVOLVED IN VISUALLY GUIDED REACHING

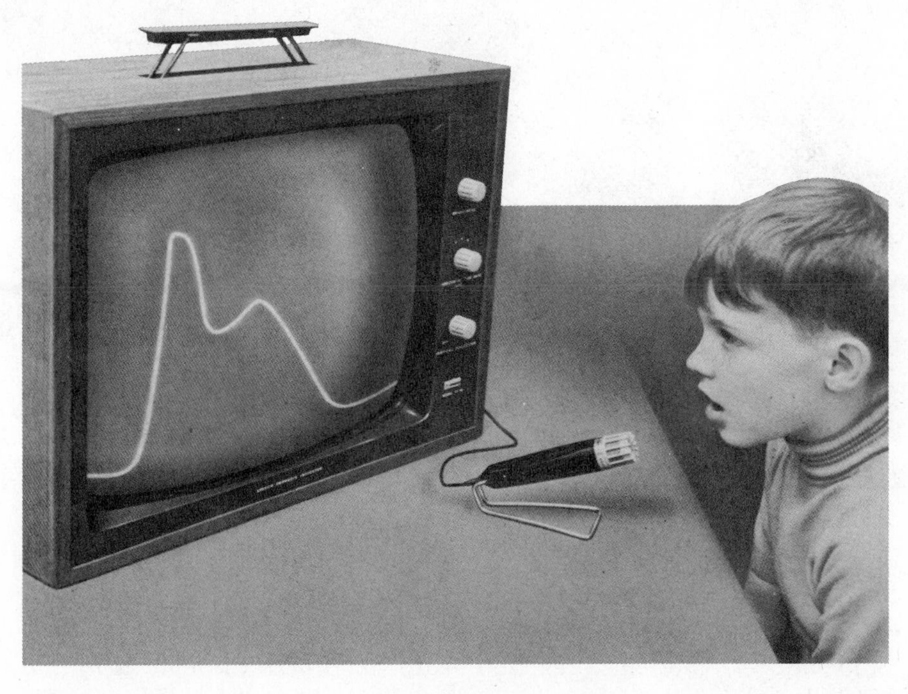

Control of behavior requires *feedback* of information about ongoing responses. Visual feedback helps a deaf child learn to control his speech sounds.
(Courtesy Madsen Electromedics Corp.)

involves sense organs in your muscles, tendons, and joints. While you are not aware of most of this internal feedback, unconscious processes of coordination regulate the activities of many muscles to achieve the intended goal.

Feedback occurs in social behavior too. Suppose, for example, that you join a new group where you hope to make friends. You make some statements about current social issues, and this elicits expressions of opinion from other members of the group. You then examine your opinions in relation to theirs, and very likely you attempt to reduce the differences among these opinions, perhaps by changing your own or perhaps by trying to persuade others to change theirs. What actually will occur depends upon a number of social factors, including the prestige of the others, the size of the discrepancy between your views and theirs, and your personal characteristics, especially your tendencies to conform or to maintain independent judgments. Feedback in social situations is complex, but in order to understand social behavior, we must be attentive to the continual interactions between the individual and his social environment.

Learning

Feedback is essential for most of the adaptive modification of behavior that we call **learning.** Many, many years of research have made it abundantly clear that much of human behavior is learned—a result of training and practice. "Precisely that behavior which is widely felt to characterize man as a rational being or as a member of a particular nation or social class is learned rather than innate" (Dollard & Miller, 1951, p. 25).

Learning changes behavior—in areas as diverse as motor skills and academic performance.
(Van Bucher, Photo Researchers; Erich Hartmann, Magnum)

Acquisition of language and culture are obvious examples of learning, and learning is also involved in facial expressions and motor skills and even, as recent research has shown, in internal bodily functions. For example, digestion and blood circulation—and hence emotional reactions—are modified through learning. Detailed discussion of the learning process is presented in Section Six of this book, Chapters 18 and 19. At this point we merely want to stress the importance of learning and, in the following paragraphs, to introduce some of the major principles of learning which appear in many parts of the book.

Reinforcement

The consequences of behavioral acts often feed back upon the individual, causing him to change his behavior—a process called **reinforcement.** Responses are strengthened if they are rewarded (reinforced)—that is, similar responses are likely to occur again in the same setting. A hungry rat in a maze makes a left turn at a choice point and finds food at the end of the runway. The food is the reinforcer; the behavior has been rewarded. The next time the rat is in that maze he is more likely to turn left at that particular choice point.

Analogously, a two-year-old, in the process of learning to say words, is being coaxed by his mother to say "cookie." She holds a cookie before him, and after several attempts he makes a sound somewhat like "cookie." The delighted mother hugs the child affectionately and gives him the cookie as a reward. Her embrace and the cookie are reinforcements; the response of saying "cookie" has been reinforced. The next time the child sees a cookie, he is likely to repeat the word.

The more often the rat is rewarded for turning left, or the child for saying cookie, the greater the likelihood that these responses will be made again. On the other hand, if the response is

ART AND PSYCHOLOGY

For centuries, artists have portrayed and interpreted major aspects of human experience with insight and imagination. During the last hundred years, psychologists have sought to achieve a scientific understanding of many of the same human experiences. Today artists and scientists not only carry on their own endeavors, but each group provides material for the other.

Whether you are alone or with others, your behavior is strongly influenced by social norms.

At the Moulin Rouge, Henri de Toulouse-Lautrec
Helen Birch Bartlett Memorial Collection
Courtesy of the Art Institute of Chicago

Motivations and emotions are major topics in the study of personality.

The Cry, Edvard Munch
National Gallery, Oslo

The effects of early mother-child relationships on later behavior are studied by the developmental psychologist.

Mother and Child, Pablo Picasso
Courtesy of the Art Institute of Chicago

Intelligence, intellectual development, and the acquisition of knowledge are the concerns of the cognitive psychologist.

The Young Governess, Jean-Baptiste-Simeon Chardin
Andrew Mellon Collection
Courtesy The National Gallery of Art, Washington, D.C

The search for general principles of learning and memory is the task of the psychologist of learning.

Scholars of the Northern Ch'i Collating the Classics (detail), attributed to Yen Li-pen, ca. 11th cy Sung Dynasty
Denman Waldo Ross Collection
Courtesy Museum of Fine Arts, Boston

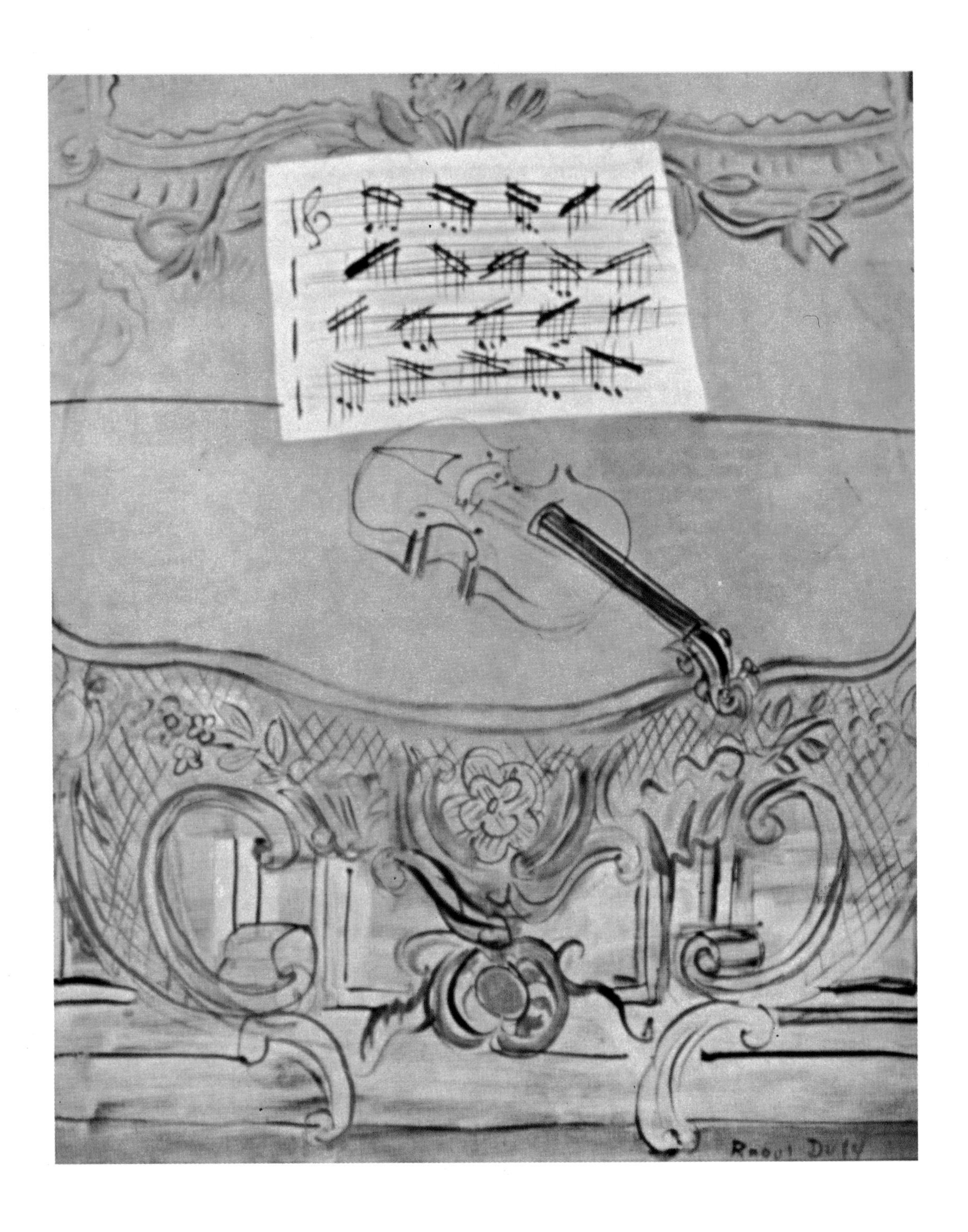

Understanding how patterns of sight and sound are captured by sensory systems and interpreted is the province of the psychologist of perception.

The Yellow Violin, Raoul Dufy
From the Sam and Ayala Zacks Collection

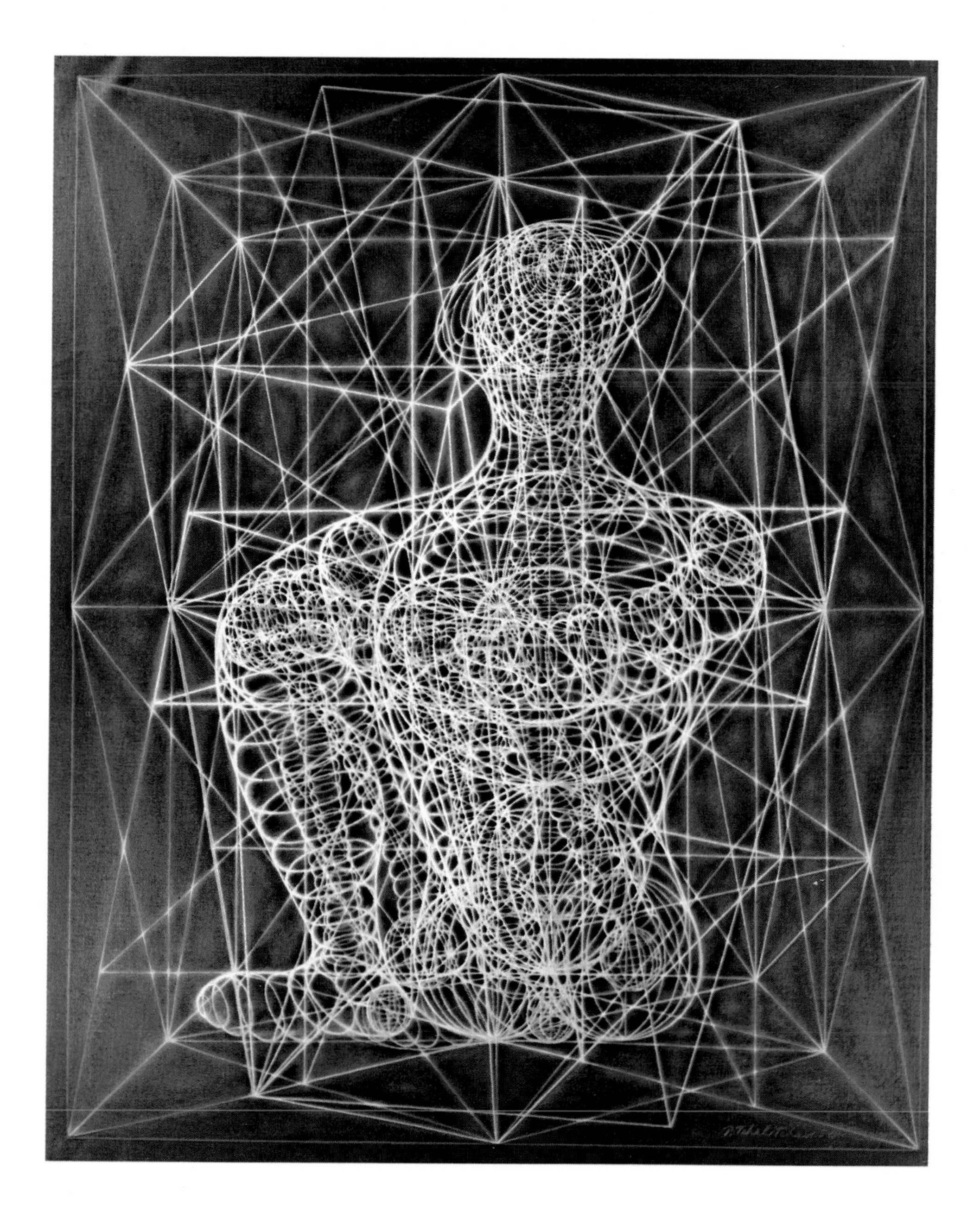

The nervous system has been described as a scheme of lines and nodal points. If its activity is represented by points of light, some are stationary and flash rhythmically, while others stream in trains. The brain is "an enchanted loom where millions of flashing shuttles weave a dissolving pattern, always a meaningful pattern though never an abiding one" (C. S. Sherrington). Discovering these neural patterns and investigating their functions are concerns of the biological psychologist.

Mercure, Pavel Tchelitchew
Collection of Mrs. L. B. Wescott,
photo by Michael Ciavolino

Most of the population of the earth is not human; the comparative psychologist studies the wide range of animal behavior both because of its intrinsic interest and because of its potential contributions to the understanding of human behavior.

The Peaceable Kingdom, Edward Hicks
Collection of Edgar William and Bernice Chrysler Garbisch

not followed by reinforcement, the probability of repetition decreases; this process is called **extinction.** If the rat running the maze does not find a reward (food) at the end of the maze, he is less likely to run the next time. After many experiences of nonreinforcement, he may not run at all. In technical terms, the response has been extinguished.

Clearly much of our learning involves reward, but does *all* learning occur through reinforcement? Some theorists suggest that the answer to this question is "yes," that reinforcement is involved even in cases where no experimenter, parent, or other person delivers rewards. For example, without receiving any external rewards, the infant learns how the shape of an object changes as it moves or as it is seen from different angles; he also learns that objects persist even when they are lost from sight. It has been suggested that in these cases of early perceptual learning, the reinforcement is

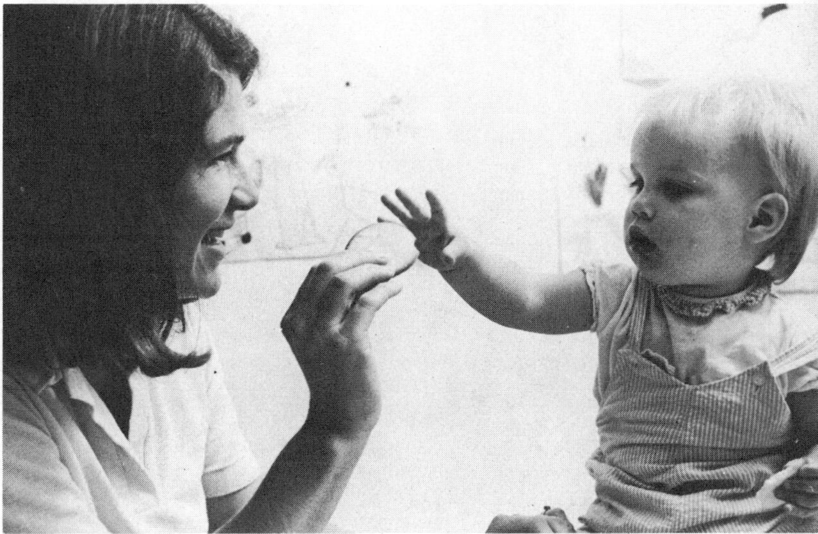

Animals and humans will repeat responses that bring *reinforcement.*
(Courtesy U.S. Navy; Ted Polumbaum)

internal—that reduction of uncertainty is reinforcing to the child. This is a plausible argument, although it is a difficult one to test. And, as we shall see, external manipulation of rewards does not seem to be important in many cases of human and animal learning (see p. 469). Consequently, many current investigators are focusing on the *processes* of learning, without regard to reinforcement. Much current research stresses information processing by humans and animals—that is, how information is taken in, assimilated to previous knowledge, stored in memory, and retrieved (see p. 450).

Motivation

Practically all behavior, everything we do—learning, working, studying, playing, solving problems, even perceiving—is **motivated;** that is, most responses are determined not only by environmental conditions but also by states within the organism—needs, drives, desires, wishes, wants—and they are generally directed toward some goal or goals. Some motives or drives are called **primary drives** because they are not dependent on learning for their basic motive force (although learning may affect the social expression of these drives). An example is hunger, a primary drive to obtain food, which is based on unlearned biological needs. Other motives, sometimes called **secondary drives,** are learned or acquired desires for particular goals such as attention, affection, approval, power, money, acceptance, or achievement. For purposes of this brief discussion, the important point is that motives, needs, or desires impel the individual to action. Basically, the topic of motivation deals with the question of *why* animals and human beings do what they do.

We are not always consciously aware of why we are doing what we are doing. On the contrary, all of us at some time or other do things for reasons that we do not understand and cannot state; we are sometimes driven by *unconscious* motives.

Motivation is obviously related to reinforcement. Food will not function as a reinforcer if the animal is not hungry. The child who wants neither a cookie nor attention will not learn to say "cookie" given these "rewards." In short, the motive determines what reinforcement will be appropriate or effective.

Differences in motivation can help to explain different reactions to the same stimulus or situation. For example, if a child has little or no desire for academic success—if he is not "achievement motivated"—he will not work for grades in school. Another child,

Motivation includes primary drives that are biological and more complex ones that are social in nature.
(Gaston Le Page, National Audubon Society; Ted Polumbaum)

no more intelligent and having no better educational background, may be highly motivated to achieve and he will work hard to get good grades.

Heredity-Environment Interactions

While we have been concentrating primarily on the role of learning in shaping and changing an individual's interactions with the environment, we cannot ignore the critical hereditary determinants of behavior. Since ancient times men have been asking, "Which contributes more to human behavior, heredity or environment?" The question is the core of the long-lasting controversy between the proponents of **nativism** and the proponents of **empiricism.** In its extreme historical form, the nativist position held that most behavioral tendencies are innate, inborn—in effect, "wired into" the organism as part of its biological makeup. In contrast, the empiricists viewed behavior as resulting almost entirely from training, learning, and past experience, and they minimized the constraints imposed by heredity.

Few contemporary psychologists hold either of these extreme positions. Instead, most accept the view that the individual's behavior is the outcome of *complex interactions* between his hereditary potentials (nature) and experimental and environmental factors (nurture).

We can of course ask questions about whether heredity or environment contributes more to specific characteristics or **traits,** such as height, intelligence, or activity level. But in most cases, the

Identical twins are often used as subjects in studies of the relative influences of *heredity and environment* on behavior.
(Susan Richter, Photo Researchers)

interaction between heredity and environmental forces is so complex that it is extremely difficult, or impossible, to disentangle their separate contributions. Certainly individual differences in height and in activity level are attributable in large part to hereditary factors. But even when considering these variables, we must remember that individual or group differences arise within specific environments. In different environments, the genetically influenced differences might have been reduced or enhanced. An individual's height *is* influenced by nutritional, as well as genetic, factors; his activity level is influenced by the environment in which he grows up.

For most aspects of human behavior, the interaction of nature and nurture is as yet poorly defined. To what extent is aggression an inherent part of man's nature and to what extent is it a learned response, shaped and maintained by reinforcements? To what extent are individual and group differences in intelligence determined by heredity and to what extent are they due to differences in experience? Many important questions of this sort are still unanswered (and some of them may not be answerable at all) but research has produced some suggestive findings and psychologists are learning how to look for more precise answers.

Research itself is a continuing feedback process, involving attempts to understand behavior, tests of hypotheses, modifications of ideas to achieve a better fit between hypotheses and findings, and new attempts to check new ideas. We will see this cyclical process in action in many sections of the text, as psychologists attempt to gain a more accurate and more complete understanding of human and animal behavior.

SUMMARY

The psychologist often begins his work by posing significant social or personal questions, which he then formulates as specific hypotheses that can be tested objectively and reliably. These are accepted or rejected on the basis of empirical evidence derived from objective observations, experiments, and precise measurements. Two fundamental steps characterize an experiment—the manipulation of independent variables by the experimenter and the systematic measurement of the effects (the dependent variables). Most psychological research involves experimental and control groups and, wherever possible, subjects are assigned at random to these groups. Many human psychological phenomena cannot be studied experimentally, but hypotheses about these phenomena can be tested by observing naturally occurring events and the relationships among these.

Statistical methods are necessary in order to put data into

manageable form, to quantify relationships between variables, and to interpret findings. Statistical descriptions usually include measures of central tendency, such as the mean and median, and of variability (standard deviation). Tests of statistical significance help us to determine whether a difference between two groups is trustworthy and likely to be repeatable or might simply result from errors of sampling. The coefficient of correlation expresses the degree of relationship between two variables, for example, between achievement motivation and tested intelligence.

Caution must be used in applying and generalizing psychological research findings; some findings seem to apply in broad spheres, others only in narrow spheres. Without further systematic tests, we cannot generalize psychological findings from one group of subjects to another (for example, from rats to humans) or from one situation to another (from a laboratory to a school).

Frequently decisions about psychological research involve profound ethical issues. The welfare and rights of subjects are of paramount importance to the researcher, and he must always be alert to the possibility of the improper use of the research findings and take proper precautions that this does not occur.

We begin our study of the content of psychology with brief discussions of five key concepts: feedback, learning, reinforcement, motivation, and heredity-environment interaction. Each of these concepts is important in many areas of psychology, and you will encounter them frequently in subsequent sections of the book.

RECOMMENDED READING

American Psychological Association. *A Career in Psychology.* Washington: American Psychological Association, 1970.

Descriptions of the major basic and applied fields of psychology together with information about the training required to become a professional psychologist.

Clark, K. E., & Miller, G. A. (Eds.) *Psychology: Behavioral and Social Science Survey.* New York: Prentice-Hall, 1970.

A short paperback, written under the auspices of the National Academy of Sciences and the Social Science Research Council, that reviews the field both as a social and behavioral science and as a profession dedicated to human welfare. It concludes with some recommendations for the further development of psychology.

Deese, J. *Psychology as Science and Art.* New York: Harcourt Brace Jovanovich, 1972.

Five essays on the critical problem, "Can psychology be a science?" Discusses the difficulties of obtaining psychological knowledge, respect for the knowledge we have acquired, and motivation to look for better ways of acquiring psychological knowledge.

Doherty, M. W., & Shemberg, K. M. *Asking Questions about Behavior: An Introduction to What Psychologists Do.* New York: Scott, Foresman & Co., 1970.

A short paperback that shows how your interests and concerns can be turned into meaningful research questions.

Hardyck, C. D., & Petrinovich, L. F. *Introduction to Statistics for the Behavioral Sciences.* Philadelphia: Saunders, 1969.

A sound easy-to-understand presentation of the basic concepts and methods of statistics, as applied to psychological research.

Helson, H., & Bevan, W. *Contemporary Approaches to Psychology.* Princeton, N.J.: Van Nostrand, 1967.

A relatively short handbook of research methods and techniques; good treatment of experimental methods in sensory processes and perception.

Kaplan, A. *The Conduct of Inquiry.* San Francisco: Chandler, 1964.

A clear exposition of the general nature of the scientific method and its application in the behavioral sciences.

Miller, G. A. *Psychology: The Science of Mental Life.* New York: Harper & Row, 1962.

A short readable book that presents some of the main currents of psychology in terms of the work of such pioneers as William James, Sigmund Freud, Francis Galton, Alfred Binet, and Ivan Pavlov.

SECTION TWO

SOCIAL PSYCHOLOGY

By Elliot Aronson

Preview

Several years ago I hired a young man to help me repaint my house. He was a Vietnam veteran, recently returned to civilian life, and he had taken up the craft of painting. I enjoyed working with him; he was pleasant, honest, friendly, industrious, and proud of his work. One day, during a coffee break, we were chatting about the Vietnamese war; I made the point that a great number of innocent people—including women and children, in South Vietnam as well as in North Vietnam—were being slaughtered. His answer was stated without apparent anger or vindictiveness—indeed, it was stated in a mild and matter-of-fact tone of voice . . . and it chilled me to the bone. He said, "Hell, Doc, those aren't people, those are Vietnamese." Further probing convinced me that this was no mere figure of speech; the house painter firmly believed that these people were less human than he or I.[1]

How does an individual come to acquire such an attitude? What is it based on? What function does it serve for him? How basic or permanent is it? How does it affect and how is it affected by the individual's behavior? Can such an attitude be changed? How?

These are questions that constitute much of the subject matter of **social psychology.** These and the related questions—Is a systematic attempt to change attitudes desirable? Is it ethical?—are among the most important facing society today. In this section there are data based on systematic research which will have a bearing on the answers to these questions. It will be up to the reader to decide whether the science of social psychology has reached the point in its development where definitive or even cogent answers can be given.

There are many ways of defining social psychology. On a very general level, social psychology has been defined as the study of man's relationship with his fellowman. This definition makes sense and has a touch of poetry in it. But a moment's reflection reveals that as a definition it is at once too broad and too narrow. It is too broad in the sense that the word "relationship" covers a multitude of qualitatively different events, from the love between a husband and wife to the obedience of an army recruit to the commands of his sergeant. It is too narrow in the sense that social psychological phenomena are not limited to *Homo sapiens*; while it is certainly true that man is a social animal, it is equally true that many other species are social animals as well.

[1] I first reported this incident to a large class at the University of Texas during the fall semester of 1969, just a few weeks before news of the My Lai massacre broke. It is interesting to note that in April 1971 Lieutenant Calley's psychiatric report stated that Calley did not consider the people he massacred to be people: "He did not feel as if he were killing humans but rather, that they were animals with whom one could not speak or reason." (*Time*, 1971, p. 18)

Although this section will be dealing exclusively with human social psychology, it would be prudent to try to define social psychology in a manner that does not exclude subhumans. In order to provide a more systematic and functional definition of social psychology, it might be most useful to state the kinds of problems that social psychologists typically investigate. These include such diverse topics as conformity, communication, aggression, prejudice, human attraction, opinion change, leadership, group dynamics, and propaganda. These topics are diverse but they have at least one common factor: they all involve *social influence*—one individual influencing the perception, opinions, or behavior of another. For humans, the simple fact that other people exist is profoundly important. No one is immune to the influence of others. On an obvious level we can think of how a devoted husband is influenced by the wishes of his wife, how an obedient young child is influenced by his mother's demands, or how a timid bureaucrat is influenced by the specific orders emanating from his superior. On a more subtle level we should point out the fact that not only is a child influenced by his mother but the mother is influenced by her young child as well. And on a still more subtle level, it is important to note that even an apparently "antisocial" individual like a revolutionary is influenced by the system he is attempting to overturn, and that even a hermit living in the isolation of a secluded cave is influenced by his prior associations with people.

While it is certainly the case that none of us can escape from social influence, thoughts of revolutionaries and hermits do not dominate our thoughts about the influence process. Rather, we think more about the individual yielding to the explicit or implicit pressure of the culture or subgroup to which he belongs. In short, we think about conformity. It is to this topic that we now turn.

NEW
3

3

Conformity

What is conformity?
Who conforms?
Why conformity?
What are the different levels of social influence?

What is conformity?

Conformity can be defined as a change in a person's opinions or behavior as a result of real or imagined pressure from another person or a group. In common parlance, conformity usually has some negative connotations; to be called a conformist is to be called weak, a follower, a person who cannot or will not think for himself. This connotation is bolstered by the mass media; Hollywood, for example, consistently makes heroes of the nonconformist—the dashing figure who goes his own way in spite of tremendous group pressure. And yet, a moment's reflection should make it perfectly clear that if there is to be a society at all, there *must* be a significant degree of conformity to the laws and customs of that society. A society of nonconformists is a contradiction in terms. Conformity in certain cases may be weakness, but without a basic, underlying, and willing conformity to sensible laws and values, we would have chaos. There would not be enough policemen to protect us from the looters and the rapists; we could not trust our best friends. There are those who complain of the lack of law and order, but there is an interesting question on the other side too. Why is there any law and order in the first place?

What causes people to conform to group pressure? What is the nature of this group pressure? These are very broad and complex questions. In my judgment the most useful way for a social psychologist to attempt to answer such questions is by studying a carefully constructed, carefully controlled situation which captures the basic qualities of a conformity situation. Imagine the following scene: You have volunteered to participate in an experiment on perceptual judgment. You enter a room with four other participants. The experimenter shows all of you a straight line, labeled *X*. Simultaneously, he shows you three comparison lines, labeled *A*, *B*, and *C*. Your job is to judge which of the three lines is closest in length to the test line. See Figure 3-1. The judgment is an incredibly easy one. It is perfectly clear to you that line *B* is the correct answer. But it's not your turn to respond. The person whose turn it is looks carefully at the lines and chooses *A*. You sit there in disbelief. "How can he believe it's *A* when it's clearly *B*?" you say to yourself. "He must be either blind or crazy." Now it's the second person's turn to respond. He also indicates that it's *A*. You are inclined to conclude that both of these people are blind. But then the next person responds and he also says that it's line *A*. You take another look at those lines—"Maybe *I'm* the one who's blind," you murmur inaudibly. Now it's the fourth person's turn and he also judges the correct line to be line *A*. Finally it's your turn. "Why, it's *A*, of course," you murmur. "Any fool can see that!"

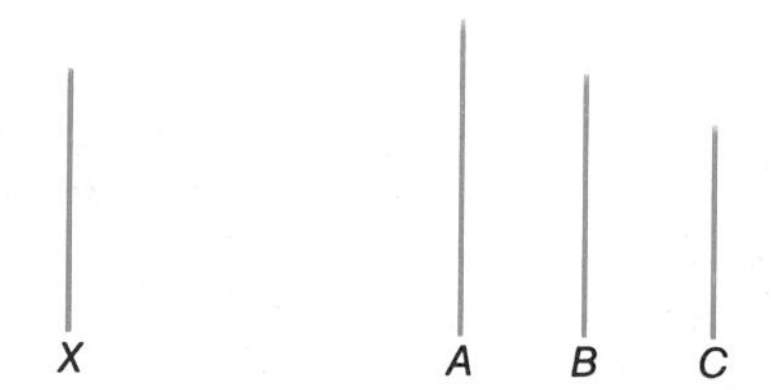

FIGURE 3-1
ASCH COMPARISON "TEST"
Subjects are asked to state which of the three comparison lines (*A*, *B*, and *C*) is equal in length to *X*.

After reading the above paragraph, the reader may disagree with my guess about what he would do. Of course, you may be right. If you actually were in such a situation, you might stand up and state your initial judgment even in the face of a unanimous opinion to the contrary. Social psychologists have no way of knowing what any single individual reader would do in this situation. But we do know how *most* people would behave because the situation described above is not a nightmarish fantasy; it is a very close approximation to a classic experimental situation designed by Solomon Asch (1951). How could the experimenter be so lucky as to have all those people making the wrong guess? He wasn't lucky, he was merely diabolical. (For a discussion of ethical constraints, see Spotlight 3-1.) In this, as in many social psychological experiments, the experimenter employed the technique of the accomplice, the confederate or "stooge." Specifically, the first four people who responded were the experimenter's accomplices who had been instructed to answer incorrectly. The purpose of the experiment was not to investigate perceptual judgment at all—it was to study the effects of group pressure on conformity.

In Asch's experiment the subjects were college students; each subject was asked to state his judgment on a series of trials in which he was presented each time with one test line and a series of lines of various lengths. On those occasions when the real subject was not put under group pressure, he always answered correctly. This result indicates that as a perceptual task the line-judging test

In the Asch line-judging conformity experiment, the naïve subject is puzzled by judgments of others (bottom left), but he finally decides, "I have to call them the way I see them."
(William Vandivert © 1955 *Scientific American*)

was a simple one. However, when faced with several fellow students who all gave the same incorrect answers, many subjects conformed to this implicit pressure from the group. There are two important data: (1) approximately three out of four subjects conformed on at least one trial; (2) of the entire series of trials, 35 percent of the responses conformed to the incorrect judgment of the stooges. Thus, although we don't know how any specific person would have responded, we do know that relatively few college students were able to resist completely the pressures to conform.

SPOTLIGHT 3-1

The Ethics of Experiments

In reading the details of the Asch line-judging experiment, the reader may have felt a twinge of pain as he empathized with the plight of the experimental subject who was being put through this procedure, or a rush of anger at the apparent callousness of the researcher. Experiments in social psychology do raise some serious ethical questions. Basically, there are two problems: deception and discomfort. We will illustrate these problems by using Asch's line-judging experiment as an example.

Deception. In the line-judging study the experimenter lied to the participants by telling them that he was interested in testing perceptual judgment. The experimenter also implied that the other people were real people behaving honestly; they weren't—they were stooges who were instructed to behave dishonestly.

Discomfort. In the line-judging experiment subjects were put into a state of conflict which was almost certain to cause them some uneasy feelings. Specifically, if an individual succumbed to group pressure, he might feel like a coward afterward; if he resisted pressure, he might worry about what the other participants were thinking about him.

Some readers may feel that research should never be done if deception is employed or if it causes subjects psychological discomfort. Others may feel that the ends are so important that they justify any means. Most social psychologists take a position somewhere between these extremes and wrestle with the ethical question while perched on the horns of this dilemma.

Why do social psychologists lie to people and cause discomfort? Are they sadists? Probably not. The major reason is that it's frequently the only way to find out the answers to important questions. For example, how *does* one find out about conformity? Well, one might simply *ask* people if they would conform in such a situation. That's been tried. You might guess what happened. Lo and behold, almost no one stated that he would have yielded if placed in a situation similar to the one in Asch's experiment. How come? People have a desire to look good. Since conformity is generally regarded as unattractive behavior, few people would admit to it—perhaps not even to themselves. By the same token, if the participants had been informed in advance that it was an experiment on conformity, then chances are they would have been on their guard. Consequently, the results would not be generalizable to a real social situation—one where people are faced with

Who conforms?

Are there differences between the kinds of people who conform and those who don't in this type of situation? Yes. The most consistent findings are that women conform more than men, that unintelligent people conform more than intelligent people, and that subjects with low self-esteem conform to a greater extent than do those with high self-esteem. This should not be construed to mean that the *only* people who conform are dumb girls who don't think very highly of themselves. A lot of bright men with high self-esteem con-

pressure to conform and are not aware that psychologists will be scrutinizing their tendency to conform. Likewise, if the subjects had been told the truth about the other people—that they were in the employ of the experimenter—the results would not have been very interesting.

Given the fact that some questions cannot be answered without the use of deception or discomfort, the experimenter must obey certain rules. First and foremost, he should not be glib about the use of deception or about causing discomfort. This means two things: (1) He should not conduct an experiment unless he's convinced that it is important—i.e., worth whatever price he must pay in terms of his own self-image as a result of lying to people and the price that the participant must pay in terms of discomfort. Since these prices are occasionally steep, most experimenters do not conduct an experiment "just to fool around" or just to see what happens. (2) He should try to design the experiment so that a minimum of discomfort and deception is employed—consistent with a reasonable test of the hypothesis.

Finally, the most important concern should be the welfare of his subjects. Thus, if a particular procedure seems to be causing a great deal of discomfort, a moral experimenter will curtail the experiment. In addition, at the end of the session the experimenter typically spends a lot of time with each subject explaining the true purpose of the study, why he's interested in the problem, and why the deception was necessary. If this is done in a gentle and considerate manner, the experimenter can provide the participant with a valuable educational experience as well as some insight into his own behavior. Most important, by taking the time and effort the experimenter can relieve whatever discomfort might have been caused by the procedures he employed.

It should be mentioned too that in the typical case the judgment of whether or not the degree of discomfort and deception is too severe is not left to a single experimenter. Most schools have committees of respected scholars who monitor the ethics of experiments at those schools; most of the research supported by funds of the U.S. Government must satisfy certain minimal ethical requirements; and, if all else fails, the American Psychological Association will "excommunicate" members who practice in violation of clearly stated ethical standards.

(For a more complete discussion of ethical issues in social psychology, see Aronson and Carlsmith, 1969.)

formed also. But there was less conformity among people with these characteristics. The picture that emerges is a coherent one and makes sense: People who have been encouraged to assert themselves and are successful learn to think highly of themselves and, consequently, have greater resistance to group pressure. In our culture, men are encouraged to assert themselves more than women; if they are intelligent, chances are that their own judgment tends to be correct more often than not. People who are correct or whose judgment is often respected tend to develop high self-esteem which, again, helps them resist pressure to conform.

The Asch experiment is a good example of an interesting kind of conformity situation—one which is subtle and also common in our society. It's a situation in which the group pressure is not explicit—but very powerful nevertheless. No one was telling the subject to behave in a particular way. No one was offering him a bribe for responding against his initial visual judgment nor was anyone overtly threatening to punish him if he didn't comply. Each accomplice was apparently doing his own thing—and by creating the illusion that they were in unanimous agreement, the accomplices served to pressure most of the subjects into doing something other than *their* own thing.

Experimental investigations of conformity to group pressure have not been limited to unimportant phenomena such as judgments of the size of a line; they have involved opinion situations and matters of fact as well. The important situational determinant of conformity in all these studies was the agreement of the majority. If all people in the vicinity are making the same erroneous judgment (whether the judgment involves the length of a line, or the life expectancy of a baby born in America, or the distance between San Francisco and New York), there is a strong tendency for people to conform—even if the correct choice is obvious and unambiguous.

Why conformity?

In the Asch situation there was no explicit punishment offered for nonconformity and no explicit reward offered for conformity. Why did many people yield to the unanimous group pressure? What was in it for them? Think about it for a moment. There are several possible reasons and these can be broken down into two broad categories: (1) It is possible that the unanimous majority managed to convince the lone subject that his perception was inaccurate. (2) The rewards and punishments could have been implicit; the lone subject, though knowing that he was correct, went along in order to please the majority or avoid antagonizing them. In other words, he was trying to live up to their expectations in order to be liked by them or to avoid being disliked.

Conformity Is Sensible

When we look at the "why" of conformity, the complexity of the phenomenon begins to emerge. There may be some real and important differences in the nature of the group pressures involved in various types of conformity. In some cases it seems reasonable to assume that conventions or customs develop and people conform to them because the conventions are adaptive and make sense in and of themselves. For example, driving on the right-hand side of the road makes sense—people do it not *simply* because everyone else is doing it; because everyone else *is* driving on the right-hand side of the road, conformity is a good way to avoid accidents. In short, conformity in this example is highly adaptive.

One can also argue that under certain conditions it makes sense to rely on other people's judgments as a way of finding out what reality is. Specifically, if you are in an ambiguous physical or social situation, you might look at the behaviors of others to help you determine what is going on. Suppose you are suddenly thrust into an exotic culture you know nothing about—and you are in the company of three anthropologists who are experts on that culture. You notice that when encountering natives wearing green turbans, all of the anthropologists invariably bow deeply from the waist. It would seem reasonable for you to conform to this behavior because the anthropologists are more expert than you about the customs of these people—one might reasonably assume that people with green turbans are noblemen and bowing to them constitutes good and reasonable behavior in that culture.

Conforming to behavior patterns of another culture may be a reasonable and appropriate response.
(UPI)

Right or Wrong—Conformity Can Be Rewarding

The difference between the group pressures in the exotic culture and those in the line-judging situation is this: In the case of the anthropologists, the conformist relies on behavior of other people as a frame of reference in an ambiguous situation—he is deciding what is right, reasonable, proper, or safe on the basis of what is being done by people who should know. In the line-judging situation it is more likely that the conformist is knowingly making errors—but is going along in order to live up to the expectations of others.

How can we be certain that this interpretation is correct and not the other, that Asch's subjects actually became convinced that the unanimous majority was correct in its judgment of the lines? How might a psychologist find out? Well, he could ask the subjects who participated in Asch's experiment. This is probably not the best way to find out; people do not like to admit that they have conformed to subtle group pressure; several might insist that their influenced judgment was correct even though secretly they really don't think so. Perhaps a better technique would be to repeat the basic situation of the Asch experiment—but allow the subject to respond in private when indicating his judgment. If the subject's actual perception of physical reality was influenced by the unanimous majority, then this influence should show up even if he answered anonymously. If, however, his actual perception was not influenced by the other people and his response coincided with the majority response in order to please or avoid displeasing the group, then his private answer should reveal less conformity. Psychologists who have compared private and public responses have found more conformity when subjects were forced to answer publicly than when they were allowed to remain anonymous (Deutsch & Gerard, 1955).

So it looks as though the conformity to group pressure in the Asch situation is temporary behavior, behavior which all but vanishes when the subject is allowed to cloak his identity from those applying the pressure. In short, it is quite clear that the subjects would not continue to see lines incorrectly after leaving the experiment. The kind of conformity produced in the Asch situation does not last beyond the presence of the group that caused it. But of course this does not mean that *all* conformity is transient. Recall the example of the three anthropologists bowing to the people in green turbans. If you made a subsequent visit to the exotic culture without the company of anthropologists and were confronted by a native in a green turban, wouldn't you bow from the waist? You would do this not because you fear to displease the people who influenced you (the anthropologists) but because the majority of experts has provided you with a model which you can regard as right, reasonable, or appropriate.

What are the different levels of social influence?

In the preceding paragraphs we described two kinds of conformity in more or less commonsense terms. The distinction between the two was based upon a difference in the person's motivation to conform and the relative permanence of the conforming behavior. We can now move beyond this "commonsense" distinction to a more complex and more useful taxonomy which applies not only to conformity, but to the entire area of social influence. Instead of using the simple term "conformity," let us distinguish among three levels of social influence: compliance, identification, and internalization (Kelman, 1961).

Compliance refers to the performance of a behavior or the statement of a belief for the sole purpose of obtaining a reward or avoiding a punishment from the person who is inducing the compliance. Remove the promise of the reward or the threat of punishment and the behavior eventually ceases. Thus, one can induce a South Vietnamese peasant to recite the pledge of allegiance to the American flag by threatening him with pain if he doesn't comply or by promising to feed and enrich him if he does. Remove the promise or the threat and the Vietnamese will cease reciting the pledge of allegiance.

Identification refers to a level of social influence based upon the individual's desire to be like the influencer. Thus, if an individual finds another person (or a group) attractive or appealing in some way, he will be inclined to accept influence from that person (or group) and adopt his values and attitudes—not in order to obtain a reward or avoid a punishment, but to be like that person. Little girls frequently put on their mother's clothes in an attempt to be like mother. As they grow older, they frequently take on their mother's values and attitudes as well—at least temporarily. (See also Ch. 9, p. 184, and Ch. 14, p. 326, for a further discussion of identification.)

Internalization is the deepest and most permanent level of social influence. A value or an attitude becomes internalized because it seems to be correct, as in the case when an individual advocating a particular point of view seems expert and trustworthy—his position makes sense and can be integrated into our value system. We tend to believe what he says because of our own desire to be right. Once a position becomes internalized, it becomes resistant to change—even if the original advocate changes his own position. Once incorporated, the position becomes independent of the person who first got us to believe it. In this sense it differs greatly from identification.

Comparison of Levels of Social Influence

Let us compare the three levels of social influence. Compliance is the most superficial and least permanent because the individual is well aware that he is performing an activity merely for the reward or the avoidance of punishment. If a gun is held to my head, I would probably say most anything that the gunholder asked me to say. But after he left the scene I would not be much affected by what I had said. This is not to say that rewards and punishments are unimportant. They are terribly important as a means of getting

Levels of social influence: prisoners of war exhibit compliance, contemporary youth identify with the stars of the rock culture, a monk, whose values are internalized, burns himself as a protest to war.
(L. to R.: James Pickerell, Black Star; Charles Harbutt, Magnum; UPI)

someone to learn and to perform specific activities. But it is a very limited form of social influence because the reward or punishment must remain present if the activities are to continue for very long.

Social influence through identification is deeper and less ephemeral than mere compliance. Continuous reward or punishment is no longer essential for the behavior or the belief to continue. Indeed, the physical presence of the person identified with is not even necessary as long as he continues to remain an important person in the identifier's life and continues to hold the beliefs in question. Even so, there may occur a change in attitudes and behavior because of a change in the person or group with whom the individual identifies. The little girl who identified with her mother and thus accepted her mother's view of life will eventually grow up; perhaps she will go off to college where she might develop strong and important friendships with a group of students who have a totally different set of beliefs. If her relationship with these new friends becomes more salient than her relationship with her mother, her values and beliefs will change through the same process—identification.

The effect of social influence through identification can also be overwhelmed by the process we have described as internalization. A person's desire to be correct is an extremely powerful force. Thus, if a person has adopted a belief through the process of identification and he is presented with an opposite belief supported by a set of facts from an unimpeachable source, he will probably change his belief. It is for this reason that internalization is the most permanent of these levels of social influence. A person's desire to be correct tends to run on its own steam; it does not depend upon constant surveillance in the form of agents of reward or punishment, as in the case of compliance, or upon the continued esteem for another person or group, as in identification.

It is important to realize that any act may be performed for any of the reasons implied in these three levels. Let us look at a simple behavior like obeying the speed limit. Society pays highway

patrolmen to see to it that people do indeed conform and obey. And people do drive more slowly when they are told that a particular stretch of highway is being carefully scrutinized by these patrolmen. This is compliance. People obey the law in order to avoid paying a fine. If this were the only force operating, and if you removed the patrolmen and informed everyone about it, no one would obey the speed limit. But the individual might also conform because his father always obeyed speed limits and/or always told him that it was good to do so. This, of course, is identification. Finally, a person might obey the speed limit because he's convinced that it's a reasonable, sensible thing to do. This is internalization.

Key Components of Compliance, Identification, Internalization

In compliance, the most important component is *power*—the power of the influencing agent to bring about the reward for complying or the punishment for noncompliance. Parents have the power to praise, give love, provide cookies, scream, give spankings, and withhold allowances; teachers have the power to paste gold stars on our foreheads or (somewhat later in our lives) flunk us out of medical school. Employers have the power to fire us or raise our salaries.

In identification, the important component is *attractiveness*—the attractiveness of the person or group with whom the individual identifies. If a person finds an individual attractive, he can be influenced by his values and behavior. Thus, if a person or group you admire announces a position on an issue (in the absence of strong feelings or information to the contrary), there will be a tendency for you to accept and adopt this position.

In internalization the important component is **credibility**—the credibility of the person providing the information. Thus, if you read a statement by a person who is highly credible—someone who is both expert and truthful—this credibility would play into your desire to be correct. Recall our earlier example of the anthropologists. Their expertise made their behavior (bowing to the people in green turbans) seem like the right thing to do. Accordingly, my guess is that this behavior (your tendency to bow to people in green turbans when in this culture) would become internalized—you would do it because you believed it to be right.

Ralph Nader's influence is based on his high credibility. (UPI)

Let us look again at the behavior of the conformists in the Asch experiment. Was their behavior an example of compliance, identification, or internalization? It is a safe bet that it was compliance. Apparently the subjects were going along in order to avoid punishment (in the form of ridicule or ostracism) by other people. If either identification or internalization had been involved, the conforming behavior would have persisted—even in the absence of the group. But conformity was rare when the subjects were allowed to respond in private.

The distinction among compliance, identification, and internalization is a very useful one, but it is limited. Most important, it should be noted that the process of internalization is not the only one which produces deep and long-lasting changes in behavior, opinions, and attitudes, as you will see in Chapter 5. There you will find some processes of unusual effectiveness in convincing the individual to change his opinions. The big difference between them and those in this chapter is that the convincing to be discussed is done not by another person—it is done by the individual himself.

SUMMARY

Conformity is a common form of social influence. It can make sense in situations where, by noticing what other people do, we are provided with valuable information about what kind of behavior is appropriate in novel situations. Conformity can be maladaptive, however, when a person blindly yields to group pressure and is thus deprived of his own individuality.

Basically, there are three levels of social influence. The most permanent is internalization. This occurs when an individual accepts influence because the induced behavior fits in with his existing value system or with what he thinks is "right." Identification occurs when an individual behaves like another person because he likes or respects that other person. Compliance is the least permanent level of social influence; a person complies in order to obtain a reward or in order to avoid punishment. The behavior of the students in Solomon Asch's experiment about judging the length of a line is an example of compliance.

4

Communication and Attitude Change

Are people aware of communications?
What's the difference between attitudes and opinions?
Is it possible to change attitudes through communication?

In the preceding chapter we discussed conformity as a special case of social influence—the change in one person's opinions or behavior as a result of pressure from another person or group of people. The influence process discussed in that chapter was largely in the form of implicit pressure—the pressure stemming from the behavior of a group of people to which the individual belonged or with whom he identified. In this chapter we will discuss social influence through direct communication.

Are people aware of communications?

We live in an age characterized by a communication bombardment in which serious and almost continuous attempts are made to influence our opinions, attitudes, and behavior. Political candidates make speeches in an effort to win our vote, manufacturers of consumer goods spend vast amounts of money on television commercials and magazine layouts in an attempt to induce us to buy their products, films are shown in public schools warning us of the dangers of drug abuse. We can be exposed to a television message sponsored by the American Cancer Society telling us why we shouldn't smoke, and at the same time we might glance at a two-page, full-color ad in a magazine on our lap telling us that smoking is a debonair, exciting, "springtime fresh," manly thing to do.

The effect of the communication media can also be more subtle and less direct. For example, a news telecast may focus on the violent behavior of individuals—college students, black militants, policemen—because "action" makes for more exciting viewing than a description of people behaving in a peaceful, orderly manner. Such coverage might influence the viewer toward the belief that almost everyone is behaving violently these days and may, accordingly, cause people to be unduly depressed about the temper of the times or the state of the nation. This may affect their vote, their tendency to contribute money to an alma mater, or their desire to visit major cities. Moreover, the fact that television has become an increasingly ubiquitous and powerful method of communication raises some additional serious political and moral problems. For example, the days have long since passed when a candidate for a major political

office can wage an effective campaign on a shoestring; a candidate can no longer rely on whistlestopping and personal appearances. In order to be effective, he must buy television time, but television time is expensive. Accordingly, a substantial political advantage may be held by a candidate who has a great deal of personal wealth or a large number of wealthy supporters. These are provocative problems but unfortunately they extend beyond the scope of this chapter. They are mentioned only to suggest some of the important practical ramifications of the material to follow. In this section we will confine ourselves to a discussion of the major factors involved in attitude formation, attitude change, and the resistance to attitude change.

Rapid information dispersal throughout the world has revolutionized communication.
(Charles Gatewood)

Successful political campaigns rely upon presenting the candidate to the public, an increasingly expensive task.
(Fred Ward, Black Star)

What's the difference between attitudes and opinions?

What do we mean by an **attitude?** Most people use the terms "attitude" and "opinion" interchangeably. There are in fact real and important differences between the two, even though it is not always easy to make the distinction. In the simplest sense an opinion is what the individual believes to be a fact. For example, it is my opinion that Mexico City is about a mile and a half above sea level and that the summer temperatures are higher in Austin, Texas, than in Palo Alto, California. Opinions are transient and cognitive; "transient" meaning that they can be changed in the face of solid evidence to the contrary, and "cognitive" meaning that they are "in the head"—thoughts rather than emotions.

An attitude is more enduring. It consists of three components: a cognitive component, an emotional component, and a disposition toward action. An attitude is usually judgmental or evaluative. If we say that a person has a positive attitude toward beautiful women, we usually mean that he has some opinions (cognitive component) about them which are favorable, that he is happy or excited in their presence (emotional component), and that he strives to be near them (action component). If a person has a negative attitude toward Jews, chances are that his descriptions of them will be less than complimentary, and probably he will not vote for a political candidate who happens to be Jewish. An attitude, thus, is more complex, having three components instead of the single cognitive feature of an opinion. But, as already mentioned, sometimes the distinction is not easy to draw. For example, a person may have an opinion about blacks—say, that they tend to be taller than Caucasians. This opinion may or may not be accurate but that doesn't concern us here. In terms of our definition, the question is whether or not it has an emotional or evaluative component and whether it implies action. In the above example, it seems unlikely. However, if a person holds the opinion that blacks are shiftless and lazy, or that Jews are money-grubbers, or that Orientals are sneaky, it is reasonably safe to assume that implicit in these opinions is an attitude—a negative attitude toward the group in question.

As mentioned earlier, simple opinions are relatively easy to change. If a person believes that American blacks are taller than Caucasians and someone shows him scientific evidence to the contrary, he will probably change his opinion. An opinion that represents the cognitive aspect of an attitude is much more resistant to change, but the specific opinion *can* be changed by irrefutable evidence to the contrary. For example, a person might have a negative attitude toward blacks which is bolstered in part by the belief that

The media of communication are diverse; the messages inescapable.
(Left, Yvonne Freund; right, courtesy VISTA)

black people are inherently stupid. If he were shown documentary evidence that blacks who grow up under favorable environmental conditions are as intelligent as whites, he may change this specific opinion (although not easily). At the same time, it is important to note that this opinion change may have very little effect on his overall negative attitude toward blacks. Attitudes—because of their emotional component—are not easy to change.

SPOTLIGHT 4-1
The Measurement of Attitudes

How do social psychologists measure a person's attitude on a specific issue? Basically, it is a matter of inducing a person to reveal his feelings on an issue; but it is not quite that simple. The question must be unambiguously phrased and it must be presented in a way that can be quantified. Let us take the question "How do you feel about drugs?" This is an example of poor phrasing. First, what is "drugs"? Marijuana? Heroin? Aspirin? Penicillin? Second, "feel" is ambiguous—does it mean "Do I enjoy them," "Do I think they're dangerous," "Do I think they're useful"? Finally, if one person answers with the word "enthusiastic" and another person answers with the words "awfully good," which person has the more powerful attitude?

This can be improved by the following rendering: "Do you agree or disagree with the following statement: Marijuana should be legalized." This would give us a fairly accurate idea of attitudes toward the legalization of marijuana. A more precise technique, developed by Likert (1932), is designed to provide fine gradations. For example:

Circle a number which best represents your agreement with the following statement: Marijuana should be legalized.

1 strongly agree
2 agree
3 undecided
4 disagree
5 strongly disagree.

One might pose a number of assertions about marijuana on the same questionnaire (e.g., "marijuana is injurious to the health," "this world would be a better place if marijuana were freely available"). By algebraically summing an individual's responses to these items, the investigator could derive a fairly precise index of a person's general views on marijuana and how he stands on this issue relative to other people.

The type of scale developed by Likert is only one way of measuring attitudes. We will mention one more type of scale—this is a scale invented by Bogardus (1925) called "the social distance scale." This measures the attitudes a person has to an ethnic, racial, or religious group by asking people to indicate the maximum closeness

Initially, opinions and attitudes are most probably learned in much the same way as other behaviors and habits are learned. (The learning process is discussed in Ch. 18.) A young child may develop a negative attitude toward excessive drinking after being exposed to an alcoholic father whose behavior within the family was destructive and abusive. Less directly, he may learn that crime doesn't pay by seeing motion pictures that depict criminals as unsavory characters who come to a bad end. Contrast to this the child of the slums who sees few movies but several impressive, well-dressed, cool characters with big cars and beautiful women—they make book or push drugs. For the child, this is living documentation that crime not only pays, it pays high. Of course, as we shall see, the process of attitude formation and change is more complicated than this. Not all of the information we are exposed to is consistent; thus, on his mother's knee, the child may have learned negative attitudes toward that they would permit people of that group to come. The degrees are as follows:

1. To close kinship by marriage
2. To my club as personal chums
3. To my street as neighbors
4. To employment in my occupation in my country
5. To citizenship in my country
6. As visitors only to my country
7. Would exclude from my country

Thus, if a person rated Chinese as 5, he would be considered to have a more "distant" attitude toward them than a person who rated them 3. Looking at it a different way, if a large group of people rated Chinese at an average of 4.3 and Germans at 1.9, one could conclude that this group prefers Germans to Chinese.

Guttman (1944) has generalized this scale beyond the measurement of social distance. For example, one could use this kind of scale to measure "sexual behavior" by presenting a list of sexual practices from hand holding at one end, through kissing and petting, and anchor the other end with some esoteric form of sexual intercourse. The key attribute of this type of scale is that, by and large, if a person agrees to item 4 (for example), you can determine how he feels on all the preceding items. Thus, a person who would not want to admit Chinese to employment in his country would obviously not want to admit Chinese to close kinship by marriage; a girl who did not go along with passionate petting would obviously steer clear of sexual intercourse.

It should be noted that one limitation with all of these rating scales is that the intervals are not equal. That is, we have no way of knowing whether the attitude of a person whose score is 4 is the same distance from 3 as the person whose attitude is 2. Thus, we cannot make the statement that one person is so much higher than another person in any absolute sense. What we are limited to is an analysis of the relative strengths of attitudes. For most research purposes, this is adequate.

black people but subsequently finds himself cheering the incredible athletic exploits of Willie Mays or Vida Blue.[1]

Is it possible to change attitudes through communication?

Let us look at the relationship between attitudes and communication in more detail. How can we best influence attitudes through communication? Suppose you wanted to concoct a communication to convince my friend the house painter that Vietnamese

[1] We speak of "attitudes" and "attitude change" as if their measurement were simple. In fact, the assessment of these theoretical constructs is a complex and sophisticated process that is briefly described in Spotlights 4-1 and 4-2.

people are human and should be treated with the same respect and dignity as Americans. How would you do it?

Basically, there are three classes of communication variables of utmost importance in attitude change. The source of the communication (who says it); the nature of the communication (how he says it); and the characteristics of the audience (to whom he says it).

The Source of the Communication

One of the most pervasive advertising ploys involves the endorsement of a product by a famous person, an individual with *prestige*. Indeed, it is difficult to turn on the television set without finding an athlete endorsing a shaving cream, a movie starlet raving about a beauty soap, or, alas, an aging actor discussing some tonic guaranteed to relieve "tired blood." One can conclude from this that advertisers have an implicit theory: the source of a communication plays an important role in attitude change.

A "Trustworthy" Communicator

This is, of course, not a recent theory. Some two thousand years ago Aristotle in his classic work on communication, *Rhetoric*, indicated that "we believe good men more fully and more readily than others." Aristotle's conjecture was systematized and subjected to scientific scrutiny in a series of experiments by Carl Hovland, perhaps psychology's most innovative investigator in the area of communication and persuasion. In one experiment (Hovland & Weiss, 1951), people were exposed to identical communications on a variety of topics. For some members of the audience the message was attributed to a source having high prestige, to others it was attributed to a source having relatively low prestige. The important fact to bear in mind is that, in this experiment, the *content* of the communication was the same for all subjects—only the identification given to the source of the communication was changed. For example, one of the messages used in this experiment argued that nuclear-powered submarines were feasible (recall that this study was done in 1951 when there was great doubt about the practicality of nuclear submarines). Some members of the audience were led to believe that the message was prepared by J. Robert Oppenheimer, the renowned physicist; others were led to believe that the message appeared in the Soviet newspaper *Pravda*, a publication of dubious credibility. The opinions of the audience were measured both before and after they were exposed to the communication. The results were clear-cut. Far more opinion change was produced by Oppenheimer than by *Pravda*. The same basic results were repeated with other topics and different "trustworthy" or "untrustworthy" communicators, as shown in Table 4-1.

Before we conclude that high-prestige communicators always have a great effect on our attitudes, we must take a closer look at the situation. What do we mean by **prestige?** Most researchers in

TABLE 4-1
NET CHANGES OF OPINION AS A FUNCTION OF THE TRUSTWORTHINESS OF THE SOURCE OF THE COMMUNICATION

	Net Change (percentage)	
Topic	Trustworthy source	Untrustworthy source
1. Are atomic-powered submarines feasible?	36.0	0
2. Should antihistamines be sold without a prescription?	25.5	11.1

Adapted from C. I. Hovland & W. Weiss, "The Influence of Source Credibility on Communication Effectiveness." *Public Opinion Quarterly*, 1951, *15*, 635-50.

this area have defined it as a combination of expertise and trustworthiness. Clearly, J. Robert Oppenheimer fits into this classification, being an expert physicist and also generally regarded as an honest and decent man; he seems to fit perfectly into Aristotle's category of a "good" man. But what does a linebacker know about shaving cream that qualifies him as an expert? Moreover, in television commercials, the trustworthiness of a communicator—any communicator—may be called into question because most of us who view commercials, if we thought about it for a moment, would probably conclude that the major reason that a person endorses a product is personal financial gain. The key phrase in the last sentence may be "*if we thought about it*"; such commercial endorsements *may* have an effect on us *because* we don't think about the intentions of the communicator. In most situations we probably attribute good intentions to other people unless we have some evidence to the contrary.

Communicators as Subtle Persuaders

We have raised two important questions: First, what does a linebacker know about shaving cream? What this question implies is this: Must a person be an expert on an issue in order to have a great effect on our opinions? Perhaps he can affect our opinions if he is simply an attractive person such as a movie star or a heroic athlete. Second, what are the intentions of the communicator? Are they important? If the selfish intentions of an otherwise attractive figure are made clear, would this decrease his effectiveness? On the other hand, if an unattractive communicator were shown to have no ulterior motive for endorsing a given position, would this increase his effectiveness?

Let us look at the second question first. How important to the audience are the apparent intentions of the communicator? In one experiment (Walster, Aronson, & Abrahams, 1966) it was dramatically demonstrated that a "bad" man (a convicted criminal) could be at least as persuasive as a respected public official if the criminal had nothing to gain by convincing his audience. Half of the members of the audience were presented with a newspaper clipping which included a strong argument that the police and courts should be given more power; the other half of the members of the audience received a newspaper clipping arguing the reverse—that police and courts had too much power and the rights of the individual accused of a crime needed more protection. Half of those people who received each clipping were also led to believe that the person making the argument was G. William Stephens, described as a prosecuting attorney who had succeeded in sending more criminals to prison than any other public prosecutor in the country. Half of the people who received each clipping were led to believe that the communicator was Joe "The Shoulder" Napolitano, a convicted dope peddler.

Imagine yourself in the situation. Suppose you had read a communication by Joe "The Shoulder" saying that the laws were too tough. How would you react? Chances are you would say, "Big deal, he's only trying to protect his own interests." Accordingly, his argument would not be very convincing. Similarly, if the prosecutor were arguing for *more* court power, you might conclude that he was out to further his own personal achievement and, again, you might be skeptical. But suppose that Joe "The Shoulder" argued for more court power. Here is a person arguing against what would appear to be his own best interests. This might be expected to increase his effectiveness because it suggests that he has no ulterior motives.

The results of this experiment showed that the greatest opinion change occurred in the conditions where the criminal argued for *more* court power and the prosecutor argued for *less* court power. Indeed, they showed that a convicted criminal who argued for more court power had slightly more impact than even a respected public servant delivering exactly the same argument. This is a particularly striking result—with some added flavor because it calls into question Aristotle's dictum that we are more likely to believe good men than men of dubious character.

We can now turn to the other question that we raised above. Is it necessary for a communicator to be an expert in order to have an effect on our opinions? Recall that most investigators in this area have indicated that expertise is a major aspect of the effectiveness of a communicator. But many advertising men believe that it's unnecessary, and so they employ athletes to endorse products like shaving cream, razor blades, and hair tonics. While it may be argued that athletes by dint of their profession know more than the average man about physical conditioning, proper diet, and even perhaps treatment of athlete's foot, it is hard to believe that they are more expert than most about razor blades.

The experimental evidence indicates that advertising men are not wasting their money—people do tend to be influenced by people they like, admire, or consider to be attractive, even if the communicators are not experts. One experiment (Mills & Aronson, 1965) demonstrated that a beautiful girl who spoke to an audience of male undergraduates was more effective in changing their opinions about the topic—specialized education—than *the same girl* when she was made up to appear physically unattractive. It should be clear that beautiful women are generally not considered to be more expert on education than unattractive women. Why, then, were more students influenced by the beautiful girl? It couldn't be that they were trying to please her, because the students knew that the girl would never see their answers on the questionnaires that they filled out after her speech. There is strong evidence to suggest that they were more influenced by the attractive girl simply because they found her attractive. They liked her and therefore wanted to be in agreement with her on an issue that she considered to be important.

The Nature of the Communication

We have discussed the importance of "who says it" for the effectiveness of a communication. We will now discuss the communication itself. There are several ways in which communications can differ from each other. Consider these three important questions:

1. Is it preferable to present *both sides* of an argument *or only the one* you are championing?
2. When two sides are presented, as in a debate or in a courtroom summation, does the *order of presentation* have an effect?
3. Finally, how does the *discrepancy* between the audience's original opinion and the opinion advocated by the communication affect opinion change?

One-Sided vs. Two-Sided Presentations

Suppose you were attempting to convince an individual or a group that your beliefs on an issue were the right ones. All other things being equal, would you be more effective if you presented only the side of the issue that you yourself favored, or would it be wise to present both sides of the argument? This is a simple question and deserves a simple answer. The world of social psychology, however, is not a simple world—rather, it is a complex and exciting one. Whether or not a two-sided argument is more effective depends on some important characteristics of the audience, specifically, their intelligence and initial opinion. Several experiments have shown that a one-sided argument is most effective when delivered to unintelligent, poorly informed people—or to people who already agree with the position you are advocating. For example, at a political fund-raising dinner, the listeners—all of them allied with the political party giving the dinner—seem to be deeply moved by and appre-

SPOTLIGHT 4-2
Attitude Change

To determine attitude change, social psychologists frequently measure the attitudes of their subjects just *before* the experimental treatment and then, once again, immediately *after* the experimental treatment. Any change in attitude could then safely be attributed to this treatment, e.g., to the nature of the communication, the prestige of the communicator, or whatever the crucial experimental treatment happened to be in a given experiment.

This technique has the virtue of immediacy. Suppose we measure a person's attitude on September 27, 1972, at 3:00 P.M., and at 3:05 P.M. he is exposed to a fifteen-minute communication; at 3:20 P.M. his attitude is measured again. We can be reasonably certain that any attitude change was due to our communication because few, if any, pertinent events other than the communication intervened between the two measures of attitude.

There are problems, however; the initial measurement of the attitude may have some effect on the subject, influencing his behavior when filling out the rating scale after the communication. Many people value consistency highly and may be reluctant to let the experimenter know their attitudes have changed. Even though the communication may have changed their attitudes, they may respond the same way they did prior to the communication.

There are many ways that researchers can avoid this problem. The simplest is to test the subject's attitudes several weeks prior to the experiment itself. This is most effective when attitude questions are embedded in a much longer questionnaire on a variety of topics. Thus, by the time the subject's attitude on the crucial issue is measured again after being exposed to the communication, his initial attitude will be less salient to him and may even be forgotten.

Of course, if several weeks elapse between the pre-experimental and post-experimental measures, events other than the experimental treatments may have modified the subject's attitude. The researcher does not know if change was due to experimental manipulation or to these other events. This problem can be avoided by the use of appropriate control conditions. For example, in many experiments we are interested in a particular effect such as the influence of the communicator's prestige. If one group is exposed to a high-prestige source and another to a low-prestige source, an outside event might affect both groups, but the *relative* difference would still reflect the impact of our experimental variable.

ciative of the "give 'em hell," one-sided approach associated with such politicians as Harry Truman and Spiro Agnew. On the other hand, if a person is on the fence, generally well-informed, and intelligent, he is often aware that there is more than one side to the issue and he tends to resist a totally one-sided presentation. For such a person, the two-sided argument has been shown to be more effective.

The Order of Presentation

Suppose you are running for political office and you are arranging to debate your opponent on television. Would it be to your advantage to state your case first or last? This is a vital question which has important ramifications throughout society. For example, in a court of law, the attorney for the defense gets to summarize his case first, followed by the attorney for the plaintiff. Does either of these lawyers have the advantage merely as a result of the order of presentation? One of the country's most successful trial lawyers, Louis Nizer (1961), contends that the lawyer for the plaintiff has a decided advantage because by summing up last he gets a chance to criticize his opponent's argument.

The situation is actually more complex than Nizer's observation would suggest. While appearing last *does* give the speaker a chance to criticize his opponent's argument, speaking first may have an advantage due to the possibility that a person's first impression may be dominant; social psychologists refer to this as the **primacy effect.** On the other hand, it could be argued that under some circumstances the last speaker may have a greater effect not only because of the opportunity to criticize his opponent's argument but also because the last piece of information heard by the listener remains more vivid and is therefore more effective than earlier information. This phenomenon has been labeled the **recency effect.**

Let's look at the research evidence. One of the crucial determinants of whether a primacy effect (first argument more effective) or a recency effect is more powerful is *time*—more specifically the length of time that elapses between the first and second communication, or the time between the end of the second communication and the assessment of opinion. Suppose that the first argument is stated and is immediately followed by the second argument; suppose further that the opinion of the audience is measured immediately after the second. Will there be much difference in the memory the listener has of the first and second arguments? Probably not, because the time factor is minimized. Because of this, there should be no advantage to either the first or second argument. Similarly, there should be no advantage to either primacy or recency if both communications were given fairly long ago so that both are approximately equally forgotten by the time the opinion is measured. About one week qualifies as "fairly long ago" in this case, but there must be one week not only following the second communication but also between the first and second communications. Otherwise the results will be different, as we shall see.

What if the person hears the first argument, then a week intervenes before he hears the second argument, and his attitude is measured immediately afterward? Here we would expect a substantial recency effect because the second argument would be much more vivid. The research evidence supports the expectation. In one representative study subjects (the "audience") were presented with condensed versions of the transcript of an actual jury trial (Miller & Campbell, 1959). Each side of the argument consisted of both witness testimony and speeches by an attorney. Of course, in the experiment, all the pro-plaintiff material was presented in one block and all the pro-defendant material in another; in the real trial, information was not so conveniently arranged, especially not the testimony of witnesses.

There is one set of conditions included in this experiment that remains to be discussed, and this arrangement is perhaps the most interesting of all because it includes the most common circumstances in an actual jury trial. It is the situation in which the first argument is presented and followed immediately by the second argument. A week is then allowed to elapse, then the "jury's" attitude is measured. This condition produced a significant primacy effect—the first argument swayed more people than the second. Thus, when little or no time is allowed to elapse between the first and second argument, the first argument has an advantage. Why? Probably because the first argument a person hears is the one he tends to believe more—and, although the effect does not show up immediately, as memory begins to decline this tendency becomes more and more prominent. This is particularly interesting not only because it is the typical case but also because it shows an effect that places the plaintiff at a disadvantage—just the opposite of the belief of Mr. Nizer, an experienced trial lawyer.

The Size of the Discrepancy

Suppose you are working at a summer camp and all of your kids are hooked on a new soft drink called "Super-cola"—they each consume eight bottles of the vile stuff per day. Suppose further that you are convinced that this is injurious to their health. Ideally, you would like them to abstain completely, but of course you would be somewhat pleased if they cut back to four or five bottles per day. Would you have a greater chance of influencing their attitude and behavior if you were to argue that Super-cola is poisonously harmful and people shouldn't drink any, or would you be more effective if you were to argue that too much Super-cola can be harmful and one should not drink more than four or five per day? This is an issue that every communicator must come to terms with. Is there a level of discrepancy between the attitudes of the audience and the position advocated by the communicator which is optimal for attitude change?

Why does a person change his attitude anyway? We have suggested several reasons and we will be discussing this issue in even greater detail in the next chapter. For now, let us make the general statement that when an individual discovers that someone else feels differently from the way he feels, it produces a feeling of discomfort—which produces a strain directed toward change. It would seem to follow, then, that the greater the discrepancy, the more intense this strain—and the more intense the strain, the greater the tendency to change attitudes. And indeed, several studies do show a simple positive relationship between discrepancy and attitude change (Hovland & Pritzker, 1957). However, other studies show a more complex trend. Attitude change increased as discrepancy increased, but only up to a point; as discrepancy became very large, there was less attitude change than with a moderate degree of discrepancy (Hovland, Harvey, & Sherif, 1957).

How can we account for these conflicting results? When results of different studies conflict, it usually is an indication that not all the important variables are being taken into account. With this in mind, one group of psychologists (Aronson, Turner, & Carlsmith, 1963) formulated the following speculation: When a person learns that his position is in disagreement with a communicator, he *does* experience discomfort—but changing his own attitude is only one of several possible ways to relieve this discomfort. One interesting alternative might be to derogate the communicator, that is, to convince himself that the communicator is stupid, misinformed, or part of a Communist conspiracy. Moreover, the more discrepant the communicator's position, the more likely it would be that the recipient might tend to derogate him. For example, if I drank eight Super-colas a day and you were to tell me that any more than five was unhealthy, this might not seem terribly unreasonable. But if you were to tell me that even one bottle per day was bad for my health, this would be so different from my own view that I might begin to think that you were some sort of a health nut. Accordingly, I might not change my attitude at all; why should I let myself be persuaded by a health nut?

This sounds like fairly reasonable speculation, but how can we be certain it's correct? The psychologists carried their speculation further. Instead of changing their attitudes, people have a tendency to derogate the communicator in high-discrepancy situations. One way to prevent this would be to use a communicator whose wisdom, expertise, and trustworthiness is beyond refute. It would be difficult to belittle such a person, and therefore, even with large discrepancies, such a communicator would produce a high degree of attitude change. Indeed, when these psychologists went back over the conflicting research in the area, they made an interesting discovery: Those experiments which demonstrated a simple and direct positive relationship (between discrepancy and attitude change) used communicators who had invariably higher prestige than the communicators in the experiments where attitude change decreased when discrepancy became very high.

In an effort to pin down their speculation, the psychologists investigated both degree of discrepancy and the prestige of the communicator. Subjects read a statement in which a person stated his opinions about a poem, opinions that were slightly discrepant, moderately discrepant, or extremely discrepant from their own opinion about the merits of that poem. When the discrepant opinion was attributed to T. S. Eliot (high prestige), maximum opinion change occurred where the discrepancy was greatest. When the discrepant opinion was attributed to a fellow college student (moderate prestige), maximum change occurred when the discrepancy was moderate and decreased when the discrepancy was greater. Figure 4-1 presents these results in graphic form along with the theoretical results which would be predicted with a *perfectly* credible or incredible communicator.

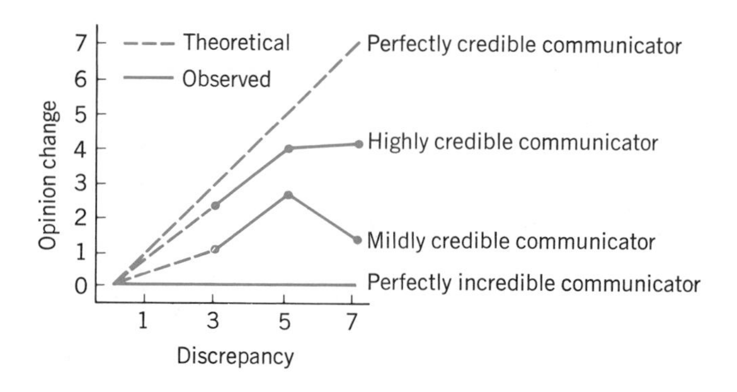

FIGURE 4-1 OPINION CHANGE AS A FUNCTION OF CREDIBILITY AND EXTENT OF DISCREPANCY—THEORETICAL AND OBSERVED CURVES

(From Aronson, Turner, & Carlsmith, 1963)

Characteristics of the Audience

All listeners or readers or viewers are not alike. Some people are easier to persuade than others. Moreover, the kind of communication that appeals to one person may not appeal to another. We have already seen, for example, that the intelligence of members of the audience as well as their prior opinion will determine whether a two-sided communication will be more effective than a one-sided communication.

There are a few other factors that play a role. For example, women change their attitudes more readily than men. This parallels the finding that women are more prone than men to conform to group pressure. Both of these results may be due to the fact that in our society women are encouraged to be more submissive and less skeptical than men. If this is the case, we may soon witness a change as women move increasingly toward giving up their traditional passive role.

Amount of Self-Esteem

The personality variable that has been most thoroughly investigated in relation to attitude change is that of **self-esteem.** Again, as was the case with conformity, if an individual feels inadequate as a person, he is more easily influenced by a persuasive communication than an individual with high self-esteem (Janis & Field, 1959). This makes good sense. After all, if a person doesn't think very highly of himself, it follows that he doesn't place a very high premium on his own ideas. Consequently, if these ideas are challenged, even by a communicator whose prestige is not terribly high, he may not be too reluctant to give them up. For an individual with low self-esteem, a communicator's prestige will *appear* high relative to his own.

The Inoculation Effect

An audience-related variable of extreme importance in evaluating attitude changes involves people's past experiences. What they have heard in the past influences how they will respond to new experiences or communications. It has been shown in an experiment that by making a mild attack upon certain established notions and then refuting the points of the attack, the established beliefs seem to withstand stronger attacks. When exposed to a full-fledged threat, the tendency of a person to respond in this way parallels the reaction that occurs when a small amount of a virus has immunized a patient against a full-blown attack by that virus. This phenomenon has been called the *inoculation effect.*

How can people be inoculated against an argument? (Ted Polumbaum)

Specifically, in this experiment a group of people stated their attitudes on several issues relating to health. They were asked to rate the extent of their agreement or disagreement with the following statements:

1. *Everyone should get a chest X-ray each year in order to detect any possible tuberculosis symptoms at an early stage.*
2. *The effects of penicillin have been, almost without exception, of great benefit to mankind.*

3. *Most forms of mental illness are not contagious.*
4. *Everyone should brush his teeth after every meal if at all possible.*

(McGuire & Papageorgis, 1961, p. 330)

These attitudes were then subjected to a mild attack—and the attack was then refuted. These people were then subjected to a *powerful* argument against their initial attitudes. Members of this group showed a much smaller tendency to change their attitudes than did the members of a control group whose attitudes had not been previously subjected to the mild attack. In effect, they were *inoculated* against attitude change. Thus, not only is it more effective as a propaganda technique to use a two-sided refutational presentation, but if it is used skillfully, such a presentation tends to increase the audience's resistance to subsequent propaganda.

Application of These Findings

How does one apply these techniques? Let us look at my friend the house painter who believes that Vietnamese are not really people. Can we induce him to change his mind by using some of the techniques we have discussed in this section? Why not simply construct a two-sided message which is attributed to a high-prestige source and which is widely discrepant from his own position—and then sit back and wait for his attitudes to change? Alas, it is not that simple. As mentioned previously, attitudes are not easy to change. Briefly stated, this is due to the fact that humans are not totally objective in the manner in which they receive and process information. This fact will be elaborated upon, and some of its exciting ramifications will be discussed in the next chapter.

SUMMARY

Communication is a natural human process, perhaps the most uniquely *human* process of all. Often communications are designed to (and sometimes do) change the attitudes of the listener or reader, whether he be an individual or a part of a mass audience. This chapter examined some of the determinants of attitude change through communication.

Some important factors of the communication process involve the characteristics of the communicator. The prestige of the communicator was seen to be among the most important; the greater the prestige, the more the influence, generally speaking. But, on the other hand, even a low-prestige communication can be effective if it is clear that the motives of the communicator are decent and not self-serving.

The nature of the communication is also important. Sometimes a one-sided argument is more effective, sometimes a two-sided presentation, depending primarily on the characteristics of the audience. Similarly, sometimes the first of two arguments is more effective, sometimes the second, and this seems to depend on timing. How discrepant an argument is from the opinion of the audience is another factor—this too is a complex factor, affecting attitudes differently, for example, if the communicator is of high or low prestige.

Finally, the characteristics of the audience must be considered. Some people are more susceptible to influence—those with low self-esteem, for example—and most communications will have greater impact with them. The listener-reader's intelligence, sex, and prior experience with the issue under debate also have been shown to affect the effectiveness of a communication, although not always in simple and direct ways. Different messages work better for different audiences.

5

Attitude Change by Self-Persuasion

Do you see what I see?
What is cognitive dissonance?
What changes attitudes?
How are attitudes formed?

Many years ago, when athletic contests were taken very seriously in the Ivy League, there was a famous football game played between Dartmouth and Princeton. It was famous not for its outcome or for any particularly spectacular plays, but rather as one of the roughest and dirtiest games in the history of the two schools. Several fights erupted on the field, there were obvious infractions of rules, much unsportsmanlike conduct, and many players were injured as a result of roughness that was far above and beyond the usual requirements. In the second quarter Princeton's star player, who had just been named to the all-American team, left the game with a broken nose. A short time later a Dartmouth player was carried off the field with a broken leg. Tempers flared and fights broke out both during and after the game.

Do you see what I see?

In the aftermath of the contest, an interesting study was conducted (Hastorf & Cantril, 1954). They showed an objective film of the game to about fifty students from each of the two schools. While viewing the film, the students were asked to write down all infractions of the rules that they noticed and which team was committing the infraction. The results showed that people do not view the same material in exactly the same way—but they do view it in predictable ways. Princeton students tended to see twice as many violations committed by the Dartmouth team as the Dartmouth students saw.

What this study demonstrates graphically is a glaring weakness inherent in a direct approach to attitude change. Where important attitudes are involved, people are not passive and objective receivers of the information that is presented; rather, they have a tendency to *distort* the message to bring it more in line with their existing attitudes. Why? In order to understand this phenomenon, it is useful to posit the existence of a motive which we will call the *need for consistency.*

Individuals' attitudes influence what each sees. (Charles Harbutt, Magnum)

What is cognitive dissonance?

In recent years several **theories of consistency** have evolved. In this chapter we will restrict our discussion to one of these theories—Festinger's theory of **cognitive dissonance** (Festinger, 1957). We have chosen this particular theory because it has generated a great deal of research and because it has been applied to a very wide range of social situations.

The core notion of the theory is extremely simple: Whenever an individual simultaneously holds two **cognitions** (ideas, attitudes, beliefs, opinions) that are psychologically inconsistent, **dissonance** occurs. Stated differently, two cognitions are dissonant if, considering these two cognitions alone, the opposite of one is the logical conclusion of the other. For example, if a person believes that cigarette smoking causes cancer and simultaneously knows that he himself smokes cigarettes, he experiences dissonance. Specifically, his cognition "I smoke cigarettes" is psychologically inconsistent with his cognition "cigarette smoking produces cancer." When there is a discrepancy between attitude and behavior, dissonance results.

Reducing Dissonance

Since dissonance is presumed to be unpleasant, the theory predicts that people will strive to reduce it. Typically this is done by adding "consonant" cognitions that are consistent with one or the other of the dissonant elements—reducing dissonance by

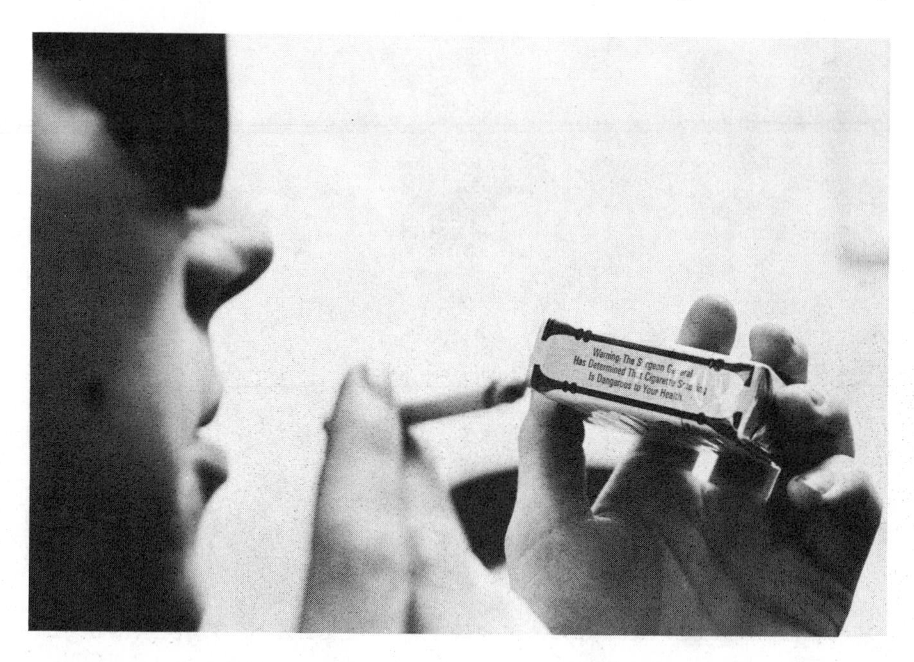

A change in attitude is often simpler than a change in behavior.
(Ted Polumbaum)

making it a smaller part of the total—or more directly, by changing one of the dissonant cognitions. Since the cognition "I smoke cigarettes" is obviously related to behavior, one of the most efficient ways to reduce dissonance in such a situation is to stop smoking. But, as many people have discovered, this is by no means easy. So a person will usually work on the other cognition. There are several ways in which a person can make cigarette smoking seem less threatening. He might belittle the evidence linking cigarette smoking to cancer ("Most of the data are clinical rather than experimental"); he might associate with other cigarette smokers ("If Sam, Jack, and Harry smoke, then it can't be very dangerous"); he might smoke filter-tipped cigarettes and delude himself into believing that the filter traps the cancer-producing materials; he might convince himself that smoking is an important and highly pleasurable activity ("You don't live longer, it just seems longer! Ha, ha"); he might actually make a virtue out of smoking by developing a romantic, devil-may-care image of himself, flouting danger by smoking. All of these techniques reduce dissonance by reducing the absurdity involved in going out of one's way to contract cancer. In effect, the individual forms or changes his attitude by a process of *self-persuasion*.

Distorting Reality

What the theory of cognitive dissonance implies, then, is that people attempt to justify their own behavior, attitudes, commitments, and associations through self-persuasion. This process of justification and self-persuasion frequently involves a distortion of objective reality. Let us look at the plight of the typical Dartmouth student watching the film of the football game. Chances are that his general opinion is that Dartmouth players are skillful, fair, and decent people because they represent his school. While watching the film, every unfair, dirty, and indecent act committed by a Dartmouth player is dissonant with this cognition. In order to reduce dissonance he either "doesn't notice" many of these actions, or tends to attribute their origin to the Princeton team.

This tendency toward self-justification frequently runs counter to the need to be correct. Recall that in the first chapter of this section we raised the question of why people conform. In the second chapter we asked why people change their attitudes. We are now able to put it all together. The most common and basic reason why people conform is that it feels good or makes sense to do so. First, there is a reward which comes from being liked, accepted, praised, and considered a regular guy and not a queer duck. Second, there is the good feeling you get from being like someone that you respect or admire. Third, there are the benefits stemming from being correct—of making wise decisions, of knowing what you're about. Finally, there is the good feeling that comes from having a good self-image, i.e., believing that you are a wise, decent, and clever human being. This last reward is the one that dissonance theory focuses on.

Although these motives are all directed to the same end, achieving rewards, they are frequently tugging in opposite directions. You will act differently, depending upon your motive. Accordingly, before being able to make a prediction of how most people will behave in a given situation, it is necessary to understand the situation. By understanding the situation, we can have a clear picture of which of the above motives will predominate.

Let us take a look at the last two that we listed. We can call these the "need to *be* right" and the "need to *appear* right." The need to be right is a very rational, functional drive. It is what motivates a person to seek impartial information, to pay attention to what is going on around him, and to make careful, rational judgments based on the facts at hand. Thus, to return to examples we used in an earlier chapter, the need to be right is what motivates a person to pay close attention to the behavior of the anthropologists around him when he is in a strange culture—and to imitate them when they bow to natives in green turbans.

The theory of cognitive dissonance implies the existence of a need to *convince* oneself that one *is* right. Far from seeking impartial information in order to satisfy this latter need, the individual is motivated to seek supportive information and reject critical information. These two needs are in constant tension. This duality is nicely illustrated by observing the behavior of people before and after making an important decision—say, for example, purchasing a new car. Before buying a new car, people are motivated to make a wise purchase. Thus, they may read *Consumer Reports,* seek information from friends who own various makes of cars, and test-drive several cars. In short, they seek to expose themselves to as much information as possible about as many makes of cars as possible. But what happens after they make a purchase? One investigator (Ehrlich *et al.*, 1957) found that individuals who had recently purchased a new car continuously read many advertisements about the brand of car they had purchased—but not about the brands they had considered and not purchased. This tendency was not present among people who had not recently bought new cars. What does this mean? Well, after buying a car, a person wants to justify himself; he wants to convince himself that he made the right choice. He no longer wants to read objective information, as he did before the purchase; he wants reassurance that he made a wise decision. What better place to find these reassurances than in advertising that presents only positive information about a given product. In order to justify the wisdom of their choice, people seek out information favorable to their choice and avoid information unfavorable to their choice.

This datum suggests still another reason why a direct information campaign is often ineffective. Not only do people tend to distort the information presented in order to bring it into line with their attitudes, values, and beliefs, but frequently they choose not to expose themselves to information which they suspect might be dissonant with these. Thus, for example, a left-wing radical would not go out of his way to hear a speech by Spiro Agnew. This is an important problem for the would-be persuader. To return to our recurring example, that of my friend the house painter, if we wanted to change the attitudes of the painter so that he no longer believed that the Vietnamese were "un-people," it would be very difficult for us to do this by using a direct communication. In the first place, if he had been informed in advance about the nature of the communication, he might choose not to listen, just as the people who had recently purchased a new car chose not to expose themselves to advertisements about other makes of cars. Such information is dissonant with his existing beliefs. Second, even if he *had* exposed himself to this

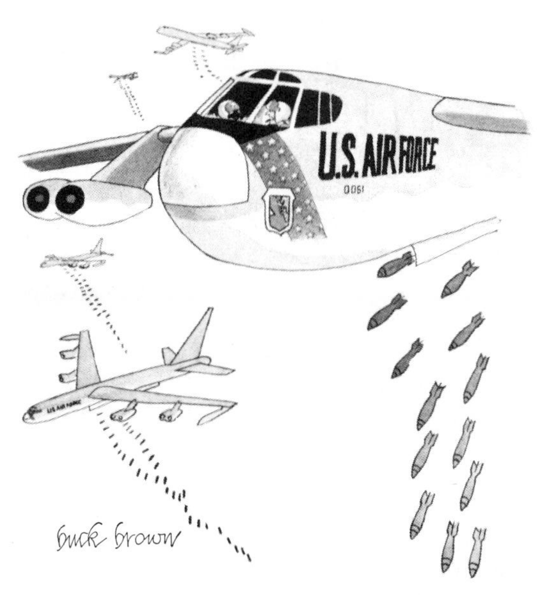

"Hell, do as I do, kid, pretend there's no one down there."

Reducing dissonance. (Drawing by Buck Brown reproduced by special permission of *Playboy* magazine; copyright © 1971 by Playboy)

information, he might tend to distort it, to change it, to bring it into line with his previous ideas in much the same way that the students watching the film of the Princeton-Dartmouth football game were able to distort what was actually happening on that film.

Dissonance-reducing behavior is defensive behavior; that is, an individual reduces dissonance as a way of maintaining a positive image of himself that makes him feel smart or good or worthwhile. Dissonance-reducing behavior can be considered irrational or malfunctional in the sense that while it *is* good for the self-image, it often prevents a person from solving very real problems in his environment. Thus, to go back to our automobile example, if after purchasing a new car a person continued to convince himself that his car was the best car ever made and exposed himself only to positive information about his car, he might fail to learn things about that car which, although negative and unpleasant, might be very useful. What if his car had a problem with brakes? Suppose the brakes tended to fail in wet and slippery weather, and that this information had been published. If the individual had either failed to expose himself to this information or minimized its importance (in order to protect his self-image), it could conceivably lead to his death.

The conflict between the needs to be right and to appear right is illustrated in an experiment involving racial attitudes (Jones & Kohler, 1958). The subjects were people whose attitudes were either in favor of racial segregation or opposed to it. These people were presented with sets of statements, some of which were in favor of racial segregation and some of which were opposed to racial segregation. Moreover, some of these statements were very plausible and others were totally implausible. Specifically, the plausible pro-segregation statement read: "Southerners will have to pay the price of lowered scholastic standards if they yield to the pressures to integrate their schools." The implausible pro-segregation statement read: "If Negroes and whites were meant to live together, they never would have been separated at the beginning of history." The plausible anti-segregation statement read: "The present inferior condition of the Negro is the result of long and effective suppression by the Southern whites." And the implausible anti-segregation statement read: "The real reason why most Southern whites oppose integration is their realization that the Negro is more capable than they are." (Jones & Kohler, 1958, pp. 316–317)

Predicting Attitude Formation

Which statements would the subjects learn and remember best? From a perfectly rational point of view, one would guess that individuals would learn the plausible statements to a greater extent than all of the implausible statements; after all, what sense does it make to fill one's head with implausible statements? For our edification, the important things to learn are statements that make some degree of sense, whether one happens to agree with that position or not. From the point of view of dissonance theory, however, people dislike hearing ridiculous arguments in favor of their own view because they can be so easily discounted that it casts doubt on the view in general. More important, every time one learns a plausible statement opposed to one's own position, dissonance is created because it suggests that there are some good arguments on the other side of the issue. The results of the experiment were consistent with predictions that would be made by the theory of cognitive dissonance: People learned the plausible statements that supported their own position to a greater extent than the implausible statements supporting those views. But for the opposing view, the results were just the opposite. They were more likely to remember the implausible support of the opposition than the plausible. It is in this case, of course, that the need to appear right and the need to be right are in greatest conflict. In most of these subjects, the need to appear right controlled their learning and memory processes.

What changes attitudes?

Insufficient Reward for an Action

The tendency to reduce dissonance is a very powerful one. We have seen how it can be used by an individual to maintain his own attitudes and to thwart attempts to change them. But just as it can be used to prevent attitude change, the same process can be utilized in order to produce attitude change. This can be accomplished by placing a person in a state of dissonance under conditions such that the path of least resistance in reducing dissonance involves a change in attitude.

One way of doing this is to induce a person to take a course of action which is dissonant with his own attitudes, values, and beliefs. Suppose Sam Schlunk is running for mayor of your town. Suppose further that you believe that Sam Schlunk is a complete idiot and would make an awful mayor. What if I induced you to stand up in a public place in the presence of hundreds of people and make an impassioned speech telling the voters that Sam Schlunk is, in actuality, a very wise and upright person who would make an absolutely perfect mayor. After having done this, you would experience dissonance: your cognition "I believe that Sam Schlunk is an idiot who would make an awful mayor" is dissonant with the cognition "I said to a bunch of people that Sam Schlunk is a wise man who would make a perfect mayor." How would you reduce this dissonance?

Perhaps the best way would be by convincing yourself that the things you said were not completely wrong; in other words, the dissonance motivates you to try to justify your behavior. The world is so constructed that reality is very rarely a matter of good and bad; there are many in-between areas to work on. You might go back over some of Sam Schlunk's previous political speeches and extract from these some small pearls of wisdom that you had previously missed. Or you might convince yourself that some of the things that Sam Schlunk was saying actually meant something other than what you previously thought he meant. The astute reader may begin to notice some similarities in this behavior to the behavior of the Dartmouth students watching the film of the Dartmouth-Princeton game. This kind of distortion could aid you in justifying your behavior of supporting Sam Schlunk's candidacy. Note what it does: it induces you to change your attitudes, opinions, and beliefs about Sam Schlunk. The fact that you made a speech supporting him is now causing you to change your attitudes.

This line of reasoning can be summarized by the statement "saying is believing"; that is, if a person states a belief, it can produce that belief in himself. Now that's a pretty bald statement and it needs some qualification. Let's turn the clock back a day; there you are, standing in the city square, and I approach you in an attempt to induce you to make a speech favoring Sam Schlunk. Let us suppose that I say, "Hey, how would you like to make a speech favoring Sam Schlunk?" You refuse. Suppose then that I pull out $50,000, hand it to you, and say, "If you make a speech favoring Sam Schlunk, you can keep this $50,000." So you take the $50,000 and you stand up and say, "Sam Schlunk is a wise man and would be a perfect mayor." Would you experience much dissonance? Probably not. The cognition "I believe that Sam Schlunk is an idiot" is, indeed, dissonant with the cognition "I have said that Sam Schlunk is a wise man," but added to that is also the cognition "I said those things in order to get $50,000." In short, the $50,000 is consonant enough with the statement that you made. There is no need to further justify your behavior by changing your attitudes. Similarly, suppose I held a gun to your head and said, "Either you make positive statements about Sam Schlunk or I'm going to blow your brains out." If you complied, you would experience no dissonance and no attitude change. The cognition that "my head will be blown off if I don't make these statements" is very consonant with making those statements.

The thrust of our argument is this: The greater the reward, the greater the probability that a person will overtly comply. But in trying to produce an actual change in attitudes, the greater the reward, the *less* likely it is that any attitude change will occur. Thus, if all I want you to do is to consent to making a speech favoring Sam Schlunk, the best thing for me to do would be to give you the largest possible reward. This would increase the probability that you will comply—that you will make that speech. But if what I'm out to attain is a change in your attitudes and beliefs, just the reverse is true. There is, of course, some minimal reward necessary to induce you to perform that behavior. Beyond that minimal amount, the less I give, the more likely it is that you will be forced to seek additional justification in the form of convincing yourself that the things you said were actually true. This would result in true attitude change rather than mere compliance. Thus, what I am suggesting is another technique to produce deep and lasting attitude change. If a person changes his attitude because he makes a public statement for insufficient reward or justification, he will maintain the changed attitude. He is not changing his attitudes because of the reward (compliance) or because

The effect of rewards on lying

an attractive person influenced him (identification). He changes his attitudes because he has convinced *himself* that his previous attitudes were incorrect. This is a very powerful and penetrating form of attitude change.

These speculations were put to the test in a classic experiment (Festinger & Carlsmith, 1959) that parallels the example that we used above. Each subject was asked to perform a very boring and laborious set of tasks. The experimenter then induced him to lie about the task; specifically, he induced him to tell another person (who was waiting to perform the task) that it was interesting and enjoyable. Some of the subjects were offered $20 for telling the lie, others were offered only $1 for telling the lie. After the experiment was over, an interviewer asked the "lie-tellers" how much they had enjoyed the tasks that they had performed earlier in the experiment. The results are shown in Table 5-1. Subjects who had been offered $20 for lying—that is, for saying that the tasks had been enjoyable—found the tasks to be dull, as did the control subjects who were not asked to lie. Subjects who had been paid only $1 for lying rated the task as an enjoyable one. In other words, people who had a lot of justification for telling a lie told the lie, but didn't believe it. But people who told the lie with very little justification did, indeed, come to believe that what they said was true.

TABLE 5-1
THE EFFECT OF REWARD ON ATTITUDE CHANGE

Condition	"Enjoyed Task"	"Willing to Participate in Similar Experiments"
$1 reward	+1.35[a]	+1.20
$20 reward	− .05	− .25
Control[b]	− .45	− .62

[a] The more positive the number, the greater the attitude change in the direction of the oral statement.
[b] Subjects who participated in the boring task but were not asked to "lie."

Adapted from L. Festinger & J. M. Carlsmith, "Cognitive Consequences of Forced Compliance." *Journal of Abnormal and Social Psychology*, 1959, *58*, 203–11.

Insufficient Punishment for an Action

Suppose you have a young child who likes to beat up his little brother and you want him to stop. Probably the best way to get him to stop is to threaten to hit him and hit him hard. The more severe the threat, the greater the likelihood that he will stop, at that moment, *while you're watching him.* That's compliance. However, he may very well hit his brother again as soon as you turn your back.

But suppose instead that you threaten him with a very mild punishment such as turning off his favorite TV program—a punishment that is just barely severe enough to get him to stop aggressing at that time. In either case—under threat of severe punishment or of mild—the child is experiencing dissonance. He is aware that he is not beating up his little brother, while also aware that he wants to. When the little brother is present, the child has the urge to beat him up and, when he refrains, he asks himself in effect, "How come I'm not beating up my little brother?" Under severe threat he has a ready answer: "I know why I'm not beating up my little brother. I'm not beating him up because, if I do, that giant standing over there (my father) is going to knock the hell out of me." In effect, the severe threat of punishment has provided the child with strong justifications for not beating up his brother, at that moment, while he's being watched.

Now consider the child in the mild threat situation; he experiences dissonance too. He asks himself, in effect, "How come I'm not beating up my little brother?" But the difference is that he doesn't have a good answer—the threat was so mild that it by itself does not provide a completely adequate answer. In this situation he

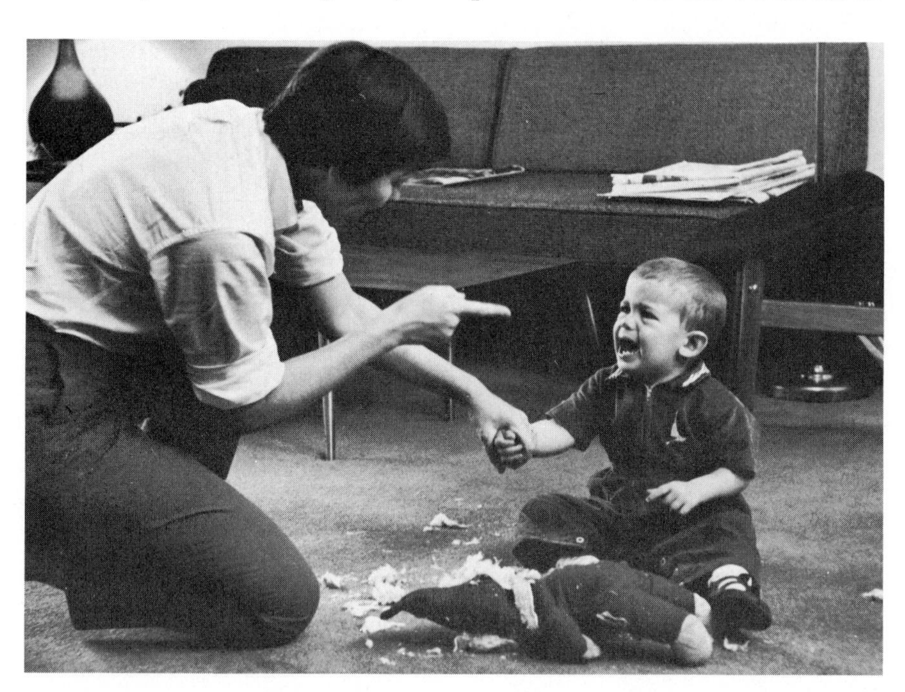

If punishment is severe, it will stop aggression, at least while the punisher is present, but a mild threat might produce a more lasting change in behavior.
(Erika Stone, Photo Researchers)

continues to experience dissonance. There is no simple way for him to reduce it by blaming his inaction on a severe threat. He must, therefore, find reasons consonant with not hitting his little brother. He can, for instance, try to convince himself that he really doesn't like to beat his brother up, that he didn't want to do it in the first place. In sum, one way to get a person to inhibit an activity is to get him to devalue it—and one way to get him to devalue it is to stop him in the first place with a mild threat rather than a severe one.

To test this notion, two experimenters (Aronson & Carlsmith, 1963) tried to influence a rather mundane value—children's toy preferences. Children were first asked to rate the attractiveness of several toys; the experimenter then told them they were not allowed to play with one of the toys, one previously rated as attractive. One experimental group was threatened with a mild punishment for transgression—"I would be a little annoyed"; the other experimental group was threatened with severe punishment—"I would be very angry. I would have to take all of my toys and go home and never come back again. I would think you were just a baby." After that the experimenter left the room and allowed the children to play with the other toys—and to resist the temptation to play with the forbidden one. On returning to the room, the experimenters found that those children who were forbidden to play with a toy under a threat of mild punishment now found the toy much less attractive while those children under a severe threat did not devalue it. As Table 5-2 shows, 8 of 12 children under mild threat gave a lower rating of the toy; of 14 children under strong threat, none lowered their ratings. The prediction of dissonance theory was supported: "I like this toy" and "I am not playing with this toy" are dissonant in both cases. In the severe-punishment group, however, the calamitous consequences of playing with the toy resolve the dissonance. In the mild-punishment group, the relative absence of such external justification makes the children change the cognition "I like . . ." into "I *don't* really like . . ." in order to reduce the dissonance.

Subsequent research has shown that this effect is a long-lasting one. Once devalued, the toy continued to remain unattractive to the children when they were retested some sixty-four days later (Freedman, 1965).

TABLE 5-2
CHANGE IN ATTRACTIVENESS OF FORBIDDEN TOY

	Rating	
Strength of Threat	Increase	Decrease
Mild	4	8
Severe	14	0

Adapted from E. Aronson & J. M. Carlsmith, "Effect of the Severity of Threat on the Devaluation of Forbidden Behavior." *Journal of Abnormal and Social Psychology*, 1963, 66, 584–88.

Temptation accompanied by a severe threat

Temptation accompanied by a mild threat

The effects demonstrated in these experiments may very well apply to more basic and important values. For example, a parent might have more success in controlling aggressiveness in a child if he used threats of mild rather than severe punishment. By doing this, he might help the child convince himself that aggression is undesirable and so bring about a lasting change in his behavior. Studies in child development suggest clearly that parents who use severe punishment to stop a child's aggression do not succeed in curtailing it in any permanent sense. Parents who punish children for aggressive behavior tend to have children who, while not very aggressive at home, display a great deal of aggression at school and at play away from home (Sears, Whiting, Nowlis, & Sears, 1953). This is what we would expect from the compliance model discussed in an earlier chapter.

The Psychology of Inevitability

Still another ramification of the theory of cognitive dissonance can best be summarized by the phrase, "The grass is usually greener in your *own* yard." If a person is committed to a particular situation or course of action, the cognition that he is about to perform that action or enter into that situation is dissonant with any knowledge he has of negative aspects of that situation. For example, in one experiment (Brehm, 1959) it was discovered that children who volunteered to eat a vegetable they disliked, and who believed that they would be eating more of that vegetable in the future, succeeded in convincing themselves that that particular vegetable was not so very bad. In short, the cognition "I dislike that vegetable" is dissonant with the cognition "I will be eating that vegetable in the future." In order to reduce the dissonance, the subjects came to believe that the vegetable was really not so distasteful as they had previously thought. In another study (Darley & Berscheid, 1967), college women volunteers were asked to discuss their sexual behavior and sexual standards with another coed whom they didn't know. Before the interview they were given two folders; each contained a personality description of a coed. Each of these personality descriptions contained a mixture of pleasant and unpleasant characteristics. Half of the subjects were led to believe that they were going to interact in the intimate discussion group with the young lady described in folder *A*, while the girl described in folder *B* would be in a different group. The other half of the subjects were led to believe that they were going to interact with the girl described in folder *B*. Before actually meeting these coeds, the subjects were asked to evaluate each of them on the basis of the personality descriptions that they had read. Those subjects who felt that it was inevitable that they were going to have to interact with the girl described in folder *A* found her much more appealing as a person than the girl described in folder *B*. Those who believed that they were going to have to interact with the girl described in folder *B* found *her* much more appealing than the one described in folder *A*. Again, the knowledge that one is going to have to spend time with another person—this feeling of inevitability—increases the positive aspects of that person or at least decreases the negative aspects. In short, people tend to reduce dissonance by making the best of a bad thing if they know it is bound to occur.

The Need to Justify Cruelty

Suppose you performed an action which caused some physical harm to an innocent bystander. If you think of yourself as a basically decent, fair, and careful person, this would arouse some dissonance. Your cognition "I am a decent, fair, and careful person" is dissonant with your cognition "I have harmed an innocent person." How could you reduce dissonance? The three most feasible directions are (1) to minimize the harm done, (2) to attempt to compensate the victim, or (3) to maximize the culpability of the victim, i.e., to convince yourself that the "innocent" bystander wasn't so innocent after all—that he did something to bring it on himself, that he's a reprehensible person, and that he deserved what he got. To reduce dissonance, a person could apply any of these lines of thought. However, to the extent that the damage done to the victim is unambiguously severe (like a serious injury or death), the one who causes the injury will be unable to minimize the damage cognitively and unable to provide adequate compensation for the victim. Therefore, he will rely heavily on the third technique; he will try to convince himself that the victim deserved what he got.

I am reminded of an article I read in the sports page of a

To reduce dissonance after unintentionally harming someone, the wrongdoer often convinces himself that the innocent victim was more to blame than he.
(Wide World Photos)

local newspaper. It seems that a defensive tackle for a professional football team had succeeded in cracking a few ribs belonging to an opposing quarterback by intentionally belting him hard after the quarterback had thrown a pass. When interviewed afterward, the tackle maintained that it was all part of the game—that the quarterback was out to "humiliate me in front of my friends" by completing passes, and, accordingly, he deserved whatever injuries he sustained.

In an experimental test of this third technique (Davis & Jones, 1960) students were cajoled into "helping" the experimenter. They were to watch another student being interviewed and then to tell the student their impressions of him—but, as a helper, they were instructed to give negative impressions: "You are shallow, untrustworthy, not very interesting, and not very attractive"—like that. The major finding in this experiment was that subjects who were induced to volunteer for this assignment succeeded in convincing themselves that they didn't like the person that they evaluated negatively. In other words, after saying things that almost certainly hurt the other student, they convinced themselves that he deserved it; they liked him less than they did before they hurt him.

As mentioned earlier, there is more than one way to reduce dissonance in these situations. One possibility not previously mentioned is that, where feasible, a person who harms someone might try to shift the blame onto a third party. If I could convince myself that, although I hurt someone, it wasn't my fault but someone else's, then I would have no need to derogate the person I hurt. This was also demonstrated in the experiment just reported: When subjects were *forced* by the experimenter to say unpleasant things to a person, they did not derogate the victim. They devalued the victim only when they were cajoled into thinking that they acted more or less on their own free will.

A word of caution: The fact that under optimal experimental conditions most people tend to devalue a victim of their own actions does not mean that *all* people behave in this manner. Some people are able to tolerate dissonance better than others. Some people can live with the knowledge that "although I am a decent and fair person, I have hurt another person—and that other person happens to be a nice guy." But most people apparently do have a difficult time tolerating dissonance and do tend to justify behavior that produces dissonance. If this weren't the case, the experiment described would not have yielded reliable results. This word of caution, of course, applies to all the experiments and conclusions stated in this chapter.

How are attitudes formed?

Perhaps we can now go back to the house painter whom we first discussed at the very beginning of the section. Recall that he firmly believed that the Vietnamese were not quite human. How did his attitude develop? There are a number of possible ways. To mention a few: (1) He might have had some unhappy experiences with a few Vietnamese people and, as a result, disliked them and generalized this dislike to all of the Vietnamese. (2) Individuals whom he respected, liked, and wanted to be like may have had a similar attitude toward the Vietnamese—and he may have adopted a negative attitude through a kind of conformity that we have labeled "identification." (3) Still a third possibility is that he came to dislike the Vietnamese and to consider them "unpeople" as a way of justifying his own oppressive behavior. Like the football player who broke the quarterback's ribs and the college students who said uncomplimentary things to their peers, the house painter may have performed some actions in Vietnam that caused him to experience dissonance. In order to reduce dissonance, he might attempt to justify these activities in the form of derogating the people whom he had caused to suffer. By stoutly maintaining, "Hell, Doc, those aren't people, those are Vietnamese," he conveniently gets off the hook; he can maintain his own self-image as a decent and fair person as he justifies his behavior which otherwise might threaten his self-image. It should be noted that once he reduces dissonance by convincing himself that the Vietnamese aren't people, he not only justifies past negative behavior, but for as long as he remains in the situation he justifies (and virtually guarantees) subsequent negative behavior as well.

Let us broaden the base of this example slightly. Suppose

you live in a culture where whites treat blacks unfairly. Let us say, for example, that the whites prevent the blacks from attending first-rate public schools, but instead provide them with a second-rate and stultifying education. As a consequence, after twelve years of schooling, the average black is less well educated than the average white and does poorly on achievement tests. Such a situation provides a marvelous opportunity for white leaders to justify their discriminatory behavior and hence reduce dissonance. "You see," they might say, "Black people are stupid (because they perform poorly on the achievement test), and therefore it would have been foolish for us to waste our resources by trying to provide them with a high-quality education." This **self-fulfilling prophecy** provides an airtight justification. So, too, is the attribution of moral inferiority to blacks: We imprison the black man in an overcrowded ghetto, guaranteeing him a situation where the color of his skin almost inevitably prevents him from participating in the opportunities for growth and success which exist for white Americans. Through the mass media he sees people succeeding and becomes painfully aware of the mountains of consumer goods that are unavailable to him. If, in his frustration, he turns to violence or if, in his despair, he turns to drugs, it is fairly easy for the white man to attribute this outcome to some sort of inherent moral inferiority rather than to the repressiveness and unfairness of white society.

Almost without realizing it, I have stumbled into the extremely complex area of prejudice—an area as important as it is complex. Accordingly, it deserves a chapter all to itself. It follows immediately.

SUMMARY

People do not digest information exactly as it is given. They have a tendency to alter it to fit their needs. One such need is self-justification—people attempt to justify their behavior and attitudes. For example, if an individual has recently invested a great deal of money in the purchase of a new car, he will tend not to notice its deficiencies—because noticing these deficiencies will suggest that he may have been stupid in his choice of a car. By the same token, most individuals are disinclined to accept negative information about their own team, their own university, or any person, object, or opinion to which they have committed themselves.

This phenomenon has been described and developed under the rubric of the theory of cognitive dissonance. This theory has led to a great deal of research with fairly wide ramifications for attitude development and change. For example, if an individual hurts someone, he will try to justify his action by convincing himself that the victim deserved to be hurt. This results in an interesting phenomenon: The harmdoer will think less of the victim *after* hurting him than before hurting him. There are other nonobvious findings from dissonance theory. If your goal is permanent attitude change, the *smallest* reward or *mildest* punishment necessary to alter the behavior related to the attitude will have the greatest effect. This is true because the individual cannot justify his actions (reduce dissonance) by pointing to the severity of threats or the size of the reward; he will tend to alter the original attitude instead. And, if it appears that future involvement with an object or person is inevitable, the individual will tend to increase the value of that object or person.

6
Prejudice

What causes prejudice?
How can the experimental method be used by social psychologists?
How can prejudice be reduced?

Ethnic **prejudice** has been defined in a number of different ways. Basically, as the term has been used by social psychologists, it can be considered to be a set of hostile attitudes directed toward a distinguishable group and based on generalizations derived from faulty or incomplete information. Thus, when we say that Sam is prejudiced against blacks, we mean that he is set to behave with hostility toward blacks and that his information about them is either totally inaccurate or contains a germ of truth which is overzealously applied to the group as a whole.

What causes prejudice?

At the close of the previous chapter we presented a brief version of one possible reason behind prejudice—namely, a need to justify one's actions and beliefs. Admittedly, that was an oversimplified version of one way in which prejudice develops and is maintained. There are others. In fact, behavioral scientists have proposed several explanations for the etiology of prejudice. It seems reasonably certain that there is no one cause of prejudice which holds true for all people—and there are undoubtedly multiple causes in even the single case. Presumed "causes" of prejudice range from broad societal factors to the operations of the narrow mind of a single individual.

On a broad social level, prejudice can be viewed as the result of economic and political forces. For example, it has been argued that intergroup hostility has been intentionally propagated to justify and foster the economic exploitation of minority groups. You need not subscribe to an exploitation theory to be aware of the fact that prejudiced attitudes tend to develop among groups that are in conflict—whether it be blacks and whites competing for scarce jobs, Arabs versus Israelis fighting about disputed territory, or Northerners versus Southerners disputing the abolition of slavery. The linkage between prejudice and job discrimination is particularly well documented. For example, in 1966, only 2.7 percent of union-controlled apprenticeships were filled by blacks—an increase of only 1 percent over the previous ten years. A recent four-city survey conducted by the U.S. Department of Labor failed to turn up a single black apprentice among union plumbers, steamfitters, sheet-metal workers, stonemasons, lathers, painters, glaziers, and operating engineers—which has prompted one commentator to observe that it is apparently easier for a black to enter an Ivy League college than it is for him to join a craft union (Levitas, 1969).

Economic and political conflict also results in the formation of unfavorable **stereotypes.** For example, in the middle of the nineteenth century, jobs were plentiful and Chinese immigrants were performing back-breaking labor on the United States transcontinental railroad. And at that time, there was little negative feeling toward

Prejudice can stem from changing economic conditions.
(Denver Public Library Western Collection)

them. Indeed, they were generally regarded as sober, industrious, and law-abiding. But after the completion of the transcontinental railroad and the end of the Civil War, employment opportunities were scarce, and the Chinese were competing for more desirable jobs. This was accompanied by a sharp increase in negative attitudes toward the

Chinese; the stereotype changed to "criminal," "conniving," "crafty," and "stupid." On a political level, the stereotype of Japanese (both Japanese nationals as well as Japanese-Americans) changed negatively as a result of the conflict during World War II, and changed again (this time positively) when Japan became one of our staunchest and most reliable allies in the '50s and '60s.

How can the experimental method be used by social psychologists?

Study of Groups

Although these observations are compelling, they are not totally convincing in and of themselves. In the complexity of the world at large, a great many events are occurring simultaneously with economic or political conflict. In order to examine prejudice and negative stereotyping more closely a less complex situation needs to be arranged. Such an environment was produced by Muzafer Sherif and his colleagues (1961) who performed an experiment on the effects of conflict and cooperation at a summer camp for boys.

Establishing a Situation

These researchers divided the campers into two separate groups, the "Bulldogs" and the "Red Devils," and attempted to knit each group into a cohesive unit by making the members of the group interdependent in most of their daily activities. For example, in order to eat, a good deal of cooperation was required within each group—in securing the food, gathering wood, preparing a fire for cooking, and dishing out the food.

Introducing Competition

Once a feeling of "we-ness" was established within each group, the researchers began to foster competitive situations between the two groups in order to determine whether animosities would develop and, if so, whether they could be reduced later. These competitions took the form of games; in order to increase tension, prizes were awarded to the winning team.

While the games began in a rather friendly manner, unpleasantness gradually began to develop. For example, at one point the Red Devils accused the Bulldogs of not playing fair and subjected them to a great deal of verbal abuse. The investigators set up a number of situations aimed at capitalizing on these tendencies. For example, they arranged a joint party and contrived to have the Red Devils arrive sometime before the Bulldogs. By the time of the party, resentment between the two groups was so high that the Red Devils cornered the most appetizing-looking refreshments for themselves—leaving mostly squashed and unappetizing-looking refreshments for the Bulldogs. When the Bulldogs arrived and saw what was going on, they were understandably miffed. The hostilities increased and name-calling soon escalated into the throwing of food, cups, tableware, and other objects.

Reducing Hostility

After the psychologists had succeeded in building within-group attraction and between-group animosity, they explored the possibilities of reducing the animosity. First, they eliminated competitive, conflict-ridden situations and tried to increase simple, noncompetitive contact between the groups. The two groups watched movies in close proximity, ate in the same dining room, and played in the same area. But once hostility had been aroused, simple contact did nothing to reduce it. Indeed, when placed in close proximity the groups *increased* their hostility toward each other.

Since cooperativeness within each group was what built strong attraction among group members, the researchers then attempted to create one large, cooperative group to see if this would reduce hostility. They formed an all-star softball team in which the best players from each group participated in the game against a group of boys from a nearby town. They also created a crisis, surreptitiously damaging the water supply system, so that all the boys had to cooperate immediately in order to repair the damage. These cooperative ventures reversed the trend of out-group animosity and increased the attractiveness of the boys for each other, regardless of group affiliation.

An Individual Approach—The Scapegoat Theory

A totally different type of explanation for prejudiced behavior focuses on what's going on inside the person. Suppose a person is angry or frustrated. These feelings result in a tendency to lash out at the source of frustration. But frequently the cause is either unidentifiable or too powerful to strike at without risk of serious retaliation. For example, if a man is insulted by his boss or a boy is pushed around by a bigger, stronger bully, a counterattack would almost certainly be dangerous. According to the **scapegoat theory** of prejudice, the individual in this instance, might *displace* his aggression by taking out his anger on an innocent but safer target. This scapegoat might be a person, an object, or an entire group. Thus, the man who was insulted by his boss might yell at his wife or kick over a wastebasket; the boy who was pushed around by a bully might slug his kid sister or pull his dog's tail. Alternatively, either might blame their troubles on some relatively powerless minority group—like Jews or blacks. This tendency is particularly common when the object of the frustration is vague or unknown. For example, if an individual is unemployed or if serious inflation is eating into his savings, at whom can he lash out? In Nazi Germany it was safe to blame the Jews; in the rural South it was safe to blame the blacks.

Individual Differences in Scapegoating

Some people get frustrated or angry more easily than others and some tend to displace aggression (choose another target)

Will the frustrated boy be able to find a victim (scapegoat) for his aggressive feelings?
(Suzanne Szasz)

more readily than others. In short, there are people whose personalities predispose them toward being prejudiced. Thus, it has been argued that because of strict and severe parental upbringing, some individuals develop deep-seated personality characteristics which increase the likelihood of the formation of certain clusters of beliefs and attitudes. Those individuals have been said to have **authoritarian personalities** (Adorno *et al.*, 1950).

In a major study of the authoritarian personality, psychologists used a questionnaire called the F-scale (*F* for fascism). It consisted of items, such as the following, with which the individual was to indicate agreement or disagreement: "Sex crimes such as rape and attacks on children deserve more than mere imprisonment; such criminals ought to be publicly whipped, or worse"; "Most people don't realize how much our lives are controlled by plots hatched in secret places"; "Obedience and respect for authority are the most important virtues children should learn." The psychologists found that people who agreed with these statements tended to show a great deal of distrust and dislike for minority groups and an inordinate degree of ethnic and national pride.

Some interesting experiments provide some support for the scapegoat theory of prejudice. In one (Weatherley, 1961), individuals who scored either high or low on measures of anti-Semitism were subjected to a procedure designed to make them angry at the experimenter. The experimenter accomplished this feat by simply assuming a nasty demeanor—by putting them down and insulting their intelligence in the course of administering a brief paper and pencil task. The subjects were angry but, as mentioned earlier, it is often dangerous to express anger directly to a high-status person. The subjects were then allowed to interact with another student, who was actually an accomplice of the experimenter. This accomplice was introduced by name and the name was either Jewish or non-Jewish.

Subjects who were highly prejudiced demonstrated more hostility toward the "Jewish" student, but not toward the non-Jewish one, than did the low-prejudice subjects. Angry at the experimenter, they displaced their aggression but only to what they considered a safer and more suitable target—a Jew.

Prejudice via Conformity

It should be clear to the reader that the two major explanations for prejudice discussed above—namely, the social and the individual—are not mutually exclusive. Rather, the two can support and strengthen each other. Still a third explanation involves conformity. It is likely that many individuals adopt prejudiced attitudes as a result of implicit or explicit social pressure. Attitude tests have shown that white college students in South Africa are more prejudiced against blacks than American students are (Pettigrew, 1958). These data are not terribly surprising. Most people would agree that if there exists a country with manifestly more anti-black prejudice than the United States, it is certainly South Africa, a country that has attitudes of segregation and discrimination written into its legal code (the policy of apartheid). What *is* interesting is that the white South Africans showed no more evidence of authoritarianism than did white Americans. Their negative feeling against blacks was probably not a result of personality structure. Moreover, the South Africans who were generally strong conformists—as tested by conformity to other social customs unrelated to prejudice—were the ones who showed the most prejudice against blacks.

If prejudiced attitudes are affected by a tendency to conform to group norms and group pressures, one might expect that as children get older they also become more uniform in their attitudes toward minority groups. It takes time to learn the rules, regulations, expectations, and prejudices of one's society. As the Rodgers and Hammerstein song goes, "You've got to be carefully taught." And, indeed, researchers have found more uniformity of anti-Semitic and anti-black attitudes among 17–18 year-olds than among 13–14 year-olds (Wilson, 1963).

What happens to prejudice when a person changes his place of residence? If conformity is a factor, one would expect individuals to show dramatic increases in their prejudice when they move into areas where the norm is greater prejudice. And this happened among some people who had recently moved to New York City. Those who came into direct and frequent contact with anti-Semitic people became more anti-Semitic (Watson, 1950).

The conformity we have in mind might be the result of the kind of explicit group pressure we described earlier in this section when we discussed Asch's experiment on the judging of lines. Recall that Asch's data indicated that conformity occurs most frequently when one's judgment is different from that of a unanimous majority.

Applying this finding to the facts of Southern prejudice against blacks, one psychologist observed that "many Southerners, faced with what appears to be solid unanimity, submit to the distortion [that is, anti-black attitudes]. But when even one respected source—a minister, a newspaper editor, even a college professor—conspicuously breaks the unanimity, *perhaps* a dramatic modification is achieved in the private opinions of many conforming Southerners." (Pettigrew, 1961, pp. 109–110)

Bigoted attitudes develop not only because of simple contact with other bigoted attitudes. They sometimes are intentionally or unintentionally fostered by a bigoted society. For example, one investigator (MacCrone, 1957) interviewed white South Africans in an attempt to find reasons for their negative attitudes toward blacks. Among other things, his respondents were convinced that most crimes were committed by blacks. What was their reason? They saw a great many black convicts working in public places, as convicts, and *no* white convicts. What the respondents either didn't realize or didn't think about was that white convicts were not allowed to work in public! In short, a society can create prejudiced beliefs by law or by custom. In our own society, until very recently, most newspapers tended to identify the race of a criminal or suspect if he was not white but very rarely if he happened to be white. Naïve readers could easily develop a distorted picture of the proportion of crime attributable to nonwhites.

It is undoubtedly true that some people are prejudiced because they are conforming to group pressures or simply because they have not been exposed to accurate or true information about the group in question. These people have been referred to as "latent liberals," meaning that their liberalization is a matter of freeing them from these pressures and misconceptions. But for many individuals prejudice does seem to fill an important personal or social need; accordingly, it would be a mistake to assume (as many people in the 1930's and 1940's did) that overcoming prejudice is simply a matter of exposing people to the truth. As we have seen, people have a way of distorting information to fit their needs. Simple information campaigns have had only limited success. One reason for this is that people tend not to listen or read material that is not congenial (dissonant) with their beliefs. For example, a series of radio broadcasts presented during World War II were aimed at reducing ethnic prejudice by presenting sympathetic informational programs about various ethnic groups. Thus, one week there was a program on people of Italian origin, the next week a program on people of Polish origin, and so forth. Who was listening? Well, the Poles listened to the program about Poles, the Italians listened to the program about Italians, and each of the other ethnic groups followed suit (Lazarfeld, 1944).

What happens if you force people to listen? There is

some evidence that, if the need to maintain the prejudiced attitude is strong enough, such a procedure might actually boomerang—the individual may misinterpret the information to fit his prejudice. To illustrate, if an individual believes that blacks are stupid and you show him a film of a highly intelligent, highly articulate black, he is apt to conclude that the fellow is a "smart-ass, uppity nigger" (see Cooper & Dinerman, 1951).

How can prejudice be reduced?

Simple information campaigns don't work. How, then do we reduce or eliminate prejudice? It should be clear from reading this chapter that there are no simple solutions to the problem of ethnic prejudice. There are, however, some intriguing possibilities based upon social psychological theory. Our belief in the feasibility of these approaches has been strengthened by some well-designed laboratory experiments. Admittedly, evidence from laboratory experiments is far from conclusive when one is dealing with a complex and highly emotional phenomenon like prejudice, but it is encouraging to note that preliminary reports from the "real world" tend to confirm the laboratory data.

Shared Coping

One possible technique has already been discussed in this chapter (the forced cooperation of the Red Devils and Bulldogs); Collins (1970) has called it **shared coping.** Recall that in our discussion of conflict as a possible cause of prejudice, we mentioned the experiment in which two groups of boys at a summer camp were intentionally placed in conflict situations until intergroup hostility developed. These hostilities were relieved after the boys found themselves in situations where it was essential for them to cooperate with each other, i.e., to join with each other in coping with a universal problem. For example, on a camping trip the truck broke down. In order to get it going again, it was necessary to pull it up a hill; and in order to pull it up the hill it was essential that both groups cooperate. After a number of these cooperative ventures, a sharp reversal of hostile feelings and negative stereotyping was observed among members of the two rival groups. Friendships developed between members of the different groups, they began to cooperate spontaneously even in noncrisis situations, and a rather relaxed atmosphere was established.

These data seem to square with common experience. For example, there are fewer incidents involving racial tensions among military personnel in combat areas, where continued cooperation is vital, than in areas that are free of crisis and where people do not have to cooperate. Clearly, it is difficult to maintain hostile feelings about someone if you are engaged with him in the common cause of fighting a war and preserving your own and his lives. Similarly, the members of integrated athletic teams become less prejudiced because of the necessity of cooperation in a common cause.

It should be clear that shared coping goes beyond mere "contact." It was once believed that if prejudice is largely the result of misinformation, then if people of diverse ethnic and racial groups came into contact with one another, prejudice would be reduced. As we have seen, contact, in and of itself, often increases prejudice—if the contact is between those of unequal status or occurs in a way or under situations which exacerbate common stereotypes, as illustrated by the contact white South Africans had with black convict workers. One of the essential characteristics of a shared coping situation is that individuals find themselves in the same situation as equal status partners.

Working together cooperatively reduces hostility and promotes friendships.
(Charles Gatewood)

A Dissonance Approach

One of the difficulties involved in the development of shared coping situations is that they don't often occur naturally. We have discussed cases in which investigators were able to engineer situations carefully so that cooperation between groups became essential. But the probability of several of these crises occurring by happenstance is remote indeed. This is especially true if we are concerned with easing interracial prejudice; in our society the races tend to be segregated into residential ghettos.

In recent years, some political progress has been made in

the direction of decreasing the segregation of racial groups. A notable example was the landmark decision of the Supreme Court which decreed that so-called "separate-but-equal" educational facilities were, in fact, unequal and therefore unconstitutional. Theoretically, it could be argued that this decision would have a profound effect on reducing prejudice. Opponents of integration have argued that you can't legislate morality; you can't make people like and respect each other simply by passing a law. In the simplest sense, this is true. As we have suggested previously, simply increasing the opportunities for contact does not in and of itself reduce prejudice—but it can set the stage for other processes to occur which might have some effect on the attitudes of the individuals involved. One of these processes might be that equal status contact, as in schools, increases the possibility of shared coping and whatever understanding can stem from that. Another possibility is that such contact, or even the anticipation of such contact, will produce a change in attitude through the operation of a process which I described in the previous chapter as the psychology of inevitability. Basically, if an individual holds the cognition that a particular event is disastrous and, at the same time, is inevitable, he experiences dissonance. One way in which he can reduce dissonance is by convincing himself that the upcoming event is not so bad as he previously imagined. In short, we change our attitudes about the events, objects, or people that we must inevitably encounter. Admittedly, it's a far cry from accepting a bowl of vegetables to changing relationships between blacks and whites. Few people are so naïve as to believe that deep-seated racial intolerance can be eliminated either by shared coping or by the reduction of dissonance in coming to terms with inevitable events. What I would suggest is that such events *can* provide the opening wedge toward producing a diminution of hostile feelings in many individuals.

Experimental Data

The data lend some support to these speculations. One investigation examined the attitudes of whites toward blacks in public-housing projects (Deutsch & Collins, 1951). Specifically, in one housing project black and white families were assigned to residential apartment buildings in a segregated manner. Each race was assigned to separate buildings in the same project. In another project the races were integrated; black and white families were assigned to the same building. Whites in the integrated project reported a greater positive change in their attitudes toward blacks (as compared to what they had been prior to moving into the project) than residents of the segregated project. It should be emphasized that the psychologists were observing a public-housing project. The world does not always become as harmonious when blacks move into private housing in white neighborhoods. Indeed, frequently, quite the contrary is true. In the private-housing situation, the white residents generally feel

Integrated public-housing projects reduce race prejudice.
(Suzanne Szasz)

that their social status and economic well-being are being threatened; consequently there is some tendency for their attitudes to become more unfavorable (Kramer, 1949). Putting both of these findings together, I would conclude that people try to adjust their attitudes to make inevitability as pleasant as possible; but if conflict, frustration, and rancor already exist in the situation, the psychology of inevitability will not, of itself, produce a positive change in attitudes. In such situations, additional work must be done to overcome the hostility that is frequently generated by desegregation. We will come back to this point in a moment. First, however, I would like to underscore the major point: One way to begin to combat prejudice is to bring the races together under conditions of equal status. Unless this is done in a manner that generates hostility and suspicion, the mere fact of desegregation leads people to accommodate their attitudes in order to make them consistent with this accomplished fact.

Observations from the Field

If my reasoning is correct, it would lead us to suggest that a particular kind of public policy would be potentially most beneficial to society—one that is the exact opposite of what has been generally recommended. In the aftermath of the 1954 Supreme Court decision there was a general feeling that integration must proceed slowly. In effect, most public officials and many social scientists felt that in order to achieve harmonious racial relations, integration should be delayed until an information campaign could be launched in order to change negative attitudes. In short, the behavior change (integra-

October 4, 1954
If people do not feel integration is inevitable, they are not so likely to change their attitudes.
(UPI)

tion) must follow a cognitive change. The present analysis suggests just the opposite, that cognitive change is frequently the result of behavioral change. Indeed, knowing what we do about the limited success of information campaigns, it could be argued that the best way to produce interracial harmony would be to launch into behavioral change. Moreover, *and most important*, the greater the speed and the greater the degree to which the public is convinced of the fact that the events are inevitable, the greater the likelihood that prejudice will decrease. But, of course, this process can be (and has been) thwarted by simply removing the inevitability from the situa-

September 7, 1971
(UPI)

tion. If people believe that the integration of schools can be circumvented, delayed, or foiled, the perception of inevitability is weakened, maybe erased. Accordingly, there will be no attitude change. For example, if the statements and actions of a governor, a mayor, or a sheriff lead a bigot to believe that there is a way to avoid sending his children to an integrated school, it should be clear that he will feel no need to reexamine his racist beliefs. In the absence of this feeling of inevitability, there will be no attitude change; the result might well be violent opposition to integration.

In a careful analysis of the process and effects of school desegregation, Thomas Pettigrew raises the question, "What leads to violence in some desegregating communities, like Little Rock and Clinton, and not in others, like Norfolk and Winston-Salem?" After noting the complexity of the situation and the probability that a multiplicity of factors are relevant, he concludes that "violence has generally resulted in localities where at least some of the authorities give prior hints that they would gladly return to segregation if disturbances occurred; peaceful integration has generally followed firm and forceful leadership" (1961, p. 105). Indeed, as early as 1953, K. B. Clark drew an identical conclusion based on desegregation in some of the border states. He found that immediate desegregation was more effective than gradual desegregation and that trouble and violence were associated with ambiguous or inconsistent policies and the vascillation of community leaders. These findings are, in turn, consistent with still earlier results based on the desegregation of military units in World War II (Stouffer *et al.*, 1949).

It should be pointed out that, ideally, maximum attitude change will occur if integration can be accomplished with a minimum of physical force. Based on our data on severity of threat (see previous chapter) I would argue that the less the force the greater the attitude change. Thus, there will be a smaller change in prejudiced attitudes if the National Guard is physically present—complete with bayonets and tanks—than if the event can proceed without force. In practice, this ideal situation cannot always be employed because of the need to protect innocent people from physical harm.

ANALYSIS OF FACTORS CONTRIBUTING TO PREJUDICE It would be a serious oversimplification to ignore other important demographic, political, and psychological factors in discussing the effect of desegregation on prejudice reduction. A careful analysis of the effects of desegregation should take into account such factors as the black-white ratio of the area, the socioeconomic status of the populace, and the traditionalism of the community (see Pettigrew & Cramer, 1959). But these factors may be less important than we once believed. In a similar vein, it was once argued that desegregation would be impossible because of the belief among social psychologists that prejudice was generally the result of a deeply rooted personality disorder which must be cured before desegregation could proceed. The evidence indicates that for the vast majority of individuals this has not been true—that instead the best way to begin to "cure" prejudice is to desegregate.

But desegregation is only a beginning. Quite frequently, rather than solving problems, desegregation *appears* to create problems. Our analysis of the way people respond to inevitability assumes that the hostile attitudes involved are based solely on misinformation. In short, our analysis does not take into account the intensity and reality basis underlying some of the existing hostile feelings. For example, bringing black and white students together for the first time in high school usually causes more initial disturbance than if they are first brought together in kindergarten, before a good deal of the negative feelings have had a chance to develop and solidify. When tension and anger already exist, additional measures must be taken to increase understanding between the individuals involved. All too often, when desegregation takes place under adverse circumstances, school authorities find themselves unprepared to cope with the resulting tension. In my own hometown in 1971, an attempt was made to overcome the *de facto* desegregation that existed in some of the high schools. Unfortunately, this was accomplished in a most inequitable manner: by closing down an almost exclusively black high school and busing the black students from their own neighborhood clear across town to a high school in a predominantly white neighborhood. Understandably, the fact that it was only blacks who were inconvenienced resulted in a great deal of resentment on the part of the black students,

Integration at an early age helps prevent a buildup of negative feelings.
(Marion Bernstein)

and there was racial violence within the high school. Eventually, tension was eased and some semblance of understanding and even harmony was created by bringing black students and white students together to discuss their feelings and problems in interracial human relations groups. In addition, a program was initiated in which small interracial learning groups were formed where participants were induced to cooperate with one another (rather than to compete) and to take responsibility for one another's learning (rather than to resent it). At this writing, the situation continues to improve.

Again, the problem of prejudice is a complex one. There are no simple solutions. It would be comforting to believe that the psychology of inevitability would produce automatic attitude change. Unfortunately, it doesn't often happen that way because, as in the example above, the resentments are often real and justified. But even in such a situation, where there were tremendous built-in problems, it has been our experience that young people can work together and by so doing can increase their empathy for each other.

PREJUDICES OF THE MINORITY This example reminds us of the fact that, for the most part, the problem of reducing prejudice has been approached as if it were a narrow one-way street; we have been talking about techniques which will reduce or turn around the negative stereotypes of minority groups held by the dominant majority. But, of course, prejudice is a two-way street. Minority group members tend to have hostile feelings against the majority group as well. As illustrated above, these are even more difficult to deal with because they are often based upon real grievances. Nonetheless, to the extent that an overgeneralization is involved, it *is* a form of prejudice, whether the grievance that some blacks feel toward some whites is justified or not, the fact that it often results in hostility directed against all whites makes it an instance of prejudice. Unfortunately, at this writing, there has been very little systematic research on the prejudices held by minority group members. Moreover, the problem of generalized hostility is broader in scope than what typically has been defined as prejudice. It extends to the feelings that any person has for any other person. That is to say, when one looks over the hill of ethnic prejudice, one sees the vast valley of interpersonal relations. When one moves beyond the problem of reducing prejudice, one encounters the broader problem of determining what makes people like and trust each other. How do we move from mere tolerance to actually taking responsibility for one another? What happens *after* schools are integrated? What happens after dissonance has been reduced and shared coping has taken place? In our day-to-day living, why is it that we like some people more than others? It is to this question that we turn in the following chapter.

SUMMARY

Prejudice is defined as a set of hostile attitudes based on and supported by generalizations derived from faulty or incomplete information. There are many causes of prejudice, among which are (1) real conflict between members of different groups, (2) the displacement of aggression aroused by dangerous or abstract forces but directed toward safe, identifiable targets, and (3) conformity to existing norms.

While some individuals, because of early childhood experience, show a greater propensity toward being prejudiced than others, it is overly pessimistic to assert that prejudiced attitudes cannot be changed short of intensive psychotherapy. At the same time, prejudice cannot be substantially reduced by simply exposing individuals to favorable information about the "out-group" because people tend to ignore or distort information that is contrary to their attitudes. Moreover, prejudice is not greatly affected by increasing contact between the individual and the group in question. Two promising techniques for the reduction of prejudice are (1) shared coping, and (2) placing individuals in inevitable situations which run counter to their attitudes.

7

Attraction: Who Likes Whom and Why

Why do we like certain people?
Whom do we like best?
Why is a reward theory of attraction too simple?
Why is a gain-loss theory better?

In the preceding chapter we saw that prejudice against a group can be reduced by certain types of direct experience with that group. But, as we have also seen, mere contact with another person is no guarantee that we will like him. In this chapter we ask, What is it about our experience with other people that makes us like them or dislike them?

Why do we like certain people?

In a sense, all people are social psychologists, although only a few of us get paid for it. We all live in the world; consequently, we all interact with other people. Through our experiences in interacting with other people we develop social psychological theories. Nowhere is this more prevalent than in an area like interpersonal attraction. I frequently consult with those of my fellow social psychologists who happen to be undergraduates in my classes. I have, on occasion, asked them what there is about their best friend that makes them like him more than they like other people. I usually get a multitude of responses; these include (1) a similarity of values, attitudes, beliefs, and/or interests; (2) some skills, abilities, or competencies; (3) some pleasant or "admirable" qualities like loyalty, pleasantness, reasonableness, honesty, and kindness.

These reasons sound like good common sense. They also

square with the results of a great deal of systematic research in the area. People like people who cooperate rather than compete, who have pleasant characteristics, who agree with them, who praise rather than criticize them, and who help rather than obstruct them.

One can include all of these aspects of attractiveness under one simple and sweeping generalization: We like people whose behavior brings us maximal reward. This proposition has been stressed by a number of theorists (see, for example, Homans, 1961). As generalizations go, this is a useful one. Although there are problems with this general statement, let us begin by looking at the wide array of situations in which it makes sense.

Rewards People Provide by Doing Favors

If you were starving and I graciously provided you with a tasty and nourishing meal, *that* would be rewarding and chances are you would like me for that. Similarly, if you were drowning and I plunged into the ocean and rescued you, chances are you would like me better than if I had walked by and simply left you to struggle on your own.

This phenomenon can be illustrated by any number of experiments. Of course, experimenters in the field of social psychology usually stop short of setting up situations where human subjects are actually starving or drowning. But, as we have seen, they attempt to set up reasonable analogues of extreme situations. In one study (Lott & Lott, 1960), children were put into three-person groups that played a game which involved choosing various pathways on a game board. Choosing the right pathways led to safety; choosing the wrong pathways led to disaster. Children were, in effect, walking single file in a mine field, except for the fact that the mine remained active even after it exploded. If the leader chose the wrong path, he was "blown up" (out of the game), and the child next in line would, of course, choose a different path. If the leader happened to choose correctly, he led the others to a successful completion of the game. The psychologists found that children who were rewarded (that is, arrived safely at the goal) showed a greater liking for their teammates who were instrumental in helping them achieve the reward than did children who did not reach the final goal. In short, we like people who contribute to our victory better than people who do not.

There are all kinds of favors that people can do for us. One class of favors involves punishing our enemies. In one experiment (Aronson & Cope, 1968) college students were placed in a situation where they were treated either kindly or cruelly by a graduate research assistant. They then chanced to overhear that assistant being chastised harshly by his supervisor for a reason totally unrelated to their own experience with the assistant. Those who had been cruelly treated by the assistant ended up with great liking for the supervisor who treated their enemy harshly. (Although we have described these experimental situations in very simple terms, measurement of such a complex concept as attraction is not easy, as you can see from Spotlight 7-1.)

Rewards Through Similarity

Another way in which people can provide rewards for others is to agree with them on some issue. If all we know about a person are his opinions on some issues, the closer his opinions are to ours, the more we like him (Byrne, 1969). Similarly, experiments have shown that the person who deviates from the opinions and attitudes of a group is rejected by that group (Schachter, 1951). Recall that in the chapter on conformity we discussed the reasons why a person conforms; one of these reasons is to be liked or to avoid being rejected. If that is their goal, it turns out that people who conform are behaving in a rational manner. While in the abstract people tend to admire and respect the individualist, when it comes right down to it, in most situations we dislike people who disagree with us and like people who agree with us. In short, we seem to be telling people: "It's fine if you are in disagreement—as long as it's not with us!"

Why do we like people who agree with us? There are three important possibilities. One is that the person who shares our opinion on an issue provides us with a kind of social validation for our beliefs; that is, he provides us with the feeling that we are right. This is rewarding and, hence, we like those who agree with us. If a person disagrees with us, this suggests the possibility that we may be wrong. This is punishing; hence, we don't like people who disagree with us.

We are more attracted to people when they agree with us because we gain rewards. (Both, Ted Polumbaum)

There is another possible reason for the relationship between similarity and liking: It is likely that we make certain negative inferences about the character of a person who disagrees with us on a substantive issue, not simply because his disagreement indicates that we may be wrong, but rather because we suspect that his opinion on that issue indicates that he is the kind of person whom we have found to be unpleasant, immoral, or stupid. For example, suppose you are a humanist and a liberal, and among your beliefs is that capital punishment should never be employed. Suppose you meet a man who tells you that he is a firm believer in capital punishment. I then come along, ask you if you liked the man, and you say "no." Am I to conclude that (1) you didn't like him because his belief suggested to you that your belief might be wrong, or (2) in your experience, you have found that people who favor capital punishment tend to be unpleasant, immoral, antihuman, bigoted, harsh, cruel, conventional, punitive, stupid wife-beaters? The data on this issue are not definitive, but they suggest that both factors play a role in determining attraction.

Still a third possibility is this: When we learn that a person holds an opinion similar to ours, it indicates that, if and when we get to know each other, *he* will like *us*. This is rewarding; hence, we like him. Let us expand on this theme.

Rewards Through Liking Us

Perhaps the greatest reward a person can bestow upon us is to like us. People like to be liked. A professional businessman and amateur psychologist named Dale Carnegie made a fortune by

Dale Carnegie's basic assumption is sound: People like to be liked.
(Suzanne Szasz)

SPOTLIGHT 7-1

How Attraction Is Measured

There are many ways to measure one person's liking for another. In one sense, attraction can be considered to be an attitude. Thus, we can measure liking for a person in much the same way that we can measure attitudes. For example, in many experiments liking is measured by two simple scales. One scale might ask the person to indicate how much he felt he would like or dislike the other person by circling a number on a seven-point scale with 7 being most positive and 1 being most negative. The other scale might ask a related question, such as whether the subject believed he would enjoy working with the other person, with 7 meaning he would enjoy it very much and 1 meaning he would dislike it very much.

Rating scales have the virtue of being easy to administer, and for this reason they are the most commonly used measure of attraction. They have one major flaw, however: They may not be totally accurate precisely because they are so easy to fill out. Specifically, since it doesn't cost a person to indicate his feelings on a piece of paper, individuals may be inclined to treat their own ratings rather casually; they may not think very deeply about their own feelings or they may be inclined to write that they like someone even when they don't—just to be a nice guy.

Because of this, social psychologists have recently begun to employ indices of attraction which require more of a commitment on the part of the person. These are called behavioral measures. For example, consider the experiment in which it was found that individuals liked a person who punished their enemies. In this study the investigators were interested in how much the subjects liked the experimenter's supervisor, who was a psychology professor. After the experiment was over, the departmental secretary told each subject that this professor desperately needed volunteers to make a number of phone calls and that he needed them right away. She asked each subject if he would be willing to volunteer to do the professor this favor. If the subject agreed, she asked him how many phone calls he was willing to make. The number of phone calls was used as an index of liking; that is, those subjects who volunteered to make 15 phone calls as a favor to the professor were considered to like him more than those who agreed to make 8 phone calls, and 8 phone calls is "more liking" than 4 or none. The assumption underlying the use of this measure is that if we like someone, it pleases us to see him happy; if we do him a favor, we increase this happiness. Therefore, the more we like him, the more favors we will volunteer to do for him, all other things being equal.

But all other things are not always equal. Perhaps one of the people in the above experiment really liked the professor a great deal and would have liked to do him a favor but was extremely busy. Accordingly, he might have volunteered to make only one or two phone calls. Thus, although he liked the professor a lot, it would not show up in his score. There are, of course, simpler behavioral measures than favor-doing. One of these is eye contact. It has been shown that when two people talk to each other they look into each other's eyes off and on for short periods, ranging from 30 to 60 percent of their interaction. The frequency of their eye contact has been shown to correlate with their expressed liking for each other (Argyle, 1967).

Still another measure of attraction is the *sociometric scale* which combines the simplicity of a rating scale with the commitment of a behavioral measure. Here, individuals are asked to indicate (on a rating scale) the extent to which they would like to have another person as a roommate, or as a work partner on a project they are about to embark on, the extent to which they'd like to sit next to him on the bus during an upcoming excursion, and so forth. While such a measure is easy to obtain, it includes a real commitment of some time to be spent with the other person. Therefore, it is unlikely that individuals would answer the question casually or haphazardly.

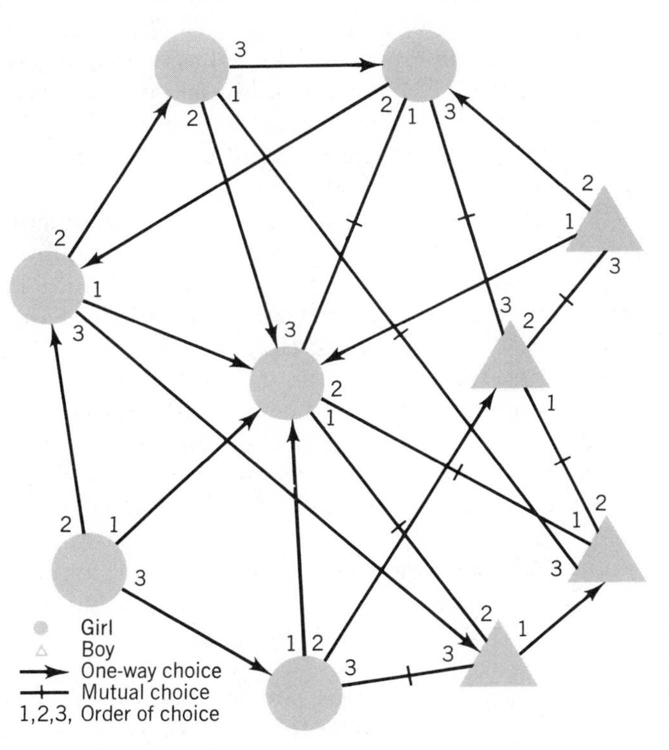

A sociogram can show the social structure of a classroom. Shown here are several students' choices of classmates they liked best, along with their second and third choices.

selling this idea. In 1937 he wrote a book called *How to Win Friends and Influence People*, which has proven itself to be one of the all-time best sellers and has been translated into thirty-five different languages. Essentially, Carnegie's advice to his readers was to be pleasant, pretend that you like the people you're talking to, that you are interested in the things that they are interested in, and "dole out praise lavishly." As we shall see, such pretense has only limited value. But the assumption behind the advice is sound: People like to be liked, and like those who like them. This has been demonstrated in numerous experiments.

The reader, a social psychologist in his own right, may be yawning by this time. Or, more likely, he may be asking with some indignation whether social psychologists don't have more important things to do with their time than performing an experiment (much less a bunch of them!) to prove something that we already know. There is something in me that's inclined to agree with the reader who feels that way. As an experimentalist, I must admit that I get a bigger kick out of doing research to test a hypothesis that is somewhat surprising and innovative than in trying to prove something that my grandmother already knows is true. And yet, I also know that we never really know something for sure unless it has been demonstrated under controlled conditions. My grandmother is a pretty good social psychologist; but so many phenomena that my grandmother knows to be true turn out *not* to be true when we put them to the test in the laboratory.

With this in mind, let us look at the phenomenon of liking someone who likes us. The reciprocation of sentiment is a common phenomenon—but which causes which? It could be that Sam likes Harry because Harry had indicated that he likes Sam; since being liked feels good to Sam and since Harry is the cause of this good feeling, Sam comes to like Harry. On the other hand, the causal sequence could be reversed. Sam could come to like Harry; then, as a consequence of this liking, he may convince himself that Harry likes him. In the complexity and hubbub of being involved in an interpersonal relationship, it is often difficult for the participants to unravel which of these causal sequences was operating. Accordingly, it does make sense for the experimentalist to attempt to arrive at a definitive answer by constructing a controlled situation and observing the relationship in a dispassionate manner.

A Test Situation

Such an experiment was constructed by two psychologists (Backman & Secord, 1959) who formed groups of people who had never seen each other before. Prior to the first meeting, each person was given a personality test and was subsequently informed that on the basis of this test certain designated people in the group would almost surely like him a lot. In actuality, the designations were made randomly. But the information they had been given had a very large *initial* effect on the feelings of the subjects; there was a strong early attraction for the people the subjects were told would probably like them. However, the effects of this deceptive information did not last for very long. After the first few meetings, the designated people were not liked better than the others. As the actual contact among people increased, each person received much more realistic information about the others and, as a consequence, their feelings changed. What the experiment demonstrated is that, all other things being equal, in the absence of information to the contrary, the suspicion that someone likes us increases our tendency to like him. At the same time, it demonstrated that this phenomenon is ephemeral; no matter how much a person expects to be liked or wants to be liked, he will usually not continue to believe that he *is* liked in the face of the continued absence of concrete evidence.

One way of looking at these data is to suggest that people need to be liked because of feelings such as insecurity, anxiety, and low self-esteem. If someone reduces these unpleasant feelings by liking us, we like him. An unusually "realistic" experiment provided graphic evidence to support this interpretation by showing that as the feeling of insecurity grows more intense, so too does our tendency to like someone who indicates that he likes us. The experiment (Walster, 1965) was performed with university coeds. Each coed arrived at a general reception room where she was greeted and asked to wait for her experimenter. While she was waiting, along came a good-looking, well-dressed male. Through a conversation between the young man and a receptionist, it was established that he was waiting to participate in a totally different experiment being conducted by a "Miss Turner." The young man, who was actually an accomplice, then struck up a conversation with the subject, indicated that he found her attractive, and asked for a date.

At this point the experimenter entered and led the young lady into the experimental room and told her that the purpose of the study was to examine the results of various personality tests which she had taken previously. The young lady was then given a contrived evaluation of her own personality. Half of the girls were led to believe that they were sensitive, original, and interesting people possessing a great deal of integrity. This information was designed to raise their self-esteem temporarily. The other girls were informed that they were immature, inflexible, and had a weak personality. This information was designed to lower their self-esteem, and thus increase their feelings of insecurity. Finally, as part of the experiment, the girls were asked to rate how much they liked a wide variety of people—a teacher, a friend, others. "And since we have one space left, why don't you also rate that fellow from Miss Turner's experiment whom you were waiting with?" The results indicated that those girls who received unfavorable information about themselves showed far more liking for the young man than did those who received favorable information about themselves. In short, we like to be liked—and the more insecure we feel, the more we appreciate being liked and, consequently, the more we like someone who likes us.

Whom do we like best?

The Relationship Between Similarity and Being Liked

As we have suggested, these two causes of attraction—similarity and being liked—are not independent of each other; i.e., one reason why we like a person with beliefs that are similar to ours may be precisely because we make the guess that if a person shares our opinion on several issues, then if he were to get to know us he would probably like us. If this is true, we would expect being liked to be a stronger force than opinion similarity. And it is. When these two variables are both present in the same experiment, being liked appears to be a more powerful determinant of attraction than similarity—although both do have an effect (Aronson & Worchel, 1966). Furthermore, it has been shown (Jones, Bell, & Aronson, 1971) that there is something *especially exciting* about being liked by someone who *doesn't* share your opinions on various issues. In one experiment, college students discovered that another person had opinions that were either similar or dissimilar to their own. After having a conversation with that person, they then eavesdropped on him while he was describing them favorably to a third party. The results showed that the students indicated the greatest liking for a person with *dissimilar* attitudes who liked them. Thus, although we generally like people who have attitudes similar to our own, if we encounter someone who likes us in spite of the fact that our opinions differ, we are inclined to infer that there must be something special and unique about us that he finds attractive. In short, "He likes me for myself—not for my opinions." Since this realization is especially gratifying, we tend to like that person most.

Attraction of Opposites

As indicated above, the relationship between opinion similarity and attraction is not a simple one. The relationship becomes even more complicated when we move from opinion similarity to consider the similarity of personality characteristics. Is it true that "birds of a feather flock together," as the old adage goes, or do you believe that other old adage, "opposites attract"? Interestingly enough, investigators who have studied the needs and values of engaged and married couples have found support for both of these possibilities (Banta & Hetherington, 1963; Winch, 1958). One possible explanation for these differences is that whether opposite personalities like or dislike each other depends on what character-

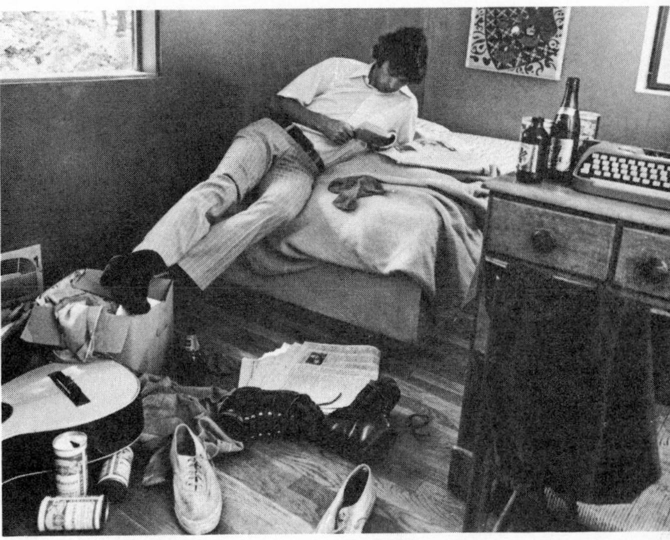

Attraction of personalities is dependent upon many variables and the values assigned to them.
(L.: Clemens Kalischer; R.: Ted Polumbaum)

istics we're talking about. For example, a person who valued neatness and tidiness to the point of turning it into an obsession might find it difficult to live with a slob. And, of course, the slob would not be too happy with an overly neat person either. It would seem reasonable to assume that neat people would flock to neat people and slobs would flock to slobs. Similarly, a person who was extroverted, needing to socialize with others, might not get along too well with an introverted person whose idea of a good time was to sit home with a good book—and vice versa. It would seem reasonable to assume that introverts would seek out introverts and extroverts would seek out extroverts. But let's look at a different set of characteristics, such as nurturance and dependency. A person who was very nurturant (likes to take care of others) and a person who had high dependency needs (likes to be taken care of) probably would get along swimmingly. In actuality, many sets of characteristics are involved in any one relationship.

Why is a reward theory of attraction too simple?

To repeat, all of the above situations lead neatly to a **reward theory of attraction:** We like people whose behavior is rewarding and we dislike people whose behavior is punishing. Although this generalization covers a wide array of human behavior, we often find that as the situation becomes more complex, it becomes increasingly more difficult for us to predict the conditions under which a person will be liked, disliked, or yawned at as a consequence of performing a specific action. The most generic reason for this difficulty is that, in complex social situations, the meaning of the term "reward" is not always clear; the social context in which the "reward" is provided can change the meaning of the reward. Consequently, the context in which a reward is given can have a great effect upon whether or not the rewarder's attractiveness is increased.

Observations of Competency

Some behaviors that might appear rewarding in one context are anything but rewarding in a slightly different setting. For example, let us look at the *competence* of another person. Being around able, competent people is usually more rewarding than being around incompetent people. People like to be right, and one way to increase the probability of being right is to be in the vicinity of people who know what they're talking about, people available for consultation. Thus, if we assume that able, competent people are more rewarding to us than incompetent people, shouldn't it follow that we would like people of extremely high ability and competence to a greater extent than people who are moderately or poorly endowed? This seems like a truism; yet, as obvious as this relationship may seem, there is some disquieting evidence that indicates that this relationship does not always hold. Experiments on group interactions, for example, have demonstrated that group members who are considered the most able are not necessarily the best liked. Other studies have shown that people who initiate the most ideas and who are generally acknowledged to be the best idea men of the group are most often *not* among the best-liked group members (Hollander & Webb, 1955; Bales, 1953).

Competency is a characteristic admired in others. (Both, Ted Polumbaum)

How come? Perhaps for most people a great deal of ability in another person makes that person appear too good, too unapproachable, too distant, too nonhuman. If this were the case, then some manifestation of fallibility (humanness) on his part might actually increase his attractiveness.

Some very tentative support for this notion can be mentioned in passing. According to a Gallup poll, when John Kennedy

Evidence of a competent man's fallibility tends to increase his popularity. (UPI)

was president, his personal popularity increased immediately *after* the abortive invasion of Cuba in 1961, commonly known as the Bay of Pigs fiasco. Here is a situation in which a president committed one of history's truly great blunders and, lo and behold, people came to like him *more*. Explanation? Perhaps President Kennedy was too perfect. He was young, handsome, bright, witty, a war hero, charming, athletic, a voracious reader, a master political strategist, an uncomplaining endurer of physical pain with a perfect wife who spoke several foreign languages, two cute kids (one boy, one girl), and a talented, closely knit extended family. Some evidence of fallibility could have served to make him more human and hence more likable. This is a possible explanation, but the real world is no place to test such a hypothesis. In the real world there are just too many things happening simultaneously, any one of which could have increased Kennedy's popularity. For example, after the fiasco occurred, President Kennedy did not try to make excuses or pass the buck. Rather, he manfully accepted full responsibility for the blunder. This action of itself could have done much to make him attractive in the eyes of the populace.

Test of a Hypothesis

The proposition that an indication of fallibility on the part of a highly competent person may make him better liked, was tested experimentally (Aronson, Willerman, & Floyd, 1966), using the disguise of an investigation of social perception. Subjects listened to a tape recording of one of four stimulus persons: (1) a near-perfect person, (2) a near-perfect person who commits a clumsy blunder, (3) a mediocre person, and (4) a mediocre person who commits a clumsy blunder. All the subjects were told that they would be listening to a person who was a candidate for the college quiz bowl and that they would be asked to rate him in terms of what kind of an impression he made and how much they liked him. The tape itself was an interview between the candidate (stimulus person) and an interviewer. It consisted primarily of a set of extremely difficult questions posed by the interviewer; the questions were of the kind that are generally asked on the college quiz bowl. On one tape the stimulus person was of very high intellectual ability and seemed to be virtually perfect. He answered 92 percent of the questions correctly. On another tape (using the same voice) the stimulus person was presented as one of average ability. On this tape he answered only 30 percent of the questions correctly. In two additional conditions (one involving the superior person, one involving the average person), the stimulus person committed an embarrassing blunder. Near the end of the interview, he clumsily spilled a cup of coffee all over himself. Thus, to repeat, there were four conditions: A person of superior ability who either blundered or did not blunder, and a person of average ability who either blundered or did not blunder. The results were clear-cut, as shown in Table 7-1. The stimulus person who was rated most attractive was the superior person who committed a blunder, while the least attractive was the person of average ability who also committed a blunder.

Again, the results of this experiment would seem to conflict with a simple reward theory. Now it may be that, after the fact, an ingenious psychologist knowing these data could explain the results in terms of a general reward theory: If a person who is perfect poses a threat, then a blundering (but competent) person is less threatening (less punishing) and, hence, overall he is more rewarding. This is a sensible explanation. But the purpose of a theory is not merely to explain results after they occur, but also—and far more important—to predict relationships. After the fact, a general reward theory can be invoked to explain any and all behavior. For example, suppose I were to state that when offered a choice between two alternatives, an individual will always choose the more pleasant. Unless I have, in advance, a clear idea of which events are pleasant

TABLE 7-1
MEAN ATTRACTION SCORES

	Blunder	No Blunder
Superior Ability	30.2	20.8
Average Ability	−2.5	17.8

From E. Aronson, B. Willerman, & Joanne Floyd, "The Effect of a Pratfall on Increasing Interpersonal Attractiveness." *Psychonomic Science*, 1966, *4*, 227–28.

and which events are unpleasant, the statement is in danger of being circular. To illustrate, suppose you said to me, "Aha! So people always choose the more pleasant alternative, eh? Then how do you explain the fact that some Christian martyrs chose to be thrown to the lions rather than recant their faith?" "That's easy," I reply, "for those people a painful death was more pleasant and more rewarding than renouncing their faith." The circularity occurs because I have defined reward in terms of the behavior I was supposed to be predicting.

The Effects of Praise

Let us now look at *praise*, which at first glance might seem always to be rewarding. But let's take a second glance. Suppose a person does a fine piece of work and his boss says, "Nice work, Joe." That phrase almost certainly will function as a reward and Joe's liking for his boss probably will increase. But suppose Joe did a very poor job—and knows it. Along comes the boss and delivers the exact same phrase in exactly the same tone of voice. Will that phrase function as a reward in this new situation? I am not sure. Joe *may* interpret this statement as the boss's attempt to be encouraging and nice even in the face of a poor performance. Because of this display of considerateness, Joe may come to like the boss even more than the case where he *had*, in fact, done a good job. On the other hand, Joe might feel that his boss is praising him out of some ulterior motive; accordingly, he might view his boss's behavior as sarcastic, manipulative, dishonest, or patronizing. Would this interpretation diminish Joe's liking for his boss or would the praise feel good anyway? What do you think?

A good deal of research has been done in this area; perhaps the best way to summarize the findings is by borrowing the title of an article written by Edward Jones (1965), the world's greatest expert on the psychology of ingratiation and flattery. The article is entitled "Flattery Will Get You Somewhere." In short, people like to hear positive things about themselves, even when they have some reason to suspect that the person might be insincere. However, we should note that, on the one hand, they like a person most if they share his positive evaluation, but if the other person is too blatant in his flattery, they don't like him at all. Nonetheless, we should stress the fact that people do tend to give the subtle flatterer the benefit of the doubt. These findings can best be illustrated by two experiments. In one (Deutsch & Solomon, 1959) subjects were presented with one of four situations: (1) a positive evaluation for a very good performance, (2) a negative evaluation for a poor performance, (3) a positive evaluation for a poor performance, and (4) a negative evaluation for a very good performance. As one might expect, the subjects liked their evaluator best in the experimental condition in which he had given them a positive evaluation for a very good performance—and the subjects disliked him most when he gave them a negative evaluation for a very good performance. But the subjects also liked him a great deal when he evaluated their poor performance positively. In fact, in this experiment, they liked him almost as much as in the condition where the subject had, in fact, performed well—even though the subjects had every reason to suspect that the evaluator should have known that their performance was, indeed, a poor one. On the other hand, in another experiment (Dickoff, 1961) the flatterer clearly was trying to obtain a favor, and subjects saw his behavior as blatant, self-motivated dishonesty. In this setting, the flatterer was disliked.

Let us reexamine Dale Carnegie's advice in the light of these experiments. People *do* like people who say positive things about them—especially when they believe that these statements are sincere. If they have good reasons for suspecting that the compliments are insincere, they dislike the complimenter. One could generalize this beyond compliments; specifically, one might make the same case in regard to doing *any* favor for another person. Generally people like favors. But sometimes they may feel their freedom is being restricted, especially when the favor-doer is in a position to benefit from that favor. For example, if you were a teacher, you might not react positively toward a student who presented you with an expensive gift just before you were about to grade his term paper. These speculations are supported by results from an experiment in which college students were asked to participate in a study (which was labeled as important) involving their first impressions of another person (Brehm & Cole, 1966). While they were waiting for the experiment to begin, the "other person" (actually a stooge) asked if he could leave the room to get a soda. When he returned, he brought back a drink for the subject as well. The question that must have arisen in the minds of the subjects was, "Why is he doing this? Is he trying to buy a better rating from me?" The actual measure of liking, however, was not the paper and pencil ratings but rather a behavioral measure. The subjects were later asked to help the stooge perform a dull task supposedly unrelated to the impression-formation experiment. Those students who had not been given the soda by the stooge were more likely to help him than those who had been given the soda.

The Effects of Having a Favor Done

Clearly, then, doing someone a favor is not a surefire way of getting him to like you. Indeed, as we have seen, under some conditions it may even backfire. A more certain way of using favors to increase your own attractiveness is by getting someone to do *you* a favor. In our discussion of the theory of cognitive dissonance we described "the justification of cruelty," in which a person caused harm to another and attempted to justify this behavior by devaluing the victim (see p. 105). By the same token, we would argue that if a person does someone a favor, he would tend to justify this action by increasing the value of the recipient. In other words, the individual will say to himself, "Why in the world did I go to all of this effort (spend all of this money, help him, or whatever) for so and so? Because he's a hell of a nice guy, that's why!" (See Spotlight 7-2 for an illustrative example by Benjamin Franklin.)

This proposition was tested in an experiment (Jecker & Landy, 1969) in which students participated in a concept-formation task which enabled them to win a rather substantial sum of money. After the experiment was over, one third of the subjects were approached by the experimenter, who explained that he was using his own funds for the experiment and was running short—which would mean that he might be forced to stop the experiment. He asked, "As a special favor to me, would you mind returning the money you won?" All of these subjects complied with the request. Another third of the subjects were approached, *not* by the experimenter, but by the departmental secretary; she asked the subjects if they would return the money as a special favor to the psychology department's research fund, which was running low. All of these subjects complied with the request. The remaining third of the subjects were not asked to return their winnings. Finally, all subjects were asked to fill out a questionnaire in which they got a chance to rate the experimenter. Those students who had been cajoled into doing a special favor for the experimenter were the ones who found him most attractive.

Why might a limited theory be more useful?

If one considers the overall mass of research on interpersonal attraction, this generalization emerges: While it is true that people like to be liked, they also like to believe that they have earned it. On the basis of this generalization (and some systematic research), a somewhat different theory of interpersonal attraction has been proposed (Aronson, 1969). Like the more general "reward theory," the **gain-loss theory of attraction** deals with the rewarding

SPOTLIGHT 7-2
Benjamin Franklin Observes the Truth of Cognitive Dissonance

Doubts have been raised whether phenomena of cognitive dissonance can be observed outside the laboratory (e.g., Tedeschi *et al.*, 1971).[1] It is therefore interesting to note the following example which occurred well before the hypothesis of cognitive dissonance was stated.

Benjamin Franklin in 1736, at the age of 30, owned a printing shop in Philadelphia and was in that year chosen to be clerk of the General Assembly of Pennsylvania. The next year he was again nominated as clerk and reappointed, but over the opposition of a new member of the House who favored another candidate. Franklin was disturbed by the opposition of this man who was wealthy, educated and talented and seemed likely to become influential in the House. What should he do about it?

(White House Collection)

"... I did not ... aim at gaining his favour by paying any servile respect to him but, after some time, took this other method. Having heard that he had in his library a certain very scarce and curious book I wrote a note to him expressing my desire of perusing that book and requesting he would do me the favour of lending it to me for a few days. He sent it immediately and I return'd it in about a week with another note expressing strongly my sense of the favour. When we next met in the House he spoke to me (which he had never done before), and with great civility; and he ever after manifested a readiness to serve me on all occasions, so that we became great friends and our friendship continued to his death. This is another instance of the truth of an old maxim I had learned, which says, *'He that has once done you a kindness will be more ready to do you another than he whom you yourself have obliged.'*"[2]

[1] J. T. Tedeschi, B. R. Schlenker, & T. V. Bonoma, "Cognitive dissonance: Private ratiocination or public spectacle?" *American Psychologist,* 1971, *26,* 685–95.
[2] Quoted from *The Autobiography of Benjamin Franklin.* J. Bigelow (Ed.) New York: G. P. Putnam's Sons, 1916. Pp. 216–17.

behaviors of others and the resulting effects on liking. But unlike reward theory, it focuses on the gain or loss of rewards, not so much on the rewards themselves. More specifically, gain-loss theory holds that *increases* in reward will have more impact than constant and invariant reward. Thus, if we take esteem as a reward, a person whose esteem for us increases over time will be liked better than one who has always liked us. This would be true even if the latter were the source of a greater overall number of rewards. Similarly, losses in rewarding behavior have more impact than constant punitive behavior. Thus, a person whose esteem for us decreases over time will be disliked more than someone who has always disliked us—even if the total number of punishments are greater in the latter situation.

Imagine yourself at a cocktail party having a conversation with a person whom you've never met before. After several minutes he excuses himself and drifts into a different conversational group. Later that evening, while standing out of sight behind a potted palm, you happen to overhear this person in conversation—talking about a person he met earlier in the evening; lo and behold, it's you that he's talking about! Suppose that you attend seven consecutive cocktail parties, have a conversation with the same person at each of these parties and, as luck would have it, chance to overhear him talking about you each time.

There are four outcomes that are particularly interesting: (1) You overhear the person saying exclusively positive things about you on all seven occasions; (2) you overhear him saying exclusively negative things about you on all seven occasions; (3) his first couple of evaluations are exclusively negative, but they gradually become increasingly positive; (4) his first couple of evaluations are exclusively positive, but they gradually become more negative. These four possibilities are presented graphically in Figure 7-1. Which situation would render him most attractive to you? The gain-loss theory would predict that you'd like him best in the "gain" condition (3) and least in the "loss" condition (4).

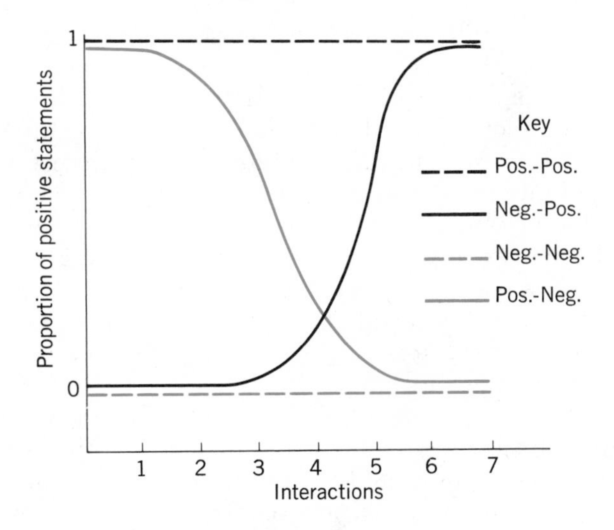

FIGURE 7-1 GRAPHIC REPRESENTATION OF EXPERIMENTAL CONDITIONS
(From Aronson, 1969)

To test this theory, two psychologists set up an experiment quite similar to the cocktail situation (Aronson & Linder, 1965).

College students interacted during seven sessions with another student, who was actually a paid confederate. After each session the subject was cleverly "allowed" to overhear the confederate evaluate her to the experimenter. The results, shown in Table 7-2, confirmed the predictions of the gain-loss theory. A person who began with negative comments about the subject and gradually became more positive was liked more by the subject than a person who made only positive comments. Also, a person who began with positive comments that gradually became negative was liked less than a person who made only negative comments about the subject.

TABLE 7-2
MEANS AND STANDARD DEVIATIONS FOR LIKING OF THE CONFEDERATE

Experimental Condition	Mean[a]	S.D.
Gain	7.67	1.51
Positive	6.42	1.42
Negative	2.52	3.16
Loss	0.87	3.32

[a] The higher the number, the greater the attraction.

Adapted from E. Aronson & D. Linder, "Gain and Loss of Esteem as Determinants of Interpersonal Attractiveness." *Journal of Experimental Social Psychology*, 1965, *1*, 156–71.

One of the implications of gain-loss theory is that once we have grown used to the goodwill (rewarding behavior) of a person (e.g., a mother, a spouse, a close friend), that person may become less useful as a source of reward than a stranger. Since a gain in esteem is a more potent reward than the absolute level of the esteem, a close friend (by definition) is operating near ceiling level and, therefore, cannot provide us with a gain. On the other hand, the constant friend and rewarder has great potential as a punisher. The greater the past history of invariant esteem and reward, the more devastating is its withdrawal. Such withdrawal, by definition, constitutes a loss of esteem. In effect, then, he has power to hurt the one he loves—but very little power to reward him.

An example may help clarify this point. After ten years of marriage, a husband and his wife are leaving their house for a cocktail party. The husband has always made a point of complimenting her, and this time is no exception: "Gee, honey, you look great!" Her response might well be a yawn. She already knows that her husband thinks she's attractive. But if the attentive husband were to tell his wife that he had decided that she was actually quite ugly,

Parents of teenagers know that their opinions are less valued than those of the peer group.
(Ted Polumbaum)

this would cause a great deal of pain since it represents a distinct loss of esteem.

Let's follow the wife: Soon after arriving at the party she is approached by a stranger who engages her in casual conversation. After a while he tells her with great sincerity that he finds her very attractive. Chances are she will not find this remark at all boring. It represents a distinct gain, makes her feel good, and increases the attractiveness of the stranger.

These speculations and data offer a bleak picture of the human condition—forever seeking favor in the eyes of strangers and being hurt by familiar people. Before we leap to this conclusion, let us discuss the impact that gain or loss of esteem has on the *behavior* of individuals—quite aside from its effect on the perceived attractiveness of the evaluator. In one experiment (Floyd, 1964) a psychologist paired young children who were either close friends or strangers. One of each pair was then allowed to earn several trinkets and was instructed to share these with his partner. Under study, really, was the perceived stinginess of the sharer. Some subjects were led to believe that the friend (or stranger) was treating them generously, others were led to believe that the friend (or stranger) was treating them in a stingy manner. These subjects were then allowed to earn several trinkets on their own and were similarly instructed to share them with their partner. As predicted, subjects showed the most generosity in the gain and loss conditions—toward the generous stranger and the stingy friend. More precisely, they were relatively stingy to the stingy stranger (why not, the stranger had behaved as they might have expected) and to the generous friend ("Ho-hum, so my friend likes me—what else is new?"). But when it looked as if they might be gaining a friend (the generous stranger), they reacted with generosity—and likewise, when it looked as if they might be losing a friend (the stingy friend), they *also responded with generosity.*

The last finding seems to be a rather touching aspect of the human condition. It suggests the possibility that individuals have some motivation toward the maintenance of stability in their relationships. Let us return to the married couple at the cocktail party. While it's true that either partner has the power to hurt the other in an important relationship, the hurt partner will be motivated to try to regain what he has lost by making himself more attractive to his spouse.

Carrying this speculation a step farther, beyond the suggestion that our close friends and marriage partners are the ones who are most apt to hurt us, we would add that it is characteristic of these relationships that the people tend to sit on minor annoyances and to keep their negative feelings to themselves. This results in the *appearance* of unambiguous esteem which can be devastated by a sudden shift in sentiment. In an open, authentic relationship, where people are more able to share their feelings and impressions — even their negative ones — *no* plateau is reached. Rather, there is a continuous zigzagging of sentiment around a line of relatively high and probably increasing esteem, leaving the partners in a situation which is reasonably close to the "gain" condition of the gain-loss experiment. In this sense, Dale Carnegie's advice can be seen as inadequate in the long run. If two people are genuinely fond of each other, the ability and opportunity to express *both* positive *and* negative feelings — openly, honestly — will probably result in a much more deeply satisfying relationship.

SUMMARY

There are a number of reasons why people like each other. Generally, we like people whose behavior is useful or rewarding to us. There are many types of "rewarding behaviors." The other person might do us a favor, or he might have similar attitudes and opinions, or he might like us. While there are complexities — we don't like favor-givers who are clearly self-serving — these behaviors usually have a clear effect.

Other behaviors are not so obviously "rewarding" but still have pronounced impact. Clumsy behavior in an extremely competent person may make us like him more, not less, for example. Increasing esteem seems to be more likely to elicit fondness than constant esteem (and decreasing esteem *less* likely than even constant dislike); these are predictions (and findings) from the gain-loss theory of attraction.

The theory of cognitive dissonance also casts light on attraction. If you want someone to like you, one way is to get him to do a favor for you. He will have to justify the favor, in many instances, by increasing his affection for you. Because it is dissonant to know you have done a favor for someone you don't like, the easiest way to reduce this tension is to change your attitudes toward the person.

RECOMMENDED READING

Allport, G. *The Nature of Prejudice.* Garden City, N.Y.: Doubleday & Co., Inc., 1958.
A classic piece of work in which one of the pioneers of social psychology takes a long, hard look at the causes and cures of ethnic prejudice.

Aronson, E. *The Social Animal.* San Francisco: W. H. Freeman Co., 1972.
A stimulating and provocative introduction to the field of social psychology, designed to acquaint the student with basic research in social psychology and to make him aware of the relevance that the field has for everyday life.

Bem, D. J. *Beliefs, Attitudes, and Human Affairs.* Belmont, Calif.: Brooks/Cole Publishing Co., 1970.
A lively and contemporary look at the way people form beliefs and attitudes and the effect that this has on their behavior.

Berscheid, E. & Walster, E. *Interpersonal Attraction.* Reading, Mass.: Addison-Wesley Publishing Co., 1969.
A scholarly and up-to-date attempt to conceptualize the research on why people like one another.

Festinger, L. *A Theory of Cognitive Dissonance.* Stanford: Stanford University Press, 1957.
In this volume one of the foremost theorists and researchers in the field presents a theory that has revolutionized the way scientists approach the area of social psychology.

Jones, E. E. & Gerard, H. B. *Foundations of Social Psychology.* New York: John Wiley & Sons, Inc., 1967.
A detailed description of the area of social psychology that presents social psychology in both its breadth and its complexity; a thorough and scholarly survey of the field.

Lindzey, G. & Aronson, E. *Handbook of Social Psychology, Vols. 1–5.* Reading, Mass.: Addison-Wesley Publishing Co.
Just about everything we know about social psychology is summarized in these 5 volumes. It does not read like a novel, but it is the most complete and most up-to-date compendium of theory and research available.

Zimbardo, P. & Ebbesen, E. B. *Influencing Attitudes and Changing Behavior.* Reading, Mass.: Addison-Wesley Publishing Co., 1969.
A highly readable look at persuasion, attitude change, and behavior change with an eye toward its relevance for current society.

SECTION THREE

PERSONALITY

By Seymour Feshbach

Preview

Personality study is the area of psychology that relates most closely to the layman's impression of psychology. It concerns what each of us is like—really like. We can best see how psychologists study this question by examining an individual biography or case study. This will introduce the kinds of questions we wish to ask about an individual and the kinds of conclusions we can draw about his personality.

In presenting this summary of the life history of Richard Paulder, we have disguised his name and other possible sources of identification but have left intact the essential factors of his life history. We first met Richard when he was a college sophomore; he was unsure about his career goals, and he sought the assistance of the counseling service in helping him define and resolve his career conflicts. He was somewhat depressed at the time, upset by a drop in his grades the previous semester, by a lack of interest in the courses he was taking, and by recent arguments that he had had with his girl friend. Also, it was the first time he had ever sought outside help, and he didn't feel comfortable with the idea. With Richard's permission, we sent out questionnaires to his parents to obtain additional biographical data as part of a research study, and we interviewed several of his classmates.

Richard was the younger of two children. His sister was an attractive and very able student who was completing her senior year at another college. Richard's early life was uneventful, marked only by continual spats with his sister. His mother notes that her daughter was a well-behaved and responsible child, much as she is now as an adult. Richard, although not a "problem" child, tended to be more buoyant and difficult. He would often hit his sister and once, when he was six, he hit her in the leg with a rock. He was severely punished by his parents, and although he had many subsequent arguments with his sister, it was the last time he ever hit her.

Richard states that both he and his sister felt closer to his mother than to his father. His father was disappointed that his firstborn was a girl and had especially high demands for Richard; Richard felt that his father liked him but at the same time was overly critical. His father's activities as a business executive kept him very busy, but he did find time to take Richard camping and fishing on occasional weekends. Richard's father was a relatively quiet man and, except for his critical comments, revealed very little about his feelings or his work experiences. Richard, in reciprocal manner, did not communicate very well with his father, but he could talk to his sister and mother. Richard's mother was an outgoing, fairly assertive woman who was very much a homemaker although she occasionally did editorial work for a magazine.

The marital relations between Richard's parents, while on the whole positive, went through a crisis when Richard was around twelve, when the parents briefly separated. Richard's sister was extremely upset and angry at the time; she got into a number of minor difficulties at school, experimented with marijuana, and stayed away from home several nights without parental permission. By the time she left junior high and entered high school, her behavior had returned to its normal pattern. In contrast to his sister, Richard displayed little reaction, other than some sadness, to the separation. In fact, he seemed to spend more time on his studies and less time with the school "crowd."

Richard was never a popular boy and during high school struck others as taciturn, isolated, and quarrelsome. However, his mother reports that he seemed to have gotten along very well with other members of a photography club in which he was quite interested; Richard also speaks enthusiastically about his activities in this club. During his senior year in high school, he had his first sexual experience with a girl whom he had known for several years. Their relationship changed when they went off to separate colleges although they remained good friends.

During his senior year and especially his first year at college, Richard seemed much more open and involved with other people. He did, however, occasionally get into severe quarrels with individuals in positions of immediate authority—a graduate student instructor, a parking attendant, a dormitory proctor. He had several close male friends and a girl friend to whom he was quite attached when he entered counseling.

The major problems in the description and study of personality can be discerned in our efforts to describe and understand Richard Paulder. How can we take account of individual differences in behavior as well as of universal human tendencies? Does a person show really general traits, or is his behavior only consistent within specific situations? How does the psychologist define, measure, and assess the major aspects of personality? Many psychologists have formulated theories of personality—efforts to explain the organization of the individual's characteristics and ways of behaving. Which of these theories—and what theoretical constructs—have proven most helpful in understanding the individual and his unique motivations, goals, and life-styles? What is known about human motivation, about the forces that incite, sustain, and direct behavior? When is behavior considered abnormal? How is abnormality diagnosed and treated? These are the questions discussed in this section of the book.

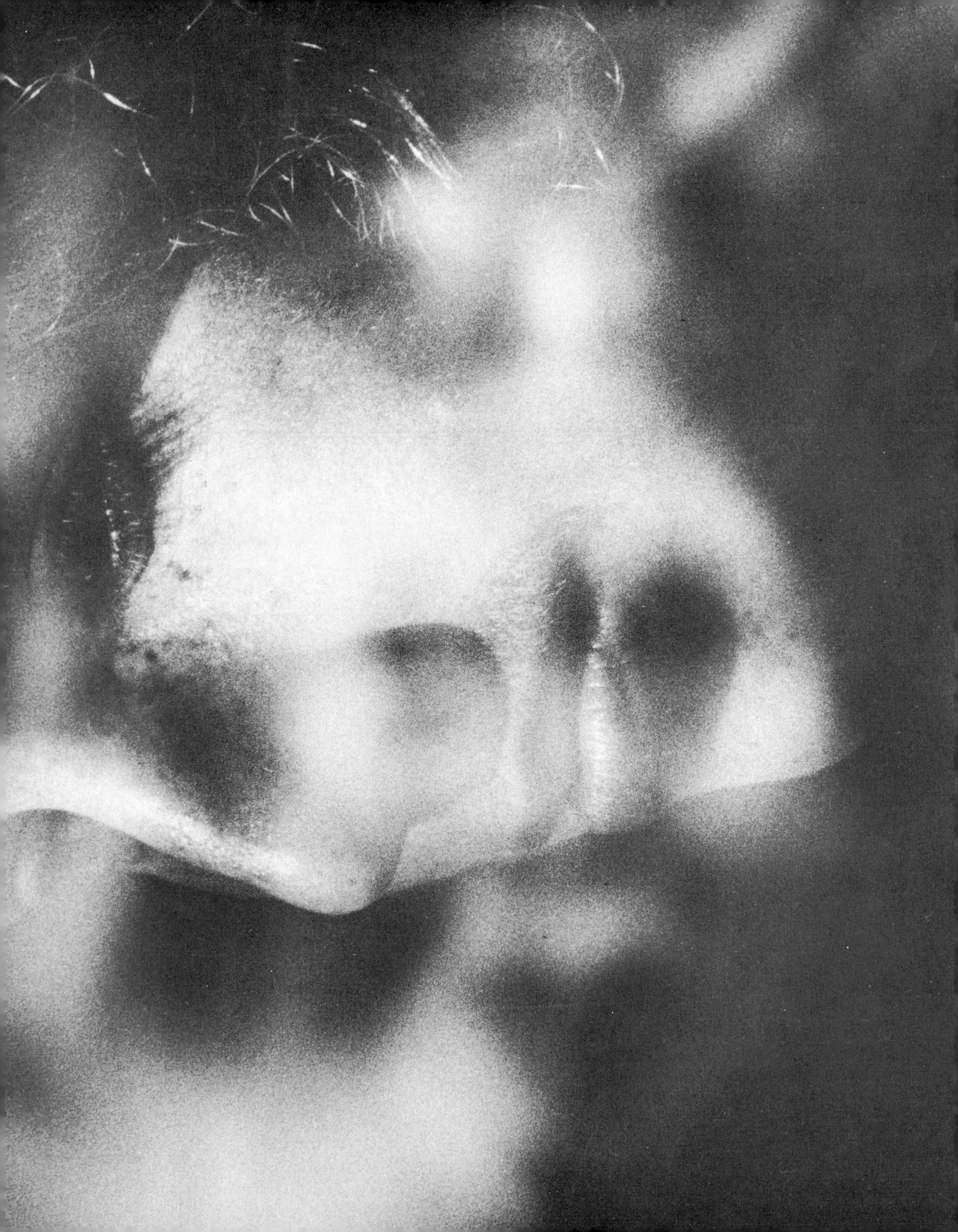

8

Personality and Assessment

Personality deals with what major issues?
What is the focus of personality dynamics?
What's involved in assessing the human personality?

Personality deals with what major issues?

Individual Differences

Recall how differently Richard Paulder and his sister reacted to their parents' separation; their reactions revealed essential personality differences. In contrast to his sister's anger and distress, Richard seemed to have responded calmly and constructively. Although both Richard and his sister shared similar aspirations for achievement and both were hardworking students, Richard's striving persisted during the family crisis while his sister's ambitions seemed to become less salient. There are, of course, many other points of similarity and difference between Richard and his sister although the ones noted are made most evident by the family crisis. One of the principal objectives of the study of personality is the determination of the most relevant dimensions of behavior along which individuals differ and the development of measurement procedures, such as tests, to assess these individual differences. These dimensions of behavior are typically referred to as **traits**. The study of traits provides a basis for the comparison of individuals and, in addition, helps account for the uniqueness of each individual (see Spotlight 8-1).

Generality and Specificity

One striking aspect of Richard's life pattern is the inconsistency in his behavior. One can well ask what is his real personality? Is he shy or open, warm or distant, aggressive or friendly, direct or devious? Richard's behavior is *consistent within a specific situation* —he was unfriendly and withdrawn in his high school classes, but

SPOTLIGHT 8-1

Uniqueness and the Rare Case

That each person is unique does not mean that individual behavior is governed by individual laws. General principles can account for individuality in two ways. First, each person can be described in terms of a unique combination of traits. For example, let us consider measures of ten personality traits, such as anxiety, introversion, generosity, aggression. Assume that each measure is independent of the others and the scores on each trait range from 1 to 10. Ten independent tests, with ten possible scores on each, yield 10^{10} or ten billion combinations, enough for a unique description of every individual on this planet, plus some allowance for the population explosion. It is through the application of a similar kind of classificatory principle that it is possible to locate and identify fingerprints that are also unique to each individual.

The second approach to the understanding of the unique and the unusual is through the application of general psychological principles and theory to a particular set of circumstances. Suppose, for example, we were to find a child who had been raised in the jungle in a band of apes. Such a child would certainly be a unique and rare individual. Nevertheless, by applying theories and principles of personality development to these unusual child-rearing conditions, we would be able to predict much of his behavior and would have some understanding of his personality.

(Ted Polumbaum)

cheerful and open when involved in photography. When in college, he had good relationships with his peers but was very aggressive with older males. There are some psychologists who feel that personality traits are quite specific to particular situations and that behavior will change as a situation changes. They feel it is a fruitless task to seek for broad, general behavior patterns that are descriptive of individuals (Mischel, 1968). Others argue that people are not chameleons, matching their behavior to particular circumstances, but that fundamental, underlying consistencies can be discerned if you analyze situations and behavior appropriately (Allport, 1961; Cattell, 1965).

Returning to Richard, one can point to certain tendencies which appear consistent over a wide range of situations and lend a unity and common dimension to his personality. One such tendency is his *need for achievement.* It is important to Richard that he excel, and he is willing to work hard for success. When a measure of achievement indicates he is not doing well, e.g., when his grades dropped, he becomes depressed and willing to accept help. He would not seek help solely because he was unhappy or had conflicts with other people. A more subtle but nevertheless dominant trait is his *ambivalence* (mixed feelings) toward authority figures. Richard chafes, most often covertly and sometimes overtly, when he is required to conform to the demands and regulations imposed by individuals in authority.

It is apparent in this description of Richard's personality that there are elements of behavior which are quite specific to the situation and others which are broader in their implications and more generally descriptive of him. Many personality psychologists have addressed their studies to the basic problem of the degree of specificity or generality of a particular behavior pattern and the factors which contribute to specificity or generality.

Organization and Structure

We have described Richard's personality as if it consisted of a number of behavior patterns that existed in isolation from each other. In delineating individual differences, it is almost inevitable that one adopts a kind of cataloging approach, enumerating a series of distinctive behaviors. Thus, Richard is described as ambitious, ambivalent to authority, given to sporadic conflict and hostile outbursts, open with women but reserved with men. The listing of traits, while often useful, does an injustice to the *unity and organization* of personality. Richard's ambition is related to his feelings toward authority. These are in turn related to his hostile outbreaks. Richard's hard work and striving is in part based upon his desire to impress authorities and obtain their approval. He is unduly sensitive to any implied criticism and resents it. This resentment may then sometimes find expression in inappropriate angry behavior. Richard's relationship to authority has the quality of a self-fulfilling prophecy: his readiness to resent authority brings about the very disapproval that he anticipates.

You can see evidence of organization and structure in Richard's behavior. And, the meaning and implication of any particular personality trait depends to a considerable extent upon this overall organization—upon the context in which that trait occurs. Richard's need to succeed has a different quality and connotation than ambition in his sister. Personality theorists are very interested in determining the interrelationships and interactions among traits. They find that some traits are loosely related while others are strongly interrelated. Some traits are central (basic) to the personality, others are peripheral. As will become evident in this chapter, personality theorists disagree about which traits are central to personality.

What is the focus of personality dynamics?

Although there is an intimate relationship between the organization and dynamics of personality, the terms refer to different aspects of personality. *Organization* refers to structure or "anatomy" of personality—how the different elements of personality are linked or go together—while **dynamics** is concerned with the function of behavior—the "physiology" of personality. You look for the purpose or objective of an act and ask *why* the individual behaved as he did. Questions of dynamics are also typically addressed to the immediate situation in which action is taking place, while questions of organization generally deal with relatively enduring and stable aspects of behavior.

The response of Richard's sister to her parents' separation provides an excellent example of motivational dynamics. Her typical behavior patterns were conformity and acceptance of parental standards. These were responses to her need for her parents' love—they were attempts to obtain that love. Her parents' separation elicited feelings of rejection, anger, and betrayal—including betrayal of the social conventions to which she so conscientiously adhered. All of these feelings were expressed in her defiant and deviant behaviors, which were superficially, but not dynamically, inconsistent with her personality structure.

Antecedents of Personality

Although the biographical data provide us with descriptions of Richard's and his sister's background, we have only suggestions as to some of the factors or causes which determined their personalities. These factors may be grouped into the following categories:

Cultural Context

Richard and his sister are products of the historical times

and culture in which they live. The values which they share and believe to be the most important as well as their attitudes toward sex, drugs, and their peer culture (the culture of people of their own age) are different in a number of respects from their parents' beliefs and from those held in other cultures. An adolescent raised in the slums of Mexico will not have the personality structure, values, and beliefs of a middle-class adolescent in Nebraska.

An individual's behavior is strongly influenced by the historical times and culture in which he lives.
(L. to R.: Courtesy SCORE; Paul Conklin, Peace Corps; Culver Pictures; George Gardner)

Social Role

There are not only differences *between* cultures (in expectations, norms, values, and prescribed modes of behavior) but also *within* a culture. Every society is structured by a pattern of social positions and corresponding **roles,** and these variations in position can have profound effects upon behavior. A mature man is not supposed to behave like a child; the behavioral demands made of a political leader are not the same as those made of the average individual; and in most societies the expectancies for women are different from those for men. The roles that we occupy shape our behavior in a direct manner in the sense that we ordinarily conform to role expectations. The business executive generally wears a suit to work. The schoolteacher follows appropriate "rules" in her relationships with her students. Our social roles also influence the way in which we perceive events. A general has a very different perception of war than a private.

To explain Richard's actions, one has to consider the behaviors expected of a child, of an adolescent, of a college student. His personality is influenced by these role expectations just as his parents' personalities are affected by their responsibilities as mother and father.

We all occupy simultaneously a multiplicity of positions in a particular society. Thus, Richard is acting in the role of a male and in the role of a son and a student. The differences in aggressiveness between Richard and his sister must be understood partly in the light of sex differences. One can, of course, push the question of causation back one step and ask whether sex differences in behavior are a consequence of culturally determined role behavior or whether they are

Patterns of behavior are influenced by society's role expectations.
(Ted Polumbaum)

a function of biological differences. This specific issue is of considerable importance in contemporary personality study.

Unique Developmental Antecedents

Practically all personality theorists agree that the child is to an important degree "the father of the man." The manner in which Richard and his sister were trained to carry out their respective roles, the unique experiences which each has encountered, and also their biological heritage have helped form their characters and shape their development. The constellation of experiences which led to Richard's suppression of aggressive feelings (toward his sister and particularly toward his father) had a profound effect on his subsequent personality development.

Children do not automatically develop adult personalities simply by growing older. The process by which the child is socialized and the manner in which these efforts at **socialization** interact with powerful biological attributes of the human organism are central theoretical and empirical issues in personality. Most of this material will be covered in the section on developmental psychology (see particularly p. 315 ff.) but there will also be some reference to these issues in the present section.

In our presentation of Richard Paulder's biography, we raised a number of questions to which the study of personality is addressed. By implication, the meaning of the term "personality" has been indicated. Although personality is not a precise concept or area, and psychologists are not in complete agreement about all of its connotations, we can propose a more formal and explicit definition of personality which you may find helpful.

Personality refers to (1) relatively enduring behavior patterns and traits that distinguish people, groups, and cultures; (2) the organization and structure of these enduring behavior patterns and characteristics; (3) the interaction between these behavior patterns and fluctuations in the individuals' internal states and the external stimulus situation.

The reader will recognize most of the elements of this definition from the previous discussion of Richard. A key phrase is "relatively enduring behavior patterns and characteristics," distinctive patterns of responses that occur frequently. However, unusual responses are not disregarded or thought to be insignificant; they often represent interactions between prominent characteristics and response tendencies and an *unusual* "external stimulus situation" (see 3 above). The sister's response to the Paulder separation is an example of an important, though unusual, response. But an unusual way of tying one's shoelaces is hardly likely to interest a personality theorist.

Finally, the definition indicates that personality is related to the universal as well as to the particular in man. There are certain needs and behavior patterns that are characteristics of all men and these, no less than the differences among men, are part of the human personality.

Enduring behavior patterns have been conceptualized in different ways in different theories of personality. As we shall see in another chapter (see p. 214 ff.), motivational constructs such as "need" and "drive" are often used to explain the direction, persistence, and intensity of behavior patterns. Other theorists use the concepts of "habit" or "personality trait" to describe an individual's typical response dispositions. Still others may use "goals," "values," or "incentives" to explain the direction of behavior. Whatever the theoretical construct employed, the theorist must have some way of measuring these needs, traits, or values. This is the topic of personality assessment, to which we will now turn.

What's involved in assessing the human personality?

Personality assessment has both theoretical and practical implications. In order to test a hypothesis about, say, the relationship between a certain trait or need and overt behavior in a particular situation, a concrete, operational definition of the trait or need is required. If we say, for example, that "high anxiety" will lead to poor performance on an exam, we must be able to distinguish those students who are anxious from those who are less so. We can do this with personality tests. Personality measures also have important practical applications. They are often used to diagnose emotional instability or mental illness or to aid in personnel selection in industry.

Standards of Measurement

For a measure to be useful, it must have certain properties. First of all, it must be *reliable*; that is, it must give approximately the same answer each time the measure is used. A bathroom scale which fluctuated wildly by as much as 75 pounds on each reading would not be very helpful if someone was attempting to keep track of his weight. The scale lacks the property of **reliability.** In the same manner, personality scales need to have adequate reliability in order to be useful. If you wanted to investigate the relationship between anxiety and performance on final examinations in a sample of college students, you might measure anxiety by a questionnaire containing such questions as, "Do your hands frequently tremble?" "Do you often feel afraid without knowing why?" "Do you feel upset when you have to talk to a group?" Suppose the questions were ambiguous or were answered at random, a student who obtained a high-anxiety score at one time might just as easily obtain a low score on a retest.

You could not discover any systematic relationships between anxiety and performance on finals—or any other behavior, for that matter—if you had to depend upon such an unreliable measure of anxiety.

Reliability is necessary, but not sufficient, to ensure the usefulness of a measure. It must also have **validity**; it must measure what it was designed to measure. Our bathroom scale would not be of much help if it gave reliable readings of some attribute other than weight (such as the size of one's feet). Thus, our measure of anxiety could yield highly consistent scores, but nevertheless be measuring something other than anxiety; e.g., sensitivity to one's own feeling, or honesty about one's feelings (Jackson & Messick, 1958; Couch & Keniston, 1960). Whether our personality measure is a questionnaire, an electronic lie detector, an astrologer's horoscope, or our own judgment, its reliability and validity must be demonstrated.

Types of Validity

Establishing the validity of a personality measure is a painstaking and often complex task. There are several types of validity research, each of which deals with a different aspect of the question, "To what extent does this test measure what it is supposed to measure?" The simplest and least important type of validity is **content** or **face validity,** the demonstration that the content of the items represents the behavior that the test is presumed to measure. For example, you could ask clinicians to judge whether or not items on our measure of anxiety really deal with behaviors indicative of anxiety—if answering "yes" to items like "Do your hands tremble frequently?" indicates anxiety. If they agree that this is the case, the scale can be considered to have a content or face validity.

A second type of validity is **criterion validity,** the demonstration of *direct* relationships between scores on the test or measure and behavior that reflects the trait being assessed. For example, one could establish the criterion validity of an anxiety measure by showing that it discriminates between people who become upset when they try to solve a new, difficult problem and those who are calm and relaxed under the same circumstances. Those who panic score higher on the anxiety test than those with low anxiety. Or you could test the criterion validity of a measure of dependency by showing that the measure could help predict which freshmen at college would visit their homes frequently or write or telephone their parents often for advice about relatively trivial matters.

Most measures of personality dimensions that relate to personality theory are validated through the procedure of **construct validity,** which is much more complex than other kinds of validations. No single behavior or assessment is used as a definitive criterion. Rather, the investigator begins with a theory or hunch about the properties of a particular trait or construct and some hypotheses about how it is manifested in behavior. He then tests his hypotheses, using his measure of the trait or construct. For example, the test-maker's hypothesis about anxiety might include the following: anxiety increases when subjects are threatened; neurotics are more anxious than well-adjusted people; anxiety is lowered by certain drugs; anxious people perform poorly in complex learning tasks. He would then test each of these hypotheses, using his test as the operational measure of anxiety. Confirmation of the hypotheses is evidence of construct validity.

In validating a test in this way, we also learn more about the construct measured and can give this construct a broader interpretation. To illustrate, the Taylor Manifest-Anxiety Scale has been used to investigate some of the theoretical properties of anxiety. The studies provide data relevant to the validity of the scale and also increase our understanding of the nature of anxiety. For example, in accordance with prediction, high-anxiety subjects have been shown to learn more rapidly than low-anxiety subjects in simple learning situations (Taylor, 1951), but do more poorly than low-anxiety subjects on difficult learning tasks (Montague, 1953). Other experiments have shown that the highly anxious subject is more vulnerable to the effects of stress than the low-anxiety subject. When required to solve a difficult task under pressure, the performance of many highly anxious subjects deteriorated while the low-anxiety subjects maintained their performance level (Feshbach & Loeb, 1959; Nicholson, 1958). These results were predicted by theory. If research data had not confirmed the prediction, we could not be sure whether the "failure" was due to an inadequate theory or to a test that was not valid. But, in fact, the predictions were confirmed; thus we can have greater confidence in both the theory *and* the test.

Techniques of Measurement

There are many different types of techniques used to assess personality constructs. These range from paper and pencil tests to physiological recordings; often the psychologist himself functions as a measuring instrument, observing, judging, and recording. In each instance a sample of behavior is recorded and is used as an indicator of a broader category of behavior. The samples of behavior might be responses to test items, changes in heartbeat, emotional reactions in an interview situation, or play activities in the schoolyard. From these samples, estimates are made of the level, degree, or intensity of a trait such as anxiety, dependency, or emotional stability.

All of us act as personality "testers" at times. Whenever we size up—"psych out"—another person, we are assessing an aspect of his personality. The *interview* is a more structured method of sizing up people. The behaviors evaluated in an interview are largely verbal, although in recent years psychologists have become attuned to the bodily movements, gestures, changes in skin color, and other indirect ways in which individuals may reveal themselves in an inter-

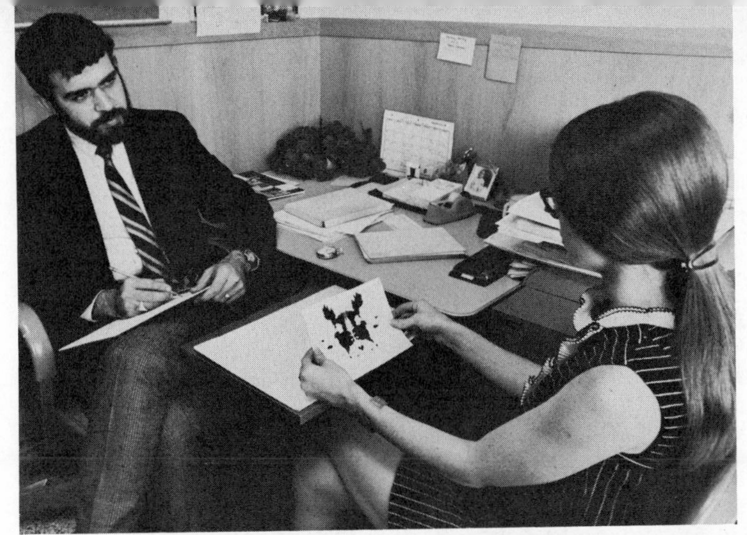

Personality is assessed by a variety of techniques.
(Top: Van Bucher, Photo Researchers; bottom left, UPI; bottom right, Suzanne Szasz)

personal situation (Mehrabian, 1969). Nonverbal cues to personality have recently been popularized as the "body language" (Fast, 1970). Since people are generally less aware of their body than of their speech and have less control over subtle body movements than over what they say, the idea that bodily movements may be sensitive indicators of feelings and personality structure is an intriguing one. Like many psychological procedures that have evoked popular enthusiasm, there is some validity to this method. However, it is easy to exaggerate the significance of some idle bodily movement. More research is needed to determine the soundness of untested propositions about body language.

Rating Scales

A **rating scale** is a very helpful instrument for quantifying the impressions obtained in an interview or in observing behavior

When people mirror one another's posture in a group, it often indicates a common viewpoint. Judging by body language, we may assume that the man in the rear prefers to remain aloof.
(Jerry Dantzic)

in a natural setting. Let us assume that the observer is asked to rate the trait of hostility; he is given a scale which consists simply of the trait name and a sequence of numbers, 1 indicating a low degree and 7 a very high degree of hostility (see Figure 8-1). In order to increase the reliability and validity of the scale, the observers usually discuss in advance the definition and scoring of the trait. Prior to using the scale, the raters are given behavioral examples of the varying degrees of hostility. Thus, indicators of "very high" hostility might be "angry remarks, gets into fights frequently"; while indicators of "very little" hostility might be "acts friendly, rarely gets into arguments."

One of the problems with rating scales is called the **halo effect:** the rater may judge an individual high on one trait simply because that person is high on another trait. Thus, if the rater finds the person he is rating to be "very friendly" he might also rate him as "highly intelligent," even though he has no good objective reason for the latter rating. There are "negative halos" as well; if the subject is unfriendly, he might be rated as unintelligent. In general, great care should be taken in the construction of the rating scale and in the training of raters in order to lessen the halo effects.

Another widely used technique related to the rating scale is the **adjective checklist.** The rater is given a long list of adjectives—e.g., active, ambitious, intelligent, friendly—and checks off those that he considers characteristic of the person he is rating. Each item (adjective) on an adjective checklist is really a rating scale with two points—0 and 1 (characteristic or not characteristic)—and permits the rater to attend to those behaviors which are most outstanding and descriptive of the individual observed. In one study, the assessment staff of a research institute rated forty graduate students in various fields, half of whom had been characterized by their instructors as outstandingly original and half as low in originality (Gough, 1960). Among the adjectives that described the highly original students were "adventurous," "alert," "curious," "quiet," "imaginative," and "fair-minded." Among those characterizing the less original subjects were "confused," "conventional," "defensive," "polished," "prejudiced," and "suggestible."

FIGURE 8-1
A SIMPLE RATING SCALE

Prior to using the scale, raters are given behavioral examples of *very little, moderate,* and *very high* degrees of hostility.

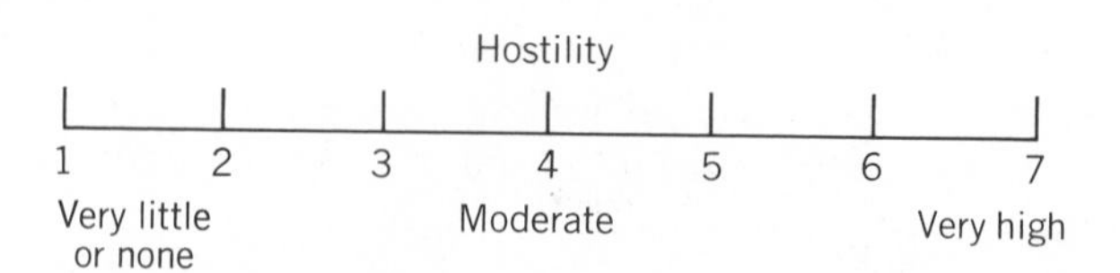

While the adjective checklist reduces the rating scale to two points, the **Q-sort** technique is a more elaborate rating procedure in which the rater is given a set of adjectives or statements. He sorts these into piles according to the degree to which they are descriptive of the subject (Block, 1961; Stephenson, 1953). The California Q set developed by Block (1961) consists of 100 statements on separate cards. Examples of these statements are:

Has a wide range of interests.

Is productive; gets things done.

Is self-dramatizing; histrionic.

Overreactive to minor frustrations; irritable.

Seeks reassurance from others.

Appears to have a high degree of intellectual capacity.

Is basically anxious.

The rater is asked to place the items in 9 piles. Cards containing statements about the subject that really "hit home" are placed in pile 9; statements that are not at all descriptive are placed in pile 1. Most of the statements are to be placed in the middle piles and fewer of the statements at the extremes, as in Figure 8-2, so that a plot of the frequencies is similar to the normal or bell curve (described in Chapter 2). An examination of the statements in the various piles provides a very rich description of the subject's outstanding, predominant qualities.

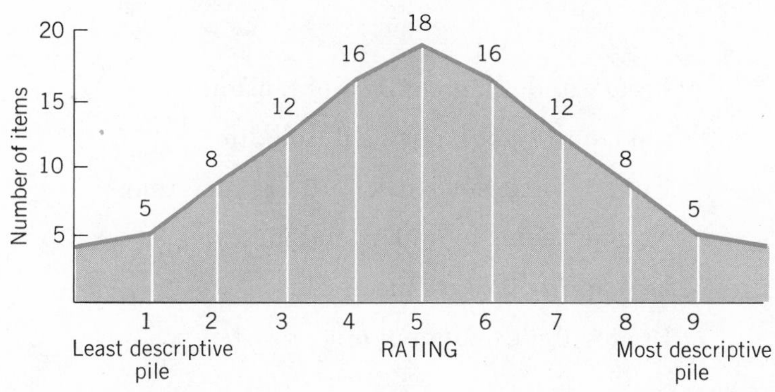

FIGURE 8-2
THE CALIFORNIA Q SORT
The number of items distributed in the nine piles of the California Q sort approaches a normal distribution.

Rating scales can also be used by the subject to describe himself; used in this way, they reflect the subject's **self-concept.** The scale becomes a self-report personality instrument, along with personality inventories. For example, we had Richard Paulder do the Q sort of himself. Two of the statements he placed in piles 8–9 (very descriptive) were "Overreactive to minor frustrations, irritable," and "Is basically anxious." In pile 2 (not descriptive) appeared the statement, "Appears to have a high degree of intellectual capacity."

Personality Inventories

Ratings of personality require that the rater really know the person being rated and that the rater has had opportunities to observe him under varied circumstances. The fact that often these requirements are not fulfilled is one of the reasons why psychologists have developed personality measures based on *self*-descriptions. In World War I, the army needed a rapid screening device for detecting individuals who would not be able to stand up to the stress of military life. To meet this need, Robert S. Woodworth developed one of the first personality **inventories,** the Personal Data Sheet, consisting of 116 questions about possible emotional difficulties (Woodworth, 1919). The subject gave a "yes" or "no" answer to such questions as "Do you daydream a great deal?" and "Do you feel like jumping off when you are on high places?" This scale has become the prototype of subsequent personality inventories.

Personality inventories can be scored easily and objectively. Every effort is made to make the questions unambiguous. The responses which the subject can make are simple and structured —yes or no, or a numerical rating.

In the years since Woodworth published his Personal Data Sheet, psychologists have been able to use this simple format to develop sophisticated personality inventories. Among the best of these instruments is the Minnesota Multiphasic Personality Inventory (MMPI), which assesses a number of personality traits. These are described in Table 8-1. There are 550 items in the MMPI which are answered true, false, or "can't say." The following are examples of some items:

I work under a great deal of tension.

I am sure I get a raw deal from life.

I like to read newspaper articles on crime.

No one seems to understand me.

Evil spirits possess me at times.

I enjoy the excitement of a crowd.

The MMPI was initially developed as a test of particular psychiatric disturbances (Hathaway & McKinley, 1943). The items in each of the subscales of the MMPI, such as depression and schizophrenia, discriminate between psychiatric patient groups and normals; for example, depressed patients obtain higher scores on the depression scale than normals. Since many psychiatric symptoms are extreme forms of tendencies that can be observed in normal individuals, MMPI scales also make useful discriminations in the personality characteristics of normal people. However, the personality

TABLE 8-1
PERSONALITY TRAITS MEASURED BY THE MMPI

Trait	Symptoms
1. Hypochondriasis	Exaggerated complaints about bodily health.
2. Depression	Self-disparaging and despondent tendencies.
3. Hysteria	Exaggerated emotional displays vying with inappropriate emotional blandness, physical impairment without an organic basis.
4. Psychopathic deviate	Impulsive, antisocial, amoral tendencies.
5. Masculinity–Femininity	Heterosexual and homosexual tendencies (applicable to males); masculine and feminine interests.
6. Paranoia	Suspicious hostile tendencies.
7. Psychasthenia	Indecision, overconscientiousness, obsessive (uncontrolled thoughts) and compulsive (ritualistic acting out) tendencies.
8. Schizophrenia	Withdrawal from other people, disturbed thinking, odd behavior.
9. Hypomania	Exaggerated feelings of excitement and elation, overactivity.
10. Social introversion	Interest in inner events.

labels for the subscales unfortunately have a distinctly psychiatric connotation and may erroneously suggest emotional disturbance rather than a score on a particular personality dimension.

In Figure 8-3 is a profile of the MMPI scores of Richard Paulder. The scales are scored so that 50 is the mean obtained by the normal, standardization population, with scores above 70 reflecting emotional pathology. Inspection of Richard's profile indicates that at the time of testing, he is quite depressed (depression scale), tends to be somewhat suspicious and resentful (paranoia scale), is conscientious and conventional (slightly elevated psychasthenia and low

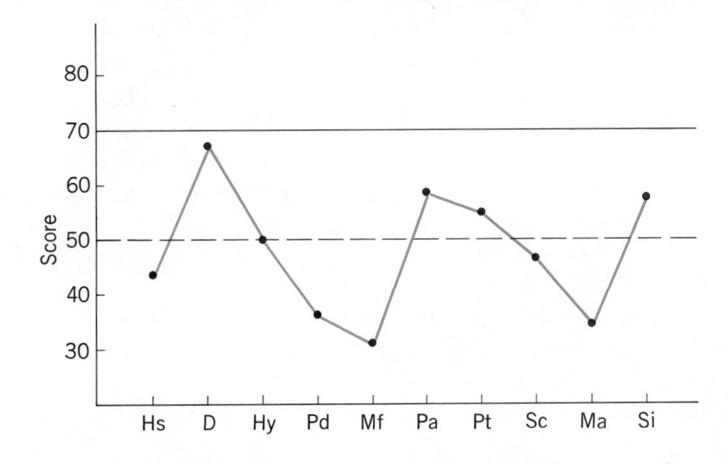

FIGURE 8-3
MMPI PROFILE OF RICHARD PAULDER
The symbols represent the following personality scales: Hs (Hypochondriasis), D (Depression), Hy (Hysteria), Pd (Psychopathic deviation), Mf (Masculinity-femininity), Pa (Paranoia), Pt (Psychasthenia), Sc (Schizophrenia), Ma (Hypomania), and Si (Social introversion).

psychopathic deviation scores), somewhat withdrawn (social introversion score), and has strong heterosexual inclinations and interests (low masculinity-femininity).

The descriptions of the personality traits measured by the MMPI, as you can clearly see from Table 8-1, are mostly descriptions of what a *high* score on a scale means, i.e., the pathological descriptions. Since the MMPI was originally designed for psychiatric diagnosis, it is natural that the pathological trends have been more thoroughly researched and interpreted. Exceptionally *low* scores have not been heavily researched, although some clinical psychologists interpret such scores. For example, low psychasthenia (scale 7) has been interpreted as a low general level of anxiety in the individual. A low score on the schizophrenia scale might indicate a very practical person, heavily endowed with "common sense." A low score on psychopathic deviate would reflect a person with a strong conscience.

In some cases, interpretations are related to the age of the test-taker. A low level of hypochondriasis – concern about health – is expected of young subjects, but among old people it may be a reflection of repression and denial. On the other hand, the hypomania scale, which measures feelings of elation, should give higher scores for young people than for old.

The MMPI has been presented as a set of independent scales designed to measure particular personality tendencies. One might also ask whether there are certain traits or personality dimensions that are common to several of these scales, that underlie the separate measures. The method of **factor analysis** is especially designed to answer this question which can be addressed to any set of personality measures. In the case of the MMPI, we begin with the ten scales and ask whether these may represent different combinations of more basic factors. An analogy may be made with chemistry in which hundreds of compounds can be analyzed and found to be combinations of only a few basic elements. Psychological "compounds" such as test behaviors can be mathematically analyzed. When factor analysis is applied to the MMPI, at least two general factors or traits are found in addition to several of less generality (Block, 1965; Tyler, 1951; Welsh, 1956). The first and most important factor appears to be a measure of *general adjustment or psychological health.* The second factor, more difficult to label, appears to measure the degree of *control over feelings and actions* which the individual exercises. General factors found in other personality measures are presented in Table 8-2.

Projective Tests

In contrast to the personality inventories, **projective tests** deliberately use vague and ambiguous stimuli such as inkblots

TABLE 8-2
PERSONALITY DIMENSIONS FOUND THROUGH FACTOR ANALYSIS

Cyclothymia (emotionally expressive, outgoing)	vs.	Schizothymia (withdrawn, emotionally restrained)
Intellectually efficient (high in general intelligence)	vs.	Intellectually deficient (low in general intelligence)
Emotionally stable (calm, emotionally appropriate)	vs.	Emotionally unstable (impulsiveness, unrealistic)
Dominance (assertive, aggressive)	vs.	Submissiveness (mild, compliant)

Leading exponents of factor analysis (Cattell, 1946; Eysenck, 1947) have used this procedure to analyze many types of inventories, rating scales, physiological measures, and other types of tests. Listed are the most important of twelve fundamental personality traits, according to Cattell, one of the leaders in this field.

and pictures. These stimuli permit a wide array of responses that are sometimes difficult to standardize and quantify. Scoring and interpretation of projective tests usually requires considerable skill and training. Advocates of projective techniques believe that these disadvantages are more than compensated for by the richness of the data yielded.

There are certain similarities between projective tests and psychoanalytic procedures. The subject is presented with a stimulus—e.g., an inkblot, a picture, a word—and is encouraged to respond with whatever association comes to mind. There are no clearly

What people see in pictures of ambiguous situations are projections of their own personalities.
(Ted Polumbaum)

correct or socially desirable answers, and so it is unlikely that the subject will disguise his true reaction. Unconscious factors have a much greater opportunity of influencing the response to a projective stimulus than the answer to a questionnaire item. Confronted with an ambiguous stimulus and attempting to give it meaning and order, the subject may reveal his innermost feelings and desires. The individual can be said to "project" onto the stimulus some part of himself. For these reasons some feel that projective tests reveal more about the individuality of people than personality inventories.

Of the many different kinds of projective measures, the Rorschach inkblot test is perhaps the best known. Designed by a Swiss psychiatrist, Hermann Rorschach (1942), this test consists of ten cards, each with an inkblot similar to the one depicted in Figure 8-4. The blots vary in shape, shading, and color, half the blots being achromatic. They were made (originally) by pouring ink on a sheet and then folding the sheet in half. The subject is shown one card at a time and is asked to state whatever the blot reminds him of. Several associations are usually given to each card. The responses given by college students to the blot in Figure 8-4 include a butterfly pattern,

FIGURE 8-4
INKBLOT SIMILAR TO THOSE USED IN PROJECTIVE TESTS

a discus thrower, an octopus, a juggler, a tumbling team, the head of a bear, an animal skin, a man caught in a trap, a nose, a human profile, and the island of Crete—and these are only a portion of the responses given to this cue card. Subjects may respond to the whole card or only to parts of the card. Their associations may be determined by the shape of the blot or may be influenced by the color and shading. Some responses are quite common, frequent associations while others may be quite rare. All of these factors enter into the scoring and interpretation of the test.

Highly trained clinical psychologists use the Rorschach test for the diagnosis of psychopathology and for the assessment of such variables as self-concept, self-control, ego strength, relationship to others, creativity, and style of coping with stress and conflict. Because the Rorschach is so flexible an instrument and so demanding of psychological skill, it has been very difficult to validate. There are many psychologists who question its utility, and currently it is less widely used than was the case ten or twenty years ago. Nevertheless, there is substantial research supporting the use of the Rorschach to assess certain dimensions such as self-control and ego strength (Klopfer, 1954; Zubin, Eron, & Schumer, 1965).

The Thematic Apperception Test (TAT), designed by Henry A. Murray (1943), is another commonly used projective test. It consists of twenty picture cards (one of which is actually blank) and the subject is asked to make up a story about each picture. Most of the pictures have one or several people in them who are engaged in some ambiguous action. Thus, one picture depicts a kneeling figure with its head resting on a bench. The figure is sometimes seen as male and sometimes as female; is perceived as crying, tired, or guilty; as being remorseful over a shooting, as being discouraged over a school failure, and so on. A second picture depicts a girl lying semi-nude on a couch with a man in a distressed posture, standing nearby. This stimulus elicits stories of illness, sexual seduction, impotence, rape, murder, and other such themes. The range of stories given to any card is great, but there are recurring themes for certain pictures; stories with sexual themes are more likely to be given to certain pictures, aggressive themes to others.

The individual's responses are analyzed to determine if there are predominant themes running through many of his stories. The method of interpretation of the TAT is comparable to that employed by the psychoanalyst in his interpretation of his patient's associations. He looks for major motivations (or *needs*), conflicts, and the methods used to resolve conflicts and satisfy needs. For example, the following themes were salient in the stories which Richard Paulder gave to the Thematic Apperception Test: intense hostility to father figures; feelings of rejection by older males; fear of punishment for aggressive behavior, strong needs for achievement and superiority; positive feelings coupled with the denial of any hostility toward women. The story he gave to a picture of a young man apparently conversing with an older man was particularly revealing:

This fellow is a college student. He wants very much to go to medical school but is worried about his poor grades. He's working about thirty hours a week on a job in addition to going to school and feels that if he could quit the job, his grades would improve. The other guy is his father. He tells his father about his situation, hoping that he will offer to pay his college expenses for at least one year. But the old man won't budge. He tells his son that he has to be responsible for his grades at college and maybe medical school is not for him.

[Question of psychologist to Paulder: "How does the son feel?"] He's as mad as hell at his father but can't tell him off.

The key assumption is made that the stories the subject tells reflect his *own* needs, conflicts, and feelings; without being aware of the process, he identifies with the principal characters in the stories and thereby "reveals" himself. While the Thematic Apperception Test is not a magic key that will automatically unlock the doors to the unconscious, it has proved to be a productive and flexible method which has helped augment our understanding of human motivation.

The TAT can be used in a clinical, subjective manner, or the content can be quantitatively analyzed to yield reliable scores on specified personality dimensions. A prominent example of the latter is its use as a measuring instrument for the "achievement motive"—the need to accomplish, to compete with a standard of excellence (McClelland *et al.*, 1953). A group of investigators first developed a reliable scoring method, reliable in the sense that anyone trained in the method would come up with almost exactly the same score from the stories. They then proceeded to obtain evidence for the construct validity of their method. For example, they showed that the amount of need for achievement reflected in the stories increased when the individual was placed in competitive situations.

Once the scoring method had been shown to be reasonably reliable and valid, estimated need for achievement was related to a number of other behaviors. For example, in risk-taking situations, individuals high in achievement motivation prefer the 50/50 chance, something neither too easy nor too difficult (Atkinson, 1958). Measures of achievement needs can even be applied to cultures. A researcher, of course, cannot get an entire tribe or nation to respond to the TAT, but popular folktales can be used and scored by the same procedures. The economic output of a nation has been shown to be related to the degree of achievement motivation reflected in their folktales (McClelland, 1961).

Studies such as these indicate that high need for achievement as expressed in stories is associated with actual behavior related to achievement. With respect to other motivations such as sex and aggression, there is a question about whether the TAT themes are *representational* or *compensational*. That is, does a high degree of TAT aggressive content indicate that the individual is overtly aggressive (representation), or does it reflect an outlet (compensation) for inhibited aggressive tendencies? This issue becomes especially important when one is trying to predict whether an individual with high TAT aggression is a good risk for release from a mental hospital or prison parole. Research indicates that high TAT aggression scores are not reliable indicators of overt aggressive behavior (Murstein, 1963; Zubin *et al.*, 1965). However, prediction of overt aggression from the TAT is considerably enhanced if one also measures the amount of inhibition of and anxiety about aggression that is reflected in responses to the TAT. Strong aggression on the TAT is associated with aggressive "acting out" behavior if inhibitory tendencies are weak (Feshbach, 1970).

Objective Measures

In an effort to achieve greater objectivity, psychologists have developed a number of procedures with primary emphasis on **behavioral samples** that can be readily quantified. In some of these, an observer notes and records behavioral incidents rather than making the kinds of inferences that are usually involved in a rating scale. In assessing a child's aggression, for example, an observer might count the number of fistfights, arguments, destruction of objects, and like behaviors in which a child participated over a particular time period (Feshbach, 1970; Lovaas *et al.*, 1965).

Ideally, a subject should be observed under many different conditions for sufficient periods of time to obtain reliable samples of his behavior. Psychological tests are, of course, shortcuts to lengthy and costly observational procedures. One can reduce the time and cost of observation by eliciting the behavior under more controlled conditions. For example, candidates for positions in the Office of Strategic Services during World War II found themselves placed in "crisis situations" (Murray, 1948). A group of candidates, armed with weapons and other military equipment, might be approaching a wide stream; one of the group would be placed in charge and given the task of bringing the men and equipment across the stream as quickly and as efficiently as possible. His performance in this standard situation was carefully observed and personality assessments were made on the basis of this.

A related method is the "stress" interview in which an individual is deliberately subjected to verbal pressure, and then his reactions are observed. The examiner may alternate between a friendly and critical attitude, pop embarrassing questions at the interviewee, and shout and demand immediate answers; all of this untoward behavior is designed to appraise the interviewee's reaction to stress (and to penetrate deception).

Another type of objective measure commonly used to assess personality is the *physiological recording*. While a person may not exhibit his true feelings verbally, or in overt actions, he will have great difficulty controlling his physiological responses, and these give an indication of his true emotional response. Try as you might to hide the fact you are embarrassed, blushing gives you away. The lie detector uses a number of physiological recordings and is based on the assumption that a "lie" will produce a marked emotional reaction.

Perhaps the most commonly used physiological measure in personality assessment is the galvanic skin response, or GSR. It reflects changes in the electrical characteristics of the skin related to sweating and, therefore, is frequently used as an indication of emotional arousal or anxiety. The electromyograph (EMG) records muscle tension and has been used in a fashion similar to the GSR, especially when muscle tension can be assumed to reflect psychological tension or stress. The electroencephalograph (EEG) records certain electrical characteristics of brain activity and has been used in personality experiments as an operational definition of the degree of cortical arousal. The EEG has been especially useful in the study of dreams (Dement, 1960), since it has been found that most people do most of their dreaming during a certain state of cortical arousal. (See p. 700 ff. for a more complete discussion of the "physiology" of dreams.)

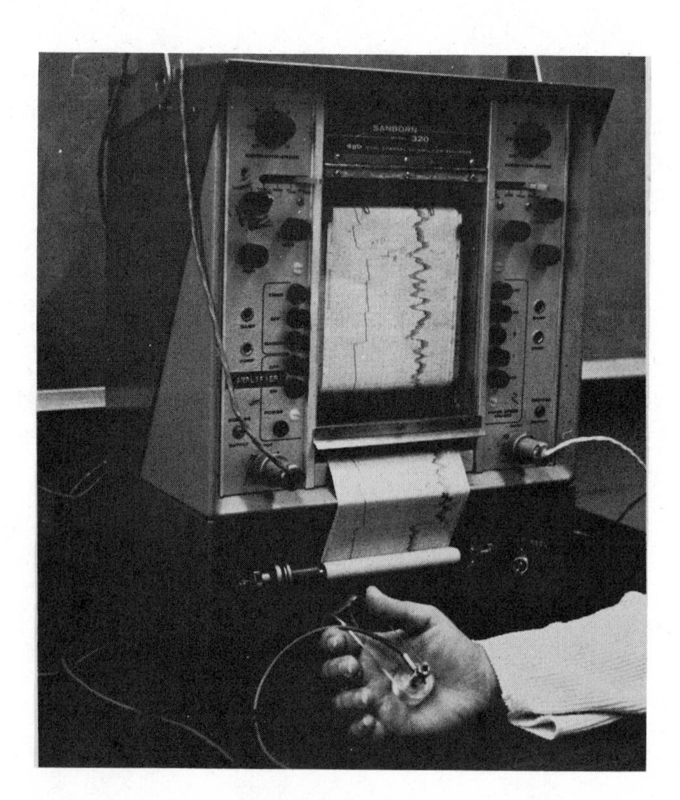

The GSR is a physiological record used in personality assessment.
(W. W. Fuller)

SUMMARY

The study of personality is concerned with the organization and patterning of people's characteristics and ways of behaving, with the basic tendencies that guide and distinguish their behavior, and with individual differences in these traits or tendencies. Personality addresses itself to such questions as the degree of consistency or generality in people's behavior and the extent to which behavior varies as a function of the different situations in which people find themselves. The interrelationships among behavioral tendencies—what types of traits or behaviors go together—are also of interest to the psychologist. In addition to being concerned with the organization of behavior, students of personality seek to ascertain the *why* of behavior, the reasons people behave as they do.

Tests and other measures of personality are needed for testing theoretical propositions about personality and, for practical purposes, as aids in diagnosis and guidance. In order for personality measures to be useful, they must be reliable—give approximately the same "score" each time they are used—and valid—test what they are supposed to test. Validity can be assessed by testing the relationship between the personality measure and a specific standard or criterion (criterion validity) or to a variety of behaviors that are theoretically related to the construct that the measure is designed to assess (construct validity).

Many different types of procedures have been used to measure personality. Some, such as the rating scale and the adjective checklist, are based on the judgments of an observer. Personality inventories, such as the MMPI, make use of the individual's self-report in response to a questionnaire. In contrast to the "yes-no" format of the personality inventories, the vague, ambiguous stimuli used in projective tests elicit responses that are presumably more reflective of individual style and unconscious motivations. Projective measures are generally less reliable than personality inventories, and it is also more difficult to establish their validity. Among the best-known projective measures are the Rorschach inkblot test and the Thematic Apperception Test, in which stories are elicited in response to the presentation of inkblots or pictures. Other personality measures make use of behavior samples that can be readily quantified. These can range from "stress" interviews to physiological responses, and include a variety of perceptual, cognitive, and motor performance procedures.

9

Theories of Personality

What did Freud mean by "psychoanalysis"?
What elements of psychoanalysis did Freud's followers reject?
What do actualization theories stress?
How do learning theories explain personality?
What is the Asian approach to personality?

In very broad terms, a theory of personality is an attempt to explain personality structure and functioning, to state why a person behaves as he does. In formulating a theory of personality, the theorist attempts to define meaningful fundamental concepts, to indicate how these concepts are related to one another, and to specify the relationship of the theoretical constructs to observable behavior. There are many personality theories, some focusing on unconscious mental forces (Freudian psychoanalysis), some on man's potential —and motivation—to better himself (self-actualization theories), and some on the ability of man to change with experience (learning theories). In this chapter we will consider each of these approaches and a few more, including an Asian approach quite different from Western theories.

What did Freud mean by "psychoanalysis"?

The greatest single figure among personality theorists is clearly Sigmund Freud, the creator of **psychoanalysis.** His impact extends far beyond psychology; one cannot understand twentieth-century intellectual thought without some knowledge of psychoanalytic theory. There are some who believe that psychoanalysis has passed its zenith and is now on the wane. Certainly psychoanalysis plays a less central role in current psychological and psychiatric thinking than it did twenty years ago, and there have always been strong voices that have cogently criticized the methods and interpretations of psychoanalysis. Psychoanalytic theory, however, is by no means relegated to history. It is a constantly changing body of thought

Sigmund Freud, originator of psychoanalysis.
(UPI)

and there are many vigorous groups in the psychoanalytic movement who are seeking new directions with a greater emphasis on the importance of social factors in personality development. In addition, many central psychoanalytic ideas have been absorbed and rephrased in other personality theories. An understanding of these theories requires an understanding of psychoanalysis and the cultural environment from which it emerged.

Sigmund Freud was born in Austria in 1856. Very early in his medical career he became interested in the nervous system. He appeared destined for a research career in neurology (Jones, 1957) and carried out several excellent neuro-anatomical investigations. His medical practice, which he began in Vienna in 1886, forced him to confront the more pragmatic problems of treating patients who suffered from such "nervous" disorders as extreme anxiety, excessive fatigue, and loss of memory. Freud at first employed conventional physical procedures in treating these patients, including massage, baths, and electric stimulation of various skin areas. When these treatments failed, he turned to hypnosis which was then employed by a number of psychiatrists including Freud's older colleague and good friend, Josef Breuer.

Freud soon became disenchanted with hypnosis too. Not

only were many patients incapable of entering a trance state, but also memories of the past (which seemed related to present difficulties) were often "lost" again upon regaining the waking state. Gradually Freud developed the method of **free association** to supplant the earlier techniques. The patient was instructed simply to focus on a symptom or an event in the past and "associate freely" to it; the patient was to say anything that came to mind, no matter how trivial or embarrassing it might seem. Needless to say, these "trivial" or "embarrassing" associations were often found to be the key to understanding the problem, for they were systematically related to the patient's underlying conflicts and to his overt symptoms. The method of free association became the cornerstone of psychoanalytic technique. It remains so even today.

By listening carefully to the patient's verbal associations, Freud detected consistent themes which on further analysis were shown to be manifestations of the patient's unconscious wishes and fears. The discovery that much of individual behavior is a compromise between wishes and fears assumed a central role in psychoanalytic theory. Freud applied this notion to a wide variety of phenomena, including the patient's neurotic symptoms, his dreams, slips of the tongue, humor, sexual behavior, and even occupational interests. In his analyses of these phenomena, he found evidence of childhood conflicts, unconscious incestuous wishes, and hostile impulses. Freud "found" much more, of course; the entire structure of psychoanalytic theory is largely based upon patients' free associations and the interpretation of these verbalizations. We turn now to some of those findings and interpretations which form the core of **psychoanalytic theory.**

Concept of Libido

Freud used the concept of **libido** to describe what he believed to be a fundamental pleasure-seeking drive which motivates us from the moment of birth. The distinctive feature of libidinally determined behavior is its erotic (sexual) quality. This quality remains even though the pattern of libidinal expression may change radically as the child matures and passes through the various **psychosexual stages.** Freud proposed that in childhood—long before mature, adult sexuality develops—the sexual impulses undergo three stages of development—oral, anal, and phallic. During the first year of life, the baby is in the *oral* stage, his libidinal impulses being gratified through stimulation of the mucous membranes of the mouth. During the child's second and third year, the *anal* stage, pleasures stemming from excretion and retention of feces dominate the child's erotic life. Sometime at the end of the third or beginning of the fourth year the child enters the *phallic* stage of development in which excitation and stimulation of the genital areas provide the primary source of erotic pleasure. Following the phallic stage libidinal impulses enter a period of quiescence called "latency"; they are reawakened, however, with the onset of puberty.

Many emotional problems which the child may subsequently experience as an adult were traced back by Freud to specific disturbances during the oral, anal, and phallic periods. As a result of these disturbances, libidinal energy becomes tied up or fixated at a particular psychosexual stage of development. It is assumed that the greater the degree of **fixation** at a psychosexual stage, the less energy the organism has available for mature relationships.

Many consider Freud's concept of libido to be the least satisfactory element of his theory. He postulated a system in which there is a fixed amount of energy, presumably innate, which becomes diminished through attachment to objects. The idea is vague and difficult, if not impossible, to test. Freud also assumed that when

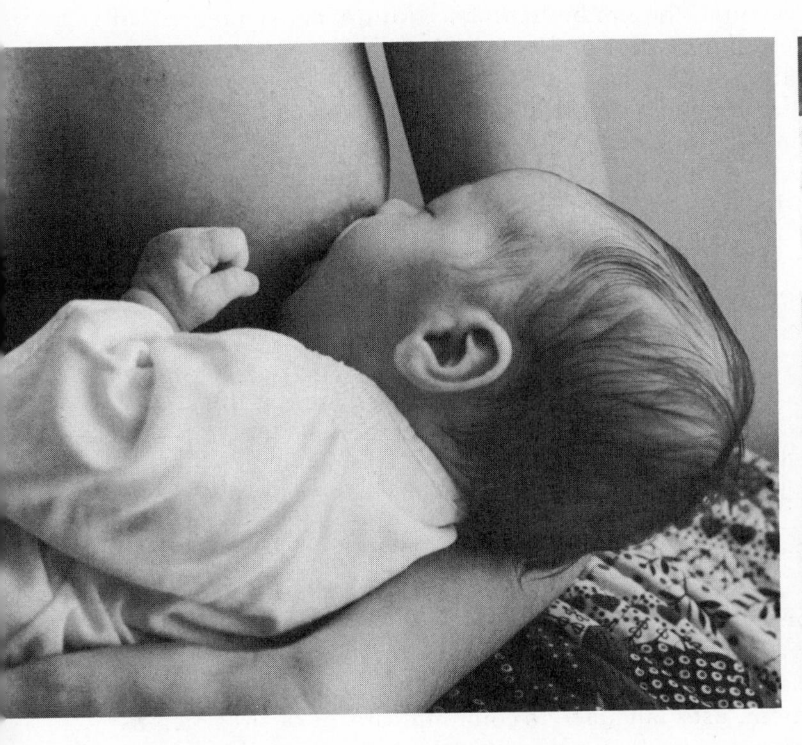

Is smoking a carry-over from the oral stage?
(Fritz Henle, Photo Researchers; Ted Polumbaum)

libidinal impulses cannot be directly expressed because of fear or guilt, tension and pressure in the energy system increase, compelling some release in the form of symptoms or antisocial behavior. Thus, from a psychoanalytic point of view, it is essential that society provide a safety valve for the indirect expression of libidinal and other impulses (e.g., aggression) whose direct expression is prohibited.

Id, Ego, and Superego

Aggressive impulses are another basic energy source and, like the libido, are biologically rooted and present at birth. Freud used the concept of the **id** to denote these primordial libidinal and aggressive drives. The id consists of unconscious impulses which seek *immediate* expression and gratification. The pressure for rapid discharge without regard to consequences to others (or to the organism itself) is referred to in psychoanalytic theory as the "pleasure principle." The pleasure principle also implies that man is basically hedonistic, seeking to maximize his pleasure while avoiding unpleasantness.

The child would not long survive and certainly could not become an effective, mature social being if he were unable to delay the immediate gratification of his impulses. He would remain savage, asocial, and amoral, governed completely by his immediate feelings and desires. The process of learning to delay impulse expression and to take into account the immediate and future consequences of behavior is referred to as the "reality principle." The reality principle governs the actions of the **ego,** which is responsible for coordinating and directing the organism's behavior, and mediates between the unreasoning id and the constraints of reality. The ego's function is to select patterns of action that will permit the maximum achievement of id impulse gratification under the limiting circumstances imposed by the real world.

In the discussion of the relationship between the id and the ego, psychoanalytic theory is often inconsistent, confusing, and illogical. It is much too easy to reify the id and ego, to treat them as two little men living in the individual's psyche, struggling for control of the helpless personality. But obviously one cannot willfully discharge aggressive, sexual, and other drives, such as hunger, with impunity. The immediate gratification of these drives often is in conflict with the demands of reality. The objects which would permit drive satisfaction are not always available (physical reality) and, even when they are, impulse expression can lead to severe punishment (social reality). The older child who in a pique of jealousy strikes his infant sibling may find that his momentary experience of gratification is followed by a sustained experience of painful punishment by his parents. It is also clear that as the child learns to discriminate objects in his environment, uses language to communicate his desires, begins to make inferences regarding cause-effect relationships—that is, as he learns to apply the reality principle—he can more effectively satisfy his needs for pleasure without being punished.

The concept of ego is used in two rather different ways in psychoanalytic theory—as a mediator or organizer and as a system of motives. Ego motives involve self-enhancement and are most clearly reflected in feelings of pride, and in strivings for status, superiority, achievement, and power. Whereas id motives are governed by biological pleasures, ego motives are based on the broader calculus of self-interest.

Human behavior is also governed by a third system of motives, the **superego,** which has an "I ought or should" rather than an "I want" (id) or an "I can" (ego) quality. This system is made up of internalized prohibitions which act to suppress id and ego satisfaction even when there is no possibility of punishment by an external agent. The superego is largely unconscious but its effects can be discerned in the feelings of guilt and pricks of conscience which almost all people experience at times. The superego robs us of pleasure and reduces efforts at self-aggrandizement. Superego emotions are in constant conflict with the id and the ego and prevent the ego from a rational resolution of opposing forces besetting the organism.

Very often, a patient's problems result from restricted and inhibited behaviors controlled by an overly strict superego; he feels guilty constantly and cannot enjoy even the most simple and acceptable pleasures (e.g., sex with his wife). So the analyst tries to restrain or weaken the superego, a fact that led many to condemn the treatments as libertine and immoral. But this criticism is rarely well founded; an irrational conscience is not moral; it is more closely associated with unthinking behaviors that have found expression in inquisitions and holy wars (kill for Christ). The irrational superego also wreaks havoc with the individual's personality, producing unnecessary conflict and anxiety because the restrictions are not based on rational considerations. At the same time, rational considerations are sometimes irrelevant to behavioral choices in which one is confronted with a conflict between one's own interests and those of others. Psychoanalysis, like some other individually oriented psychotherapeutic systems, has never adequately resolved the problem posed when social responsibility conflicts with self-interest.

The psychoanalytic theory of the development of the superego accentuates the irrational qualities of this personality structure. The theory is clearest in the case of the boy. During the phallic period, at the age of five or six, the boy's libidinal impulses are directed toward his mother. He resents his father whom he sees as a rival for the affections of the mother. Freud labeled this classic rivalry the **Oedipal conflict** (Oedipus complex) after a character in a Greek legend, Oedipus Rex, who unknowingly killed his father and married his mother. The young boy also fears that his father will retaliate by castrating him. Freud labeled this fear **castration anxiety** and considered it the prototype of all subsequent anxiety. The fear of castration normally leads to (1) repression of the boy's erotic feelings toward the mother and (2) identification with the father as a powerful figure. (The process of identification is discussed on p. 326.) Obviously, any disturbances in the resolution of this central developmental conflict would have serious and lasting effects on future personality development.

The identification process not only permits the child to express indirectly his love toward his mother with minimal anxiety but it also marks the beginnings of his internal identification of himself as a *male*. Much of the content of the superego also grows out of this identification process. The child internalizes his father's values and accepts them as his own, even though his view of these values tends to be idealized, as if the father were perfect or godlike. Neither the son nor the father can live up to these standards, completely, and this fact underlies many later conflicts. The result is that the psychoanalyst must try to weaken the superego in many patients who can neither live by, nor reject, the idealized moral demands internalized as a very young child.

The young girl is presumed to undergo a transformation at about the same time, although the situation is more complex and takes longer to resolve. Psychoanalytic theory, in fact, is much less "worked out" for females. It is believed, however, that the girl at this time begins to internalize a sense of weakness and inferiority—the concept of *penis envy* was developed to indicate this sense of being "incomplete"—and the identification with the mother is seen as a result of a kind of "shared misfortune." Only by getting a man (a husband) and bearing a male child can a woman fulfill herself.

Freud's psychology of women has been criticized as pure male chauvinism, and the criticisms are neither new nor without some basis (see Spotlight 9-1). The theory was certainly influenced by traditional views of the female role in European society. Many later psychoanalytic scholars (e.g., Thompson, 1964) preferred the concept of "privilege envy"—a social and changeable state—to "penis envy"—biological and irreversible. We shall return to this issue when the topic of sex differences in personality is considered.

Repression

One of the more provocative aspects of psychoanalytic theory is the assertion that a significant part of our behavior is governed by forces of which we are unaware. Our choice of marital partner, the vocation that we select, our hobbies, quarrels with friends, careless acts, and incompetent performances may reflect the influence of impulses and fears which remain unconscious, that is, inaccessible to our consciousness. Impulses and feelings such as shame, guilt, or fear—and memories associated with these unacceptable feelings—may also be excluded from awareness. When Freud encouraged his patients to recall painful memories and to confront unacceptable feelings, they appeared to resist his efforts. Freud hypothesized that this resistance was a function of an active, though unconscious, attempt to exclude unpleasant events and feelings from memory. He called this **repression** (see Spotlight 9-2).

SPOTLIGHT 9-1
Was Freud a Male Chauvinist?

Freud had spurned an excellent opportunity to open the door to hundreds of enlightening studies on the effect of male-supremacist culture on the ego development of the young female, preferring instead to sanctify her oppression in terms of the inevitable law of "biology." The theory of penis envy has so effectively obfuscated understanding that all psychology has done since has not yet unraveled this matter of social causation. If, as seems unlikely, penis envy can mean anything at all, it is productive only within the total cultural context of sex. And here it would seem that girls are fully cognizant of male supremacy long before they see their brother's penis. It is so much a part of their culture, so entirely present in the favoritism of school and family, in the image of each sex presented to them by all media, religion, and in every model of the adult world they perceive, that to associate it with a boy's distinguishing genital would, since they have learned a thousand other distinguishing sexual marks by now, be either redundant or irrelevant. Confronted with so much concrete evidence of the male's superior status, sensing on all sides the depreciation in which they are held, girls envy not the penis, but only what the penis gives one social pretensions to. Freud appears to have made a major and rather foolish confusion between biology and culture, anatomy and status. It is still more apparent that his audience found such a confusion serviceable.

SPOTLIGHT 9-2
A Case of Repression

One of my patients in therapy could not acknowledge any feeling of anger. He would sometimes wake up in a panic with his hands clasped around his wife's throat. Yet he stoutly maintained that his wife neither irritated nor angered him and that he had no hostile feelings toward her. As therapy progressed, he became aware of his anger toward his wife and of the source of this anger in his own feelings of inadequacy. It took many months before he could recall any situation in which his mother had behaved unfairly or irrationally. These memories had been repressed because they elicited angry feelings which he could not tolerate. At the termination of the therapy, his irrational fears and obsessive thoughts had disappeared and he felt much more relaxed. Nevertheless, he still had difficulty in acknowledging ever having experienced hostile feelings toward his mother, even after he was able to recall "forgotten" memories of his mother having unfairly and hysterically beaten him. Repression was a key defense he unconsciously employed to preserve his self-image and his image of his mother.

In a later section we shall discuss the varied and subtle defenses which human beings have employed to mitigate psychological wounds, unhappy memories, and distressing feelings (see pp. 223–226). The concepts of repression and especially the unconscious have been sources of contention and controversy. These ideas run counter to the image of "rational man" whose difficulties presumably stem only from lack of education and opportunity to live in social harmony. In addition, because unconscious forces cannot be observed directly, it is difficult to refute or confirm their influence. Most psychologists accept the idea that behavior can be influenced by internal and external stimuli of which the individual is not conscious. However, many argue that it is neither useful nor logical to hypothesize unconscious feelings and motives. While we cannot hope to resolve the philosophical and empirical controversies concerning the concept of the unconscious, it is helpful to consider some of the implications of this concept and the kinds of observations on which it is based.

The Unconscious

The **unconscious** is not a place situated deep in the recesses of the brain. It is a property of behavior. People are conscious of some of their thoughts and actions and the reasons that underlie them, while they may be completely unaware of some of their other attitudes and feelings. Richard Paulder did not know why he got into arguments with certain adults. He wasn't aware that there was a particular type of person involved, and sometimes he wasn't even aware that he was behaving in an angry, aggressive manner. Variations can occur in degree of awareness of external stimuli or internal states and of one's overt behavior.

Several different kinds of clinical and experimental observations support the notion that unconscious factors may exert significant influences on human behaviors. The phenomenon of posthypnotic suggestion is an example. The hypnotist suggests to the subject that when he wakes from hypnosis, he will experience a particular feeling or carry out a specific action. At the same time the subject is instructed to forget the bases for the feeling or action. When the subject is awakened, he will carry out the posthypnotic suggestion without apparent awareness of the reasons for his actions.

Several experimental findings also indicate that behavior can be modified without the person being aware of the source of influence. In some studies of verbal conditioning, the experimenter decided to increase the subject's use of a particular word or category of words such as pronouns or plural nouns. Every time that the subject utters the designated word category—for example, every time the subject uses a plural noun—the experimenter "incidentally" reinforces the response by nodding his head or simply saying "uh-huh." It has been shown that the subject will utter the reinforced words with increased frequency, even though he is not aware of either

Experiment of hypnosis by Dr. Charcot in Paris. Freud, who studied with Charcot, had this picture in his study. (Culver Pictures)

the change in his behavior or the experimenter's pattern of reinforcement (Greenspoon, 1955; Krasner, 1958). Students can demonstrate the efficacy of this procedure for themselves by trying it out on a friend or even an instructor.

What is especially intriguing about this phenomenon, sometimes called the Greenspoon effect, is that reinforcement can be subtly related to the subject's feelings and desires. In one experiment (Feshbach, Stiles, & Bitter, 1967), the subject was initially angered by another "subject," who in reality was a confederate of the experimenter, deliberately being insulting according to experimental design. (The real subject, of course, did not know this.) He was then asked to observe the confederate carrying out a complex task under the stress of periodic electric shock and to make repeated ratings of his emotional reactions. In between ratings the subject was asked to make up a sentence with any one of the following pronouns: I, we, they, he, she, you. He then would return to his main task of judging the confederate's emotional reactions.

The confederate was supposedly being administered electric shock on a random basis. Actually, every time the subject used the pronouns *we* or *they,* the confederate would receive a shock. Subjects who had been angered by the confederate significantly increased their use of the pronouns *we* and *they* while a control group of nonangered subjects did not. Detailed interviews of the subjects conducted after the experiment showed they had no awareness that their use of the particular words was related to the administrations of shock to the confederate.

Relatively simple behaviors like the choice of a pronoun can be unconsciously influenced by feelings and rewards; it seems likely that complex choices like the selection of a husband or wife will be affected at least in part by feelings and associations of which we have little or no awareness. For Freud, a principal goal of maturity is to bring these unconscious feelings, insofar as possible, into consciousness. Although personality theorists may differ in the importance they attribute to conscious and unconscious forces in behavior, almost all have incorporated Freud's concept of the unconscious in one form or other.

Recent Trends in Psychoanalytic Theory

A number of different theories of human personality are called psychoanalytic. Some only loosely warrant this classification while others are closely related to Freud's thought and may be considered extensions or "descendants" of his basic discoveries. The extensions have come primarily in two areas. First, since Freud had spent most of his time working out the dynamics of the id, the later developments have focused on the ego. Freud's daughter Anna, for example, developed the notion of ego defense (against threat) and delineated the mechanisms of defense that her father had mentioned but had not discussed in great detail (A. Freud, 1946). (See pp. 323–326.) Other psychoanalytic theorists (Hartmann, 1958) began to examine more closely the functions of the ego such as perception and thought; conscious cognition became a topic of increased interest.

The second trend has been a more detailed examination of the social and cultural influences on personality. Freud's thinking was strongly influenced by his training in medicine and biology, and more recent studies in anthropology and sociology began to cast doubt on the generality of some of his concepts. His view of the development of the female personality has been criticized as being too biological, not taking into account the powerful influence of the social milieu.

Erik Erikson

A good example of both trends is found in the writings of Erik Erikson (1950). Erikson views the early stages of development in terms similar to those of Freud, but he examines these stages from the perspective of the particular kinds of ego processes involved rather than in terms of biologically determined libidinal tensions. An emphasis on ego processes leads naturally to considerations of social and cultural forces, for the ego is the "mediator" between the personal needs and the demands of social reality. In addition, Erikson does not see the pattern of personality as essentially completed and unchangeable by the time the child enters school. He extends his analysis of development to embrace the full life span from infancy to maturity.

Erikson proposes eight **psychosocial stages** in personality formation. Each stage is critical in the development of certain fundamental personality characteristics, and earlier stages prepare the way for the later ones. The stages and the attendant personality dimensions are presented in Spotlight 9-3.

The personality dimensions described are related to psychosocial crises. Each stage involves crises. If the crises are adequately resolved, the individual acquires a healthy component of personality (e.g., trust or initiative); if the crises are not adequately resolved, a negative quality is generated (e.g., mistrust or guilt). Let us take one specific example. In the earliest stage, the oral-sensory

SPOTLIGHT 9-3

Erikson's Eight Stages of Man and Their Implications for Personality Structure

Psychosocial Stages	Personality Dimensions
1. Oral-Sensory (first year)	Basic trust vs. Mistrust
2. Muscular-Anal (ages 2–3)	Autonomy vs. Shame and doubt
3. Locomotor-Genital (ages 3–5)	Initiative vs. Guilt
4. Latency (ages 5–12)	Industry vs. Inferiority
5. Puberty and Adolescence	Identity vs. Role confusion
6. Young Adulthood	Intimacy vs. Isolation
7. Adulthood	Generativity vs. Stagnation
8. Maturity	Ego integrity vs. Despair

stage, the infant interacts primarily with its mother, and the "goal" of the interaction is primarily food supply. It is the infant's first interaction with the social world. Is the "world" to be trusted or not? Are basic needs fulfilled generously and with affection, or is the world instead harsh and unpredictable, giving supplies grudgingly, without

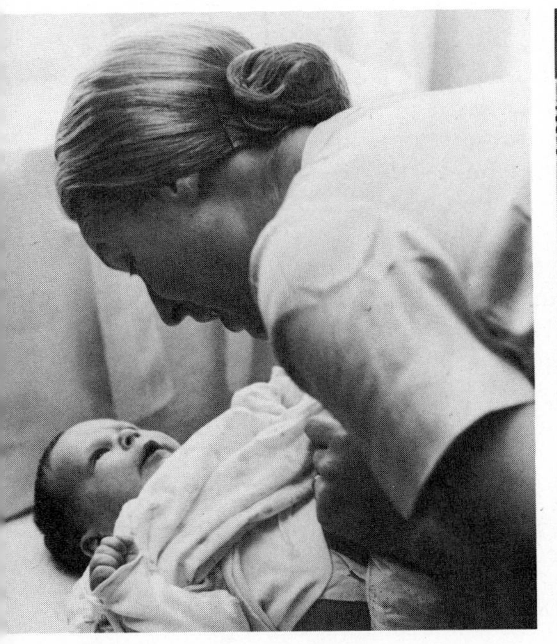

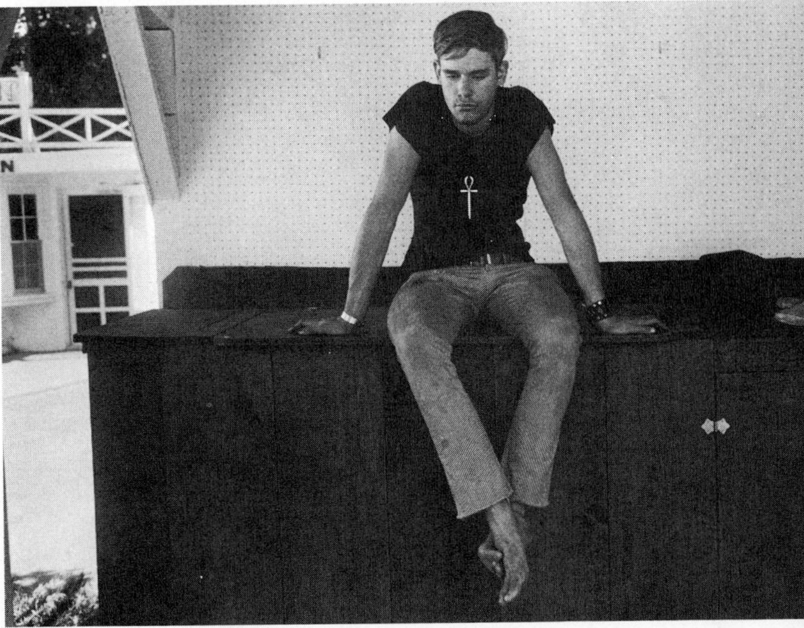

According to Erikson's theory, each of eight stages of life is critical for the further development of personality. (Suzanne Szasz, Photo Researchers; Charles Gatewood)

Personality development, according to Erikson, extends into maturity and involves the resolution of psychosocial crises.
(Ted Polumbaum)

love? According to Erikson, the infant develops during this period a *basic sense of trust*, or mistrust, toward the world (which is of course composed almost entirely of one person—his mother—at this time). He becomes a "trusting" or a "distrusting" person. This is not to say that later events cannot alter the basic dispositions, only this is his first experience of expectations fulfilled or unfulfilled and thus it is of critical importance.

Erikson's thoughtful analysis is especially appealing to contemporary readers because of his emphasis on factors determining a sense of identity and relationships with other people. If sexual problems can be said to have been the predominant hang-up in the Victorian era, then problems of confusion in identity and feelings of isolation from other human beings can be said to be the predominant hang-ups in modern, technologically advanced Western societies. Erikson's writings speak to these problems.

Erikson, like Freud, sees conflict as an inevitable dimension of the human struggle but has a less tragic or pessimistic conception of the outcome of the resolution of conflict. Self-insight and control have an important role in Erikson's model of the human skills and capacities that are needed to cope with the inevitable vicissitudes and dilemmas of living. But these are substantially augmented and amplified by the attributes acquired by a positive resolution of each developmental stage. Thus, in the mature person, the following attributes, or virtues have evolved (Erikson deliberately chooses moralistic terminology): hope, will, purpose, and competence—the rudiments of virtue developed in childhood; fidelity—the adolescent virtue; and love, care, and wisdom—the central virtues of adulthood (Erikson, 1964). These "virtues" are reminiscent of Old and New Testament preachings, and it is probably not accidental that the ideal model of man as conceived by Erikson has its counterpart in Western religious thought.

What elements of psychoanalysis did Freud's followers reject?

There are a number of personality theories that appear to be psychoanalytic and obviously owe a great debt to Freud's original thinking, but which deviate in certain fundamental respects from the classical psychoanalytic model. The clearest examples of such theories are those of Alfred Adler, Carl Jung, and Otto Rank—all early associates of Freud who eventually decided that some of Freud's most basic concepts had to be revised. Because of their dissent on some basic issues, they separated (or were separated) from Freud with his request: "Do not call your theory psychoanalytic."

In one form or another, both early and later dissent from Freud took the form of rejection of his postulate concerning human motivation: that it is sexual in nature (libido). The alternatives to libido theory proposed by Adler (1930), Jung (1959), Rank (1945), and later dissidents such as Fromm (1941), Horney (1937), and Sullivan (1953) are diverse; Spotlight 9-4 provides a brief description, reflecting only part of the original thinking and contribution of these theorists.

Freud gave his first university lectures on psychoanalysis at Clark University, Worcester, Mass., in 1909. These were arranged by Psychologist G. Stanley Hall (center), President of Clark University. The others are disciples of Freud: Carl Jung (seated right) and, standing, left to right, A. A. Brill, Ernest Jones (who later wrote Freud's biography), and Sandor Ferenczi. (Culver Pictures)

Change of Emphasis

Still, among the dissenters from Freud, certain general themes emerge. The need for relating to others, for loving and being loved, as developed in the writings of Horney, Fromm, and Sullivan, has a quite different connotation than Freud's needs for libidinal gratification. These theorists emphasize interpersonal relationships, and the erotic aspects are seen as only one component of these relationships.

Another dimension of interpersonal relationships, sometimes conflicting with the need for relatedness, is the need for separateness, for independence. This basic human motivation, first emphasized by Rank (1929; 1945), appears in different forms as a critical aspect of human striving in the writings of the psychologists listed in Spotlight 9-4. Fromm, in particular, but also Adler, Jung, and Rank, suggested that needs for relatedness and independence can function in harmony in the mature individual and can be satisfied by appropriate interpersonal relationships.

The concept of a need for independence requires a "*self*" that is asserting its independence. The self and the self-concept have many other motivational attributes, expressed, for example, in the needs for self-esteem, for power, or for approval and reassurance. The concept of self as a fundamental source of human motivation is reflected in Adler's concept of the individual's striving toward perfection and in Jung's postulation of a striving for self-actualization.

Jung's Concepts

Carl Gustav Jung, one of the greatest and most erudite contemporary thinkers, formulated a distinctive model of man, which has had a significant impact on modern thought. Jung places much greater stress on the role of man's aims and aspirations in determining his behavior than Freud did. In Jung's writings, the ultimate goal toward which each individual is striving is **self-actualization,** the realization of his aims and potentials, and this goal directs man's development and destiny.

In the actualized personality, according to Jung, there is an acceptance and integration of opposing forces and tendencies. There are many opposing forces to be balanced. Each of us, for example, has both masculine and feminine tendencies, and the integrated personality balances aggressiveness with sensitivity. A similar integration must be maintained between opposing tendencies toward introversion and extroversion, personality orientations first discussed in detail by Jung. **Introversion** refers to attention to one's inner thoughts and feelings: the subjective world. **Extroversion** refers to the tendency to direct one's attention outward toward the objective world and is reflected in the social, gregarious actions of men. Unlike some psychologists who have seen these tendencies as personality types, Jung considered all men to have both dispositions. An integrated

SPOTLIGHT 9-4

Suggested Alternatives to Libidinal Motives

Alfred Adler	Will to power, feelings of inferiority, and striving toward superiority or perfection.
Erich Fromm	The expression of one's human nature, as contrasted to animal nature; and as reflected in the needs for relatedness to and transcendance from other people and physical nature, identity, and a stable frame of reference for perceiving and comprehending the world.
Karen Horney	Basic anxiety, as reflected in exaggerated needs for love (moving toward people), for independence (moving away from people), and for destruction (moving against people).
Carl Jung	Striving for self-actualization, as reflected in integrating the "wisdom" of the personal and collective unconscious with the products of conscious experience.
Otto Rank	The struggle for independence, with separation anxiety being the primary source of conflict.
Harry Stack Sullivan	The need for security in conjunction with the need for biological satisfactions; postulation of a self-dynamism as a major motivational outgrowth of the need for security.

personality, in his view, is one in which the need for social contact and the need for privacy and reflection are both satisfied. He further proposes that if one tendency is exaggerated, the other will somehow manage to express itself, in dreams, in psychopathological symptoms, or in overt action (acting out). This view is similar to Freud's notion concerning the individual's need for some sort of discharge of repressed impulses.

One of Jung's most original and most intriguing concepts is the **collective unconscious.** Extending the overriding concept of balance to the more global aspects of personality, Jung felt there must be integration among the conscious, the personal unconscious (similar to Freud's conception of the unconscious), and the collective unconscious. The collective unconscious is conceived to contain the psychological "residue" of man's ancestral past; it consists of certain innate ideas, feelings, and attitudes called **archetypes.** For example, all of our ancestors had experience with males and females. According to Jung, some of this experience is passed on to us, and in a woman, there is an archetype of a male called the "animus." (In a man, the archetypical female is called the "anima.") Thus, to some extent and in certain ways, a woman has ideas and attitudes about men *innately.* How she responds to a particular man is in part a function of this archetype and in part, of course, a function of the actual man.

The suggestion of a racial inheritance based upon the acquired experiences of the species is not acceptable to modern geneticists. However, the notion of innate emotional and behavioral dispositions to particular stimuli, such as fear of the dark, fear of strangers, and attachment to warm objects, is not incompatible with biological theory. The collective unconscious may be viewed as innate predispositions to particular feelings and beliefs resulting from repeated experiences over many generations. The collective unconscious is essentially universal, reflecting the evolutionary history of *Homo sapiens.*

What do actualization theories stress?

Just as there are many different views of personality that are considered psychoanalytic, in basis if not in name, so are there varied conceptions of human behavior that can be grouped together under the label of **actualization** theories. These theories share a number of broad characteristics, of which the following are the most important.

Common Emphases

1. They assume that human beings have a self-actualizing tendency, similar to that proposed by Jung, which guides their behavior. Activities that are self-actualizing, that help man realize his aims and potentials, are fulfilling, satisfying, and self-enhancing, while activities incompatible with the self-actualizing strivings are frustrating.

2. There is an emphasis on present experiences as determinants of behavior, in contrast to the psychoanalysts' preoccupation with the critical influence of the past. This focus on the present has several roots. One is the philosophical theories of existentialism, concerned with the *now* as compared to the distant future. Another is

the field theory of the late Kurt Lewin, one of the most seminal individuals in the history of psychology. Lewin's is essentially a psychodynamic formulation in which the variables determining behavior are all in the present situation (Lewin, 1935). Both the future and the past are to be understood in terms of their present psychological representation. Lewin emphasized the forces and constraints induced by *situations*, an emphasis reflected in the writings of a number of actualization theorists (Goldstein, 1939; Rogers, 1959).

3. Cognition is emphasized. Actualization theorists begin with the premise that people think and perceive; therefore, understanding of the individual's thoughts and perceptions is essential to understanding his behavior. In the case of Richard Paulder whom we discussed at the beginning of the section, what matters is not the objective situation but how he perceives himself, his opportunities, and the attitudes of his girl friend and authority figures. The effects of early experiences, such as the anger and resentment generated by his father's punishment, are important only insofar as they influence his current perceptions.

4. Actualization theorists stress the *positive* forces in personality. Psychoanalysts working with Richard Paulder would focus on his unconscious resentments, his fears, and the maladaptive defenses he uses to cope with his unacceptable feelings. Actualization theorists would see Paulder in the light of his struggle to assert his independence, his strong aspirations for achievement, his willingness to work hard for his goals, and his need for affection and acceptance especially by an older man. The psychoanalyst tends to perceive the individual as beset by socially unacceptable impulses and preoccupied with the problems of reducing the tensions generated by these impulses. In contrast, the actualization theorist sees the individual as engaged in a valiant effort to achieve understanding of himself and of others, and searching for novel, creative modes of expression.

5. The love relationship is seen as a positive force which has a very special role. For the psychoanalyst, love is a direct or derivative manifestation of the libido. For the actualization theorist, erotic feelings are either ancillary to or a consequence of love but are not a necessary component. The primary qualities of the love relationship are intimacy and mutual acceptance. The feelings of closeness and warmth that are expressive of intimacy can be manifested in many types of human relationships, even in essentially religious experiences. Mutual acceptance is reflected in shared high regard, in openness, trust, spontaneity, and noncritical attitudes. There is a wide distance, indeed, between these descriptions of a mature love relationship and the Freudian model.

Rogers' Unconditional Positive Regard

Now let's look at some prominent actualization theorists who have had a major impact upon the investigation of personality. A

Carl Rogers, originator of client-centered therapy.
(Courtesy Dr. Carl Rogers)

core concept in Carl Rogers' theory is the *actualizing tendency*, defined as "the inherent tendency of the organism to develop all its capacities in ways which serve to maintain or enhance the organism" (Rogers, 1959, p. 196). Of particular importance is self-actualization, the maintenance and enhancement of the self-concept. According to Rogers, human beings have a basic need for positive regard from others in the form of warmth, love, and acceptance; and this is usually offered on a conditional basis. Typically, the individual receives love or recognition as a result of some particular behavior. Consequently, his perception of himself, and his self-esteem, may become inappropriately attached to particular actions and to the evaluations of other individuals. But the truly healthy personality perceives his whole self in a positive manner, and is not so concerned with specific actions and traits.

In order to attain this level of adjustment, the individual needs the experience of **unconditional positive regard**, of being valued for himself regardless of the degree to which specific behaviors are approved or disapproved. The love of a parent for a child often has an unconditional quality. A mother may disapprove of her four-year-old's aggression toward a younger sibling or of his sloppy table manners, but she nevertheless will communicate her fundamental love and acceptance of the child. According to Rogers, one should criticize the action, not the person. He developed a psychotherapeutic approach, **client-centered therapy**, in which a key element is the therapist's manifestation of unconditional positive regard for the client. The Rogerian therapist is accepting, friendly, and empathic. He conveys to the client an understanding of the client's perception of his feelings and problems. Through the therapist's acceptance and empathy, the client becomes able to accept himself—his experiences and his real feelings. He had previously distorted or denied the truth because it conflicted with self-perceptions that were based on the *conditional* regard of others.

Maslow's View of the Healthy Person

Abraham H. Maslow (1954), another eminent actualization theorist, contrasted two broad categories of human motives—*growth motives* and *deprivation motives*. The first kind is characterized by a push toward actualization of inherent potentialities, while the other is oriented only toward the maintenance of life, not its enhancement. Deprivation motives are arranged in a developmental hierarchy. The first are physiological needs—for water, food, sleep. These are followed by safety needs, characterized by the avoidance of pain and discomfort (e.g., the child needs shelter or is uncomfortable until his diaper is changed). When these needs are satisfied, the needs for belongingness (for love and intimacy) become significant and these, in turn, are superseded by needs for esteem (approval of others and of self). Satisfaction of needs lower in the hierarchy makes possible the pursuit of needs that occur higher in the hierarchy.

Only when the individual's survival needs are satisfied—when he is not "hung up" in their pursuit—can his actualization tendencies be expressed strongly. On the basis of his observations, Maslow (1963) maintains that truly healthy, self-actualizing people share certain common qualities. These include:

1. Efficient perception of reality.
2. Spontaneity and unconventionality of thought rather than unconventionality of behavior.
3. Acceptance of themselves, of others, and of nature.
4. Independence from their environment and an affinity for solitude and privacy.
5. Concern for basic philosophical and ethical issues.
6. Continued freshness of appreciation for ordinary events, e.g., sunsets and even, at times, the workday moment-to-moment business of living; the ability to discriminate between means and ends but enjoyment of means as well as ends.
7. Ability to experience "the oceanic feeling" which has elements of great ecstasy, awe, and both power and helplessness.
8. Genuine desire to help others in conjunction with deep ties with relatively few people.
9. Truly democratic orientation, a philosophical sense of humor and creativeness.

Abraham H. Maslow, proponent of a humanist psychology. (Courtesy Mrs. A. H. Maslow)

You may well question whether these characteristics are a consequence of a psychological process called actualization or the reflections of Maslow's particular value system. And how could one designate in a consistent manner individuals who display these idealized attributes? The student may accept Maslow's criteria of the healthy personality while having a different kind of person in mind than Maslow has. Nevertheless, Maslow's descriptions have called attention to significant dimensions of experience and behavior that other personality theorists have neglected. The fact that Maslow was elected president of the American Psychological Association in 1967 indicates that his humanistic approach was viewed favorably by many psychologists.

How do learning theories explain personality?

There are many theories of personality that emphasize the learning process, and differences among these theories are as acute as differences among the various psychoanalytic theories. Still, they have certain common properties. The strategy of the learning theorists is to begin with empirically established, basic principles of learning and then to build a model of personality and of complex behavior made up of these simple elements. The learning theorist begins with a narrow brush and gradually extends his sweep. (The student is referred to Chapter 18 for a detailed description of learning processes.)

Shaping through Reinforcement

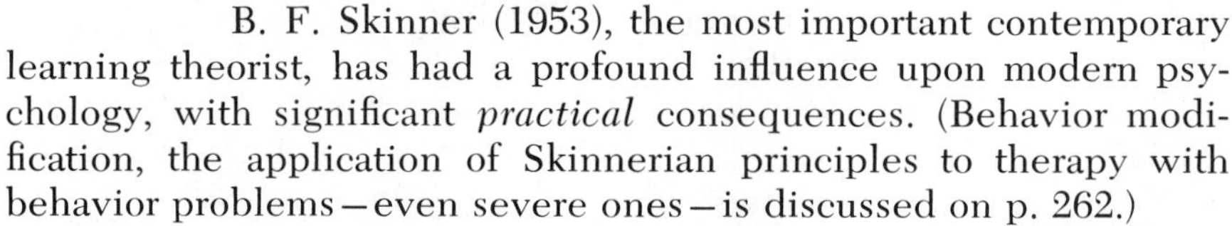

B. F. Skinner (1953), the most important contemporary learning theorist, has had a profound influence upon modern psychology, with significant *practical* consequences. (Behavior modification, the application of Skinnerian principles to therapy with behavior problems—even severe ones—is discussed on p. 262.)

B. F. Skinner, whose learning theory has been applied to personality and psychotherapy. (Jill Krementz, courtesy B. F. Skinner)

The principal thrust of Skinner and his adherents has been to establish links between a stimulus situation and an individual's response. These links come about or are strengthened when the response is rewarded or reinforced. The process of **reinforcement** increases the probability of a response being emitted when a particular stimulus is present. The response is then said to be under stimulus control. A response of this type is called an **operant** or **instrumental response.** If a child is given a piece of candy frequently after he pets a particular dog, he will pet that dog whenever he sees it. Petting the dog becomes an operant response when the stimulus of the dog is presented.

A Skinnerian, in examining Richard Paulder's behavior, would select a particular pattern of behavior—say his tendency to quarrel with authority figures—and look for the elements in the situation which reinforce his verbal aggressive responses. Perhaps when Richard is quarrelsome, authority figures pay him more attention or, on some occasions, may satisfy Richard's complaint. The reinforcement for Richard's behavior can be subtle or obvious. These quarrels may eventually result in some type of punishment to Richard. However, the closer a reward or punishment occurs in time to a response, the stronger is its effects. Consequently, the positive reinforcement, which is more immediate in this situation, will prove more powerful than the punishment that may come later.

Skinnerian analyses tend to employ basic, narrow units of behavior which can then be *shaped* into more complex segments. To improve a student's study habits, for example, one might initially get him to read at his desk for only a five-minute period. The reinforcement might be food, money, or attention. Gradually the length of study period would be increased, step by step, with systematic reinforcement at each step in the process.

A Push-Pull Theory

It will be noted that Skinner's model makes minimal assumptions about any processes occurring *within* the individual. He is essentially seen as having been shaped by past interactions with the environment. The social learning approach of Miller and Dollard (1941), based upon Hull's theory of learning, makes use of both "push" and "pull" concepts. Critical to this theory is the concept of internal motivational states or **drives.** Most human drives, through the processes of learning and association, can be aroused by a variety of internal and external cues or signals. In Richard's case, a male authority figure has become a cue or signal, eliciting internal feelings of anger and aggressive drive. A related cue which elicits aggressive drive is criticism, which Richard cannot accept without resentment. What Richard or anyone else learns to do when he is angry depends on which responses are most effective in relieving the feelings of anger; in other words, in reducing the aroused drive. As in the Skinnerian model, the individual learns those behaviors that are rewarded or reinforced—in this instance, quarreling, and, to a lesser extent, avoidance and withdrawal.

The critical concepts in the Miller-Dollard analysis are *cue, drive, response,* and *reinforcement.* Note that the response that results in a reduction of drive and is thus rewarded is more likely to occur again when the same or similar situation reoccurs. In this theoretical analysis there are also internal, mediating responses. These responses are usually elicited by external stimuli (cues). And they may also have drive functions. Thus, internal responses such as anger, fear, or sexual feelings, may be conceived of as mediating responses which can motivate or drive the organism and, at the same time, serve as distinctive cues eliciting certain overt responses. For example, during Richard's high school years, members of his family often elicited his anger, a mediating response, which in turn evoked another mediating response, fear. He apparently resolved these conflicting tensions by avoiding people who were "reminders" (re-evokers) of the disturbing conflict and concentrated on his studies. Through the ingenious application of these concepts, Miller and Dollard have shown how many psychoanalytic propositions can be reconciled with a more rigorous learning orientation (Dollard & Miller, 1950).

Learning by Imitation

Other learning theorists stress the fact that responses can be learned through *imitation* or *modeling.* A number of studies show that children can acquire a variety of behaviors (e.g., aggressive responses or positive approaches to an animal they previously feared) through imitation of models (Bandura & Walters, 1963). (See pp. 12, 334 for descriptions of these studies.) This is true even though the imitated responses are not directly rewarded. In contrast to shaping, imitation may result in very rapid acquisition of new responses.

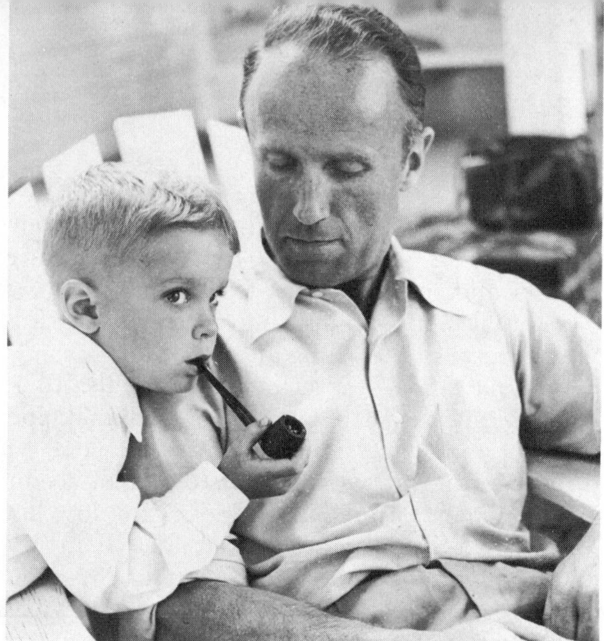

Many responses are learned through imitation or modeling.
(Suzanne Szasz)

What is the Asian approach to personality?

While psychoanalytic, actualization, and learning theorists use different terms and deal with different phenomena of personality, they all share a "Western" framework. This can be contrasted to the approaches to personality associated with important Asian religious and philosophical traditions. Of the theorists cited, Jung and perhaps Maslow can be considered as intermediaries, although still more Western than Eastern in outlook. Eastern conceptions of behavior are no less varied and complex than Western, and an adequate description of Asian psychologies goes well beyond the scope of this chapter. We will only briefly comment on that aspect of Eastern psychology which appears to offer a conception of personality that differs greatly from the Western theories we have considered.

One striking feature of Eastern theologies is their concern with consciousness and the liberation of consciousness (Murphy & Murphy, 1968). In that very important sense, they are much more psychologically oriented than Western religious thought. As in Western tradition, activities of the mind are more highly valued than activities of the body. However, the "higher" level of man is itself arranged in a hierarchical manner. Above the body are the senses, while the mind is greater than the senses. And above the mind is the intellect, with the self being greater than the intellect. The true self is imperishable and unchanging. The qualities of the self are complex and paradoxical. Of particular psychological interest is the notion of the self being a witness rather than an actor. The notion of the ego or individual causing events is illusory; people are not seen as agents of action. True mastery of the self can only be achieved when man acts without being *involved* in action. The following stanzas from the Bhagavad-Gita may help convey these ideas:

But who takes delight in the self alone,
The man who finds contentment in the self,
And satisfaction only in the self,
For him there is found (in effect) no action to perform.

He has no interest whatever in action done,
Nor any in action not done in this world,
Nor has he in reference to all beings
Any dependence of interest.

Therefore unattached ever
Perform action that must be done;
For performing action without attachment
Man attains the highest.

The Eastern goal of achieving a higher level of consciousness through meditation requires a theory of personality different from those of the Western tradition.
(G. Nanja Nath, Black Star)

From a Western perspective, these conceptions of human personality have the effect of diminishing interest in achievement, encouraging a fatalistic and passive attitude toward experience, and turning the individual's energies inward. While effective action (in the Western sense) in the real world is not discouraged, self-actualization is achieved internally rather than through externally directed efforts. According to this Asian view, the highest level of personal fulfillment is the achievement of a state of consciousness in which, through meditation and concentration, the individual becomes aware of the true Self. This state is difficult to describe and has been characterized as having the qualities of empty space, a lack of consciousness of individuality, of body, and of specific thoughts. Feelings of serenity, well-being, and sometimes ecstasy appear to accompany the achievement of this state.

SUMMARY

Questions about personality cannot be answered simply. Consequently, there are many theories that attempt to explain personality structure and dynamics. Of these various theoretical alternatives, the most influential has been the psychoanalytic, formulated and elaborated by Sigmund Freud. Freud proposed that human beings were motivated from birth by a fundamental, biologically rooted sexual energy which he called "libido." The primary modes of expression of libidinal impulses change as the child progresses through the oral, anal, and phallic periods during the first five years of life. Toward the end of this developmental period, libidinal impulses are typically directed toward the parent of the opposite sex. Freud maintained that the personality of the adult was basically determined by the pattern of resolution of these conflicts and the child's experiences during the early stages of psychosexual development. Freud also maintained that the child repressed the painful aspects of these conflicts and that much of human motivation occurred at an unconscious level.

Other psychoanalytic theorists such as Carl Jung, Erik Erikson, Alfred Adler, and Erich Fromm have differed from Freud in placing greater emphasis on cultural determinants of behavior and in proposing alternative motives to the libido as basic to human striving. These psychoanalysts also tend to place greater stress on the positive forces in personality, a theme that is particularly central to the writings of the actualization theorists. The latter assume that human beings have a self-actualizing tendency which guides behavior, they also emphasize the importance of *present* experience and cognitive factors—as contrasted to the role of early childhood and unconscious emotional influences—in determining behavior. Among the most prominent actualization theorists are Carl Rogers and the late Abraham Maslow. Rogers' many contributions include an alternative therapeutic approach to psychoanalysis, called client-centered therapy, while Maslow focused his attention on the hierarchy of human motivations and the characteristics of the truly healthy, self-actualized person.

In contrast to the psychoanalytic and actualization theorists, the learning theorists attempt to use simpler, empirically established principles of behavior in their explanations of human personality. B. F. Skinner and his adherents see behavior, in both its simple and more complex forms, as largely a function of the specific reinforcements or rewards received for making particular responses in the presence of particular stimuli. Miller and Dollard emphasize the role of drives and drive reduction in personality and behavior. Their work has provided a bridge between psychoanalytic theory and learning theory interpretations of personality.

A very different conception of personality is provided by Asian religious and philosophical traditions, which have addressed themselves to states of consciousness and the procedures through which higher levels of consciousness can be achieved.

10

Motivation and Emotion

How do theorists define personality?
How important is motivation?
Why does man have conflict?
How does an analysis of aggression help us understand motivation?

How do theorists define personality?

The history of the study of personality is the history of a search for the key dimensions of personality—variables that are fundamental to an understanding of individual behavior. Such key dimensions must be of wide **generality:** They must apply to most, if not all, individuals and, most important, these variables must influence behavior in a wide variety of situations. The opposite of generality, as we mentioned in Chapter 8, is **specificity.** To repeat what was said there, some psychologists feel that human behavior is a function primarily of the situation and that the search for general characteristics of individuals is fruitless. Probably the majority of personality psychologists, however, consider personality attributes useful and important, and though they might differ significantly in which characteristics they view as most valuable, they are committed to the search for generality.

Approaches to Personality

This search has typically been focused on motivational and emotional variables. Motives, needs, and emotions, both innate and learned, are key concepts for most personality theorists and researchers. It would not be misleading to say that most personality psychologists feel that if they could understand the "why" (**motivation**) of behavior, they could predict the "what" of behavior with much greater precision. Thus, this chapter on the search for general, key concepts will be dominated by considerations of motivation and emotion.

Still, many scientists feel that other characteristics of the individual are more important—or, at least, must supplement motivational constructs—in explaining personality. Some discuss biological variables such as constitution, physique, or sex. Others have considered not the "why" of behavior but the "how" of behavior in studies of expressive movements (handwriting analysis is such an approach). A large and growing number of psychologists have turned to cognitive variables, trying to understand the way an individual thinks or processes information. Before we discuss the motivational and emotional approach to the search for key dimensions, therefore, we will briefly consider some of the alternatives.

In some ways, each person is like *all* others; in some ways, like *some* others; and, in some ways, like *no* other person.
(Charles Gatewood)

Biological Variables

PHYSIQUE Interest in human physique as a key to personality has waxed and waned over the centuries. Literature abounds in references to differences in body build from which differences in personality are inferred. Shakespeare, for example, made his jolly characters fat (Falstaff) and his scheming characters lean (Cassius). While the relationship between physique and personality is an imperfect one, there is some slight scientific basis for Shakespeare's intuitions. For example, Sheldon (1942) identified three primary components of body build—**ectomorphy** (roughly defined as lean-

Do the body builds of Cassius and Falstaff tell us anything about their personalities?
(Both, Culver Pictures)

ness, linearity), **mesomorphy** (muscularity), and **endomorphy** (roundness fatness). (See Figure 10-1.) People who were predominantly ectomorphic were found to be highly sensitive and introverted while mesomorphs (highly muscular, solidly built people) showed assertive, competitive characteristics. High degrees of endomorphy (rounded body builds) were related—as in Falstaff's case—to easygoing sociability.

How can one account for the correlation between body build and personality? Sheldon hypothesized that physique and temperament are both manifestations of underlying biological variables. It may also be that people are behaving in accord with cultural expectations. The fat man is jolly because he is supposed to be jolly. Perhaps certain kinds of physique *facilitate* success in particular behaviors. Thus, the mesomorph's strength may increase

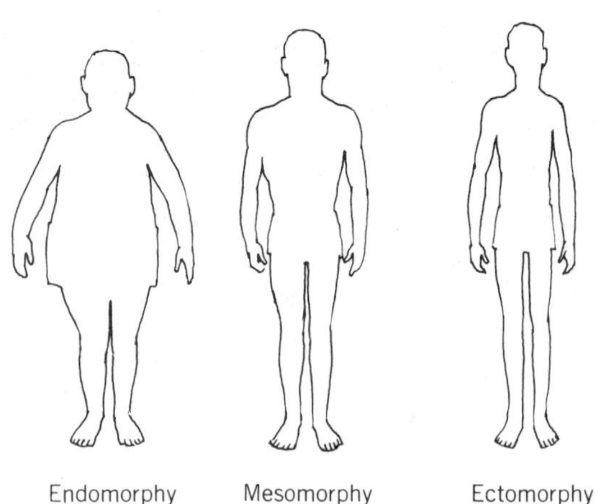

FIGURE 10-1
BASIC BODY TYPES

the likelihood of his being reinforced for being assertive and aggressive. Or perhaps behavior also influences body build—the relaxed, sociable, and jolly fellow is likely to develop a rotund appearance.

GENETIC FACTORS Sheldon's views on the relationship between biological factors and personality were generally considered intriguing but perhaps a bit "odd" by American psychologists. As a group, personality theorists tend to emphasize motivation and learning, and while some motives may be biological, temperament and other resulting personality attributes are seen largely as the result of experience, not constitution. More recent advances in our knowledge of genetics, however, spurred renewed interest in the biological roots of personality. Specifically, the question is asked: To what extent is personality inherited?

The study of twins is important in the search for genetic factors. Twins are of two types: identical and fraternal. Identical twins develop from *one* fertilized ovum and have identical heredities, but fraternal twins developing from two ova, have different genetic makeups. In one carefully executed study, Gottesman (1963) compared thirty-four pairs of each kind, all high school students. Each twin was given the Minnesota Multiphasic Personality Inventory (MMPI) and another personality questionnaire. I.Q. scores on each subject were also available. The results showed that identical twins resembled each other much more than fraternal twins in I.Q., in introversion-extroversion, and in aggressiveness, moodiness, dependency, and shyness.

Identical twins (developed from one egg) resemble each other more in some personality characteristics and in appearance than do fraternal twins (developed from two eggs).
(Both, Suzanne Szasz)

The findings provide some evidence of hereditary influences on several of the personality dimensions. The relationships are only moderate, and you might argue that the findings can be given a learning interpretation if you assume that identical twins have more similar learning experiences than fraternal twins—for example, that identicals are more likely than fraternals to be raised in the same ways and in a similar environment. Nevertheless, the evidence that pairs of identical twins are, on the average, more similar in scores on personality and interest measures than fraternal twins, together with the data on genetic differences in behavior of animals (Williams, 1967), strongly suggests that some aspects of personality are influenced by genetic factors. In general, however, environmental factors seem more important than genes in accounting for individual differences in personality traits.

SEX DIFFERENCES The question of biological determinants of personality has direct relevance to current controversies, stimulated by the women's liberation movement, concerning the behaviors and social roles of men and women. Much of the rationale for defending the traditional role assumed by women is based on the assumption that women are *constitutionally* more emotional, more dependent, more passive, and less assertive and aggressive than men.

Prior to answering questions concerning the cause of sex differences in personality, one must first establish what these

In many situations, boys in our culture are more active than girls.
(Van Bucher, Photo Researchers)

differences are. A number of studies have indicated that by nursery-school age boys behave more aggressively than females, a pattern which extends into adulthood (Bennett & Cohen, 1951; Feshbach, 1970). By high school and college age, girls seem to be more dependent and conforming than males (Barry, Bacon, & Child, 1957).

Consistent sex differences have also been found on cognitive measures which assess whether the individual makes perceptual judgments independently and analytically or in ways that show dependence on the appearance of the "field" or immediate environment. (Witkin *et al.*, 1962). On one of these measures, the rod and frame test, the subject is shown only a rod contained within a square frame and is required to adjust the rod to the vertical as the frame tilts. The degree to which the tilt of the frame influences the judgment of the verticality of the rod can then be determined (see p. 407). Men make fewer errors and work more rapidly than women (Maccoby, 1966; Witkin *et al.*, 1962), indicating that women are more "field dependent." This dependency is related to social dependency and conformity (Witkin *et al.*, 1962). Girls tend to be superior to boys in a number of cognitive functions, for example on tests of verbal ability. They also learn to speak at an earlier age than boys (Maccoby, 1966). It should be pointed out, however, that there have been reports of important exceptions to each of these sex differences in personality and intellectual ability (Anastasi & D'Angelo, 1952; Dundsdon & Fraser-Roberts, 1957; Iscoe *et al.*, 1964).

Even the greater aggressiveness found for males has been questioned. In her famous monograph "Sex and Temperament in Three Primitive Societies," Margaret Mead (1935) described striking variations among societies in the aggressive behavior displayed by the two sexes. Working within a relatively small geographical area in New Guinea, she found one tribe in which both males and females were violent and aggressive; a second in which both sexes were mild and unaggressive; and a third in which there was a real reversal of the pattern of our own culture, the women being more aggressive and the men more mild and dependent. Several experiments conducted with American middle-class boys and girls have reported data indicating that girls are more indirectly aggressive than boys (Feshbach, 1969; Feshbach & Sones, 1971). While they made less use of physical aggression, girls were more likely than boys to reject another child or to act unfriendly. Under some circumstances girls will behave more aggressively in a direct manner, with an unmistakable hostile message. In one experiment in which college students were placed in an apparent competitive situation and given an opportunity to retaliate against their competitor with electric shock, the use of strong shocks was greatest among girls who were led to believe their opponents were males.

There are many unresolved issues about sex differences

in personality and some questions have only begun to be explored. One must therefore be cautious in making generalizations. Even in traits in which the sexes differ, there are marked *individual* differences within each sex and great overlap between boys and girls. Perhaps the culture reinforces sex differences that are rooted in biologically based tendencies.

The relationship between personality attributes and sexual behavior is also not well understood. Perhaps certain sex differences in personality facilitate heterosexual attraction and sexual competence. But it is clear that the specific sex-typed behaviors—e.g., playing with dolls versus playing ball—are strongly influenced by cultural norms which are conveyed to the child by parents and by peers whom the child can observe and imitate. The processes in-

Men and women of today who break from societal roles demonstrate that sex differences are largely determined by their culture.
(Bell System)

volved in the establishment of sex identity and the development of distinctive sex interests will be discussed at greater length in the chapter on personality development (see p. 328).

In any case, the results of psychological and anthropological research indicate that both males and females are capable of a great variety of behaviors. Individual differences and cultural definitions and prescriptions probably play a greater role than biological differences in determining men's and women's ways of expressing emotions and their occupational and professional choices.

Expressive Behavior

Both the psychologist and the layman have been interested in the possibility that the way we move may express our personalities. We have already mentioned "body language" (p. 165), and handwriting analysis remains a popular parlor performance. In a pioneer experiment, men and women who scored at the extreme of an inventory measure of social dominance were asked to carry out a series of motor tasks including walking, drawing geometrical figures, handwriting, and gripping a pencil as strongly as possible (Allport & Vernon, 1933). The men high in dominance wrote and drew more rapidly, covered more space on a page, and exerted more pressure on a pencil than those low in dominance. Fewer reliable differences in expressive movement, however, were found between women high and low in dominance. The suggestion that aspects of handwriting may reflect personality traits is especially intriguing, but there is little evidence to support the graphologist's claim that specific handwriting signs are associated with particular personality characteristics. The interpretation of handwriting bears many similarities to the interpretation of projective tests. It contains a core of validity but is subject to many sources of error.

Cognitive Dimensions

In recent years, psychologists have been interested in investigating variations in personality as expressed in cognitive functions. An example is the dimension which runs from "field independent" to "field dependent" to which reference was made earlier. (See also the discussion on p. 406.) A rather different dimension has been described as perceived "internal" versus "external" control of reinforcement (Rotter, 1966). This personality dimension refers to the person's tendency to perceive himself as able to influence and control events or as someone who is largely controlled by outside forces. It is a trait which operates at both the cognitive level (how one thinks about his world) and at the decision process level (how one decides to act). A useful measure of this dimension is a twenty-three item forced-choice inventory, referred to as the I-E (for internal-external) scale. The following sample of items is illustrative. The subject is asked to choose the alternative in each pair with which he agrees.

a. *Without the right breaks, one cannot be an effective leader.*
b. *Capable people who fail to become leaders have not taken advantage of their opportunities.*

a. *I have often found that what is going to happen will happen.*
b. *Trusting to fate has never turned out as well for me as making a decision to take a definite course of action.*

a. *Sometimes I can't understand how teachers arrive at the grades they give.*

b. There is a direct connection between how hard I study and the grades I get.

In each instance alternative *a* is the "external" response. The student may find it difficult to choose between alternatives, but he should keep in mind that it is the total score rather than the choice on any individual item that is important. The utility of the scale has been demonstrated in many different kinds of situations. For example, black students who were willing to participate in such civil actions as a march on the state capitol or a "Freedom Ride" score significantly more *internal* on the I-E scale than those students who were uninterested in participation (Gore & Rotter, 1963). Also, nonsmokers were found to be more "internal" than smokers (Straits & Sechrest, 1963). In addition, among smokers who had quit, fewer "internal" males resumed smoking compared to males who felt less control of their own destiny (James, Woodruff, & Werner, 1965). A wide scope of behaviors appear to be influenced by differences in the expectancy of internal versus external control of reinforcement.

The question of locus of control, whether internal or external, can be seen as related to specific situational factors as well as to personality. For example, the perceived difficulty of a task is an important determinant whether we attribute our success or failure to internal or external factors. When we are successful at difficult tasks, we are more likely to attribute our success to internal factors; in contrast, we tend to blame failures in easy tasks on external factors (Weiner & Kukla, 1970).

One can view cognitive processes as fundamental determinants of behavior without the assumption that the individual is conscious of these processes. George Kelly (1955) proposed that much of behavior can be understood if we consider each person a sort of scientist—observing the world, formulating his own personal theory of personality and social interaction, and then acting on the basis of predictions he makes from his theory. Each individual has his own set of theoretical constructs—called "personal constructs"—which are much like the traits of the personality psychologists—although these may be accepted with much less systematic "testing." For example, another person can be labeled as good or bad, happy or sad, masculine or feminine. If you see him as good and sad, you may be disposed to give help or sympathy. If you see this person as bad and sad, you might do nothing. People use different numbers and kinds of personal constructs. Those with few constructs are less "cognitively complex" and tend to see most of the world and its problems in simple black and white terms. Richard Paulder might be said to use one particular kind of construct in relation to figures of authority—"critical or accepting"—resenting those seen as critical. Quite different behaviors could be expected from people who view authority figures primarily as "just or unjust."

How important is motivation?

Human Motivation and Emotion

As we have indicated, the search for the key general dimensions of personality has been focused primarily on human motives and emotions. In psychoanalytic theories the basis of behavior is the energy of libido, and the key to personality is the patterning of this motive force. How this motive force is expressed depends on the psychosexual stage of development the individual has attained, the resolution of the Oedipal conflict, and other significant events in childhood. The id, ego, and superego represent distributions of libido for certain purposes. Emotions reflect the expression or suppression of libido, e.g., guilt when id impulses conflict, anxiety when the ego is threatened by strong id impulses, and hostility when the satisfaction of libidinal aims is thwarted. Projective tests as well as other types of tests have been used to assess these personality dimensions.

Other theories are also based on motivation dimensions. Actualization theories stress such drives as the needs for self-actualization and for positive regard. Learning theories might emphasize acquired drives (learned motives) like fear, which is both drive and emotion. Some theorists have gone so far as to say that personality *is* motivation. In any case, the description of general motivational dimensions has so far dominated the history of personality theory and research.

Elements of Motivation

There are three characteristics of behavior that can be explained by motivational concepts:

Direction

1. People rarely behave at random: there are reasons for their actions; there is *direction* guiding their behavior. They eat when they are hungry; they work hard for money, status, or creative goals, avoid putting their hand in a flame because it hurts, and sometimes coldly and painstakingly humiliate someone because of envy or vengeance. Motives such as hunger, fear, and revenge steer the individual toward particular goals. The organism is capable of using *different responses* to achieve the *same* goal. A rat may press a lever, run down a lengthy alley, or jump over a water hazard in order to obtain a food pellet. A student may study arduously, cheat on an examination, ingratiate himself with the teaching assistant, all in order to obtain a high grade in a course. These behaviors which are instrumental to the attainment of a goal are referred to simply as "instrumental responses."

Persistence

2. Closely associated with the directionality of motivated behavior is its *persistence* in the face of obstacles and competing interests. A suitor in love with a girl may be repeatedly rebuffed and yet persist in his pursuit while varying his instrumental behaviors—sending flowers, telegrams, growing a beard, cutting his hair, giving up poker, and so on.

Intensity

3. The passion of the suitor is not only manifested in the persistence of his behavior but also in its *intensity*. When dating this girl, he seems excited; he embraces and kisses her with passion. One sees much less evidence of excitement when he is in the company of a girl in whom he has little interest.

Why does man have conflict?

External Stimuli vs. Internal Drives

There are a number of different explanations of these motivational attributes. One major distinction between approaches concerns the extent to which behaviors are seen as "pulled" by external stimuli or as "pushed" by internal needs and drives. Psychologists who favor "pull" theories see the organism as essentially *reactive*. Behavior is largely elicited by environmental stimuli and controlled by these stimuli. What appears as internally determined direction is really a sequence of stimulus-response links that have been formed through prior learning. A child who sees a toy in a store may tug at his parent's sleeve, ask for the toy, cry when his request is denied, and finally stop crying when his parent yields and buys the toy. The pull theorist, in describing this situation, would not use subjective motivational explanations, such as the child *wants* or *desires* the toy. Rather, the toy might be described as an "incentive," or simply as a stimulus, that elicits a succession of responses which the child has learned to make through prior reinforcement.

The push theorist views the organism as actively *initiating* and *directing* its behavior. The direction is provided by internal motivational states, which are variously labeled by such theoretical constructs as motives, drives, desires, and needs. In many instances, motivated behavior appears to have elements of both reaction and initiation.

Primary Drives

Motives such as hunger, thirst, sex, and pain avoidance are closely correlated with physiological states and are called **primary drives.** These physiological or primary drives usually arise from a physiological imbalance, occurring when the organism lacks food or when there is a biochemical disturbance due to tissue injury. At the physiological level an organic need is present. When there is a state of physiological imbalance, physiological and behavioral changes typically occur which are designed to reduce this imbalance and maintain the organism at a level of physiological equilibrium. This state is called *homeostasis*. Unfortunately, an organic need does not always result in a primary drive. The inhalation of carbon monoxide produces an organic need for oxygen. The organism, however, is not driven to engage in any particular behavior that will lead to the restoration of oxygen. Some primary drives seem not to be directly related to tissue needs. For example, animals seem to have innate *exploration* and *stimulation-seeking* drives; they are strongly motivated to explore their environments and they seek novel stimuli. These drives are also clearly manifested in human infant behavior, but there is controversy about whether these are primary in the case of humans. Some psychologists maintain they are; others consider these drives to be learned or secondary.

Secondary Drives

Many human motives are not rooted in a physiological, homeostatic condition, but are acquired in the course of the organism's development. These are referred to as learned or **secondary drives.** When we consider secondary drives, more questions arise. How do human beings acquire new drives? What initiates them? How are they satisfied? What happens if the drive is not expressed? What happens if two secondary drives are in conflict?

Of course, even the physiological or primary drives have important *learned* components. How we satisfy our hunger drive is very dependent upon the foods to which we have been exposed. Some people abhor eating snails while others relish them. The goal objects that satisfy the hunger drive are influenced by learning and so are the states of being hungry and ceasing to be hungry. The noon bell rings and we suddenly feel famished; the aroma from the kitchen reaches us while working at our desks, and we feel hungry. We may approach a meal with gusto, discover that an especially unappetizing dish is served, and lose our appetite. The regulation of a physiological drive such as hunger is clearly dependent upon many psychological factors, including the effects of learning.

The role of learning is even more pronounced in the human's sex drive and in his sexual behavior. The psychological and the hormonal and other physiological mechanisms that influence sexual behavior are detailed in Chapter 25. A wide array of stimuli, varying from the perception of a nude part of the body to watching a romantic movie, can *acquire* the property of arousing sexual impulses. Individuals can learn to find many different kinds of objects and activities sexually attractive and satisfying—heterosexual or homosexual relations, masturbation, exposure of the genitals, or even the handling of an object (a fetish) such as a shoe.

Development of Secondary Drives

Several mechanisms have been proposed to explain the development of secondary or acquirable motives or drives. Conditioning is one mechanism, as Neal Miller (1948) has shown particularly vividly for fear motivation. Miller placed a rat in a two-compartment apparatus, with one compartment painted white and the other black. When the rat was in the white compartment, he was given a series of brief electric shocks through the metal bars of an electric grill in the floor. This shock produced agitated, fearful behavior. When the rat was subsequently placed in the white box, he reacted with agitation although he was no longer being shocked;

such reactions were not observed in the black box. The fear responses, originally associated with the shock, became *conditioned* to the white compartment. (See discussion of conditioning in Chapter 18.)

Miller then showed that the learned fear response operates in the same way as the primary drive of pain avoidance. The animal showed directed, persistent, and excited behavior when he was in the white compartment. Then Miller placed a wheel in the white compartment. Turning the wheel opened a door separating the white and black compartments. The fearful rats readily learned to turn the wheel which opened the door, permitting them to race into the safety of the black compartment. Note that the rat was never shocked while learning to turn the wheel. The reinforcement was the *reduction of fear* (by escape from the white compartment) rather than the reduction of the primary drive of pain.

Fear created by shock persists over a long period. It is difficult to decondition or unlearn fear because it has a built-in reinforcement mechanism—namely, escape from the feared stimulus is reinforcing. This fact has important implications for pathological behavior in humans. Imagine a girl who has had a traumatic sexual experience. The fear induced by this experience motivates her to avoid sexual overtures. Avoidance of sex is reinforcing in the sense that it reduces fear. But then she is avoiding the very situation that can reduce her fear of sex—namely, a positive sexual experience. A vicious cycle which maintains her fear is established. In the next chapter we shall discuss some of the methods used for interrupting this cycle and reducing irrational fears.

The process of **conditioning** provides an important basis for the development of many secondary drives. The newborn infant probably does not automatically love his mother, but very early he learns to associate his mother with the primary drive satisfaction she supplies: food, warmth, support, relief from pain. (See also the discussion on p. 315.) The mother becomes a sign or symbol of these gratifications. When the baby is hungry or upset, her mere presence is comforting. In short, the mother becomes a *reinforcer*. The child becomes attached to his mother. He enjoys being with her and seeks her out even when he is not hungry or upset. Where formerly she was instrumental to primary drive satisfaction, she, as an individual, has now become a source of gratification. This process is the basis for Allport's (1937) theory of the functional autonomy of acquired motives. Allport cites as an example a sailor who initially goes to sea in order to make a living but subsequently becomes so fond of sailing that he would sail even after attaining wealth. The means (sailing) that was instrumental to an end or satisfied a primary need (obtaining food and shelter) has become an end in itself. The motivation to sail has become part of the person's ego system or self-concept and, Allport assumes, it will persist independently of the drive with which it was originally associated.

How does an analysis of aggression help us understand motivation?

The analysis of aggressive behavior provides an excellent example of the various issues that have been raised regarding human motivation. **Aggression** can take many forms—fighting, torture, burning, a nasty remark, or an angry grimace. Why do people engage in such destructive activity? One answer to this question is that aggressive behavior is a manifestation of *aggressive drive*, that people, like other animals, have a need to aggress. This was Freud's view and is also the view of some students of animal behavior (see p. 842). The particular form in which aggression is expressed is dependent upon prior learning. Another, contrasting answer is that aggressive behavior is a habit (rather than a drive) that has been reinforced. A preschool child finds that by pushing or hitting his peers, he gets a bicycle he wants to ride. He is displaying instrumental aggressive behavior—aggressive behavior that brings him something he wants. Later on, aggression may be instrumental in the attainment of sex, food, safety, and other goals.

Both answers are partially correct, for aggression has both *instrumental* and *drive* components. The thief who assaults his victim to rob him of his money is carrying out an instrumental aggressive act. The mugger who assaults his victim simply because he wishes to hurt him is expressing an aggressive drive; we call this kind of behavior hostile aggression.

Reinforcement of boys' aggressive behavior may produce successful businessmen.
(Ted Polumbaum)

Frustration and Aggression

Freud maintained that the aggressive drive is innate, a vestige of our animal inheritance, and, like sex and hunger, due to internally generated biochemical changes. Systematic observations of animals, discussed more extensively in Chapter 28, provide evidence of innate aggressive tendencies but do not support the notion that there is a generalized drive to attack. Rather, studies of animal aggression indicate that only certain situations and stimuli—"invasion of territory," threatening gestures, competition for food—have a high probability of eliciting anger and attack reactions. Thus, in contrast to the Freudian position of innate aggressive drives, the animal observations suggest that aggression is linked to external stimulus events which act as provokers or releasers.

The frustration-aggression hypothesis is an important modification of the innate aggressive drive theory. The hypothesis (Dollard *et al.*, 1939) states that every frustrating event produces an instigation to aggression and the strength of the individual's aggressive drive is a function of the number and type of frustrating events he has encountered. This simple formulation provides a quantitative basis for accounting for individual and group differences in the strength of aggressive drive; it helps provide a uniform theoretical integration of aggressive phenomena as diverse as lynchings and violent fantasies. It also offers a more optimistic outlook concerning the possibility of reducing the prevalence of violence in human affairs.

Subsequent research and analysis revealed deficiencies in the original frustration-aggression formulation, however, and the initial hypothesis has been revised. This revision reflects the increasing importance that psychologists give to *cognitive* factors in explaining human motivation. How we *perceive* and *think* about events are powerful determinants of feelings and actions. In reviewing the following factors that need to be taken into account in relating frustration to aggression, the student may think about how some of these same factors affect other motives.

1. TYPE OF MOTIVATION First we must define **frustration.** A frustrating event is any obstacle which blocks or interferes with the organism's striving toward a goal. However, not all goals are of equal importance. Physical pain usually elicits more aggression than the blocking of goal attainment (Buss, 1963, 1966). Frustration of self-esteem motives through insult and humiliation is often a much more powerful provocation than the frustration of primary drives (Feshbach, 1970; Maslow, 1941; White & Lippett, 1960; Worchel, 1960).

2. INTENTIONALITY We respond differently when we believe that someone deliberately frustrated us than when we believe

that the frustration was accidental. Think of your reaction when you feel you have been deliberately tripped and compare it with your reaction to being tripped accidentally. Intentional frustration elicits much more aggression than unintentional frustration. One reason for Richard Paulder's aggressiveness was his tendency to interpret any frustration at the hands of authority as having been deliberate and intended. Closely related to intentionality is the degree of arbitrariness or unfairness of a frustration (Cohen, 1955; Pastore, 1952). A failure on an examination will seem less frustrating and produce less anger if you feel that the grade was fair than if you feel it was arbitrary and unrelated to your actual performance. To state this relationship in the terms of internal versus external locus of control (see p. 211), if you attribute the failure to internal factors, such as your own lack of ability, preparation or effort, you will be much less angry than if you attribute it to external factors such as the grader's carelessness or malice.

3. RELATIVITY OF FRUSTRATION Frustration and its effects are a function of the difference between what one wants and what one can get, not simply of the absolute level of deprivation. Frustration is relative to one's expectations. An income of $4,000 a year may provide a family only a marginal level of subsistence. However, this income level may be less frustrating to a family who expects to be on a minimal living standard than an income of $18,000 to a family who aspires to a higher standard of living. Moreover, an increase in material gains and in privileges is sometimes accompanied by increased dissatisfaction. Thus it is true that blacks in American society have a higher standard of living and enjoy more civil rights than they did thirty years ago. But this has led to greater articulation of black consciousness and refusal to accept subordinate status; frustration may have been heightened as income and opportunity grew because expectations also increased and at a faster rate than the tangible benefits.

A related process arises from the relationship between intensity of motivation and proximity to a goal. Motivation to attain a goal increases as one gets closer to a goal; this has been called the **goal gradient.** Therefore an obstacle close to the goal is much more frustrating than the same obstacle at a distance from the goal. Compare the frustration of a runner who trips and falls at the beginning of a race with his level of frustration when he trips and falls five yards from the finish line and victory is almost within his grasp. Frustration occurring close to a goal will produce more aggression than frustration occurring at a distance from the goal.

4. ALTERNATIVE RESPONSES TO FRUSTRATION Aggression is only one of many responses to frustration (McClelland &

Apicella, 1945). For example, frustration can be the impetus for problem solving and creativity. Demosthenes, working to overcome his speech impediment, became a great orator. Other possible responses are the adoption of a substitute goal or sometimes simply giving up.

Responses to frustration can be markedly influenced by learning. In one experiment, seven- to nine-year-old children were given a series of training sessions in which half the children were praised for aggressive behavior and the other half for cooperative, task-oriented responses (Davitz, 1952). After seven sessions, the children were placed in a frustrating situation—a movie they were seeing was interrupted just as it approached the climax and, in addition, they had to return a candy bar they had been given. After the frustration, the children had a free play session. Those who had been previously trained to respond constructively displayed cooperative reactions while the group that had been rewarded for being aggressive displayed much more aggression.

This study is one of a number of investigations which indicate that the rewards and punishments which society metes out for aggressive behavior have profound influence on responses to frustration. People raised in families in which their aggression was reinforced are more likely to behave aggressively than people raised in situations in which aggression was discouraged. So, in predicting the probability of an individual's aggression, we must consider the history of both past frustration and the encouragement received for aggressive behavior. "Encouragement" can take more subtle forms than praise or the material rewards for successful aggressive actions. The father who beats his son because of the son's aggressive behavior is delivering a conflicting message. While ostensibly punishing aggression, the father is acting aggressively himself. Thus, he serves as an aggressive model which his son may imitate. As we have seen, children who have been exposed to an aggressive model are much more likely to behave aggressively than children who have not been exposed to such a model (Bandura, Ross, & Ross, 1961, 1963) (see p. 12).

Social and situational variables can also markedly influence whether or not we feel angry and how we behave when we are frustrated and angry. In a classic experiment (Schachter & Singer, 1962), college students were initially injected with either epinephrine (adrenalin) or a placebo, a salt solution that had no medical value or side effects. Epinephrine increases blood pressure and heart rate, resulting in palpitation (rapid heart beat), tremors, and sometimes accelerated breathing. Some subjects given epinephrine were informed about epinephrine and its effects; others were kept ignorant or misinformed of its side effects. Following the injection, the experimenter introduced the subject to a stooge who presumably had received the same injection. The subject and stooge were then given a series of questionnaires to complete, during which time the stooge either behaved in a euphoric, happy, and moderately silly manner or in an angry, irritated, hostile manner. In answering questions about their reactions to the injection, the subjects in the epinephrine informed condition were uninfluenced by the stooge's responses. Because of the information given them, they did not need to rely on the behavior of someone else to "interpret" their own feelings. However, the behavior of the uninformed subjects and the feelings they reported were markedly affected by the stooge's emotional reactions. The degree of these subjects' feelings of happiness or anger directly related to the euphoria or anger displayed by the stooge. This effect was particularly pronounced for subjects who showed a clear-cut physiological response to the drug. Clearly anger and euphoria are in part influenced by *cognitive* interpretations of the aroused physiological states. Anger and aggression are not simple manifestations of an internal drive state but are strongly influenced by external, environmental stimulus factors.

The Reduction of Aggression

According to psychoanalysts, aggressive impulses will be expressed in a socially destructive form unless the ego "defends" against them. The expression of angry impulses must be distinguished from instrumental aggressive acts. There is no evidence that instrumental aggression in the form of war or murder is either a psychological or biological necessity.

The reduction of an impulse by expressing it directly or indirectly, particularly in verbal ways or in fantasy, is called **catharsis.** Can thought and fantasy reduce anger and overt aggression? This question has been the topic of considerable research and controversy. What are the effects of the kinds of aggressive fantasy children engage in when they are exposed to violence on television and in other mass media? Does the portrayal of violence on television act as a catharsis for aggression or does it, as many contend, stimulate aggressive behavior? The predominant research finding has been an increase in aggression rather than a reduction of aggressive impulses following exposure to aggressive actions on films (Bandura, Ross, & Ross, 1963; Hartmann, 1969; Lovaas, 1961; Mussen & Rutherford, 1961; Walters & Thomas, 1963). (See pp. 12, 333.) In all these studies, brief film sequences of aggressive behavior were employed in laboratory settings. In two studies that used lengthier motion pictures, there was little evidence of either enhancement or reduction of aggression (Albert, 1957; Emery, 1959).

It is difficult to generalize from these studies to the natural viewing situation where so many more variables are operating. In a naturalistic study, television exposure was experimentally varied over a six-week period (Feshbach & Singer, 1971). The subjects were boys ranging in age from ten to seventeen, who were either attending a private school or living in a detention home. Within each institution boys were randomly assigned to a television schedule containing predominantly aggressive programs or to a control treatment of predominantly nonaggressive programs. All subjects were required to watch a minimum of six hours of television a week and were permitted to view as much television as they wanted but they could see only programs from the designated list. Measures of aggressive personality attributes, and aggressive fantasy (stories) were administered before and after the six-week experimental period. In addition, daily ratings of aggressive behavior were submitted for each boy by his immediate supervisors.

The results indicated that the differences in television exposure had little effect upon boys attending private schools, perhaps because these boys have many intellectual resources and also engage more frequently in other kinds of fantasy activities, such as reading. But subjects in the boys' homes who had viewed aggressive programs displayed significantly *less* verbal and physical aggression toward peers and toward authority than the group who saw predominantly nonaggressive television programs. These cathartic or aggression-reduction effects were especially pronounced for boys who were initially impulsive and aggressive.

These experimental findings suggest that the observation of aggression on television may under some circumstances help control and moderate the expression of aggressive impulses in some children who have strong aggressive tendencies. The findings must be interpreted with considerable caution and cannot be generalized to girls and to younger children without further testing. A recent series of investigations conducted under the auspices of a federal agency suggests that there are a number of circumstances in which the depiction of violence on television may encourage aggression in children. These diverse results point to the complexity of variables influencing the responses to violence in television and the need for extending laboratory research to more naturalistic settings in which the effects of varying ages, backgrounds, and personalities are studied.

Conflict and Defense Mechanisms

Aggressive drive is of particular interest to students of human motivation because, like sex drive, it is subject to many social prohibitions. As a result, the arousal of both these drives is frequently accompanied by feelings of anxiety and guilt, and these are *incompatible* with the individual's desire to satisfy his aggressive or sexual impulses. In brief, the individual is in a conflict. Psychological conflict, a very human state of affairs, poses a number of basic motivational questions. How does the individual cope with and reduce the conflict? What happens to an impulse when its direct expression is inhibited? Is the expression of impulses critical for psychological adjustment?

Much of our understanding of methods of coping with

prohibited impulses is derived from the work of Sigmund Freud and his followers, in particular his daughter, Anna Freud. The conflict-resolving mechanisms—which may be used in dealing with conflicts involving many kinds of motives including sex, aggression, envy or pride—are known as the **defense mechanisms.** We all use these mechanisms to some extent to deal with our conflicts and anxieties. For Freud, the key defense employed by the ego is **repression** which, as we have seen (see p. 184), refers to the unconscious exclusion from awareness of unacceptable impulses and ideas. Other common defense mechanisms are defined below.

In **denial,** unacceptable impulses and associated ideas are simply denied, i.e., the individual refuses to believe that he has such impulses. For example, one patient could not express any feelings of anger toward his mother and would deny or make light of actions toward her that others would construe as arbitrary and selfish. Unwillingness to check up on physical or mental symptoms that might be indicative of serious illness is another example of denial, as is the tendency of combat veterans to engage in banter and jest as they go into battle (denial of fear).

Reaction formation is the manifestation of behavior that is directly opposite to unconscious feelings and attitudes. For example, a parent may defend against unconscious feelings of resentment toward an unwanted child by reacting with overly solicitous affection toward him. Extreme hostility to homosexuals can be a reaction formation against latent homosexual impulses. A literary prototype of the use of this defense is seen in Charles Dickens' Uriah Heep, whose unctuous politeness and humility were barely concealed reactions against strong feelings of arrogance and envy.

How can one distinguish between a genuine expression of feeling, a deception, and a reaction formation? Clinically, behavior arising from reaction formation is exaggerated, inflexible, and often inappropriate. In addition, the reaction formation may permit partial gratification of the repressed impulse against which the individual is defending. The overly solicitous parent is also harassing the unwanted child, and the antihomosexual, in his efforts to censor homosexual literature and movies, becomes intimately acquainted with these very materials.

In **projection,** the individual attributes to others his own unacceptable, repressed feelings and ideas. For example, if he is unable to accept his own hostile impulses, he frequently sees others as hostile. This mechanism is often manifested in social prejudice—for example, hostile whites say blacks are aggressive. When frightened, children are more likely to see other children as frightened and adults as threatening (Murray, 1933; Feshbach & Feshbach, 1963). Projective tests were developed largely on the assumption that people will project their *own* feelings onto the ambiguous picture or inkblot.

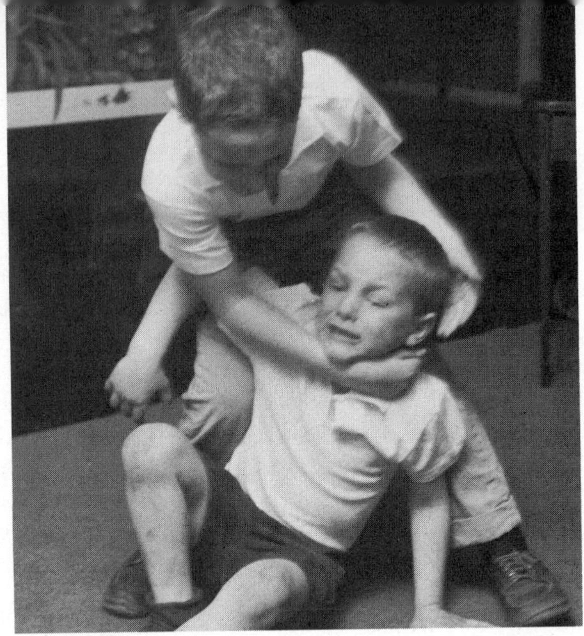

Displacement. Bobby beats up Ricky who is smaller than he. So Ricky, frustrated and angry at Bobby, beats up Fred who is still smaller. Fred, in turn, beats up little Tom.
(Suzanne Szasz)

Displacement is the expression of repressed feelings toward an innocent target. (See p. 113 for a discussion of the relationship between displacement and prejudice.) Richard Paulder displaced his hostility toward his father onto authority figures. In this instance, there was a modification of the object of the feeling. Displacement may involve the response as well as the object; for example, hostile dreams may be a displacement for the direct expression of hostility.

Sublimation is a form of displacement in which an unacceptable or unsatisfied impulse is expressed in a socially acceptable form. Ungratified sexual impulses may be expressed in highly approved ways in lyrical poetry or in painting. Surgery may be a socially acceptable means by which hostile, sadistic impulses can be partially gratified. It would be absurd, however, to suggest that surgery is *necessarily* a form of sublimated hostility. The point here is that *some* people may utilize the constructive behavior of surgery to satisfy ordinarily destructive impulses.

There are many other defenses against painful, anxiety-producing feelings and thoughts. We are all certainly familiar with—and use—**rationalization** of shortcomings that we are reluctant to admit—justifying our behavior in such a way that it appears rational, giving a "good" rather than a "true" reason for our actions, blaming circumstances rather than ourselves for failures ("I missed the ball because the sun was in my eyes"). Anxiety-arousing impulses may undergo **intellectualization** so that they can be discussed in an elaborate, detailed manner, avoiding the feelings involved in the conflict. In **isolation,** the individual defends himself from anxiety-arousing ideas, by keeping them in psychological "compartments," separated from related thoughts and attitudes.

Sublimation.
(Ted Polumbaum)

Defenses vary in their psychopathological consequences. **Regression,** in which the individual adopts an earlier, immature model of functioning when confronted with a difficult conflict, can result in seriously inappropriate behavior. In contrast, sublimation is a much more adaptive defense.

Defenses can be highly specific reactions to particular conflict situations or may become generalized traits, central to the

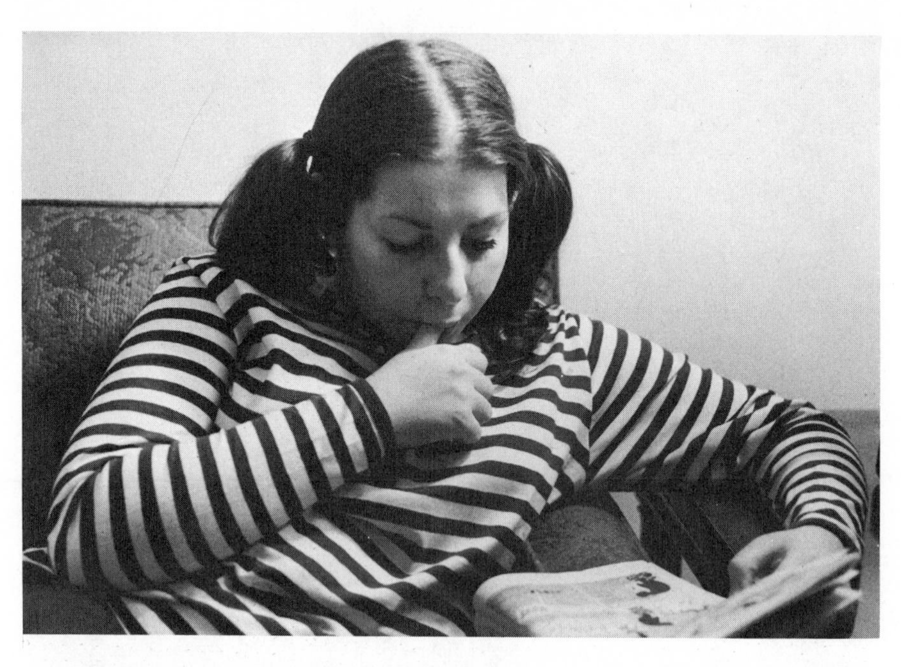

Regression.
(Van Bucher, Photo Researchers)

individual's personality structure. Thus projection is a key mechanism employed by the paranoid individual who is overly suspicious and sensitive (see p. 240). The role of defense mechanisms in other patterns of neurotic adjustment will be further considered in the next chapter, which deals with psychopathology.

The Freudian view of how individuals deal with conflict between motive and reality or between two motives is only one of many approaches to the understanding of conflict. A related but different approach is based on the observation that, when in conflict, some people tend to avoid or repress the conflict, while others tend to become unduly sensitive and excessively preoccupied with the conflict. The former have been called "repressors," and the latter, "sensitizers" (Byrne, 1964).

SUMMARY

In their search for *basic* dimensions of personality—dimensions of the widest generality and most central—psychologists have focused on physique and genetic factors, on thinking and perceiving, and, most importantly on motivational dynamics and feelings. Studies of physique have provided some evidence of moderate relationships between body build and personality characteristics, and studies of twins strongly suggest that genetic factors influence aspects of personality. Cognitive style variables closely related to personality include field dependence (or independence) and generalized expectancies of internal or external control of reinforcement.

In studying the properties of human motivation, it is useful to distinguish between primary drives such as hunger and thirst, which are closely correlated with internal physiological states, and secondary drives such as fear, aggression, achievement striving (need achievement), and affiliation. Whether a motive is primary or secondary, it is important to determine the antecedent conditions which give rise to the motive, the behaviors the organism uses in satisfying the motive, and the conditions that are associated with satisfaction or reduction of the motive. In addition, the consequences of suppression or thwarting of the motive and of motivational conflict have been studied. Frustration has been proposed as a highly significant antecedent of aggressive drive. Such cognitive factors as the intentionality and arbitrariness of the frustration and the individual's prior expectancy are important determinants of the degree of aggressive drive elicited by a frustrating situation. A person's aggressive behavior, in addition to being influenced by his aggressive drive, is markedly affected by his history of rewards and punishments for aggressive actions, by social norms, and by the models he has encountered. Aggressive drive may be reduced through direct or indirect aggressive acts (catharsis) or through modification or elimination of the antecedent stimuli which had evoked the aggressive motivation.

Defense mechanisms are designed to reduce conflicts about aggression and about other important human motives. Among the common defense mechanisms are repression, denial, reaction formation, projection, displacement, and sublimation.

11

Psychopathology and Therapy

How have conceptions of mental illness changed?
What do we mean by "abnormality"?
How many kinds of mental disorders are there?
What are the goals of therapy?

In our discussion of normal personality, we made frequent references to abnormal behavior. Some theories of personality, such as psychoanalysis, can be applied to both the psychologically disturbed and the psychologically adjusted individual.

The study, assessment, and treatment of the abnormal, the psychopathological, and the mentally ill—individuals whose behavior is irrational, inappropriate, bizarre, or uncontrolled—is **psychopathology**, an important specialty within psychology. Although all areas of psychology have a bearing upon the study of psychological disturbances, clinical psychologists are most immediately concerned with these problems. The clinical psychologist is a specialist in psychological methods of treatment for the emotionally disturbed, in the use of psychological tests in diagnosis, and in methods of research and evaluation.

Mental patients occupy more hospital beds than any other patient group in the United States; the number of seriously disturbed patients is between 1 and 2 percent of the total population. It is estimated that about one in ten individuals will develop a severe mental disorder sometime during his life, and this does not include the problems that occur with senility.

How have conceptions of mental illness changed?

Mental disturbances are by no means a phenomenon of recent history. It does not appear that the stresses of contemporary life have produced an increase in mental illness—at least in those types severe enough to require hospital admission. Rates of hospital admission for 1840 and 1940 are surprisingly similar (Dunham, 1966; Goldhamer & Marshall, 1949). Primitive societies seem to be no less vulnerable to the more severe forms of psychopathology than the more developed societies (Dohrenwend & Dohrenwend, 1967). The basic nature of psychopathology appears to be similar in different cultures, although the symptoms may assume different, more or less exotic, forms. For example, in the syndrome "amok," the Malaysian native is suddenly seized with a fit of rage and runs madly about slashing at people with his dagger. An Ojibwa Indian with the disorder called "windigo" believes that he is possessed by a cannibalistic monster. He sees his family and friends taking on the characteristics of edible animals; he may commit suicide or ask others to kill him in order to avoid destroying others. (I once saw a patient who believed that an unwanted child to which she had given birth resembled a wolf. The patient was hospitalized in order to prevent her from harming the child.)

Mental Illness

Of course, conceptions of mental illness and its treatment have changed tremendously in the course of Western history. In ancient Egypt, Israel, and Greece, it was generally believed that madness was due to possession by evil spirits, yet as early as approximately 400 B.C., Hippocrates, the Greek physician, proposed that mental illness was due to a disease of the brain and should be treated like other diseases. While this notion was accepted for many centuries in the Arab world, the prevailing view of psychological derangement in Europe during the Middle Ages was that of possession by demons. Treatments varied from prayer to flogging, all designed to drive out the devils that resided in the afflicted person's body. Between the fourteenth and sixteenth centuries, thousands of the mentally ill, especially women, were accused of witchcraft. Church and state combined in a joint effort to pursue and punish these presumed agents of the devil, and many were burned at the stake (Lea, 1939).

Even after the belief in witchcraft declined, the mentally ill were still treated with scorn and abuse, often isolated, locked in cellars and attics or, if seen as dangerous, confined in lunatic asylums where they were kept in chains and controlled with whips. Severe shocks were sometimes applied, supposedly for therapeutic purposes, hot irons were applied to the head and patients were lowered into a

In the sixteenth century some of the insane were viewed as demon-possessed and burned. Later Philippe Pinel unchained the insane and viewed them as patients needing treatment.
(Both, The Bettmann Archive)

snake pit or tossed from a high cliff into the sea (Zilboorg & Henry, 1941). Among the more ignominious aspects of the treatment of the mentally ill (in a history filled with ignominy) was the public display of the mentally ill for a fee. As late as the eighteenth century, Londoners could amuse themselves by watching the lunatics at the Bethlehem asylum. The term "bedlam" is derived from the popular pronunciation of Bethlehem and refers to wild, disorganized activities such as those which took place there.

By the end of the eighteenth century, several enlightened leaders in Western Europe began to demand more humane treatment for the insane. The most eminent of these was the French psychologist Philippe Pinel (1745–1826) who reorganized the historic Salpetrière hospital in Paris, removed chains from the patients, and trained the attendants to regard the insane as patients who needed treatment rather than as brutes who needed coercion. He also introduced the psychiatric case history, a simple classification of mental disorders, and systematic record-keeping. Pinel's ideas subsequently spread throughout the Western world.

Early in the nineteenth century, American Quakers established several hospitals for the mentally ill but the great majority were still confined in almshouses, jails, and cellars where they were "chained, naked, beaten with rods, and lashed into obedience" (Dix, 1843, p. 4). Dorothea Dix, a Massachusetts schoolteacher, became a prime mover in the founding or enlarging of over thirty state hospitals and, in addition, extended her activities to Europe. Nevertheless, primitive practices persisted in the treatment of the mentally ill. In 1908, Clifford Beers, a former mental patient, published a book,

At Bedlam hospital, visitors amused themselves by watching psychotic patients; notice the chains on the patient in the foreground. (Culver Pictures)

A Mind That Found Itself, describing his illness and recovery. Beers hoped to eliminate the stigma associated with mental disorders and to modify the widespread belief that mental disorders were incurable. To further these aims, he established the National Committee for Mental Hygiene which encouraged the early recognition and prevention of mental illness and stimulated the development of child guidance clinics, while still working for the improvement of conditions in mental hospitals.

Mental Health

The mental health movement is still very active in the United States and, although there have been significant changes in most mental hospitals, there is a need for continued effort to improve treatment of the mentally ill. Recent anthropological and social-psychological studies of the mental hospital as a community, indicate that the hospital situation itself—and the practices employed there—often prolongs and exacerbates emotional disturbances. Efforts must be made—and in some places they are being made—to restructure mental hospitals so that patients have greater choice and greater responsibility. In **milieu therapy,** the hospital patient is encouraged to interact with other patients and to relate to the staff on a more informal, human level rather than as simply "patient" and "caretaker" (Sanders *et al.*, 1967). In some hospitals there are wards in which efforts are made to change the behavior of chronic hospitalized patients by reinforcing desirable responses directly—for example, by granting extra privileges and various material benefits to a patient when he tries to help another patient (Ayllon & Azrin, 1968).

A number of programs have also been initiated to maintain the patient in the regular community. Special "halfway houses" have been established where the discharged patient can live or visit as he is adjusting to life outside the hospital. Outpatient clinics, sheltered workshops, and home visits provide additional support to the newly discharged patient. Ironically, these programs are reversing the previous trend to take the patient out of the community and put him in a hospital, a trend started by people like Dorothea Dix whose motivations were of the most humane sort. In those days, of course, the community had little understanding of mental illness; increasing knowledge and a more sympathetic attitude have removed some of the stigma of psychological maladjustment. Now it is possible to treat some cases of mental illness within the community.

Mental Disorders and Organic Diseases

Until Freud's time and contributions, most psychiatrists believed that mental illness was the result of a malfunction of some bodily process—particularly in the brain. The idea that mental illness has an organic basis, referred to as the "somatogenic hypothesis," was bolstered by the discovery late in the nineteenth century, that the disease of general paresis was caused by syphilis. The symptom complex of paresis included defective speech, disturbances in memory, lack of insight, grandiose and unrealistic self-descriptions, and deterioration of motor functions. The mental disturbance increased and was accompanied by motor paralysis which fairly rapidly led to death. Postmortem examinations of paretic patients revealed destruction in the brain and other nerve tissue. The critical clue was provided by the statistical observation that 65 percent of paretics had a known history of syphilis; this illness was found in only 10 percent of other mental patients.

This finding excited the hope that similar infectious agents could be found for other forms of mental illness. The first task was to identify other symptom **complexes** that characterize groups of patients. A fundamental step in this direction was made by the German psychiatrist Kraepelin (1855–1926). Through painstaking study of hundreds of case histories of hospitalized patients, he identified and defined two major mental diseases: **manic-depressive psychosis** and **dementia praecox,** now more generally called **schizophrenia.** The manic-depressive symptom complex was primarily characterized by abrupt changes in mood in which patients might display extreme euphoria and excitement (mania) or deep melancholy (depression). The dementia praecox (schizophrenia) classification consisted of the grouping of a variety of symptom patterns which displayed two common threads; early onset, often in adolescence (praecox), and marked deterioration and disturbance in thinking (dementia). The classification of mental disorders has been greatly elaborated since Kraepelin's original work, although these two categories include almost two thirds of the resident population of mental hospitals.

But no physical disorder has been found to explain these mental disturbances. The general consensus today is that while these disorders may well be associated with abnormal biochemical or neural processes, there are no clear physical causes—at least none as clear as in the case of paresis. And, as we shall see, abnormal experiences are clearly part of most patients' histories. Probably there is an interaction between biological (including genetic) and environmental factors, and those with a biologically "weak constitution" require less disturbed environments to become severely mentally ill.

The distinction between "biological" and "psychological" is not so absolute in human functioning as it is in some theoretical accounts; there are **psychosomatic reactions,** physical problems "caused" by mental conflicts (e.g., many ulcers) and **somatopsychic illnesses** in which mental conflicts are "caused" by physical problems (e.g., paresis). Sometimes it is difficult to determine in an individual case whether the physical or mental disorder is primary. (See Spotlight 11-1.)

SPOTLIGHT 11-1

What Made the Hatter Mad?

The curious character of the Mad Hatter in *Alice in Wonderland* was not a pure invention. Like many of Lewis Carroll's characters, this one was based on shrewd observation. Hatmakers in Carroll's time did tend to show eccentric and irrational behavior. Later it was found that their abnormal behavior was caused by damage to the nervous system; this developed because of use of a mercury compound in treating felt for hats. Once this was clear, use of the mercury compound was discontinued in hatmaking, but neural damage due to mercury still causes behavioral problems and is a reason for ecological concern. For example, newspapers recently reported the case of a woman whose failing memory and difficulties of concentration were treated unsuccessfully by psychiatrists for several years. Finally it was found that she had a toxic concentration of mercury in her body, apparently due to a diet high in swordfish. The cooperative investigations of several specialists are often necessary to reveal the true nature of a particular case.

(Culver Pictures)

What do we mean by "abnormality"?

When we speak of "abnormal" behavior, we often speak as if the concept of **abnormality** was easily defined. But in fact there are many definitions of abnormality, each with some merit, none without some shortcomings. How we define it, of course, is a matter of no small importance; the definition of abnormality has implications for therapeutic treatment, legal proceedings, and social acceptability.

The word itself—*ab-normal*—implies a deviation from a norm. Using a statistical criterion, the norm could be considered the average, and "abnormal" would describe the infrequent or rare instance. If we accept this definition, we can easily apply quantitative measures, such as test scores, in making diagnoses. For example, we have discussed the MMPI (p. 168), which yields ten scores; exceptionally high scores are considered indicative of pathology. The disadvantage of the statistical criterion, taken literally, is that it does not differentiate between the exceptionally gifted and the exceptional lack of talent. A moron and a genius are both "abnormal." In the MMPI, where a score of 50 on any scale is average or normal, a score of 70 or above is indicative of pathology; a score of 30 or below, however, is equally abnormal by a statistical criterion. Yet we rarely interpret the "low" exceptions, for these point to the abnormally cheerful, the exceptionally trusting, or the extremely considerate individuals.

For reasons such as these, social criteria are often added to the statistical criterion in making judgments about whether an

The concept of abnormality must be precisely defined. Each culture has its own norms which differ from culture to culture.
(Ted Polumbaum)

individual is pathologically abnormal and in formulating plans for care and treatment. The genius is statistically abnormal, but he is socially valuable; the imbecile is considered pathologically abnormal—he contributes little and may require expensive care. The use of social criteria makes the concept of normality culturally relative—an anti-Hitler intellectual might have been considered pathologically abnormal in Germany in the late 1930's or early 1940's.

To avoid cultural relativism, many have sought to define abnormality in terms of certain basic characteristics and deficiencies. These are presented in Spotlight 11-2. The consistent inability to cope with one's environment is the basic overriding criterion, with the emphasis on *inability*. All of us at times may *choose* to behave in an extraordinary manner—to reject a Hitler, to refuse to conform, to express an impulse—but those who have no choice, who *cannot control* their inappropriate emotions or actions, are considered pathologically abnormal.

SPOTLIGHT 11-2

Some Criteria of Abnormality

1. *Inadequate Reality Testing*
Impaired cognitive functioning, that is, disturbances in thinking, in perception, in memory, in judgment, and in the ability to communicate in a coherent manner.

2. *Inappropriate Affect or Feelings*
Emotional expression not reasonably related to eliciting stimuli. Includes irrational fears, anger without provocation, and persistent feelings of depression which are only remotely related to current experiences.

3. *Inability to Exercise Voluntary Control over Behavior*
Tendency to act on impulse. The most serious manifestations of lack of control are aggressive outbursts, but more subtle manifestations are found in conflicts between conformity and nonconformity to social norms regarding dress, language, marriage, and the like. What matters is not the specific behavior as such, whether the individual conforms or does not conform, but rather the degree of voluntary control exercised over this behavior. A person can also suffer from *overcontrol*, from rigidity and inhibition, and a lack of spontaneity.

4. *Deficient Social Functioning*
High degrees of egocentricism, lack of interest in other people, incapability in forming stable, close emotional ties. Absence of social awareness. Excessive distrust of, and negativism toward, other people. Inability to assume a socially responsible role.

From the individual's own perspective, a critical indicator of mental disorder is *psychological distress*. It is when he feels persistently anxious, tormented, at odds with himself and others, that he is likely to recognize that he has a psychological difficulty and seeks help. For milder disturbances, self-reports of psychological distress may be the only evidence of psychopathology.

The legal definition of abnormality differs from the psychological definitions in that its purpose is not to describe behavior disorders but to excuse certain individuals from the punitive sanctions in criminal law. The term **insanity** is a legal rather than a medical concept. The legally insane are not considered responsible for their actions, where responsibility is defined as the capacity to exercise a free and rational choice.

How many kinds of mental disorders are there?

The label "mental illness" has been applied to a wide variety of behavior deviations. Spotlight 11-3 shows the ten major classifications or diagnostic categories used by the American Psychiatric Association. It should be noted, of course, that the categories are more easily distinguished in theory than in practice, and diagnoses are often difficult and tentative.

A major distinction is made between psychoses and neuroses. A **psychosis** is a major behavior disturbance typically characterized by personality disintegration and loss of contact with reality, where a **neurosis** is not so severe. The neurotic can usually function fairly adequately in society, although he may have morbid fears and anxieties, unusual compulsions or other severe hang-ups. In some cases, the neurotic disturbance is not an isolated symptom but a deep-seated personality trait. The individual is then said to have a neurotic character structure or personality disorder. In other cases, the emotional disturbances produce physical symptoms ranging from a minor rash to serious heart dysfunction; such cases are classified as psychophysiological disorders or, as they are more commonly known, psychosomatic illnesses. These categories include most of the troubled individuals a clinical psychologist is likely to encounter; we will discuss each in more detail.

The Psychoses

Schizophrenia

The diagnosis of schizophrenia covers a broad array of the most puzzling and profound symptoms such as bizarre speech and ideas, a split between affect and thought, and strange behaviors. There are schizophrenics in every culture and they include about 1 percent of the general population (Slater, 1968). In the United States, about 20 percent of first admissions to public mental hospitals are schizophrenics, but since they are difficult to treat, they stay in the hospital longer than most patients; hence they constitute over 50 percent of hospitalized patients. It strikes males and females with equal frequency and the peak incidence rate occurs between the ages of twenty-five and thirty-five.

SPOTLIGHT 11-3

Classification of Mental Disorders

Classification	General Description
1. Mental Retardation	Subnormal intellectual function, originating at birth or early childhood; learning ability and social maturation are impaired.
2. Organic Brain Syndrome a. Nonpsychotic b. Frequent psychotic syndromes: senile dementia (disease of aging), alcoholic psychosis, general paresis (due to syphilitic infection), cerebral arteriosclerosis	Disorders related to impairment of brain tissue function; impaired orientation, memory, comprehension, etc. Unstable and shallow affect.
3. Psychoses Schizophrenia (major thinking disturbance. Social withdrawal; regressive and bizarre behavior) Affective disorders (extreme depression or elation dominates mental life) Paranoid states (delusions, persecutory or grandiose, dominate mental life)	Impairment in mental functioning sufficient to grossly interfere with meeting demands of daily life; deficits in perception, language, or memory; profound alterations of mood; hallucinations and delusions.
4. Neuroses Anxiety neurosis Hysteria Phobias Obsessive-compulsive neurosis Depressive neurosis Neurasthenia Depersonalization syndrome Hypochondria	Anxiety is primary symptom; may be experienced or controlled through unconscious mechanisms; no gross breaks with reality or gross personality disorganization.
5. Personality Disorders Some subtypes include: Paranoid personality Schizoid personality Antisocial personality Homosexuality Fetishism Voyeurism Alcoholism Drug dependence	Deeply ingrained, usually life-long maladaptive behavior patterns; includes generalized personality and character disturbances; also, more focused symptomatology as in alcoholism, sexual deviation, drug addiction.

(Continued next page)

Classification	General Description
6. Psychophysiological Disorders Subcategories are the various bodily areas and functions that can be affected by psychological factors; e.g., skin disorders as in neurodermatitis; respiratory disorders as in asthma; cardiovascular disorders as in hypertension and migraine	Physical disorders of presumably psychogenic origin; physical symptoms caused by emotional factors and usually involving a single organ system.
7. Special Symptoms	Patients manifesting single specific symptoms which are not part of a broader mental disorder; e.g., tics, speech disturbances, sleep disorders, learning disorders; can be very specific.
8. Transient Situational Disturbances	Transient disorders occurring in individuals without an underlying mental disorder, and representing an acute reaction to extreme environmental stress.
9. Behavior Disorders of Childhood and Adolescence Examples of subcategories are: Hyperkinetic reaction Withdrawing reaction Runaway reaction	Behavior disorders, occurring in childhood and adolescence, that are more resistant to treatment than transient situational disturbances but more transient than psychoses, neuroses, and personality disorders.
10. Conditions without Manifest Psychiatric Disorder and Nonspecific Condition	Individuals who are psychiatrically normal but have problems sufficiently severe to warrant examination and treatment.

Adapted from Official Manual of American Psychiatric Association, 1968.

There are several major types of schizophrenia, distinguished by symptom clusters. While we will focus our attention on these symptoms, you must realize that each patient is a whole person, and, though he is seriously disturbed, he has resources as well as psychological difficulties. Most schizophrenics are *not* raving maniacs or bizarre comics as some Hollywood films suggest. The patient is not always "out of it." Only some of his ideas are delusional, only some of his language is unintelligible. He hallucinates only part of the time, and not necessarily every day or even every week.

I am reminded of a relevant personal experience. After

a day consulting at a state mental hospital, I was invited to join one of the staff in an indoor tennis game. There were several players already on the court but since I was a guest, they courteously invited me to play in the next doubles match. During the course of the match, the players were very solicitous and encouraging. (I was unaccustomed to the court and only a modest player.) I was completely taken unaware when, at the conclusion of the game, I found out that my opponents, whom I believed to be staff members, were actually patients.

The primary symptoms of the *simple* schizophrenic are social withdrawal, loss of interest, and emotional apathy. The onset and development of the simple schizophrenic reaction is a gradual, insidious process. Friends and family may be unaware of the extent of disturbance until the withdrawal from people and outside interests becomes extreme. The disorder may begin, as in the case of one adolescent, with quitting school and lounging around the house, doing nothing. He proceeded to spend more and more time in his room, rarely speaking even to his family. At the time he was hospitalized, he would lie in bed most of the day, had not shaved or bathed for several months, and would respond to questions only with anger or monosyllables. Many simple schizophrenics are able to maintain marginal adjustments without hospitalization. A substantial number work in solitary occupations or become vagrants or prostitutes.

The *hebephrenic* schizophrenic's reactions resemble the common stereotype of the psychotic—silly mannerisms, inappro-

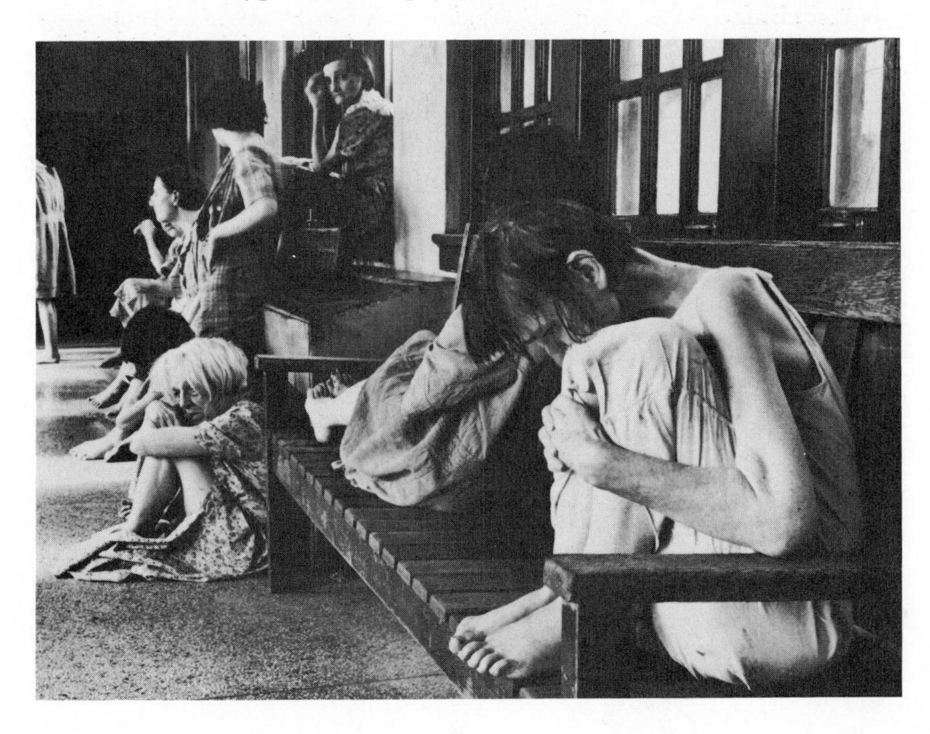

Catatonic-schizophrenics may at times manifest postures such as these.
(Jerry Cooke, Photo Researchers)

priate affect, hallucinations, and unsystematized bizarre delusions. Hebephrenics will often giggle at unpredictable times and talk to themselves or to fantasied companions. One patient, when asked how she felt, stated, "My heart is rock-a-bye; he wants me to grow high." Perhaps relevant to this remark is the fact that several years previously, the patient reluctantly underwent an abortion.

In contrast to the hebephrenic, the *catatonic* schizophrenic is either in a stupor or displays extreme excitement. His speech, often repetitive, is difficult to comprehend. In the stuporous state, patients may assume a peculiar posture or rigid stance for hours on end. They are unresponsive and uncommunicative; in some cases, the patient remains mute for several years and appears to be completely oblivious of his surroundings. However, at some subsequent time, he may repeat conversations and events that occurred while he was ostensibly out of contact. During outbreaks of excitement, the patient can become dangerous to himself and others. The catatonic, in his passivity and unresponsiveness, often impresses one as being resistant and negativistic.

A *paranoid* reaction is another important category of schizophrenic behavior. The distinguishing characteristic of the paranoid is delusions of persecution or of grandeur. He believes that people are plotting against him, and he misinterprets and distorts situations to conform with this belief. One patient believed that he was marked for destruction by the Martians and accused several of his acquaintances of being in league with the Martians. He claimed that the extra radios which they had in their homes were evidence of this collusion with his enemies. Another patient felt that people were resentful of him because of his secret powers which enabled him to dominate the mind and body of whomever he chose.

These delusions were supported by hallucinations. The first patient heard "messages" being sent over the radio while the second heard God speaking to him. While auditory hallucinations are the most common, some patients report strange body sensations, disturbing odors, and peering eyes. The paranoid often assumes that other people's conversations and actions refer to him—an implicit kind of grandiosity.

The paranoid patient tends to be overly sensitive, egocentric, and suspicious; he is quite capable of acting on the basis of his delusions and committing serious offenses. One paranoid killed his local grocer, a Jew, because he believed that Jews were organized in a conspiracy to destroy the United States and that it was his special mission to defend his country. He was very effective in hiding his psychosis until the murder. Paranoids maintain better contact with their environment than other schizophrenics; they are more aware of what others think (Silverman, 1964). Examination of the patient revealed subtle indicators of psychopathology such as the absence of affect in connection with his ideas and actions, a poorly organized and illogical delusional system, and overelaborate speech which, on analysis, made only partial sense.

Related to the paranoid schizophrenic reactions are the psychotic reactions labeled the "paranoid states." These states are described in Spotlight 11-4.

SPOTLIGHT 11-4

Paranoid States

Common to both paranoid schizophrenics and paranoid states are persecutory and grandiose delusions and the notion that others are talking about them (ideas of reference). However, in the paranoid state, the delusional system is well organized, the patient's feelings of distress or anger are more closely related to his distorted judgments and beliefs, and thought processes outside of the delusional area are relatively intact. Many people misinterpret events because of their suspicion and egocentricity. They are characterized as having paranoid personalities but are not psychotic. The paranoid state, in contrast, entails a serious break with reality.

Individuals who suffer from a paranoid state psychosis sometimes assume leadership roles in a society because of their single-minded, inflexible, and emotional attachment to a delusional system which has partial cultural support. It has been proposed that Adolf Hitler was such a case, and clinical studies of the other top Nazi leaders suggest serious psychopathology in many of them. It must be emphasized that adherence to a particular belief system or ideology is not, in and of itself, a manifestation of psychopathology. However, some ideologies, especially those emphasizing real or unreal conspiratorial threats, may attract paranoid personalities and paranoid psychotics.

(Wide World Photos)

Theories of Schizophrenia

While our knowledge of schizophrenia is substantially greater than it was when Kraepelin first described it, the disorder still remains very much of an enigma. Research on schizophrenia has been concerned with two principal questions: (1) What are the psychological and physiological processes underlying the schizophrenic symptoms? (2) What are the origins of the schizophrenic reaction?

Studies indicate that the schizophrenic is not able to screen or filter effectively the internal and external stimuli that impinge upon him. His impaired judgment and perception are not due to intellectual dullness or to defective vision or audition, but he is not able to select the relevant cues in his environment to which to respond or to filter his associations to these cues. The schizophrenic either filters out too much and responds with a highly *concrete*, impoverished association (e.g., he states that a book and a newspaper are similar because they both are made of paper) or he filters out too little and his associations are loose and overinclusive (e.g., a book and a newspaper are similar because, as one patient said, "they live to eternal damnation"). Often the filter is a clearly personal one (e.g., the book and newspaper are alike "because I own them both"). Similar patterns of thinking disturbances can be the result of severe stress, and several investigators see both the marked social withdrawal and the impaired thought process of the schizophrenic as reactions to the stress of chronic anxiety (Mednick, 1958; Rodnick & Garmezy, 1957; Venables, 1966).

It is also possible that these disturbances are brought about by endocrine or neurophysiological malfunctions. For example, it has been proposed that the schizophrenic suffers from an inherited neural integrative defect, which has been labeled "schizotaxia" (Meehl, 1962). This defect is assumed to be a *necessary* but not *sufficient* condition for the development of schizophrenia. Schizophrenia may be a consequence of both a schizotaxic predisposition and an unfavorable family environment, particularly a disturbed mother-child interaction. While it is presumed that most schizotaxics will not develop schizophrenia, they remain carriers of the genetic defects.

There is considerable evidence supporting the hypothesis that schizophrenia has a genetic basis. The incidence of schizophrenia in the families of schizophrenics is much higher than in the families of normals. In addition, children of schizophrenic mothers who have been reared in adoptive homes are more likely to become schizophrenics than other children who are adopted (Heston & Denny, 1968). The incidence of schizophrenia in identical twins—(twins with the same genetic inheritance) and fraternal twins (twins developing from two different fertilized eggs) has been compared. The percentage of cases in which *both* twins suffered from schizophrenia is significantly higher among the identical twins than among the fraternal, suggesting that genetic factors play an important role in the development of the disorder (Rosenthal, 1970).

While the identical-twin studies and the adoption studies provide substantial evidence for a genetic factor in schizophrenia, a complex of environmental factors is also involved. The families of schizophrenics tend to be characterized by marked discord (Lidz, 1967). Clinical studies suggest that the child's relationship with the mother may be a critical variable in the development of schizophrenia. One prevalent view, the double-bind hypothesis, suggests that the schizophrenic as a child is exposed to contradictory messages from the mother; for example, she might *say* "I love you" but couple the verbal statement with "cold" kisses and other signs of rejection. Since there is no rational way the child can cope with these conflicting communications, he responds with confusion and withdrawal, precursors to a subsequent schizophrenic reaction.

Because of the complex nature of the schizophrenic reaction, all of these hypotheses may have some degree of validity. Some explanations may be more applicable to certain schizophrenic conditions than to others. For example, some of the data from twin studies suggest that heredity factors are less important in the moderate than in severe schizophrenic reactions (Gottesman & Shields, 1966).

Treatment of Schizophrenics

The cure for schizophrenia is as elusive as its causes. None of the treatments that are currently in use is overwhelmingly effective, but some significant advances have been made. The advent of **chemotherapy** in the form of the tranquilizer drugs such as chlorpromazine has produced a striking change in ward behavior of many schizophrenics and in the length of time patients spend in mental hospitals. These drugs can relax tensions and dissipate anxiety without interfering with attention, memory, and other cognitive functions. The patient becomes less impulsive and agitated and can be entrusted with more responsibility and privileges. Many patients who had been incoherent become capable of discussing their problems, hence more accessible to psychotherapy and to outpatient management. They can leave the hospital sooner than patients did years ago. As a result, the number of patients residing in mental hospitals has dropped since 1955, although the number of admissions has not.

In contrast to the changes in patient behavior produced by chemotherapy, the various psychotherapeutic approaches have proved to be relatively ineffective in treating schizophrenics. Therapists who are more empathic and insightful, as well as accepting and active, in their patient relationships are more likely to be effective in their therapy with schizophrenics (Whitehorn & Betz, 1960).

Certain techniques based on research in learning, particularly operant conditioning (see p. 244), have shown considerable promise for the reduction of many schizophrenic symptoms and the modification of behavior on hospital wards. The therapist, working with conditioning techniques begins by delineating clearly the specific symptoms he wishes to modify and the specific behaviors he wishes to encourage. The desired behaviors are then systematically reinforced while the symptoms are ignored or mildly punished. These techniques have limited effectiveness and they lay no claim to curing schizophrenia. However, as Spotlight 11-5 indicates, they sometimes produce impressive improvements in patient behavior.

SPOTLIGHT 11-5

Use of Operant-Conditioning Techniques in Modification of Schizophrenic Behavior

In one study designed to produce changes in apathy, the patient was reinforced whenever he made a positive social interaction (helped another patient) or made a desirable personal hygienic response (brushed his hair). Among the reinforcements used were verbal praise and tokens, which could later be exchanged for various amenities. The patients placed on this experimental program displayed a marked improvement in behavior over the two months of the program in comparison to a control group which showed little change over the same time period (Schaefer & Martin, 1966).

Quite striking improvements in behavior were found following the initiation of a "token economy" in a psychiatric hospital ward. The tokens served as a kind of substitute for money. Performance of a desired behavior—cleaning floors, grooming oneself, serving meals—was reinforced with tokens which could then be exchanged for such privileges as a comfortable bed, desired foods, cigarettes, a pass, or an opportunity to see a physician or psychologist (Ayllon & Azrin, 1965).

Affective Disorders

The distinguishing characteristic of the affective psychoses is a persistent disturbance in mood. It is so extreme that it interferes with rational judgment. The depressed patient feels personally unworthy and the future seems hopeless. The elated psychotic, in contrast, denies any evidence of mistakes or misfortune. His optimism and feelings of grandiosity are boundless and unrelated to the real world in which he lives. Most patients hospitalized for an affective disorder are depressed. About one fifth suffer from periods of euphoria and elation alternating with periods of depression.

The manic-depressive reaction, which usually begins in early adulthood, is characterized by *severe* mood swings. Mood changes—ups and downs—are, of course, a quite normal occurrence. The patient in a manic state is more than simply elated; he acts as if he were under extreme pressure: overexcited, easily distractible, jumping from one idea to another. His excessive activity is often accompanied by weight loss and insomnia. His gaiety has a thin veneer, however; it is rapidly transformed into anger and arrogance when he is frustrated.

In the depressive phase of the manic-depressive psychosis, the patient manifests a completely opposite pattern of be-

Severe changes in mood characterize the manic-depressive.
(Ted Polumbaum)

havior. He feels sad, worthless, and guilty, and he can be suicidal. (See Spotlight 11-6.) His motor reactions are significantly retarded; he seems lethargic and apathetic. The depressed patients can also become quite agitated, displaying excessive worry and anxiety. Reduced sexual interest, indecisiveness, and inability to concentrate also accompany depression, and there may be delusions and preoccupations with somatic complaints.

Before becoming psychotic, victims of affective disorders are characteristically conforming, conscientious, and socially responsible. When they fall short of the high standards they set for themselves, or feel they have disappointed parents or others they love, they react with discouragement, self-criticism, and guilt. All of these behavioral tendencies become exaggerated in the psychotic episode. The manic reaction can also be seen as an overcompensation for the underlying despair. At the same time, a genetic predisposition may play a role in the manic-depressive reaction patterns (Rosenthal, 1970). If one of a pair of identical twins is a manic-depressive, the chances that his co-twin will also be a manic-depressive are 7 out of 10, while the rate is only 2 out of 10 for fraternal twins.

The prognosis for affective psychotic reactions is quite

favorable and many patients recover spontaneously. The manic-depressive patient, however, is subject to recurrent episodes. Drugs specifically developed for the manic and depressed states are very helpful during the acute phases of the disorder. The severely depressed patient who is resistant to psychotherapy may be responsive to **electroconvulsive shock therapy.** This treatment consists of inducing a convulsion, rendering the patient briefly unconscious, through the administration of electric shock to the brain. We do not

SPOTLIGHT 11-6

Suicide

There are many possible reasons for committing suicide: hopelessness, guilt, depression, shame, hostility, and attempts to punish others. Suicide is not necessarily a manifestation of psychopathology. It can be heroic; a captured spy who takes lethal poison rather than endanger his nation's safety. Or it may be an expression of conformity to social norms; traditionally many Japanese who had disgraced their family or social group committed hara-kiri.

In the United States suicide is the tenth-ranking cause of death, with an annual rate of 11 per 100,000. Although the rate of suicide tends to increase with age, it is the fifth most important cause of death among the 15- to 24-year-old age group, more common among college students than among others this age. Suicide rates are markedly influenced by social factors such as nationality and religious affiliations. Catholics, for whom suicide is a mortal sin, have lower rates than Jews or Protestants. Proportionally more whites than nonwhites commit suicide, and three times more males than females, although women make many more suicide attempts than men.

A hopeful aspect of the suicide problem is that, whatever the underlying reason, in most instances, people who commit suicide reveal their intention before the suicide act. (N. W. Farberow & E. S. Shneidman, Eds., *The Cry for Help.* New York: McGraw-Hill, 1961.) Centers have been established in many cities throughout the United States to provide emergency help via twenty-four-hour telephone service to those contemplating suicide. Anyone with suicidal thoughts is encouraged to call one of these centers and speak to someone about his problems and fears.

(Van Bucher, Photo Researchers)

yet have a clear understanding of why the procedure is often effective for alleviating depression.

The Neuroses

All of us fall short of achieving a fully efficient and adaptive level of psychological functioning. We may get angry without apparent reason, need assurance that we are loved, conceal from ourselves and others the motives for our behavior, and occasionally feel intense anxiety. In the neurotic, these needs and feelings become so exaggerated and persistent that they interfere with social adaptation and produce extreme personal misery. The neurotic, unlike the psychotic, is aware of his unhappiness, even if he is unaware of the underlying reasons. He usually recognizes his "symptoms" and would like to get rid of them. And, most important, the neurotic's thought processes are not so disorganized as the psychotic's. He has a better grasp of reality and does not have hallucinations or delusions.

Intense anxiety appears to be a common element of all neuroses. Neurotic reactions are interpreted as either direct manifestations of anxiety or as behaviors which help avoid the pain of anxiety. Thus impaired concentration, insomnia, inability to make a decision, and sexual impotence may be manifestations or direct consequences of anxiety. In contrast, compulsive rituals (such as hand washing), amnesias, and exaggerated social conformity may be ways of reducing anxiety. (See discussion of defense mechanisms in the previous chapter, p. 223.)

Hysteria

A young woman was referred for psychological study by a throat specialist who could find no physical basis for her extreme hoarseness. The woman was very upset by her symptom because she hoped to obtain a lead part as a singer in a musical comedy. After several sessions with a psychologist, it became apparent that she had been extremely anxious about the possibility of being rejected for the part. The development of the laryngitis enabled her to avoid the anxiety and the threat to her self-image which rejection would have entailed. She recovered her voice after five weeks of treatment (unfortunately, after the part had been given to someone else).

This young woman was suffering from a symptom of **hysteria** (often referred to as a "conversion reaction"), the impairment of some bodily function for psychological, as contrasted to organic, reasons. Included in this category are cases of hysterical blindness, deafness, paralysis of the limbs, anesthesia, and the well-known writer's cramp. The hysteric does not deliberately put on or fake his symptoms; the conversion process is an unconscious one.

Another extreme type of hysterical disturbance is "dissociative reactions," in which components of the individual's personality are excluded from his conscious functioning. Amnesia for past events and dual personalities are examples of dissociative reactions. In fugue states the individual "loses" his memory and escapes problems by running away—perhaps even starting a new life, unaware of his former identity. In dramatic cases of dual or multiple personalities, one personality assumes the moral, superego, "Dr. Jekyll" role while the other takes on the more negative, id-dominated, "Mr. Hyde" aspects (Thigpen & Cleckly, 1957).

Phobias

Phobias are irrational, intense fears of specific objects and situations that persist despite the individual's recognition that the fears are groundless—at least from a rational point of view. Some phobias can be extremely disabling. *Acrophobia* (fear of high places) and *claustrophobia* (fear of closed places), for example, greatly limit the individual's freedom of movement.

According to psychoanalytic theory, phobias are displaced reactions, substitutes for the fear of repressed impulses. For example, "Little Hans," a classic case of Freud's, was a five-year-old boy who would not go into the street because of a persistent fear that he would be bitten by a horse. After detailed investigation of the case, Freud concluded that the phobia was a symbolic expression of his fear of castration by his father.

Learning theories would suggest a conditioning explanation of phobias. In the case of Little Hans, a clinical psychologist using a learning approach would look for a previous association between a horse and a frightening event; such an association would explain how the sight or thought of a horse would evoke fear. (See discussion of the acquisition of fear in the previous chapter, p. 215.) In fact, Little Hans was involved in a traumatic incident in which he was almost run over by a horse.

Obsessive-Compulsive Neurosis

Obsessions are recurrent thoughts, words, or impulses that a person cannot control. One patient was obsessed with exag-

Lady Macbeth's hand-washing compulsion was an outward sign of her guilt feelings.
(Culver Pictures)

gerated doubts as to whether he had locked the door of his house whenever he left it. On one occasion, he returned six times to check the door to see if it was "really" locked.

This same patient also had many **compulsions,** repetitive motor acts that the individual feels impelled to carry out. For example, he had a compulsion to wash his hands repeatedly "to get rid of the germs," much like Lady Macbeth trying to cleanse her hands of the bloodstains of the murdered king. The patient, like most obsessive-compulsive neurotics was a rigid, guilt-ridden individual, trying to control impulses that he could not consciously accept.

Psychophysiological Disorders

Psychological stimuli can elicit strong emotional responses and thus produce marked changes in bodily reactions. A sudden fright can produce a sharp increase in heart rate, a rise in blood pressure, changes in respiration, and digestive upsets. Prolonged stress can result in maladaptive reactions which are manifested in physical symptoms such as gastric ulcers, asthma, high blood pressure, migraine headaches, and eczema.

Some recent and exciting research on psychophysiological processes has important therapeutic implications. Heart rate, blood pressure, and stomach contractions have been assumed to be involuntary, stereotyped, psychological and physical reactions, controlled by the autonomic nervous system. (Voluntary responses, such as movement of arms or torso are controlled by the central nervous system. See Chapter 23, p. 653, for a more detailed description of the autonomic and central nervous systems.) "Autonomic" has been taken to mean automatic, as if these responses automatically changed when the individual experienced conditions such as stress. However, a series of ingenious experiments with rats has demonstrated that it is possible to change many of these physiological reactions through the application of operant-conditioning procedures (Miller, 1969; Dicara, 1970). The animals were first injected with curare, a drug which blocks the action of the skeletal muscles, which are under central nervous system control, but involuntary, autonomically-controlled reactions continue. A number of physiological recording instruments were hooked up to the animals. To increase stomach contractions, the experimenter rewarded or reinforced the animal whenever the recording instrument showed a spontaneous increase in these contractions. And the number of contractions increased. Furthermore, by systematic application of reinforcements whenever a desired response was made, rats were taught to modify heart rate, blood pressure, rate of urine formation, frequency of stomach contractions, and amount of blood in the right ear!

Operant-conditioning procedures have also been successfully applied in training heart beat and galvanic skin responses in human subjects (Engel & Chism, 1967; Greene, 1966). These findings suggest the possibility that in the future disorders such as high blood pressure and gastric ulcers may be treated by operant-training methods.

Personality Disorders

Many individuals who do not display clear-cut, isolated symptoms have personality styles and character structure that reflect emotional disturbance. These individuals, unlike neurotics, do not perceive themselves as being disturbed. They may seek psychological help because others recommend it or because of problems such as inability to keep a job or a spouse. Because their problems and ways of adjusting are so ingrained, they do not respond readily to therapy and may require years of treatment. The therapist must first help the patient to see that he has a personality problem; only then can he begin to help the patient change his behavior. Many personality disorders appear to be counterparts of neurotic and psychotic disturbances. Some of these are listed in Spotlight 11-7.

SPOTLIGHT 11-7

Personality Disorders Related to Neuroses and Psychoses

1. The *paranoid personality* is an individual who is suspicious of others, hypersensitive to slights, egocentric, hostile, and very self-righteous.

2. The *schizoid personality* is shy, aloof, emotionally cold, and frequently asocial, avoiding social interactions that are fear-arousing.

3. The *hysterical personality* is self-dramatizing and given to role-playing, with superficial and often misleading emotional accompaniment. Hysterical women, for example, are frequently overt flirts but basically frigid and sexually repressed.

4. The *obsessive-compulsive* personality is typically rigid, orderly, and strict in his adherence to social convention, preoccupied with schedules and regularity, overcontrolled and overintellectualized. His disturbance becomes apparent when the situation calls for a change in behavior and he is utterly inflexible and responds with irritation.

The Antisocial Personality

Antisocial (or **sociopathic**) **personalities** are people who lack a sense of responsibility and morality, are unable to develop attachments to other people or feel empathy for them, and find it difficult to delay impulse gratification. They hunger for excitement, are concerned with their own immediate satisfactions, unrestrained by remorse, regardless of the consequences for others. They seem unable to profit from the "lessons" of experience. Some can be quite charming and adroit in their exploitation of others, appealing to the sympathy of their victims, lying unhesitatingly, and acting contrite—then promptly pursuing their errant ways. Other sociopaths are less charming and can, in fact, be quite hostile and cruel. Many become juvenile delinquents and criminals (but many professional criminals are not antisocial personalities and are capable of loyalty, warmth, and responsible behavior toward their family or their own cultural group).

The sociopath is very difficult to treat because he lacks insight and a desire to change. He is unable to establish the kind of trusting relationship that is required for effective psychotherapy.

Sexual Deviancy

The definitions of "normal" and "abnormal" sexual behavior are very much subject to social values and changing social norms. While the official classification of mental disorders by the American Psychiatric Association includes **homosexuality** as a personality disorder (see Spotlight 11-3), this view is currently being actively contested by many clinicians and, most especially, by homosexuals who maintain that they are not abnormal or mentally ill. Many homosexuals suggest that it is not their behavior but the attitudes of society that require modification.

Gay liberation.
(Charles Gatewood)

According to the data of the Kinsey survey of sexual behavior (1948), 37 percent of adult males had had at least one homosexual experience to the point of orgasm, but the proportion of males who could be properly described as fundamentally homosexual was less than 8 percent. There are considerably fewer female homosexuals (lesbians). Homosexuals seem to be biologically normal and cannot be discriminated from heterosexuals on the basis of established physical and hormonal tests; recently, however, some investigators claim that more precise hormonal or genetic analyses show possible differences in a relatively small sample; these claims must be subjected to further research attention before they can be accepted with confidence.

Among the psychological explanations of homosexuality, some focus on the patterning of sexual behavior through conditioning. Others point to the importance of the family constellation—specifically, a dominating mother and an inadequate father—and support their claim with many clinical studies.

Other forms of sexual deviance include fetishism—the attainment of sexual gratification through attachment to an inanimate object—found only among males. Voyeurism and exhibitionism are also male deviations, rarely observed in females. The voyeur is sexually stimulated and relieved by peeping at females while they are nude or undressing. The exhibitionist essentially reverses this pattern in that he obtains sexual pleasure when a woman observes his erect penis. Both the voyeur and the exhibitionist are insecure men who are fearful of the sex act and will rarely molest or harm women.

Drug Addiction

ALCOHOLISM Alcohol is the most widely used and the most socially acceptable of the psychoactive drugs. When taken in moderate doses, it can produce relaxation and a "high." When taken in large doses, it can be extremely toxic. Heavy drinking results in defective cognitive and motor functioning; driving while drunk is the most important cause of auto accidents. Alcoholism can disrupt family relationships and lead to occupational difficulties; it can produce irreversible liver and brain damage and eventual psychosis.

The term **alcoholism** is restricted to heavy, regular drinkers who are unable to control their alcoholic intake. Once having started to drink, alcoholics cannot stop; they are compelled to continue until intoxicated.

Four percent of American adult males and about 1 percent of females are alcoholics. Typically alcoholism starts with increased social drinking, followed by surreptitious drinking and increasing signs of emotional dependence on alcohol. The final phases of alcoholism are marked by solitary drinking, long drinking bouts, and a physiological dependence. At this point, the alcoholic may suffer delirium tremens, a state marked by confusion, tremors, and disturbing hallucinations. Also, because the alcoholic generally eats poorly, he may have a vitamin deficiency that produces degeneration of brain tissue.

Alcoholism is the complex result of a number of interacting factors. Social variables determine the extent to which alcohol is available and is approved. Personality traits are of paramount importance. The tendency to become addicted to alcohol and to use it as an escape from anxiety and the pressures of daily living is associated with underlying dependency, exaggerated emphasis on masculinity (in males), repressed hostile tendencies, and inadequate impulse control. But the correlations between personality traits and alcoholism are small, so there is little reason to postulate an "alcoholic personality."

Alcoholism has proved to be very resistant to psychological treatment. In therapeutic-conditioning procedures, which have had some success, alcohol is paired with nausea-inducing drugs or with a painful electric shock in order to induce an aversion to alcohol (Frank, 1967; McBrearty *et al.*, 1968). In group therapy, a group of alcoholics meets several times a month to discuss their drinking and emotional problems. This form of therapy is employed by Alcoholics Anonymous (AA), an organization run by alcoholics who have stopped drinking. The members also are encouraged to seek each other's support when they have an emotional problem or an urge to drink. In addition, considerable emphasis is placed on religious values. While no precise statistics on the effectiveness of AA are available, it appears to be effective for many alcoholics.

NONALCOHOLIC DRUG USE, ABUSE, AND DEPENDENCE

Until the last ten or fifteen years, the use of nonalcoholic drugs was not a major social problem in the United States. Drugs have been used for centuries in many cultures to relieve tension and pain, to achieve heightened sensations and feelings of pleasure and well-being (euphoria), to produce mystical experiences, and to expand consciousness. Opium and its derivatives, very potent addictive drugs, were prominently used drugs in Western medicine late in the last century. But even marijuana use, now so pervasive, was very largely limited to people in the urban ghettos. Then in the mid-sixties came the psychedelic revolution, and the use of drugs—many kinds of drugs—became very widespread, especially in the eighteen to thirty age group.

And, as you would expect, people who had hardly been aware of the existence of drugs became worried about their possible harmful effects and about why young people were using them. Many parents were concerned and threatened by their children's use of drugs, not only because of possible damaging effects but because drug use is often regarded as a mark of alienation from society or

Drug use has become associated with membership in a counterculture.
(Ted Polumbaum, *Life* magazine © 1972 Time Inc.)

membership in a counterculture that rejects the establishment and the middle class's values such as the accumulation of wealth and the pursuit of occupational success. Or parents may feel guilty if they believe their child's use of drugs reflects personal maladjustment or basic feelings of insecurity.

There is no reason to believe that everyone who tries drugs like marijuana, or uses such a drug occasionally, is emotionally maladjusted, alienated, or trying to escape his problems. Most young people do not feel that they have to have drugs; they use them because they are curious and they like some of the effects. After extensive study of the drug culture around the Berkeley campus of the University of California, one sociologist concluded that

> *While a profound state of dissatisfaction with the larger society and [its] values . . . usually precedes extensive experimentation with marihuana, the dissatisfaction by itself is not an explanation for use. Many alienated young people do not resort to drug use. Two other things must be present: the person must be in the setting where drugs are available and he must be introduced to drugs by someone [usually friends] he holds in esteem. (Carey 1968, pp. 51, 52)*

The youth who belongs to groups in which drug use is prevalent is likely to experiment with drugs but this does not mean that he will become dependent upon them. What drugs mean to the individual depends upon his personality and his personal history as well as on the way that drugs are used in his own social groups. Some become heavily dependent upon the use of drugs because of their own personal, neurotic needs. But most people who try drugs and use them occasionally do not become dependent upon them.

From the social and psychological points of view—which may be quite different from the legal point of view—the use of drugs becomes a problem only when it is damaging to the user himself or to society. The criteria of drug abuse are impairment of the individual's functioning, inability to mobilize his energy and direct himself, undermining of his moral restraints, or criminal and violent behavior.

We can only understand the problem of drug abuse if we know something about the characteristics of the most widely used drugs and their effects, both positive and negative. There are four major types and each has its own properties, characteristics, and effects.

1. *Hallucinogens.* These include a varied group of drugs such as marijuana and LSD that can alter visual experience, producing hallucinations and other perceptual changes. They typically induce a euphoric state but some can bring about unpleasant mood changes as well. Users may become *psychologically* dependent on the drug, that is, they may feel that they must continue to use the drug to ease tensions or to feel good. But the drugs do *not* produce *physiological* dependence or addiction—the body does not become dependent on chemical effects of the drugs as it does with heroin.

Marijuana, the dried flowers and leaves of the hemp plant, is undoubtedly the most frequently used illegal drug. Roughly half the men and a third of the women in the United States between the ages of eighteen and twenty-four have tried marijuana, and a fourth of the men in this age group have smoked it fifty or more times. The effects of the drug are those of a mild intoxicant, inducing mild euphoria, increased awareness, greater openness to other people and to colors, tastes, smells, and sounds. The feelings produced are typically relaxation, peacefulness, and freedom from anxiety, not hostility, although "bad trips" can occur and produce great anxiety. Time perception may be altered so that the individual focuses clearly only on the present, responding in immediate, natural ways. In the words of a twenty-one-year-old part-time artist who frequently used marijuana:

> *. . . you notice many things, you become very interested in the little details. For instance, you may have noticed things like handles, or bottles, or pebbles, and children's attitudes, and you'd find that children aren't so young as you think and that you aren't as old as you think and that you don't become an adult if you don't understand that you aren't going to become any greater than a child. (Carey, 1968, p. 54)*

The hazards of marijuana have probably been exaggerated. In one experimental test of the effects of small amounts of the drug, first-time users showed slight impairments in motor and cognitive functioning. However, habitual users showed no such impairment—and in some cases their performance improved even though they thought they were doing poorly—although they did report feeling high (Weil, 1968).

Of course large amounts of marijuana may have different, adverse, effects. The "stoned" driver may suffer from perceptual distortion, loss of sense of direction, poor judgment, and poor reflexes and thus become as much of a traffic hazard as the drunk driver. And it has been suggested that chronic, heavy use of marijuana, like heavy use of alcohol, may lower the individual's level of productive activity and may produce psychotic reactions. But there is no evidence that the use of marijuana leads to criminal behavior, delinquency, sexual excitement, or addiction. Nor is there any scientific basis for the popular belief that using marijuana leads to using heroin.

LSD (lysergic acid diethylamide) is a potent—and, under some circumstances, dangerous—drug that is frequently used by college students. It was first used in psychiatric research and treatment and originally called a "psychotomimetic" because it produced a variety of psychosislike experiences. While the drug is no longer used in this kind of research, it is still sometimes used by psychiatrists in treating alcoholism and neuroses, because it may aid in establishing rapport with chronically withdrawn patients and it may help them to verbalize memories and feelings that they could not otherwise talk about.

The drug is now called **psychedelic,** meaning "mind manifesting," opening the mind to new experiences and sensations. About thirty minutes after a small quantity of LSD is ingested, the "trip" begins, and the drug's influence generally lasts approximately eight to twelve hours. Effects are highly individual and unpredictable, depending on the social setting as well as the age and personality of the user. Mood changes and heightened emotionality are the first obvious effects; intense happiness or unhappiness can be stimulated by the most casual remarks of others, and sensitivity to all kinds of stimuli is tremendously enhanced. Tactile and visual distortions, including vivid hallucinatory experiences, occur, and the distinction between self and the environment may become blurred. Later the user is likely to become introspective, extremely suggestible and, in some cases, paranoid. Many LSD users are convinced that they have achieved greater self-understanding and that creativity is enhanced by the drug, but there is little evidence to support this view.

Bad trips may occur among habitual LSD users or among those trying the drug for the first time. These may be characterized by confusion, paranoia, feelings of omnipotence or invulnerability, and, in some cases, panic reactions, a sense of helplessness, overwhelming intense anxiety, fear of losing control and going crazy. There may be recurrent reactions after the trip is over, a spontaneous return of per-

The mental and emotional states of the LSD user are revealed in artwork, as in this drawing done by one on a "mind-manifesting" trip. (Lawrence Schiller, Magnum)

ceptual distortions or feelings of unreality, often accompanied by panic and anxiety. Heavy users of LSD have sometimes become so preoccupied with subjective experiences and sensations that they withdraw from normal social activities, lose their critical judgment, and seem unable to mobilize themselves or to make plans. Essentially they "drop out" of the culture.

2. *Stimulants.* Amphetamines or pep pills, including dexedrine sulfate (dexies) and methamphetamine (speed or meth), have an energizing and psychologically stimulating effect. They are used for weight control (through reduction of appetite) and for counteracting fatigue and depressive moods, and occasionally by athletes trying to enhance their performance in contests and by students staying up late to study. These drugs produce feelings of euphoria, increased alertness, restlessness, motor and verbal activity, irritability, and wakefulness. These effects may be accompanied by irrationality, paranoia, and anxiety.

Prolonged and heavy use of amphetamines can be very dangerous and addictive. Tolerance for the drug builds up rapidly, so that the pill-popper has to take more pills at shorter intervals, to reach the same high, to combat depression and fatigue. Unfortunately, many adolescents—speed freaks or meth heads—ingest or inject large quantities of these drugs several times a day. These people keep on the go all the time, not eating or sleeping for several days, often manifesting paranoid symptoms. Sometimes they have to take sedatives, barbiturates, or tranquilizers to calm their nerves. Finally, exhaustion sets in and the user may sleep for a day or more; after that he is likely to be quite depressed. To escape the miserable "down" he takes amphetamines again. A cycle is begun and psychological dependence on the drug develops.

Paranoid symptoms—especially fear, suspicion, and delusions of persecution—are fairly common among heavy users of amphetamines and these may be accompanied by compulsive behavior that the victim repeats hour after hour apparently without boredom or fatigue. For example, one victim of amphetamine psychosis set a table, constantly rearranging his fork and knife for hours.

3. *Sedatives.* This group includes habit-forming barbiturates such as Seconal (reds), Nembutal (yellow jackets) and Amytal (blue heavens), which have a relaxing and, in larger doses, sleep-inducing effects. The chronic user becomes too dulled to cope with his problems adequately; hence the drugs serve as an escape. In taking barbiturates, the user risks the dangers of a lethal overdose. In addition, the physiological effects of withdrawal from the drugs are extremely debilitating and can, in fact, be fatal.

4. *Opiates.* This group includes opium, the parent drug, and morphine, heroin, and codeine, opium derivatives. The most popular is heroin and no drug is more potent in producing euphoric effects, and relief from pain, tension, and anxiety. Initially, the major effect is only a pleasant high that lasts about four hours. But the drug is dangerously and severely addicting. In the United States the vast majority of drug addicts use heroin and heroin addiction is of the classic type—a compulsion to use the drug and a tendency to increase the dose as one gets more "hooked." Psychological and physical dependence on the drug have enormous detrimental effects on the user and on society. The habit becomes the dominant motif in the addict's life, and in order to support this expensive habit, he may be forced to resort to theft, prostitution, or other illegal activities. His social contacts, conversations, and thoughts revolve around drugs, especially the next "fix." Even sexual activity diminishes because, contrary to popular belief, heroin inhibits the sex impulse.

After taking heroin steadily for a period of several weeks, the user is hooked and requires the drug in order to feel normal and to avoid withdrawal symptoms. If he is deprived of it, he experiences intensely uncomfortable withdrawal symptoms, beginning with feelings of tension, restlessness, and nervousness. These become progressively worse as time goes by, and, within twenty-four hours of withdrawal, most habitual users are acutely miserable, shivering and experiencing intense cramps and pain in the back and extremities. Arms, legs, and feet twitch almost constantly. Symptoms are most intense in the second or third day after withdrawal and then decline for the next week. The remaining complaints are likely to be nervousness, insomnia, and weakness, which may not disappear for a period of weeks or months. A single dose of the drug during the withdrawal period will produce a prompt and pronounced reduction of these disturbances.

The heroin addict is extremely resistant to treatment. About 90 percent of hospital-treated addicts who kick the habit become addicted again within a period of about six months after discharge (Hunt & Odoroff, 1963). The Synanon movement, founded in 1958 by a former alcoholic, Charles E. Dederich (who had been helped by Alcoholics Anonymous), has provided a promising treatment approach. The addict becomes part of an autocratic structure of former addicts who guide him until he develops the inner resources to control the habit on his own. A special group therapy technique is employed in which the addict is given direct and sometimes harsh feedback about the consequences and meaning of his present behavior.

More recently a number of drugs, such as methadone, have been developed which substitute for or block the action of heroin. While these may also be habit-forming they are much less expensive, can be prescribed by a physician (under appropriate conditions), and are generally less damaging to the individual and to society.

What are the goals of therapy?

The treatment of mental disorders has been considered at various points in this chapter; chemotherapy, milieu therapy, shock therapy, operant-conditioning procedures, and group therapies have been mentioned. There are as many **psychotherapies** as personality theorists. We shall here briefly consider four major therapeutic approaches used by psychologists. Most therapies are variants of one or another of these approaches: psychoanalysis, client-centered therapy, group therapy, behavior modification.

Psychoanalysis

The goal of psychoanalysis as a therapy is to uncover and resolve the emotional problems, usually stemming from the patient's childhood, that are the causes of his symptoms. The process is a long and costly one. Standard psychoanalytic treatment involves seeing the analyst an hour a day, four to five times a week for a period of from two to five years and sometimes more. The analyst uses the technique of free association (see p. 180). The patient's resistance (the silences and the blocks in his associations and discussion) provide clues to those areas of conflict which the patient finds painful and which he attempts to avoid. Psychoanalysts interpret the patient's resistances as well as the content of his associations and his dreams.

As treatment progresses, the patient develops an intense emotional response to the analyst called the **transference neurosis**—he transfers to the therapist characteristics of significant figures in his childhood (e.g., his father) and reenacts with the therapist, major childhood conflicts that remain unresolved. The transference neurosis has a paradoxical effect. It temporarily interferes with the patient's progress but it is the key to the successful resolution of his conflicts. Through the analyst's interpretation of the transference neuroses, the patient acquires insight into the inappropriateness of his emotional reactions and into the nature of his psychological defenses. Thus, in working out his feelings toward the analyst, the patient may be able to resolve some of his basic conflicts.

It is very difficult to obtain convincing evidence of the effectiveness of psychoanalytic treatment. There is little doubt that it has proved helpful to many people. However, questions have been raised as to its utility in a great many cases. It is a costly treatment which relatively few people can afford and which is inaccessible to the great majority of the psychologically disturbed who are in need of treatment.

Client-Centered Therapy

The client-centered therapist attempts to help the client accept his feelings and open up to experiences that he has been dis-

Contrasting styles of individual psychotherapy: psychoanalysis and client-centered therapy.

(P. 260: Van Bucher, Photo Researchers; p. 261: Ted Polumbaum) torting or shutting out (Rogers, 1951). A therapist using this approach is nondirective; he does not provide advice to his client or offer interpretations of the client's verbalizations and behavior. Rather, he demonstrates his **unconditional positive regard** for his client, recognizing and clarifying the client's feelings. In so doing, he conveys to the client that he empathizes with him and truly understands and accepts his feelings.

The client is seen as the central agent in therapy; the therapist essentially provides a warm, accepting environment in which positive growth can take place. From the very first therapeutic hour, the client is informed that the hour is his to talk about whatever he pleases. The client may at first find it difficult to take all the initiative. However, he soon adapts and begins to express his feelings which, at first, are predominantly negative ones of inferiority, guilt, anxiety, and anger. When these feelings are accepted and clarified, positive feelings of love and self-respect begin to emerge along with the achievement of insight. As the patient feels better about himself and becomes aware of other alternatives than those he has been pursuing, he relinquishes his neurotic behavior patterns and engages in more positive modes of action.

Client-centered therapy is much less time-consuming than psychoanalysis, frequently being terminated with six to fifteen contacts (Rogers, 1942). While several studies indicate that client-centered therapy has a positive effect, there are many clients who are not helped by this treatment mode and who might benefit from other types of intervention.

Behavior Modification

In recent years there has been a rapid increase in the use of therapeutic techniques based on learning principles. In contrast to more traditional therapies that focus on childhood antecedents, internal psychological processes, and insight, behavior modification procedures are designed simply to reduce or eliminate undesirable behavioral symptoms, and to increase the probability of productive activities. The use of these procedures is known as **behavior therapy.**

There are many instances in which **operant conditioning** can be used effectively in modifying behavior problems. For example, in a case of a socially withdrawn nursery-school child, teachers were advised by a clinical psychologist to make a concerted effort to watch the girl and to reward her with maximum attention whenever she approached, or played with, another child. At the same time they did not reward withdrawal behavior but tried to extinguish these responses by paying no attention to the child when they occurred. (Under ordinary circumstances, sympathetic teachers would probably do the opposite, that is, notice her and give her particular attention when she was withdrawn.) Almost immediately after the treatment began, the child's behavior changed drastically. She began to interact with other children actively and spent relatively little time in isolated

This behavior therapist rewards an autistic child's speech sounds.
(Allan Grant)

activities. Even after the reinforcements were discontinued, she continued to spend most of her time interacting with other children and in general became a happier, more confident, and more sociable child.

Operant techniques have also been used with considerable success in work with autistic children. Those who are in the severely psychotic state of **autism** are extremely withdrawn and so unresponsive to social stimuli that they have not learned to speak, which makes conventional "talking" therapies of little use. To make matters worse, many are self-destructive; they may do things like banging their heads on a table, so hard that they often have to be fitted with gloves, football helmets, or even straightjackets for protection against themselves. Behavior therapists working with these children have used systematic and carefully controlled programs of rewards (food, attention, and affection, for example) to increase the incidence of meaningful speech and social responsiveness. Punishment is sometimes necessary (but effective) in reducing aggressive and self-destructive behavior while friendly and responsive acts are reinforced.

In **systematic desensitization,** the therapist attempts to teach the patient how to relax in situations that typically produce anxiety. First, the patient is taught how to relax. Then the anxiety-provoking situation is introduced, but only gradually, never exceeding the patient's capacity. For example, if the problem is an extreme fear of heights, the person might be asked to *imagine* looking out of a second-story window—while relaxing. Gradually the imagined height is increased to the third story, the fourth story, until finally the person can visualize himself on top of the Empire State Building—while relaxing. Often this imaginal activity is enough, but in some cases, the therapist may actually take the patient to a high building, having him actually look out of a first-story window, then a second-story window, and so on to the top. The procedure was effectively applied to a nine-year-old girl who suffered night terrors, severe abdominal pain and fear of separation from her mother (Lazarus, 1960). Immediately prior to the appearance of the girl's symptoms, a school friend had drowned, a playmate had died of meningitis, and she witnessed an accident in which a man was killed. But these factors are not critical to the process of behavior modification. The behavior therapist first trained the girl to relax and then had her imagine increasingly long periods of separation from her mother. Each new step was introduced only after she could manage the previous step without anxiety. The girl's symptoms were eliminated after only five sessions.

Often desensitization procedures are combined with operant techniques. In one case of a nine-year-old boy who exhibited an extreme fear of school, the fear was reduced by desensitization.

The boy was taken to school for a short visit, accompanied by his therapist who tried to allay his anxiety by talking with him, trying to make him feel relaxed, telling him jokes, and distracting him. In the second stage of the treatment, the boy was rewarded with various tokens for remaining in school on his own; the longer he remained the more tokens he received. He could then trade these in for valuable prizes. The treatment proved to be very effective in overcoming the boy's school phobia.

Behavior therapies appear to be quite effective for eliminating specific neurotic symptoms such as phobias and nervous mannerisms. They are less applicable to the personality disorders and to the modification of neurotic styles of behavior and of neurotic symptoms which are manifestations of deep-rooted conflicts.

Group Therapies

Within the last two decades, therapy in groups rather than in therapist-patient pairs has become increasingly common. It has long been thought that interaction in small groups of five to fifteen people could be advantageous. Since many psychological problems exhibit themselves in interpersonal relations, activity in a group setting allows the therapist to observe directly such behaviors as hostility, nurturance, and anxiety and the means by which the individual copes with threats and frustrations.

A group setting may be highly effective in modifying or eliminating maladaptive behaviors. Group members, interacting under a qualified therapist's leadership, may help each other to gain insights into their problems and conflicts and to achieve new perspectives. The group is also like the real world in many ways; it is a social situation in which one can "try out" new behaviors and new means of adjustment. The group can be a kind of laboratory where new skills can be tested and refined in an understanding environment before they are applied in everyday life. And along with the changed behaviors, the perception of oneself often becomes more positive as the individual interacts with others in the group and begins to feel more competent. At best, then, **group therapy** can help produce a self-assured individual with confidence in his abilities to cope with a world that had been confusing and anxiety-producing.

There are also potential disadvantages to group therapy. Many psychologists feel that the interactions in groups are too superficial to be of much use, especially if the patient's conflicts are deep-seated. For some individuals, the group's focus on their defensive tactics can be highly threatening and could be more harmful than helpful. Today more and more groups are probing complex personality dynamics, in many cases without anyone in the group who is qualified to recognize or treat serious psychological breakdowns. Attacks on a person's defenses may produce breakdowns, and many psychologists worry about the apparent disregard for such potentially devastating events.

Therapeutic groups today can be categorized on the basis of their goals and the characteristics of group members. On the one hand, there are what might be termed the "traditional" groups with members who experience some degree of emotional maladjustment, or neurosis. The goal of these groups is to promote adequate or normal adjustment. Included in this category are groups organized to combat a specific problem such as alcoholism or drug addiction. On the other hand, there is an increasing number of groups with the goal of self-improvement for its members, members who may not be emotionally disturbed. These groups include sensitivity groups and encounter groups. A **sensitivity group** is one in which the goal of the participants is to recognize and become sensitive to the emotional response their actions produce in others. An **encounter group** gets its name from the belief that if people really communicate with each other, are open and honest, and "encounter" one another, the natural human "growth" forces will become operative. This encounter will result in self-actualization—ideally, full self-actualization—and enrichment of the personality. The philosophies of many of these groups are based on the writings of Carl Rogers and Abraham Maslow.

Important variants of the types already discussed are activity groups (Slavson, 1943), role-playing groups (Moreno, 1946), and family groups (Satir, 1964). Activity groups are like "clubs" organized to pursue common interests such as painting or dancing,

Sensitivity training strives to make participants more aware of their feelings and those of others. People must be loosened up before self-erected barriers can be lowered.
(Van Bucher, courtesy Wagner College Psychology Dept., Photo Researchers)

but the enhancement of personality, rather than the activity per se, is of central interest. It is said that activity groups are especially useful for overly withdrawn or overly impulsive people and for problem children in general.

Role-playing groups are designed to produce insight by having the individual improvise a scene or drama about personally disturbing situations. J. L. Moreno's psychodrama is the most commonly known form of role-playing. For example, an adolescent girl might be asked to "play" herself in a scene portraying her and her overprotective mother arguing about the time the girl must be home after a date. (Another member of the group would play her mother.) Presumably, the psychodrama promotes open expression of feelings and conflicts. The girl might also be asked to play the role of mother in the same scene, promoting empathy and understanding; this technique is called "role reversal."

In family groups, the therapist may meet with all members of the family at the same time. Very often, the problems of an individual in a family—a child, for example, or a wife—cannot be clearly understood unless the therapist sees the interactions within the family. For example, a child's emotional problems may stem from his interactions with his parents. They may be overly dominating or overly critical. Or they may have too high standards for the child. These parental characteristics might be extremely difficult to detect ordinarily, but they may become apparent in family group therapy sessions. Then they can be discussed, and, with the resulting increased insights of the family members, the child's problems may be ameliorated.

You should be aware that it is, unfortunately, extremely difficult to evaluate the general effectiveness of any of these kinds of therapy. Therefore, it seems appropriate to give you some words of caution in closing this section. Many people feel they can benefit from psychotherapy and many can. But one must be careful in selecting the kind of therapy that is most likely to benefit him. There are many fads in therapy and any new approach is likely to be greeted with enthusiasm and to gain many adherents. Often case reports of therapeutic success sound convincing. But the fact is that a hard second look usually leads to a less optimistic appraisal. There has been relatively little controlled research on the effectiveness of particular kinds of psychotherapy because of the complexity of problems. Generally these research findings indicate that the therapy technique has less success than its adherents think. Anyway, by the time a proper evaluation is completed, the technique is likely to have lost popularity, only to be replaced by another therapy approach—also of unknown value. The moral of this is simple: If you seek psychotherapy or guidance, choose your therapist with great care; check on his record and credentials (Meltzoff & Kornreich, 1970).

SUMMARY

Mental illness is a very significant contemporary problem, but it is not a new one. The ancients wrote about it and it appears to be common in simpler societies, as well as in sophisticated urban cultures. Attitudes toward mental illness have changed slowly over the centuries, from a belief that such disorders were caused by possession by the devil to the view that they reflect underlying illness and should be treated as such. Conceptions of mental disorders are still in flux. Some theorists regard psychopathology as a reflection of problems of living or of maladaptive habits rather than as an illness.

Mental disturbances vary in degree and in types of symptoms manifested. The most severe are the psychoses, and the most common psychosis is schizophrenia, a diagnosis that embraces a wide range of diverse behaviors, including profound thought disorder and social withdrawal. The causes of schizophrenia are not yet established. There is evidence of genetic determinants and unfavorable family environment, and related social and experiential factors also have a significant role in the development of the disorder. Chemotherapy has reduced markedly the time schizophrenic patients spend in mental hospitals, and the application of operant-conditioning principles in hospital wards has produced some dramatic modifications in patient behavior and schizophrenic symptoms.

The affective disorders, such as manic-depressive psychosis, are characterized by severe disturbances in mood. Extreme elation or, more typically, extreme depression, dominate the patient's attitudes and thoughts. Judgment and motivation are seriously disrupted. Genetic predispositions appear to contribute to manic-depressive reactions and people with certain kinds of personality characteristics seem to be especially vulnerable to this disorder. Many patients suffering from affective psychoses recover spontaneously while others are responsive to drugs or to shock therapy.

The neuroses are characterized by intense emotional discomfort and by symptoms which the individual recognizes as maladaptive. Examples of the many types of neurotic symptoms are amnesia, loss of sensory or motor function (without organic basis), phobias, and obsessive recurrent thoughts and compulsive repetitive actions. People who do not have neurotic symptoms may have personality disorders; that is, personality style and character structure that reflect emotional disturbance. Included are antisocial personalities who lack a sense of responsibility or morality, drug addicts, and alcoholics.

The therapeutic approaches used in the treatment of the neuroses and the personality disorders are closely linked to the personality theories described in the first chapter of this section. Psychoanalytic therapy is directed toward uncovering early childhood conflicts and helping the patient, through interpretation of his resistances, to achieve insight into the unconscious motivations responsible for his symptoms. In client-centered therapy, in comparison, the patient is the active participant and the therapist offers little or no interpretation. Instead, he is accepting and empathic as he tries to clarify the client's feelings. The techniques of behavior modification are based on learning theory and rely on various types of conditioning procedures. They appear to be quite effective in eliminating specific neurotic symptoms and maladaptive behavior. More recently, a number of group therapeutic approaches, such as sensitivity and encounter groups, have become popular. These are intended to enhance self-actualization among normal participants by encouraging the recognition and open expression of feeling.

RECOMMENDED READING

American Psychological Association. Special Issue: Testing and Public Policy. *American Psychologist*, 1965, *20*, 857–93.
This publication provides a thought-provoking discussion of the issues involved in the practical application of tests and provides a guide to their proper use.

Cronbach, L. J. *Essentials of Psychological Testing.* (3rd ed.) New York: Harper & Row, 1970.
This excellent text reviews the principles underlying psychological testing and also the major psychological tests.

Dollard, J., & Miller, N. E. *Personality and Psychotherapy.* Paperback. New York: McGraw-Hill, 1950.
Demonstrates the application of Hullian learning principles to complex human behaviors.

Erikson, E. H. *Childhood and Society.* New York: Norton, 1950.
Erikson's earliest volume, considered by many to be one of the most important contributions to psychoanalytic theory.

Feshbach, S. "Dynamics and Morality of Violence and Aggression: Some Psychological Considerations." *American Psychologist*, 1971, *26*, 281–92.
This paper provides a theoretical analysis of aggressive behavior, summarizes some pertinent experimental data, and, on the basis of theory and data, draws some inferences regarding the evaluation of various manifestations of violence in contemporary life.

Freud, A. *The Ego and the Mechanisms of Defense.* New York: International Universities Press, 1946.
This volume by Anna Freud extends psychoanalytic theory and offers a detailed and interesting account of the sundry psychological mechanisms people use to avoid shame, fear, guilt, and conflict.

Hall, C. S., & Lindsey, G. *Theories of Personality.* New York: Wiley & Sons, 1970.
This standard text provides excellent summaries of the views of the leading personality theorists.

Hilgard, E. R. "Human Motives and the Concept of the Self." *American Psychologist*, 1949, *4*, 374–82.

This paper by an eminent experimental psychologist offers an important rationale for an examination of the self-concept as a basis for understanding human motivation.

Hollingshead, A. B., & Redlick, F. C. *Social Class and Mental Illness: A Community Study.* New York: Wiley, 1958.
Includes some provocative data regarding the relationship between psychiatric diagnosis and the patient's income level.

McClelland, D. C. *The Achieving Society.* Princeton: Van Nostrand, 1961.
This interesting study indicates how projective measures of motivation can be fruitfully applied to the study of complex social phenomena.

Monroe, Ruth. *Schools of Psychoanalytic Thought.* New York: Holt, 1955.
Offers a detailed, comprehensive summary of psychoanalytic concepts and theories; it also traces the changes and developments in psychoanalytic theories.

Rogers, C. R. *Client-Centered Therapy.* Boston: Houghton Mifflin, 1951.
A readable presentation of the nondirective psychotherapeutic approach initiated by Rogers.

Watts, Alan. *Psychotherapy: East and West.* Ballantine Press, 1969.
While the title suggests that the book is limited to psychotherapy, it provides an interesting and readable comparison of Eastern and Western conceptions of man.

Zilboorg, G., & Henry, G. W. *A History of Medical Psychology.* New York: Norton, 1941.
The authors present a thorough and well-written overview of the history of conceptions of mental illness and the changes that have taken place in the treatment of mental illness.

Zubin, J., Eron, L. D., & Schumer, F. *An Experimental Approach to Projective Techniques.* New York: Wiley, 1965.
An excellent reference for the student who wants to find out more about the validity of various projective techniques.

SECTION FOUR

DEVELOPMENTAL PSYCHOLOGY

By Paul Mussen

Preview

To help students acquire some feeling for young children, I frequently ask them to make observations in a nursery school and to record and interpret the behavior of one or two children. One of my students made his observations in a large sunny, well-equipped playroom in a nursery school where sixteen four-year-olds were playing. Here is his account of a brief interaction between two boys.

In a sandbox in one corner, Jimmy and Ollie are busily engaged in a game of Cowboys and Indians, using small plastic toys. A new teacher approaches the corner. Jimmy, the taller of the two, a good-looking, blond, blue-eyed boy, smiles brightly at her and greets her with a loud "Hi." Ollie, a shorter, dark-haired, dark-eyed boy, looks up shyly and tentatively, says nothing and quickly turns his attention again to his own activities. The teacher says, "Hello, boys," and moves on.

In his play activities, Jimmy is ebullient, moves very rapidly, jumps about, and shouts frequently and loudly as he explains the events of the game and gives his companion orders. "Get that other gun for this guy or they'll get him," he shouts.

Ollie is much more quiet, deliberate in his movements, and apparently absorbed in his awkward attempts to assemble a small plastic stagecoach. He is playing quietly and apparently contentedly, but in response to Jim's last loud command, he stands up, brushes the sand off his pants, and gets out of the sandbox. "I don't wanta play anymore. You make too much noise." He turns slowly and walks off, heading in the direction of the slide on the other side of the room.

(Richard Fauman)

(Richard Fauman)

Like the student who made the observations and wrote the report, you are undoubtedly struck with the vast differences between these two middle-class four-year-old boys—differences in their patterns of reactions, personality characteristics, interests, and motives. Take a few moments to speculate about the possible sources of these differences. You probably ask yourself questions such as these: To what extent were these boys "born different," endowed by nature—by genetic or constitutional factors—with different personality characteristics and abilities? Or can each boy's behavior and motives be attributed to what is generally called "nurture"—that is, to environmental factors, early experiences, training, and learning? Are the characteristics we observed at age four likely to be stable and enduring, or will they change?

Actually, we all ask these questions about ourselves and about others, particularly when we (or they) do things we cannot readily understand. Thinking about the human aspects of pressing social problems also leads us to consider the same kinds of issues. Why do some people become delinquents, criminals, or drug addicts? What accounts for the lack of academic motivation and the high percentage of school dropouts among children and adolescents from poverty-stricken families? Why are some people intolerant and prejudiced toward foreigners or people of other races, while others are egalitarian in their attitudes and behavior?

In a sense, we are all aware that if we want to understand people we must know something about their development and the forces that influence and shape behavior. If we know what these forces are and how they operate, we may be able to use this knowledge for socially constructive ends, for the betterment of human welfare and society.

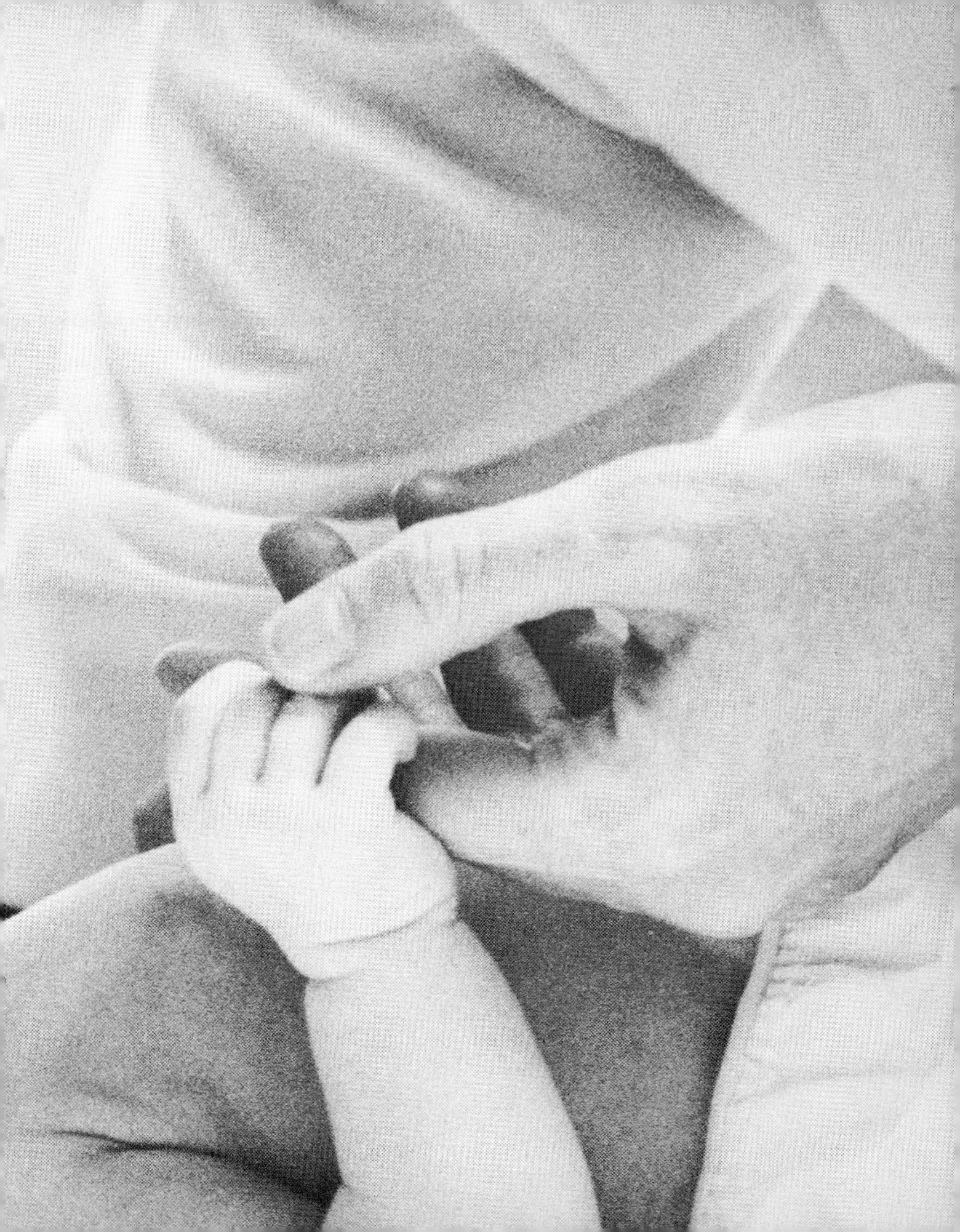

12

What Is Developmental Psychology?

How has developmental psychology developed?
Which research methods are used?
What has research yielded?

Broad general questions about "how people become what they are"—how they acquire their personality styles, motives, goals, and social behaviors—are the central concerns of the science of developmental psychology. The major objectives of the field are the *description* of age changes in behavior and psychological functions and the *explanation* of the processes accounting for these changes, i.e., the biological and environmental factors that determine them.

How has developmental psychology developed?

Although many of the problems are still unsolved, the fundamental questions about development have been asked for centuries. In the fourth century B.C., Plato suggested that individual differences in abilities and aptitudes are, at least to some degree, inborn. However, he also believed that early childhood training may have significant impacts on later motivations and occupational adjustments.

The seventeenth-century British philosopher John Locke asserted that the mind at birth was a **tabula rasa** or blank slate. The child's development and subsequent personality were shaped and molded by teaching, learning, and experience. Jean Jacques Rousseau, the French philosopher writing about a century after

Locke, had a much different view. In his opinion, the young child is a "noble savage" with an innate sense of justice and morality. The restrictions imposed by society and "the typical interventions of parents and teachers mar and distort the natural succession of the changes of childhood; the child that man raises is almost certain to be inferior to the child that nature raises."

Each of these philosophers was convinced that his conception of human development was valid and used his theory as a basis for giving advice about how to raise children. Locke, for example, told parents to begin instructing their children in self-denial from the very earliest infancy and to treat their children "as rational creatures." In the area of developmental psychology, theory and practical action have often been very closely linked.

These early philosophers did not test their theories scientifically. They speculated, but they did not conduct research. And their observations were casual rather than systematic. But beginning late in the eighteenth century, a few educators, philosophers, and biologists began to make observations and records of early growth and changes. In the next century, a number of baby biographies were published, each of them an account of the development of one child, generally the author's son or daughter, niece or nephew. One of these was by Charles Darwin who used his careful observations of his own son's development as evidence in support of his theory of human evolution.

These baby biographies were very interesting and provocative, but they were not scientific works. The writers were undoubtedly biased in their observations, lacking in objectivity, and probably selective in their perceptions, seeing what they wanted to see in the child's behavior. Furthermore, since each biographer observed only one child, it is difficult to determine whether his "conclusions" are applicable to others.

The systematic study of developmental psychology began with the work of the American psychologist G. Stanley Hall at the beginning of this century. He attempted to study "the contents of children's minds" by administering questionnaires about their feelings, attitudes, and emotions to large groups of children of different ages. From their responses he traced the changes in children's behavior and thoughts as they grew older; that is, he was able to determine *age trends* in these functions.

With the establishment of developmental psychology as a scientific discipline, investigators turned their attention to many phenomena of growth and change, and they devised more precise and objective methods for their studies. A major advance came in 1903 when the French psychologist Alfred Binet was asked by Paris school authorities to help identify mentally retarded children at an early age. To accomplish his goal, Binet constructed the first useful intelligence

Charles Darwin, left, and G. Stanley Hall, right.
(L., courtesy of the American Museum of Natural History; R., Culver Pictures)

test consisting of a series of tasks involving judgment, comprehension, and reasoning, the essential components of intelligence. These were then administered to large samples of children between the ages of three and eleven. By measuring these subjects' performances in these tests, Binet was able to derive *age norms* (average performance at particular ages). By comparing a particular child's test performance with the norms, Binet could determine whether the child was average for his age, accelerated, or retarded. (For a more complete account of intelligence testing, see Chapter 15.)

In constructing a useful intelligence test, Binet demonstrated that objective measurement (or quantification) could be applied in the investigation of complex psychological functions. This opened the door for scientific research on many other aspects of development such as perception, motor abilities, language, thinking, reasoning, and, finally, motives, emotions, conflicts, and mechanisms of adjustment. For example, by means of careful and objective studies, the exact nature and step-by-step development of motor activities such as grasping, block building, sitting, and walking have been established. Psycholinguists, interested in the psychology of language, have traced language development with a great deal of precision from the earliest utterances of crude infantile sounds to communication in complex grammatical sentences. The stages of intellectual development from the infant's earliest perceptions and reactions to adult thinking and reasoning ability have been spelled out in some detail (see particularly pp. 299–306). And while our understanding of emotional and social development is far from complete, research methods in these areas have improved, some important facts have been accumulated, and valuable insights have been achieved. These are just a few examples. The major research findings in these and other areas of developmental psychology will be discussed in detail in the next two chapters.

Which research methods are used?

Developmental psychologists differ in their approaches to research and choose the methods which in their opinion will yield the most accurate and significant information about the problem they are studying. *Observation* is the fundamental method. Some observations are made in naturalistic or "real-life" settings such as in nursery school, on the playground, or at home; this is **naturalistic observation.** Suppose a researcher was interested in the development of sympathy or altruism in children of nursery-school age. He might work with a sample of children, observing them for several short periods as they played in school and on the playground and recording all acts of helping, sharing, or expressing concern and sympathy.

Other observations can be made more precisely and in greater detail under *standardized, controlled* conditions. Suppose you want to study the early development of reactions to strangers. You could choose thirty infants—ten (five boys and five girls) at the age of thirty weeks, ten at forty weeks, and ten at sixty weeks. You could

Psychologists observe nursery-school children perform in standardized situations (left) and in free play.
(Suzanne Szasz; Van Bucher, Photo Researchers)

have the child's mother bring him into a cheerful, comfortable room, settle him in a highchair, give him some toys, and play with him for five minutes. After this time a stranger enters the room, talks briefly with the mother and, after this, the mother leaves. If the whole episode is filmed, there will be a complete objective record of the children's reactions to the entry of the stranger and to the mother's leaving. These can then be analyzed carefully, noting the frequency and amount of such behaviors as temper tantrums, crying, smiling, interest in toys, continuing play, screaming, throwing things down, and destroying objects. Comparisons of the records of children of different ages would serve as a basis for describing age trends in the development of reactions to mother-absence and to strangers.

Wherever possible, *experimental manipulation* of the relevant variables is used to discover the mechanisms underlying changes in behavior. To illustrate, suppose you want to test the hypothesis that a child is more likely to imitate your behavior if you are warm and friendly toward him rather than cold and unresponsive. You could work with two groups of nursery-school children, assigning subjects at random to each group, so that there would be no significant differences between groups in such factors as age, grade placement, sex, intelligence, socioeconomic class. You would then lead each child in one of the groups into a playroom where he is free to play with a set of attractive toys for ten minutes. While he is playing, you have a great deal of interaction with him, talking with him, expressing interest in what he is doing, showing approval and affection frequently. With each child in the other group, you behave in a much more matter-of-fact way, letting him play with the toys for ten minutes, but remaining distant and aloof, attending to some work you brought with you.

Following this interaction, you lead the subject to another room to show him how to play a fascinating but somewhat complicated game with a pinball machine. During your demonstration you could do some things that have nothing to do with the game; for example, you might drum on the table, walk around the room in a very stiff way and repeat some irrelevant phrases ("Hey, what do you think about that?"). At the end of this session, leave the child alone to play with the game. A few minutes later, bring another child into the room, introduce him, and ask the subject to show the new child how to play the game. All this time the child would be observed through a one-way screen and his imitations of your behavior would be recorded. If the hypothesis is valid, the children in the group with whom you had warm nurturant interactions would imitate more of your behavior—even the irrelevant aspects—than the other group would.

This experiment permits you to evaluate clearly and precisely the effects of warmth and nurturance on tendency to imitate.

Actually, this particular experiment has not been conducted, so we cannot be sure of what the results would be. But other similar experiments demonstrate that warmth and nurturance on the part of the model do in fact elicit more imitative behavior (Bandura & Huston, 1961; Mischel & Grusec, 1966). (See also pp. 327–328.) Naturalistic observations of imitative behavior might also yield some valuable data about these effects, but it would be difficult to measure them as accurately or objectively as you could in the experiment.

Unfortunately, there are many critical problems that cannot be studied by experimental manipulations. For example, developmental psychologists want to understand the effects of different kinds of child-rearing practices on children's personality, adjustment, and social behavior. But parent-child relationships cannot be manipulated simply for experimental purposes. Mothers and fathers can hardly be expected to handle their children harshly or permissively just so some psychologist can assess the effects of their treatment. Other methods must be utilized to investigate questions of this sort.

Parents can be interviewed about their methods of dealing with their child's problems, their use of punishment, the amount of freedom the child has, and similar matters. On the basis of the interview data, child-rearing techniques can be *rated* as permissive, authoritarian, punitive, warm, or democratic. The relationship between these child-rearing practices and the child's personality (evaluated from observations and tests) can then be examined. Unfortunately, however, the interview technique has many shortcomings. The parents may not be good observers of their own behavior, memory may be selective or distorted, and reports may be biased.

A naturalistic method, a **home visit,** is sometimes used to assess some of these variables. The specially trained home visitor goes to the child's home for a specified period, say two hours, and observes the family members in their normal interactions. These observations, recorded carefully, are the bases for rating or scoring variables such as degree of parental authoritarian control or permissiveness. Unfortunately, the presence of the home visitor may have an inhibiting effect on the behavior of the family. If the observed interactions are not natural or spontaneous, the behavior sample can hardly give an adequate or valid picture of family life.

In **structured observation** a parent and child are brought together in a standard setting and presented with a novel task or problem that requires interaction between the two. For example, a mother might be given educational materials or toys and told to teach her child how to use these. This kind of situation provides a very small sample of habitual, natural interactions and gives the researcher opportunity to observe (and rate) a variety of behavior patterns such

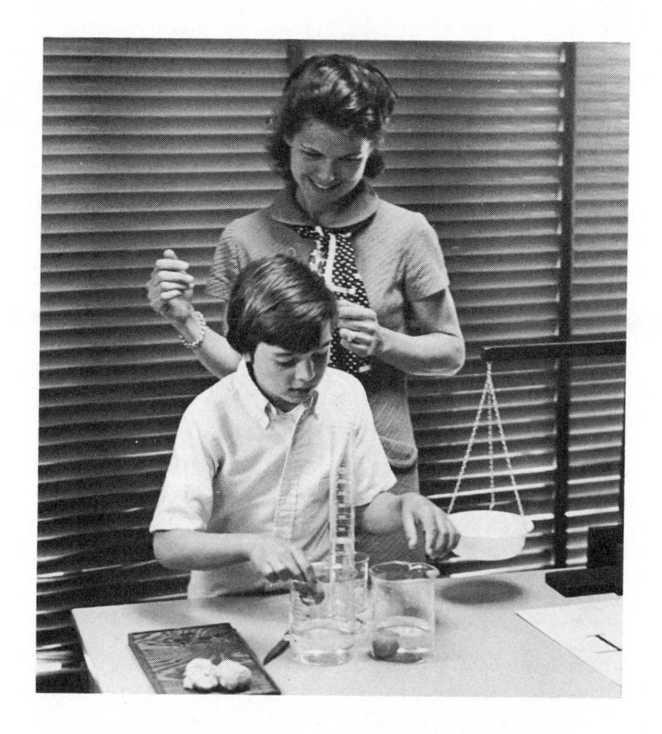

By observing a mother and her son in a structured situation, we can learn a great deal about mother-child interactions.
(Richard Fauman)

as these: the mother's directiveness in teaching, her ability to motivate the child, her use of praise and disapproval, degree of control, degree of supportiveness, methods of enforcing rules, and permissiveness in allowing the child to make and correct his own mistakes.

Longitudinal Studies

There are two basic approaches to the study of human development. In a **longitudinal study** the same children are followed up and studied over an extended period of time. They will be observed, tested, and interviewed at specified intervals; for example, every six months or every year between the ages of four and sixteen. A broad range of behaviors may be assessed: intellectual functions, personality characteristics, and social attitudes and opinions. Analysis of the results would reveal age trends in the development of these functions. But much more can be done with the longitudinal data. Longitudinal studies are needed to study the influence of early experience on later behavior, to evaluate the effects of rejection during the first few years of life on emotional adjustment during later childhood and adolescence. The study of individual trends in development requires longitudinal study. Unless the same individuals are observed and tested repeatedly at different ages, it is not possible to determine whether characteristics such as high intelligence or neurotic traits are stable and consistent, and hence predictable from earlier to later age periods. Obviously, the longitudinal method is a very useful one, but it is expensive, time-consuming, and difficult to use.

Cross-Sectional Studies

A more common research method, the **cross-sectional study,** may be contrasted with the longitudinal. The investigator selects groups of children of different ages and collects data only once. An investigator could use either the cross-sectional or longitudinal method to trace the growth of reasoning ability. If he used the cross-sectional, he might select a group of twenty children at each of six ages—four, six, eight, ten, twelve, and fourteen. Then, by comparing the average performances of the different age groups in reasoning tests, he could define age trends in this ability. If he used the longitudinal method, he would work with the *same* group of children, testing them first at age four and again at ages six, eight, ten, twelve, and fourteen.

Since the cross-sectional method is less expensive and less complicated, it is more likely to be used in this kind of study and, in fact, in most developmental research.

What has research yielded?

Complexity of Development

As you search more intensively for the explanations—for the processes underlying growth and change—you become aware of the enormous complexity of all developmental phenomena. Every aspect of development is influenced by many factors that are interrelated in intricate ways. Consider a relatively simple characteristic like height. Height is largely determined by genetic, constitutional factors. If a boy's parents are tall, he is likely to be tall. But state of health and nutrition may also have marked effects on physical growth. Early in this century, it was discovered that Japanese-Americans born and raised in the United States were taller and heavier than their Japanese-born parents and brothers and sisters reared in Japan. This difference was undoubtedly due to better nutrition and health in America. Other physical attributes such as weight and physiological reactivity (tendency to sweat and change in heart rate in response to emotional situations) are also partially determined by genetic factors. But again, nutrition, health, and psychological adjustment may be significant influences. Obesity may be a result of overeating which stems from feelings of anxiety or strong dependency needs.

The development of psychological functions is even more complicated and affected by many more factors. Intelligence, as measured by standard intelligence tests, is to some extent determined by hereditary factors—although the precise contribution of heredity to intelligence is not known (see p. 366); but your performance on intelligence tests may be very substantially influenced by your motivations, by the amount of stimulation you received in infancy, and by the quality of early mother-child interactions.

Personality characteristics are shaped and modified by innumerable forces. A child's **achievement motivation**—his desire to do well in whatever he undertakes—has been shown to be related to a wide variety of factors including sex, social class, ethnic background, position in the family, intelligence, parental encouragement of independence and competence, and many others. Among American children, high achievement motivation is more characteristic of boys than of girls, of first or only children than of later-born children, of middle-class than of lower-class children, of those of Jewish than of Italian background.

Aspects of development are interrelated, interact, and affect one another; changes in one function have repercussions on others. As the child grows in height and weight and as his intellectual capacities increase, his perceptions of himself and of the world about him are modified. These changes may be reflected in his personality characteristics—such as increased self-confidence—and in relationships with others. These, in turn, may affect later intellectual functioning and personal adjustment.

Because of the enormous complexities of developmental processes, we must be very cautious in making generalizations from research findings, especially if we want to apply these findings to particular individuals. Consider, for example, the evidence that, in American culture, democracy in the home, warmth, and understanding generally have positive effects on the child's personal development (Baldwin, 1949). These factors foster the growth of self-confidence, independence, leadership, creativity, good social adjustment, and happiness. But these effects may be significantly different in other cultures or modified under certain conditions. What would happen if the child, brought up in a democratic home and encouraged to think independently, found himself in a more authoritarian culture that stressed conformity, obedience, and suppression of individuality rather than self-expression and independence? The child's excellent adjustment, established early, might be undermined.

Or, to take another example, a boy who has acquired adequate self-confidence as a result of early treatment in his family may be very slow in maturing physically. He may therefore be regarded by others as immature, and he may begin to feel inadequate and inferior; his early-established sense of security may deteriorate markedly. On the other hand, boys who mature rapidly are more likely to have positive self-concepts and good social adjustment in adolescence—in many cases, in spite of unfavorable early relationships with their parents (Mussen & Jones, 1957). In brief, generalizations about the effects of different kinds of parent-child relationships are applicable to many cases, but not to all. In applying these generalizations to individuals, you must consider additional factors that may alter outcomes of good or poor early family interactions.

Some General Principles

In spite of the enormous complexity of developmental phenomena, and the difficulty of understanding these, some broad principles of human development have been established.

1. Development is, to a very great extent, orderly and predictable, proceeding in an unvarying sequence. The head, eyes, trunk, arms, legs, heart, lungs, genitals, and other organs of all fetuses emerge and develop in the same order and at approximately the same prenatal ages. All fetuses can turn their heads before they can extend

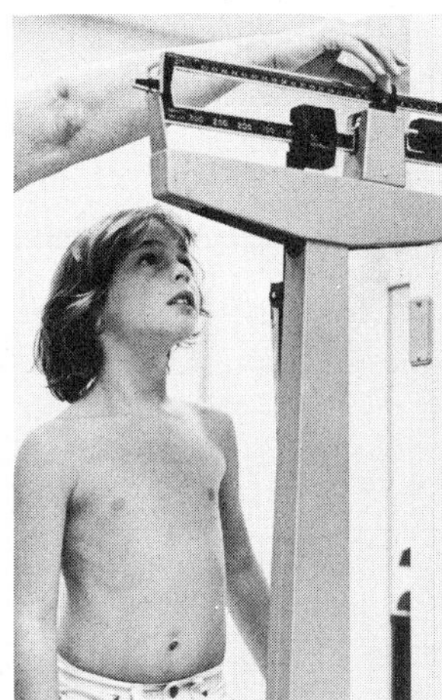

Development depends upon complex relationships between experiences and maturation.
(Left & center, Ted Polumbaum; right, Judy Polumbaum)

their hands. After birth, the baby's motor and cognitive abilities develop in regular, patterned ways. Every child lifts his head from a prone position before he sits up, sits before he stands, and stands before he walks. The successive stages of speech development are similar in all children. Babbling precedes talking and certain sounds are invariably uttered before others; for example, the aspirate *h* (as in house) occurs before consonants *n*, *l*, and *b*.

2. Although development is continuous, it is not always smooth or gradual. There are spurts in physical growth and in some psychological functions. Height and weight increase extremely rapidly during the first year and again during adolescence. The growth of the genital organs is very slow during childhood but accelerates tremendously during adolescence. Size of vocabulary rises sharply during the preschool years, and many motor skills improve markedly at the same time. The abilities to think logically, to formulate scientific hypotheses, and to solve complex problems emerge and develop quickly during adolescence.

3. The child's experiences at early stages may significantly affect his later development. The infant who lives in a very dull, unstimulating environment is likely to perform poorly in tests of intellectual functions later on. "Inadequate mothering" (too little

warmth, love, and attention) in the first year may lead to an emotional instability and maladjustment during adolescence.

4. There appear to be **critical or sensitive periods** in the development of body organs, physical attributes, cognitive functions, and personality or social characteristics. If the course of normal development is interrupted or interfered with at one of these periods, the child may suffer permanent deficiencies or malfunctions. A severe virus infection or German measles (rubella) at a certain point in a woman's pregnancy—at a critical period in the fetus's development—may produce mental defects in the infant or irremediable damage to the baby's heart, eyes, or lungs.

Erikson considers the first year of life a critical period for the development of trust in others (Erikson, 1950). (See p. 318.) If the infant does not receive sufficient gratification and love from his mother at this time—if he does not learn to trust and depend on her—he may not ever acquire a sense of trust in others. Consequently, he may have persistent difficulties in his relationships with others. As we shall see later, there is evidence to support Erikson's notion (see p. 319).

5. Two basic though complex processes are involved in all developmental changes: **experience** (learning or practice) and **maturation** (the physical, neural, physiological, and biochemical changes that take place *within* the organism as it grows older). These two processes almost always interact so it is difficult to determine the

Creeping and first steps. (M G M Documentary)

precise contributions of each of them to development. Clearly, changes in body proportions and in the structure of the nervous system in early infancy depend on maturational processes rather than on the child's experiences. But the development of motor skills and cognitive functions depends on both maturation and experience—and on the interaction between them. For example, the age at which the child first sits, or walks is largely determined by maturation rather than by experience or practice. Restrictions on practice do not ordinarily retard the onset of these skills, except in extreme cases. Some Hopi Indian infants are kept bound to cradleboards most of the time for the first three months of their lives and for part of each day after that, but they begin to walk at the same age as other children. Furthermore, you cannot teach a baby to sit or stand or walk unless he is sufficiently mature, that is, unless his muscular apparatus has ripened to a certain point. Of course, once acquired, these basic motor skills improve with experience and practice. Walking becomes better coordinated, waste movements are eliminated, and steps become longer, straighter, and more rapid.

Babies do not talk until they attain a certain level of maturity—until they are "ready" to talk—regardless of how much coaching they may be given. But the language the child acquires and his verbal facility are strongly dependent on his experiences—on what language he hears others speaking and on the encouragement and rewards he gets for talking.

SUMMARY

For many centuries, philosophers and writers speculated about problems of development—growth and change in abilities, skills, personality styles, motives, goals, and social behavior. Scientific work in the field did not begin until the beginning of the twentieth century, however, when G. Stanley Hall used questionnaires to study "the contents of children's minds" and Alfred Binet constructed the first useful intelligence test.

The major goals of scientific study of developmental psychology are the description of age changes in behavior and psychological functions and the explanation of the processes underlying these changes. A variety of methods is used in research in this field. Observations may be made in naturalistic settings such as the school, playground, or home, or under standardized, controlled conditions. Experimental techniques are employed wherever possible, but many critical problems of developmental psychology cannot be studied experimentally. For example, ethical and practical considerations would preclude the experimental study of the effects of parental neglect on the personality development of children. Structured observations, interviews, and home visits may provide data that are valuable in investigating such problems.

In longitudinal studies the same children are followed up and studied (observed and tested) over an extended time span. Cross-sectional studies involve children of different ages who are studied at only one period. In investigations of the growth of psychological functions, such as perceptual or reasoning abilities, either the cross-sectional or longitudinal method can be used. Longitudinal data are required, however, to study the relationship between the early influences and later behavior.

Almost all aspects of psychological development are influenced by many interrelated factors—genetic, constitutional, social, and familial. Development in one function is likely to have repercussions on others. Thus, as a child becomes more self-confident, his intellectual functioning is likely to improve. When considering one particular aspect of development, we must constantly be aware of the interrelatedness of all aspects of development.

While much of development is orderly and predictable, it is not always smooth and gradual. Many functions, such as language, develop very rapidly at some periods and more slowly at others. The child's experiences at one developmental stage may significantly affect later developments. All developmental changes seem to involve both experience (learning or practice) and maturation (physical, neural, and biochemical changes within the organism).

13

Growth and Cognitive Development

What do we know about physical growth?
Is there a pattern of intellectual development?
How do moral judgments evolve?
Is language acquired only through learning?

The expression "the miracle of growth" is a cliché. Yet early growth is so swift and dramatic, and the underlying processes are so poorly understood, perhaps "miracle" is the proper word after all.

To a very great extent, the infant's early growth and change are dependent on biological, maturational forces. The development of the fetus ordinarily proceeds according to a biological "program," although the mother's illness or malnutrition may adversely affect the course of development. The newborn's needs, sensory capacities, and motor abilities are not learned, and neither are most of the sensory, motor, and cognitive abilities that emerge shortly after birth. In considering the critical importance of biological forces, however, we must not lose sight of the fact that, from the very early days onward, experience and learning interact with growth and maturation in shaping behavior. As we shall see, the very young infant's contacts with his environment and the people in it, particularly his mother, influence the child's development profoundly. Even very young infants can be conditioned and can learn. And the baby is not simply a passive organism that is molded and shaped by environmental forces. Infants are *active* in learning, in processing and filtering environmental stimuli, and in adapting to the world. This is particularly clear in Piaget's observations of intellectual development, which we will discuss later in this chapter.

What do we know about physical growth?

During the first year of life, the child's body increases in size and weight at a faster rate than at any other time. On the average, boys weigh about seven pounds at birth and girls weigh slightly less. The baby's weight doubles during the first six months and almost triples in the first year. Body length—about 20 inches at birth on the average—increases over one third, to about 28 or 29 inches, by the end of the first year.

The proportions of the body also change rapidly, becoming more like the adult's. The newborn baby, or **neonate,** has a disproportionately large head and very short legs; his head makes up a fourth of his total height and is already about 60 percent as large as it will be when he is an adult. After birth the head grows less than other parts of the body, constituting about a tenth of the individual's total height in adulthood. The neonate's legs however, are only about a third of his height, but they grow a great deal, and account for about half of the adult's total height (see Figure 13-1).

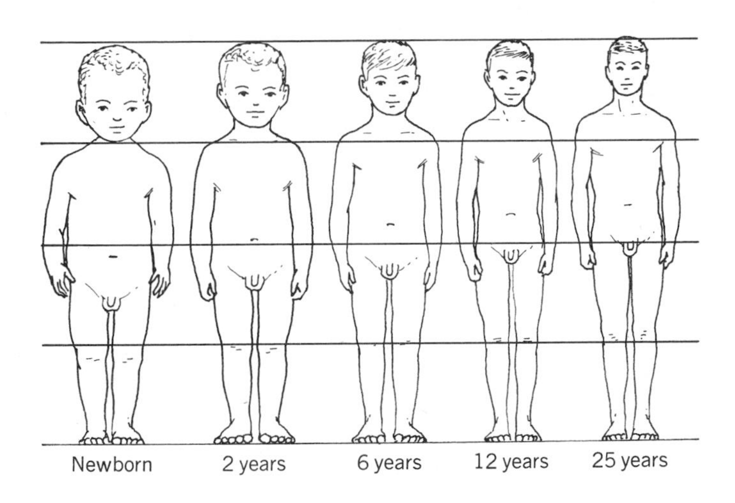

FIGURE 13-1 BODY CHANGES IN FORM AND PROPORTION

(Redrawn from Jackson, 1929, p. 118)

Natural Growth of Neonates

Some basic biological needs are present from birth—needs for oxygen, for elimination, for food and drink, for temperature regulation—and must be satisfied if the infant is to survive. It is fortunate, therefore, that he has **reflexes** that gratify some of these needs in a self-regulatory way, that is, without voluntary control or active participation by the infant or by others. Thus, reflex breathing responses provide the neonate with the oxygen he needs and reflex sphincter action takes care of his needs for elimination. Automatic physiological reactions generally keep his body at a relatively constant temperature, and chemical and physiological balances are maintained through sleep.

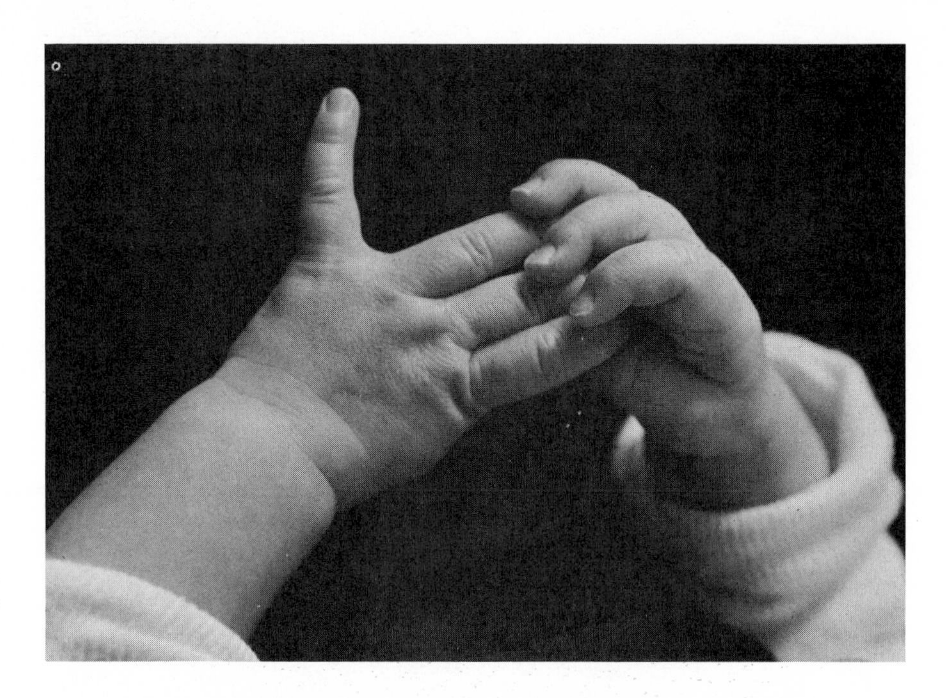

Certain reflexes and responses are characteristic of all babies.
(Wayne Miller, Magnum)

Other reflexes present from birth on—or developing very shortly afterward—also assist in the infant's survival and adjustment. For example, a newborn only two hours old will follow a moving light with his eyes; his pupils will dilate in darkness and constrict in light. He can cry, cough, turn away, vomit, lift his chin, flex his muscles, extend his limbs, smack his lips, and chew. The grasp reflex, which is strong at birth, consists of a tight closing of the hand when it is stimulated by pressure on the palm. Sudden stimulation by loud noises or other kinds of strong stimuli may elicit a "startle response," throwing the arms wide apart, throwing the head back, and extending the legs.

Hunger and thirst needs (both satisfied by milk) are not relieved by means of automatic responses alone, however. Neonates generally have well-developed sucking reflexes and will suck at a nipple or a finger inserted into the mouth. Furthermore, an "orienting reflex"—turning the head in the direction of the bottle or nipple and looking for it—appears very soon after birth. But the infant is dependent on his mother to supply milk to satisfy his hunger and thirst needs, and interactions with the mother during feeding are the infant's first social relationships. These experiences may have significant effects on later personality development, because the feelings of gratification, tension reduction, pleasure, warmth, security, and comfort that are associated with feeding become attached to the mother as a person. By generalization, these feelings may be extended to others (see p. 316).

Individual Differences

We have been discussing universal characteristics of neonates, characteristics they all share. But neonates are not all alike; there are also vast individual differences in temperament, activity level, irritability, and strength of response. These are manifested at birth and are probably determined by genetic and constitutional factors. Some infants are extremely active and restless, thrashing their arms continually, crying loudly, kicking their legs with great vigor, and sucking with great energy. Others are much more placid and quiet, move about less, nurse less vigorously, and sleep more peacefully. Some infants show a startle reaction to rather weak stimuli, such as gentle stroking or sounds or light flashes of low intensity, while others show this reaction only in response to strong stimulation. Pain sensitivity also varies from child to child, girls generally responding more readily to mild pain stimulation than boys do.

These biologically determined characteristics may have vast implications for the child's future development; they affect the child's approach to the world and to new experiences and, thus, influence what and how he learns. In addition, the way his parents and others treat the infant will depend, to some extent, on his temperamental characteristics.

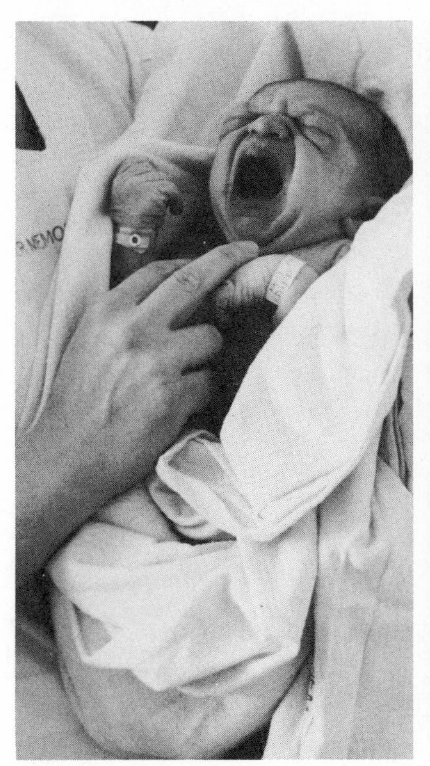

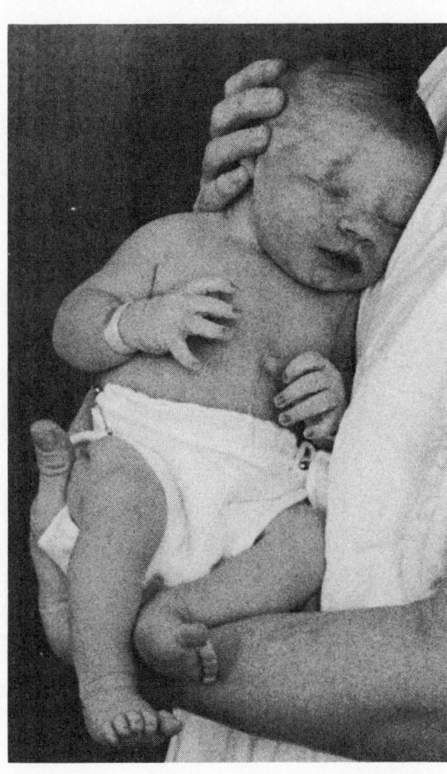

Individual differences are present from birth.
(Both, Eve Arnold, Magnum)

Sensory Development

The neonate's sensory system functions relatively well and improves very rapidly. Infants as young as fifteen days of age can discriminate differences in brightness and color. Coordination and convergence of the eyes, which are necessary for visual fixation and for depth perception, begin to develop immediately after birth and are fairly well established by seven or eight weeks. From the age of sixteen weeks onward, the infant is capable of adjusting his eyes so that he can focus on objects that are near or far, accommodating just as an adult does.

Neonates are sensitive to differences in loudness of sounds. If a tone is sounded and then made louder or softer, a neonate may respond physiologically—for example, with changes in gross body movements and in rate of heartbeat and breathing. He also reacts to differences in taste, sucking in response to sweet substances and grimacing in response to sour ones.

Not all stimuli are equally likely to attract attention. Infants are more likely to attend to, and look longest at, stimuli that move or have a great deal of contour (black edge on white background). Even a five-day-old baby sucking on a nipple is likely to stop sucking momentarily if a light begins to move in his visual field. Apparently attention to movement and contrast is unlearned. Within a very few months, however, the infant's experience begins to affect these responses. Attention becomes more selective; he attends more to familiar and meaningful stimuli than to others. When four-month-old infants are shown schematic diagrams that vary in degree of similarity to the human face (see Figure 13-2), they pay most attention to those that are like the human face and thus are most familiar (Kagan, 1970).

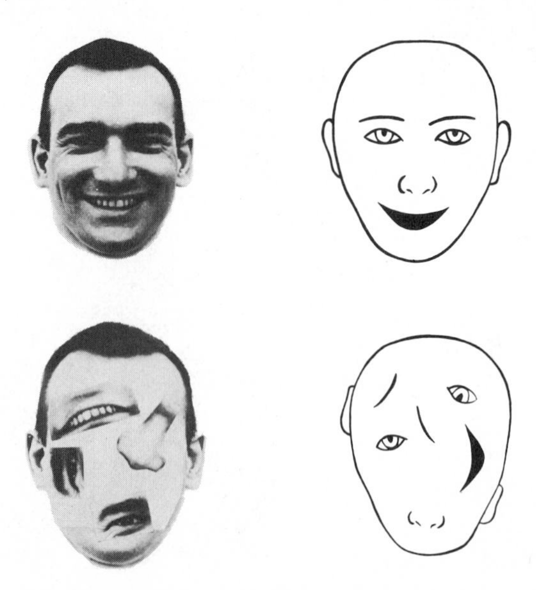

FIGURE 13-2
FACELIKE STIMULI SHOWN TO INFANTS
(From Kagan, 1970)

Motor Development During the First Year

After the neonatal period, motor skills improve at an impressive rate. In general, development follows a **cephalocaudal** or head-to-foot direction; that is, responses involving the head region develop before those of the lower parts of the body. The infant becomes capable of visual fixation before he can coordinate his arms and hands in reaching and grasping, and these skills precede standing and walking. Similarly, motor activities involving more central parts of the body generally develop before those involving the peripheral segments (the so-called **proximodistal** or outward direction of the development)—arm and forearm can be used effectively before wrists, hands, and fingers can. The infant's earliest movements are massive, diffuse, and undifferentiated but gradually become more refined, differentiated, and precise (a trend from **mass to specific**, or from *large to small* muscles).

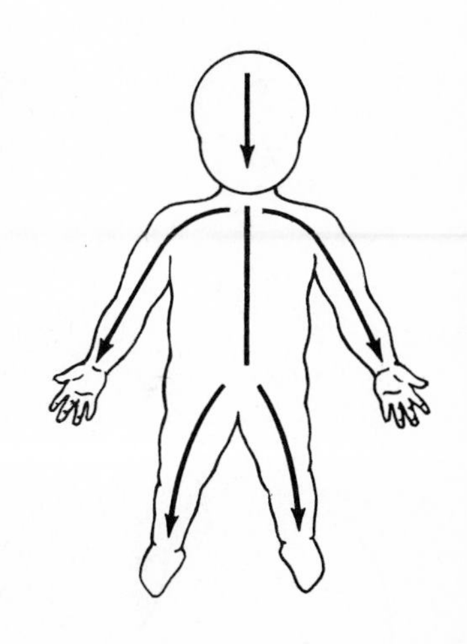

In reaching for a toy, the twenty-week-old baby moves slowly, crudely, and awkwardly, making many unnecessary movements of the shoulders, upper arms, and elbows. With further development, useless motions are eliminated; reaching becomes more direct, and the movements of the wrist, hand, and fingers become more refined and precise.

Motor skills such as grasping, manipulating objects, crawling, creeping, and walking develop in invariant sequences or stages. The stages in the development of locomotion have been carefully delineated and are illustrated in Figure 13-3, which gives the average age that children attain each stage.

Dr. Nancy Bayley of the Institute of Human Development of the University of California made extensive and detailed studies of the motor abilities of young children and devised a motor scale consisting of eighty-one items (Bayley, 1969). To standardize the scale, she administered the items to a very large representative sample of children between one and twenty months of age in the United States. Then, for every item, she determined the *norm* or age placement (average age at which children could perform the task). Some of the first-year items are presented in Table 13-1, together with the norms. The scale provides the basis for evaluating whether a particular child's progress in motor development is average, accelerated, or retarded (Bayley, 1969).

Learning in Neonates

The preceding discussion has emphasized progress in perceptual abilities and motor skills that are attributable to maturation, to processes that seem to be wired or "built into" the organism. But even very young infants can be conditioned and they do learn from experience. Several dramatic studies of infant learning have been reported recently.

In one experiment, a three-day-old newborn was directly conditioned to turn his head toward the right side in response to the sound of a bell coming from that direction. This is how it was accomplished. A bell was sounded to the right of the neonate's head. Each time he responded by turning his head in the direction of the sound, he was presented with a nipple to suck on and he received milk. If he did not respond this way during the first few trials, the experimenter touched the right corner of the infant's mouth lightly, thus eliciting head turning to the right, a reflex response to this stimulation.

In each experimental session, the sound of the bell was

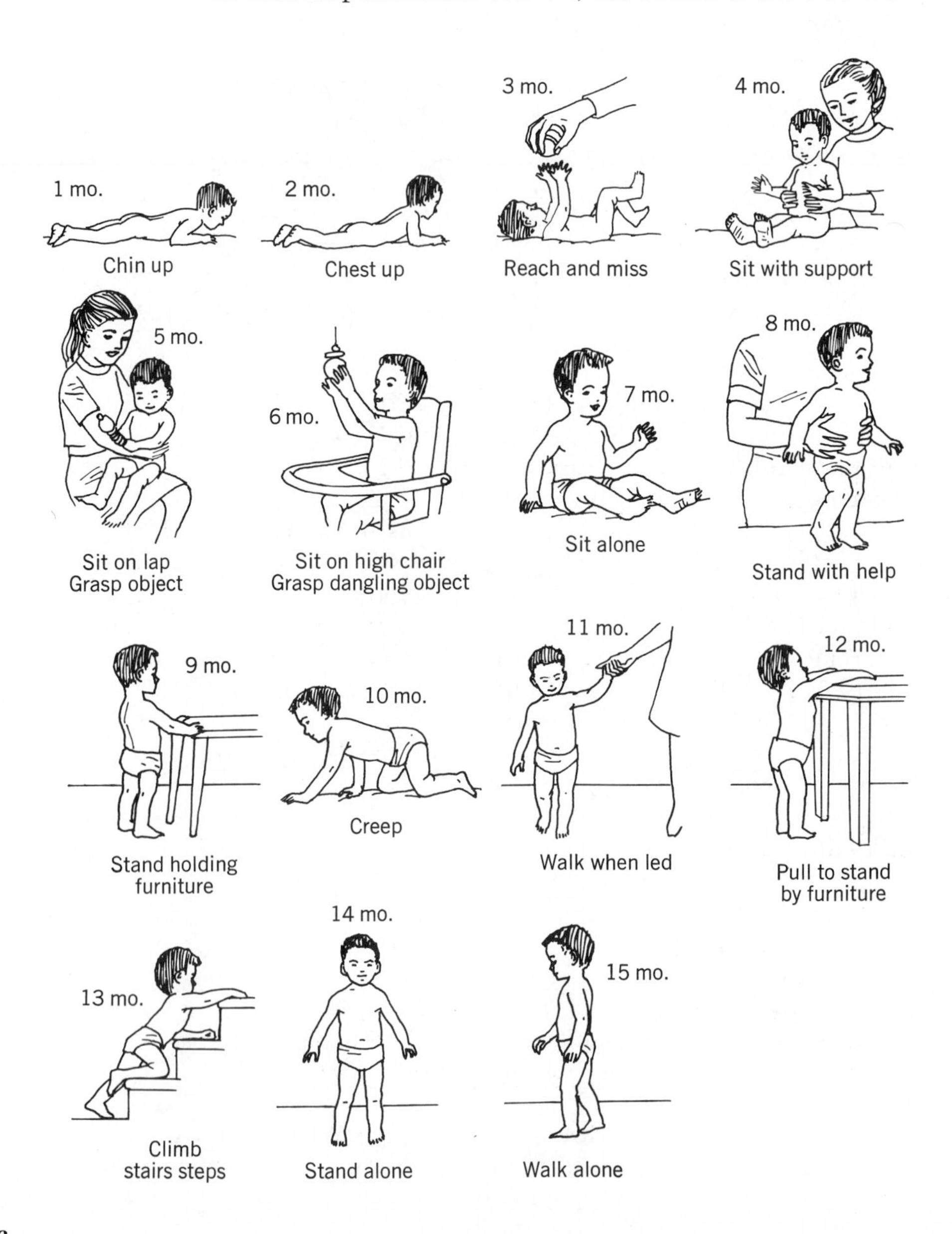

FIGURE 13-3 DEVELOPMENT OF POSTURE AND LOCOMOTION IN INFANTS
(Redrawn from Shirley, 1933)

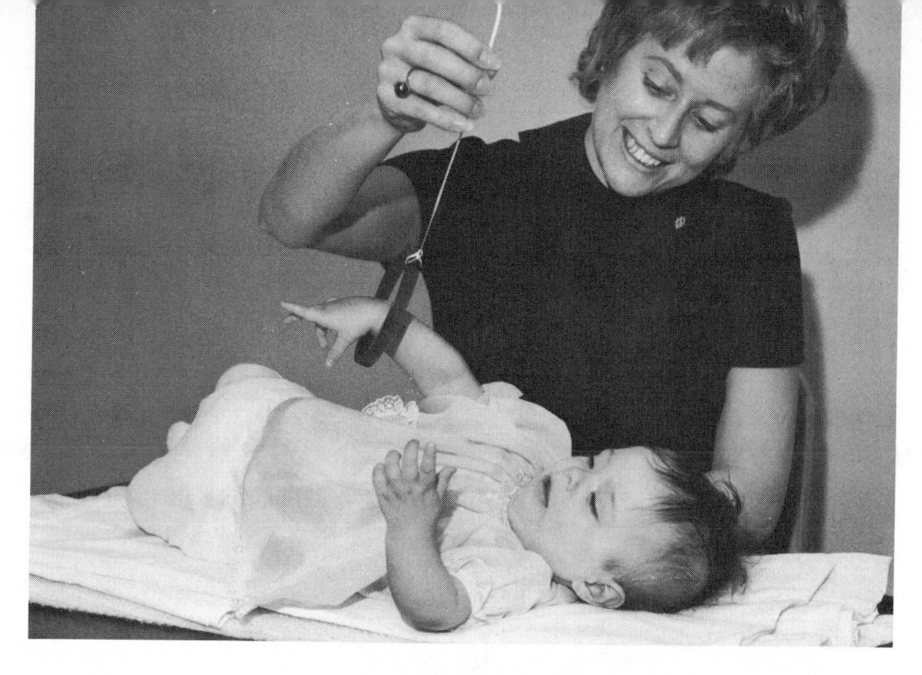

Testing to see if the baby will reach for the dangling ring is a three-month item of the Bayley Scales of Infant Development.
(Courtesy John Schutz and the Institute of Human Development, University of California, Berkeley)

paired ten times with receiving milk. During the first sessions the infant sometimes turned his head to the right when the bell sounded; sometimes he did not. However, after seventeen or eighteen such experimental sessions—a total of about 177 trials—the infant had learned to turn his head in the right direction every time the bell sounded. In other words, the neonate's head-turning response had been conditioned to the sound of the bell; an association had been formed between an external stimulus and a neonatal response (Papousek, 1967).

TABLE 13-1
SOME ITEMS FROM MOTOR SCALE OF THE BAYLEY SCALES OF INFANT DEVELOPMENT

Item	Age Placement (months)
Crawling movements	0.4
Holds head erect: vertical	0.8
Sits with support	2.3
Turns from back to side	4.4
Pulls to sitting position	5.3
Sits alone 30 seconds or more	6.0
Early stepping movements	7.4
Raises self to sitting position	8.3
Fine prehension of pellet (pincer-like movement)	8.9
Walks with help	9.6
Walks alone	11.7
Throws ball	13.3

N. Bayley. *Bayley Scales of Infant Development.* New York: Psychological Corporation, 1969.

Other experimenters have demonstrated that a three-month-old infant can learn to increase the frequency of vocalizations and smiling if these responses are reinforced (rewarded). During the experimental sessions an experimenter rewarded the infant every time the infant vocalized spontaneously. The rewards were smiling at the infant, making "tsk" sounds, or touching his abdomen lightly. After he had been rewarded, the infant's frequency of vocalizations increased over what it had been during a baseline period before the experimental treatment and reinforcement. When the experimenter stopped giving the rewards, the frequency of the infant's vocalizations decreased to the baseline level (Rheingold, Gewirtz, & Ross, 1959).

In another study, a four-month-old infant's smiles—in a sense, his first real social responses—increased after an adult rewarded him immediately for smiling. The rewards were picking him up, smiling back at him, and talking to him. When these rewards were discontinued, the frequency of the smiling response diminished significantly (extinguished) and protest responses (crying, kicking, howling) increased. Clearly, adults have a significant degree of control over the behavior of infants—both by giving rewards and by withholding them (Brackbill, 1958).

In a recent experiment, Professor Jerome Bruner and his colleagues at Harvard University's Center for Cognitive Studies demonstrated that very young infants can learn to "regulate" or to "control" reflex responses if such regulation has satisfying consequences. Specifically, they showed that infants could learn to suck at different speeds in order to produce changes in their environment. Each subject, an infant four, five, or six weeks of age, was seated in a well-padded chair with a pacifier in his mouth and placed in front of a panel of colored light bulbs. The lighting of the bulbs and play of lights (a light show) could be controlled (through an electrical system) by the infants' sucking. Amazingly, these very young infants learned to suck in longer bursts when longer sucks brought displays of lights. Or, if the conditions were reversed so that harder sucking turned off the lights, they learned to desist. Moreover, they learned to respond *immediately*—that is, during the very first experimental sessions—to these changes produced by their own acts. The speed of this learning was so striking that Bruner and his co-investigators do not believe that they are simply shaping infants' responses by rewards. Rather, they maintain that there is some kind of *inherent predisposition*—in effect, a built-in program of action in the mind—that permits babies to pick up rules extremely rapidly and to establish relationships between what they do and see.

This interpretation is far different from the one proposed by learning theorists who view the infant's behavior as being shaped and molded bit by bit by environmental events, particularly by

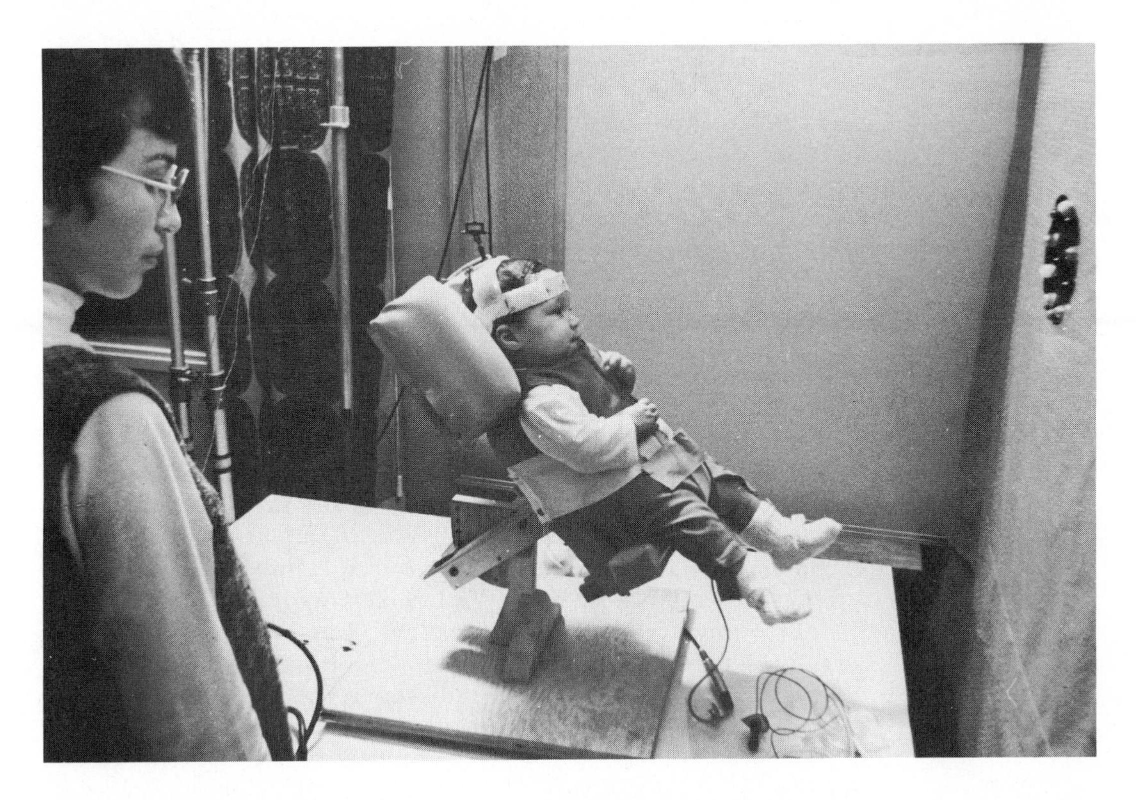

Young infants can learn to turn on a "light show" by sucking hard on a nipple connected to an electronic device.
(M G M Documentary, courtesy J. Bruner)

rewards. In Bruner's explanation, the baby's own initiative, activities, and intentions are vitally important in learning and development. In this sense, Bruner's ideas are closer to those of Piaget, whose work we will discuss next.

Is there a pattern of intellectual development?

Piaget's many years of research in the area of intellectual development have yielded a brilliant and influential theory. The theory is derived largely from his own acute observations, first of his own children during infancy—using both naturalistic and informal experimental techniques—and from extensive observations and interviews with children whom he presented with problems to solve.

Piaget views **intelligence** as the ability to adapt to the environment and to new situations, to think and act in adaptive ways. His demonstrations point up clearly the *active and creative nature of children's thinking*. From the very start, the infant is curious about his environment; he does not simply wait for events to happen; rather, he searches and seeks to be stimulated and excited. Curiosity and intellectual activity are characteristic of the child throughout his development.

Piaget's Cognitive Stages

Intellectual development is divided into four major periods or stages: the sensorimotor (birth to 2 years); preoperational (2 years to 7 years); concrete operational (7 years to 11 years); and formal operational (11 years and over). The age ranges for these stages are only approximate, and there are wide individual differences. What is important is the *regular, invariant order of succession of the stages.* There are no reversals, no "skipping" of stages. The child does not reach the stage of concrete operations without first going through the preoperational stage, for example.

This should not be interpreted to mean that Piaget believes that the sequence of cognitive stages is innately determined or that each stage evolves simply as a consequence of maturation. Nor is cognitive development viewed as the direct result of learning or environmental determination (shaping) of responses. Rather, Piaget sees cognitive development as the result of the interaction between the structure of the organism and the environment. That is, at each stage, the individual has certain organizing and structuring tendencies and these determine how the child interacts with—or "operates on" —the environment and his experiences. Clearly, experience is a necessary element in cognitive development, but it does not direct or shape this development; the individual *actively* selects, orders, organizes, and interprets experience and gives it significance. "His experiences feed back upon the present [mental] structure, and eventually, in ways that are . . . little understood, the present structure is *qualitatively* altered to become the structure of the next [more advanced] stage" (Langer, 1969, p. 100, italics ours).

Sensorimotor Period

During the first eighteen months, approximately, the child perceives and performs motor actions, but he does not have mental representations of the world or thought processes that depend on symbolic language. The development of the infant's intelligence is seen in the progress from vague awareness and simple — and often gross—reflexes to more distinct, precise perceptions of the environment and increasingly more systematic and well-organized responses. The **sensorimotor period** ends with the development of the most primitive form of representation, which Piaget calls **imagery** (Piaget, 1952).

Piaget subdivides the sensorimotor period into six developmental stages. These stages are traced and summarized in Spotlight 13-1, and each stage is illustrated by one of Piaget's own observations. From these observations, you can see that the child makes a great deal of progress in adaptation during the sensorimotor period. But even at the end of this period he can deal only with what he perceives and what he can manipulate concretely. He does not yet use symbols or psychological operations.

Cognitive abilities develop in a regular order. A child deals with the concrete before he understands the abstract.
(Suzanne Szasz)

One of the most important achievements of this period is the development of the concept of the permanence of objects. The young infant does not really have any sense of objects as distinct from himself, and when an object disappears, it no longer exists . . . for him. Observing one of his own children, Piaget noted that she would reach out for something she wanted, but when he concealed it with his hand she immediately ceased to reach. But by the time the child is about a year old he will follow the movements of a desired object and, when it disappears from view, he continues to search for it. He has achieved the concept of **object permanence,** the notion that objects continue to exist even though they are no longer immediately visible (Piaget, 1952).

Preoperational Period

With the beginnings of real language at about two years of age, the child enters the next major stage of intellectual development, the **preoperational period.** He becomes capable of imitating an absent model and of creating symbols, that is, of representing objects by images and words. In his play, a stick becomes an airplane, a basket is used as a ship. The ability to treat objects as symbolic of other objects is an essential characteristic of this stage.

SPOTLIGHT 13-1

The Sensorimotor Period

There are six stages in the sensorimotor period. The characteristics of each stage are summarized here, and each is illustrated with some of Piaget's observations of his son Laurent. Note the infant's *active* role throughout. "His curiosity does not let him wait for environmental events to happen; rather he searches them out and seeks levels of stimulation and excitation. When some environmental event occurs the infant does not register it passively, but instead interprets it. It is this interpretation, not the event itself, which affects his behavior." (Ginsburg & Opper, 1969, p. 70)

During *Stage 1*, approximately the first month of life, the neonate depends heavily on his reflexes for interaction with the environment. He exercises his reflexes actively, and as a result they rapidly become modified, elaborated, and more efficient.

Piaget observed Laurent's sucking at twelve days of age:

> As soon as his cheek comes in contact with the breast, Laurent applies himself to seeking until he finds drink. His search takes its bearings immediately from the correct side, that is to say, the side where he experienced contact. (Piaget, 1963, p. 26)

Stage 2 is that of "primary circular reflexes" (approximately one to four months). If the infant by chance behaves in a way that produces a pleasurable result, he immediately attempts to repeat this behavior. For example, the child finds that sucking his hand is enjoyable, so he begins to make active efforts to insert his hand into his mouth.

At one month and four days of age, Laurent was "not completely satisfied" after a meal and

> . . . his right hand may be seen approaching his mouth. . . . But as only the index finger was grasped, the hand fell out again. Shortly after it returned. This time the thumb was in the mouth. . . . I then remove the hand and place it near his waist. . . . After a few minutes the lips move and the hand approaches them again; . . . the hand enters the mouth, the thumb alone is retained and sucking continues. I again remove the hand. Again lip movements cease, new attempts ensue, success results. (Piaget, 1963, pp. 51–53)

During *Stage 3*, "secondary circular reactions" (approximately four to ten months), the infant begins to crawl and to manipulate objects, and he is clearly interested in the external environment. He actually reproduces interesting and enjoyable events that he initially discovered by chance. For example, Piaget arranged things so that when Laurent moved his arm a string attached to his hand shook a rattle hanging in his crib. Laurent could see it and hear it. For the first few days of the experiment the string was attached to the right arm and Laurent gradually began to swing this arm to shake the rattle. Then

> At three months, ten days, I attached a string to the left arm. . . . The first shake is given by chance: fright, curiosity, etc. Then, at once, there is coordinated circular reaction: . . . the right arm is outstretched and barely mobile while the left swings. . . . It is therefore possible to speak definitely of secondary circular reaction. (Piaget, 1963, pp. 160–61)

Laurent's behavior was clearly intentional; and, furthermore, he seemed to perceive the connection between his own actions and the results he desired. His goal, repeating the interesting events he has just experienced, motivated and directed his actions.

Further advances in cognitive ability occur in *Stage 4*, "coordination of secondary schemes" (approximately ten to twelve months), when the infant coordinates his intentions with simple problem solving. A previously learned response can be applied in order to achieve a goal. If someone shows the infant a desirable toy and then hides it behind a pillow, he will knock the pillow down to reach the toy.

At nine months, seventeen days,

> Laurent lifts a cushion in order to look for a cigar case. When the object is entirely hidden the child lifts the screen with hesitation, but when one end of the case appears Laurent removes the cushion with one hand and with the other tries to extricate the objective. The act of lifting the screen is therefore entirely separate from that of grasping the desired object and constitutes an autonomous "means," no doubt derived from earlier and analogous acts. (Piaget, 1963, p. 222)

In *Stage 5*, "tertiary circular reactions" (approximately twelve to fifteen months), the baby begins to search for novelty. He has an active sense of curiosity and invents new ways of dealing with problems. There is considerable experimentation—trial and error—in attempting to attain goals and, in this way, new means are discovered. His activities are more deliberate, constructive, and original.

> Laurent discovered in "exploring" a case of soap, the possibility of throwing this object and letting it fall. Now, what interested him at first was not the objective phenomenon of the fall—that is to say the object's trajectory—but the very act of letting go. He therefore limited himself, at the beginning, merely to reproducing the result observed fortuitously. (Piaget, 1963, p. 268)

Stage 6, achieved at approximately eighteen months, marks the real beginning of thought — acquisition of the capacity to think about objects or events that are not immediately observable and to construct "mental images." The child begins to "think out" a problem before attempting to solve it, using ideas and images to invent new ways of accomplishing goals. By "internal experimentation," a kind of mental exploration of ways and means, he considers objects in new relationships to one another.

At sixteen months of age,

> Laurent is seated before a table and I place a bread crust in front of him, out of reach. Also, to the right of the child I place a stick about 25 cm. long. At first Laurent tries to grasp the bread without paying attention to the instrument, and then he gives up. I then put the stick between him and the bread; it does not touch the objective but nevertheless carries with it an undeniable visual suggestion. Laurent again looks at the bread, without moving, looks very briefly at the stick, then suddenly grasps it and directs it toward the bread. But he grasped it toward the middle and not at one of its ends so that it is too short to attain the objective. Laurent then puts it down and resumes stretching out his hand toward the bread. Then, without spending much time on this movement, he takes up the stick again, this time at one of its ends (chance or intention?), and draws the bread to him. . . . After one or two seconds . . . he pushes the crust with real intention. (Piaget, 1963, p. 335)

As this account demonstrates, the infant makes enormous strides in cognitive ability within the first eighteen months. He progresses from an undifferentiated state in which he hardly separates himself from the environment and is capable only of reflex action to a level of a problem-solving, inventive individual who can mentally represent objects and events. These developments are gradual and continuous; transformations are not sudden.

Piaget's experiments show that the preoperational child does not understand the notion of conservation.
(The New York Times)

But preoperational thought is superficial, primitive, and confused. It is generally **egocentric;** the child has difficulty taking the point of view of another child or adult. As he sees it, the sun and the moon follow *him* around. If you ask a three-year-old child walking away from his home to show you where the house is, he is likely to point in the direction behind himself. Ask him the same question on the return journey, and he again will point behind himself. His home is conceived as being in a fixed position relative to himself.

In solving problems, the preoperational child concentrates on only a single feature of an object or event and neglects other important aspects. He does not see the relationships among various aspects of the objects or events. This is neatly demonstrated in Piaget's conservation experiments. A four-year-old is shown two identical glasses filled equally high with grape juice. After the child has agreed that there is the same amount of juice in the two glasses, the liquid from one glass is poured into a taller and thinner glass, reaching a higher level than it did in its original container. When asked to compare the amount of drink in the two glasses, the child is likely to say that the tall narrow container contains more than the other one. For him, the amount of drink is equal to its level in the container. Clearly, in this situation the child has concentrated solely on the height of the liquid in the glass. He does not consider height and width in relation to each other; he does not realize that the increase in height is compensated for by the decrease in width. His thought is dominated by his one perception, the perception of height (Inhelder & Piaget, 1958, 1959).

Period of Concrete Operations

Two or three years later, the same child, now in the **period of concrete operations,** will respond quite differently. The seven-year-old will say immediately that the amount of liquid in the tall narrow glass is exactly the same as the amount in the lower wider glass, because "nothing was added or taken away," or because "what it gained in height, it lost in width." By this time, the child has achieved the concept of **conservation,** the notion that the quantity of liquid remains unchanged in spite of changes in its appearance.

During this stage the child's thought is much more solid and flexible, and he becomes capable of logical processes or what Piaget calls "operations." For example, he is able to classify, to form groups of objects with common characteristics. The preoperational child can of course group some things together—for example, he can sort red and blue blocks into separate piles—but according to Piaget he does not think of them as "classes" in the abstract sense. In the concrete operational stage, the child has a more advanced notion of class, particularly when concrete objects are involved. He sorts objects by defining properties and understands the relationships between class and subclass. If a four-year-old child is shown ten brown beads and four white beads and asked, "Are there more brown beads or more beads?" he is likely to say, "More brown beads." The child in the stage of concrete operations understands that brown beads are a subclass of beads and he will answer as adults do, that there are more beads than brown beads (Inhelder & Piaget, 1959).

During the period of concrete operations the child also becomes capable of handling relational terms. The preoperational child does not understand such terms as longer, higher, wider; he tends to think absolutely. In Piaget's words, "He does not realize that a brother must necessarily be the brother of somebody, that an object must necessarily be to the right or left of something or that a part must necessarily be part of a whole, but tends to think of all these notions existing in themselves absolutely." If a preoperational child is given ten sticks which differ in size, and asked to arrange them in order of size, he either arranges them incorrectly or solves the problem only with a great deal of difficulty. If he succeeds, he does so by frequently rearranging his ordering, shifting sticks from one position to another. The operational child does the task easily and his ordering seems to have an overall plan or strategy. This ability to see relationships and to order things (called **serialization**) is necessary for learning and understanding arithmetic. The achievements of the operational period reflect the child's increased ability to reason in a systematic and logical way, from premise to conclusion, with the result that he can create and follow rules.

Period of Formal Operations

The most advanced stage of intellectual development, that of **formal operations,** begins at approximately age twelve and lasts through adulthood. The preadolescent begins to think in abstract terms, to reason by hypothesis, and to use adult logic. Earlier, in the stage of concrete operations, the child thinks in terms of objects, perceptions, and representations of these. Now, in the final stage of intellectual development, he can *think about thinking*, he can evaluate his own and others' ideas and thoughts. The discussions of adolescents are frequently concerned with beliefs, values, and abstractions like liberty and freedom. They are concerned with the world of thoughts and ideas which complements the world of rules, of symbols, and of objects with which they dealt at previous stages.

The ability to think in terms of logical propositions appears at this time. The adolescent can clearly follow the argument that "if A is true, then B must follow," while younger children cannot. At the stage of formal operations, the adolescent has the basic intellectual equipment of a scientist. Deductive reasoning and consideration of the full set of possibilities are cardinal features of the adolescent's thinking. In working out a problem, he will not be content, as the younger child is, with the first solution he thinks of; instead he analyzes the problem and formulates hypotheses about possible outcomes, about what *might* occur. He may develop many hypotheses and they may be complex ones because he tries to take into account all possible combinations of eventualities in an exhaustive way. He then proceeds to test his ideas, either in reality or mentally, by experiments that support some hypotheses and disprove others. In short, the adolescent becomes capable of highly abstract, objective, scientific modes of thought (Inhelder & Piaget, 1959).

How do moral judgments evolve?

Just as there are age trends in the development of thinking and reasoning, there appear to be universal and regular trends in the development of moral judgments, the cognitive aspects of morality. This has been demonstrated in studies in America and in other cultures (Swiss, Belgian, Chinese, Mexican, Israeli, Hopi, Zuñi, Sioux, Papago), conducted by Lawrence Kohlberg of Harvard University and his colleagues (Kohlberg, 1963, 1969). To test moral judgment, Kohlberg devised a series of stories that present moral dilemmas and asked subjects to react to these. Here is an example.

In Europe, a woman was near death from a special kind of cancer. There was one drug that the doctors thought might save her. It was a form *of radium that a druggist in the same town had recently discovered. The drug was expensive to make, but the druggist was charging ten times what the drug cost him to make. He paid $200 for the radium and charged $2,000 for a small dose of the drug. The sick woman's husband, Heinz, went to everyone he knew to borrow the money, but he could only get together about $1,000 which is half of what it cost. He told the druggist that his wife was dying and asked him to sell it cheaper or let him pay later. But the druggist said: "No, I discovered the drug and I'm going to make money from it." So Heinz got desperate and broke into the man's store to steal the drug for his wife. Should the husband have done that?*

It is not the content of the subject's responses that is evaluated; rather it is the thought structure or reasoning underlying his responses. (Careful analysis indicates that there are six *developmental stages of moral judgments*, grouped into three broad levels. At the *premoral* level, the child is guided by an orientation toward obedience and punishment (Stage 1) or naïve selfish satisfaction of needs (Stage 2). At the level of the morality of *conventional order*, moral judgments are based on the approval of others – what Kohlberg has called "good boy" morality (Stage 3), or reliance on authority and doing one's duty (Stage 4). At the level of *principled morality*, conformity to shared standards of rights or duties are the bases of moral judgments. Morality is viewed in terms of contractual obligations and democratically accepted law (Stage 5), or is marked by an orientation toward conscience and individual principles as directing agents (Stage 6). Spotlight 13-2 describes the levels and stages briefly and gives examples of responses illustrating each stage with a response to the story given above (Heinz's dilemma).

The sequence of development of these stages appears to be universal. Thus, in all cultures studied, most ten-year-olds give Stage 1 moral judgments, and Stage 2 responses are the next most frequent. At age thirteen, the "good-boy" Stage 3 responses predominate. American sixteen-year-olds' responses are most frequently at Stage 5, with Stage 4 responses the next most common, and Stage 1 the least frequent. Very few subjects give Stage 6 responses.

Apparently moral judgments, like other cognitive functions, evolve in a regular, predictable order. According to Kohlberg, the thought structures underlying these stages "emerge from the interaction of the child with his social environment rather than directly reflecting external structures given by the child's culture. . . . While these successive bases of a moral order do spring from the child's awareness of the external social world, they also represent active processes of organizing or ordering this world." (Kohlberg, 1969, p. 386)

We have been considering the cognitive aspects of conscience and morality. The development of moral *behavior* will be discussed in the next chapter (see p. 330).

SPOTLIGHT 13-2

Levels and Stages of Moral Development

Levels and Stages	Illustrative Responses to Story of Heinz Stealing the Drug
Level I *Moral value resides in external happenings, in bad acts, or in needs rather than in persons and standards*	
Stage 1: Obedience and punishment orientation. Egocentric deference to superior power or prestige, or a trouble-avoiding set.	It isn't really bad to take it—he did ask to pay for it first. He wouldn't do any other damage or take anything else and the drug he'd take is only worth $200, he's not really taking a $2,000 drug.
Stage 2: Naïvely egoistic orientation. Right action instrumentally satisfies the self's needs and occasionally the other's. Orientation to exchange and reciprocity.	Heinz isn't really doing any harm to the druggist, and he can always pay him back. If he doesn't want to lose his wife, he should take the drug because it's the only thing that will work.
Level II *Moral value resides in performing good or right roles, in maintaining the conventional order*	
Stage 3: Good-boy orientation. Orientation to approval and to pleasing and helping others. Conformity to stereotyped images of natural role behavior, and judgment by intentions.	Stealing is bad, but this is a bad situation. Heinz isn't doing wrong in trying to save his wife, he has no choice but to take the drug. He is only doing something that is natural for a good husband to do. You can't blame him for doing something out of love for his wife. You'd blame him if he didn't love his wife enough to save her.

Is language acquired only through learning?

As we have seen, the child's cognitive abilities take great strides forward when he acquires language. Language is generally involved in the cognitive processes of abstraction and concept formation and, in fact, in almost all higher mental processes such as thinking, planning, reasoning, remembering, judging, and solving problems. A fuller discussion of the relationship between language and cognition appears in Chapter 16.

A major part of the child's learning—at home, in the neighborhood, in school, and from the mass media—depends on

Stage 4: Orientation toward authority and maintaining social order. Orientation to "doing duty" and to showing respect for authority.	The druggist is leading a wrong kind of life if he just lets somebody die. You can't let somebody die like that, so it's Heinz's duty to save her. But Heinz can't just go around breaking laws and let it go at that—he must pay the druggist back and he must take his punishment for stealing.

Level III *Moral value resides in conformity by the self to shared or sharable standards, rights, or duties*

Stage 5: Contractual legalistic orientation. Recognition of an arbitrary element in rules or expectations. Duty defined in terms of contract, general avoidance of violation of the will or rights and welfare of others.	Before you say stealing is wrong, you've got to really think about this whole situation. Of course, the laws are quite clear about breaking into a store. And, even worse, Heinz would know there were no legal grounds for his actions. Yet, I can see why it would be reasonable for anybody in this kind of situation to steal the drug.
Stage 6: Conscience or principled orientation. Orientation to principles of choice, involving appeal to logical universality and consistency, to conscience as a directing agent, and to mutual respect and trust.	Where the choice must be made between disobeying a law and saving a human life, the higher principle of preserving life makes it morally right—not just understandable—to steal the drug.

Adapted from:

L. Kohlberg. "Moral and Religious Education and the Public Schools: A Developmental View." In T. Sizer (Ed.), *Religion and Public Education.* Boston: Houghton Mifflin, 1967.

J. Rest. "Level of Moral Development as a Determinant of Preference and Comprehension of Moral Judgments Made by Others." Symposium: Recent Research in Moral Development. Society for Research in Child Development, March 1969, Santa Monica, California.

language. So does practically all social communication. For these reasons, it would be difficult to overestimate the importance of language in the child's intellectual development.

The process of language acquisition is not yet fully understood. Clearly, environmental conditions and learning make powerful impacts. Babies learn to speak the language they hear around them. Some parents stimulate language development more than others do. However, most **psycholinguists** (psychologists interested in psychological aspects of language and its development) feel that learning cannot fully explain the amazingly rapid development of the child's comprehension and use of language, particularly

The babbling of babies, which becomes refined into language, is not the result of learning.
(Ted Polumbaum)

his early mastery of grammar. Babies begin very early to generate—to invent and construct—*new* sentences (or phrases that serve as sentences) that they have not heard previously and could not have learned by imitation.

Maturational processes loom large in early language development. Deaf babies utter the same elementary speech sounds (phonemes), and at about the same time, as children who hear normally. Babies coo and babble (repeat the same sound over again like "ma-ma-ma") from about the third month until about the end of the first year, apparently just for their own amusement. Imitation of adult speech does not generally begin until after approximately nine months, but new sounds are not learned by imitation. The baby imitates only those sounds that he has already uttered spontaneously.

In language development, comprehension precedes performance. At about ten months of age, the average baby will respond to simple commands, but the average baby does not speak his first word—generally a single or duplicated syllable (ma-ma)—until some time around the end of the first year. A single "word" may function as a whole sentence; "ma-ma" may mean "where is mamma" or "I want mamma."

Marked individual differences in every aspect of speech development—in frequency and variety of speech sounds emitted, duration of the babbling period, and vocabulary development—are apparent from earliest infancy onward. These are undoubtedly attributable in part to variations in rates of maturation, but environmental stimulation plays an important role. Orphan infants, living in unstimulating institutional environments, make fewer and less varied sounds than infants living in families where they get more attention and stimulation. And, as we noted earlier (p. 298), if an infant is rewarded for vocalizing, his rate of vocalization will increase. Infants between the age of six months and a year in middle-class families produce more frequent sounds and a greater variety of sounds than laboring-class babies, presumably because middle-class parents are more likely to reward and encourage their vocalizations (Irwin, 1948).

The young child's effective vocabulary (words spoken or understood) increases at a tremendous rate after the first year. The average one-year-old has an effective vocabulary of 3 words; by fifteen months the average is 19; by eighteen months, 22; by twenty-one months, 118; by two years, 272; by three years, 896. For the next two years, he adds about fifty new words each month, so that by the age of five, the average child has over 2,000 words in his vocabulary (Smith, 1926). (See Figure 13-4.)

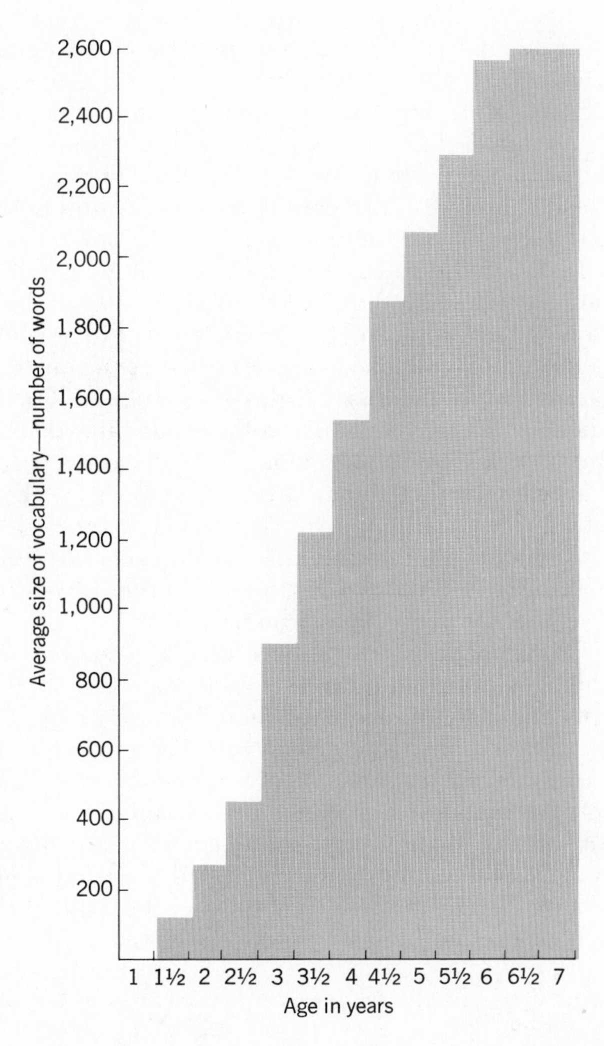

FIGURE 13-4
AVERAGE VOCABULARY SIZE OF TEN SAMPLES AT VARIOUS AGES
(From Smith, 1926)

The most impressive linguistic accomplishments—and the most difficult to explain—are the early mastery of syntax or grammar and, related to this, the young child's ability to create new sentences. At approximately eighteen months, children begin putting two words together in simple sentences. There is a kind of grammatical structure to these two-word utterances, some rules of word order. Typically, a word, called a "pivot," is singled out, fixed in a particular position, and many other words—called "open words"—are appended to it. For example, a pivot word might be the child's name, Bobby, and his first sentences might be "Bobby go," "Bobby up," "Bobby toy," "Bobby mommy," and "Bobby eat."

The development of pivotal constructions is slow at first and then becomes more rapid during the third year. The number of open words grows more rapidly than the number of pivots. While open words occur alone, pivot words do not ordinarily appear in isolation; they are always in the same position, initial or final, relative to other words. It should be noted that the child *generates* (creates) many of his two-word sequences; he has not heard them before.

As the child acquires a greater vocabulary, he puts longer strings of words together and he does this following grammatical rules. These are quite complex; yet even three- or four-year-olds master many of the fundamentals and generate complex new sentences. Listen to the speech of a four-year-old; you will be amazed at how grammatical it is. Word order is correct, plurals are formed properly, and past, present, and future tenses are expressed accurately. Of course, the child will make some errors but even these suggest that he has acquired the basic rules of grammar. For example, a nursery-school child may tell his mother that "the teacher bringed some white mouses to school today." The words "bringed" and "mouses" are not correct forms, so we can be sure that he is not imitating adult speech. But, in using these words, the child shows that he knows the rules for forming the past tense and plural. He has simply overgeneralized these rules, treating irregular words as though they were regular (Brown, 1965; Chomsky, 1967).

Systematic study shows that the speech of children between the ages of two and three is a kind of "systematic reduction of adult speech," largely accomplished by omitting such terms as articles and prepositions which carry very little information. In other words, youngsters are capable of producing many new sentences, that are not just imitations of things they have heard, and these are likely to be briefer than adults' sentences. Yet these reduced sentences reveal that the youngsters have acquired the basic grammatical structure of the language and that they understand the rules that govern the construction of new sentences (Ervin, 1964).

SUMMARY

Many of the newborn's needs, sensory capacities, and motor abilities appear to be biologically programmed or prewired. There are marked individual differences among infants in temperament, activity, and irritability.

Reflex activities gratify many needs in self-regulatory ways, helping the infant to survive and adjust to the external world. He is dependent on his mother to satisfy his hunger and thirst needs, however. The child's interactions with his mother during feeding may have significant impacts on his later personality development.

During the first few months the infant's sensory and motor abilities improve tremendously rapidly, and in fixed, invariant sequences or stages. In general, motor development follows a cephalocaudal or head-to-foot direction, and activities involve more peripheral segments (proximodistal or outward direction of development). Movements also become more refined, differentiated, and precise.

From the very earliest days onward, infants are capable of learning and conditioning. Neonates as young as three days can be conditioned to turn their heads in the direction of the sound of a bell. At four weeks of age, they can learn to "regulate" or "control" their sucking responses in order to bring about satisfying consequences. And, by twelve weeks, they can learn to smile and vocalize more frequently if they are rewarded for making these responses.

Piaget's brilliant work demonstrates that children's thinking is, from the very start, active and creative. According to his theory, intellectual ability develops in a sequence of four major periods. During the first eighteen months (approximately), the child is in the sensorimotor period, perceiving and performing motor actions but operating without thought processes or symbolic language. In the preoperational period, approximately two to seven years, symbols, images, and words are used but thought is superficial, primitive, and egocentric. During the stage of concrete operations, the child's thought becomes much more flexible and there is evidence of some logical operations—ordering things, classifying objects, and understanding the relationships between classes and subclasses. In the final stage, formal operations, which begins at approximately age twelve and continues through adulthood, the individual can think in abstract terms, reasons by hypothesis, and considers all possible outcomes in solving problems. He "thinks about thinking" and evaluates his own thought processes.

Moral judgments, the cognitive aspects of morality, also progress through a regular series of stages. Language development proceeds extremely rapidly after the first year, grammatical or syntactic rules seem to be acquired very early, and even two-year-olds have the ability to generate their own new sentences.

14

The Development of Personality and Social Behavior

What makes us what we are?
How does socialization proceed in the second year?
What effect do home atmosphere and child-rearing practices have on the nursery-school child's personality?
What is the role of peers as agents of socialization?
How stable are the personality characteristics of childhood?

What makes us what we are?

It would be difficult to overestimate the influence of social experiences in the formation of the child's personality and character. But this does not mean that biological and cognitive factors play no role in shaping personality and social development; in fact, such factors are of great significance. Consider, for example, the possible effects of temperamental differences that are determined by biological (genetic and constitutional) factors. If the infant is very responsive, vigorous, and active, he reacts readily and participates energetically in his environment. Thus he exposes himself to more different situations and learning experiences than does a less responsive and active child. And, very important, parental reactions may be determined to a large extent by the infant's characteristics. The parents may be very responsive to an energetic attentive infant, but relatively unresponsive to a quiet placid one (Thomas *et al.*, 1963).

Analogously, social experiences as varied as living with older brothers and sisters or visiting a museum may evoke different reactions depending on the child's intelligence, curiosity, and creativity. And, again, parental reactions may be influenced by the child's intelligence and cognitive ability. A parent who places a high value on intellectual achievement may be very disappointed if his offspring is of average ability and his treatment of the child may reflect this disappointment.

Agents of Socialization

Socialization is a concept of central importance in the following discussion. The term is a very broad inclusive one and refers to all the social experiences that affect the development of the individual's personality, motives, values, attitudes, opinions, standards, and beliefs. Included are all aspects of parental behavior (directed toward their child), training in school, imitation of peers, religious teaching, communication in the mass media, and major social events such as war, depression, social unrest. The **agents of socialization** are all those individuals and institutions that participate in socialization—parents, teachers, neighbors, ministers, friends, characters in stories, movies, and television (Mussen, 1967). It should also be clear that the process of socialization is not restricted to childhood; it is a lifelong process. Learning the role of "young adult," for example, is socialization, and later the role of "mature adult" demands new adjustments. Our occupational and adult family roles similarly entail socialization.

To make the concept of socialization more real, think about your *own* development and the people and events that helped shape this development. Why are you what you are today? Think about your parents—were they permissive? authoritarian? What long-lasting effects have they had on your personality? Your brothers and sisters, friends, teachers you liked or disliked, and other adult influences—how have they affected you? Now we can proceed to look at some general findings about factors affecting socialization.

Attachment and Dependency

Practically all normal infants in all cultures seek to be close to their mothers and seem most comfortable when they are with them. These responses are behavioral manifestations of attachment and dependency. Other manifestations are the baby's clear differentiation between his mother and other people, his orientation toward her, smiling at her, seeking her out and following her, and trying to make physical contact. **Separation anxiety**, marked distress when she leaves, and fear of strangers, a temporary reaction related to the child's disappointment at seeing a stranger when he expected to see his mother, are also signs of attachment and dependency.

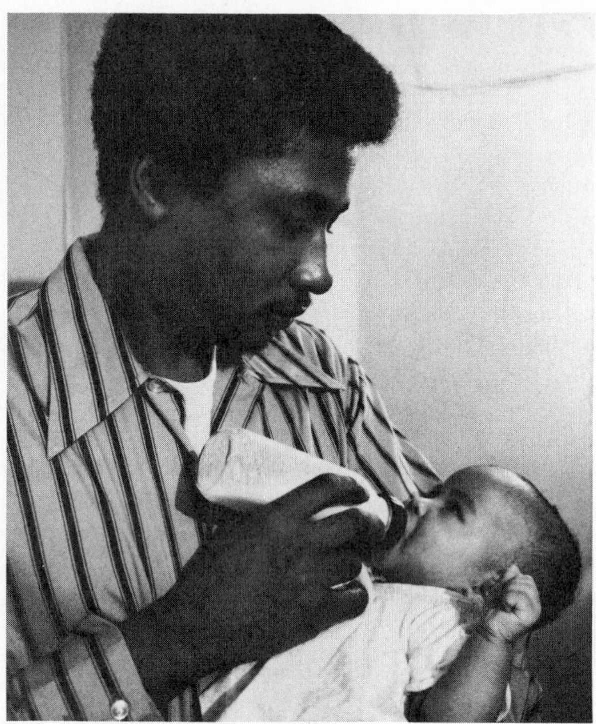

Parent-child attachment can be observed in all cultures. Is it learned or instinctual? (Georg Gerster, Rapho Guillumette; Van Bucher, Photo Researchers)

Studies in vastly different cultures—for example, in Scotland and in Uganda—show that **attachment** to the mother generally emerges clearly by six or seven months of age and becomes more intense during the next three or four months (Ainsworth, 1967; Schaffer & Emerson, 1964). There are, of course, pronounced individual differences in the age of onset of attachment behavior. One child studied in Scotland showed clear attachment by four months of age, but some infants did not manifest signs of attachment until after their first birthday.

A number of different explanations of the origin of attachment and dependency have been offered. Social learning theorists argue that these are learned or conditioned responses, the results of repeated associations between the mother's presence and gratifications and rewards such as food, warmth, and security. Consequently, the mother becomes a stimulus that signifies satisfaction, pleasure, comfort, and contentment. For this reason, the infant seeks her out, approaches her, and stays close to her.

Other theorists, influenced by ethological research (see p. 821), consider attachment and dependency to be instinctual rather than learned. In a classic series of studies, Professor Harry Harlow and his colleagues at the University of Wisconsin placed infant monkeys in cages with "mother" monkeys constructed of wire mesh

(Harlow & Zimmerman, 1959; Harlow & Harlow, 1966). Some of the infants were nursed from a bottle attached to the chest of a plain wire-mesh "mother"; others were fed from a bottle attached to a "mother" who was covered with terry cloth. When the infant monkeys were free to go to either "mother," almost all of them, including those who were always fed from the wire mother, chose the terry-cloth one and spent a great deal of time clinging to her. And almost all infants ran to the terry-cloth mother when frightened. These findings may be interpreted to mean that the clinging response, a manifestation of attachment and dependency, is instinctive rather than a product of association and learning.

Clearly, questions about the origin of attachment and dependency cannot be answered definitively, since there is some empirical support for both theoretical positions. In any case, almost all infants develop attachment to their mothers, although there are vast individual differences in the *intensity* of this attachment, and these are attributable to the infant's experiences and learning in his interactions with his mother. Some mothers are extremely responsive to their babies' expressions of dependency and attachment; others respond only to the infant's most urgent demands. Infants are likely to form strong and secure attachments to highly attentive mothers who devote a great deal of time to them and respond immediately to their

The infant monkey prefers the terry-cloth "mother," even though he nurses from a wire "mother."
(Courtesy H. F. Harlow)

cries by picking them up and taking care of them. Mothers who are less attentive and less responsive, giving only routine care, evoke only weak attachments from their infants (Schaffer & Emerson, 1964).

These maternal reactions to the infant's attachment and dependency needs may have significant enduring effects on his adjustment. Infants brought up in emotionally cold and unstimulating environments where they receive only impersonal care do not readily form attachments to others. Compared with infants who form strong attachments to their mothers, they are less healthy, less alert, less happy, and less interested in other people and in social stimuli like smiles and cooing.

If unsatisfactory mother-child relations last less than six months, and the infant subsequently experiences more gratifying interactions, his behavior and adjustments may improve considerably. Orphan infants were removed from the institution where they were handled very impersonally for the first few months of their lives and placed in a home where they received individualized, responsive care and attention. Soon they formed attachments to **surrogate** (substitute) mothers and their performances in mental tests improved dramatically (Skeels, 1966).

A very interesting, humane experiment provides further impressive evidence that early responsiveness and warm intimate "mothering" have beneficial effects on babies' behavior. A kindly lady psychologist became the "mother" of eight babies in an orphanage for eight weeks. She attended to them personally for eight hours a day, performing all the necessary functions such as bathing and diapering them, playing with them, smiling, cooing, and talking to them. Eight other infants, a control group, were handled in a routine, impersonal, although kindly way by the staff of the institution. These had very little individualized attention and interaction with adults.

After the eight-week experimental period, there were pronounced differences in the social behavior and responsiveness of the two groups of infants. The infants who were personally cared for by the mother surrogate became attached to her and were generally friendly and outgoing. They vocalized, cooed, and smiled when the experimenter-mother or strangers smiled at them or talked to them. The controls were much less sociable (Rheingold, 1956).

According to Erik Erikson, the individual's basic sense of trust—or its opposite, mistrust—has its roots in these early mother-child interactions and attachments (see also p. 188). The way the infant is fed, handled, and comforted by his mother is "a prime source for the development of trust. At around four months of age a hungry baby will grow quiet and show signs of pleasure at the sound of an approaching footstep, anticipating (trusting) that he will be held and fed. This repeated experience of being hungry, seeing food, receiving food and feeling relieved and comforted assures the baby that the world is a dependable place." (Erikson, 1953, p. 219)

The infant who has a responsive, nurturant mother seeks her out and approaches her; in Erikson's terms, he *trusts* her. This basic sense of trust then generalizes to others. But if the infant is frustrated in his relationships with his mother, if **nurturance** is lacking, he begins to mistrust her. This mistrust may generalize to others, laying the groundwork for future difficulties in forming social relationships and, in extreme cases, for withdrawal or schizophrenia.

Enduring psychological damage may result from unsatisfactory early relationships with a mother or a mother substitute. In one longitudinal study, two groups of orphans had markedly different social experiences during infancy. One group had foster parents and individualized nurturant care from very early infancy onward. The other group of children, raised in an orphanage for the first three years, were handled impersonally and without individualized mothering, although most of them were adopted later on (Goldfarb, 1943b; 1944; 1945a, b). In later childhood and adolescence, those reared in foster homes were intellectually superior and better adjusted socially and emotionally, than those who spent their first three years in an orphanage (Goldfarb, 1943b). Those from foster homes performed better on all intelligence tests, especially those involving concept formation, reasoning, and abstract thinking. Observations, tests, and interviews showed that they were more mature and more independent. They also manifested much better self-control, less aggression, less distractibility, and less hyperactivity than the institution-reared children. The latter were more dependent on adults, demanding attention and asking for help unnecessarily, lied more frequently, and had temper tantrums. As adolescents, they seemed to be distant from others, emotionally detached, withdrawn, and unresponsive. Apparently they had not, in Erikson's terms, developed a basic sense of trust.

How does socialization proceed in the second year?

As the baby becomes more intelligent and acquires more motor skills, he becomes more independent, and he wants to test out his new abilities. He is interested in exploring the world around him—investigating objects and events, walking, running, climbing, jumping, carrying, picking things up, and throwing things down. The quest for autonomy seems to be a dominant theme during the second year, when the child can get around on his own.

His earliest socialization was centered about his helplessness, dependency, and attachment. In the second year, the child begins his socialization for independence and for facing some of the demands of reality. While exercising new skills, he must learn that some objects are to be avoided, expensive lamps and dangerous

Overprotection may be a crucial factor in the child's early personality development.
(Ted Polumbaum)

electric plugs, for example. And there are some things that he is not permitted to do even if he feels capable of doing them. Also during this period the child usually acquires bowel and bladder control.

Parental Reactions to Independence

Most parents welcome the child's emerging independence and increasing maturity, but some feel threatened and discourage his explorations and initiative. Parental reactions are the child's most significant socialization experiences during the second year, and they exert profound influences on his subsequent development.

Maternal Overprotection

Overprotective mothers are easily recognized. They are generally highly affectionate, warm, and nurturant with their infants, but do not really want them to grow up or to become independent. They try to keep their children dependent upon them by "tying them to their apronstrings," never letting them out of sight, discouraging their exploration and experimentation. Overprotective mothers who are also overindulgent have offspring who are disobedient, impudent, excessively demanding, and tyrannical. These children have learned that these characteristics are very effective in manipulating their mothers; hence, they become habitual responses that are generalized to their interactions with others. In their play with peers, these children are aggressive, bossy, impolite, and "show-offs" (Levy, 1943).

In some cases maternal **overprotection** is accompanied by domination, rigid discipline, and overcontrol. Children who are treated this way soon learn to be submissive and compliant with their mothers and, by generalization, with others. They tend to be shy, withdrawn, inhibited in investigation and experimentation, afraid to initiate activities or to act independently. As you would expect, they find it difficult to establish or maintain friendly relationships with other children. Spotlight 14-1 presents a brief case history of two cases of maternal overprotection.

Independence Rewarded

Fortunately, most parents are pleased about their child's growing independence and encourage his initiative, exploration, and experimentation. Having been rewarded for such activities, their children are motivated to investigate new places and new things, to test out their developing abilities and skills, and to attempt to solve challenging problems. In brief, children of this age ordinarily begin to develop such fundamental motives as curiosity, autonomy, independence, achievement, mastery, and competence, and these motives become stronger and more salient.

A simple observational study shows how maternal rewards for curiosity and achievement may shape the child's motivation and behavior. Thirty nursery-school children were observed, first, interacting with their mothers and then playing spontaneously at home and at school. Some of the mothers praised their children lavishly or rewarded them generously whenever they did things

If the child's explorative behavior is encouraged and rewarded, she will continue to show exploration and initiative.
(Richard Fauman)

SPOTLIGHT 14-1
Maternal Overprotection

Here are two cases of overprotected boys who after a clinical evaluation received treatment. In the first case, maternal overprotection was accompanied by great indulgence; in the second, by overcontrol. Note how different the behavioral outcomes were.

Case 1
Overprotection Plus Overindulgence

An only child, male, age 10 years, 11 months, I.Q. 146; superior in all tests, including school achievement. Height 56 inches; weight 93½ pounds—10 pounds overweight.

Evidence of Overprotection

Excessive contact: The patient gets constant nagging attention from the mother, with added devotion from the grandmother in his first four years. Mother stopped numerous social contacts to devote herself to the patient.

Patient was bottle fed to the age of 21 months. He was always given his own way in infancy, if not by mother, then by grandmother; whenever refused, he always commanded obedience by screaming and throwing temper tantrums.

Mother still wants to bathe him, but he locks the bathroom door. She stays outside and gives him directions for bathing. She always gets his hat and coat for him when it is time for school in the morning; he angrily snatches it from her, but is very cross if she does not get it.

Patient's Behavior

Patient is disobedient and impudent at home. He is disobedient in regard to homework and bedtime, leaving home and coming in at will, or reading hours after bedtime, eating meals when he pleases, refusing to answer when spoken to. He is sullen and impudent to both parents, taunting, teasing, and bullying them. Persistently repeats demands for toys or money.

Patient has no chums. Although he is not barred from the group, he is unpopular. "He hangs around on the edge of the group and talks a lot." When playing, he wants to be a leader and have his own way.

Case 2
Overprotection Plus Overcontrol

The patient is 13 years, 4 months

independently, accomplished some worthwhile goal, or tried new activities. In free play situations, these children spent much of their time and energy in activities that revealed their interest in mastery, achievement, and competence (e.g., painting, making clay models, reading books). Children whose mothers did not encourage independence and initiative showed much less interest in these kinds of activities (Crandall, Preston, & Rabson, 1960).

The effects of early rewards for independence persist. A study of the determinants of achievement motivation in boys between eight and ten years of age demonstrates this. The strength of each subject's achievement motivation was measured by means of a projective personality test in which the subject told stories about situations that were described to him (for example, "Two men are standing by a machine . . . one is older"). It was assumed that if a boy's stories stress overcoming obstacles and accomplishing worth-

old, male, the second of two siblings. I.Q. 114; all tests indicate superior intelligence. Height 58.5 inches; weight 103 pounds. He is somewhat shorter and about 13 pounds heavier than the median.

Evidence of Overprotection

Mother says he was very close to her as a baby—that is, to age seven—since she never let him go out without her, not even with his father or another adult.

His schooling was delayed until he was seven, because the mother did not like him to leave her. "She has always kept him in very close range and was afraid to have him mix with other children for fear of diseases and the things he might learn from them."

Mother walks to high school with him. When father wanted to make him go to school—Grade 1—after patient pleaded not to, the mother interfered, kept him at home several days and said he was not feeling well. Mother's plan of overcoming his unhappiness in school—the present problem—is to "simply sacrifice everything and take him out of school and go with him some place where she could be with him all the time . . . and maybe next fall he would be able to come back to school."

When patient was sent to camp—at age 12, mother became anxious, visited him the second day, found his feet were wet, and took him home. Mother still prepares special food for him since he is always a fussy and finicky eater.

Patient's Behavior

The patient is timid, shy, and reserved. He never plays with other boys, lacks any social initiative or ambition, and prefers to stay home all the time. Boys call him "sissy," tease him, and take things away from him; he never fights back. He is timid and seclusive in school.

When he could not get his own way, he threatened to jump out the window. He fakes illness to keep from going to the present school. He usually whines and sulks, although he never has temper tantrums and never even used cross words with his mother.

Abstracted from David Levy, *Maternal Overprotection.* New York: Columbia University Press, 1943.

while goals, the boy himself has high achievement motivation.[1] (See also p. 285 on achievement motivation.)

The subjects' mothers were then asked questions about early independence training. Compared with mothers of low-achievement boys, mothers of high-achievement boys reported that they expected earlier self-reliance and independence from their sons and gave them more frequent and substantial rewards for independent accomplishment during their early years. Apparently early training contributed to the development of an enduring strong motive to achieve (Winterbottom, 1958).

[1] Actually, there is good evidence that this assumption is valid. Boys who show high achievement motivation in this test are highly concerned with doing well in school, and according to their teachers are more independent, more strongly motivated toward success. They are also more likely to express pride in their accomplishments than boys who score low in the achievement-motive tests.

What effect do home atmosphere and child-rearing practices have on the nursery-school child's personality?

As the child grows and makes further advances in ability and understanding, his interactions with his parents become more extensive, more complex, and more subtle. By the time the child is in nursery school, parental handling of specific needs such as hunger are less salient in determining the child's personality and behavior. But general global features of the home atmosphere and parental attitudes become more critical. We refer to qualities like warmth, protectiveness, acceptance, criticism, affectionateness, punitiveness, friction, permissiveness (or restrictiveness), democracy (or authoritarian control), firmness of discipline, and parental involvement with the child. These home and family variables significantly influence children's social behavior, personality characteristics, and attitudes, as a number of investigations demonstrate.

In one study, conducted at the Fels Institute in Yellow Springs, Ohio, subjects were carefully observed in nursery school and then rated on a wide variety of personality characteristics, such as aggression, dependency, creativity, cooperation, leadership, and originality (Baldwin, 1949; Baldwin, Kalhorn, & Breese, 1945). A home visitor visited each subject's home, saw him in interactions with his parents, and assessed the home atmosphere on thirty carefully defined scales, for example, protectiveness, affectionateness, acceptance, and severity of penalties. These home ratings fell into clusters or groups of related variables—democracy in the home, control, indulgence, restrictiveness, and activity.

Democracy vs. Control

In *democratic* homes, parents are characteristically permissive, encouraging their children's curiosity and self-expression. Family decisions and rules are generally formulated on the basis of family discussions. In contrast, homes high in *control* are restrictive and rules are formulated and communicated by the parents. There is little discussion of problems or disciplinary procedures. As you might anticipate, children from these two types of homes showed profound contrasts in personality. *Democratic homes* produced outgoing, active, competitive, original, curious, planful, self-assertive, and aggressive children. In nursery school, they tended to be leaders, participating energetically in activities, expressing themselves freely, and occasionally behaving in nonconforming ways. Children from *highly controlled* homes were conforming, socially unaggressive, well-behaved, quiet, lacking in curiosity and originality, and inhibited in self-expression.

Clearly the behavior that the children manifested in school was a generalization of the responses rewarded and learned at home. Curiosity and spontaneity, rewarded by democratic parents, were carried over into nursery school. And so were the conformity and acquiescence to parental demands, as well as suppression of curiosity and self-expression, that the children of highly controlling parents learned at home.

In another study, conducted at the University of California, nursery-school children were intensively observed and then rated on self-control, curiosity about new and exciting stimuli, self-reliance, warmth, and general mood (predominant degree of pleasure and enthusiasm) (Baumrind, 1967). Two contrasting groups of children were selected for further study—one consisting of the most mature, competent, content, and independent, and the other of the most immature, highly dependent, most lacking in self-control and self-reliance. Researchers then visited the children's homes, observed parent-child interactions in structured situations (see p. 282), and interviewed the parents. Using these data, they rated four dimensions of parent-child relationships: control, maturity demands (pressures on the child to perform at his ability level and freedom to make some decisions on his own), clarity of parent-child communication, and parental nurturance (warmth toward the child and involvement with him).

The parents of the most mature, competent children proved to be high in all four dimensions. They were effective in balancing nurturance and control, high demands and clear communications. In dealing with their children they were supportive, loving, conscientious, secure, and respectful of their children's independence. At the same time they held firm in their own positions and were explicit about the reasons for their decisions. Their attempts to control their children's behavior were integrated with teaching and reasoning. In contrast, the parents of the least mature children were low in control of their children, although they, too, were warm and nurturant. They tended to be overprotective, lax in discipline, made relatively few demands, and did little to motivate, teach, or encourage self-reliance or independence.

Although these two studies were done at different times and places, and used different research techniques, they yielded findings that are highly consistent. Parents who are warm, supportive, and nurturant and, at the same time, encourage their children's independence and responsibility promote the development of competence, interest in others, outgoingness, self-control, and self-reliance. Parental nurturance, accompanied by high degrees of control or firmness and high maturity demands (but *not* authoritarian discipline, high punitiveness, or overprotection) foster the development of maturity and competence in children.

Identification with Parents

As the previous discussion demonstrated, learning and reward can account for the child's acquisition of many personal and social qualities. But these processes cannot explain all of the characteristics and responses that the child adopts. Some of his complex behavior and patterns of response, personal characteristics, motives, and attitudes seem to emerge spontaneously, without direct training or reward, without anyone teaching them, and without the child intending to learn. A more subtle process, identification, is involved (see Mussen, 1967).

In a previous chapter on social psychology, the term "identification" was introduced to describe a process of conformity more effective than "compliance" and less than "internalization" (see p. 69). In developmental psychology, **identification** has a broader connotation. Specifically, as used here, the term will include most of the phenomena of internalization as well as those of identification. And remember also that we are speaking here of the broad developmental trends in the child, not of the formations of specific attitudes in adults.

Let me illustrate the concept of identification by telling of a recent experience. I was visiting a nursery school attended by the three-year-old son of an old friend. I had not seen the boy since he was an infant, and he did not look like his father. Nevertheless, it was very easy to pick him out of the thirty pupils. His facial and hand gestures and his way of moving were clear duplicates of his father's. He had the same slouching posture; used the same quick, deliberate steps in walking; and swung his arms in the same, somewhat stiff manner. Talking with the youngster, I discovered that he used his father's patterns of inflection when he spoke, pausing frequently between words as his father did, and using expressive gestures very much like that parent's.

It is not likely that my friend had taught his son to walk, move, and speak as he did. Nor is it likely that he rewarded the child directly for emulating his behavior and mannerisms. Nevertheless, the child adopted the responses, through identification with his father.

Identification may be regarded as a desire or motive to be like another individual. When the boy identifies with his father, he begins to think, behave, and feel as though his father's characteristics are his own. In identifying with his parent, Freud said, the child "attempts to duplicate in his own life the ideals, attitudes, and behavior of that parent." The person or group with whom the child identifies is referred to as the model or **identificand.**

Identification is a fundamental mechanism of personality development and socialization. Through identification with his parents, the child acquires many of these adults' characteristics, reactions, attitudes, emotions, feelings, and ways of thinking. He

Identification with parents is a basic mechanism of personality development.
(Nat Farbman, *Life* magazine © Time Inc.)

believes he absorbs some of their strength and adequacy; hence, he feels himself to be more secure and self-controlled.

In addition, identification with parents lays the foundation for the child's adaptation to the society in which he lives. His parents are, after all, representatives of their own culture and, by identifying with them, the child acquires the temperamental qualities and skills that are typical and approved in his culture. The American middle-class child becomes competitive and achievement-oriented; the Hopi child becomes cooperative and democratic; the Chinese child, dependent and acquiescent; Mundugumor boys in New Guinea, harsh and aggressive.

It has been hypothesized that the motivation to identify with a model is rooted in satisfactions derived from interactions with that model. That is, if a model gratifies a child's needs, he becomes associated with feelings of satisfaction, pleasure, and comfort. He is viewed as rewarding, and so are the behavior and characteristics he manifests; in learning theory terms, he as a person, his qualities and actions, acquire reward value for the child. By identifying with the model, believing that the model's characteristics and behavior are his own, the child is then able to experience the feelings of gratification that he originally associated with the model; in a sense, he becomes a source of his own rewards.

Evidence from several research studies supports this hypothesis. Children are more likely to identify with a parent and emulate his behavior if he is gratifying, warm, and easygoing. The mothers of a group of kindergarten girls were interviewed about their child-rearing practices, and on the basis of their responses, they were categorized as nurturant (warm, giving, attentive, gratifying to the child) or nonnurturant. Each mother was then asked to teach her daughter to solve some maze problems. During the teaching sessions, the mother—the model in this situation—acting on instructions, made a number of responses that had nothing to do with solving the mazes. For example, she drew her lines very slowly, hesitated at each choice point, commented before each trial ("Hmm, let's see now"), and made unnecessary marks such as loops in her tracing. The daughters of the nurturant mothers imitated many of these irrelevant incidental behaviors, while the daughters of the nonnurturant mothers copied relatively few. In other words, mothers who are warm and gratifying foster more identification—and more emulation of their behavior—than mothers lacking in these qualities (Mussen & Parker, 1965).

Freud emphasized two major products of identification with parents that are of particular relevance for later personality and social development. These are (1) *appropriate sex-typing*, the adoption of personality traits, social and emotional behavior, and attitudes considered appropriate to the individual's own sex in his own culture, and (2) *superego or conscience*, the organization of the individual's moral standards, judgments, ideals, attitudes, and values (Mussen, 1969).

Sex-Typing

Almost all cultures assign different roles to men and women, and expect the two sexes to behave differently and to manifest different personality characteristics. The definitions of masculine and feminine behavior vary from culture to culture, however, and they may change from time to time within a culture. Consider how things have changed since Victorian times when women were supposed to be dependent, submissive, and noncompetitive—and most of them were. In brief, sex differences in characteristics such as aggression, submissiveness, and dependency are determined mainly by cultural prescriptions and hence can be modified; they are not inherent in the biological structure of the two sexes, not innate or immutable (see p. 209). **Sex-typing,** then, refers simply to the acquisition of the patterns of behavior characteristics, attitudes that are *defined* as appropriate for males and females by the individual's own cultural group. Such patterns are acquired, in large part, by the child's identification with the same-sex parent.

The relationship between identification with the father and sex-typing in boys was demonstrated in a study of five-year-olds who were given a projective test of sex-role preference (Mussen & Distler, 1959, 1960). In this test the child is first presented with a

Much sex-typing is dependent upon the culture. (Marc Riboud, Magnum)

card on which is drawn a stick figure called IT, whose sex is ambiguous. The subject then is given a set of cards showing a variety of toys, objects, clothes, and activities ordinarily regarded as masculine or feminine and is asked to choose "the ones IT would like best." It is assumed that highly sex-typed boys choose more masculine toys and activities, while the less masculine boys choose more feminine ones.

The ten most masculine and the ten least masculine boys, judged from the test, were brought into a **doll-play** situation and given dolls representing a mother, a father, and a boy, together with some simple toy furniture. Each boy made up endings, in play, to a number of incomplete stories, such as this one:

The boy is having fun with his toys. Mommy and daddy say it's time to go to bed. . . . The boy says, "I don't want to go to bed." Then he throws a toy on the floor and breaks it. What happens?

In making up doll-play stories, the child reveals his own feelings about himself, his mother, and his father. Portraying the story father as nurturant, warm, tender, loving, and rewarding (or as punitive, rejecting, and hostile) indicates that he perceives his own father in these ways.

Participation in competitive games in childhood prepares the way for adult competitiveness.
(Leonard Kamsler)

The father perceptions of highly masculine boys were vastly different from those of the least masculine boys. The highly masculine saw their fathers as much more nurturant and rewarding. In addition, interviews with the boys' mothers indicated that the fathers of these boys *were* warmer, more affectionate, more interested in their sons and spent more time with them than did the fathers of boys low in masculinity (Mussen & Distler, 1959, 1960). These findings clearly support the hypothesis that masculine sex-typing in boys is based on identification with their fathers.

Conscience Development

In one important study extensive interviews with mothers of nursery-school children were the source of information about child-rearing practices and also about the children's reactions to doing "something wrong"—breaking something, hitting someone, taking something without permission (Sears, Maccoby, & Levin, 1957). The strength of the child's conscience was evaluated on the basis of the mother's reports of his reactions—confessing, feeling guilty, apologizing, trying to make reparations, lying, denying the wrongdoing. Warmth of the mother was found to be positively related to the strength of the child's conscience. Boys who had accepting fathers manifested more guilt following wrongdoing and higher levels of conscience development than boys with rejecting fathers.

Generosity is also related to identification. Nursery-school boys who were generous in an experimental situation, readily sharing prizes they had earned with other children, portrayed their fathers in doll play as warm, giving, nurturant, and loving. These kinds of father perceptions were significantly less frequent among boys who were not generous (Rutherford & Mussen, 1968).

Inadequate warmth and affection from parents may result in failure to establish strong parental identifications during early childhood, and this may have some persistent damaging effects on the child's adjustment. The child who does not acquire the characteristics, motives, attitudes, and ideals essential to adjustment and happiness in his own culture, may become, and remain, socially and emotionally insecure. A boy who does not identify with his father or with other males is not likely to adopt masculine attitudes and behaviors; he may, in fact, become effeminate and in some cases homosexual. Delinquent or criminal behavior may be a consequence of failure to identify with one's parents and to incorporate their moral and ethical standards.

Parents are generally the child's first models or identificands; as he matures, he adopts more of their characteristics. As the child's social world expands, he finds other models to identify with—peers, teachers, ministers, heroes from fiction, movies, and TV. Behavior patterns that are the products of identifications with parents may be altered and new patterns of thought and behavior may emerge as a consequence of these new identifications. Our adult personality structure is the product of a long series of identifications. In some respects we are like our parents, in other respects we are like admired peers, teachers, and even fictional characters.

Parent-Child Relations and Self-Concept

Positive, favorable **self-concepts** and feelings of self-esteem are necessary conditions for personal happiness and effective social functioning. Youngsters possessing these characteristics are active, self-confident, and independent, expressing themselves freely and spontaneously, experimenting with new ideas and activities, and approaching people and tasks with the expectation of success. In contrast, children lacking self-confidence tend to be anxious, apprehensive, inhibited about expressing their own opinions, self-conscious, and withdrawing. They feel helpless, lonely, and inferior, devaluing themselves and their accomplishments. Furthermore, their social interactions are limited, their initial school adjustments are difficult, and academic work is discouraging to them.

The roots of high and low self-esteem are found in the child's home background and relationships with parents. Tests and interviews show that the parents of self-confident children have more positive self-concepts, are stable emotionally, self-reliant, and effective in child-rearing. They hold high goals for their children, provide sound models, and are consistently supportive, accepting, and affectionate. When family plans are made, the child is typically consulted and encouraged to participate fully in discussion; his opinions and rights are clearly respected. At the same time, these parents have clearly established rules and enforce them consistently, generally using reward as a preferred way of modifying behavior.

Punishments, when invoked, are straightforward, appropriate, and perceived as justifiable by the children. In brief, parents of high self-esteem children establish a reasonable balance between protectiveness and support on the one hand and the encouragement of independence and autonomy on the other.

In contrast, mothers of children low in self-esteem tend to be emotionally distant and rather inattentive and neglectful in their treatment. Low self-esteem children tend to be either indifferent or hostile to their parents (Coopersmith, 1967).

What is the role of peers as agents of socialization?

When they enter nursery school, children begin to spend more time with other children their own age and their social interactions begin to increase in scope, complexity, and intensity. **Peers** begin to play increasingly important roles as agents of socialization, acting as rewarders and punishers of responses, and as models for imitation and identification. Consequently the young child's behavior, attitudes, and motivations may undergo significant modifications as a result of his peers' reactions. The extent of change will depend on many factors, especially the social and personality characteristics he has already acquired—his outgoingness or withdrawal from social contacts; his dependence or independence from parents; willingness to try new activities; dominance or passivity in social interactions. Popular nursery-school children are both givers and receivers of rewards more frequently than those who are disliked, so they are most likely to influence their peers and, in turn, to be influenced by them (Hartup, 1970).

Peers participate in the child's training in many ways. Responses that bring rewards from peers are likely to be repeated and thus to be strengthened. Some behaviors learned at home may bring punishment from peers—selfishness or dependency, for example—and these responses may be weakened or extinguished. In brief, peers' reactions may be an important determinant of whether the child maintains or modifies responses he established earlier at home.

Aggressive behavior is frequently rewarded by peers in nursery school—unfortunately, from some points of view. If children yield to an aggressive child's wishes, withdraw from conflict, and permit him to attain what he wants, they reward his aggressive behavior. Consequently, highly aggressive children are not likely to become less aggressive because they attend nursery school; however unaggressive children are likely to become more aggressive if they are active socially. The latter may be frequent victims of aggres-

Peers are important agents of socialization.
(Van Bucher, Photo Researchers)

sion at first, but eventually they counterattack and their aggression is likely to be successful (rewarded). Subsequently, their assertive and aggressive reactions are likely to become stronger and more frequent. Children who are unaggressive and also socially withdrawing are not likely to show significant increments in aggressive activities, because they do not counterattack and hence get no rewards for aggression (Patterson, Littman, & Bricker, 1967).

Peers serve as models whose behavior, both desirable and undesirable, is readily imitated. Kindergarten children who are at first mild-mannered are likely to become more assertive if their companions in play use force and threats to attain goals. Children readily imitate specific behavior patterns of aggression, such as striking objects, screaming, or destroying things, after they see peers making these responses (Bandura, Ross, & Ross, 1961). (See p. 12.)

Fortunately, positive social behavior can also be acquired or strengthened through contact with peer models. If they play with peers who are socially more mature, children are likely to become more cooperative, to seek common purposes and activity, and to use requests and suggestions rather than force in dealing with others (Hartup, 1970). They may also become more generous. In one experiment, children observed a very altruistic peer model sharing prizes he won for solving some simple problems. When the subjects later solved puzzles and won prizes themselves, they also generously

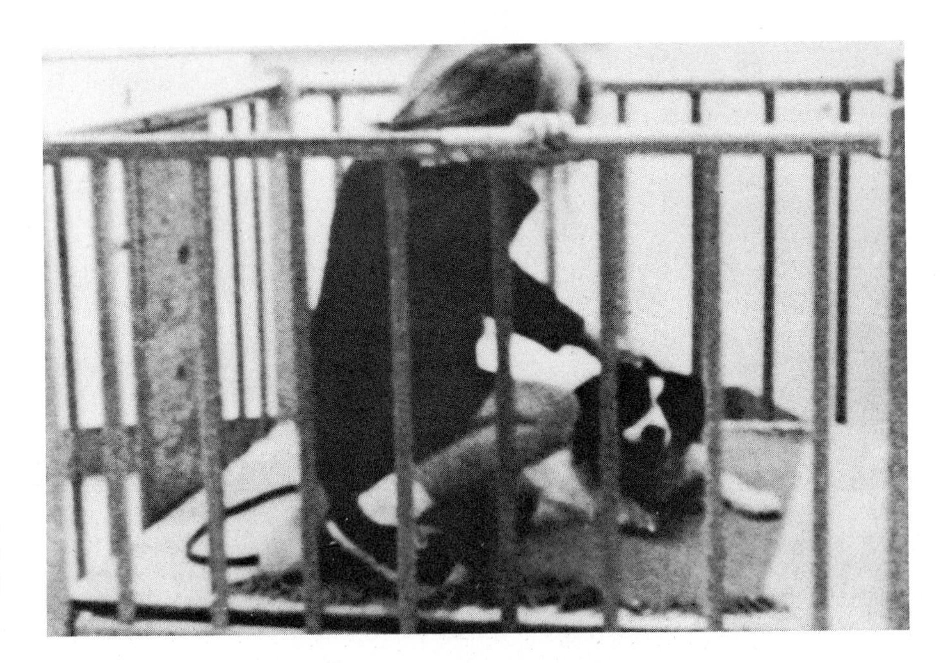

This child was able to overcome her fear of dogs by observing a peer playing freely with a dog.
(Courtesy A. Bandura)

shared their prizes with others. Control subjects who were not exposed to the model were not nearly so generous (Rosenhan & White, 1967).

By serving as models of adaptive behavior, peers can in effect serve as psychotherapists, helping to reduce a child's maladaptive responses. A group of children between three and five years of age who had excessive fears of dogs participated in eight "treatment" sessions in which they observed a four-year-old peer model playing with a dog and petting him. In each successive session, the model stayed with the dog for a longer period of time and interacted with the animal more intensively. A control group of children with equally severe fears of dogs were not exposed to the model. The day after the "treatment" series was completed, all the children were tested to determine whether they were willing to approach the animal, play with him, or climb into a playpen with him. The children who had observed the fearless model showed very little fear of the dog and approached him readily. A month later these gains were still evident and approach responses were generalized from the familiar dog to an unfamiliar one. The controls, however, remained fearful and avoided the dog (Bandura, Grusec, & Menlove, 1967).

Peers become even more influential teachers and models during the elementary school years when the child spends a great proportion of his time away from the family—a proportion that increases steadily from kindergarten through high school. Most children of school age are eager to relate to others and to become members of a peer group. If they are in an unfamiliar social setting—for example, if they have just transferred to a new school—they make strong efforts to initiate social contacts with other children.

In middle childhood the peer group provides excellent opportunities for learning many kinds of social responses the child cannot acquire as readily at home. For example, peer groups provide training in interacting with larger groups, in relating to leaders, and in leading others. Children help each other to become more confident and knowledgeable, more aware of the interests, attitudes, behavior, and skills expected of their own groups. Thus they assist the child in adapting to the broader social world.

The peer group can also provide the child with psychotherapy, and aid in achieving better personal adjustment. Peers can help the child to find new and effective ways of dealing with feelings of hostility, dominance, dependence, and independence. A child may be very much reassured—and his tensions and anxieties may be reduced—when, through discussions, he discovers that others share his problems, conflicts, and feelings.

The peer group seems to be more influential in contemporary American culture than in most other societies, or in the America of earlier times. For example in Mexico, children are much more oriented toward their families and are much less concerned with their peer group's attitudes, judgments, and behavior. On the other hand, there are societies, such as Israeli *kibbutzim* (communal settlements) and the Soviet Union, in which children are as much—or perhaps even more—concerned with peer approval as with their family's reactions.

The rapidity of social change in American society may account, in part, for this great increase in peer influence. In the children's view, parents are set in their attitudes and do not know how to swing with the changing times and the changing customs. Consequently, children are more likely to look to their peers for guidance today than they did in earlier times when social change was more gradual.

The influence of peers, particularly of close friends, is greater at adolescence than at any previous age. In our society the pressures on the adolescent, the adjustments he must make, and the problems he faces are numerous, varied, intense, and concentrated. Conflicts with parents, often rooted in contradictory emotions and feelings, are intensified—yearnings to be independent but needing to be dependent, respect for parents' standards but acceptance of peers' values. Parents may not understand these problems and conflicts, so inevitably the adolescent turns to his peers for support, approval, and security. He needs others of his own age to serve as models, teachers, therapists, and critics.

How stable are the personality characteristics of childhood?

Continuity of Childhood Traits

The study of personality development during childhood would probably not be very fruitful or meaningful if the traits displayed at that period were transient or highly subject to change. For the developmental psychologist, the question of stability or persistence of personality structure is a critical one. Empirical evidence supports the popular view that many of the personal qualities and social attitudes established by the time the child is ten are likely to be carried over into adolescence and adulthood. Studies of maladjusted adults seeking treatment in clinics and hospitals illustrate dramatically the relationship between early and later maladjustment. Emotionally disturbed adults generally have histories of intense conflicts, feelings of rejection, and inadequacy during childhood; adult maladjustment often seems to be an extension of early established maladjustment.

Within normal (nonclinic) populations, too, many personality characteristics persist from childhood into adolescence and adulthood. In one longitudinal study seventy subjects were studied from birth through adolescence. When they were young, they and their parents were interviewed and observed in their homes, in nursery school and day camps, and in elementary schools. Each of the subjects was rated on a variety of critical personality characteristics such as dependency, aggression, withdrawal, mastery, and achievement. A psychologist working independently and knowing nothing about the subjects' early development interviewed the subjects in depth when they were adults and then rated them on the same variables (Kagan & Moss, 1962).

A substantial number of characteristics were found to be stable from childhood to adolescence and adulthood. Some of these were characteristics that have been traditionally sex-typed. For example, in our culture at least, boys are generally more aggressive than girls, and girls are more dependent. And, interestingly, the longitudinal data showed that boys who were aggressive at early ages—throwing temper tantrums and displaying rage—became adolescents and adults who angered easily and were verbally aggressive when frustrated. Dependency was a more stable trait for girls than for boys. Girls who were highly dependent on others during childhood were more closely tied to their families during adolescence and, as young women, they were closer to their mothers and relied on others to help them solve their problems. A girl who achieved relative independence from her family during adolescence was likely to continue to be independent and self-sufficient.

Several other traits related to social and emotional adjustment were also carried over from earlier to later periods. The motivation to achieve, especially in the intellectual area, proved to

Personality characteristics observed in childhood carry over into later life.
(Clemens Kalischer)

be one of the most stable aspects of a child's personality. Preschool children who showed interest in mastering intellectual skills were likely to be highly motivated for achievement during school and concerned with intellectual competence in adolescence and adulthood. The child who was inhibited and apprehensive in his relationships with peers during the early school years was likely to become an adult who is tense and uncomfortable in social interactions (Kagan & Moss, 1962).

Clearly, then, many personality characteristics established early in life are stable and enduring; the child's personality is a reasonably good predictor of what he will be like as an adolescent and adult.

Adolescent Development and Adjustment

In Western societies, **adolescence** is often a period of particular stress and conflict. This is because the adolescent faces a whole host of adjustments, many of them very difficult ones, practically simultaneously. The physiological changes of adolescence—rapid body growth, sexual maturity, increases in sex hormones—often precipitate special problems and doubts related to self-concept, sexual identification, and relationships with others. At the same time, our society makes numerous demands on the individual and it is expected that these will be met within a very short period of time: achieving independence from his family; establishing satisfying, give and take relationships with his peers of both sexes; and deciding on, and preparing for, a meaningful vocation. Meanwhile, he must develop a philosophy of life, a set of moral principles and standards having some order and consistency that will guide his decisions and actions in many matters. Most basic, he must develop a **sense of identity.**

Erik Erikson speaks of the **identity crisis** as the major psychosocial problem of adolescence. The adolescent, trying to "find himself," must arrive at some satisfactory answer to the question, "Who am I?" To achieve an effective personality and basically adequate adjustment, he must regard himself as an individual—a self-consistent, integrated, unique person, worthy of the recognition of others.

The identity the adolescent seeks to clarify is who he is, what his role in society is to be. Is he a child or is he an adult? Does he have it in him to be someday a husband and father? What is he to be as a worker and an earner of money? Can he feel self-confident in spite of the fact that his race or religious or national background makes him a person some people look down upon? Overall, will he be a success or a failure? By reason of these questions adolescents are sometimes morbidly preoccupied with how they appear in the eyes of others as compared with their own conception of themselves. (Erikson, 1953, p. 215)

By adolescence the child has identified with many people, incorporating the traits of a number of different models. Now he must integrate and synthesize past identifications, dropping some, and strengthening others. Earlier identifications and past learning and experiences form the basis for the new and unique sense of **ego identity** that emerges, but "the whole has a different quality than the sum of its parts" (Erikson, 1959, p. 90). It may be defined as

the accrued confidence that one's ability to maintain inner sameness and continuity (one's ego in the psychological sense) is matched by the sameness and continuity of one's meaning for others. Thus, self-esteem . . . grows to a conviction that one is learning effective steps toward a tangible future, that one is developing a defined personality within a social reality which one understands. (Erikson, 1959, p. 89)

According to Erikson, the subjective components of a sense of ego identity are a feeling of comfort with one's own body, a sense of knowing where one is going, and "an inner assuredness of anticipated recognition from those who count." If he achieves a sense of identity, the adolescent will have some certainty about himself, feel less self-conscious, and harbor less self-doubt. The individual who fails to acquire an adequate sense of ego identity suffers **ego diffusion**; he has not found himself. He is unable to integrate his various part identities into a coherent sense of self and he is uncertain of himself and of where he is going.

Even in the best of circumstances, most adolescents experience some ego or identity diffusion. Contemporary Western culture is characterized by enormous complexity and incredibly rapid social change; the adolescent therefore encounters many different values, choices, and models. To complicate matters even further, many parents have great difficulty in understanding their adolescent children's needs and in serving as effective models or guides. This seems almost inevitable—

Because of the rapidity of the rate *of change, today's adolescents and their parents have grown up in markedly different worlds. . . . When the developmental experiences that shape our personalities, and the social changes that must be confronted, vary markedly from adults to young people, from parents to their children, generational differences [the so-called generation gap] in cultural values and outlook—even in knowledge—tend to be magnified. (Conger, 1971, p. 1106)*

While there undoubtedly *is* a generation gap between the average parent of today and his adolescent offspring, the extent of the gap may be exaggerated in the thinking of many. Adolescents may be strongly dependent on peers as models and guides at this period—and peer influences may often seem the dominant ones—but parental influences are still very significant. This is especially true if parents have established good relations with their children earlier and continue to be supportive and affectionate during adolescence.

A penetrating analysis of the recent voluminous literature on adolescence led Professor John Conger of the University of Colorado Medical School to conclude that the decline of parental influence is not so great as is often supposed. Some of his arguments are given in Spotlight 14–2.

What is right for a particular adolescent is not an easy decision. Some adolescents become scornful and hostile toward obvious faults in the "established" society—this is natural, common, and healthy—while others may look rather strenuously for faults in themselves: self-doubt and uncertainty. Others react more extremely. They may attack the whole of society as rotten and corrupt. Or they may withdraw completely into their own subjective world of drugs or schizophrenia. Or both.

Happily, for our society at least, the vast majority of adolescents respond in the less extreme fashions. Probably those who will have the greatest ultimate impact are the ones who neither accept yesterday's customs and morals blindly nor reject totally both the good and the bad in our way of life. They will be somewhat uncertain about themselves and somewhat doubtful about society's "wisdoms"; but they will be responsibly independent (Conger, 1971). If they use drugs, including alcohol, they will do so judiciously, not in a way that severely damages their problem-solving capacities. The adolescent who has achieved ego identity has a sense of his own worthiness, a sense of where he's going and where society should go, and he operates on the basis of reality, not "pipe dreams." He has confidence in his ability to differentiate between desirable and undesirable attitudes and goals, together with a generally optimistic view of his future.

SPOTLIGHT 14–2

Parental and Peer Influences—A False Dichotomy?

There is a well-worn cliché that at adolescence the young person turns away from his parents and becomes the captive of his peers. There can be little doubt that the peer group assumes increasing importance during adolescence, as dependency on the family decreases, and also that a number of recent social changes—including the decline of the extended family and neighborhood and increasing age segregation—have tended to heighten peer-group dependence (Constanzo & Shaw, 1966; Tuma & Livson, 1960). However, a number of recent studies indicate that this cliché also contains a considerable element of mythology, at least as applied to most adolescents.

In the first place, there is usually considerable overlap between parental and peer values because of commonalities in their backgrounds—social, economic, religious, educational, even geographic. Thus, for example, a white, Catholic, lower-middle class "ethnic," blue-collar adolescent's peers in one of our larger cities are likely to share more common values (e.g., educational, vocational, sexual, social, political) with his parents than with their own upper or upper-middle class WASP contemporaries (Mussen, Conger, & Kagan, 1969). In this sense, then, peers may actually serve to reinforce parental values.

Second, as has been demonstrated (Brittain, 1963, 1969; Larson, 1970), neither parental nor peer influence is monolithic. The weight given to either will depend to a significant degree on the adolescent's appraisal of its relative value in a specific situation. For example, peer influence is more likely to be predominant in such matters as tastes in music and entertainment, fashions in clothing and language, patterns of same- and opposite-sex peer interaction, and the like; while parental influence is more likely to be predominant in such areas as underlying moral and social values, and understanding of the adult world (Douven & Adelson, 1966).

It is also important to recognize that in many instances where the peer group assumes an unusually dominant role in the lives of adolescents, it is likely to be due as much or more to the *lack* of attention and concern at home, as to the inherent attractiveness of the peer group. Thus in a recently completed study of younger adolescents, it was found that those who were strongly "peer oriented" were more likely than those who were "adult oriented" to hold *negative* views of themselves and the peer group (Condry, Simon, & Bronfenbrenner, 1968).

"They also expressed a dim view of their own future. Their parents were rated as lower than those of the adult-oriented children both in the expression of affection and support, and in the exercise of discipline and control. Finally, in contrast to the adult-oriented group, the peer-oriented children report engaging in more antisocial behavior such as 'doing something illegal,' 'playing hooky,' lying, teasing other children, etc." (Bronfenbrenner, 1970).

These investigators conclude that "the peer-oriented child is more a product of parental disregard than of the attractiveness of the peer group—that he turns to his agemates less by choice than by default. The vacuum left by the withdrawal of parents and adults from the lives of children is filled with an undesired—and possibly *undesirable*—substitute of an age-segregated peer group."

Somewhat similar findings have emerged from a very recent investigation of seventh-, ninth-, and twelfth-grade boys and girls. Parental influence was greatest where "parent-adolescent affect" (i.e., the quality of the parent-child relationship, as measured by parental interest and understanding, willingness to be helpful, amount of shared family activity, etc.) was highest. Furthermore, adolescents with high parent-adolescent affect were significantly less likely than those with low affect to see a need to differentiate between the influence of their parents and their best friends (Larson, 1970; Bowerman & Kinch, 1959).

Not surprisingly, parental influence was found to be greatest at the sixth-grade level, and least at the twelfth-grade level. Interestingly, it was also found that at the seventh-grade level, the extent of parental influence was only minimally a function of the quality of the parental relationship. At later grade levels, however, where the potential impact of peer group influence had increased significantly, parent-adolescent affect assumed markedly increased importance as a determinant of parental influence. In short, a parent may be making a serious mistake if he thinks that because he can influence his children at the beginning of adolescence without concerning himself with the quality of the relationship with his children and his contributions to it, he will continue to be able to do so in middle and later adolescence.

Finally, we tend to overlook the important fact that the need for rigid conformity to *either* parents or peers varies enormously from one adolescent to another. Thus, more self-confident, more autonomous (democratically reared) adolescents may be able to profit from the views and learning experiences provided by both parents and peers, without being strongly dependent on either, or being unduly troubled by parent-peer differences. Ironically, the adolescent who has gained most confidence in his own self-image as a result of such child-rearing techniques, and who is least concerned with popularity, "and goes his own way may find that his peers flock around him as a tower of strength" (Stone & Church, 1957).

Abstracted from J. J. Conger. "A World They Never Knew: The Family and Social Change," *Daedalus*, 1971, *100*, 1105–38.

References

Brittain, C. V. "A Comparison of Rural and Urban Adolescents with Respect to Parent vs. Peer Compliance," *Adolescence*, 1969, *13*, 58–68.

Brittain, C. V. "Adolescent Choices and Parent-Peer Cross-pressures," *American Sociological Review*, 1963, *28*, 385-91.

Bowerman, C. E., & Kinch, J. W. "Changes in Family and Peer Orientations of Children Between the Fourth and Tenth Grades," *Social Forces*, 1959, *37*, 206–11.

Bronfenbrenner, U. *Two Worlds of Childhood: U.S. and U.S.S.R.* New York: Russell Sage Foundation, 1970. Pp. 101–02.

Condry, J. C., Jr., Simon, M. L., & Bronfenbrenner, U. "Characteristics of Peer- and Adult-Oriented Children." Unpublished manuscript, Department of Child Development, Cornell University, 1968.

Constanzo, P. R., & Shaw, M. E. "Conformity as a Function of Age Level," *Child Development*, 1966, *37*, 967–75.

Douvan, E. A., & Adelson, J. *The Adolescent Experience*. New York: Wiley, 1966.

Larson, L. E. "The Relative Influence of Parent-Adolescent Affect in Predicting the Salience Hierarchy Among Youth." Paper presented at the annual meetings of the National Council on Family Relations, Chicago, October 1970.

Mussen, P. H., Conger, J. J., & Kagan, J. *Child Development and Personality*. 3rd ed. New York: Harper & Row, 1969.

Stone, L. J., & Church, J. *Childhood and Adolescence: A Psychology of the Growing Person*. New York: Random House, 1957. P. 291.

Tuma, E., & Livson, N. "Family Socioeconomic Status and Adolescent Attitudes to Authority," *Child Development*, 1960, *31*, 387–99.

SUMMARY

"Socialization" is a concept that refers to the vast range of social experiences that influence the development of the individual's personality, motives, values, attitudes, opinions, and beliefs. Individuals and institutions that participate in socialization—parents, teachers, neighbors, friends, peers—are agents of socialization.

Almost all infants show attachment to their mothers during the first year. The mother's reactions to the infant's attachment and dependency have immediate and enduring effects on the child's adjustment. Warm, responsive, and intimate "mothering" fosters sociability, alertness, and positive attitudes in the child, while cold impersonal care produces only weak attachments and less interest in other people and in social interaction.

The child's socialization for independence and for facing the demands of reality begins during his second year. Parents who reward the child's growing independence and initiative stimulate the development of motives such as curiosity, autonomy, achievement, and competence.

Global features of the home atmosphere and parental attitudes—for example, democracy, control, or permissiveness—are powerful determinants of the nursery-school child's behavior and adjustment. Children from democratic homes are outgoing, active, competitive, original, and self-assertive; while those from highly controlled restrictive homes tend to be conforming, well-behaved, quiet, and lacking in curiosity and originality. Highly mature and competent nursery-school children have parents who are supportive, warm, loving, and secure, as well as firm and reasonable in their own positions.

Identification, the drive or motive to be like another person, is a fundamental mechanism of personality development and socialization. Children are motivated to identify with models with whom they have gratifying relationships. Through identification, the child acquires many of his parents' characteristics, reactions, attitudes, and ways of thinking. Two major products of identification are sex-typing (the adoption of personality traits, behavior, and attitudes appropriate to the individual's own sex, as these are defined in his culture) and conscience development.

Peers are also important agents of socialization. They act as "teachers" by rewarding (and punishing) responses and serve as models for imitation and identification. Both desirable responses, such as generosity, and undesirable behavior, such as aggression, may be acquired or strengthened by imitating peers. Peer influence seems strongest during adolescence, but parental influence continues to be highly significant at this period.

RECOMMENDED READING

Conger, J. *Adolescence and Youth: Psychological Development in a Changing World.* New York: Harper & Row, 1973.
A discussion of the major facts and theories regarding adolescence, emphasizing the problems of this period of life and the personal and social factors related to adjustment.

Flavell, J. *The Developmental Psychology of Jean Piaget.* New York: Van Nostrand, 1963.
A comprehensive, definitive account of Piaget's theory and research.

Ginzburg, H., & Opper, S. *Piaget's Theory of Intellectual Development.* Englewood Cliffs, N.J.: Prentice-Hall, 1969.
A brief introduction to Piaget's major concepts of cognitive development with rich illustrative material taken from Piaget's observations.

Goslin, D. (Ed.). *Handbook of Socialization Theory and Research.* Chicago: Rand McNally, 1969.
In-depth discussions of theories and approaches to socialization together with summaries of research in the development of personality and social behavior.

Kessen, W. *The Child.* New York: Wiley, 1965.
The history of the field of child development presented in a series of excerpts from the writings of major contributors to this field.

Langer, J. *Theories of Development.* New York: Holt, Rinehart and Winston, 1969.
A short authoritative survey of the major theories of child development.

McCandless, B. *Children: Behavior and Development.* New York: Holt, Rinehart and Winston, 1967.
A general text in child psychology emphasizing intellectual development, socialization, and school adjustment.

Mussen, P. (Ed.). *Carmichael's Manual of Child Psychology* (3rd ed.). New York: Wiley, 1970.
A comprehensive, advanced treatment of the major theories and research areas of child psychology, each chapter written by a recognized authority in his field.

Mussen, P. H., Conger, J. J., & Kagan, J. *Child Development and Personality* (3rd ed.). New York: Harper & Row, 1969.
A comprehensive textbook on child development that stresses learning, cognition, and socialization.

SECTION FIVE

COGNITIVE AND EDUCATIONAL PSYCHOLOGY

By David Elkind

Preview

Roger B. is a thirteen-year-old boy referred to family court for setting fires. The following paragraph describes the psychologist's description of his intellectual functioning:

Roger attained a verbal I.Q. of 110, a performance I.Q. of 106, and a full-scale I.Q. of 109. His performance was, however, quite uneven. He did best on tests requiring rote learning and least well on tests requiring reasoning and abstraction. He did most poorly of all on a test which presupposes sound judgment in practical situations. The picture is of a verbally facile young man who appears rather impulsive and unthinking in practical situations.

This paragraph illustrates two different related approaches to the study and assessment of human intellectual ability, namely, the quantitative and the qualitative. The *quantitative* approach, reflected in the I.Q. score, is useful since it tells immediately where the individual ranks in brightness in comparison to others his own age. In this case, the score tells us the boy is of high average intelligence, which means that we can rule out retardation as a factor in his behavior. It also suggests that he should be able to do most schoolwork without difficulty.

The *qualitative* statements about particular mental abilities give us a "richer," more suggestive picture of this particular young man's intellectual strengths and weaknesses. In practice, qualitative and quantitative approaches are often combined—as in our example—but they have not always been combined in research investigations and have somewhat different historical antecedents.

In the first chapter of this section, we will discuss the quantitative approach—the origin and development of intelligence testing, one of the great achievements of modern psychology. As we shall see, the mental-test approach, which emphasizes individual differences, has been the source of many critical social questions and not a few controversies. We will review a number of controversial issues that have stimulated a great deal of research, including questions about the best way to measure general intelligence, the basic nature and structure of intelligence, the stability of I.Q., the hereditary and environmental determinants of intelligence, and the nature of intellectual functioning in later life.

Researchers and theorists interested in the qualitative aspects of cognition and intelligence have not usually been concerned with assessing differences between people. Rather, they have turned their attention to the essential components of intellectual activity such as thinking, reasoning, abstraction, concept formation, comprehension, and problem solving. They have explored development and age changes in these abilities as well as their verbal, social, and personality determinants. And, since language plays a significant part in intellectual activity, many researchers and theorists have been concerned with the acquisition of language and its relationships to intelligence and intellectual functioning. These topics are the subject matter of Chapter 16. Of course, you have already been introduced to an outstanding example of the qualitative approach to intelligence in an account of Piaget's view of mental growth and the stages through which new, qualitatively different mental abilities emerge in the course of development (see p. 299).

Educational psychologists draw heavily on the quantitative approaches to intelligence and other findings from research on cognitive functions in their research and in their applied work in the schools. In diagnosing and treating cases of learning difficulties or school behavior problems, the school psychologist also uses the facts, theories, and methods of clinical, personality, and developmental psychology. The related fields of educational and school psychology, and the work done by people in these fields, are described in Chapter 17.

15

Human Intelligence and Its Measurement

What were the beginnings of human ability measurement?
What issues have been raised by testing intelligence?
How do tests reflect differences in theories of intelligence?

What were the beginnings of human ability measurement?

The measurement of human abilities has a relatively short history. It began with the work of Sir Francis Galton in the latter part of the nineteenth century. Galton, strongly influenced by the theory of evolution proposed by his cousin, Charles Darwin, was convinced that human abilities were inherited and variable and that they could be assessed by scientific methods. Furthermore, Galton and others who followed his lead believed that the higher order mental abilities, such as reasoning and problem solving, could be inferred from measures such as rate of tapping, strength of handgrip, estimation of the length of a line, and other simple motor and perceptual tasks. This approach grew out of Galton's not unusual belief that complex ideas and mental skills depended on simple perceptual or motor abilities. An idea comes from a sensation, does it not? Therefore, superior perceptual abilities mean, ultimately, superior reasoning. In his "anthropometric laboratory" individuals were measured on a variety of simple tests of perception, motor skill, and memory. Some of Galton's tests, or variations of them, are still in use today.

Another early worker, probably the most prominent in the field of the assessment of intellectual ability, was a French psychologist, Alfred Binet. Binet was asked by the school authorities to devise a test that would help in the early detection of mentally retarded children, especially in distinguishing between retarded children and those with sufficient ability but with low motivation. Unlike Galton, Binet believed that to evaluate intelligence, you must devise *direct* measures of complex processes such as reasoning and problem solving, the ability to use past experience to solve present problems, and the ability to adapt to new situations—you cannot simply infer complex processes from simple skills. So, in 1905, Binet and his colleague Theodore Simon published the first Binet-Simon scale, measuring *not* perceptual-motor skills but "reasoning, judgment, and imagination" (Binet & Simon, 1908).

Alfred Binet, who devised the first real intelligence test, 1905.
(Culver Pictures)

This was the first of three scales published by Binet and Simon, the last in 1911, shortly before Binet's untimely death. In developing their tests, they were concerned with two major criteria. First, since mental ability improves with age during the school years, a good mental-test item should be **age-graded;** that is, it should be easier for older than for younger children. Therefore, in selecting items for the test, Binet chose items in which success was related to age; more older than younger children passed the item. Thus, an item that 15 percent of 6-year-olds can pass, 60 percent of 7-year-olds can pass, and 100 percent of 8-year-olds can pass, would be placed at age level 7. The percentage of children at a particular age who passed a given item was the measure of its difficulty, a *psychological* rather than a *physical* scale. Second, performance on a test should be related to school achievement; that is, children who were considered bright by their teachers should perform better on these tests than children regarded as dull.

The Binet-Simon scales were very good ones, judging by the second criterion mentioned above (while Galton's and similar scales were poor) and, because of this, these scales were quickly adopted in other countries. In America, Lewis Terman of Stanford University was largely responsible for the translation and revision of what came to be the most widely used intelligence test in America, the Stanford-Binet, published in 1916, revised in 1937, and again in

Lewis Terman, who made important revisions to the Binet-Simon scales.
(Culver Pictures)

1960 (Terman & Merrill, 1960). The Stanford-Binet samples a wide variety of cognitive functions such as memory, verbal and mathematical reasoning, comprehension, vocabulary, and ability to abstract.

Binet repeatedly emphasized the importance of expressing the measurement of mental ability in psychological rather than in physical units. Indeed, in the second version of the Binet-Simon Intelligence scale (1908), Binet introduced a purely psychological dimension for describing a subject's level of intellectual functioning. This psychological measure, also adopted for scoring the Stanford-Binet, was the mental age (M.A.), derived in the following way. In the tests, items are grouped according to the age at which a substantial proportion of children pass them. In the 1960 Stanford-Binet there are six items, tapping a variety of functions, at each age level. Thus the eight-year-old level consists of the following items: defines eight words, such as orange, gown, eyelash; answers from memory questions about a short story read to him; tells what is foolish about some absurd statements (e.g., "A man had flu twice. The first time it killed him, but the second time, he got well quickly." Why is that foolish?); names similarities and differences in pairs of objects such as an airplane and a kite; answers questions involving comprehension such as "What makes a sailboat move?"

In administering the tests, the examiner first presents easy tasks—usually those for an age level lower than that expected for the child—in order to build rapport, motivation, and confidence. He then determines the child's **basal age,** the mental age level at which he passes all the tests. Tests for higher age levels are then given in order; and the child is credited two months for each additional test item passed. This is added to the basal age. The total number of items passed by the child could thus be expressed in years and months; a test score expressed in this way is the **mental age.**

Suppose, for example, an eight-year-old passes all the tests for age level eight; his basal age then is eight. He is next given the items of age level nine and he passes two of these, thus earning an additional four months of mental age (two months for each item). At the ten-year-old level he passes one item and thus earns two more months of mental age credit. He fails all the tests at the age eleven level. His mental age therefore would be eight years and six months.

Intelligence Quotient

To express the test results in a way that would indicate immediately how bright a child was—whether he was accelerated or retarded relative to his agemates—Terman adopted a concept from the German psychologist William Stern. This was the **intelligence quotient** or I.Q., expressed as the ratio of the mental age to the chronological age of the child

$$\text{I.Q.} = \frac{\text{M.A.}}{\text{C.A.}} \times 100.$$

The ratio is multiplied by 100 simply to remove the decimal point. Thus, if a child 8 years old has a mental age of 8, his I.Q. is 100 (average). If he has a mental age of 7 his I.Q. is 88. And if he has a mental age of 10, his I.Q. is $\frac{10}{8} \times 100$ or 125.

The I.Q. scores of all children—of the total population—fall into a normal distribution with a mean (average) of 100 (see p. 34). The percentage of children in the standardization sample of the 1960 Stanford-Binet falling at various I.Q. levels is given in Table 15–1. As that table shows, 47 percent of the population falls into the I.Q. range between 90 and 109. Approximately 1 percent have

I.Q.'s of 140 or over and only 3 percent fall below 70, into the mental deficient range (Terman & Merrill, 1960).

TABLE 15-1
PERCENTAGE DISTRIBUTION OF I.Q.'S AND CLASSIFICATIONS

I.Q.	Classification	Approximate Percent in Standardization Sample
140 and above	Very superior	1
120–139	Superior	11
110–119	High average	18
90–109	Average	47
80– 89	Low average	15
70– 79	Borderline	6
69 and below	Mental defective	3

In the years since its popularization by Terman, I.Q. has been one of the most used and abused concepts within psychology. Test-makers such as Binet and Terman were careful to emphasize that the M.A. and the I.Q. were psychological measures, different in many respects from physical measurements. A person with an I.Q. of 120, for example, does not have "twice as much" intelligence as a person with an I.Q. of 60. Despite the fact that an I.Q. is expressed in numerical terms, it is no different, in principle, from the rank positions accorded contestants in a beauty contest. Although everyone might agree who was the most beautiful contestant, it would be impossible to quantify how much more beautiful she was than any other. An I.Q. test can tell us who are the brightest people but not how much brighter, in unit terms, they are than the rest.

Over the years since its introduction, the I.Q. has been a useful clinical and educational tool. In general, the I.Q. correlates well with academic performance. For example, I.Q.'s in grade nine correlate highly with achievement tests in reading, English, history, biology, and geometry (correlations between .50 and .70). The I.Q. predicts fairly accurately how well a child will do in school. The case of Roger B. which introduced this section shows how a qualitative examination of test performance can also be of significance in suggesting remedial action. Unfortunately, however, the public is not sufficiently aware of the limitations and cautions that have to be exercised in interpreting I.Q. data. Too often the I.Q. is taken as some fixed, unchangeable value to be gloated over or to bemoan. In fact, however, the I.Q. is neither fixed nor inexorable; the test measures present ability—not inborn capacity. Nor is the I.Q. score a sure predictor of success or failure in life. The difficulties in using the I.Q., therefore, do not reside in the score itself but rather in its misuse and misinterpretation.

The Wechsler Scales

While the Stanford-Binet remains the standard instrument for intelligence testing with young children, it is less frequently used today with older children and adults. In 1939 the Wechsler-Bellevue intelligence scale was introduced, and this scale is much easier to administer and to score than the Binet (Wechsler, 1939). It has the added virtue of providing a picture of the subject's *pattern* of performance—his intellectual strengths and weaknesses. The Wechsler scale is divided into two subscales, a verbal scale and a performance scale. While the items in the Stanford-Binet tests are grouped according to difficulty level, with each level containing a sampling of cognitive functions, the items in the Wechsler are grouped into subtests of various types, a total of eleven scored subtests. The *verbal scale* includes tests of Information (items such as "How many weeks are there in a year?"), Comprehension (questions such as "Why should we keep away from bad company?"), Digit Span (repeating digits forward and backward), Similarities ("In what way are air and water alike?"), Arithmetic (simple arithmetic problems), and Vocabulary. The *performance scale* includes five subtests. In the Picture Arrangement test the story is told in three or more cartoon panels presented in random order; the subject must piece them together in a way that tells the story. Each of the pictures presented in the Picture Completion test has something missing from it; the subject tells what is lacking. In the Block Design subtest, the subject uses small blocks to copy a design that has been made and presented to him by the examiner (see Figure 15-1). In Object Assembly, the subject is given parts and required to discover how they go together to form such objects as a profile, hand, or elephant. The Digit Symbol test requires the subject to learn a code symbol for each number and to fill in the code symbol in a series of blank spaces under the numbers.

A subject's score on these subtests gives an immediate picture of his intellectual strengths and weaknesses. In standardizing the scales, the average score (scaled score) for each subtest was set at 10. The subject's scores in the eleven subtests make up a **test profile** which indicates the evenness and unevenness of his performance, as well as his level of functioning in different kinds of cognitive tasks. It is this pattern of performance which the clinician used in writing the report on Roger B. that introduced this section. A copy of Roger B.'s test record is shown in Table 15-2, and a profile or psychograph of the record is shown in Figure 15-2.

TABLE 15-2
ROGER B.'S WISC PROFILE

	Raw Score	Scaled Score
VERBAL TESTS		
Information	23	14
Comprehension	15	9
Arithmetic	12	10
Similarities	13	10
Vocabulary	59	15
(Digit Span)	(12)	(12)
Sum of Verbal Tests		58
PERFORMANCE TESTS		
Picture Completion	13	10
Picture Arrangement	30	9
Block Design	25	11
Object Assembly	24	10
Coding (Digit Symbol)	62	14
(Mazes)	—	—
Sum of Performance Tests		54

FIGURE 15-1
BLOCK DESIGN SUBTEST
This task is one of the performance tests of the Wechsler scales.
(Ann Zane Shanks, Photo Researchers)

There are now three Wechsler scales, the WAIS (Wechsler Adult Intelligence Scale), WISC (Wechsler Intelligence Scale for Children—ages 7 to 16), and most recently the WPPSI (Wechsler Preschool-Primary Intelligence Scale) for children ages 4 to $6\frac{1}{2}$ (Wechsler, 1939, 1949, 1963). The Wechsler scales are currently the most widely used individual tests of intelligence in America.

Although the Stanford-Binet and the Wechsler scales differ greatly in content, scores from the two tests are highly correlated. Stanford-Binet I.Q. correlates about +.80 with the verbal scale of the Wechsler Intelligence Scale for Children (WISC), +.65 with the performance scale, and +.80 with the full scale.

Group Tests

The success of individual tests of intelligence, partic-

FIGURE 15-2
PROFILE (PSYCHOGRAPH) OF ROGER B.'S WISC SUBTEST SCORES

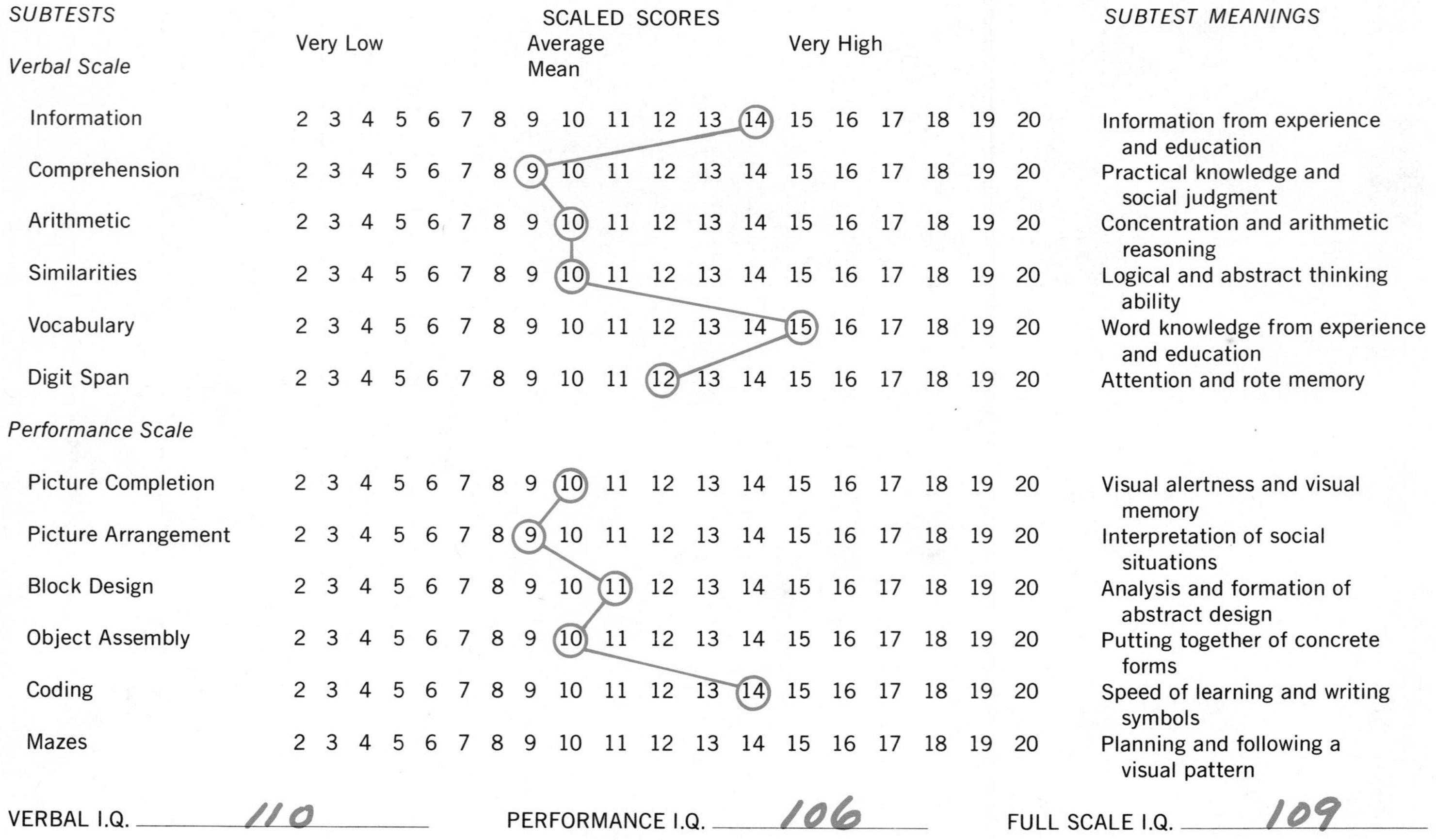

SUBTESTS	SCALED SCORES Very Low — Average Mean — Very High	*SUBTEST MEANINGS*
Verbal Scale		
Information	2 3 4 5 6 7 8 9 10 11 12 13 14 15 16 17 18 19 20	Information from experience and education
Comprehension	2 3 4 5 6 7 8 9 10 11 12 13 14 15 16 17 18 19 20	Practical knowledge and social judgment
Arithmetic	2 3 4 5 6 7 8 9 10 11 12 13 14 15 16 17 18 19 20	Concentration and arithmetic reasoning
Similarities	2 3 4 5 6 7 8 9 10 11 12 13 14 15 16 17 18 19 20	Logical and abstract thinking ability
Vocabulary	2 3 4 5 6 7 8 9 10 11 12 13 14 15 16 17 18 19 20	Word knowledge from experience and education
Digit Span	2 3 4 5 6 7 8 9 10 11 12 13 14 15 16 17 18 19 20	Attention and rote memory
Performance Scale		
Picture Completion	2 3 4 5 6 7 8 9 10 11 12 13 14 15 16 17 18 19 20	Visual alertness and visual memory
Picture Arrangement	2 3 4 5 6 7 8 9 10 11 12 13 14 15 16 17 18 19 20	Interpretation of social situations
Block Design	2 3 4 5 6 7 8 9 10 11 12 13 14 15 16 17 18 19 20	Analysis and formation of abstract design
Object Assembly	2 3 4 5 6 7 8 9 10 11 12 13 14 15 16 17 18 19 20	Putting together of concrete forms
Coding	2 3 4 5 6 7 8 9 10 11 12 13 14 15 16 17 18 19 20	Speed of learning and writing symbols
Mazes	2 3 4 5 6 7 8 9 10 11 12 13 14 15 16 17 18 19 20	Planning and following a visual pattern

VERBAL I.Q. 110 PERFORMANCE I.Q. 106 FULL SCALE I.Q. 109

ularly the Stanford-Binet, led many workers to design tests that could be given to large groups of subjects at the same time. Such group tests were needed because individual testing was expensive and time-consuming and because the detailed information derived from an individual test was unnecessary when only rough screening of many individuals was required. Such was the case in 1914 when America prepared to enter World War I.

World War I created a demand for a means of group intelligence testing.
(The Bettmann Archive)

At about that time, Arthur S. Otis was working on a group test of intelligence, and he turned his work over to a group of psychologists appointed to construct a mental test for rapid screening of Army recruits. With the Otis tests as a basis, the psychologists created the famous Army Alpha tests of mental ability (Yerkes, 1921). The Alpha proved extremely useful in screening recruits. For example, about eight thousand men were discharged because of limited ability; others were assigned to "special" battalions because of either very low or very high test scores. The value of the Alpha test was demonstrated by the fact that it was highly correlated with measures such as officers' ratings of ability and rank eventually attained.

One finding was a surprise to many Americans—almost a third of all men tested were illiterate. Since they could not read or write, they obviously could not be tested with the Alpha. A second test that did not use language and did not require reading ability, the Beta, was created for use with illiterates and foreigners who could not read English (Yerkes, 1921). Scores from the Beta also proved useful and demonstrated once again the difference between ignorance (lack of knowledge) and lack of intelligence. Many illiterates were highly intelligent; they simply had not had the opportunity to learn to read.

In World War II, improved versions of Alpha and Beta were used. The new Alpha was called the Army General Classification Test, and recruits scored much higher, on the average, than the soldiers in World War I. This was not due to the new test items. A representative sample of World War II soldiers tested on the *old* Alpha scored much higher than World War I soldiers had. The difference was sizable: only one sixth (16 percent) of the soldiers in World War I scored as high as the median score of World War II soldiers. Better education probably accounts for much of the difference, and factors such as better nutrition, health, facility with the English language, and more "test experience" probably played a part.

Infant Tests

With the rapid growth of the testing movement in America, particularly during the 1920's, interest in assessing the I.Q. of young infants (below age two, the youngest age test in the Stanford-Binet), mounted rapidly. In part this interest grew out of the natural curiosity of parents who were anxious to be assured that their children were "normal." There were practical considerations as well. If mental retardation could be detected early, parents could be better prepared for the fact that their offspring might not talk or walk at the usual ages and might require special education. Such tests would be also useful in placing infants for adoption. It is usual in adoption procedures to try to match infants as closely as possible to the adoptive parents. Such matching usually involves matching coloration (giving brunette infants to brunette parents) and socioeconomic and educational background of real and adoptive parents. With infant intelligence tests, parents and adoptive children could be matched with respect to intelligence as well.

The father of infant tests in America was Arnold Gesell. To assess infant mental abilities, Gesell employed a variety of simple tasks, which he arranged in order of difficulty; that is, according to the age at which the item was commonly passed by a standardization group (Gesell, 1928). After Gesell introduced his infant intelligence scale, a number of other workers introduced other similar scales aimed at improving Gesell's procedures.

Among the most notable of the currently used infant tests, in addition to the Gesell, are the Bayley Scales of Infant Development, which were developed after many years of research. The latest version of these scales was published in 1969 (Bayley, 1969). Sample mental-scale items, together with their age placements (norms), are given in Table 15-3. (Chapter 13 presented the motor items in the Bayley scales.)

TABLE 15-3
EXAMPLES OF INFANT INTELLIGENCE TEST ITEMS FROM BAYLEY SCALES OF INFANT DEVELOPMENT

Item	Age Placement (months)
Responds to voice	0.7
Visually recognizes mother	2.0
Turns head to sound of rattle	3.9
Lifts cup with handle	5.8
Responds to verbal request (e.g., to wave bye-bye)	9.1
Turns pages of book	12.0
Points to shoes (or other clothing) on request	15.3
Imitates crayon stroke	17.8
Uses 2-word sentence	20.6
Names 3 objects shown to him	24.0

N. Bayley. *Bayley Scales of Infant Development.* New York: Psychological Corporation, 1969.

The infant tests differ in many important respects from intelligence tests devised for children and adults. Tests for older subjects inevitably involve a great deal of language; tests for infants do not. Indeed, many of the infant subtests, such as following an object with both eyes, have no parallel in the tests designed for adults. In brief, the abilities measured by the infant tests are vastly different from those measured by the Binet or the Wechsler scales. Not surprisingly, therefore, test scores earned in the first year or two do not correlate highly with later tests of intelligence and are not good predictors of later intellectual ability. Infant tests are most useful in detecting the extremes of mental ability and retardation.

New Approaches

The Binet and the Wechsler scales, along with various group tests of intelligence, have become rather staple items in the practicing psychologist's armamentarium of materials. Psychology and society have not stood still, however. New ideas and new social problems highlight unfulfilled needs in the domain of testing. New tests are emerging to meet these needs.

One of the major problems of intelligence tests such as the Binet and the Wechsler is that the content of many of the test items presupposes a particular background of experience. For example, one item asks the child, "What should you do if your mother sends you to the store for a loaf of bread and the store doesn't have any?" Children on an Indian reservation where there is only one store will answer this question differently from children who live in a city where there are many grocery stores close to one another. For the Indian youngster "return home" would be a correct answer whereas "go to another store" would be correct for a child living in the city; yet "return home" was, until recently, scored as incorrect—as if all children live in the city.

Other parts of the test also pose special problems for young people with backgrounds different from those of the standardization group (the group on which the norms are based). For example, many children have very poorly educated parents and live in homes without books or magazines; such children are likely to have a more limited vocabulary than children whose homes are intellectually more stimulating. That is to say, children with equal potential ability could perform differently on intelligence tests because they have had different experiences at home.

These problems have become especially prominent in recent years when the plight of disadvantaged minority children has been brought to the forefront of social and psychological concerns. Standard tests are biased against such children not only in terms of the content, as described above, but also because of the fact that successful test-taking requires certain attitudes toward tests, interpersonal skills, and verbal skills that a child living in the ghetto may not acquire. Minority-group children may, for example, feel uncomfortable and shy with a stranger who looks and talks differently compared with the people they know best. Ghetto children acquire many practical abilities useful for coping with ghetto life, but these abilities rarely include techniques for handling test situations.

Some attempts have been made to construct **culture-fair tests,** that is, tests less culturally biased than those already available. Many such tests, including the Leiter International Performance

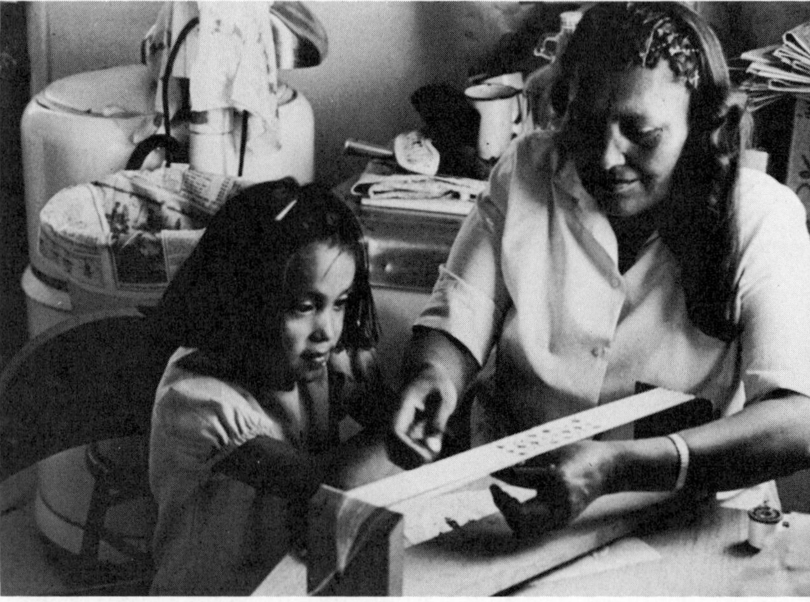

Intelligence may be manifested in many ways. (L., National Archives; R., Bob Towers, courtesy ACTION)

Scale (Leiter, 1950) and the Peabody Picture Vocabulary Test (Dunn, 1965), employ pictures in the belief that these reduce some of the difficulties present in existing tests. Such culture-fair tests, however, on the whole, have been unsuccessful. Perhaps they cannot be successful, in principle. There cannot really be a culture-fair test because every individual is in part at least a product of his culture, and his intelligence is in part knowledge of that culture. His performance will always be affected by his background and experience, no matter what the nature of the test. Perhaps more important than culture-fair tests, therefore, are culture-fair *interpretations*, which take into account a subject's background and experience in evaluating the meaning and significance of his test scores.

Another movement in testing derives from our burgeoning knowledge about cognitive growth that has been provided by Piaget and the growing body of information about language development (see pp. 299 and 308). Some investigators have tried to develop intelligence scales using tasks related to Piaget's stages of mental development. But these tests tap only the reasoning abilities of children and hence give a narrower picture of mental development than standard intelligence tests. The same holds true for new tests devised to assess the language abilities of children. In the long run, progress in the testing movement probably depends as much upon improving and expanding the range of existing tests as it does on introducing entirely new instruments.

What issues have been raised by testing intelligence?

The use of mental tests has raised many questions about I.Q. constancy, possible genetic determinants of I.Q. differences, mental growth after maturity, and mental development in exceptional children. These have been the starting points of extensive research projects.

Stability of the I.Q.

The I.Q. is essentially a rank; there are no true "units" of intellectual ability. It is, however, important to know whether the measure is relatively stable or, in other words, whether individuals tend to maintain their relative intellectual standing over time. If the I.Q. is relatively stable, we can fairly confidently make long-range predictions about an individual's future intellectual status, and these can be used in educational and vocational planning.

Many studies indicate that for a large proportion of the population the individual's relative intellectual standing is in fact stable. It does not change radically from test to retest, even over a fairly long time span. This has come to be known as **I.Q. stability.** While infant tests are not very good predictors of later intelligence, tests given during preschool and after, when language functions are well established, are highly correlated with later tests. For example, Stanford-Binet scores at age four correlate .70 with mental-test scores at age sixteen. In general the child who is superior in intelligence at age six remains so; the child who is inferior at this age generally scores low at later ages (Honzik, Macfarlane, & Allen, 1948).

This does not mean that every individual's standing is fixed; some change markedly from one time to another. The correlations between a test given between the ages of six and nine and a second test given later on depends on the interval between tests. The correlation between tests given a few days apart is +.91; with an interval of three years, the correlation is +.84. It drops still lower with longer intervals between tests. Significant changes in I.Q. are more likely when there are longer intervals between tests. At least 10 percent of children change at least fifteen points during an interval of six to eight years.

The most relevant data on individual changes in I.Q. come from longitudinal studies in which the same subjects are tested repeatedly over a long time. Figure 15-3 shows the intelligence test results of repeated tests of three subjects of the longitudinal Guidance Study at the Institute of Human Development at the University of California at Berkeley. The three children had very similar I.Q.'s at age four, but two of them changed markedly over the years (Honzik, Macfarlane, & Allen, 1948).

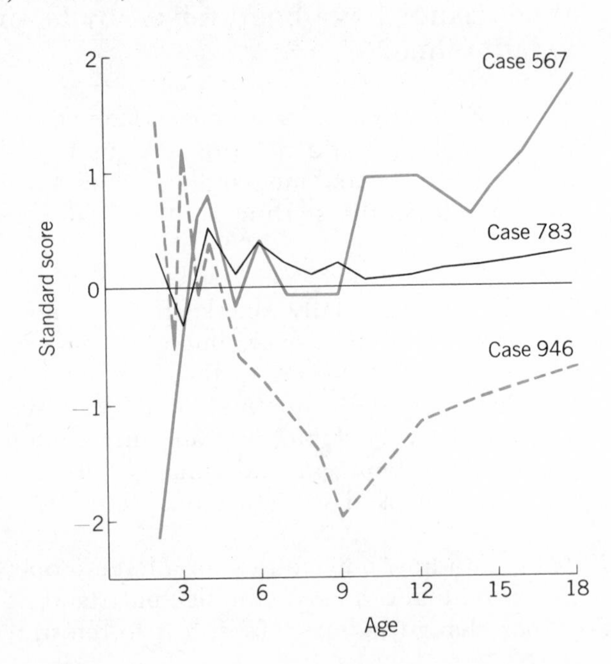

FIGURE 15-3
A LONGITUDINAL STUDY OF I.Q.

The graph shows I.Q. scores of three children on successive tests (plotted in standard scores with the mean for children in this study taken as 0).
(From Honzik, Macfarlane, & Allen, 1948)

The histories of the three children whose I.Q. test scores are shown in the figure suggest causes of change but at the same time show that simple causal hypotheses may be inadequate. Case 783 changed very little in I.Q. through the years, although he had poor health, was insecure, did poorly in school, and had a number of symptoms of emotional disturbance. Case 946 scored as low as 87 and as high as 142. She was the daughter of unhappily married immigrant parents who were divorced when the girl was seven. When she was nine her mother remarried but the girl was very insecure and unhappy at home. When she became better adjusted in her family, her I.Q. scores rose. Case 567 showed consistent improvement. In her early years she was sickly and shy, but after age ten her social life expanded and she became very much involved in music and sports. These changes were reflected in her improved test scores.

Gains or declines in I.Q. also appear to be correlated with personality and emotional factors. Among children with the same I.Q. at an early period, those who gain are likely to be vigorous, emotionally independent, aggressive, nonconforming, curious children who are actively engaged in exploring their world and are interested in intellectual pursuits (Sontag, Baker, & Nelson, 1958).

Changes in a child's intellectual standing may occur if there is a major change in environment—and in opportunities for learning—either from good to bad or vice versa. This was dramatically demonstrated in one study in which a small group of children were removed from a foundling home where they were given physical care but little else. The babies were placed in a home for mentally retarded girls who "adopted" the infants and raised them with much love and care. At the time they were removed from the foundling home their I.Q.'s were in the sixties (in the mentally defective range). Retested after years with their surrogate mothers, these youngsters attained close to normal or average I.Q. scores, and thirty years later the majority of them were leading normal productive lives. Here is a rather remarkable demonstration of change in I.Q. associated with a dramatic change in environment. A control group who had not been adopted but remained in the foundling home presented a much different picture as adults. Most of them were living in institutions of one sort or another (Skeels, 1966).

A change in the other direction is often observed among minority children such as native Americans (Indians) and blacks. While these children may score close to average intelligence when they are young, they score increasingly more poorly as they grow older; they seem to undergo a kind of progressive retardation (see also p. 421). The reasons for this are not entirely obvious. One possible factor is motivational. As minority children grow older, they become increasingly aware of their low status in the larger society (a situation that is hopefully changing today) and the lack of opportunity available

Children reared in unstimulating environments are likely to be deficient in cognitive functioning.
(George W. Gardner)

to them, even with an education. As a result, they lose interest in academic matters. Exposure to societal prejudice may have had a retarding effect upon intellectual growth.

In general, people tend to retain their relative intellectual standing when they grow up in an environment that provides the opportunities and nourishment to maximize mental growth. When, however, a child growing up in an optimal environment moves to a less favorable one or vice versa, then there may well be very large shifts in intellectual performance. In short, there is nothing fixed or immutable about the I.Q. score.

Genetic Determinants of I.Q.

In recent years there has been a rebirth of interest in the hereditary and biological determinants of human behavior, and as a consequence, a new look at genetic factors in intelligence. It is important to distinguish between the generally accepted notion that **heredity** contributes to intellectual ability and the idea that intelligence is somehow established at conception and is therefore unchangeable. Most psychologists agree that heredity sets limits, but these limits are flexible—or even elastic—so that they can be stretched considerably under special circumstances.

The evidence for the role of heredity in intelligence is of several sorts. One kind of evidence comes from studies of the I.Q. scores of parents and their children. On the average, the correlation between the I.Q.'s of parents and their natural children is on the order of .50, but between parents and their adopted children, it is about .25. Even more impressive are the data from identical and fraternal twins. The I.Q.'s of fraternal twins correlate about .55, while the I.Q.'s of identical twins (who have the same genetic makeup) correlate about .90. Even if reared apart in different environments, the I.Q.'s of identical twins correlate .75. A summary of studies of this kind is presented in Figure 15-4.

Although such evidence clearly suggests that intelligence is strongly influenced by genetic factors, it is also clear that environmental factors—including everything from diet to education—play a role. Partly because of environmental determinants, children's I.Q.'s tend to be closer to the average I.Q.'s than their parents' are. Extremely intelligent parents will have intelligent children, to be sure, but the children on the average will be slightly less intelligent, closer to the mean for the general population. Children of parents with extremely low intelligence will tend to be brighter than their parents—again, closer to population mean. This phenomenon is called **regression to the mean.** An extremely intelligent person, for example, probably represents an extremely fortunate coincidence of many genetic factors related to high I.Q. *and* a highly favorable environment; it is unlikely that his child will be as fortunate.

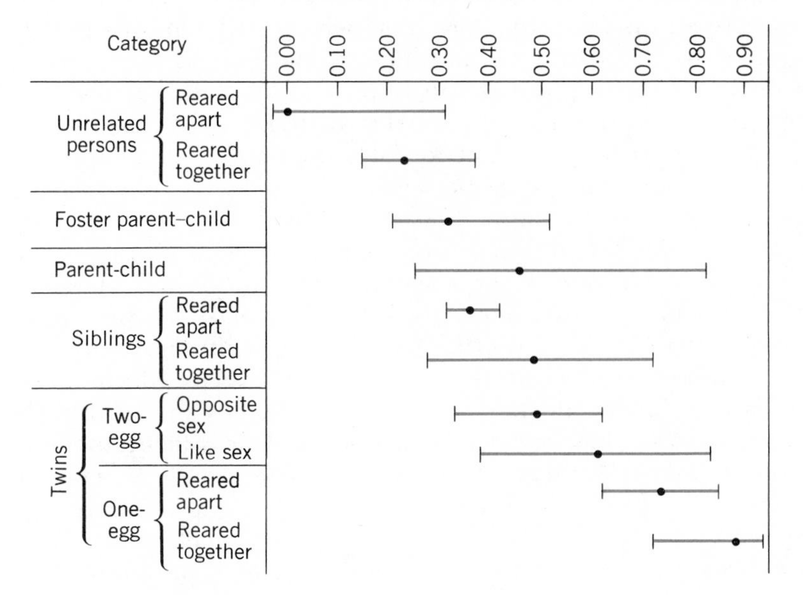

FIGURE 15-4 CORRELATION COEFFICIENTS OF INTELLIGENCE TEST SCORES

Test scores from 52 studies are of pairs of people of different degrees of genetic similarity. Median coefficients are shown by large dots on the horizontal lines, which represent the ranges. (From Erlenmeyer-Kimling & Jarvik, 1963)

One of the most consistent findings with regard to intelligence testing of black and white Americans is that blacks on the average score ten to fifteen points below whites on most of the standard measures of ability. Obviously, this does not mean that every black is less bright than every white. Rather, what it means is that 33 percent of blacks are brighter than 50 percent of whites. Put differently, intelligence is randomly distributed in a normal curve for both blacks and whites and the differences *within* each group are much larger than the difference *between* the two groups. Many blacks earn high scores.

What factors could account for the finding that blacks score lower on the average? It has been suggested that this difference may be attributable to genetic differences between the groups, but most psychologists believe that black-white differences in I.Q. can readily be explained in terms of environment and experiential, rather than genetic, factors. For one thing, whites and blacks live in vastly different environments and have different experiences, on the average. They react differently to the content of the tests and to being tested. In addition, societal prejudices against blacks—and the blacks' awareness of their status in society—stifle intellectual motivation. Furthermore, black children have few role models who have used intellectual skills and education to get ahead in the world.

A few examples may help to make concrete how environmental factors can affect intellectual growth. Recent studies suggest that protein deficiency during a mother's pregnancy can have lasting negative effects upon her offspring's intellectual ability. The relevance of these findings to the data on black-white intelligence is clear. Blacks are on the average poorer than whites and more likely to have poorer diets, diets that include high proportions of fat, starch, and carbohydrates, with low amounts of protein—just the reverse of what is required for optimum intellectual growth. Likewise, the diet of the infant after birth is important for later intellectual development. At least some of the differences between black and white children in test performance could be due to these nutritional differences.

Perhaps the most important factor contributing to black-white differences in test performance is related to the generally low socioeconomic level of most blacks. Lower class families provide restricted experiences and little intellectual or cultural stimulation for their children. Those factors are consistently related to intellectual retardation. Finally, despite the positive changes in racial attitude, prejudice against blacks is still a fact of life. It is difficult to motivate the black child to learn and to get an education if he is not convinced that it will lead to greater rewards—a better job, a more prestigious position, or greater self-esteem. The possible effects of any genetic differences cannot be separated from these effects of differential nutrition, differing environmental stimulation, and inequality of opportunity.

Still, the observed I.Q. differences between races have frequently been interpreted as *genetic* differences in the past. The issue is a highly emotional one, for obvious reasons, and it is complicated. "Race" itself is defined socially, not genetically; someone with all white ancestors except for one black great-grandfather—who is, genetically, mostly white—is still labeled black. So the basic term "race" is indefinite from a genetic point of view. And "intelligence"

—what it is, how it should be measured, and whether present tests are "fair" to all groups—also remains a somewhat indefinite theoretical construct. Nevertheless, the relationship between race and intelligence remains a current controversy, as may be seen in a recent form of the old debate, reviewed in Spotlight 15-1.

One final point must be made before we leave this issue. Intelligence tests measure only a limited sample of human abilities. They were, moreover, devised by whites for white populations. It is possible that other tests, designed by and for blacks using the vocabulary and concepts of black culture would produce quite a different picture, namely, that blacks on the average are brighter than whites. In the end, therefore, the question of whether blacks perform less well than whites on intelligence tests will have to be qualified with some statement as to the kinds of knowledge and language sampled by the test in question.

Experience, environment, heredity, nutrition, motivation, all are factors affecting I.Q. scores.
(L., courtesy VISTA; Paul Conklin)

Mental Growth After Maturity

Most investigators agree that intelligence grows very rapidly in the early years, but more slowly with increasing age. Intelligence test performance ordinarily reaches its peak in late adolescence or early adulthood, and at this period people seem to stop acquiring new intellectual powers. For example, immediate memory span grows until the age of fifteen but not after that. The average fifteen-year-old can repeat seven digits, and so can the average fifty-year-old. Other items of the Binet scale also level off at about the same age. Early studies indicated rather sharp decreases in mental abilities,

SPOTLIGHT 15-1
Race and Intelligence

The question "Is intelligence inherited?" is an old one, and by now we have a probable answer: "Yes, to some extent." This answer of course applies to intelligence as measured by general I.Q. tests such as the Stanford-Binet or the Wechsler scales. Scores on these tests clearly are related to genetic variations; e.g., your I.Q. is probably closer to that of your brother or sister or parents than it is to that of some unrelated person. Indeed, one of the better estimates of an infant's I.Q.—before direct testing is possible—is the average I.Q. of his parents. But variations in environmental experiences, including everything from the health of the pregnant mother (which affects the prenatal environment) to educational opportunities, broadly conceived, also clearly affect measured I.Q. The research evidence supports the hypothesis that both genetic and environmental factors are important.

Recently, sophisticated statistical techniques for estimating the *relative* contribution of heredity and environment—which is *more* important?—have permitted a number of scientific publications that are highly controversial. The controversy is partly about methodological issues, but the most heated arguments develop when the findings are used to suggest that blacks are genetically inferior in intelligence compared to whites. Needless to say, there are many in our imperfect society who are eager to discover and publicize any "scientific" conclusions that support their bigotry and justify their discriminatory behaviors. So the question—and the answers—have profound social implications.

Arthur R. Jensen recently raised the possibility of inferiority of the blacks in the prestigious *Harvard Educational Review* (Jensen, 1969). In essence, these are the facts cited in support of his suggestions: (1) Analysis of numerous studies of blood relatives, especially those of identical twins raised in different environments (same heredity, different environments), leads to the estimate that approximately 80 percent of the variation in I.Q. can be accounted for by genetic factors. In other words, heredity is *far more important* than environment in determining I.Q. scores. (2) Numerous studies have shown that blacks, on the average, score lower than whites in I.Q. If intelligence is largely inherited, this fact alone could lead to the conclusion of black genetic inferiority. But Jensen used a third fact as well: (3) Special, remedial programs designed to increase the I.Q.'s of disadvantaged children—mostly blacks—have not been generally effective. This evidence, he suggests, supports the notion of high heritability of I.Q. scores because it shows how little impact results from changing the environment and educational program.

Many psychologists have reacted to Jensen's publications by saying that his analyses are overinterpreted and misleading. For example, even if one concedes that intelligence is 80 percent heritable in the white middle class—the group from which almost all of the subjects in important twin studies were drawn—one cannot assume that the same estimate holds for blacks or for lower social classes. Indeed, recent evidence indicates that I.Q. scores are determined much more by environment in these cases (Scarr-Salapatek, 1971a). A white middle class child is much less likely, in other words, to be "held back" by the lack of opportunity or by overt discrimination (environmental factors), and thus his I.Q. score might more directly reflect his genetic endowment. As Herrnstein (1971) points out, if everyone had truly equal opportunity, variations in I.Q. would have to be largely determined by genetic factors.

But even if you were willing to concede that I.Q. is to a great degree heritable in both groups, blacks and whites, you could still not conclude that I.Q. differences *between* the groups are the result of different heredities. To clarify this point, consider this relevant analogy to a population of corn seeds and their height and productivity. Suppose you take one hundred seeds of varying genetic characteristics and randomly assign them to two groups. You would then have two subgroups of equal genetic potential on the average. (Recall that random assignment assumes this. See p. 28.) Now plant one group in rich soil, the other in poor sandy soil. *Within* each plot, your corn plants will vary in height and productivity, and these variations will be almost entirely a result of genetic differences in the seeds (almost 100 percent heritability). Plants in poor soil, however, will be—on the average—shorter and less productive than those in rich soil. These average differences *between* the two plots will be almost entirely a function of environmental (soil) differences. It would be nonsense to assert that the seeds planted in poor soil were genetically inferior. Now consider the average differences between the living conditions of whites and blacks and the pervasive nature of prejudice and discrimination in the United States. The analogy between poor and rich soil and the environmental conditions in which black and white children are raised—on the average—becomes very meaningful.

Jensen's thesis has also been criticized on the grounds that the statistics used to estimate the relative contributions of heredity and environment in intelligence are, in essence, correlations. Recall that correlation coefficients reflect a similarity in *ordering* but not in absolute level (see p. 38). For this reason, they can be highly misleading. For example, many studies have demonstrated that the I.Q.'s of adopted children correlate much higher with the I.Q.'s of their natural parents than with those of their adoptive parents. This finding supports a genetic hypothesis. But these results have often been misinterpreted as meaning the adopted child's I.Q. is closer, in absolute terms, to the I.Q. of his natural parents. This is not the case. Consider three children adopted by one family but coming from three disadvantaged families where the average I.Q.'s of the mother and father were 86, 95, and 101. The average parental I.Q. of their new environment was, say, 115. After several years, the children are tested and score 106, 115, and 121, each child scoring 20 points above his parents' average, each much closer in absolute terms to the average I.Q. of his *adoptive* parents. Still, the correlation with natural parents' I.Q., which reflects ordering, is high. The child of the dullest natural parents is the least intelligent in the new family and the child of the brightest parents is the brightest. But the correlation masks the fact that each child scores considerably higher than his real parents (higher than you would predict on a purely genetic basis) presumably because he grew up in a richer intellectual environment. And it is not uncommon to find an average increase in I.Q. of about 20 points among adopted children, compared with their natural parents (Skeels & Skodak, 1949). Environmental changes obviously have significant impacts on I.Q.

The question of how heredity and environment *interact* is perhaps a more meaningful one than the question of which is *more* influential. No doubt there are genetic factors in general intelligence, but without environmental support or stimulation, the genetic factors could not possibly produce their effects. Consider another appropriate analogy. Tuberculosis could be judged to be highly heritable by the standards used to estimate the inheritance of intelligence. If one identical twin has tuberculosis, the other is very likely to have it; this is the situation that has been found in 87 percent of identical twins with TB. However, this figure drops to 26 percent for fraternal twins, who may share the same—or very similar—environments but do not have the same heredities (Hebb, 1966). We cannot conclude that TB is inherited, for in this case we *know* the direct cause of the illness is environmental—a bacillus. We can conclude, at most, that some form of *susceptibility* to TB is inherited. The environment and the genetic factors *interact* to produce the disease itself.

The same is very likely true of intelligence. An individual's *potential* intelligence may be inherited but certainly the environment determines whether or not that potential is actualized—and to what degree. In the environment the average black encounters, he is less likely to actualize his full potential, and thus, any assertion that measures of "functional intelligence" (I.Q. scores) reflect genetic differences is suspect. Perhaps Sandra Scarr-Salapatek (1971b, p. 1228) most accurately reflects the views of most psychologists:

> To assert, despite the absence of evidence, and in the present social climate, that a particular race is genetically disfavored in intelligence is to scream "FIRE . . . I think" in a crowded theater.

References

Hebb, D. O. *A Textbook of Psychology.* 2d ed. Philadelphia: Saunders, 1966.
Herrnstein, R. I.Q. *Atlantic,* 1971, *228* (3) 44–64.
Jensen, A. R. "How Much Can We Boost IQ and Scholastic Achievement?" In *Environment, Heredity, and Intelligence.* Reprint Series No. 2. Cambridge, Mass.: *Harvard Educational Review,* 1969.
Scarr-Salapatek, S. "Race, Social Class, and I.Q." *Science,* 1971a, *174,* 1285–95.
Scarr-Salapatek, S. "Unknowns in the I.Q. Equation." *Science,* 1971b, *174,* 1223–28.
Skodak, M., & Skeels, H. M. "A Final Follow-up Study of 100 Adopted Children." *Journal of Genetic Psychology,* 1949, *75,* 85–125.

especially after the age of forty. These data were based on "cross sections" of the population, i.e., comparisons were made between the test scores of people aged 21–30, 31–40, 41–50, and so forth. Later, in the 1950's, a few studies reported scores of the *same* individuals tested at different ages (longitudinal data); the results were strikingly different. In fact, some investigators reported an *increase* in some abilities with age.

Both types of research turned out to be somewhat misleading. With cross-sectional data, comparisons were made between individuals born in 1885 (age sixty when tested in 1945) and people born in 1925 (age twenty in 1945). There are great differences between the two cross sections in diet, health care, and educational opportunities, especially during the youthful, formative years. These undoubtedly affected their intelligence test performance differentially. Longitudinal studies, on the other hand, were expensive, and finding subjects for later follow-up testing was difficult. The early longitudinal studies were often done on college students, whose continuing education may have accounted for the unusual increases in ability, especially in early adulthood. More sophisticated longitudinal studies produced results such as those shown in Figure 15-5, which showed that Wechsler scores increased through age twenty-six, after which they leveled off and remained unchanged through the age of thirty-six.

Recent careful analyses of data from both types of research suggest that whether a particular kind of mental ability is maintained or declines in adulthood depends upon *both* the intellectual function *and* the person. One cannot really generalize about the course of mental growth. Tests that require speed, close attention, and concentration seem to show decreasing scores earliest (in the

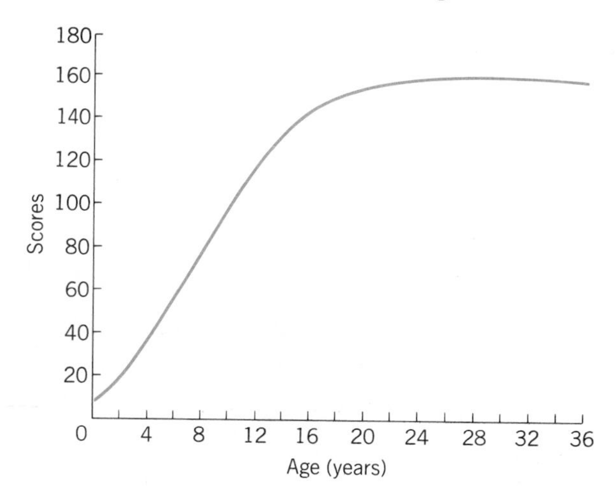

FIGURE 15-5
CURVE OF THE GROWTH OF INTELLIGENCE

This curve is based on data from a longitudinal study. The scores are units of growth derived from a method of absolute scaling. (From N. Bayley, "Development of Mental Abilities," in P. H. Mussen, Ed., *Carmichael's Manual of Child Psychology,* Vol. *1,* 1970, p. 1176)

mid-twenties or even earlier). Abilities such as deductive reasoning—abilities that appear relatively late in life—decline more rapidly than tests of abilities such as language, vocabulary, and rote memory, which show little decline with age. The rate of decline of specific abilities is influenced by the individual's occupation. Scientists and logicians would probably show little deterioration in deductive reasoning, although this function ordinarily declines relatively early. On the average, bright people and those in more intellectually demanding occupations do not decline in mental ability as early as others do. Teachers, writers, artists, and scientists maintain their productivity, if not their creativity, into their later years with little apparent loss of acumen. Persons of lesser ability are likely to lose some of their mental alacrity earlier. Physical health is also a factor; among old men, those in optimal health show relatively little deterioration in intellectual test scores, while those with chronic ailments decline significantly.

Motivation must also be taken into account in considering the course of mental growth after maturity. Every college teacher has encountered highly motivated students of middle age or older whose motivation to learn more than compensated for somewhat lessened mental acuity. Because of their maturity and desire to get the most out of their courses, these students are often a delight to teach and are exuberant witnesses to the fact that intellectual prowess and achievement are not solely the province of the young.

It should be noted that this discussion pertains *only* to performance on intelligence tests. People do not lose their accumulated knowledge as they grow older and, in fact, continue to acquire more information, interests, and—hopefully—wisdom. What the older person has gained from greater experience often more than compensates for the diminished speed and efficiency of his intellectual functioning. On the basis of his experience and wisdom, an older person may be more competent in many ways than a younger person who is more alert and adaptable, and hence, performs better in intelligence tests.

Mental Development in Exceptional Children

So far we have discussed mainly individuals in the broad middle ranges of intellectual ability. What about the intellectual futures of those at the extremes, the mentally retarded and the gifted? Recent research has laid to rest some long-standing myths about both groups of individuals.

The diagnosis of **mental retardation** commonly involves some statement about the determinants of the retardation. The usual distinction is between the endogenous (genetically determined) retarded and the exogenous (environmentally determined) retardation. In many cases, the endogenously retarded have significant physiognomic and sensory deficits as well as low intelligence, poor coordination, and physical problems; the mental deficit is part of a larger picture of total organismic deficit. (See Spotlight 15-2.)

Among the exogenously retarded, such physical and physiological correlates of retardation are generally absent. Retardation can be produced by a variety of traumas which affect the delicate tissues of the brain, including insufficient oxygen during the birth process, prolonged high fever, injury, or a disease such as encephalitis. In recent years it has been recognized that many children suffer from "minimal brain damage," which can be quite selective in its effects. Premature babies, for example, may later show perceptual problems and reading difficulties although they show no other signs of retardation or defect.

A different sort of exogenous retardation is **pseudoretardation.** Such retardation is present in individuals who perform at the retarded level because of severe emotional and/or social deprivation. One disturbed young man's I.Q. was 60 when he first came for psychiatric treatment, but it was 125 after some of his problems were relieved. Pseudoretardation is a frequent phenomenon among ghetto children and others who have been deprived of all but the most minimal forms of intellectual stimulation.

SPOTLIGHT 15-2
Down's Syndrome or Mongolism

Some varieties of mental retardation are produced by genetic abnormalities that occur in the process of cell division during the embryonic period of fetal growth. It is believed today that in some cases of incomplete separation, the new cells may have one too many or too few chromosomes. Cells with too few chromosomes tend to die but those with too many may continue to thrive and produce a viable individual with an abnormal number of chromosomes in all of his body cells. Individuals with an extra chromosome in their cells manifest a form of mental retardation known as "Down's Syndrome" or "mongolism." The syndrome includes the following features: thick tongue with many fissures, flattened face, extra eyelid folds, physical deficits, and defective intelligence (I.Q. between 20 and 60). Such children sometimes grow up to be semi-independent individuals who can do certain types of menial work. This tends to be the exception, however, and most such individuals tend to die young because of congenital defects such as heart disease.

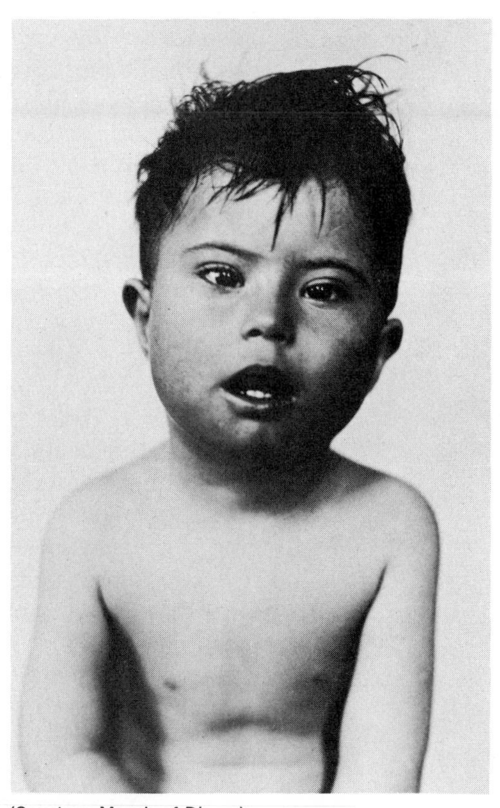

(Courtesy March of Dimes)

A final point about the retarded has to do with the so-called **idiot savant.** It was long believed that many retarded persons had one special ability or talent that was average or above. Some apparently retarded people were very good at puzzles while others could repeat any melody they heard and still others had remarkable memories for numbers or figures. Recent advances in diagnosis, however, suggest that many of these individuals were probably not retarded but rather were suffering a particular form of psychosis called **autism** with symptoms, such as muteness and extreme withdrawal, that resemble those of mental retardation. The special abilities, in these cases, were clues to general but unrealized potential rather than nature's attempt to "compensate" the mentally limited person. Still, there are also some cases of true idiot savants. By concentrating all of his (limited) ability and energy on one simple task, the retarded child or adult may become quite proficient at that one task.

When we look at the other end of the spectrum, at the extremely gifted person, we again find little evidence of "compensation." The intellectually gifted person is usually not weak physically, with poor health and limited eyesight—the bookworm myth; rather, he tends to be gifted in the physical as well as in the intellectual domain. The gifted are, on the average, taller, better coordinated, and less subject to illness than those of lesser ability. Likewise, gifted people tend, on the average, to realize their ability and to attain high positions in their vocations. There are, of course, many exceptions to this rule but the general trend is quite clear and consistent.

A few additional remarks about the gifted need to be made. First, recent studies suggest that in some cases the factors that operate to produce gifted children also appear to be operative in the production of mental retardation. For example, the incidence of mongolism increases with the age of the mother; the incidence of extremely bright and gifted children also increases with the age of the mother. Apparently the hormonal and endocrinal changes that increase the probability of mongolism also increase the probability of giftedness among the offspring.

Second, recent work suggests that intelligence, as measured by standard tests, and creativity, as assessed by public recognition, are related but not in a simple, direct way. Many creative writers and artists, for example, do not have exceptional mental ability, and many who are extremely gifted intellectually are not especially creative in the artistic sense or within their occupations. While there is *some* relationship between intelligence and creativity, it is important to remember that an intelligent person is not necessarily creative and that a creative person is not necessarily intelligent. (See p. 400 for a discussion of creativity.)

How do tests reflect differences in theories of intelligence?

When Binet and Simon began work on their intelligence scale, they started from a fairly broad conception of what **intelligence** was, namely: "To judge well, to comprehend well, to reason well, these are the essentials of intelligence." As new and different tests came into existence and as new statistical procedures were devised, a variety of different conceptions of intelligence began to prevail. Each investigator constructed his test to assess intelligence as he conceptualized it. The situation became so ambiguous that Edwin G. Boring once (in 1923) seriously proposed that intelligence be defined as "what intelligence tests measure."

Spearman was among the first of the mental testers to

propose a general theory of intellectual development, a two-factor theory of intelligence (Spearman, 1927). He argued that there was a **general intelligence factor,** *g*, which all individuals have, but in differing amounts. This *g* factor—which is genetically determined, according to Spearman—played a part in all intelligence test performance. In addition to *g*, however, there were also *specific* or *s* factors, for particular abilities or forms of tests (arithmetic and vocabulary tests, for example). A person's intelligence could thus be described in terms of the magnitude of the *g* and *s* factors.

Spearman's theory has been called a theory of general intelligence because it assumes that there is some common factor in all intelligence functioning. Other investigators, however, disputed the general theory of intelligence and proposed that intelligence test performance is a product of many different and separate factors. Such theories, called **multi-factor theories,** have been proposed by men such as Thurstone and Guilford.

Thurstone is perhaps best known for his test of Primary Mental Abilities (PMA), which is still in widespread use in schools (Thurstone, 1938). Thurstone argued on the basis of factor analysis of many kinds of intelligence tests (see p. 170 for more on factor analysis) that there was no underlying general intelligence but rather a system of interrelated **primary mental abilities.** While it is difficult to say precisely how many primary mental abilities there are—there appear to be different numbers for children and adults, for example—the following seven factors (primary abilities) have been found in many studies:

1. *Verbal comprehension* (*V*) The ability to understand words.
2. *Space* (*S*) A visualizing ability such as that exhibited in the accurate reproduction of a design from memory.
3. *Perception* (*P*) The ability to see quickly similarities and differences between pictures of objects.
4. *Number* (*N*) The ability to work with numbers and to compute.
5. *Memory* (*M*) The ability to recall verbal stimuli such as words.
6. *Word fluency* (*W*) The ability to think of words quickly—for example, in public speaking or in doing crossword puzzles.
7. *Reasoning* (*R*) The ability to find an underlying rule or structure in a series, for example, a sequence of numbers; in some studies, inductive and deductive reasoning were distinguished.

Spotlight 15-3 gives two items from a test for young children, one for word meaning (*V*) and the other for perceptual speed (*P*).

SPOTLIGHT 15-3
Test Your Primary Mental Abilities

The following two items are from the Test of Primary Mental Abilities for ages five and six, written by Thelma Gwynn and L. L. Thurstone.

The first row of pictures is from the test of word meaning. The instructions are: "Mark the picture that answers this question: Which one do you look at if you want to know how cold it is? Mark it."

The second row is from the test of perceptual speed. The instructions are: "In every row of pictures you are to do two things. First mark the picture all by itself in the little box. Then find the picture in the big box which is exactly like the picture in the little box and mark it too. Work fast. Do as many as you can on these two pages before I tell you to stop. Are you ready? Begin!"

Thurstone's primary mental abilities were not completely independent of one another; they were significantly intercorrelated. Because of this, some psychologists suggest that Thurstone's results did not contradict Spearman's notion of *g*, or general factor of intelligence, present in all intellectual tasks. But Thurstone's research did suggest that there are many components of intelligence. Unusual ability (or disability) in a particular aspect of intelligence may be important in individual diagnosis. For example, a person may be weak in one particular area such as arithmetic ability (*N*), even though he is *generally* high in intellectual abilities. Such information is useful for planning a course of study or a career.

The work of Thurstone and other investigators was the basis of *hierarchical theories of intelligence* (Burt, 1949; Vernon,

1950). According to these theories, there are an almost infinite number of very specific abilities that can be grouped into a few "primary mental abilities." These few abilities, in turn, are all influenced by a general factor—*g*, in Spearman's terms. People high in the general factor can be expected to be slightly above average on all intellectual tasks, but a better picture of their strengths and weaknesses can be obtained by measuring the specific primary mental abilities. These theories also suggest that if a specific ability is needed for a particular job, such as the ability to spot discoloration of eggs before marketing, it is preferable to test this ability directly—rather than rely on a more general predictor such as a score on a general intelligence test.

One notable investigator remains unconvinced that there is a general factor in intelligence. In denying the existence of a single general factor, Guilford (1967) even suggested that there are at least 120 unique intellectual abilities! In the past, he asserted, psychologists tended to confuse different aspects of intelligence. For example, as we have seen, Thurstone uncovered a verbal (*V*) factor and a spatial (*S*) one, and these were related to the *content* of different tests—the verbal and nonverbal tests. But other factors like reasoning (*R*) had little to do with content; they reflected what one *does* with content.

Guilford distinguished among four kinds of content: *semantic* (verbal material where "meanings" are critical); *figural* (the traditional nonverbal material, mostly pictures, but also including auditory content); *symbolic* (mostly letters and numbers); and *behavioral* (interpretations of human behavior). "Operations" refer to what you can do with content, and there are five categories: *cognition* (essentially knowing, as one knows the meaning of a word); *memory* (retaining information); *convergent production* (producing one "correct" answer); *divergent production* (like creativity; producing many possible answers to questions, such as "How many uses can you think for a brick?"); and *evaluation* ("judging" wisely).

In addition to the types of content and operations, Guilford suggested that intellectual abilities can also be distinguished in terms of the *products* resulting from the particular operation on the specific content. In other words, the final outcome (answer or answers) can be one of six types: *a unit* (e.g., a word), *a class of units* (e.g., a noun), *a relationship between units* (e.g., similar), *a system of information* (e.g., a plan), *a transformation* (e.g., a change), or *an implication* (e.g., a prediction).

Each unique ability is a combination of a type of content, an operation, and a certain product. With four contents, five operations, and six products, therefore, there are a total of 120 abilities ($4 \times 5 \times 6$); this theory is shown graphically in Figure 15-6.

A few examples may clarify Guilford's model. A vocabulary test has *semantic* content, calls for *cognition*, and the product is a discrete chunk or *unit:* "What is an albatross?"—"It's a bird."

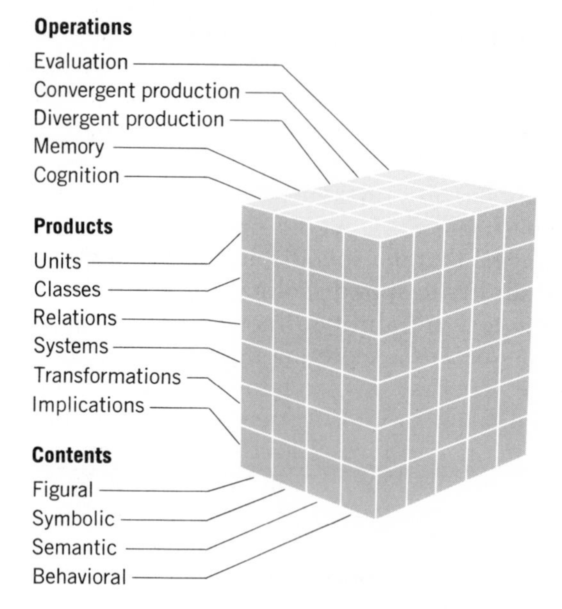

FIGURE 15-6 REPRESENTATION OF GUILFORD'S MULTI-FACTOR THEORY

Each "cell" of the cube represents a unique intellectual ability.
(From J. P. Guilford, 1967, p. 63)

Now consider the following item: Find the concealed name of a sport in the sentence, "He found a Mongol for his bride." The answer is "golf." According to Guilford, the content is symbolic (letters), the operation is convergent production (find the right answer), and the product is a transformation (a change from the originally presented material).

Suppose you ask someone to reproduce a map presented earlier. What would you call such a test, using Guilford's system?

Guilford's model of intellectual abilities was based partly on the results of previous studies, but not entirely. Like any good theory, it pointed up certain gaps in our knowledge and thus directed future research. More specifically, of the 120 abilities hypothesized, about 40 had been verified at the time the model was proposed; fairly good tests of these abilities had been devised and research (e.g., factor analysis) had shown them to be relatively distinct components of intelligence. Guilford and others then set out to devise and validate tests of the other abilities, and some ten years later (1967), another 40 had some research support. Research on the remaining, unverified 40 abilities predicted by the model continues today.

Guilford's theory of intelligence is respected but by no means universally accepted; it is still controversial. But multi-factor theories, in general, raise some interesting questions, not the least of which has to do with the hereditary basis of intelligence. If there are 120 (or more) unique intellectual abilities, it makes little sense to ask if global "intelligence" is inherited. Each individual ability must be investigated. The little evidence we now have indicates that some abilities are highly dependent on genetic factors while others are not.

SUMMARY

The measurement of human intelligence began in the latter part of the nineteenth century with the work of Galton and Binet. The tests devised by the French psychologist Alfred Binet, in which he stressed reasoning and problem-solving abilities, were found useful in diagnosing mental retardation and in predicting scholastic achievement. The Binet tests became widely used and revisions such as the Stanford-Binet are still used today. The concept of intelligence quotient (I.Q.) was developed to describe an individual's mental age as a ratio of his chronological age. An I.Q. of 100 indicates average mental ability.

A second important intelligence scale is the Wechsler. Because it is made up of a number of verbal and performance subtests, it can give a clearer picture of specific strengths and weaknesses. Group tests such as the Army Alpha enable the investigator to test a large number of people at the same time. Intelligence tests for infants have been devised, but assessments before the age of two have not been successful in predicting later achievements, except at the extremes of mental ability.

Intelligence tests seem to be unfair to disadvantaged minority children, who have had experiences different from those of the standardization group and who have not had parallel experiences in test-taking. Available tests work best with white middle-class children or adults, and scores from other populations must be interpreted cautiously. Attempts to create a culture-fair test have been unsuccessful but more important are culture-fair interpretations.

One of the questions frequently asked about I.Q. is "How stable is it?" Generally, the I.Q. is fairly stable over the years, but major environmental changes can produce significant increases in test scores; and, in at least some components, older people (over age forty) show decreases. General intelligence is clearly determined by both genetic and environmental factors; the relative contribution of each class of factors remains controversial. One of the most controversial issues has been the suggestion that differences between races in mean I.Q. are due to genetic differences.

There are various theories of intelligence depending upon the theorist's definition of what intelligence is. Some theories focus on a general factor, such as Spearman's *g*, presumably common to all intellectual performance. Others have described a set of between five and ten primary mental abilities. Still others posit even more distinct components of intelligence, up to 120. One popular theory of intelligence is the hierarchical, which suggests that a few primary abilities influence performance in a large number of specific tasks. These primary abilities, in turn, share a general common factor that could be called general intelligence.

16

Thought and Language

What is distinctively human about thought?
What do we know about language?
To what extent do thought and language depend on each other?

Human thought and language are capacities that most prominently mark the distinction between man and other animals. The ability to think about the consequences of an action before acting, and to change plans on this basis, is an evolutionary advance of such magnitude that philosophers for centuries refused to consider man as part of the animal world. Thought and language permit abstractions that can lead to intelligent decisions in situations never before encountered. We can consider the past and conceptualize the future in ways no other animal can. We can also "make a mountain out of a molehill" or see a "tempest in a teapot." For better or for worse, human thought and language are among the most significant features of human behavior.

Thought as it has been typically studied by psychologists could be defined as the acquisition and manipulation of symbols and ideas. Studies of concept formation, for example, are designed to investigate the acquisition of verbal symbols or concepts. The manipulation or use of symbols in thought is the focus of studies of reasoning and problem solving. The ability to use symbols in an original and socially valuable manner is called creativity, and individual differences in this ability have been central concerns of a number of interesting investigations. Recently, individual differences in cognitive style have been investigated; cognitive styles are presumed to be fairly general, stable ways of solving problems that apply regardless of the specific content of the thinking. For example, some people seem to arrive at a solution to a problem intuitively while others use a more analytic approach.

Closely related to thinking are the processes of symbolization known as *language*. It is quite clear that language and thought affect each other in many ways. Presumably, frequent or necessary thoughts eventually become identified verbally as words in a language system. On the other hand, a language system might facilitate certain kinds of thought and inhibit others. One investigator (Whorf, see p. 410) noted that Eskimos have in their language several different words for different kinds of snow. He suggests that they therefore think differently about snow compared to people with only one word, "snow."

Still, the relationship of thought and language is not a simple one. People may use a word accurately with little or no "conceptual" understanding, as a young child may use the term "brother" for his but no one else's brother. And one may have a concept with no verbal label, as children seem to understand "pressure" (the need to push hard to open a door that sticks) even though they do not know or understand the concept. Philosophers, linguists, and psychologists have debated the issue of the thought-language relationship for centuries, but the controversy continues. We will examine some of the research and some of the prominent theories relating to thought and language; then you can make your own judgments.

What are main characteristics of thought?

Concept Formation

Concepts are indispensable tools of mental activity and make up the "content" of human thought. When you think, you generally use concepts. Some of them may be quite concrete—like desk; some are abstract—like comprehension. What is a **concept?** Generally speaking, the term refers to a response made to a class of objects or phenomena that have certain common characteristics; usually—but not always—these responses are verbal "labels." When the child can use the label "dog" in a discriminating way in response to four-legged animals that bark and have fur, we generally assume he has learned the concept of "dog."

Concrete Concepts

Psychologists who have studied **concept formation** have often dealt with concepts in which the common characteristic is a dominant perceptual feature. In a classic study Hull (1920) presented subjects with packs of cards containing Chinese symbols (called characters). The characters were given a label, like "oo" or "na," assigned on the basis of a common aspect of the character. Somewhere embedded in the following "oo's" is the symbol shown last:

The subject was instructed to give the proper label when each character was presented. If he did not respond within a certain time, or if he gave an incorrect response, the experimenter told him the correct answer. The first time through a set of characters, of course, no correct replies were possible, but the subjects quickly learned the concepts after that. Learning was facilitated by emphasizing the embedded element (say by outlining it in a different color). This procedure facilitated learning to a greater extent than presenting the elements in isolation.

In a similar type of experiment subjects had to learn to associate arbitrary labels such as "relf" and "fard" to different kinds of pictorial stimuli (Heidbreder, 1946). The subjects learned the nonsense words associated with concrete objects (faces, buildings, articles of clothing) more quickly than they learned the ones associated with geometric forms or with numbers. In brief, concepts were more easily attained if they had "thinglike" qualities. Heidbreder, like Hull, also found that more perceptually prominent features—those that "stand out"—were more easily learned as concepts.

Concepts as Mediators

Much of the more recent work on concept formation focuses on concepts as mediators, such as verbal labels, mental images, and associations, that can be presumed to serve as bridges linking the same response to a number of different stimuli. For example, dogs come in many shapes and sizes, but a child who has acquired the concept of "dog" is likely to respond to these myriad stimuli in the same way; if his previous experience with dogs has been positive, he is apt to pet all animals he labels "dog." The verbal mediator allows him to behave appropriately to new stimuli (unfamiliar dogs) on the first encounter.

An excellent experimental paradigm demonstrating the role of mediating processes in concept formation is the **reversal shift** problem (Kendler & Kendler, 1967). The subject is presented with two squares at a time and has to learn to choose one of them. The squares vary in size (large and small) and color (black and white). (See Figure 16-1.) The subject is consistently reinforced or rewarded (given a marble) for choosing in terms of *either* color or size. If color is the relevant dimension, the subject would be rewarded every time he chose the darker square regardless of its size. The size dimension would be irrelevant in this instance; that is, it is not used in making the correct discrimination. In a reversal shift, the subject must learn to *reverse* his responses, to do exactly the opposite of what he has done previously in the same situation. After learning to choose the black square, for example, the child is confronted with a new problem in which he must learn to choose the white square to obtain the reward. In a *nonreversal* shift, the subject would be required to choose on the basis of what was previously the irrelevant dimension; in our example, he would have to make his choice—and be rewarded

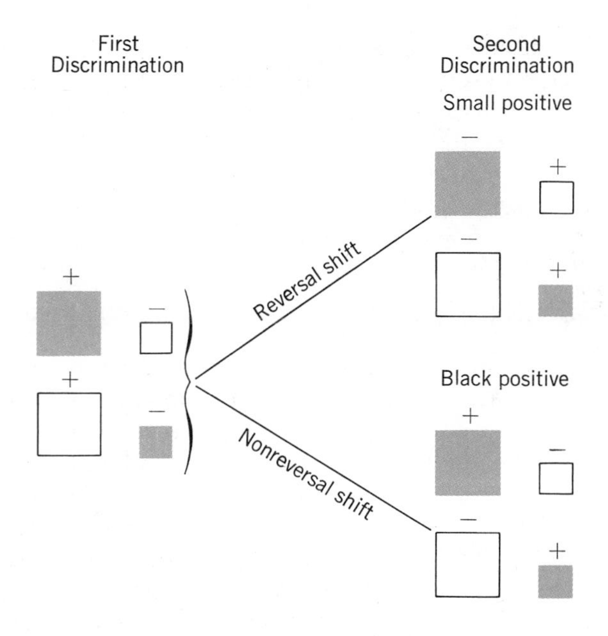

FIGURE 16-1 EXAMPLES OF A REVERSAL AND A NONREVERSAL SHIFT
In a reversal shift, the subject first learns to select the large stimuli; then he is reinforced for selecting the small stimuli in the second discrimination. In a nonreversal shift, he must respond to another dimension (color or brightness) in the second discrimination.
(From Kendler & Kendler, 1962)

for it—on the basis of size (large or small) rather than of color.

You might think that it would be easier to switch from black to white choices, the reversal shift, than to begin considering a previously irrelevant dimension. And, in fact, the reversal shift is easier for children over seven and for adults, probably because they can use verbal mediators. That is, they can tell themselves that "color is the important thing" so when they find that black is no longer rewarded, they try white. However, younger children and animals, lacking the ability to use verbal mediators, have great difficulty with reversal shifts and do better on nonreversal shifts. Apparently, to do the opposite of what you have been trained to do is easier if you use verbal mediators like "color" to identify the critical dimension.

Verbal mediators typically represent *abstract concepts* as contrasted with the more *concrete* commonalities among objects (perceptual properties such as red or round) investigated in the Hull and Heidbreder studies (pp. 383 and 384). The concept "brother," for example, is abstract; one cannot simply look at two males and see that they are brothers; the concept refers to a rule or principle, that brothers have the same parents. During World War I psychologists found that many soldiers suffering brain injury could use concrete but not abstract concepts. Since this deficiency could be used to diagnose the presence and extent of the injury, a variety of tests were devised to assess ability to use abstract concepts.

One of these tests was the Object Sorting Test, devised by Goldstein and Scheerer (1941). The content of this test consists of a variety of familiar objects common to most people's everyday environment—a spoon, knife, hammer, matches, pipe, apple, cigar, and ball. The subject is asked to sort the objects into groups that are alike or the same in some way. This is an easy task for normal subjects. The objects can be grouped on the basis of several characteristics: color, material they are made of, what they can be used for, and many more. Brain-injured subjects tend to group on the basis of very specific or concrete attributes, such as color. Another task in the test, once the subject has made his first grouping, is to group the objects again in a new and different way. Normal subjects can do so with ease; brain-injured subjects have great difficulty.

Young children have similar difficulties with such tasks, presumably because they have not yet reached the stage in which they can use abstract concepts easily. This developmental trend from concrete to abstract concepts is also seen in responses to the "similarities" subtests included in many general intelligence tests. Similarities tests have items such as, "In what way are an orange and a grapefruit alike?" The question can be answered in terms of rather concrete commonalities (they are both round) or in more abstract terms (both are fruits). Older children and adults give more abstract answers, while younger children give more concrete ones.

Derived Concepts

Another type of concept that has been studied by psychologists is what has been called a **derived concept.** Derived concepts are those which are formed or constructed out of concepts already in the subject's repertoire. The concept of speed, for example, is derived from the combination of the concepts of time and distance. The lower order concepts from which the higher order concept is derived have been called "fundamental concepts." The distinction between derived and fundamental concepts is, however, relative because concepts which are derived themselves can be fundamental to other concepts. The concept "American Protestant," for example, is derived from the concepts of American and of Protestant, which are themselves derived from core fundamental concepts such as person, religion, and country.

Some ground-breaking research in the study of derived concepts was done by Bruner, Goodnow, and Austin (1956). These investigators were concerned with how subjects acquire three different kinds of derived concepts—conjunctive, disjunctive, and relational concepts, each involving a different way of combining attributes. They presented their subjects with the eighty-one cards shown in Figure 16-2. Note that each card is made up of figures and borders, and cards can vary in four attributes. The figures vary in three attributes: *shape* (square, circle, or cross), in *color* (red, green, or black), and in *number* (single, double, or triple). In addition, the *number of borders* varies (one, two, or three). Each card in the array exhibits one value of each of these four attributes. We may speak of a concept in terms of the defining properties of some subset of cards. For example, "all cards with one red figure" is a concept, so too is "all cards with two figures and/or with circles," and so is "all cards possessing the same number of figures and borders" (Bruner *et al.*, 1956, p. 41). These three examples involve three different kinds of concepts, and their definitions may be simplified by reference to Figure 16-2.

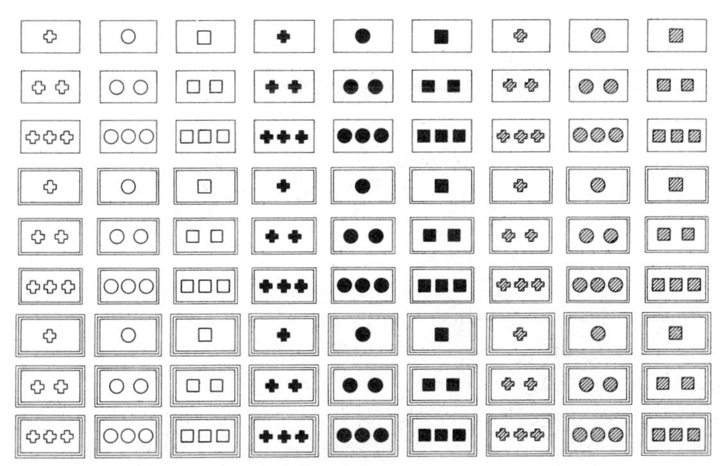

FIGURE 16-2 CARDS USED IN STUDYING DERIVED CONCEPTS

Cards vary in four attributes: color, shape, and number of figures, and number of borders. Outlined figures are in green, solid figures in black, striped figures in red.
(From Bruner, Goodnow, & Austin, 1956)

A **conjunctive concept** is defined by the joint presence of several attributes; all examples of the concept have one or more attributes in common. The concept "WASP," for example, refers to the combination of white, Anglo-Saxon, and Protestant. In the stimuli presented in the figure, one conjunctive concept would be "three red circles," which includes all those circles which come in threes and are also red. In logic, the process of forming conjunctive concepts is called "logical multiplication," and is illustrated in Figure 16-3A.

Disjunctive concepts are derived by combining fundamental concepts which have no common members; that is, examples of the concepts have any one of several characteristics rather than all of them. The concept "children" refers to "boys" or "girls" (or three- or ten-year-olds). Classes are not overlapping. In the cards shown in Figure 16-2, a disjunctive concept would be exemplified by a concept that referred to "three" things, *or* "red" things, *or* "round" things. In logic, disjunctive concepts are said to be arrived at by "logical addition," as illustrated in Figure 16-3B.

In a third type of derived concept, the **relational concept,** the relation between attributes, rather than the attributes themselves, is important (e.g., the "taller" figure). The concept "right side" does not refer to any particular class members but merely to a relation to other objects, and, in the forms shown in Figure 16-2, any one of the forms or colors could be on the "right side" of the card. Relational concepts are often difficult to define because, more often than not, they do not involve a physical characteristic but rather a psycho-

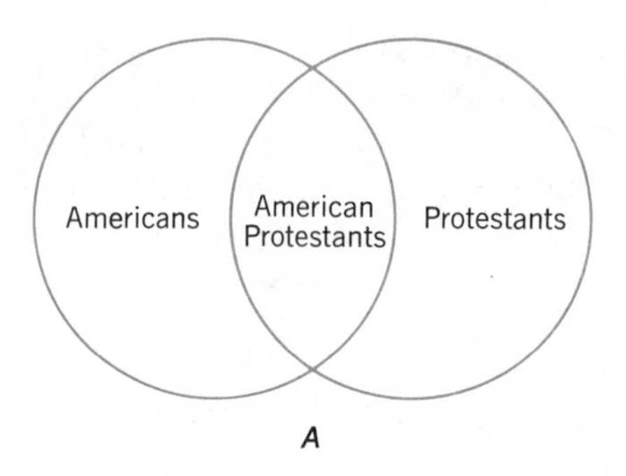

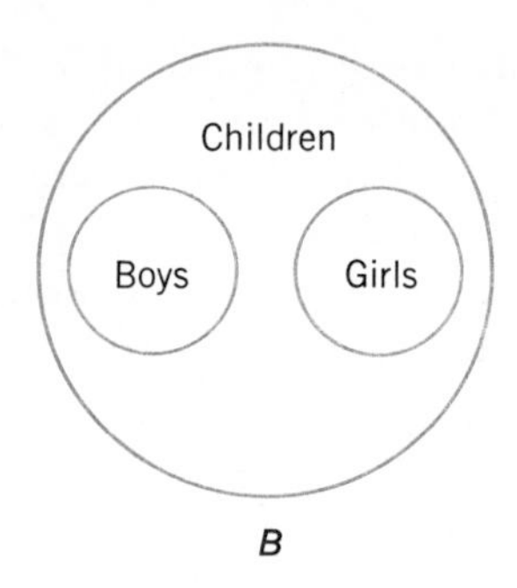

FIGURE 16-3
CONCEPTS DIAGRAMMED
A—Conjunctive concept
B—Disjunctive concept

logical attribute imposed upon the materials ("rightness" or "leftness" do not exist in things the way color and form do, and whether something is on the right or left is always relative to the subject).

In the study of Bruner and his colleagues, subjects were told explicitly what their task was: to find out which cards on the board before them were the positive cards and which were negative; that is, which exemplified and which did not exemplify a concept that the experimenter had in mind. (See Figure 16–2.) They were also informed about whether the concept was disjunctive or conjunctive, and these terms were fully explained. The subject could choose one card at a time in any order he wished and after each choice the experimenter would tell him whether the card was positive or negative. Suppose, for example, that the experimenter's concept was the conjunctive one "red circles." If the subject pointed to a card with three crosses, he could be informed that this was incorrect, a negative instance. If however, he pointed to a card with three red circles, he would be told that this was a positive instance. He would then point to another card and, if that card had any red circles, he would again be told this was a positive instance. The procedure continued until he found the correct concept.

The ease or difficulty of acquiring a concept was found to be partially a function of its complexity (for example, the number of dimensions employed in it—color, shape, number, spatial position) and also of its logical structure. Other things being equal, conjunctive concepts were easier to acquire than relational concepts, and disjunctive concepts were the most difficult of all to learn. These investigators also found that subjects approached the task in different ways and employed certain characteristic strategies, as described in Spotlight 16-1.

Reasoning

When we speak of **reasoning** we generally have in mind the rule aspect or the *modus operandi* of the thinking process. With the exception of dream and reverie states, our thinking usually moves in clear directions and according to certain rules which, by and large, are the rules of logical discourse. We are rarely *conscious* of our

SPOTLIGHT 16-1

Typical Strategies in Concept Attainment

In concept attainment studies, such as the one described in the text (Bruner, Goodnow, & Austin, 1956), subjects typically employ a variety of strategies in their attempts to guess the correct concept. Two major types of strategies are scanning and focusing.

If you are using a *scanning strategy,* you formulate a hypothesis about what the correct concept might be. Suppose you are shown a card with three red circles and two borders and are told that this is a "positive" instance of a conjunctive concept. You then know that the correct concept is three, or red, or circle, or two borders—or some combination of these attributes. In the simplest of scanning strategies, called "successive scanning," you test each possible hypothesis in turn. For example, "three circles" is possible, so you might first choose a card with three green circles with one border; your first hypothesis predicts that this will be called positive. If it is not, that hypothesis is no longer tenable, and you might try another possibility, say "red objects." Each hypothesis among the remaining possibilities is tested in turn until the correct one is discovered.

If you use a *focusing strategy,* you would focus on the individual attributes in the card designated positive. In the simplest focusing strategy, called "conservative focusing," each attribute is tested in turn. In our example (three red circles with two borders), you might first test the number to see if "three" is a relevant attribute; you would choose a card with two red circles and two borders. If this is called positive, number is irrelevant. Then you focus on color, choosing a card with green circles and two borders. Suppose this card is negative, red is relevant. Then shape is considered by choosing a card with red crosses and two borders. Say this too is negative; circle is relevant. Finally, the number of borders is tested by choosing a card with red circles and one border. If this choice is positive, you know the concept is "red circles."

In situations like this, the focusing strategy is more frequently used because it is effective and it puts less strain on the memory. But in other situations, successive scanning or more intricate forms of scanning and focusing strategies might be preferable. If you were limited to only two guesses, the conservative focusing strategy would not seem quite so attractive.

reasoning processes and of the extent to which they govern our everyday judgments and conclusions, however. Like Molière's character who was surprised to discover that he had been speaking prose all of his life, we are all a little amazed to discover how rational most of our thinking turns out to be.

Reasoning in Adults

Studies of reasoning in adults have been primarily concerned with formal logical reasoning, that required by syllogisms, and with errors in logic. For example, one investigator studied the problem of whether more abstract or more concrete material is handled more logically. She presented college students with syllogisms that were logically identical, but phrased in terms of familiar words, letters, or unfamiliar (esoteric or made-up) words. Subjects were to choose the correct conclusion from the three possibilities suggested for each syllogism. Here are some examples:

A. *All the people living on this farm are related to the Joneses; these old men live on this farm; therefore,*
(1) *these old men are related to the Joneses;*
(2) *all the people related to the Joneses are these old men;*
(3) *some people related to the Joneses are not these old men.*
B. *All* X*'s are* Y*'s; all* Z*'s are* X*'s; therefore,*
(1) *all* Z*'s are* Y*'s;*
(2) *all* Y*'s are* Z*'s;*
(3) *some* Y*'s are not* Z*'s.*
C. *All lysimachion is epilobium; all adenocaulon is lysimachion; therefore,*
(1) *all adenocaulon is epilobium;*
(2) *all epilobium is adenocaulon;*
(3) *some epilobium is not adenocaulon.*

In each example (1) is the valid conclusion.

Syllogisms utilizing familiar words—the most concrete—were the easiest to solve logically; those using symbols or letters were significantly more difficult, and those with unfamiliar terms were the most difficult (Wilkins, 1928).

Another interesting early discovery was the "atmosphere effect" of a syllogism. The words "all," none," or "some" in the premises create a global impression or "atmosphere" that seems to call for a corresponding conclusion. Thus, syllogisms with positively stated premises (e.g., All *A*'s are *B*'s, All *A*'s are *C*'s) tend to elicit choices of positively stated conclusions—and negatively stated premises (No *A*'s are *B*'s) elicit negative conclusions—even if these are invalid (Sells, 1936).

Personal convictions may also affect an individual's response to syllogistic reasoning, especially in the case of propositions involving controversial issues. A syllogism can be constructed, for example, in which the logically correct (valid) answer is factually false. "All men are immortal. I am a man—therefore I am immortal." One of the other possible responses to this syllogism might be "I am mortal," which is true but not logically valid. When the topic of the syllogism is controversial and deals with strong personal beliefs, logic is less likely to determine the choice of conclusions. For the premises, "Abortion is a right of women" and "The rights of women should be protected by law," the logical conclusion is that abortion should be legalized. But people with strong attitudes against abortion are likely to see this conclusion as invalid. For the premises,

"Abortion is murder" and "Murder should be prohibited by law," the logical conclusion is that abortion should be prohibited. People strongly favorable to abortion would be more likely to see this conclusion as invalid.

The research evidence as a whole does not speak well for the rationality of man. One typical finding is that, for controversial items, personal beliefs determined most of the chosen conclusions; for neutral items, the atmosphere effects dominated. For both neutral and controversial items, logic was a less important factor than either atmosphere or personal conviction in the determination of a subject's choice of conclusion in syllogistic reasoning.

Reasoning in Children

Studies of reasoning in children have been more varied than those with adults and reflect more concern with mediating processes. Several investigators (e.g., Kendler & Kendler, 1962) have used a basic experimental design that requires the subject to combine two different experiences in order to reach a desired goal. For example, in learning to use the apparatus shown in Figure 16-4, the child is *first* taught that if he presses a button on the left, a steel ball will be delivered; pressing the button on the right brings a marble.

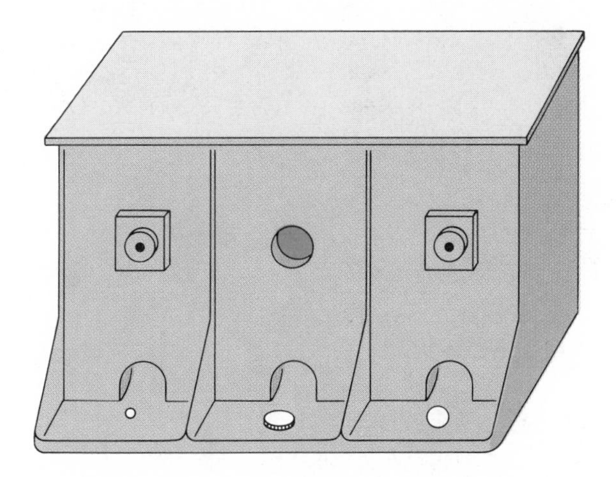

FIGURE 16-4 APPARATUS TO STUDY REASONING

By pressing the button on the left, the subject can get a steel ball, which when placed in the center hole will produce a charm. Preschool children have difficulty solving the problem of how to get a charm.

After he has learned this, the center section is opened and the side sections closed; the child then learns that if he puts a steel ball into the center hole, an attractive charm drops out of the slot at the bottom; if he inserts a glass marble, nothing happens. Finally, all three sections are opened and the child is instructed to get the charm. All he has to do is press the left button (which he knows will yield a steel ball), and then put the steel ball in the center hole to get his charm. Can he combine these two bits of learning in order to solve the problem? Young preschool children have difficulty. For some reason they do not associate the steel ball that comes from pushing the button on the left with the steel ball that gets the charm. Children over seven or eight and adults solve this two-part problem easily.

Some more recent studies have related these data about reasoning to theories of concept formation. Perhaps the younger children fail to solve the two-stage reasoning problems because they lack verbal labels that might function as mediators. Perhaps if the child was taught to say "ball" when the steel ball was delivered after he pressed a button and "ball" again when the steel ball was inserted in the center section to get the charm, this verbal label would serve to mediate the necessary association between these two actions. This was done in one study, and while performance did improve, the increase in number of correct solutions was much less than expected, at least for nursery-school children. These data led to the hypothesis that there are three stages in verbal mediational processes. In the *preverbal stage*, the child does not have or under-

When children begin to use verbal mediators, they can solve problems by reasoning. (Kingsley Fairbridge)

stand the words necessary for solution. In the *verbal deficiency stage*, the child seems to know the appropriate words, but the verbal labels do not mediate behaviors to similar stimuli. In our example, the child might spontaneously say "ball" when the steel ball comes out after a button press, and "ball" when he inserts the steel ball in the top hole to get a charm, but he still does not solve the two-part problem readily. The third stage could be called the *verbal mediation stage*, in which words are both available *and* effective in mediating responses. The last stage is characteristic of most school children and, of course, adults.

Taking a more cognitive approach to children's reasoning, Donaldson (1962) used a variety of tasks or problems of which the following is an example:

Five boys, Jack, Dick, James, Bob, and Tom, go to five different schools in the same town. The schools are called North School, South School, East School, West School, and Central School.

Jack does not go to North, South, or Central School.
Dick goes to West School.
Bob does not go to North or Central School.
Tom has never been inside Central School.
1. What school does Jack go to?
2. What school does Bob go to?
3. What school does James go to?
4. What school does Tom go to?

Children's errors fell within a few more or less circumscribed categories. Some were *structural* and really reflected the child's failure to grasp the problem and what was required for a solution. Other errors were *arbitrary* in the sense that the child did not sufficiently attend to the data with which he was provided. Last but not least were *executive* errors; the child understood the problem and the manipulations required for its solution but for one reason or another failed to execute the required operation. Such executive errors may be attributed to "some defect of concentration, of attention, or of immediate memory" (Donaldson, 1962).

A third approach to reasoning in children derives from an educational and pedagogical perspective. In one study (Suppes & Hull, 1961) children between six and eight were presented with simple problems in logic. They were given two or three premises after which they were required to judge whether or not a particular conclusion followed from them. A control group solved the same problems but did not have the initial premise of the arguments. The number of correct answers for the experimental group ranged from 71 percent at age six to 86 percent correct answers at age eight. The correct judgments for the control group was only 52 percent. Such studies suggest that, in teaching, children should be given complete, rather than partial arguments; the full line of reasoning should be explicit.

Problem Solving

Although **problem solving** has been studied from the beginnings of scientific psychology, the classic work on human problem solving was carried out during the 1930's by Karl Duncker (1945). He began his investigations with the premise that thinking arises when an individual is blocked from attaining some desirable goal. Thinking in this situation involves devising a solution that will fulfill two aims: (1) it must bring out the desired goal and (2) it must be practical in the sense that it is workable. To study how individuals go about solving problems, Duncker devised a number of tasks, which he presented to subjects. Spotlight 16-2 shows an example of a typical protocol—the complete record of the task and ways of attacking the problem.

SPOTLIGHT 16-2

Duncker's "Inoperable Stomach Tumor" Problem

When Duncker presented the following problem to college students, he asked them to think out loud, and he (the experimenter) then provided clues which would lead them to the correct solution.

> Given a human being with an inoperable stomach tumor, and rays which destroy organic tissue at sufficient intensity, by what procedure can one free him of the tumor by these rays and at the same time avoid destroying the healthy tissue which surrounds it? (Duncker, 1945, p. 1)

1. Send rays through the esophagus.
2. Desensitize the healthy tissues by means of a chemical injection.
3. Expose the tumor by operating.
4. One ought to decrease the intensity of the rays on their way; for example—would this work?—turn the rays on at full strength only after the tumor has been reached.
   (Experimenter: False analogy; no injection is in question.)
5. One should swallow something inorganic (which would not allow passage of the rays) to protect the healthy stomach walls.
   (Experimenter: it is not merely the stomach walls which are to be protected.)
6. Either the rays must enter the body or the tumor must come out. Perhaps one could alter the location of the tumor—but how? Through pressure? No.
7. Introduce a cannula.
   (Experimenter: What, in general, does one do when, with any agent, one wishes to produce in a specific place, an effect which he wishes to avoid on the way to that place?)
8. (Reply:) One neutralises the effect on the way. But that is what I have been attempting all the time.
9. Move the tumor toward the exterior. (Compare 6.)
   (The Experimenter repeats the problem and emphasizes, ". . . which destroy *at sufficient intensity*.")
10. The intensity ought to be variable. (Compare 4.)
11. Adaptation of the healthy tissues by previous weak application of the rays.
    (Experimenter: How can it be brought about that the rays destroy only the region of the tumor?)

Goal-Direction

In analyzing protocols such as the one in Spotlight 16-2, Duncker found that the solution process involved putting forth a series of concrete proposals. Usually these proposals were more or less impractical, as in the example, with the exception of the last one. But Duncker argued that they were *not* random or meaningless; the proposals would meet the demands of the problem had they been practical. Were it possible, for example, to send rays through the esophagus, then it would be a correct solution. Duncker thus emphasized the *goal-directed* nature of problem solving.

Perhaps it seems elementary that problem-solving attempts would be goal-directed. But what seems simple often turns out to be complex upon further investigation. Studies of the "intelligence of animals" began almost a century ago, and the early researchers, such as Thorndike (1898), found little evidence of goal-direction in the problem-solving behavior of hungry cats and dogs, for example, in learning to push a lever that would open their cage door and give them access to food outside. At first the hungry animals made many random responses, such as thrashing about and running around the cage. In the course of these random behaviors, some movement or action would accidentally trip the lever. Gradually, this effective response became more frequent and others less so, but many incorrect, ineffective responses were repeated even after the correct solution had been discovered and used. Thorndike proposed that the correct response was only gradually "stamped in" or strengthened, automatically, mechanically, as the animal was rewarded.

Insightful Behavior

The behavior of Thorndike's cats and dogs gave little indication of **insight**—the sudden recognition of the nature of the problem and its correct solution. Later studies, however, have indicated that higher animals such as apes do use insight in solving problems. Wolfgang Köhler (1926) worked with a most intelligent chimpanzee named Sultan. One day Sultan had a short stick with him in his cage and Köhler placed some fruit outside the cage, too far away to be reached by hand or with the short stick. Also outside the cage was a long stick, too far to be reached by hand but close enough to be pulled in by the short stick. Sultan first tried to reach the fruit with his hand and then with the short stick. Failing, he paused and looked about, saw the long stick, and then rather suddenly took his short stick and used it to scrape the longer one toward the cage. Then he used the long stick to get the fruit.

Köhler concluded that Sultan's use of the stick in this way in this situation, to solve new problems, was clear evidence of goal-directed, insightful behavior. Many psychologists at the time agreed. Some, however, asked whether previous experience might not have been necessary for the apparently insightful performance. Sultan was a captured chimp who spent the early part of his life in the natural jungle habitat. Ethologists observing chimpanzees in this kind of setting have found that chimpanzees do use twigs and branches as primitive tools. Later, working with primates born in captivity, psychologists found that if animals have not had this kind of experience—if they have never used a stick before—they will not show "insightful" performance. Slow trial and error learning invariably precedes complex problem solving.

The apparent insight of the chimp depends on his past experience with trial and error.
(Courtesy Yerkes Regional Primate Research Center)

Research on human problem solving, such as Duncker's, also gives evidence of goal-directed and insightful behavior. The question is not whether problem-solving activities are random trial and error *or* insightful and goal-directed. Both types exist. Which type prevails is a function of many variables: the nature of the problem, the species under study, the age of the subjects, and many others. Of particular interest to psychologists are developmental trends. Very young children, like lower animals, tend to approach many problems in a random, trial and error manner, while older children and adults perform with more insight. Why is this so? The development of language and the corresponding increase in the ability to use abstract concepts is one possible reason.

Another reason is that many animals, including men and chimpanzees, can apparently "learn to learn." In fact, one eminent psychologist, Harry Harlow, believes that insight depends on previous trial and error experiences (Harlow, 1949). He demonstrated this in several experiments in which monkeys solved a series of discrimination problems. For each problem, the animal was presented with two objects that differed in size, shape, and color—a green square and a red circle, for example. If he chose the correct object, he was immediately reinforced, because he found some raisins or peanuts under it. The pair was presented over and over, in different positions, but the reward was always under the same object. When it was clear that the monkey had learned the correct object—when he chose this one on every trial—a new pair of objects was presented. The animal was given another series of trials in which the correct choice was immediately rewarded and trials were continued until this problem was mastered. Animals were presented with a long series of discrimination problems, 344 in one experiment. The animals' problem-solving behavior changed dramatically as they acquired more experience. The first problems presented were solved with a great deal of trial and error, and the solutions were arrived at gradually. After more experience, however, the animals showed a kind of insight; toward the end of a long series, they would reach a correct solution after one, or very few, trials. They had "learned to learn," they knew how to deal with this type of problem; in Harlow's terms, they had developed a "learning set" (Harlow, 1949).

Analogously, in his first attempt to set up a chemistry laboratory experiment, the student ordinarily exhibits a great deal of inefficient, trial and error activity. After some experience, however, he can set up experiments quickly and efficiently, even though he is using new, different apparatus and chemicals. He has learned something of general applicability: how to handle laboratory equipment and chemical substances.

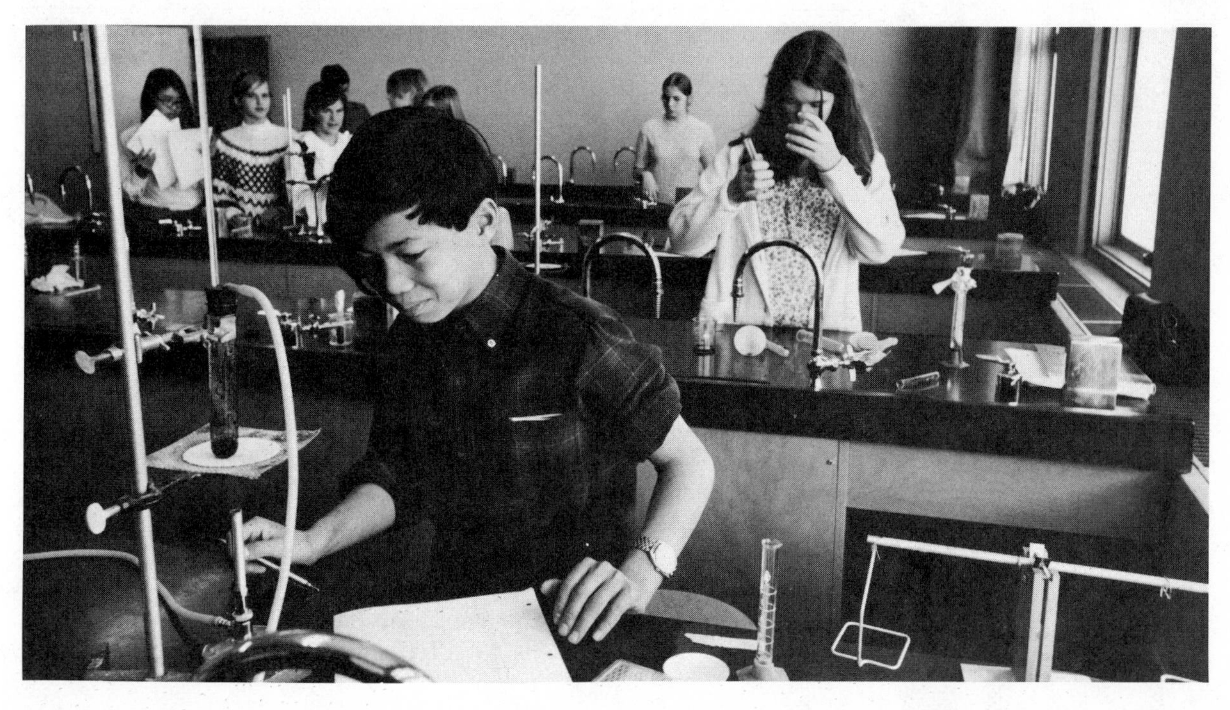

A student's first attempts to set up laboratory experiments involve a great deal of inefficient, trial and error activity.
(Van Bucher, Photo Researchers)

Functional Fixedness

One of the characteristics that impede human problem-solving behavior has been called **functional fixedness,** an inability to see the multiple potential uses of a particular object or technique. A man who needs a screwdriver and is holding a dime in his hand shows functional fixedness if he does not recognize that the dime could be a screwdriver as well as a coin.

An individual who decidedly did *not* demonstrate functional fixedness was a man who, according to newspaper accounts, was taken from his car, robbed, and locked in the trunk. When breathing became difficult, he recognized his spare tire as "a source of air" and by slowly releasing the "spare air," he managed to survive until help came.

Functional fixedness is a kind of *set* or predisposition to act in a specific routine way. At times when flexibility is important, sets can blind people to other information. A good example is the water jar problem devised by Luchins (1942). In this task the experimenter tells the subjects that they are "to figure out, on paper, how to obtain a required volume of water given certain empty jars as measures." The subjects were then shown the problem given in Table 16-1. They were asked for the solution to problem 1, which was written on the blackboard. Then problem 2 was put on the board and

TABLE 16-1
LUCHINS' WATER JAR PROBLEMS

	Problem	Given the Following Empty Jars as Measures A	B	C	Obtain the Required Amount of Water
Examples	1	29	3		20
	2	21	127	3	100
Developing the Set	3	14	163	25	99
	4	18	43	10	5
	5	9	42	6	21
	6	20	59	4	31
Tests	7	23	49	3	20
	8	15	39	3	18

the subjects were again asked for their solutions. The answer was then illustrated in both a written and a verbal form; verbally "one fills the 127-quart jar and from this fills the 21-quart jar once and the 3-quart jar twice. In the 127-quart jar there then remains the 100 quarts of water" (Luchins, 1942).

Inspection of the problems shows that the method to solve problem 2 also suffices to solve problems 3 through 6. If the jars are designated *ABC* from left to right, then the solution has the formula $B - A - 2C$. Or, in words, "Fill the middle jar and use it to fill the left jar once and the right jar twice—this will leave the required amount in the middle jar." While the same method can be used to solve problems 7 and 8, they can be solved much more simply. In the case of problem 7 the solution is symbolized by $A - C$ while in problem 8, the solution is symbolized by $A + C$. All of Luchins' subjects, however, proceeded to solve the problem by the more difficult and circuitous formula $B - A - 2C$. Their *set* to solve problems in this manner precluded the recognition of the much simpler solution.

Computer Models of Thought

Thinking, reasoning, concept formation, and problem solving generally involve activities such as "processing" and sorting information, abstracting common features of a set of stimuli, and combining and reorganizing information in new ways, all according to certain rules (e.g., rules of logic or scientific inference). These are the kinds of activities high-speed computers can perform. Hence it is not surprising to find that there have been a number of interesting attempts to model *general* thought processes by means of **computer simulation.**

A computer *model* is an attempt to reproduce human behaviors, not to improve on human capabilities. A computer cannot solve a problem unless it is given a "program," a specific detailed set of instructions, for its solution. In writing such a program, the programmer breaks the problem down into its component parts and programs the computer to put them together in precisely defined ways. For example, a computer can be "instructed" (programmed) in the rules of logical inference. Give the properly programmed computer a set of syllogisms and it will draw the logically correct conclusions.

Early computer simulation models tried to reproduce the thinking of the perfectly logical man. And with simple tasks, like making logical inferences or playing tic-tac-toe, this is not too difficult. You can tie but never beat a good computer program of tic-tac-toe. Chess-playing computers, on the other hand, will usually lose to human chess experts, but only because the brain of a chess expert takes many more factors into account, some of which the expert cannot even describe. The computer cannot be programmed with such unspecifiable factors. But even if the computer had all the necessary information to win at chess or to exceed human capacities for intelligent behavior generally, it would be a poor model of human thought. Humans get impatient and bored with a problem after awhile; they choose *adequate* solutions while the rational computer chooses only *optimal* solutions. Humans "give up" after a series of failures; the computer keeps trying.

Most of us are at best part-time logicians. Factors other than logic and rational thought exert strong influences on our problem-solving efforts: personal beliefs and atmosphere effects (see p. 390), self-confidence or lack of it, impatience, level of aspiration—and many others. Hence, it is very difficult to construct computer models of how people *actually* think. To "think" like a real person, the computer would have to be programmed in such a way as to take all of these factors into account.

More recent computer models of thought have attempted to give more consideration to motivational and emotional influences on human problem solving (e.g., Simon, 1967). With such models, the computer takes variables like impatience or discouragement into account by working toward a solution to a problem only for a limited time, then "giving up" (stopping operations), and using the best solution among those already formulated—which probably will not be the optimal solution. Or it might be programmed to give up after a certain number of failures in its attempts at solutions.

It is important to note that in order to model thinking on the average imperfect human, the computer must be programmed in accordance with a *theory* of human thought. If the responses of the computer do not match those of an average subject, the theory with which the computer is programmed is called into question—the program becomes a kind of rigorous test of the theory or hypothesis. Writing a computer program requires step-by-step specification of an overall process such as problem solving. Simply trying to do this may indicate where we lack sufficient knowledge, where we don't really know what the next step is. Thus, computer models have a unique potential for breakthroughs in the understanding of human thought. It is too early to say whether these breakthroughs will actually occur, but it is certain that computer models will become more ubiquitous and more sophisticated.

Creativity

Some people say intelligence and creativity are synonymous, since both involve cognition or thought; others say the two are completely different. What is the relationship between the two, if any? What distinguishes the creative person from the ordinary?

Consider the relevant distinction between convergent and divergent thinking. **Convergent thinking** applies to questions that have one correct answer, e.g., "What is the capital of Nebraska?" or "What is the best way to milk a cow?" **Divergent thinking** is reflected in answering questions such as, "How many uses can you think of for a kitchen knife?" or, "How are these two objects—a potato and a carrot—alike? List as many ways as you can." (Guilford, 1964)

Many psychologists believe this distinction is necessary to the understanding of **creativity.** By their reasoning, traditional intelligence tests do not assess creativity because they are designed to measure only convergent thinking, the extent to which the individual follows accepted patterns of thought. On the vocabulary test of most intelligence scales, for example, the subject's score reflects how closely his definitions of particular terms correspond to the dictionary definition. Tests of creativity assess divergent thinking, the extent to which the individual's thinking is innovative or unique and diverges from customary thought patterns.

Many different measures of divergent thinking have been devised. One employs a kind of anagram test; subjects are told to create as many words as they can from the letters of a word like "generation." An originality score is devised on the basis of the number of *uncommon* responses (not occurring more than once in a hundred responses) (Barron, 1957). A similar test, called the "Unusual Uses" requires the subject to think of uses other than the common one for particular objects such as a "brick." Responses are then scored on a five-point scale of originality by a team of raters (Guilford, 1964).

In one study, a large sample of entering freshmen at Duke University was asked to list as many uses they could think of for common objects such as a shoe, as many meanings they could imagine for abstract drawings, and as many similarities they could see in pairs of common objects such as "potato-carrot" (Wallach & Wing, 1969). The number and uniqueness of their responses were unrelated to their scores on standard I.Q. tests, but were correlated with creative achievement in the fields of art and writing, as assessed by criteria such as prizes won in painting and story competitions.

If one defines creativity as divergent thinking, therefore, it appears general intelligence and creativity are quite different variables—at least among people who are high in intelligence.

Some other tests of creativity are based on the assumption that creative people have more unusual or unique (remote) associations to stimuli. If this is true, they should also be able to *use* these uncommon associations. Consider the following question: "What fourth word is related to these three: rat, blue, cottage?" The answer is "cheese." Properly classified, this question asks for convergent thinking (find the one correct answer), but the correct answer depends on divergent thinking (to answer correctly, the person must think of a number of different, fairly uncommon associations to each of the three words). One test of creativity, the Remote Associates Test, is made up of items like these (Mednick, 1962).

It is misleading, however, to suggest that all psychologists consider creativity and general intelligence as independent concepts. Some, such as Guilford, consider divergent thinking as a neglected aspect of intelligence (see p. 379). Others see divergent thinking simply as the ability to make unusual verbal associations, and, as such, consider it a very limited aspect of creativity.

Characteristics of Creative Persons

Another way to approach the question of creativity is more direct: what are the characteristics of people who are generally recognized as being very creative? What are internationally famous

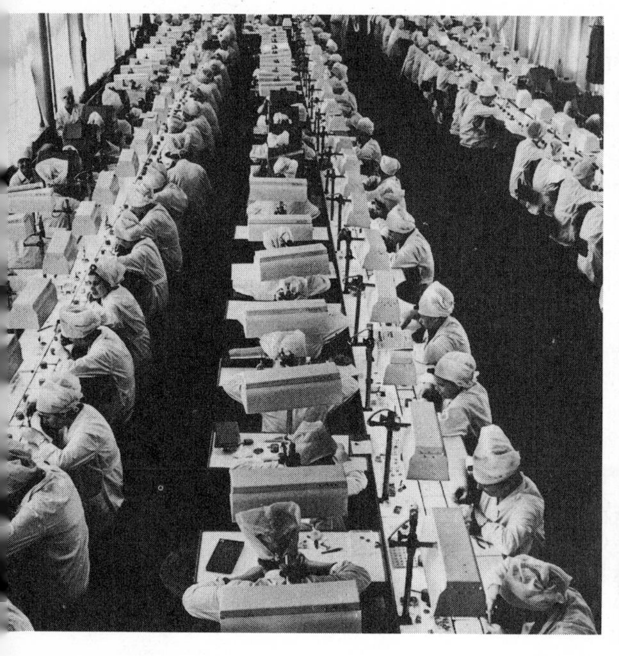

What personality characteristics do you associate with creativity?
(SOVFOTO; Charles Gatewood)

creative writers such as Truman Capote, Norman Mailer, MacKinlay Kantor, Frank O'Connor, and Kenneth Rexroth really like? One psychologist (Barron, 1957) convinced a number of people engaged in creative work to spend three days in a research center taking tests and undergoing extensive interviews. The writers mentioned and many others participated. Some of them were rated by professional writers as highly creative; others were less creative. Mathematicians and architects of varying degrees of creativity were also studied.

After the interviews and tests were completed, staff members of the research center rated the subjects on a large number of personality dimensions. Table 16-2 gives the correlations between some of the personality items (rated by Q sort; see p. 166), and degree of creativity. In general, the highly creative subjects were judged to be independent, nonconforming, unconventional in thought and action, rebellious, moody, flexible, self-accepting, and relatively lacking in self-control, responsibility, and dependability. They reported less of a sense of well-being than the less creative subjects and were less concerned with "making good impressions." Creative writers and creative research scientists were remarkably similar in personality, in spite of the differences in their professional work. It must be remembered that these findings represent trends only and that they do not characterize any one creative person completely. Indeed, one of the predominant characteristics of creative people is that they are original and do not fit into general types, categories, or pigeonholes.

TABLE 16-2
Q-SORT ITEMS CORRELATED WITH CREATIVITY

Q-Sort Item	Correlation with Creativity Rating
Thinks and associates to ideas in unusual ways: has unconventional thought processes.	+.64
Is an interesting, arresting person.	+.55
Tends to be rebellious and non-conforming.	+.51
Genuinely values intellectual and cognitive matters.	+.49
Appears to have a high degree of intellectual capacity.	+.46
Is self-dramatizing; histrionic.	+.42
Has fluctuating moods.	+.40
Judges self and others in conventional terms like "popularity," "the correct thing to do," "social pressures," and so forth.	−.62
Is a genuinely dependable and responsible person.	−.45
Behaves in a sympathetic or considerate manner.	−.43
Favors conservative values in a variety of areas.	−.40
Is moralistic.	−.40

Creativity, Intelligence, and Personality

As we have seen, creativity as measured by the number and uniqueness of ideas is not highly correlated with intelligence, at least not in people who are above average in I.Q. The independence of these two traits makes it possible to identify people who are high in one but not the other, people who are high in both, and people who are low in both. In one extensive study, the personalities and social behavior of these four "types" were thoroughly investigated (Wallach & Kogan, 1965).

The subjects were 151 fifth-grade pupils who were average or above average in intelligence and generally from middle-class families. In general, high creativity was associated with self-awareness, openness to experience, and stimulation from both internal and external sources. Girls who were highly intelligent *and* creative were successful in school and in their relationships with peers. They were self-confident and popular with their friends, free of anxiety about having unconventional ideas. Highly creative girls of lower intelligence had little self-confidence and tended to be cautious and hesitant in social situations. Those who were highly intelligent but low in creativity were sought out by their peers but seemed to be a bit aloof and cautious with others. Spotlight 16-3 summarizes the evaluations of the children in the various groups.

SPOTLIGHT 16-3

Characteristics of Children Higher and Lower in Creativity and Intelligence

Higher Creativity

Higher Intelligence	Lower Intelligence
These children can exercise within themselves both control and freedom, both adultlike and childlike kinds of behavior.	These children are in angry conflict with themselves and with their school environment and are beset by feelings of unworthiness and inadequacy. In a stress-free context, however, they can blossom forth cognitively.

Lower Creativity

Higher Intelligence	Lower Intelligence
These children can be described as "addicted" to school achievement. Academic failure would be perceived by them as catastrophic, so that they must continually strive for academic excellence in order to avoid the possibility of pain.	Basically bewildered, these children engage in various defensive maneuvers ranging from useful adaptations such as intensive social activity to regressions such as passivity or psychosomatic symptoms.

Abstracted from M. A. Wallach & N. Kogan, *Modes of Thinking in Young Children.* New York: Holt, Rinehart and Winston, 1965.

Stages in the Creative Process

When creative people tell about how they arrive at their ideas, a common pattern emerges that seems to hold for most intellectual endeavors. It must be remembered, however, that our ability to reconstruct our own mental processes is subject to error. So while the phases of the creative process outlined below do occur, they probably do not invariably occur in the sequence described here. To illustrate these stages we will use material provided by Watson in his book *The Double Helix* (1968), in which he describes how he and his colleague Crick finally solved the mystery of the secret of how the genetic code works.

The first "stage," *preparation*, involves acquiring all

possible information about a problem. Watson has described his preoccupation with the problem of finding the structure of the DNA molecule. The first step toward a solution was immersing himself in any and all of the available information about the structure of molecules gleaned from laboratory and library research. This period of intensive preparation set the stage for the next phase.

There was a period in the search for the double helix in which work seemed to be going nowhere; there were many blind alleys. During this period Watson and Crick went on ski trips and engaged in other relaxing activities. This was the **incubation stage** during which the material Watson and Crick had acquired could be absorbed and assimilated. To the creative person, the incubation period often appears to be a rather barren and unproductive time, but it is in fact very important. Creative writers often "go to sleep" on a problem and awaken with a solution. Undoubtedly there is a great deal of unconscious mental activity during this stage.

After the period of incubation there is a rather sudden **illumination stage** wherein new ideas arrive quite unexpectedly. In the case of Watson and Crick the idea of a double helix came suddenly after Watson had attended an old movie in which there was a spiral staircase. Of course, such sudden insights can turn out to be quite misleading, although in the first glow of "illumination," the idea seems perfect. Many people get so infatuated with new ideas that they act on them immediately without going through the final all-important stage of *verification.*

The notion that the DNA molecule was a double helix had to be tested. Watson and Crick constructed a physical model of the molecule and then did the experimental tests that supported the predictions based upon the double helix hypothesis. Their results were confirmed by other investigators and both men won the Nobel Prize in chemistry. While the actual process of discovery is more complex than the one just described, the phases of preparation, incubation, illumination, and verification have been noted in the histories of other creative productions.

Cognitive Styles

Ego psychology was a development of psychoanalysis which sought to explore the origins and development of the cognitive, thinking, and rational functions of the mind. One aspect of an individual's ego functioning is his approach to cognitive tasks. Stable characteristic approaches and ways of handling problems have been called **cognitive styles.**

Reflectivity-Impulsivity

Some people are *impulsive* in solving problems; they act on the basis of the first solution that comes to mind with little consideration for its adequacy. Others are *reflective,* thinking about many possible solutions, evaluating alternatives, censoring their ideas, and weighing the products of their thinking. Individual differences in **reflectivity-impulsivity** are evidenced as early as age two and seem to be consistent and stable over time (Kagan, 1966).

In a test for reflectivity-impulsivity, the Matching Familiar Figures test, the child is asked to select one stimulus from six variants that is identical with a standard (Kagan, 1966). (See Figure 16-5.) The time it takes the subject to make his first choice (response time) and the number of errors before choosing the correct response are the two variables scored. At every age between five and eleven there is a negative correlation between response time and errors; those who are fastest in responding tend to make the most errors—they are the impulsive ones. Reflective children respond more slowly and make fewer errors.

In tests of recall of word lists, impulsive children are more likely to report words that did not appear in the original list. When reading aloud, impulsive children make more errors than reflective children, and in tests of inductive reasoning they respond more quickly and make more errors.

Leveling-Sharpening

In a classic study on remembering, Sir Frederick Bartlett (1932) noted that when a story was passed around from person to person it underwent certain transformations. Some of the unusual elements of the story became more common or usual, while other unusual aspects were increasingly accentuated. Bartlett called the regularization phenomenon "leveling" and the accentuation phenomenon "sharpening." Later researchers suggested that some individuals tend to "level" (see similarities among things and make them alike), and others are more likely to "sharpen" (to accentuate differences) in handling cognitive problems.

Suppose, for example, subjects are seated in a darkened room and asked to make judgments about the sizes of a series of squares of progressively increasing size. Some subjects (levelers) tend to see new stimuli as very similar to those previously presented, often missing an actual change, while others (sharpeners) notice changes quickly and accurately (Holzman & Klein, 1954).

The tendency to level or to sharpen seems to be a generalized one, applicable to many cognitive performances. For example, sharpeners (as assessed by simple tasks such as size judgments) are superior to levelers in recalling stories they heard years earlier (Holzman & Gardner, 1960), and levelers are more likely to simplify the grammatical structure of verbal materials they are asked to recall (Livant, 1962).

Field Independence and Dependence

Perhaps the best-known of individual differences in cognitive styles is **field independence** or **dependence.** Field-dependent people rely on external stimuli (stimuli in the "field" around them) for their judgments, and field-independent people rely more on internal cues. An illustrative situation—one in which the distinction was first observed—is a pilot flying in a cloud or fog. Some pilots in such a situation (without instruments) emerge from the cloud upside down (and thoroughly surprised). Such pilots would be called field dependent. Without external cues, they literally could not tell "up" from "down." Field-independent pilots did not rely so heavily on the view (or lack of it) and estimated their position in relation to the ground by using cues emanating from their own bodies.

In a laboratory test of this style, subjects sat in complete darkness facing a luminous rod that was surrounded by a luminous frame. Both the rod and the frame could be tilted independently, and the subject saw them first in a tilted position. Then, while the frame remained tilted, he was told to direct the experimenter to move the rod until it appeared vertical to him. Some subjects adjusted the rod so that it appeared vertical in the context of the visual frame (field) that surrounded it. Other subjects ignored the orientation of the frame and directed the experimenter to align the rod so that it was vertical with respect to their own body position. The first solution was called field dependent, the second field independent (Witkin *et al.*, 1962).

Field dependence or independence, as measured by the rod and frame test, turned out to be related to a number of other vari-

FIGURE 16-5 MATCHING FAMILIAR FIGURES

Response time and errors in matching figures indicate degree of impulsivity or reflectivity.

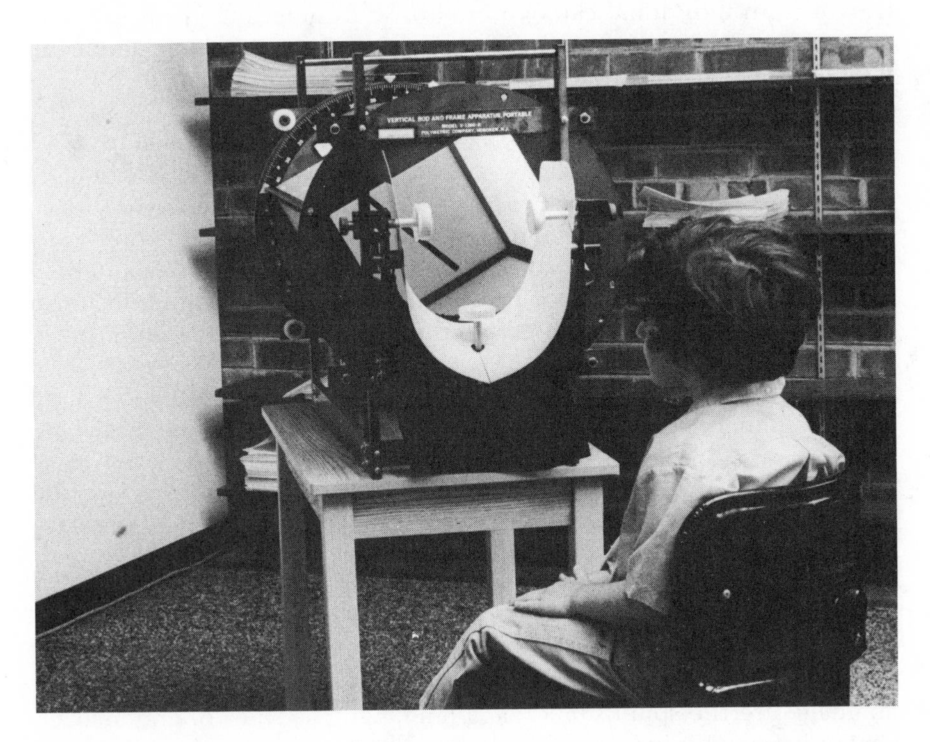

In the rod and frame test, the subject indicates when the rod, which can be adjusted, is vertical, that is, "straight up and down." (Richard Fauman)

ables. Women tend to be more field dependent than men, and young children are, on the average, more field dependent than are older ones. Field-dependent people are more likely to change their opinions when they learn that these are different from the opinions of an authority. Furthermore, field-dependent people tend to be socially oriented; they are good at remembering people and faces and gravitate toward occupations involving contact with people.

The cognitive-style approach to human thinking is a valuable one because it brings us closer to the unique individual. It is important to remember, however, that no one is consistently impulsive or reflective, field dependent or field independent in all situations. The notion of cognitive styles is a useful one if we remember that it is basically a typology that never fits any one individual perfectly.

What do we know about language?

Man, as we saw in the last section, is a *knowing* organism who seeks to acquire, store, and utilize his past and present experience for future ends. But man is also a *showing* organism in the sense that he seeks to express how and what he thinks and feels about himself and about his world. Although there are many different ways in which an individual can express himself, including gesture, facial expression, and posture, language is by far the dominant mode in which humans show their feelings and thoughts.

The Nature of Language

If we look at language from a broad perspective, it is obvious that it is part of what we call a society's "culture." Language is basically an arbitrary sign system that is institutionalized within a society; it is part of the unique complex of thinking, expression, behavior, and technology that distinguishes one culture from another. English, for example, is part of the culture an American child must acquire, just as Japanese is a part of the culture a Japanese child must learn.

Despite the diversity of human languages, linguists find certain commonalities both in content and in form. Almost all languages, for example, have words for trees, sun, sky, moon, animals, and other universal aspects of human experience. It is this commonality of conceptual content that makes translation from one language to another possible.

In addition to content similarities, there are also structural similarities. All languages have certain basic components, which are organized in a hierarchical structure. Since language is first and foremost a system of spoken signs, the essential components of a language are the sounds, and each language has rules of grammar or syntax for combining sounds into meaningful utterances.

Since sound and meaning are separate, linguists distinguish between deep and surface structure of language. The **deep structure** is the underlying meaning or thought, while **surface structure** refers to the overt sounds. The same meaning (deep structure) may be expressed by different patterns of sound (surface structure). "The child ate the cake" and "The cake was eaten by the child" have the same underlying meaning but are expressed by vastly different sound patterns. Conversely, the same patterns of sound (surface structure) may have different meanings (deep structure). Thus the sentence "They are entertaining guests" may have two quite different meanings: "Some people are hosts to visitors" or "These people are fun to have as guests."

Language Structure

All languages have distinctive basic sounds including vowels, consonants, tones, relative intensities, durations, and pauses. These basic sounds do not convey any meaning in themselves, but they are combined to form the meaningful units of a language and give it the unique sound qualities that distinguish it from other languages. The basic sounds of a language are called **phonemes.** The English language uses about forty-five phonemes. Some languages contain fewer; others contain many more.

When phonemes are combined in a sequence to yield an utterance that conveys meaning, we have the next higher order component in the language system, the form. Forms can be of varying length; *dog* has fewer phonemes than *raspberry*. Any form or meaningful unit that cannot be broken into smaller forms is called a **morpheme.** Morphemes may be words, prefixes, or suffixes. The words *work, house,* and *good* are single morphemes; so are the prefixes *un* and *re* and the suffixes *ism* and *ed*. All of them contain meanings and contain only one form. The words *worked* and *goodness* each consist of two morphemes, the root word plus a suffix (*ed* indicating past tense and *ness* indicating quality of being).

The next higher component in the language system is the *construction*. A construction involves an arrangement or pattern of forms such that any particular form in the construction is replaceable by another form. Phrases and sentences are all constructions according to this definition. In the noun phrase *red truck* the construction can be changed in numerous ways—*blue truck, red car, blue car*—all of which are noun phrases. Likewise in the sample sentence *I run home,* the construction remains the same whatever pronoun, verb, and nouns are substituted for the ones in the sample.

It should be noted that the nature of language is hierarchical. Constructions are made up of forms, and forms, in turn, are made up of distinctive basic sounds or phonemes. Each language system has its own rules (grammar or syntax) by which forms can be combined to make other forms and constructions can be combined to make still other constructions.

To what extent do thought and language depend on each other?

The term "thinking" refers to many kinds of activities that involve the manipulation of concepts and symbols, representations of objects and events. Usually thinking has a purpose, the discovery of the best solution to a problem. In the broadest sense, thought reflects man's propensity to know, to understand, and deal with his world. Since language is a very important source of symbols, and thought generally involves symbols, psychologists have long been intrigued with the relationships between thought and language.

Language plays a major role in cognition, thinking, and reasoning. Remember that in reversal-shift learning (see p. 385), the ability to use verbal mediators—attaching verbal responses or labels to stimuli and using words to give oneself instructions—facilitates the child's ability to solve the problem. Many other studies also suggest that the ability to use language is highly correlated with the ability to deal with concepts and relationships. But this does not mean that language and thought are identical or even that language is a necessary condition for thinking and problem solving. As we shall see, the relationships between language and thought are intricate, extraordinarily complex, and not yet fully understood. The essential question is that of specifying the extent to which language and thought depend on each other. There are three more or less distinct theories dealing with this issue: isomorphism, reductionism, and interactionism.

Isomorphism

The term "isomorphism" means "identical in structure." Applied to the language-thought issue, isomorphism implies that language and thought are structurally similar, if not identical. There are a number of proponents of this position, but we shall deal here only with some prominent theories, those of Whorf, Vygotsky, and Skinner.

Whorf

According to the "linguistic-relativity hypothesis," offered by Benjamin Lee Whorf (1956), our language largely determines the ways we perceive and think about the world we live in. In essence, the isomorphism between language and thought is attributable to the direction given our thoughts and perceptions by language.

In support of his hypothesis, Whorf used evidence from Indian and Eskimo tribes. Eskimos, for example, have several different words to describe different kinds of snow. Therefore, Whorf maintained, Eskimos *think* about snow in a way different from people whose language contains only a single word for snow. Similarly, investigators working on a Navajo reservation (Carroll & Casagrande, 1958) observed that Navajo verbs for actions such as "to pick up," "to drop," and "to hold in the hand" vary in form depending upon the material being handled. If the object of the verb "to pick up" is a round thin thing, Navajos use a verb different from that used if the object is long and flexible. On a simple sorting task in which children could sort objects on the basis of either shape or color, Navajo-speaking children generally sorted on the basis of shape, whereas English-speaking Navajo children sorted on the basis of color. Presumably the fact that Navajo grammar requires the child to pay attention to shapes and forms makes him more likely to think and categorize on the basis of these aspects of his environment.

Although it is clear that language influences and directs thought, there is little evidence that it actually determines what and and how we think. Most American skiers, for example, differentiate many kinds of snow, even though English does not include simple names for all of the distinguishable varieties of snow. Indeed, skiers may make up words to describe previously unlabeled types of snow. Similarly, young children, adolescents, and even adults constantly invent new words or appropriate old words to convey the unique quality of their experience (e.g., "groovy," "heavy"). Such observations make it difficult to maintain the notion that language determines thought, as proposed by the linguistic-relativity hypothesis.

Vygotsky

The Russian psychologist Vygotsky had a somewhat different approach to the issue of isomorphism between language and thought (Vygotsky, 1962). In his view, at least some forms of thought are forms of speaking, a kind of "inner" speech. For example, a young child often "thinks out loud" by "talking to himself." Between the ages of about three and seven, these behaviors decrease in frequency. According to Vygotsky, the speaking is "interiorized," i.e., out-loud speech is replaced by silent, inner speech—which we call thoughts. Thus, like Whorf, Vygotsky believes that language often determines the structure of thought. Whorf, of course, stressed the influence of language on the thought of all people in a particular culture, while Vygotsky emphasized the developmental aspects—how and why thought comes to take on the form of the language system.

Vygotsky's hypothesis is contradicted by much the same evidence that makes it difficult to accept the Whorfian view. In addition, many theorists, Piaget, for example, have proposed that the increasing ability to solve problems "in the head" is not merely a result of the internalization of language or even of progress in language learning; instead, they suggest that higher levels of mental abilities develop (see p. 299) and replace more primitive forms of thought. Such theories (and much research) indicate that language development is often dependent on changes in the nature and scope of thought processes rather than the reverse. Moreover, Vygotsky's theory cannot explain the fact that many deaf children show normal intellectual and cognitive abilities in spite of considerable retardation in the acquisition of language (Vygotsky, 1962).

Skinner

Basically, Skinner's position is that language, no less than thought, is *behavior* and can be understood in terms of behavioral principles. Words are first and foremost responses, and the words that occur in particular situations will depend upon the environment and the reinforcement history of the speaker. For Skinner, language is more complex than other forms of behavior, but it is as predictable and modifiable, in principle, as the pattern of bar-pressing by a rat that receives direct reinforcement (a pellet of food) every time he presses a bar.

At the same time, however, Skinner acknowledges that verbal behavior is unique in one respect; namely, it is instrumental in producing reinforcements indirectly rather than directly. The rat that presses the bar is rewarded *directly* for his act by a food pellet; when the young child says "water" (or something that sounds like it), his mother gets the water and brings it to him. The reinforcement for verbal behavior is produced through the intervention of another person.

In describing verbal behavior, Skinner introduces the concepts of mands and tacts. Any verbal behavior that directs some other person to action (request, demand, or command) is a **mand.** Mands are usually elicited in the presence of an audience which has reinforced such behavior in the past. A child, for example, easily discriminates between two uncles, the one who always responds to his request for ice cream and the one who does not. After awhile, the child will make the request in the presence of the reinforcing uncle but not in the presence of the nonreinforcing uncle. If saying "please" when stating a mand ("please give me some ice cream") has produced reinforcement, the child is more likely to include this word in future mands.

Skinner defines **tacts** as verbal behaviors that are elicited by nonhuman stimuli in the environment. When a child informs his mother that "the spaghetti water is boiling over," he is responding to physical events. The statement is likely to be reinforced by the parent's expression of "thanks." The physical environment partly determines the tact; the child learns to match his words and the external events as closely as possible. By and large, mands benefit the speaker whereas tacts benefit the listener. By rewarding the tacts, however, the listener helps strengthen the speaker's "information giving" (tacting) and increases the frequency of occurrence of tacts.

According to Skinner, the meaning of verbal behavior has to be defined in terms of the conditions of performance and reinforcement; meaning resides in what the verbal behavior does or accomplishes. If a child says "get me water" and the parent does so, the parent's behavior provides the behavioral meaning of the verbal response. For Skinner, therefore, the problem of meaning is not "What do words represent?" but rather "What do words do?" This is another way of saying that, for Skinner, language and thought are, first and foremost, behaviors.

Reductionism

When we use words and concepts, our thinking is strongly influenced by the meanings we attach to these. Hence, the problem of the relationship between language and thought could be approached by *reducing* words and concepts to some rather basic dimensions of meaning that can be measured quantitatively and objectively.

The denotative meaning of a word is the actual object or action it represents; connotative meanings are the associations called up when the word is used. Such associations are frequently emotional or evaluative—expressing some kind of feeling or preference—and vary from individual to individual. The word "mother" denotes a specific individual, but to some it connotes a warm kindly woman and to others a cold aloof one.

Osgood and his associates developed the **semantic differential** as a way of studying connotative meanings of words and concepts. Thus, the connotative meaning of a concept like teacher may be determined by giving subjects a series of seven-point scales and asking them to rate the concept on each of the scales. The end points of the scales are bipolar adjectives such as good–bad or beautiful–ugly, as shown in Figure 16-6. When a large number of individuals have rated a series of concepts, we can arrive at the semantic space of the concept for any particular individual or for the group as a whole (Osgood *et al.*, 1957).

Good		X						Bad
Cruel					X			Kind
Masculine			X					Feminine
Pleasant	X							Unpleasant
Active					X			Passive
Beautiful			X					Ugly
Unsuccessful			X					Successful
Hard				X				Soft

FIGURE 16-6 RATING SCALES USED FOR CONCEPT "TEACHER"
The semantic differential consists of scales for evaluating words and concepts.

Of course, a tremendous variety of scales would be derived by including scales made of many bipolar pairs such as dark–light, sharp–dull, and brilliant–stupid. Actually, different scales frequently elicit similar responses. Thus, concepts rated as pleasant (rather than unpleasant) also tend to be rated as kind (rather than cruel) and sweet (rather than sour). These scales and others like them are positively intercorrelated and form a cluster that represents an underlying evaluative factor, essentially indicating how good or bad the concept is regarded.

Research with the semantic differential—applying it to wide varieties of concepts and dimensions and to different groups of people—consistently points to three more or less independent factors or basic dimensions. In addition to the *evaluative factor*, there is a *potency factor* (represented by scales such as strong–weak, heavy–light, and hard–soft) and an *activity factor* (represented by scales such as fast–slow, active–passive, and excitable–calm). In other words, most concepts have connotative meanings pertaining to evaluation, potency, and activity. These are apparently basic factors to which much of our thinking and language can be reduced.

Interactionism

In a third approach to the problem of the relationship between language and thought, they are regarded as separate systems which are, nonetheless, closely interrelated. Taken separately, each system can be described in terms of certain elements and rules. Thus, Piaget (1952) has provided a model of thought which involves elements (operations) and rules of logic (see p. 305), while Chomsky (1965) has proposed a transformational grammar that formulates rules linking underlying thought or meaning (deep structure) and sounds (surface structure).

The problem of language and thought from the interactionism standpoint, then, is to assess the nature of the interconnections between the two systems. Some relevant studies deal with the dependence of language upon the development of thought, while others show how language plays a determining role in mental processes. All these studies demonstrate the multiple and complex ways in which the linguistic and cognitive systems interact.

Piaget maintains that to understand a child's language you must understand his ways of thinking; the meaning children attach to words is, in part, a function of their level of mental development. Words such as "same" and "different," "more" and "less," and "right" and "left" may be used appropriately by children in some instances, but the words do not mean exactly the same things they mean to adults.

An illustration may help to make this point concrete. Suppose children at different age levels are presented with identical beakers filled to equal heights with colored liquid (as in Piaget's conservation experiments discussed in Chapter 13, p. 304). The liquid from one container is then poured into another, which is much taller and thinner than the first. Young children under the age of five or six typically agree that the amounts of liquid are equal when in identical containers, but say that the two quantities are no longer "the same" when they are in two differently shaped containers. After the age of six or seven children recognize that the change in appearance does not reflect a change in amount.

For the young child the terms "more" and "same" do not have the same meaning as they do for older children and adults. For him "same amount" means "same height" or "same width." If the two liquids differ in either or both of these dimensions, the young child regards them as unequal. The child's difficulty in understanding "same," "more," and "less" derives from cognitive immaturity, the inability to coordinate height and width mentally so as to arrive at a concept of quantity that incorporates both. The young child's limited understanding of words thus derives from limitations in his mental operations.

A recent experiment clarifies this relationship between mental operations and language (Sinclair, 1969). The investigator worked with three groups of children. One group was entirely lacking in notions of "conservation." They did not regard the liquid quantities in the example above as the same when poured into other containers; the second group was at a transition stage, and the third group had clearly attained conservation. These children then did some tasks involving verbal description and verbal comprehension. For example, they were shown two dolls, one holding four large red balls, the other holding only two small red balls, and asked "Is this fair?" and "Why not?" They were also asked to state the difference between two pencils, a short thick one and a long thin one. There were significant differences among the three groups on the description tasks. About 90 percent of the children who were lacking in conservation used absolute terms in their descriptions ("one doll has a lot," "the other has few," "one pencil is big," "the other is little") and did not employ comparatives. Among the children who had attained conservation, however, 80 percent used *comparative* terms in their descriptions. Of the two pencils they said, "One is fatter and smaller and the other is bigger and thinner." Children at the intermediary stage were somewhere in between.

These results suggest that, in some domains, thought and conceptual development determine language usage. Further evidence of this is found in the observation that it is only when children attain the level of "formal operations," at age eleven or twelve (see p. 306), that they spontaneously begin to use abstract categorical terms such as "belief," "intention," and "nationality." The use of these abstract words and expressions waits upon the development of the high-level mental abilities.

Language, however, also affects thought in important ways. We know that words are not absolutely essential to thinking, for many deaf children who are severely retarded in language acquisition reason and solve cognitive problems very well. But language very frequently *facilitates* thought. Certainly it would be much more difficult to solve many problems if we had to rely on direct manipulation of objects and images. Symbolic systems such as language permit us to solve complex problems rapidly, efficiently, and accurately. In some ways, language is to thought as mathematics is to science, an indispensable tool and handmaiden.

The influence of language on cognitive process was clearly demonstrated in a study in which two groups of subjects viewed the stimulus figures shown in Figure 16-7. One group saw the figures described by the words on Word List I while the other group saw the figures paired with Word List II. Later the subjects were asked to reproduce the figures from memory. As the figure shows, the reproductions were much more like the verbal labels associated with the figures than the original figures were.

There are, of course, many other obvious influences of language upon thought. Propaganda and advertising of all sorts are attempts to influence thinking by the use of words. Names of cars and of movie stars are often selected with the thought of their "appeal to the consumer." A skilled actor can move an audience to tears or to rage, and the religious evangelist can promote a conversion experience, both through the use of language.

A Practical Problem of Language Learning

Minority-group children—blacks, Mexican-Americans, and native Americans (Indians)—suffer major language handicaps. The majority of schools in America are middle-class oriented and the principals and teachers have middle-class values, attitudes, and behavior. They speak a particular English dialect, standard English, which is characteristic of the middle class. Written English also represents this dialect. American schools, well suited for middle-class children, may be much less appropriate for children from minority or lower socioeconomic groups whose values, attitudes, and language differ significantly from those of the prevailing culture.

Some educators and psychologists have maintained that minority children, especially blacks, use a language that is simpler grammatically, less differentiated, and more concrete than the language used by middle-class whites. The black child appears less willing or able to use language; he is more likely to speak in very short sentences and to reply to questions with one-word answers. His pronunciation and vocabulary may be so different from standard English that teachers may have difficulty understanding him.

But linguists who have studied the language of black children intensively, observing them in their homes and neighborhoods, find no reason to consider them deficient in language. In fact, with friends and family, black children express themselves with a

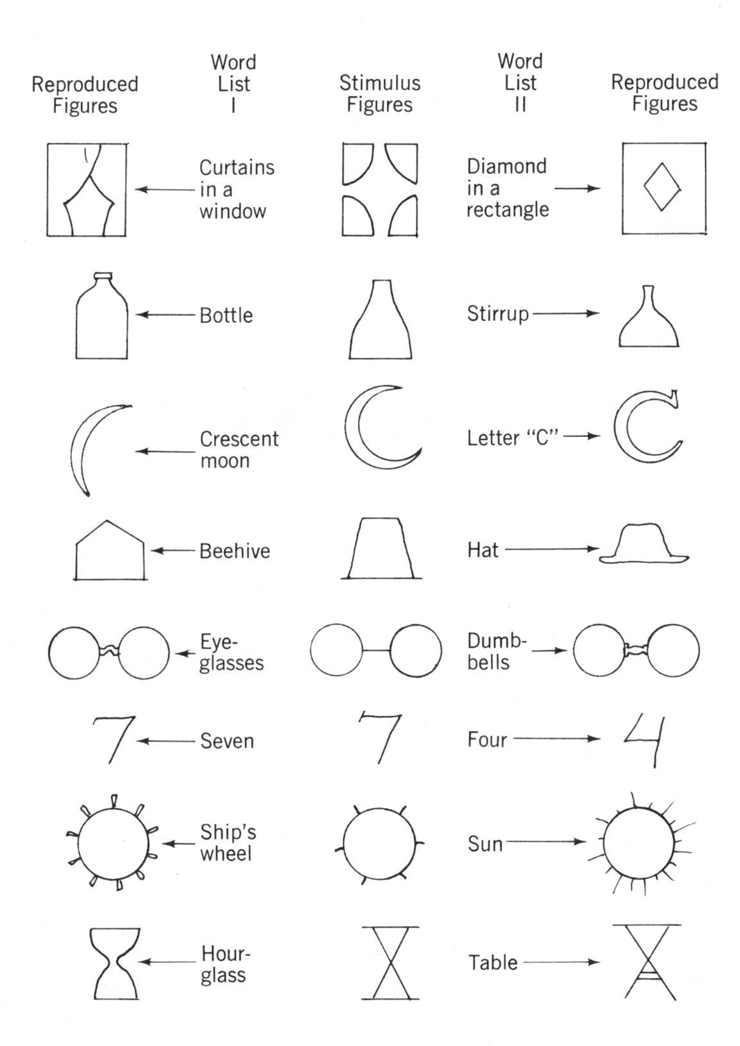

FIGURE 16-7
TEST OF VISUAL AND LANGUAGE INFLUENCES
The figures in the outer columns, drawn from memory, are more like the verbal labels than the stimulus figures, which were to be reproduced.
(From Carmichael, Hogan, & Walter, 1932)

great deal of richness, ease, and fluency; and they play many language games. Nor is there any evidence that their language is less differentiated or complex than the whites' (Houston, 1970).

Black children's deficiencies in standard English are hardly evidence that they cannot handle the language. Clearly, they understand standard English, and if this language becomes a major and significant part of their environment, they can master it. It has been suggested that black children have a language of their own and must be taught standard English as a second language or dialect, not as a refinement or superior form of the language they already speak.

Related problems have been met by Mexican and American-Indian children who also come to a school where they must speak a language different from the one used at home. In the past it was always the child who was forced to accommodate to the language of the school, and this often worked to his educational detriment. Fortunately this situation is changing, and many schools in the southwestern United States now have Spanish and Indian-speaking teachers who teach English as a second language. Hopefully this approach will remove one of the inequalities in the educational opportunities of minority groups.

SUMMARY

Thinking is an evolutionary advance that permits the acquisition, storage, and utilization of immediate and past experience for more effective adaptation. The process is aided by the use of symbols in the form of language, especially at the higher levels of abstract thought. Symbolization aids in defining concepts, which are the content of human thought. Basic to the thought process is concept formation, whereby responses are evoked by diverse objects or ideas which share some characteristics, often perceptual features like "redness." This is the most concrete type of concept. Abstract concepts are those in which the common characteristic is not immediately obvious but where the elements are generally related by a rule or principle rather than by a perceptual property. An example is the concept "mother." Derived concepts are combinations of more fundamental concepts. "Textbook" is a derived concept because it is the conjunction of two smaller concepts, "book" and "teaching instrument."

In many ways, concept formation is a prerequisite to reasoning, the logical patterns of thinking. Reasoning can be influenced by an "atmosphere effect," so that premises elicit an invalid response. Personal convictions also affect the adequacy of reasoning when the material is controversial.

Discovering how to attain a desired goal is known as problem solving. Both trial and error and insight are used in solving problems. One of the biggest hindrances to effective problem solving is functional fixedness, which is a set or predisposition that limits thinking when flexibility and ingenuity are called for.

In recent years there has been considerable interest in evaluating creativity. Since intelligence tests focus on convergent or conventional thinking, new tests measuring divergent (nonconventional) thinking have been devised to assess this characteristic element of creativity. It has been found that creative people have certain personality characteristics in common. They tend to be more independent, unconventional, flexible, and self-accepting than noncreative people. The process of creative thinking generally involves the successive phases of preparation, incubation, illumination, and verification. A particular individual may be gifted with both creativity and high intelligence or with neither or only one. The relationship between them is complex. Different personality configurations are associated with different combinations.

There are also marked individual differences in how people form concepts, reason, and solve problems; their cognitive styles differ. Some individuals are reflective and think before acting, whereas others are impulsive and act before thinking. Some are field independent and make judgments on the basis of internal cues, whereas others are field dependent and make judgments primarily on the basis of external cues.

As thinking is a basic process to all people, so is language. Despite the diversity of human languages, there are a few basic concepts of structure and content common to all. All languages have a surface and a deep structure (sound and meaning). The basic element of the surface structure is the phoneme.

Linguists have studied the problem of the relationship between language and thought. Three theories have been proposed: isomorphism, reductionism, and interactionism. A practical problem relevant to today's society is the difficulty minority-group children have in acquiring the standard English spoken and written in the schools. Linguists suggest that these children do not have a language deficiency; they are essentially bilingual with standard English as their second language.

17

Educational Psychology

Why is this applied science everchanging?
What is the relationship between motivation and academic performance?
Who develops innovations in teaching?

Item. *Earl is disruptive in the classroom and is working far below his intellectual potential, so the school psychologist is called in for help. After giving Earl some tests, the psychologist decides that a therapeutic program involving "behavior modification" is called for. The program is put into practice and after a couple of weeks there is a marked change in Earl's behavior and he relates better to teachers and to his peers.*[1]

Item. *Professor E. is asked to evaluate the effectiveness of an innovative experimental school in producing creative, high-achieving children. In the course of the evaluation, Professor E. and his colleagues discover that scores on their tests of creativity are strongly affected by the motivation and expectancies of children while taking the tests.*[2]

These are but two examples of the many diverse activities of educational and school psychologists. In this chapter we will survey the field of **educational psychology,** sampling some of the activities and problems with which educational psychologists are daily confronted.

Why is this applied science everchanging?

Educational psychology is a very broad field of applied psychology that utilizes the theories, findings, methods, and instru-

[1] This case is described in greater detail later in the chapter, p. 433.
[2] This research is described later in the chapter, p. 442.

ments of psychological science for educational purposes. Educational psychologists engage in a wide variety of activities, including research, educational testing, counseling and guidance, consultation with teachers and parents, and work with handicapped children. There is a continual search for new knowledge, followed by testing and evaluation of the new data. The rapid development of technology, for example, has made a profound impact upon the theories and methods of educational psychology, resulting in an ongoing revision of the concepts of education.

Educational Research

Educational research follows the same principles and methods employed in all research and is distinguished only by the fact that it is concerned, for the most part, with practical issues in education. Among these are investigations of various tests and scales, evaluation of educational programs, assessments of "classroom atmosphere" and "teacher style."

An example of an important educational research issue may help to make concrete the nature of investigations of educational issues. One problem of acute social significance in recent years has to do with the effects of preschool education upon the later intelligence, academic achievement, and social adjustment of children. Children of low-income families begin school with an initial disadvantage in that *their* experiences do not equip them to perform adequately in cognitive tasks. To make matters worse, they suffer a kind of "progressive retardation," falling still farther behind others as they go through school. Great efforts are being made to raise the educational and intellectual levels of these children through compensatory educational projects – for example, the Headstart program sponsored by the Office of Economic Opportunity. These programs are now being evaluated, and the question being asked is: Can enriched preschool programs offset the cognitive and social disadvantages found in the first grade? The problem, like so many others in educational-psychological research, appears to be simple and straightforward, but in fact it turns out to be very complex.

To illustrate, consider the conflicting and ambiguous results of the following studies. The first example pertains to the effects of preschool attendance on children's school adjustment. Some researchers (Allen & Masling, 1957; Cushing, 1934) have found that children who attended nursery school were more popular and spontaneous in kindergarten and first grade than children who had not attended nursery school. Other investigators, however, found no difference between nursery and non-nursery-school attenders with respect to their prestige and spontaneity in kindergarten and first grade (Bonney & Nicholson, 1958; Brown & Hunt, 1961). Such conflicting results may be due to many different factors; nursery schools vary tremendously in their facilities, in their programs, and in the competence of the teachers. Any or all of these factors could account for the fact that experience in one nursery school facilitates social adjustment more than attendance at another nursery school.

Even more significant than social effects are the possible effects of nursery-school attendance on intellectual and cognitive functioning. Again the conflicting results indicate how complex the evaluation problem is. Some studies have reported moderate but consistent and enduring gains in intelligence test scores of children who attend nursery school (as contrasted with children who do not); others indicate that children who attend nursery school achieve slight and only temporary gains; still others indicate that nursery-school attendance produces no significant gains in intelligence, temporary or enduring.

An interesting recent study suggests that gains in intelligence test scores by nursery-school children, when they occur, may be attributable to heightened motivation and better **test-taking attitudes** rather than to actual changes in intellectual ability (Zigler & Butterfield, 1968). The researchers felt that the poor performance of disadvantaged children on intelligence tests (see p. 308) is, in large part, due to what they called "debilitating motivational factors." These include wariness of adults combined with strong motivation to secure adult attention, little motivation to be correct just for correctness' sake, and willingness to settle for low levels of achievement. If these motivational factors can be positively influenced by nursery-school experience, the experience can lead to better test performance.

To examine this possibility, culturally disadvantaged children from two nursery schools were compared with a control group of children who did not attend nursery school. All children were given *two* intelligence tests at the beginning of the nursery-school year and two again at the end of the school year. One of the tests was administered in the standard way—that is, according to the prescribed rules—the examiners remaining neutral but friendly toward the children throughout the test. The second intelligence test was administered according to "optimizing procedures," procedures involving pleasant social interactions between the child and the examiner, allowing the child considerable success experience with easy items, minimizing the child's wariness of the tester, and trying to motivate him to achieve.

The study yielded a number of interesting results which are shown graphically in Figure 17-1. First of all, in the testing at the beginning of the school year, the disadvantaged children performed much better under *optimizing* than under standard conditions. This difference, the largest noted in the study, suggests that standard procedures often undercut the culturally deprived child's intellectual potential to perform. When he is especially motivated, he *can* do

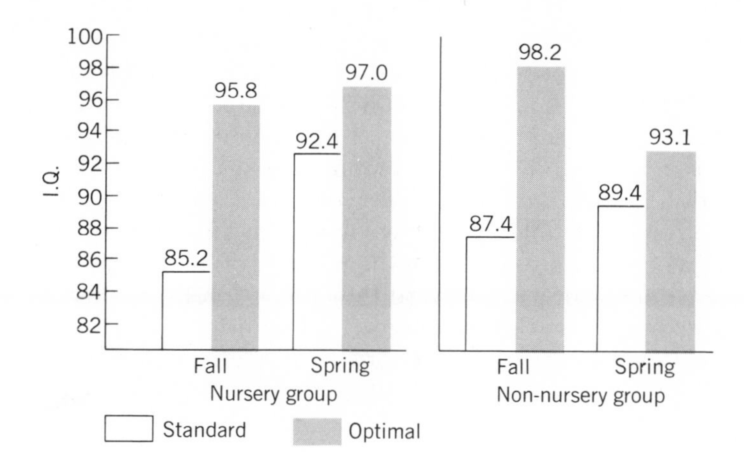

FIGURE 17-1
EFFECT OF MOTIVATION ON I.Q. SCORES

Shown here are mean I.Q.'s of nursery and non-nursery groups for standard and optimal fall and spring testings.
(From Zigler & Butterfield, 1968)

better on the test. Furthermore, the children who attended nursery school showed significant gains in I.Q. from the beginning to the end of the year (seven months), while the other children did not. But this gain was manifested only in the tests given under standard conditions, not in the tests given under optimizing conditions.

By the end of the school year, the nursery-school children's average I.Q., measured by standard testing, had increased significantly over that achieved under standard conditions in the fall testing. This was not the case for the other children. Apparently, when he enters school, the disadvantaged child is lacking in motivation to do well in cognitive tasks—and perhaps in attention and emotional readiness as well—so that he does not display his full ability when tested under standard conditions. But the "debilitating motivational factors" appear to become ameliorated after several months of attendance at nursery school, and this results in much better performance under standard testing procedures. From this it might be concluded that nursery-school attendance modifies the attitudes and *motivations* of disadvantaged children, rather than their cognitive abilities. Nevertheless, there is little doubt that "the demonstrated improvement in their standard I.Q. indicates that these children were generally more competent by the end of the nursery-school year" (Zigler & Butterfield, 1968).

Some other studies indicate that, with conscientious effort on the part of nursery-school teachers and special individual attention, some of the adverse effects of early deprivation can be overcome. For example, the Early Training Project, directed by Gray and Klaus at George Peabody College and sponsored by the U.S. Office of Education, yielded some encouraging findings. The subjects of the study were black preschool children from poverty-stricken families in the South. Some of the children, the experimental groups, attended two or three special summer sessions of preschool, while two groups of controls did not attend preschool or receive any special training. The preschool program was designed to promote stronger motivation toward achievement and to facilitate the development of characteristics related to achievement—persistence, ability to delay gratification, and interest in schoolwork. In addition, the mothers of the experimental subjects met weekly with specially trained black teachers who attempted to make them aware of the children's motives and to encourage them to reward the child's intellectual accomplishments. At the end of the training period, children who had attended preschool were markedly superior to the controls in tests of intelligence, vocabulary, language ability, and reading readiness (Gray &

Some preschool programs can have significant and long-lasting effects on academic performance.
(Van Bucher, Photo Researchers)

Klaus, 1965; Klaus & Gray, 1968). What is most interesting and novel about the study is that the subjects have been followed for a number of years to see if the early (preschool) gains were maintained. The results of the follow-up are modest but encouraging. After twenty-seven months, the experimental subjects had maintained their gains, and after five years—at the end of the second year of public school—positive effects of early training were still apparent. The control subjects who had no special preschool training actually showed decreases in I.Q. scores—a usual phenomenon among disadvantaged children, called **progressive retardation**—up to the point of school entrance. The findings on the experimental groups are most encouraging, for they suggest that it is possible to create programs that will have enduring benefits. This requires "starting with children at a relatively early age and . . . providing a program that is specifically planned in accordance with the deficits to be expected in such children" (Klaus & Gray, 1968, p. 54). "Intervention programs, well conceived and executed, may be expected to make some . . . lasting changes" (Klaus & Gray, 1968, p. 64).

Nevertheless, the investigators warn, "Such programs . . . cannot be expected to carry the whole burden of providing adequate schooling for children from deprived circumstances; they can provide only a basis for future progress in schools and homes that can build upon that early intervention" (Klaus & Gray, 1968, p. 64).

Although the question of the effects of preschool programs upon intelligence and academic achievement has been intensively and extensively researched, the results are far from consistent, and no overall generalization can be made. Whether or not a program will be beneficial for a child will depend upon many factors, such as (1) the age at which the child begins the program; (2) the intellectual quality of the home environment from which he comes; (3) the quality of the program, including the nature of the materials and the skill of the teacher(s); (4) the kind of school program the child attends after the preschool; and (5) the composition of the group of children in the program.

Given the variety of factors just cited, we will generalize and say that the earlier a child enters a preschool program the more significant will be its effects. Second, the greater the disparity between the intellectual stimulation of home and school, the greater the impact of the school; that is, a stimulating school will have more marked effects on children from very unstimulating homes. Third, the better the facilities and equipment of the school and the skill of the teacher, the more enduring and significant will be the effects on the child. Fourth, if the elementary school program perpetuates the qualities of the preschool program—in terms of educational materials and characteristics of teachers—the preschool experience will have a greater impact. And, finally, the greater the orientation of the classroom group toward learning, the greater its reinforcement of the individual's learning and development. While this list does not exhaust all the factors that influence the effects of preschool experience, it indicates the complexity of a "simple" educational research problem.

Educational Testing

More testing goes on in schools than in any other institution of our society. Children are tested for reading readiness, scholastic achievement, intelligence, personal adjustment, and for vocational and college aptitude. The construction of most of the tests used, as well as their administration, scoring and interpretation, is the work of educational psychologists. Let us look at some of these kinds of tests and testing situations in more detail.

An innovation with far-reaching effects has been the widespread use of standardized testing.
(Van Bucher, Photo Researchers)

Achievement tests, such as the Metropolitan Achievement Tests (Hildreth, Bixler, *et al.,* 1953) and the Stanford Achievement Tests (Kelley *et al.,* 1953) are nationally standardized group tests designed to assess basic academic skills such as word recognition, reading comprehension, and arithmetic operations. Most of these tests are scored in terms of a grade-level index for each child; the grade-level index is the mean grade level of all children in the normative sample who attained that score. A child beginning the fourth grade in school who attains a reading comprehension score of 5.0 is one year ahead of the average fourth-grader in this skill.

Academic achievement tests can be useful indices of how children are progressing and of the effectiveness of particular schools, programs, and school districts. The misuse of achievement tests and test findings is, however, a constant problem. Some teachers, who know the tests are coming, may train children specifically on the material that will be assessed. In such cases, the test scores are clearly invalid since the scores presuppose that the test material will be new to the child and present a genuine challenge. Tests are also misused when the results are taken as reflecting the *limits* of the child's *ability* rather than as an imperfect index of his *current functioning*.

In addition to achievement tests, school psychologists (particularly at the high school level) may also administer **vocational aptitude and interest tests.** Some of these tests, such as the Strong Vocational Interest Test, may be used in educational and vocational guidance to suggest possible directions for the student. The Strong Vocational Interest Test blank lists hundreds of activities, both vocational and avocational, and the subject is asked whether he likes, is indifferent to, or dislikes each one. Included are such diverse topics and activities as geometry, hiking, being a pilot, and discussing philosophy. People in particular occupations tend to enjoy very much the same sorts of activities. Therefore, the reasoning goes, a young person who has the interests typical of a particular occupational group will probably enjoy work in that occupation. For example, high school girls who enjoy what nursery-school teachers enjoy—whether this is hiking, attending movies, or folk dancing—would be advised to consider preschool teaching as an occupation while students with other interest patterns are counseled that they do not have the same kinds of interests as preschool teachers.

What is the relationship between motivation and academic performance?

Diagnostic Testing and Evaluation

Educational psychologists often work with problems of diagnosis and evaluation of school problems such as learning disorders, underachievement (poor school performance despite good intelligence), truancy, or problem behavior in the classroom. To understand each case the psychologist interviews the child, his parents, and his teachers, and, in addition, administers individual tests of intelligence, achievement, and personality. He is particularly interested in the child's *motivations*, which may be critical determinants of school maladjustment, academic failure, or school problems.

Emotional instability, conflicts with parents, and inadequate self-concepts interfere with the child's academic performance and with his school adjustment. Children who have not acquired adequate achievement motivation do not do well in school, even if they are highly intelligent. But in evaluating this motivation, the psychologist must differentiate between real interest in learning, and doing well in school in order to avoid failure and disapproval. The child with genuine motivation to achieve enjoys mastering subject matter and his environment, whether or not this mastery brings external rewards. The anxious, driven, striving child is more concerned with avoiding failure and with pleasing his parents than he is with learning for its own sake.

Not surprisingly, the child's past experiences of success or failure in school influence his aspirations and achievement goals. This has been established in a number of **level of aspiration** studies. In these studies, each subject is given a series of tasks (e.g., puzzles, word tests) and asked, after each trial, how well he expects to do on the next trial. The question is whether or not the child sets reasonable goals—goals near or slightly better than his last performance. Children who have been generally successful in school set positive but realistic goals. In contrast, many children with histories of school failure set unreasonable, unrealistically high goals, while others set their goals very cautiously, much below the levels they have already achieved. For the latter, failure has led to demoralization and fear of further failure; they consequently aspire to very little.

Many children have acquired unusually intense fears of failure. They doubt their ability to learn their schoolwork and to pass tests; they are easily discouraged and they cannot concentrate on their work. Excessive anxiety, a common symptom of maladjustment in both adults and children (see p. 223), may hamper learning and thinking and lead to withdrawal of interest in school, resulting consequently in school failure.

The anxious child needs guidance and encouragement from an authority such as the teacher or counselor. He is hesitant to deviate from the safe approved way of doing things and is more likely to "go to pieces" when he encounters extra stresses. There are some school tasks in which anxious—but not excessively anxious—children actually perform better than their nonanxious peers of equal intelligence. These are learning tasks involving simple clearly structured materials, tasks requiring a cautious diligent approach and a great deal of checking and rechecking. Anxiety sometimes fosters this kind of approach. But in tasks requiring originality, judgment, flexibility, creativity, and spontaneity, less anxious students are superior. They also perform better under stressful conditions.

Problems Uncovered

Many school problems may be attributable to nonintellectual motivational factors such as those we have just been discussing. Often, of course, both ability and motivation are involved in the cause of a problem. In fact, the child's adjustment to school is affected by all of his characteristics—his biological equipment, his ideas and abilities, his motives, conflicts, attitudes, and values.

Consider *reading difficulties,* among the most common of school problems. Such difficulties seem to be nonspecific symptoms, a little bit like fever, produced by a wide range of antecedents, including inadequate motivation, immaturity, minimal brain damage, parental pressure for achievement, anxiety, inappropriate teaching methods, emotional instability, or perceptual defects. Psychological testing aids in diagnosing the underlying factors and in formulating treatment plans. A child with minimal brain dysfunction or perceptual defects might, for example, benefit from special kinds of sensorimotor training while the emotionally disturbed child might benefit most from psychotherapy.

Underachievement is a problem that is most frequently encountered in the junior and senior high schools. The underachieving young person usually has average or better than average intelligence, as measured by standard tests, but is doing poorly or failing in school; he is not working up to his intellectual potential, at least not in school. He may, however, be an avid sports fan and know every player on his favorite ball club together with each player's batting average and much more. In many ways underachieving students are highly selective learners.

There are many different reasons for underachievement, and the school psychologist, by means of interviews and tests, attempts to arrive at the particular factors operative in each case. Emotional instability is a frequent source of underachievement, particularly in boys with poor father identification. Such boys may develop a poor self-concept, have low self-esteem, doubt their own ability to achieve success in school, and lack the security necessary to accomplish as much as they could.

Specific causes of underachievement must be determined on an individual basis. One case referred to a school psychologist was a boy with an I.Q. of 142 who was failing school. Inquiry revealed that his father was dead; his mother was an alcoholic who was entertaining strange men in their home. The boy was so preoccupied with his personal problems that schoolwork had little interest for him. Some bright children are underachievers because school bores them; others may be embarrassed because they are slow in physical maturation. The school psychologist seeks to uncover the reasons for underachievement and to do whatever he can to remedy the situation. Sometimes he counsels the young person himself. Sometimes the remedy is more appropriately handled by a clinical psychologist or by a community agency such as a family service organization.

Closely related to the problem of underachievement is

truancy. Many truants have a history of repeating one or more grades in school. Responsible for their truant behavior is failure in school, which is often a function of low intelligence. The low intelligence in many cases is at least a partial function of intellectual deprivation; unsatisfactory home situations, broken homes, or poverty hinder intellectual growth. Whatever the cause of low intelligence, a child with a functional I.Q. of from 80 to 90 finds school progressively more difficult. He has trouble keeping up with his peers of average or better intelligence, but he is too "intelligent" to be placed in special classes. By the time he reaches junior high, repeated failure and humiliation become too much to bear, and he may refuse to go to school.

Underachievement and low intelligence are important factors leading to truancy. (Marion Bernstein)

Another frequent cause of truancy is **school phobia,** fear of school. While intense emotional aversion to school can appear at any point in the young person's academic career, school phobia is most frequent during the early elementary school years and again early in adolescence. In many cases there is a history of school phobia in the family; the mother or siblings may have experienced similar difficulties.

Usually some or all of the following patterns underlie this condition. One of the parents, usually the mother, tends to be isolated and lonely and, although she tells the child to go to school, manages to communicate her wish that the child stay home and keep her company. The children tend to be rather passive, compliant, and sensitive to parental needs. It has been suggested that what such children fear is not school but rather that something will happen to their mother in their absence. Beneath their passivity, many school-phobic children have an intense desire to be independent and to be free of parental domination. Hence, a counselor who encourages and applauds the child's independence strivings may achieve rapid and dramatic results. Some phobic students who have avoided school for months return to school after a single counseling session.

Counseling

So far we have spoken of kinds of children who come to the attention of the school psychologist and some of the diagnostic problems with which the psychologist is confronted. Although many school psychologists refer children with problems to child guidance clinics or to clinicians in private practice, many school psychologists counsel children in the school setting. In counseling, school psychologists employ much the same range of techniques as the child clinical psychologist does in the clinic. Some of the most effective procedures will be described briefly.

Play therapy is a technique based on the assumption that a child's unconscious wishes, conflicts, and fears will often be revealed in his play activities. This is particularly true for children below the age of nine or ten. In play therapy, the counselor may give the child toys such as dolls which represent father, mother, or chil-

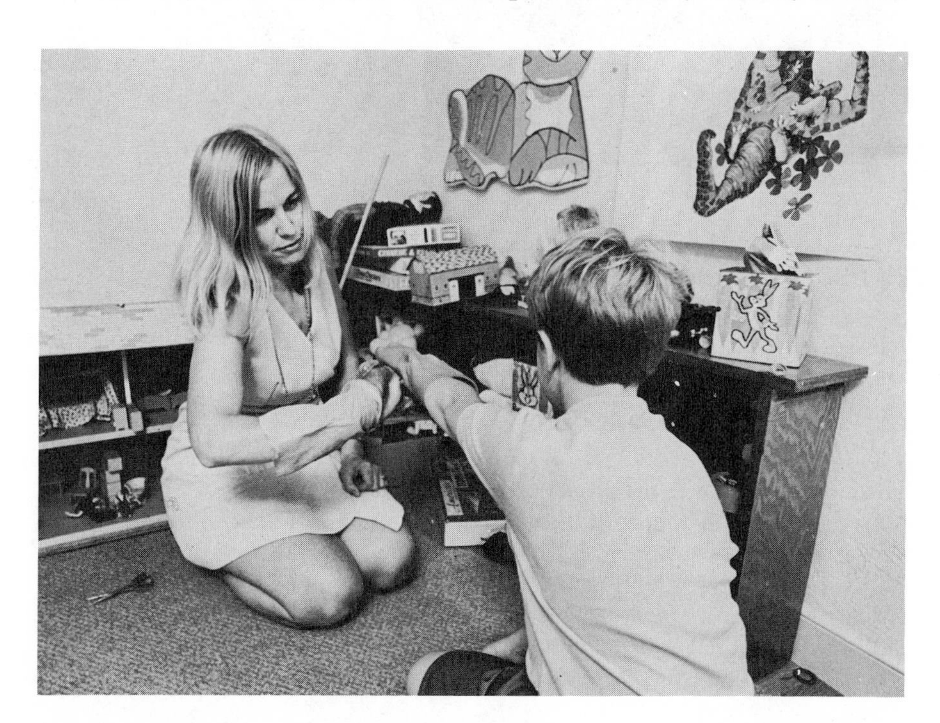

Play reveals problems; it also allows a counselor opportunity to aid the child in working out those problems.
(Dan Bernstein, courtesy Wellesley Human Relations Service)

dren. The counselor then allows him to play freely, and observes his play. Interpretation of his play may help the child become aware of his problems and how to deal with them more adaptively. If, for example, the child's play reveals that he feels rejected or pushed by his parents, the counselor may interpret this and encourage the child to discuss his feelings openly. New insights and more adaptive ways of reacting may emerge from such discussions. The efficacy of play therapy, like that of all psychotherapy, will depend upon such factors as the seriousness of the child's problem and the cooperation of parents in changing their ways of interacting with the child.

Another procedure, often employed with adolescents, is a kind of **group therapy** in which six or eight troubled young people and a counselor meet at regular intervals to talk over problems. (See p. 264 for a more detailed discussion of group therapy.) Often such groups become quite cohesive and continue to meet even though some members leave the group and are replaced by others. In one high school I know of, a group has been going for six years, and those who leave the group are instrumental in selecting their replacements.

Through group therapy sessions adolescents may achieve better understanding of themselves, their problems, and their relationships with others.
(Van Bucher, courtesy Wagner College Psychology Dept.; Photo Researchers)

During the group meetings, the students voice their feelings about themselves, their parents, their friends, and the school. The group's reaction to this expression of feeling often helps the individual young person to see himself and his problems from a broader, less self-centered perspective. This, in turn, may help the student to handle his problems more constructively.

A different kind of treatment widely used in the schools

is **behavior modification,** a procedure employed when a child displays relatively *specific* behavior patterns that are disruptive (see also p. 262). Suppose a child continually interrupts the class by getting up and making disturbing noises. In behavior therapy aimed at modifying this behavior, the school psychologist would work with the teacher to instruct her as to how to treat the youngster. He might suggest that she and the other children ignore the child's disruptive behavior as much as possible, but reinforce any instances of cooperative behavior. Teachers and children might be urged to compliment and accept him when he is well behaved, and to ignore him when he makes a nuisance of himself. The following is an example of a behavior-modification approach to a conduct problem in a school child.

Earl was a nine-year-old boy in the second grade. He was referred to the university clinic because of marked hyperactive behavior and academic retardation. He was described as being in almost continuous motion in the classroom and impossible to control unless he was in the immediate physical presence of the teacher. He was easily distracted, would work on his lessons for short periods of time or not at all, and leave his desk and wander around the room. He was extraordinarily disruptive to the other children in the classroom and, although he relieved their boredom, by and large they avoided him.

Previous to his adoption at age three, Earl had been treated with extreme brutality by his natural parents and later by his grandparents. His medical records showed a skull fracture which he received at less than one year of age, and at age four he was referred for neurological examination because of recurring convulsions and motor incoordination.

The therapeutic procedure began when the boy was observed for a period of time. Most of his hyperactivity was categorized as talking, pushing, hitting, pinching, looking about the room, looking out the window, moving out of his location, tapping, squirming, handling objects, and the like. Conditioning sessions followed a baseline observation period. The procedure brought fellow classmates into the situation. They were told that Earl had trouble learning things and one reason he was not learning was that he moved around and did not pay attention. Every time a light which was placed on his desk would flash, Earl had earned a penny or a piece of candy. This occurred for every ten-second period during which Earl had been attentive. The counter attached to the light would keep score. At the end of a period, the pennies and candies which Earl had earned would be divided among all of the class. In short, the program was such that Earl received a feedback (a flash of light and the counter) reinforcement for himself plus support or even social pressure from his peers. That is, Earl's good behavior became meaningful not only to himself but also to those around him, who no longer reinforced him with laughter or social approval for his disruptive behavior. Quite the contrary they reinforced his good behavior. [Figure 17-2 illustrates the sharp decrease after baseline of disruptive responses under the training program.]

A telephone call to Earl's parents four months after the study indicated that the teachers in school reported him to be much "quieter."

For the first time, other children came to his home to play and he was making progress in a remedial reading program. (Patterson, 1965, pp. 370–373)

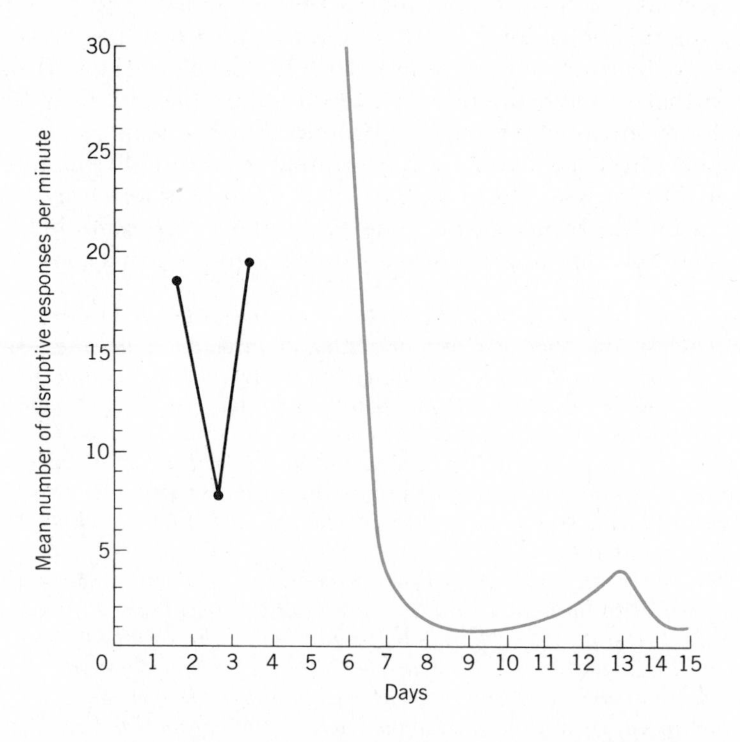

FIGURE 17-2
EFFECTS OF BEHAVIOR MODIFICATION PRACTICES ON DISRUPTIVE BEHAVIOR
(Adapted from Patterson, 1965)

Who develops innovations in teaching?

In these days of rapid social and educational change, psychologists have also been at the forefront of efforts to improve and modernize instruction, to make it more efficient, more appealing, and more meaningful. The vast possibilities of programmed instruction and automated teaching are being explored in many research centers and there seems little doubt that this kind of teaching, particularly **computer-assisted instruction (CAI)**, will be very widely applied in the future.

Programmed Instruction

The first teaching machine was invented by the psychologist Sidney L. Pressey about fifty years ago. Multiple-choice questions were presented in a slot in the machine and the student answered by pressing a button corresponding to his answer. If he chose the correct answer, the next question appeared in the slot; if his choice was incorrect, the original question remained until he found the right answer. The number of errors was recorded mechanically so that a total score was immediately available.

Many years later, B. F. Skinner began to use teaching machines in what became known as **programmed instruction.** The program for a course in arithmetic, for example, is a carefully planned set of materials that are arranged in a sequence beginning with elementary problems and progressing in small steps, up to relatively complex ones. Items are presented mechanically in the order that has been proven most effective in teaching, each new step being presented only when the learner is "ready" for it. Nowadays, computers are frequently used in programmed teaching, referred to as computer-assisted instruction (CAI). (See Spotlight 17-1.)

Basic to all programmed instruction is a curriculum, a body of materials in a particular subject area such as English or geography which the student is to learn. The curriculum in turn consists of units of instruction (see Figure 17-3), which are to be learned in a specified or programmed sequence and over a given period of time. A curriculum also includes a series of tests for measuring the student's progress and teacher aids for use in helping children

Jim had 13 marbles and lost 7 of them.
How many does he have now?

T see TS

	USE	DO	DONE
a.	Worksheet pencil Worksheet 1	Do the worksheet. Check work.	

FIGURE 17-3
A UNIT OF PROGRAMMED INSTRUCTION
(Redrawn; original unit is copyright © 1970 by Westinghouse Learning Corp.)

master the curriculum. The preparation of the curriculum is the most difficult and the most important part of the instructional system and the success of such programs depends on the knowledge, experience, and imagination of those who have developed the curriculum.

SPOTLIGHT 17-1

Computers as Teachers

The electronic computer has had a tremendous impact on American society. It computes and mails our bills; it sets type for many of our newspapers; it guides a man to the moon. In psychology it has proven to be an invaluable research instrument not only aiding in mathematical computations but also as a testing device. In Chapter 16, the use of computer programs as models of human intelligence was discussed (p. 399). It has also been applied in actual classroom situations as a partial substitute for teachers.

The computer has several advantages in teaching. For one thing, it has infinite patience. Unlike human teachers, it never gets frustrated or angry. It never has a "bad day." A second advantage is that it can keep *complete* records of everything the student has done and make use of this prior experience to present to the student a unique and individual program of study expressly designed for him.

Basically, the computer does three things. First, it displays the material to be learned to the student. Second, it records the response of the student to the material. Third and most important, on the basis of the responses (and certain program rules), the material to be presented next is adjusted so that the learning process will be maximally effective.

Psychological research enters the picture most clearly in the third state; this research provides the "certain program rules." In other words, there must be a theory of instruction. If the student is learning multiplication tables or a foreign language, the format is usually paired associates. The foreign word is displayed and the student is asked to give the correct English equivalent—typing it usually, although the ability of the computer to accept verbal responses is a near-reality. Or 2×2 is presented for the response "4." The anticipation method in serial-order

learning may be the format for learning the alphabet. In either case, in order to optimize learning, a theory of paired-associate or serial-order learning is required.

Computers are quite expensive. A method of individualized instruction that can be utilized with less expensive materials was developed by B. F. Skinner, the "father" of operant conditioning. Some question is presented, a response is asked for, and the student is informed whether or not his response is correct. For example, Holland and Skinner (1961) have prepared a course in psychology in book form. One item is phrased as follows: "In the conditioned eyeblink reflex just described, the ringing bell becomes the ______ ______." The student turns the page to discover "conditioned stimulus" is the correct response. The sequence of items is such that a high degree of success is experienced (almost continuous reinforcement), and the student is led step by step to quite intricate considerations. This approach has been called "programmed instruction," even though the programs may be used in "teaching machines" other than computers. Again, the instruction is individualized, at least in the sense that each student can work at his own rate. The computer has the advantage of being able to record and use the student's record of success and failure. It can adjust to give more practice where there are difficulties, less where no problems arise, something a book or other simple devices cannot do.

CAI has also been used widely in teaching elementary school subjects. In the program formulated by Patrick Suppes of Stanford University, computers assist teachers of arithmetic by drilling large numbers of students for short periods each day (about five or ten minutes per student) on arithmetical problems and keeping records of their progress. Relatively large numbers of students in grades one through 6 have been exposed to computer-assisted "drill and practice," and evaluations show that students do, on the average, learn more from the experience, but not much more than they would if conscientiously drilled by a teacher.

Although books are much cheaper, computers give a much more patient and individualized treatment to each student. Some remarkable results have been achieved (Atkinson & Wilson, 1969), but, as the recent review points out

> . . . despite a great variety of more or less successful trials of computer-assisted instruction (CAI) on a small scale, the revolution in the classroom predicted by the most ardent proponents of CAI has yet to take place (Hammond, 1972, p. 1005).

The use of computers in instruction is hardly likely to decrease, however. This fact raises the question of what is to happen to the human teacher. It is a simple question but it has no simple answer.

> Primary education is perhaps the most difficult challenge for CAI because of the importance accorded to the teacher-pupil interaction in primary schools. Hence the computer is usually considered as an addition to the normal educational experience, rather than as a replacement for the teacher. . . . Computers have been used both to enrich primary education by providing opportunities for conceptual learning that are not available in the normal curriculum and to relieve the teacher from routine but necessary educational chores. (Hammond, 1972, p. 1005)

Generally, teachers in schools using such systems appear to be quite pleased with the results of CAI. The dull and dreary rote learning is handled by the computer, and they are free to spend their time on the more interesting aspects of teaching: encouraging students to reason, create, and so forth. But it is not unlikely that such tasks could also be handled by computers if we knew enough about such processes. It will take much time to learn enough to make such programs feasible, and even then, the cost might make their use impracticable. No one knows the answers for sure. One writer on the subject recently noted that

> despite the seeming vitality of efforts to develop CAI systems, as evidenced by the many diverse approaches to this goal, there remains considerable skepticism in many parts of the educational community as to the future role of the computer in education (Hammond, 1972, p. 1006).

What do you think?

References

Atkinson, R. C., & Wilson, H. A. (Eds.) *Computer-Assisted Instruction.* New York: Academic Press, 1969.

Hammond, A. L. Computer-Assisted Instruction: Many Efforts, Mixed Results. *Science,* 1972, *176* (4038), 1005–06.

Before a student begins a unit of instruction he takes a test—really a pretest—to determine his standing in the subject and his readiness for the curriculum. The student puts his answers on an answer sheet that can be scored by a computer, which also determines the point at which the student should be introduced into the curriculum, that is, the unit of instruction with which he should start. This material is then reported to the teacher who can assign instructional units accordingly. Once into the curriculum, the child moves along the sequence at his own rate. At various points within or between instructional units, the student takes tests to assess his progress.

The computer also provides a variety of different reports for the teacher, noting the unit of instruction the student is working on, the objectives of that unit, and his progress as indicated by his scores on various achievement tests included in the unit. Reports of this kind inform the teacher about how each child is doing and indicate whether he needs special attention. If a child is doing very poorly, he can be given remedial materials. Accelerated students can be provided with supplementary enrichment activities. In addition to individual reports, the teacher also gets reports on the progress of the group as a whole.

One type of computer-assisted instruction, called "automated teaching," involves having the child working directly at a computer console. In automated teaching the student sits in front of a TV screen and a typewriter keyboard; he may also wear earphones.

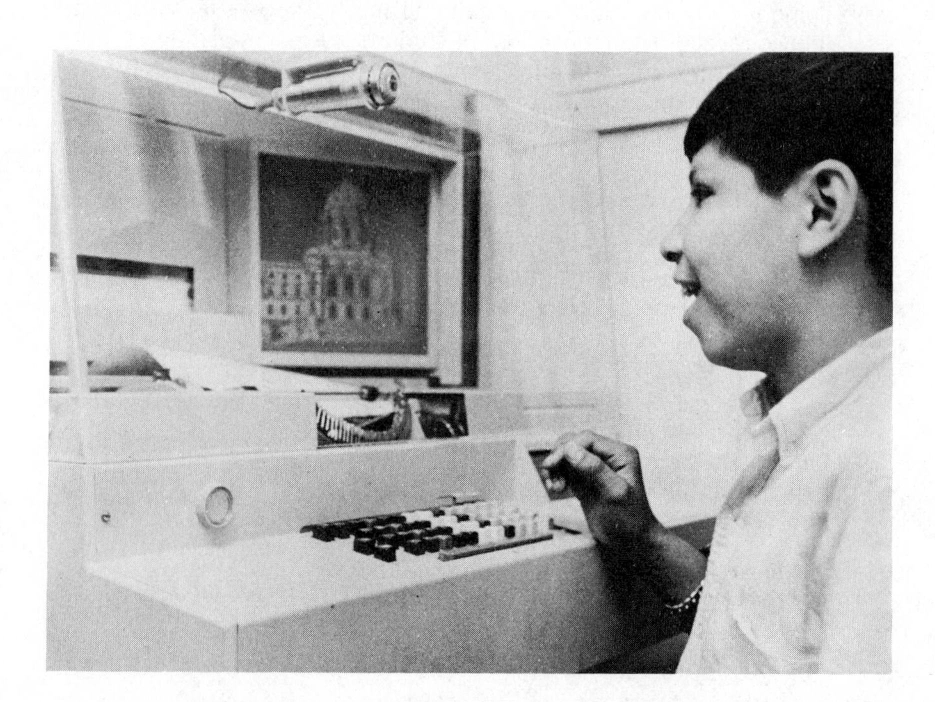

An advantage of computer-assisted instruction is the individualization of the program to the student.
(Courtesy Responsive Environments Corp.)

The computer presents instructions, explanations, questions, or pictures on the TV screen, and auditory messages may be received through the earphones. The student responds to the computer's questions and instructions through the keyboard. The computer evaluates his response immediately, moving on to the next item on the instruction program if the student gives the correct response. If his answer is not correct, the computer analyzes the nature of the student's difficulty and then, acting almost as a tutor, presents supplementary remedial material or a review of earlier work. It may also give the student some additional practice. The system can be used to teach subjects as varied as basic arithmetic and thermodynamics.

Since CAI has so many obvious advantages for both students and teachers, it is likely that the schools in the future will make greater use of these kinds of programs. The great problem of CAI is not dependent upon computer technology as much as it is upon human ingenuity and resourcefulness. CAI programs are only as good as the curriculums they employ.

Teacher Training

Psychologists have also contributed knowledge and techniques to improve the training of teachers. One of the most important recent innovations is the use of videotape systems. Because TV tapes are easy to make and do not need to be processed like film, they are extremely flexible tools. Tapes of experienced teachers at work can demonstrate the scope and variety of effective teaching styles. More important, prospective teachers can be taped during practice teaching and can see for themselves in a later replay, exactly what they did to earn a supervisor's criticism or praise.

Child psychologists can aid teacher education simply by presenting the rapidly growing fund of information on the physical, intellectual, and personality development of children. The work of Piaget (see p. 299) is particularly noteworthy. Learning psychologists, who have been instrumental in the development of many new techniques such as CAI, also provide new insights on the nature of learning. Almost every brand of psychologist has something to offer, and programs for training teachers are integrating psychological knowledge to an increasing degree.

One result is the increased concern with the personality and emotional sensitivity of teachers. Many programs use encounter or sensitivity groups to help teachers understand themselves and their pupils better (see p. 265). Both beginning and experienced teachers can benefit from carefully conducted group experiences. Unintentional but offensive personal mannerisms may become apparent, new approaches to honest communication can be tried, and, in general, the knowledge that all teachers suffer some degree of frustration can relieve some of the emotional strain of "personal failures."

Preschool Education

One of the most rapidly growing areas in education today is that directed toward preschool children (three- to five-year-olds). The reasons for this trend are many and complex. One of the most significant reasons, however, is the growing independence of American mothers. Women who are also mothers are eager to put their education, talents, and abilities to use, and no longer accept the notion that a mother should always stay home with her children when they are young. An increasing number of mothers are therefore demanding and getting day-care and educational facilities for young children. It is likely that, in the future, free preschool education and day-care facilities will be provided for all parents who desire it for their children.

While there is no question about the need for expanded and higher quality day-care and preschool programs, there is controversy about what is the best kind of program. At least three program models of preschool education have evolved out of different needs, different social climates, and different conceptions of the child. Before evaluating the relative efficacy of these programs, it might be well to describe the three different models.

Schools in the *home model* embody the goals of keeping children safe and healthy. Teachers are mother substitutes and fulfill the mother's duties and responsibilities while the child is in her care. A nursery school in the *clinic model* seeks to correct any personality or socialization problems; teachers in such schools see themselves primarily as therapists and focus their activities on helping the child resolve his tensions and anxieties. A relatively new pattern for preschool programs is the *instructional model.* In such programs, the teacher views her task primarily as that of instructing children in skills and information that will prepare them for further learning in the elementary school.

We have already described some of the difficulties in assessing the efficacy of instructional preschool programs on the child's later intelligence and academic performance; studies of different program models add still more complexity to the problem. In general, research suggests that the teacher's personality and style—her sense of humor or lack of it, her zest and warmth—are more important than whether her role is that of mother substitute, therapist, or teacher. Whatever the teacher's goals may be, she is likely to be more successful if she is appealing to children.

One investigation (Connors & Eisenberg, 1966) was focused on the instructional practices of thirty-eight experienced teachers who participated in a summer Headstart program for preschool children. Teachers' remarks and behaviors, recorded at regular intervals by trained observers, were scored in terms of the goals they seemed designed to serve. For example, a teacher's remark,

"Good job, Billy," was rated as serving the goal of "enhanced self-concept." Other remarks and behaviors were categorized as "encouraging consideration for others," "encouraging intellectual growth," and "encouraging neatness." Teachers' personality and style were also rated on warmth versus coldness, permissiveness versus restrictiveness, activity versus passivity, and variety versus lack of variety. The Peabody Picture Vocabulary Test was administered to the children at the beginning and at the end of the program to assess their intellectual progress.

Results showed that teachers who were rated high in both "encouraging intellectual growth" and in warmth were most successful in the sense that their pupils made the greatest gains on the intelligence test. Other studies point in the same direction. In one (Prescott & Jones, 1969), teachers rated high in level of interest and involvement in their activities were found to be most effective. The findings suggest again that what counts most is what *kind of a person* the teacher is, not what kind of school she is in or the role she is supposed to fill.

> *Positive responses from children are highly related to encouragement from teachers. They are also related to teacher emphasis on verbal skills and to lessons in consideration and creativity and pleasure, awe and wonder. They are* negatively *related to restriction, guidance, and lessons in control and restraint and rules of social living. (Prescott & Jones, 1969)*

While the teacher's style is important, its impact will vary with the characteristics of the children in her class. The complex interactions between teacher personality and student personality were clearly demonstrated in one study (Hill, Powell, & Feifer, 1960) of elementary school teachers and their pupils. The teachers were rated as either *turbulent* (outspoken and objective in evaluation and status-striving) or *self-controlling* (practical, dominant, orderly, and dependent upon authority) or *fearful* (plagued with anxiety resulting from fear). Students were categorized as *conformers* (high in social orientation, strict control of impulses, emphasis on mature behavior) or as *opposers* (pessimistic, intolerant of ambiguity, disappointed and frustrated in self, in others, and in objects) or as *waverers* (anxious, ambivalent, fearful, floundering, and indecisive) or as *strivers* (ambitious, hardworking, and school achievement oriented).

Standard achievement test results of children were analyzed to determine what kinds of teachers were most effective or ineffective—and with what kinds of students. *Self-controlling* teachers were most effective, that is, produced the greatest achievement, regardless of the students' characteristics. *Turbulent* teachers were very successful with *conformers* or *strivers,* but not with children classed as opposers and waverers. Finally, *fearful* teachers were effective with children classed as *strivers,* but were less successful than other teachers with other children. Apparently, the strivers will work hard and achieve regardless of teacher style. However, the performances of other children is much more dependent on the teacher's style.

Symbiosis of Psychology and Education

In recent years psychology and education have moved increasingly closer together. Prominent child psychologists have been appointed to professorships in schools of education and psychologists are becoming increasingly involved in educational organizations such as the American Educational Research Association and the National Association for the Education of Young Children. On an informal level, increasing numbers of psychologists and educators collaborate in research training and evaluation projects.

The closer relationship between education and psychology is an expected development, for education is a natural proving ground for psychological theories of learning and motivation. Psychologists are also discovering that the classroom is not simply a proving ground; problems that arise in the schools lead to generating psychological hypotheses and theories that are worth testing. Close cooperation between psychologist and educator can prove to be beneficial to both: the psychologist can benefit from the ready access to children in natural settings, who can serve as subjects for testing his hypotheses; teachers and schools can utilize the information generated by the research.

Consider the following study (Elkind, Deblinger, & Adler, 1970), which was suggested by some surprising findings from an evaluation of an innovative "experimental" public school. The "experimental" school was a nongraded, multiracial, inner-city school that included "interest areas" such as shop, art, and science to which children could go during the afternoon periods. The mornings were given over to instruction in basic school subjects. The school thus provided a happy compromise between free and structured learning opportunities. Children who had attended the innovative school for several years were matched with regular public school children equivalent on variables such as socioeconomic level and parental motivation. The groups were tested on a variety of measures including some tests of creativity. Contrary to expectations, the children in the regular public school did better on the creativity measure than the children in the innovative public school.

The effectiveness of the innovative school might have been brought into serious question were it not for an observation of an alert investigator. He noted that the children in the regular school seemed to enjoy the testing session very much and sought to prolong it, whereas the children in the innovative school found the testing dull and were eager to return to their stimulating classrooms. This consideration suggested the hypothesis that children who are taken from an interesting activity (to which they will return after the test) will seem less creative (produce fewer responses on a test of creativity) than children who come to the testing from a boring activity (to which they know they will return).

This hypothesis was tested in the following way. Three tests of creativity were employed, and each had alternate equivalent forms. Each child took one form of the test when he was interrupted while engaged in an *interesting* activity and the other form when interrupted while engaged in *uninteresting* activity. The *interesting* condition, determined by the child's own interests, included playing games, drama, science, reading, art, gym, music, shop, and social studies. The subject was told, "Would you please come with me. I have a few games [actually, the creativity tests] I would like to play with you. After we finish, you can complete whatever you are doing or are working on now." The child's groans, grimaces, and foot dragging that followed the examiner's request gave evidence that the ongoing activity was indeed interesting.

The *uninteresting* activities consisted of circling all of the *n*'s or *6*'s on two pages of letter and number combinations. The tasks were administered in the classroom. After the child completed the first page of the uninteresting task (about ten to fifteen minutes) he was given instructions about leaving to "play games" and returning to the uninteresting activity afterward. Again, behavioral evidence supported the view that these tasks were indeed uninteresting. The children complained while doing the task and called it "stupid." With few exceptions, the children were delighted when their participation in the "games" was requested.

The results support the hypothesis that performance on creativity measures is influenced by the ongoing activities interrupted by the test procedures. When children were temporarily removed from an uninteresting activity, they were almost twice as creative as when they knew they would return to an interesting activity. This finding held equally true for boys and girls, for children at different age levels, and for children from different ethnic groups.

This study illustrates how educational problems can generate research studies which have both applied and theoretical consequences. From the applied point of view, the study suggests that the circumstances from which children are taken for testing affect their performance. And, from a theoretical point of view, the results suggest that creativity, as measured by standard tests, is not a fixed ability but can be affected by the individual's emotional and motivational state.

SUMMARY

Educational psychologists engage in studies directed toward the resolution of practical educational problems. Their research is difficult and complex; for example, despite the fact that there have been numerous studies on the effects of nursery school on intellectual ability and achievement, no simple generalization can be made.

School psychologists do a great deal of testing for purposes of guidance—intelligence, achievement, aptitude, and interest testing. They also help to diagnose and treat a number of behavior problems, typically truancy, underachievement, school phobia, and reading retardation. These conditions rarely have a single cause but many relate to family disturbances, slow physical maturation, or low self-esteem. Treatments involve a variety of techniques including play therapy, group discussion, or behavior modification.

In recent years educational psychologists have been instrumental in developing programs for individualized instruction, many involving computers. Programs of computer-assisted instruction (CAI) allow the student to work at his own pace, with his progress automatically recorded and reported to the teacher. The teacher is freed to help the slow child or enrich the program of the bright child.

Psychologists contribute to teacher training by presenting educationally relevant psychological theories and research and by using psychological techniques to facilitate the learning of teaching skills (e.g., by using videotape systems for direct and immediate feedback) and interpersonal sensitivity (by group experiences). More sophisticated approaches to evaluating teacher effectiveness have related the *styles* of teachers and students. Students classified as "strivers" learn from all teachers, and "practical, orderly" teachers are effective with most students. But many students learn more from one type of teacher than from others, and many teachers are most effective only with certain types of students.

In general, psychology and education both benefit from their interaction. We have listed some of the benefits to education, but psychologists gain too by noting the success or failure of applications of basic research findings in an important applied setting. Failure—finding the results don't work in practice—suggests deficiencies in the basic conceptualizations. One example was the discovery that scores on creativity tests are strongly affected by students' level of interest in the tests, which, in turn, varies with activities they are engaged in before and after the testing.

RECOMMENDED READING

Barron, F. *Creative Person and Creative Process.* New York: Holt, Rinehart and Winston, Inc.
Barron's summary of many different studies of creativity gives many insights into the backgrounds and personalities of creative people.

Cronbach, L. *Essentials of Psychological Testing.* 3d ed. New York: Harper & Row, 1970.
A comprehensive and sophisticated treatment of psychological assessment procedures and techniques.

DeCecco, J. P. *The Psychology of Learning and Instruction.* Englewood Cliffs, N.J.: Prentice-Hall, 1968.
A comprehensive text designed for teachers in training; covers a wide range of research and issues pertaining to education together with practical applications for the teacher.

Ellis, H. C. *Fundamentals of Human Learning and Cognition.* Dubuque, Iowa: Wm. C. Brown Company, 1972.
In this comprehensive book Ellis takes up a wide range of issues including learning, memory, language, and problem solving. The discussion is informed and instructive.

Environment, Heredity and Intelligence. Cambridge: Harvard Educational Review Reprint Series, 1972.
A compilation of articles concerned with arguments for and against racial differences in intelligence and various types of compensatory education programs.

Hayes, J. P. (Ed.). *Cognition and the Development of Language.* New York: Wiley, 1970.
Collection of solid papers which present the latest thinking on language acquisition and its relation to cognition.

Hess, R. D., & Bear, R. M. (Eds.). *Early Education: A Comprehensive Evaluation of Current Theory, Research and Practice.* Chicago: Aldine, 1968.
The subtitle of this book describes pretty well the nature of the articles included within it.

Manis, M. *An Introduction to Cognitive Psychology.* Monterey, Calif.: Brooks/Cole, 1971.
A relatively non-technical treatment of cognitive psychology, which includes discussion of cognitive development as well as treating topics such as psycholinguistics and computer simulation of human intelligence.

Vernon, P. E. *Intelligence and Cultural Environment.* London: Methuen, 1969.
Vernon presents a thoughtful, balanced, and well-documented discussion of intelligence tests and testing in the context of cross-cultural investigations.

SECTION SIX

LEARNING AND MEMORY

By Bennet B. Murdock, Jr.

Review and Preview

As you are already well aware, learning is a key concept in psychology. It is one you have encountered frequently. In fact, you know quite a bit about learning, especially about the application of learning principles in explaining or theorizing about social behavior, development and functioning of personality, and thinking and problem solving. In these areas, learning principles are used in a general way.

In contrast, specialists in the psychology of learning, while acknowledging the importance of learning in everyday life and in social behavior, concentrate on detailed, precise, fine-grained analyses of the learning process. In their research they are rigorously experimental and most of them are concerned with theoretical issues. The research and theories of psychologists working in the related areas of learning and memory are the subject matter of this section.

Before beginning this in-depth analysis of learning, it seems appropriate to bring together some of the facts and principles of learning that have been presented in earlier sections of this book. Reinforcement is one of the most widely used concepts in psychology. Responses are strengthened if they are rewarded or reinforced—that is, these responses are likely to occur again in the same setting. Responses that are not reinforced will be extinguished, that is, they will be less likely to occur subsequently in these situations.

According to B. F. Skinner, probably the most influential contemporary American learning theorist, reinforcement is the key factor in shaping and forming responses, that is, in learning. Skinner's theory is simple in structure and, perhaps for this reason, it has been widely applied. Earlier we discussed some dramatic examples of the application of reinforcement in psychotherapy, specifically in the technique of behavior modification (see p. 262). In this technique, the therapist (or teacher) attempts to modify a patient's (or child's) maladaptive behavior by rewarding (reinforcing) his positive, socially-desirable responses while disregarding (not rewarding) his undesirable or neurotic behavior. These techniques have produced some dramatic changes in behavior. A more complete explication of Skinner's theory will be given in this section.

For Skinner, then, what follows a response is most important; he is not concerned with the internal forces—motives, drives, and needs—that instigate goal-directed behavior. These motivational variables do loom large in other theories, notably those of Clark Hull and his disciples who were the leading learning theorists of the 1940's and 50's. In Hull's view, drives and reinforcements are the critical concepts, and the two are intimately related; reinforcement is defined in terms of drive reduction. A hungry (that is, motivated) rat turns right in a T-maze and finds food at the end of the alley. Food is a reinforcement because it reduces hunger, which is a primary, biologically-determined drive. The response of turning right has been reinforced; consequently, the rat is more likely to turn right again the next time he is at that point in the maze.

Hull's theory appealed to many psychologists who saw its vast implications for social psychology, personality, developmental, and educational psychology. The theory seemed helpful in explaining the acquisition of important secondary social drives, called "learned" drives. The process of acquiring secondary drives was illustrated earlier in an account of an experiment in which a rat learned to fear a white compartment of a box because he received electric shocks whenever he was there. Subsequently, the rat learned to turn a wheel that opened a door that allowed him to escape from the white compartment (see p. 215). The reinforcement was the reduction of fear, a learned drive. Another learned drive is an infant's love for his mother. This is not a primary drive according to learning theory; rather it is learned on the basis of the association between the mother's presence and the infant's feelings of satisfaction that stem from food, warmth, support, and relief from pain—all supplied by the mother. The mother begins to stand for gratification—that is she acquires reward value—and, when the baby is hungry or upset, her mere presence is comforting. She becomes a social reinforcer, the child becomes attached to her, and he frequently seeks her out even when he is not hungry or upset.

The concepts of generalization and mediation (often called "mediated generalization" or "verbal mediation") are also derived from Hull's theory. These concepts are helpful in explaining why some responses are learned relatively easily and why some problems are readily solved. According to the principle of generalization, the behavior learned in response to one stimulus is likely to be transferred to—generalized to—similar stimuli. For example, if the child has learned to make friendly outgoing responses to his mother, he is more likely to make such responses to other friendly-appearing females. And, after a child has learned a label—a verbal mediator—applying to an object or an event, he is likely to respond in the same way to all stimuli having the same label (see p. 383). If he has learned to smile and be polite to someone called "uncle," he is likely to react this way to other men whom he hears called "uncle."

Clearly this kind of learning theory is flexible and useful in explaining the acquisition and development of many kinds of behavior. Yet some of the most interesting and exciting phenomena of learning cannot readily be explained in terms of motivations and reinforcement. For example, most of your own current learning is not motivated by primary biological drives or reinforced by drive reduction. Animals, too, as we will see in Chapter 18, can learn well under conditions of no drive and no reinforcement. They may learn their way around a maze, but they may not actually show their learning—that is, they may not run the maze correctly—until they receive a reward for performing. The concept of latent learning refers to learning without reward and highlights the distinction between learning and performance (see p. 469).

You have also encountered other instances of learning without reward. Recall, for example, that a child may acquire many complex responses, including aggressive behavior and generous behavior, simply by observing models and imitating their behavior (observational learning). (See p. 333.)

In other learning experiments, and in some problem-solving situations, subjects give evidence of insights, achieving solutions *suddenly*—as contrasted to trying one response after another (trial and error) and gradually zeroing in on the correct (rewarded) solution. Actually, insight solutions probably depend on previous experience *and* a perceptual reorganization of the field, a new way of looking at the stimuli. Furthermore, there is abundant evidence that we form learning sets, that is, we "learn to learn." After experience with certain kinds of learning tasks or problems, we handle related ones much more rapidly and efficiently.

Motivation and reinforcement, traditionally the key concepts of learning, no longer seem adequate to explain all the phenomena of learning. And they are no longer the primary interests of learning psychologists. It should not be inferred from this that motivation is no longer an important topic in psychology. It is a primary concern of social, personality, developmental, and educational psychologists who study man in the social world and want to investigate the question of why he acts as he does. For example, the theory of cognitive dissonance discussed in Section Two is concerned with the motivation or drive that results from holding two incompatible beliefs. And, as we shall see later, biological psychologists investigate the bodily mechanisms underlying basic drives such as hunger and thirst. Reinforcements—social rewards or basic physiological mechanisms—are also being intensively studied in other areas. Social psychologists who espouse dissonance theory see any act that results in dissonance reduction (drive reduction) as likely to be learned. This could account for acquiring a changed attitude. Thus, the concepts of motivation and reinforcement have been removed from the area of learning to other areas of psychology.

What then are the issues on which the contemporary learning psychologist focuses his attention, the questions with which this section will deal? Essentially, they are the issues of associationism and information processing. How is an "association" formed? How is it stored? Why is it sometimes "lost"? Is it really lost, or is it just not retrievable? Do different processes affect retention of information in the short term—the first few seconds—as compared with retention over the long term—hours, days, and years? How, exactly, does one retrieve information stored in memory? These are questions you are about to encounter. The research is exciting, for it involves basic aspects of the workings of the human mind.

SN75325N
7223A

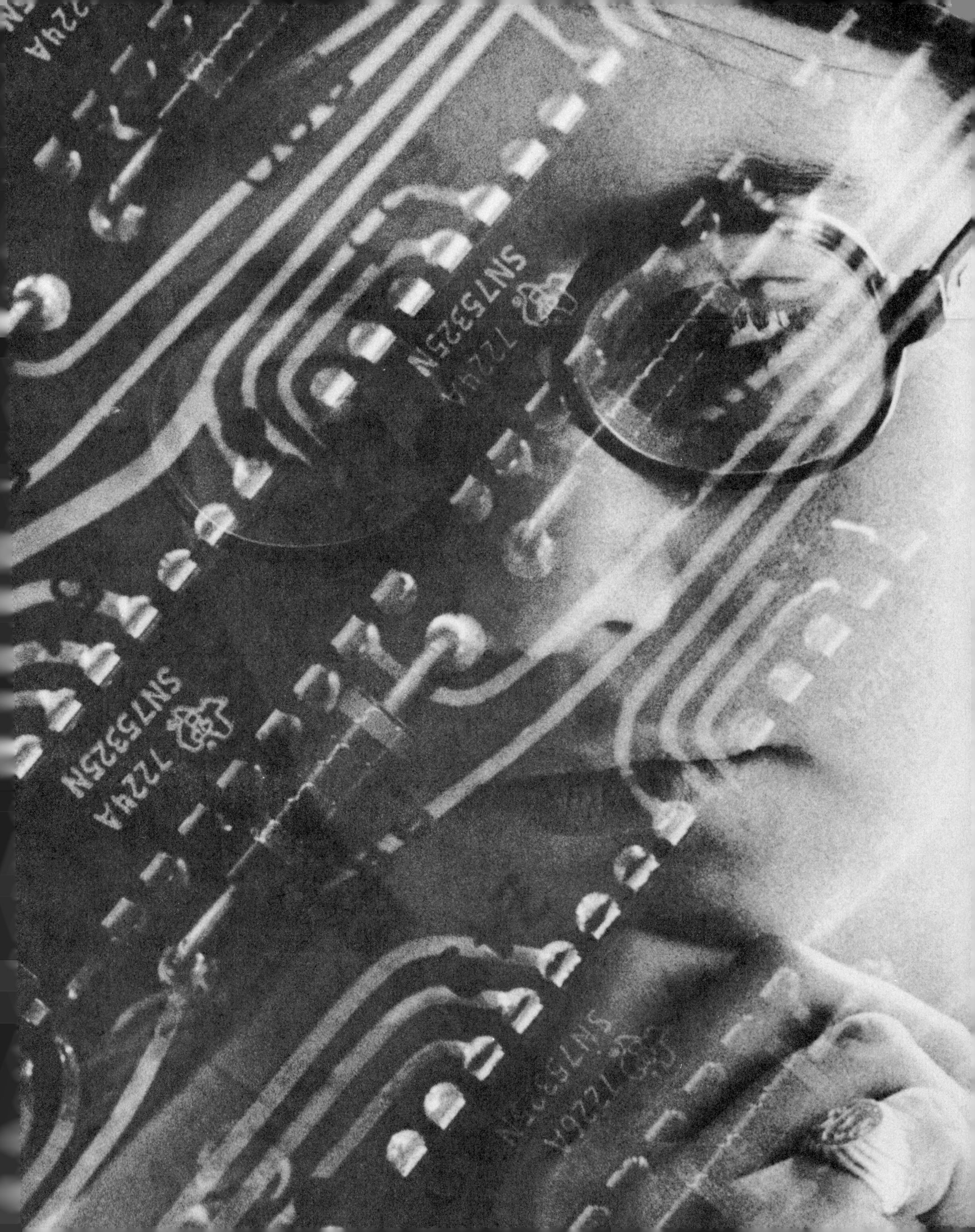
SN75325N
7224A
SN75325N
7224A

18 Learning

What do single associations reveal about learning?
How are sets of associations learned?
Does past learning help or hinder new learning?
What are the current issues of learning psychology?

How does an individual come to modify his behavior through experience? The process is called **learning,** and this process is the topic of concern in this section. The goal is to understand something of the principles underlying changes in behavioral response, changes that are often quite complex. The newborn human infant, for example, has a very limited set of effective behaviors; he is dependent on the aid of parents for his very survival. Somehow, in a period of fifteen to twenty years, the exceptionally complex repertoire of skills of the adult develops. Some of these changes are relatively simple, such as basic discriminations; when faced with a green traffic light, the adult "goes," but if the light is red, he "stops." Other changes are much more complex, such as the integrated skills of a businessman, an opera star, or a professional football player. Even the organization of day-to-day living involves so much knowledge and so many different habits that it is difficult to imagine how one could have learned so much in so short a time.

By now psychologists have collected considerable data and have formulated and tested hypotheses on learning principles. There is still much unknown and what has been discovered indicates how much more there is to know. Simple answers to simple questions invariably produce a host of more complex questions; we do not realize the extent of our ignorance until we gain a little knowledge. The result is that questions about the learning process are continually increasing in number, in depth, and in breadth. The scientist must dig deeper into basic principles underlying the "basic" principles already discovered, and he must simultaneously expand his observations to related questions (an increase in breadth), for he knows that in the answers there lie parts of the puzzle. In this chapter, therefore, you will find some of the current attempts to understand quite intricate phenomena. For instance, we already know that following a response with a "reward" (reinforcement) is likely to increase the probability of that response; but how does giving a reinforcement only after every twenty-fifth response affect the probability? At the same time that we are digging deeper, we are expanding "horizontally." Moving on from the early work on simple, single associations, we are now amassing evidence on more complex collections of associations, including skills.

What do single associations reveal about learning?

The first concept to be discussed in a chapter on learning should be **association.** In a sense, what we learn are associations. The red traffic light becomes *associated* with the response of stopping. The linebacker learns to associate small muscle movements in the opponent's quarterback with a particular direction in which the play will be run. These associations were not present at birth; they developed through experience; they were learned. Clearly we have not explained anything by using the word "association." We have not described the nature of the bond nor have we given any details of its development—we have simply stated that there is a relationship between a stimulus (S) and a response (R) such that an S-R pair exists now where it did not before. An association is to the learning psychologist what the "atom" is to the physicist and what the "gene" is to the geneticist. All are essential concepts. They are necessary for communication—rather than explanatory concepts—and they describe what it is we endeavor to explain. These basic concepts represent goals that we set, not goals we have achieved.

Classical Conditioning

Classical conditioning refers to the formation of a single association by means of a procedure developed by Ivan Pavlov, a Russian physiologist, in the early 1900's. Pavlov's special field of study was the digestive secretions of the body, for which he received the Nobel Prize in 1904. Salivation was one of the bodily secretions under study. In order to obtain a precise measure of secreted saliva under varying conditions, Pavlov inserted a small tube into the salivary glands of his experimental animals, which were usually dogs (see Figure 18-1). Thus, when the dog salivated, the fluid was routed into Pavlov's measuring cups. By this method, he could determine not only when salivation occurred but also how much and at what rate. For the time—indeed, even for today—it was a remarkably clear and rigorous estimate of response strength.

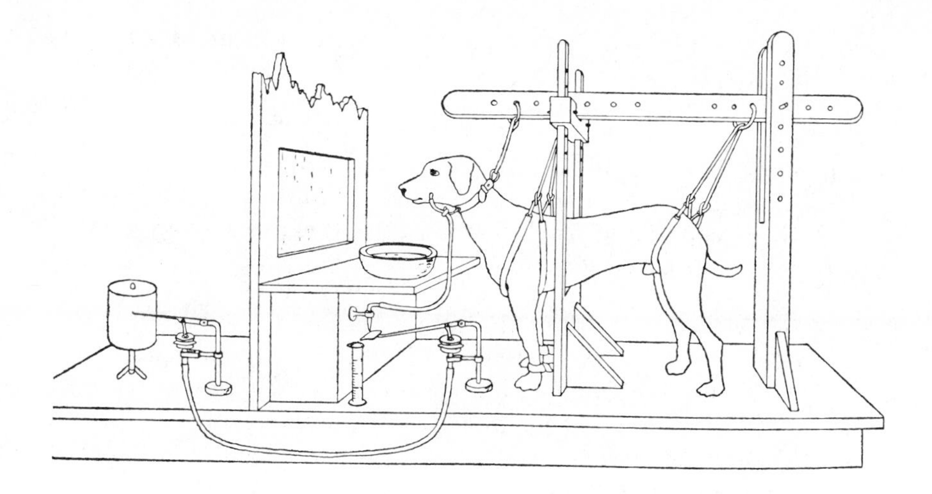

FIGURE 18-1 PAVLOV'S CONDITIONING SITUATION

This drawing is from the first major account in English of Pavlov's experiments on conditioning the salivary response in dogs.
(From Yerkes & Morgulis, 1909)

"Psychic Secretions"

In the course of his studies of salivation, Pavlov noted secretion of a particular type which he called "psychic secretions." If food is placed in the mouth of an animal, it will secrete saliva automatically—this is an innate, not a learned, response. But the dogs in Pavlov's apparatus soon began to salivate to other stimuli as well. The *sight* of food, for example, the sight of the person who fed them, and even the feeder's footsteps in the hall were enough to elicit salivation. These associations had to be learned. They were in effect "anticipations" of food in the mouth. Since the response (salivation) was not controlled by the simple reflex connections, some higher neural processes had to be involved. It was as if the mind took over control of the reflexive act—hence, "psychic" secretions—as if the "thought" of food was sufficient to produce the same response as food itself.

Psychic secretion was hardly a new and unexpected phenomenon. Pavlov had witnessed it in his earlier studies of the digestive secretions of the stomach, and even the phrase "the mouth waters" dates back at least to the sixteenth century. That psychic secretions involved associations of a response to a "new" stimulus was similarly common knowledge (Rosenzweig, 1959). In physiological research, these "deviant" responses were generally considered a nuisance, much like unexpected noises, sights, and smells that could distract the animal from his true purpose, which was to be an experimental subject in the study of automatic bodily reflexes. Great efforts were made to eliminate or at least to control these secondary influences. Pavlov's genius lay in his decision to study the "nuisance" phenomena directly and in his careful and brilliant experimental programs. That classical conditioning is sometimes called Pavlovian conditioning is testimony to the impact of one man's endeavors.

Ivan Pavlov, pioneer investigator of conditioning.
(Library of Congress)

Pavlov called the innate automatic responses (e.g., salivation to food) *unconditional responses* since they happened uniformly and without any special requirements. He called responses acquired through training (e.g., salivation in response to hearing a tone) *conditional responses* since they occurred only under certain conditions. If a particular tone is to elicit salivation in the dog, that tone must be followed by the food in repeated instances. Such "conditions" do not apply to the automatic reflex; food must be placed in the mouth, of course, but such a stimulus will cause salivation on all occasions including the very first.

All this terminology with the root word "condition" had a salutary effect on the subsequent research. Pavlov set out to discover the exact nature of the *conditions* in which a previously neutral stimulus could come to elicit a response. Early theorists knew well enough that the sight (or thought) of food was often enough to elicit salivation; they even speculated that past pairings of the sight of food with food itself was responsible, but they did not take the next step. If the sight of food causes salivation because of its relationship with the actual presentation, then it should be possible to associate an unrelated stimulus to the same response: a bell or buzzer, for example, or a flash of light. Pavlov took the next step.

Because of a somewhat unfortunate early translation of the Russian into English, the terms "conditional" and "unconditional" are typically rendered "conditioned" and "unconditioned." If the S-R pair is natural or reflexive (does not require learning), the stimulus is called the **unconditioned stimulus** (US) and the response the **unconditioned response** (UR). If the S-R association develops from experience, the stimulus is called the **conditioned stimulus** (CS) and the response the **conditioned response** (CR). For example, food in the mouth is a US to salivation (UR); the sight of the experimenter might become a CS to the same response, now called CR. The process of classical conditioning was conceived as one in which a new stimulus (CS) is substituted for another (US) in provoking the response (UR, changing to CR).

Stages of Classical Conditioning

According to the procedures developed by Pavlov, as presented in Figure 18-2, there are three stages to classical conditioning. Figure 18-3 shows changes in response strength during the three stages. The first stage involves choosing two stimuli, one of which is a US to the response of interest, the other clearly not (we hope to make it our CS later). We must therefore, in Stage 1, demonstrate that US does reliably elicit UR and that CS as yet does not. CS may well produce a response, if only an orienting response, but our concern is that it does not naturally produce UR.

The US-UR pair used in most of Pavlov's experiments was food-salivation, but others serve equally well. Much research has been done in humans using the eyeblink caused by a puff of air directed at the eye. Other research has studied emotional responses,

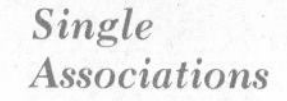

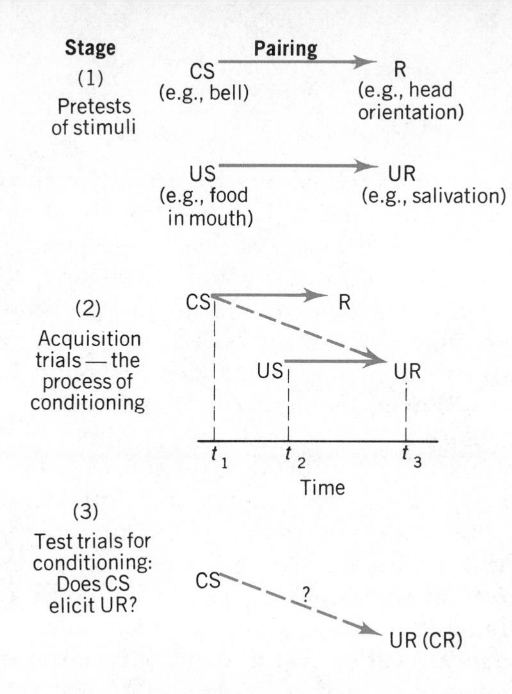

FIGURE 18-2
PROCEDURES FOR CLASSICAL CONDITIONING

Stage 1 is to ensure that CS does not initially evoke UR. Stage 2 is the paired presentations of CS and US during which the conditioning is gradually established. Stage 3 is the test to see if CS does evoke the response. If it does, then UR has become CR and so demonstrates learning. If Stage 3 is continued, extinction will result, i.e., CS will no longer elicit CR.

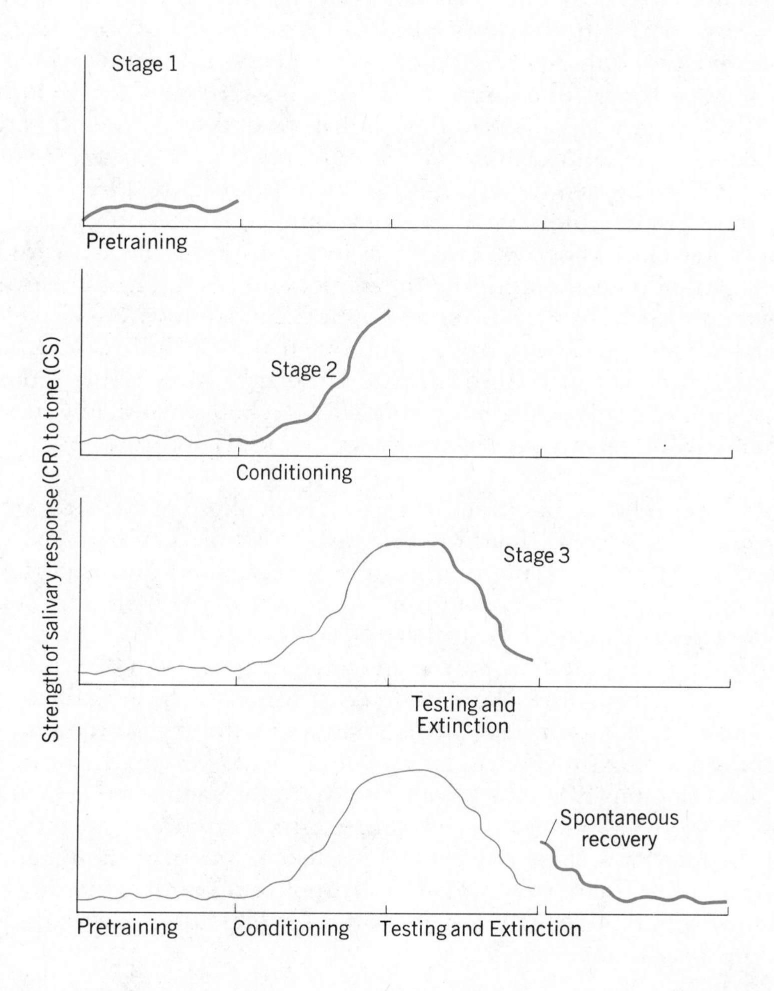

FIGURE 18-3
THREE STAGES OF CONDITIONING

Response strength of CR is plotted in the various stages. Also illustrated is spontaneous recovery of some response strength which occurs when CS is presented some time later (say 24 hours) after extinction is seemingly complete.

such as fear, that can be triggered by a US, a loud noise or an electrical shock. The CS in research has typically been a light or a tone; these simple stimuli have the advantage of being susceptible to rather precise description in terms of intensity and frequency.

Stage 2 in classical conditioning represents the learning process: the **acquisition** pairings (trials). Say that CS is a pure tone and that UR is salivation. Then Stage 2 might consist of the brief presentation of the tone, followed by the food stimulus (US), which elicits salivation. This pairing is repeated several times. If CS forms an association with the response, it can be demonstrated in Stage 3; here the CS is presented but the US is not, so if UR (CR now) occurs, the CS-CR bond can be said to be in effect. The tone now elicits salivation whereas it did not before. Conditioning has been accomplished.

The trials of Stage 1 are usually called pretests. Those of Stage 2 are called conditioning trials, acquisition trials, or, simply, trials. Stage 3 trials are called test trials if their purpose is to test the CS alone to see if the association has been formed. But they are also *extinction* trials. If the tone produces salivation but is *repeatedly* presented without the US (food), as in Stage 3, eventually the response will cease following CS—it will be *extinguished.* A tone is fine if it "means" food is coming, but if several tones sound and no food comes, the anticipatory salivation stops.

The acquisition trials depicted in Figure 18-2 represent only the most common and effective sequence of CS and US. Exactly what is the most effective, of course, is a question to be answered by experimental investigation, and the meticulous research of Pavlov was directed to this end. It was found that if CS precedes US—if the tone precedes food—conditioning occurs, but if the CS follows US, little or no learning results. More precisely, it can be shown that the optimal sequence is to have CS precede US by a half second; any interval longer or shorter will produce a weaker conditioned response.

Spontaneous Recovery

The acquisition and extinction phenomena are not the only characteristics of learning that can be studied in classical conditioning. After a response has been extinguished and a period of time has elapsed, the conditioned response may *spontaneously recover*—regain some of its strength (see Figure 18-3). Why this occurs is not known for certain, but in many cases it appears to be some kind of fatigue effect in the extinction stage; it is as if the organism still has some "association" left but is unable to exhibit it at the end of a fatiguing set of extinction trials. The next day, however, the refreshed organism demonstrates the remaining strength. Spontaneous recovery is of theoretical importance, of course, since any theory worth considering must somehow explain it; it is also of practical significance—you may think you have eliminated a response through extinction only to find it spontaneously recovered later. Several additional extinction sessions may be necessary.

Generalization

Another feature of conditioning is **generalization.** Once a CR has been established, not only will CS elicit it, but so will a variety of other stimuli. These other stimuli are marked by their *similarity* to the CS. The conditioning has generalized to other stimuli along a dimension of stimulus similarity. For example, suppose a dog learns to salivate to a tone of a certain frequency, say 500 cycles per second (written 500 Hz or hertz); he will then also salivate to similar-sounding tones such as 480 Hz or 520 Hz, even though these tones have never been paired with US-UR in any acquisition trials. The more "similar" to the original CS, the more response strength demonstrated, as indicated in Figure 18-4. A tone of 2400 Hz would elicit very little, if any, response.

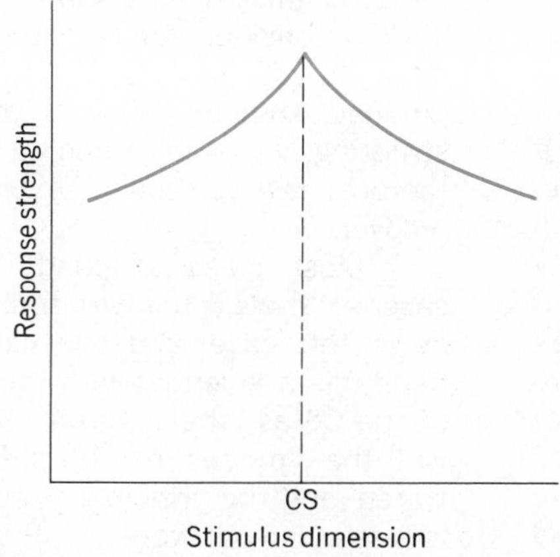

FIGURE 18-4 GENERALIZATION GRADIENT

The CS denotes the original training stimulus; the test stimuli are similar to CS but at different points along the stimulus dimension. The farther removed from CS, the weaker the resulting response strength.

Generalization is in part a failure of discrimination. Sometimes it is very important, in the laboratory or in real life, that fine discriminations be made. To establish greater discrimination, you present the CS *with the US* repeatedly, and, on other trials, you present stimuli that differ somewhat from the CS *without the US*. Thus, in our example, a tone of 500 Hz would be presented repeatedly *with* food, while tones of 480 and 520 Hz would be repeatedly presented *without* food. Thus the CR to 480 and 520 would disappear but the CR to 500 Hz would remain. A finer discrimination would thus be achieved.

This is another way of saying that the generalization curve in Figure 18-4 will be much sharper, with steeper gradients, after discrimination training. It is not an unimportant feature of conditioning. Consider the real-life example of a person with a conditioned fear response to snakes who lives in a region populated by many snakes, some of which are not only harmless but immensely useful to the environment. If he does not learn to discriminate among snakes, his life will be one of constant terror and the environment might well suffer by his fear-induced destruction of harmless reptiles. (The relevance of classical conditioning for "real" problems is also discussed in Spotlight 18-1.)

SPOTLIGHT 18-1
Classical Conditioning Outside the Laboratory

Experiments on classical conditioning in the psychologist's laboratory may sometimes seem unreal and not very relevant, dealing as they do with dogs with surgical inserts, precisely-measured pure tones, and the like. Surely the need for precision and rigor in scientific experiments is clear, but the principles thereby determined are not easily integrated into our understanding of everyday human behavior. As a more homely illustration, we can give an example, a true case history of a young girl's encounter with a large dog.

The girl was six years old at the time. She and her parents had just arrived at a small New England inn and were outside, about to enter the dining room. A dog, a large St. Bernard, was sitting some forty yards from them. Suddenly, without warning, the dog gave a fierce bark and charged directly at the small girl. Her unconditioned response was naturally one of fear and she ran screaming to her parents. The dog charged by, within a few feet, in fierce pursuit of his real target, a squirrel in the parking lot.

It was several minutes before the parents could quiet the girl's anguish, but the remainder of the day passed without incident. The next day, however, provided ample evidence that the encounter had not been without effect. The neighbor's dog, a Collie, appeared. It did not bark or charge; it simply entered the girl's field of vision. The girl broke into tears and ran home. Throughout the week, various neighborhood dogs evoked a similar reaction, until finally the girl was afraid of even leaving the house for fear of seeing a dog—almost any dog, although the bigger, the more terrifying. A psychotherapist would have diagnosed her condition as a phobia, an extreme and unnatural fear. Therapy was clearly needed. Luckily the parents were psychologists and had little trouble alleviating this phobia. If you were the parent and knew the principles of classical conditioning, what would you have done? Can you imagine the form of the "therapy"? Consider these questions, too: What do you think, precisely, the unconditioned stimulus was? If you are constructing in your mind a reasonable therapy, have you considered spontaneous recovery?

Most classical conditioning takes several "trials," not one traumatic event as in this case, and one cannot be too happy as a scientist with the description of the CS as "the sight of a St. Bernard." But the "procedure" is fairly well illustrated, and the principle of generalization is also clearly at work.

Finally, as we have already seen in preceding sections, this example is by no means unique or unusual. Many of us have phobias, if only the mild variety. Psychotherapists treat people with severe cases. But in any case, there is increasing acceptance of the view that a high proportion of phobias are conditioned responses in the classical-conditioning mold and are treated accordingly, with extinction procedures if possible. There is a lot of Pavlovian conditioning in the normal (and abnormal) world.

We should mention the concept of "response strength," which we have used more or less intuitively in our discussion of basic principles. It is obviously desirable to know something about how strong a response is, in addition to knowing simply whether it occurs at all.

After training with one particular CS, such as a 500 Hz tone, you can test generalization by measuring the strength of response to other stimuli, such as tones of 480, 460, 520, and 540 Hz. Several measures are typically used to estimate response strength. One is the *probability of occurrence* of a CR, i.e., the proportion of test trials on which CR occurs; the more probable a response is, the stronger it is. A second measure is *latency*—the time between the presentation of CS and the beginning of CR—and a shorter latency usually suggests a stronger response. A third method is to estimate the *intensity* of the response more directly if such a measure is appropriate. In salivation it is; more saliva is considered a stronger response than less. A fourth possibility is called *resistance to extinction*. A stronger CR will presumably take more extinction trials before it disappears. Thus, there are many ways to estimate response strength, and though the operations are different, producing different numbers on different scales, in most cases the measures are conceptually interchangeable. In other words, generally speaking, a stronger CR is more likely to be given in response to CS, has a shorter latency, occurs in greater degree, and takes more trials to extinguish. The statements made here about classical conditioning will apply regardless of the response measure one chooses to use.

Operant Conditioning

Pavlov was the "hero" of classical conditioning. The hero of operant conditioning is an American psychologist, B. F. Skinner, and the impact of the discovery of a second type of conditioning may well exceed that of the first. **Operant conditioning** is defined as conditioning in which the response is determined by what *follows* it (unlike classical conditioning in which the *preceding* stimuli are important). In layman's language, operant conditioning applies to those cases in which someone *does* something in order to *get* something. He pulls the knob on the vending machine to get a candy bar; he says nice things to his father in hopes of getting the car this weekend; he studies German in the expectation of a better grade. In other words, he *operates* on the environment in some way—hence the term "operant"—in order to achieve some goal or reward.

B. F. Skinner
(Jill Krementz)

Operant responses Skinner called "emitted responses," to distinguish them from the elicited responses in classical conditioning. This is not to say that no influential stimuli precede an emitted response, only that these stimuli are not the prime consideration. In many cases it would be difficult if not impossible to specify a stimulus, a US, that would automatically "elicit" responses of the type mentioned. The prime consideration is the stimulus following.

Reinforcement as Key to Association

The single most important principle in operant conditioning is that **reinforcement** following a response will increase the probability of that response in the future. A reinforcement is a stimulus, an attractive one in some sense, and most people would call it a reward (but "reward" is a term with too much surplus meaning for technical use). There are *positive reinforcers*, like food and water, which will increase the probability of response if they are present following the response (assuming the organism is hungry or thirsty), and there are *negative reinforcers*, like electric shock, which increase response strength if they are *removed* following the response; taking aspirin alleviates pain so the probability of taking aspirin when pain "strikes" increases.

So much is perhaps common sense, even though the technical details in even the simplest case are more complex than the casual observer might imagine. But there is a simple prescription: wait for the response you want, reinforce it, and the association will build in strength. Now add a pinch of complexity: Suppose the response you want is *never* "emitted," then what? You could wait for years before your white rat would stand up on his hind legs and press the bar in his cage (hooked up to a food delivery mechanism). Skinner developed a technique for these very situations; it is called **shaping** or the method of successive approximations. Say you want to train a rat to play basketball. You set up a small hoop in his cage and throw in a small ball—you want him to pick it up and drop it through the hoop. Don't bother to wait for the first natural occurrence; it will never come. But you can train him by successive approximations. First, any sign of attention to the ball (looking at it, moving toward it) is reinforced. Then greater "involvement" is reinforced (moving closer and closer). Soon he must touch the ball to get his reinforcement; then he must pick it up; then he must carry it; then he must carry it toward the hoop; then he must carry it to the hoop; and finally,

Operant-conditioning techniques are used in training animals.
(Courtesy U.S. Navy)

The animal performs to receive a reward; reinforcement encourages repeat performances.
(Russ Kinne, Photo Researchers)

he must pick it up, carry it to the hoop, and drop it through. And there you have it. It's surprisingly easy to train him once you know how. (See Skinner's article, "How to Teach Animals," in *Scientific American,* December, 1951.)

Here is another complexity. What happens if you reinforce not every single correct response but only every other one? every tenth response? every twentieth response? It is certainly a rare case, especially in real life, where every single response gets reinforced. Take the gambler in Las Vegas, for example, responding furiously to the promised reinforcement from the "one-armed bandit." He doesn't win every time, but there is **partial reinforcement.** Is there a difference in behavior with an intermittent schedule of reinforcement? Yes, there is, and most of what we know about the effects of various schedules is due to Skinner's thought and research.

Reinforcement Schedules

There are four basic families of **reinforcement schedules.** There are actually six but the first two are special cases in which every single response is reinforced (continuous reinforcement) and no response is reinforced—called "extinction," just as in classical conditioning (it results in decreased probability of response). The four basic intermittent families are fixed-ratio, variable-ratio, fixed-interval, and variable-interval. A *fixed-ratio schedule* operates to deliver a reinforcement once every so many responses; every tenth time the correct response is made, for example, would be a 10:1

fixed-ratio schedule. A *variable-ratio schedule* delivers one reinforcement every so many responses but only *on the average;* a 10:1 variable-ratio schedule might "pay off" after 8, then 12, then 10—in the long run, on the average, the ratio is 10:1. A simple slot machine works on a variable-ratio schedule. It can't pay every time and, if it paid *exactly* every tenth time, the house regulars would make a fortune. The schedule is therefore variable.

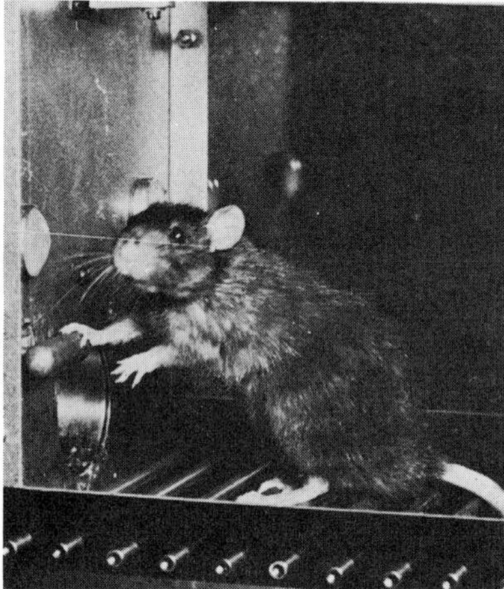

Operant behavior of three species.
(Left and center, courtesy B. F. Skinner; right, George W. Gardner)

Interval schedules are based on time intervals rather than the number of responses. A reinforcement is delivered for the first response after an interval of elapsed time, say one minute or five minutes or thirty. Again, *fixed-interval* means the interval is always exactly the same and *variable-interval* means the interval varies around some average period. As an example, though he did not use the technical terms, a writer on religion recently suggested that preachers stop using twenty-minute sermons all the time and use five, ten, twenty, thirty, or thirty-five minutes as the topic demands. He suggested that, as an added benefit, churchgoers would always pay more attention because they would never be sure when the point would be made (or when they would have to wake up to sing the next hymn!). He was suggesting changing from a fixed-interval schedule to a variable-interval schedule.

He was also suggesting that behavior is different under different schedules, and research supports his assumption. In laboratory studies of operant conditioning, the most common measure of response strength is the probability of response—more specifically, what is measured is the rate of response. In a typical experiment, a rat presses a bar or a pigeon pecks a key that activates a **cumulative recorder,** a kymographic type of instrument that makes a horizontal line when there is no responding and "jumps up" vertically a small

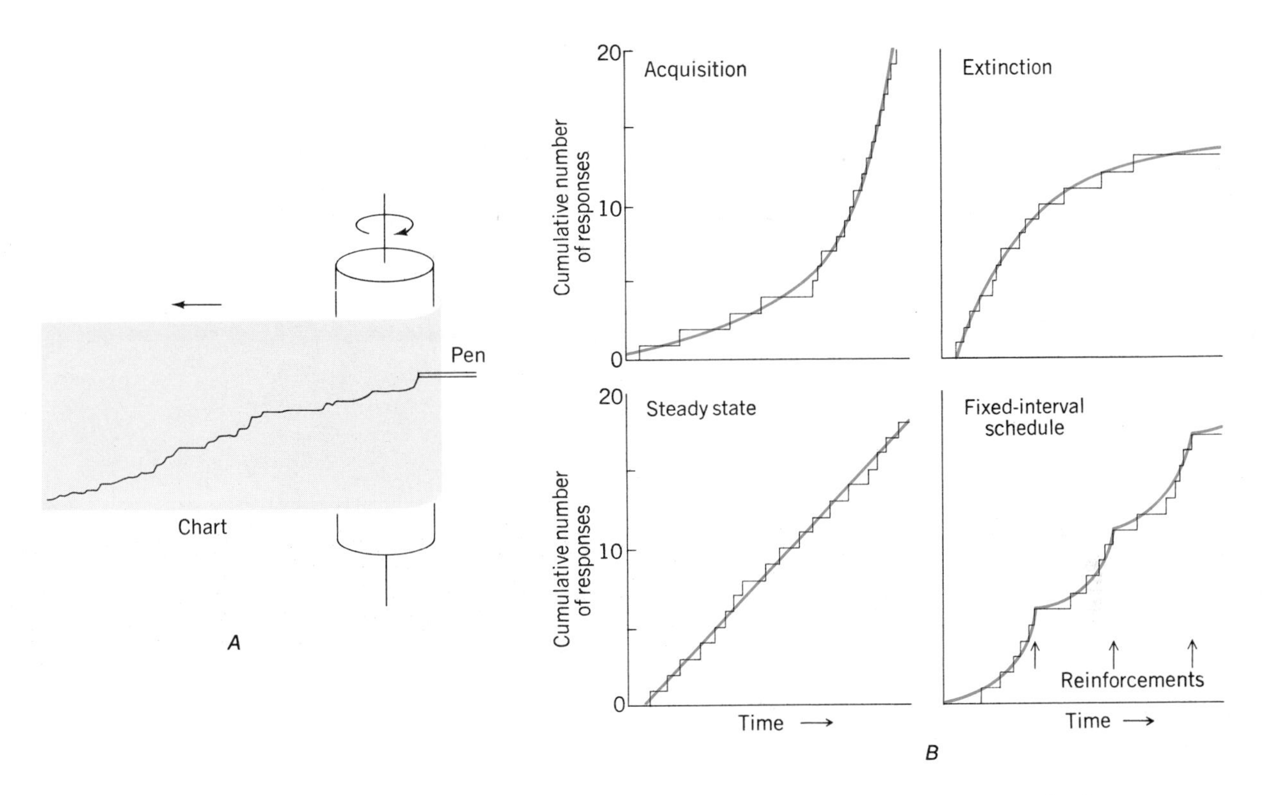

distance each time a response is made. Figure 18-5A shows a picture of such a device and Figure 18-5B some of the typical records. Note that a fixed-interval schedule produces a funny kind of record that includes "scalloping"—a slow rate of response immediately following a reinforcement increasing to a very fast rate immediately preceding the time for the next reinforcement. Variable schedules, both of the ratio family and the interval family, produce records more like the one labeled "steady state"—a more or less constant rate of responding. "You never know when the sermon will end, so you pay attention throughout."

Although operant conditioning deals with emitted responses and therefore with the stimulus following the response (the reinforcement), it is not unaffected by preceding stimuli. Although the prior stimuli may not elicit the response, as US does UR or CS does CR, they often provide information or cues that affect the operant response. For example, if your phone rings, it is a cue that if you pick it up, you will be "reinforced" by hearing someone's voice. Such informative preceding stimuli are called **discriminative stimuli** because they signal the availability (or nonavailability) of reinforcement if the response is made. In the laboratory, one can flash a green light to indicate that the food-delivery mechanism is in operation and a red light to indicate that it is not. Eventually the pigeon

FIGURE 18-5
CUMULATIVE RECORDER AND RECORDS

Every response moves the pen up a notch on the recorder, as the paper moves to the left at a constant speed. The tracing steepens as the frequency of response increases. The curves on the right show that rate of response is speeding up and slowing down for acquisition and extinction, respectively. The slope is constant during steady-state responding. The "scalloping" is characteristic of FI schedules; after reinforcement the responses start slowly but gradually pick up speed.

or human will respond only when the green light has flashed. In real life many responses will gain a reward only under the proper circumstances; hitting a man is unlikely to gain a reward unless the cues are right—a boxing ring surrounds you, for example.

By using discriminative stimuli properly, the scientist can increase his control of a response. He can increase the probability of that response in one situation and decrease it in others. A child-training specialist (a mother, for example) has similar desires for **stimulus control** of a response; to "romp and play" is an encouraged set of responses on vacation in the woods, but the same set is decidedly discouraged in other situations such as in church. The mother tries to teach her child to discriminate between the cues identifying each situation.

Punishment

Finally we consider a procedure that is the direct opposite of reinforcement. Suppose you use **punishment** after a response, depriving the subject of something that he wants or causing him pain, discomfort, or injury. Reinforcement, we know, results in the increased probability of a response. Does the opposite procedure result in the opposite effect, a decreased probability of response? In short, is punishment for error an effective aid in learning? Folklore would seem to indicate that it is, but actually the research issue is a complicated one that is not yet fully resolved.

Experimental data do make it clear, however, that punishment is *not* as effective as experimental extinction in eliminating habits. Punishment may result in temporary *suppression* of a response, but the response is not really weakened. This was demonstrated in an experiment in which two groups of rats learned to press a bar in a Skinner box to get food (the reinforcement). After the bar-pressing response was learned, the rats were given extinction trials in which food was withheld. For the first few extinction trials, one group of rats was shocked (punished) through the floor every time they pressed the bar. No shock was administered during the rest of the extinction trials. The other group of rats received no shock during the extinction trials; food was simply withheld. The effects of the punishment proved to be short-lived. The animals that had been shocked made fewer bar-pressing responses only during the time that they were being punished and shortly thereafter. In the later part of the extinction trials their rate of bar pressing was the same as it had been previously (before the shock), and by the end of the experiment they made as many responses as the nonpunished rats. In short, punishment led to temporary suppression of the response but did not weaken it.

Punishment may be effective in changing behavior, however, by forcing the individual to find a desirable alternative response that may subsequently be rewarded. From the point of view of modifying behavior, this may be a very important consideration.

For example, a father can punish his son for throwing rocks at windows and for a time at least the son will suppress this response; he will stop throwing rocks. In the meantime, the boy may learn other ways of "releasing excess energy" or "attracting attention"; he may learn to play baseball (a more socially acceptable way of breaking windows). If no adequate substitute response is learned, however, the son may soon revert to his old habits with undiminished intensity. Simply punishing children for undesirable behavior is not enough. They must at the same time be given an opportunity for practicing and being reinforced for more desirable responses. In fact, under some circumstances, punishment may serve to strengthen or "fix" a response rather than to eliminate it, perhaps because of the fear and anxiety attached to the punishment. Punishing a child for stuttering may actually increase the frequency of this behavior.

Furthermore punishment for some particular behavior, especially if it is repeated, may lead to self-punishment or "guilt feelings." While guilt is basically a human emotion, many lower animals seem to exhibit "guilty" behavior after performing a response that has been punished in the past. Some psychologists have viewed such behaviors as conditioned responses to the stimuli present *after* the response. For example, a dog leaps up at the window and knocks a vase to the floor. The sight and sounds of shattering glass (CS) have been paired with a sharp painful slap (US) on his nose, leading to flinching and withdrawal (UR). Now if the dog knocks something down, he flinches and slinks away (CR) even before he is slapped. He "looks guilty." Guilt and anxiety become associated with the forbidden response although they were not present until the forbidden behavior had occurred. Since these are unpleasant feelings, the individual may suppress anxiety- or guilt-producing responses. Avoiding these feelings, like avoiding punishment, may be rewarding. But again the fact that the response is suppressed does not mean it is weakened or unlearned. Guilt or anxiety, like punishment, will have little long-range effect on behavior, unless the individual has an opportunity to acquire a new response. For example, an individual may be punished or feel guilty about overeating, which is his response to anxiety. However, unless he learns new ways of handling his anxiety, the overeating response will not be suppressed for long. He may continue to feel guilty about overeating but he will continue to overeat.

Latent Learning

Much human and animal learning occurs with no use of the primary reinforcers such as food, drink, sex, and pain avoidance. Some psychologists hold to the universality of reinforcement; they explain these modifications in behavior in terms of **secondary reinforcements** (see Spotlight 18-2). Others have denied the necessity of reinforcement altogether. One such dissenter was Edward C. Tolman, who instead stressed the learning of **cognitive maps**—even in rats.

SPOTLIGHT 18-2

Secondary Reinforcement

If we had to rely entirely on primary reinforcements such as food, water, avoidance of pain, and even sex, little of everyday learning could be explained. Why does the student study or the secretary type? In some "eventual" sense, perhaps their behaviors could be related to basic necessities, but what bridges the gap between immediate reinforcement and this "eventual" reward? What are the immediate reinforcements?

A concept that offers an answer goes by the name of "secondary reinforcement." In laboratory studies, the concept can be most easily demonstrated with operant conditioning, though classical conditioning shows similar effects. If a previously neutral stimulus is consistently associated with a primary reinforcer, the neutral stimulus itself will acquire the power of reinforcement—it will become a secondary reinforcer. For example, an animal in an operant-conditioning situation performs a response, then receives food from a food-delivery mechanism. This mechanism usually makes some noise as it releases the pellet of food—a click. This sound becomes reinforcing; an animal will work just to hear it. (If the click sounds too often without food, of course, gradually the secondary reinforcer will lose its power and return to its previously neutral status.)

In the study of human behavior, thought and language add to the complexity of the issue. But such generally effective techniques such as giving praise or giving money for behaviors considered appropriate are typically interpreted in terms of their secondary reinforcing powers. They have no intrinsic value, but they are commonly associated with the basic satisfactions of life.

Approval from peers is a powerful secondary reinforcement in learning to read.
(Charles Gatewood)

Consider, for example, the following study of **latent learning** in rats (Tolman & Honzik, 1930). Three randomly selected groups of rats were run in a large maze with twelve T-shaped choice points as shown in Figure 18-6A. Each rat in each group was placed in the start box after several hours of food deprivation. As he came to a choice point, a door closed behind him, preventing him from retracing his steps, so each rat eventually reached the end box. Animals in one group received a food reinforcement in the end box, while rats in the other two groups found the end box empty.

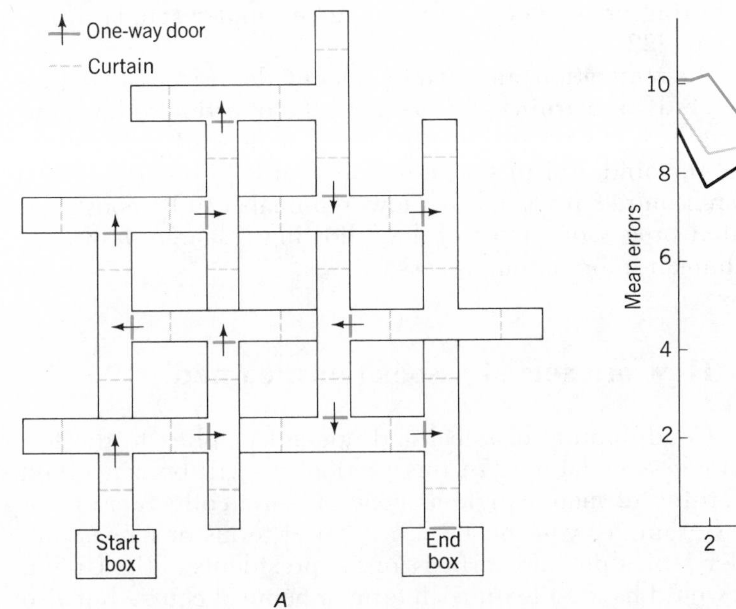

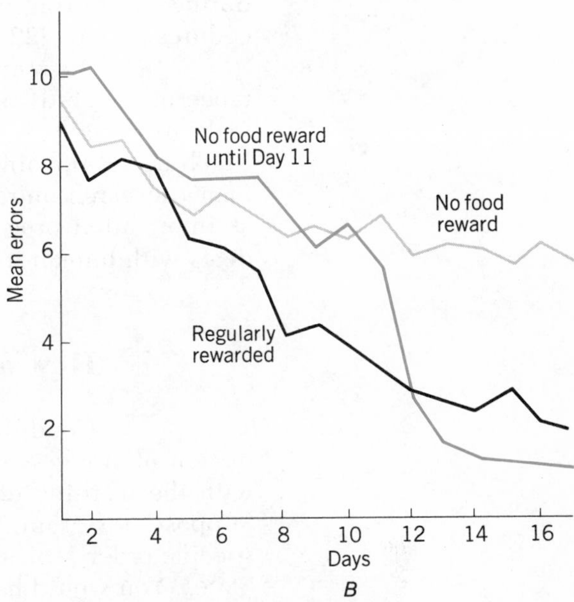

FIGURE 18-6
LATENT LEARNING

A. A complex maze is used to study learning in rats.
B. When one group of rats (shown by the dark colored line) found food in the end box of the maze for the first time on Day 11, their performance on Day 12 was just as good as that of the rats that had received food every day. Reward brought to view the latent learning that had been occurring on the earlier trials.

Each entry into a blind alley at a choice point was counted as an error. By the end of ten days (one trial per day) the reinforced rats were making on the average less than half the errors of the first day, while the other rats showed only a slight reduction in errors. On Day 11, one of the two nonreinforced groups suddenly encountered food in the end box. The question was, had they learned something in the past ten days, something *latent* (not exhibited in overt behavior)? If so, we could expect them to perform with only a few errors on Day 12. If not, we would expect a *gradual* improvement in performance until they *eventually* equaled the efficiency of the reinforced rats. As Figure 18-6B shows, the improvement of the "not-reinforced, then-reinforced" rats is sudden and dramatic; the data support the notion that these rats learned a lot but did not exhibit their learning until there was incentive to do so. This is latent learning.

Tolman concluded from studies such as these that reinforcement was not essential to learning. What animals learned was not "responses," he claimed, but "cognitive maps" which *could* be put to use *if* the incentive was introduced. What he was saying, in effect, was that the important questions in learning concerned the information presented and how the animal processed it. Whether "knowledge" was exhibited in behavior might well be a function of whether or not a reward was contingent on behavior, but the "increase in knowledge" was a separate issue. (We have considered the distinction between knowledge and performance elsewhere. For example, a child may do well or poorly on an intelligence test depending on whether he is given special encouragement and motivation during the testing or whether the test is given under standard procedures. See p. 422.)

As motivation and reinforcement decreased in importance in the study of learning and memory, the question of how animals (especially humans) process information became paramount. Much of the remainder of this section will deal with this topic. Tolman's research on rats revealed that lower animals can be construed as information processors; most of the following research, however, deals with human information processing.

How are sets of associations learned?

Conditioning, classical and operant, applies to the formation of single associations. In this section we will be concerned with the learning of many single associations in a collection or set. Suppose, for example, you must learn a list of terms or names in a specific order—the alphabet, perhaps, or the presidents of the United States. You would have to learn each term or name of course but also the order, that *b* follows *a* and precedes *c* and that Eisenhower falls between Truman and Kennedy. There is no single association to be made but a collection of them. Such a task is called **serial ordering.** Another task might be to learn **paired associates.** Here the procedure involves the presentation of terms in pairs as in learning a language, "Spanish word–English equivalent," over a set or vocabulary of such pairs. A third type of learning is called **free recall,** which is the same as serial ordering except that the order is not important. Suppose you were on a TV show and they offered you $10 for each vice-president you could name, in any order. That would be a free-recall task.

Sometimes these procedures or tasks are lumped under the designation **rote learning,** which has a rather dreary connotation to most people. It's an unfortunate connotation. These basic learning tasks are not only fundamental to most so-called creative endeavors—what kind of mathematician would you be if you had not learned the multiplication tables?—but also they are simple enough, clear enough, and regular enough to provide us with situations in which we can gain

A student learns verbal associations with material presented on a memory drum; the psychologist records correct anticipations and errors. On the right is a closeup of the memory drum.
(Van Bucher, courtesy Wagner College Dept. of Psychology, Photo Researchers; closeup courtesy Ralph Gerbrands Company)

considerable knowledge about the essential processes of learning. Following are some of the facts and principles psychologists have discovered.

Serial Ordering

To repeat, serial ordering is a procedure in which a string or list of items is presented to the subject one by one and he is asked to reproduce them in the same order. In laboratory studies, such lists are usually words or **nonsense syllables.** A nonsense syllable is a collection of letters that has no obvious meaning. Examples are "CEV" or "GZL." Hermann Ebbinghaus, who began his study of learning and memory in the previous century, was the first to use nonsense syllables, largely in the hope that they would be "meaningless" and thus of value in studies of the formation of associations where none existed prior to the practice sessions. It was a somewhat forlorn hope. Many nonsense syllables have clear meanings: JFK, for example, or LBJ, and of course your own initials. The **association value** of an item in a list, whether a word or nonsense syllable, quickly became an important variable in research; it is roughly defined as the degree of meaning an item has for the subject. The reason for its importance is obvious—one is after all not likely to forget his own initials, no matter where in the list they occur. Any material that is already highly meaningful—that has many associations—is more readily learned than less meaningful material.

Hermann Ebbinghaus, the first person to measure memory.
(The Bettmann Archive)

There are two common methods of testing in serial ordering, the study-test method and the anticipation method. In the study-test method, items (words or nonsense syllables, usually) are presented to a subject, who then attempts to repeat the items in the same order. In the anticipation procedure, the first item is presented, then time and opportunity is given for the subject to anticipate what the following item will be (which of course would be impossible in the first round); then the second item is presented and the subject is asked about the third, and so on through the list. The advantage of the anticipation method is that, supposedly, one can isolate and analyze the formation of each individual association in the set (*A* to *B*, *B* to *C*, *C* to *D*, etc.). But the more precise research of recent years is concerned with the exact time spent in studying the prior association and in anticipating the next. Because one cannot know how much of the interval between items in the anticipation method is spent on each task, the anticipation method has declined in popularity.

One of the most obvious factors affecting serial-order learning is the timing of the items—how long each item is shown and the time interval between items. In studies of effects of other variables on serial-order learning, these timing factors must be carefully controlled.

The single most important finding from research on serial-order learning is that items in the middle of a list are learned more slowly than items either at the beginning or at the end of the list. Graphically, this fact is represented by a bowed or U-shaped curve when a measure of learning (e.g., number of errors) is plotted against the position in the list (see Figure 18-7). The first and last items in the list are learned quickly and most of the errors occur in the middle positions. This finding holds regardless of the length of the list—in Figure 18-7 lists of 8, 13, and 18 items show the same effect.

This **serial-position effect** is very commonly found. Indeed, if an experiment fails to show the effect, that in itself would be extremely surprising. Moreover, the serial-position effect has given us a psychological law—perhaps not so precise as physical laws, but reasonably consistent. It is called the **Hunter-McCreary law,** which states that in any list of a particular length the *proportion* of errors at any serial position is always the same.

To give a concrete example, suppose you learn two lists, one in which you learn to order the names of twelve of your friends and the other in which you learn to order twelve nonsense syllables. The names of your friends (in an order) will be much easier to learn, that is, you will make fewer *total* errors before getting it perfect. But the *proportion* of errors at each serial position would be approximately the same in both cases.

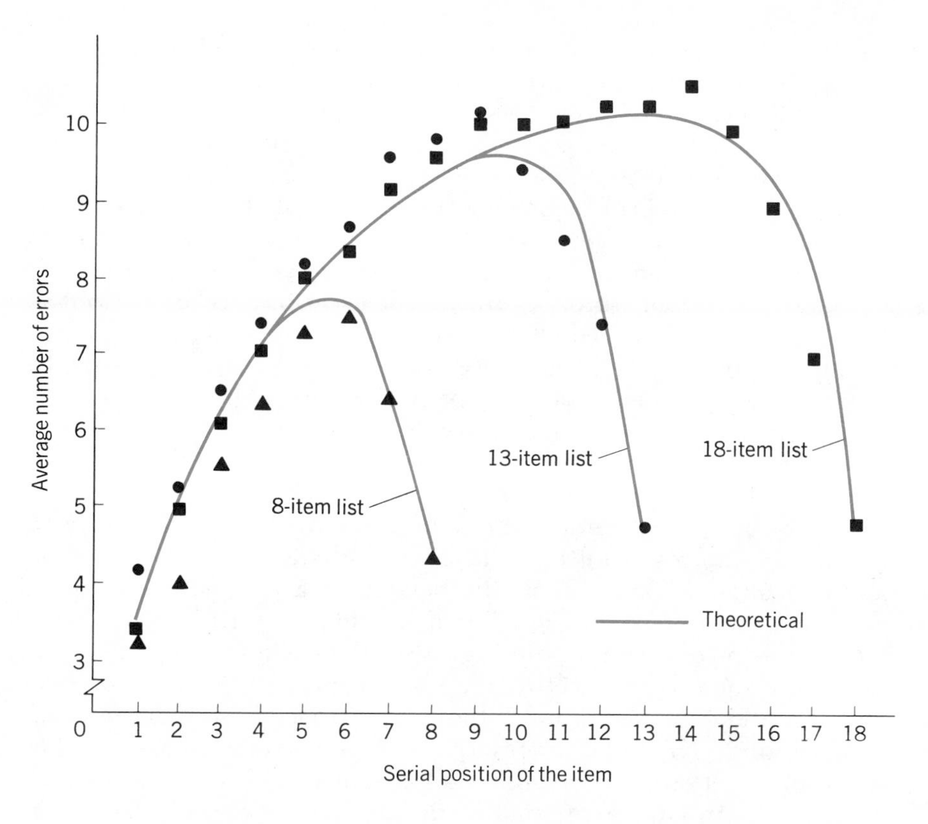

FIGURE 18-7
BOWED SERIAL-POSITION CURVES

Curves are for list lengths of 8, 13, and 18. The data points are actual experimental values, and they are fitted by smoothed theoretical curves. In all cases, there are fewest errors for items in the beginning and end of the list and most errors for items in the middle part of the list.
(After Atkinson, 1957)

The Hunter-McCreary law is a good example of the lawfulness of behavior. Unfortunately we do not yet have a good explanation for these regularities. On the other hand, the identification of constancies in behavior is in itself scientific progress. One cannot explain a phenomenon before it has been shown to be regular and lawful—that has been the history of all science. We will in later sections discuss other findings that *might* be used to account for the serial-position effect, at least in part. Perhaps you can keep this "puzzle" in mind and later try your hand at an explanation. Should you develop a satisfactory explanation, you would probably not only get an A in this course, you would also earn the respect of thousands of psychological investigators. In a young science like psychology, such a feat is not beyond the realm of possibility.

Paired Associates

In paired-associate learning, items are presented two by two rather than singly. In your next exam in this course, for example, the instructor might present one item of a pair and ask you for the other. "The Hunter-McCreary law" is presented and you are supposed to supply its paired associate, in this case its definition. Or in a German class, you are given "Ich" and asked to supply "I," the

English equivalent. In the laboratory the pairs might be arbitrary. I tell you that whenever I say "inspire" I want you to say "legend." In most cases, a collection of these pairs is presented.

A somewhat surprising discovery led to the formulation of a very important principle of paired-associate learning—the **total-time hypothesis.** This states that in learning a list of paired associates the *total* study time is important but how this time is *distributed* has little or no importance. For example, suppose you are to learn a list of eighteen pairs of words. If you can learn it in five "go-throughs" (trials) spending four seconds per pair, the hypothesis states that if you spend only two seconds per pair per trial, you will need ten trials. In other words, you need 20 seconds per pair no matter how you go about it. Five trials at four seconds per pair, ten trials at two seconds per pair, or twenty trials at one second per pair—the result is always the same.

Approximately—the total-time hypothesis is only approximately correct, and one can even find situations in which the approximation is rather poor. But science is a pragmatic endeavor, and one exception is not enough to discredit an assertion. Exceptions add to the puzzle, often pointing to ways in which the original assumption should be revised, but the "approximate laws" of psychology are still useful until they are replaced by more precise formulations. The total-time hypothesis does encompass a wide range of situations and organizes a vast amount of research data.

In any case, some of the implications of the total-time hypothesis are worth discussing. There is no quick and easy way to learn paired associates; the more time you spend the more you will learn, but there is no way to learn without spending the time. Second, there appears to be little advantage to "distributed" practice or to "massed" practice. The issue of the **distribution of practice** has been a controversial one. Students have often been advised that distributed practice is preferable to a concentrated effort: "study one hour a day for a week, don't cram for seven hours the night before the exam." Such advice appears sound in certain cases—skill learning, for example (see p. 485)—but in other cases, such as learning a language, the advice might be less appropriate. One must consider the task before applying such generalities.

A related issue concerns the motivation to learn. It is perhaps universally accepted that a student with higher motivation will learn more than one with little motivation. But the matter is not quite so simple. Clearly a student motivated to learn French will spend more time at his studies and hence learn more. There is little evidence, however, that a highly motivated student will learn more *if* both he and the poorly motivated student study for equal amounts of time. (The relationship between motivation and learning is complex; see Spotlight 18-3.)

SPOTLIGHT 18-3

Motivation and Learning

One of the implications of the total-time hypothesis is that motivation does not affect paired-associate learning in a direct way; if the time spent on study is held constant, the poorly motivated will learn as much as the highly motivated. Great care must be taken before generalizing this finding beyond paired-associate learning. On the other hand, additional evidence can be cited; the area of "incidental learning" shows similar results.

Incidental learning is to be contrasted with "intentional learning." As you read this page, you *intend* to learn the facts and principles of psychology; if the instructor asks you to identify "the first word on page 36" or the color used in a certain illustration, you would be rightfully upset with his pedagogic techniques, but you might be able to answer correctly. This is incidental learning. In laboratory studies of incidental learning, the general conclusion is that intent to learn leads to better results as you would expect. But not because of motivation (the intention). Rather, it appears that the intention to learn leads to more frequent rehearsal of the material. If frequency of rehearsal is equated, then incidental learning is as effective as intentional learning.

No psychologist would suggest that motivation does not affect behavior, and none would assert it has no effect on learning, at least indirectly. But as the broad concept of motivation is refined by accumulating data and changing theories, more and more of the effects are being defined with great precision. So motivation may be translated into an effect on time spent studying, for example, or an effect on rehearsal frequency. As another illustration, take the hypothesis that a more highly motivated animal will work faster—run faster in a maze, for instance—if he is hungrier than another. That is a fact easily demonstrated. But the speed of running can be considered as an aspect of the conditioned *response,* and one could easily devise an experiment in which highly motivated animals ran very slowly. All that is required is an operant-conditioning procedure whereby the animal is not reinforced unless . . . (can you complete the sentence?).

Nevertheless, it is equally inaccurate to say that no psychologists feel that motivation directly affects learning. Obviously it is a complex issue. The interested reader can consult Cofer and Appley (1964) or Haber (1966).

As a final consideration, it should be clear that *mediation* plays a role in paired-associate learning (as well as in learning more generally). Mediation means that the association between a stimulus and response is not direct but mediated by one or more "interrelating" associates. (In Chapter 16, p. 384, for example, mediating associations were discussed as "concepts," abstractions of the thing itself; the pair "orange-grape" might be remembered because they are both fruits.) Some people attempt to formulate arbitrary associations to aid in learning paired associates. For example, if one were asked to learn the pair "XFZ-2," he might imagine an "eXcessively Fat Zebra smoking 2 cigars" to help himself remember. It takes time (some of the total time) to think of such mediators, and they require storage space in memory over and above that for the items themselves. Mediators can be very useful in learning lists of paired associates, but it is unlikely that such an approach would aid the learning of a foreign language.

Free Recall

The word "free" in free-recall tasks refers to the freedom to repeat the items in any order. In serial ordering, the correct order is necessary or required; in free recall, the order is not demanded.

Free-recall experiments allow the investigator to study the *natural* organizational processes in learning. Suppose the following list is presented: FORD, JANE, DATSUN, PINK, MARY, ORANGE, LOUISE, BLUE, BUICK. If subjects are asked to recall freely (in any order), they typically cluster by categories—automobiles come together, as do girls' names and colors.

In lists with no obvious basis for categorization, subjects still tend to group. That is, they invent or discover some means of forming useful classifications of the items. Subjects who organize the material in some way generally learn more rapidly than those who do not. Learning and *organization,* in other words, are apparently two highly related processes; the controversy now centers on which is cause and which is effect. (See discussion on p. 492.)

Free-recall learning also demonstrates a regular and systematic **learning curve.** Years ago psychologists were interested in finding the "true learning curve": they wanted to graph a measure of learning against the number of trials (amount of practice) in such a way that would uniquely specify the progress of learning in its "true" form. Unfortunately, learning curves have been and are quite variable for different tasks. The learning curve for free recall, however, is close to the smooth function the early investigators were seeking (see Figure 18-8).

This typical curve in Figure 18-8 can be described as an exponential function rising quickly at first and then leveling off. It can be defined quite precisely with mathematics and, in more comprehensive terms, it can be shown that such a curve would result if, on each trial, the subject remembered all of his previously recalled words plus a constant fraction of the previously unlearned items. In the figure the fraction is one third. Thus, after one trial, the subject remembers one third of the 30 items—10 items. After the second trial, he retains these 10 and adds a third of the remaining 20 (6.7, on the average over several subjects)—16.7 items, and so on. Obviously there are variations for the individual and even for whole experiments, but this curve occurs regularly enough to be called the free-recall curve of learning. The value of the constant fraction may vary too; it is the general shape that reappears frequently.

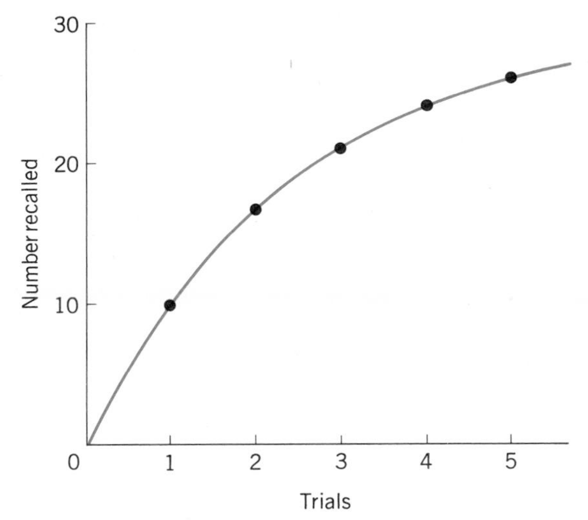

FIGURE 18-8
EXPONENTIAL LEARNING CURVE OF SINGLE-TRIAL FREE RECALL

On each trial the subject remembers all the items previously recalled plus a constant fraction of the number of items yet to learn. The learning curve is simply the smooth function drawn through the points representing number recalled on each successive trial.

Still, the search for the true learning curve now seems unrealistic. Learning curves for serial-order learning and paired-associate learning are quite different from the free-recall curve. This is not the only difference. There is a serial-position effect in free recall, but it is quite different from that found in serial-ordering experiments. The total-time hypothesis developed in paired-associate experiments does not seem to apply to serial ordering. We are coming to appreciate the many differences among various types of learning, but we do not yet have a good synthesis.

Does past learning help or hinder new learning?

What we have learned in the past can affect our learning in the present. That is the concept described in psychology as **transfer of training.** Having learned to drive a car with a standard transmission, for example, enables one to learn to drive a car with an automatic transmission perhaps more rapidly than someone starting from "scratch." This is *positive transfer;* but the driver with the previous experience might step frequently on an imaginary clutch pedal, a wasteful and ineffective behavior—this is *negative transfer.*

It was not too long ago that students were required to learn Greek and Latin under the assumption that such "disciplined" training would transfer (positively) to more "relevant" studies. Although it is difficult to conduct conclusive research on such a problem, most experiments testing this assumption offered little support, even when the transfer was fairly direct, as with Latin to English vocabulary. There are indications, however, that we can learn how to learn (see Spotlight 18-4).

SPOTLIGHT 18-4
Learning to Learn

Suppose you are faced with a triangle and a circle and are asked to choose one. The experimenter has arbitrarily decided to reward you for one choice only. Perhaps reward lies with a choice of the "left" or the "right," or perhaps with the triangle (or circle) regardless of position. You would experiment a little until you had unearthed the proper clue, but in so simple a task, it would not take long. For a monkey, however, or for a very young child, such a task is more difficult.

Harry Harlow, a psychologist, offered this choice to monkeys (1949). After several trials they were able to solve the problem, but Harlow did not stop there. He offered a similar choice to the same monkey, this time involving new geometric shapes or reversing the "correct" choice in the previous task. The monkey solved this problem, and then still another task was presented, and so on, until literally hundreds of similar tasks had been solved, all of the same general type (two stimuli, one correct and the other incorrect). After several such tasks, monkeys were solving each new task swiftly, typically taking no more than two trials. (The first choice is always random; if it is correct, you stay with it; if it is not rewarded, you switch.)

Harlow was researching what he called "learning sets," meaning subjects could "learn to learn"; they apparently learned not the specifics of the task, but how to approach it—how to get the necessary information and how to apply it to solve the problem at hand.

These ingenious experiments, which have also been applied to human subjects (children) with similar results, have affected the thinking of psychologists on many issues. To cite just two examples, the positive transfer from previous learning (as in school) is now being considered more frequently than before in terms of learning a general approach to problems, rather than in terms of the specific facts that may have constituted the original learning task. A whole range of topics such as "insight" and "hypothesis-testing" is illuminated, especially if the subjects are animals. If one of Harlow's monkeys were observed only on the 300th task, the quick solution might be called insight following effective hypothesis-testing (even if the surprised observer did not believe animals capable of such "higher" activities). Harlow has given us a glimpse into the events preceding such abilities.

The monkey is learning which object hides the peanut in the Wisconsin General Test Apparatus.
(Courtesy H. F. Harlow)

Laboratory studies can yield more precise evidence on the question of transfer. We will discuss three common paradigms used in transfer studies. ("Paradigm" is used in the sense of a general pattern or arrangement of experimental conditions.) In the first, you learn a list of paired associates. Then you learn a second list with all the stimulus words exactly the same as in the first list, but all the "correct" responses are completely new. This paradigm is labeled *A-B, A-C* to indicate the stimuli are the same but the proper responses change (see part I of Table 18-1). This arrangement yields negative transfer, as you might well expect. Subjects who have previously learned List 1 have more trouble with List 2 than those with no prior experience, because when a stimulus word is presented, there is some conflict between the previously learned associate and the new one.

Another negative-transfer paradigm is labeled $A\text{-}B_r$, which is illustrated in part II of Table 18-1. The stimulus words are the same in both lists, but here the responses are rearranged (hence the subscript *r*). Again, those who learn List 1 first have trouble with List 2 — negative transfer.

An example of a positive-transfer arrangement is the three-stage chaining paradigm *A-B, B-C, A-C*, illustrated in part III of Table 18-1. Someone who had learned the first two lists would have an easier time learning the third than a subject without that experience. When GALLANT is presented from List 3, the experienced subject presumably thinks of THEREFORE because of the association formed from learning List 1, and this thought triggers (as the next link in a chain) LEGEND from List 2. LEGEND, of course, is the correct response for GALLANT in List 3.

TABLE 18-1
TRANSFER PARADIGMS

I. *A-B, A-C* (negative transfer)

List 1	*List 2*
GALLANT-THEREFORE	GALLANT-LEGEND
INSPIRE-UNTIL	INSPIRE-STANDING
COCKTAIL-PURSUIT	COCKTAIL-BRIEFLY

II. $A\text{-}B_r$ (negative transfer)

List 1	*List 2*
GALLANT-BRIEFLY	GALLANT-LEGEND
INSPIRE-LEGEND	INSPIRE-STANDING
COCKTAIL-STANDING	COCKTAIL-BRIEFLY

III. *A-B, B-C, A-C* (positive transfer)

List 1	*List 2*	*List 3*
GALLANT-THEREFORE	THEREFORE-LEGEND	GALLANT-LEGEND
INSPIRE-UNTIL	UNTIL-STANDING	INSPIRE-STANDING
COCKTAIL-PURSUIT	PURSUIT-BRIEFLY	COCKTAIL-BRIEFLY

Typical lists for three transfer paradigms: *A-B, A-C*; $A\text{-}B_r$; and *A-B, B-C, A-C*. In I and II, learning List 1 impairs learning List 2, but in III, learning List 1 aids learning List 3. Note that I and III are quite similar, differing by the inclusion of a mediating list in III. These lists are only illustrative. In an actual experiment, lists would be longer than three pairs, and the order would be varied haphazardly from trial to trial.

In the *A-B*, *B-C*, *A-C* paradigm, the second list in a sense mediates the other two. Because of the *B-C* associations, *A-B* transfers more readily to *A-C*. Similar mediation effects can be shown from associations already "built-in." For example, in one experiment (Russell & Storms, 1955) only two lists were used to obtain the chaining effect described above. In List 1, the stimuli were nonsense syllables and the responses were common words. In List 2, the stimuli were the same nonsense syllables and the responses were different words but associated in our culture with those in List 1. List 1 might have the pair ZIL-OCEAN and then List 2 would have ZIL-DRINK. Both "ocean" and "drink" will elicit the response "water" in a free-association situation, and presumably because of this mediating influence, List 2 is learned faster by subjects who have learned List 1 compared with those who learned similar lists with no such mediating associations. The built-in associations help to produce positive transfer even though the paradigm (*A-B*, *A-C*) is one that usually produces a great deal of negative transfer.

Transfer and Interference

Interference is a topic one usually finds in the memory chapter of a textbook, not in the learning chapter. But its close relationship with negative transfer suggests that we would do well to discuss the two concepts in conjunction.

There are two types of interference designs, as shown in parts II and III of Table 18-2. One is for the study of **proactive interference:** a subject learns one list (designated *A-B*) and then learns a second list (*A-C*); proactive interference is indicated by the difficulty in *remembering* the second list. ("Proactive" means "acting forward" and suggests that memory for the first list "acts forward" to interfere with the memory for the second.) Note the similarity of this paradigm with that for negative transfer, shown in part I of Table 18-2. In negative transfer, subjects learn two lists also, and the effect is indicated by difficulty in *learning* the second list.

In **retroactive interference** (retroactive: acting backward), subjects learn two lists but are tested for their memory of the *first* list to see if the second has interfered. This paradigm has no direct counterpart in transfer designs, but it is relevant to interference theory. Explanations of interference phenomena are more common than those of transfer effects, and we introduce some of these explanations here, for their own sake as well as for the light they can shed on learning and transfer.

Let's consider the possibilities logically. Subjects who learn one list (*A-B*), and then learn a second list with the same stimuli but different responses (*A-C*), generally perform poorly on *A-C* compared to a control group without the prior *A-B* learning. This is true if you test the learning of *A-C* (transfer) or if you test memory of *A-C* (proactive-interference procedure). Why? Interference theory sug-

TABLE 18-2
TRANSFER AND INTERFERENCE PARADIGMS

Condition	*Task 1*	*Task 2*	*Test*
I. Negative Transfer	*A-B*	*A-C*	Learning of Task 2
Comparison group	Nothing or an unrelated list: *X-Y*	*A-C*	Same; learning is more rapid
II. Proactive Interference	*A-B*	*A-C*	Later: memory of Task 2
Comparison group	Nothing or an unrelated list: *X-Y*	*A-C*	Same; memory is superior
III. Retroactive Interference	*A-B*	*A-C*	Later: memory of Task 1
Comparison group	*A-B*	Nothing or an unrelated list: *X-Y*	Same; memory is superior

Typical experimental arrangements for negative transfer, proactive interference, and retroactive interference. Each is defined in terms of a comparison between an experimental and a control group. For proactive interference and negative transfer, the critical difference between the experimental and the control group comes in Task 1; for retroactive interference, the difference is in Task 2. Note the similarity of the arrangements for proactive interference and negative transfer.

gests the following: In learning *A-C*, the *A-B* associations conflict with or *interfere* with the *A-C* associations; hence, slower learning or poorer memory.

But what is interference? In a rather literal surface sense, there may be response competition. You are given the stimulus word and two responses come to mind, one from List 1 and one from List 2. With only a limited time to respond, you might choose the wrong one or become uncertain and fail to respond at all (blocking). But this interpretation is oversimplified, as is shown by a classic study of **retroactive inhibition** (Barnes & Underwood, 1959). (The term "inhibition" has become conventional here, although a more general term such as "interference" might be preferable.)

In this experiment, each subject learned a list of eight paired associates until he could correctly anticipate all eight pairs on a single trial. Then four groups were randomly formed and given 1, 5, 10, or 20 practice trials on the second list, which used the same stimuli but different responses (*A-B, A-C*). The goal was to examine how the varying degrees of practice on the second list affected *memory for the first list*—i.e., retroactive inhibition. But the test trials gave each subject the stimulus and asked *explicitly* for the associates from *both* the first and second list; an unlimited time to respond was allowed. This method, called the "modified method of free recall"

(MMFR) differs from typical test methods that ask only for the first list and give limited response time. The rationale for MMFR is that it should alleviate or even eliminate the problems of literal response competition. If response competition is the only factor, the *A-B* list should be remembered fairly well, equally well in all four groups. The results are shown in Figure 18-9. Clearly, removing the factor of response competition did not eliminate the retroactive-inhibition effect, and the more trials on List 2, the less of List 1 was remembered. Somehow the responses from List 2 "displaced" those from List 1. (A control group not included in Figure 18-9 learned List 1 but not List 2; they remembered almost all of List 1.)

The results are clear-cut, but what is the interpretation? Historically, psychologists have thought in terms of unlearning or **extinction.** They consider the S-R pair in terms of classical conditioning; if the S (CS) is presented frequently and the original R (CR) is no longer appropriate (reinforced), extinction occurs. The original associates are unlearned.

For example, it is not difficult to explain retroactive inhibition in terms of unlearning. You learn *A-B*, and then *A-C;* as you are learning *A-C*, *A-B* becomes unlearned, so a later test of *A-B* shows poorer memory. But how about proactive inhibition? Here you learn *A-B*, then *A-C*, and are tested for memory on *A-C*. If MMFR is used, direct response competition should not be much of a factor, and unlearning cannot be a factor because nothing happens between the time List 2 is learned and List 2 is tested. Memory of *A-C* should be perfect, or nearly so. In fact it is not, clearly not.

One possible explanation is that **spontaneous recovery** has occurred (see p. 460). The *A-B* associations are extinguished temporarily but recover some of their strength as time passes. When the test on *A-C* is made some time after learning *A-C*, some of the *A-B* associations have returned to interfere. Up to a point there is increasing spontaneous recovery as the time interval between the extinction (*A-C* learning) and the test increases, so we would expect the proactive-inhibition effects (decrements) to increase as this interval increases. Such has been shown to be the case.

But now look at the control group for proactive inhibition. They should not be expected to forget anything because, in essence, they learn only List 2 and then are tested on List 2. They in fact do forget less than the group that learned *A-B* first, but they do not perform perfectly. Interference theorists have found it necessary to invoke still another concept to explain this loss—the concept of "extra-experimental interference." Presumably, when a student comes in the laboratory to learn a list, he already has through real-life experience a number of associations to the stimuli. These extra-experimental associations allegedly recover over time to produce the forgetting shown by the control group.

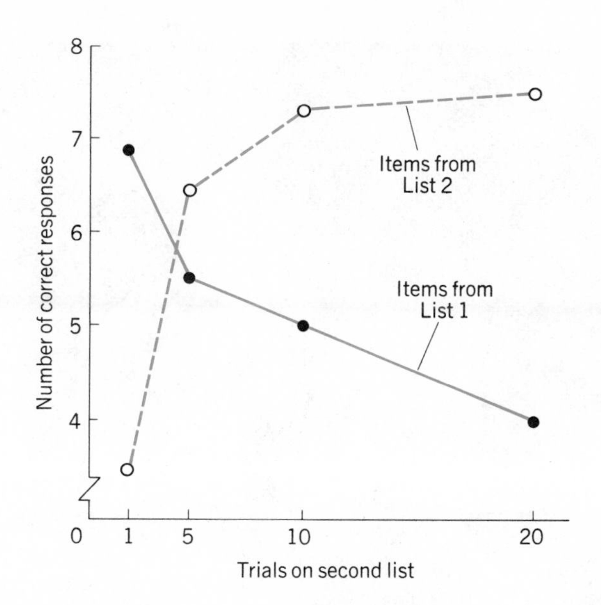

**FIGURE 18-9
EFFECTS OF RETROACTIVE INHIBITION**

Clearly, the more trials on the second list, the less the recall on List 1; this indicates retroactive inhibition even with the modified method of free recall.
(From Barnes & Underwood, 1959)

While this explanation is ingenious and plausible, it has been difficult to document. However, interference theory is currently undergoing revision, and it has been useful in summarizing and integrating many of the experimental findings in retroactive inhibition and proactive inhibition—hence, also in the area of transfer phenomena.

Skill Learning

When we speak of learning in daily life, very often we refer to a complex collection of associations that develop over a fairly long period of time. A neighbor is learning to weave rugs; her son is learning judo. To trace the development of each association involved in such skills would be an impossible task, and it is for this reason that the *basic* principles of learning are studied more effectively in the somewhat simpler tasks we have already discussed. Certainly these principles *apply* to the more complex learning, but the principles could not have been obtained by studying intricate skills in the first place.

Nevertheless, direct investigation of skill learning has much to offer. Simple applications of basic principles to complex situations often fail to take into account all the necessary considerations, and the best way to discover oversimplification is to test the predictions with more complicated learning tasks. By doing this, the investigator often collects unexpected data. The failure to confirm a prediction based on simple principles can lead to refinement and extension of the basic theory as well. Discrepancies between the simple and the complex cases represent an important source of questions for theory and research.

Skills are complex collections of associations that are developed over rather long periods of time.
(P. 486, Charles Gatewood; p. 487, Maria Thal, courtesy Ford Foundation: Charles Gatewood)

One of the principles most frequently demonstrated in the direct investigation of skills is that distributed practice is preferable to massed practice. To perfect some athletic skill, for example, practicing one hour a day for five days would yield better results than practicing five hours all at once. This statement stands in direct contradiction to one we made earlier in regard to paired-associate learning, in which the total-time hypothesis was applied; five hours of practice on paired associates is equally effective with massed or distributed study—it is the total time, and no other factor, that is important.

Why is there this discrepancy? Certainly the answer lies somewhere in the complexity of skills. Even a simple skill involves some classical conditioning, some operant and serial-order learning, paired-associate learning, some free recall, a lot of transfer, both negative and positive, and mediation effects in abundance. In such an enormous collection of associations organized in quite intricate ways and developed over a long period of time, trying to apply basic principles of all sorts may lead to conclusions that only seem to be contradictory. To learn to be a consular officer, for example, may require the learning of a large number of skills. Foreign language is

one, and the total-time hypothesis might apply rather directly for this learning. But there are so many other tasks to be learned for the job (e.g., how to fill out numerous forms, procedures to be used in international transactions, how to attend to the welfare of foreigners abroad) that massed practice might well produce fatigue and inefficiency, information overload, distractions, and other disadvantages.

One discrepancy between simple and complex cases can serve as an illustrative example of the value of studying both kinds of cases concurrently. For many years, textbook descriptions of skill learning talked of a "learning plateau," that is, ability increased up to a point (the plateau) after which no further improvement could be expected. It was as if some sort of psychological or physiological limit had been reached. Athletes often "experience the plateau": they learn rapidly at first and then, as they become more skilled, improvement is less pronounced, less rapid. Finally, they reach a point where more practice seems to have no effect at all. Numerous experiments in psychology seemed to demonstrate the same phenomenon.

This principle of skill learning was difficult to reconcile with results from the study of simpler examples of learning. There are so many single associations to be learned in the complex skills that it is hard to accept the notion that one cannot learn more. In addition, many types of associations (free recall, for example) showed no evidence of plateaus when studied in the simpler situations.

We now have good evidence that the so-called plateau in skill learning is nothing more than a statistical apparition. A psychologist named Fitts studied a number of skills in exceptional detail, in one case where practice effects were observed over seven years. On the basis of his results, which conflicted with previous findings, he formulated a law. **Fitts' law** states that the relationship between performance and practice of a skill is a power function. In other words, when one is beginning to learn, performance improves rapidly, but as skill increases, the same amount of improvement takes much more practice. Consider, as an analogy only, the numbers 10^1, 10^2, and 10^3. Suppose we take the exponents as estimates of skill: levels 1, 2, and 3. To get from level 1 to level 2—10 to 100—90 numbers intervene. To get from level 2 to level 3, 900 numbers intervene. The greater number of numbers between levels can be used to represent the greater amount of practice required as skill increases. The plateau is never reached; there is always improvement with practice. It just seems as if there is no more improvement because it proceeds so slowly, ever more slowly. An assembly-line worker may double his output in the first year; to double it again may require ten years; to double it a third time may require a thousand more years. Time runs out, of course, but there is no evidence that skill stops improving with practice.

What are the current issues of learning psychology?

Now that we have discussed specific topic areas, let us examine two of the most significant general issues in the field of learning psychology. The first is called the **pluralism** issue and deals with the question of whether or not all learning is the same. The second is the **continuity** issue; it asks about the fundamental nature of an association. Is an association formed gradually with practice, continuously increasing in strength, or does each single association either exist or not, all-or-none fashion?

Obviously, both issues are matters of central concern for any learning psychologist, whatever his specialized domain. They have long been matters of controversy and remain so today.

The Issue of Pluralism

Is learning all of one type (this is the monistic position), or are there several discrete phenomena lumped under the general heading of learning (this is the pluralistic position)? One recent classification listed seven different types of learning: classical conditioning, operant conditioning, chaining, multiple-discrimination learning, concept learning, principle learning, and problem solving (Gagne, 1965). At the other extreme from **pluralism,** one could argue that the principles of classical conditioning are (or could be) sufficient to account for all known types of learning, the concept of **monism.** This monistic position is the "official" Russian one (Pavlov was Russian).

Because it is impossible to discuss all facets of the pluralism issue, we will restrict our attention to two of the most common manifestations: (1) whether classical and operant conditioning are two distinct processes or only one; (2) whether association principles and organizational principles are antithetical or complementary.

Classical vs. Operant Conditioning

On the surface, it would appear that classical and operant conditioning are quite different processes. In classical conditioning, the response is controlled by the stimulus preceding it (the US or CS), and, in operant conditioning, the response is controlled by the stimuli following it (reinforcement). Many psychologists have suggested that classical conditioning applies to certain types of responses and operant conditioning to others. The involuntary bodily responses to certain stimuli include the commonly known reflexes that control salivation, eyeblinks, knee jerks, breathing, heart rate, and other such actions typically regulated without conscious thought. In other words, these UR's are elicited by clearly defined US's and generally are subject to classical conditioning. In contrast, the voluntary bodily responses, those under conscious control, have no clear US; what is the automatic stimulus to talking or running? These are generally subject to operant conditioning. It is not an uncommon theoretical position, therefore, to assert that there are at least two types of learning, of voluntary and involuntary responses, affected by operant and classical conditioning respectively.

Those who would assert the opposing position (that there is really only one type of learning) argue that we have little basis for distinguishing between two types, despite their surface differences. Consider the similarities between the US in classical conditioning and the reinforcement in operant conditioning. In each case, presence of these stimuli results in acquisition of an association and absence results in extinction; operationally, very similar processes seem involved.

Let us be more precise. In classical-conditioning paradigms, the CS is presented, and *no matter what the animal does* the US is subsequently presented. In the operant-conditioning paradigms, the experiment delivers the reinforcement (US) *only if the animal makes a desired response.* Consider then the following sequence of events: CS, then R, then US, then UR (see Table 18-3). In classical conditioning, R is usually ignored and interest focuses on CS-UR associations. In operant conditioning, R is all-important and

US is contingent on its presence. UR is ignored. For example, food is commonly used as a US in classical conditioning and as a reinforcement in operant conditioning. When used as reinforcement, it produces salivation just as readily as when used as US, but the experimenter is not interested in this. He is interested in the response preceding the US. When food is used in classical conditioning, responses of various types do occur before US, but the experimenter is not interested. He delivers the "reinforcement" (US) regardless of the response. In some cases, the animal salivates after CS and before US, in which case the experimenter is proud to have found his CR, but the response of salivation could be as well termed "instrumental"—an active preparation for the US (food) rather than a passive response to it. In short, the superficial difference between the two types of conditioning seems less pronounced on closer examination, and many of the differences may be credited to the experimenter's interests—and therefore his procedures—instead of different underlying processes (see Table 18-3).

This singular or "monistic" view of learning raises certain questions. What about the view that classical conditioning applies to involuntary responses and operant to voluntary responses? For many years, the monist's position was suspect because of considerable evidence that involuntary responses could not be conditioned by operant procedures. A person could not control his blood pressure in order to gain a reward, for example.

Dramatic new research by several investigators, however, has shown that the chief impediment to operant conditioning of involuntary responses was not an innate inability but poor experimental techniques. In one study (Miller & Banuazizi, 1968), rats were trained to modify such involuntary responses as heart rate or intestinal contractions by using careful techniques that included reinforcement by direct electrical stimulation to the brain (see Chapter 25, p. 717).

Similar studies have been accomplished with humans, training them to control heart rate, blood pressure, body temperature, and brain waves, to name a few. It has been possible to train some people simultaneously to raise the temperature in one hand and to lower it in the other (presumably by controlling dilation and constriction of blood vessels). Here the problem in the past had been one of feedback; the subjects could not control their involuntary responses because they could not know what was going on inside their body. If they can actually *see* or *hear* their internal responses by means of electronic recording devices, they can learn to control them for reinforcement. For example, a temperature recording device can be attached to the fingertips of each hand and connected with two large dials—one for each hand—so that the subject can easily monitor his finger temperatures. When such feedback is made available, some subjects can learn in a few sessions to raise finger temperature in one hand and lower it in another, producing a difference of about 10° F.

TABLE 18-3
A DIAGRAMMATIC VIEW OF THE ONE-TYPE-OF-LEARNING APPROACH

A. Learning in general works on this sequence:

$$S_1 \rightarrow R_1 \rightarrow S_2 \rightarrow R_2$$

B. Classical conditioning

$$\frac{S_1}{CS} \rightarrow \frac{R_1}{(r)} \rightarrow \frac{S_2}{US} \rightarrow \frac{R_2}{UR}$$

$$CS \rightarrow CR$$

S_1 is systematically presented
R_1 is of no interest
S_2 is delivered regardless of R_1; is reinforcing in an operational sense
R_2 "becomes" the CR

C. Operant conditioning

$$\frac{S_1}{(s)} \rightarrow \frac{R_1}{R} \rightarrow \frac{S_2}{S} \rightarrow \frac{R_2}{(r)}$$

S_1 and R_2 are of no interest
R_1 is the operant (or CR)
S_2 is the reinforcement and is delivered only when R_1 occurs

A. The general sequence of stimuli and responses. B. The foci of interest in classical conditioning. C. The foci of interest in operant conditioning. Are there different processes involved in the two types of learning, or do the "two" types merely reflect different interests, focusing on different aspects of the same general process?

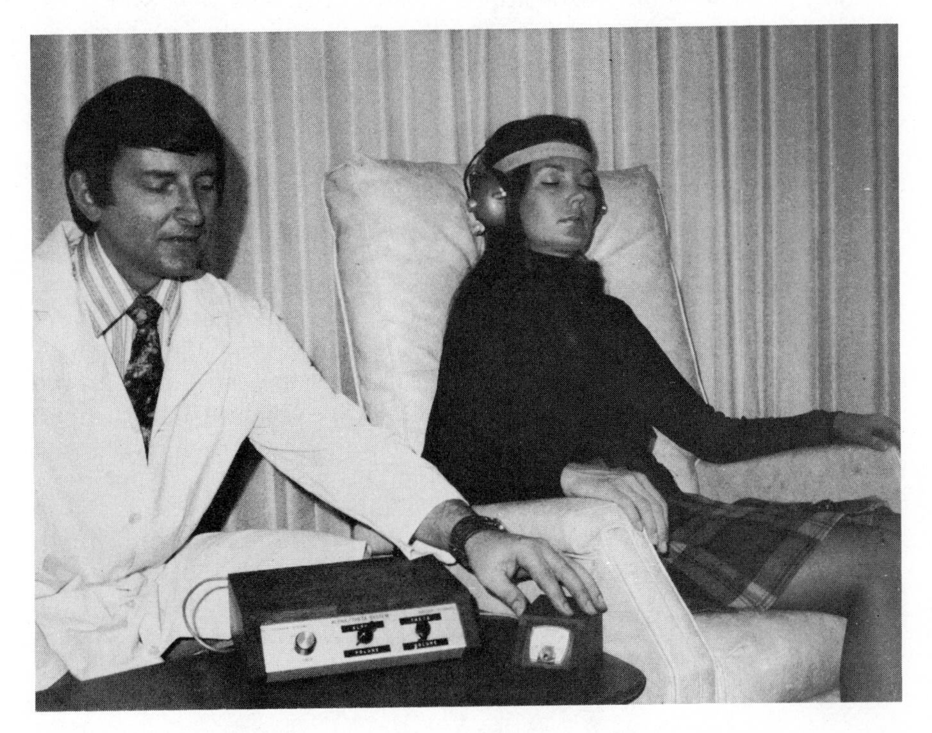

By using operant conditioning and biofeedback (for example, an auditory indication of internal bodily responses), a person can learn to control some aspects of electrical activity of the brain or autonomic responses.
(Courtesy Dr. Thomas H. Budzynski)

Such experiments have exciting medical implications. Drugless control of high blood pressure, for example, might be highly desirable for patients suffering from hypertension. In the world of learning theory, the monist's position has been strengthened by fairly clear evidence that at least one of the pluralist's assumptions is in error. There is no simple partitioning of voluntary and involuntary responses conditioned only operantly and classically respectively.

Needless to say, however, the issue is far from resolved. Differences in facts and principles among various surface types of learning—among serial-order, paired-associate, and free-recall learning, for instance—strengthen the pluralist position. In addition, the monist is also typically an associationist, suggesting that all learning can be explained through principles of association. This view is criticized by theorists who see a need for other principles, especially organizational principles. We now turn to this issue.

Association vs. Organization

The association is the basic building block for learning psychologists, as we have seen. In explaining more complex types of learning, extrapolation from the principles of classical or operant conditioning is commonly used. For example, if you were to ask an associationist what he understood to be the "meaning" of a word, he would most likely answer in terms of the word's "association value," that is, meaning is construed in terms of what the subject associates with the stimulus word—what responses and how many associates. The more associations a subject makes to a word, the greater its meaning and the greater its association value for him.

For many situations, association value is an easy and apt measure. There is clear and abundant evidence that "meaningfulness" as estimated by association value has a significant effect on rote learning; the greater the meaningfulness, the faster the learning. However, many people feel this definition of meaning does not capture the true and essential characteristics of meaning.

There are many possible criticisms of the associationistic view of meaning. Here we will consider an organizational criticism which proposes that much of what we understand of a word derives from (1) the position or context of that word in a greater organization or arrangement and (2) the rules that give meaning to the position regardless of the particular word. (See Chapter 16 for a more complete discussion of language and meaning.) For example, the sentence "They are eating apples" is ambiguous because we do not know whether "eating" is supposed to be an adjective or a verb (Neisser, 1967). If we did know, the meaning would be clear—the meaning would come from the rules of grammar, not entirely from the word itself.

The association versus organization debate is clearly evident in the study of language learning. It is at least possible to devise an associationistic interpretation of language development:

babbling reinforced or extinguished by parents so that common usages are strengthened and uncommon usages weakened. More recent data, however, seem to give strong support to organization hypotheses—rule induction as opposed to specific associations. Still, the issue is unresolved, perhaps primarily because language learning is fairly complex, and one cannot be sure that associations do not in some way account for the so-called organizational principles.

Even in simpler tasks organizational effects are not easily dismissed. We have seen in the section on free-recall learning that the subject's organization of the items has a marked impact on his learning rate. Consider, for example, the experiments that involve what is called "part-to-whole transfer." Subjects first learn a list, say of twelve words, and are asked to recall them in any order; the list is designated "noncategorized," meaning it has no simple a priori basis for categorization selected by the experimenter. Subjects will still impose their own organization on such a list, even if we do not know precisely what "rule" is used. Now the subjects are presented with a second list of twenty-four words, twelve of which are the same as the first and twelve of which are new (in completely scrambled order, of course). An associationist would predict positive transfer since, after all, the twelve words of List 1 are repeated in List 2, so whatever associations are needed have already formed; only the twelve new words need to be learned. Actually, however, the control subjects who have learned a prior list of twelve words, none of which is repeated in List 2, learn the second list of twenty-four faster; they start slowly (the experimental group does better on the first trial) but soon overtake their "privileged" competitors, even though—for them—all twenty-four words are completely new.

Findings such as these may be interpreted as supporting the organizational point of view. The argument here is that the subjects in the experimental group suffer because, when presented with List 2, they try to add the twelve new words to the structure or organization they have already devised for the twelve old words; the new words may not fit very well. The control group, by contrast, starts fresh, and therefore these subjects have a better chance of creating an *optimal* organization for the twenty-four items.

Thus, the evidence supports the pluralist in this aspect of the issue: two types of learning, associationistic and organizational. Nevertheless, the associationist-monist can broaden his conception of "associations" to include hierarchies, a kind of organization, and make many of the same predictions as the organization theorist. So the controversy continues. We will meet it again in the next chapter on memory (see p. 518).

The Issue of Continuity

The basic continuity issue concerns the concept of response strength: Is it discrete or continuous? Are associations formed in an all-or-none fashion, or is the formation incremental, gradually increasing in strength from very weak to very strong? The obvious and common answers are all on the side of continuity, a gradual increase in strength. The typical learning curve, to the extent that such a curve exists, shows a gradual and continuous increase in response strength plotted against trials; this is true for a wide variety of tasks, simple and complex, and for a wide variety of response measures. You have seen such curves in Figures 18-7 and 18-8.

Nevertheless, in the 1930's several investigators adopted the view that learning is noncontinuous, that each item is learned in all-or-none fashion. These all-or-none theorists held that learning consists of the formation, testing, and confirmation of hypotheses. Their research on this question dealt mainly with rather complex behavior, such as learning of mazes that included many choice points. At each choice point the rat had to make a hypothesis about whether a right turn or a left turn was correct. Each hypothesis was presumed not to vary in strength; it was either correct or not. The overall learning curve for the maze looked gradual, but this was held to occur only because so many hypotheses were involved.

For a clearer test between the continuity and noncontinuity positions, the situation was simplified to learning which of two stimuli was correct. The rat had to learn to go to one stimulus rather than to the other. For the first few trials, the animals behave at chance level. Their odds of being correct are 50/50. According to the all-or-none theorist, the animal has not yet found the correct hypothesis—he has learned nothing. The continuity theorist, on the other hand, would suggest some strengthening of the correct association over these first few trials, but not enough to be exhibited in behavior yet. Suppose at this point we reverse the stimuli for an experimental group, making the correct stimulus incorrect and the previously unrewarded stimulus the proper choice. Because he believes that "some strengthening" has occurred, the continuity theorist would predict *negative transfer*; that is, slower learning for the animals that got the reversal than for controls. The all-or-none theorist would predict no difference between experimentals and controls. The results of such experiments usually showed that animals with the brief prior experience did learn more slowly than control animals with little or no relevant prior experience. This evidence of negative transfer from the few initial trials to the later reversal trials supported the continuity position.

More recent studies on this problem have been done with human paired-associate learning, but the basic issue remains unresolved. Some results favor the all-or-none assumption (Atkinson, Bower, & Crothers, 1965), although the majority of psychologists probably hold to the continuity hypothesis. In any case, it is fairly clear that the all-or-none hypothesis gains support mostly from very simple experiments involving a choice between two stimuli and does not apply as well to more complex tasks.

There is perhaps a lesson in the history of this issue. The earliest studies were phrased in rather definite and uncompromising terms, in spite of the fact that the data were from relatively imprecise experiments in rather complex situations. As the research became more rigorous, the issue was not resolved, but we learned more about the problem in general—ways of phrasing the issue mathematically, for example. In addition, the issue is now being reformulated as one that pertains really to memory rather than learning: Are memory traces all or none, or do they gradually increase in strength? This is progress; the question has been reduced to more manageable proportions. It now seems surprising that this issue could have been seriously investigated in so complex a situation as animal maze learning. The answers simply cannot be seen there. It is an issue that calls for the most careful and precise control of experimental variables.

Finally, the trend to see learning issues in terms of memory is hardly restricted to the discrete versus continuous learning controversy. It seems unlikely that any aspect of learning can be understood very well until we understand memory. Most learning psychologists, therefore, could today be more properly called memory psychologists, for the current focus—in theory and in research—is clearly on memory. It is to this topic that we turn in the next chapter.

A Note on Reinforcement

Not too many years ago a theoretical discussion of the nature of reinforcement would have constituted a very large section of a chapter on learning. Reinforcement obviously affects learning, and its effect is quite important. Why? What is reinforcement essentially? These are still important questions, but more and more they are becoming the province of the biological psychologist (see Section Eight for our discussion of the issue).

Operationally, reinforcement is defined as an event that increases the probability of a preceding response. Food, for example, is reinforcing for a hungry animal and water for a thirsty organism. Why? Early answers were dominated by conceptions of *drive reduction*; hunger is a drive produced by bodily needs and food reduces that drive; hence, food is reinforcing to the hunger drive. Some more recent answers have turned to the effects of reinforcement on the memory trace in the brain. Another recent discovery was that one could reinforce an animal by direct brain stimulation; no food, no water, no sex, no praise—just an electrode implanted in certain brain areas. What this means, of course, is that the "why" answers have typically been phrased (correctly) in terms of underlying body functions: the physiology of hunger and thirst and the biology of brain function, for example. These answers must come from the biological psychologist.

Much of the most recent research on learning and memory has been done on human subjects in precise verbal learning situations. In such situations, reinforcement is rarely a prime concern; usually the subject is simply told that he is right or wrong, either verbally or by presentation as in anticipation methods. This is reinforcement, to be sure, but the investigator is not overly concerned with the "drives" or the "drive reduction"; he is studying variables that affect the rate of learning or the impact on memory. So reinforcement is a topic of decreasing interest in human learning and memory (although it remains current in other fields such as biological and comparative psychology and even personality).

SUMMARY

Learning is the process by which an organism modifies its behavior as a result of experience. The experience can be in the form of a single association, the most simple type of learning, or sets of associations.

The formation of single associations has been studied by classical- and operant-conditioning techniques. Classical conditioning begins with a natural pairing: US-UR or unconditioned stimulus—unconditioned response. By repeatedly pairing a CS (conditioned stimulus) with a US, CS eventually comes to evoke UR or some related response, now called the conditioned response (CR). Repeated presentations of CS *without* US lead to extinction; the CR no longer follows.

Unlike classical conditioning where the response is dependent upon the preceding stimulus, in operant conditioning, the response is controlled by the stimuli *following* it—the reinforcement. Results differ according to the schedule of reinforcement; the schedule can be expressed as a ratio of the number of reinforced responses to total responses or, if the time between reinforcements is the important variable, as a temporal interval.

More complex learning tasks involve a combination of associations, as can be seen in the three types of rote learning. These are serial ordering (learning a list in order), paired associates (two-by-two pairings), and free recall (no order requirements). Performance can be tested by either the anticipation method, which uses one item of a pair as a cue, or by the more traditional study-test method.

Serial-order learning is characterized by the serial-position curve—middle items are learned more slowly—and the related Hunter-McCreary law, which states that the proportion of errors at any position is the same over a wide range of material. In paired-associate learning, the total-time hypothesis states that learning is a function of the total study time but not of how that time is distributed. Free-recall learning introduced the notion that organization imposed by the subject aids acquisition.

Sometimes prior learning helps in new learning (positive transfer), but at times it may hinder (negative transfer). Interference theory seeks to explain transfer effects, including the notions of proactive and retroactive inhibition. Operationally, negative transfer and proactive inhibition are clearly related, and the explanation of one increases our understanding of the other. In a theoretical explanation, proactive inhibition can be seen as interference from the spontaneous recovery of associations learned in the prior inhibiting list.

Skill learning is difficult to investigate because of the complexity of the associative structure. One discovery that has been made is that skills do continue to improve with practice, although progress becomes progressively slower. Fitts' law says that the rate of improvement is a power function.

Two of the most significant issues in the field are the plurality issue and the continuity issue. The plurality issue encompasses the many forms of the question of "one versus many kinds of learning." We considered just two aspects of this issue: Are classical and operant conditioning in essence the same or are they different? There are good arguments on both sides of this question. Theory and research are also somewhat equivocal on the second aspect of association principles versus organization principles. It seems clear that the associationist, if he is to remain so, must do better in interpreting organization effects within his scheme.

The continuity issue asks whether response strength increases gradually (continuously) or all at once, from none to all. Early forms of the issue were resolved in favor of the continuity position, but later and more precise experimentation has reopened the debate.

19

Memory

What are the processes and stages of memory?
How is memory tested?
What have we discovered about memory?
How have memory theories integrated the data?

How does an individual remember his past? This is the question of memory, and philosophers have puzzled over the answer for centuries. William James, the great American psychologist-philosopher, explained it in terms of learning—associations are formed and brought back by reexcitation. James was much more precise in his descriptions of the formation of associations than he was in his discussion of reexcitations. Historically, this has been the typical approach. It was believed that if we truly understood the learning process, we would understand memory also, ipso facto. Is not the extinction curve of learning also a forgetting curve of sorts? Does not learning involve laying down a memory trace? Is not memory the indication of learning? Are not the two processes intimately related?

The close relationship between learning and memory can hardly be denied, but in recent times research emphasis has shifted to memory. Similarly, the underlying assumption is more accurately rendered as, if we can understand memory, then we will understand learning also. There are many reasons for the shift. Among them is the relatively permanent character of the unit of study in memory—the memory trace or **engram.** Learning may be viewed more as a process and memory more a result, something that stays around for further examination. Progress in biological psychology, for example, has dovetailed nicely with behavioral studies of the engram.

In this chapter we will begin by considering some of the basic processes and stages in memory. Next there will be a brief section on experimental methods, which describes some techniques for testing memory. The following section examines what research has revealed on seven different aspects of memory. The concluding portion of the chapter summarizes two general theories of memory that attempt to systematize the major findings.

What are the processes and stages of memory?

Encoding, Storage, and Retrieval

It is generally agreed that there are three processes involved in memory: encoding, storage, and retrieval. The first process, **encoding,** involves the registration of the basic information. When you are looking at a painting, hearing a friend's phone number, or seeing or hearing a paired associate, this information is temporarily registered or encoded through the operation of sensory receptors and internal nervous circuits.

Storage, the second process, reflects the fate of the information encoded. How long does the information stay with us? In what form? Where? Is storage a *passive* process ("stored" books are passive—they do not lose or gain content) or is it an *active* process (as skin is maintained by adding cells)?

Retrieval is the third process of memory and describes the utilization of stored information. Thus, if I were to ask the name of your third-grade teacher, it is not enough that it was originally encoded and stored; you must be able to find it and retrieve it from your mental storehouse. Even if it is there, somewhere, it is still possible you will not come up with it; it is *inaccessible.* **Inaccessibility** should be distinguished from **unavailability.** If information is "lost," it is unavailable, not simply inaccessible at the moment. Thus, if a book is misplaced in a library or if its catalog card is out of order, the book is inaccessible; but if the book is not in the library (discarded or stolen), then it is unavailable. The use of the words "find" and "lose" is only metaphorical; the exact nature of the retrieval process we will examine later.

Since memory depends on these three processes—encoding, storage, and retrieval—the failure to remember something does not tell us much about where the fault lies. Perhaps it was never encoded. Perhaps it was encoded but not kept in a permanent store, and so it is unavailable. Or maybe it was encoded and stored but is currently inaccessible. In everyday situations it is often impossible to pinpoint the precise source of the memory failure, but the psychologist can discriminate these processes more rigorously in the laboratory.

For example, to separate encoding from storage and retrieval, an investigator might present a list of items to be learned and give a memory test *immediately* after the presentation. If the subject can reproduce the items then, it must have been encoded. More specifically, we can test *some* items this way and then assume that if *they* were encoded, the others were too. We can later test the other items for storage and retrieval.

Actually whether or not an item is encoded is seldom a problem in studies of memory; for our purposes, we can consider all information encoded and thus focus our attention on other issues, such as the distinction between storage and retrieval. However, the nature of the encoding process is still a matter of controversy; the question of *what* is encoded is a debated issue to which we shall return.

Memory and Decision

We have discussed three processes involved in memory, but memory is only one of two stages in the information-processing system. The other is the decision stage. For example, if you are asked for some information that may or may not be in your memory, you first check your memory. On the basis of what you find there, you decide to respond "Yes," "No," or "I'm not sure." Memory might not provide clear information—"My third-grade teacher? Let's see. Johnson?"—so your actual response is based partly on a decision about the amount of information recovered and partly on how valid you feel this information is. The amount of information required to make a definite decision can vary considerably among individuals. You know the different types: the person who is "absolutely certain" no matter how foggy the memory and no matter how many times his absolute certainty has been proved absolutely wrong in the past. At the other extreme is the person who is unwilling to commit himself no matter how clear his memory—"I can't be sure." So there are at least two stages in the information-processing system, one involving memory, the other decision, as diagrammed in Figure 19-1. Obviously, identical memories could result in different responses because of variations in decisional processes, as we will see more clearly in the following section on recall and recognition memory tasks.

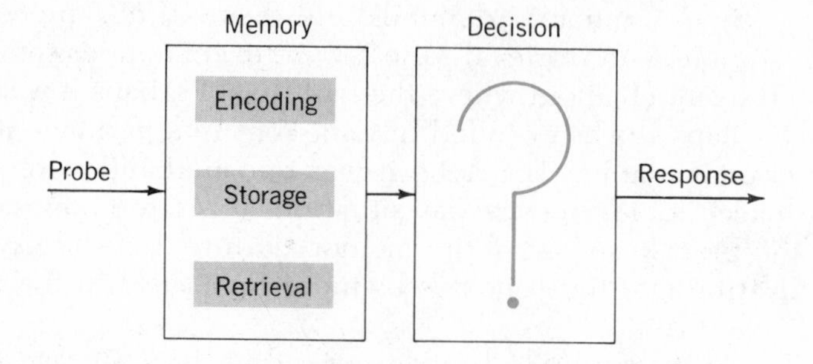

FIGURE 19-1 THE TWO STAGES OF INFORMATION PROCESSING

When a probe item is presented, information in the memory stage is activated as a function of what has been encoded, stored, and retrieved. The output from the memory stage is fed into a decision stage, which then produces a response.

How is memory tested?

Recall and Recognition

Recall and recognition are the standard methods of testing memory. "What was her name?" asks for **recall**; "What was her name—Alice or Jane?" asks for **recognition.** In school examinations, memory for course content is tested by such items as essay questions or definitions—recall tasks—or by multiple-choice and true-false questions that call for simple recognition of the correct answer. More precisely, recall methods ask you to retrieve a certain item from your memory and aids your search only by giving pointers or cues. "What was her name?" identifies what is to be remembered, but you are left to your own resources to dredge up the correct response.

Recognition methods are of three main types, each using a different kind of probe question. The first is a simple yes-no question, in which a possible reply or response is presented and you are to describe it as true (yes) or false (no). "Her name was Jane. True or false?" A second type presents several possible responses and you are asked to choose the correct one; it is called the multiple-alternative forced choice method or, more commonly, multiple choice. The third type is called batch testing, in which a batch or collection of items are randomly intermixed and the subject is asked to identify the "correct" items. For example, you could be presented with a list of city names and asked to identify state capitals. Some would actually be state capitals (targets) while others would not (lures).

When a person is presented with a recognition task, presumably some sort of *comparison* process begins. The item (one of the batch, one of the alternatives in multiple choice, or the single possibility in yes-no tasks) is compared with the information in memory. The results of this comparison process form the input to the "decision system," as indicated in Figure 19-1, and eventually a response ensues. A clear "match" of the presented (probe) item and something in memory should result in a positive response, and a clear "no match" in a negative response. Where there is some doubt, the response will probably rely more heavily on characteristics of the decision system, and this will be discussed in the section on signal detection theory. The comparison process in recognition memory is purely hypothetical, of course, since no one has ever observed it directly. By clever and careful experimentation, however, we can learn something of its nature—see Spotlight 19-1.

In recall methods no comparison is possible because no potential "matches" are given. Here, presumably, some sort of search process begins. With the aid of the pointers provided by the probe question ("What was the name of your third-grade teacher?"), the individual searches his memory for relevant information and transmits this information to the decision system. Presumably the decision system seeks to define the acceptability of the proposed response. If acceptable, the response is made, but, if not, a second search begins; these search cycles continue until an acceptable alternative is generated or until the decision is made to stop the search and to respond "I don't know."

Again the search process is hypothetical, and the metaphor may not be optimal. What does seem reasonably clear is that *something* different goes on in recall and recognition; we try to represent this difference by the use of the concept of "comparison" for recognition and "search" for recall.

SPOTLIGHT 19-1
The Comparison Process

The comparison process presumed to occur in recognition memory tasks is not directly observable, but recent studies have demonstrated some of its characteristics (Sternberg, 1969). Here is the situation: The experimenter presents a short list of items very quickly and then a single test item. For example, he gives a list of five digits—8, 3, 7, 4, 9—and then a test or probe item—for example, 3. The subject's task is to respond "yes" ("this is one of the items in the preceding list") or "no" as quickly as possible. Half of the test items are correctly designated "yes" (positive probes) and half "no" (negative probes). The dependent variable is reaction time, how long the subject takes to answer. The independent variable, that which is expected to affect the response measure, is set size, the number of items in the presented list: 1, 2, 3, 4, or 5.

The results, as plotted on the graph, show a constant (linear) relationship between set size and reaction time. The longer lists produce longer reaction times. The interpretation of the results we will state blatantly, then explain: In the comparison process, subjects compare the probe with each of the list items in a *sequential* (serial) and *exhaustive* fashion.

The term "sequential (successive) comparison" is used in contrast to simultaneous comparison. We believe that comparison in the experiment is sequential because of the fact that subjects take longer to produce a response the longer the list of items; each additional item in the presented list adds a relatively constant amount to the reaction time, as shown in the graph. If subjects compared items simultaneously, they could respond as rapidly with five alternatives as with two. The finding that comparisons are made sequentially is perhaps intuitively plausible. But the data also suggest that the comparison process is *exhaustive,* and this is a little surprising. "Exhaustive" means the comparison process proceeds item by item (sequentially) through the entire list, *regardless* of whether a "match" is found in one of the first few items. In the example we gave with the items 8, 3, 7, 4, 9, and the positive probe 3, "exhaustive" means the subject does not stop when he comes to the 3 in the list. Instead, he continues to compare the probe with 7, 4, 9, before answering "yes."

How do we know this? Consider the alternative possibility, that comparisons are *not* exhaustive and stop when a match is made. With negative probes (items not in the list, for example, 6), each additional item in the set would add a constant amount of time; all must be scanned, for none affords a match. With positive probes, however, we would expect the

Recall and recognition can be utilized to distinguish between storage and retrieval processes in memory. Many times a subject cannot *recall* information, that is, reproduce it by himself, but he can *recognize* the "answer" if it is presented to him. In such cases, failure of recall is clearly a retrieval problem—the information was available but inaccessible, for the success of recognition indicates the information was stored.

curve to rise more slowly than for negative probes as is illustrated in the panel on the right. In a set of five items, for example, sometimes the match would come on the first comparison, sometimes on the second, the third, or the fourth, and sometimes on the fifth. On the average over many trials, the positive match would be made on the third comparison. Thus, with positive probes, a list of five items should show the same reaction time that is required for a list of three items with a negative probe—*if* the comparison process stops when a match is made. This is clearly not what we observe, so the hypothesis of exhaustive comparison is thereby strengthened.

Incidentally, the data also indicate that the comparison process is extremely rapid in this particular task. Extrapolation suggests that about thirty comparisons can be executed in one second, since each additional item adds 35-thousandths of a second or less to the reaction time.

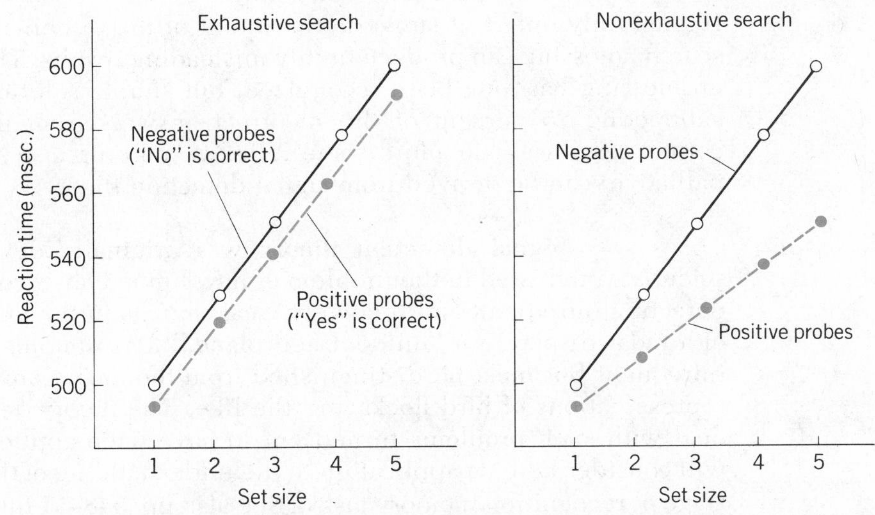

The graph on the left shows actual data averaged for a number of subjects and lists of items. The graph on the right shows how the results would appear if the search with positive probes terminated whenever the subjects found a match.

Even within recall tasks, the difference between storage and retrieval can be demonstrated. The recall pointers (probes) identify what is to be remembered, and some pointers are better than others. If instead of simply asking you the name of your third-grade teacher, I specify in addition her appearance, the number of syllables in her last name, and the first letter of the last name, I am providing more "help." If you could not remember at first but do remember with the enriched clues, the failure before was clearly a retrieval problem, not a storage deficiency.

Increasing the likelihood of retrieval (given that the information has actually been stored) by using recognition or by enriching recall cues raises another problem: guessing. If I say your third-grade teacher's last name has one syllable and begins with S, you might guess "Smith"—and you might be right, even though you actually had absolutely no memory (storage) for her name. Someone who never went to your school could probably generate the same guess with equal facility. With recognition tasks the problem is even more pronounced. Say you and I take a multiple-choice test of 100 four-alternative items and each of us knows 60 of them; the others we know nothing about. You answer the 60 and leave the others unmarked; your score is 60 percent. I answer the 60 and guess (choose randomly) on the remaining 40. By chance alone, I will get 10 correct, so my score is 70 percent, even though we have equal knowledge. It's not only unfair, it subverts the intent of the examination. In research, guessing can produce highly misleading results. The problem of guessing has long been recognized, but simple solutions such as subtracting 25 percent of the incorrect answers from the total of correct responses, do afford some relief. A more precise solution (or palliative) can be derived from signal detection theory.

Signal Detection Measures

Signal detection theory was originally developed by scientists interested in the problem of how human observers go about detecting infrequent and relatively weak signals in the visual clutter of a radar display. An "unidentified plane," for example, is not only infrequent but must be distinguished from the more common visual representations of bird flocks and the like. The theory developed to deal with such problems turned out to have wide applications. We will consider here its application to the understanding of the decision stage of recognition memory tasks. (See also pp. 548–51 in Chapter 20 on perception.)

In the typical recognition memory experiment we present a probe item and ask whether or not the item is familiar (has been learned previously). The answer is partly a function of memory and partly a result of a decision process—"Should I say 'yes,' 'no,' or 'not sure'?"—and we cannot without additional analysis distinguish between the two systems. If we are willing to make certain reasonable assumptions about the general nature of the decision system, then signal detection theory can give us an answer.

We could use for illustration words from a list previously learned in the laboratory, words related to prior learning outside the laboratory, or any one of a number of recognition tasks, but for relevance to educational testing problems, let us use the true-false question as example. In this case, a statement is presented, e.g.,

Checking products on a conveyor belt requires signal detection.
(Elliott Erwitt, Magnum)

"Skinner is noted for his research on classical conditioning," and you are asked to respond "true" if correct and "false" if not. Presumably what happens when a student is faced with this statement is a comparison process in which he tries to match this statement with information in his memory. From that process comes an estimate of familiarity (in this case, in the sense of plausibility), and he feeds that estimate into his decision system for final processing. Figure 19-2, by the use of the **signal detection measures,** depicts the assumed nature of the decision system.

The most general assumption is simply that the estimate of familiarity (plausibility) from the memory comparison process is placed on a dimension running from very low familiarity to very high. The individual then sets up a **criterion** (point β) of how much familiarity is necessary before he is willing to answer "true"; if the particular item exceeds that value, he will respond "true." The criterion level, β, varies among different subjects—some require a higher estimate of familiarity before responding positively—but the value of β in any case is clearly part of the decision system; it has no direct relationship to the memory processes.

The second basic assumption of signal detection theory concerns **distribution.** In somewhat simplified terms, this means that if you took the estimates of familiarity of all the really true items in a test and plotted them as in Figure 19-2 (frequency against degree of familiarity), you would have a distribution with some "trues" fairly low in familiarity, some high, and most bunching in the middle of those extremes. The resulting descriptive curve is "normal" or bell-shaped. A similar distribution and curve could be created for untrue statements, similar in form but (hopefully) lower in average familiarity.

Note that in Figure 19-2B the two distributions *overlap.* Some of the true statements are *lower* in plausibility than some of the most plausible untrue statements (you might have noticed this fact on your last exam). The degree of overlap would be an important consideration, since the more overlap, the more difficulty one has in

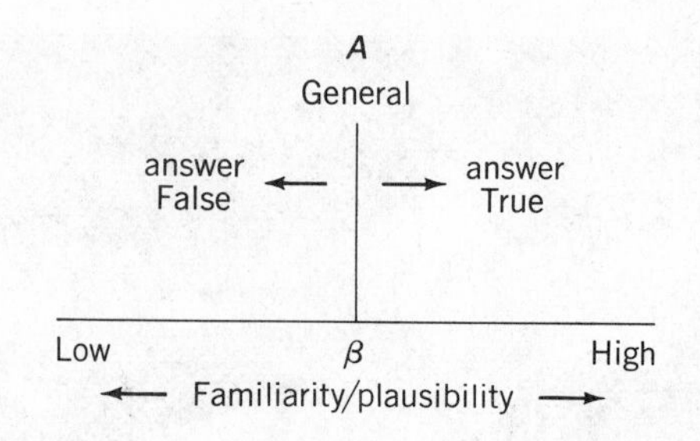

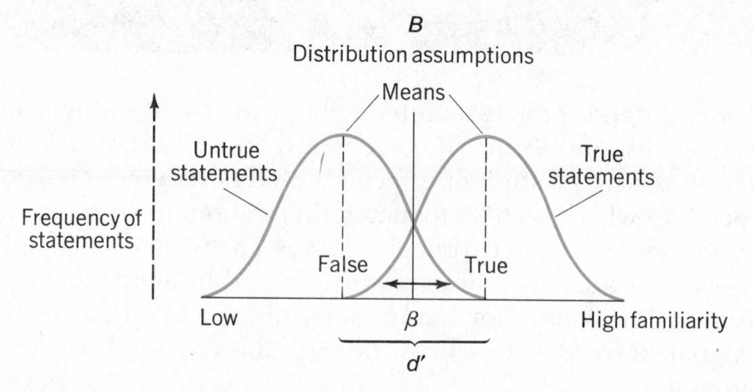

FIGURE 19-2 SIGNAL DETECTION MEASURES

A. Highly familiar or plausible items are designated "true," highly unfamiliar items "false." β represents the criterion or cutting point for the degree of familiarity the subject *decides* is necessary and minimal for an answer of "true."
B. Actually "untrue" items (negative probes) and actually "true" items (positive probes) both vary in familiarity, presumably forming relatively normal distributions differing in mean value. The difference in means of the two distributions is d'. Usually d' is small enough that some overlap between the distributions occurs, and this makes it impossible to set a cutoff point (β) that will permit a correct response for every item.

discrimination between yes (true) and no (false) items. One estimate of overlap is the difference (d') between the average familiarity value for true items and that for untrue statements—the less the difference the more the overlap.

The distributions of familiarity are clearly part of the memory process, just as the decision criterion is clearly part of the decision process. The individual familiarity values that together form the distributions come directly from memory. Someone who studied long and hard for the exam, for example, does better because the familiarity of true statements is greater for him; there is more relevant information stored in memory; d' is greater, meaning there is greater separation between the distributions of the true and untrue statements. The ideal case would be if there were no overlap at all; then one could set his criterion β at a point somewhat higher than the most plausible untrue statement and lower than the least plausible true statement, and he would then get 100 percent correct. But the typical case is not ideal and some overlap is usually found. The student is then faced with a dilemma. Suppose he sets his criterion too low (the β line would move to the left on graph 19-2B). Then he might identify most true statements as indeed true, but he will also call a large number of false statements "true." If he sets his criterion too high, a large number of true statements will be called "false." There are rational methods of determining an *optimal* criterion, but they are outside our present discussion.

The point we wish to make is that the statistics d' and β can be estimated in any actual experiment (or test). (Exactly how is indicated to some extent on pp. 550–51.) The point of these calculations, however, is that by observing the effect of any experimental treatment on β and/or d', we can discover whether the treatment is affecting memory (d') or decision (β) or both. Needless to say, this is tremendously useful information. For example, giving more practice trials would probably affect d' more than β. Telling a student there will be a "correction for wild guessing" would affect β. These are fairly obvious examples, but the general procedures have produced much information of use to the memory psychologist, the educational psychologist, and—as we shall see—the psychologist interested in perception.

In the previous chapter we discussed several experimental methods (rote-learning techniques) that are also used in studies of memory (see pp. 474–84). Most prominent among these are the study-test method, the anticipation method, and the modified method of free recall (which asks for the associates from *both* lists in a two-list sequence and gives more response time). For more precise investigations, two additional techniques have been developed recently: the distractor technique and the probe technique.

Distractor Technique

The **distractor technique** was devised to study memory for a single item. Suppose I read you a nonsense syllable CQF, wait twenty seconds, and ask you to recall that item. In the twenty-second wait, you might repeat to yourself over and over CQF, CQF, CQF . . . until it is time to recall. This intervening (an uncontrolled) rehearsal makes it difficult for me to study forgetting—there won't be any. Therefore, in the distractor technique, I give you something to do during the wait, something to occupy your attention and thus preclude rehearsal. A very commonly used distractor activity is counting backwards by threes, starting with a number given by the experimenter following the presentation of the target item.

Probe Technique

The **probe technique** was designed to overcome "output interference." If a subject is asked to recall all of the items in a long list, he may forget some of them during the process of recall itself—hence the term "ouput interference." In the probe technique, only one item is requested with a probe (pointer) similar to those we have discussed in previous sections: "What is the third word?" "What word followed RECLUSE?" or the like. By asking for only one randomly selected item, output interference is eliminated. Rehearsal is less of a problem using the probe technique because of the long original list; any item can be the target item but the subject does not know which one until the probe is given, so rehearsal of the target item is unlikely.

These two techniques, the distractor and probe techniques, have been valuable additions to the scientist's repertoire. In particular, they have been extremely useful in the study of memory over short periods of time.

What have we discovered about memory?

We have already discussed some general assumptions about memory processes and stages and some of the experimental tools used in testing those assumptions. By using the experimental technique, including appropriate controls, observations are obtained. The experimenter now has experimental data, also known as empirical phenomena, to analyze. We will summarize some of the findings pertaining to seven empirical phenomena—seven facts in search of a theory. As you read through these summaries, try to observe relationships or trends, and notice any apparent inconsistencies. This is the same type of procedure used by those who have tried to integrate the various findings into a general theory of memory. We will examine two of these theories in the following section.

1. Memory Span

Suppose you were presented with a collection of items to be remembered after a single presentation—say, an unfamiliar telephone number with seven digits. Could you remember it? Suppose we try ten digits, similar to a phone number plus area code. What we are trying to determine is the *number* of items you can consistently recall after the one presentation. This value is called your span of immediate memory or, simply, your **memory span.**

Memory span is determined by presenting collections or lists of different lengths. Most people can recall all members of collections up to size 5 and most fail on collections over size 9. Lists of size 7 are recalled perfectly on the average about 50 percent of the time, and that percentage of perfection is arbitrarily defined as the

Carefully controlled experiments have yielded valuable data on memory processes. (Ted Polumbaum)

memory span. The value of memory span varies somewhat with different people but not much. It varies somewhat with different material but not much; in fact, to the surprise of many, the memory span for a collection of zeros and ones (to be recalled in order) is about the same as for a list of unrelated words (to be recalled in order). Because of the amazing regularity of this list size – 7 plus or minus 2 – some have called it a magic number; by this they mean it must refer to something in the memory system that is very basic – not that it will bring you good luck!

As we will see later in the section on memory theories, some have taken the memory-span data as the basis for a theoretical memory system that has a limited number of immediate storage "bins" into which any kind of "chunk" of information can be placed for further processing. In any case, the memory-span facts are basic to any understanding of memory.

2. Forgetting Curves

Curves, as you know well by now, are meant to provide a graphic representation of some process – in these chapters, of learning or memory processes. Forgetting curves represent the amount of material forgotten (or remembered, if you prefer) plotted against some other important variable such as time or serial position in a list. Just as psychologists have historically been interested in the "true" learning curve (see p. 478), they have also tried to somehow depict the "true" curve of forgetting. For similar reasons, both quests have been more or less abandoned; in both cases, curves for different methods and for different tasks produce quite different pictures.

Prior to the more sophisticated experimental techniques of recent times, forgetting curves were often plotted against a time measured phrased in terms of "days since learned." The curves showed that forgetting was most rapid in the first day or two, then leveled off to a less rapid memory decrease over the next month or so. It came as somewhat of a shock, therefore, to read reports of studies done with the distractor technique; subjects were forgetting a considerable amount within twenty *seconds!*

We would do well here to distinguish between **short-term memory** and **long-term memory**; it is an important distinction both for methodological reasons and for some theoretical models. As we have mentioned, the distractor and probe techniques make possible investigations of the fate of memory in the first few seconds after presentation of material. The older techniques – say, asking for recall after a delay of days or weeks – provide information on memory over the long term. The results of short-term memory studies do not always fit neatly with those from long-term observations. Theories of memory must deal with these discrepancies in some fashion; our purpose here is simply to point out the discrepancies – and the similarities, too.

One of the discrepancies is the evidence that material can be forgotten very quickly. Figure 19-3 presents a family of curves for lists of different lengths presented only once. The lists are made up of familiar items—for example, digits or letters of the alphabet. The distractor technique was used to prevent rehearsal. The vertical axis of this graph (probability correct) is estimated by using the proportion of subjects who recalled the entire list correctly after the number of seconds shown on the horizontal axis. After only a few seconds, practically no one could recall all items in a seven-item list; after five seconds, almost all had forgotten at least one of the members of a six-item collection. Only with the very short lists, one or two items, does perfect recollection extend beyond twenty seconds.

A free-recall forgetting curve is shown in Figure 19-4. In this situation, a subject is given a single trial with a list of items. Each item is presented individually for a second or two in the window of a memory drum (see p. 473). The subject is then asked to recall as many of the items as he can. In this example there are three cases: a list of 20 items, each presented for one second (designated 20-1); a list of 40 items, each presented for one second (40-1); and a list of 40, each presented for two seconds (40-2). The probability of recall, expressed as a percentage, is shown on the vertical axis, and, on the horizontal axis, the serial position, the rank order of the item in the list. Note that the items presented in the first few positions and those presented in the last few positions are favored in recall over those in the middle of the list; this is called the serial-position effect. The **recency effect** (better recall of the items presented last) is more pronounced and extensive than the **primacy effect** (better recall of the first items). The differences between (1) a 20-item list and a 40-item list and (2) a one-second presentation and a two-second presentation are clearest in the middle range.

3. Interference Effects

We have already discussed the "interfering" effects of prior learning (proactive inhibition) or later learning (retroactive inhibition) in the learning chapter. They were described primarily as effects on memory and as empirical phenomena, they are important for any theory of memory, so we will consider them again here.

Recall that in proactive-inhibition procedures, a subject learns List 1, then List 2, and then is tested for his memory of the second or more recent list. Generally he shows poorer memory than someone who has not learned the first list (or who had some control procedure). In retroactive-inhibition procedures, subjects learn both lists but are tested for their memory of List 1. They generally show poorer memory than those who have not learned the second list.

These interference effects also occur in studies of short-term memory in which the probe technique is used. Figure 19-5 illustrates proactive and retroactive interference for a five-word list.

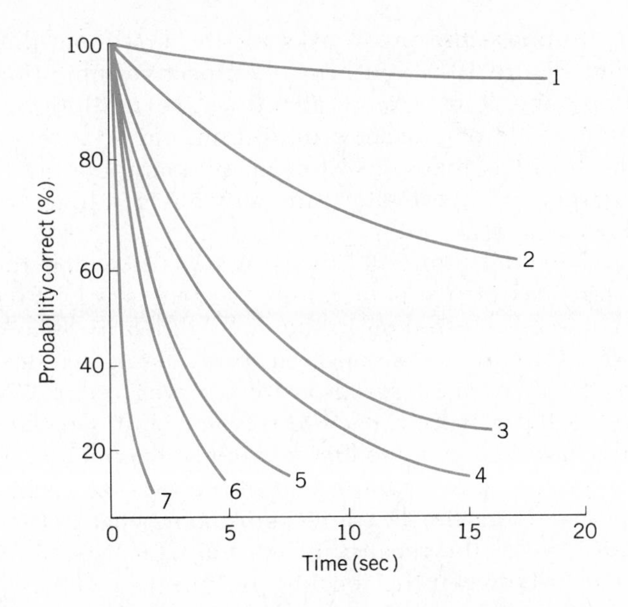

FIGURE 19-3 SHORT-TERM FORGETTING

The probability that an item will be recalled correctly is plotted as a function of the duration of the retention interval. Each curve is identified by the number of chunks to be remembered, shown at the lower ends.
(After Melton, 1963)

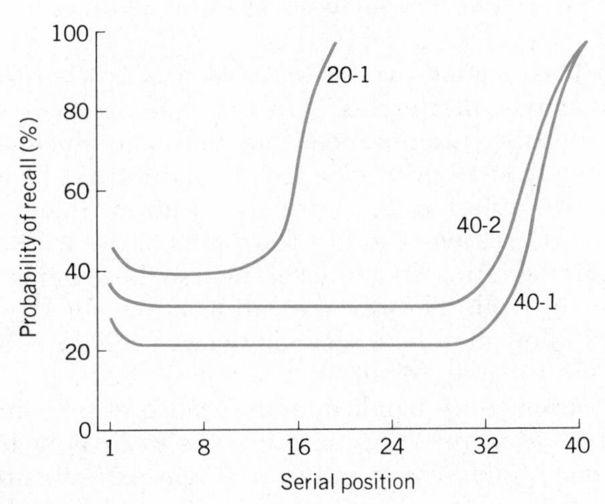

FIGURE 19-4 SERIAL-POSITION CURVES OF SINGLE-TRIAL FREE RECALL

Forgetting curves are for lists of 20 or 40 words with a presentation time of 1 or 2 seconds per word. All curves show a primacy effect, a recency effect, and a flat middle section. The longer the list or the shorter the presentation time per item the lower the curve.
(After Murdock, 1962)

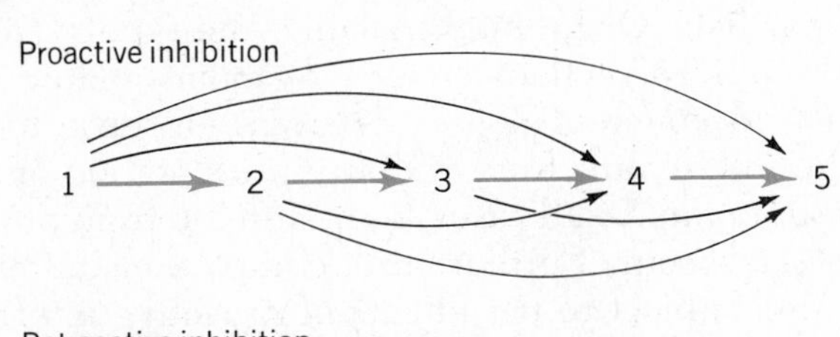

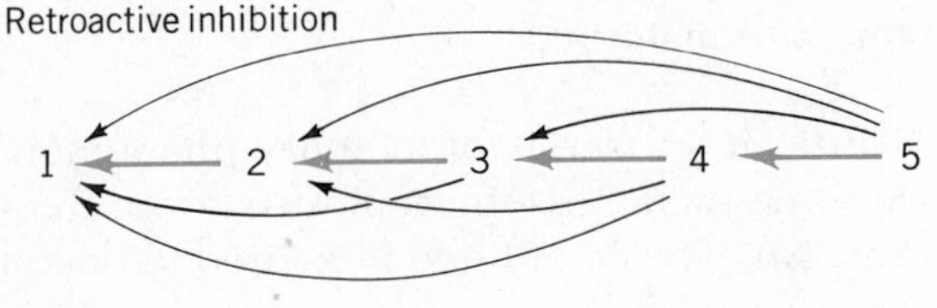

FIGURE 19-5 PROACTIVE AND RETROACTIVE INHIBITION

Each item exerts proactive effects on items following it and retroactive effects on preceding items. The first item of the list suffers no proactive inhibition from other items in the list—this explains the primacy effect. The last item suffers no retroactive inhibition—this explains the recency effect. Proactive effects can also extend from one list to another.

Suppose the probe asks for the first item; then, as you can see from Figure 19-5, you have no proactive inhibition (no preceding items) and four "units" of retroactive inhibition. The fifth word has four units of proactive inhibition and no retroactive inhibition. The third has two units of each. By manipulating list length and probe target, an investigator can study any combination of interference effects.

Now let's turn to the situation in which the subject learns several lists of words or numbers successively. First he will learn one list and be tested on it; then he will learn a second list and be tested on that one; and so on for a series of lists. Under such circumstances the shape of the serial-position curves (see p. 475) changes progressively—there is a primacy to recency shift. On the very first list, the subject remembers the first few items much better than he remembers the items in the middle part of the list—this is the primacy effect; he remembers the last few items somewhat better than the middle ones—this is the recency effect. On later lists, however, this relative balance between the recency and primacy effects shifts, the subjects showing a clear recency effect but much less of the primacy effect.

This change over successive lists is the result of accumulating proactive interference. On the first list there is no prior learning, so proactive interference is negligible for the first few items, hence a relatively large primacy effect. On later lists, the associations from earlier lists interfere—proactively—with all items, and so the primacy effect decreases. The last few items of the list being tested, however, suffer no retroactive interference, so these items are remembered relatively well. The serial-position curve for these last lists will therefore show more of a recency than a primacy effect.

Fortunately, even after we have learned a great deal, we are not permanently handicapped because of proactive interference. "Release from proactive interference" can be achieved by a number of techniques even within a single experimental session. For example, the experimenter might introduce a long delay between two of the later lists. Or he might change the type of material to be remembered from polysyllabic words to monosyllabic words, from abstract nouns to concrete nouns, or from nonsense to meaningful stimuli. Or he might shift from auditory presentation of the material to visual presentation. In all cases, some release from proactive interference seems to occur. Furthermore, complex meaningful material is generally less subject to the effects of proactive interference than is simple or nonsense material.

4. Repetition Effects

Fourth in our series of memory phenomena that require explanation are some puzzling effects of repetition. Repetition affects memory; it helps. No experiment need be cited to document that fact, although careful experimentation has shown us how much and in what way repetition aids memory. In this section we will focus on two rather unexpected discoveries, findings that have puzzled and continue to puzzle memory psychologists.

The first is called the **Hebb repetition effect.** In an experiment ostensibly on memory span, Hebb presented list after list of digits and tested the subject's memory after each. Without the subject's knowledge, however, one of the lists was repeated from time to time during the long session. Figure 19-6 gives typical results; clearly the memory for the repeated list improved with repetition, especially when compared with memory for the unrepeated lists. This improvement is known as the Hebb repetition effect.

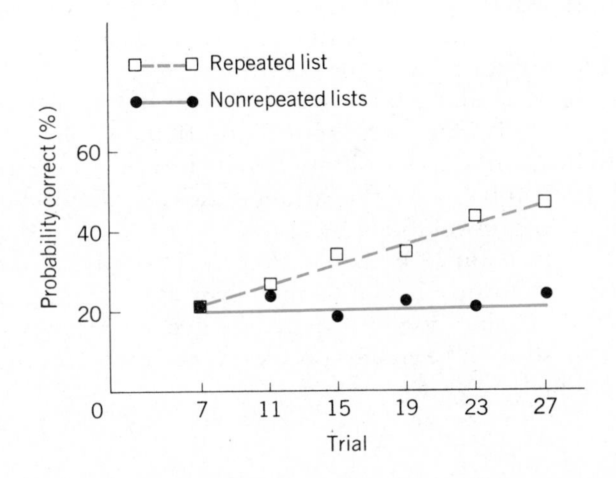

FIGURE 19-6
HEBB REPETITION EFFECT
The benefits of repetition are obvious. The dotted line represents an experimental group who had a list repeated on the trials indicated. The control group had a different list each trial. The difference increases with the number of repetitions.
(After Melton, 1963)

Hebb did not expect to find this effect, however reasonable it may sound to you. He did not expect it because he attached great importance to the distinction between short-term and long-term memory. Hebb believed that material that is relatively meaningless to the subject (such as experimental lists of numbers) would not be committed to long-term storage; if there was enough time between repetitions, therefore, the short-term memory trace should die out and no residue would remain—hence the prediction of no effect of repetition. But his results showed that there was a residue and that it could build up with repetition, even though the subject was not aware that the key list was being repeated.

Other "two-memory" theorists were not surprised at the finding, but they were pleased with the *technique*. Hebb's procedure afforded them a neat and fairly precise method of studying repetition effects in short-term memory. Figure 19-6 shows results when a list is repeated every fourth presentation. Other research shows that the greater spacing between repetitions of a list, the smaller the benefit.

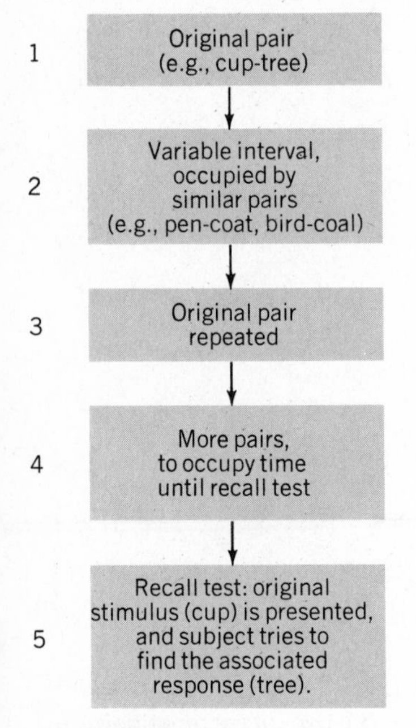

FIGURE 19-7
STEPS OF PETERSON PARADOX STUDIES

The second puzzle is called the **Peterson paradox** and states that spaced repetitions are better for memory than massed repetitions. This has been found in studies in which the same pair of items is presented twice during a trial, separated by a time interval. Then, in subsequent trials using different items, this time interval is varied. To be specific, five steps are used, as shown in Figure 19-7. On a given trial (1) the experimenter presents a pair of words to be associated (e.g., CUP – TREE), (2) then he gives a few other pairs of the same general kind (e.g., PEN – COAT; BIRD – COAL), (3) then presents the original pair again, (4) then gives more items to occupy the time until the recall test, and (5) finally the original stimulus is given as a probe (CUP) to see whether the subject can recall the associated response (TREE). Then, in subsequent trials the interval between repeated presentations (Step 2), and the interval between the second presentation and recall (Step 3) are varied systematically. Data are collected for many subjects.

Results show that as the interval between the two presentations (Step 2) is *increased* (up to a point), the subject does better on the recall test. Figure 19-8 shows results from a typical experiment of this sort. The probability of recall increases as the number of items between the two presentations increases.

Why is this a paradox? Well, why should a longer interval between repetitions facilitate memory? If anything, the longer the interval, the more forgetting should occur by the time of the second presentation. The more you forget, the more you remember? That is a paradox!

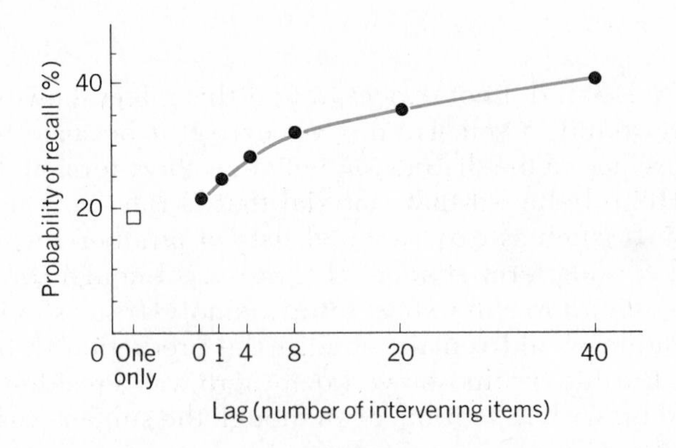

FIGURE 19-8
PETERSON PARADOX

The probability of recall for an item increases as a function of the lag. The "one only" point indicates memory for a single presentation; all other points are for repeated items. The steepest increases are at short lags, but even at lag 40 the curve seems to be rising.
(After Melton, 1970)

The Peterson paradox also contradicts the Hebb repetition effect, as you may have noticed. The paradox states that the longer the interval between repetitions, the greater the effect, while Hebb's procedure shows exactly the opposite, the greater the spacing, the smaller the positive effects of repetition. The experimental conditions are quite different in the two cases (lists vs. paired items, for example), but we do not know precisely the basis for the contradiction. We have here two contradictory but (each in its own way) well-substantiated principles of memory; it should be proof enough that psychology offers ample opportunity for the young scientist with a good mind and an eye for careful research.

5. Similarity Effects

It has long been known that learning two sets of similar materials produces more mutual interference (less memory) than two dissimilar sets. Students studying for final exams, say, in French, psychology, and sociology, might well be advised to position their French studies between the other two.

In more recent studies of memory, the word "similarity" has been used more precisely. The words "happy" and "carefree" are similar in a "meaning" or semantic sense; the words "blink" and "drink" are also similar but in their sounds, not in their meanings; they are acoustically similar. One of the first important discoveries in this field was that long-term memory was affected by semantic confusion but short-term memory seemed to be unaffected.

Additional research soon required some revision in this simple notion that one memory system was affected by similarity and the other was not. More specifically, it was discovered that **acoustic similarity** has a considerable effect on short-term memory even though **semantic similarity** has relatively little effect. For example, suppose your short-term memory span was tested either with lists such as CUFF, ROUGH, SNUFF, BUFF, and TOUGH or with lists such as SUNNY, HAPPY, CHEERFUL, CAREFREE, and PLEASANT. Lists of the first kind (CUFF, ROUGH, SNUFF . . .) yield rather poor memory spans, which is why we say that they suffer from acoustic confusion. In short-term memory a semantically similar list (SUNNY, HAPPY, CHEERFUL . . .) would probably give results no different from lists of unrelated words.

A few years ago, therefore, investigators concluded that there were two different memory systems, each affected by similarity of a different type. Short-term memory is affected by acoustic similarity, and long-term memory is affected by semantic similarity. But even this view encounters problems, as research continues. As an example, long-term memories often show the "tip-of-the-tongue" phenomenon—you can almost remember a word, but not quite. Your attempts to retrieve the word—the close guesses—often yield words similar in sound rather than meaning. This would indicate that there are some acoustic-similarity effects in long-term memory, even though the semantic effects are most prominent there.

6. Auditory vs. Visual Presentations

Effects due to the mode of presentation of the to-be-remembered material are called **modality effects.** Since the eye and the ear are our two main avenues of communication with the external

The method of presentation can influence memory.
(Burk Uzzle, Magnum)

world, the most commonly studied modes are visual and auditory presentations. The question asked is this essentially: Is an individual more likely to remember something he sees than something he hears? Or maybe there is no consistent difference.

One of the great problems in such research is choosing material that is equivalent for the two senses. A picture is better suited to the visual sense and music is designed for listening. Words are at least equivalent on an information dimension—GALLANT, LEGEND, and INSPIRE at least mean the same whether heard or read—so verbal material is typically used in these studies. In most early investigations, which were mainly of long-term rote learning, the data led to the conclusion of "no difference"—the number of trials required to attain mastery of the material or the total time spent in study to mastery were the same whether the material was presented visually or auditorily.

Research on short-term memory, however, has revealed some interesting discrepancies. A typical experimental finding is shown in Figure 19-9, plotting serial-position effects for auditory and visual presentations. Auditory presentation is superior but only toward the end of the list; the recency effect, in other words, is greater for the auditory than for the visual mode.

How can a theory of memory explain these differences between results of auditory and visual presentation? We have one more set of phenomena to present first, before we unveil the theories.

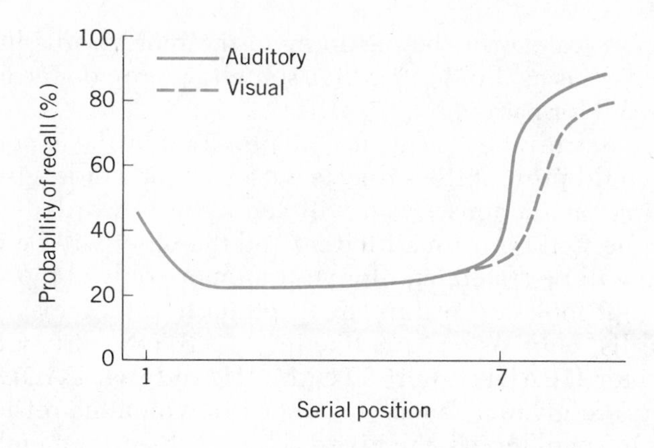

FIGURE 19-9 MEMORY FOR AUDITORY OR VISUAL MATERIAL
Memory for an auditory or visual presentation does not differ, except for a greater recency effect for the auditory mode. The difference decreases as presentation time per item increases.
(After Murdock & Walker, 1969)

7. Factors Influencing Retrieval

Retrieval is one process of memory, the process of finding and using information from memory storage. As we have seen, when discussing memory failure, we must be careful to distinguish between storage problems and retrieval problems. If the desired information is in storage, it is *available* although it may be momentarily *inaccessible*. When one speaks of factors influencing retrieval, therefore, he is talking about the determinants of accessibility—availability is assumed, at least until the evidence becomes overwhelming that there is no relevant information in storage.

We can review a few factors influencing retrieval from previous discussions. The method of soliciting information from memory, for example, can be quite important. Recognition tests elicit greater memory than recall tasks. Within different recall tasks, those with the greatest amount of "pointing" information produce the most evidence of remembering—"Your third-grade teacher, whose last name starts with *J*" is more likely to gain the correct recall than simply, "Your third-grade teacher."

If we wish to be very precise, we can distinguish between a pointer or probe—that which gives just enough information to identify the target memory—and **retrieval cues,** which supply additional clues to the target. In the above example, "third-grade teacher" is the probe; all these pointers are necessary, for it wouldn't do to say "Name a teacher" or "Name someone you knew when you were in the third grade." To add that her last name begins with *J*, on the other hand, is unnecessary but helpful—it is a retrieval cue.

Organizational cues seem to function as beneficial retrieval cues, even if the organization is supplied by the subject. Suppose you give a subject fifty words, each written on a 3 × 5 card, and tell him you are investigating how people categorize things. He is to sort these cards into as many categories as he wishes, up to seven, on whatever basis he likes. When he has completed the task and without prior warning, he is asked to recall as many of the fifty words as he can. The more categories he has formed, the more words he will remember. It seems as if the categories somehow provide retrieval cues to the stored information.

Retrieval cues can also be provided by the experimenter. Thus, one could present the subjects with a list of words, giving them the following instructions: "You will see a list of words in pairs. In each pair, one will be in small letters and the other will be in capital letters. You will be tested later for your memory only of those in capital letters, but look at those in small letters too; they may help you later." The list consists of pairs like leg-MUTTON, dirty-CITY, girl-SHORT, vigor-HEALTH, hurt-STOMACH, and soar-EAGLE. Later, the subjects are given a "cued" recall test in which the retrieval cues (the words in small letters) are given. These subjects remember many more of the target items than subjects who go through exactly the same procedure but are asked to recall the target items without being given the cues.

This seems to be an obvious finding. But there is more. It has also been demonstrated that subjects can use these paired cues more effectively than they can use other cues you might ordinarily expect to be more effective. One might think that for the subject who could not recall SHORT, the cues "tall" (opposite) or "small" (similar) might jog his memory. They don't. But the cue "girl," which was paired with SHORT in the original list, does. Results such as this suggest that an effective retrieval cue must be stored with the target at the moment of encoding. This is another fact to be considered by any potentially satisfactory theory of memory.

We have now surveyed enough facts and basic principles. Let us turn to the integrative attempts, the "models" of memory that purport to aid our understanding of memory and direct our future investigation.

How have memory theories integrated the data?

It should be clear by now that one of the primary considerations of any current theory of memory is the apparent distinction between short-term and long-term memory. The experimental observation of the course of memory in the first few seconds after material is presented, made possible by recent methodological advances, has produced data that are not easily integrated into older theories of long-term memory. Long-term memories are more susceptible to interference from confusions between items that have similar meanings; short-term memories are more likely to exhibit detrimental effects with items that sound the same. More generally, memory for presented material shows extremely rapid decline using short-term procedures—a matter of seconds—and somehow a theory of memory must integrate this fact with the retention of material over years—as shown by long-term studies.

Thus, perhaps the most common theory of memory today is the type that postulates two kinds of memory and suggests the means by which short-term storage is or can be converted to long-term storage. This type of theory we will consider in two particular manifestations: Broadbent's "filter theory" and Atkinson and Shiffrin's "buffer model." The first was one of the earliest two-memory theories and was thus influential in guiding the direction of subsequent research and theories. The Atkinson and Shiffrin buffer model is representative of current formulations. But, although two-factor theories may dominate the present scene, we should at least point out the fact that there are current and respected theories that make no distinction between "types" of memory.

Broadbent's Filter Theory

British psychologist D. E. Broadbent in 1958 impressed the psychological world with a carefully constructed theory of "information processing" with general relevance not only to memory but also to attention, perception, and certain information-processing skills such as vigilance (e.g., watching radar screens for significant information). Among the most impressive features of this **filter theory** was the distinction between short- and long-term storage systems in memory.

Consider "information" to be processed as an input from the external world—action on the television screen, material presented by an experimenter, or whatever. The first impact on the organism is on his *sense organs*, as shown in Figure 19-10. According to the theory, this sensory information next goes to a *short-term storage system*. Memory from this store decays very rapidly without further processing. Further processing, however, is not random; it is directed by a *selective filter* which favors some material over the rest. (Note in Figure 19-10, many arrows go into the filter but only one points out.)

To oversimplify a bit, the filter is included in the theory

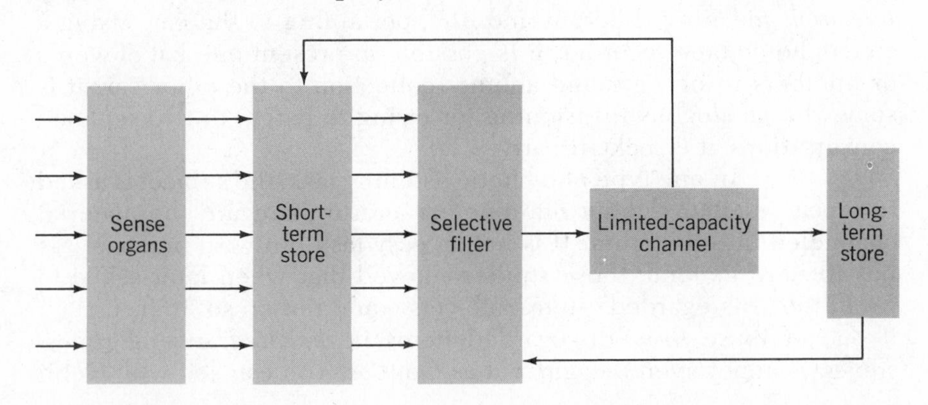

FIGURE 19-10 BROADBENT'S FILTER THEORY

Arrows indicate the flow and amount of information through this system. The information bottleneck is the limited-capacity channel, which attends to only one thing at a time. The filter must select material that will pass into the channel when there is an opening. Information may either be recirculated back through the short-term store for rehearsal or deposited in long-term memory.
(After Broadbent, 1958)

because the human information-processing system cannot possibly handle *all* of the information transmitted to it from the outside world. It has a *limited-channel capacity*, which means its abilities to process information to a useful form are limited. The filter acts to ensure that these limited capacities are not overloaded. It selects the most relevant information for further processing, much as a tuning mechanism on a radio selects a certain signal for amplification. The amplified material, if amplified enough, then goes into *long-term memory storage.*

There are two feedback or "backward-going" loops in Figure 19-10, and these require explanation. One goes back from the "channel" to the short-term store. In brief, this loop is meant to represent rehearsal and repetition; if something is relevant and "gets through" but is not very strong, it recycles to increase strength before going into long-term storage. In ordinary language, if some important information is transmitted (that pretty blonde's phone number), you repeat it over and over to make sure you don't forget it. The second feedback loop goes from long-term storage to the filter; it is meant to represent the influence of already stored information on the selectivity of the filter or, in layman's terms, "that which is relevant (relates to previous experience) is to be tuned in."

In evaluating Broadbent's theory, we should remember that it was an *early* attempt to make sense out of the discrepancies between results from short-term and long-term memory experiments. Indeed, it was in large part the data from Broadbent's own experiments that made the issue cogent, and his theory did much to stimulate the interest in the distinction. Most of the empirical evidence on short-term memory is no older than ten years. In this light, it is surprising how well the filter theory has held up over the years; the newer theories do not contradict Broadbent's model so much as they extend and amplify it.

Many of the empirical data used to formulate the filter theory came from studies of **dichotic listening,** where a subject hears a different message in each ear. The term "dichotic" is from the Greek root *dich* meaning different and *otic*, pertaining to the ear. Using a stereophonic tape recorder, it is possible to present one list of words or numbers to one ear and another collection to the other ear; it is somewhat analogous to listening (or trying to listen) to two separate conversations at a cocktail party.

In one type of dichotic listening task, the subject is asked to repeat all items going into one ear and to disregard the material channeled into the other. It is not an easy task but with practice it is possible. In general, these studies showed that when later asked to recall the "disregarded" items subjects could not do so. In fact, even if one of these to-be-disregarded items is *repeated* several times, subjects cannot even *recognize* it as familiar. You can see why Hebb

In dichotic listening, a person can attend to words in one ear and ignore the different message that reaches the other ear. Such experiments have provided clues to short-term storage of information.
(Van Bucher, courtesy Univ. of Florida Clinical Psychology; Photo Researchers)

was surprised to find *his* repetition effect (see p. 513). Only if the dichotic presentations are *suddenly* stopped and the subject is *immediately* queried can he recall even the last item or two on the unattended channel. Evidence of this kind led Broadbent to postulate a short-term storage system with rapid decay *before* the filter; see Figure 19-10. Only material attended to is retained for any length of time, i.e., filtered through to long-term storage.

In a second type of dichotic listening task, the subject is asked to repeat all items from both ears. Suppose we deliver to the left ear the digits 2, 7, 3 and simultaneously to the right ear 4, 1, 8. What will the subject report? It depends on the rate of presentation, how fast the items are delivered. If the rate is relatively slow, he will report either *pair by pair* (2, 4; 7, 1; 3, 8—the two first items first, then the two second items, and so forth) or *by ear* (2, 7, 3; 4, 1, 8—all the left-ear, then all the right-ear items). If the presentation rate is increased, a point is reached where, if subjects can report at all, they report only *by ear*; that is, first the items presented to one ear and then the items presented to the other ear. This effect is attributed to difficulty in switching attention rapidly. What is of interest to us, however, is the implication—in theory terms—that the channel (or ear) reported second must be stored temporarily in the short-term system while the first channel is being fed directly through the filter. If this is a reasonable explanation and if the short-term store does show rapid decay, we would expect memory failures for the second channel. The data show that the information given in the channel (or ear) reported first is usually correct; the channel reported second is usually wrong, at least in part.

Shortly after the Broadbent model was published, some dramatic new data were reported which seemed to provide considerable support for Broadbent's notion of a short-term store with rapid decay. An experimenter, Sperling (1960), flashed three lines of three letters each on a screen for a brief time. Immediately following the disappearance of these stimuli (just a small fraction of a second later), he gave a probe indicating which of three lines was to be recalled. Under these circumstances memory for letters was two to three times better than "normal," that is, two to three times better than it would be if memory were tested a second or two after the stimuli disappeared. There appears to be a brief "sensory memory," which has been termed **iconic memory** (see Spotlight 19-2).

While these experiments gave support to some of Broadbent's hypotheses, they also instigated new controversies; the time period covered was *so* short. Theorists who liked to think in terms of two memory storage systems had pegged short-term memory as applicable to time periods measured in seconds, but a quarter-second! This was too short. Some began thinking in terms of three systems and called the first very brief storage the *sensory* (preperceptual) store. Others argued this preperceptual store, if it exists, is not a *memory* problem, since information in it (by all reports) is not encoded—the material must be reported literally, without change, something like a sensory "afterimage" you "see" if you stare at a bright light and then close your eyes. Most investigators of memory ignore these very short fraction-of-a-second effects and measure only effects occurring in intervals of a second or more. It remains controversial whether events in the very brief sensory store are important determinants of long-term memory.

Simply by positing two kinds of memory storage systems, the Broadbent filter theory was able to integrate and direct much of the research on short-term memory. With two stores, the governing principles of each were subject to study; if the principles were found to be discrepant, why not? They apply to two different systems. We entered a period of scientific investigation that sought in large part to discover discrepancies. As we have seen, many differences were found. So it is only fitting that later theories of memory were devised that not only distinguished between two memory stores but also explained in more detail the relationship between the two. It is to such a theory that we now turn our attention.

The Atkinson-Shiffrin Buffer Model

There are a number of more sophisticated theories that could be chosen as a representative current model, and in most respects these theories are quite similar. The one we have chosen to examine is called the **buffer model,** for reasons that will become ap-

SPOTLIGHT 19-2
How Sensory Memory Fades in Less Than a Second

You may have experienced this problem: You see a telephone number given briefly on a television screen and as you write the first digits down, the latter ones fade from memory. If you could have started with the last digits, you would surely have had them correct, but then you might have lost the first digits. The whole number was probably available for a brief moment, but during the time required to write down part of it, the rest of it vanished.

Sperling (1960) found an ingenious way to test memory *immediately* after a visual presentation. He flashed a 3 X 3 block of letters, like the one shown here, on a screen for 50 milliseconds (one-twentieth of a second)—a very brief presentation. After the letters disappeared, there was rather poor memory for the brief visual stimulus. In response to a probe, subjects typically recalled about three or four of the nine letters correctly—only about 30 or 40 percent. Sperling then used a tonal signal to instruct the subjects which row to recall—a high tone meant the top row, a middle tone signaled the second row, and a low tone was for the bottom row. If the tone was simultaneous with the flash, the row was reported with about 75 percent accuracy. If the tone was given 150 msec after the flash, accuracy was about 60 percent; at 300 msec after, about 55 percent. Apparently a fleeting visual memory could be scanned to find the information specified by the tonal signal. (This has been called "iconic memory" from the Greek word *eikon,* likeness or image.)

But the fact that the subjects were able to recall, with great accuracy, whichever row was designated *immediately* after the stimulus had disappeared, indicates that they must have had most of the letters in all three rows accessible right at the start. So forgetting can be measured over a one-second duration, as the graph demonstrates.

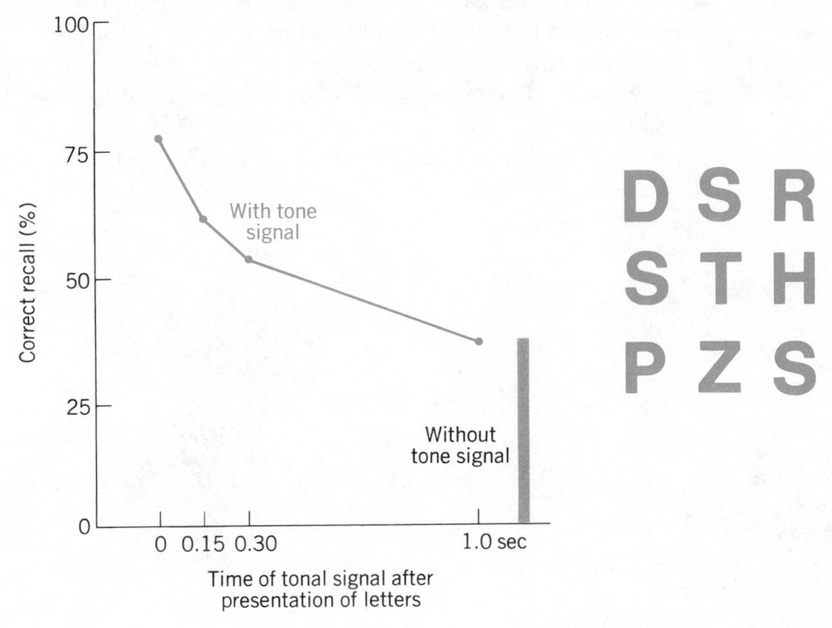

parent. It was formulated and developed by Stanford psychologists R. C. Atkinson and R. M. Shiffrin and their colleagues (Atkinson & Shiffrin, 1968, 1971).

The buffer model is shown diagrammatically in Figure 19-11. It has three storage systems, the first of which is the sensory registration system or sensory store, reflecting the evidence for the very short (quarter-second) preperceptual stage discussed above. The other two stores represent short-term and long-term memory—the short-term store (STS) and the long-term store (LTS).

The focus of the buffer model theory is on the control processes in the short-term store. In this model what happens in STS is most significant in considering memory as a whole: STS accepts the information coming in from the sensory registration system, and STS delivers *some* of that information to LTS. STS is the key link. What happens to the information in STS?

The key concept in this system is the rehearsal buffer, from which the model takes its name. Broadly defined buffer means "protector," so the term is meant to signify a process that protects the LTS from incoming information. Through rehearsal of the incoming material, the buffer keeps the information "alive" until LTS can efficiently accept it. This rehearsal process prevents rapid decay and eventual loss. The rehearsal, of course, does not need to be conscious or overt.

The buffer was also conceived as a structural entity. We could think of it as a file box with a certain number of slots. Chunks of information can be placed in these slots and then they will be rehearsed. Chances of the chunks' going into the LTS will be greater as the amount of rehearsal increases.

The number of slots is thought to be very limited. It is a somewhat analogous situation to a basketball team. Five starting positions are up for grabs and possibly a hundred men show up for the first day of practice. Once the five best men have been chosen, they can add to their advantage because they get the game experience. But

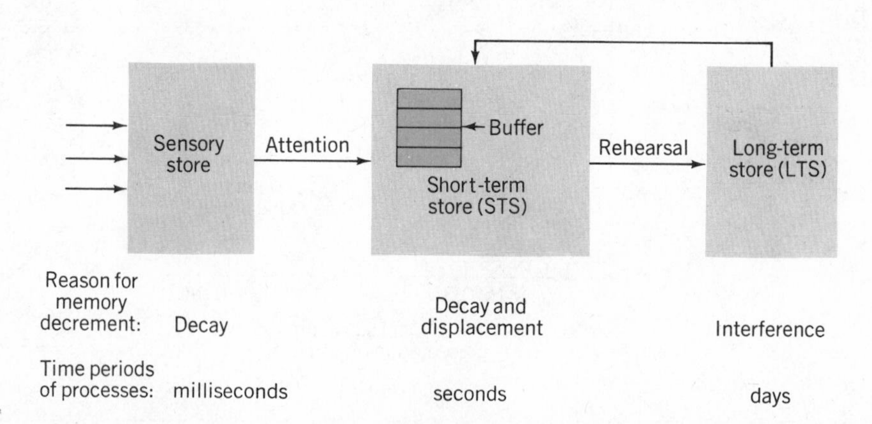

FIGURE 19-11 THE BUFFER MODEL OF MEMORY

Various sensory stores receive input, but attention determines what enters the short-term store. Here material passes through a rehearsal buffer. Rehearsal transfers information to the long-term store. The forgetting mechanism and time values are shown below each store.

(After Atkinson & Shiffrin, 1968)

if a new man comes along, he may displace one of the starters; he has to displace if he wants to make the starting team—you can't simply increase your team size to six. Similarly, much memory information "fights" for a spot in the rehearsal buffer but only a few items can be chosen. In some sense, the chosen few are chosen on the basis of importance to the individual. If new information comes in, it can displace some of the old information from the buffer.

The main reason for memory loss in STS is *decay*, a simple decrement in the strength of the memory trace over time. Information in the buffer is protected from decay by rehearsal; if it is displaced, it becomes subject to the same forgetting process that affects other STS material not in the buffer.

Decay also occurs in the sensory store but much more rapidly. In the sensory store one must speak in terms of a fraction of a second; in STS, the time period discussed is in terms of several seconds. In LTS, we speak of days, months, and years, and here the main reason for memory loss is believed to be *interference*—we cannot remember because some similar association is interfering—though certainly other reasons can be demonstrated (such as destruction of nerve cells in injuries or through aging). There is some question whether interference should be called memory loss, which would imply loss from storage; many interference effects, as you have learned, might better be explained in terms of retrieval problems.

The arrows in Figure 19-11 deserve some comment. Transfer from the sensory store to STS is seen primarily in terms of *attention*, which is a little more sophisticated way of saying that "importance" determines not only what gets into the buffer but also what gets in STS at all. Rehearsal of course is a prime determinant of transfer from STS to LTS, and this arrow is so represented. But there are also considerations that may be lumped under the general heading of "coding." Information that can be classified according to the established categories in LTS will be "passed" more easily. Coding is also significant with new information—it must be classified in some way. LTS has been likened to a permanent filing cabinet of large capacity, and anyone who has tried to file his own material knows the problems: Here's a letter with content on the integration of *A* and *B* on the basis of some creative new ideas (*C*); you have an *A* file and a *B* file, no *C* file; where do you put the letter? If it can't be easily filed, it is almost impossible to retrieve later.

There is also an arrow feeding back from LTS to STS. This is an impoverished representation of the fact that there is a constant interaction between the two systems. LTS affects what in STS is deemed important, both for attention and rehearsal. LTS also feeds information into STS—like an activated file—so the behavioral output of memory is presumed to be coming from STS, even in the ordinary cases where the information comes from LTS and not from the senses.

To illustrate application of the buffer theory, we can consider an experiment on free-recall memory. A list is presented to be recalled later in any order. Two groups of subjects, however, differ in *when* they are asked to recall; one is asked to do so immediately after presentation; the other only after several seconds. The distractor technique is used to fill the waiting period. Results from such an experiment are shown in Figure 19-12, plotting percentage of recall against serial position of the item in the presented list. Note that the results are essentially the same for both groups *except* for the items at the end of the list; in delayed recall the recency effect is eliminated.

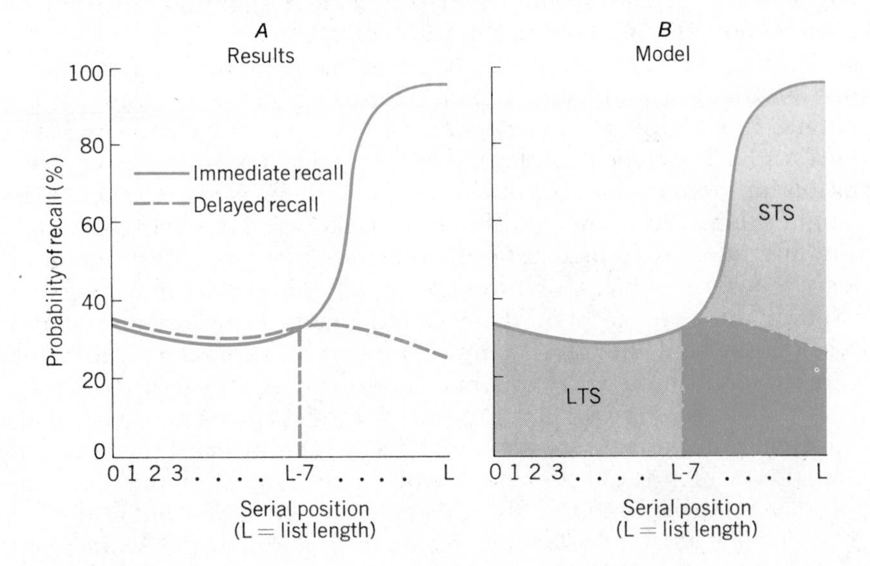

FIGURE 19-12
IMMEDIATE AND DELAYED RECALL: RESULTS AND THEORETICAL MODEL
A shows the effect of the distractor technique upon the serial-position curve of free recall. Recall after the distraction (delayed recall) has no recency effect. *B* interprets this effect according to the buffer model. Items can either be in STS (upper right corner), LTS (lower left), or both. The interpolated distraction eliminates the STS effect but the LTS component is unchanged.
(After Glanzer, 1972)

How does the buffer model account for such results? Figure 19-12B is a graphic representation of the theoretical interpretation. The flat middle portion of the serial-position curve is attributed to information retrieved from LTS; this interpretation holds for both groups. The recency effect, on the other hand, extends over approximately the last seven items, and only the immediate-recall subjects show this effect. This portion of the curve is affected by information in STS but *only* if the recall is asked for *immediately*, before STS transfers its information to LTS.

You already have learned that memory span is around seven items, and here we see the recency effect to extend to a similar number. This "magic number" (7 ± 2) is believed to reflect the limited number of slots in the rehearsal buffer, though not exactly (mathematically, three or four slots can account for a seven-item effect). Consider a serial-order task. As a subject goes through a list, the first four items go into STS slots; the fifth item must displace one of the first four, and subsequent items displace others, at a regular rate based on the actual presentation rate. The amount of time in the buffer, which determines how much information goes to LTS and therefore probability of recall, is equal for all middle items. It is slightly longer for the first few items (the second does not displace the first because there are still unfilled slots available) and this accounts for the slight primacy effect. But the *last* four items are being actively processed in STS when immediate recall is requested so they have the advantage that shows up in the experimental measure, percent recalled. If recall is delayed for just a few seconds, however, the buffer "dumps" the list items and presumably gets filled by distractor material, hence there is no recency effect. In fact, since the last two or three items (before the distractor activity begins) have less than average time in the buffer, the buffer theory predicts a slight *negative* recency effect, as shown in Figure 19-12.

Now consider the other facts and findings presented in this chapter. Memory-span data we have already mentioned; they are seen as representing the number of slots in the buffer. The section on forgetting curves considered the very rapid memory decrement using the distractor technique and the primacy and recency effects in the serial-positions curve; both phenomena were discussed above.

Interference effects (proactive and retroactive inhibition, in particular) in LTS can be seen as a sort of competition at the moment of attempted retrieval, but in STS, they must be viewed in terms of displacement—"knocking out" information put in previously (retroactive effects) or "leaving no room" for material coming later (proactive effects). One has to make a further assumption to account for the similarity effects: The "file system" in STS is based on simple classifications such as sounds and, therefore, acoustic similarity causes confusion in the buffer. In LTS, semantic coding by "meaningful" linguistic file categories is more prevalent, so semantic similarity causes more problems there.

Everything considered, the buffer model provides a reasonably good interpretation of most of the empirical data we have gathered. Repetition effects remain somewhat of a puzzle. The findings on retrieval processes that might pose problems—for example, the evidence that retrieval cues are stored in STS with their target—represent a vein of research that is still too new to be well integrated into any theory. These phenomena are not so well explained, but they are not incompatible with the buffer model; future formulations of a buffer model might well be devised to handle these facts.

Modality effects, however, present a more immediate problem. As we have seen, the recency effect is generally greater for auditory presentation than for visual presentation, even though the remainder of the serial-position curves are the same for the two senses. (Review Figure 19-9.) In terms of the buffer model, this means there is no difference in LTS, only in STS. *But if there is a difference in STS, why doesn't it show up later in LTS?* In other words, if visual information is handled less well in STS (a less prominent recency effect), why isn't visual information less likely to be rehearsed and thus less likely to go into LTS (showing decreased probability of recall in the midrange of the serial-position curve)? This is a puzzle for the buffer model.

But perhaps we are too demanding. The buffer model is very good in integrating many findings, better than most theories. No one has set forth a theory yet that can explain everything. Each new theory represents an advance and, if it is precisely and rigorously phrased, as is the buffer model, it points the way to an even more sophisticated model. The buffer model is popular because it explains much that has been confusing. It is likely to remain popular until a better model of memory comes along.

SUMMARY

Memory involves encoding, storage, and retrieval of information. Encoding is the initial registration in memory, storage is reflected in the persistence of information over time, and retrieval refers to utilization of stored material. One must be careful to distinguish the source of memory difficulties. Apparent forgetting may mean the material was never encoded; it may mean the information was not stored (it is unavailable); or it may reflect retrieval difficulties (it is inaccessible).

One way to distinguish between storage and retrieval is to note results from different tasks. Recognition tasks provide possible responses for the individual and require a relatively simple comparison process; generally more information is remembered this way than with recall procedures, where the information must be generated by the subject (presumably by a more involved search process). So if something cannot be recalled but can be recognized, clearly the recall problem was one of retrieval—recognition shows the material was available, however inaccessible.

Another major distinction must be made, between *memory* and *decision* systems, if we are to make sense of behavior related to the processing of information. That is, if a person says he does not remember something, that does not necessarily mean memory is at fault—he may remember at least some part of the material but *decide* to indicate ignorance for various reasons. On the other hand, he might indicate knowledge, say by choosing the correct alternative in a multiple-choice test, when in fact he has none—he was guessing.

Signal detection theory provides a means of distinguishing between memory and decision processes. Two statistics, d' and β, can be computed from a subject's performance in a recognition task. The first, d', estimates the degree to which the subject can distinguish between old (previously seen) and novel stimuli and thus reflects comparisons with memory. The second, β, indicates the degree of familiarity the subject requires before he is willing to report "yes" or "true," and thus reflects his decision criterion. Factors that affect memory, such as amount of training, will usually change d', while factors that affect decision criteria, such as instructions to be very cautious or not, correlate with β.

To aid in gathering data on memory, new techniques have been developed recently. The distractor technique tries to prevent rehearsal by having subjects do something (e.g., count backward by threes) between presentation and recall. The probe technique presents a list of items but asks for only one of them by means of a directed probe. Both techniques give evidence of substantial forgetting within a few seconds after presentation.

Experimental findings cover many topics. Memory span is about 7 ± 2 chunks of information. Of the two forgetting curves discussed, one shows the rapid loss of information using the distractor technique, and the second shows the three main parts of a serial-position curve: the primacy effect, the less frequently-remembered middle items, and the recency effect. Interference effects (proactive and retroactive inhibition) were briefly reviewed, and the proactive interference effects were seen as a possible explanation of the primacy-to-recency shift that occurs when many lists are presented in one session.

Sometimes data indicate apparent contradictions. The Hebb repetition effect is improved memory after several repetitions of a list; the closer together the repetitions, the greater the effect. The Peterson paradox suggests that the farther apart the repetitions of items, the greater the memory.

Similarity effects of greatest concern are confusion between words that sound the same (acoustic similarity), which occurs most often in studies of short-term memory, and between words that mean the same (semantic similarity), which occurs more frequently in long-term memory. Modality effects are differences observed when nothing but the sensory mode is varied: auditory presentation consistently results in better memory than visual presentation, but only in the last few items of a list (recency effect). This finding is one of the most difficult to integrate into a general theory. Retrieval effects include increased probability of recall when retrieval cues are stored with their target at the moment of presentation.

After information is gathered, theorists attempt to tie the data together by formulating a coherent theory of memory. Broadbent's filter theory was an early attempt to distinguish between a short-term memory store with rapid decay and a long-term memory with more permanent storage. Evidence for the theory from dichotic listening tasks included (1) an inability to recall material presented to the ear the subject had been previously instructed to disregard and (2) forgetting of material to the ear that was reported second when the subject was to report both channels. Taken together, these findings give support to the notion of a short-term store before the filter, a store characterized by rapid memory loss through decay. Later experiments gave additional support, but some became so precise that they were able to demonstrate considerable loss in the first quarter-second after presentation.

This latter finding led some theorists to postulate three storage systems, as in the Atkinson-Shiffrin buffer model. The first or sensory store is conceived as a sensory registration system with very brief storage capabilities. The second store is called the short-term store (STS), with somewhat longer capabilities. Information that gets to STS is subject to fairly rapid loss through decay *unless* it is protected in the rehearsal buffer. Through rehearsal and coding, material is transferred to the long-term store (LTS), where it remains relatively impervious to loss, though it may become inaccessible through interference or confusion.

The central explanatory concept in buffer theory is the rehearsal buffer itself. It is viewed as a file with a limited number of slots in which material is protected from STS decay by rehearsal. The number of slots is related to the number of items (or chunks of information) defining the memory span. Although the buffer theory can explain most of the empirical phenomena it does encounter difficulty explaining modality effects. In general, the explanations concern themselves with assumptions about what material gains access to buffer slots, and when. Displacement (of one chunk by another) in a slot is an important consideration because "time in slot" determines amount of rehearsal and eventually storage in LTS. This, in turn, is measured by probability of later recall. The buffer model is not a perfect theory, but it does a very good job of integrating what we know, and it explains much that had previously been confusing. It has the further advantage of showing us where the main gaps in our knowledge exist.

RECOMMENDED READING

Broadbent, D. E. *Decision and Stress.* London: Academic Press, 1971.
An extensive review of the experimental and theoretical work on human information processing, with an updated version of filter theory.

Ebbinghaus, H. *Memory: A Contribution to Experimental Psychology.* New York: Dover reprint, 1964.
Still a classic and well worth reading.

Howe, M. J. A. *Introduction to Human Memory.* New York: Harper & Row, 1970.
A brief introduction, simply and clearly written, which covers much of recent work in the field.

Kintsch, W. *Learning, Memory, and Conceptual Processes.* New York: Wiley, 1970.
Probably the best review of the verbal learning and memory area currently available.

Marx, M. H. *Learning: Processes.* New York: Macmillan, 1969.
An advanced-undergraduate to graduate-level survey of conditioning, rote learning, transfer, and motor learning.

Neisser, U. *Cognitive Psychology.* New York: Appleton-Century-Crofts, 1967.
A serious and scholarly review of the higher mental processes from a cognitive point of view. Particularly good in synthesizing a large number of experimental findings into a coherent theoretical framework.

Norman, D. A. *Memory and Attention.* New York: Wiley, 1969.
A very readable introduction to the topics of memory and attention from an information-processing viewpoint, with emphasis on broad issues and an overview of how the system might work. Howe and Norman make a good complementary pair.

Skinner, B. F. *Walden Two.* New York: Macmillan, 1948.
A novel applying principles of operant conditioning to a utopian community.

SECTION SEVEN

THE PSYCHOLOGY OF PERCEPTION

By Michael Wertheimer

Review and Preview

An environmental event occurs in the presence of a person or an animal. How do we know if he saw it or heard it? What did he perceive, exactly? Would the perception of two people be the same or different? If different, why? Do factors such as one's culture or his motivational state affect the percept?

In this section we focus on questions like these, all encompassed by the topic of **perception.** In other sections of this book, perception is often simply assumed. In most learning and memory studies, for example, the stimuli are presented in such a way that the investigator can be reasonably sure that they register and are encoded—then he can focus on the processing of information *within* the system.

The section on social psychology starts with an experiment on conformity in the judgment of line lengths (p. 62). This experiment was set up so that almost all subjects would have reached the same perceptual judgments if no social pressure had been involved. The experimenter had tested and chosen stimuli with large enough differences so that he could be sure of the response that a subject would give by himself. The experimenter also made sure that the subject perceived the responses of the others, who were actually confederates of the experimenter. Social pressure arose when the subject believed that his own perceptions and those of the others did not agree. We have learned that perceptions of other people usually agree with our own—at least when the stimulus situation appears to be clear-cut and when none of us suffers from an obvious sensory defect (such as color blindness or deafness).

But we also know that in complex situations people's perceptions often differ. These differences may be related to group membership and allegiance, as when students at two colleges, watching the same movie of a football game between their teams, see significantly more rule infractions by the opposing team than by their own (p. 92). Some differences in perception are so consistent and stable that they have been labeled "cognitive styles" or even "personality traits" (p. 405). Some people determine whether a target is vertical by referring chiefly to surrounding objects (and are therefore called "field-dependent" individuals) whereas others determine verticality by reference to cues from their own body (and thereby show "field independence") (see p. 406). This difference has been found to be related to many social behaviors, such as conformity.

In our discussion of perception we will start with instances where most people tend to agree and where relatively few factors determine the perceptual results—where the stimuli themselves are rather simple and uniform. Thus Chapter 20 will include such topics as the perception of visual brightness and hue and auditory loudness and pitch. Research on these aspects of perception has progressed to the point where certain relations between stimulus conditions and perceptual responses can be stated quantitatively. This chapter will stress vision and audition but will also take up some features of the other senses.

Then we will proceed in Chapter 21 to an examination of how *relations among parts of the stimulus field* are important in determining the perception—contrast between parts of the field, pattern and organization of forms, and movement. Why are certain parts of a complex stimulus field perceived as belonging together in a coherent form or pattern? How, on the contrary, can knowledge of perceptual laws be used to hide or camouflage objects? What are characteristics of forms that are "good" and distinctive versus forms that are "poor"?

In Chapter 22 we will consider the creative role of the perceiver. We will also take up perceptual phenomena that are less stable and are more subject to personal variables of set, attitude, motivation, and personality. Chapter 22 concludes with a discussion of how hereditary and environmental factors interact in producing perceptual abilities, some of which are present in early infancy and some of which develop only after prolonged experience. This is an examination of the problem of nativism and empiricism in the context of perception.

Whether the determinants of perception are clear and reliable or complex and variable, we will find the perceiver actively engaged in the processing of environmental stimuli. "His curiosity does not let him wait for environmental events to happen; rather he searches them out and seeks levels of stimulation and excitation. When some environmental event occurs [he] does not register it passively, but instead interprets it. It is this interpretation, not the event itself, which affects his behavior." You may remember this quotation; it appeared in Chapter 13 (p. 302) but with the words "the infant" instead of "[he]." This is the Piagetian description of the active role that the infant plays in interpreting his environment. We will see that the adult too is constantly forming perceptual hypotheses and testing them in feedback interactions with his environment.

Before starting Chapter 20, on the following pages we will look at several phenomena of visual perception. Each relates to discussions in the chapters of this section. For further examples of interesting perceptual phenomena, look also at the figures of the color section on perception.

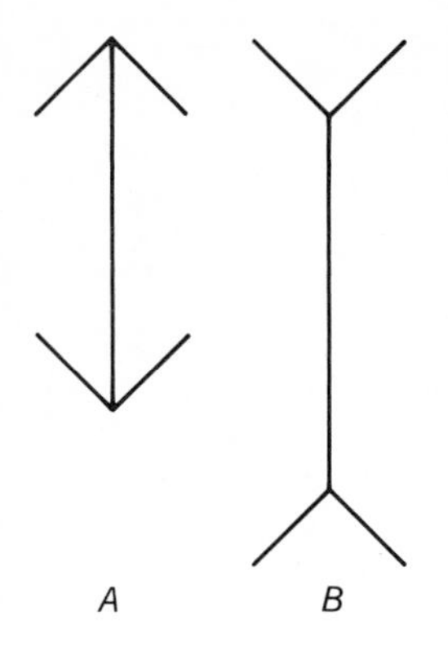

FIGURE 1

Which vertical line is the longer? Line *B* seems longer, but they are equal. The magnitude of the illusion appears to vary among cultures. See pp. 617-618.

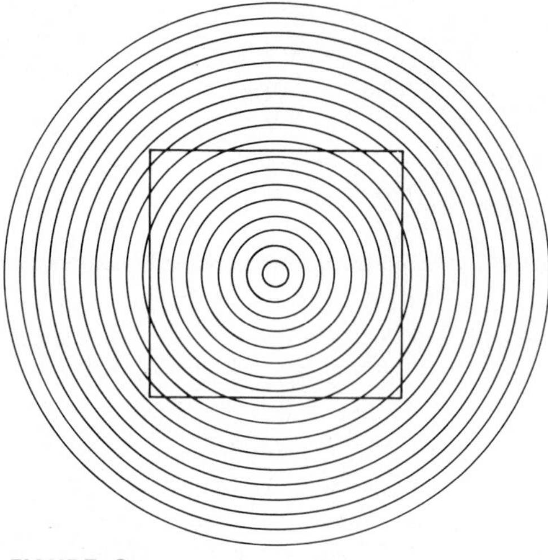

FIGURE 2

Are the sides of the square straight? Check for yourself. The sides appear curved because of the contrast with their background. See the discussion of contrast on pp. 570-572.

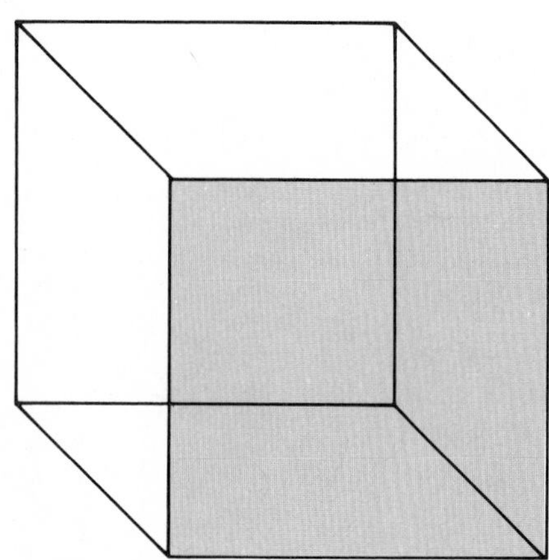
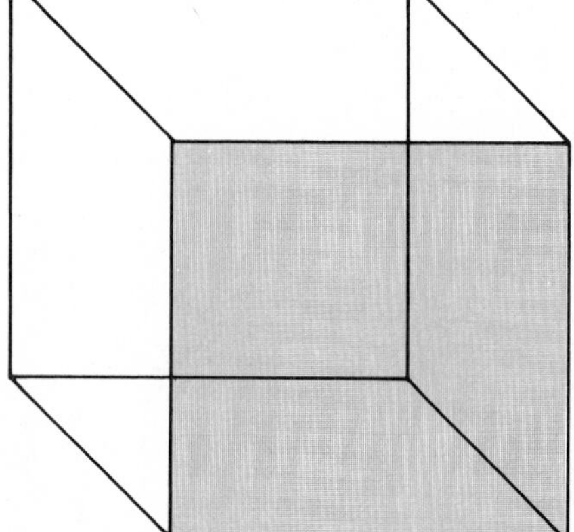

FIGURE 3

Is the colored face of this cube at the front or at the rear? Your answer will change suddenly if you stare at the cube for a while. See the discussion of hypotheses in perception on pp. 601-605.

FIGURE 4

This picture is called "My Wife and My Mother-in-law." Which do you see? Look again for the other face. You can prepare a friend to see either of the two faces by using the pictures on p. 614. (If you find it difficult to see a second face here, you can check there for the other.)

FIGURE 5

Look at the gray ring. Then place a pencil over the black-white boundary and note that the two halves of the ring no longer seem the same shade. You can "pull" the darker gray into the left half by slowly moving the pencil in that direction. What happens when you move the pencil in the other direction? This is another contrast effect. See pp. 570-572.

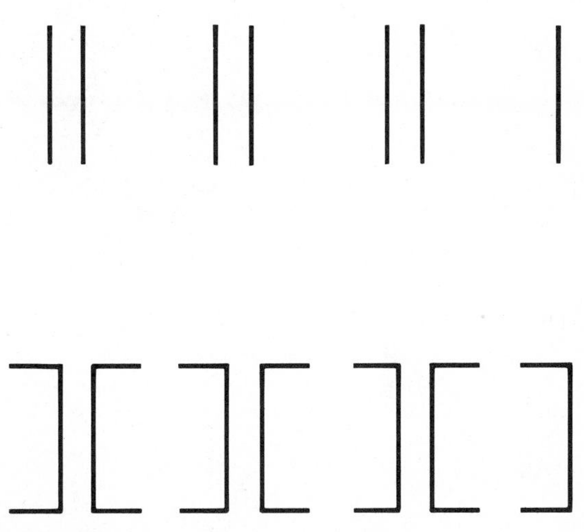

FIGURE 6

Is the odd line to the left or to the right in the upper and lower sets of lines? Note that the two sets are identical except for the horizontal extensions in the lower set. But the change affects what you see as "going together." See p. 587.

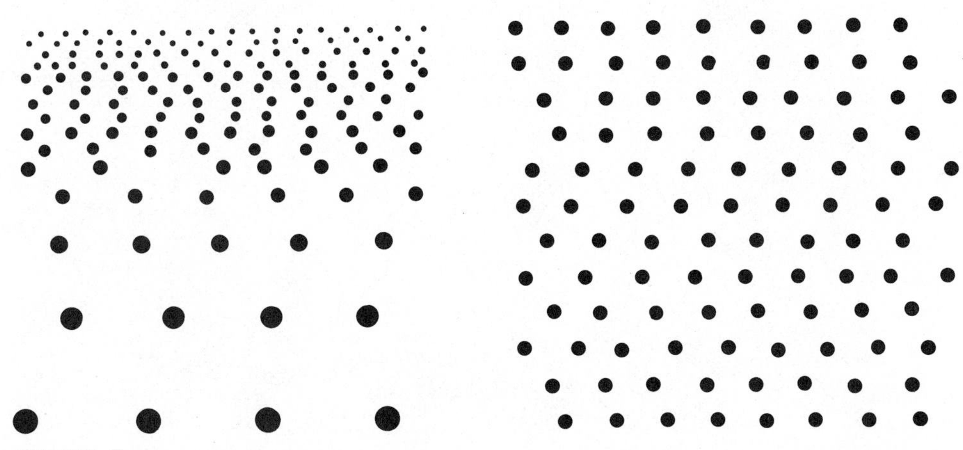

FIGURE 7

Notice that one pattern appears to recede from you, whereas the other seems to stay in the plane of the page. Depth perception is discussed on pp. 594-597.

The perception of infants (and animals) who cannot tell you what they see can be studied by observation of their behavior in carefully designed situations. Studies of young animals (including infants) tell us much about the contributions of hereditary and environmental factors to perception.

FIGURE 8

A baby's eye movements can be observed while he looks at patterns such as these. Do you think he spends more time looking at one than at the other? This is discussed on p. 625.

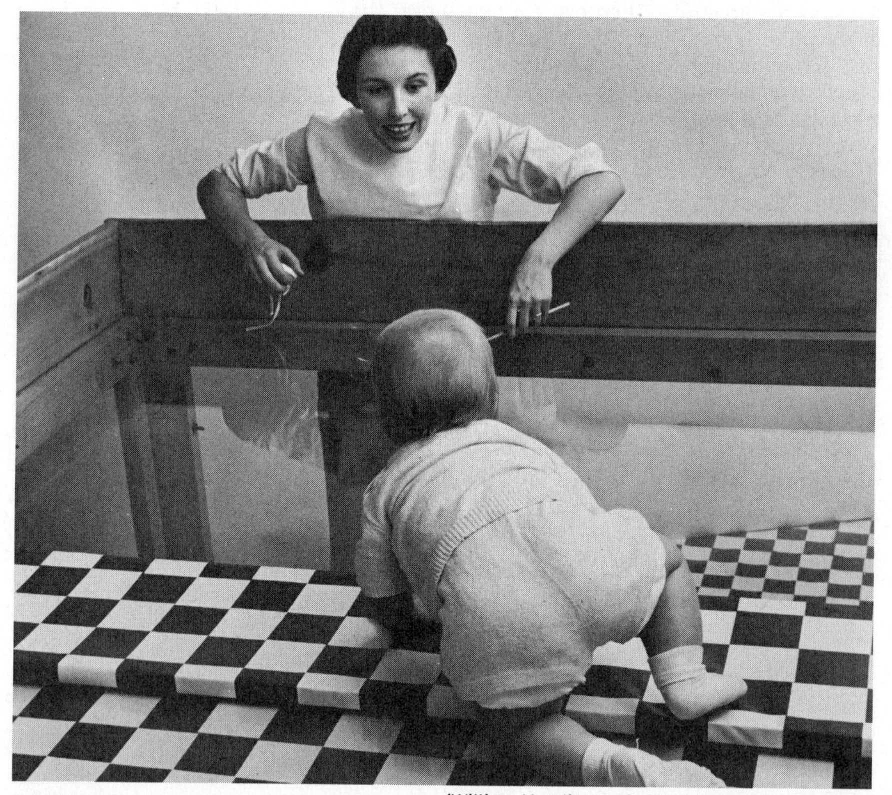

FIGURE 9 (William Vandivert; © 1966 *Scientific American*)

Can the baby perceive depth? Do you think he will crawl onto the transparent surface over the drop? See pp. 621-623.

FIGURE 10 **FIGURE 11**

Does Figure 10 have two or three prongs? You get different answers from looking at the different ends. Now look at Figure 11. What is your point of view—upward, downward, or sideward? As with Figure 10, small portions of Figure 11 allow a clear answer, but there is no single answer for the figure as a whole. Even some portions are "impossible"; look at the stairway near the top of the drawing. One man is walking up while the other, although facing in the same direction, is walking down the stairs. There is no danger of their bumping into one another, however, because they exist in two different worlds!

See the discussion of hypotheses in perception on pp. 601-605.

("Relativity" by M. C. Escher, courtesy Escher Foundation, Haags Gemeentemuseum, The Hague)

FIGURE 12

What is a blind spot and what can be "seen" in it?

With your right eye closed, stare at the square at the upper right. Move the book back and forth about one foot from the eye. When the upper circle disappears, its image is falling on the blind spot of your left eye. See color Figure 8.

Now do the same thing with the lower square. This time, when the lower circle falls on the blind spot, the line is seen as continuous. Why? When the book is held nearer or farther than the critical distance, the lower circle is seen to interrupt the line.

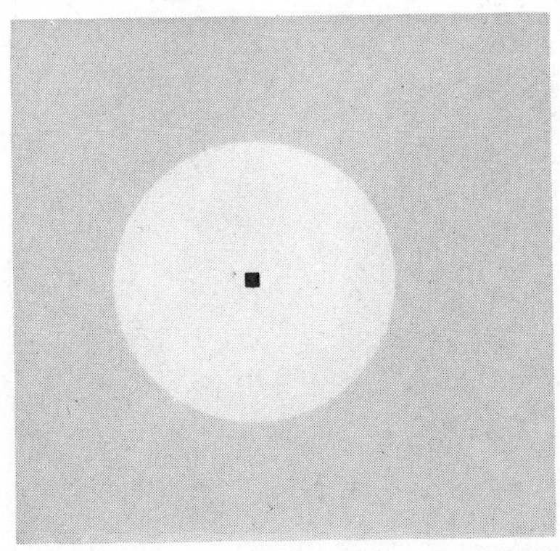

(After Cornsweet, 1969)

FIGURE 13

Stare at the small black square in the left box for a minute and the disc will fade away. If you then shift your focus to the *X*, the disc will reappear. In the second box, the disc does not fade so quickly. The eye, like the other sense organs, responds best to sharp differences in stimulation. See pp. 570-574.

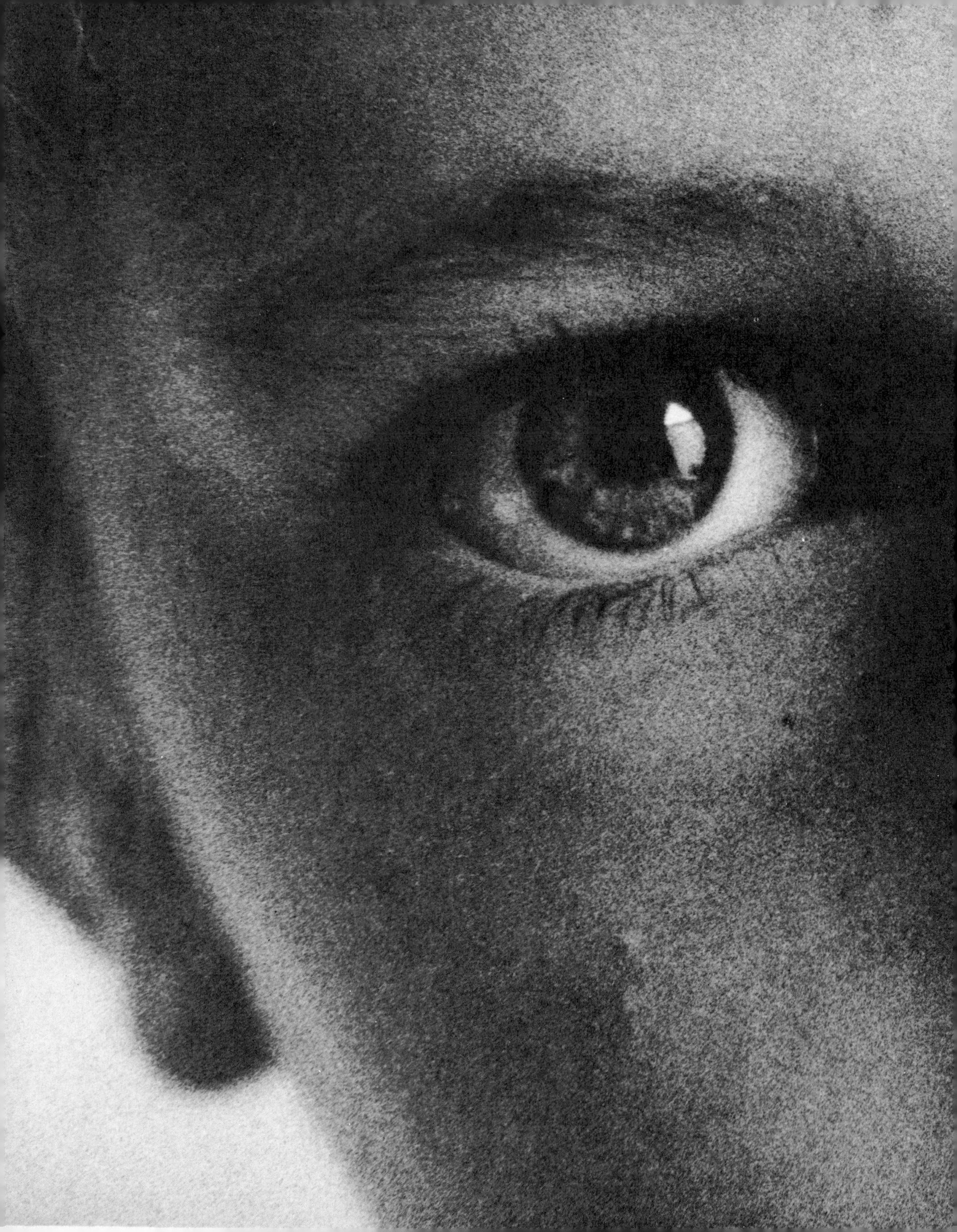

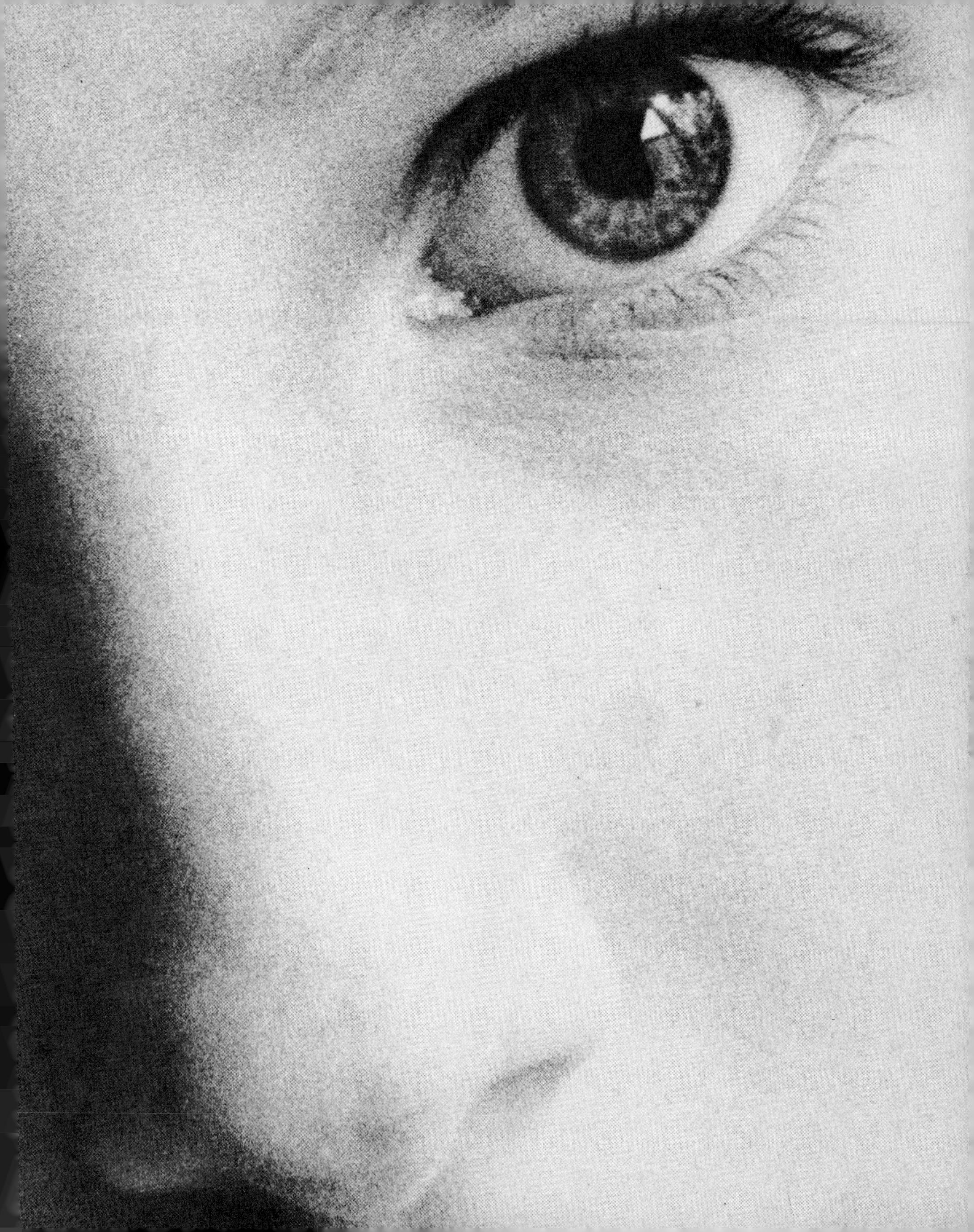

20

Sensory Aspects of Perception

How does psychophysics relate the physical and psychological worlds?
How sensitive are we, absolutely?
How sensitive are we, relatively?
How do our sensory systems function?

When you look at a patch of color or listen to a note, how is your experience related to physical characteristics of the sensory stimulus? What are the relationships between the *physical dimensions* of the stimulus and the *psychological dimensions* of your experience?

How does psychophysics relate the physical and psychological worlds?

Philosophers and scientists wrestled with such questions for many centuries, but an obstacle stood in their way: How could perceptions be measured? The physical intensity of a light could be quantified—two candles obviously yield twice as much light energy as does one—but how could the experience of brightness be measured? A major breakthrough occurred in 1860 when Gustav Theodor Fechner published a book, *Elements of Psychophysics,* describing methods for measuring psychological quantities such as the strength of a **sensation.** Fechner tried to use these methods to develop a general law relating physical and psychological magnitudes. It turned out that the light of two candles looks less than twice as bright as the light of a single candle. Before we consider the general laws of **psychophysics,** let us try measuring brightness ourselves.

Measurement of a Psychological Quantity

In Figure 20-1, each line includes a black square, a gray square, and a white square. For purposes of rating, consider the black square to have the brightness rating of zero and the white square to have the brightness rating of 20. Using these as anchor values, now assign a brightness rating to each of the gray squares. It will help if you use the following procedure: Prop the book open to Figure 20-1 in such a way that the lighting falls evenly on the page with no glare. Now make a table and assign a number between 0 and 20 to each gray square. Complete your ratings before reading on.

Table of Ratings

A ______	C ______	E ______
B ______	D ______	F ______

Figure 20-2 presents means of ratings of the gray squares made by twenty students; the means are represented by the black dots. The figure also gives the **albedo** (the percentage of light reflected) of each of the squares, including the black and white squares. Plot your own ratings to see where they fall on the graph. On the colored line running up from *A*, put a dot at the height for your rating of *A*, according to the scale at the left; then do the same for your judgments of the other squares. Now draw a line connecting your successive ratings from left to right across the graph (*D*, *F*, *B*, *A*, *C*, *E*).

Probably your ratings do not agree exactly with those printed in the figure, and they may not make a smooth graph. Some variability is to be expected, since you probably have not had much practice in making such judgments and since the printing processes cannot reproduce the original grays exactly and uniformly. But which line do your ratings resemble more closely—the curve connecting the black points or the diagonal line in the figure? The diagonal line is what would occur if your perception of brightness had increased directly and linearly with the amount of light reaching your eye from the page. If that had been the case, then *C* (which reflects about 40 percent of the light) would have been judged about half as bright as white (since the page reflects about 80 percent). Instead of following this linear function, your ratings probably all fell above the diagonal and made a bow-shaped line.

Fechner's Law

This method of rating is called "category rating," and was worked out in the present century. The psychophysical methods that Fechner devised are somewhat more complicated and will not be described here, but they yield results similar to those of direct estimation. Based on his results, Fechner proposed that the intensity of perception is related to the logarithm of the physical intensity of

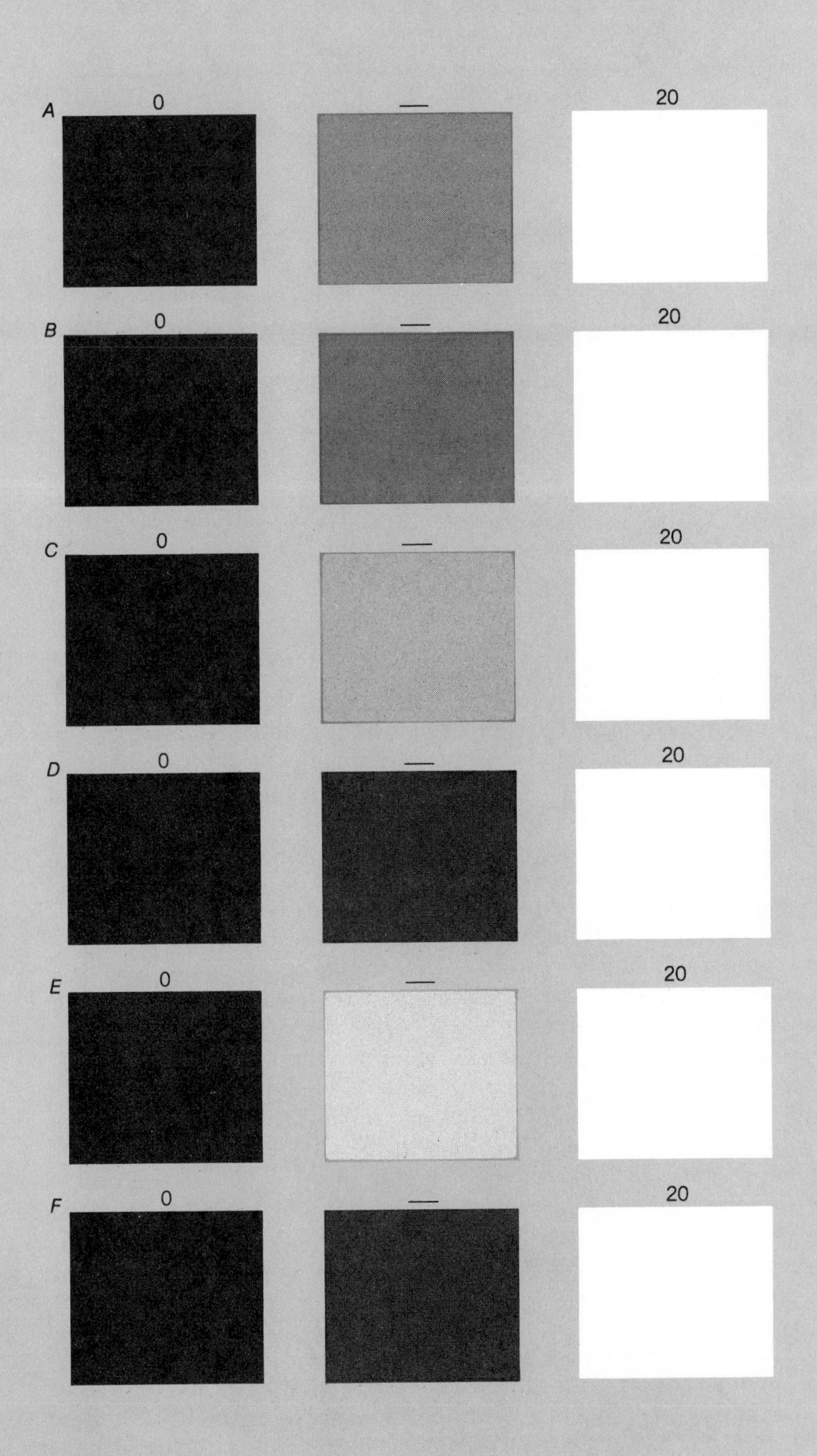

FIGURE 20-1
RATING THE BRIGHTNESS OF VARIOUS SHADES OF GRAY
Follow the directions on p. 544 and do these ratings before proceeding farther.

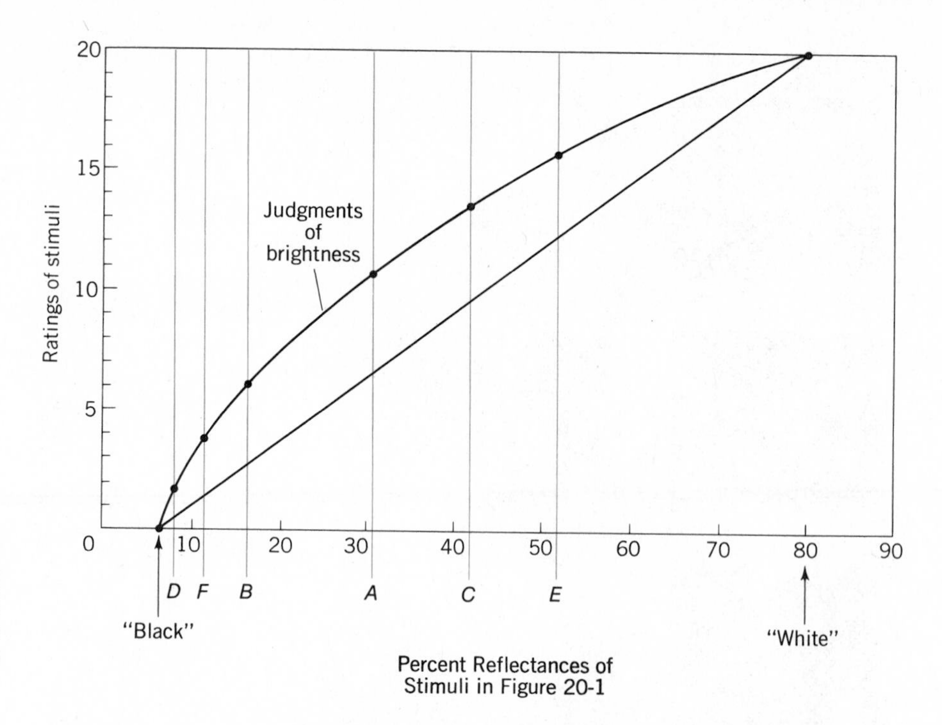

FIGURE 20-2
RATINGS OF GRAYS
These are mean values for a group of students who rated the gray squares in Figure 20-1. Compare your ratings with these.

the stimulus. This can be expressed by the following formula: $\psi = k \log \phi$, where ψ (psi) stands for the psychological magnitude, ϕ (phi) is the physical magnitude, and k is a constant for a given sense and experimental condition. This rule, which came to be known as **Fechner's law,** provided a serviceable approximation for many senses—visual brightness, auditory loudness, strength of taste, and others.

Because our perceptions of intensity increase (approximately) with the logarithm of the strength of the stimulus, many physical scales use logarithmic units. For example, even before Fechner, astronomers classified stars' intensities in "magnitudes" of about equal steps of perceived brightness. When the intensities were later measured physically, each magnitude was found to be one log unit removed from the next; the astronomers had devised a logarithmic scale of brightness without planning to do so! Intensity of sound is measured in decibels, another logarithmic physical unit. Sixty decibels represents *ten times* as much sound power as 50 decibels and is *one hundred times* as powerful as 40 decibels. The Richter scale, used to measure the intensity of earthquakes, is also logarithmic; an earthquake that registers 9.0 is ten times as powerful as one that registers 8.0.

Stevens' Power Law

More precise measurements have shown that the relation between stimulus intensity and perceptual intensity is not exactly logarithmic. A mathematical relation known as a **power law** affords a better fit for many sets of data. According to this rule, perceptual magnitude increases in proportion to the physical intensity raised to a given power:

$$\psi = k\phi^n.$$

Here n is an exponent that is fixed for a given sense and experimental condition. As before, ψ stands for the psychological magnitude, ϕ for the physical intensity, and k is a constant. The power law relation between perceived intensity and stimulus intensity is sometimes known as Stevens' law, named for the American psychophysicist S. S. Stevens.

Using the power law formulation, we can show that the senses differ from each other in how rapidly the strength of experience rises when the intensity of the stimulus is increased. The exponent n reflects this aspect of the relation between sensation and stimulus. For the judged length of a line in vision, the exponent is 1.0; that is, apparent length increases directly, linearly with physical length. This linear relation between apparent and physical length is shown by the one-to-one relation in the graphs of Figure 20-3. On the other hand, for many senses the exponent is less than 1.0; for a point source of light presented to the dark-adapted eye, $n = 0.5$, and for loudness, it is 0.3. The slow increase in loudness with sound intensity is shown by the lower curves of the graphs. In a few cases, sensation increases more rapidly than stimulus intensity; for judgment of weights lifted by the hand, $n = 1.4$, and when electric shock is applied to the fingertips the sensation increases rapidly with shock strength—$n = 3.6$.

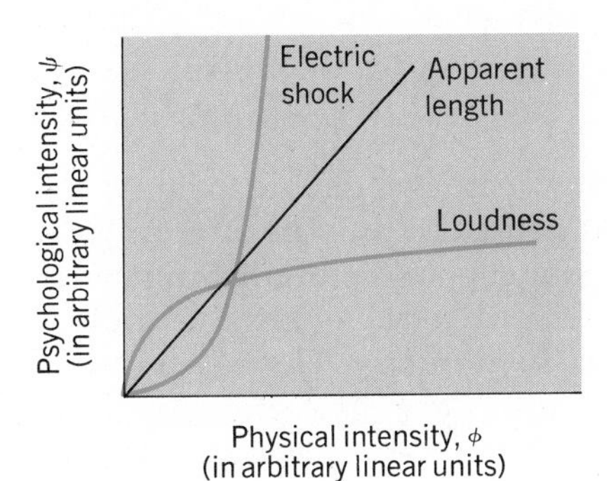

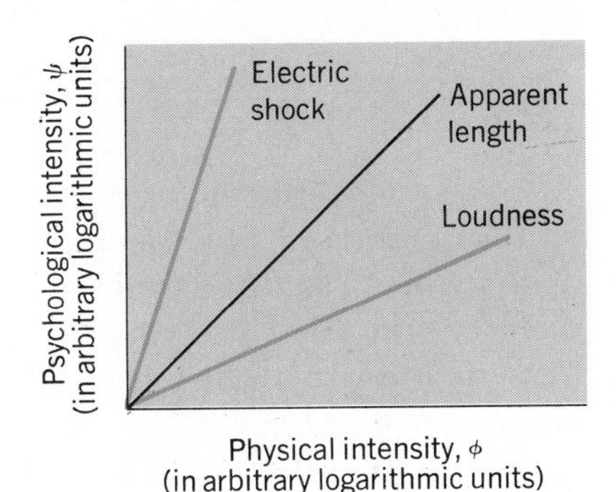

FIGURE 20-3
HOW SOME PSYCHOLOGICAL MAGNITUDES (ψ) VARY WITH SOME PHYSICAL MAGNITUDES (ϕ)
On the left data are plotted on linear coordinates; on the right, on double logarithmic coordinates. The fact that all the functions become linear in the second graph is a demonstration of Stevens' power law.
(After Stevens, 1962)

How sensitive are we, absolutely?

Did the telephone just ring in the next room? Is there a smell of gas in the house? Did you just see that shooting star? Our senses are very acute and under good conditions we can detect amazingly small amounts of stimulus energy. The weakest stimulus that can be detected is called the **absolute threshold**; the absolute thresholds for several senses are shown in Table 20-1. Actually, threshold determinations form a distribution, as shown in Figure 20-4. Some stimuli are so weak that they are almost never reported; some are so strong that they are almost always reported, and in between are stimuli that are detected on some trials but not on others. The usual convention is to take the stimulus intensity that is detected on 50 percent of the trials and to call that the absolute threshold, but it may be better to think of a threshold zone, as indicated by the colored region in Figure 20-4, rather than of a single precise value.

TABLE 20-1
THE ABSOLUTE THRESHOLDS OF SOME SENSE MODALITIES

Sense	*Absolute Threshold*
Vision	Candle flame at a distance of 30 miles on a dark clear night (about 10 quanta of light energy)
Hearing	Tick of a watch 20 feet away, in a quiet setting (about .0002 dyne/cm^2)
Taste	One teaspoon of sugar dissolved in 2 gallons of water (about one part in 2,000); saccharine, about one part in 1,000,000
Smell	A single drop of perfume diffused in the volume of air in an average three-room apartment (about one part in 500,000,000)
Touch	The wing of a bee falling on your cheek from a distance of 1 centimeter

After Galanter, 1962.

Theory of Signal Detection

Between two people, how can we decide who is the better perceiver? The **theory of signal detection** provides the answer. This theory was discussed earlier as a means of distinguishing memory from decision processes (p. 504). The theory can also be applied to perception, where in fact it had its beginnings. The reasoning is similar to that in memory studies. In both areas, investigators often deal with a verbal report from their subjects: "Yes, I saw it" (perception) or "Yes, I saw it before" (memory). Such reports are partly a function of a *decision* by the subject to say "yes" or "no," and psychologists would very much like to know to what extent the person's attitude (influencing his decision) affects the report. In a perceptual task, two different subjects might both "see" a "faint hint" of a stimulus, but one might report "no"—being very cautious—while the other, being more impulsive, might report "yes."

Suppose we want to know if a subject can detect a certain weak tone. We might present a "warning"—a light perhaps—

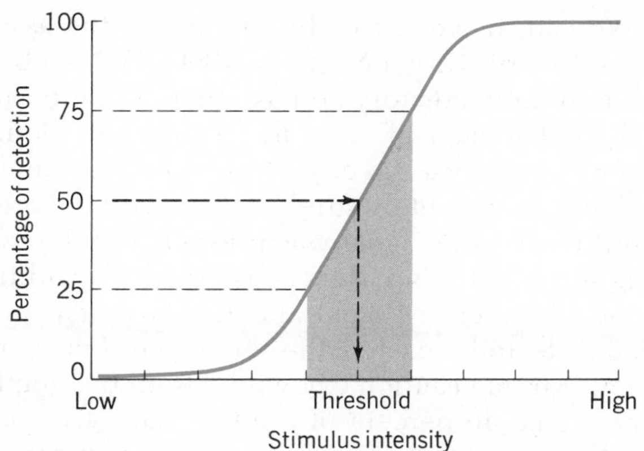

FIGURE 20-4
THRESHOLD ZONE
The absolute threshold is often defined as the intensity at which the stimulus will be detected on 50% of the trials. You can also think of the threshold as a zone or region surrounding the 50% report intensity.

indicating that in the next two-second period, there will either be a faint tone or nothing at all. Suppose the subject says yes 90 percent of the time when a tone is actually present. This fact, by itself, might be (mis)interpreted as meaning he can detect our weak signal; we must look also at the trials on which no tone was present. If he says yes on 90 percent of those, our conclusion that he is detecting the signal is untenable. It appears that he is saying yes 90 percent of the time, regardless of whether or not the stimulus is present.

Generally, if a weak signal is detectable, the percentage of "hits" (saying yes when the stimulus is present) is greater than the percentage of "false alarms" (saying yes when no signal is presented). This is perhaps common sense. But now suppose we are to compare two subjects to see which has the better perceptual sensitivity. A question like this has great practical significance. Imagine a situation in which *you* must choose a man to monitor one of the radar screens in our national defense system. Person *A* scores 90 percent correct when a signal is really there and says yes 50 percent of the times when no signal is present. Person *B* "hits" on only 60 percent of the signal trials but gives a "false alarm" on only 20 percent of the no-signal trials. Whom would you choose to monitor the radar screen?

Obviously, person *B* is more cautious, and this attitude results in fewer hits—but also in fewer false alarms. We could instruct him to be less cautious or, equivalently, instruct person *A* to be more cautious. Our instructions would depend on the situation—false alarms could be disastrous if what is being detected is "enemy bombers," but they would not hurt as much if the stimulus is "defective merchandise." In the latter case, we might want a very high hit rate, i.e., we don't want many of our products going out to the public in defective condition, even if the high hit rate means a large number of false alarms—items we have to check even though they are in perfect condition. It is possible to train our perceiver to give us a high hit rate or a low false-alarm rate. We can modify his attitude easily enough. But who is the better perceiver? Can we answer that?

We can, if we are willing to accept the assumptions of signal detection theory (Green & Swets, 1966). We can bring persons *A* and *B* back into the laboratory and ask them to perform our yes-no detection task under each of, say, five conditions defined by the degree of cautiousness we specify—from "Be extremely cautious; don't say 'yes' unless absolutely sure" to "Say 'yes' if there is the most remote possibility that the signal was present." Each of the subjects is given a long series of trials under each of the five conditions. Figure 20-5 shows the hits (vertical axis) and the false alarms (horizontal axis) of two subjects under each of the conditions. For example, under the condition of extreme caution (shown by ● on the graph) subject *A* recognizes the signal 40 percent of the time and gives a false alarm (says "yes" when no signal is given) only 10 percent of the time; subject *B* shows a hit rate of 30 percent and a false-alarm rate of 12 percent. As the figure makes clear, when instructions call for less caution, the hit rate goes up and so does the false-alarm rate; this is true for both subjects. The responses of the subjects determine the bowed curves illustrated in Figure 20-5. If a person could not detect the signal at all, his performance would be represented by the diagonal line; he would say "yes" the same percentage of times regardless of whether the signal was present (hits) or not (false alarms).

These curves are called receiver-operating-characteristic curves—ROC curves for short. Just as the bowing of the curves indicates *some* detection (% hits > % false alarms), a curve that bows *more* than another indicates that that "receiver" is *more* sensitive than the other. So if person *A*'s curve is more bowed than person *B*'s, person *A* would be judged more accurate, better at perceiving, and more suitable for the job at the radar screen.

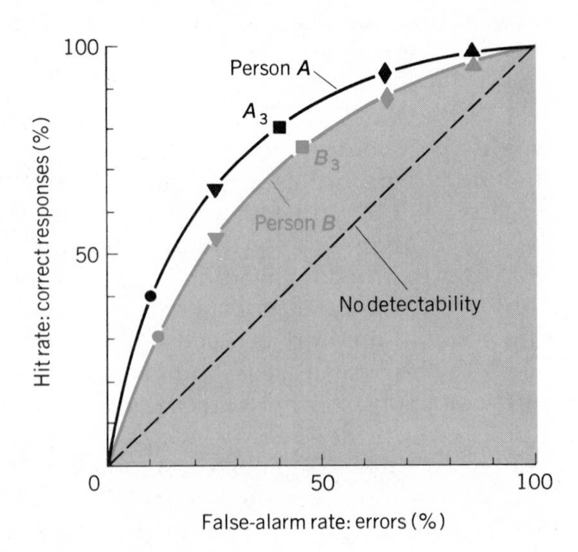

FIGURE 20-5 COMPARISON OF ROC CURVES

For any given error rate, person *A* scores more hits than does person *B*, so *A* is the better observer. The five conditions are shown by different symbols, with ● indicating extreme caution and ▲ indicating the least amount of caution.

The degree of bowing in a curve can be defined mathematically with a statistic called d' (dee prime), which reflects the area under the curve. Thus, in Figure 20-5, d' for subject B is the shaded area. A curve that is very bowed has more area beneath it, so d' is greater than for a slightly bowed curve. This single statistic, then, can be used as an estimate of a subject's sensitivity, i.e., his overall ability to detect a signal of a given strength. Similarly, if two stimuli are used, one stronger than the other, we can draw an ROC curve for each stimulus, and d' would be greater for the stronger signal. This of course would indicate that the stronger stimulus is more easily detectable.

Thus, signal detection theory gives us a way of estimating the perceptual ability of a subject or the relative detectability of, say, a weak tone compared to a weak flash of light. And these estimates are independent of the subject's attitudes or any factors (other than the stimulus intensity) that might influence his *decision* to report "yes" or "no." As such, the theory is obviously of immense value to perception psychologists.

We have presented signal detection theory here in a slightly different fashion from that in the chapter on memory (see p. 504). It would be instructive to read both presentations at one sitting, for together they give a more complete picture of the signal detection approach in psychology. In the memory presentation, d' was introduced in its more theoretical form; there it was shown to reflect the difference in familiarity between the means of two distributions of true and untrue statements (see Figure 19-2). Applying this kind of reasoning to sensory stimuli, for example weak tones to be detected, these two distributions would be the varying intensities of (1) background noise, and of (2) background noise plus a signal (see Figure 20-6). If the signal is relatively strong, then the difference, d', between the two distributions in Figure 20-6, will be great and the ROC curves, like the ones in Figure 20-5, will be strongly bowed. It is quite feasible to work out the ROC curve for a person and then to compute d' from it. The distributions of (1) background and of (2) stimulus plus background are harder to obtain, but when we compute d' from the ROC curve, we can assume that we are also estimating the difference between means in the underlying distributions of background noise and of stimulus plus background.

The decision criterion, β, reflects the intensity of a sound the subject is willing to report as "yes, there was a tone," and this criterion is affected by his attitude. By distinguishing d' and β, signal detection theory allows us to study the important *basic* characteristics of either perception (to what degree is the signal detectable?) or memory (to what degree was the item stored?)—separate from the decision to be cautious or not in the judgments.

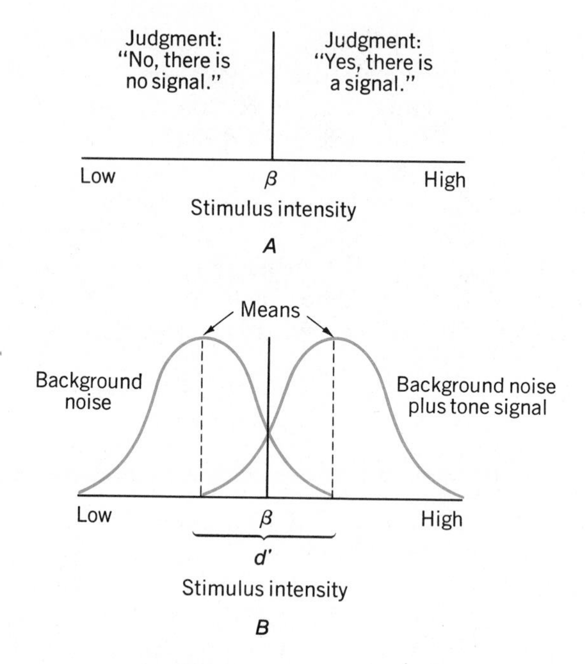

FIGURE 20-6 SIGNAL DETECTION MEASURES

A. When the intensity of the stimulus is high, the subject answers, "Yes, there is a signal." When the intensity is low, he answers, "No." β represents the criterion or cutoff point for the amount of intensity the subject *decides* is necessary and minimal for an answer of "Yes."
B. Both among trials when there is only noise and among trials when there is actually a signal, the stimulus intensity varies. This presumably forms two relatively normal distributions—one for background noise alone and the other for noise plus signal. The difference between means of these distributions is d'. Usually d' is small enough that some overlap between the distributions occurs, and this makes it impossible to set a cutoff point (β) that will permit a correct response for every trial.

How sensitive are we, relatively?

Often we want to know whether two stimuli are effectively the same or whether there is a just noticeable difference between them. Do these two color chips match? Is this violin tuned correctly? What is the lowest line on the eye chart for which you can distinguish the letters accurately? Is one of these lights slightly brighter than the other?

Weber's Law

In the middle of the last century, the German physiologist E. H. Weber worked on the ability to perform such discriminations; he measured what are called **difference thresholds.** Weber found that it is the relative amount of change, not the absolute amount, that determines perceptibility. For example, Weber observed that even though you can just notice that it has gotten brighter if one candle is added to 60 that are already lit, you will not notice the addition of one candle to 120. It would take at least two more candles before you can detect that it has gotten brighter. Comparably, if 300 are already burning, you would have to add at least five more candles to notice that it is any brighter. This principle, which Fechner later called **Weber's law,** can be symbolized by the simple formula

$$\frac{\Delta I}{I} = k.$$

This equation states that the smallest detectable increment in the intensity of a stimulus (ΔI or delta I) is a constant *proportion* (k) of the intensity of the stimulus already present (I); in the example of brightness above

$$\left(\frac{1}{60}, \frac{2}{120}, \frac{5}{300}\right), \text{ or } k = \frac{1}{60}.$$

This law holds very well in the middle ranges of intensity, though it breaks down somewhat at the extremes (at very low and very high intensities you have to add a bit more than the formula indicates in order to notice a change). The constant k is different for different dimensions, but can be readily determined by discovering by what proportion a stimulus must be changed in order to yield a **just noticeable difference** (or *jnd,* as it is often symbolized). This fraction turns out to be about 1/10 for the intensity of a tone, 1/7 for pressure on the skin, 1/50 for lifted weights, 1/5 for the saltiness of a liquid, and 1/333 for the frequency of a tone, to list a few. One could argue that Weber's law was one of the first clear demonstrations of relativity in psychology.

How do our sensory systems function?

Now let us consider some of the special features of the different sensory systems. We will take up vision first and in greatest detail, then we will turn to audition, and finally we will say a bit about other senses.

Vision

The visual system, consisting of the eyes and a whole series of intricate associated neural structures, is sensitive to only a very narrow band of the electromagnetic spectrum (which contains X-rays, radar, and radio waves as well as the visible spectrum—see Figure 20-7). Nevertheless, the visual system performs a whole host of functions. It organizes the wealth of information it receives (as we shall elaborate in the next two chapters); it can discriminate a wide range of brightnesses, can detect minute differences in form, discriminate among thousands of colors, and even mediate various experiences that don't reflect "real" input, such as afterimages. Let us take up each of these functions in turn.

The wide range of intensities over which the eye can function is shown in Figure 20-8. The most intense light that the eye can bear is over *ten billion* times as intense as the dimmest light you can see when your eyes are adapted to darkness. In logarithmic terms, this range is expressed as "10 units" and reflects the "total" range of sensitivity. At any one time, however, the "effective" range of sensitivity is much less (about 2 logarithmic units—where the most intense light is about one hundred times as intense as the dimmest). This is

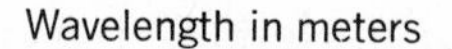
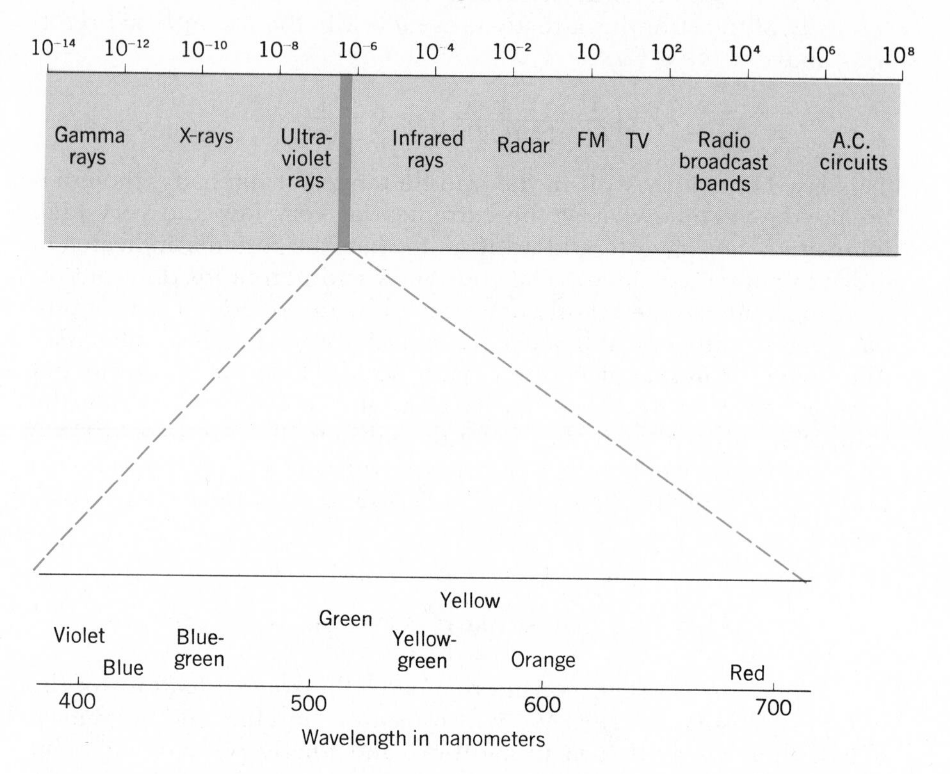

FIGURE 20-7
THE ELECTROMAGNETIC SPECTRUM AND THE VISIBLE SPECTRUM

The lower part, the visible spectrum, is an expansion of a small region of the upper electromagnetic spectrum. It is only this narrow range—from about 400 to 700 nanometers—that the visual system processes as light.
(After Chapanis, Garner, & Morgan, 1949)

because of adaptation of the eyes to the average level of stimulation at that time by such processes as an increase or decrease in pupil size and biological changes in the sensitivity of receptor cells. If our eyes are adapted to intense stimuli, we can distinguish between a very intense and a moderately intense stimulus. But if we are adapted to weak light, as when we come out of a dark movie theater at midday, the lights around us will all be relatively intense and will "hurt"; few of them can be distinguished until our eyes readapt to our new environment.

What Determines Brightness?

The main determinant of the perception of brightness is the *intensity* of the stimulus, but brightness is also a function of the *wavelength* of the light. Different parts of the visible spectrum yield experiences that differ in brightness as well as in color; the middle of the visible spectrum appears brighter than the ends at the same light intensity. Figure 20-9 shows that the curve of relative brightness is different in the light-adapted and the dark-adapted eye. As the eye adapts to darkness, its relative sensitivity shifts toward the shorter wavelengths. That part of the visible spectrum that produces the experience of "green" appears brightest to the dark-adapted eye, while the yellow wavelengths look brightest to the light-adapted eye. You

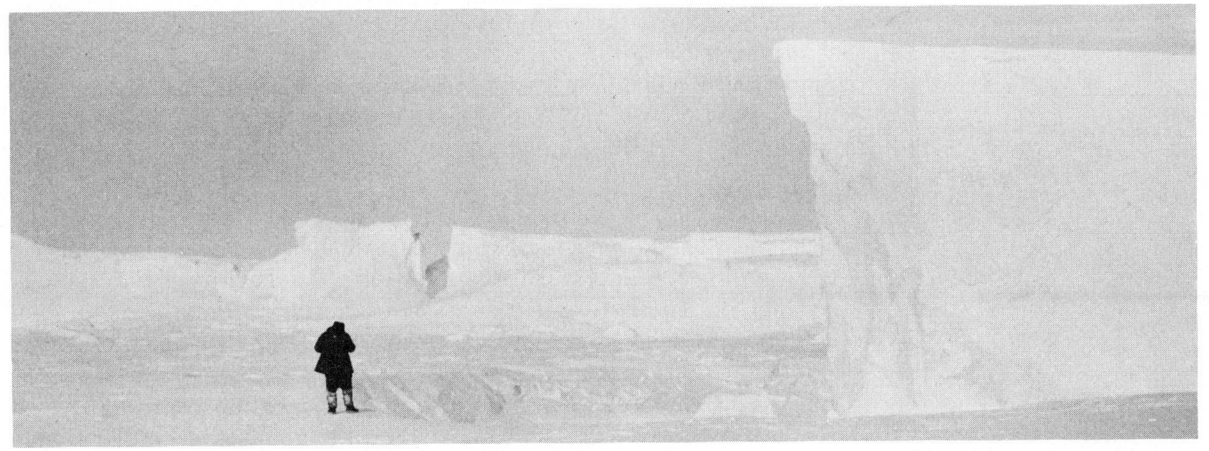

Glare from snow and ice results in a most intense stimulus to the eye.
(Coast & Geodetic Survey)

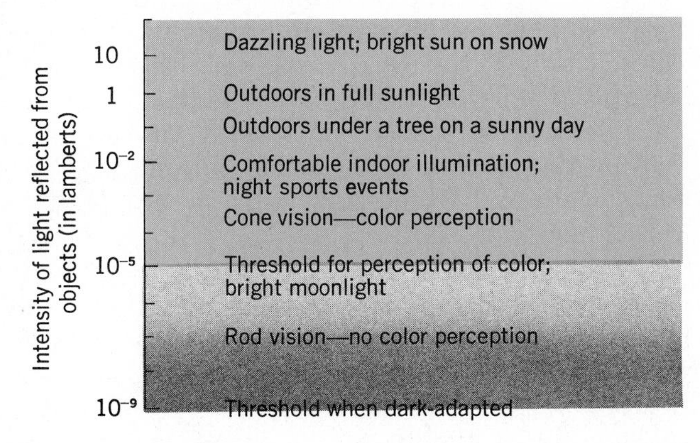

FIGURE 20-8
EYE'S RANGE OF SENSITIVITY TO LIGHT

The range from the most intense to the weakest visible stimulus is over ten billion times, or over 10 logarithmic units (10^{10} lamberts). At any one time, however, the eye adapts to the prevailing level of illumination and can discriminate over a range of only about 2 log units (10^2 lamberts).

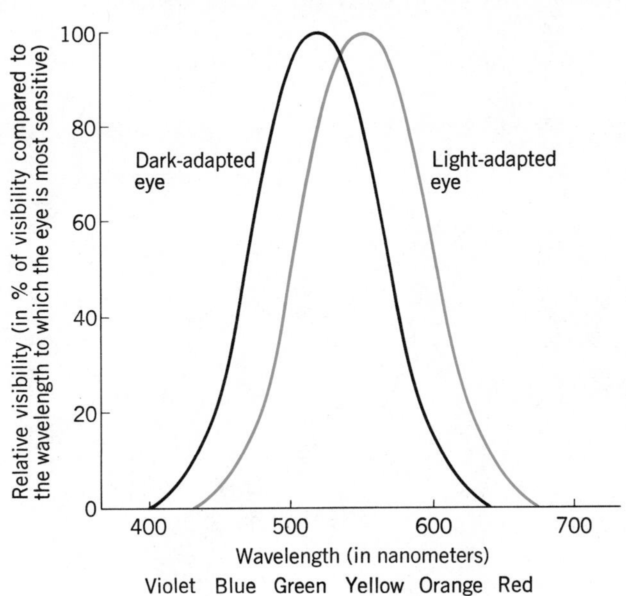

FIGURE 20-9
BRIGHTNESS AS A FUNCTION OF WAVELENGTH OF LIGHT

Note that the sensitivity curve of the light-adapted eye is different from that of the dark-adapted eye. The former is maximally sensitive to wavelengths around 550 nanometers (a slightly greenish-yellow), the latter to wavelengths around 510 (in the green portion of the spectrum).

may have noticed that some colors seem to "come out" at night or that clothing bought inside a store seems literally to change color outside in bright sunlight. These effects are caused by changes in brightness of certain colors as the eye adapts to changes in the predominant level of illumination.

VISUAL ACUITY The doctor's eye chart, designed to estimate your need for glasses, is a test of the resolving power of the eye. In more technical terms, your visual spatial **acuity** is being measured. If you can distinguish at 20 feet what the normal eye can distinguish at 20 feet, your vision is 20:20. If you can distinguish only at 20 feet or less what the normal eye can see at 200 feet, your vision is 20:200 – and you should be fitted with corrective lenses.

Psychologists use a variety of methods to study visual acuity (see Figure 20-10). They are interested in how acuity varies when the image is projected on different parts of the retina. As Figure 20-11 indicates, acuity is greatest at the center of the retina, the **fovea,** and drops sharply when you focus slightly to the left or right of the stimulus. In other words, your vision looking straight ahead might be 20:20, but for objects slightly off in the periphery, your vision is much poorer, something like the 20:200 of a near-sighted person for objects in direct focus.

These statements, however, apply only to vision in reasonably intense stimulation. The cells in the center of the retina are blind at low illuminations, so in darkness acuity is better slightly to the periphery. This means, among other things, that if you want to get the clearest possible image of a faint star or a distant dim light at night, you should look slightly to one side of it rather than directly at it.

Notice also in Figure 20-11 that in one area of the retina

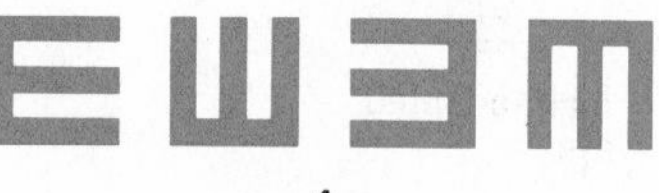

FIGURE 20-10 PATTERNS FOR MEASURING VISUAL ACUITY

In *A*, the viewer must indicate which way the letter *E* is pointing, in *B*, where the break in the circle is. In *C*, he reports the letters that he can read, and in *D* he must indicate which line is broken. Typically, method *D* yields the best (most discriminating) acuity measures.

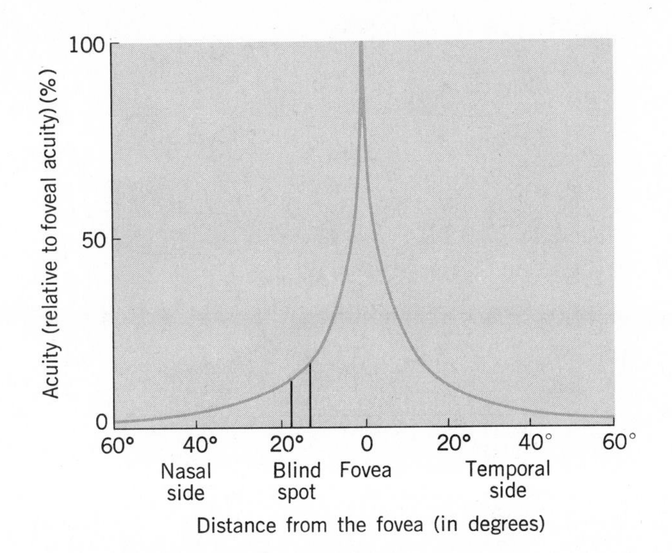

FIGURE 20-11
HOW VISUAL ACUITY VARIES ACROSS THE EYE

In daylight vision, acuity is best in the center of the retina, the "fovea." Taking foveal acuity as 100, and then testing acuity at other positions, we find that it drops off rapidly toward the periphery. That is why we use the fovea to look at objects and to read. Acuity is zero at the blind spot, the place where the optic nerve leaves the eyeball and where there are no retinal receptors.

acuity drops to zero. This is the blind spot of the eye where the "transmission lines" of the retinal receptors all congregate and exit from the eye to transmit their messages to the brain. Every eye has a blind spot, though we are rarely aware of the fact. Figure 12 in the preview shows you how to demonstrate its existence in your own eyes.

THE DOUBLE RETINA The difference between the locus of best acuity for the light- and dark-adapted eye and other differences (such as those represented in Figure 20-9) indicate that the human eye is functionally two different eyes—one for bright light and color vision and the other for dim light. From biological research, we know that there are actually two different sets of receptor cells in the retina—"cones" for daylight color vision and "rods" for dim light.

In addition to the differences already mentioned, many others exist between the eye that has been exposed to the dark for a long time and the eye that has been in daylight. The completely dark-adapted eye cannot see colors; it is sensitive only to differences in intensity. Only the light-adapted eye sees colors.

The shift from the light-adapted to the dark-adapted eye takes a long time (it is not complete even after one hour in total darkness), but the shift in the other direction goes quite quickly: the eye is fully light-adapted within only about two minutes after going from a dark movie theater into the bright sunlight. The shift in sensitivity between the dark- and the light-adapted eye is of an extraordinarily large order of magnitude. The dark-adapted eye is about a hundred thousand times more sensitive than the light-adapted eye.

As Figure 20-12 shows, the increase in sensitivity during adaptation to darkness is quite rapid at first, and then slows down;

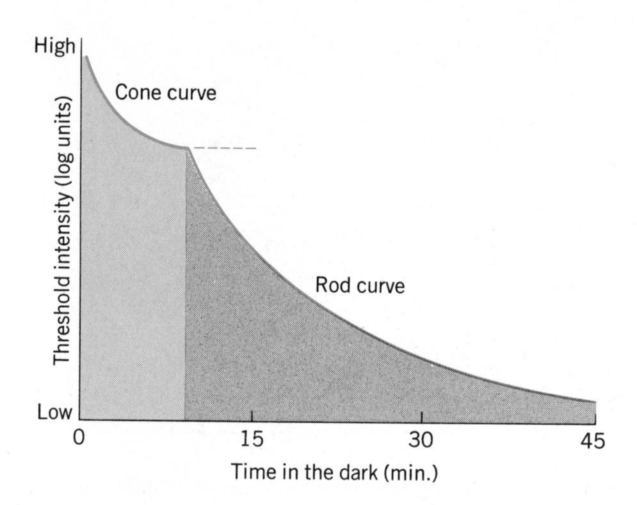

FIGURE 20-12 THE DARK-ADAPTATION FUNCTION

The curve shows the threshold intensity (the smallest amount of light energy that can be detected) as a function of length of time in darkness. The rate of increase in sensitivity rather closely parallels the rate at which sunlight fades at dusk. Note also the discontinuity in the curve, due to adaptation of the cones first and then of the rods.

furthermore, there is a discontinuity after about ten minutes in the dark. The first part of the dark-adaptation function is due to the adaptation of the cones, the later one to the adaptation of the rods. But we are getting ahead of ourselves; we will consider this duplex function of the eye in more detail in the section on biological psychology.

What Determines Color Vision?

The eye adapted to daylight can discriminate a very wide range of colors, hues, and tints. In fact, our language does not come close to having enough words to identify all of the different colors that the eye can distinguish. This ability to discriminate colors is not distributed evenly across the retina. The center of the retina, the fovea, on which is focused whatever it is that you are looking directly at, is the retina's most sensitive part. The periphery of the eye, on which is projected what you in effect see "out of the corner of your eye," turns out not to have any color discrimination at all. As a stimulus is gradually brought in from far out in the periphery toward the fovea, you at first detect only that something is moving, and can't tell its color, shape, or brightness. Next comes an area in which you can tell how bright the visual stimulus is, but still can't tell its color or its exact shape. Next, as the stimulus moves farther in, its shape becomes clearer, and you can distinguish blues from yellows, but can't tell reds from greens. Finally, you get to the region in which shape is clear and all of the color discriminations are possible, including the red-green distinction. You can test this with a partner by having him look straight ahead and try to describe small colored objects as you bring them in from his side toward the center of his field of vision.

WAVELENGTH EFFECTS The perception of a specific color or hue, for people who are not color-blind, is directly related to the wavelength of the visual stimulus, as shown in Figure 20-7. Most of the objects in our world are colored the way we perceive them because they reflect to our eyes the wavelengths related to their colors. Rarely does an object reflect a pure (unmixed) wavelength, but the dominant wavelengths determine the experience of hue. A leaf looks green because it reflects more of the wavelengths in one region of the spectrum than in the other regions. (We could say that the leaf reflects principally "green" wavelengths, if we were careful to note that the wavelengths themselves are not green but that these wavelengths [around 500 nm] are most apt to evoke a response of "green" in human observers.) Similarly, a bluebird's feathers look blue because the pigment in them absorbs most wavelengths and selectively reflects back into your eyes more of the "blue" region of the spectrum. Selective absorption and reflection also explain why an apple looks red and an orange, orange; indeed why anything appears to have the color it has.

By superimposing visual stimuli of various wavelengths, we can study how the eye responds to mixed colors. If we place a red filter in front of a projector, this filter removes proportionately more of the "nonred" wavelengths emitted by the lamp, and transmits onto the screen a light whose composition includes a relatively high intensity of the wavelengths in the "red" part of the spectrum. Comparably, a green filter does the same thing for the "green" wavelengths. What happens, now, if we project a circle of "red" light upon a screen in such a way that it is superimposed upon a circle of "green" light? What will be the result of adding the "red" and the "green" wavelengths? If the wavelength composition of the "red" and the "green" lights are chosen appropriately, their addition will produce a response of yellow, as you can see in color Figure 1.

The result of mixing lights is quite different from mixing pigments, as in water colors. Colored lights *add* their dominant wavelengths to the mixture, while colored pigments *subtract* (i.e., absorb) wavelengths other than those that give the pigment its particular hue. Compare color Figures 1 and 2 to see the difference. The **law of complementaries** states that complementary colors are those that when added produce an experience of white or gray (depending on brightness); examples are shown in the **color circle** (Figure 20-13); any two colors directly opposite each other in the circle (e.g., yellow and blue-violet) are complementary. If lights of these colors are added, the result will be white. If, however, the two colors are not directly opposite, the hue resulting from the combination will be midway between the two on the color circle. In a **subtractive mixture,** as results when an artist mixes blue and yellow paints, the result is a pigment that looks green. A number of the principles of **additive color mixture** are efficiently summarized in the color circle (see Figure 20-13 and color Figure 3). All of the colors in the circle are equally bright; gray is located at the center of the circle, and the hues are arranged around its circumference. The caption of the figure gives some of the laws of color mixture that the circle symbolizes.

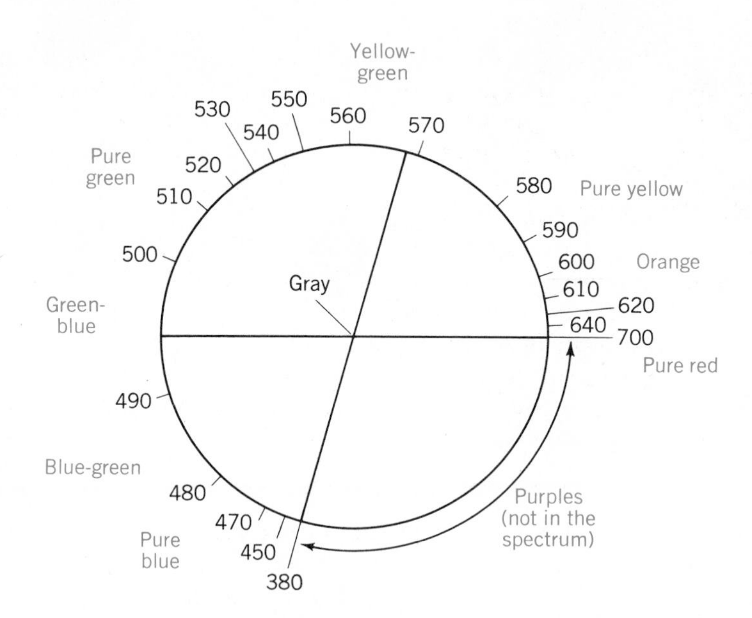

FIGURE 20-13
THE COLOR CIRCLE

The hues (and their corresponding spectral wavelengths) are arranged around the circumference of the circle; saturation decreases toward the center of the circle. Colors located opposite each other are complementary; if they are mixed in the right proportions, the mixture will look white or gray. Mixtures of colors that are not opposite each other on the circle yield intermediate colors lying on a straight line connecting the two mixed colors. Colors in the upper left sector have no complementary hues in the spectrum. All the colors in the circle, including the center neutral gray, are equally bright. Unequal mixtures of complementaries yield the color of the dominant component at a reduced saturation.

PSYCHOLOGICAL RESPONSES The circle conveys information about two of the three main psychological dimensions of color, hue and saturation. **Hue** is the dimension that distinguishes red from yellow or green from blue. **Saturation** refers to the richness versus paleness of color; it is the dimension that varies, for example, from red to pink to gray. As you go from the periphery of the color circle to the center, saturation decreases. The color circle omits the third dimension of color—**brightness** (or where a color falls on the white-black dimension). The third dimension can be added to the color circle, yielding a **color solid**, which contains all discriminable colors within its volume (see Figure 20-14). The solid is a double cone, with white at the top and black at the bottom. It is narrow at the top and bottom and wider in the middle, because very bright and very dark colors (those close to white or to black) cannot be as saturated as those of moderate brightness can be. The circle forming the bases of both cones is tilted, with yellow closer to white and blue closer to black, because a maximally saturated yellow is brighter than a maximally saturated blue. Also, yellow is never as saturated as is a rich blue or green or red, so the cones are not symmetrical around the vertical axis.

Color experiences are not produced only by stimulation with particular wavelengths of light. Pressure on the eyeball, the ingestion of various toxic substances, minute electric currents applied to the eye, or a blow on the head can all yield the experience of highly-saturated, brilliant colors. This shows that the color arises within the observer and is not given by the visual stimulus.

Prolonged exposure to particular stimuli can also lead to the experience of colors after the initial stimulation is terminated. If you stare at a brilliant red patch for about a half-minute and then

PERCEPTION

FIGURE 1
ADDITIVE COLOR MIXTURE

Three projectors cast circles of red, green, and blue light, and these are made to overlap on a colorless background. The areas of overlap show what hues result when different wavelengths are added to each other in this way. For example, red light plus green light yields yellow. Where all three circles overlap in the center, the addition of red plus green plus blue yields white.

FIGURE 2
SUBTRACTIVE COLOR MIXTURE

Pigments absorb light, and different pigments absorb different parts of the spectrum. A red pigment absorbs light from most of the spectrum and allows chiefly "red" wavelengths to be reflected back to the observer's eye. When pigments are mixed, the mixture absorbs the wavelengths absorbed by each of the pigments; therefore the more pigments are used, the darker the mixture appears. The combination of red, yellow, and blue pigments (in the center) absorbs almost all the light and therefore appears black. Note that this effect is the opposite from addition of lights above where all three lights together yield white.

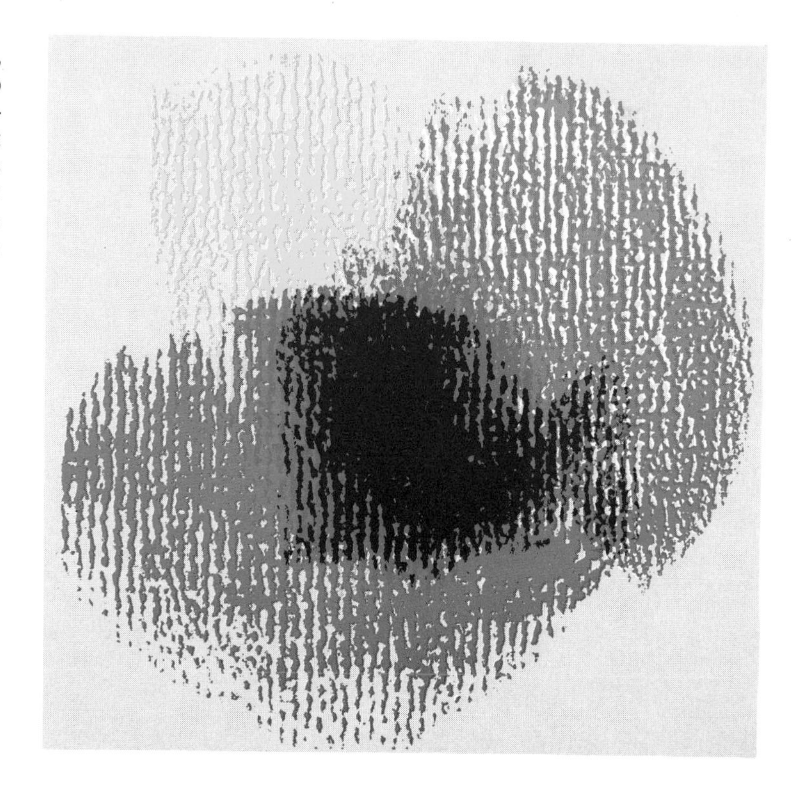

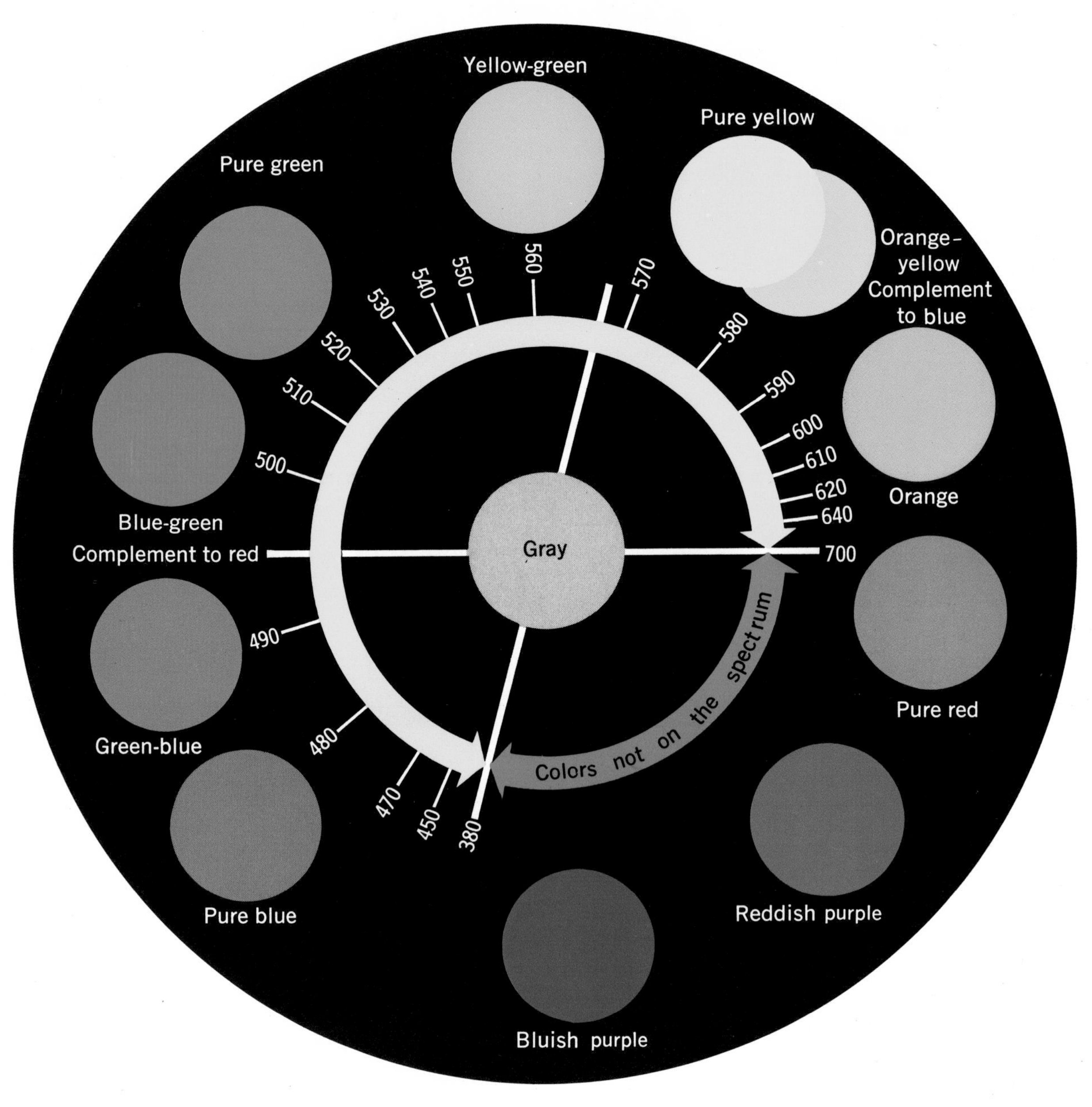

FIGURE 3
THE COLOR CIRCLE

All the hues of the rainbow, and more besides, are placed in order around the color circle. Complementary hues are placed directly opposite each other; thus green-blue (produced by light of wavelength 490 nanometers) is the complement of orange (607 nm). Green has no complementary hue in the spectrum; its complement is purple, which cannot be produced by a single wavelength of light. Two complementary lights, if added together in the proper proportions, will produce neutral gray. If you stare at any of the discs of color for half a minute and then shift your gaze to a neutral background, you will see an afterimage of the complementary hue.

Courtesy National Bureau of Standards

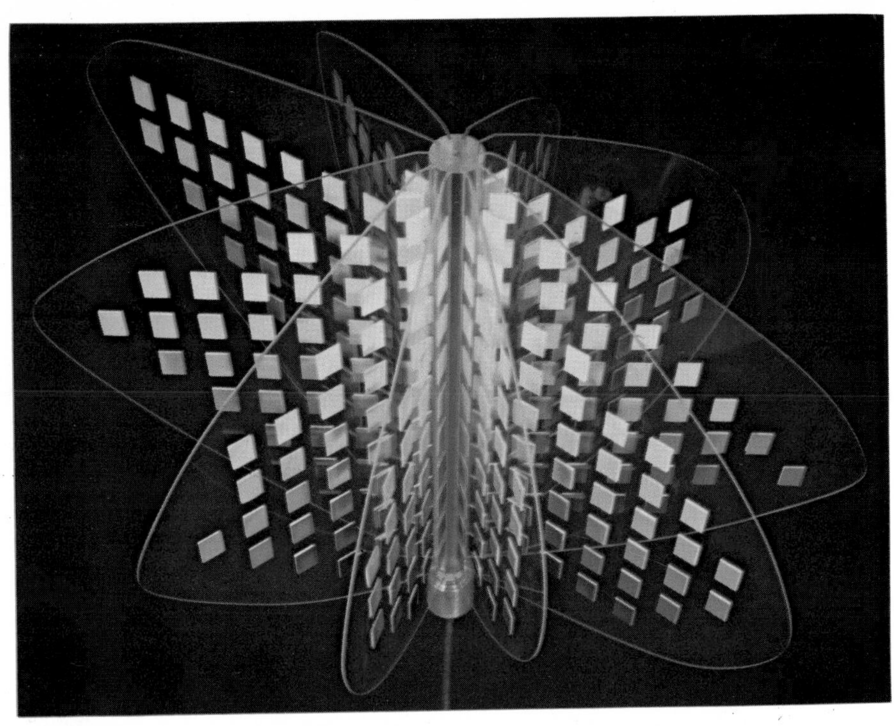

FIGURE 4
THE COLOR SOLID SHOWS THE THREE DIMENSIONS OF COLOR

Hue varies around the perimeter of the color solid, as it does in the color circle on the opposite page. **Saturation** varies from the perimeter to the center; that is, colors are rich and vivid at the outside but become paler as you follow any radius in toward the center. **Brightness** varies along the vertical axis. The color circle is a horizontal section through the color solid.

A vertical section through the color solid is shown below. It has brighter colors toward the top and darker colors toward the bottom, richly saturated colors at the edges and neutral gray in the center, and the yellow hue to the left is the complement of the blue hue to the right.

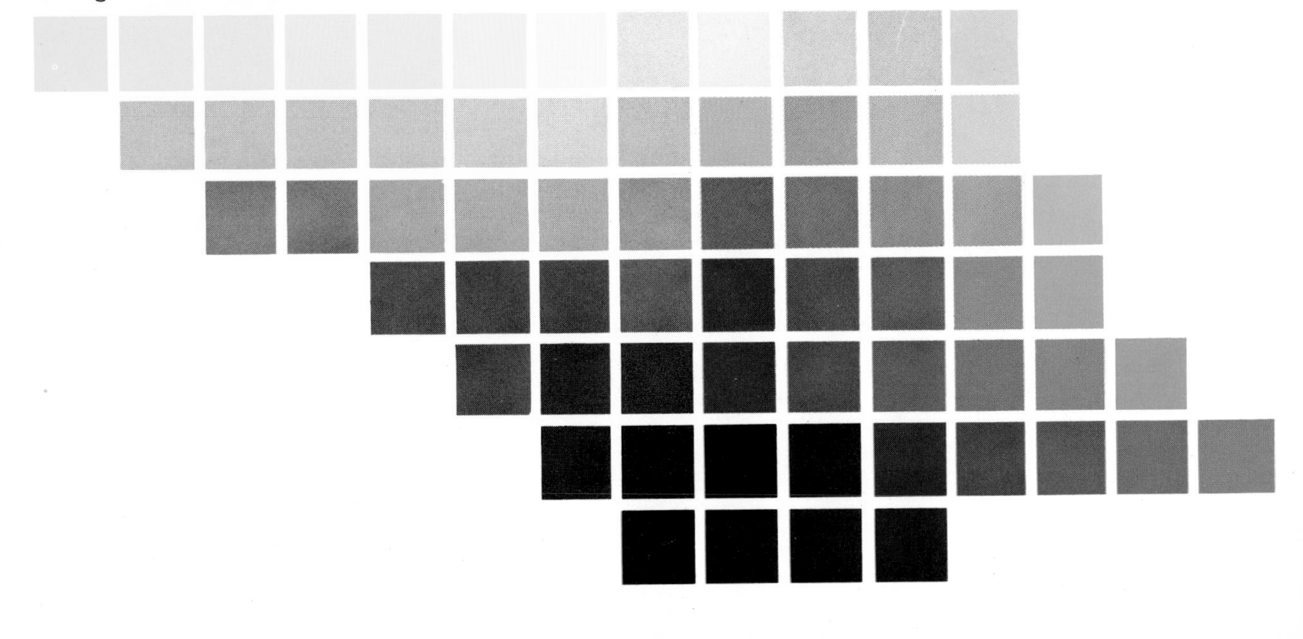

FIGURE 5
SIMULTANEOUS COLOR CONTRAST

The three gray circles are identical physically, but they appear to have slightly different hues because they are on three different backgrounds. The hue induced in each circle is the complement of the hue of the background. This effect is enhanced if you blur the contour separating circle and background somewhat — by squinting your eyes or by laying a piece of onionskin paper over the figure.

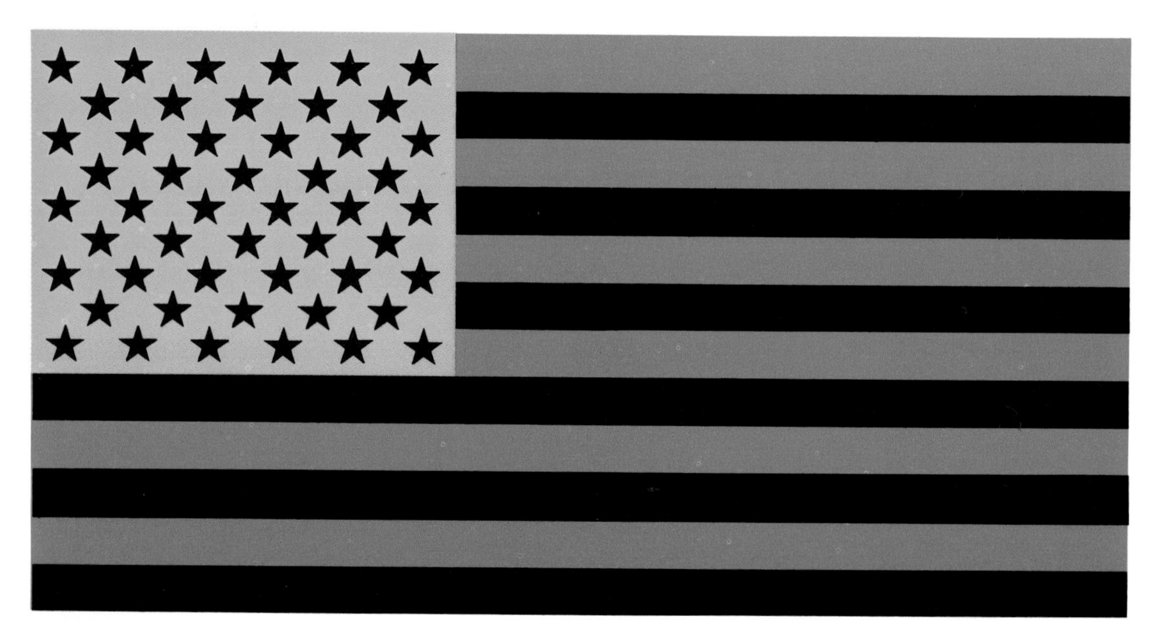

FIGURE 6
AN AFTERIMAGE AMERICAN FLAG

Keep your eyes fixed on the bottom right corner of the orange field for about thirty seconds, then quickly shift your gaze to a point on a neutral (gray or white) surface. The complementary afterimages of the colors will yield a more familiar experience.

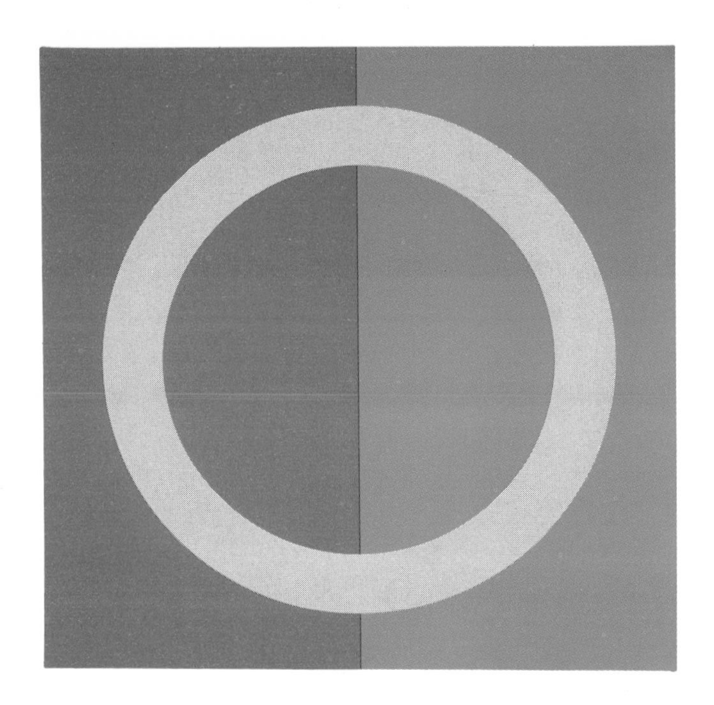

FIGURE 7
SIMULTANEOUS COLOR CONTRAST

First look at the gray circle and see whether its left and right halves appear the same or different from each other. Then separate the two halves by laying a pencil along the vertical line between the red and green backgrounds, and compare the two halves of the circle again. Now move the pencil back and forth a little to the right and a little to the left of the midline and observe what happens. It appears that color contrast depends not only on the colors but also on the way in which the figure is divided.

FIGURE 8
THE BLIND SPOT

How many apples do you see? It depends on how you look. This figure allows you to locate the blind spot (the place where nerve fibers leave the eyeball; there are no receptor cells where this "cable" goes through the retina). The figure also shows how a pattern is "filled in" or "completed" across the blind spot. Close your left eye and look at the yellow apple, holding the book about fifteen inches in front of your eyes. Adjust the distance until the red apple disappears. Does this leave a "hole" in the checkered background or does it appear to be continuous? Now repeat the procedure, closing your right eye and looking at the red apple. The fact that the background pattern appears continuous when the apple disappears is an example of the principle of Prägnanz discussed in Chapter 21.

FIGURE 9
DAY VISION AND NIGHT VISION

The eye perceives differently in daylight and at night. At daylight levels of illumination, the cone receptors of the eye function and we see different hues. In dim illumination the rod receptors of the retina take over; they are color-blind and so we see only varying shades of gray.

"Sunday Afternoon on the Island of La Grand Jatte" by Georges Seurat
Helen Birch Bartlett Memorial Collection, Courtesy of the Art Institute of Chicago

FIGURE 10
DOTS ORGANIZED INTO FORMS

When you look at the enlarged detail from this pointillist painting by Seurat, you can see that it is made up of small juxtaposed spots of different colors. But when you look at the painting from a distance, the dots seem to merge together and you see forms clearly. This can be understood in terms of the principles of perceptual organization and of figure formation.

FIGURE 11

Our perceptions of the world — how do they depend on these factors:

- — the stimuli that reach our sense organs?
- — our active attempts to organize and understand the flux of sensory information?
- — our sensory and neural mechanisms?

Findings and theories concerning the first two questions are discussed in Section 7 (Chapters 20–22), and the third question is taken up in Chapter 24 of Section 8.

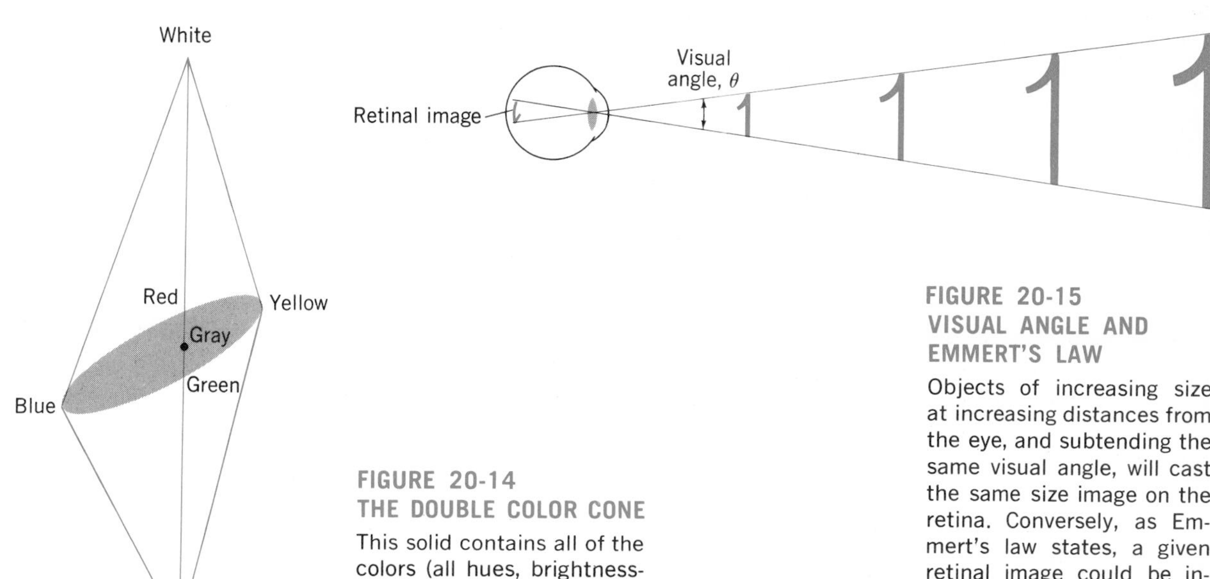

FIGURE 20-14
THE DOUBLE COLOR CONE

This solid contains all of the colors (all hues, brightnesses, and saturations), and it illustrates how the colors are related to each other.

FIGURE 20-15
VISUAL ANGLE AND EMMERT'S LAW

Objects of increasing size at increasing distances from the eye, and subtending the same visual angle, will cast the same size image on the retina. Conversely, as Emmert's law states, a given retinal image could be interpreted as due to any of an infinite number of "objects" of various sizes at different distances from the eye, as long as they all subtend the same visual angle, θ; the apparent size of the "object" will increase directly with its apparent distance.

look at a neutral gray or white section of wall or at a blank sheet of white paper, you will see floating there mysteriously an eerie green **afterimage** of the red object. Comparably, a strong yellow stimulus will produce a blue afterimage. (The color circle in Figure 20-13 helps to predict these effects; a **negative afterimage** is always complementary in color to the inducing stimulus.)

A rather striking instance of a negative afterimage is the complementary-colored American flag in the color section (Figure 6). The size of such negative afterimages, incidentally, varies with the distance of the surface upon which they are "projected." You can demonstrate this readily for yourself by developing a good afterimage, and then projecting it on the page of a book, on a near wall, and on a farther wall. The farther away you project it, the larger it seems to be.

The fact that the apparent size of an afterimage is directly related to its apparent distance is known as **Emmert's law.** This law is readily explained. The afterimage is due to a kind of "fatiguing" of particular retinal cells by the inducing stimulus. If this local retinal image is projected at different distances, it must correspond to "objects" of different sizes, since the same visual angle corresponds to different sizes at different distances (see Figure 20-15). In other words, a large tree far away might produce the same size image on your retina as a small tree close by, but the large tree looks larger nevertheless. So when the same image is projected on a near or far screen, that on the far screen looks larger. (See the discussion of constancies in perception in the next chapter, p. 574.)

Hearing

Just as the human visual system is capable of some astounding achievements, so too is the auditory system. Just as the visual system can respond to a very small number of quanta of light, comparably the auditory system can, under optimal conditions, respond to a vibration of the eardrum as minute as one tenth the diameter of a hydrogen atom.

While the visual system is sensitive to a particular narrow band in the electromagnetic spectrum, the auditory system is tuned to a range of wavelengths in a different spectrum, that of pressure waves. These waves, composed of successive condensations and rarefactions of the medium that is carrying them—usually the molecules of the air—are typically produced by a vibrating body. The simplest kind of a sound vibration consists of a single frequency, as occurs when a tuning fork is struck. In this case, the condensations and rarefactions of the air molecules can be described by a simple mathematical function—the sine function of trigonometry. Sine waves are shown in Figure 20-16. A complex sound, such as that of a musical instrument or the human voice, can be analyzed into the sum of a number of sine wave components; the amplitude and frequency of each of these components can be specified, so as to provide a complete

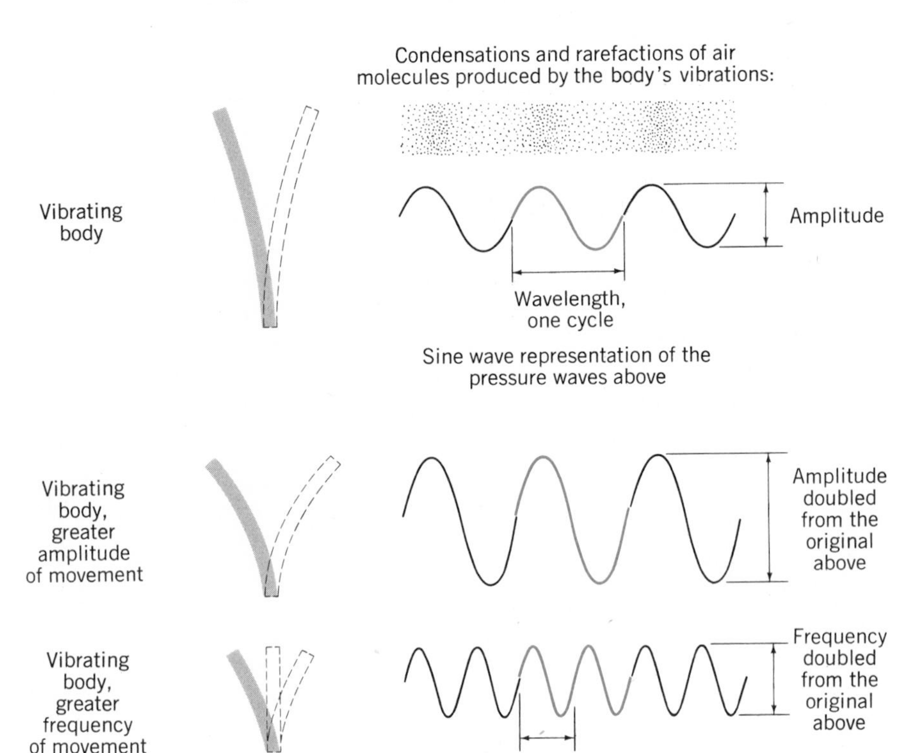

FIGURE 20-16
THE AUDITORY STIMULUS
A vibrating body produces pressure waves in the surrounding medium. Here a pure tone with a single frequency of vibration is shown. The larger the vibration, the greater is the amplitude of the waves. The more frequent the vibration, the more closely spaced are the waves (that is, the shorter is their wavelength).

physical description of the sound. The amplitude of the sound wave is usually measured in **decibels** (db), and the **frequency** of a tone is measured in **hertz** (Hz) or cycles per second. If you are not familiar with the basic physics of sound, study Figure 20-16.

A complex sound can be analyzed into a pattern of frequencies at various intensities. For example, the rustling sound produced by a six-year-old stomping enthusiastically through a pile of leaves is a noise composed of many different simultaneous frequencies at fairly low intensities. A foghorn has more low-frequency components than high-frequency components, while the sound of a whistling teakettle has more high- than low-frequency components. A musical tone, by contrast, has a much more circumscribed sound spectrum; energy is present only at a certain frequency and its multiples (see Figure 20-17). Middle C, for example, has the frequency of 256 Hz (or cycles per second). This fundamental frequency is the same whether middle C is played on a piano, on a violin, on a clarinet, or sung by the human voice, but there is also energy at some of the overtones (the frequencies that are multiples of the fundamental tone; for middle C they are 512, 768, 1024, 1280, and so on). The relative intensities of the various overtone frequencies differ among the various instruments; that is what gives them their **timbre** or distinctive sound quality.

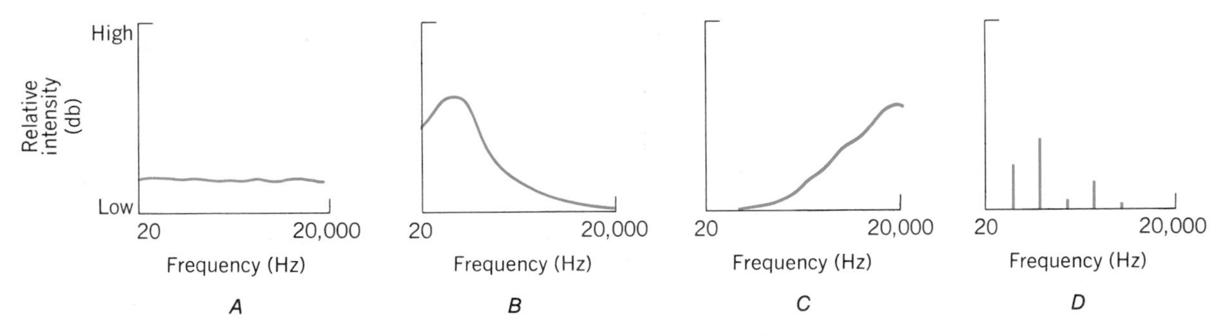

FIGURE 20-17 FREQUENCY COMPOSITIONS OF SOME COMMON SOUNDS
Shown are approximate sound spectra, showing the amplitude or relative intensity of various frequencies present in the sound, for *A*, a child rustling leaves; *B*, a nearby foghorn; *C*, a whistling teakettle; and *D*, a tone played on a musical instrument.

What Determines Loudness?

A major determinant of **loudness** is, of course, the **intensity** or amplitude of the stimulus. Stimulus intensity is measured in decibels, a logarithmic scale, and the intensities of several common sounds are shown in Figure 20-18. Note that some are near or exceed the threshold of pain, the level of intensity that most subjects report as "hurting." Prolonged exposure to high intensities can result in damage to the auditory system, and in laboratory animals prolonged exposure to very high intensities (around 150 db) has resulted in death.

But loudness does not increase linearly with sound intensity, just as brightness does not increase linearly with light in-

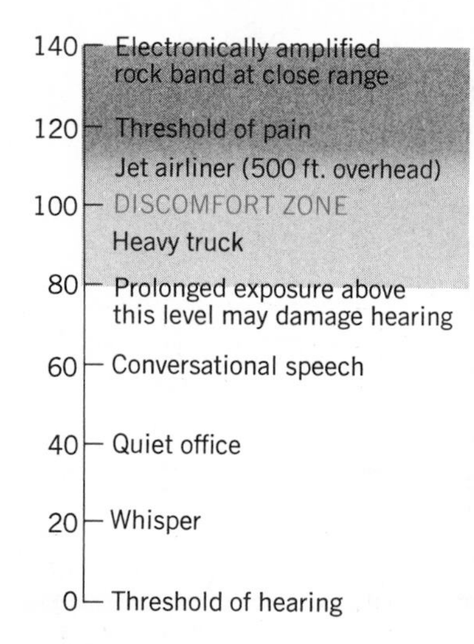

(Elliot Landy, Magnum)

FIGURE 20-18
INTENSITIES OF SOME COMMON SOUNDS

The stimulus intensity is measured in decibels.

tensity. Furthermore, just as brightness varies with the wavelength of light, so loudness also varies with the frequency of sound. Figure 20-19 shows how the threshold of hearing varies with the frequency of sound. A sound of 40 db intensity is inaudible if its frequency is much below 100 Hz; it is just about at threshold intensity at a frequency of 100 Hz, and it is about 40 db above threshold and within the range of conversational speech if its frequency is around 2,000 Hz.

The way in which loudness varies as a function of intensity is shown by Figure 20-20. Note that as intensity is increased above threshold, loudness increases very slowly at first and then (above 70 db) it rises rapidly. Because the decibel scale is useful in telephonic and engineering applications, it is sometimes believed that

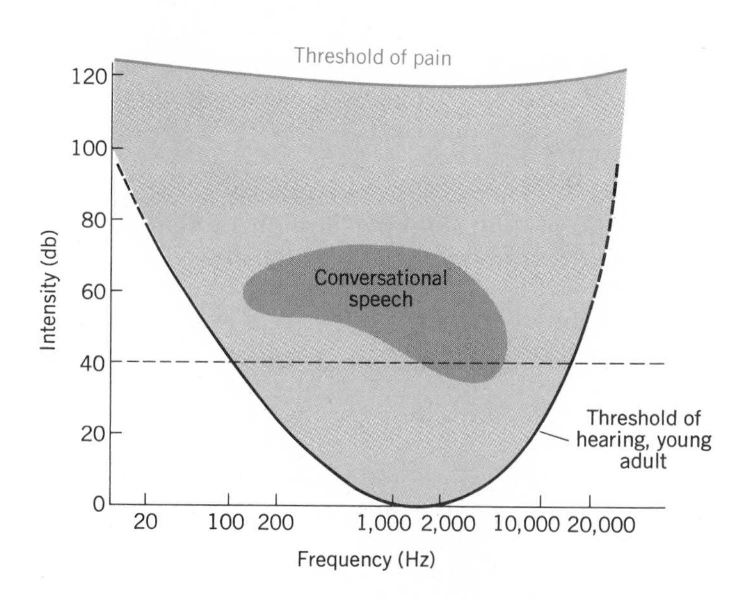

FIGURE 20-19
THRESHOLDS OF HEARING

The black line shows the minimum intensity required at each frequency in order for the tone to be barely audible. The darker central region shows the range of frequencies and intensities within which most speech sounds occur. If sound is too intense, as shown by the colored line at the top of the diagram, it becomes painful, and if prolonged can damage the inner ear. The dotted line at 40 db shows how loudness varies with frequency of sound: at frequencies below 100 Hz, a 40 db sound is below threshold, at 200 Hz it is about 20 db above threshold, and at 1,000 Hz it is 40 db above threshold.

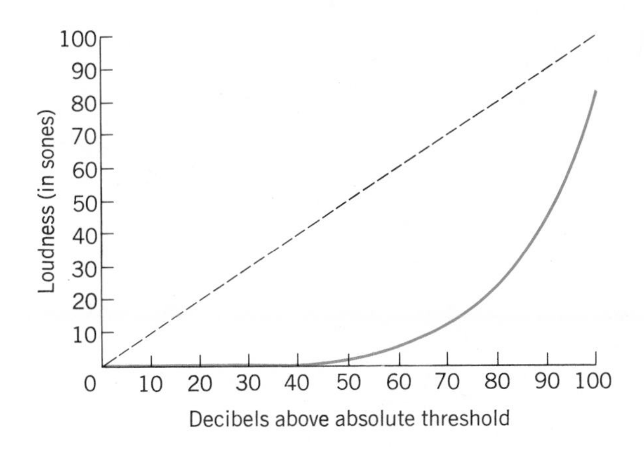

FIGURE 20-20 LOUDNESS AS A FUNCTION OF SOUND INTENSITY

The colored line represents judgments of loudness of a 1,000 Hz tone. A sound of 40 db intensity was taken as the standard; that is, a 1,000 Hz–40 db tone was assigned the loudness value of 1 sone. Note that loudness does not vary linearly with intensity in decibels; if it did, the loudness function would be the linear dashed line, but this is far from representing judgments of loudness.

it accurately represents perceived loudness, but this is clearly not the case. Fechner's law predicted a logarithmic response, like that shown by the dashed line in Figure 20-20. A more accurate representation is given by Stevens' power law, with an exponent of 0.3: Loudness = k Sound Intensity$^{0.3}$.

What Determines Pitch?

Besides loudness, the other main dimension of auditory experience is **pitch,** how low or how high the tone sounds. The frequency of the acoustic stimulus is the primary determinant of pitch, although stimuli of the same frequency sometimes sound higher or lower if intensity is varied. To provide a standard for pitch, a sound with a frequency of 1,000 Hz and an intensity of 40 db is said to have a pitch of 1,000 mels. (The name of the unit, the mel, comes from "melody.") That pitch is not a linear correlate of frequency is shown in Figure 20-21. A doubling of frequency in the middle range results in a greater change of pitch than does doubling at the lower or higher audible frequencies. It turns out that a tone of 2,200 Hz is judged as about twice as high as one of 1,000 Hz, and one of 4,000 Hz sounds about three times as high as one of 1,000 Hz; a tone of 550 Hz sounds about half as high as a 1,000 Hz tone, and one of 300 Hz, about a quarter as high as a 1,000 Hz tone, and so on.

The way that pitch changes with intensity is somewhat complex. Tones below about 800 Hz decrease in pitch as their intensity is increased; the lower the frequency, the steeper the drop in pitch with increased intensity. Conversely, tones above about 3,000 Hz increase in pitch as intensity increases, and this increase is steeper the higher the frequency.

We experience tones, even pure tones, as having qualities or attributes over and beyond pitch and loudness. Thus, one can, for example, speak of the "volume of a sound," not in the sense of its loudness, but of how much space it seems to fill. A low-intensity, high-frequency tone seems to be rather small, while an intense, low-frequency tone seems to be quite large. Thus while the "volume"

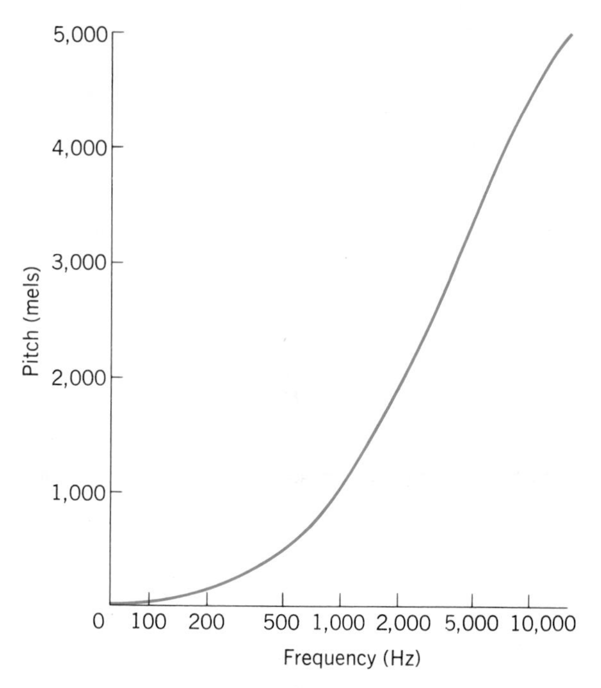

FIGURE 20-21
PITCH AS A FUNCTION OF FREQUENCY
This curve was generated by a magnitude estimation procedure. A tone 40 db above threshold, at 1,000 Hz, was defined as having a pitch of 1,000 mels; corresponding mel values of the other frequencies were determined by magnitude estimation. While the pitch of a tone increases with its frequency, the relationship is not linear (even with frequency represented logarithmically, as here).
(After Stevens, Volkmann, & Newman, 1937)

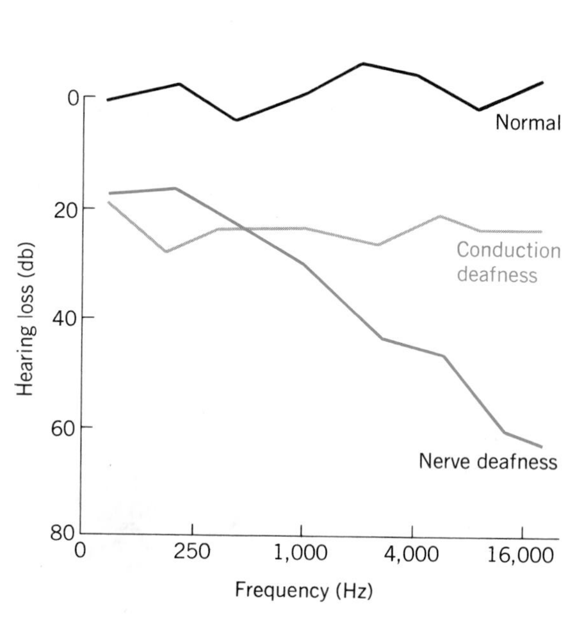

FIGURE 20-22
AUDIOGRAMS OF NORMAL AND HARD-OF-HEARING INDIVIDUALS
The figure shows how much each test frequency has to be increased in intensity, relative to the average normal individual, in order for the tone to be heard.

control knob on a television set or radio actually controls the intensity of the sound, it also affects the volume in the sense we have described. One can also speak of such things as the apparent "compactness or density" of a sound, a dimension which is yet a different function of its frequency and intensity.

Weber's law holds for the intensity of sounds about as well as for the intensity of the visual stimulus. A greater absolute change in intensity is required at higher levels of intensity than at lower ones in order for us to notice that the loudness has changed. For changes in intensity to be perceived as comparable, they must be in about the same proportional relation to the original intensity.

DEAFNESS Everyone becomes somewhat deaf as he gets older; the main form that the deafness produced by aging takes is a raised threshold for the higher frequencies. Clinically, two kinds of deafness can be distinguished (see Figure 20-22 for the pattern of hearing loss involved with each). A pattern of fairly uniform loss across all frequencies is usually due to some defect in the sound-conduction mechanism in the middle ear, such as a broken eardrum, malfunction of the ossicles in the middle ear (the tiny bones that transmit the vibrations from the eardrum to the cochlea of the inner ear, where the sound energy is transduced into neural activity), or stoppage of the auditory canal or the Eustachian tube. The other pattern, much greater loss at the higher frequencies, is typically due to damage to the neural mechanisms mediating hearing or, more commonly, to damage to the receptor cells in the cochlea of the inner ear. The mechanisms of the inner ear are described and discussed in the chapter on biological mechanisms of perception (Chapter 24; see especially Figure 24-8 and pp. 680–81).

Other Senses

We have, of course, other senses besides vision and hearing. Much is now known about smell, taste, and the many different modalities of skin senses, as well as senses such as kinesthesis and equilibrium, and various other internal modalities such as pain.

Smell and taste usually cooperate in our experience of *flavor*, and other modalities are involved as well. It is usually hard to distinguish the relative contributions of smell, taste, muscular awareness of texture, warmth, and cold, and still others. Among the interesting findings with these senses is that smell adapts very rapidly; within a matter of minutes after entering an environment imbued with an odoriferous substance, we are no longer aware of the smell, or at least the smell seems to be much less strong. Taste also adapts quite quickly. This rapid adaptation may well be one of the reasons why meals in most cultures typically consist of several different foods; the variety of flavors keeps the sensory input interesting.

Kinesthesis, our awareness of the position of our limbs and joints and of the status of our muscles, is a modality essential to our ability to get around in the environment, to walk, to stand erect, to hold objects, and the like. Our awareness of gravity, and of changes in the direction of motion of our bodies, depends upon tiny receptors deep in the inner ear—organs that are also involved in sensations of dizziness and nausea. Since conditions of weightlessness produce an altered state of stimulation of the organs of equilibrium, much attention has recently been devoted to these mechanisms in the atypical gravitational and equilibrium conditions produced by space travel.

There are at least four distinguishable skin senses: touch, pain, warmth, and cold. Exploration of a small area on the skin, millimeter by millimeter, reveals that some spots are sensitive to none of these four sensations, some to only one, some to two, some to three, and some to all four. This spatial localization of the skin senses suggests that different receptors may underlie these four sense modalities, some stimulated by changing the shape of the surface (touch), some sensitive to tissue damage (pain), some stimulated by an increase in skin temperature (warmth), and some sensitive to a decrease in skin temperature (cold). The search for these different receptor elements has a long history, but, as yet, none have been unequivocally identified.

Pain also comes in several varieties. There is the sharp, bright pain of a pinprick, as contrasted with the dull ache of a sprained ankle. A stomachache or a headache are something else still. Tissue damage is obviously a determinant of pain in many situations, but different types of pain appear to have quite different physical causes—and often respond quite differently to various drugs used to alleviate pain. The total picture is very complex. The perception of pain depends often on what other stimuli are present; for example, pain is typically less if there is concurrent auditory or vibratory stimulation, a fact that has been applied in dental practice. A hypnotized subject told simply to feel no pain can endure events that would be unbearable to nonhypnotized subjects (Hilgard, 1969), and people have undergone serious operations with no more aid than hypnotically-induced anesthesia. A man rescuing his family from a burning house may fail to notice his own painful injuries. In some cases of intractable pain, a brain operation—prefrontal lobotomy—has been used as a last resort; some of the patients report that after the operation the pain is unchanged but that it doesn't bother them as much as it did before. Dogs raised in isolation provide a striking example of the importance of prior experience. Such animals respond to a painful stimulus, such as a burning match, but have great difficulty in learning to avoid it. Unless restrained, they will expose themselves time and again to painful situations. An attempt to solve some of the puzzles of pain in terms of its neural mechanisms is described in Spotlight 24-3 (p. 684).

SUMMARY

Psychophysics studies the relation between the physical dimensions of the stimulus (such as the frequency and intensity of a tone) and the psychological dimensions of the corresponding sensation (such as the loudness of the tone). Fechner's discovery of psychophysical methods in the last century made this field accessible to objective study. The results of investigations with these methods established that the sensory modalities do not operate additively or linearly; rather, they follow laws like these:

Weber's law: $\Delta I/I = k$. The smallest detectable change in stimulus intensity (ΔI) is proportional to the intensity of the stimulus already present (I).

Fechner's law: $\psi = k \log \phi$. The intensity of the perception (ψ—psi) is proportional to the logarithm of the intensity of the stimulus (ϕ—phi).

Stevens' power law: $\psi = k\ \phi^n$. The intensity of the perception is proportional to the physical intensity raised to a given power (n).

The human eye is sensitive to only a narrow range of the electromagnetic spectrum, with the yellow region being the brightest for the light-adapted eye, the green the brightest for the dark-adapted. The light-adapted eye can discriminate a large number of hues and brightnesses. The periphery of the eye is color-blind (and so is the entire dark-adapted eye). As you move in from the periphery toward the fovea, a zone is reached where discrimination of blue and yellow becomes possible; still closer to the fovea, discrimination of red and green occurs. The color circle summarizes many laws of additive color mixture (such as the law of complementaries); mixture of paints is subtractive color mixture. The colors of negative afterimages are complementary to the colors of the original stimuli that produce them. Visual acuity is sharpest at the fovea in the light-adapted eye (but slightly to one side of the fovea in the dark-adapted), and falls off steeply toward the periphery.

Any sound can be analyzed into its frequency components. Pitch is determined by the intensity as well as by the frequency of the sound, and so is loudness. Pitch increases with the frequency, but not linearly: the slope of the function is steeper in the middle frequencies than at very low or very high ones. The pitch of high-frequency tones increases with increasing intensity, but the pitch of low-frequency tones decreases with increasing intensity. The loudness of sounds increases approximately with the logarithm of their intensity, but the power law gives a more accurate representation of the findings. Loudness increases as frequency rises, reaching a maximum at about 2,000 Hz, then decreases again. In addition to pitch and loudness, tones have qualities like volume and density.

Smell and taste both adapt quickly, and it is often hard to distinguish what part of flavor is smell, what part taste, and what part due to still different modalities (such as temperature sense and kinesthesis). The equilibrium and gravitational senses have received a research emphasis recently because of the significance of understanding them better for purposes of space travel. The skin senses, touch, pain, warmth, and cold, are functionally clearly distinguishable, but separate sensory receptors for them have not yet been discovered despite a century-long search.

21
The Relativity of Perception

How does context affect our perception?
How do we perceive movement?
How do we organize what we see?
How does space perception equip us to live in a three-dimensional world?

In this chapter we examine how perceptions are affected by relations among various stimuli. Relational considerations will not be entirely new; although the last chapter discussed perception of simple stimuli, we were introduced to Weber's law, which describes a just noticeable difference as a function of *relative* change—not absolute change. We also demonstrated how negative afterimages (remember the American flag in color Figure 6) depend upon the relation between present and past stimulation.

Now we will focus on the relativity of perception. Perceptual contrast and constancy are two particularly clear-cut demonstrations of the effects of *stimulus context* on perception, and we will examine these phenomena in some detail. An example of contrast was given in preview Figure 5; the same gray ring is seen as darker or lighter depending on its contrasting relation with the surrounding white or black. On the other hand, we speak of constancy effects when percepts are similar or identical even though the actual physical stimuli are quite different; a person does not appear to shrink as he moves away from you, even though his image on your retina becomes much smaller. After contrast and constancy, we will consider the perception of movement. Next we will examine how various collections of stimuli are perceived as belonging together, that is, what aspects of the stimulus array lead the perceiver to group certain parts together into coherent figures instead of seeing only a fragmentary and disparate mosaic. Finally, we will discuss sensory processes that lead to the perception of three-dimensional space.

How does context affect our perception?

Perceptual Contrast

In **perceptual contrast,** the percept of the same stimulus is substantially altered by the *surround* or *context.* The context can either be other stimulation occurring at the same time (*simultaneous* contrast) or it can be the preceding pattern of stimulation (*successive* contrast). In general, perceptual contrast operates in such a way that a *difference* between a particular area and its surround, background, or context is enhanced. This exaggeration of a difference is not limited to vision. Water of an average temperature feels cool to a hand previously held in warm water, warm to a hand previously held in cold; a tone can sound loud if preceded by silence but soft if it follows very loud stimulation; a moderate weight may feel heavy if preceded by a series of lightweight stimuli, light if preceded by heavy ones. Figure 21-1 shows a size contrast effect; the two colored circles in the middle of the two groups of circles are actually equal in size, although the one surrounded by larger circles appears smaller than the one surrounded by smaller ones. In the same way, a beagle may look fairly large in a pack of toy poodles and chihuahuas, but small if socializing with collies and St. Bernards.

Whenever the stimulus differs from its context, contrast effects are at least possible. The straight lines in preview Figure 2 look curved in the context of concentric circles. Color Figure 5 illustrates color contrast effects, where the identical gray circle takes on the hue complementary to the surround. This fact is flagmakers' knowledge, and thus you will often see flags and pennants in complementary colors; the blue in a context of yellow is "bluer than usual" because of contrast.

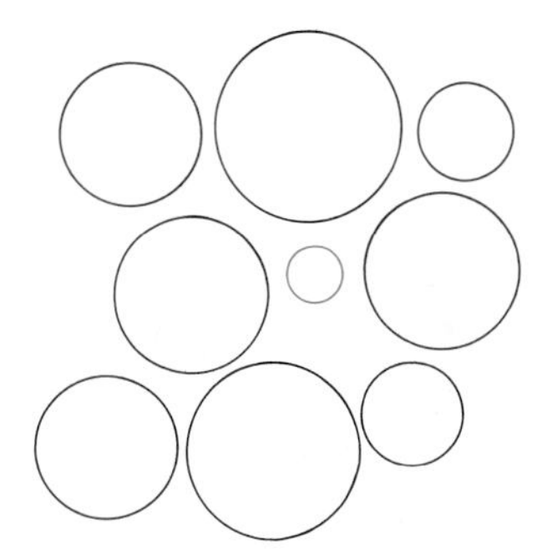

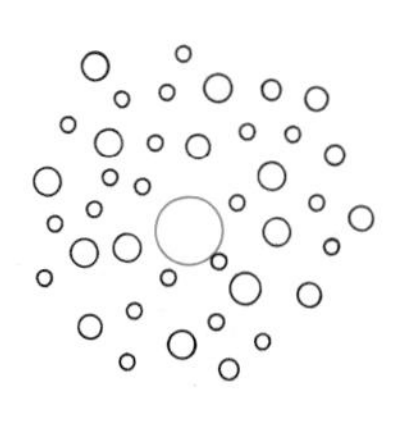

FIGURE 21-1 SIMULTANEOUS SIZE CONTRAST

Simultaneous Contrast

In such phenomena as simultaneous brightness contrast (preview Figure 5), the strength of the contrast effect depends upon the magnitude of the difference between the critical area and its surround and upon the area of contrasting background—other things being equal. These "other things," which we depict as equal but which rarely are in real life, include the configuration of the stimulus. For example, in Figure 21-2 the small gray triangle in A looks darker

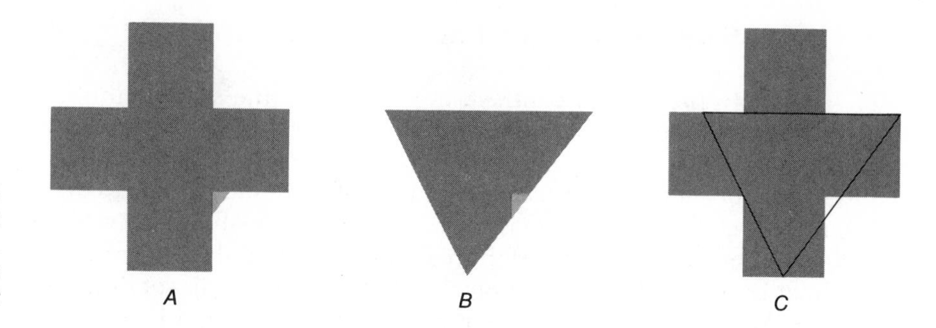

FIGURE 21-2 RELATIONAL DETERMINATION OF SIMULTANEOUS BRIGHTNESS CONTRAST

The small gray triangle in *A* is of equal intensity to that in *B*, but it looks darker. Why? Actually, *B* is simply a part of *A* as diagram *C* shows.
(After Benary, 1924)

than the same triangle in *B* despite the fact that the area of the black surround is greater in *A*. The reason for this is that we perceive the figure in *B* as a large dark triangle with a small lighter one on top of it and the figure in *A* as a dark cross with a piece attached. Thus our little gray triangle is seen as "lying on" the black background in *B* and "lying on" a white background in *A*. In contrast to the "white background" in *A*, therefore, it looks darker, and in contrast to the "black background" in *B*, it looks lighter. These atypical contrast effects depend on the complex processes that govern our perception of figures, some of which will be discussed in this chapter.

Preview Figure 5 provides another illustration of how configurational variables can affect contrast. When the figure is first viewed, it tends to be seen as a reasonably-uniform gray ring on a background, the left half of which is black, and the right half of which is white. According to the principle of simultaneous contrast, one might expect the left half of the gray ring to look lighter than the right half, but the *unity* of the ring seems to be sufficient to overcome this effect. If the perceptual unity of the ring is destroyed by placing a pencil along the contour separating the black and white backgrounds, then the left half-ring looks noticeably lighter than the right half. You can even "pull along" the induced contrast effect to some extent by slowly moving the pencil to the right or left. Even though a bit of white background might begin to become visible as you move the pencil to the right, the small amount of gray ring on the white background still continues to look light, because it continues to be perceptually organized as "belonging to" the perceptually-homogeneous left portion of the ring. Similarly, if you move the pencil to the left, you can "pull" the apparently-darker right half-ring partly over onto the black background. (For more on simultaneous contrast, see Spotlight 21-1.)

Figural Aftereffects

Successive shape and size contrast effects have been studied systematically during the last several decades. Thus, a particular set of distortions of the perception of a figure can be produced by prior stimulation with another figure; such **figural aftereffects** have been demonstrated to occur in several modalities (vision, hearing,

SPOTLIGHT 21-1
Mach Bands

A particular simultaneous brightness-contrast effect has been named after a nineteenth-century scientist, Ernst Mach, who first studied it intensively. (Mach's name has also been given to high velocities—Mach 2 means twice the speed of sound.) The Mach effect is the appearance of distinct lines or bands at places in a stimulus array where there are abrupt changes in the intensity gradient. The information-processing system increases the degree of discontinuity contained in the array; the band at *X* in the figure looks darker than the dark part of the array to the left of it, the band at *Y* lighter than the light part of the array at the right. So we perceive an exaggerated version of the physical stimuli.

Recently, lateral inhibitory mechanisms have been discovered in the retina which can account for Mach bands, for contour enhancement (the fact that a dark area looks darker near a light area, a light area lighter near a dark area), and for other simultaneous—and possibly some successive—contrast effects. Phenomena comparable to visual Mach bands have been observed in audition, too (Carterette, Friedman, & Lovell, 1965). Current research is providing exciting clues to the physiological mechanisms underlying many complex perceptual processes (see the chapter on the biological psychology of perception, especially pp. 670–71).

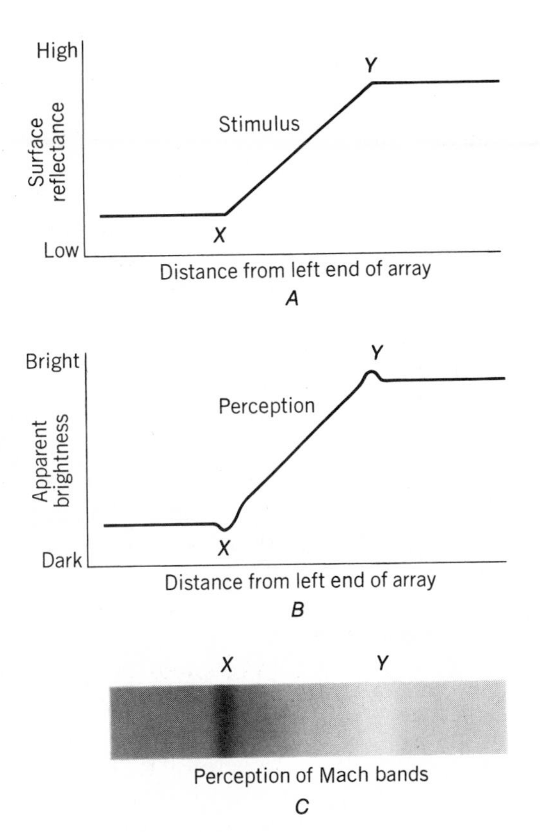

Illustrated above are Mach bands. *A* shows the distribution of light intensity along the array; *B* and *C* show the appearance of the array. A dark band is seen at *X*, a light band at *Y*, even though there are no such lines in the stimulus. (Based on Ratliff, 1965)

touch, kinesthesis), and they follow certain predictable regularities. Figure 21-3 can be used to demonstrate a figural aftereffect which produces a distortion in perceived *size*. Stare at the *X* between the two circles in *A* (the inspection figure) for about one minute. Thereafter, immediately shift your gaze to the *X* in the center of *B* (the test figure). Which of the two circles in the latter observation looks larger?

FIGURE 21-3 FIGURAL AFTEREFFECT PRODUCING A SIZE DISTORTION

Stare at the *X* in figure *A* for about sixty seconds, then stare at the *X* in figure *B*. The left-hand circle will look larger than the right-hand circle in *B*, even though both circles are the same size.

(To convince yourself that the apparent size difference really isn't just the way the figure is drawn and *is* due to the preceding exposure to *A*, you might repeat the experiment, but quickly turn the book upside-down before you look at the *X* in *B*.) A given circle looks larger if its image falls on a place on the retina previously stimulated by a small circle than if its image falls on a place on the retina previously stimulated by a large circle. Analogous phenomena can also be demonstrated in the tactual-kinesthetic modality. If you rub a curved edge such as the rim of a cup or the edge of a phonograph record for a minute or so, then rub a straight contour like the edge of a table, the straight edge will seem to be curved in a direction opposite to the curvature of the object you rubbed just before (such effects work better if you keep your eyes closed during the experiment). These results are predictable. Most people, when presented with situations such as these, will respond in the same way you did. See Spotlight 21-2 for a discussion of the effects of prolonged perceptual distortion.

Perceptual Constancy

The perceptual constancies are, in a way, opposite to perceptual contrast effects. In contrast effects, the *same* stimulus at the receptor is perceived as *different* in different contexts; in **perceptual constancy,** *different* stimuli are essentially perceived as the *same*. We tend to perceive the stable enduring properties of the objects around us, even though the patterns of physical energies impinging upon our sense organs are anything but stable and enduring. For example, as we mentioned earlier, a person is perceived as being the same size even if he is walking toward us or away from us, even though our retinal images of him change considerably. Obviously, this is a very efficient form of functioning, and makes it much easier to deal with the environment than would be the case if the percept always accurately reflected the ever-changing sensory stimulation of our receptors.

In general, our percepts correspond more closely to the object than to the stimulus at the sense organ. But constancy is by no means perfect. Usually, we perceive a kind of compromise between the object—sometimes called the **distal** (remote) stimulus—and the stimulus at the sense organ—called the **proximal** (near) stimulus. The compromise perception usually falls much closer to the distal object than to the proximal stimulus.

SPOTLIGHT 21-2

Effects of Prolonged Perceptual Distortion

Ivo Kohler at Innsbruck, Austria, has been engaged for years in a series of experiments in which subjects wear goggles that distort the visual field in various ways (Kohler, 1962). The course of adaptation to such altered visual input is studied, sometimes over a period of several weeks or longer, during which the only visual experience the subject has is through the distorting goggles. Then the goggles are removed, and the course of readapting to the usual input can be followed. For example, if the lenses produce apparent curvature of vertical lines, successive contrast effects occur. When the goggles are finally removed, vertical lines now look curved in the opposite direction.

A particularly dramatic finding was obtained in an experiment in which the subject wore spectacles with split-color lenses. Yellow glass made up the right half and blue glass the left half of each lens, so that when the subject looked to the right, the world looked yellow, and when he looked to the left, it looked blue. Soon, as in other experiments, adaptation to the altered visual input occurred and everything looked reasonably normal. But when the spectacles were removed, for a time the world looked blue when the subjects turned their eyes to the right and yellow when they looked to the left. That is, colors complementary to those of the spectacles were induced in subsequent vision, depending upon which way the eyes were turned. An interesting aspect of this finding is the implication that not only visual input but also some kind of input from the muscles controlling eye direction affects the percept.

Size Constancy

Consider size constancy, for example; estimates of actual size are quite accurate up to moderate distances, but they break down at greater distances. Houses, people, trees, and cars seen from the top of a very tall building, from a mountain, or from an airplane, do look tiny; but they do not look as much smaller than they do from closer up as the reduction in the size of their image on the retina alone would require. Figure 21-4 shows the geometry of the situation.

If the available cues indicating the distance of the object are clear enough, size constancy may be almost perfect for distances up to a mile or so, at least for adults (Gibson, 1950). Size constancy at great distances is less clear-cut in eight-year-old children in the sense that their compromise perceived size is farther removed from distal size, and somewhat closer to retinal image size than that of adults (Zeigler & Leibowitz, 1957). However, some degree of size constancy already exists for near objects (three to nine feet away) in infants as young as two months old (Bower, 1966). Of course, information about distance of the objects must be available in order for size constancy to occur.

FIGURE 21-4
HOW THE SIZE OF THE RETINAL IMAGE VARIES

The same size retinal image can be produced by an infinite number of different distal sizes (1, 2, 3, and 4 are examples), as long as they all subtend the same visual angle. The same size distal object (4 and 5) casts a larger image the closer it is to the eye. Compare this figure with Figures 20-15 and 21-18.

Size constancy.
(Drawing by Gahan Wilson, reproduced by special permission of *Playboy* magazine; copyright © 1971 by Playboy)

"Excuse me for shouting—I thought you were farther away."

Brightness Constancy

Size constancy is dependent upon the integration of at least two types of information: the size of the retinal image of an object and its distance from the observer. Brightness constancy depends upon a similar integration; it can be seen to be a perceptual conclusion about (1) the amount of light falling on an object and (2) the percentage of this light that is reflected to the eye.

Brightness is a function of the intensity of the visual stimulus, as we have seen (p. 546). But a black (low reflectance) object in bright light can reflect as much light as a white object in low illumination; that is, 8 percent reflectance of a lot of light may equal 80 percent reflectance of a little. How is it, then, that we don't see a black object in sunlight as white? Our judgments of light or dark as applied to objects is primarily a function of albedo, the percentage of light reflected. How do we respond to albedo in varying illuminations?

Why does a piece of chalk look white in a dark corner and an asphalt road dark in sunlight, even though the chalk reflects less light to our eyes than the asphalt?

The great nineteenth-century scientist Hermann von Helmholtz suggested that many perceptual integrations reflect unconscious inference. In the case of brightness constancy, this would mean that we get information about the intensity of general illumination and take this information "into account" in interpreting the input from any particular object in that area. This hypothesis can be applied to other constancies as well. In size constancy, for example, we note the size of the retinal image but take into account the apparent distance.

More recent investigators, notably James J. Gibson (1950, 1966), have pointed out that the total stimulus input at any time usually contains enough information to make these inferences or unconscious calculations. Such calculations, however, would be extremely complex and would take a tremendous amount of past experience to learn. But young children with little past experience and animals with relatively little intellectual capacity (chickens, fish) show certain constancies in perception. Furthermore, under some circumstances, constancy can break down even if full knowledge of the stimulus situation is available to the observer (see Spotlight 21-3).

Rather than attributing perceptual integrations to inferential processes, current investigators often think in terms of cortical "feature extractors," which respond to relative rather than absolute stimulus information. There is a good deal of psychobiological research, some of which will be reviewed in Chapter 24, showing that certain neural circuits respond most actively to specific information about one part of the stimulus field—only to slanted lines, for example—and some of these respond only to *relative* differences—to "lighter" rather than to "light" (see p. 671).

It appears that what is crucial for brightness constancy is the *ratios* of the intensities of light in different parts of the stimulus field. Figure 21-5 presents two arrays that are identical in structure. Both *A* and *B* consist of a small disc within a larger ring, with the intensity of white light in both the ring and the disc independently variable. If the illumination of the ring in *A* is at an intensity of 100 (arbitrary) units, and the disc at an intensity of 50, in an otherwise dark field, the ring will look white and the disc light gray. The experimental question is, If the outer ring illumination is set at 40 in *B*, how intense should the inner disc be, in order to look just as bright as the disc in *A*? If perceived brightness simply corresponded to the local intensity, then the illumination of the disc in *B* would have to be 50 units, the same as in *A*. But an intensity of 50 turns out to make the disc in *B* look much brighter than the disc in *A*. Instead, as repeated experiments have shown, the disc in *B* must be illuminated

SPOTLIGHT 21-3

A Case of Breakdown of Brightness Constancy

You can demonstrate for yourself that brightness constancy is not simply a result of unconscious inference. Cut a circle, about six to eight inches in diameter, out of a piece of nonglossy black cardboard. Suspend it, using fine black thread, in an open doorway at eye level. Now set up a projector so that it illuminates the disc but not the door frame or the wall; place the projector somewhat to one side so that the observer cannot see the wall that is lit up in the next room. Part *A* of the diagram shows how the setup looks to the observer, and part *B* shows the arrangement from above.

When the projector is off, there is nothing remarkable about the setup. You see a black disc hanging in a doorway. When the projector is turned on, however, suddenly the disc looks white. If perception of brightness were a matter of taking all relevant factors like illumination into account, your *knowledge* that the projector is on should result in a veridical percept, that is, of a black disc in high illumination. But that is not the way it works. By changing the ratio of the amount of light coming to you from the disc relative to the amount of light coming to you from the background—the walls of the room visible behind the disc—you have changed the apparent brightness of the disc.

Now if a small piece of white paper is held immediately in front of the disc so that it too is illuminated by the projector, the disc snaps back to its black appearance. Why? Apparent brightnesses depend upon stimulus *ratios.* The piece of white paper reflects much more light into your eyes than the disc; what determines the brightness of the disc now is the relation between the amount of light reflected from it and the amount of light reflected from the piece of white paper.

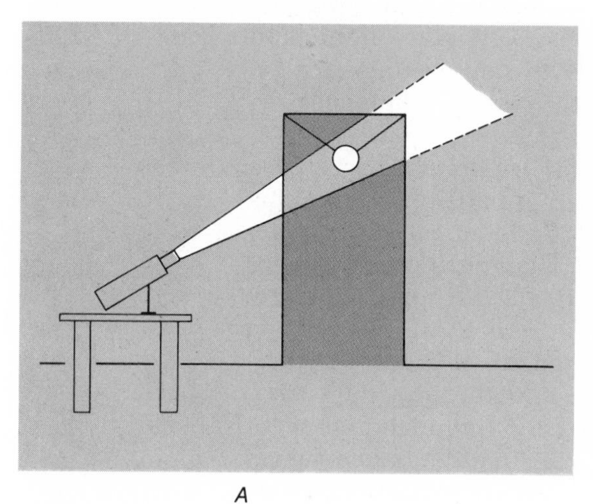

A

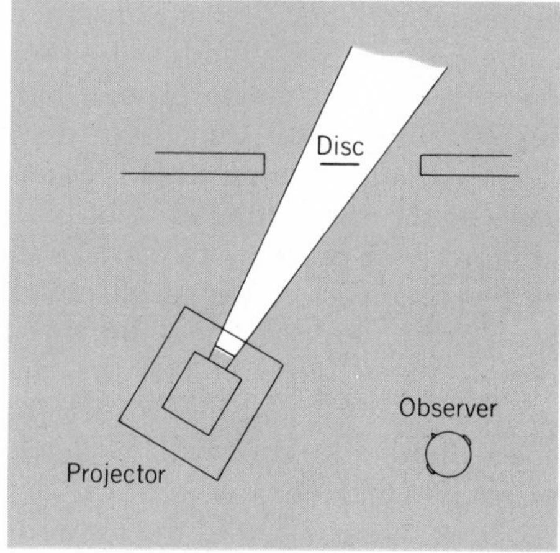

B

(After Gelb, 1929)

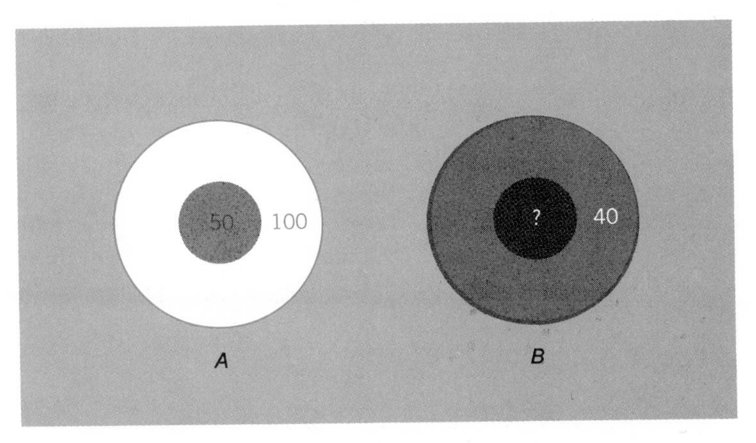

FIGURE 21-5 THE RELATIONAL DETERMINATION OF BRIGHTNESS

How many units of illumination are needed in the inner circle in *B* to make it look just as bright as the inner circle in *A*, which has an illumination of 50 units?

with about 20 units if it is to look just as bright as the disc in *A*. In other words, it is the *ratio* of the critical intensity to the surrounding intensity that seems to determine brightness: 50 is to 100 as 20 is to 40. This generalization holds over a broad range; we can change the intensity of the ring in *B* and predict reasonably well what intensity the disc will have to have in order for it still to look just as bright as the disc in *A*. For a ring intensity of 50, the disc intensity must be about 25; for a ring intensity of 500, the disc intensity should be about 250, and so on.

Note how well relational perception accounts for brightness constancy. If the proportion of the light falling on any surface that is reflected into the eyes remains constant (that is, as long as the surface's albedo does not change), the apparent brightness of an object *relative to its surround* does not change with changes in the absolute amount of illumination. The experiment described in the preceding paragraph provides a pretty good analogue for the everyday situation: you don't, after all, have a single object in isolation, with nothing else in the stimulus field; virtually always you see various objects of different albedo in a complex spatial relationship. While the amount of light reflected from any one surface may vary over time as the illumination changes, the *proportion* of the light falling on it that it reflects (that is, its albedo), relative to the albedos of the surrounding objects, does not change.

Such a relational approach has also been applied to the understanding of size constancy. As you walk toward a building, for example, the *relative* sizes of the images cast on your retina by the windows and doors of the building do not change, though each is expanding. It appears as though size constancy depends upon a tendency for the perceptual system to analyze perceived size not according to the magnitude of the retinal image but according to the relative sizes of the retinal images of various objects or parts of the visual field.

We have focused here on size and brightness constancies, but there are many other constancies as well. Just to cite one, there is shape constancy. A rectangular door or table looks rectangular even though we are rarely in a position in which the sensory input is truly rectangular. The retinal image of an opening door, for example, or of a table near eye level, is really a trapezoid—the edge nearer us casts a longer image than the edge farther away—but the door and table still "look" rectangular. Gibson (1950, 1966) has suggested that relations to other objects in the visual field can explain shape constancy (and other constancies), just as it can explain size and brightness constancies.

How do we perceive movement?

The naïve view that our eyes passively register the "real" size or brightness or shape of an object in our visual field should by now be suspect. How about the naïve view of movement? An object moves, and the image on our retina moves, and that's all there is to it. Do you now suspect this view?

In one sense, the naïve view of movement is correct, although *how* it could be has been a puzzle until quite recently. Consider what happens "out there" and at the sense organ when, for example, a car passes by on the street. For the sake of illustration, assume that your eyes are focused on a point below eye level on the trunk of a tree across the road from you. At first, certain cells on your retina are stimulated by the gray of the tree trunk. Then, as the car passes between you and the tree, those same cells are suddenly stimulated by the light reflected to your eyes from the passing car; after the car passes they are again stimulated by the tree trunk. Any individual retinal cell receives one stimulus at one time (from the tree), a different one at another time (from the car), then the first one again (from the tree). So at one time any nerve cell fires more or less vigorously than at another. How can we, under these circumstances, perceive any movement? The neural processes mediating such perception are just of a "yes-no" or "more-less" kind.

The answer is that the retina receives information from a broad visual field, so the car stimulates cells on one side of the retina before it stimulates others, and cells at higher stations in the nervous system receive inputs from different parts of the retina. So the relative timing of stimulation at different retinal positions provides information about movement. Some central cells are specialized as "motion detectors" to utilize such information.

The Relativity of Perceived Motion

Perception of speed, like perception of brightness, size, and other attributes, appears to be largely a relative matter. We do not see speed in an absolute sense, but always how fast something is moving in relation to something else. Figure 21-6 is a diagram of two rectangular apertures, behind each of which a continuous strip of paper moves to the right. Every part of the diagram on the right is two times the size of its corresponding part in the left-hand diagram; assume that the two apertures are physically much farther separated in space than they are in the figure so that the observer cannot see both of them at once, but must look first at one and then at the other. How fast must the paper move behind the large opening in order for it to look as though the dots are moving to the right in that one just as fast as the dots are moving in the small one? If the same paper speed is used for both, it looks as though the dots in the large framework are moving much more slowly than the dots in the small framework. In order to make it look as though the speed of the dots in the larger diagram is the same as the speed of the dots in the small one, the paper speed in the large one will have to be about two times as fast as the paper speed in the small one. The perception of speed, in other words, seems to follow principles very similar to those obtaining in the constancies: it is *relative* displacement that counts.

The apparent *direction* of motion also depends upon

FIGURE 21-6
THE RELATIONAL DETERMINATION OF APPARENT SPEED
Apparent speed varies with the size of the stimulus.
(After Brown, 1931)

(William M. Graham, Photo Researchers)

relational, interactive processes. The framework within which motion occurs plays a substantial role in the perceived direction of motion. If, for example, on a partly cloudy day, you look up at the sky to try to determine the direction in which the clouds are moving, the apparent direction will depend greatly upon the characteristics of other stationary and moving things visible at the same time. If you are standing near a building as you look up and can see the edge of the roof of the building, the clouds will often seem to be moving in a direction that is at right angles to that contour. The perceived direction of motion also tends to be economical; in ambiguous situations apparent motion is such as to yield the smallest apparent displacement per unit time that is consistent with the physical stimulus conditions.

Figure 21-7 illustrates an experiment that demonstrates this principle. In both cases, assume a rectangular aperture, behind which a continuous strip of paper is moving in the direction indicated by the arrow. Even though the paper is actually moving from left to right in *A*, it looks as though a series of stripes is slowly moving upward; similarly, in *B*, even though the paper is actually moving upward, it looks as though the stripes are moving to the right.

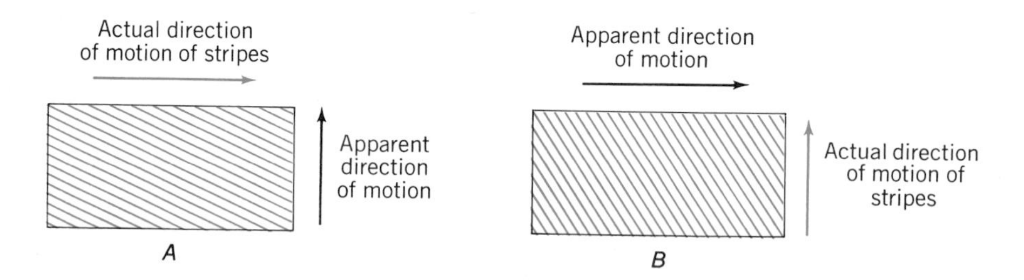

FIGURE 21-7
THE RELATIONAL DETERMINATION OF APPARENT DIRECTION OF MOTION
(After Wallach, 1935)

The perception of motion, then, like many other aspects of perception, is economical. We perceive that pattern of motion which entails the least change. If we obtain successive views of a rotating object (Figure 21-8), it would be possible to see a sequence of flat patterns whose shape is changing; but a percept of a single rotating three-dimensional object of unchanging shape is simpler, and this is the typical output when such incoming information is processed. Shape constancy, then, can play a significant role in the perception of motion.

FIGURE 21-8
DEPTH FROM MOTION
Successive views of a changing, flat, two-dimensional pattern can result in the perception of a stable, rotating, three-dimensional object.
(After Wallach & O'Connell, 1953)

Induced and Apparent Motion

There is not a perfect correspondence between which part of the physical stimulus actually moves and which part is perceived as moving. Generally, the enclosing framework is seen as stationary and smaller parts contained within it are seen as moving. On a windy moonlit night, with variable clouds, it can look as though the clouds are standing still while the moon goes scudding across the sky in a direction opposite to that of the actual motion of the clouds. A laboratory analogue of such induced motion is shown in Figure 21-9. If a spot of light is cast upon a screen, and the screen is slowly moved to the right, it appears as though the screen is stationary while the spot seems to move to the left (Duncker, 1929).

It is even possible for such apparent motion to be induced in the observer himself. If you are sitting in a stationary train, and a train on the next track is moving slowly, you may get the uncanny impression that the train outside the window is really stationary, while the train you are on is moving in the opposite direction. In this case, you and the railroad car in which you are sitting have become the "contained," enclosed part of your perceptual field and the train outside the window has become perceptually part of the larger, apparently-stable rest of the world. Such an effect has also been demonstrated in the laboratory (Duncker, 1929). The observer sits in a small cylindrical enclosure formed by hanging a curtain from the rim of a large wheel suspended horizontally above. The curtain has vertical black and white stripes. If the wheel is rotated slowly in a clockwise direction, the observer perceives the curtain as stationary and himself as turning in a counterclockwise direction! It is a strange perception, since the sense of motion is not stimulated in the way it normally would be if the observer were actually being rotated, but the effect of the visual framework is strong enough to overcome this sensory incongruity. Here movement of the observer seems to be the simplest hypothesis by which he can account for the change that is occurring. Spotlight 21-4 discusses our perception of causality in motion.

Apparent movement, that is, perceived motion in the absence of actual physical displacement in the image on the retina, is often indistinguishable from real motion. There are many different kinds of apparent motion; we have already touched on a few just above, in the discussion of induced motion. Motion can even be per-

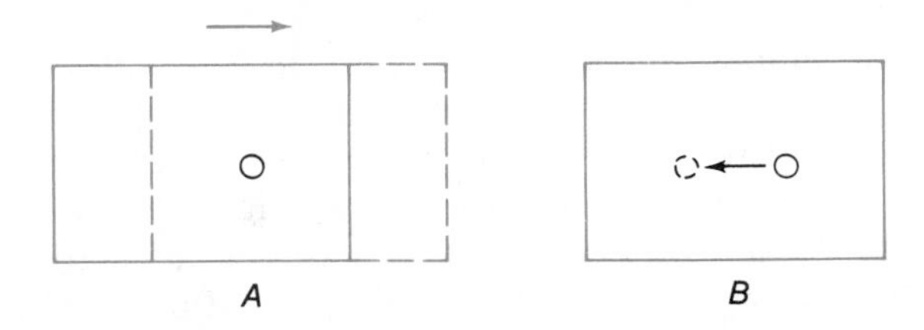

FIGURE 21-9 THE RELATIONAL DETERMINATION OF MOTION
If a spot of light is projected from a fixed point upon a screen which is moved to the right (*A*), the screen appears stationary while the spot is perceived to move to the left (*B*).

SPOTLIGHT 21-4
Perception of Causality

Simplified arrangements have been devised for the study of the perception of causality in motion. Under what conditions does it look as though two events are "causally" related? For example, when a billiard ball strikes another billiard ball, why does it look as though the motion of the first causes the motion of the second? Through techniques of animation, or by using a large disc rotating behind a screen with a narrow horizontal slit on it (Michotte, 1963), it is possible to produce stimulus patterns such as the one illustrated in the diagram. Initially, both squares are stationary. Then square *A* moves to the right until it comes to rest next to *B;* square *B* then moves to the right.

Our perception of causality in this kind of a setup is sensitive to very slight changes in time, speed, and direction, and it seems to be surprisingly independent of experience. Thus, for example, if *B* is made to move faster than *A,* if *B's* motion begins as long as one-half second after *A's* motion ceases, or if *B's* direction is "unusual," seeing this set of events a thousand times will not result in a convincing perception of *A's* motion *causing B's.* This phenomenon raises some interesting questions about the role of past experience in perception, which we have already touched on and to which we shall return in the next chapter. Suffice it to say at this point that the perception of causation, like the perception of movement, depends upon complex interactive relations in the stimulus pattern and not primarily upon past experience.

ceived in stimulus patterns in which nothing is being displaced. One way to do this is to remove the framework entirely, say by having a stationary pinpoint of light in a completely dark room. When there is no framework with respect to which the pinpoint can maintain a stable relationship, the light soon appears to move all by itself. This phenomenon has been called **autokinesis,** a term whose Greek roots mean "self" and "movement."

Another way to get a physically stationary object or field to appear to move makes use of a successive contrast phenomenon in motion. If you stare at a waterfall for a minute or so and then rapidly shift your gaze to dry terrain nearby, it will appear as though the bushes, leaves, and dirt are eerily floating upward.

A comparable, quite dramatic movement aftereffect can be obtained by staring at the center of a rotating spiral for thirty to sixty seconds (see Figure 21-10). If the spiral is rotating in one direction, it appears to be contracting; if it is rotating in the other direction, it appears to be expanding. If the spiral is stopped, it will now appear to shrink if it was expanding before, to expand if it was shrinking before. This aftereffect can even be applied to your friend's face, which

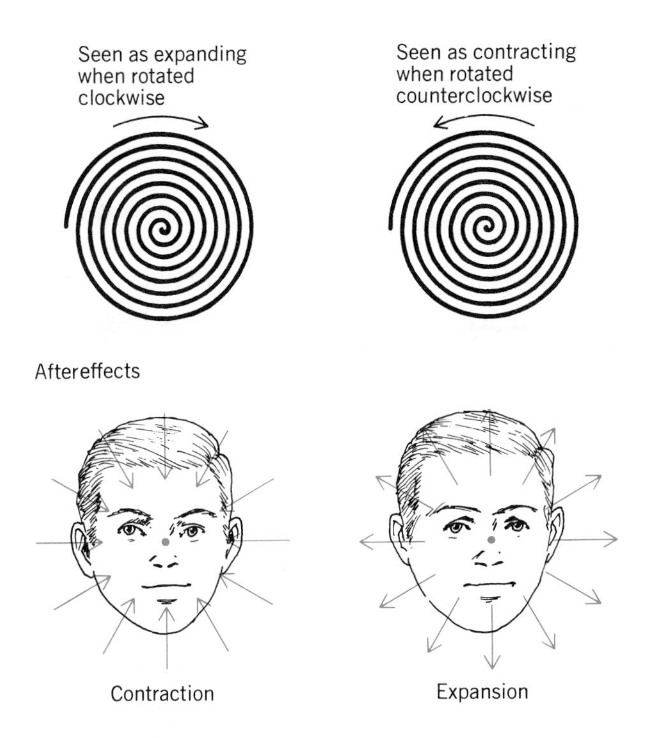

FIGURE 21-10 AFTEREFFECTS OF SPIRAL EXPANSION OR CONTRACTION

When the spiral is rotated clockwise, it appears to expand. If, after a minute of observation, the spiral is stopped, it will appear to contract. If you shift your gaze quickly to your friend's nose, his face will appear to contract too.

will appear to shrink after you have looked at an expanding spiral for some time.

Whenever you watch a movie, you are, of course, experiencing apparent motion; the film is just a rapidly presented series of still pictures. Setups far simpler than movies can be used to study the determinants of this kind of apparent movement, called **stroboscopic motion.** The simplest consists of two lights. If these two lights go on and off on an appropriate schedule, it will appear as though a single light is *moving* back and forth. (Neon display lights often illustrate this fact.) With such a setup, one can investigate the optimal time and space intervals for producing stroboscopic motion. It has been found that if the time interval is too short, the observer reports two simultaneous flashes; if the time interval is too long, the observer reports two successive flashes. Optimal apparent motion is typically obtained with a time interval of thirty to sixty milliseconds between the turning off of one and the turning on of the other (Wertheimer, 1912).

How do we organize what we see?

A fundamental question in perception is how different parts of a stimulus array are perceived as belonging together in a coherent form or pattern. The receptor cells transduce the stimulus into many separate electrical impulses. How is this mosaic of disparate messages integrated by the information-processing system into our awareness of coherent figures? The principles of perceptual organization have been thoroughly studied by a group calling themselves **Gestalt** psychologists (Wertheimer, 1923). (*Gestalt*—a German word—translates roughly as "configuration." Parenthetically, we should also mention that the currently popular "Gestalt" therapy bears only a rather oblique relation to the traditional Gestalt principles, which were formulated primarily in the areas of perception, learning, thinking, and problem solving.)

Principles of Perceptual Grouping

One Gestalt principle states that parts of the stimulus pattern that are *similar* to each other tend to be perceived as belonging together. This is the **law of similarity.** Part *A* of Figure 21-11 does not develop an overall coherent pattern, although there are occasional sets of two or three similar squares that are grouped together. Part *B* provides a regular pattern, and is typically seen as sets of squares of the same color going from upper left to lower right. Still more cohesive are *C* and *D*, which yield compelling impressions of vertical columns and horizontal rows, respectively. There is the same number of squares of each color in each of the four patterns, but the haphazard arrangement of *A* yields no strong organization, while the

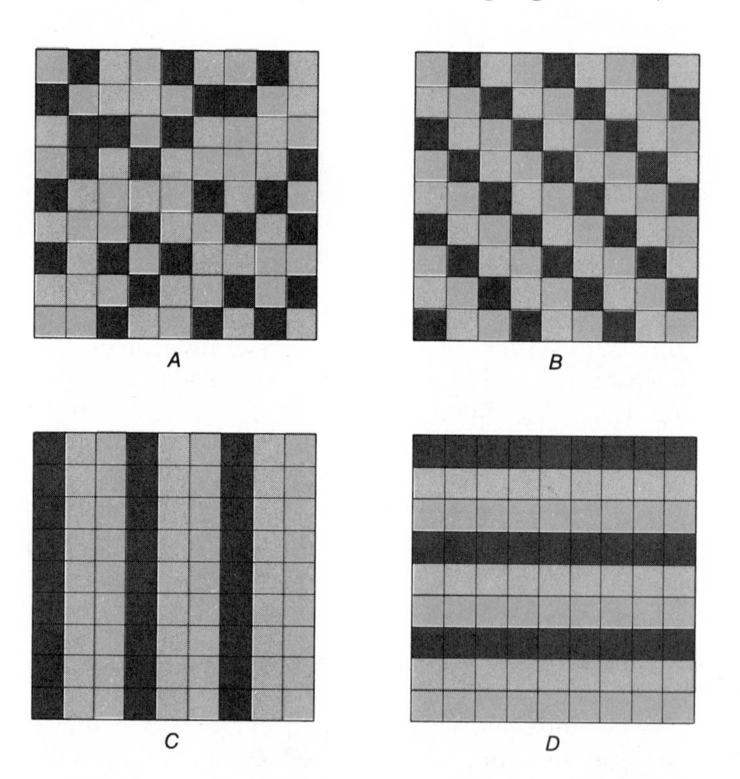

FIGURE 21-11 SIMILARITY AS A PRINCIPLE OF PERCEPTUAL ORGANIZATION

Pattern *A* yields no clear overall coherence, but *B* appears to be composed of diagonals running from upper left to lower right. *C* is seen as vertical columns, and *D* as horizontal rows. In all cases, there are 27 squares of each color. The squares of a given color tend to "go together" in perception, especially when *proximity* and *good continuation* favor this.

systematic configuration of especially patterns *C* and *D* does yield strong perceptual units. This combination of *similar* elements *near* each other can produce quite cohesive units, as patterns *C* and *D* show.

Pattern *A* in Figure 21-12 is another illustration of **proximity**; this time the elements, identical in color and form, are perceptually paired by virtue of their nearness to each other. But in pattern *B* these pairs are "destroyed" by adding a few horizontal lines. This illustrates the effect of **closure** on the perception of "belonging together." That is, in *B* we spontaneously perceive four "closed" squares plus two lines, rather than five pairs of lines as in A. If closure is partial, as in preview Figure 6, we tend in a sense to complete the closure; thus Figure 6 is perceived as quite similar to Figure 21-12. See also preview Figure 12B, which shows the almost automatic effect of closure in a line, part of which is not seen at all because of the eye's blind spot.

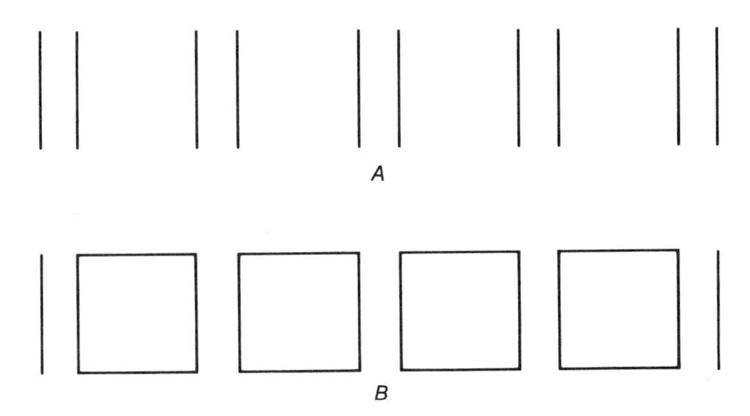

FIGURE 21-12 CLOSURE AS A PRINCIPLE OF PERCEPTUAL ORGANIZATION

Following the principle of proximity, pattern *A* tends to be described as five pairs of vertical lines. But the same vertical lines are perceived differently in *B;* now the second and third are generally described as belonging together, as part of the same rectangle; so are the fourth and fifth, and so on. Even partial horizontal lines, as in preview Figure 6, are enough to suggest closure.

Parts of the stimulus array that move together or in other ways have a **common fate** (getting brighter at the same time, having an object approach them, and so on) also tend to be perceived as a group. The marchers in a parade are distinguished from the people watching the parade; the marchers are walking in step while the onlookers are stationary or are moving about aimlessly. Figure 21-13 illustrates the same principle with abstract dots. Pattern *A* consists of an undifferentiated row of nine equally spaced dots; proximity and similarity are the same, so the set does not break down systematically into subgroups. Closure plays little role in this pattern. Now three of the dots suddenly move up and to the right, as in *B*, and then return to their original position in *C* so that again there is just an undifferentiated row of nine equally spaced dots (*D*). But the common motion of the three dots yields a strong perceptual bond among them while they are moving; even for some time after their motion ceases they remain perceptually segregated as a group distinct from the rest.

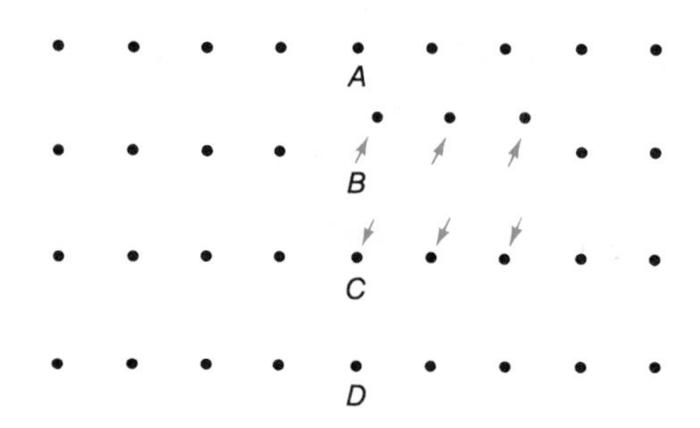

FIGURE 21-13 COMMON FATE AS A PRINCIPLE OF PERCEPTUAL ORGANIZATION
Parts of the field that move together are perceived as belonging to the same group.

A frog, salamander, or other creature with protective coloration may be quite indistinct in its natural surround—until the animal *moves* as a unit.

The two patterns in Figure 21-14 are typically organized spontaneously into curves and lines that are *continuous*. On the basis of proximity, *A* could be seen in such a way that the two straight lines on the left "belong" to the bottom left section of the curved line, while the remaining right-hand vertical line could "belong to" the remainder of the curve, but such a percept is not typical, nor possible without effort. Similarly, pattern *B* usually looks like a curve of circles sweeping up to the right from the lower left, crossing another curved line of circles undulating down to the right from the upper left (notice that this percept goes against the principle of proximity for some of the circles near the crossing point). Generally, figures look "better," more aesthetically satisfying and more regular, if they are construed in one particular way than in any of a large number of other ways that might be consistent with the sensory input.

FIGURE 21-14 GOOD CONTINUATION AS A PRINCIPLE OF PERCEPTUAL ORGANIZATION
The spontaneous grouping in *A* typically is of three sides of a square and a curved line; in *B* of two lines of circles crossing each other.

Law of Prägnanz

This principle of economy of organization, which we have met several times in this section, has been summarized in the **law of Prägnanz,** which states that any whole will be as "good" as the prevailing conditions allow. (*Prägnanz* is a German word with no exact equivalent in English; in the sense employed here, it means roughly the tendency to assume a characteristic or distinctive form.) **Goodness** in this formulation means such things as regularity, symmetry, simplicity, and stability. The perceptual constancies can be seen as consistent with the law of Prägnanz, as can some of the phenomena of motion perception. Over the years since the law of Prägnanz was first proposed, various researchers have attempted to state it in a more precise and quantitative form. For example, it has been proposed that the less the amount of information needed to define a given organization as compared to other alternatives, the more likely is it that the input will be perceived according to that organization (Hochberg & McAlister, 1953). Thus preview Figure 3 can be seen as a cube in perspective, or as a complex set of triangles and quadrilaterals lying in the same plane; it requires less information to specify it as a cube. Recent experiments have demonstrated that such assumptions predict rather effectively how both simple and complex inputs will be construed (Attneave & Frost, 1969; Garner, 1970). See Spotlight 21-5 for examples.

The other principles of organization in perception can be seen as special cases of the law of Prägnanz. Consider the principle of proximity in the auditory mode, by way of illustration. If you tap a table with a pencil according to this pattern—.. .. ..—a rhythm of repeated pairs of taps will be perceived. If you use this pattern—... ... ...—a percept of triads occurs. Why? Because of temporal proximity, of course. But, also, predicting what will follow two taps in the first example (a pause) and what will follow two in the second (another tap) is not too difficult; there is little uncertainty—and uncertainty is the opposite of having information. Thus, little uncertainty means much information, and much information means goodness in the sense implied by the law of Prägnanz. In this case, goodness is a function of proximity relations, but any of the other principles—similarity, continuity, closure—can be seen in the same light as providing information about "what comes next."

Camouflage

On occasion, as in Figures 3 and 4 in the preview, alternative organizations are about equally good and both are consistent with the input. Under such conditions the percept may fluctuate between the alternatives, or characteristics of the perceiver (his set, motivation, or past experience) may result in the dominance of one of the alternatives.

The decisive role of past experience in perception of ambiguous material is illustrated by our ability to read handwritten (cursive) writing. Although the basic principles of organization can help us understand how separate words are perceptually segregated, they do not help much in trying to understand where one *letter* leaves off and the next one begins. The series of loops, circles, lines, and curves is broken down into separate letters on the basis of our past experience with this style of writing. Handwritten material in an alien language—of which we are ignorant—looks very different from script in English. We "see" a series of letters strung together in English, but in the alien script, we are hard pressed to say where one letter ends and the next one begins.

On the other hand, if the organizational factors—similarity, proximity, closure, and so on—are such that the information-processing system constructs an unequivocal percept, then the role of past experience is reduced or even eliminated. This is one way to hide "real" units, as in camouflage. What do the drawings of Figure 21-15 look like to you? To most observers, *A* is a somewhat regular collection of sticks or lines, and most people are somewhat startled when told that it contains the name of a month. In the same way, pattern *B* looks like a mildly interesting arrangement of a few circles, a couple of triangles, and a rectangle; it doesn't immediately make the observer think of the digits specifying a particular year.

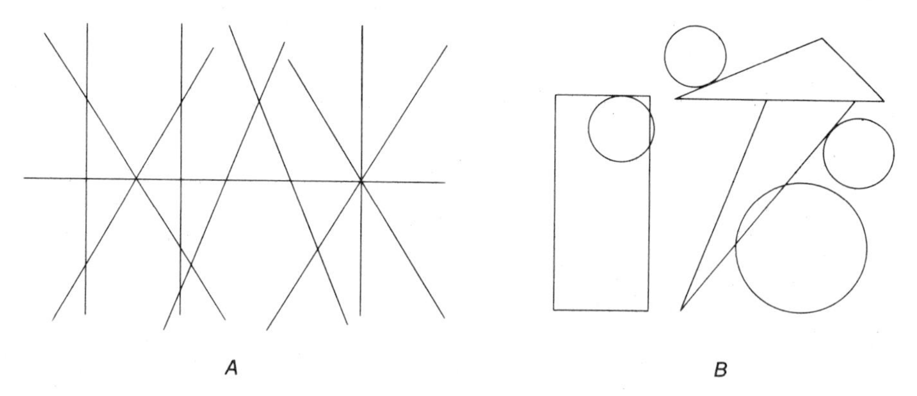

FIGURE 21-15
CAMOUFLAGE
The principles of organization are used to camouflage.

Figure 21-16 gives away what Figure 21-15 camouflaged. Figure 21-16, you will note, actually contains *more* "clutter" than the first. But there is obviously more to camouflage than simply cluttering; successful camouflage is an application of the principles of organization in perception. (Which principles can you identify in Figure 21-15?) Probably you have never before seen the particular patterns in Figure 21-15, but you have seen capital letters and digits, words and numbers, thousands upon thousands of times in the past. You begin to realize the small effect of past experience when pitted against a few simple perceptual principles.

Figure and Ground

Perceptual units are generally seen as figures on or against a background. There are some interesting differences between a figure and its ground. For one thing, the figure always is seen as in front of or on top of the ground, and the ground seems to com-

SPOTLIGHT 21-5
Quantifying Goodness of a Figure

Suppose a psychologist gave you a sheet of graph paper ruled in 4,000 squares (50 rows by 80 columns) and asked you to guess whether each square should be black, brown, or white in order to make a pattern the psychologist has arbitrarily designated correct. This pattern is not shown to you. Your task is to start at the lower left square and to proceed along the bottom row, then to start at the left end of the second row, and so on. After each guess, you are told if you are correct and, if necessary, you can make a second or third guess on that square. You keep a record by filling in the black and brown squares with pencils, and leaving the white ones blank.

If the pattern is the one shown in the figure here, your task is relatively simple. After a few errors at the beginning of the first row, you find that the next cell is "always" white. Then at column 21, you discover that the cells are now brown. When you work your way up to row 21, you find that there are no more brown squares, but that a black region begins at column 40 and ends at column 71. Even the tapering sides of the black area don't cause much trouble, because you find that the slope is regular and that the two sides are symmetrical. The pattern is simple and it does not take many errors to figure it out. All the squares of one color are contiguous and all the contours are regular. When six subjects performed this task, their errors ranged from 13 to 26, and around 20 errors in 4,000 guesses isn't bad!

At first blush it might seem that something as abstract as the "goodness" of a figure would be difficult to quantify. But the number of errors in a task like the one above is one way to proceed. A good figure is one that elicits relatively few errors in prediction. By this measure, good figures tend to be relatively simple, symmetrical, and therefore easy to describe.

A good pattern has still other quantifiable characteristics. One could, for example, have a number of people rate the pattern according to goodness and use the average rating as an index (Garner & Clement, 1963). People can do this fairly reliably; you might try it yourself on the patterns below. Each is made up of five dots distributed over three rows and three columns. Rate each pattern on a 7-point scale where 1 stands for a very good pattern, 4 is a mediocre pattern, and

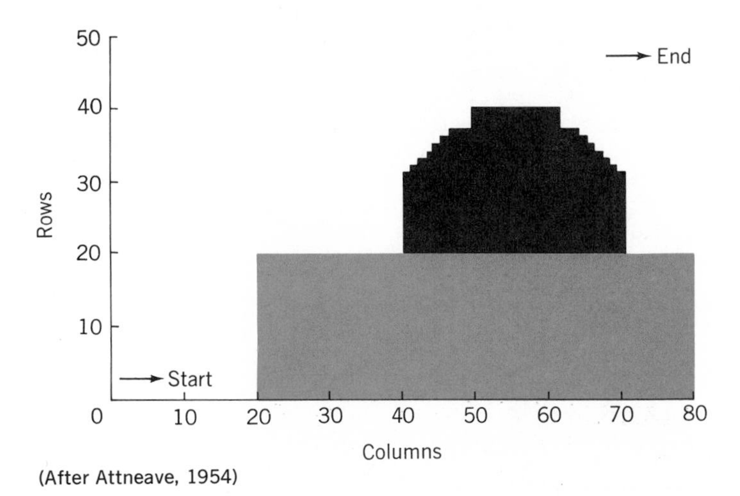

(After Attneave, 1954)

7 is a very poor pattern. You can give the same rating to more than one pattern, and you can use any number from 1 to 7. Complete your ratings before reading on.

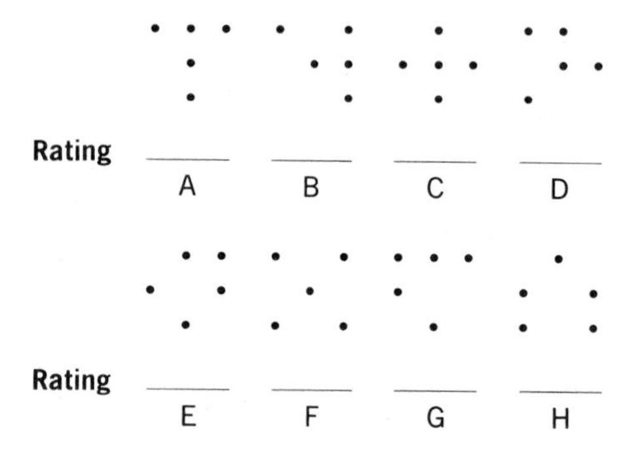

The average ratings of the dot patterns given by a group of subjects are shown in the table. How well do your ratings compare with these means?

In the study from which the averages were obtained, the subjects were given 90 such dot patterns in random order, not just the 8 that you rated. Another group of subjects were asked to take all 90 patterns and arrange them into about 8 groups so that the patterns within a group were "similar"; it was explained that the number of patterns in different groups need not be the same. The mean group sizes are also shown below, and you can see that the higher the rating, the smaller the group to which the pattern seemed to belong; that is, the "better" figures seemed to be more *distinctive*. The correlation between ratings and sizes of the similarity groups over all 90 patterns was high—0.88. Thus, distinctiveness and lack of similarity to other patterns is another quantifiable aspect of a good figure. Also, distinctiveness, ratings of goodness, and the number of errors in "predicting" the pattern are highly correlated. Many of the principles of organization discussed in this chapter can be related to these measures. In a figure that can be seen in two ways, the figure with the higher index of goodness is the one most people will see most of the time. This is the law of Prägnanz in more formal mathematical dress.

TABLE—DOT-PATTERN RATINGS

Patterns	Mean Ratings of "Goodness"	Mean Size of Group of Patterns Judged Similar	Patterns	Mean Ratings of "Goodness"	Mean Size of Group of Patterns Judged Similar
C	1.0	9.4	E	3.0	15.4
F	1.0	8.2	B	3.4	14.5
A	1.6	9.8	G	4.8	16.8
H	1.7	12.7	D	5.5	15.7

From Garner & Clement, 1963.

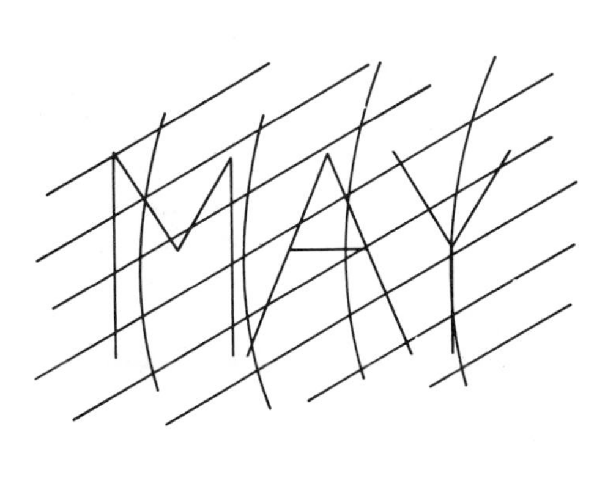

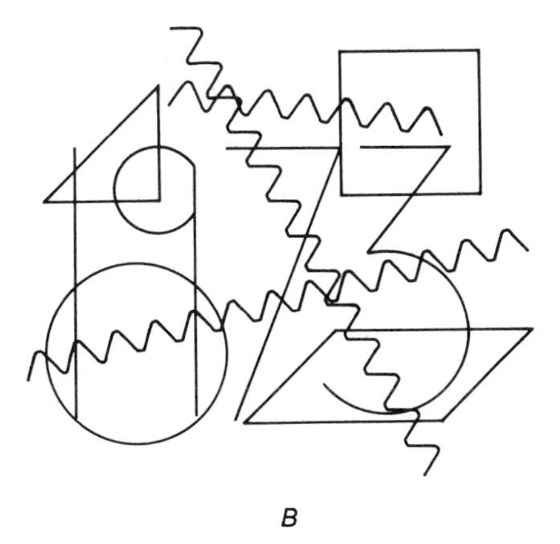

A B

FIGURE 21-16 UNSUCCESSFUL CAMOUFLAGE

This figure is a giveaway of what was hidden in Figure 21-15.

plete itself behind the figure. The figure is typically more salient not only in perception, but also in memory. In terms of appearance, the contour or line separating figure and ground is seen as belonging to the figure, not to the background. Since the background typically looks as though it continues behind the figure, it does not seem to have an edge or a contour where it meets the figure. Finally, in certain ambiguous configurations (such as Figure 21-17, which can be seen as either two profiles or a vase), the contour appears to "belong to" whichever part of the pattern is seen as figure at the moment.

The principles of perceptual organization help to describe how the mosaic of neural activity in the visual system gets transformed into the perception of solid objects in particular spatial relationships to each other. These principles of object organization do not help much, however, when it comes to the question of how these perceptual units acquire meaning—"This is a chair and so is this quite different-looking object, but that is a table." Object identification depends to a great extent upon past experience, which we will discuss in the next chapter.

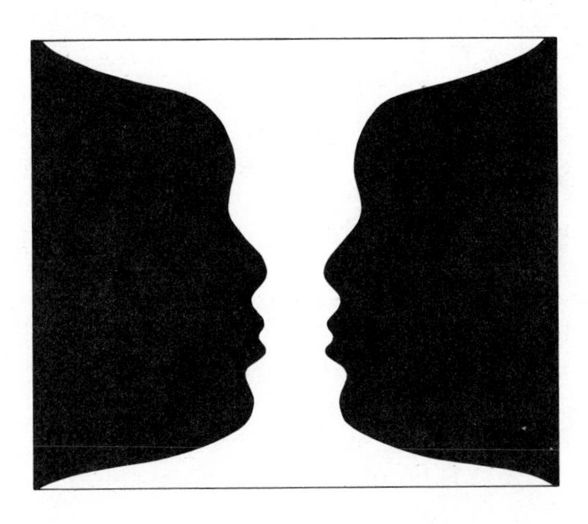

FIGURE 21-17 TWO PROFILES OR A VASE?

You see either two black profiles against a white background or a white vase on a black background. At any given moment, you can see only one of the alternatives. The shape of the contour depends on which one you are seeing, and in each case the figure stands out in front of the background.

How does space perception equip us to live in a three-dimensional world?

Perceived visual and auditory patterns are located in three-dimensional space. We see a table in a particular space, and hear a voice as coming from a particular location. Different species perceive spatial locations more or less accurately, depending upon the requirements of their ecological niches. Chapter 27 on comparative psychology tells how man reflects primate evolution for accurate perception of visual space; this developed in monkeys so that they could leap unerringly from branch to branch. Here we want to ask, How does our information-processing system yield awareness of objects located in three-dimensional space? This question has a long history. How can it be, for example, that stimulation of the retina, a two-dimensional surface, gives rise to a three-dimensional view of the world?

Depth Perception

One answer is that we see with two eyes, not just one, and each of our two eyes receives a slightly different image—this is **binocular disparity.** The visual system uses these two views to yield a percept of depth or of three dimensions. (Try playing ping-pong with one eye closed.) The stereoscope, invented in the nineteenth century, quickly became a popular parlor amusement; looking at two slightly disparate pictures gave a perception of three dimensions or "3-D." In the twentieth century, 3-D movies became a similar fad, using the same principles. Spotlight 21-6 presents some demonstrations of effects produced by binocular disparity. It would help if you were to make the observations described there before reading farther.

The depth achieved with *A* and *B* and with *B* and *C* in Spotlight 21-6 might be attributed in part to our experience in looking at simple geometrical objects. Each eye gets its own view of the object and then, it used to be believed, these two slightly different views are "put together" by the brain to yield a perception of depth. Quite recently, however, a radical new advance has occurred in our understanding of binocular vision. One of the major contributions to this advance was the development of random-dot stereograms by Julesz (1964) (*D* and *E* of Spotlight 21-6). To construct one of these figures, say *D*, each little square in a large field is made either black or white, as determined by a random process, so there is no observable pattern. The paired field, *E* in this case, is identical to *D*, except that certain sections are shifted horizontally from the rest of the figure in order to provide for binocular disparity. A percept of depth in *D* and *E*, therefore, cannot be attributed to past experience, since we have never seen such patterns before.

Research with such patterns has led to several novel conclusions. Not only is familiarity not essential, but even perception

SPOTLIGHT 21-6

Binocular Depth Perception

These diagrams illustrate how depth perception results from our two eyes getting slightly different inputs. Try this experiment. Put the book down flat, take a manila folder or a piece of cardboard about twelve inches long and place it vertically between *A* and *B* along the dotted line. Now put your head on the upper end of the cardboard so your left eye sees only *A* and your right eye only *B* (you can cover *C* with a piece of plain paper). Stare "through" the page, focusing farther away, until the two figures fuse; a solid appearance should result. Is the point of the pyramid directed toward or away from you? Next, cover *A*, move the cardboard between *B* and *C*, and look with your left eye at *B* and your right at *C*. Fuse, and what do you see? Why do you suppose this occurs?

Figures like *A*, *B*, and *C* are familiar, so experience might be supposed to play some role in your perceptions of them. Now look at the "random-dot patterns" of figures *D* and *E* (Julesz, 1964). Does either *D* or *E* show any recognizable pattern? Put the cardboard between them, stare into space and achieve binocular fusion of *D* and *E*. Don't be discouraged if this takes some time. What depth perception occurs as you continue to stare at the center of the merged figure?

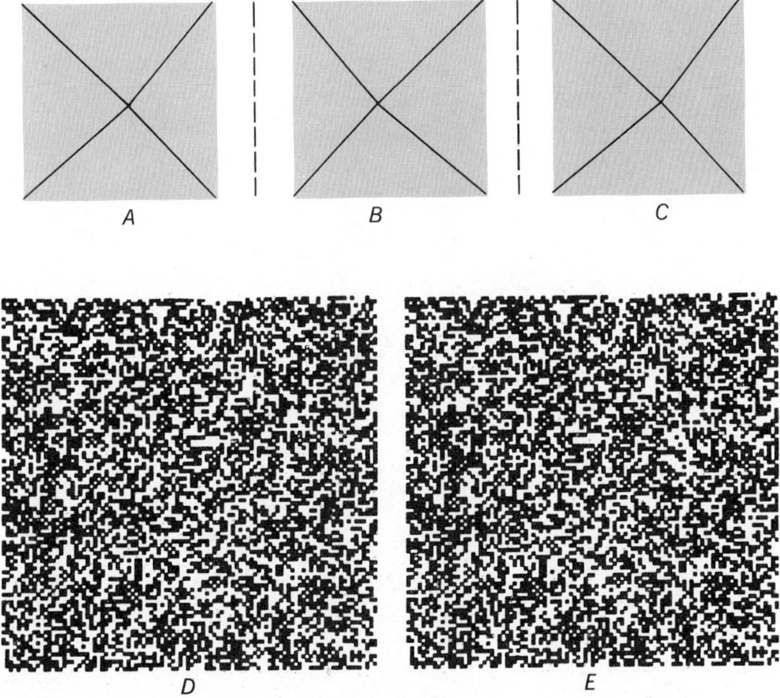

D and *E* © Bell Laboratories and *Scientific American*.

of form is not required for perception of depth. In *D* and *E* you cannot see form until depth perception occurs. Before these studies, it had been thought by many that one must perceive form first; that is, you must perceive a figure before trying to "locate" it in three dimensions. This does not seem to be the case, and some researchers (Bishop & Henry, 1971) conclude that the underlying neural mechanisms for depth perception operate *earlier* in the processing of visual experience than do the mechanisms for form perception.

Binocular disparity is clearly a factor in depth perception, but it is not the only factor. A man who loses vision in one eye is able to perceive depth, increasingly so as he comes to rely less on the lost binocular cues. Artists, especially an artist-scientist like Leonardo da Vinci, discovered some of the secrets of monocular (one-eye) depth perception long before psychologists appeared on the scene. They had to produce a percept of depth from a two-dimensional canvas, just as the psychologist had to explain 3-D effects from a 2-D image on the retina.

Linear perspective is a monocular cue to depth often used by painters (see Figure 21-18). The retinal images of a set of parallel railroad tracks are separated more the closer they are to us—that is, they are *not* parallel in the image we receive—but we tend to perceive them as parallel, extending off into 3-D space.

Observe how the artist conveys the dimension of depth. (The Bettmann Archive)

FIGURE 21-18
PRINCIPLE OF LINEAR PERSPECTIVE

This classic engraving by Brook Taylor, 1811, is a study in the eye's perception of converging lines. It shows how the solid block at the left can be projected onto the flat surface of the window.
(From p. 73 of M. H. Pirenne, *Optics, Painting and Photography*. Cambridge University Press, 1970.)

The painter also uses the fact that an object casts a smaller image on the retina the farther away it is. Gradients of size can produce a strong depth effect, as illustrated in preview Figure 7. We also see more detail in nearby objects than in distant ones, and near objects are seen more clearly than are far ones—partly because more air (including dust particles, etc.) obscures the farther objects. Scattering of light by the air varies for the different wavelengths, so that far objects seem less red and more blue than do nearby ones. All of these observations were put to good use by Renaissance artists like Da Vinci.

One monocular cue that cannot be used in a two-dimensional painting is **motion parallax.** This term refers to the fact that as you move your head, or as you walk or ride, near objects change their positions rapidly in your visual field while far objects remain still, or move less. Furthermore, the images of objects nearer to you than the point on which your gaze is fixed move in the opposite direction from the one in which you are moving, while objects farther away than the point of fixation move in the same direction as you are going. Relative distance can be perceived when motion parallax alone provides information, but this kind of perception must be integrated over time. We are far from a full understanding of the physiological processes involved.

Auditory Localization

Just as there are monocular and binocular cues to visual space, so there are monaural (one ear) and **binaural** (two ears) **cues** to auditory space. From stimulation of either ear alone, we can get some idea of the distance of a sound source if we know something about the intensity and the sound spectrum at the source: the less intense the sound, the farther away the source must be; and the greater the relative damping of high frequencies relative to low frequencies, the farther away the source must be, since high frequencies are propagated through space less well than low ones (think of the sound of a foghorn nearby as against one far away). But, just as the differential location of the two eyes yields the powerful cue of retinal disparity, so too a most significant aspect of our auditory space localization equipment is the sheer fact that our two ears are separated by a few inches. This means that the pattern of stimulation of the two ears at a given moment in time is usually slightly different, unless of course the sound source is directly in front of the observer (or directly above him, or directly behind him or, for that matter, is located anywhere on the surface of a plane that perfectly divides the right from the left half of his body). If the sound comes, say, from the right of the observer, the right ear will receive a slightly more intense stimulus, some of the frequency components may be damped a bit for the left ear, and the right ear will receive the stimulus a tiny fraction of a second earlier than the left ear will. The auditory sensory apparatus and the brain are organized so that these binaural differences result in a perception of a sound source located in a particular direction from the observer—in this case, to the right.

The ability to localize sound adds to both our acuity and our enjoyment of sound. In a noisy situation, we can hear voices or other signals better when we can localize them and attend to them separately from the background. In the case of music, sound localization allows us to attend separately to the different instruments in an orchestra; this is why stereophonic records are deemed preferable to monaural ones.

Localization raises some interesting questions. Consider the listener in a concert hall; sound reaches him not only directly from the source but is also reflected to him from the ceiling, the walls, and other surfaces. Reflection takes time, so that the same sound is reaching the listener at slightly different times, and a reflected tone reaches him at the same time as a more recent tone from the source directly. Why is it, then, that we don't hear a confused jumble of direct sounds, echoes, and reverberations coming from the orchestra, the ceiling, and the walls? The answer is that the direct sound partially inhibits the reflected sounds, and there is also a "backward inhibition" of the later-arriving reflected sounds on the direct sound (von Békésy, 1971). That is, a reflected sound that arrives about 60 milliseconds later (because it has followed a path about twenty meters longer) can

The acoustical engineer who designs such concert halls needs to be both a physicist and a psychologist. (The New York Times)

inhibit perception of the original sound. (In vision also, if two stimuli are presented in succession, the second can "wipe out" the first if the interval is about 60 msec.) If the interval becomes as long as 120 msec, then two separate distinguishable sensations occur. In other words, if you are in a room with "poor" acoustics, annoying echoes and reverberations are indeed a problem. The physical problems of room acoustics, therefore, are resolved if "echo delay" is kept within bounds the auditory system can handle; echoes need not be totally eliminated. A good acoustical engineer is part physicist, but part psychologist too.

SUMMARY

Perception is dependent on relations among stimuli. In perceptual contrast, a percept varies according to its relations with the surround. The same size stimulus seems small in the company of large objects, large in relation to tiny objects. A light stimulus on a dark background looks white and, on a bright background, may look dark, even black. These are examples of simultaneous contrast, where perception of the stimulus is affected by other stimuli simultaneously present. There is also successive contrast, in which the preceding stimuli affect the perception of a particular stimulus. Figural aftereffects are examples of successive contrast; a given circle looks large after a series of small circles, small after large circles.

Perceptual constancy is the opposite of contrast in the sense that constancies refer to percepts that remain the *same* in spite of *differing* stimulation, not to differing percepts of the same local proximal stimulus. Brightness constancy, for example, means that a "white" object looks white in both dim and bright light, even though in dim light it may reflect less light than a "black" object in sunlight. Brightness constancy is dependent on the ratio of light reflected from various parts of a stimulus array. An object that reflects twice as much light as its surround will be perceived as about equally bright in dim light and sunlight.

Perception of movement may be fairly direct, a result of activity in cells of the central nervous system called "motion detectors." Speed, however, is clearly relative; how fast does something move in relation to the motion of something else? Apparent direction of movement also depends upon relational, interactive processes; in what direction, relative to some point of reference, does something move? Apparent movement can be induced in several ways, such as eliminating all "points of reference." A stationary pinpoint of light in a dark room appears to wander about for this reason.

Perceptual grouping or figure formation can be described in terms of a number of Gestalt principles. Similarity, proximity, closure, continuity, and common fate, all can be subsumed under the law of Prägnanz, which states that the organization of any configuration tends to be as "good" as the prevailing conditions allow. When a figure can be perceived in different ways, it will usually be seen as the "best" possible form.

Although past experience often influences perception greatly, its role is limited when basic perceptual principles are sufficient to determine the percept. For example, figures can be camouflaged by breaking up their perceptual organization; these effects are strong enough to erase the influence of familiarity. The principles of perceptual organization describe how the stimulus input gets segregated into figure and ground. The figure appears to "own" the contour, while the ground seems to continue behind the figure; the figure is also remembered better than the ground.

The location of objects in visual or auditory space often depends on differential cues from the two eyes (binocular) or the two ears (binaural). But cues from one eye (monocular) or one ear (monaural) also suffice to localize a stimulus in many cases. For example, even with one eye, objects nearer to us show finer grain, more detail; even with one ear, a nearby foghorn sounds louder, and it has a higher pitch than one farther away, because higher frequencies travel less well through air.

22

The Creativity of Perception

Is perception a hypothesis?
How do we recognize patterns?
How do attention and motivation affect perception?
How do hereditary and environmental factors interact to determine perception?

This chapter will stress the active role of the perceiver. We have already seen that both the characteristics of a single stimulus (Chapter 20) and its relations to other stimuli (Chapter 21) affect perception. But of all the stimuli reaching our sense organs, only a small fraction are acted upon, and this "acting upon" is very much a function of the perceiver's characteristics—attention, past experience and memory, and social and cultural factors. The active role of the perceiver is also a very creative one; we do not simply accept or reject a percept that is entirely determined by stimulus characteristics. Instead we create percepts from the information we have, and this information is partly sensory, partly personal, and partly social. We may even create a percept with no sensory input at all, as in the case of hallucinations. Some people claim to be able to perceive accurately without having to receive sensory information; this is discussed in Spotlight 22-1 on extrasensory perception.

Is perception a hypothesis?

Consider what happens when our sense organs are affected by an energy change in the environment. First of all, we now know that the effective stimulation does not cease immediately with the offset of the physical stimulus. For up to a second after the offset of, say, a brief presentation of nine or ten letters, the perceiver retains

SPOTLIGHT 22-1

Extrasensory Perception?

There are many accounts of individuals "knowing" something that could not have come from sensory information in the usual sensory channels. Most of these anecdotes involve events in which something happens to loved ones—a serious injury, some sudden good fortune, a death, and the like. Even dogs have been reported to have acted strangely when some important event occurred in the life of their distant masters.

Individual anecdotes are colored by coincidence, error, misinterpretation, and unintentional fabrication; hence most psychologists are not convinced of the reality of **extrasensory perception** (ESP) on the basis of the evidence from such accounts. More convincing would be clear-cut laboratory evidence obtained under well-controlled conditions.

There are three main kinds of phenomena typically considered ESP: **clairvoyance,** sensing something when the physical stimulus cannot affect the sense organs (e.g., "seeing" the message inside a sealed envelope); **telepathy,** one person "reading" another person's thoughts; and **precognition,** or perceiving some event in the future. Another class of phenomena often discussed in connection with ESP is **psychokinesis** (or PK), which concerns the effects of mental events on physical ones, or "mind over matter." PK involves no sensing or perception; it is more like a "motor" act. Examples would be concentrating upon a particular number to make the appropriate faces come up when dice are thrown, projecting an imaginary image onto unexposed photographic film to make the image emerge when the film is developed, or praying to make a plant grow taller.

The scientific case for ESP is based on empirical findings that, under the ordinary canons of scientific credibility, are relatively sound. The most widespread method for studying ESP uses a deck of twenty-five cards, each with one of five different symbols: a circle, a star, wavy lines, a square, or a cross. In a test of clairvoyance, the subject, who cannot see the cards, guesses what each card is. Telepathy is tested in the same way, but with a "sender" concentrating upon each card as he turns it over; the subject, who cannot see the cards, acts as "receiver." In a test of precognition, the subject guesses beforehand what the order of all twenty-five cards will be; then the deck is shuffled, and the correspondence between the actual order of the cards and the subject's predictions is determined. This last procedure could also be used as a design for studying psychokinesis, if the intent of the subject is to influence rather than to predict the cards' subsequent order.

In such tests, the number of guesses that would be correct by chance is five out

almost all of the information in the display in a form called the **icon** (Neisser, 1967). The icon is a rather literal reproduction of the stimulus array, like an afterimage, a brief period of "photographic memory" that all of us can achieve. But this period is very brief, and if the information is to be processed further, it must be encoded in some way. Here perceiver characteristics become important. Some of the stimof twenty-five. Some experimenters have reported subjects averaging about seven correct over a long series of trials; such results would be highly unlikely, in a statistical sense, to have occurred purely by chance (Rhine & Pratt, 1957). Some of the early studies contained serious methodological flaws; for example, some of the early sets of ESP cards were printed with such force that the impression on the face of the cards could be faintly seen on their backs; there was no control to avoid the possibility of recording errors which made the subjects' performance appear better than it actually was; and data from runs in which the subject had done especially poorly, because he was "tired," were discarded. But later studies with more careful controls still reported results somewhat better than chance.

Why then is ESP not universally accepted? For one reason, it is a little disconcerting for a critical scientist to be told that only those who "believe in ESP" can obtain positive results—yet this seems to be the case. Furthermore, consistent achievement of an average of ten or more correct has never been reported in any carefully controlled experiment, so even if there is statistical evidence for a small effect, that effect is small indeed. Another source of disbelief is the fact that as the procedures have become better controlled, not only in ESP but also in PK studies (Girden, 1962), the results get worse rather than better. That is, the better controlled the ESP experiment, the smaller the proportion of high-scoring subjects. In most research, the opposite is true; as irrelevant factors come under control, an effect should be enhanced.

There is another problem with ESP; it "makes no sense." There is no coherent theory to explain such phenomena even if one were to admit their existence. Indeed ESP phenomena, if accepted, would call for serious revision of established theories in physics and psychology. These theories have the support of vast quantities of empirical findings, and one should not give them up without strong reason. The experiments of ESP advocates do not constitute "strong reason" by any means.

This problem has been long recognized by the more serious proponents of ESP, and some have even tried to explain ESP as a function of physical phenomena like "space-time warps." Strange as this concept may sound, it is a more acceptable approach for scientists than to use terms like "occult" or "supernatural." And with physicists talking of particles moving backward in time and having negative energy, it is perhaps not strange at all. But, for the present, most psychologists are not convinced about the reality of ESP.

ulus information must be lost, but the selection of that which is to be further acted upon is by no means random. Material that is important (in a personal sense) is favored, and habits play a role, too; we retain best letters on the left of a display partly because we have learned to read from left to right.

In any case, the perceiver is now left with reduced information and must create a percept. This constructive, creative act can be seen as the forming of a hypothesis about "what is out there" (Bruner, 1957; Gregory, 1966; Solley & Murphy, 1960). For example, it has been suggested that many visual **illusions,** such as the "arrowhead illusion" in preview Figure 1, stem from this creative act. As Figure 22-1 illustrates, the configuration of lines in the illusion is one we often see in corners. If the corner of a room, say, is far away, we get a view much like line *B;* if it is close, the view is more like line A. Thus if one of two equal lines is seen as close (*A*) and the other is seen as far (*B*), which is *really* longer? Why *B*, of course, as we know from the discussion of size constancy (p. 575). It's a hypothesis generated by information about (1) line length, (2) the angle of the horizontal lines, and (3) past experience with such configurations. But it's a percept, not simply a judgment; line *B* actually *looks* longer. You have constructed a percept from ordinarily reliable information, a percept that can be called illusory only in the barren and arbitrary world of controlled experiments. In real life, *B is* usually longer.

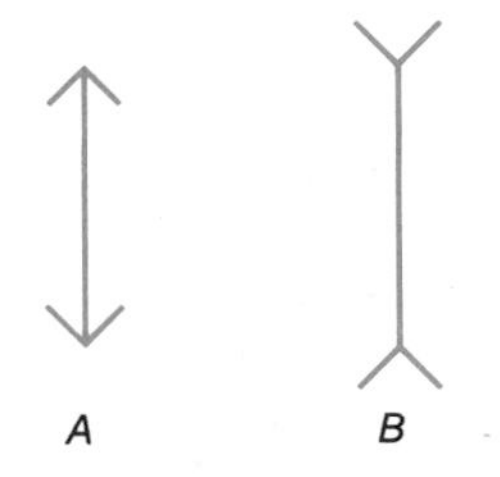

FIGURE 22-1 MÜLLER-LYER ARROWHEAD ILLUSION

This illusion may occur because the two patterns (*A* and *B*) are interpreted as corners of objects that are equal in visual angle but are near, as in the left photo, or far.

(Philip Clark, from *The Intelligent Eye,* by R. L. Gregory, © 1970 by Weidenfeld & Nicholson, London.)

If this view of this illusion is correct, we should be able to test it in cultures with few corners where people live in round houses. These people would be expected to see lines *A* and *B* as more nearly equal. Such studies have been done, and the results are generally consistent with the hypothesis theory of perception; see p. 617.

There is of course another stage in the perception process, and that is the verbal report of the person describing what he sees or hears or tastes. Perhaps this stage is not best defined as perceptual, but we rely on these reports to study the percept. Decision processes enter here. The subject may see something but report that he has not. Signal detection theory (pp. 504, 548) has helped distinguish perception from decision in many situations, and the fact that subjects may decide not to report what they perceive has been used in experiments on conformity (p. 62). So the perception psychologist must remember that verbal reports and percepts are not the same thing.

The selection of information from the icon, the creation of a percept from many types of information, and the possible decision to report not quite what he perceives, all illustrate the active role of the perceiver. There are other phenomena we could mention; characteristics of the perceiver, for example, determine where he is in the environment, in which direction he is looking, and so forth. Thus, the perceiver can literally decide in many cases which physical energy changes he would like to affect his sense organs.

How do we recognize patterns?

The creative role of the perceiver is well illustrated by pattern recognition, a complex task that has been investigated in depth. How does our information-processing system go about such fundamental tasks as recognizing meaningful patterns like the letter *A*? The task seems very simple until you start to think about it or to specify how a machine could be programmed to perform it. We have little difficulty recognizing *A* printed or handwritten, large or small, erect or tilted. But reading handwriting is something no inanimate system—even large computer resources—can perform very well yet. Thinking about the problems of pattern recognition has gone through three stages, each representing a more complex and more adequate solution (Neisser, 1967). The three hypotheses have been called (1) template matching, (2) feature analysis, and (3) analysis-by-synthesis.

Template-matching means comparing the stimulus with a fixed standard form (the template). This is what a machine does when it "reads" the curiously shaped magnetic numerals that appear at the bottom of most bank checks. The bank machine has no problem about various forms of the numerals, because these are standard, and so are their size, orientation, and position. If any of these stimulus aspects were changed, the machine could no longer function. Obviously, our human perceptual mechanisms must be more flexible than this in order to categorize properly all of the variety of stimuli that we recognize as instances of *A*. More complex template-matching systems have been elaborated, but they still have limited capacities.

Feature analysis works by extracting parts of patterns—such as horizontal strokes, vertical strokes, or arcs of circles—and finding which combination of features is characteristic of any particular pattern. Thus, *A* is made up of two oblique lines converging at their tops and joined somewhere between top and bottom by a horizontal line. Note that this description holds equally well for large and small *A*'s, for fat and thin *A*'s, for *A*'s placed anywhere in the visual field, and it even holds if the pattern is tipped somewhat (but not if it is tipped very far). Describing the features of a written letter is more difficult but entirely feasible. Computer programs have been written that can discriminate printed letters on the basis of feature analysis, but "reading" varied samples of handwriting seems so far to be too difficult to be accomplished in this way. Still, feature analysis does seem to play a role in human perception; we will see in the section on biological psychology that there is evidence that particular cells in the brain serve as "horizontal line detectors," "vertical line detectors," "angle detectors," and so on (see pp. 671–72).

Analysis-by-synthesis implies a more creative role for the perceiver. Neisser (1967) compares the process with the paleontologist who sees a mass of bone chips, dirt, and rocks, extracts a few fragments he considers important—and then reconstructs a dinosaur! The perceiver similarly takes in sensory information, selects some of it as important and discards some as irrelevant, and then—using information from memory, too—constructs his percept of a particular letter or meaningful pattern. Various strokes and arcs are synthesized and tested (as in hypothesis testing) to see if they form a letter in the alphabet. If so, does it fit with other letters to make a word in the

In perceiving we reconstruct the world around us from bits and pieces of information, somewhat as an archaeologist reconstructs artifacts of the past.
(Courtesy University Museum)

language? Does this word fit with other words to make a reasonable sentence? It should not be thought that this process is slow, deliberate, and conscious; in most cases, it is presumed to be rapid and automatic; it is presumed to be happening, for example, as you read a handwritten letter from a friend.

Analysis-by-synthesis, perhaps in combination with feature analysis and even some complex template-matching, seems a better description of the perceptual processes involved in pattern recognition than those that preceded it. The view is obviously related to notions of percepts as hypotheses (see p. 601), and though almost certainly wrong in some details, it represents an important advance in perception theories of pattern recognition.

A number of experimental situations have been designed to explore further the active role of the perceiver. For example, in one study subjects were presented with a series of slides of a common object; the first slide was badly blurred and each successive slide was clearer than the one preceding it (Bruner & Potter, 1964). The subject was asked to try to name the object each time. If a subject gave a wrong identification of an object on an early blurred slide, he often did not recognize it correctly until it became quite clear—clearer than would have been required to recognize it at the outset. That is, once a wrong percept was formed, it had to be dislodged before the correct perception could be achieved.

Speech Perception

An example that is still closer to everyday experience comes from the perception of speech. When a person talks to us in our own language, it is clear that he is uttering a series of words; we can tell where one word ends and where the next word begins. This is not the case with an unfamiliar language; there all the words seem to be jumbled together in a hurried flow with few distinct breaks. Actually, analysis of the acoustic patterns of speech shows that words in English are no more separate and distinct than are words in other languages; some pauses in the middle of words in an English sentence are longer than most of the transitions between words. The separateness of words in a familiar language occurs not in the stimulus but rather in our perceptual reconstruction of words and phrases. We implicitly recognize this when we aid the verbal perception of people with a poor command of English, such as foreigners or young children, by introducing artificial gaps between words as we speak.

An ingenious experimental procedure suggests that we process (or synthesize or reconstruct) sentences in rather long chunks of words. In the experiment, a click is superimposed on a tape-recorded sentence, and the subject must identify exactly where in the sentence it occurs (Ladefoged, 1959; Ladefoged & Broadbent, 1960). Subjects make rather large errors in timing the click, usually locating it at a major grammatical break, even if this is not signaled by an acoustic gap or pause. The interpretation is that as the listener analyzes the sentence by synthesizing it, he processes or constructs it in rather large chunks that are difficult to interrupt by other perceptual processes. To make sure that it is not an acoustic feature in the sentence that seems to "call for" the click, one group of investigators constructed pairs of sentences with a special property (Garrett, Bever, & Fodor, 1966). The final portions of both sentences were identical—actually taken from the same strip of recording tape—but the first parts of the sentences were different, and this required a different grammatical structure in the last part. Here is an illustrative pair of such sentences, with the identical parts in italic:

1. As a direct result of their new invention's *influence the company was given an award.*
2. The retiring chairman whose methods still greatly *influence the company was given an award.*

In sentence (1) the major grammatical break is just after *influence*, whereas in (2) it follows *company*. When a click was delivered simultaneously with the first syllable in *company*, it was usually heard much earlier in (1) than in (2), near the main grammatical break in each case, even though the italic portions of both sentences were acoustically identical. Thus, the perceived place of the interruption was largely determined by how the listener constructed or construed the sentence.

Research in speech perception, then, has provided a wealth of information about pattern recognition. If you stop to think about it, the recognition of spoken messages, in their acoustic and linguistic intricacy, is quite a remarkable accomplishment on the part of the sensory system and the brain. The information that is processed, and the meaning that is derived from it, is really incredibly complex.

The basic information in a speech stimulus is contained in the frequencies of the component sounds, their intensities, and the changes in frequencies and intensities through time. If this information is electronically recorded, one gets a speech spectrogram such as the one in Figure 22-2. This kind of "visible speech" contains the main auditory information of speech. In fact, people can learn to read such signals; a few deaf people have attached to their telephone an apparatus which yields visible speech, enabling them to "hear" (see) the auditory message and, therefore, to hold conversations. Deaf children usually have trouble learning to speak properly because they cannot monitor (hear) their own speech sounds. But with electronic recording devices, the deaf child can see the discrepancy between his vocalizations and those his speech therapist wants him to make. Supplying this feedback to the deaf child greatly facilitates his learning.

Perception of words is, of course, pattern perception. That is, we can recognize the word "dough" whether the speaker says it quickly or slowly (alters it in the time dimension), whether the

Speech is composed of a series of patterns, and the perception of words and sentences involves pattern recognition. Speech therapy can aid children with impaired hearing to perceive and replicate speech patterns.
(Van Bucher, Photo Researchers)

speaker uses a high or low pitch (alters it in the frequency dimension), loudly or softly (intensity), and whether it is spoken by a man or a woman, a child or an adult (complex qualitative changes). Furthermore, in these cases the various sorts of distortions can also be recognized in the visible speech portrayal.

In Figure 22-2, we have a visual representation of the sound of a particular speaker saying "dough." The initial *d* sound is represented by the initial inflections and the *o* sound by the horizontal concentrations of frequencies (formants). Had he said "dee" instead of "dough," a different picture would emerge. One of the striking findings of such research has been that there is no pattern uniquely representative of the initial *d* sound. The inflections at the beginning of "dee" are quite different from those at the beginning of "dough," as shown in Figure 22-3. English-speaking people have little problem recognizing this initial *d*; a computer would have considerable problems.

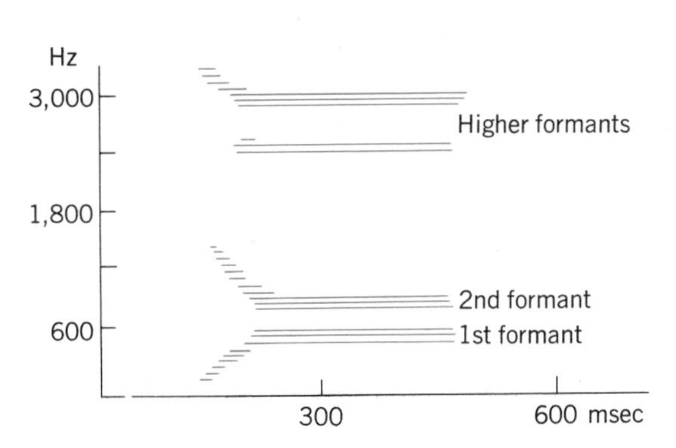

FIGURE 22-2
VISIBLE SPEECH

The *d* sound of the word "dough" is represented as inflections at the beginning, and the *o* sound by the concentrations of frequencies (formants) depicted as horizontal bars. Most of the energy is concentrated in the first two formants, and these are sufficient for recognition of the sound if the higher frequencies are filtered out as they are in Figure 22-3.

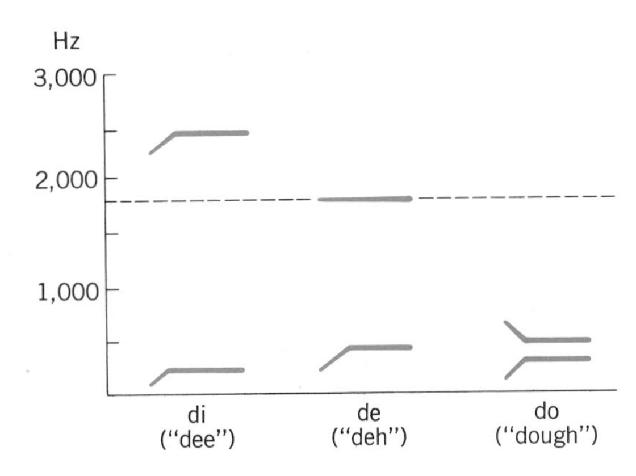

FIGURE 22-3
SIMPLIFIED SPEECH SPECTROGRAMS

The inflections at the start (left end) of each formant bar represent the *d* sound. Note that in the case of the upper formant the slope of this initial part varies with the height of the formant; it seems to start with reference to the frequency of 1,800 Hz. We recognize all these patterns as *d*, whether they move up or down.
(Modified from Liberman *et al.*, 1967)

Impossible Figures

Now that we have examined how we perceive by forming and testing hypotheses, it is worth reconsidering the two "impossible figures" that we inspected in the preview. One (Figure 10, p. 539) seemed to have three prongs at one end but two prongs at the other, with an inexplicable transition between the two. The other was the drawing "Relativity" by M. C. Escher (Figure 11, p. 539); each part could be understood, but no single overall perspective held for the whole drawing. In both figures we try to see the two-dimensional drawing as an indication of a three-dimensional object or scene. But no hypothesis about a three-dimensional object will fit all the information in either figure, so in a sense these figures cannot be perceived. The figures are intriguing because they baffle our attempts to find hypotheses that will fit all the parts together into a self-consistent percept.

How do attention and motivation affect perception?

Selective Attention

The central nervous system is constantly bombarded by messages from the sense organs; the input at any moment is so complex that it is impossible for us to attend to all of it. So perception works selectively. We pay attention to some part of the input, and not to other parts. Assuming that you have shoes on at the moment, you probably were not aware of the pressure of your right shoe on your foot until it was brought to your attention by this sentence. Comparably, there probably were various sounds stimulating your ears just now which were not in your awareness until you were led to pay specific attention to them. By shifting your **set,** as in becoming aware of the pressure of clothing or in listening for sounds, you can affect what it is that you will notice. Set is just one of the characteristics of the perceiver that can determine attention.

Motivation can also play a role; if you are very hungry, you become more likely to notice the smell and sight of food. A hungry person may be quite aware of the restaurant across the street, but not notice the menswear shop next door, while the man looking for a shirt might notice the clothing store but not be aware that there is a restaurant next to it.

Past experience also structures which aspects of the input will be noticed. Thus the artist, the geologist, the rock climber, and the child from the city will each notice different aspects of a particular cliff in the Rocky Mountains: its aesthetic proportions, its strata, the best route for ascent, or its sheer overwhelming bulk.

It is not only characteristics of the perceiver that determine attention, of course. Characteristics of the stimulus also play a major role. Other things being equal, stimuli which are particularly intense, which move, or which are new and unusual are more likely to be noticed. Repetition is another principle of selection in perception; repetition of a stimulus attracts attention, as long as it does not occur too frequently. All of these come down to a basic principle of *contrast:* anything which differs markedly from routine input is more likely to be noticed. A colored picture in a black and white magazine will stand out, as will a black and white figure in a full-color context. Similarly, a few lines of type set at a slant on a page in a newspaper, flashing lights, or an ad printed upside-down will catch the viewer's eye. So will a PHRASE PRINTED IN CAPITAL LETTERS embedded in regular type.

All these principles of course can be, and are, imaginatively used in advertising. You could easily find examples that use motivation to gain our attention, that, for example, use sex to get us to read or hear the company's message—which often is totally unrelated to sex. Television commercials often employ intense or unusual stimuli, rapid changes, and other devices based on the principle of contrast. The use of such stimulus characteristics attracts the attention of children—even if they have not yet learned to speak. Some of these same devices are being used for more noble purposes by educational programs such as Sesame Street.

Shutting Out Stimuli

When you attend to one input, you "shut out" others, meaning that attention is selective. There is considerable debate, backed by much research, on the nature of this selective process. For instance, does "shutting out" occur at the level of the peripheral sense organs, or does selection occur later in the more central or cortical processing of information? The first possibility, sometimes called sensory gating, is supported by a study involving recordings of neural (electrical) activity in sensory systems (Hernández-Peón, Scherrer, & Jouvet, 1956). Electrodes were implanted in cats' heads so as to pick up neural activity in the auditory nerve. A series of clicks was sounded; each click produced a burst of neural activity that was recorded by the electrodes. Then a glass jar containing mice was placed in front of the cat; the neural response to the continuing clicks was greatly diminished. When the mice were removed, the neural response to the clicks regained its former magnitude. The interpretation was that the new and interesting visual input inhibited the neural activity in the auditory channel. More broadly, the suggestion was that selective attention operates, at least in part, at the peripheral sensory level.

Attending to Only One Ear

If we put an earphone headset on a subject, we can present one message to one ear and another to the opposite ear; this is called **dichotic stimulation**—from the Greek roots *dich,* meaning in two parts, and *otic,* pertaining to the ear. This setup has proved to be valuable in the study of selective attention. For example, one investigator (Treisman, 1960) instructed her subjects to "shadow" one of the messages—repeat it out loud as he heard it. By and large, subjects could perform this task quite well. It was noted that material coming into the other ear—to which the subjects were not attending—was rarely retrievable; it was as if this message had been gated out by conscious intention induced by the instructions. (See pp. 520–21 for dichotic phenomena and short-term memory.)

Expectation and context also play a role, however. If in the middle of a sentence, the two messages were switched, the subjects could not maintain attention to one ear. For example, consider the following messages:

Left ear: SITTING AT A MAHOGANY / three POSSIBILITIES . . .

Right ear: Let us look at these / TABLE with her . . .

The subject was instructed to shadow the left ear, but when the messages were switched (at the slash), the subject followed the message to the right ear for one word. (The words in capitals were the subject's report.)

Other experiments with a similar technique have provided further evidence that *some* information does "get through" the "unattended" channel after all (Cherry, 1953). For example, subjects did notice the change when a low-frequency tone replaced prose or when a man's voice was substituted for a woman's in the *unshadowed* message. Further, if the unshadowed message was identical to the shadowed one, subjects noticed that it was the same, even if one message lagged behind the other by several seconds. Whether or not we will notice a stimulus depends upon such things as familiarity, even if the stimulus is coming along a channel that seems to be "shut down." Thus a subject who is shadowing prose presented to one ear will notice his name presented to the other ear (which the subject is supposed to be ignoring), a finding that fits well with common sense (Moray, 1959). Even sleeping subjects respond more to their own name, as measured in physiological recordings, than they do to other names (Oswald, Taylor, & Treisman, 1960).

That the message in the unattended ear can be processed in a complex way, even though the subject is intentionally shadowing the input to the other ear, was shown in another ingenious recent experiment (Korchin, personal communication). The investigator had subjects listen to, repeat, and write down a list of unrelated words presented to the right ear while another list of words was given simultaneously to the left ear. Among the words presented to the right ear were several homonyms such as "see (sea)," so that the subject had to make a choice whether to write "see" or "sea"—even though subjects were usually unaware that a choice was involved. Each homonym was paired with a specially chosen word in the other, unattended ear. For example, when "see (sea)" was delivered to the right ear, half the subjects had the word "wave" in their left earphone, while the other half had "look." These "unheard" words in the other ear definitely influenced what was written down, although the effect did not occur for each subject on each homonym. Subjects tended to choose the homonym that was suggested by the simultaneous word in the other ear. We will see a little later (p. 616) that personality characteristics help to determine how much the subject is influenced by such unconscious stimuli.

Effect of Motivation

The selectivity of perception can obviously be affected by motivation, as we have seen in the ability of subjects to shadow one ear if instructed to do so. We have also noted unintentional deviations when, for example, messages are switched. Motivation to attend to something, of course, is not by itself a guarantee of success. Subjects motivated by instructions can *focus* attention better on inputs (e.g., auditory vs. visual) and targets (e.g., violin vs. flute) than on stimulus dimensions such as intensity (Treisman, 1969).

So perception is affected by both ability and motivation. We have said much about perceptual abilities, and now we can note some findings of motivational effects. Keep in mind, however, that ability and motivational factors rarely operate in isolation in everyday real-life situations.

Set and expectation are motivational factors we have just discussed. Figure 22-4 displays a pattern that is reported as a capital letter *B* if preceded by other capital letters, but as the number 13 if the subject is "set" for two-digit numbers.

FIGURE 22-4
AN AMBIGUOUS FIGURE
If this pattern is shown to a subject after he has seen a series of single capital letters, such as *F, R, M,* he will tend to report it as the letter *B*, but if it follows presentation of a series of two-digit numbers, like 24, 36, 87, he will tend to report it as the number 13.

Effects of set have also been demonstrated with the ambiguous picture, "My Wife and My Mother-in-law," that you saw in the preview; it is repeated here as Figure 22-5A. When students looked at this figure with no special preparation or set, 65 percent saw a young woman turning her head away over her right shoulder and 35 percent saw an old hag. Two other groups of students were shown the ambiguous drawing only after they had been given special preparation (Leeper, 1935). Group *B* was first shown Figure 22-5B, which was drawn to emphasize the young woman. After fifteen seconds of inspecting this drawing, they wrote out descriptions of it. Group *C* was shown Figure 22-5C (the old woman), and wrote descriptions of that one. The students in each group were then shown the ambiguous figure and were asked to describe it. In Group *B*, which had seen the drawing of the young lady, all 25 subjects saw the young lady in the ambiguous figure. In Group *C*, 30 of the 31 subjects saw the old woman and only one saw the young woman. No statistical tests were needed to demonstrate the significance of these results.

Motivational factors can also affect attributes like the judged size of an object. Estimates by children of the size of poker chips increased as the chips were made valuable to them (because

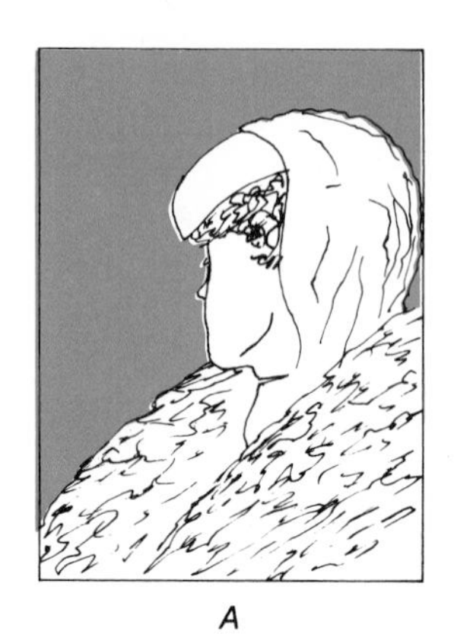

FIGURE 22-5
MY WIFE AND MY MOTHER-IN-LAW
A is an ambiguous figure. Subjects who see *B* first, later see a young woman in *A;* subjects who have seen *C* first, see an old woman in *A.* (Leeper, 1935, after Boring, 1930)

they could be used to get candy); these estimates decreased again when the chips lost their value (when they could no longer be turned in for candy) (Lambert, Solomon, & Watson, 1949). The mean estimated height of a stranger introduced to classes at an Australian university increased as a function of the status attributed to him. When introduced as "Mr. England, a student from Cambridge," he was judged to be 5 ft. 10 in. tall; as "Mr. England, lecturer in psychology from Cambridge," 5 ft. 11 in. tall, while as "Professor England, from Cambridge," his mean estimated height increased to over six feet (Wilson, 1968).

Children overestimate the sizes of coins, with the degree of overestimation increasing with the value of the coin (Bruner & Goodman, 1947); furthermore, children who are reasonably well off tend to overestimate the size of coins less than children from economically less-advantaged families (see Figure 22-6). Similarly, people tend to overestimate the size of paper currency, depending upon its value. Thus, if subjects are asked to draw true to size a $20, a $5, and a $1 bill, the $20 bill will be drawn largest (on the average), and the $5 bill will be drawn larger than the $1 bill. Apparently, then, the "value" a subject places upon an object can influence its apparent size for him.

Perceptual Defense

If there is a stimulus we do not *want* to see, is it harder to recognize? To study defensive processes in perception, a typical procedure has been to expose a list of words one at a time in a **tachistoscope,** a device for presenting visual stimuli at very short durations. Each word is first exposed for such a brief time that it cannot be recognized. The length of exposure is gradually increased, until the subject can report the word correctly. Under these conditions, common and socially acceptable words are recognized at exposures substantially shorter than those required for various taboo words (like unprintable four-letter words) interspersed within the rest of the list (McGinnies, 1949). These results were taken as evidence of "perceptual defense" —the person's refusal to see unwanted stimuli.

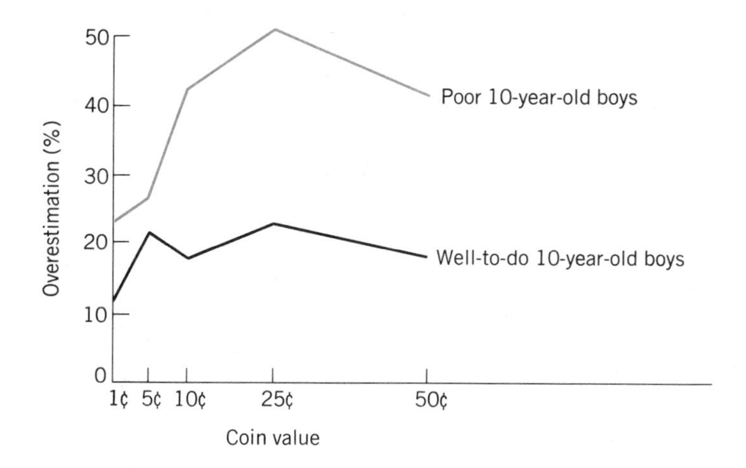

FIGURE 22-6 THE EFFECT OF COIN VALUE ON THE ESTIMATION OF COIN SIZE
When asked to judge the size of coins, ten-year-old boys tended to overestimate the sizes of coins more, the greater the value of the coins. Moreover, boys from poorer families, for whom the coins were presumably more valuable than they were for boys from families that were better off, overestimated the sizes of the coins more than did the boys from well-to-do families.
(After Bruner & Goodman, 1947)

Other investigators were quick to point out that subjects may be hesitant to say such words out loud in the social setting of an experimental psychology laboratory, at least until they are *very* sure of the correct response. Still others suggested that the effect could be explained simply by the "commonness" of the stimuli; words that are uncommon, as estimated by word counts in magazines and newspapers, take longer to recognize even if they are not "taboo." In reply, the advocates of the defense hypothesis pointed out that publications do not provide good estimates of the frequency of four-letter words, which may be frequent in speech. More recent work (e.g., Minard, Bailey, & Wertheimer, 1966) has introduced intricate controls for possible "response bias" and some apparently defensive effect remains. This perceptual effect may well be related to some of the Freudian defense mechanisms that were discussed in the section on personality (see p. 222).

Person Perception

During the last two decades or so, psychologists have begun investigating perception of people; such research has been labeled "person perception" or "impression formation." How do we come to judge others as kind, generous, cold, beautiful, or intelligent? Such impressions are often quite compelling, and they can be formed as soon as we see someone for the first time. Since many of these attributions of particular characteristics to other people are not directly perceivable—they are judgments, sometimes tenuous—many psychologists have felt that it would be wiser to call this area "person cognition" rather than "person perception."

It has been demonstrated experimentally that the processes of person cognition are very complex and that interaction plays a major role in these impressions. A particular act performed by the same person in two different contexts may lead to very different impressions of what the act means about the person's personality. In one study (Lambert, Hodgson, Gardner, & Fillenbaum, 1960) residents of Quebec who were fluent in both French and English were recorded reading passages in each language. English-speaking listeners were asked to rate a large number of speakers on traits such as likability, sincerity, and reliability. They were unaware that each speaker appeared twice, once in English and once in French. The same speaker reliably received more favorable ratings when he spoke English than when he spoke French. Our impressions of others depend in an intricate, interactive way upon expectations we hold ourselves, upon what the other person does, upon our relationships to each other, and a host of other factors (Beach & Wertheimer, 1961).

How individuals employ unconscious material in forming impressions of others was investigated in some other recent experiments (Korchin, personal communication). The dichotic-perception technique, described earlier, was used. In the right earphone, a subject heard and shadowed (repeated aloud) a story about a young man named Harry. Harry went from his small town to the big city. He took up city ways and began to forget about his home. His girlfriend at home began to hear from him less often. Would he remain loyal to her? While the subject was following this story in the right ear, he was told to ignore sentences in the left ear. For some subjects, the sentences in the left ear were favorable to Harry: "Harry is good," "Harry is kind," "Harry is thoughtful," and so forth. For other subjects, the sentences were neutral. And for other subjects, the sentences in the left ear were unfavorable: "Harry is bad," "Harry is selfish," "Harry is inconsiderate," and so on.

When the presentation ended, subjects were asked to complete the story and to fill out adjective checklists about Harry. Subjects who received unfavorable or neutral material in the left ear gave similar responses, but subjects who received favorable material were significantly more favorable to Harry—both in the ways that they concluded the story and in the adjectives they used to describe him. Checks made after these procedures showed that subjects were not aware of the content of the messages to the left ear; nevertheless, their personality judgments were influenced by it.

Personality characteristics of the subjects were found to predict how strongly they would be influenced by the unconscious input to the left ear. Subjects who were found on other tests to be field dependent—relying heavily on external rather than internal clues in forming judgments—were apt to be more strongly affected by the unconscious material. The experiment was also carried out with mental-hospital patients who were well enough to be cooperative subjects. Most schizophrenic subjects gave results similar to those of normal subjects, but paranoid schizophrenics were much more influenced by the unattended sentences. Paranoids, you will recall, are characteristically suspicious of their environment and highly alert to it. Thus, personality variables both within and outside the normal range had measurable effects on person perception.

Cultural Effects

There may be cultural differences in perception that cannot be attributed to differences in perceptual acuity. These may be further instances of the creativity of perception. Some social psychologists have proposed that perceptual illusions may be used to measure cultural differences; they assume that the magnitude of the illusions depends upon the kinds of perceptual judgments a particular culture demands or values highly (Rivers, 1901). In one extensive study (Segall, Campbell, & Herskovits, 1963), almost two thousand people from seventeen different cultures were asked to estimate the lengths of lines in the four illusions shown in Figure 22-7. In all four, the two lines to be judged are equal in length, although they tend to appear unequal. For each subject, the amount of illusory discrepancy was recorded.

The results of most interest and generality can be best described by classifying subjects as either European (including United States subjects and South-African whites) or non-European (in this study, mostly black Africans), and by classifying illusions as "horizontal-vertical" (*C*, *D*) or "involving acute and/or obtuse angles" (*A*, *B*). On the average, Europeans made larger errors on illusions involving acute and obtuse angles, but non-Europeans made larger errors on horizontal-vertical illusions.

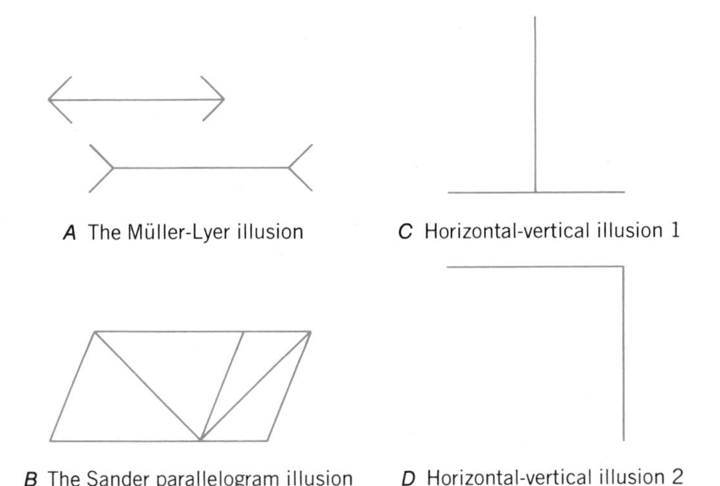

FIGURE 22-7 ILLUSIONS USED WITH SUBJECTS OF SEVERAL DIFFERENT CULTURES

Subjects of some cultures tend to make relatively larger errors in judging illusions involving acute and obtuse angles (*A* and *B*), whereas subjects of other cultures tend to make larger errors on illusions involving horizontal and vertical lines.
(From Segall, Campbell, & Herskovits, *Science*, 1963)

The investigators interpreted these results as reflections of cultural demands learned in response to typical visual environments. Most Americans and Europeans live in settings with a great many rectangular objects—books, buildings, tables, and television screens. People in such environments tend to see obtuse and acute angles as representing three-dimensional objects in perspective. For example, they may see a parallelogram as a rectangle extending away from them, like a book lying on a table. Accustomed to inferring the "true" lengths of lines that are foreshortened by perspective in three-dimensional figures such as buildings, they make similar but incorrect inferences in two-dimensional figures.

Most of the non-European groups in this study lived in dwellings that have few regular angles, but many lived in open countryside where the terrain is flat. The investigators reasoned that their exaggeration of the vertical lines might come from experience in such an environment. The vertical line might be interpreted as a road or some natural feature stretching away into the distance, in which case the line might be assumed to be longer than it looks. Whether these explanations are correct or not, the data suggest measurable and characteristic differences in perception among people of different cultures. A cautious attitude toward such studies is indicated, however, since cross-cultural research is fraught with methodological problems, including those of communication between experimenters and subjects.

How do hereditary and environmental factors interact to determine perception?

In this section of the text, we have repeatedly referred to the role of past experience in determining perceptual responses. In some contexts the role of experience has been crucial, while in others it has been negligible. The question of the extent to which perceptual processes are "built into" the organism (the nativist position) and the extent to which they are learned (the empiricist position) has a long history. Although there have been over three hundred years of speculation and dispute on the topic, full-fledged psychophysical investigations into this issue began as recently as the 1950's (Hochberg, 1962). Modern comparative psychology has been important in showing that a wide range of possibilities actually exists among different animal forms—from those that show mature perceptual abilities from birth to those whose perceptions develop through interaction with the environment. Advances in knowledge of genetic coding have suggested limitations in the degree to which bodily structures and behavior can be determined by hereditary mechanisms; some information may need to be supplied by the environment.

Deprivation of Visual Experience

For a time it looked as though a fruitful way to study the development of perception would be to raise animals without visual experience and then to test their visual discrimination. If they could discriminate from the start, then their ability would be innate; if discrimination emerged only slowly over many trials, then it would be learned. Rats raised in the dark turned out to show unimpaired visual form discrimination (Hebb, 1937), which supported the nativist position. But then experiments were performed with chimpanzees raised in the dark for several months after birth. When these higher animals were tested, they showed little or no ability to see. This seemed to support the empiricist position—until it was found that dark-raising does not allow the retina to develop normally; the animals were almost blind (Chow, Riesen, & Newell, 1957). In subsequent experiments, animals were raised instead with diffuse occluders over the eyes so that they could see light but not form. In this case the retinas did not degenerate and the animals could readily discriminate light from dark, but they still showed little or no ability to discriminate visual forms (Riesen, 1961).

Psychobiological research (to be described in the next section, p. 677) indicated that these animals did not develop normal cortical cells that react specifically to lines, angles, and forms. They did not have biologically abnormal retinas, but biological differences at higher levels could be detected. Thus, it appears that we cannot test the nativism-empiricism problem in this way; a higher organism deprived of certain normal experiences during early development is biologically different from an animal that benefits from normal sensory experiences.

Adaptation to Rearranged Sensory Input

In 1897 Professor George Stratton of the University of California surprised his students and colleagues by wearing odd eyeglasses that made everything look upside-down. He wore these spectacles from morning till night, whenever he had his eyes open; after a few weeks he could walk around easily and perform skilled tasks guided by vision.

More recently, a psychology professor at Innsbruck, Austria, performed a similar experiment upon himself. After several weeks of adaptation, he was able to carry on his usual routines, even riding his bicycle through the twisting, steep streets of the area (Kohler, 1964). This certainly shows that visual orientation and space perception can be modified by experience with rearranged sensory input—although it appears likely that adaptation is more proprioceptive (movement) than visual (Harris, 1965; Rock & Harris, 1967). No subject has ever reported that the visual world "looks right" even after weeks of experience with such rearranged input; it just becomes easier to get around in the peculiar-looking world.

How does all this relate to the normal development of perception? Although the drastic changes caused by reversing lenses are unusual, all of us have had to modify eye-hand coordination as the length of our arms increased with age. As another example of normal adaptation to altered sensory input, we described earlier how localization of sound is based on differential stimulation of the two ears; this also changes during development as the head grows and the ears move farther apart. Some changes that accompany increased age are not necessarily adaptive; see Spotlight 22-2.

SPOTLIGHT 22-2

Space Perception in Chicks

Chicks improve the accuracy of their pecking between the ages of one and four days. Is this improvement a matter of learning?

Eckhard H. Hess performed an ingenious experiment to find out (1956). To measure the accuracy of their pecking, he allowed young chicks to peck at a brass nail embedded in modeling clay; the pecks left little indentations in the clay, providing a convenient record of their behavior. The pattern of pecks made by a one-day-old chick is represented by *A*, while the pecks of a four-day-old chick are shown in *B*. Clearly, the older chick did much better than the younger one. One might guess that the older chick had learned to improve his accuracy in the first few days of his life: when he was pecking at grains, he got food if he hit, but didn't get food if he missed.

To find out whether this kind of reinforcement was indeed responsible for the improvement, Hess made special hoods that were placed on the heads of some chicks as soon as they were hatched. The hoods were fitted with prisms that were held in front of the chicks' eyes, in such a way that visual objects were displaced seven degrees to the right. Compare the pecks of a one-day-old chick (left) and a four-day-old chick (right) wearing the hood. The left-hand record shows that the prisms had their intended effect: the pecks are clearly displaced to the right. But look at the right-hand record. The pecks are indeed more tightly clustered, as in the normal chick's record, but they are still clearly displaced to the right. These rather surprising results show that the visual space perception of young chicks, and the improvement in their pecking behavior, is not dependent on learning; it is a matter of maturation.

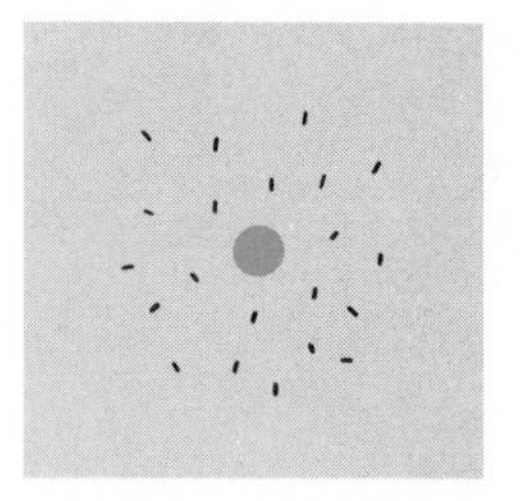

A One-day-old chick

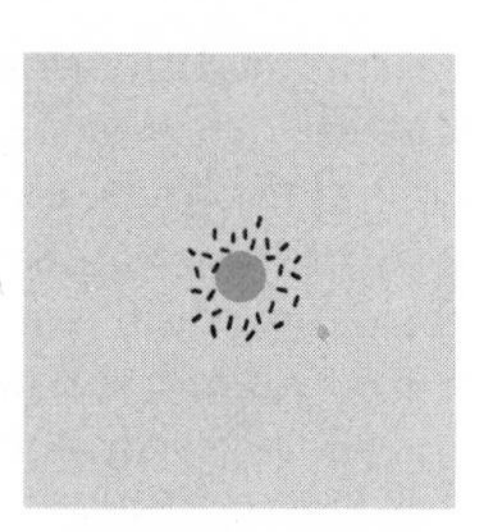

B Four-day-old chick

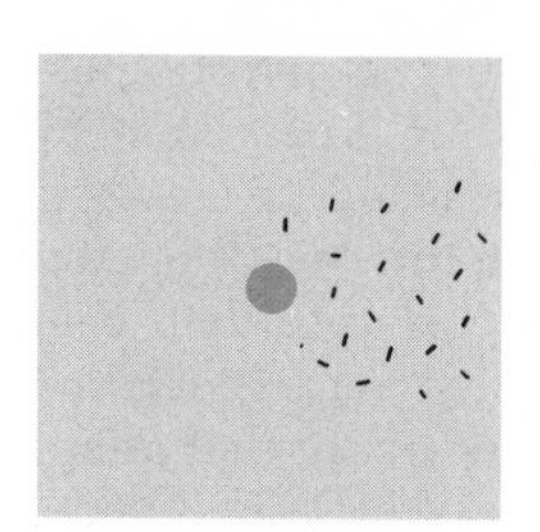

A One-day-old chick wearing prisms

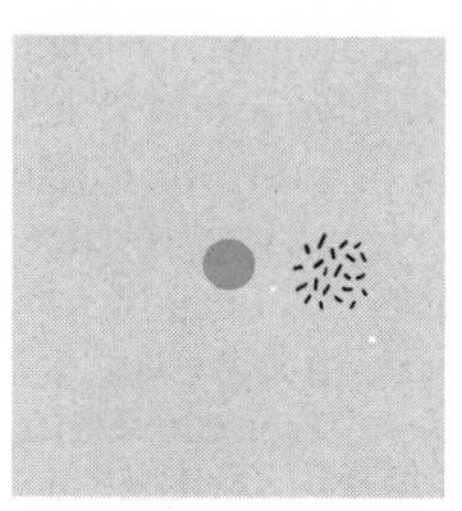

B Four-day-old chick wearing prisms

For more than a decade Richard Held has studied the effects of rearrangement of sensory input in man and in other mammals. In man, adaptation to a visually rearranged environment occurs when the person can make bodily movements and see their perceptual effects. Mere passive exposure to the rearranged conditions does not seem to be sufficient. For example, you can adapt comparatively quickly to "upside-down" glasses when you can move around while you wear them, but just sitting and looking through them does not help you to adapt. But is active movement necessary for the *original* development of visual perception and visual-motor coordination? To answer this question, Held and Hein designed an animal experiment (1963).

Pairs of kittens were raised in the dark with their mothers until the kittens were about ten weeks of age. Then they received three hours a day of visual experience in the apparatus shown in Figure 22-8. The active member of the pair could walk around in its yoke turning in one direction or the other. The other member of the pair was carried passively in its gondola. The mechanical linkages assured that both would get much the same stimulation. For example, when the active kitten turned toward the wall, the gondola also swiveled toward the wall. Neither animal could see its own body or the other animal, but both saw the stripes on the wall and on the central pillar. When not in the apparatus, the kittens remained in the dark with their mothers. After several days, their space perception was tested.

FIGURE 22-8 TESTING SPACE PERCEPTION

The kitten on the right has opportunities to explore the environment actively; the kitten on the left is exposed to it passively. How will they compare on visual space perception later on?
(Ted Polumbaum)

How do you test visual space perception in animals? One convenient method is by use of a **visual cliff** (Gibson & Walk, 1960); this is illustrated in Figure 22-9 and also in preview Figure 9. The animal is placed on a narrow central platform where it can step down an inch or so to a large pane of glass. On the "deep" side the animal can see down through the glass to a patterned surface thirty inches below; on the "shallow" side the pattern is just below the glass. Many species of animals, including young children, have been tested on the visual cliff. They almost invariably go to the "shallow" side. Babies

FIGURE 22-9
SIDE VIEW OF THE
VISUAL CLIFF

A newborn goat will not cross to the "deep" side of the visual cliff.
(William Vandivert © 1966 *Scientific American*)

do that as soon as they can crawl, which has led some investigators to think that some aspects of depth perception must be innate. The kittens in the Held and Hein experiment were tested after they had been in the visual exposure apparatus for as little as three sessions or as many as twenty-one sessions (9 to 63 hours). Six tests were given to each kitten on two successive days.

The results are shown in Table 22-1. Every kitten that moved actively in the apparatus stepped to the shallow side on every trial. No kitten that moved passively showed any consistent discrimination between the two sides. There is no need to perform statistical tests when results are so clear-cut. Other tests showed that the passive kittens had normal pupillary responses to light and could follow moving objects with their eyes, but they had not developed depth perception or other responses to visual space.

In a latter experiment (Hein, Held, & Gower, 1970), each kitten was given both active and passive experience, but one eye was open and the other occluded in the active condition and the other eye was open in the passive condition. These kittens were later tested on the visual cliff, with each eye separately. When a kitten used the eye that had been open during active locomotion, it typically chose the shallow side on each of eight trials. When it used the other eye, it typically chose the shallow side only five out of eight times. So, using

TABLE 22-1
TESTS ON THE VISUAL CLIFF AFTER ACTIVE OR PASSIVE EXPERIENCE

Pair Number	Age in Weeks	Total Exposure in Apparatus (hr)	Active Kittens		Passive Kittens	
			Number of Descents			
			Shallow	Deep	Shallow	Deep
1	8	33	12	0	6	6
2	8	33	12	0	4	8
3	8	30	12	0	7	5
4	9	63	12	0	6	6
5	10	33	12	0	7	5
6	10	21	12	0	7	5
7	12	9	12	0	5	7
8	12	15	12	0	8	4

From Held & Hein, 1963.

each animal as its own control, we see that perception of depth had developed with the eye used in active locomotion but not in the eye used only during passive movement. Note too the lack of transfer of learning from one eye to the other. That is, in normal cats as in normal people, a task learned with one eye can be performed with the other eye. In these experimental kittens, however, the two eyes had never been used together—one or the other had been covered whenever the kittens were in the light—and the kittens had not acquired the "normal" ability to recognize with one eye what had been seen with the other.

Species Recognition

Seagulls probably look pretty much the same to you, unless you happen to be a bird watcher or an ethologist—or a seagull. Actually, there are several species that differ clearly in coloration, especially of the head and bill. How do the chicks of different species come to recognize their own kind?

The chicks of various species of gulls get food in the nest by pecking at the bill of the parent; this is called the "begging response." In response to the chick's pecking, the parent disgorges food. Different species of gulls have different colors of heads and bills. How well can the chick recognize the adult of its own species? Is this discrimination innate or learned? Hailman (1967) worked on these questions with two species of gull. In the laughing gull the adult has a black head and a red beak; in the herring gull the adult has a white head and a yellow beak with a red spot at the end of the lower bill.

In controlled tests, chicks pecked from their first day at any long vertical rod. The color was not very important. On their first day, herring gull chicks pecked about as much at a model head of an adult laughing gull as at a model of the head of a herring gull. During the first few days, however, they came to devote an increasing percentage of responses to the model of their own parent (see Figure 22-10). These were chicks who lived with their parents except for the time spent advancing science; they were fed ordinarily by their parents. So the increasing discrimination pictured in Figure 22-10 could be due to learning; they were being reinforced for pecking at a herring gull in "real life." But there is also the possibility that an innate response is maturing, like the pecking accuracy of chicks described in Spotlight 22-2. A controlled laboratory experiment was necessary to distinguish between these two possibilities.

Three groups of newly hatched laughing gulls were used. They were fed by hand for a week, using an operant-conditioning procedure. Chicks of one group were shown a laughing gull model and given a piece of food whenever they pecked at the model. The second group was treated similarly but with a herring gull model. The third group was fed without any model. Occasional nonreinforced tests were made with both models. Each of the first two groups showed an increasing proportion of pecking directed to the model associated with food, while the control groups did not develop a preference for either model. Thus, the gull chicks were hatched with sufficient form perception to see the parent's bill and sufficient motor control to peck it, but their preference for one or another adult model was learned through reinforcement.

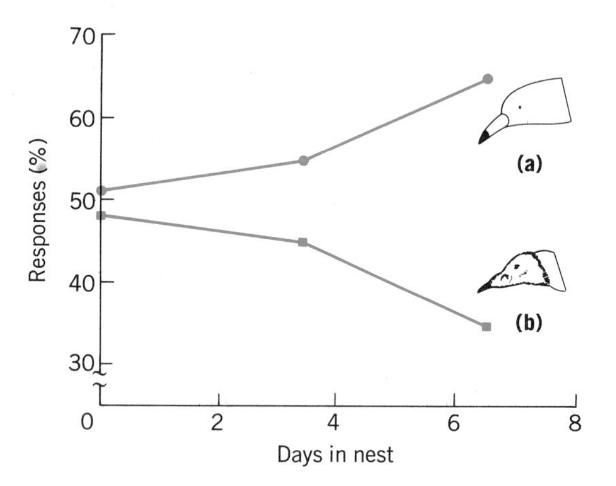

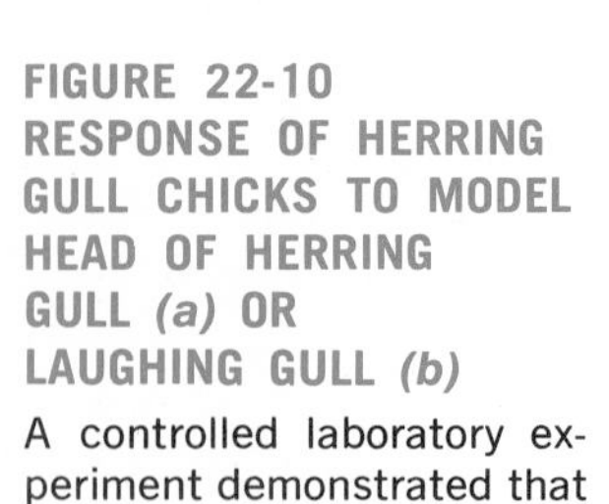
FIGURE 22-10 RESPONSE OF HERRING GULL CHICKS TO MODEL HEAD OF HERRING GULL *(a)* OR LAUGHING GULL *(b)*

A controlled laboratory experiment demonstrated that this naturally occurring preference is learned through reinforcement.

The ability to recognize their own species develops quite differently in different kinds of birds. This is consistent with Anokhin's principle of **systemogenesis**, presented in Chapter 2—that sensory and motor capacities of different species vary in their development according to the requirements of the life of the animal being considered. Thus fowl such as ducks that are hatched by the mother do not require an inborn capacity to recognize the mother. At the start they have a tendency to follow and become attached to (imprinted on) any moving and sound-emitting object, even if that object happens to be a kindly old ethologist like Konrad Lorenz (see p. 781). In nature this tendency usually results in the ducklings becoming attached to the mother, but in experimental situations they may become imprinted on objects as diverse as a scientist or an electric train. On the other hand, a cuckoo or cowbird requires an innate recognition of its own kind, because eggs of these species are laid in the nests of other birds. The cuckoo grows up exclusively with members of another species, yet it manages to recognize another cuckoo when the time comes to mate.

Development of Perception in Children

In children, as in other animals, some perceptual abilities are present from birth whereas others develop through experience. A kind of primitive space perception can be demonstrated with newborn babies. When an observer snapped his fingers to one side of the baby's head, some babies consistently responded by moving the eyes and even the head in the direction of the sound (Wertheimer, 1961). This means that there is coordination between hearing and eye movements at birth, and perhaps also a crude awareness of auditory space.

Other experiments have been done with young babies by suspending stimuli such as those of Figure 22-11 over the crib and measuring the time the child looks at each pattern (Fantz, 1963). It turns out that *A* receives the least attention, *B* somewhat more, and *C* the most. (This is true whatever their relative positions, which must, of course, be counterbalanced in such experiments.) Differences in "complexity" of a stimulus pattern lead to differences in interest, even with the very young.

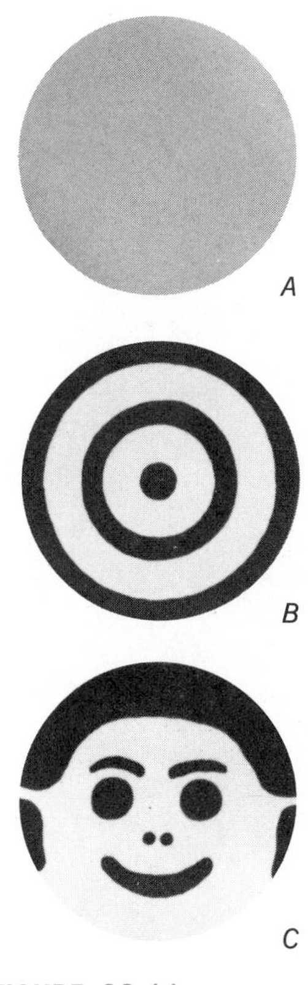

FIGURE 22-11 VISUAL STIMULI USED WITH NEONATES

(David Linton; © *Scientific American*, May 1961)

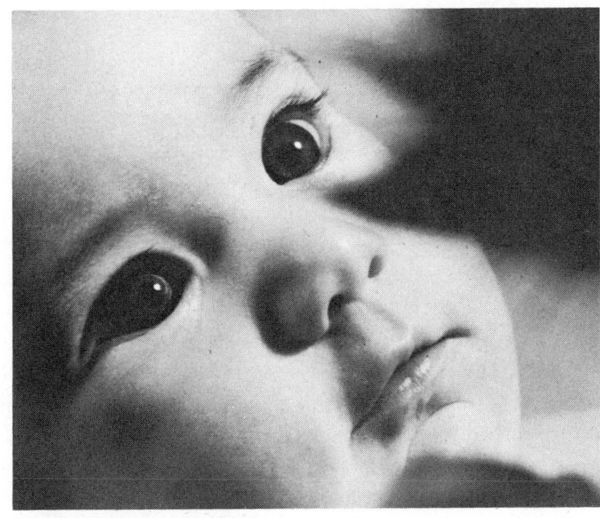

(Charles Harbutt, Magnum)

Nativism vs. Empiricism

It should be clear by now that the old controversy of whether perception is innate or learned is no longer much of an issue in psychology. Some perceptual abilities in some species seem to be innate, and some appear to result from experience, but what is innate in one species may be learned in another. Moreover, innate capacities are significantly influenced by experience, and learning is significantly influenced by genetic capacity. Thus, psychologists have more or less abandoned the old controversy as a pseudo-issue; instead they concentrate on understanding how innate and experiential factors *interact* to produce the behavior patterns we observe. "Nativism versus empiricism" has become "heredity *in interaction with* environment," and this is a scientific advance of no small magnitude.

SUMMARY

Perception is a constructive activity on the part of the organism, with the information-processing system yielding synthetic impressions of the perceptual world by integrating the sensory input. The creative and fundamentally illusory nature of most normal perception (illusory in the sense that the percept does not correspond precisely with the characteristics of the physical stimulation of the receptor surface) raises the question of the veridicality of perception: How is it that our perceptions correspond so well with the objects in the real world within which we move and behave?

Part of the answer lies in hypothesis testing. That is, if perception often involves construction of a percept that is a sort of hypothesis about what's really "out there," then this hypothesis can usually be tested by acting as if the hypothesis were true. If you reach for an imaginary object, the lack of tactile feedback is a new input, and ordinarily you will revise your percept-hypothesis. In adapting to new or rearranged sensory input, we normally move around and thereby vary the input in order to test hypotheses about the new environmental conditions.

The recognition of patterns is a complex task. Explanations in terms of template-matching and feature analysis can account for some phenomena, but neither seems able to explain the power and flexibility of our pattern recognition. A current hypothesis is analysis-by-synthesis; that is, the perceiver recognizes an object (which may be visual or auditory or in some other sensory modality) by actively synthesizing his percept of it from a portion of the available sensory information (plus information stored in memory); if possible, this provisional percept is then checked further against other sensory information or knowledge of the situation.

Constructing a percept on the basis of insufficient information can sometimes make it more difficult to recognize the true pattern. In one experiment, a series of progressively clearer pictures of objects was projected, and subjects who made early wrong guesses took longer to achieve the accurate percept.

Speech perception also involves pattern recognition, and our knowledge of grammatical structure strongly influences how we perceive a spoken sentence. Speech can be displayed visually on a cathode-ray tube, from which it can be literally read. Some patterns that look quite different sound quite similar (*d* in different words). Thus, the pattern recognition capacities of the human are quite complex and quite amazing.

Because we must select from all the various inputs impinging on us at any given time, attention is an important feature of perception. Set and expectation, past experience, and motivation are all determinants of attention. Attention can operate peripherally, determining where the sense organs are directed, and many effects of attention occur in later, more central processing.

There are many motivational effects on perception. A valued stimulus, such as a piece of money, may be overestimated in size. An unpleasant stimulus may not be recognized as quickly as a neutral one—this is perceptual defense.

Forming impressions of people is a perceptual-cognitive activity. Subjects often use information of which they are unaware in their judgments of others. Some of the information can be classed as "cultural," and people generally give more favorable ratings to persons speaking in their native tongue—even in comparison to the same person speaking in a foreign language. Cultural differences in the judgment of illusions suggest that people may organize percepts partly on the basis of the typical visual experiences in their culture.

The nativism-empiricism controversy arises again within the context of perception. In the face of research evidence, much of the controversy now seems irrelevant to an understanding of human and animal behavior. Animals deprived of normal experience lose some of their innate capacities. Normal experience (moving around) is necessary for the utilization of capacities (depth perception) that may be at least partly innate. Some species recognize their own kind through experience and some do so instinctively, and the requirements of life for each species can explain into which category a particular species falls. Most psychologists, therefore, are less interested in taking a strong nativist or empiricist stand than they are in exploring the subtle interactions of heredity and environment in specific behavioral patterns.

RECOMMENDED READING

Beardslee, D., & Wertheimer, M. (Eds.) *Readings in Perception.* New York: Van Nostrand-Reinhold, 1958.
Selected classical papers from the earlier literature on perception.

Gibson, E. J. *Principles of Perceptual Learning and Development.* New York: Appleton-Century-Crofts, 1969.
An award-winning survey of theories of perceptual learning which also reviews what is known about perceptual development.

Gibson, J. J. *The Senses Considered as Perceptual Systems.* Boston: Houghton Mifflin, 1966.
Presents a detailed account of how the perceptual systems work as information-seeking devices.

Gregory, R. L. *Eye and Brain.* New York: McGraw-Hill, 1966. Paperback.
A delightful, authoritative, profusely illustrated popular account of perception that deserves to be a best seller.

——— *The Intelligent Eye.* New York: McGraw-Hill, 1970.
Another fascinating book by Gregory with many intriguing illustrations.

Haber, R. N. (Ed.) *Contemporary Theory and Research in Visual Perception.* New York: Holt, Rinehart and Winston, 1968.
An advanced collection of recent important papers in visual perception.

——— *Information-Processing Approaches to Visual Perception.* New York: Holt, Rinehart and Winston, 1969.
An advanced collection, mostly of quite recent, important papers, sampling the new information-processing orientation to perception.

Lowenstein, O. *The Senses.* Baltimore: Penguin, 1966. Paperback.
A brief introduction to the psychology of sensation, written for the layman, including interesting details about the sensory capacities of animals.

McCleary, R. A. (Ed.) *Genetic and Experiential Factors in Perception.* Scott, Foresman, 1970. Paperback.
A collection of representative papers on the nativism-empiricism problem in perception.

Neisser, U. *Cognitive Psychology.* New York: Appleton-Century-Crofts, 1967.
An award-winning presentation of the analysis-by-synthesis theory of information-processing, with a wealth of detail and careful surveys of evidence; a work that has already left a major mark on the field of perception.

Pirenne, M. H. *Optics, Painting and Photography.* Cambridge, England: The University Press, 1970.
A detailed analysis of linear perspective and space perception, richly illustrated with ingenious experiments and art reproductions.

Stevens, S. S., & Warshofsky, F. *Sound and Hearing.* Life Science Library. New York: Time Incorporated, 1965.
A very readable and profusely illustrated account of hearing in man and animals, whose first author is one of the leading investigators of psychoacoustics.

Von Fieandt, K. *The World of Perception.* Homewood, Ill.: Dorsey, 1966.
A thorough, traditional coverage of the field with a European flavor, and including material on perception of art.

SECTION EIGHT

BIOLOGICAL PSYCHOLOGY

By Mark R. Rosenzweig

Preview

Biological psychology is one of the newest ways to study behavior. People have always had to know a great deal about human behavior in order to live together, but accurate knowledge of bodily mechanisms of behavior is recent and still incomplete. Writings that are thousands of years old—such as those of Confucius, or Buddha, or the writers of the Old Testament—show many insights into human nature that still strike us as applicable or even sometimes as being surprisingly modern, but descriptions of the nervous system written even fifty years ago are hopelessly outmoded. Some psychologists such as B. F. Skinner claim that psychologists should study only behavior and not its bodily mechanisms. But from the time psychology became an independent discipline—about one hundred years ago—many psychologists have devoted themselves to studying the bodily bases of behavior as well as their manifestations in action.

Combining behavioral techniques with those of other biological sciences is advancing our understanding of many aspects of behavior. The other sections of this book consider many central problems about behavior: how individuals differ in temperament, how behavior changes through learning, how perception reflects the outside world accurately in some cases and how it leads to distortion or illusions in other cases, and the extent to which nativistic or empiristic interpretations are valid. In this section we will see how biological techniques are helping to solve these and other important behavioral problems.

Let us look at a few specific examples of research in biological psychology before we go farther. Brief answers, printed upside down, follow the questions, and each of these topics will be taken up in later chapters of this section.

FIGURE 1

What neurological procedure can tame a lynx?

Removal of a small area in the base of the temporal lobes on both sides of the brain tames wild animals. In some cases this area can become abnormally active in human beings and cause pathological aggressive behavior. This will be discussed on p. 714.

(Leonard Lee Rue III, National Audubon Society)

(Courtesy A. Kling)

(Courtesy H. F. Harlow)

FIGURE 2

Some young monkeys usually behave like little ladies, while others frequently wrestle like little boys. Is there a biological basis for their difference in temperaments?

(Courtesy N. E. Miller)

FIGURE 3

Why does this rat press the lever repeatedly, hundreds of times per hour, for hour after hour?

Some sex differences occur in the absence of "culture" (Harlow). These differences in temperament can be modified by early hormonal treatment. See discussion on p. 709.

Each press causes a brief electrical shock to be delivered through the implanted electrode to a "reward" region of the brain (Olds & Milner, 1954); see p. 717. Brain processes involved with reinforcement of behavior are being studied.

(Courtesy J. M. R. Delgado)

FIGURE 4

How did the brain scientist halt the bull?

Pressing a button on a little radio transmitter in his hand, he caused an electrical signal in a wire implanted in an inhibitory region of the bull's brain (Delgado, 1965). See p. 716.

FIGURE 5

Why doesn't this man's left hand know what his right hand is doing? When the examiner places one hand in a particular position, the subject cannot copy it with his other hand.

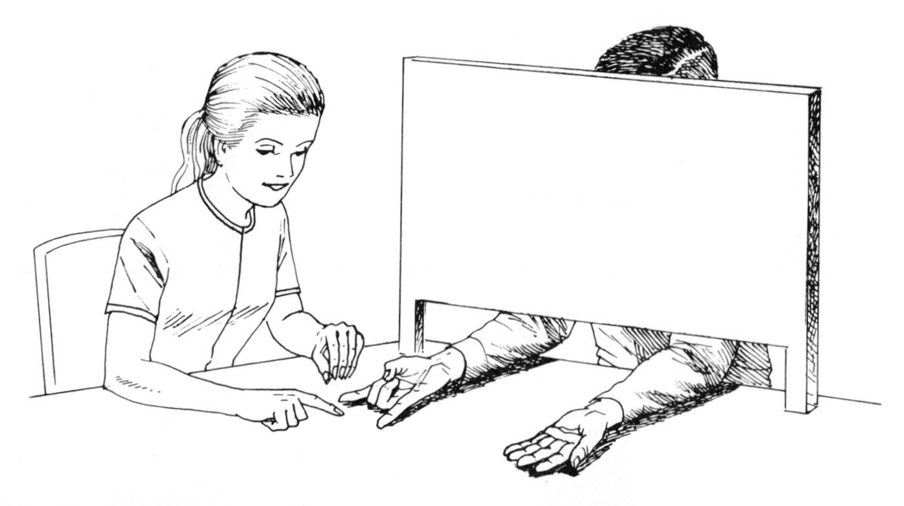

Most people can perform this task easily, but this man has had his corpus callosum transected in a surgical procedure; this is the band of fibers that connects the two cerebral hemispheres. Such people seem, in some ways, to have two separate minds. Research with these subjects is helping to reveal the different roles of the two hemispheres and how they interact; see pp. 741–742.

(Courtesy N. E. Miller)

(Ted Polumbaum)

FIGURE 6

What unexpected facts about obese people have been discovered by extending research on animals that were made obese by physiological techniques?

Obese people are *not* more inclined to start eating than are people of normal weight, but they do not have an effective shut-off mechanism. Their taste preferences do not change after eating as do those of normal-weight people. The obese eat fewer meals, but their meals tend to be longer. These and other findings were first suggested by observations with rats made obese by lesions of the brain; see p. 697.

(Courtesy Stanford University Medical Center's Sleep Disorders Clinic)

FIGURE 7

Sleep researchers sometimes want to waken a subject during a dream. How do they know when to awaken him?

The patterns of electrical brain waves change from dreamless sleep to dreams. By watching the ongoing recordings, researchers can tell how deep sleep is and whether dreams are occurring. Nightmares have been shown in this way to be a different state. See discussion on pp. 700–706.

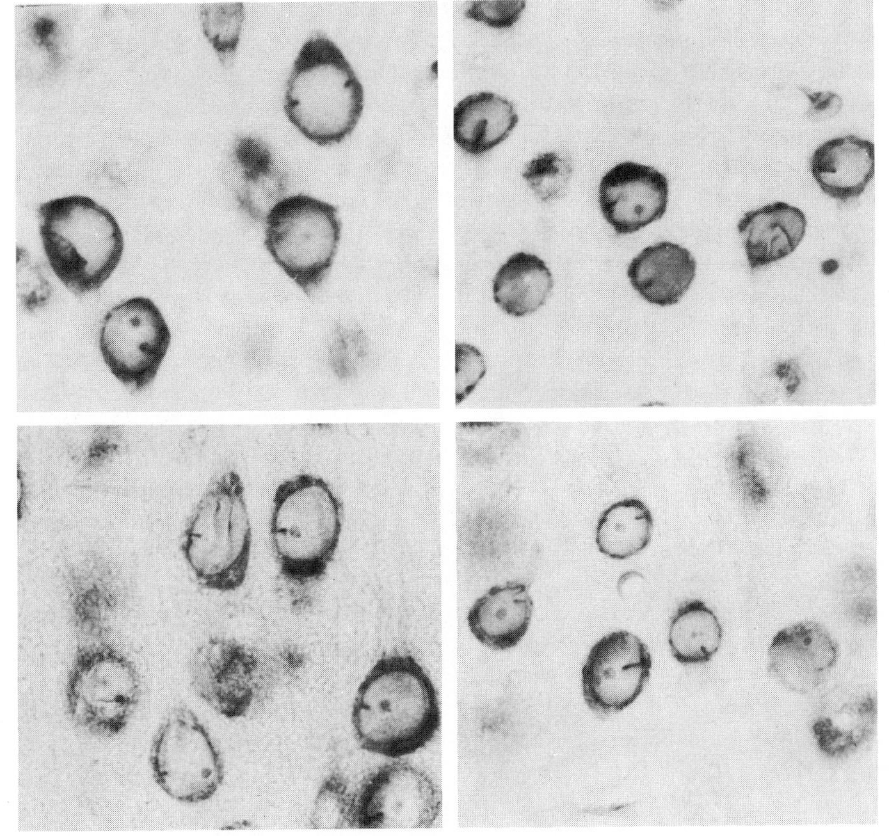

(Courtesy M. C. Diamond and M. R. Rosenzweig)

FIGURE 8

What behavioral treatment made the brain cells shown in the left column larger than those in the right column? The photographs are of rat cerebral cortex stained to show the nuclei of neurons; enlargement, 1,000 times. The top pair came from brains of two brother rats; the bottom photos, from brains of another pair of brothers.

The left-column rats were kept in an enriched environment with varied opportunities for informal learning, while their brothers, on the right, were kept in an impoverished environment. This behavioral treatment causes many changes in the brain. (Rosenzweig, Bennett, & Diamond, 1972). See discussion on p. 734.

Understanding the bodily processes involved in kinds of behavior as those just illustrated—aggression, social interaction, problem solving, visual perception, and learning—has long been part of the program of psychology. Even before psychology became a formal discipline, some physiologists and philosophers speculated on the neural bases of behavior. Johannes Müller, a German who was the first person to hold the title "Professor of Physiology," included behavioral topics in his 1834 *Human Physiology*. But Müller was a vitalist—he thought that a special life principle was necessary to account for the processes of living matter. A few of his students, men not yet thirty, made a pact in 1845 to compel acceptance of a natural science basis for all life processes: "No other forces than common physical chemical ones are active within the organism." We will see the names of three of these physiologists later on—Hermann von Helmholtz, Emil Du Bois-Reymond, and Ernst Brücke—for they and their students did much to realize their aspiration. They helped to establish the mechanisms of basic bodily activities. Without these principles, progress could not have been made on the physiology of complex behavior.

The difficulty of trying to cope with a problem when you don't know its basic principles was illustrated in a science fiction story that I read a few years ago. In the story, scientists were baffled about the function of metal objects from outer space. One scientist said, "These things probably work by some principle that we don't even know. Even a great scientific mind like Aristotle couldn't have discovered the function of a radio, if one could have been placed in his hands." It occurred to me that while Aristotle never examined a radio, he did examine and dissect brains. How successful was he in understanding them? The answer shows the progress since his time—Aristotle suggested that the brain acts as a refrigerating unit to cool the hot blood coming from the heart!

Realistic conceptions of how the brain works had to await discoveries of the nineteenth and twentieth centuries—the electrochemical nature of nerve impulses established by Du Bois-Reymond (around 1860), the identity of nerve cells and synapses (1890), and the nature of synaptic transmission (1940's and 1950's). Similarly, while doctrines of bodily fluids or "humors" go back to antiquity, knowledge of hormones dates from this century; the term "hormone" was coined in 1906.

As the principles of neural activity were discovered, they were applied first to sensory and motor processes; the organs involved in these processes are peripheral (near the surface of the body) and are therefore relatively accessible. Only recently have improved techniques permitted investigators to observe directly processes occurring deep in the brain and to manipulate them.

Early attempts to treat higher mental processes in terms

of neural function were bound to be largely speculative. One such attempt was the essay "Reflexes of the Brain," published in 1863 by the great Russian physiologist Ivan Sechenov who had studied with Helmholtz and Du Bois-Reymond. Sechenov later inspired Pavlov in his research. Even Sigmund Freud, who studied with Brücke, tried his hand at an explanation of human behavior in terms of neural function before he turned to psychoanalysis.

In the twentieth century, views of underlying bodily mechanisms, dominated by the reflex model, became less rigid and more flexible: Pavlov showed that reflexes could be trained or conditioned, and the American psychologist Clark Hull showed that trained responses display variability. By now, biological psychology is fully engaged in what Donald O. Hebb has called the second American Revolution in psychology. The first, according to Hebb, was behaviorism. The second is the attempt to establish an equally objective study of higher mental processes.

Chapter 23 takes up some of the most basic aspects of neural and hormonal functions. This provides background necessary for the other chapters of this section. Chapter 24 shows how biological methods are providing answers to some of the questions raised in Chapters 20–22 on perception: How are we able to discriminate brightness, color, and form? How do different parts of the brain participate in different aspects of perception? How do the two ears make different connections to brain centers, accounting for some of the phenomena of dichotic perception? Chapter 25 deals with motivation. It takes up the different brain processes that occur in wakefulness, sleep, and dreaming. It shows how brain processes are related to aggressiveness, sex behavior, obesity, and reinforcement. Then Chapter 26 shows how investigators are trying to find out what happens in the brain during learning and how memories are stored in the brain.

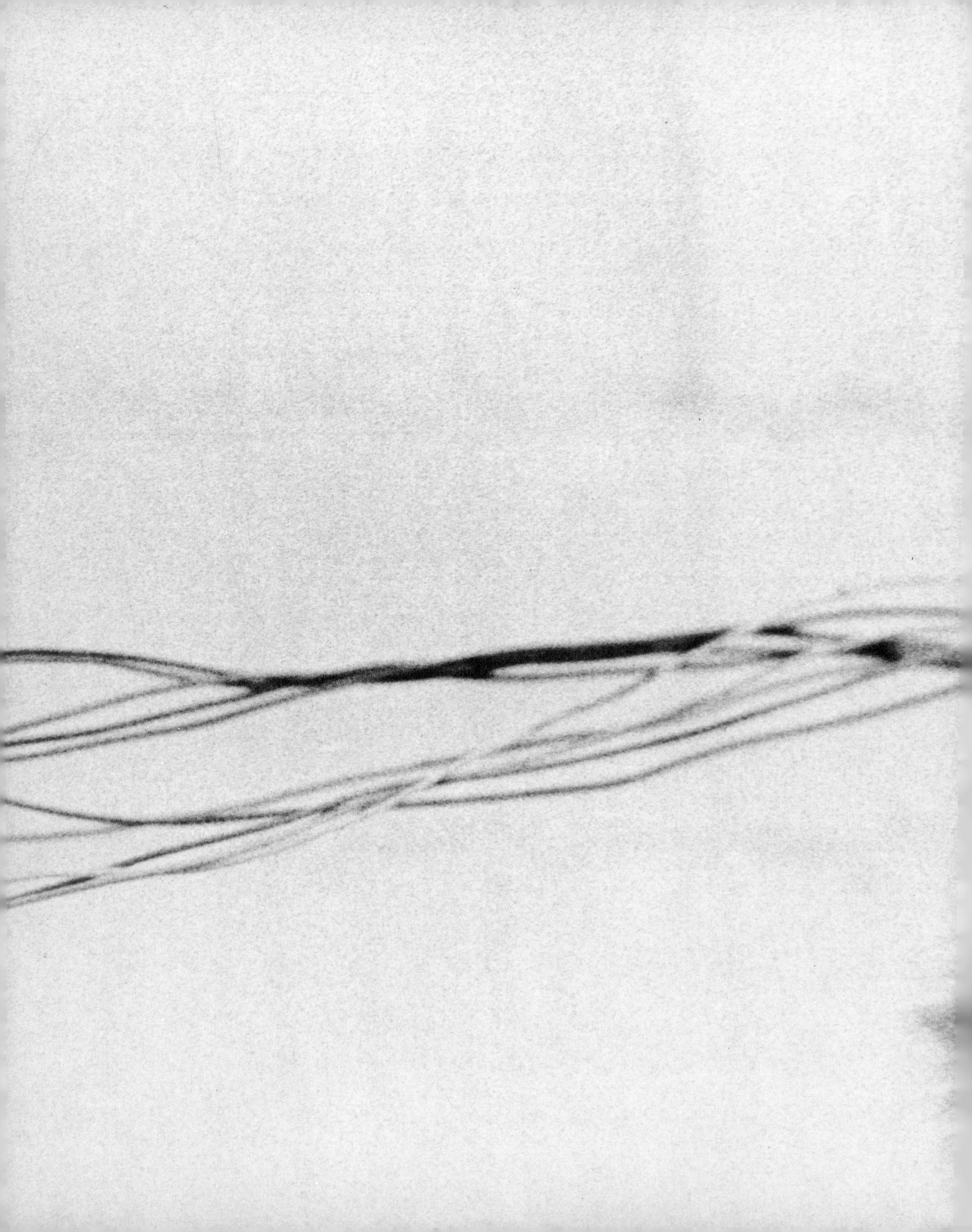

23

Neural and Hormonal Integration of Behavior

How do nerve cells transmit information?
How does the hormonal system work with the nervous system?
How does observable behavior depend on activity of muscles and glands?

All behavior depends on integration of processes within the body, and the two chief systems of integration are the nervous system and endocrine (hormonal) system. Any behavior—perceiving the world around us, an emotional response, satisfying basic needs—requires such integration. These integrative systems are therefore fundamental to understanding the bodily bases of behavior.

To be specific, let us consider what happens when a skier sees a red flag on his course and swerves around it. First, the skier *sees* the flag; this entails capturing the stimulus with the sense organs. The skier sees a *flag;* in biological terms, the neural impulses from the sense organs are transmitted by a series of relays to brain centers where various features of the stimulus are extracted and analyzed. Information from memory, structural and chemical changes induced by past experience, are integrated with the incoming information.

The skier *swerves;* as a result of the processes underlying the seeing of the flag, certain patterns of activity occur in the motor areas of the brain, leading to muscular responses. Parts of the endocrine system are also stimulated, leading to changes in heart rate, blood circulation, and metabolic activity. Before the skier completes his turn, he may adjust his response. Feedback stimulation from the muscles and endocrine activity is integrated with the changing visual information and provides a basis for modification of ongoing behavior.

The skilled performance of the skier involves not only complexly patterned movements of the skeletal musculature but also coordinated responses of internal organs and glands.
(Margaret Durrance, Photo Researchers)

These processes are complex but, especially in cases of well-practiced behavior, they can occur very rapidly. The person is not consciously aware of most of them, but they can be studied by behavioral and biological methods.

The information used for these complex neural and hormonal integrations is transmitted by nerve cells in the form of small electrical and chemical changes called **nerve impulses** or **action potentials.** Nerve impulses are much the same wherever they occur, and their properties are basic to the biological understanding of behavior. Let us consider briefly how they work.

How do nerve cells transmit information?

Basic Physiology of Neurons

A nerve cell or **neuron** is a little transparent bag with a somewhat leaky wall and an irregular shape. Your brain is made up of an enormous number of neurons, about ten billion of them. A neuron is like other cells of the body in some respects, but it also has specialized features that allow it to convey messages rapidly from one part of the body to another. Like other cells, the neuron has a nucleus and various other specialized parts that manufacture materials and carry on metabolic functions. Unlike most other kinds of cells, most neurons have a complex shape with many branches, and many neurons are much longer than any other cells in the body. For example, sensory neurons from your big toe run up your leg and into the spinal cord in the middle of your back, so these neurons are over a meter long (depending on your height). Certain other neurons in the spinal cord and in the brain are much shorter, being much less than a millimeter in length. Shapes of some of the variety of neurons are shown in Figure 23-1. Whatever their shapes, most neurons have the same parts. There is a cell body, an **axon** for conducting nerve impulses, and usually several other branches that are called **dendrites.** (Unless you have already studied the nervous system, you should study the figures in this chapter carefully; they contain a great deal of basic information.)

Now let us consider how the neuron works. Investigators have found out by recording and amplifying the tiny electrical charges that occur in neurons and by analyzing chemically the fluids inside and around the neurons. The neuron is constantly active to keep a special chemical balance; it pumps out positively charged sodium ions (Na^+) that diffuse in from body fluids, and it lets potassium ions (K^+) and chloride ions (Cl^-) enter. Because of active processes, more negatively charged particles (ions) exist on the inside of the cell wall (membrane) compared to the outside, and the balance of charges results in a small electrical potential or difference across the membrane. The outside is usually charged positively with respect to the inside, a little less than one tenth of a volt (more precisely, about 70 millivolts). This is the resting state of the neuron, as shown on the left in Figure 23-2.

If an electrical or chemical stimulus is applied to the membrane and this reduces the charge by only a slight amount, the pumping action reverses. Now sodium ions are carried in through the membrane, so that the outside becomes negative with respect to the inside. This change then itself stimulates the adjacent stretch of membrane. The newly stimulated section, in turn, rapidly alters its charge and stimulates the next portion. So the change sweeps down the fiber as a wave of electrical negativity.

Figure 23-2 illustrates these events as they are recorded when a small wire (electrode) is placed in contact with a neuron cell body or axon. The cylinder in the upper part of the figure represents a stretch of axon. The small potentials can be amplified and displayed on a cathode-ray screen, which operates much like an ordinary television screen. The lower part of the figure shows how such a recording appears. Such recordings provide much information about neural activity. Because the rise and fall of the action potential are so rapid

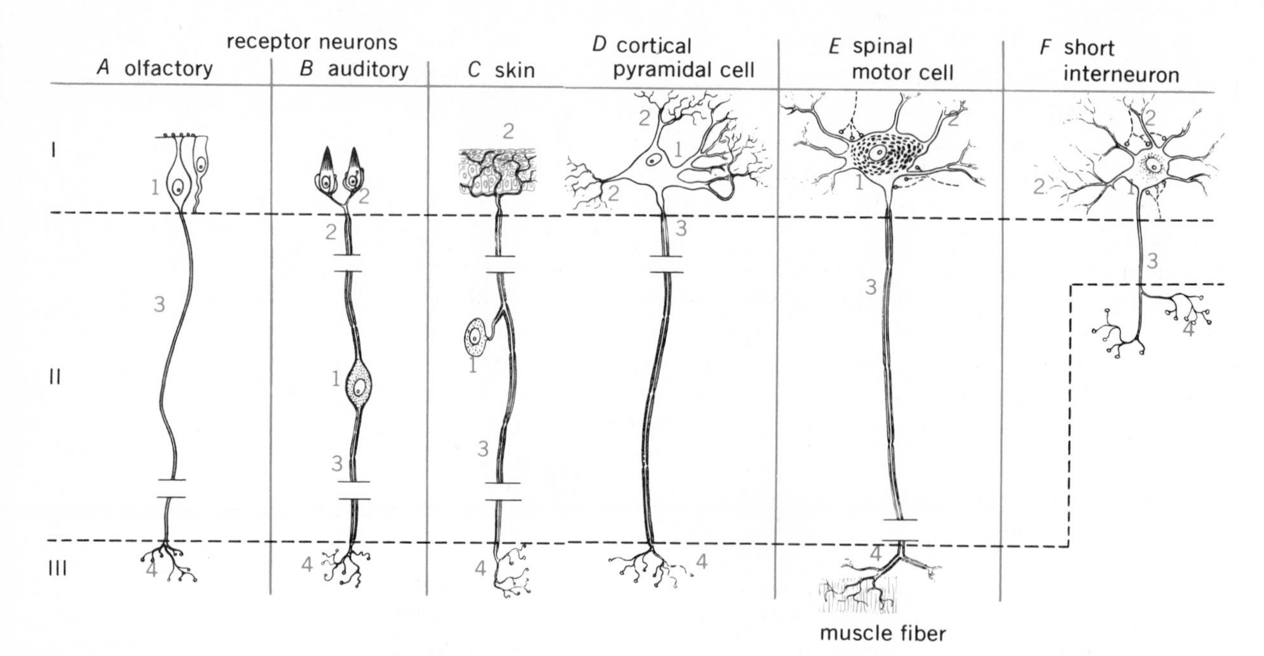

	Functional	Anatomical
I	Input zone	Dendrites, and sometimes also cell body
II	Conducting zone	Axon, and sometimes also dendrites
III	Output zone	Axon terminals

1	cell body
2	dendrites
3	axon
4	axon terminals

FIGURE 23-1
SHAPES OF NEURONS

Each type has a cell body which contains the nucleus. In addition, each neuron has one or more branches. Neurons receive stimulation from other neurons or from sense receptors; the input to some neurons is directly to the cell body as in the olfactory neuron (*A* in the figure), in some cases to branches called dendrites (*C*), and in some cases to both cell bodies and dendrites (*D–F*). Conduction of the nerve impulse takes place along the axon in many types of neurons (*A, D–F*), but in some types of neurons the dendrites also conduct (*B, C*). Neurons deliver impulses to other neurons or to muscles or glands; this output always occurs over terminal branches of axons. In many cases the branches of a neuron are very long so breaks have been indicated in diagrams *A–E* to allow us to show both ends of the neuron and the cell body without including long stretches of axon.

(only about a millisecond), it is sometimes called a "spike potential" or simply a spike.

For a model of some aspects of neural activity, you can think of what happens if you hold a match under a paper straw. If the match is not too close, the paper may turn brown along a stretch, but that is all; this is like small electrical variations in the neuron that are too weak to trigger a full-blown response. But with greater heat, the paper bursts into flame. If this happens, then the burning section soon ignites the next portion, and the fire travels to the end of the straw, each section igniting the next. This is like the full-blown nerve impulse. In the neuron, the impulse travels rapidly; the fastest fibers carry impulses at about 100 meters per second (roughly 220 miles per hour).

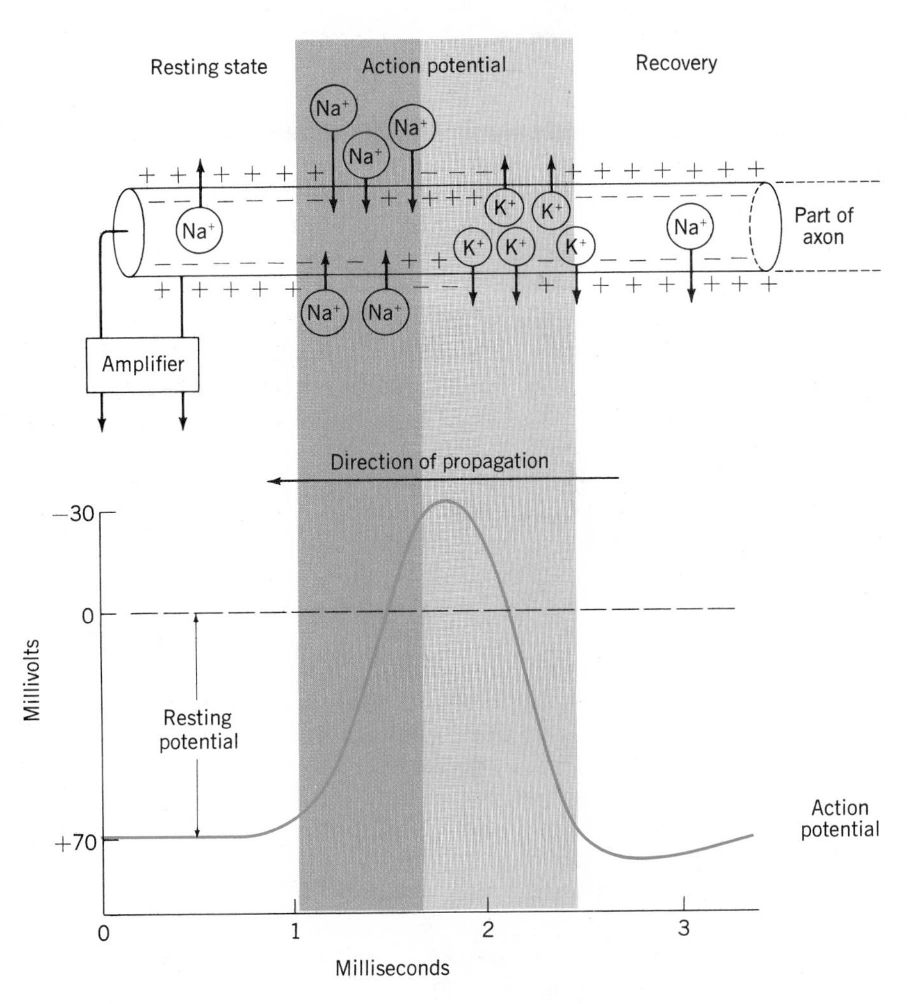

FIGURE 23-2
THE NERVE IMPULSE OR ACTION POTENTIAL

The upper part of the figure represents a stretch of axon of a neuron. The lower part shows a recording of the potential (voltage difference) between the inside and outside of the axon. At the left of the figure, the neuron is in a resting state. The cell actively pumps some ions out (for example, sodium—Na^+) and pumps other ions in; this creates a resting potential of about +70 millivolts. When an impulse is conducted, sodium ions are actively pumped in, as the diagram shows in the area of dark shading; this causes the potential to reverse to about −30 millivolts. Then potassium ions (K^+) rush out, and the potential drops back close to the resting level, as shown in the lightly shaded area.

Surprisingly, the neuron restores itself to its usual state in about a millisecond. It is as if a new straw formed out of the ashes. Thus the neuron can carry several hundred impulses per second or, in some cases, even 1,000 per second. All impulses in a given neuron are of the same size and speed, although neurons differ from each other in the amplitudes of their impulses and in their rates of conduction. Using the analogy of the straw, it is clear that straws of the same size and composition will burn at the same temperature and rate, but straws that differ in size and composition will burn differently from each other. When an electrode with a fine tip is put into contact with two or three neurons, you can usually identify which impulses come from which neuron because the impulses consistently differ in amplitude.

It should be clear that the stimulus only starts the impulse and does not supply the energy to conduct it along the neuron. The neuron provides the energy, just as the paper straw does when it continues to burn after the match is removed.

Synaptic Transmission

The place where one neuron makes functional contact with another is called a **synapse** (from Greek words meaning "clasp together"). Diagrams of synapses are given in Figures 23-3, 23-4, and in color Figure 7. The term "synapse" refers to both the end button of an axon and the receptor membrane under it. In a few locations in the nervous system, the electrical activity in one neuron can stimulate directly the next neuron across the synaptic gap. In most locations, however, the gap between two neurons is bridged by a chemical **transmitter agent,** which is stored inside the end button in tiny globules called **synaptic vesicles.** When a nerve impulse reaches an end button, it causes some vesicles to release the transmitter agent into the synaptic gap. The transmitter agent combines with a receptor chemical in the receiving cell. This chemical reaction sets up an electrical change that may be strong enough to excite the second cell. In certain cases the second neuron is not excited but is inhibited; that is, it becomes less susceptible to excitatory influences from other sources.

Several chemical transmitter agents have been identified and more will probably be found. One such chemical is **acetylcholine;** it occurs at many places in the nervous system. Chemical transmission is relatively slow; it takes a millisecond or more to stimulate a neuron across the synaptic cleft. This doesn't seem like much time, but the "gap" is only about 20 billionths of a millimeter wide, so the rate of transmission is quite slow.

Synaptic transmission accounts for several characteristics of the nervous system. For one thing, the synaptic junctions allow switching so that messages can be routed into one channel or another, depending on how impulses from different neurons converge. It usually takes many impulses converging on a neuron to fire it. A specific pattern of input may be required, and this provides a means of integrating sensory information and of detecting sensory patterns, as we will see shortly. Another feature of synaptic action is that the chemical transmitter agents are specialized; some effects are excitatory and others are inhibitory. This permits control in both directions, like the use of both the accelerator and the brakes in a car. The chemical nature of most mammalian synapses has the further consequence of making them susceptible to various chemical agents, some natural and some artificial; examples of such chemical effects at the synapse are shown in Figure 23-4.

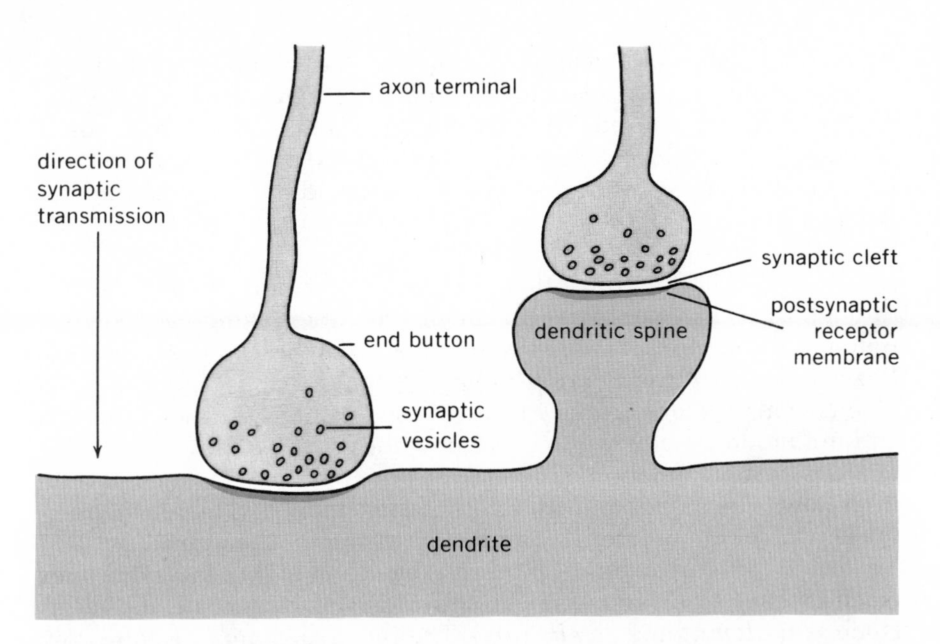

FIGURE 23-3
HOW IMPULSES GET FROM ONE NEURON TO ANOTHER

When a neural impulse reaches the end button of an axon, some synaptic vesicles discharge their contents into the synaptic cleft. The transmitter substance combines with a receptor chemical in the receiving cell. This chemical reaction sets up an electrical charge that may excite or inhibit the receiving cell.

Certain drugs that alter moods and emotional states can probably be understood in terms of their activities at synapses. These include both drugs that mimic psychotic states—such as LSD—and drugs that alleviate psychoses, such as chlorpromazine. LSD in its chemical structure resembles a synaptic transmitter called "serotonin," and serotonin has been linked to mood and emotion. There is recent evidence that when LSD is given to rats, it accumulates rapidly in certain cells in the midbrain and medulla. It may act like the transmitter and overstimulate these brain cells.

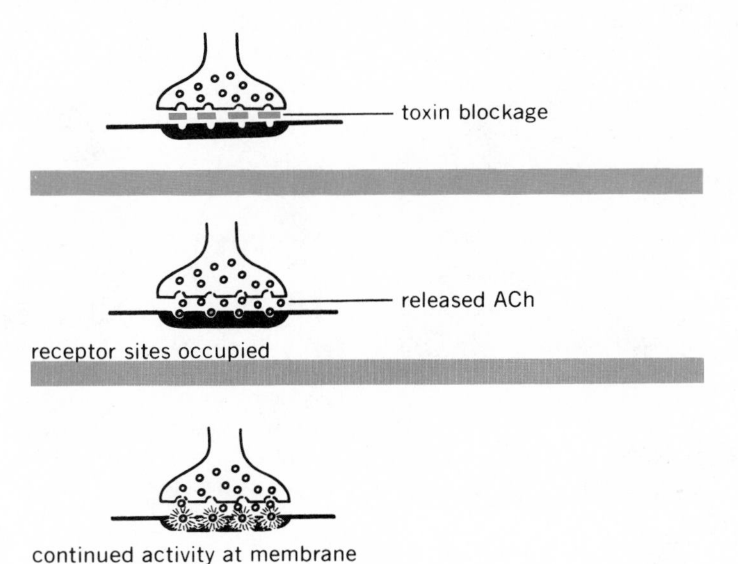

FIGURE 23-4
EFFECT OF DRUGS ON SYNAPTIC ACTIVITY

The diagram shows synapses where acetylcholine (ACh) is the chemical transmitter. Certain drugs can block release of ACh (1), can block its receptor chemical in the receiving cell (2), or can prolong its activity (3). Other drugs affect synapses where different chemical transmitters are active.

1. Botulinus toxin (which can form in improperly canned vegetables) blocks the release of ACh from the end button. The result can be a fatal paralysis.
2. Curare (a South American Indian arrow poison) occupies the receptor sites in the postsynaptic membrane and prevents ACh from acting. This also results in paralysis.
3. Certain nerve gases destroy the enzyme (acetylcholinesterase or AChE) that normally inactivates ACh. This causes a buildup of ACh, which blocks further transmission across the junction. This too causes paralysis.

Chlorpromazine—a drug that has helped greatly to reduce the numbers of hospitalized mental patients—works on neural circuits where noradrenalin is the synaptic transmitter. Chlorpromazine blocks the release of noradrenalin at the synapse. This results in fewer neural messages traversing synapses, and the effect is tranquilizing.

Basic Geography of the Nervous System

The neurons that we have been describing run all through the body, but by far the greatest number of them are concentrated in the central nervous system, that is, the brain and spinal cord. Basic anatomy of the **nervous system** is portrayed in Figures 23-5 to 23-8 (see also color Figures 1 to 7). These diagrams are meant only as an introduction. Later we will see how these specialized parts of the nervous system function, so don't try to master the anatomical relations now. The names and sites will become more and more meaningful as you see them later in connection with their functions.

Neuroanatomical terms range from highly inclusive ones (such as *central nervous system* and *brain*) to rather specific terms (such as *thalamus* and *cerebellum*). The block diagram in Figure 23-5 indicates how some of the most frequently used terms relate to each other, and the positions of the main structures are shown in the succeeding figures. In particular, Figure 23-6 indicates how the main parts are named in accordance with the divisions that are seen in

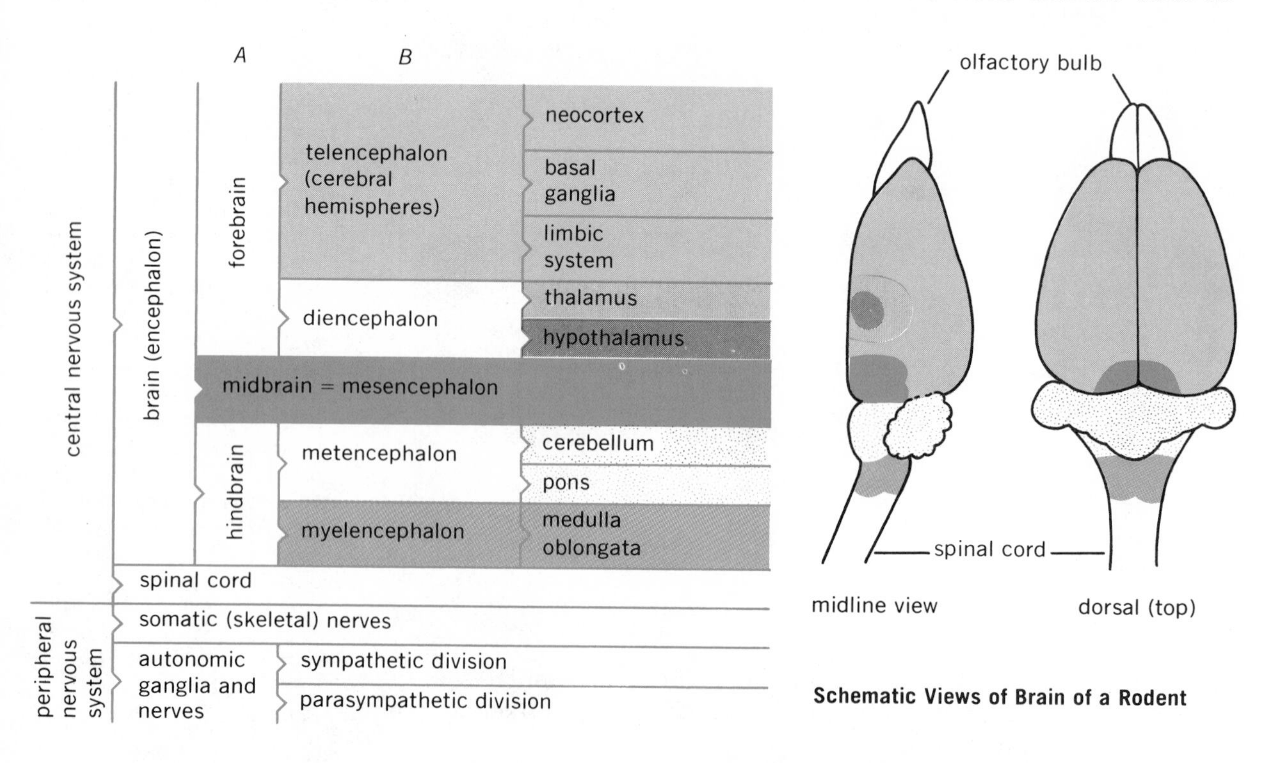

FIGURE 23-5 SUBDIVISIONS OF THE NERVOUS SYSTEM
The table shows increasing specificity of terms from left to right. The subdivisions listed under *A* become apparent early in the embryonic development of the brain; those under *B* are seen later in development, as shown in Figure 23-6.

front

back

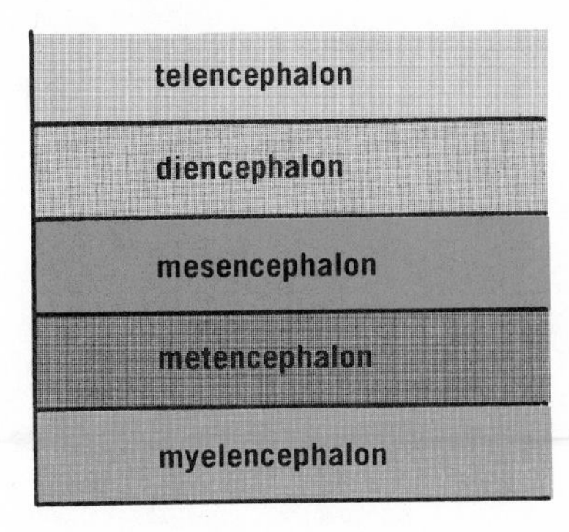

A

forebrain

midbrain

hindbrain

B

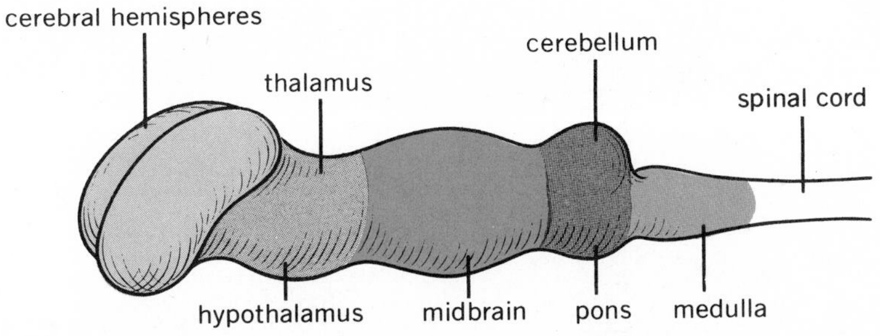

C

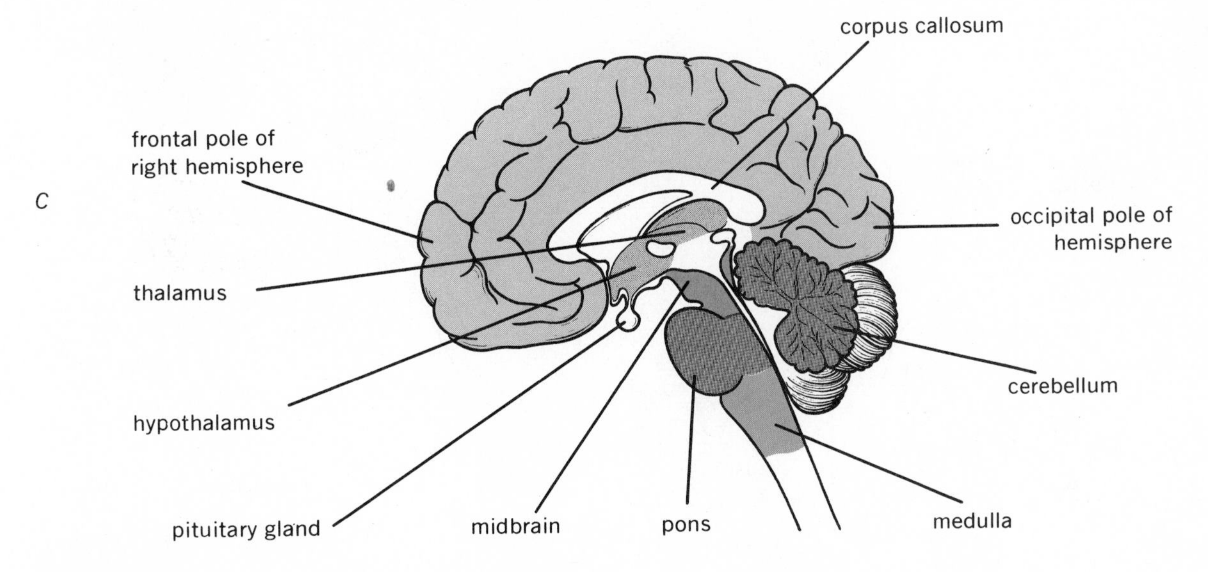

FIGURE 23-6
EMBRYONIC DEVELOPMENT OF THE HUMAN BRAIN

A. In a very young embryo, the primitive tubular brain develops three subdivisions—forebrain, midbrain, and hindbrain.
B. With further development, there are five main subdivisions that will persist in the adult brain. "Encephalon" is the Greek word for brain, and the five subdivisions, from front to back, are called respectively the telencephalon, diencephalon, mesencephalon, metencephalon, and myelencephalon.
C. The right hemisphere of the adult human brain is viewed from the midline after the left hemisphere has been removed.

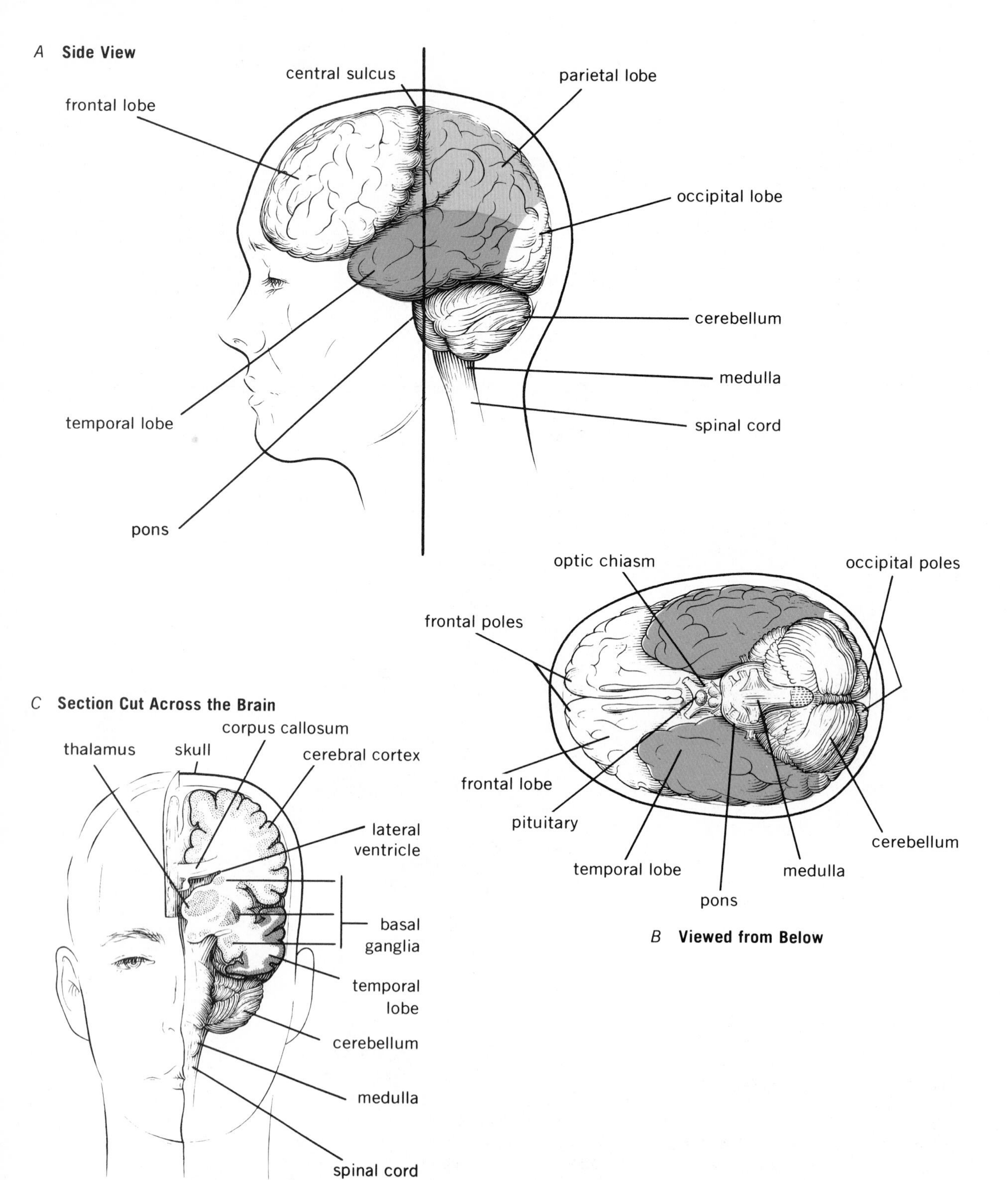
A Side View
central sulcus
parietal lobe
frontal lobe
occipital lobe
cerebellum
medulla
temporal lobe
spinal cord
pons
optic chiasm
occipital poles
frontal poles
C Section Cut Across the Brain
corpus callosum
thalamus
skull
cerebral cortex
frontal lobe
pituitary
lateral ventricle
cerebellum
temporal lobe
medulla
pons
basal ganglia
B Viewed from Below
temporal lobe
cerebellum
medulla
spinal cord

FIGURE 23-7
THREE VIEWS OF THE HUMAN BRAIN

View *A* shows some of the main surface features of the human brain as they would be seen if the skin, muscles, and skull were transparent. The cerebral hemispheres are usually divided into four main lobes—frontal, parietal, occipital and temporal. The vertical line shows the cross section of drawing *C*.

View *B* shows the brain as seen from below. The pituitary gland is in the center of the drawing, attached just below the hypothalamus (refer back to Figure 23-6). Just behind it can be seen the pons, which got its name from the Latin word for "bridge" because many of its fibers bridge between one side of the cerebellum and the other. Just ahead of the pituitary gland, the optic nerves cross, forming the chiasma (named after the Greek letter Chi—X).

View *C* shows how the brain would appear if the left side of the head were removed back to about the ear. The cerebral cortex, or "gray matter," starts at the surface and goes down to a depth of a few millimeters. Inside this is "white matter," composed mainly of neural fibers that are insulated with light-colored fatty material. One large band of fibers, the corpus callosum, interconnects the two cerebral hemispheres. Buried deep in the brain are structures such as the basal ganglia and the thalamus, which we will consider later.

early development of the brain. Very early in embryonic life, the primitive neural tube develops three thickenings at the head end; these are called the forebrain, the midbrain, and the hindbrain. As the embryonic brain becomes more complex, the **forebrain** subdivides into the **telencephalon** and the **diencephalon** (or tween brain); the telencephalon grows into the large **cerebral hemispheres,** and the diencephalon includes the **thalamus** and **hypothalamus.** The **midbrain** (or mesencephalon) remains relatively small in the human brain, overshadowed by the large growth of the forebrain and the hindbrain. The **hindbrain** subdivides into the metencephalon and the myelencephalon (or medulla oblongata); the metencephalon includes the large **cerebellum** and the **pons.**

The main parts of the brain and their anatomical relations are quite similar in all mammals. We can see this from the paired diagrams of the human and rat brains in Figure 23-8. The human brain is, of course, much larger than the rat brain, but in both cases the brain weighs about 2 percent of the total body. In the human brain, the cerebral hemispheres are relatively large, and the outer bark (the **cerebral cortex** or "**gray matter**") has many folds. The rodent cortex, in contrast, is smooth and has no fissures.

Two thirds of the cortex in the adult human brain lies buried in fissures; if it was spread out flat, the cortex of the average human brain would cover over two square feet. Beneath this surface layer of gray matter there are millions of nerve fibers running to and from the cortical cells; each fiber is covered with a fatty insulating sheath. When this fibrous part of the brain is exposed, the insulating sheaths give it a white shiny appearance, and it is therefore called **white matter;** see Figure 23-7C and color Figure 5.

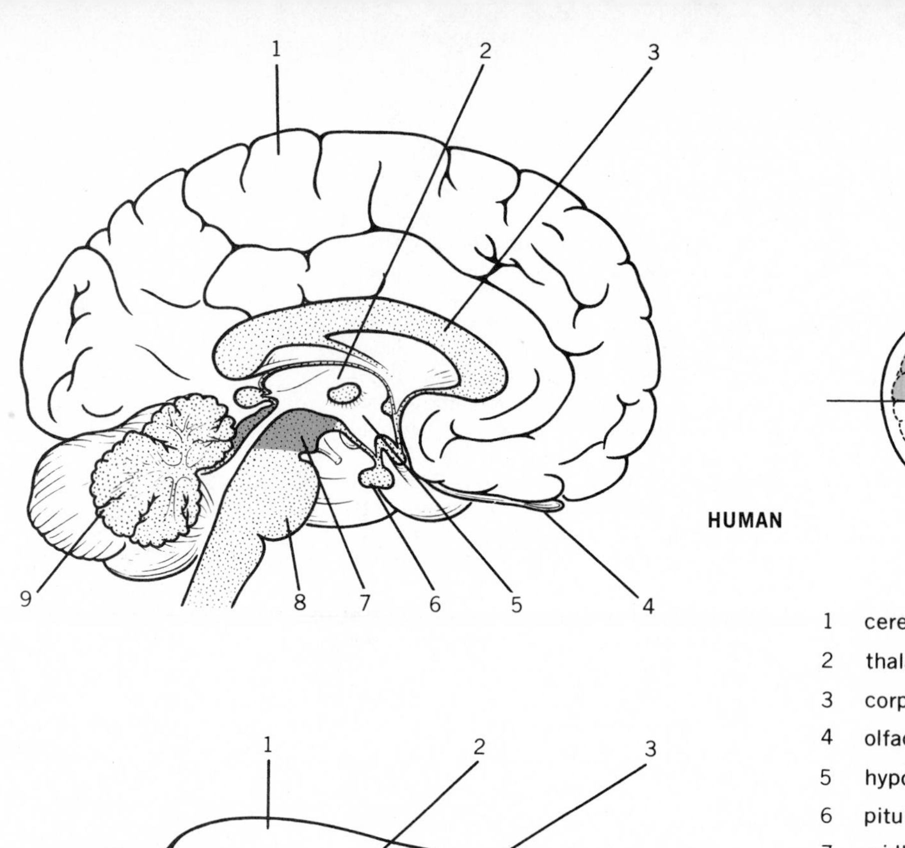

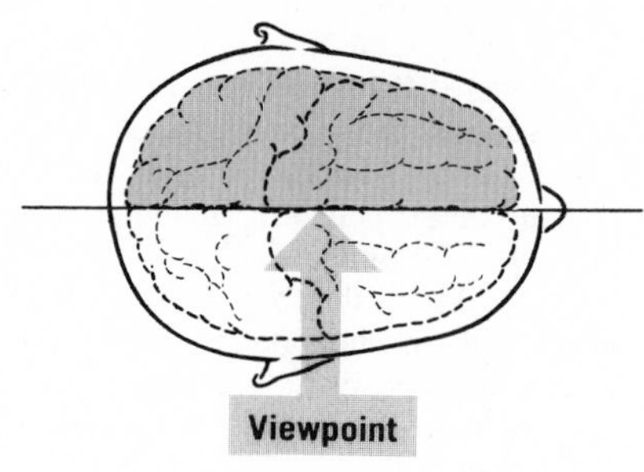

1 cerebral hemisphere
2 thalamus
3 corpus callosum
4 olfactory bulbs
5 hypothalamus
6 pituitary gland
7 midbrain
8 pons
9 cerebellum

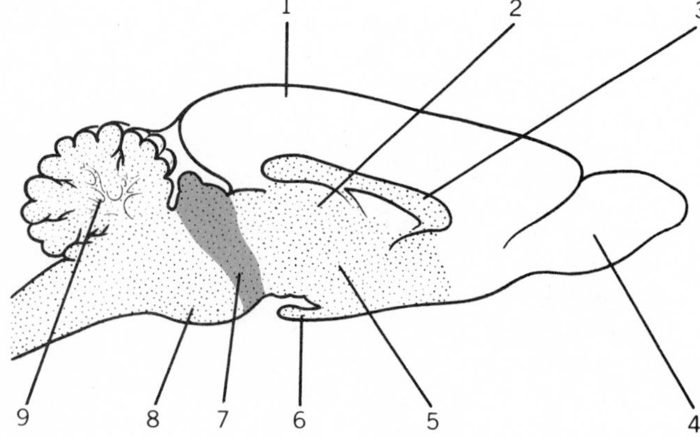

RAT

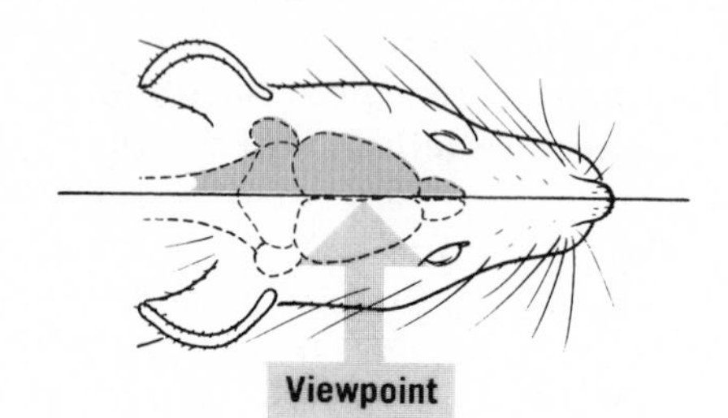

FIGURE 23-8
COMPARISON OF HUMAN AND RAT BRAIN STRUCTURES

The brains shown here have been cut along the midline of the body, and one half has been removed, as shown in the small diagrams. This allows you to see structures along the midline of the brain. The parts that were cut are shown stippled in the midline views. The rat brain has been enlarged about six times in relation to the human brain.

The main parts of the brain are in similar positions in man and rat (and in all species of mammals). The relative sizes of some parts differ considerably, however. Note that the cerebral hemispheres occupy a much greater proportion of the human brain than they do in the rat, whereas the rat has the relatively larger midbrain and much larger olfactory bulbs.

How does the hormonal system work with the nervous system?

In addition to the nervous system, the **endocrine glands** also integrate behavior. These glands secrete **hormones**—special chemical messengers that are carried throughout the body by the bloodstream. This system is closely related to the nervous system, since the secretion of some endocrine glands is controlled neurally and several hormones modify the excitability of neural cells. Beyond this, some neurons employ a hormone as their synaptic transmitter—norepinephrine, also secreted by the adrenal gland. And a major endocrine gland, the **pituitary,** is partly an outgrowth of the brain and is joined to its base. The location of the major endocrine glands is shown in Figure 23-9, along with the main functions of these glands.

In our case of the skier, secretion of the hormone epinephrine (also called adrenalin) by the **adrenal medulla** facilitates his activity and high metabolic level. It helps to redistribute the blood supply to his skeletal muscles and away from the internal organs, and it increases heart rate and blood pressure; it releases blood sugar from the liver into the bloodstream, making a ready supply of energy available; it causes the blood to clot more quickly in case of injury.

In many of these activities, the hormonal system works in conjunction with the nervous system, and each system depends in part on the other. The rates of secretion of certain endocrine glands, the posterior pituitary and the adrenal medulla, are directly controlled by the neurons that innervate them. Other endocrines are controlled chemically, several of them by secretions of the anterior pituitary gland, which is therefore often called the "master gland." For example, the pituitary manufactures some hormones that directly stimulate the release of sex hormones from the gonads. The anterior pituitary in turn is controlled in part by the secretions of the endocrine glands it influences (a **feedback** relationship) and in part by secretions of special cells located in the base of the brain. These cells are governed by adjacent neurons.

Here is an example of neural-hormonal interaction in the control of mating behavior: in some female birds, the sight of a courting male leads to neural activity and then to secretory activity, which increases the output of a certain specialized hormone by the anterior pituitary. This hormone stimulates the gonads to increase the level of hormones circulating in the blood. These hormones selectively affect both certain brain cells and cells in the reproductive tract. The hormonal influence on the brain cells makes the female more ready to engage in copulatory activity. Thus there is a neural-hormonal-hormonal-neural sequence of events that underlies the female's response to the male's courtship and that helps to coordinate the behavior of the pair. We will consider hormonal influences on behavior further in Chapter 25 on biology of motivation (see pp. 706–12).

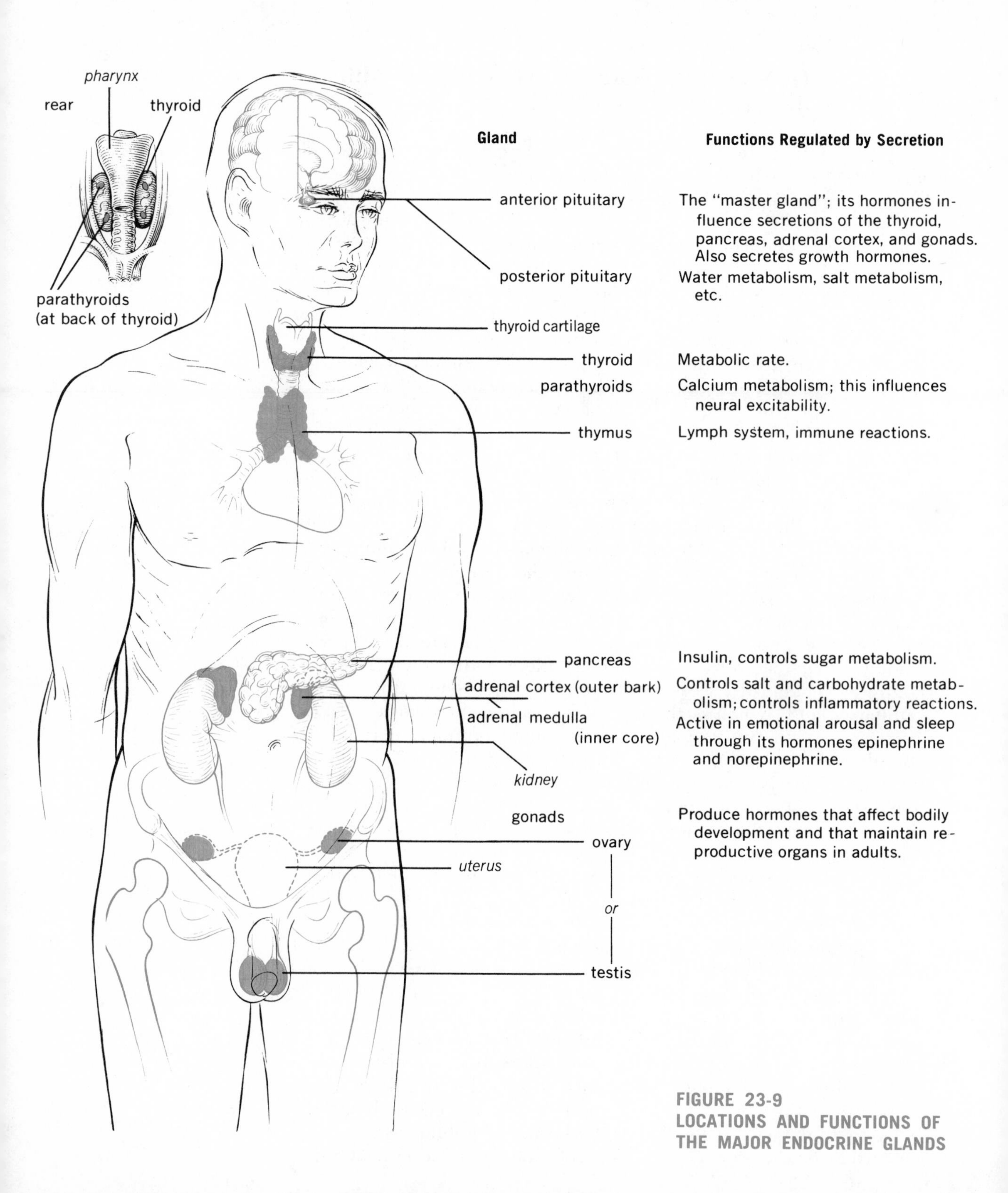

FIGURE 23-9
LOCATIONS AND FUNCTIONS OF THE MAJOR ENDOCRINE GLANDS

How does observable behavior depend on activity of muscles and glands?

The processes that we will take up in the next three chapters—perception, motivation, and learning—are usually inferred from observable behavior of people or animals. The smiles and frowns we see, the voices we hear, the touches we feel, the swerving of the skier around the flag—all these are the products of muscular activities. Certain other responses are glandular; cold air on the skier's eyes may cause him to secrete tears from his tear glands. Therefore, before going on to the next chapters, it will be helpful to consider briefly motor behavior. ("Motor" is a term used to indicate the behavioral or output functions of the body—muscles and glands and their direct control—as contrasted with the "sensory" input functions or the inner "associative" activities.)

The muscular systems of the body are controlled by the nervous system. A muscle will contract if you stimulate it electrically, but you can use a weaker current if you stimulate the motor nerve that runs to the muscle. The motor neurons form special junctions with muscles; impulses in these neurons lead to the discharge of a transmitter chemical which excites the muscle.

When muscles are mentioned, you probably think first of muscles in your arms or legs, muscles that you can move voluntarily. There are also many other muscles that are usually not under voluntary control but that nevertheless function in coordination with ongoing bodily activities; these muscles include those of the heart, the stomach and intestines, the blood vessels, the iris of the eye, and the little muscles in the skin that raise the hairs, causing "gooseflesh" when they contract.

Central Nervous System

We will consider first the control of the skeletal muscles (so-called because they move the arms and legs and other visible parts of the body around the joints). Under microscopic examination, these muscles have a striped appearance, so they are also called "striate muscles." Most of the muscles inside the body cavity—in the intestines and blood vessels—have a uniform appearance, so they are called "smooth muscles." The skeletal muscles are controlled by neurons whose cell bodies are inside the spinal cord. The smooth muscles are controlled by neurons outside the spinal cord—the so-called "autonomic" nervous system, which we will discuss a little later.

The motor neurons in the spinal cord are affected by excitatory and inhibitory impulses from many levels. For example, when a muscle is stretched—when a doctor taps below your knee with a rubber mallet or when a skier's leg drops a little over a hollow in the snow—a special type of receptor cell within the muscle is stimulated by the stretch. When these receptors are activated, they send impulses along sensory nerves to the spinal cord and up to the brain. Some of these impulses stimulate motor neurons that send impulses to the muscle that was stretched, and these impulses cause a reflex contraction of the muscle. This quickly restores the initial posture of the leg. This reflex integration occurs within a single level or segment of the spinal cord (see Figure 23-10), but it is also modulated by nerve impulses from other levels of the cord and by impulses from the brain. The exact origin of these impulses has been pinpointed in the brain.

A surprising finding was made in 1870 during the Franco-Prussian war when two German doctors stimulated exposed brain tissue of a wounded soldier, using weak electrical currents. They found that different sites of stimulation regularly led to different precise muscular responses. Careful mapping was then done on animal brains by a number of investigators, and it was found that points along a strip of tissue would yield restricted motor responses when *weak* stimulation was employed; stronger currents gave only gross convulsive responses.

A map of the human *motor* cortex is given in Figure 23-11, along with a map of the *sensory* (input) representation of the skin surface. Note that the size of each motor subregion is related to the precision with which we can control that part of the body. Thus the fingers, lips, and tongue have large representations, whereas the trunk, although it is much larger, has a rather small representation in the motor cortex. Similarly the size of the sensory surface is related to the precision of sensitivity on the skin. For example, on the finger-

FIGURE 23-10 NEURAL CONNECTIONS IN A SPINAL REFLEX

One of the 22 segments of the spinal cord is shown. At each segment there is a spinal nerve on each side of the cord; just before the spinal nerve joins the cord, it divides into two roots—the dorsal (back) root and the ventral (front) root. Sensory impulses come in from receptors in the body (in skin, muscles, joints, etc.) through the dorsal spinal root. Motor neurons have their cell bodies in the gray matter in the ventral side of the cord, and their axons go out to skeletal muscles through the ventral spinal root. Insulated sensory and motor fibers run up and down within the cord in columns of white matter. There are millions of fibers and connections at each segment.

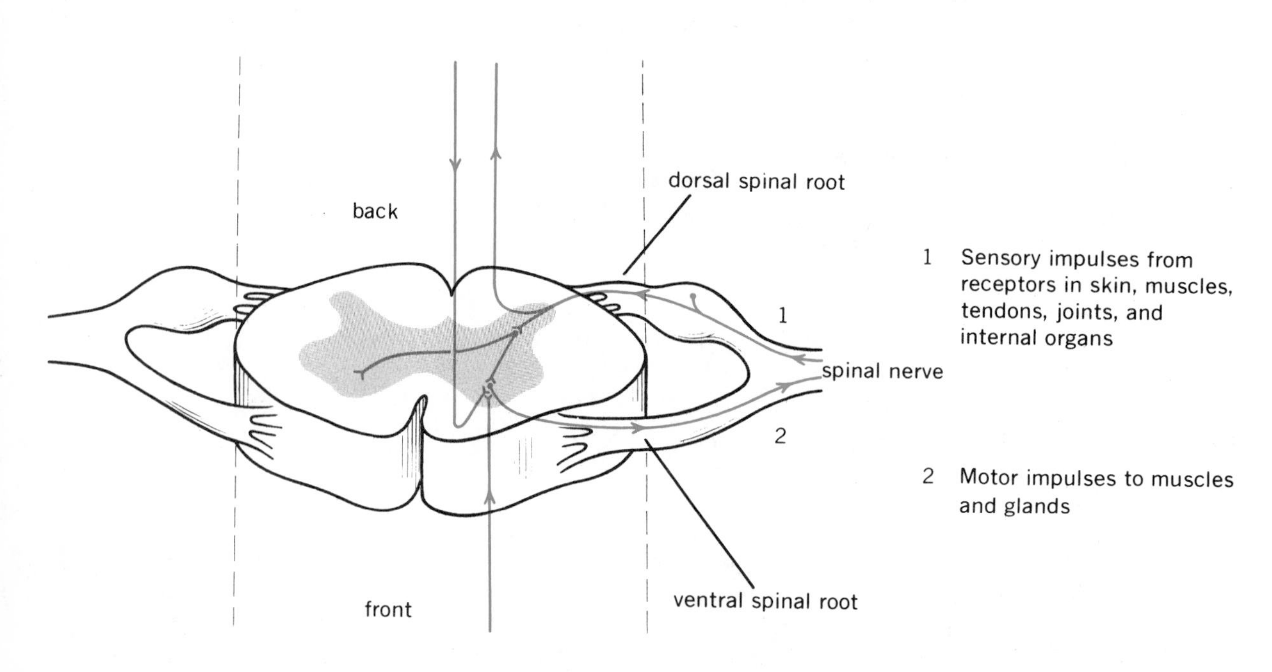

Motor Cortex

wrist
shoulder
hip
little
elbow
trunk
knee
ring
hand
ankle
middle
index
thumb
toes
neck
brow
eyelid
and eyeball
face
lips
vocalization
salivation
jaw
tongue
mastication
swallowing
motor outflow to spinal cord

Somatosensory Cortex

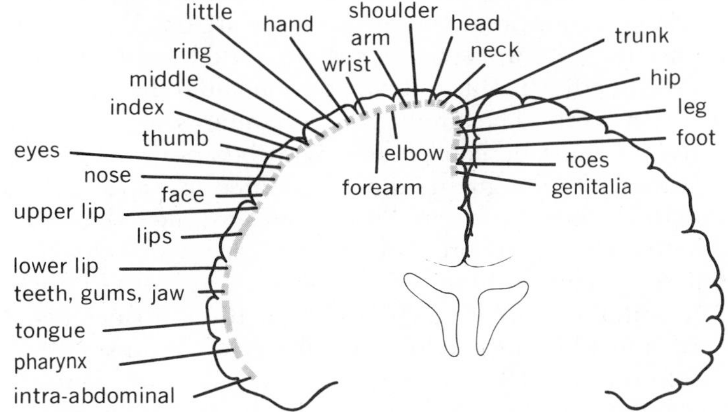

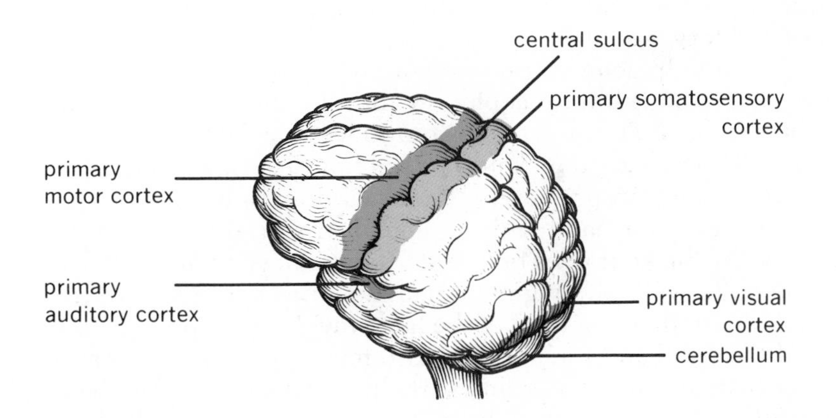

FIGURE 23-11 HOW THE MUSCLES AND SKIN ARE REPRESENTED AT THE CEREBRAL CORTEX

The **primary motor cortex** sends impulses to the muscles. This area is shown in darker color on the lower part of the diagram; it is located just ahead of the central sulcus, which is a major fissure or groove in the cortex. Each muscle is represented in a particular strip of motor cortex, as is indicated by the names of body parts or movements on the upper diagram; this shows a cross section of the brain through the motor cortex. Most motor functions are represented symmetrically in the two cerebral hemispheres, impulses from each hemisphere going to muscles on the opposite side of the body. Control of speech muscles, however, is located only in the left hemisphere of most people.

When the skin is stimulated, some of the resulting neural impulses reach the **primary somatosensory cortex.** This area is located just behind the central sulcus and is shown in light color on the diagram. Each section of skin is represented in a particular strip of sensory cortex, as is shown on the cross section in the middle diagram. Here too, each side of the body connects with the opposite side of the brain.

(Based on Penfield & Jasper, 1954)

tips and on the lips you can accurately distinguish points that are separated by a millimeter or two, but on the back you cannot distinguish points unless they are centimeters apart. The fingertips and lips, compared to the back, have large representations in the sensory cortex.

The motor connections are largely, but not completely, "crossed-over." Most axons from the left motor cortex cross over to the right side and end on or near spinal motor cells that run to muscles on the right side of the body. Similarly, most motor fibers originating in the right side of the brain help to control muscles on the left side of the body. This is why damage to one side of the brain can cause paralysis on the other side of the body. The muscles for speech, in most individuals, are controlled by the left hemisphere of the brain, but in a few percent, speech is controlled by the right hemisphere; and in an occasional person, both hemispheres are used in speech.

There are complex circuits in the brain that provide for the elaborate coordinated movements of which we are capable, such as walking, making a turn in skiing, or writing a word. These might be thought of as neural "programs," analogous to computer programs. As these motor programs run off, they are constantly being monitored for accuracy by the sensory systems, and this feedback allows corrections and adjustments to be made. Consider the coordination required to say a word. The tongue alone contains many muscles, and their activities must be coordinated with others in the larynx, throat, lips, chest, and diaphragm in order to produce speech sounds. For example, the difference between "time" and "dime" depends partly upon whether the vocal cords are left relaxed or are tensed during the initial consonant; in both words the cords are tensed during the vowel. The initial consonant lasts less than 100 milliseconds, and the vocal cords must be in the correct position during most of that time, so that the timing must be accurate to about 10 msec (one hundredth of a second). Certain types of damage to the brain may impair such coordination or even make speech impossible. Speech sounds are monitored by hearing, so that normal speech is difficult to attain for a deaf person who lacks auditory feedback.

To help achieve precise control of movements, there is also sensory feedback from receptors within the muscles and in the tendons and joints. This is called "proprioception" (perception of one's self). When you go to pick up a pencil from a desk, you normally use both visual and proprioceptive feedback to steadily reduce the distance between your hand and the pencil. If you eliminate visual feedback by closing your eyes before starting to move your hand, you can still do quite well, although you may sometimes miss the pencil.

Skilled movements of the hand involve not only the musculature of the hand and forearm, but also muscles of the upper arm, shoulder, chest, and neck. For any particular movement of the hand (reaching forward, reaching with the palm up, etc.), there is a different

BIOLOGICAL PSYCHOLOGY

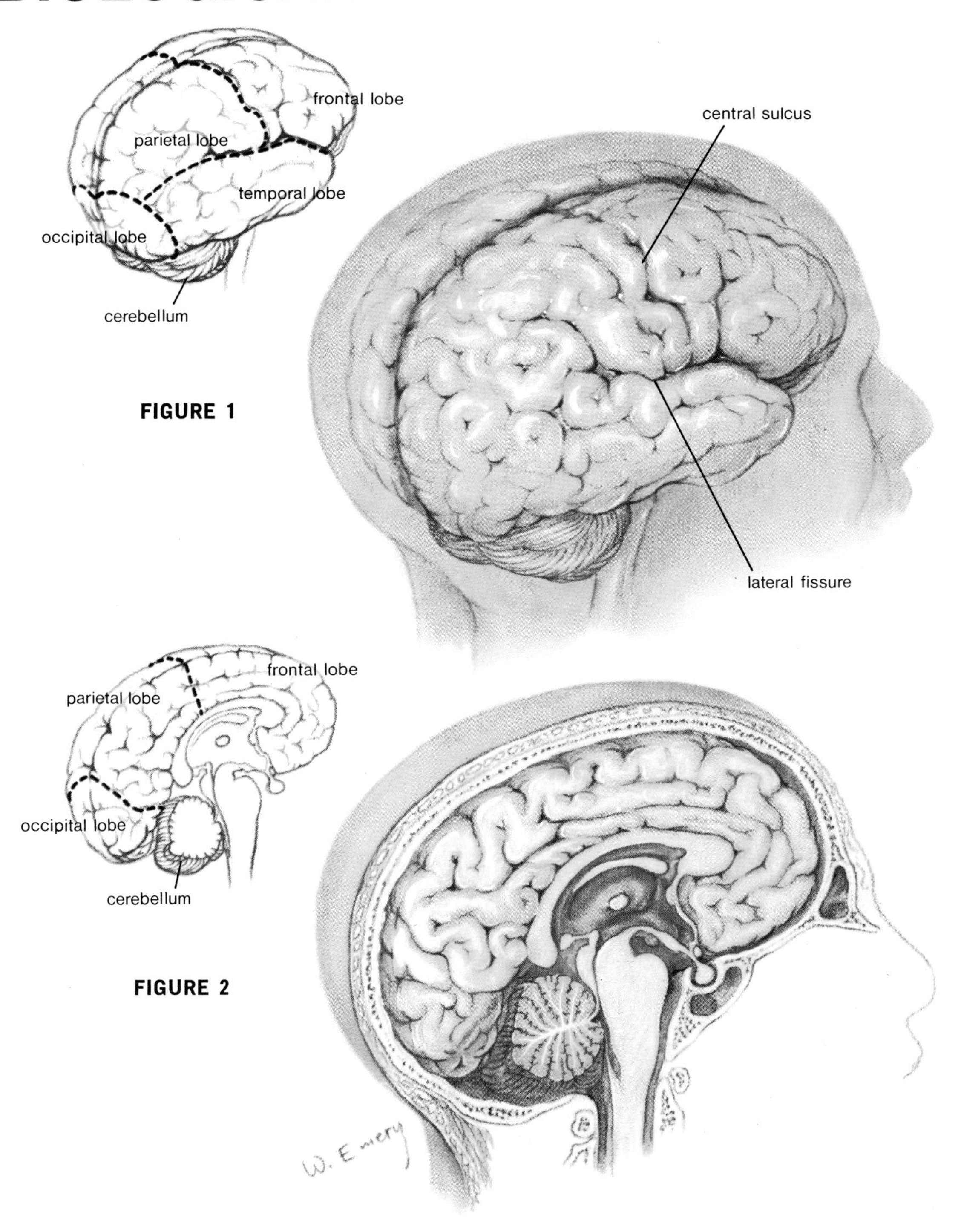

The adult human brain is seen from the right side and slightly from the rear in Figure 1. In Figure 2, the right half of the brain has been removed, and the left half of the brain is seen from the midline. The small drawings identify the lobes of the brain.

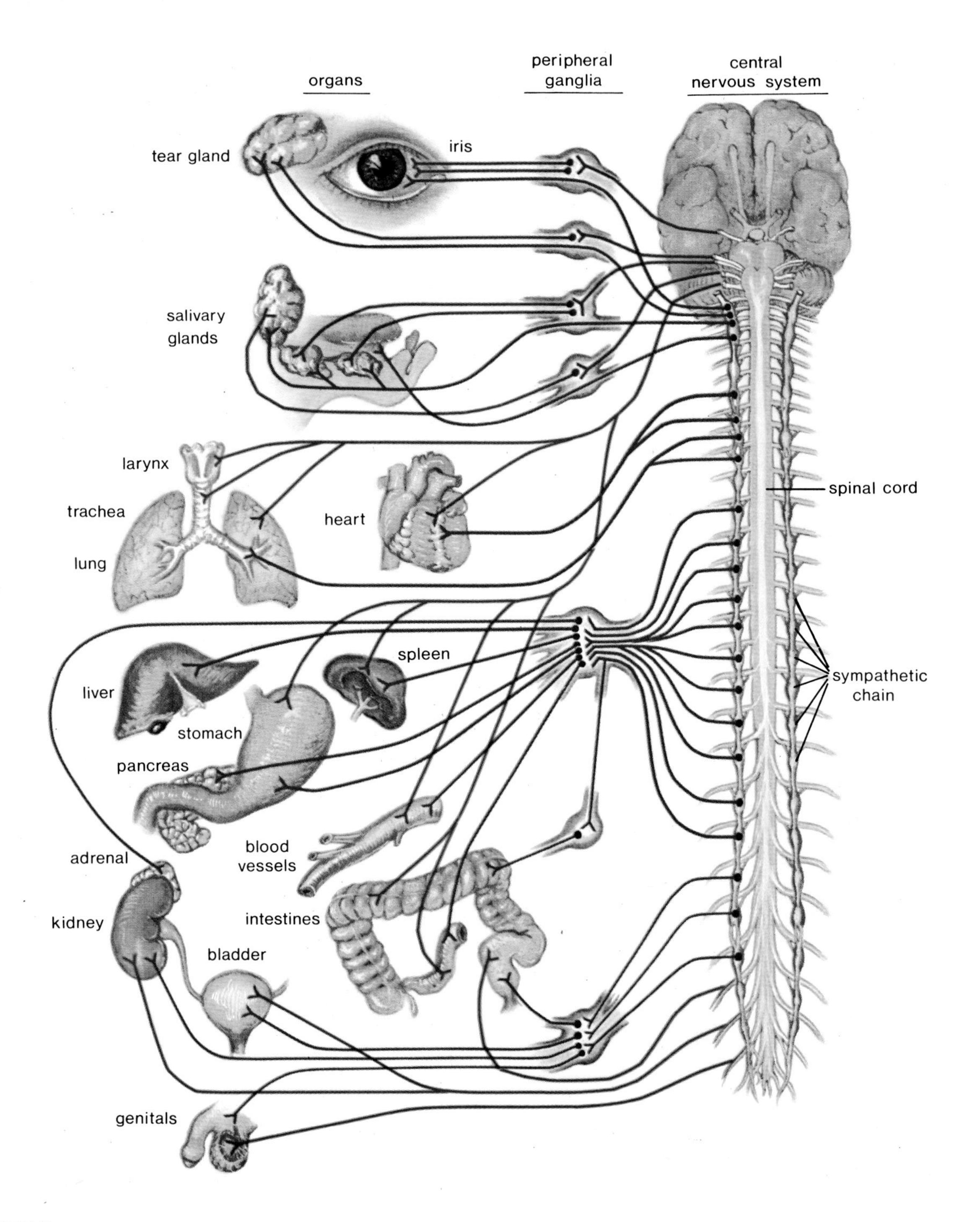

FIGURE 6

The autonomic nervous system controls the activities of many internal organs. Autonomic activities have recently been found to be modifiable by learning, as discussed at several points in the text.

Fibers of the sympathetic division of the autonomic system are shown in red; they arise from the chains of spinal ganglia on either side of the spinal cord. Above and below the sympathetic fibers, fibers of the parasympathetic division branch off from cranial or spinal nerves. The parasympathetic division is shown in green.

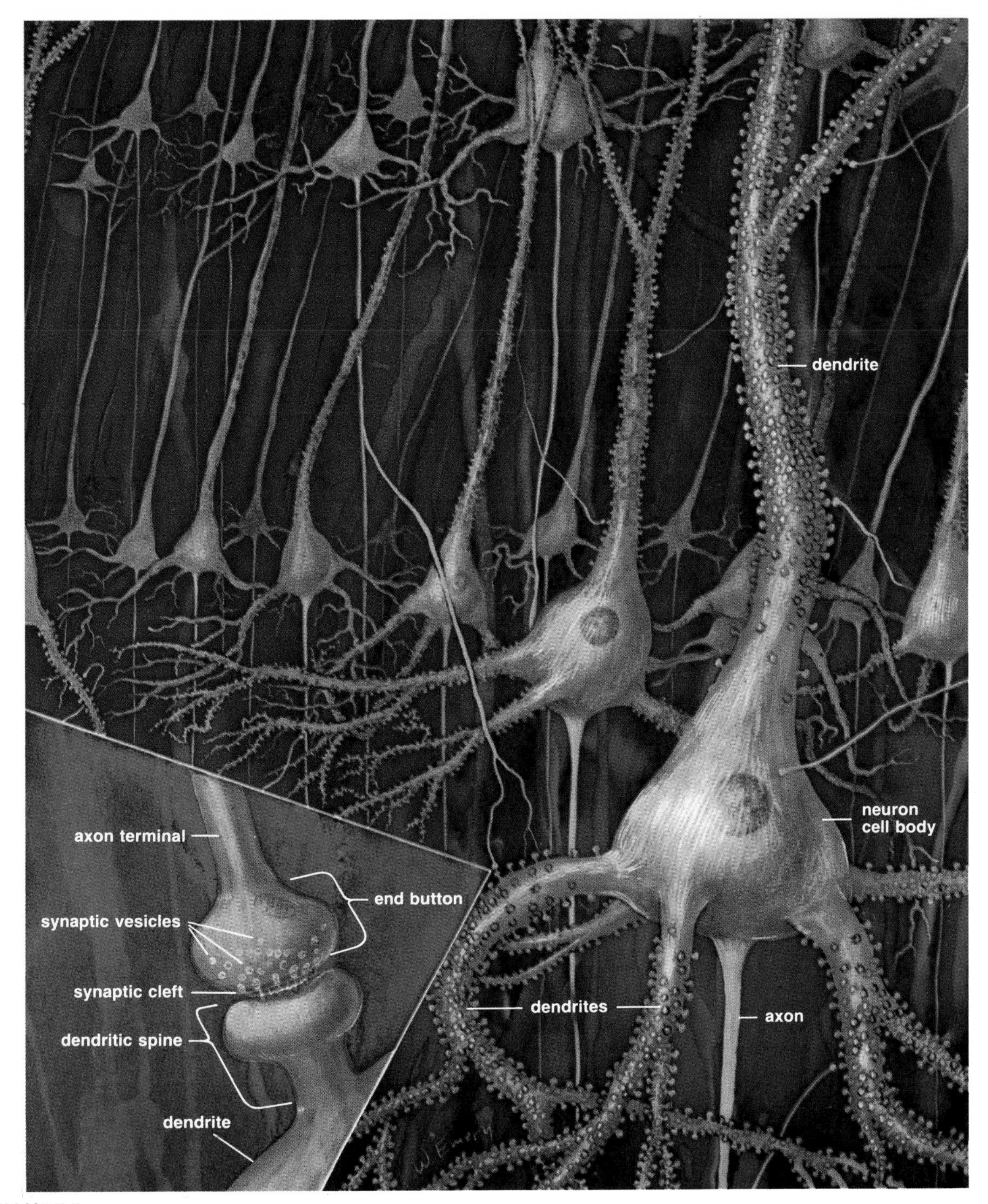

FIGURE 7

Some of the complexity of structure of the cerebral cortex with its columns of neurons is suggested here. Each neuron has a single axon to send out impulses and many branching dendrites to receive inputs from other cells. Only a few synaptic junctions are shown here, although a cortical pyramidal cell (like those shown) may receive thousands of contacts. The nearby neuron is enlarged about 500 times. The synaptic junction at the lower left is enlarged about 10,000 times.

COMPARATIVE PSYCHOLOGY

(From *Science Year, The World Book Science Annual.* © 1970 Field Enterprises Educational Corporation.)

FIGURE 1
When a troop of African savannah baboons travels in dangerous territory (above), juvenile baboons and females with infants stay close to the dominant males at the center of the group. The bolder juvenile males and young adult males walk in the vanguard and at the sides of the troop. When a leopard threatens (below), dominant males lead a mass attack and the rest of the troop flees. Chapter 28 contrasts this troop organization with that of other baboon species who live in one-male groups.

(Phyllis Dolinhow)

FIGURE 2
The antelope watch alertly from a distance, but do not flee from the two female lions and cub.

(Phyllis Dolinhow, taken at Gombe Stream Reserve)

FIGURE 3
In this chimpanzee group there is close physical contact. Adults sit quietly, juveniles wrestle, and an infant manipulates a small branch.

(Phyllis Dolinhow, taken at Gombe Stream Reserve)

FIGURE 4
This is part of a troop of forest-dwelling baboons. An adult male (center) gives an open-mouth threat to an off-camera intruder. A female (upper right) grooms a juvenile while infants play in the grass.

(N. Smythe, from National Audubon Society)

FIGURE 5
A dead-leaf praying mantis has successfully captured a fly. The mantis uses mimicry to camouflage itself from potential prey.

(N. Smythe, from National Audubon Society)

FIGURE 6
A stick insect sits in relative safety while feeding on a guava leaf. This "walkingstick" uses mimicry to conceal itself from predators.

pattern of activation of these associated muscles (see Spotlight 23-1). Movement at each joint in the body is controlled by at least two muscles, so that motion can be made in both directions. For example, a finger can be raised (extended) or lowered (flexed). The muscles that control these oppositely directed movements are called "antagonists" in that they work in opposite directions. In controlled movements, however, both muscles contract and the motion results from delicate shifts in balance of the relative activation of the two; we might think of this as "cooperative antagonism."

Autonomic Nervous System

The motor neurons that control the heart, smooth muscles, and glands are located outside the spinal cord. They seemed to early neuroanatomists to be almost a separate nervous system, and the processes they controlled seemed to be autonomous and independent of voluntary control, so this motor outflow was named the **autonomic nervous system.** We now know that this is simply a part of the motor system and that it is controlled by neural impulses from the brain and spinal cord. The autonomic system has two divisions, which work antagonistically for some functions and cooperatively in others, as shown in Table 23-1. The **sympathetic division** generally predominates when the skeletal musculature is active—it routes blood to the

TABLE 23-1
SOME FUNCTIONS OF THE TWO DIVISIONS OF THE AUTONOMIC NERVOUS SYSTEM

Organ or Function	*Sympathetic Division*	*Parasympathetic Division*
Pupil of eye	Dilation	Constriction
Tear glands	———	Secretion
Salivary glands	———	Secretion
Sweat glands	Secretion	———
Body hair	Hairs raised (piloerection)	———
Heart rate	Increased	Decreased
Blood vessels		
In skin	Constriction	———
In striate muscles	Dilation and constriction	———
In smooth muscles	Constriction	———
In heart	Dilation	Constriction
Adrenal medulla	Secretion	———
Liver	Sugar liberated	———
Stomach	Mainly inhibition of secretion and peristalsis	Mainly stimulation of secretion and peristalsis
Intestines	Inhibition	Increased tonus and movement
Rectum	Inhibition	Defecation
Bladder	Inhibition	Urination
Genital organs		
Female	———	Tumescence
Male	Ejaculation	Erection

SPOTLIGHT 23-1
An Artificial Arm Controlled by Thought

Newspaper stories with titles like the above appeared a few years ago. They referred to the current development of superior artificial limbs that an amputee can use with little or no special training. The artificial arm seems to do whatever the user intends. The operation of motors in the artificial arm is actually controlled by the pattern of activity in the intact muscles of the shoulder, chest, and neck. Electrical signals are recorded from these muscles, and a small electronic circuit determines what pattern is being produced. According to this pattern, the different motors in the artificial arm are operated with more or less force. Feedback occurs both visually and from the pull of the artificial arm on the rest of the body.

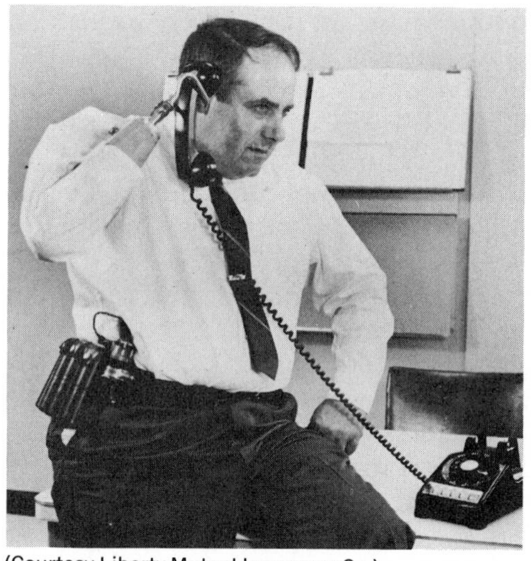

(Courtesy Liberty Mutual Insurance Co.)

Researchers are now attempting to provide more complete feedback of the movements and stresses within the artificial arm. To do this they are placing various detectors within the arm that produce stimulation in the form of touches or vibrations on adjacent patches of skin. This gives more adequate feedback, but the amputee has to learn how to interpret and use it.

skier's skeletal muscles, speeds his heart beat, releases sugar from his liver, and causes secretion of adrenalin. The **parasympathetic division** predominates in restoration of bodily energy—for example, it promotes digestion.

The motor neurons of the sympathetic division are located in two chains, one on either side of the spinal cord (see Figure 23-12). Corresponding to each segment of the spinal cord is a cluster of autonomic cell bodies and synapses; such a clump of neural tissue is called a **ganglion.** The motor neurons of the parasympathetic system are located still farther away from the spinal cord and close to the organs they innervate. (See color Figure 6.) Although the actions of the smooth muscles are often thought of as involuntary, control over many of them can be learned. For example, control of urination and defecation are learned. As mentioned in the sections on personality

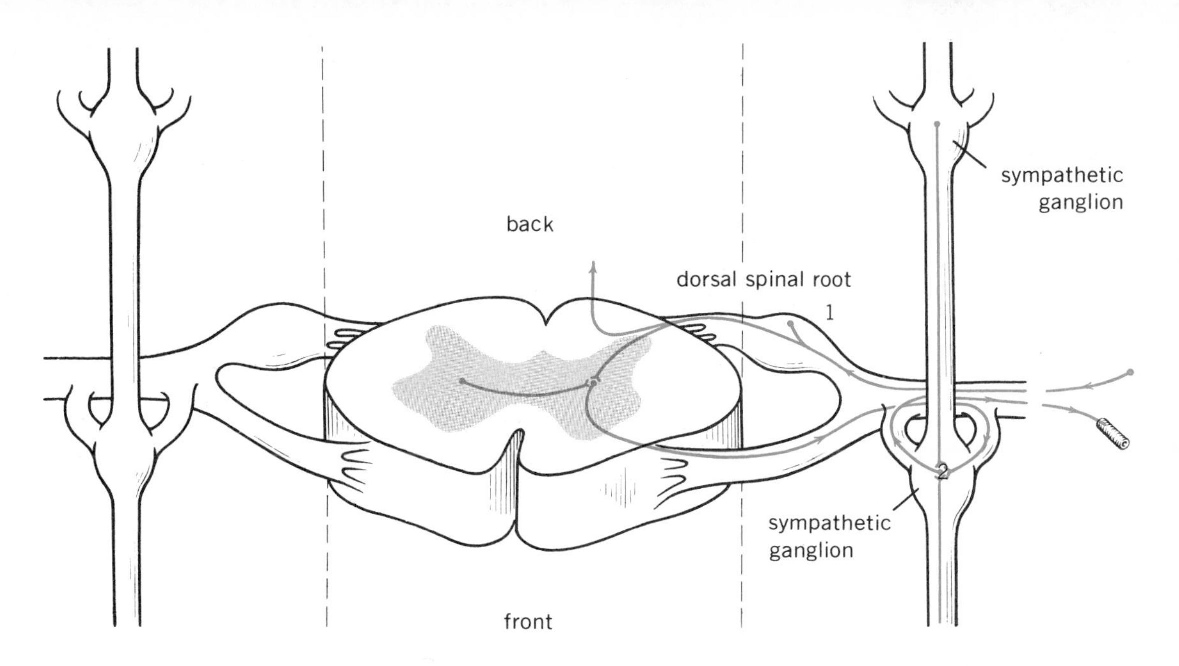

1 Sensory impulses from receptors in internal organs and skin; e.g., cold receptor in skin

2 Responses of smooth muscles and glands; e.g., constriction of blood vessel in skin

FIGURE 23-12
AUTONOMIC REFLEX CONNECTIONS

Two chains of autonomic neurons run along the two sides of the spinal cord. (These sympathetic chains were omitted for the sake of simplicity from Figure 23-10.) As an example of an autonomic reflex, consider what happens when cold receptors in the skin are stimulated. Impulses run to the spinal cord; there some make connections with cells that send axons out the ventral root to sympathetic ganglia. The sympathetic impulses constrict blood vessels in the skin and thus protect the body from losing too much heat.

(p. 249) and learning (p. 490), many autonomic functions can be brought under control by operant conditioning. By this means, new relations can be established between internal responses and emotional or motivational conditions.

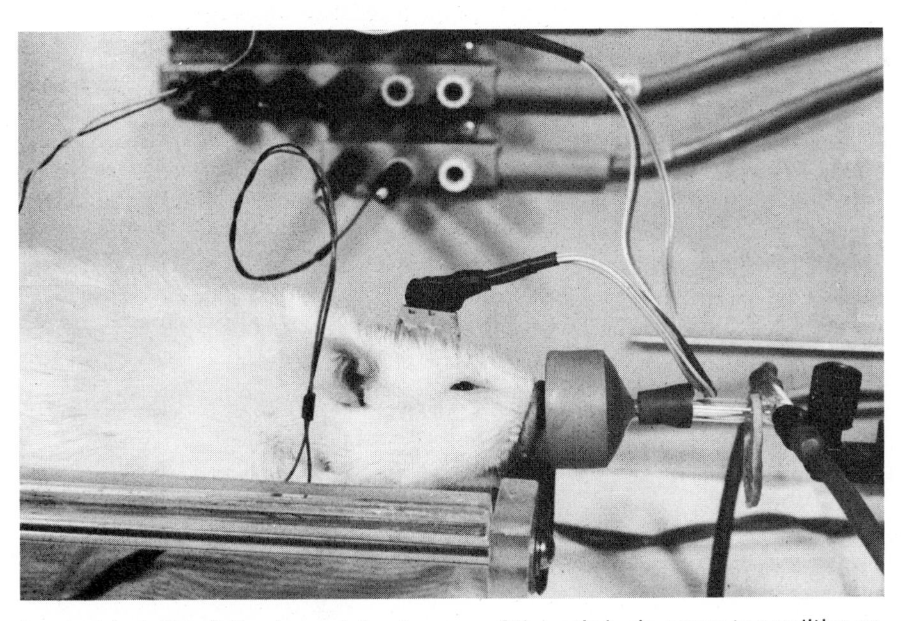

An electrical stimulation to a reinforcing area of the rat's brain serves to condition an autonomic response. (Courtesy N. E. Miller)

SUMMARY

Complex behavior requires the integration of many simultaneous bodily processes, and this is accomplished by the neural and endocrine systems. The basic physiology of neurons can be summarized: neurons conduct bioelectrical potentials along their membranes. At the synaptic junctions with other neurons, chemical transmitter compounds are released to bridge the narrow synaptic gap. The chemical activity at some synapses excites the postsynaptic neuron, whereas at others it inhibits. To be activated, a neuron requires a preponderance of excitatory incoming messages over inhibitory messages. The fact that many neurons receive inputs from hundreds or thousands of other cells allows these neurons to integrate a great deal of information. The endocrine glands also are at work. In many cases the neural and hormonal systems work together, each influencing the other, and sequences of behavior may include both neural and endocrine steps.

Skilled movements require the coordinated activity of many muscles; this means accurate timing of the contractions of certain muscles and of the relaxation of others. The muscles are represented in the primary motor cortex, principally in the contralateral or "opposite-side" cerebral hemisphere. The size of the cortical representation of a muscle is related to the precision of control of its motion. Muscular coordination demands the participation of the motor cortex, other motor centers within the brain, and peripheral neurons. These motor circuits appear to develop and to store elaborate "programs" of acts. Feedback from sensory receptors within muscles, tendons, and joints allow monitoring and correction of behavior in progress.

The autonomic division of the nervous system controls the heart, certain glands, and the smooth muscles in internal organs and in blood vessels. The sympathetic division of the autonomic system generally predominates when a person is active; many of its functions help the body to expend energy. The parasympathetic division predominates during the restoration of bodily energy; for example, it promotes digestion. Thus, the nervous system coordinates the activities of the skeletal muscles with the activities of the heart, smooth muscles, and glands. Many autonomic functions can be conditioned, thereby establishing new relations between these responses and emotional or motivational states.

24

Biological Processes in Perception

How do we capture and encode visual stimuli?
How do we capture and encode auditory stimuli?

No machine yet devised comes close to matching your ability to recognize faces, to identify spoken words, or to make your way over rugged terrain. This is true in spite of the fact that there are artificial sense organs that are more sensitive than our eyes or ears or touch receptors. The fact is that we do not sense and perceive just with our sense organs but also with our nervous systems. The perceptual processes occur very swiftly, so that the perceiver can adjust to a rapidly changing world. The skier must adjust in a fraction of a second to changed angles and surface characteristics that he sees ahead or that he feels through receptors in his joints and tendons. The listener can identify two hundred words a minute (and most of these involve several distinctive phonemes or sound segments). It used to be supposed that these complex decisions involve elaborate judgments or inferences too fast to follow introspectively, but it now appears that there are many automatic neural processes by which information is extracted from the sensory flux.

A great deal of progress has been made in recent years in understanding the brain processes of perception. Some of this progress has come from new or improved ways of recording the electrical activity of individual cells in the nervous system. Some has come from increased precision in making surgical interventions in the nervous system. And much has come from combining ingenious and careful behavioral tests with electrophysiological and surgical procedures.

This chapter will take up some of the main processes that allow us to see and hear. It will increase your understanding of some of the aspects of perception treated in Chapters 20 to 22. We will discuss only a few of the topics raised in those chapters—chiefly the discrimination of quality (hue and pitch) and perception of form and space.

In many fundamental ways all the senses work similarly, once the initial processes of capturing the stimuli have occurred. For each type of stimulus energy—light, sound vibrations, mechanical energy on the skin, odors—a special receptor is needed. Each type of receptor converts stimulus energy into electrical energy, and this stimulates sensory neurons. Different aspects of the stimulus—its spatial distribution, its quality, its intensity—are coded into patterns of neural impulses. These are then decoded in specific parts of the nervous system. Since we will take up vision first, we will spend the most time on it, in order to develop the basic principles of neural processes in perception; many of these principles apply to other senses as well.

How do we capture and encode visual stimuli?

The visual receptor cells are tiny light meters, the rod and cone cells in the retina at the back of the eyeball. There are millions of rods and cones in each retina. These cells contain special **photopigments**; these chemicals are altered and produce an electrical potential when they capture photons, packets of light energy. This electrochemical change builds up an electrical potential that stimulates the neural cells that touch the receptor cells in the retina. (In all senses when the receptor cells are stimulated, they produce what is called a **generator potential.**) This electrical response of the receptor cells amplifies the weak energy of most stimuli and turns it into a form capable of exciting neurons. It is the generator potential rather than the external stimulus that actually stimulates the sensory neurons.

Most human beings have three different color chemicals in three different sets of cones and a fourth chemical in the rods. The three cone chemicals have different wavelength sensitivities; that is, one chemical responds most strongly to the shorter visible wavelengths (which most people see as blue); another responds best to medium wavelengths (seen as green); and the third has its response peak in longer wavelengths (seen as yellow). The colors that we see are not determined directly by these chemicals but by neural processes that extract information about the relative intensities of different wavelengths of light. The rods have a very sensitive chemical; this plus certain neural features of the rod system allows it to operate in very weak light.

Now let us see how the excitation of the receptor cells

results in the transmission of neural impulses to many brain centers and how the patterns of impulses are decoded in the visual centers to permit discrimination of hue, brightness, form, and space. There are several successive stations of the visual system; it will be helpful to take an initial look at the anatomy of the visual brain in Figure 24-1.

How can nerve impulses convey all of the information that you gain as you look around the room or that the skier sees as he rushes down the slope? How are color, brightness, form, and position encoded into nerve impulses? Two types of codes are employed: (1) which neurons are excited or inhibited, and (2) how frequently the excited cells fire impulses.

Discrimination of Color

Determining *which neurons* are affected is one way of encoding what receptors have been stimulated. If a fly alights on your right hand, sensory impulses run up the axons in the right arm, reporting stimulation of the skin. The fact that the impulses do not run along the fibers from the left arm or the right leg enables you to detect where the stimulation occurred. Even at the same position, different qualities can be coded by which neurons are stimulated. If a drop of warm water falls on your hand, temperature receptors as well as touch receptors in the skin are stimulated. Some impulses travel up the nerve fibers that are reserved for messages about warmth while others go up the touch fibers. In vision, which fibers are affected helps to determine color, position, and many other aspects of the perception.

The three types of cone receptors and certain neural connections in the retina are shown in Figure 24-2. The nerve cells next in line, those that "pick up" the messages from the cones, are called **bipolar cells,** because the cell bodies have extensions at the two ends or poles. The bipolar cells fall into three classes, the activity of each class reflecting the absorption spectrum of one of the three cone photopigments. Therefore light in the long wavelength end of the spectrum (red, orange, and yellow) tends to stimulate the long-wavelength cones and the long-wavelength bipolar cells more strongly than the medium-wavelength and short-wavelength cells.

After the bipolar cells come neurons called **ganglion cells;** their cell bodies are in the retina and their axons make up the **optic nerve.** These cells fire impulses spontaneously, five to ten spikes per second. Most ganglion cells are excited by certain bipolar cells but are inhibited by others. Thus, the ganglion cell at the left in Figure 24-2 is excited by connections from long-wavelength (yellow) bipolars and inhibited by impulses from short-wavelength (blue) bipolars; it is therefore called a Yellow Plus–Blue Minus cell ($Y+$, $B-$). The next ganglion cell in the figure responds in just the opposite way—positively to blue and negatively to yellow ($B+$, $Y-$). Similarly, there are cells that fire to green and are inhibited by red ($G+$, $R-$), and there are

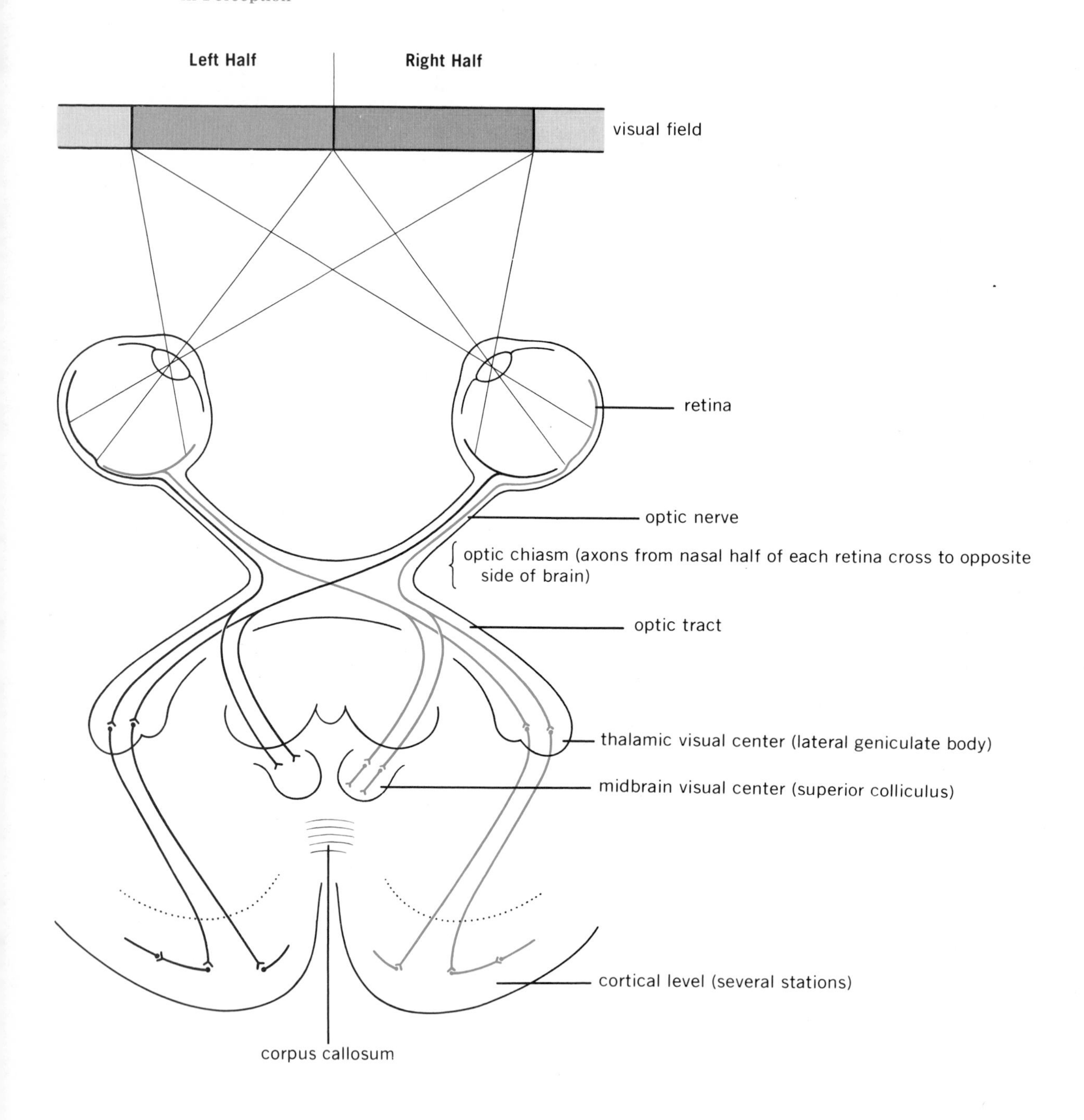

FIGURE 24-1
MAP OF THE HUMAN VISUAL SYSTEM

This diagram shows some of the main pathways in the visual system. Note that the left half of the visual field (in color) stimulates the right half of each retina and sends neural impulses to the right half of the brain.

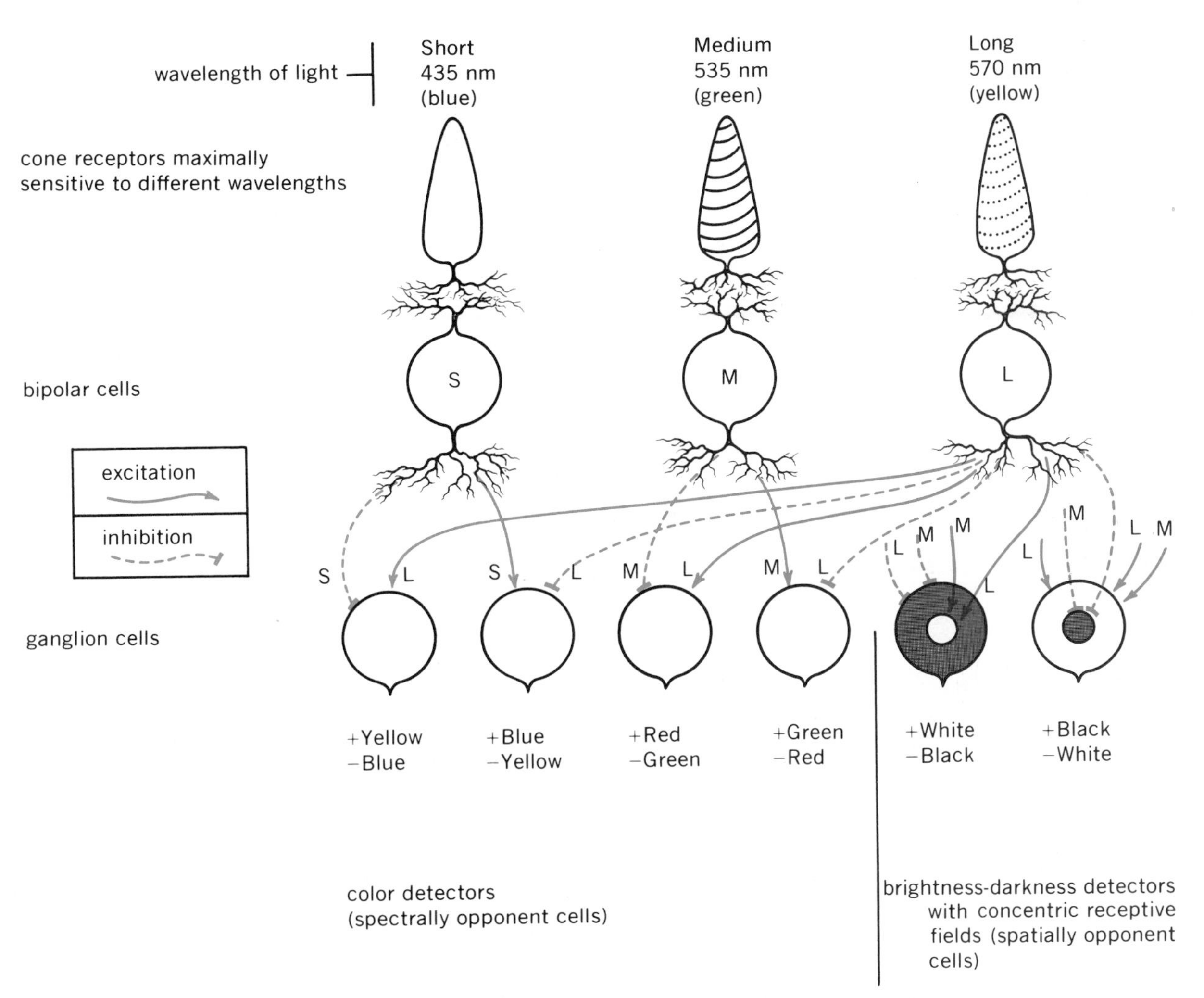

FIGURE 24-2
RETINAL SYSTEMS FOR DETECTING HUE AND BRIGHTNESS

The human retina contains three types of cone receptors. Each can be stimulated by any wavelength of visible light but is most sensitive to one of the three wavelengths shown at the top of the diagram. The receptor cells make contact with neurons, the bipolar cells. Each neural bipolar cell is excited by only one type of cone. The bipolar cells, in turn, synapse on the next set of neurons, the ganglion cells. The axons of the ganglion cells run out of the eye and form the optic nerve. The ganglion cells fire impulses spontaneously and can be excited to a higher rate of activity by certain bipolar cells and inhibited by other bipolar cells.

There are six main populations of ganglion cells: four kinds detect color, while the other two detect brightness or darkness. The color-detecting ganglion cells, unlike the bipolar cells, cannot be excited by all wavelengths of light; they are inhibited by part of the spectrum. For example, a Yellow Plus–Blue Minus cell (like the ganglion cell at the left of the diagram) fires faster than its spontaneous rate if the stimulus energy is mainly in the long wavelengths, but it stops firing if the light energy is concentrated in the short wavelengths.

The two types of ganglion cells that detect brightness differences have concentric receptive fields. For a Black Plus–White Minus cell (like the ganglion cell at the right of the diagram), a light in the center of its field inhibits, while an off-center light excites.

(Modified from De Valois, 1969)

also their opposites ($R+$, $G-$). These four types of cells are called **spectrally opponent,** since each is excited by light in one part of the spectrum and inhibited by other wavelengths. They discriminate wavelengths and permit us to differentiate hues.

Two other types of ganglion cells do not show spectral opposition, but instead respond to the distribution of light in space. One type is excited by most wavelengths of light—but only when that light falls in the center of the **receptive field** of the ganglion cell. (The receptive field of a cell is that part of the visual field where stimulation alters the cell's activity—either excites it or inhibits it.) Light falling a little to one side or the other of the center of the receptive field inhibits this type of cell. Such a cell is therefore excited most strongly by a small circle of light positioned in just the right part of the visual field. When a larger stimulus is given, or if the whole visual field is illuminated, there will be inhibition from the surrounding area and less activity than if just the center were stimulated. Such a cell is called White Plus–Black Minus. The opposite kind of cell is inhibited by light in the center of its receptive field and stimulated by light in the surrounding area; this is a Black Plus–White Minus cell. These White-Black cells can be thought of as having **spatially opponent** receptive fields. The White-Black cells are the main determiners of brightness but they are color-blind.

These six types of comparison—four for hue and two for brightness—are made at peripheral sites in the sensory pathway, and the results are transmitted to the stations farther along the nervous system. In no case is there a direct channel from the receptors to the cortex.

The spectrally opponent cells can be called color cells more appropriately than can the primary receptor cones. The fact that a particular cone is active does not by itself tell us anything about the hue of the stimulus, but the fact that a given spectrally opponent cell is active tells us a good deal. Each cone responds to some extent to light from any part of the visible spectrum, although it is most sensitive to a particular part of the spectrum (Figure 24-3). Therefore, a weak response in a "yellow" cone can be caused either by weak energy at a long wavelength or by strong energy at a short wavelength. But an opponent cell responds positively to a limited region of the spectrum and is inhibited by light of other wavelengths, as you can see in the parts *B* and *C* of the figure. A Yellow Plus–Blue Minus cell will not respond to blue; it is inhibited by blue. Thus the neural connections sharpen the selectivity of the response. We will see later that this is also true of other senses; for example, cells in the auditory tracts discriminate among frequencies of sound much more precisely than do the receptor cells in the inner ear.

Discrimination of Intensity

The visual system codes for brightness of the stimulus in terms of frequency of spikes; that is, for White Plus–Black Minus cells, the brighter the light, the more spikes the optic nerve axons carry per unit of time. But there are some special features of this relation that are worthy of a more detailed examination. For example, we are sensitive to very small differences in intensity, yet we can function over a very wide range of stimulus intensities.

The brightest light you can stand is about ten billion times more intense than the weakest light you can see (as was shown in Figure 20-8 in Chapter 20). The cones are sensitive only to the stronger intensities in this range. For weaker illumination, another set of retinal receptors—the rods—comes into operation. They do not participate in color discrimination, but they extend visual sensitivity down to a very low level of illumination. In fact, your eyes could hardly be any more sensitive than they are; under optimal conditions a human observer can detect a light flash of only a few photons, the minimal packets of light energy. However, at these lowest levels, below "bright moonlight," it is a colorless visual world.

Mechanisms Assisting Discrimination of Intensity

Although your total capacity for discriminating brightness gives a ratio of ten billion to one (brightest to darkest), your operating capacity at any given moment is considerably less, giving

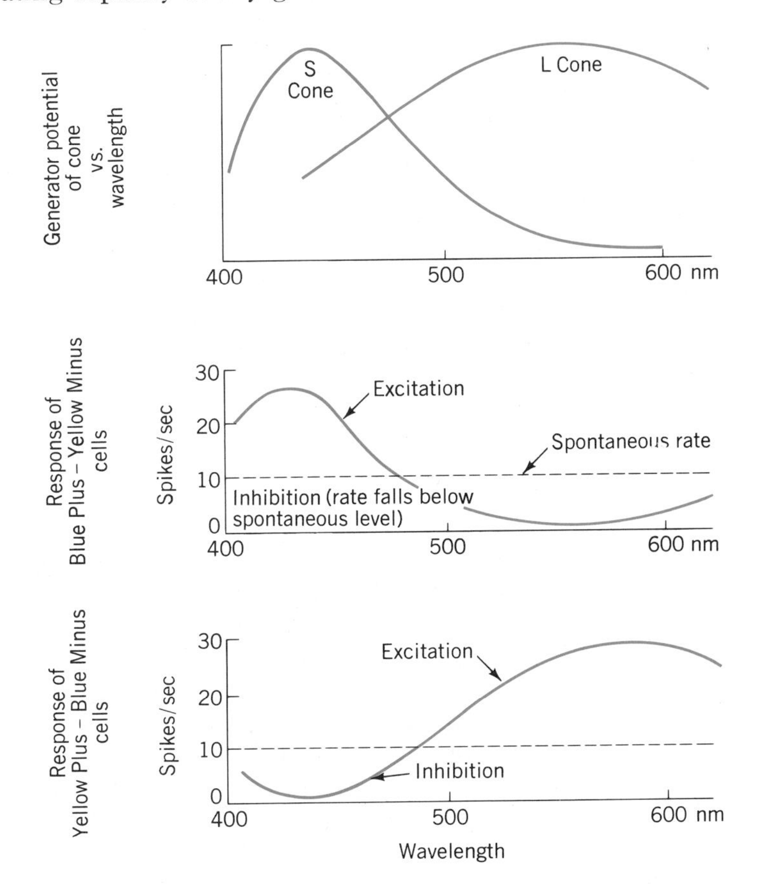

FIGURE 24-3 COLOR DISCRIMINATION

Because of their neural inputs, each ganglion cell is "turned on" by certain wavelengths and is "turned off" by other wavelengths. The bottom graph shows the response of a Yellow Plus–Blue Minus ganglion cell; it is just the opposite of the middle graph, which is for a Blue Plus–Yellow Minus ganglion cell. The top graph shows the strength of the generator potential evoked in a cone that prefers short wavelengths (S cone) and in a long wavelength cone (L); each shows some response all across the spectrum.

a brightest-darkest ratio of about a hundred to one. Your entire ability to discriminate light intensities is thus devoted to a relatively small part of the total range, and your discrimination can be much finer than if it had to be spread across the entire range.

How does the visual system perform this feat? Several mechanisms are involved. The pupil adjusts to the prevailing intensity of light and regulates how much light reaches the retina. In very weak light the pupil becomes about sixteen times larger than it is in very bright light. Cameras employ a similar mechanism in the diaphragm or *f* stop.

A second mechanism is the use of two sets of receptors, the rods and the cones. The rods function in dim light. As many as a hundred rods may connect with a single bipolar cell. This convergence aids sensitivity, because stimulation of any of the rods within the group will excite the bipolar cell. While their convergence promotes sensitivity, it is gained at the cost of reduced spatial acuity. Responding to any one of a group of rods, the bipolar cell cannot tell exactly where the stimulus occurred. Night vision then is not as spatially acute as is day vision where less convergence occurs. There is much convergence in the rod system but less in the cone system; the human retina contains about 120 million rods but only about 6 million cones. Above the level of moonlight the cones function, and when the cone system is active it inhibits the rod system. A photographic analogue to the two types of receptors is the use of more or less sensitive films.

A third mechanism is the receptive field organization that we described above for the White–Black cells. This enhances relative differences between parts of the field, to whatever level of illumination the eye is adapted. This spatial interaction of excitatory and inhibitory effects has no analogue in photography, but there is one in television where the receiving elements have inhibitory connections to each other. You may have noticed that where a television camera picks up a very bright light—such as a flashbulb at a press conference or the flame of a satellite booster at blastoff—there appears to be a dark cloud around it.

Finally, there are mechanisms of adaptation. One type is chemical and another is neural. Bright light tends to bleach the photopigments so that the retina is less sensitive; in dim light the regeneration of the photopigments keeps up with the bleaching so that a maximum of stimulation can occur. Neurally there is inhibitory feedback, so that activity tends to reduce sensitivity. Adaptation in vision is very effective: when you look at something for a minute or so, the chemical and neural adaptation would so deplete or inhibit the receptors that the object would disappear—if it were not for the fact that your eyes always tremble slightly. This normal tremor changes which receptors are stimulated and thus counteracts adaptation. If the object we see is *in* the eye, however, and "trembles" just as the receptors do, then the object does fade. For example, there are numerous blood vessels between the retina and the pupil, but we usually do not see them because of adaptation.

Cells in the optic nerve can fire no more frequently than about 100 spikes per second, but this is enough to account for the range of brightness that we can see at any given time. The effective range of light intensities that we can discriminate at any moment (the operating range) is only about 100 to 1 (see Figure 24-4). Sometimes this range is in the bright part of the total, sometimes the range includes only lower intensities, but wherever it is, it is interpreted by essentially the same cells. In other words, to know how fast a cell is firing tells you how much stimulation it is receiving *relative* to other cells, but tells you nothing about the *absolute* brightness. In terms of what you experience, inputs above the operating range are seen as "white" and those below as "black."

This fact helps to explain some of the effects pointed out in Chapter 21 on perception. Black objects usually remain black, and white remain white in spite of major changes in illumination. But interesting illusions can be created if we conceal the relation between the illumination of the object and the illumination of its field (see Spotlight 21-3, p. 578).

Within the operating range, your impression of brightness does not increase in direct linear proportion to the amount of light energy of the source. As shown in Chapter 20, your perception of brightness follows approximately the logarithm or power law function

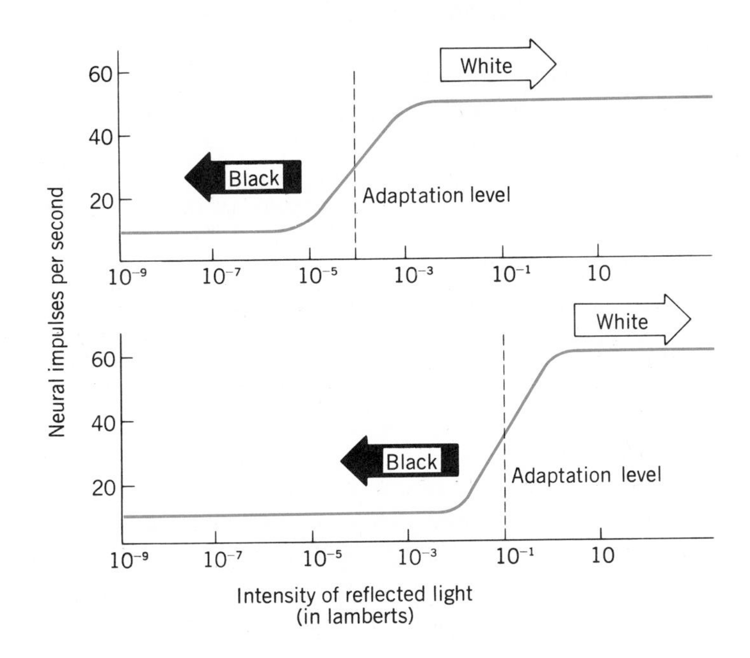

FIGURE 24-4
PERCEPTION OF BLACK AND WHITE

The level of illumination to which the eyes are adapted at any given time can change over a broad range. Any surface looks white if it reflects back about one logarithmic unit more light than the current adaptation level; any surface looks black if it reflects back about one log unit less light than the current adaptation level.

of the stimulus intensity—the exact form of the function is still a matter of dispute. This nonlinear relation between stimulus and response is determined by the rods and cones. The receptor cells produce a generator potential that is approximately logarithmically related to the stimulus intensity.

Contrast and Enhancement of Contours

How bright one part of the visual field looks is dependent on the brightness of neighboring parts of the field. A gray patch looks darker where it touches a white patch and lighter where it contacts a black patch. (This was demonstrated in Figure 5 in the preview to perception.) Such contrast sharpens borders or contours—lines between two "things." The outer shape or contour of something communicates a great amount of information; line drawings and cartoons, for example, make their point with little else.

The contrast and sharpening effects in vision are known to depend on complex interrelations among retinal cells as well as among cells higher in the visual system. Understanding of these mechanisms has been aided by the study of a simpler system where the units are readily accessible and where only one type of interaction among units occurs. This is the compound eye of the horseshoe crab, *Limulus*. This eye has about a thousand separate units or ommatidia (from the Greek for "little eye"). (See Figure 24-5.) Each ommatidium is innervated by a single neuron. Soon after leaving the ommatidia, the neurons are interconnected by side branches that form a network. Through this network, any neuron that is activated inhibits its neighbors, and the closer they are, the stronger the inhibition. It is relatively easy to record the activity of one or more individual neurons from this compound eye.

If a narrow beam of light is focused on one ommatidium, then the neuron from that unit fires impulses. The stronger the light, the faster the rate of firing; the rate is roughly proportional to the logarithm of light intensity. If the light is maintained on unit *A* and a second light is focused on unit *B*, the rate of firing in *A* promptly falls, just as if the light on *A* has been dimmed. If the light on *A* is then extinguished, the rate of firing in *B* rises. Thus each unit inhibits its neighbor.

To study contrast, investigators illuminated one half of the compound eye and prevented light from reaching the other half; this is diagrammed in Figure 24-5. Recording from units at various locations then revealed that the *greatest* rate of neural firing is found just to the lighted side of the light-dark boundary, while the *lowest* rate of firing is found just to the dark side of the boundary. Farther to either side of the boundary, the rates of firing are intermediate. Since the rate of firing is more or less proportional to the logarithm of intensity of light, what does the observed pattern mean? The eye responds as if the light were brightest just inside its boundary and as

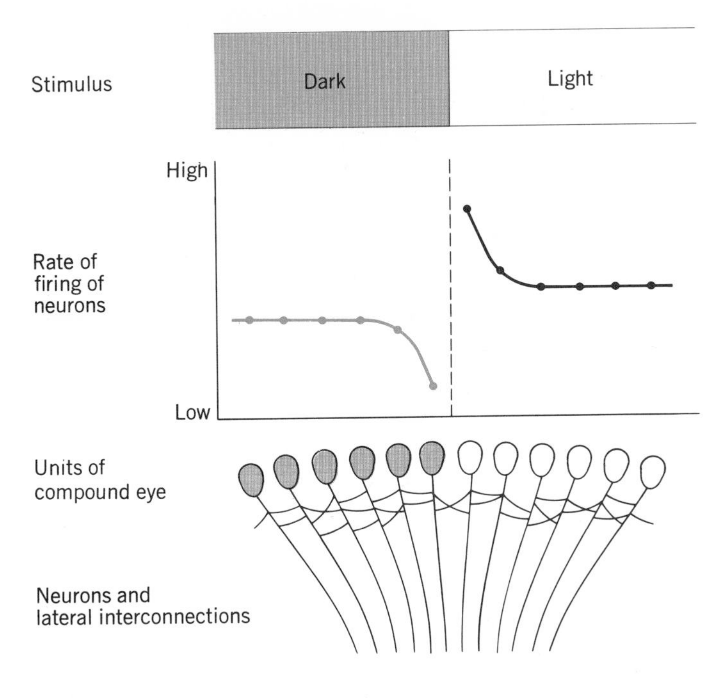

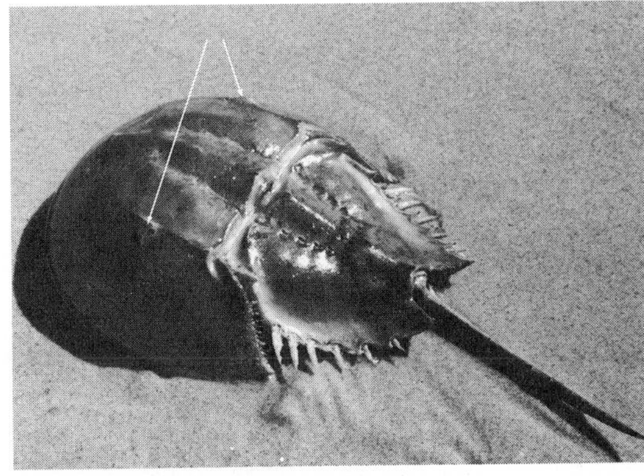

(Gordon S. Smith, National Audubon Society)

FIGURE 24-5
STUDY OF CONTRAST IN A COMPOUND EYE
Each unit or ommatidium in the compound eyes (location shown above) of the horseshoe crab can be recorded separately. The graph shows the rate of firing of neural impulses depending upon the position of the ommatidium with respect to the light-dark boundary. The greatest difference in firing rates occurs at the boundary. This contrast effect is caused by the mutual inhibition among units. (Adapted from Ratliff & Hartline, 1959)

if the surrounding area were darkest just outside the boundary. It is clear that differences in rates of firing are enhanced at the boundary between the light and dark areas.

Discrimination of Form

As impulses travel up the visual pathways of a mammal, there is more and more specific detection of form. During the last ten years investigators have found that some cells in the visual system respond *only* when *special shapes* or even *special movements* are presented in the visual field. To study such phenomena, the investigator inserts a microelectrode, whose fine tip records from only a few cells—ideally only one. Then the experimenter presents various stimuli and tries to determine which stimulus evokes the greatest amount of activity in the cell (see Figure 24-6).

Recording Receptive Fields

Cells at lower levels in the visual system—ganglion cells in the retina and some cells in the thalamus—respond to specific but rather simple stimuli. They have roughly circular receptive fields such as *A* in Figure 24-6. But as one moves up the line to the brain cells involved in perception, discrimination becomes finer, more precise. Many cells respond best to a particular position and orientation—a bar at a particular angle, such as *B*. Another cell may best be stimulated by a line a little to the left of center in the visual field and

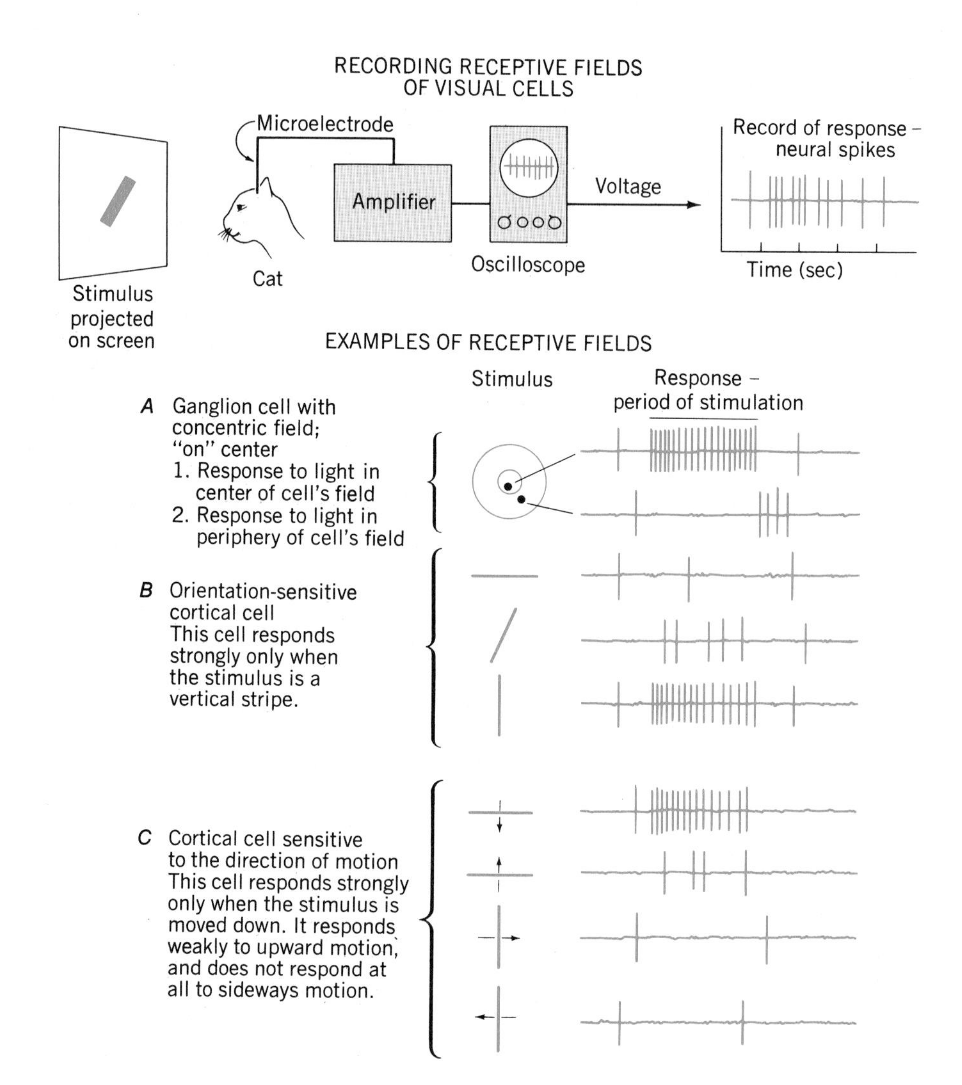

FIGURE 24-6
CORTICAL CELLS' REACTIONS TO SPECIFIC STIMULI

at a 45° angle; a third cell will respond only to a horizontal line at a particular position in the lower right quadrant, and so on. Such cortical cells receive inputs from several neurons located closer to the receptor—we noted in the previous chapter that many neurons will fire only when several converging inputs are active simultaneously—and these lower cells probably show a physical arrangement (in combination) that resembles the form of the effective stimulus. For example, in the case of *B* in Figure 24-6, the cells that feed into this unit probably have their receptive fields aligned vertically to each other. Illuminating a broad area will not stimulate such a cortical cell, because this will inhibit the cell just as much as it excites it. This is why many cells in the visual cortex do not respond when the lights in the room are turned on. This lack of response to general illumination puzzled many early researchers. They thought that the cells in the visual cortex ought to respond to *any* visual stimulus, but now we know that most cortical cells are much more demanding.

Cells that are close together in the primary visual cortex respond to stimulation in the same area of the visual field but often respond to quite different stimuli. This means that the primary cortex does "map" the visual field, each region of cortex receiving information from a specific part of the field, but that within the map different cells represent different sorts of visual input—hues, brightness or darkness, angles, and so on. Two neighboring cells may then respond very differently, so detailed electrical recording does not support the commonsense (or scientific) notions that what you see is accurately represented in the large-scale distribution of activity across the surface of the brain. Even the gross mapping may, however, prove useful in providing some vision to the blind by electrical stimulation of the brain (see Spotlight 24-1).

Some cortical cells act as if they could be fired only through other cortical cells. For example, some respond only to two lines joined at an angle (a corner), as if two "line detectors" fed into

SPOTLIGHT 24-1

Artificial Eyes

We have artificial limbs; why not artificial eyes?

Recent experiments show some success in giving vision to a totally blind person by delivering electrical stimulation directly to the primary visual cortex. When a point on the cortex is stimulated, the person reports "seeing" a glowing spot in a particular part of his visual field. If two points are stimulated in succession, the person can report their relative positions in his visual field. If several points are stimulated, the person sees a pattern of luminous spots, somewhat like a sign made up of light bulbs.

Following developmental work on monkeys, a blind woman had an array of electrodes implanted through the skull (Brindley & Lewin, 1968). When patterns of stimulation were fed into the electrode array, the subject could identify several of them by "sight"; for example, she could discriminate "7" from "?". The device did not work as well as was hoped, but plans have been developed to improve the system. It should be noted that the electrodes were rather large and each probably activated hundreds of cortical cells. Therefore a system of this sort cannot utilize the highly differentiated receptive fields of single cells but depends on the grosser spatial map of the visual cortex.

New hope for the blind, as the *Reader's Digest* might put it, may be far in the future, but even the crude and partial success of these studies is adding useful scientific knowledge, not only for the blind but also for an understanding of the normal visual system as well.

the "corner detector." Some cortical cells respond only to lines of a specific "tilt" or orientation but respond to such lines placed anywhere in a relatively large area of the visual field, as if they were "abstracting" a common feature of a number of different and specific inputs. It appears that these generalized "orientation detectors" can be fired by the more specific cortical cells, each of which requires not only the angle but also a fixed position. In general, cortical cells that are both complex and yet highly specialized have been found with increasing frequency in recent years. One researcher discovered cortical cells in the monkey's temporal lobe that fired best to a precise stimulus, such as the shape of a hand or a forceps; the cell responded to that stimulus regardless of its orientation or its location within a wide extent of the visual field (Gross, Bender, & Rocha-Miranda, 1969).

The way that functions are distributed among brain regions is not necessarily the same for all species. Rather complex processes that occur in the brains of mammals may occur peripherally in sensory systems of somewhat simpler animals. For example, in the frog, which does not have a cerebral cortex, shape discrimination occurs in the ganglion cells of the retina. Thus one type of cell in the frog retina will react only to small roundish moving stimuli such as the insects the frog eats; these retinal cells have been called "bug detectors." It is not that the frog sees and ignores stationary bugs; his visual system simply does not respond to such stimuli.

Effects of Brain Lesions on Form Vision

Electrical recording or stimulation is not the only means of studying the functions of biological tracts and centers related to vision. Another method is to study the behavioral effects of localized cuts or destruction of the brain—brain lesions. We will consider successively the effects of lesions in the three cortical regions most concerned with form vision (see Figure 24-7): (1) The *primary visual cortex* is where the signals from the eyes first reach the cortical level; this is often called the "striate area" because one layer of this cortex is a light-colored strip running parallel to the surface. (2) From the primary visual cortex, axons run to the surrounding area called the *secondary visual* (or circumstriate) *cortex*. (3) The last region lies at the base of the temporal lobe and is therefore called **inferotemporal cortex**; here some of the most complex visual integrations seem to occur.

Localized lesions in the primary visual cortex produce both localized and more general effects. The visual field is "mapped" rather precisely on the primary visual cortex, and a partial destruction of this area results in blindness for the corresponding part of the field. This blindness (called a "scotoma") is not a black patch, for blackness is just as much a result of an active process as is whiteness. Instead the scotoma is simply an area in which nothing is seen. The patient is not aware of a blind spot—until a visual object vanishes into it—just

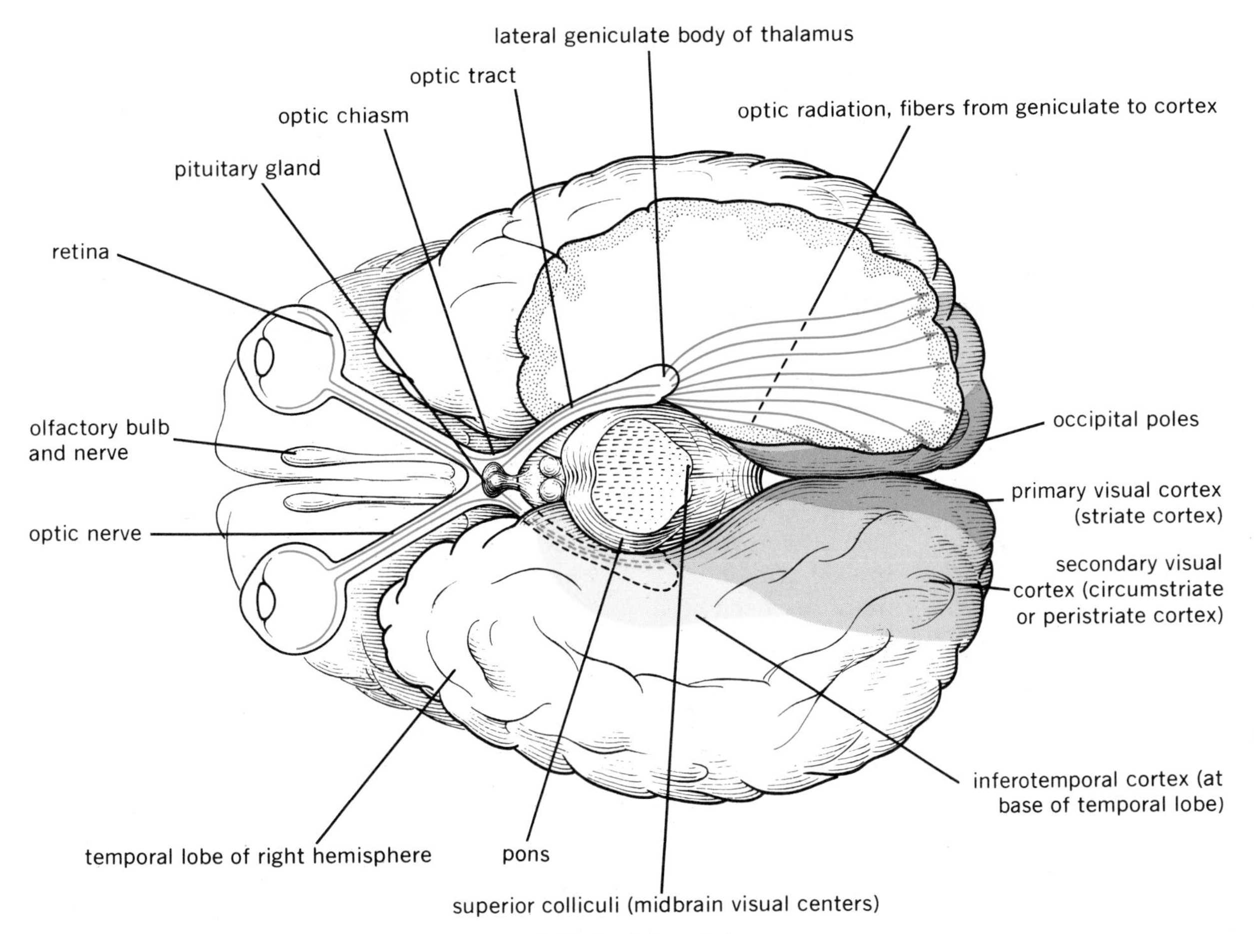

FIGURE 24-7 VISUAL PATHWAYS AND CENTERS IN THE HUMAN BRAIN

The visual pathways and centers are shown in color. Parts of the brain have been removed to reveal visual structures: the left temporal lobe (in the upper half of the diagram) has been largely cut away to reveal the thalamic visual center and axons running from it to the cortex. The cerebellum has been removed to show regions of the visual cortex. The brain stem has been cut across at the level of the midbrain visual centers.

as you are not aware of your blind spot unless you look at a stimulus like Figure 12 in the preview to perception (p. 539). To this extent, destruction of part of the primary visual cortex results in a sensory defect; there is simply no vision in that part of the field, although vision elsewhere is relatively normal.

Localization of function in the visual cortex is not quite so simple, however, because even the localized "sensory" lesion does have other effects. For example, the ability to distinguish a flickering light from a steady light is somewhat impaired throughout the visual field whenever any part of the primary visual cortex is injured.

The effects of a lesion in the secondary visual cortex (the circumstriate area) are still a matter of dispute. There is no hole in the visual field, but there is a decrease in the accuracy of discriminating shapes or sizes of objects. Therefore, some investigators speak about *perceptual* damage here, in contrast to the *sensory* damage resulting from lesions in the primary visual cortex.

When a lesion is made in the inferotemporal region, there is impairment in various complex visual tasks. For example, there are difficulties in learning series of discriminations between paired objects and also difficulties in responding positively or negatively to one object of the pair. A monkey with this type of lesion can learn to respond to one stimulus in a pair if that one is rewarded and the other is not. But the monkey with the inferotemporal lesion does not improve its rate of learning over a long series of new problems of the same general type. A normal monkey "learns to learn" discriminations of this sort, taking several trials for the first pair, fewer for the second (different) pair, and still fewer for subsequent pairs to the point that it requires but a single trial to identify the correct or rewarded one (see p. 480). Also, the normal monkey who has learned to discriminate can then do so with only one of the two stimuli present; it will respond to the correct one and will refrain from responding to the wrong one. A monkey with inferotemporal cortex destroyed cannot perform correctly when only one of the pair is presented; it must have both present in order to respond correctly. The impairment seems to be in processing and perhaps also in long-term storage of information. Some investigators conclude that the functions damaged here are *conceptual*, as opposed to the *perceptual* and *sensory* damages described in the previous paragraphs.

There are still problems left to unravel. For example, some visual tasks are disturbed by lesions anywhere in the cortex, including regions usually assigned to other senses or to motor function. One such task involves finding hidden figures, where a simple drawing is embedded in a more complex picture. (Examples of hidden figures were shown on p. 590.) Any cortical lesion impairs the ability to detect the hidden figure, even when the cells in this area do not have visual receptive fields.

Thus the two techniques of studying cortical function in vision—plotting receptive fields and studying behavioral effects of cortical lesions—yield results that are parallel to some extent but that do not mesh perfectly. Both methods reveal increasingly complex functions as one goes from primary visual cortex to secondary (circumstriate) cortex to inferotemporal cortex. But the highly complex receptive fields of the inferotemporal region would not have led us to suspect that monkeys deprived of this region can still learn to discriminate objects when they are presented simultaneously. Nor would the failure (to date) to find visual receptive fields in cortical cells outside these areas have led us to guess that lesions there would impair detection of hidden figures. Thus, while we can identify parts of the brain that are important in form vision, and while we are finding something about the ways in which they work, there is still much to be investigated on these problems. A related question is the extent to which form vision is inborn or is acquired through experience; see Spotlight 24-2.

SPOTLIGHT 24-2

Beyond Nativism and Empiricism

Recent biological research suggests a new answer to the long-disputed question of whether form perception is inborn (the nativist position) or acquired through experience (the empiricist position). Previously, much attention had been paid to cases of people who were born with cataracts and who were able to see for the first time as adults when the cataracts were removed. Most of these case studies indicated that these people very quickly saw differences in color and could sense where an object was, but they could not immediately identify objects or discriminate distances. Only gradually, over weeks and months, did some people learn to identify faces and objects and to see them in depth; others gave up the attempt and never acquired useful form vision. These findings suggest that learning plays a more significant role in form perception than do the inborn capacities. But another possibility is that visual proficiency is inborn but can be lost during the period when cataracts cover the eyes. Recent research supports this third possibility.

Hubel (1967) found that newborn kittens had cortical visual receptive fields rather similar to those of adult cats. But if the eyes were covered for the first two months, then many cortical cells did not respond to visual stimulation of the eyes, and some cells gave abnormal responses. The longer the eyes were occluded, the less well did the cats regain useful vision. Such effects applied only to the early developmental stages; in an older cat, the eyes can be occluded for months, and vision will return very rapidly when the eyes are uncovered.

If only one of a kitten's eyes is covered for several weeks, later testing shows that the kitten can no longer discriminate forms *with that eye.* Similarly, a child can lose the use of an eye for form vision if he relies on the other eye. This often occurs if the two eyes do not converge—do not aim at exactly the same place. In such cases of cross-eyes or divergent gaze, there would be double vision if the input from one eye was not suppressed. But even with normal convergence, a child may begin to use only one eye, and acuity then declines in the other. If this is detected, the treatment is to put a patch over the favored eye for a period each day to force the use of the neglected eye; unless this is done, loss of form vision through the neglected eye will result.

It appears that, in the typical case, rather normal organization of visual connections is present at birth. This is the nativist position. But the normal organization of visual connections also seems to *require experience* to confirm it and perhaps to strengthen it. This is an empiricist position. Apparently, then, *inborn* visual systems need *experience* to be confirmed and retained. This finding is a new and relatively precise demonstration that the extreme empiricist and nativist positions have become outmoded.

Visual Perception of Space

How does the skier see the position of the slalom gates? How do you see the location of a book in order to pick it up? It might seem that solving the problems of visual form (what is it?) would also solve the problems of visual space (where is it?). Since forms are extended in space, don't we perceive and discriminate space if we perceive and discriminate form? Research has demonstrated that the two abilities are rather different, as William James suspected when he wrote his *Principles of Psychology* in 1890. Let us consider first a few examples to illustrate the difference between perceiving form and perceiving space and location. Then we will consider evidence that at least some of the neural circuits that detect space are different from those that detect form.

The accuracy of your discrimination of position is quite good in the periphery of the visual field even though your acuity for form is poor. If you detect a small movement out toward one edge of your field, you move your gaze in that direction very quickly and accurately; then you examine what is there. But if you try keeping your eyes directed straight ahead, you realize that you cannot discriminate shapes very well out to the side. For example, look at the center of this page while you wiggle a finger tip around the middle of the opposite page. You can see very well where the moving finger tip is, but can you read the words around it? Form discrimination is accurate in the center of the field and falls off rapidly as the target is moved to either side or above or below; that is why you have to move your eyes to identify objects and to read. Space discrimination does not deteriorate nearly so rapidly away from the central region, and this enables you to know *where* objects are before you can tell *what* they are. Your spatial perception allows you to duck a rapidly approaching object before you can tell whether it is a stone or a bird or a snowball.

Recent experiments show that, in at least some mammals, the visual midbrain is involved in discrimination of space but not of form. (The visual part of the midbrain consists of the paired **superior colliculi**, shown in Figure 24-7.) Separating form perception from spatial perception has only been attempted recently with animal subjects; the two abilities were often confused in the past. Schneider (1969) has clarified this issue, testing three groups of hamsters—normal animals, animals with the primary visual cortex removed, and animals with the superior colliculi removed.

The hamsters were tested both for orientation to a moving stimulus (where is it?) and for recognition of visual patterns such as a triangle and a circle (what is it?). The moving stimulus was a sunflower seed—a favorite food for hamsters—waved back and forth in the experimenter's hand. Normal hamsters soon learned to come and get the seed, and hamsters with the visual cortex removed also oriented to the motion and learned to take the seed. But hamsters with the superior colliculi removed were first judged to be blind by this test because they found the food only by smell or touch.

The hamsters were then tested in a device where they could approach two adjacent transparent panels; behind each panel was a different test pattern. Pushing the panel in front of the correct pattern produced a reward, but pushing the wrong panel led to removal of the animal to the start position and no reward on that trial. The positions of the targets were exchanged irregularly so that the problem could not be solved by learning simply that one side was always correct. Normal hamsters soon learned to approach and push the panel in front of the correct target. Hamsters with the visual cortex removed never performed above a chance level; they did not discriminate the visual patterns. The hamsters lacking the superior colliculus approached the wrong panel as often as the correct one, but they learned to *press* only the correct one. In other words, they could not orient to the position of the target, but once they faced it they could recognize whether it was right or wrong.

What is the interpretation of this experiment? The moving-stimulus test was meant to be a test of space perception; the normals and the hamsters with no primary visual cortex passed this test. The animals with midbrain lesions failed. The conclusion is that these particular midbrain structures are necessary for space perception. The second test was one involving form perception, the perception of patterns. Normals passed, of course; but here the hamsters with midbrain lesions passed too and those with no primary visual cortex failed. The primary visual cortex is necessary for form perception.

The general conclusion is that different brain regions are responsible for the two functions, form and space perception. Whether or not this conclusion holds for animals other than hamsters and in other space- or form-discrimination situations remains a vital topic of research. But the separation of function has been demonstrated in one animal, and more recent evidence (in monkeys, for example) suggests the same distinction of form and space perception exists in others as well.

How do we capture and encode auditory stimuli?

As you listen to words, you extract information in much the same way as you do when you see objects. Auditory stimuli have both tonal qualities (which are analogous to hues in vision) and intensities (analogous to luminous intensity); spoken words are auditory patterns (just as written words are visual shapes), and you can localize auditory stimuli in space. The auditory stimulus is a different kind of energy from the visual stimulus, so a different kind of receptor organ is needed to capture it and to transduce it into neural impulses. From that point on, however, many of the processes in the auditory tracts and centers are similar to what we have just considered in the visual system.

The Auditory Receptor

The inner ear is like a specialized strip of skin which is sensitive to mechanical vibration just as your fingertips can detect vibration of an object that they touch. But the ear of course is far more sensitive to both frequency and intensity of vibration than is the skin. As was pointed out previously in the perception section (p. 565), both the frequency and the intensity of vibration of a sound determine the pitch—whether it is low (a bass) or high (a soprano)—and both the intensity and the frequency also determine loudness.

The sensitivity of the auditory receptors is really quite amazing. Most young people can hear sounds as low in frequency as 20 Hz and as high as 20,000 Hz. (Hz stands for hertz, a unit of frequency equal to one cycle per second; see Figure 20-17.) We can hear such incredibly weak sounds—if our ears were any more sensitive, we would be bothered by hearing air molecules colliding! But we can also listen briefly to intense sounds without damage to the ear. Let us look at the receptor that accomplishes the first steps in capturing and discriminating sounds.

Sound is transmitted from the eardrum through a series of three little bones (or ossicles) that span the middle ear and that contact the inner ear (or **cochlea**) (see Figure 24-8). The cochlea is a fluid-filled tube that is coiled. (This is why anatomists named it "cochlea," from the Greek word for snail.) Running down the length of the cochlea is a partition that divides it into upper and lower chambers, as shown in *B* and *C*. During one half of a cycle of sound vibration, when the last of the ossicles presses in on the membranous oval window in the upper chamber, the fluid in the cochlea is displaced and the round window in the lower chamber bulges out (as shown in *B*). In the next half of the cycle, the ossicle pulls out and the round window bulges in (as shown in *C*). These movements of the windows and the fluid cause the partition to ripple up and down; a traveling wave moves along it. Something like this happens when you hold a cord that is secured at the other end and you snap your end up and down; you see a wave travel from your end to the far end. The greatest amplitude of up-and-down motion of the partition occurs near the windows when the frequency of vibration is high; the greatest amplitude occurs near the far end when the frequency is low; so the place of maximum movement is related to frequency of the stimulus. Also, the more intense the vibration, the greater the overall amplitude of movement of the cochlear partition.

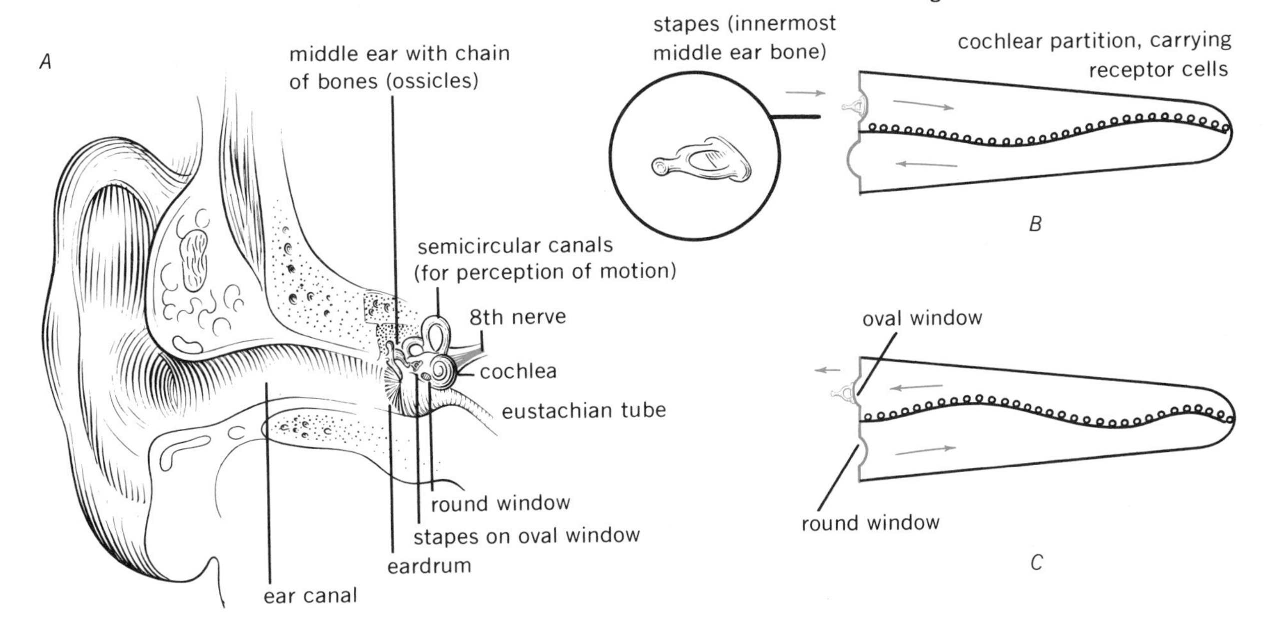

FIGURE 24-8 ANATOMY AND FUNCTION OF THE EAR

On the partition sit the auditory receptor cells, the "hair cells," and they are stimulated by the traveling waves of motion that sweep along the partition. When stimulated, the hair cells develop an electrical potential, and this excites or inhibits the primary auditory neurons. This generator potential is such an accurate transformation of acoustic energy into electrical energy that it is called the "cochlear microphonic," because it acts just like a microphone. In fact, when an electrode is put on the cochlea of an animal, and the electrical signal is amplified and fed into a loudspeaker in another room, listeners there hear clearly what is said into the animal's ear.

Auditory Discrimination

In hearing as in sight, perceived intensity (loudness) is approximately a logarithmic function of stimulus intensity. It requires about ten singers to sound twice as loud as one singer. That is why the intensity of the auditory stimulus is usually given in logarithmic units, decibels. The rate of impulses in the auditory nerve shows that the logarithmic transformation between stimulus intensity and bodily response has already occurred by this level. Just how the transformation occurs between the linear cochlear microphonic and the logarithmic rate of impulses is not yet known.

Pitch Discrimination

How can you discriminate low pitches from high ones? In other words, how does the auditory system encode information on the frequency of vibration caused by the incoming stimulus? For many years debate centered on two possibilities. One was called the "telephone hypothesis," which suggested that the system worked simply as a direct and exact transmission—if 100 Hz came in, 100 impulses per second were sent to the brain. Analysis of the complexities was presumed to occur only in the higher centers. The second hypothesis was based on the "traveling waves" in the cochlea. Because different incoming frequencies produce their greatest effect (most up-and-down stimulation) at different places along the cochlear membrane, this "place hypothesis" asserted that different cells fired for different frequencies.

Now we know that both hypotheses are correct in different parts of the total range of frequencies. For low frequencies, the neurons do follow the rate of vibration, transmitting this information in rather direct fashion to the higher auditory centers, telephone fashion. In other words, this finding indicates that analysis of low frequencies must be accomplished in the brain, rather than peripherally in the cochlea. For higher frequencies this method would not be possible, because auditory neurons can fire up to only about 1,000 impulses per second, whereas we can hear tones up to about 20,000 Hz. Even if several fibers took turns firing, this would permit following the stimulus up to only a few thousand cycles per second. Here is where the traveling waves in the cochlea play their role.

The hair cells located at the point of maximum amplitude of the traveling waves produce the strongest generator potentials. The nerve cells coming to this point are stimulated strongly, and they send inhibitory impulses to the nerve cells on each side. Thus the neural mechanism sharpens the rather broad mechanical discrimination performed by the cochlea (see Figure 24-9). This is quite similar to the sharpening of visual contours achieved by inhibition in the retina.

Such phenomena in vision, hearing, touch, or other senses are caused by **lateral inhibition**—strongly excited cells send impulses that inhibit their neighbors on both sides (which is why the inhibition is called "lateral"). This produces excitation that is highly sharpened (localized). You can demonstrate lateral inhibition to yourself by putting a pencil point on the underside of your forearm and vibrating the pencil strongly up and down, keeping it in contact with the skin. You will see that the skin moves for several centimeters around the pencil point, but your feeling of the movement is much more restricted around the point. Now move the pencil point a centimeter away on the skin and vibrate it gently, so that the skin there moves only as much as it did in the first case. You clearly feel the pencil vibrating in the second position. The movement there was strong enough to have been felt when the pencil was in the first position, but lateral inhibition prevented your feeling any place but the center of maximum stimulation.

Cells in the auditory centers show "receptive fields" for sound (see Figure 24-9). In many cases this means that a cell will be stimulated by a narrow band of frequencies, whereas its spontaneous activity will be inhibited by adjacent frequencies. Such cells permit the discrimination of sound frequencies. Furthermore, in the part of the total frequency range where discrimination is best, there tend to be more cells responding to these frequencies and their tonal ranges are narrower than elsewhere in the scale.

Neural activity representing one sensory modality may even be able to inhibit activity of another modality. This intersensory inhibition has been used to explain some methods of suppressing pain; see Spotlight 24-3.

Neural Coding for Sound Patterns

Most of the sounds that we listen to include many frequencies and in definite patterns. When different musical instruments play the same note, each instrument can be recognized because it gives not just the fundamental frequency but also a characteristic pattern of overtones or harmonics. Bird songs, animal cries, and words are also patterns of frequencies. Each pattern can be described according to the frequencies, their relative intensities, and the changes in time of frequencies and intensities.

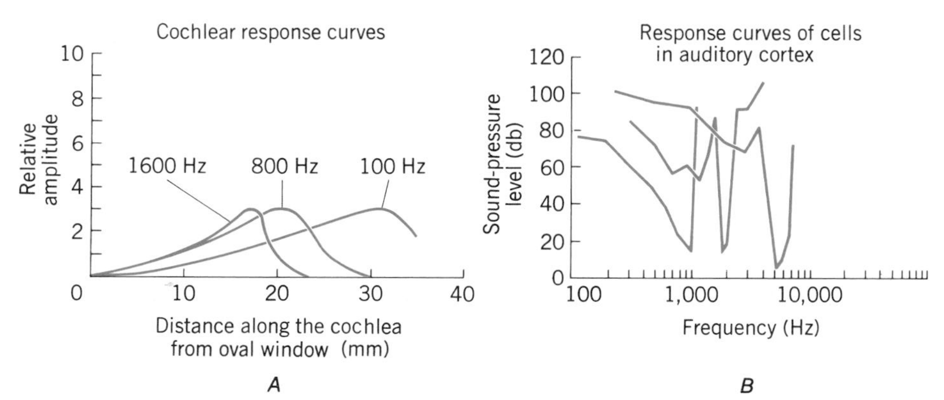

FIGURE 24-9
FREQUENCY DISCRIMINATION

A. Within the cochlea, the traveling waves show different maxima, depending upon stimulus frequency, but this tuning is broad. The amplitude of movement in the cochlea is shown for three different stimulus frequencies. These rounded curves for the auditory receptor are somewhat like the broad response curves of retinal receptors shown in Figure 24-3.
(After Békésy, 1947)

B. Some neural cells in the auditory system show sharp tuning, responding strongly at one frequency and weakly or not at all to nearby frequencies. Shown are response curves for three different cells in the auditory cortex of the cat.

Other types of specificity are also shown in auditory receptive fields, for example, responding only to a given pair of frequencies, or responding only to a tone that rises in frequency, or responding only to a tone that comes from a particular direction with regard to the head.
(Redrawn from Hind *et al.*, 1961)

SPOTLIGHT 24-3
Acupuncture or Music to Block Pain?

Pain is a puzzle. We cannot specify a unique stimulus, because many widely different stimuli can cause pain. Unlike vision or audition or touch, we cannot specify the sensory receptors or the brain centers involved in pain. There are wide individual differences in sensitivity to pain and in tolerance for pain, and these make it difficult to generalize from one subject to another. Even procedures used to relieve pain are not uniformly effective: in a large study of relief of pain after surgery, patients were given morphine at some times and at others were given a placebo (a substance made up to look like a drug but without any pharmacological properties). About a third of the patients gained greater relief from the morphine than from the placebo; about a third got as much relief from the placebo as from morphine; the final third could not be helped by either the placebo or by morphine in doses considered safe to use.

We do know that many nerve impulses that usually lead to pain perception are carried by slow-conducting axons of small diameter. These small axons are more sensitive to chemical blockade than are larger diameter fibers. So when neural activity is blocked chemically, for example by an injection of novocaine, the small fibers are affected first, causing a period of *analgesia* (lack of feeling of pain) before the onset of *anesthesia* (lack of all feeling in the bodily area affected). Even if "pain" impulses get to the spinal cord and to the brain, the perception of pain may be blocked centrally. For example, in an automobile accident a person may extricate himself from the wreckage and help others without being aware of injuries that are felt as painful only later. Hypnosis is another example of altered cerebral activity that is effective in preventing pain in many dental and medical procedures. It was largely abandoned for this purpose when chemical anesthetics were introduced in the 1840's, but it is making a comeback.

To try to encompass some of these complex features of pain, a "gate-control theory" has been formulated (Melzack & Wall, 1965). This hypothesis holds that at certain spinal synapses and at unspecified cerebral ones, the impulses in small "pain" axons can be inhibited by the larger, faster impulses serving touch, vibration, and other senses. Such blockade of "pain" impulses can be demonstrated by recordings made in the spinal cord.

It has long been known that pain can be prevented or reduced by stimulating other senses. Recently some surgical procedures have been performed successfully without chemical anesthesia by having the patient wear earphones and allowing him to choose either music or wide-spectrum noise and to control the intensity of the sound. Another procedure now being tested in the West is the ancient Chinese practice of acupuncture—inserting needles into certain regions of the body and vibrating them. Explanations of acupuncture have ranged from Oriental philosophical concepts ("altering the balance of Yin and Yang") to hypnotism. Chinese physicians state that acupuncture is effective in preventing pain in animals, so that they are inclined to doubt the older philosophical explanations. Recently two Chinese-American physicians have used the gate-control theory to explain how acupuncture blocks pain. The combination of the ancient technique and the recent theory may provide a key to unlocking the puzzle of pain.

Just as investigators have found complex receptive fields in the visual system that suggest coding for elements or patterns of form, so some cells in the auditory system also have complex requirements. Some can be stimulated only by a combination of two frequencies (and finding such cells obviously requires a great deal of searching by the experimenters). Some cells respond only to a stimulus that is rising in frequency; others to a falling tone. Much research is being done along this line, recording from the brains of experimental animals. Investigators are hopeful that it will reveal how auditory patterns are analyzed and recognized. Meanwhile, unexpected evidence of specialization of cells in hearing has come from the study of auditory discrimination in human beings.

Conflict Between the Ears

If your hearing is reasonably normal, you can hold a telephone to either ear and understand your caller. But what if you wore a headset with a different conversation in each ear? You could attend to either ear, following that conversation accurately and with scarcely no interference from the other ear. Such **dichotic hearing** is discussed in Chapter 22, p. 611, in relation to perception and personality. Recordings of receptive fields of cells in the auditory cortex show that some cells respond chiefly or exclusively to stimulation of the right ear and some to stimulation of the left ear. Most auditory cells respond more strongly to the contralateral ear (the one on the other side of the head), since the majority of the fibers from an ear cross to the other side in the brain stem. Apparently in attending to one ear or the other, you can select those circuits that respond to the desired ear and can partially inhibit the other channel.

What happens if you try to listen to two different words delivered simultaneously, one to your left ear and the other to your right? When the ears are put in conflict in this way, most people report a larger percentage of right-ear words correctly than of left-ear words. The right-ear channel goes more directly to the left hemisphere speech area; words put into the left ear stimulate the auditory cells in the right hemisphere, and impulses must then be relayed over the corpus callosum to the left hemisphere for verbal analysis. The slight delay of the more roundabout route (only a few milliseconds) is enough so that the left-ear signals find the word-analysis mechanisms already occupied by the right-ear words. This problem does not arise in normal hearing but only when different words are very accurately synchronized to arrive simultaneously at the two ears. (It also does not occur when you *select* which of two ears to listen to, since then the other channel is apparently inhibited lower down in the system.)

Recent anatomical evidence also indicates a predominance of verbal auditory function in the left hemisphere of human beings. The secondary auditory area (so-called "association" cortex) is larger in the left than in the right hemisphere for most people (see

Figure 24-10). We saw earlier that the motor control of speech is also vested in the left hemisphere of most people. On the other hand, perception of music and of other nonspeech sounds depends more on the right than on the left hemisphere.

Spatial Hearing

We saw in Chapter 21 that an ability to hear the direction from which a sound comes is dependent on slight differences of stimulation of the two ears. Now we can note how such stimuli are analyzed neurally. Auditory receptive fields of some cells are very sensitive to small time differences. Not only do some cells respond chiefly or exclusively to one ear or the other, but some respond best when two ears are stimulated with a particular time difference between them. Only with the correct *difference* in time of arrival at the ears will impulses summate simultaneously at the cell and cause it to fire maximally. Thus small dichotic time differences can be detected and made use of in the auditory system. Auditory discrimination of direction appears to be already "wired in" to the neural circuits at birth, in human babies. Snapping the fingers to one side or the other of the newborn baby will often cause it to move its head or eyes to the side of the stimulus—an orienting reflex that would be impossible without inborn localization abilities.

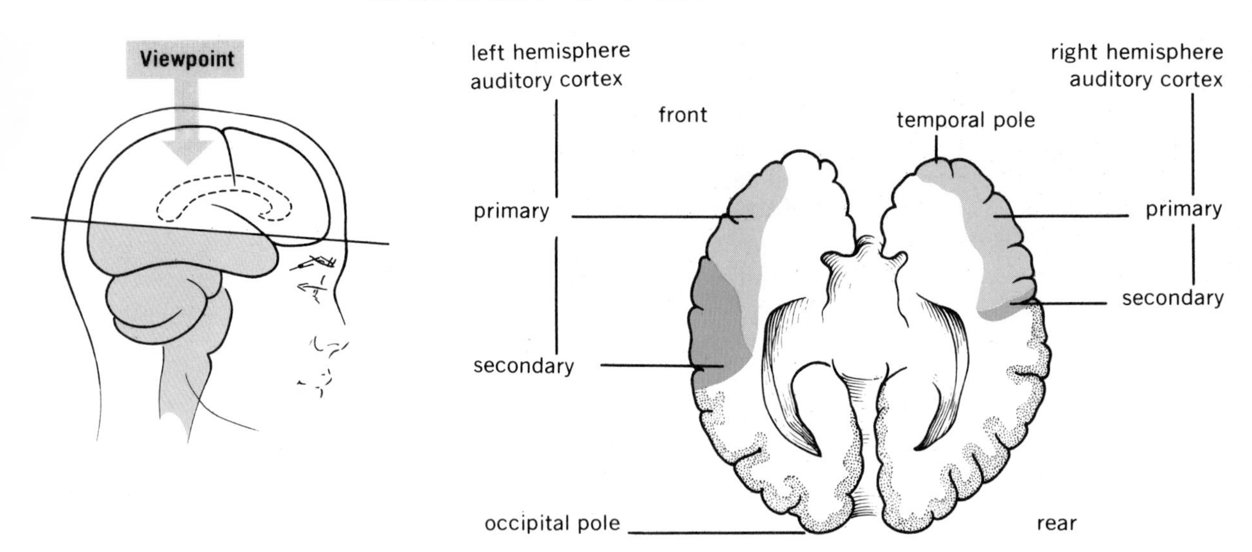

FIGURE 24-10
SIZE OF AUDITORY CORTEX IN EACH HEMISPHERE

The auditory cortex is situated on the upper surface of the temporal lobe. The primary auditory cortex is shown in light color, and the secondary auditory cortex is in dark color.

Investigators measured the size of the secondary auditory cortex in 100 adult human brains. They cut through the brains as shown in the left diagram in order to expose the upper surface of both temporal lobes. The diagram on the right shows this section in a typical brain. The secondary auditory area is seen to be considerably larger in the left than in the right hemisphere, and the majority of brains showed such a difference.
(From Geschwind & Levitsky, 1968)

SUMMARY

Our survey of perception reveals many similarities among different sensory modalities. Each has sensitive receptors to capture its own special kind of stimulus energy. Each type of receptor cell generates an electrical potential when it is stimulated, and this can excite the neurons, so all stimuli are converted into the common currency of nerve impulses.

From each receptor, impulses are distributed rather widely in the nervous system, over successive relays of neurons. And impulses from a number of different receptors converge on any particular central cell. This divergence and convergence permits different central cells to extract different combinations of information. Thus some visual cells extract information about hue, others about position, others about shape, and others about motion. Some auditory cells extract information about frequency of sound, some about intensity, and some about difference in time of arrival of sound at the two ears. Both excitatory and inhibitory influences combine in most of these processes.

In some cases, stimuli in one sensory modality can inhibit responses to stimuli in another modality. This is the basis of the "gate-control theory," which attempts to account for some of the complex features of pain perception.

Many complex functions are built into the nervous system so that responses can be made automatically. Thus, perceiving the direction of a light or a noise does not, as was long supposed, require complex unconscious judgments, assembling and comparing the different information reaching the eyes or the ears. Rather, a particular combination of information may be extracted by certain specific cells whose input connections provide just that combination of stimuli; for example, certain cells in the visual cortex respond only when the stimulus is a horizontal line, and certain cells in the auditory system respond only when the stimulus arrives at the left ear a particular fraction of a millisecond before it reaches the right ear. Some of these connections are available at birth, but they may nevertheless require early use and experience if they are to persist. Other specific connections are undoubtedly formed later as a result of individual experience.

25

Biological Processes in Motivation

Eating and drinking—How do neural circuits regulate them?
Wakefulness, dreamless sleep, and dreaming—How does neural activity produce one state or another?
Sex behavior—What are the roles of hormones, neural circuits, and experience?
Aggression—To what extent can biological research help to explain and control it?
Reinforcement—What is it in terms of neural activity?

During a single day a person may engage in many varied sorts of behavior—skiing or sex, dreaming or drinking, fighting or feeding, listening or learning. Which types of activity occur depend upon both internal conditions of the body and external stimulation.

What we respond to at any given time depends greatly on our motivational state. Electrical recording from the brain is helping to determine how this selectivity works. Furthermore, it has been found that electrical and chemical stimulation of specific regions of the brain can alter the motivational state, especially if the brain stimulation is coupled with appropriate external stimulation. What we learn depends not only on the external situation but also on the strength of our involvement and on the consequences or reinforcing aspects of the situation. Recently investigators have found that direct stimulation of certain brain regions is strongly reinforcing.

Some motivational states ensure the relative constancy of internal bodily conditions, whereas other motivations govern relations of the individual to the world around him. Eating and drinking, for example, serve primarily to maintain metabolic processes and fluid balance, although the ways in which they are performed may also serve social functions and may express one's personality. Behavior that is primarily directed to relations with the external world includes attention, sex, aggression, and curiosity. We will consider both sorts, starting with eating and drinking as examples of internal regulation. The brain mechanisms governing eating and drinking have been explored rather thoroughly, and they will help us in the study of mechanisms of other motivational states.

Our understanding of biological processes in motivation has been rapidly changing during the last thirty years. Since the 1940's more and more specific "motivational" locations have been found in the brains of experimental animals. It began to appear as if each kind of motivated behavior was regulated by a different small area in the brain region called the "hypothalamus" (see Figure 25-1). Activation of one location in the hypothalamus led to hunger and the onset of eating behavior, whereas activation of another nearby site led to satiety and cessation of eating; stimulating a specific locus led to thirst and drinking; another was the center for sex behavior; activity at one locus induced wakefulness, stimulating another led to sleeping, and stimulating still another produced dreaming; stimulating one center led to aggressive behavior, whereas another caused pleasure and reinforcement. Now, however, it begins to appear that the different functional sites are only parts of complex circuits and that circuits for different behaviors may overlap in part. Furthermore, activation of a given small brain region may evoke different behaviors depending upon the external stimulus situation, as we shall see. Some of the functions of the human hypothalamus are described in the neurological case of Spotlight 25-1.

Eating and drinking—How do neural circuits regulate them?

Eating

Most adults control their weight amazingly closely. Even though your food intake goes up or down with your expenditure of energy—you need more food when you ski and less when you are studying—your weight probably remains nearly constant. This constancy isn't a matter of watching the scales and making deliberate choices, for it is found in human societies where people do not weigh themselves and also among animals. This is remarkable if you consider that if you gained only an ounce a day, you would gain over twenty pounds in a year.

To study this more closely, Jean Mayer and colleagues (1956) measured body weights, calorie intakes, and physical activity in males of a racially-homogeneous Bengali community in India.

SPOTLIGHT 25-1

Effects of a Small Hypothalamic Tumor in a Human Being

Most of our knowledge of the functions of the hypothalamus comes from animal experimentation. This is because brain damage in humans caused by accidental injury or by disease usually invades several different parts of the small but complex hypothalamus, and it is therefore difficult to assign the various symptoms to particular regions of the hypothalamus. A recent case involving a small sharply localized tumor in a woman's brain showed that results of the animal experiments could help in interpretation of human motivated behavior; it also reflected the multiple functions of the hypothalamus (Reeves & Plum, 1969).

The patient was a twenty-year-old bookkeeper. She came to the hospital because about a year previously she had developed an abnormal appetite so that she ate and drank large amounts and gained weight rapidly. During the same period she had frequent headaches and her menstrual periods had stopped. She was mentally alert, performed her work well, and did not show any emotional abnormalities.

Another year passed and her family brought her back to the hospital because of changes in her behavior. She was often uncooperative and at times attacked people around her. She was confused and sometimes could not remember correctly. She would not attempt arithmetic calculations. Tests showed reduced endocrine function, involving the gonads, the thyroid gland, and the adrenal cortex. An operation revealed a tumor at the base of the brain, but its position did not permit removal of the tumor. The outbursts of violent behavior became more frequent, especially if food was withheld. Toward the end of her hospitalization, she had to be fed almost continuously in order to keep her reasonably tractable, and she was eating about 10,000 calories a day. When she died, three years after the onset of her illness, the position of the tumor was determined precisely; it is shown in Figure 25-1.

The tumor had destroyed a part of the hypothalamus called the "ventromedial nucleus" ("ventro"—on the belly side; "medial"—along the midline). In animal studies that we will soon take up (p. 694), destruction of the ventromedial nucleus has been found frequently to cause overeating and obesity. In some species, such as the cat, the same operation usually makes the animal display rage behavior more frequently and more readily than a normal animal does. Hypothalamic areas particularly involved in sexual receptivity and in mating behavior are also found nearby (p. 709), but in the case of this patient, the reduced gonadal function was probably caused by interruption of pathways by which the hypothalamus regulates the pituitary gland. This would also explain the observed decreases in thyroid and adrenal cortex function, since these endocrine glands are also regulated by the anterior pituitary gland (see Figure 23-9). The causes of the confusion and the disturbances of memory are not clear, although hypothalamic structures have been implicated in learning and memory, as we will see in the next chapter.

This case shows how a small tumor—about the size of the last joint of the little finger—because of its location in a critical region of the brain could affect a variety of motivated behaviors, eating, aggression, and sex. The neurologists who reported the case conclude, "The findings provide a close functional correlation between the human and homologous lower mammalian ventromedial hypothalamic structures."

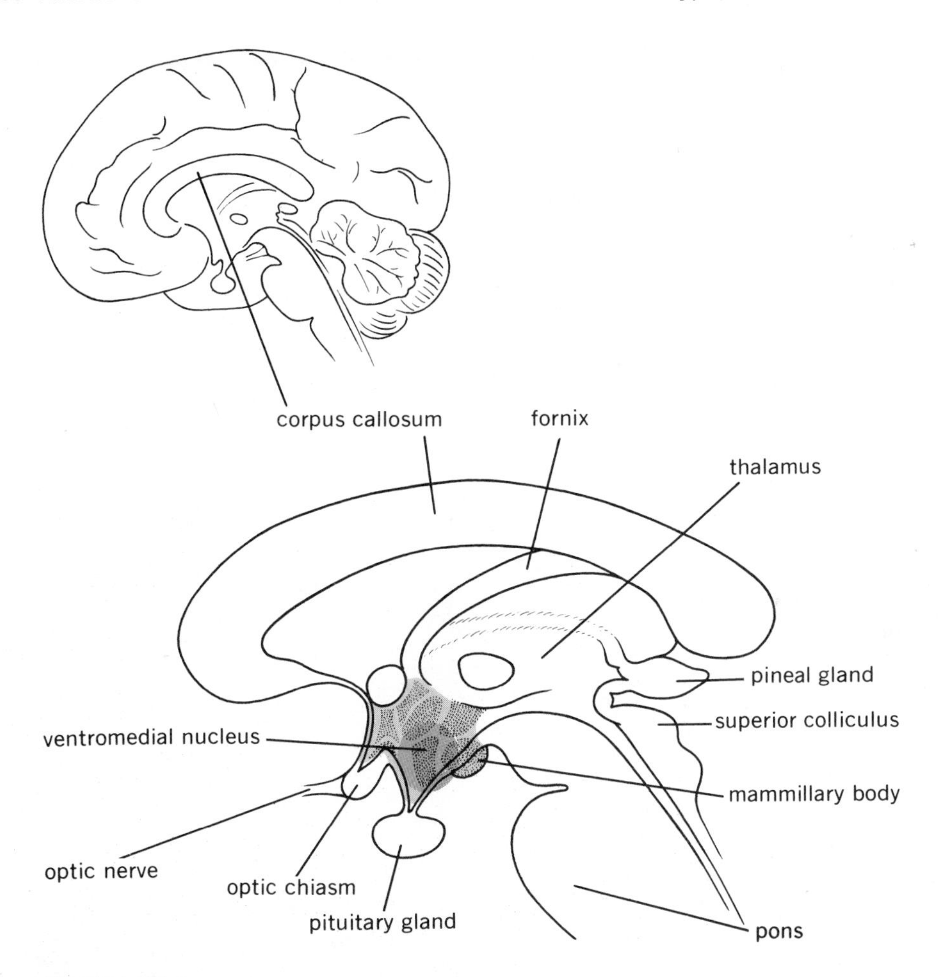

FIGURE 25-1
THE HUMAN HYPOTHALAMUS AND NEARBY STRUCTURES

The entire hypothalamus is shown in color. The darker oval shows the location of the tumor; it extends somewhat beyond the boundaries of the ventromedial nucleus of the hypothalamus. The position of the region within the brain is indicated on the upper diagram, which presents a medial section of the brain.
(Modified from Figure 3, Reeves & Plum, 1969)

Starting with clerks who did light work and going to men performing medium and heavy work, the daily calorie intake went up steadily with the energy expenditure, so average body weights were practically identical for all these classes of workers; this is illustrated in Figure 25-2, to the right of the dashed line in *A* and *B*. The data to the left of the dashed line show a very different relation. The sedentary men ate more than was necessary for their level of energy expendi-

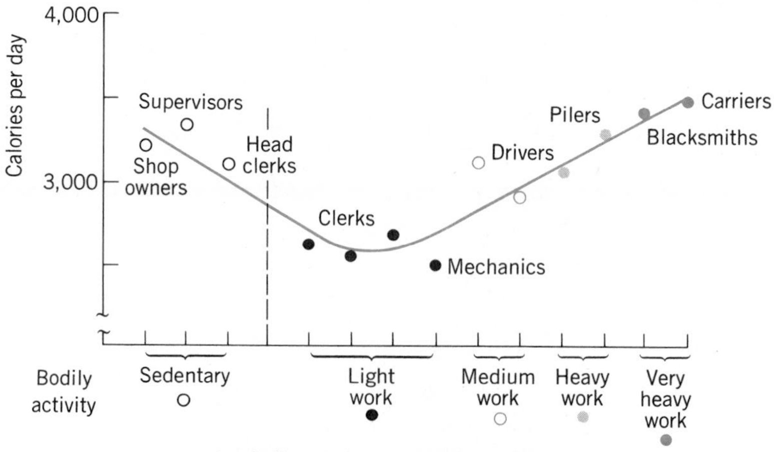

A Daily calorie intake and type of work

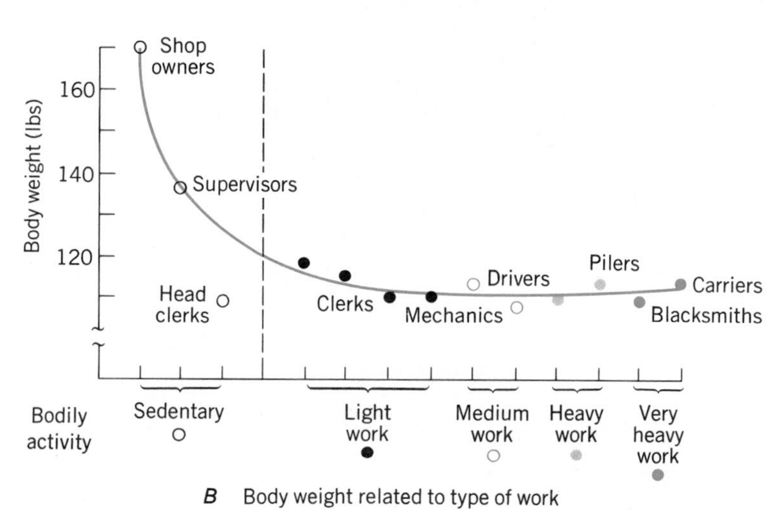

B Body weight related to type of work

FIGURE 25-2 RELATIONSHIP OF FOOD INTAKE AND ACTIVITY

When work ranged from light to heavy—as shown to the right of the dashed line—intake was proportionate to energy output, and body weight remained constant. But among sedentary people, food intake was as high as among heavy workers, and body weight was greater than among heavy workers. (Modified from Mayer, 1956)

ture, and the shop owners and supervisors were the heaviest groups of all. So, weight control broke down when activity was reduced to a minimum.

Mayer and colleagues also demonstrated a similar phenomenon in rats (1954). When rats were forced to run on a treadmill, the more they ran per day, the more food they took in, up to the point of exhaustion; body weight remained relatively constant over a wide range of activity. But when rats were confined to small cages and given no opportunity to exercise, their food intake went up and they put on excessive weight, just as did the sedentary men. The need for exercise, therefore, seems less related to "burning off calories" than to stimulating basic weight-control mechanisms.

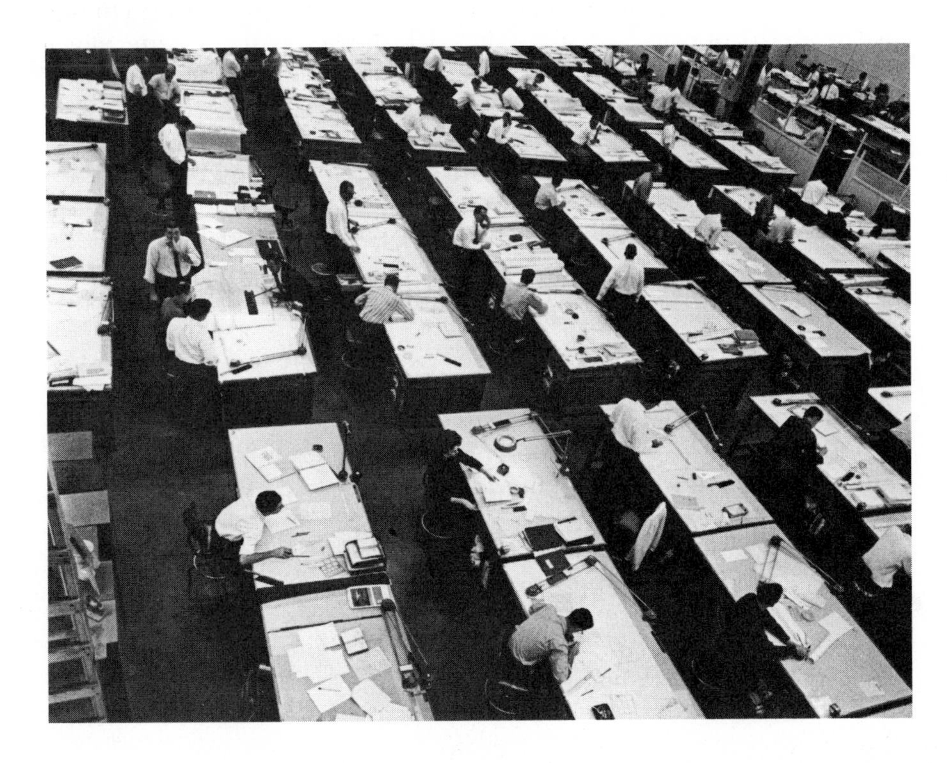

Research has shown that when people are involved with sedentary tasks, weight control may break down. (Elliott Erwitt, Magnum)

Within normal ranges of activity, how are needs and intake balanced so well? At one time this question used to be answered in terms of appetite and sensations of hunger, but we now know that there are several different mechanisms at work. These include (1) monitoring of food supplies in the body, (2) monitoring of eating behavior, and (3) learned controls. The fact that there are several mechanisms baffled investigators for many years and made critical experimentation difficult; if one mechanism was impaired, the experimental subject could still get along with the others. The existence of multiple mechanisms is typical in brain function; it endows the individual with considerable resiliency against accident or disease.

Monitoring of Bodily Supplies

There is good evidence that mammals receive feedback from both the stores of body fat and the rate at which blood sugar is consumed. Information about the state of food supplies in the body is collected in the hypothalamus, a small region in the base of the brain (see Figure 25-3). Small precise lesions in two different parts of the hypothalamus can affect eating quite differently. When lesions are made in one precise brain location of a normal adult rat (or cat or monkey), the animal will overeat voraciously. This location is the **ventromedial nucleus of the hypothalamus.** Weeks later, the animal's weight may reach a plateau at a high level where it is maintained. In a human being, destruction of the ventromedial nucleus by a tumor also leads to obesity, as Spotlight 25-1 showed. An opposite effect has been produced in animals by a lesion only a few millimeters away from the ventromedial nucleus. If a normal rat is operated on to produce lesions in the **lateral nuclei of the hypothalamus,** this animal will stop eating and drinking. (To be effective, the operation must be done in both lateral nuclei, one on each side of the midline.) Unless it is nursed carefully and tempted to eat with highly palatable moist food, the rat with its lateral nuclei destroyed will die of starvation and dehydration. If the rat is brought through this critical phase, it will eventually maintain its weight but at a level lower than normal.

Originally these results were taken to mean that the lateral nuclei of the hypothalamus constitute a "feeding center," whereas the ventromedial nucleus is a "satiety center," which signals that the body has enough food and therefore inhibits eating. These conclusions would explain why an animal would stop eating if the lateral nuclei were destroyed and why an animal would overeat and gain weight if the ventromedial nucleus was destroyed.

A new interpretation of these results has been suggested in the last few years because of further experiments. Some rats were first overfed until they reached a very high weight. Then lesions were made in the ventromedial hypothalamus (VMH), which causes vora-

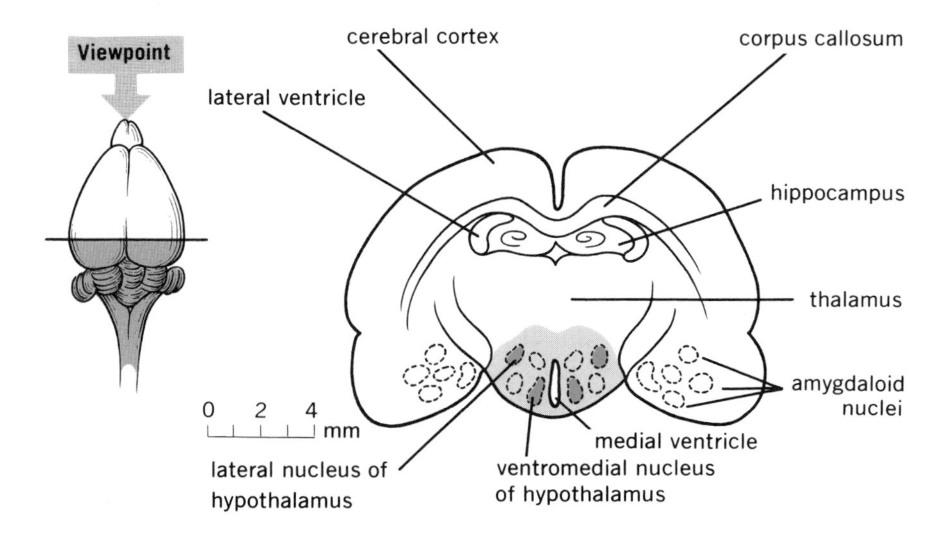

FIGURE 25-3 REGIONS IN RAT BRAIN WHERE LESIONS CAN INDUCE OVEREATING OR STARVATION

Shown here is a cross section of rat brain transecting the hypothalamus. The small dorsal view to the left shows where the section was made. The hypothalamus is shown in color at the base of the brain, and two of its several nuclei are labeled—the ventromedial nucleus, close to the medial ventricle, and the lateral nucleus. Lesions of the VMH usually cause overeating; lesions of the LH usually cause undereating or starvation.

cious eating in the normal rat, and the "fat" rats were then allowed to eat whatever they wished. Instead of gaining weight, the rats *lost* some weight; their weight fell to a plateau *below* that of the high preoperative level but *above* that of their normal weights (Hoebel & Teitelbaum, 1966). (See Figure 25-4.) Other experimenters then tried underfeeding rats until their weights were considerably below normal. The experimenters then made lateral hypothalamic (LH) lesions and allowed the "skinny" rats to set their own intake. These animals quickly started eating again, and gained weight, whereas rats of normal weight lose when they sustain LH lesions. The underfed animals with LH lesions gained, however, only to the level of the plateau to which normal rats fell (Powley & Keesey, 1969). (See Figure 25-5.)

It appears then that the lesions may not directly determine gain or loss of weight but rather set the reference level or target

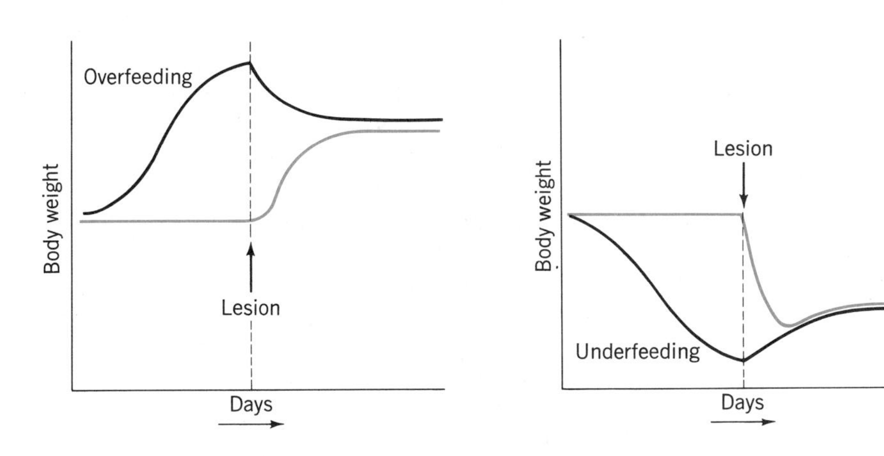

FIGURE 25-4 EFFECTS OF VMH LESIONS ON BODY WEIGHT

When normal rats receive lesions in the ventromedial nuclei on both sides of the hypothalamus, they usually gain weight rapidly, as is shown by the colored line. But if rats have been made overweight before the operation (as shown by the black line), they lose weight postoperatively until they reach about the same plateau as the other VMH operates.

FIGURE 25-5 EFFECTS OF LH LESIONS ON BODY WEIGHT

In normal rats, lesions in both lateral hypothalamic nuclei cause a rapid drop in weight, as shown by the colored line. But if rats have been underfed before the operation (as shown by the black line), they gain weight postoperatively and reach the same rather low plateau as the other LH operates.

around which weight is regulated. Setting the level high (VMH lesion) means that previously normal animals will gain weight but that animals that are already grossly overweight will lose, if they are given the chance to determine their own intakes.

But lateral hypothalamic lesions do more than set the target body weight to a lower level; they also knock out the normal response (eating) when utilization of blood sugar (glucose) falls to a low rate. Usually a low rate of use of blood sugar means that this basic substance is in short supply in the body. Glucose use is believed to be monitored by certain hypothalamic cells. Giving insulin drives down the glucose in the blood, and it also induces eating in the normal rat. But insulin has no effect in the LH-lesioned rat, even after the animal has apparently recovered from the operation and is maintaining its long-term weight. This means that the mechanisms of response to fat reserves (which affect weight) and those to glucose levels are independent, since the LH-lesioned animal recovers its ability to respond to fat reserves but never recovers its response to glucose levels. Spotlight 25-2 shows how research based on the animal model has led to new information about obesity in human beings.

As we consider other motivational mechanisms, we will see that many of them involve multiple systems and multiple channels for each system. Evolution seems to have provided "back-up" capacity, as engineers do in space vehicles, so that failure of one mechanism will not necessarily put the whole organism out of operation. It should also be noted that the brain circuits from different mechanisms often pass through the same brain regions, so that even a small precise brain lesion may interfere with more than one function.

In addition to the central monitoring of fat reserves and of glucose metabolism, there is also monitoring of more peripheral processes, including taste and smell, the motor acts of ingesting food, and loading of the stomach. Taste and smell are certainly important in determining what is acceptable as food and what is desired. A newborn baby accepts milk readily but will not accept either water or solid food; neither will a newborn rat pup nor an adult rat that has just had a lateral hypothalamic lesion. But the operated rat can be induced to take soft palatable food, such as moist chocolate chip cookies, and thus can be encouraged to eat again. The rat with a ventromedial hypothalamic lesion, although it eats more than a normal rat, is quite finicky; a small addition of bitter material or other adulteration is enough to make it reject food that a normal rat would accept.

Feedback from Eating

Experiments with both human and animal subjects show that the acts of eating and the effects of loading the stomach are also monitored. This feedback information provides a signal to stop eating after a normal meal has been consumed and before any of the nutritive material has been absorbed into the bloodstream. If it were not for such information, people would consume far too much for their needs; they can eat much faster than they can absorb. But the central monitoring of food supplies already absorbed and the monitoring of eating still give only a part of the complex picture of the control of eating behavior. There is one other aspect that must still be considered, even in a brief presentation—the roles of development and learning in relation to eating.

Development and Learning in the Control of Eating

We noted just above that human babies and rat pups will accept only milk when they are young, but their food preferences change as they grow older. In the rat pup this occurs rapidly, since maturation is rapid. At about the age of fourteen days, the rat pup becomes able to maintain its body temperature; it is just about this age that it begins to crawl out of the nest frequently; it will drink water

SPOTLIGHT 25-2

New Findings on Human Obesity, Inspired by Research with Animals

The many and varied observations on eating and obesity that have been made with animal subjects since the 1940's have recently inspired psychologists and physiologists to make novel observations on human subjects.

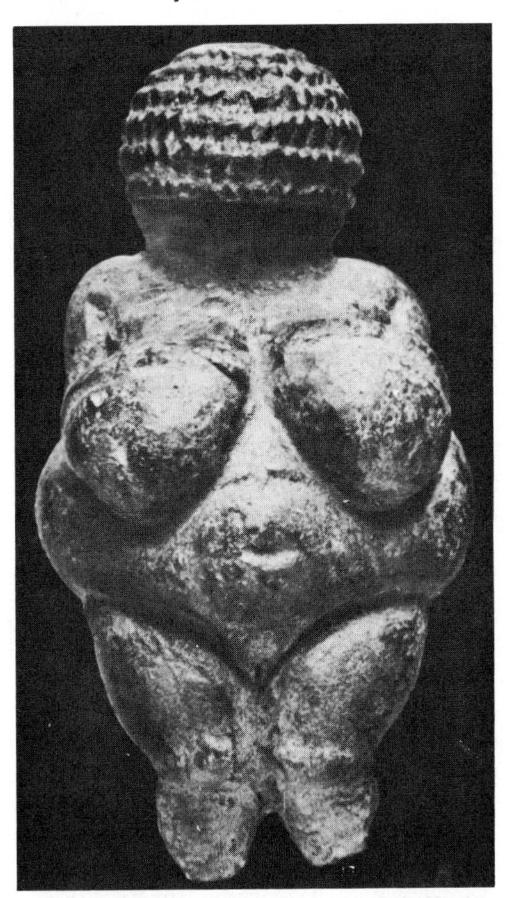

Obesity is not new. The "Venus of Willendorf," a stone age figure, indicates that obesity was recognized and perhaps even revered.
(The Bettmann Archive)

Preview Figure 6 introduced such research with rats. Rats made obese by hypothalamic lesions differ in many ways from normal controls: the obese rats eat a somewhat greater amount per day, eat *fewer* meals per day, eat more per meal, eat faster, and are less active. Which of these characteristics do you suppose are also true of fat people as compared with people of normal weight? The psychologist Stanley Schachter (1971) surveyed the research literature and found that each of these facts is also true of obese humans. He and his collaborators then ran experiments to see whether other findings on obese rats would also hold for obese humans.

One often-repeated observation has been that fat rats will actually eat less than normals if the taste is made slightly bitter or if it takes effort to obtain the food. To test whether this last characteristic would be observed with humans, the psychologists tested eighty students, one at a time. Each student sat at a desk, ostensibly to fill out a questionnaire. On the desk was a bag of almonds; the experimenter helped herself to a nut, invited the subject to do the same, and then left the room for fifteen minutes. For half of the subjects the nuts had shells on them; for the other half, the shells had been removed. The presence or absence of shells had no effect on the forty normal-weight students—about half ate nuts in either case—but it was of crucial importance for the obese. Nineteen of twenty obese subjects ate the shelled nuts, but only one of the twenty ate when the shells still had to be cracked!

Schachter also cites a study made

(Continued)

on extremely obese persons who were hospitalized to reduce their weights. Given a bland unappealing liquid diet, the obese people readily cut their caloric intake and lost weight. Normal subjects when given the same diet maintained their caloric intake and kept their weight up. When the formerly obese individuals left the hospital and reentered the world of attractive cues to eating, they all became obese again. Thus the obese seem to be stimulus-bound; that is, they are strongly influenced by external stimuli but they are relatively unaffected by cues arising from within their own bodies.

Recent confirmation that the obese are stimulus-bound has come from research done independently in France (Cabanac, 1971). Normal subjects usually rate the taste of sugar as pleasant, but this is changed by drinking a concentrated solution of glucose. About fifteen minutes after taking the glucose, normal people rate the taste of sugar as neutral or even slightly unpleasant; these lowered ratings last an hour or more. Obese people, however, continue to rate sugar as pleasant even after drinking the concentrated glucose solution; they remain responsive to the external stimulus and are scarcely affected by their altered internal state. This helps explain why the obese eat prolonged meals, continuing to eat even after they have taken in large quantities of food—they are unresponsive to internal signals from the food they have already ingested. When normal subjects dieted and lost weight, they also rated sugar as being just as pleasant after taking the concentrated glucose as before taking it. Thus the obese people act in this respect like subjects who are below their target level for weight. We saw that brain lesions can shift the target weight up or down; why the obese have an elevated reference level is not yet known.

that it finds and will gnaw on solid food. The rat pup eats voraciously and gains weight rapidly. In fact, making a lesion in the ventromedial hypothalamus of the young rat does not increase its rapid intake of food or increase its already rapid weight gain. Recent experiments suggest the hypothesis that the high secretion of growth hormone acts to inhibit the activity of the ventromedial hypothalamus and thus sets the target weight at a high level (Wade & Zucker, 1970). Later, at about forty days of age, the production of estrogen (a "female" hormone) causes a clear drop in the target weight level of the female rat.

Learning also governs eating from the very start. Human babies and other young mammals *learn* many aspects of nursing behavior. For example, babies can learn either of two ways of obtaining milk from a nipple: either suction or pressing the nipple between the tongue and the palate. An artificial nipple was made that could be set to give milk in response to one or the other behavior and to require a particular magnitude of the appropriate response. Babies promptly learned to perform the type of response that brought food (Sameroff, 1968).

Later in life, people and animals may adopt special food or taste preferences or shift established preferences as bodily needs arise. For example, during pregnancy and lactation appetites often change because of unusual needs. Mineral-deficient children may eat plaster or clay. Animal experiments demonstrate that rats that are made deficient in thiamine (vitamin B) or in calcium or in magnesium will then prefer a novel diet to the deficient one; this is true whether or not the novel diet contains the substance that has been lacking in the previous diet. As between two novel diets, one containing the missing material and the other not, rats then learn to choose the adequate diet, at least in the cases of thiamine and calcium. There are exceptions, however; not in every case has evolution provided a mechanism to get the organism out of a difficulty into which it has fallen. But in many natural circumstances, trying out novel foods will permit animals to overcome a deficiency (Rodgers, 1967).

Ingestion of food also depends upon ingestion of water and vice versa, as we will see in the next section.

Drinking

Water intake is normally controlled by two independent monitoring mechanisms. One type of monitoring is for osmotic pressure in the blood. (The osmotic pressure is determined by the concentration of substances, such as salts, dissolved in the blood.) The saltier the blood, the more readily a person or animal will drink, if this system is working normally. The other type of monitoring is for volume of fluid outside the body cells, mainly in the bloodstream. Hemorrhage or other loss of body fluid causes need for water (and readiness to drink) by this route.

Monitoring for osmotic pressure is probably done by brain cells in a special region of the hypothalamus. Some of the best evidence that monitoring is done here comes from the following experiment. Tiny tubes were implanted into the brains of anesthetized experimental animals by a surgical procedure. Later, very small amounts of fluids could be put into the brains of awake animals and their behavior could be observed. Putting a tiny drop of salty solution into this region led promptly to drinking of water. Injecting a solution less salty than body fluids led to cessation of drinking.

Monitoring for fluid volume seems to involve a complex peripheral route. When blood flow through the kidney is reduced (and this usually occurs when fluid volume is lowered), a series of chemical substances is released into the blood. One of these chemicals, the final one in the series, has been shown to evoke drinking when injected in tiny amounts into any of several brain regions (Epstein *et al.*, 1969).

Both types of control (for osmotic pressure and for fluid volume) are abolished when the lateral hypothalamic area is destroyed. This is one reason why animals often do not regain eating behavior after such lesions; they become so dehydrated and weakened that they can no longer eat. That is why *moist* as well as palatable food is needed to nurse the animals back to eating.

Some animals do, in fact, recover from LH lesions. Does

this mean that there is still a further system for monitoring the water supply? Careful observation of "recovered" LH-lesioned rats shows that they never drink unless they are eating. Furthermore, they do not drink large draughts at the beginning or end of a meal, as normal rats do; they take repeated small draughts during the meal. The same pattern of frequent small draughts is seen when normal rats are deprived of their salivary glands. Injecting water into the stomach (which meets bodily need but leaves the mouth dry) does not stop this pattern of drinking-with-eating, but injecting water into the mouth does. It may be concluded that the LH-lesioned rat learns to drink in order to swallow dry food and that this, quite by accident, meets its needs for water (Kissileff & Epstein, 1969).

Learning is important in the water intake of the normal individual too. The presence of a bodily need for water does not lead to drinking unless suitable stimulus conditions are present, and these are mainly learned. The individual has to learn to identify water and where it can be obtained. Once this learning has occurred, then the presence of the bodily need can lead to a long sequence of behavior, which results in obtaining water—leaving the room and walking down the corridor to the water cooler, or going to the kitchen, or hiking down a trail to the spring.

The drinking mechanism thus includes parallel activating circuits and also feedback loops to stop intake. Drinking occurs only if the organism is aware that a potable fluid is present and if either of the monitoring systems signals a bodily water deficit, or if the mouth is dry. The behavior of drinking then leads to signals that soon stop further drinking even before water is absorbed from the stomach into the body. This peripheral feedback system gauges the amount of water ingested, and when this is equivalent to the bodily need, it shuts off drinking so that too much water is not taken in.

Wakefulness, dreamless sleep, and dreaming—How does neural activity produce one state or another?

Now we go from regulation of internal bodily states to regulation of relations with other organisms and with the external world. In regulation of both internal states and external relations, the behaviors occur only when there is an appropriate combination of internal condition and external stimulation. Also, learning plays an important role in external regulations, just as it does with regard to processes of regulating eating and drinking.

Wakefulness, Sleep, and Dreams

Wakefulness is of course the state in which we interact directly with others; but sleeping is a much more active and varied state than was believed a few years ago. Current research is providing clues to the puzzle of why we sleep. **Dreams** represent a special type of sleep activity, and evidence now indicates that all people dream, whether or not they remember their dreams. The physiological accompaniments of dreaming occur in all mammals and birds but not in reptiles. Each of these three states—wakefulness, dreamless sleep, and dreams—is characterized by its own special pattern of brain waves, and each can be induced by localized stimulation of the brain. Discovery that electrical activity of the brain continues throughout the day and night—during rest as well as active behavior, during sleep as well as during waking—was a decisive refutation of the old concept that organisms are inactive until stimulated by events in the environment.

What different patterns of brain waves and muscular activity occur as a wakeful person becomes drowsy, falls asleep, and then dreams? Many subjects have been studied by attaching electrodes to the head and other parts of the body and recording the tiny electrical potentials of brain (the **electroencephalogram**) and of muscle. (See Figure 7 in the preview.) Many species of animals have also been investigated in the same way.

The waking person has an irregular electroencephalogram (EEG) with waves of rather high frequency (around thirty per second) and low amplitude (see Figure 25-6). The musculature

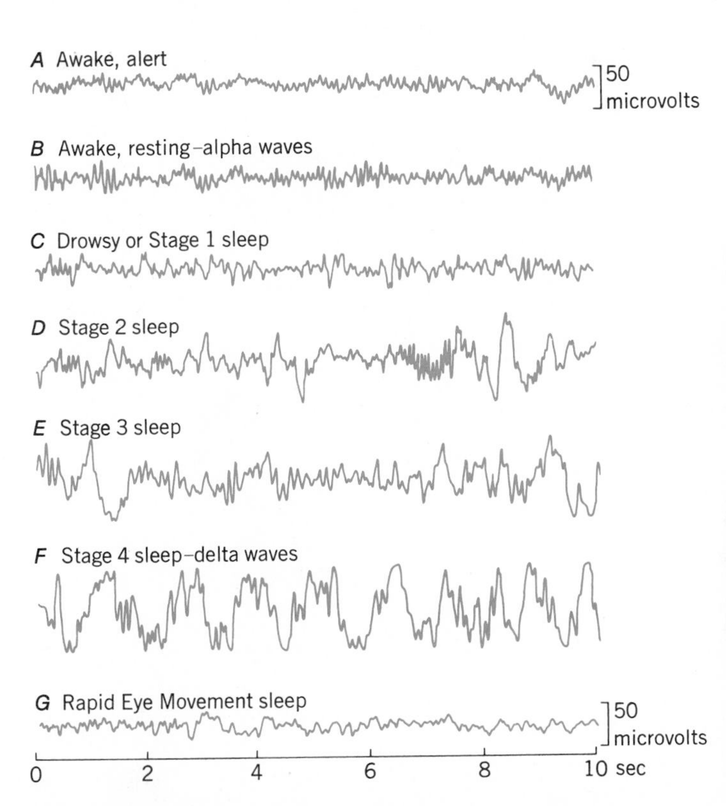

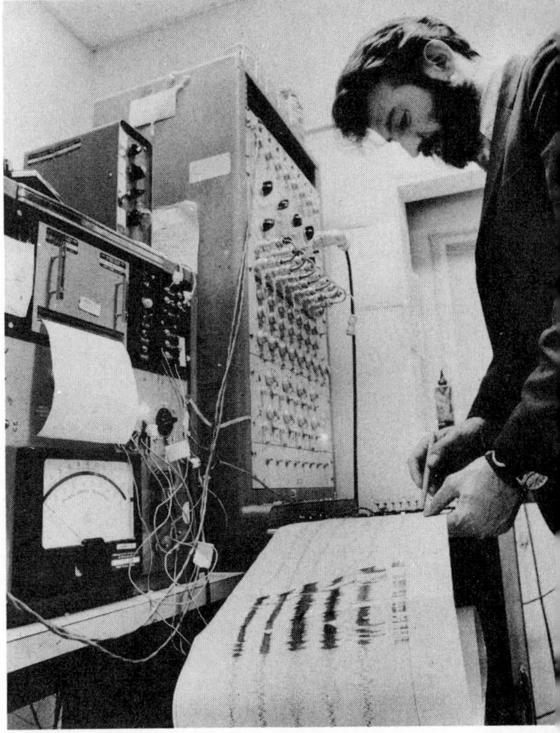

FIGURE 25-6 BRAIN-WAVE PATTERNS IN WAKING, QUIET SLEEP, AND DREAMING

The EEG records on the left show that the electrical activity of the brain has characteristic patterns that vary with the state of the person. When a person is awake and mentally active, the EEG record shows relatively rapid waves of low amplitude, as in *A*. When a waking person is relaxed, and especially if his eyes are closed, there may be an 8–12 Hz rhythm called alpha waves (*B*). As a person becomes drowsy and falls into deep sleep, the EEG waves become slower in frequency and larger in amplitude (*C*–*F*). During dreaming, the EEG pattern (*G*) resembles that of wakeful activity (*A*) or of drowsiness (*C*). (Photo courtesy L. Fehmi) usually shows considerable tension. As a person becomes drowsy, the EEG becomes larger in amplitude and more regular, and a ten per second rhythm called the "alpha rhythm" may appear; the muscles become more relaxed. With the onset of sleep, the EEG shows irregular large waves of only a few cycles per second.

After perhaps ninety minutes of sleep, a paradoxical pattern may appear: Although the person continues to sleep, his EEG resembles the waking state with fast, low-voltage waves. In the cat, the pattern is even more paradoxical because, in spite of the aroused EEG, the animal seems behaviorally to be more deeply asleep—the neck muscles relax completely so that the head cannot be held partly up as it is in other phases of sleep, and the animal is harder to awaken than in other phases of sleep. There may be considerable small motor activity—twitches, smiles, or frowns—but inhibition predominates. In animal subjects, stimulation of the motor cortex usually causes precise bodily movements during either waking or slow-wave sleep, but these impulses are actively inhibited during what is now often called **paradoxical sleep.** Thus, during paradoxical sleep the brain may be active as it is during waking, but most of the motor outflow is clamped off. But while most muscles relax during paradoxical sleep, the eyes move rapidly under the closed lids. This can easily be seen through the thin lids of a baby's eyes, and babies a few weeks old show this paradoxical or **rapid eye movement (REM)** sleep during about 80 percent of their sleeping time. Adults spend about 20 percent of their sleeping time in this stage (see Figure 25-7). Both baby boys

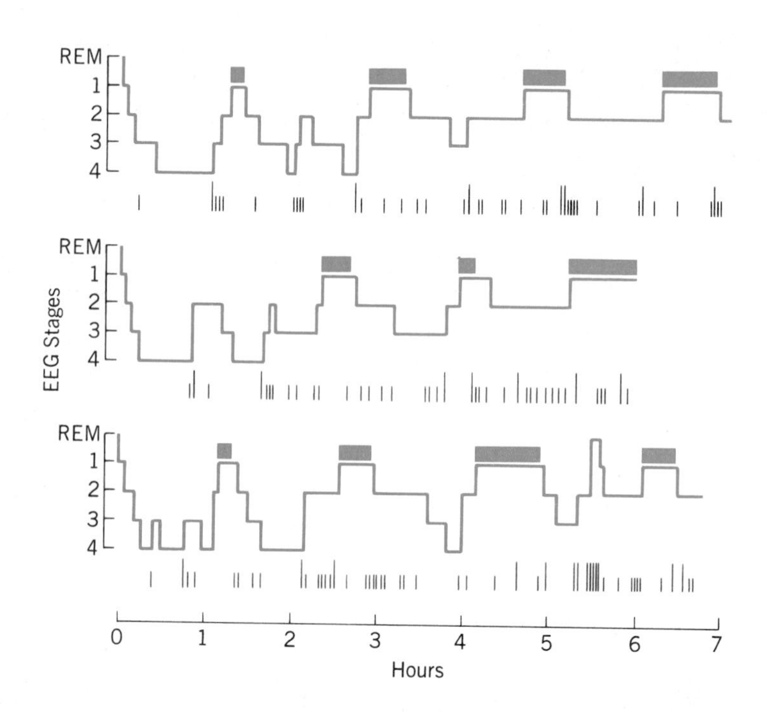

FIGURE 25-7
DREAM PERIODS DURING A NORMAL NIGHT

These typical EEG records from all-night recordings of adults show fairly regular cycles from EEG Stage 1 through 2 and 3 to Stage 4, and then in reverse order to Stage 1. The deepest sleep, Stage 4, tends to occur only early in the night. The first occurrence of Stage 1 is usually brief and is not accompanied by rapid eye movements; subsequent occurrences of Stage 1 last longer and rapid eye movements can usually be observed. REM periods are shown by the colored bars. If a person is awakened during REM sleep, he usually reports dreaming; during other stages of sleep, dreams may occur, but they are much less frequent. Body movements are shown by the vertical lines at the bottom of each graph—long lines for large movements and short lines for minor movements. Bodily activity is absent in Stage 4 sleep and tends to occur in lighter stages and at transitions between stages.
(Modified from Dement & Kleitman, 1957)

and men often show erections of the penis during this phase of sleep.

Because the cat is an animal that sleeps for long periods of time, as any cat owner can testify, more research on sleep has been done on the cat than on any other animal, including man. Some accounts attribute to human beings all the findings made with cats, so it is well to be aware that the patterns of electrical and motor activities in sleep show real differences between cat and man, as summarized in Table 25-1.

If a child or adult is awakened during paradoxical sleep and is asked to report what he was experiencing, he will almost always report a dream, a vivid concrete experience. This is true even of people who ordinarily do not remember their dreams the next day. By this means investigators are making far more complete collections of dreams than were previously available. During slow-wave sleep the person can often report experiences too, but these tend to be more abstract and conceptual: "I was thinking of my work," or "I was driving."

In normal adults, the periods of paradoxical sleep occur about every ninety minutes and last about twenty minutes. There are individual differences in this periodicity, and changes in the course of

TABLE 25-1
DIFFERENCES BETWEEN CAT AND MAN IN PATTERNS OF RAPID EYE MOVEMENT SLEEP

	Cat	*Man*
Eye movements during REM sleep	Very rapid, unlike waking movements	Slower than shifts in fixation during waking but similar in form
Electroencephalographic (EEG) pattern	Extremely fast and activated	Resembles the somewhat slowed and random pattern found at the initial transition from waking to sleep
Muscle tonus	Great drop in tonus	Subtle and irregular changes
Thresholds of arousal	Elevated, so sleep is especially deep during REM periods	Somewhat lower than in other phases of sleep, so REM sleep is not deep

From F. Snyder, 1971.

sleeping are proving important in the study of changes in personality and mental health.

Brain Regions Involved

As in other kinds of motivation, the hypothalamus seems to be involved in sleep and wakefulness. If the posterior hypothalamus of a cat is destroyed, the cat will sleep (or be "sleepy") continuously. Stimulation of the posterior hypothalamus produces wakeful behavior.

Much research on sleep is done on cats, but there are differences between sleep of cats and of human beings, as Table 25-1 describes. (Jerome Wexler, National Audubon Society)

As relatively broad "states of being," sleep, wakefulness, and all the degrees within each are affected by activity of a variety of brain regions. Regions in the brain stem are also involved. For example, insomnia is produced in cats by severing part of the brain stem, the pons (see Figure 25-8). These cuts prevent impulses from the pons from reaching more forward brain areas. Further and more precise research has revealed a small collection of nerve cells and fibers in the middle of the pons (and also higher, in the midbrain) that produce the same effect (Jouvet, 1967). Other small regions were discovered in the "dorsal" pons—the "top" of this region in the normal posture of a cat. Destruction of these points abolished that stage of sleep characterized by rapid, low-voltage brain waves and which we have termed "paradoxical." The locations of these regions are given in Figure 25-8.

The neuron interconnections in the region controlling paradoxical sleep utilize a chemical transmitter at the synapse different from that used in controlling "light" sleep. For this reason, some drugs affect one kind of sleep more than the other. Barbiturates, for example, block transmission of chemicals at the "paradoxical" synapses and therefore prevent paradoxical sleep and suppress dreaming.

Nightmares

Study of the brain activity of people subject to **nightmares** has recently brought us to a new understanding of this phenomenon (Broughton, 1968). Heretofore it was commonly assumed that a nightmare was simply a bad dream; Freud, who made great progress in interpreting the meaning of dreams (see p. 180), considered nightmares to be extreme cases of "anxiety dreams." That is, nightmares were thought to be dreams in which a person's mental conflicts, facing less repression than in the waking state, came to consciousness even if only in weird distorted images. If nightmares were dreams, then they would be expected to occur during paradoxical sleep. Recent research shows that they do not. Instead, like certain other disturbances of sleep—sleep-talking, sleep-walking, and bed-wetting—nightmares occur either in the deepest level of nondreaming sleep or, more often, during sudden arousal from deep sleep. They seem to be disorders of arousal before the person has regained waking contact with his environment. There is lack of coordination, confusion, and usually amnesia for the occurrence. If anything is remembered, it is usually only a scene, not a prolonged episode as in the case of a dream. During paradoxical sleep there may

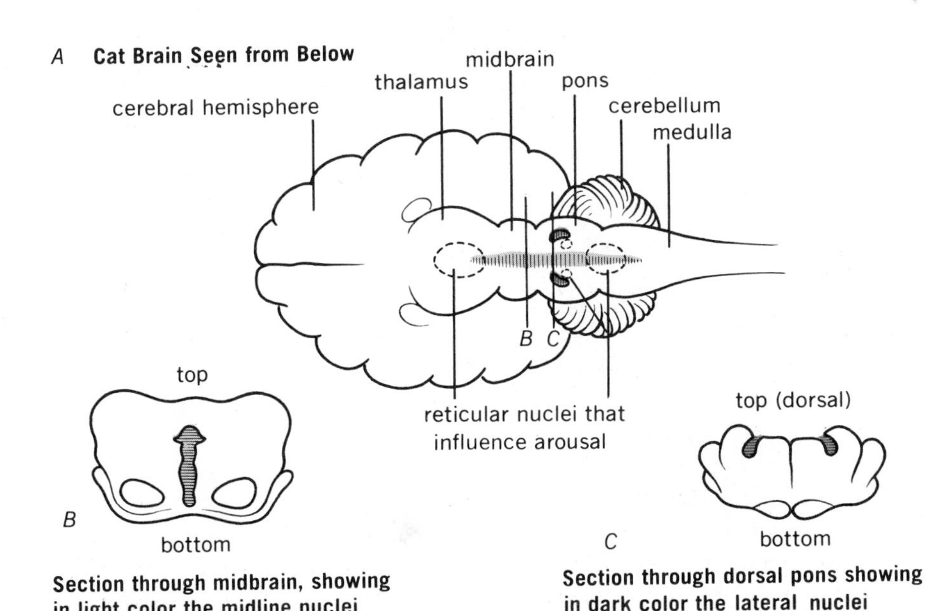

FIGURE 25-8
BRAIN AREAS OF THE CAT INFLUENCING SLEEP AND WAKEFULNESS
(After Jouvet, 1967)

be bad dreams accompanied by anxiety and these may even waken the sleeper, but a nightmare seems more pathological and out of control; the heart rate may rise dramatically.

Since nightmares occur during a particular stage of slow-wave sleep, they can be controlled by the use of drugs that reduce the amount of time spent in this stage. When nightmares are overcome in this way, the person reports a general increase in well-being. This finding is inconsistent with Freud's belief that nightmares are only a symptom of a deep-seated mental conflict, and therefore removing only the symptom (and not the cause) would result in the appearance of a new symptom. But this does not seem to happen when nightmares are chemically suppressed.

Why We Sleep

This recent research, while it has told us a great deal about sleep, has not made clear why we spend about one third of our adult lives asleep. In fact, it has allowed us to reject certain hypotheses. For example, the fact that the brain is active during sleep shows that sleep is not required in order to permit the brain to rest. Nevertheless, more sophisticated versions of the possible restorative functions of sleep continue to be put forth (e.g., Oswald, 1970). What seems to be a significant lead has come from another direction—comparative psychology, discussed in Section 9. Some animal forms have evolved to be most efficient during the light phase of the daily cycle (e.g., primates, dogs, and deer); some have evolved to be most efficient in the dark part of the daily cycle (e.g., cats, rats, and bats). Perhaps sleep and its brain mechanisms evolved in order to keep animals quiet and inconspicuous during the part of the daily cycle when they were least efficient and most apt to fall prey to other forms. Sleep will continue to pose research problems for the foreseeable future.

Sex behavior—What are the roles of hormones, neural circuits, and experience?

Many differences in bodily structure and behavior can be traced back to whether individuals have the female (XX) chromosomal pattern or the male (XY) chromosomal pattern. These chromosomes direct the production of different amounts of the **sex hormones.** The **androgens** (so-called "male" hormones) are actually secreted by both sexes, and so are the **estrogens** (so-called "female" hormones). The difference between the sexes is a relative one: the blood of an adult man contains about five times as high a concentration of androgens as does the blood of an adult woman; around the time of monthly ovulation, the blood of a woman contains about ten times as high a concentration of estrogens as does the blood of a man (Turner, 1971).

These hormones clearly affect the development of sexual characteristics of the body—the genital organs, the breasts, the distribution of body fat, even the bony structure. Do they also lead to the development of sexual organization in the brain? Many investigators believe that the brain becomes female or male, just as the body does. But this is still a matter of dispute, as we will see. Does the continuation of sexual activity in the adult depend upon hormonal functioning? This depends upon the species of mammal, as we will discuss. What regions of the brain are especially involved in mating behavior? Does learning play an important role in development of mating behavior or is this largely an "instinctive" activity that requires little or no learning?

More work has been done on the sexual behavior and anatomy of the rat than of any other species, so we will start with the rat, but we will frequently refer to other species, including man. However, one must use great caution in generalizing among species, because no two species are exactly alike in these respects; even other rodents such as the mouse and the guinea pig differ considerably from the rat. Patterns of mating behavior in the rat and in other species are described in Chapter 27 on comparative psychology, p. 818.

Hormones and Development

Both female and male anatomical potentialities exist in the fetal rat; there are originally two systems of ducts—one that could develop into parts of the female reproductive tract and another that could develop into parts of the male reproductive mechanisms. The fetal rat ovary produces very little hormonal secretion, but the fetal testis releases into the bloodstream a fetal morphogenic testicular substance (FMTS) that affects both duct systems. This hormone, which is not one of the adult sex hormones, causes the male duct system to develop and prevents growth of the female ducts, which eventually disappear. When there is no FMTS, as in the genetic female, the male system disappears whereas the female tract develops normally. If FMTS or androgens ("male" hormones) are administered artificially at the proper stage in fetal development, a genetic female rat will develop male genitalia.

Now let us consider the brain. Some investigators have suggested that neurally, too, the individual originally has the potentialities of both sexes but that only one or the other system can develop, just as in the case of the reproductive tracts. In support of this hypothesis, they describe the results of secretion or administration of androgen during the first few days after birth in the rat (Levine, 1966). Presence of androgen during this *early* period, either normally or by injection, increases the probability of male mating behavior in *adulthood* in the male and, to a somewhat lesser degree, even in the female. This mating behavior is neurally directed, at least at the final motor level. It is as if the early influence of the male hormone caused the nervous system to become "male." If there is no androgen during the early postnatal period, certain female mating responses will occur in adulthood, such as the arching of the back and raising of the rump (**lordosis**) when the rat is primed with female hormones and stimulated by another rat mounting it or by the experimenter touching it on the back. The absence of androgen early in life is normal in the female and can be produced in the male either by castration or by injection of chemical compounds that combat androgens.

Other researchers disagree with this interpretation. One (Beach, 1971) has argued that the nervous system probably is not masculinized or feminized but retains the capacity for both masculine and feminine behavior. Some adult female rats are not only receptive to males but will also frequently mount other females; an occasional male rat that mounts females and exhibits the full mating pattern will also respond receptively to other males. Many adult male rats that do not spontaneously show receptivity and lordosis can be brought to do so by a series of high-dosage injections of estrogen ("female" hormone). This indicates that the nervous system of the adult male rat has not lost this female neural pattern even if it was not being used. The difference between the sexes in this regard may not be absolute but rather one of degree.

Direct evidence of differences in brain anatomy between adult male and female rats has been reported recently. In four brain regions, the two sexes were found to differ significantly in the size of nuclei of nerve cells (Pfaff, 1966). Furthermore, when male rats were castrated at seven days postnatally, the adult brain measures were either intermediate between male and female or differed significantly from males but not from females. In these respects, male hormones must normally influence brain development. In a hypothalamic region important in controlling ovulation, adult male and female rats have been found to differ in the number and pattern of synaptic connections (Raisman & Field, 1971).

The Estrous Cycle—Behaviors, Hormones, Brain Regions

The adult female shows a cycle of **estrus** or receptivity to the male; in the rat this cycle is four to five days long whereas in the rhesus monkey it is about twenty-eight days long. The peak of receptivity occurs around the time of ovulation; that is, when an egg is released from the ovary and is available for fertilization. The cyclical changes involve several behavioral aspects, several hormones, and different brain regions. Behaviorally, at estrus the female is not only more receptive but she is also more attractive to the male. The receptivity of the female monkey has been found to depend partly upon androgens produced in the female's adrenal cortex; injecting androgens increases her receptivity more than does injecting estrogens. On the other hand, the male monkey's responsiveness to the female is governed chiefly by the estrogen level of the female; injecting estrogen into the female increases the male's mating behavior whereas injecting her with androgen has little effect on the male's response (Herbert, 1970). A regular cycle of vaginal and ovarian changes normally accompanies the changes in receptivity, but they can be shown to depend upon somewhat different neural circuits. Lesions in the mammillary body of the brain (at the posterior boundary of the hypothalamus, see Figure 25-1) abolish sexual receptivity although the cycling of ovarian function and vaginal changes persists. Conversely, lesions in the anterior hypothalamus abolish ovarian function, but receptivity continues if the estrogen normally supplied by the ovary is replaced by injection.

Sex-Linked Behaviors

Many kinds of behavior are **sex-linked** even though they are not involved in mating. Women are more sensitive to tastes than are men; female rats have a significantly greater preference for sweet tastes than do male rats. Among monkeys, young males differ from young females in their patterns of play. The young males show much more of the following kinds of social behavior than do the females: rough-and-tumble play, threatening acts, pursuit play. (See also preview Figure 2.) Rough play is also characteristic of little boys as compared to little girls. In the case of human children, we sometimes wonder whether the difference may not be learned or enforced through cultural sanctions. In the case of infrahuman primates, we can

Rough-and-tumble play like this is characteristic of young male monkeys and is shown much less frequently by young females. But females that receive androgen prenatally engage in significantly more rough-and-tumble play than do normal females.
(Courtesy H. F. Harlow)

be sure that this difference arises without cultural intervention, especially since it is seen even when young monkeys are raised with no adult present (Harlow, Harlow, & Suomi, 1971). Of course, in children, differences may be reinforced by social patterns. The genetic difference can be influenced by early hormonal treatment: Administering androgen prenatally produced female monkeys with male-like genitalia and with relatively male-like behavior; they engaged in more rough-and-tumble play than did normal females, although less than normal males (Phoenix, Goy, & Resko, 1968). Some aspects of temperament are therefore strongly conditioned by sex. Here the role of male hormones seems to be one of *organizing* neural structures in early development rather than of *activating* patterns of behavior. The sexually-different play patterns in young monkeys occur even though there is practically no secretion of sex hormones. On the other hand, hormones may activate sex-linked patterns in the adult. For example, cases of extreme aggressiveness in people are sometimes treated successfully by using drugs that counter male sex hormones.

The fact that style of play is sex-linked does not mean that experience has no influence. When male monkeys were raised in isolation, they did not show normal play behavior even when they were later placed with other young monkeys. As "therapy," some previously isolated males were placed with females who had had social experience and who exhibited normal female-monkey play patterns. In the social group the males gradually began to play, and as soon as they did, they showed the typical male patterns (Harlow & Suomi, 1971). In other words, experience in the group induced play, but the type of play was determined by genes and early hormonal developmental influence. Here, as in many examples of perceptual behavior, neither an exclusively nativistic nor an exclusively empiristic explanation can account for the observed facts.

Hormones and Continuation of Sex Behavior

In the adult rat of either sex, removal of sex hormones abolishes mating behavior. Sex hormones are therefore said to have an *activating* function in adulthood, whereas earlier they had an *organizational* influence on bodily structure. In dogs and cats, the female becomes unreceptive when the supply of ovarian hormones is removed, but the male may continue to mate for some time, or in the case of some animals, indefinitely. In adult men and women, sexual drive and activity may continue in spite of loss of sex hormones through illness or age, but individuals may react quite differently. Thus, as one goes from rat to dog to man, up the phylogenetic scale, there appears to be an evolutionary trend toward relative independence from hormonal control.

Even in the rodent, however, individual differences in mating behavior cannot be explained solely by hormonal levels. This was demonstrated originally for the guinea pig (Grunt & Young,

1952) and then confirmed with the rat (Beach & Fowler, 1959; Larsson, 1966). Figure 25-9 shows ratings of three groups of normal male guinea pigs on sexual activity; some showed high drive, some medium drive, and some were low in drive. When the animals were castrated, sexual activity gradually declined to a low level and the individual differences disappeared. Then the hormone testosterone was restored by injection, and the differences in sexual activity reappeared, even though all animals received the same dosage. Those that had been low were low again, and this was true even in the last stage of the experiment when the dosage of hormone was doubled. So the differences among the groups could not be attributed to differences in their production of hormone.

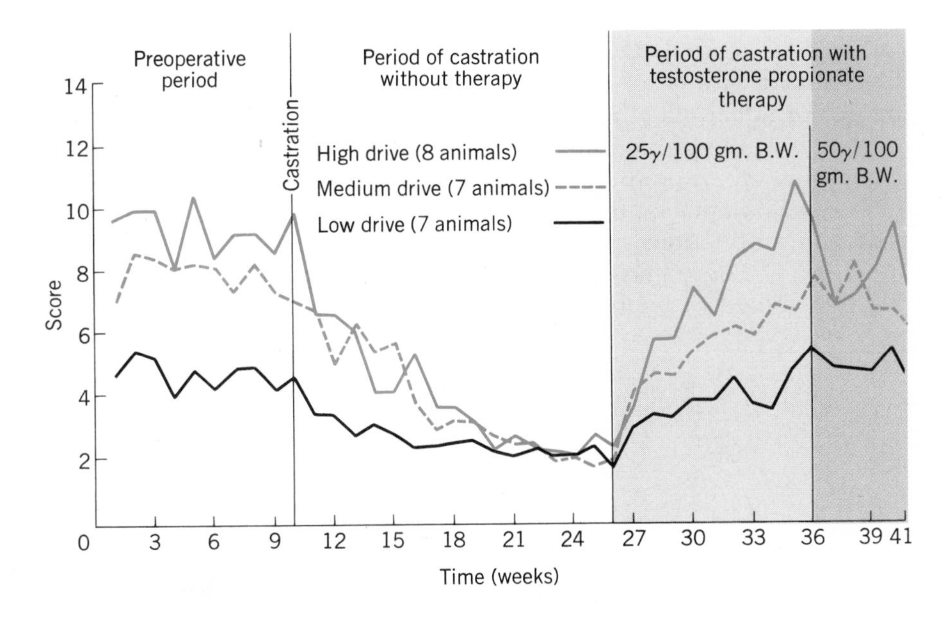

FIGURE 25-9 HORMONES AND SEX BEHAVIOR

After castration of guinea pigs reduced sex activity, the same amount of testosterone was given to each animal, beginning at week 26 (the light-colored area). The group that had shown high sex activity before the operation became high again; the animals that were originally low remained the lowest. Doubling the amount of hormone (darker shading) did not increase the ratings.
(From Grunt & Young, 1952)

Localized Uptake of Hormones

Since hormones are spread throughout the body by the bloodstream, it may seem surprising that the sex hormones seem to affect only the reproductive tract and very localized parts of the brain. The answer is that these affected regions selectively take up the hormones. By analogy, radio waves spread widely through space, but only a receiver that is tuned to a particular station will capture those signals. In the case of hormones, we can demonstrate this tuning by injecting into a female animal estrogen that has been "tagged" with radioactive atoms. Then, tissue samples taken later show that the radioactivity is concentrated in the pituitary, in parts of the hypothalamus, and in the vagina.

A variant of this procedure can be used to stimulate brain centers without affecting the reproductive tract. In this case a small pellet containing hormone can be implanted in the anterior hypothalamus of an animal whose ovaries have been removed. The hormone is at high enough concentration in the hypothalamus to induce receptivity. But its concentration in the bloodstream is too low to affect the reproductive tract.

Role of Experience

Experience with other animals is important in developing an animal's mating behavior, but it is not yet clear whether this is really learning or whether a hormonal effect is involved. In rats (Gerall, Ward, & Gerall, 1967), dogs (Beach, 1968), and monkeys (Missakian, 1969), males raised in isolation are clumsy and ineffective when given a chance to mate with a receptive female. The males seem motivated and attempt to mount, but they orient poorly and are unsuccessful. It is not yet known how much or what kind of prior experience is needed. Dogs allowed only minimal (fifteen minutes a day) contact with other dogs during their first year are normal in mating. A hormonal effect may be important here since male rats reared for fifteen weeks alone (or with other males) showed retarded development of the reproductive system as compared with those with heterosexual contacts; the latter animals appeared to have the greater androgen production.

There may be a sex difference in the amount of learning that is involved in sex behavior and in the role of the cerebral cortex.

A male monkey raised in isolation is clumsy and ineffective when given the opportunity to mate with a receptive female. Social experience is clearly important for normal development of mating behavior.
(Courtesy H. F. Harlow)

In humans, the male is often said to be aroused by a wider range of stimuli than the female. This may indicate more learning and more varied learning concerning sex on the part of the male. In the rat, the male is more impaired in mating by sensory loss or by cortical lesions than is the female. This may have to do chiefly with the more active roles of males in most mammalian species: the male more often initiates mating and pursues, while the female is relatively passive or receptive. Nevertheless, estrous females of many species will approach males to initiate mating. It may be that this active female behavior is just as dependent on the cerebral cortex as is male behavior; only experimental tests will answer this question. (See also pp. 819–20.)

Aggression—To what extent can biological research help to explain and control it?

Emotions are sometimes considered to be purely subjective states, to be studied only through one's own introspections or through verbal reports of other people. But we are learning a great deal about brain processes involved in emotion, from studies of both human and animal subjects. Emotional behavior has been found to involve not only changes in experienced mood but also changes in sensory systems and motor response patterns, as we will see. As an example, we will consider violent or aggressive behavior, on which much research has been done in recent years. Let us start with a case report:

Paul M., a handsome muscular 20-year-old, came voluntarily to Boston City Hospital because he was afraid that he was "going wild" and "didn't want to hurt anybody." Shortly before this he had gone wild in his own apartment. He had ripped plaster off the walls with his bare hands and had smashed a mirror; then with pieces of the mirror he had cut deep gashes in his chest and abdomen. Further information pointed to brain damage as the cause of the violent behavior. For one thing, Paul reported that just before his rampage at home, he had suffered a spell of unconsciousness from which he awoke dazed and violent. Five months earlier he had had an attack of grand mal epilepsy. (In a grand mal epileptic seizure the person falls unconscious, his limbs may contract repeatedly; he may salivate, bite his tongue, urinate or defecate. The electroencephalogram shows a characteristic pattern of very large spikes during this time. The seizure may last from 30 seconds to 5 minutes, and after it is over, the person is often confused, tired and sleepy.) Paul's seizure occurred after prolonged use of stimulant drugs, although other factors in his history may also have contributed to brain damage.

While his previous behavior had often been aggressive and antisocial, Paul had always kept it within limits. But after his grand mal seizure, this changed. He experienced dreamlike states which convinced him that he was losing his mind, and he could no longer restrain his violent impulses toward other people or even himself. Neurological tests led to a diagnosis of mild brain damage, and Paul was placed on medication used to prevent seizures. Since being on medication he has had no violent outbursts, and he says that he feels once again in control of himself. (Mark & Ervin, 1970)

In this case anticonvulsant drugs are keeping the attacks under control. The drugs have little effect on normal excitability of neural tissue, but they inhibit neural responses that are abnormally large. In some cases, however, drugs do not work and operations have been used to remove injured or abnormal brain tissue. The brain operations grew out of animal experiments that started from a broad investigation of a large area of brain called the **temporal lobe.**

Surgical Techniques

In the 1930's experimenters found that removal of a large part of the temporal lobe in monkeys resulted in a variety of changes in behavior including tameness. Gradually, through more precise experiments, the tameness was found to be due to removal of a little almond-shaped group of nerve cells lying under the cortex near the front tip of each temporal lobe; this nucleus is called the **amygdala** (from the Greek for "almond"). (See color Figure 3.)

In a number of laboratory animals, removal of the amygdala on both sides of the brain resulted in tameness. Schreiner and Kling (1956) decided to test this further by operating on a lynx, a savage member of the cat family. The lynx was so vicious that it could not be removed from its cage (see preview Figure 1). It was injected through the bars of the cage with an anesthetic agent, and then the small amygdaloid nuclei were destroyed on both sides. As soon as the anesthesia wore off, the lynx was found to be tame. When other animals were put in its cage, the lynx behaved like a kitten. It could be petted or fed by hand. Spotlight 25-3 describes a situation where only portions from the right half of the temporal lobe were removed.

The animal experiments encouraged a few neurosurgeons to try similar operations on humans whose attacks of violence were not controlled by anticonvulsant drugs. One of the pioneers has been a Japanese doctor who has made it possible for some "criminally insane" patients to leave the hospital and return home. One patient said after his operation, "Now I can't get mad even if I want to." In order to destroy the right tissue and no more than is necessary, the neurosurgeons may insert several electrodes and map the responses of the awake patient to electrical stimulation of different points within the brain. Even points that are near each other may elicit quite different emotional experiences. Thus, electrical stimulation at one point

SPOTLIGHT 25-3

A (Surgically) Split Personality

A dramatic experiment was the preparation of a monkey with a split personality—surgically split down the middle by transection of the corpus callosum. With its left eye open, the monkey reacted to an approaching person with its usual wild and aggressive behavior, but with only the right eye open, the monkey responded placidly (Downer, 1962). What the experimenter had done was to split the brain by transecting most of the tracts that connect the two hemispheres. The optic chiasma was among the tracts cut, so that input from the right eye was restricted to the right hemisphere and input from the left eye, to the left hemisphere. In addition to splitting the brain, the experimenter removed part of the right temporal lobe, including the amygdala. Thus, depending on which eye was open, the approaching person was perceived by the normal left hemisphere or by the surgically-tamed right hemisphere. (Split-brain preparations have also yielded illuminating results in the study of learning, see p. 741.)

in a patient's brain brought a report of a pleasant calm feeling; when stimulated at another point, the patient reported a strange detached sensation of "looking on" at the world. With stimulation at another point, only a few millimeters away in the middle of the amygdala, he reported pain in his teeth, then in his face, and he felt that everything was "going wild." Subsequent surgical destruction of this area of the amygdala in both hemispheres brought an end to attacks of violence that had plagued the patient for seven years (Mark & Ervin, 1970, pp. 92–97).

Stimulation of the brain in animal subjects can elicit aggressive behavior predictably, and this procedure can be used to study sensory changes as well as motor patterns involved in this behavior. For several of these studies, experimenters have selected cats that do not spontaneously attack rats or mice; such a cat will normally remain quiet in its cage with a rat. When stimulated in particular hypothalamic sites, however, the cat will attack. Stimulated in one site, the cat will promptly bite or strike the rat. Simultaneous recording from sensory cells in the visual cortex demonstrated that some receptive fields are altered by the hypothalamic stimulation that induces attack (Flynn, Edwards, & Bandler, 1971). This suggests that perception is altered during emotion—perhaps the cats "see red."

Biological Methods of Controlling Aggression

Some recent studies indicate that many people with records of repeated violent crimes suffer from brain disorders. It is possible that prevention of brain injuries at the time of birth and during childhood may be a major preventive step in overcoming individual acts of violence. Drugs are helpful in controlling many cases of pathological violence. Usually anticonvulsants are used, but drugs that combat "male" sex hormones are also being used to reduce aggressive behavior in some cases. Brain operations can be carried out where drugs are ineffective. A further possible method being tried is to train subjects to control their brain waves and keep them from showing the pattern of large spikes in the electroencephalogram that trips off an attack.

A direct way to stop aggression, tested in animal subjects but unlikely to be used in a human patient unless all other means fail, is to stimulate an inhibitory brain region whenever aggressive behavior begins. A dramatic demonstration of this was given by the neurophysiologist José Delgado of Yale when he stopped a bull charging at him (Figure 4 in the preview of this section). The bull had been operated on in advance to place an electrode in an inhibitory region of the brain, and this was connected to a small radio receiver implanted under the skin of the head. With a small hand-held radio transmitter, Delgado could then send a signal to halt the bull's charge. A similar setup has been studied in Delgado's laboratory for social control of aggression among monkeys. The most aggressive member of a group is outfitted with a radio receiver and brain electrode, as was the bull. In this case, however, it is the cagemates that can send the inhibitory signal. When the aggressive animal starts to act up, its companions can press a button on the wall which sends a radio signal and "turns off" the aggression.

The use of biological methods to control pathological aggression has given rise to discussions of the ethics involved. Many concerned individuals have challenged the use of brain operations on a number of grounds; one of these is the difficulty in obtaining informed consent of patients who are suffering from brain malfunctions. There is also legitimate concern that techniques devised to cure pathological aggression may be misused to suppress nonconformity or political dissent. Clearly these problems are complex, and they call for a searching evaluation of the alternatives.

Reinforcement—What is it in terms of neural activity?

Animals will work hard to get electrical shocks to certain parts of the brain (Olds & Milner, 1954); they will work hard to avoid shocks to other parts (Delgado, Roberts, & Miller, 1954). These two effects, both announced in 1954, have led to hundreds of studies that may help to explain brain mechanisms of reinforcement.

Electrical Self-Stimulation of the Brain

A misplaced electrode led to the first observations of the positive reinforcement qualities of brain stimulation. When James Olds and Peter Milner at McGill University were testing the effects of stimulating an "activation" region in rats during maze performance, they noticed that one rat acted differently from the others—it tended to remain wherever it was in the maze when the brain stimuli were delivered or even to run back from the goal to the place where it received the stimulation. After this unexpected effect was repeated several times, the experimenters checked on the position of the electrode and found that the tip was in the **septal region** (see Figure 25-10). Rather than just discarding their observations with the misplaced electrode, Olds and Milner were intrigued and decided to investigate further. They implanted electrodes in the septum in other rats. Since the stimulation seemed to be reinforcing, they made it possible for the rats to stimulate their own brains. Each press on a pedal or bar sent a brief shock to this part of the brain. Some rats pressed the bar at amazingly high rates—for example, 2,000 presses per hour for twenty-four hours. (See preview Figure 3.) Other brain points were not reinforcing; the rat would press the bar occasionally as it moved about in the small enclosure, but it did not seem to do so deliberately. Other points were aversive or negatively reinforcing; that is, after the rat had pressed the bar once or twice, it would carefully avoid pressing it again.

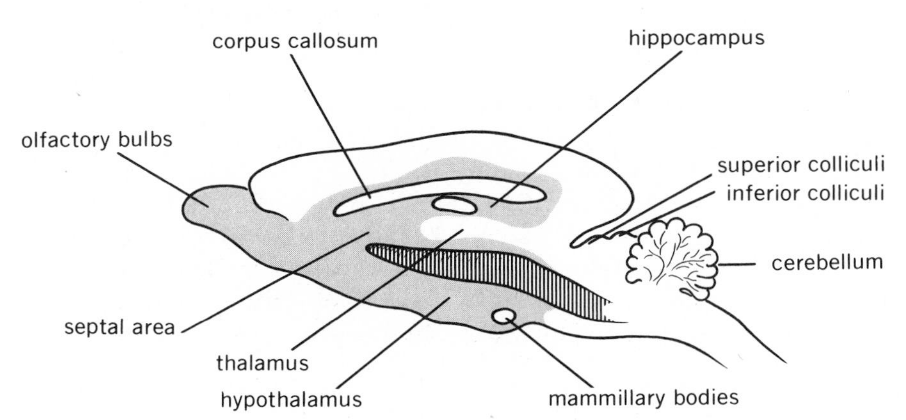

FIGURE 25-10 REWARDING AND PUNISHING REGIONS IN RAT BRAIN

Shown in this medial section of a rat brain are areas where electrical stimulation is rewarding (colored) or punishing (striped). Rewarding effects are found in a band of cortex just above the corpus callosum, in the hippocampus, septal area, olfactory bulbs, and hypothalamus. Punishing effects are found in the medial brain stem tracts and nuclei. Neutral or weak effects are found in the unshaded areas. (Modified from Olds, 1958)

Mapping the locations of such points in many rats showed that a large part of the rat brain gives positively reinforcing effects and a relatively small part yields negative effects (see Figure 25-10). The brains of other species also have been mapped in this way, and they reveal similar basic phenomena but with species differences. Rodents show relatively large positive areas. The cat has rather small positively reinforcing areas, and the effect is not so strong as in rodents. Some observations of this sort have also been made in human psychiatric patients in the attempt to relieve depression (Sem-Jacobsen & Torkildsen, 1960; Bishop *et al.*, 1963). Some of these patients have reported that stimulation of certain brain regions brings warm or pleasant feelings. Even on the basis of the early animal experiments, some investigators were referring to these brain regions as "pleasure centers." Further work suggests a rather different interpretation, as we will see next, but this field remains active and changing; more surprises and new interpretations must be expected.

Stimulation-Bound Behavior

How can we put together the facts about animals controlling the stimulation of their own brains and the observations on brain stimulation that evokes or alters behaviors suggestive of changed motivational states? It will be recalled that stimulation of particular hypothalamic sites was reported to evoke eating or drinking or male sex behavior when the appropriate goal object was present. Different types of behavior have also been produced in other experiments; these include gnawing, hoarding food pellets, and stalking and attacking. The term **stimulation-bound behavior** refers to behavior that is elicited by direct stimulation of the brain and that appears like normal motivated behavior; often it lasts only as long as the brain stimulation continues. It turns out that a brain site that yields stimulation-bound behavior is almost certain to result in frequent self-stimulation when the animal is allowed to control the stimulation. Since the two sorts of behavior are related, how can stimulation-bound behavior help us to understand more about the brain mechanisms of reinforcement?

Stimulation-bound behaviors have been considered by many investigators to be *motivated,* rather than simple elicited motor acts, because of their apparent purposiveness and flexibility: (1) The behavior will not be shown unless the appropriate goal object is present. (2) During stimulation animals will perform a learned task in order to obtain the goal object. (3) The animal will tolerate painful or unpleasant stimuli in order to reach the goal object. Therefore many psychologists have concluded that the brain stimulation activates specific neural circuits underlying "hunger" or "thirst" or "sex motivation."

Recently doubts have arisen about this interpretation (Valenstein, Cox, & Kakolewski, 1970). The brain regions for different stimulation-bound behaviors were found to overlap when the same animals were tested with different goal objects. That is, an electrode site that induced a rat to go to food and eat when food was present would induce going to water and drinking when that was present. Often two electrodes spaced rather widely apart in the hypothalamus would elicit exactly the same behavior. Furthermore, careful examination of the behavior showed that it was not always as purposive and flexible as normal motivated behavior. For example, animals eating in response to brain stimulation did not readily switch to another familiar food when the first food was removed; in fact, many switched eventually to stimulation-bound drinking. Animals showing stimulation-bound drinking sometimes continued to lap at the tube even when the water was removed, so that something other than satisfaction of an induced need could maintain the behavior.

On the other hand, other experimenters have found equally compelling evidence for the motivational interpretation of stimulation-bound behavior. The normal motives of hunger and thirst are affected by depriving the animal of food or water, and these normal motives decrease with intake of food and water. Can the same phenomena be demonstrated with the "stimulated motives"? Devor and his colleagues (1970) found brain sites that could evoke either eating or drinking, and they studied how the thresholds for these behaviors varied with deprivation or intake of food or water. They found that depriving the animal of food lowered the electrical threshold for evoking eating but did not alter the threshold for evoking drinking; feeding the animal raised the threshold for stimulation-bound eating but again did not change the threshold for drinking. Similarly, manipulating the water balance altered the brain thresholds for drinking but not for eating. Thus, in these experiments, the eating and drinking elicited by electrical stimulation are affected separately and appropriately by external events, just as are normal eating and drinking.

We can summarize present understanding in this way: It appears that brain stimulation evokes behavior that is prepotent or ready to be tripped off at the time. The prepotency is based partly on the current state of bodily need, partly on the goal objects present, and partly on training to respond to one or another type of goal object. Since the stimulus electrode touches only a small part of a complex circuit, it is not surprising that in some cases the evoked behavior does not show all of the characteristics of normal motivated behavior.

A combination of self-stimulation and stimulation-bound behavior has been tried in a few experiments, and this may be especially reinforcing. Thus rats which ran a maze to receive brain stimulation performed better when they also received food in the goal area (Mendelson, 1966). In another experiment, rats received a reinforcing brain shock whenever they reached either end of a chamber, so they shuttled back and forth from end to end. When the chamber contained small wooden pellets that the rats could carry in their mouths, they preferred to do this, taking a pellet to one end, dropping it, and carrying another pellet back to the other end (Valenstein, Cox, & Kakolewski, 1970). Such carrying behavior is natural for rats, and here it seemed to add to the effectiveness of the reinforcing situation.

A Formulation of Reinforcement

It appears from the foregoing observations that stimulation or activation of particular regions of the brain is positively reinforcing. This stimulation can occur in several ways. Certain stimuli are reinforcing independently of biological consequences. Thus the sweet taste of saccharine and the salty taste of lithium are rewarding even though neither has any nutritive value. The motor acts of eating lead to satisfaction and cessation of ingestion long before the food is digested and the bodily need is made up by metabolism. The direct electrical activation of circuits involved in consummatory behavior is reinforcing even if the full response pattern is not acted out. Similarly perhaps, if we activate certain brain patterns by thinking about desirable activities, this can be gratifying. Depending upon the person, thinking about eating or sex or money or sports or a hobby may be a pleasant way to spend time, and conditions which favor such reveries may themselves become reinforcing. When the feedback of motor response patterns is added to the localized brain stimulation, the strongest activation of the circuits underlying reinforcement is achieved. Such is a current formulation of brain mechanisms of reinforcement. We can expect to see both further applications and further developments of the biological psychology of reinforcement during this decade.

SUMMARY

The biological bases of motivated behavior are being investigated actively. Findings that can be applied to human behavior have been made in control of eating, aggression, sex, dreams, and nightmares. Concepts of motivation and reinforcement are steadily becoming fuller and more adequate to interpret and predict human and animal behavior.

The central and lower regions of the brain are particularly important for motivational aspects of behavior. They facilitate or inhibit patterns of behavior that help to regulate both the internal bodily economy and relations with the external world. Cells in these regions acquire information both about internal bodily conditions—by monitoring metabolism and hormones—and about the external world, including especially the presence of goal objects. Often there are multiple mechanisms to achieve a particular end, as we saw in the cases of control of food and water intake. This multiplicity endows the organism with resilience in case of injury or disease, but it also makes it difficult to perform crucial experiments, since shutting off one major pathway may not impair behavior as long as another pathway functions. The multiplicity of control also permits feedback to stop consummatory behavior before its metabolic consequences have occurred.

Stimulation of these motivational regions does not initiate stereotyped motor patterns, as was the case in motor centers. Rather, the behavior is relatively flexible and purposive. Nevertheless, doubts have been raised recently as to whether such stimulation induces true motivational states or whether it simply helps to trip off behavior that is prepotent at the time.

Motivation and learning are complexly interrelated, since much motivated behavior is learned, and since much learning depends upon reinforcement. Activation of many motivational regions of the brain appears to be reinforcing; that is, it will favor the behavior that led to such reinforcement. Such activation can occur through certain types of sensory stimulation, through physiological internal stimulation, or by artificial electrical or chemical stimulation. It appears that the strongest reinforcement is obtained when stimulation occurs in the presence of a goal object and the motor pattern of consummatory behavior can be run off.

26

Biological Psychology of Learning and Memory Storage

Does biopsychological research support multi-stage models of memory?
How are memories stored in the brain?
Where in the brain do learning and memory storage occur?
What are the basic assumptions of a model of memory processes?

The challenge of understanding learning and memory from a biological point of view has proved to be more difficult than investigating the biological bases of perception and of motivation. Nevertheless, considerable progress has been made in recent years, and active research is motivated by both theoretical and practical considerations. Clearly, no theory of behavior would be complete without an understanding of the mechanisms of learning and memory, since, as we have seen in other sections of this book, the adaptability of behavior is important in every area of psychology. Practically, we hope that further understanding of these biological processes will help to alleviate the impairment of people who suffer from deficiencies in learning and memory—retarded children, people whose memory is impaired by brain damage, and those who suffer from senile decline of learning ability. Perhaps research in this area will not only help to overcome deficiencies but will also help to promote superior capacities.

This chapter will discuss the following questions:

1. What light does biological research on learning and memory shed on the behavioral studies and theories discussed in previous chapters? We will see that evidence from a variety of biopsychological studies is consistent with multi-stage models of memory, and, indeed, biological psychologists had independently suggested hypotheses of this sort.

2. What is the biological form of the "memory trace" or **engram**? Are there different biological mechanisms of storage for different stages in the memory processes or for memories of different lengths (short-term, intermediate-term, and long-term memories)? You may have seen newspaper reports that chemists are beginning to extract "memory molecules" from the brains of animals that have been trained and even to synthesize such molecules; we will evaluate these reports critically.

3. Are some parts of the nervous system especially concerned with learning and with memory storage, just as there are parts especially involved in perception and in motivational processes? Where in the brain does memory storage occur?

4. Can biological procedures modify the rate of learning and the permanence of memory? We will see that both improvement and impairment can be achieved. We will consider some conditions under which people seem unable to learn.

At the end of this chapter we will describe a hypothetical model to suggest how neural action potentials and chemical processes at synapses might work in storing short-term and long-term memories in the brain. The model will also suggest how both basal regions of the brain and the cerebral cortex are active in memory storage.

Does biopsychological research support multi-stage models of memory?

At the end of Chapter 19 on memory, it was shown that much of our current knowledge about human verbal memory can be represented by multi-stage storage models, such as the buffer model of Atkinson and Shiffrin (1968). According to this model, information obtained by a person may be in any of three types of storage: the sensory store (from which loss is very rapid, in milliseconds), the short-term store (from which items are lost in seconds unless they are rehearsed), or the long-term store. Information is transferred from the short-term to the long-term store by being processed through the rehearsal buffer which has a limited capacity.

Biopsychological research has also led to multi-stage models to encompass results for both animal and human memory. Let us examine how behavioral and biological theorizing converge.

Perseveration-Consolidation Hypothesis

The buffer model is essentially an elaboration of the perseveration-consolidation model that was proposed for verbal learning in 1900 by Müller and Pilzecker, and that has ever since influenced biological hypotheses about memory. In some of their verbal learning experiments, Müller and Pilzecker trained subjects in one session and had them come back for tests of recall at later sessions. They requested the subjects not to rehearse the material between sessions, but some subjects reported that they had been unable to keep themselves from rehearsing. This suggested to the experimenters that perhaps all subjects rehearse, whether consciously or not. They then hypothesized that perseverating (that is, rehearsing or keeping up activity with regard to the items) is a necessary process to consolidate memory (to transform it into a stable, long-lasting form).

This perseveration-consolidation hypothesis was brought back to prominence in a biological form by Hebb (1949) as the "dual trace" hypothesis. Hebb proposed that memory traces may take either of two forms. He hypothesized that there was first an active form consisting of circulating neural impulses and then a structural form, involving new synaptic junctions. Furthermore, the structural, anatomical form of memory trace is achieved only if there has been sufficient neural activity. The idea that neural activity can lead to the formation of new or more efficient synapses and that memory can be stored in this way was actually first proposed about eighty years ago (Tanzi, 1893), but biopsychological research of the 1940's and thereafter gave this theorizing new meaning and importance. This research studied first the effects of head injuries on memory loss in humans and then the effects of experimental treatments that impair or improve memory in animals.

Retrograde Amnesia

A driver whose head is injured in an automobile accident often cannot remember the actual impact, although he can remember approaching the intersection where the accident occurred. An analysis of hundreds of cases of brain concussion which left the patients unconscious for a period of time showed that there was typically an **amnesia** for the events just before the injury (Russell & Nathan, 1946). In about three quarters of these cases this amnesia obscured the period of one to several minutes before the accident. This type of amnesia is usually called **retrograde,** as if the injury worked backward on the previous registration of information, although undoubtedly it actually worked forward and affected memory storage. Presumably the accident stopped the process of rehearsal and also physiological events that are necessary for transfer of material to the long-term store. Put in another way, the short-term memory trace is fragile and can be impaired by treatments that leave long-term traces intact.

Post-Trial Treatments

While observations about effects of head injuries have provided valuable information about memory processes, experimentation with animal subjects has yielded more specific findings and has permitted more powerful tests of hypotheses. Such animal experiments, begun in the late 1940's, have used a variety of procedures administered shortly after training trials to impair or to improve memory. These treatments include electroconvulsive shock to the brain or the use of various drugs.

Let us consider an example of an experimental design that is currently in frequent use. It is called a one-trial passive avoidance task—"passive avoidance" means that on the recall test, the animal can avoid punishment if it simply remains passively in the start area and does not venture into the other part of the apparatus. In the single training trial, the animal (usually a mouse or a rat) is placed in a small chamber that connects through a small doorway, to a larger chamber. The time it takes the animal to step into the large chamber is recorded automatically. Once it is in the large chamber, the mouse receives a footshock through the floor bars until it runs back to the "safe" start area. It is then returned to its home cage. When the mouse is put back into the apparatus for a test, it shows its memory by remaining in the start box and passively avoiding the far chamber. Whether the test occurs a day, a week, or even a month after the training trial, the mouse either refuses to go through the doorway or it waits minutes before doing so.

Yesterday when the mouse stepped from the black starting chamber into the white compartment, he received a shock through the floorbars. What determines whether he will step through today? (Courtesy J. Flood)

But interference with brain processes just after the training trial can prevent the establishment of such long-term memory. An effective type of treatment is to give **electroconvulsive shock (ECS)** to the head. ECS makes the animal unconscious briefly, and during this time it usually shows some convulsive movements of the limbs. A mouse that received ECS shortly after the training trial appears to have forgotten the footshock; on a retest it promptly steps through to the area where it received footshock. Furthermore, the closer the ECS follows the footshock, the more completely the memory is disrupted (see Figure 26-1). In the experiments, some mice receive ECS immediately after the footshock, and others after delays of minutes or hours. The subjects that had the longer intervals between footshock and ECS were more likely to show memory for the punishing situation—that is, a larger percentage of these subjects refused to step through the doorway (Kopp, Bohdanecký, & Jarvik, 1966).

These results are consistent with the consolidation hypothesis, but there are still problems that cause investigators to be cautious about accepting it. Let us note a few of these problems that illustrate the complexities of behavior and of research in this area:

1. It has recently been found that even if an animal

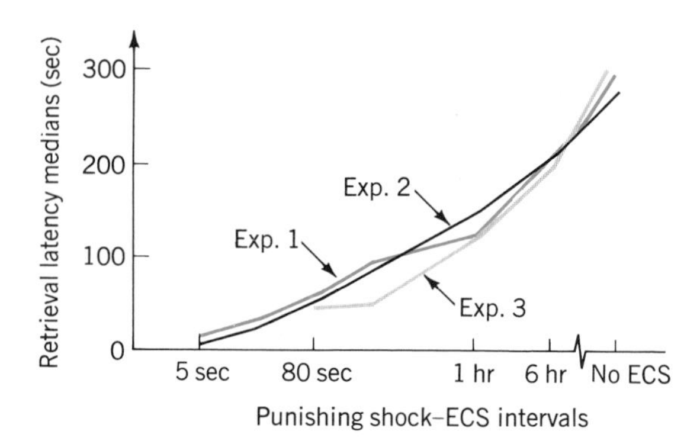

FIGURE 26-1
AMNESIA FROM A BRAIN SHOCK

Data are results of three experiments with 141 mice to test the effect of ECS upon memory. Mice that received ECS 5 seconds after the training trial showed a high degree of amnesia at the test trial 24 hours later—they stepped into the compartment in an average of 5 seconds. Those mice that received ECS 80 seconds after training showed a mean latency of 50 seconds on test—still considerable amnesia. In fact, even mice that received ECS six hours after training showed some amnesia; their mean latency was 195 seconds, whereas controls that received no ECS waited almost 300 seconds before entering the lighted compartment.
(After Kopp, Bohdanecky, & Jarvik, 1966)

appears to show complete amnesia so far as one measure of response goes, it may still show memory by another measure. Thus, a rat that steps promptly through the door to be shocked may nevertheless have a higher than normal heart rate indicative of an emotional response. In another experiment, rats could make a choice and step through to either of two different chambers. In whichever one a rat entered, it received footshock, and then it was given ECS. On retest the rats stepped through again and thus appeared to show amnesia for the footshock. But most rats did not step into the chamber they had chosen originally, and thus they revealed memory by avoiding the place in which they had received the footshock (Carew, 1970). We know that subjects learn many different responses in even an apparently simple situation. It is probable that some of these memories are more easily disrupted than others. Even the more resistant responses are disrupted when there is a very short interval between training and footshock.

2. Many investigators had hoped that these experiments would reveal *the* time course of consolidation of long-term memory (consolidation being measured by the increasing resistance of memory to interference as the interval between the trial and the ECS was lengthened). But the time courses that were found actually varied greatly among experiments. Some investigators found that if they delayed ECS by more than ten seconds after the trial, there was no impairment of memory (e.g., Chorover & Schiller, 1966). Others found that they could produce impairment with ECS given hours after training (e.g., Kopp *et al.*, 1966; McGaugh, 1966). The stronger the disruptive treatment, the longer you can delay giving it after the learning trial and still interfere with the animal's memory. Life and research might have been simpler if there were only one fixed gradient of memory for all behaviors, but the facts show this is not the case.

Another kind of support for the consolidation hypothesis comes from research on facilitation of learning by the use of excitant drugs such as pentylenetetrazol and strychnine sulphate (see Figure 26-2). In this case the behavioral task is usually one that requires a number of daily sessions to learn—a maze, for example. The animal is given an injection of a stimulant drug shortly after each training session. If the drug is given after the trial, then it cannot affect behavior during training but only affects the cerebral afteractivity. It has been found that several excitant drugs can speed the course of learning. That is, the drug-injected animals reached the criterion sooner and with fewer errors than did controls. This is sometimes called retrograde facilitation of memory, since the post-trial treatment appears to work back on the training session, although it actually works forward on formation of the memory trace. Further experiments showed that the more closely in time the drug injections follow the daily learning trials, the more they facilitate learning. This was found

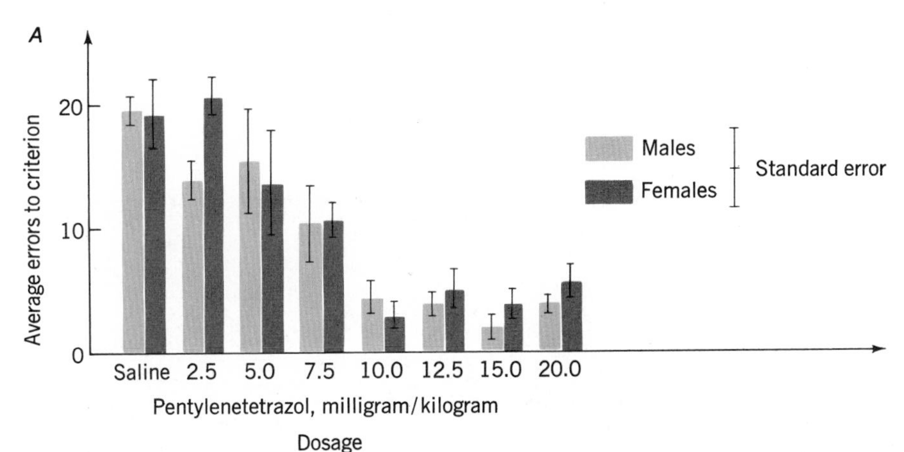

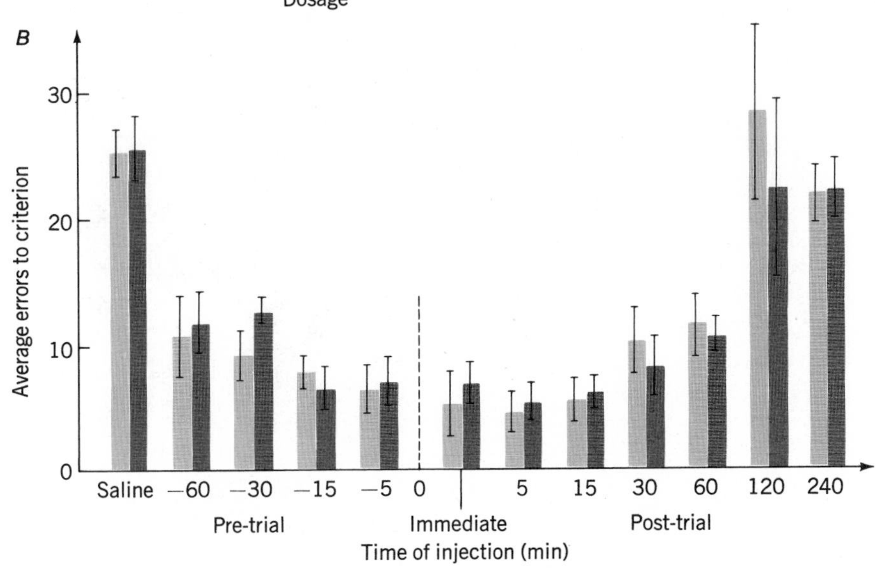

FIGURE 26-2
BRAIN STIMULATION AND LEARNING INCREASES

Giving small doses of certain stimulant drugs before or after each daily learning session can help rats to learn a maze faster than control animals do.

A. With increasing dosage of the drug, there are progressively fewer errors to reach criterion, until the optimal dosage—for these subjects and for this task. A separate group of subjects was tested with each dosage.
(Krivanek & McGaugh, 1968)

B. Improvement could be obtained—for these subjects and for this task—if the drug was given as much as 60 minutes before daily trials or as much as 60 minutes after daily trials. Somewhat different time courses have been reported in other studies.
(McGaugh & Krivanek, 1970)

by using several groups, each receiving drugs at a different interval after the learning sessions. Positive effects are obtained even with a one-hour delay between training and drug injections (see Figure 26-2). Thus chemical facilitation of neural activity appears to aid consolidation just as disruption by ECS appears to impair it. For some effects of drugs on human learning, see Spotlight 26-1.

Two Kinds of Memory

Certain biopsychological observations and experiments support the distinction between processes underlying short-term memory and longer-lasting memories. Some senile patients and others suffering from certain brain diseases seem to be unable to form new long-term memories, although they retain their old memories and they can form new short-term memories. Such patients can carry on a conversation, so it is clear that they retain their language habits, but they forget the conversation completely a few minutes after it is over. Similarly, they remember their families and their friends of earlier times, but they are unable to retain the names of new people they meet.

How are life-long memories stored in the brain?
(Ted Polumbaum)

SPOTLIGHT 26-1

Effects of Drugs on Human Learning and Memory

Recently doctors have been prescribing small doses of excitant drugs to many school children who seem to be overactive or "hyperkinetic." For unknown reasons, these drugs often quiet down an overactive child, although they would excite a normally active child or an adult. It has also been reported that the drugs enable the previously overactive child to concentrate better and to learn more.

Some researchers suspect that the improvement in learning may be independent of the quieting effect of the drug. Perhaps most children would learn better with small and well-controlled doses of certain excitant drugs, but we are not likely to find out soon. It is obvious that there are important social and ethical barriers to research of this sort with human subjects, especially if their behavior is normal and does not call for therapy.

One possible and justifiable avenue for further research with human subjects would be to test the effects of administering the drugs after class to overactive children who need help. Just as in previous animal studies, this might allow a separation between effects during the learning session (improved attention and concentration) and effects on consolidation of memory. If post-session administration improves memory, then effects on attention and concentration are not required (although they might help too). The other clearly feasible avenue of research is to learn more about these effects with animal subjects.

While excitant drugs can, under some conditions, improve learning and memory, depressant drugs can impair them. A striking example is that under appropriate doses of some general anesthetics, a person can converse or even show short-term memory for novel items, but the memory is lost after anesthesia wears off. (This again supports the distinction between processes of short-term and long-term memory.) For example, the drug scopalamine may be used during childbirth, so that the mother can respond to the doctor's directions and help with the birth. But afterward there is no memory of the event. Experimental studies have confirmed this, showing only poor memory afterward for items that were learned well during the anesthetic state (Osborn *et al.,* 1967). Intelligent behavior and consciousness are not enough to guarantee that lasting memories are being laid down.

In a few cases such inability to form new long-term memories has been caused inadvertently by brain operations. One surgeon tried to treat patients with severe epileptic seizures, which could not be controlled by medication, by removing tissue from the bottom of both temporal lobes including part of the lower cortex called the **hippocampus** (see Figure 26-3); this is an old region of cortex in evolutionary terms. Patients who had this operation no longer had seizures, but neither could they form long-lasting memories. They retained memories that were formed before the operation; and they

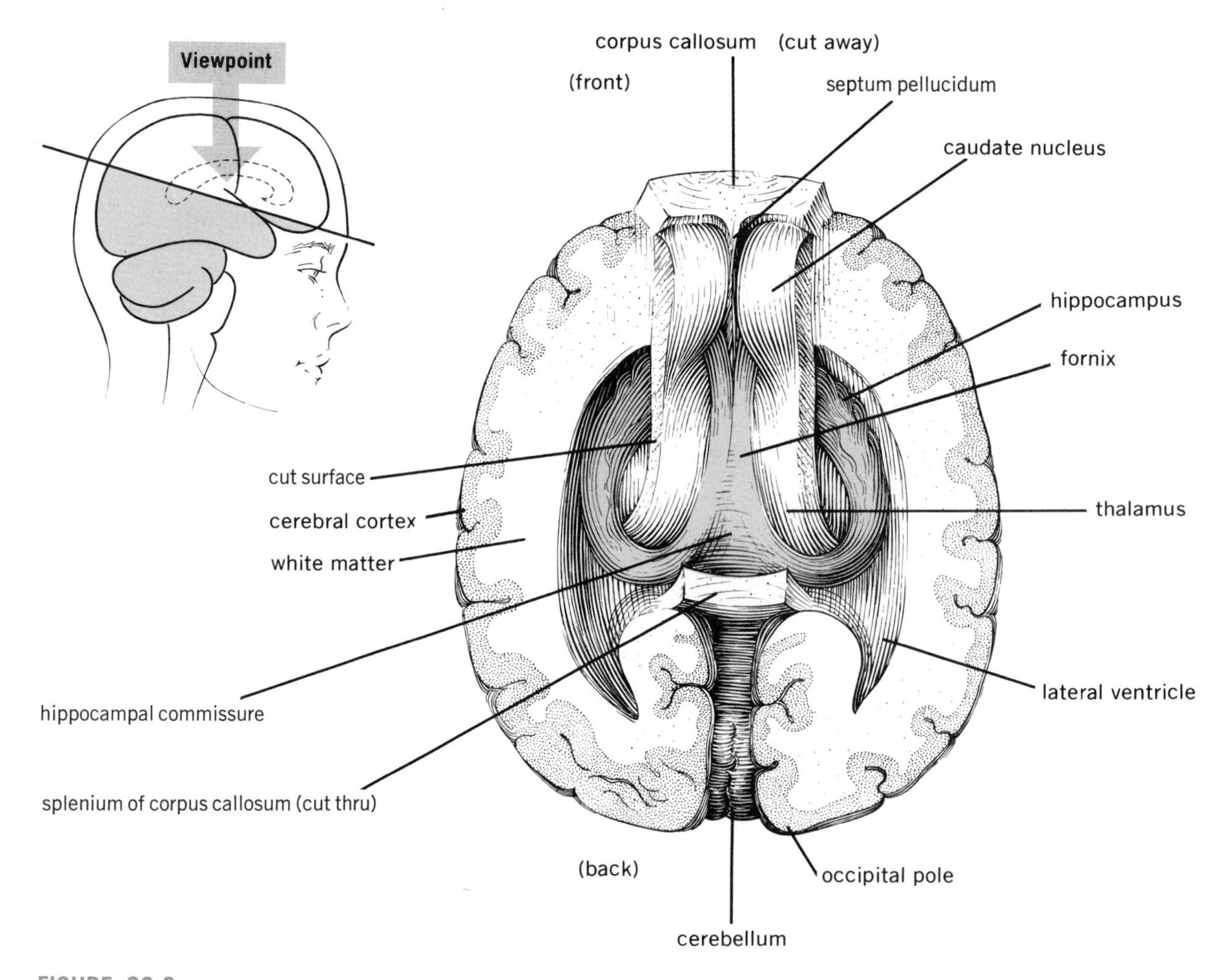

FIGURE 26-3
THE HIPPOCAMPUS—OLD CORTEX IMPLICATED IN MEMORY STORAGE
The brain is cut to show the position of the hippocampus and other structures. The upper portion of the cerebral hemispheres is removed, as indicated by the small diagram at the left, and the cross section is viewed from above. The corpus callosum has been cut and most of it removed, exposing the lateral ventricles, which normally are filled with cerebrospinal fluid. The hippocampus curves around the floor of the lateral ventricles. The large caudate nucleus (named for its long tail) is one of the basal ganglia.

could form new short-term memories so they could carry on a conversation, which requires remembering only the last few sentences. But if a visitor left the patient and came back a few minutes later, the patient would greet him as if he had not been there earlier. Such a patient seems to live in a short present time span, but with memories from the distant past. Occasionally he may show some awareness that he suffers from a reduced time span. One such patient would sometimes say anxiously, "Right now, I'm wondering, have I done or said something amiss? You see, at this moment everything looks clear to me, but what happened just before? That's what worries me. It's like waking from a dream; I just don't remember." (Milner, 1966)

A few animal experiments have also indicated that short-term or intermediate-term memories may be present even when there is no evidence of long-term memories. In the passive avoidance experiments that we reviewed above (p. 725), the recall tests were usually conducted twenty-four hours or longer after the training trial. Recent experiments have included some groups tested a few hours after training as well as the usual group tested at twenty-four hours. Under some conditions, retention is shown for a few hours but not for a longer period (Geller & Jarvik, 1968; Agranoff, 1967). Presumably the ECS or the drug that interfered with consolidation of long-term memory did not abolish the intermediate-term memory process. Thus, such results support the idea that different brain processes underlie memories of different durations.

How are memories stored in the brain?

The ancient Greeks could do no better than liken the brain to a tabula rasa or blank wax tablet on which experience engraves its messages. John Locke, the eighteenth-century philosopher, returned to this image. By that time, however, most philosophers followed Descartes in thinking of the nerves as narrow tubes that conducted thin fluids, "animal spirits," that caused the muscles to contract. Learning in this hydraulic system was thought to occur by enlarging tubes and turning valves so that the fluids tended to go in one direction rather than another. By the middle of the nineteenth century, the bioelectrical nature of the nerve impulse was recognized, but neurons were supposed to merge into each other anatomically, so it was not known what kept neural messages separate. In 1890 the synapse was recognized, and in 1893 it was hypothesized that learn-

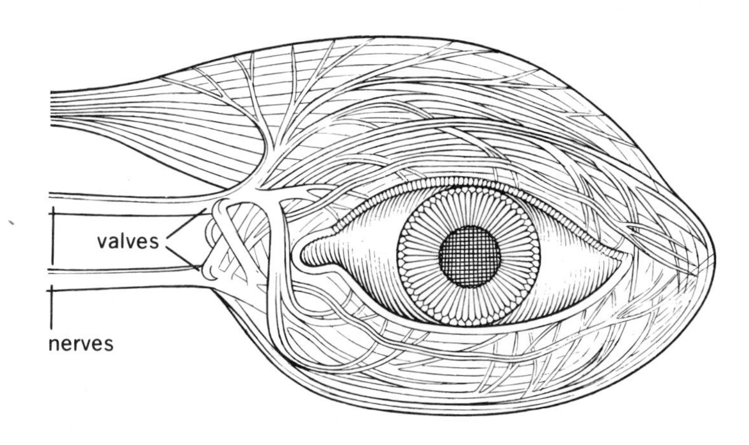

The drawing illustrates Descartes's concept of the nerves as hollow tubes with valves to control the flow of neural fluid. The nerves are portrayed as branching extensively around the eye and the eye muscles.

ing might involve changes in synapses or even growth of new synapses. In the last few years research techniques have allowed us to test this anatomical hypothesis, and we will soon look at some of the results.

Another possible kind of storage might be in the electrical rhythms of the brain. Recording of these rhythms was begun in the 1920's by means of the electroencephalogram (EEG). (Examples of such recordings during waking and sleep were shown in Figure 25-6.) An accidental observation in 1935 showed that the EEG could be conditioned. Two French psychologists were studying the fact that shining a light in the eyes usually blocks the ten-per-second electrical rhythm (the alpha rhythm) recorded from the back of the head. They were making repeated recordings of this phenomenon when, on one trial, the switch clicked but the light did not go on—nevertheless the subject's alpha rhythm ceased. Instead of ignoring this one "bad trial," they decided to investigate the unexpected result. It turned out that the blocking of the alpha had been conditioned to the click that had consistently accompanied the onset of light. Once these findings were published, other investigators confirmed and extended the results. Today studies of conditioning of electrical activity of brain regions or even of single brain cells are being carried on in many laboratories.

Possible chemical mechanisms in memory storage are also under active investigation. In the 1950's it was shown that hereditary information is encoded in molecules of DNA (deoxyribonucleic acid); these molecules make up the chromosomes that had already been identified as the genetic material in the nucleus of every cell in the body. Once the "genetic code" had been solved, it was suggested in 1958 by the Swedish neurochemist Holger Hydén that memory might also be encoded chemically. He suggested that memory might be stored in molecules of RNA (ribonucleic acid). RNA is involved in using genetic information from DNA to govern the synthesis of proteins along the forms laid down by heredity. Since the late 1950's there has been much research to determine whether changes in RNA or synthesis of protein are required for memory storage.

Now let us review in more detail the studies on possible anatomical, electrophysiological, and chemical ways of storing memories.

Anatomical Changes

During the last decade a few groups of investigators have shown that the brain is more plastic chemically and anatomically—more subject to experience—than had been supposed. A group at Berkeley has demonstrated that putting rats in enriched or impoverished environments for a few weeks brings about significant changes in a number of anatomical as well as chemical brain measures (Bennett *et al.*, 1964; Rosenzweig *et al.*, 1972a). The enriched condition (EC) is a large cage provided with stimulus objects or "toys" and housing ten to twelve rats (see Figure 26-4). The impoverished condition (IC) is simply a small individual cage with no stimuli beyond

FIGURE 26-4
EFFECT OF EXPERIENCE ON BRAINS OF RATS

In most laboratories, rats live in colony cages like those shown above. A relatively enriched environment, like that below, leads to enhanced development of brain chemistry and brain anatomy. A restricted environment with each rat housed singly (right) depresses brain development. (Courtesy M. R. Rosenzweig)

the usual cage environment. The animals from enriched and impoverished conditions are compared with those from the standard colony (SC) condition where animals live three per cage. Being placed in the EC cage for two hours a day over a thirty-day period is sufficient to produce statistically significant changes in the brain. When EC rats are compared with brothers kept in IC, the EC rats have heavier and thicker cerebral cortices and larger neuronal cell bodies and neuronal nuclei. The larger nuclei were depicted in Figure 8 of the preview. The EC rats also have an increased number of dendritic spines, the little projections that occur on certain branches of neurons. (See color Figure 7 for spines and synapses.) (See Table 26-1 for effects.) These effects are extremely reliable, some of them having been found in experiment after experiment over a thirteen-year period (see Figure 26-5). The larger neuronal nuclei of enriched-experience as compared to impoverished-experience rats suggests that animals in EC have more active neurons than littermates in IC. (Somewhat analogously, it turns out that well-fed rats develop larger neural nuclei in the ventromedial hypothalamus than do underfed rats. On some measures, EC goes up and IC goes down, as compared to the SC baseline.

The tiny synaptic junctions can now be visualized in detail with the high magnifications afforded by electron microscopes. So we are beginning to be able to test hypotheses about synaptic changes with learning—hypotheses that were proposed in the 1890's,

TABLE 26-1
BRAIN MEASURES IN WHICH SIGNIFICANT CHANGES HAVE BEEN PRODUCED BY PUTTING RATS IN DIFFERENTIAL ENVIRONMENTS FOR SEVERAL WEEKS

Type of Measure	Direction of Change +, EC greater than IC −, EC less than IC
Anatomical measures	
Weights of brain sections	+
Thickness of cerebral cortex	+
Number of glial cells per unit of cortex	+
Size of neuronal cell bodies	+
Size of neuronal nuclei	+
Number of dendritic spines	+
Cross sections of synaptic junctions	+
Number of synaptic junctions	−
Biochemical measures	
Acetylcholinesterase activity per unit of tissue weight	−
Cholinesterase activity per unit of weight	+
RNA per unit of DNA	+

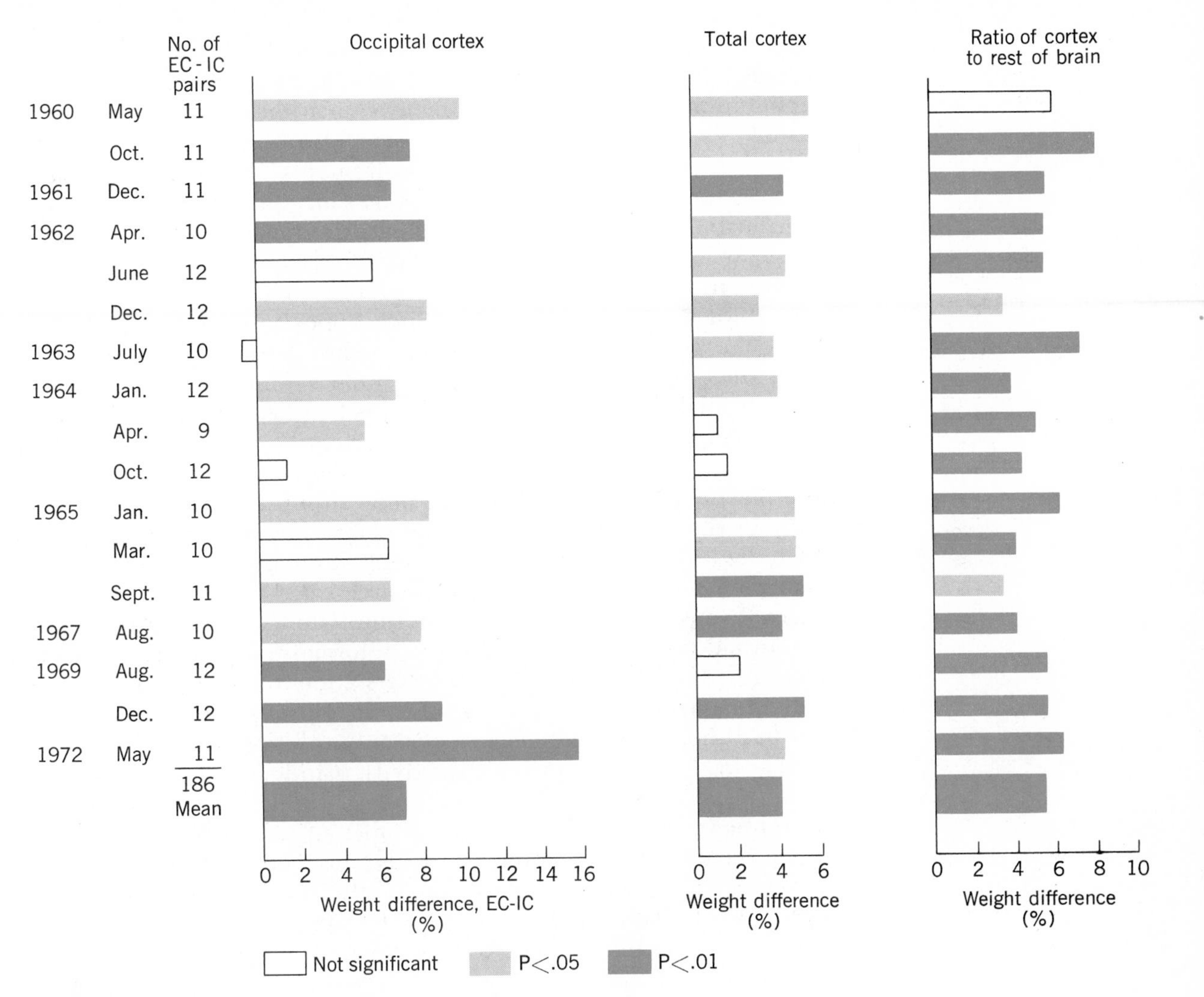

FIGURE 26-5
EFFECT OF EXPERIENCE ON BRAIN WEIGHT

The figure shows results of 17 experiments conducted from 1960 through 1972 with male rats of the Berkeley S_1 strain. The animals were put in the differential environments at 25 days of age and removed at 105 days of age. Percentage differences between enriched (EC) and impoverished (IC) groups of each experiment are shown. Most of the differences are statistically significant, especially for the ratio of weight of cerebral cortex to weight of the rest of the brain.

almost as soon as the synapse was discovered. At that time it was suggested that learning might promote the formation of new or larger and more effective synaptic junctions among neurons. This would have the effect of "wiring in" new circuits in the brain, in addition to those provided innately. A few theorists have also suggested that increased specificity of brain circuits could be achieved by systematic elimination of undesired or random connections among neurons.

Information can be increased either by additive or subtractive processes, just as an artist can make a figure either by joining and shaping lumps of clay or by cutting away marble to reveal the statue within.

Recent counts and measurements of synapses indicate that both positive and negative changes may be induced through experience. Thus, rats given enriched experience showed, in comparison with impoverished-experience littermates, larger but fewer synapses in a particular part of the cerebral cortex (Møllgaard *et al.*, 1971; West & Greenough, 1972). Such opposite effects in size and number of synapses have also been reported from experiments in which some animals were prevented from seeing while others had normal visual experience. We can expect to hear more about such detailed brain measures and learning during the next few years.

From these studies we can see that the brain is much more plastic anatomically than had been supposed. It is tempting to conclude that learning causes these changes and that they are associated with memory storage, but scientists are professional skeptics. Some point out that most of the research cited here has dealt with effects of sensory stimulation or opportunity to learn (EC) rather than with formal training. Experiments with formal training have, in fact, shown less clear cerebral results. Others argue that the results might be due to associated variables. That is, the enriched condition differs from the impoverished condition not only in opportunities to learn, but also in the amount of bodily activity it induces, in the handling of the animals, possibly in stress, and so on. Control experiments have already demonstrated that a number of such related variables cannot account for the cerebral effects obtained, but that does not prove that the effects are due to learning. In brief, evidence is mounting for the hypothesis that anatomical changes underlie long-term memory storage, but it is not yet conclusive.

Electrophysiological Changes

Animals with electrodes implanted in many regions of the brain have been studied during various sorts of training procedures. When the animal is learning that one stimulus is a signal for reward while another stimulus signals no reward, the electrical responses to the stimuli are very widely spread throughout the brain. As conditioning progresses, these patterns of electrical responses change (John & Killam, 1959; John, 1967). The fact that many parts of the brain are involved is understandable, since most learning undoubtedly involves a number of sensory and motor patterns. As the animal becomes proficient in making trained discriminations among stimuli and in performing the required response efficiently, the patterns of activity in the brain become restricted to a few regions.

During such conditioning, investigators have observed that specific learned patterns of electrical brain activity (called "tracer patterns") sometimes appear spontaneously between trials. For example, if a light flashes on and off seven times per second to signal reward, electrical activity at this frequency sometimes occurs in the brain when no stimulus is being presented, most commonly when conditioning is improving rapidly; it drops out after the conditioned response has become fully established. This spontaneous appearance of learned patterns is reminiscent of the perseveration (rehearsal) of verbal material that Müller and Pilzecker observed at the beginning of the century. It is consistent with the hypothesis of a memory trace made up of reverberating neural impulses, but it also implies some other mechanism of storage, since the tracer pattern dies out and then reappears. Some other form of storage must exist to make it possible for the tracer rhythm to start up again.

Microelectrode techniques are also being used to study electrical activity of single cells while rats are learning which stimulus is the signal of reward. Recent work indicates that early in learning changes occur in cells in the brain stem reticular formation (see Figure 25-8) and in reinforcing areas of the hypothalamus. Later in the learning process other changes occur in the cerebral cortex (Halas, Beardsley, & Sandlie, 1970).

Neurochemical Changes

Much of the current work on neurochemical changes during learning involves ribonucleic acid (RNA). RNA controls and directs the formation of protein in cells; since protein synthesis is responsible for the growth of cells and the production of transmitter chemicals at the synapse, it is a logical place to look for "memory" substance.

A number of influential studies conducted at North Carolina (Adair *et al.*, 1968; Kahan *et al.*, 1970) indicate that, as predicted, the synthesis of RNA increases in brain cells with training. The investigators conditioned mice to avoid an electric shock by jumping to a shelf when a light and buzzer were activated. Typically, thirty trials were given over a fifteen-minute training period. Another group of mice (the control group) received exactly the same light, buzzer, and shock, but there was no shelf to which they could jump to escape (i.e., for them there was no task to learn). In order to measure RNA synthesis during the experiment, the animals were injected thirty minutes prior to training with a compound that is used by the body to synthesize RNA. The compound was made radioactive to "tag" it and thus permit later measurement of how much had gone into RNA during training. After the training session the RNA in the brains was extracted and the radioactivity was measured. In mice sacrificed immediately after training, there was increased incorporation of the radioactive tracer into the RNA of the nervous tissue, significantly more than in the control mice. This increase occurred chiefly in the diencephalon, which includes the thalamus and hypothalamus.

If formal training leads to the formation of more RNA, this should later lead to more protein. Evidence of increased protein synthesis during avoidance training in rats was found in a well-designed and carefully executed study (Beach *et al.*, 1969). Brother animals were assigned to experimental or control conditions. The learning task was similar to the one described above in which the experimental rats had to respond to the light-buzzer signal in order to avoid shock. Each set of rats was sacrificed only three minutes after the conditioned rat had made its first avoidance response. The increase of protein synthesis was found in certain areas (the hippocampus, basal cortex, and septum) of the trained animals but not in the controls. There were no differences in other brain areas or in the liver. It is surprising that increased protein synthesis was found after only a brief training session.

The effects on RNA of prolonged differential experience, lasting for weeks, has been studied recently in rats (Rosenzweig, Bennett, & Diamond, 1972b). Some animals were kept in groups in an enriched environment while others were confined singly to restricted-experience cages, as was described above (see Figure 26-4). The enriched-experience rats, as compared to their impoverished-experience littermates, showed an increase of RNA per cell in the cortex as well as an increase in protein. It is interesting that in the *prolonged* experiments, the largest chemical changes are found in the cerebral cortex, whereas in the *brief* experiments they are found in the lower brain areas. This suggests a similarity to results of recent microelectrode work which also indicates a sequence of changes from heightened activity in lower brain areas early in learning to heightened activity in the cortex later in learning.

Speculation about the possible role of RNA in memory storage has led some investigators to attempt to transfer memory from one animal to another by transferring brain chemicals. This controversial research is discussed in Spotlight 26-2.

Where in the brain do learning and memory storage occur?

A variety of procedures have been employed to attempt to determine what parts of the nervous system are most important in learning and memory storage. These procedures include comparison of capacities of animal forms with different types of nervous systems, removal of cerebral tissue or severing of cerebral tracts. We have already seen some indications of localization in our discussions of electrical recording from different sites within the nervous system during conditioning and localization of anatomical and chemical changes in the brain as consequences of training.

SPOTLIGHT 26-2
Can Memory Be Injected?

A great deal of publicity has been given in the last few years to reports of what might be termed memory by injection. Animals can be trained in a habit, for example, to go to the lighted part of an apparatus in order to avoid shock or to press one of a pair of levers in order to obtain food. Chemical extracts can then be made from their brains and these can be injected into other animals who have had no experience with the task. When tested in the apparatus, the naïve recipients then appear—according to some reports—to show the effects of the training given to the donor animals, as though the naïve animals had acquired by injection the memories of the donor animals.

If memory could be injected, this would afford a wonderful tool for working on the chemistry of memory. Neurochemists could analyze the brain extracts, and using behavioral tests, could determine which chemical components were effective in producing the same results as training. The next step would be to synthesize the active compounds—to manufacture memory molecules! If this could be done, then animals—and perhaps eventually students—could acquire knowledge by the spoonful or by the syringeful.

So far, however, the reports of the basic phenomena remain controversial; many investigators have been unable to produce the alleged effects in their own laboratories. I took part in a large-scale unsuccessful effort of this sort (Byrne *et al.,* 1966), but a few laboratories have reported consistent successes (see chapters in Byrne, 1970). Unless and until an effect can be produced reliably, it is not under control, and little can be done with it. For the present, at least, the only route to memory is through learning.

Learning in Simpler Nervous Systems

A large brain like that of a mammal is not required for learning and long-term memory storage, since these phenomena are found even in insects. Maze learning and conditioning have been claimed even in the primitive planarian (flatworm). Even part of a relatively simple nervous system can learn, since conditioning has been demonstrated in a single ganglion of an insect. To show this, the experimenter takes from the body of a locust a segment that contains two legs and a neural ganglion with sensory and motor connections to the legs. If one leg is then shocked whenever it is lowered, it will soon be kept raised most of the time, while the other leg will be lowered as often as before.

Apparently it does not require much neural tissue to learn, in a simpler animal, but that does not guarantee the same is true in a complex animal. As we saw earlier, form perception is accomplished in the retina in the frog, but in a mammal the cerebral cortex is required (see p. 674). The spinal cord of a mammal is certainly more complex than the nervous system of an insect, yet experimenters have not found clear evidence of conditioning in the spinal cord. When connections between the brain and spinal cord are severed, learning can still be accomplished in the upper parts of the body served by the brain, but no learning is achieved by the lower parts of the body, even though the spinal circuits still support many reflex functions. If a person's spinal cord is severed in the middle of the back, he can still learn mental and manual skills, but he loses all control of his legs; although spinal reflexes of the legs persist, no new reflexes of the legs can be learned.

Mammalian Nervous System

Widely divergent hypotheses have been proposed about the loci of learning within the mammalian brain. Pavlov believed that conditioning requires the presence of the cerebral cortex and that it involves the creation of "temporary connections" within the cortex. These connections he thought extended from sensory to motor areas of the cortex, creating new "reflex arcs." On the other hand, the distinguished neurologist Wilder Penfield proposed that the fundamental connections in learning and conscious processes occur in the basal center of the brain (the diencephalon) and that the cortex only elaborates the sensory and motor detail. Although the complete answer to this problem is not yet available, investigators have been able to test and to discard as incorrect the hypotheses of both Pavlov and Penfield. The methods employed in these experiments have been to test behavior after either the removal of brain tissue or the severing of brain tracts.

Some conditioning can be obtained in mammals even after all cerebral cortex has been removed. For example, a dog with cortex removed can learn to lift its paw whenever a light flash occurs in order to avoid shock. Such conditioning occurs slowly and irregularly, however, because such animals tend to be distractable and irritable and they do not have keen sensory discrimination. But the evidence is clearly antagonistic to Pavlov's claim that the cortex is necessary. When cortex is present, it is employed in conditioning, but the learned connections do not run horizontally through the cortex from sensory to motor areas, as Pavlov supposed. This is shown by the fact that cross-hatching the cortex with knife cuts, thus severing connections between cortical areas, has little effect on retention or on sensory or motor performance. Instead, the connections employed in the learned behavior appear to loop under the cortex or they go up and down between thalamus and cortex.

Learning can be restricted to a single cerebral hemisphere by putting the cortex of the other hemisphere temporarily out of function. This is done by treating the cortex of one hemisphere with potassium chloride or with a strong localized electrical shock that has the effect of temporarily "depressing" its function. When a rat is placed in a maze or other learning situation with one hemisphere depressed (e.g., the right), it can learn with the other, the left hemisphere. If it is later put back in the apparatus with the left (trained) hemisphere depressed, it shows no memory for the problem. Tested later with the right hemisphere depressed but the left functioning, it again shows that it had learned. In brief, memory for this learning seems to be confined to one hemisphere. If, however, the rat is once tested with both hemispheres functioning normally, the memory then spreads rapidly to the right hemisphere and thereafter either one shows the memory (Bureš & Burešová, 1970).

The fact that memory can be confined to one hemisphere in these experiments refutes Penfield's hypothesis that learning occurs in the basal core of the brain. Since the diencephalon has connections with both hemispheres, any learning occurring in the base of the brain should be available to whichever hemisphere is functioning, but this was not found. **Split-brain** subjects, to be described next, also show learning restricted to a single hemisphere.

Split-Brain Research

The two hemispheres of the cortex can be permanently disconnected by transecting the **corpus callosum,** the main interhemispheric tract of nerve connections. This is done occasionally in patients suffering from severe epilepsy to prevent it from spreading from one side to the other and incapacitating the person. Results of hemisphere disconnection were first studied extensively in animals. For example, cats have had both the callosum and the **optic chiasm** sectioned so that each eye is connected only with the hemisphere on its own side. Such a cat can learn with the left eye that ∨ stands for reward but that ∧ does not, while with the right eye it can learn to go to ∧ rather than to ∨. (See Figure 26-6.) Each hemisphere is ignorant of what the other has learned (Sperry, Stamm, & Miner, 1956). This again refutes the hypothesis of learning in the diencephalon, since this remains intact. Incidentally, it is worth noting that, in the cat,

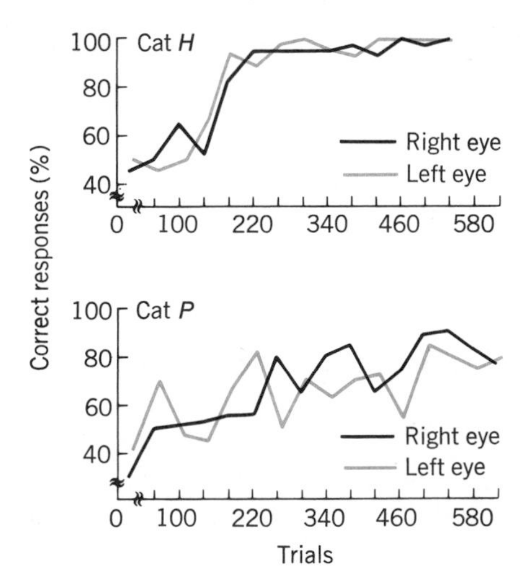

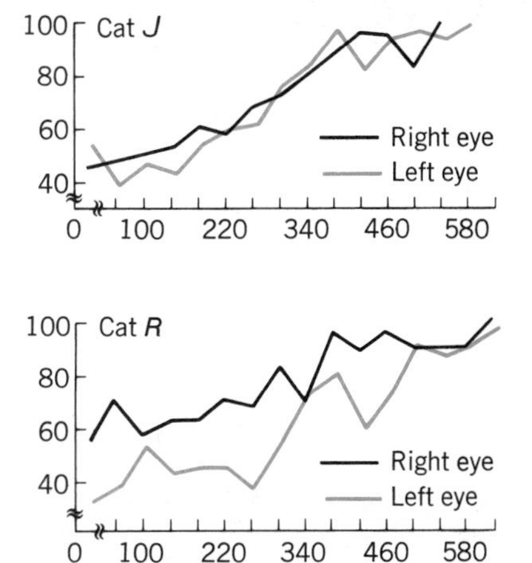

FIGURE 26-6 LEARNING BY SEPARATED HEMISPHERES IN THE SAME HEAD

The brains of cats were split—both the corpus callosum and the optic chiasm were transected. After the operation, when one eye was covered, only the opposite hemisphere received visual input. The two hemispheres of a cat could thus be trained separately, and the graphs demonstrate that the two hemispheres of each cat had similar learning curves. (Modified from Sperry, Stamm, & Miner, 1956) the independent learning curves of the two hemispheres are as similar as if the two hemispheres were identical twins.

In human split-brain patients, the hemispheres not only function separately but unlike the case of the cat, they also function somewhat differently (Gazzaniga, 1970). Certain tasks can be carried out by either side. Thus, such a person can understand even fairly complex instructions with either hemisphere. For example, a split-brain woman could touch a few objects without seeing them and then signal with her raised fingers how many were there. This could be done accurately with either hand, so long as the same hand did both parts of the task. (Each hand, its sensory and motor connections, is associated with only one hemisphere.) But if she was asked to touch with one hand and to signal with the other, she could not perform the task, since with the corpus callosum transected, neither hemisphere has access to the memories in the other. A similar disability was shown by the split-brain man in preview Figure 5. For some tasks one hemisphere is superior to the other, as we noted in the case of dichotic hearing, p. 685, and in the case of perception of form and space, p. 686; for most people, the left hemisphere is superior in perception of speech, whereas the right hemisphere is superior in perception of music, form, and space.

Electrical and Chemical Localization

You will recall that recording from many electrode sites during conditioning has shown widespread activity early in the training. Learned electrical patterns occur in sensory tracts, in the cerebral cortex, the midbrain reticular formation, the hippocampus, and other diverse sites. Later, when conditioning has been accomplished, the patterns showed a more restricted distribution. Since most learning involves a variety of sensory and motor adjustments, especially while the subject is trying to find what the problem is about, it is not surprising to find many brain areas participating in the early stages.

Short-term training experiments show chemical changes chiefly in the diencephalon, whereas long-term experiments with differential experience show effects chiefly in the cerebral cortex (see p. 734). Other recent studies employing quite different techniques (Paolino & Levy, 1971) also suggest that short-term memory processes are chiefly subcortical, whereas the formation of long-term memories requires the participation of the cerebral cortex.

What are the basic assumptions of a model of memory processes?

A hypothetical model is useful to suggest how neural potentials and chemical processes might work in storing memories in the brain and how different regions of the brain participate in memory storage. This model should not be taken as being correct—it goes beyond existing data in some ways and is undoubtedly over-simple in other ways—but it illustrates current thinking about these problems.

The model assumes that learning occurs through changes in connections among neurons. For simplicity, we will consider only changes occurring through transforming nonfunctional synapses into functional connections. Let us suppose that a given synapse can exist in three functional states, as illustrated in Figure 26-7. The receptor proteins on the dendritic side may be in a form that blocks conduction (symbolized by △ in *A*). In this form they will not respond if the transmitter substance is released from the end button, so no impulse will be conducted across the synapse. Or the receptor proteins may temporarily be in a conformation (symbolized by ⊔ in *B*) that accepts and reacts with the transmitter chemical. In this case the impulse can bridge the synaptic gap. There may be some spontaneous shifts of molecules from one form to the other; the receptive form (⊔) tends to go back to the unreceptive form (△) but sometimes the reverse change also occurs. There are many proteins that can shift from

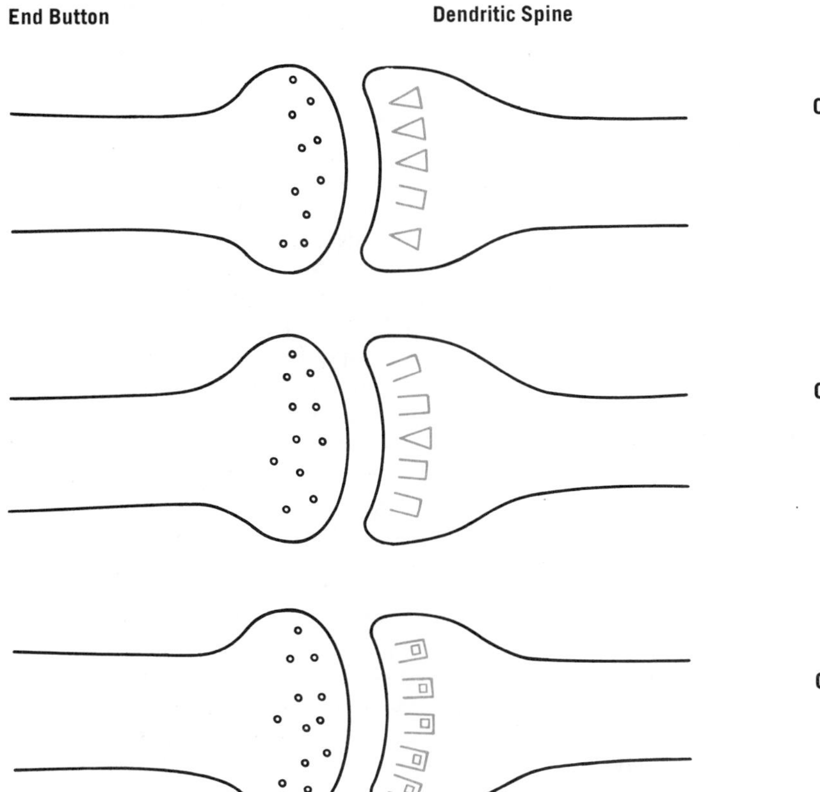

PROPERTIES OF SYNAPSE

Conformation *A*

Relatively stable
Little connectivity
Nonfunctional pathway

Conformation *B*

Unstable
Temporary connectivity
Functional pathway
(Short-term memory)

Conformation *C*

Stable
Permanent connectivity
Functional pathway
(Long-term memory)

FIGURE 26-7
A MODEL FOR SYNAPTIC EVENTS IN SHORT-TERM AND LONG-TERM MEMORY
(Modified from Glassman, Machlus, & Wilson, 1972)

SPOTLIGHT 26-3
Are Memories Formed During Sleep?

You may have seen ads for a tape recorder device with a small speaker that fits under your pillow and "teaches" you while you sleep. Psychologists have tested whether "sleep learning" actually occurs. Part of the problem turns out to be defining whether the subject is actually asleep. Retention is good for material learned just before going to sleep, perhaps because there is relatively little interfering learning going on then. So the recording will be helpful if you turn it on as soon as you go to bed, especially if the sound keeps you awake long enough to accomplish some learning. Once you fall asleep, you may be awakened by a change in stimulation, as when the recorder goes on or off. If learning occurs at these times, again it is not truly "sleep learning." To obtain a definitive answer, investigators have used EEG recordings to monitor the state of sleep, as we described in the last chapter, p. 701. If verbal material (short sentences) is presented only when the person is in deep slow-wave sleep, and if he remains deeply asleep, there is no memory for the material at later tests. But if presentation of the sentences causes the person to awaken for thirty seconds or more, as shown by his EEG, then he can later remember the material (Koukkou & Lehmann, 1968). The conclusion of several such studies has been that while you may learn from the recorder, this cannot truly be called "sleep learning."

But, if you are a person who remembers dreams, you may properly ask if dreams are not material learned during sleep and retained afterward. Yes, they certainly are, but the ones that people remember are usually only a small proportion of the total. How many dreams do you remember from a night, on the average? There are many people who rarely remember any. Individuals differ in this, but it is rather unusual to remember more than one dream from a night, although the average young adult has each night about

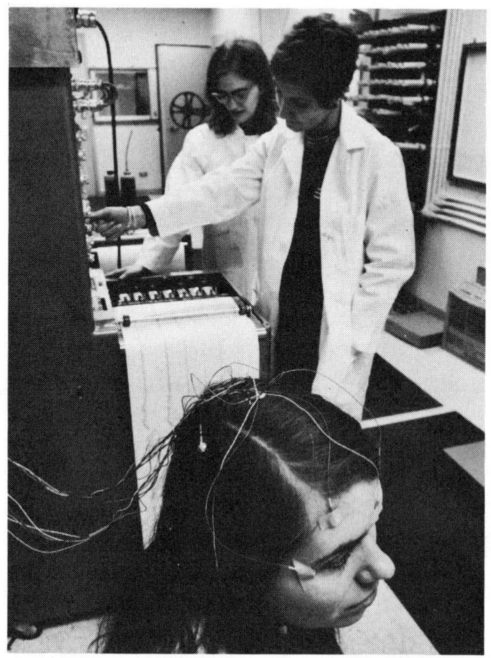

(Van Bucher, Photo Researchers; courtesy NYU Research Center for Mental Health)

five fairly long periods of sleep thought to be "dream" sleep (rapid eye movements—REM—and fast, low-voltage brain waves). If awakened several times during the night in successive REM periods, a different dream will usually be reported on each occasion. But if a person is awakened only a few minutes after the end of an REM period, usually he has no dream to report. It is likely that the only dreams that are remembered are those that cause a person to awaken briefly or those that are followed by a period of light sleep. Just as with material presented experimentally to a sleeper, if deep slow-wave sleep follows a dream, then the dream is unlikely to be retained in long-term memory. Thus sleep may be somewhat like the state of light general anesthesia in which thought processes are carried out and short-term memories are formed, but in which conditions oppose the consolidation of long-term memories.

one shape to another and thus change their functional properties—for example, the visual pigment molecules in the rods and cones behave this way.

If occasional impulses arrive at a synapse like *A*, they find it nonfunctional. However, if a strong volley of impulses arrives at *A*, the few active receptor molecules will respond repeatedly and their potentials may induce neighboring molecules to enter the receptive state too. Then the synapse as a whole becomes functional, as in *B*. As long as impulses keep arriving, and for a short time thereafter, the synapse remains functional; but when activity (stimulation and rehearsal) ceases, the synapse soon again becomes nonfunctional. This temporary opening of a neural pathway could serve to explain the formation and rapid decay of a short-term memory.

Now let us add one more assumption: While the receptor proteins are in a temporarily responsive form, they can be converted to a permanently responsive form (symbolized by |□| in *C*). This is brought about by arrival of molecules (symbolized by □) manufactured by neurons in basal areas of the brain. They could be conveyed across synaptic junctions from such neurons or perhaps they are transported in the bloodstream like hormones. If certain emotional or motivational events occur during or shortly after training, it is known that the circuits that have recently been activated will tend to become permanent. The present hypothesis explains this by supposing that "reinforcement molecules" from the basal brain can consolidate patterns of neural activity that are accompanied or followed by desirable consequences or by favorable internal states. They would also consolidate any pattern that occurred frequently enough, so that sheer repetition or rehearsal would ensure permanence of the neural connections. This would provide a basis for long-term memory. Further anatomical changes in size and number of synapses could also follow.

According to the model, learning would involve early electrical activity throughout the brain and early chemical events in the basal brain. In higher brain centers the early unstable changes in receptor conformation could not be detected, but the later stable chemical changes supporting long-term memory could be measured. Such a model provides a molecular basis for the formation of neural pathways for both short-term and long-term memories. In the model, it is also possible to have short-term memory without formation of long-term memory (if the "consolidation" molecules do not arrive at the active receptor sites). Drugs that allow learning to occur but that interfere with formation of long-term memory (see p. 729) might act by preventing the manufacture or release of "consolidation molecules." The idea that synapses exist in different functional states is very likely to be related to mechanisms of memory even if the results of future research show that other specific processes are involved.

SUMMARY

Biopsychological research on learning and memory has led to multi-stage and multi-process hypotheses, just as has the research on human verbal memory that was discussed earlier in Chapter 19. That is, the findings have been interpreted as indicating that memory is first in a form that can easily be destroyed and that does not last long. A more durable memory may then form or "consolidate." One type of evidence for this hypothesis is that head injury often produces retrograde amnesia for a period of several minutes before the accident. Careful timing of interfering events can be achieved in animal experiments in which electroconvulsive shock is used to disrupt cerebral activity following the training trial. The rapidity with which memory becomes impervious to the electroconvulsive shock varies with the training situation and with the strength of the shock. Learning can also be facilitated by giving a stimulant drug after each training session, and this provides another sort of evidence for the consolidation hypothesis.

The hypothesis that there are different brain processes for short-term and for long-term memories is supported by observations of senile patients and by sufferers from certain brain lesions. These patients retain their old long-term memories but cannot form new ones. Since they can form short-term memories that last for seconds or minutes, they can carry on a conversation normally, but a few minutes after it is over, they have forgotten it completely.

The biological forms of the memory trace or engram is a subject of much current research. Changes in electrical activity of the brain, changes in neurochemistry, and changes in neural and synaptic structure have all been proposed as mechanisms of the memory trace, and evidence for each of these types of change has been reported. Since there are very likely different brain processes that underlie short-term, intermediate-term, and long-term memories, it is not surprising that a variety of types of cerebral changes are found. After training lasting only a few minutes, changes in RNA and protein synthesis have been reported. For long-term memory storage, anatomical (structural) changes seem likely, and these have been reported in experiments that last for days or weeks. Among the anatomical changes observed are alterations in size and number of the tiny synaptic junctions. It seems probable that the anatomical changes found after relatively prolonged experience may be the cumulative result of many successive episodes of increased synthesis of RNA and protein, such as are seen in the brief experiments.

The brain processes underlying learning and memory can to some extent be localized within the nervous system. Even animals with simple nervous systems can learn, but in mammals learning seems to occur principally in the cerebral hemispheres. Conditioning can be obtained after the cerebral cortex is totally removed, but no very fine discriminations can be achieved then. When the cortex is present, it seems to play a major role in learning. Different types of learning are restricted to different functional regions of the cortex. Learning and memory can be restricted to one cerebral hemisphere either by inactivating the other hemisphere or by cutting the major fiber tracts between the two hemispheres. Thus, in a split-brain person or animal, one hemisphere may have memories that are inaccessible to the other. Several sorts of evidence suggest that, at least in nonverbal training, short-term memory processes are chiefly subcortical, whereas the formation of long-term memories requires participation of the cortex.

Various biological states have major effects on learning and memory. Carefully controlled doses of excitant drugs can facilitate learning, as experiments with both man and other mammals have shown. On the other hand, under an appropriate dose of some anesthetic agents, a person may be able to converse and to learn novel items; yet he has no memory for these materials at a later time. In other words, short-term memories were formed but no long-term ones. During deep slow-wave sleep, it appears that no memories are formed, despite some commercial claims to the contrary. Some dreams may be remembered from the rapid eye movement, fast-wave stage of sleep, but most dreams seem to be forgotten within minutes after they have ended. Thus, anesthesia and sleep are cerebral conditions that appear to oppose the consolidation of long-term memories.

A hypothetical model has been proposed to show how different chemical changes at synapses can account for both short-term and long-term storage of memory. The model is useful because it offers a way of tying together several aspects of learning and memory and because it illustrates current thinking in this area.

RECOMMENDED READING

Calder, N. *The Mind of Man.* New York: Viking Press, 1970.
A fascinating account of current research on brain and behavior by a science journalist who visited laboratories around the world in 1970; many illustrations.

Gray, J. *The Psychology of Fear and Stress.* World University Library. New York: McGraw-Hill, 1971. Paperback.
A short readable account of emotional behavior and its biological bases.

McGaugh, J. L., Weinberger, N. M., & Whalen, R. E. *Psychobiology: The Biological Bases of Behavior.* San Francisco: W. H. Freeman Co., 1967. Both paperback and hardcover editions.
A collection of 45 articles reprinted from the *Scientific American* magazine, reflecting much of the scope of biological psychology. Readable and well illustrated.

Mark, V. H., & Ervin, F. R. *Violence and the Brain.* New York: Harper & Row, 1970. Both paperback and hardcover editions.

A readable account of research and case studies. The authors, a neurologist and a psychiatrist, conclude that many violent individuals suffer from brain dysfunctions that can be treated medically.

Milner, P. M. *Physiological Psychology.* New York: Holt, Rinehart and Winston, 1970.

A textbook for upper division courses; rather difficult. Many references.

Noback, C. R., & Demarest, R. J. *The Nervous System: Introduction and Review.* New York: McGraw-Hill, 1972. Paperback.

A concise introduction to neuroanatomy. The second author is a medical illustrator, and the drawings are clear and numerous.

Oswald, I. *Sleep.* Middlesex, England: Penguin, 1970. Paperback.

A lively, succinct, and reasonably up-to-date account by a psychologist-psychiatrist who has specialized in research on sleep.

Singh, D., & Morgan, C. T. *Current Status of Physiological Psychology: Readings.* Belmont, California: Brooks/Cole, 1972. Paperback.

A collection of 27 recent articles that reflect the range of research in current biological psychology.

Stevens, L. A. *Explorers of the Brain.* New York: Knopf, 1971.

The dramatic history of attempts to understand the brain, starting with 18th-century pioneer investigators but emphasizing the present century.

Teyler, T. J. *Altered States of Awareness.* San Francisco: W. H. Freeman Co., 1972. Paperback.

A collection of 14 articles reprinted from the *Scientific American* magazine, emphasizing changes in awareness and their brain mechanisms; topics include dreaming, boredom, drug-induced states, split-brain humans, and meditation.

Thompson, R. F. *Foundations of Physiological Psychology.* New York: Harper & Row, 1967.

A textbook for upper division courses. It includes material on related basic sciences; rather difficult. Many references.

——— *Physiological Psychology.* San Francisco: W. H. Freeman Co., 1972. Paperback.

A collection of 46 articles reprinted from the *Scientific American* magazine, showing considerable overlap with McGaugh *et al.*, but more recent.

Wilson, J. R. *The Mind.* Life Science Library. New York: Time, 1964.

A rather simple account of behavior and its neural mechanisms; profusely illustrated with photographs and diagrams.

SECTION NINE

COMPARATIVE PSYCHOLOGY

By Stephen E. Glickman

Preview

We live on a planet with 3,200 species of mammals, 8,600 species of birds, 20,000 species of fish, and several hundred thousand species of insects. In the comparison of these species—in their similarities and differences—there is much knowledge to be gained. The ways in which man, for example, is like all animals, the ways in which he is like some other animals, and the ways in which he is unique—this is information to be gained from a **comparative psychology.** Each individual species with its abilities and social interactions is of interest in its own right, and the need to know something of the interdependencies among species is reflected in the current concern about ecology. To provide knowledge on these issues is the goal of comparative psychologists.

The study of human and animal behavior was to be markedly affected by the publication in 1859 of Darwin's theory of **evolution through natural selection.** Darwin maintained that the variety and changes in animal form and function came about because, in any generation, some individuals possessed **selective advantages** that increased the chances of their survival in their environment. For example, a stronger or swifter individual is more likely to survive and reproduce, passing on those characteristics to his offspring. So natural selection operates, generation by generation, to bring about more adaptive bodily structure and behavior. The interaction between the demands of the environment and the responses of organisms can be seen as an ongoing feedback process. Although Darwin's original theory was concerned mostly with the evolution of anatomical structures, interest in the evolution of behavior came soon after. If human arms evolved from the same ancestral line as the limbs of mammals or the wings of birds, why should not our brain—and thus our thought processes and behavior patterns—be a product of evolution?

In its earliest stages, comparative psychology was heavily influenced by the implications and assumptions of evolutionary theory. One approach, which flourished in the United States, involved a search for humanlike characteristics in animals. Since great plasticity of behavior is most characteristic of man, scientists began looking for plasticity and flexibility in the behavior of animals. The resultant studies were usually of learning abilities, and they were conducted primarily in the laboratory, where careful experimental manipulations were feasible. General principles of learning, thought to apply to many species, were formulated. The popular book by B. F. Skinner, *Beyond Freedom and Dignity,* is in this tradition of generality of principles and of continuity of behavior among species.

A second line of investigation was directed at clarifying the ways in which the unique behavior patterns of different species adapted them for survival in particular ecological slots. Toward this end, a group of European and American zoologists began investigating the behavior of animals in their natural habitats; this approach has been termed **ethology.** Recently, some ethologists have begun to look for such behaviors in man. Popular books by Desmond Morris (e.g., *The Naked Ape*) and by Konrad Lorenz (e.g., *On Aggression*) reflect this tradition.

Thus we had, for many years, one group (chiefly in Europe) investigating differences among various species and another (chiefly in America) concerned with continuity and similarity. The first group worked primarily in the field, the second primarily in the laboratory. Today we are witnessing a synthesis of these two traditions, a true comparative psychology interested in both similarities and differences. Laboratory studies are valued for their potential for answering questions about the effects of a particular variable on behavior—effects that would be difficult if not impossible to isolate in field observations, where many factors vary all at once. But the comparative psychologist also knows that the artificial laboratory setting can lead to distortions and misinterpretations. So both laboratory and field studies are necessary; they can supplement each other.

The findings of comparative psychology are relevant to many topics. The nativism-empiricism issue has been discussed in several chapters, and the relative contributions of genetic predispositions and of learning is an important question in this section as well. As in other areas (e.g., perception), we no longer ask whether a particular behavior is inherited *or* learned; rather we inquire about the development of behavior and about the interaction of the genetically-determined neurochemical substrate *and* the effects of the environment. Results from comparative studies also shed light on many ecological issues. Without empirical knowledge, the best of intentions can sometimes lead to a cure worse than the disease. For example, as an alternative to the chemical control of pests, "biological controls" have been suggested: Rather than try to poison a pest, we introduce a natural predator. This prevents pollution and saves the other innocent animals. Such a noble purpose was behind the importation of the mongoose to the West Indies in the nineteenth century; it was brought in to prey on the rats that were causing great crop damage. It indeed did the job; the mongoose drove the rats from the fields and, to some extent, into houses! The mongoose then turned its predatory talent toward the poultry of the farmers and became a significant pest in its own right. If you have never seen a mongoose in the zoo, it is partly because the West Indian story is known and most countries that do not have mongooses have placed strict bans against importing them.

In this section, we will focus first on individual behavior. Chapter 27 deals mainly with studies of learning in various species, their similarities and their differences, studies done largely in the laboratory. In the concluding chapter, the social life of animals is our primary concern. Cohesion and dispersion will be the central concepts. They encompass cooperation and competition, mating and aggression—we might even say, love and hate—in the animal world.

27

Adaptation and Learning in Evolutionary Perspective

How did the primates evolve?
Does intelligence vary systematically among animal species?
Are principles of learning really the same in earthworm, fish, rat, and man?
Does behavior consist of fixed patterns of action, characteristic for each species?
What factors limit animals' adaptive behavior?

Are animals intelligent? How well can they learn? Are the processes of learning the same in all species? Is there a continuity between lower animals and man? By studying animals can we understand something of man; by studying man can we understand something of other animals? These questions that were raised by Darwin's theory of evolution all deal with continuity of behavior among animals. But Darwin's theory raised other questions as well, questions that stressed differences and discontinuities among species: What are the survival advantages of a particular adaptation to a particular **habitat?** Why did the evolution of behavior of a particular species take one direction and not another? Do different species in different environments learn differently?

Since Darwin's time, many scientists have worked on the first set of questions and others have focused on the second. Which set a scientist is trying to answer influences the type of research he does and the type of conclusions he derives from his empirical evidence. Today we see these two lines of research coming together, each qualifying and sharpening the other. In American psychology in particular, the first approach—the search for continuity, similarities, and general principles of learning—has been paramount for nearly three quarters of a century. In contrast, European studies tended to stress differences among species, often emphasizing the "innate" or species-specific behaviors that adapt the "lower" animal to his environment. (Since we will be discussing many species in this section, Spotlight 27-1 tells how species are classified and named.)

It is a matter of conjecture why the American emphasis was on *learning* rather than on **adaptation.** Were Americans more interested in man, and less in animals, so that they sought knowledge of human abilities in their research on animals? Was it un-American and undemocratic to study "lower," "simpler" animals with "innate" **instincts,** and American to study sources of change, flexibility, and the ability to learn no matter what one's heritage? Were animals studied only because they could be subjected to precise experimental control? Why did most European scientists focus on adaptation and instinctive behavior patterns? These questions, however interesting, belong to a treatise on the social psychology of science. We will describe only the findings that have emerged from the two traditions and some from the more recent synthesis.

How did the primates evolve?

Before we begin to examine the search for continuity and for discontinuity in behavior of animal species, it will be worthwhile to consider the evolution of the **primates,** which includes man. We will illustrate some of the principles of evolution and then show how both generality and specificity of adaptation arise. This section will summarize some of the main developments in the "family history" of the primates and will treat selection pressures that have led to specifically human traits and capacities (Washburn, 1968; Colbert, 1961).

Basic Adaptations

The primate order had its origins in a group of insect-eating mammals (insectivores) that lived some seventy million years ago. The basic primate adaptations were in the structure of the front and hindlimbs, which permitted locomotion and existence in the trees. This arboreal life in turn permitted an escape from ground-dwelling predators and gave access to new food supplies of fruits and leaves. The earliest primates were members of the infra-order prosimians, and some of the existing members of this group (e.g., the tree shrews and lemurs) display the same characteristics found in their long-extinct ancestors, including a relatively small brain with a proportionately large representation of sense of smell, an elongated skull, and eyes spaced rather widely apart.

Life in the trees exerted new selective pressures and led to changes from the prosimian characteristics. Development of vision

SPOTLIGHT 27-1
Taxonomy: How Animals Are Classified and Named

In order to permit identification and categorization of the millions of living and extinct forms of life, biologists have devised a taxonomic system in which any organism can be classified by a two-word sequence; the first word designates the general category or *genus* and the second, the specific group or *species*. For example, the domestic cat and dog are known as *Felis catus* and *Canis familiaris* respectively, as shown on the bottom line of the table. Each, in addition, belongs to broader *family* groups—the Felidae and the Canidae—as shown on the third line from the bottom. The family of the Canidae include the wolves, foxes, and coyotes, as well as the domestic and wild dogs. Note that the wolf and the dog both belong to the genus Canis and differ only in their species, the wolf being *Canis lupus* and the dog being *Canis familiaris.* Both the Canidae and the Felidae are members of the *order* Carnivora, which are marked by a certain tooth structure common to this group of meat-eating mammals. Relationships among the carnivores are shown on the next page. The order Carnivora is, in turn, one of twenty-one orders containing living members of the *class* Mammalia (**mammals**). The class Mammalia is part of the *phylum* Chordata, which in turn is included in the broad *kingdom* Animalia (animals).

It is important to recognize that this classification system is not based on superficial similarities; it is an attempt to categorize on the basis of descent from a common ancestral group. Thus, in external appearance, sharks are more similar to dolphins than dolphins are to dogs. However, the dolphins and dogs are properly placed together in the class Mammalia, while sharks are in the class of the cartilaginous fish, Chondrichthyes. (See the figure, p. 759.) An ancestral group common to both dolphins and dogs made the crucial adaptations for maintenance of a

CLASSIFICATION SYSTEM SHOWING SIMILARITIES AND DIFFERENCES

Common Names	Timber Wolf	Domestic Dog	Domestic Cat	Bottle-nose Dolphin	Bull Shark
Kingdom	Animalia	Animalia	Animalia	Animalia	Animalia
Phylum	Chordata	Chordata	Chordata	Chordata	Chordata
Class	Mammalia	Mammalia	Mammalia	Mammalia	Chondrichthyes
Order	Carnivora	Carnivora	Carnivora	Cetacea	Squaliformes
Family	Canidae	Canidae	Felidae	Delphinidae	Carcharhinidae
Genus	Canis	Canis	Felis	Tursiops	Carcharhinus
Species	Canis lupus	Canis familiaris	Felis catus	Tursiops truncatus	Carcharhinus leucas

At each level of classification, vertical lines separate animals that differ; thus the wolf and dog differ only in their species, while the shark differs from the other four animals in not being a mammal.

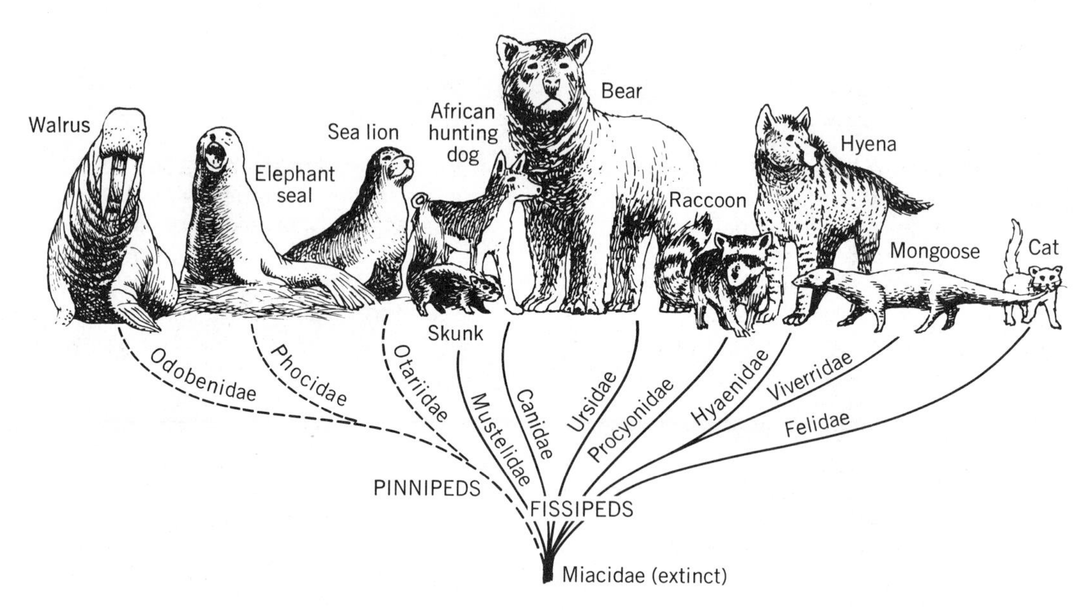

Relationships of Living Carnivores

constant internal temperature (warm-bloodedness), nursing of the young by the mother, and breathing through the lungs; the ancestors of the shark and other cartilaginous fish did not make these adaptations. The similar shapes of the shark and dolphin are now seen as the result of a common environment, the sea, which favors fishlike body structures, even in mammals like the dolphin whose ancestry and internal structures are quite different from those of the shark.

As members of the order Carnivora, the Felidae and Canidae also are viewed as developing from a common ancestral group, the Miacidae. The Miacidae were an assemblage of small mammalian carnivores who lived tens of millions of years ago, and all of the species that once comprised this family are now extinct. Although possessing certain traits in common by virtue of common ancestry, the Felidae and Canidae are classified as separate families because they show major differences both in structure (e.g., true cats have retractable claws) and in behavior. For the most part the cats evolved as solitary hunters, leading a generally asocial

rather than smell was favored, particularly stereoscopic vision, which is crucial for good depth perception (see Chapter 21, p. 594). Stereoscopic vision requires an overlap of the two visual fields; natural selection therefore operated to bring the eyes closer together at the front of the head. There was also selection for specialization of the limbs for better arboreal locomotion and grasping. Over a span of many millions of years, these evolutionary pressures produced the forms that we classify as monkeys (see Figure 27-1). Prosimian ancestral

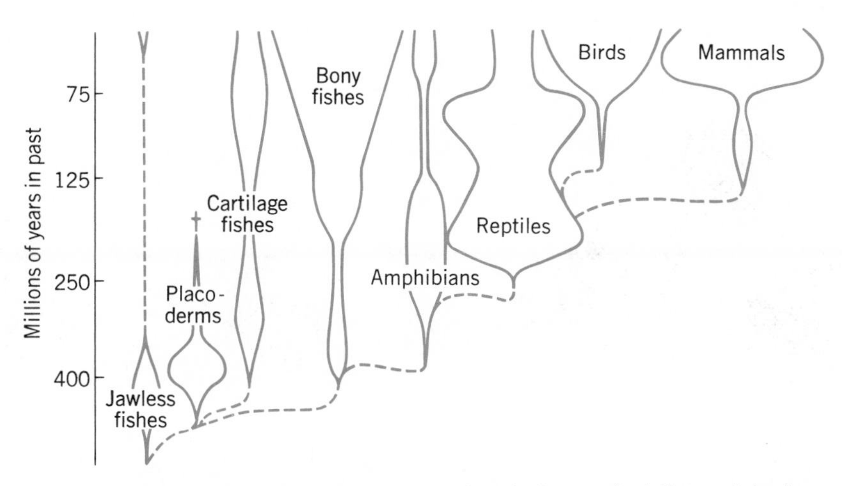

Illustrated are the broad outlines of the historical record of the vertebrates. For each vertebrate class, the width of the pathway is proportional to its known variety in each of the geological periods in which it lived.
(From Simpson, 1949)

existence (although there are exceptions such as the lion). In contrast, virtually all of the Canidae are highly social animals, frequently including communal hunting techniques as part of their behavioral repertoire.

The species designation is the basic unit of modern taxonomy. Although at one time any given species was viewed as being typified by a single ideal specimen, modern concepts emphasize the variability found within an interbreeding population of animals. Thus, the domestic dogs are categorized as a single species despite the wide variations in appearance of different breeds. As Lerner (1968) has indicated, one would probably not normally mate a Saint Bernard with a Chihuahua, but they could theoretically produce fertile offspring, and they share many common recent ancestors.

Within a species, we may find subgroups with varying degrees of distinctive genetic characters that can be used to define them as subspecies. With sufficiently long time spans, appropriate geographical isolation of subspecific populations, and with different selective pressures operating on those populations, new species may eventually emerge.

groups independently gave rise to the "Old World" monkeys of Asia and Africa and the "New World" monkeys of the Americas. The development of monkeylike characters from geographically-disparate prosimian ancestors is one of the most striking examples of "parallel" evolution: in two different places, common selective pressures, operating on a common ancestral stock, ultimately produced similar characteristics in species evolving independently. Of course, one would not expect the results of such parallel evolution to be identical.

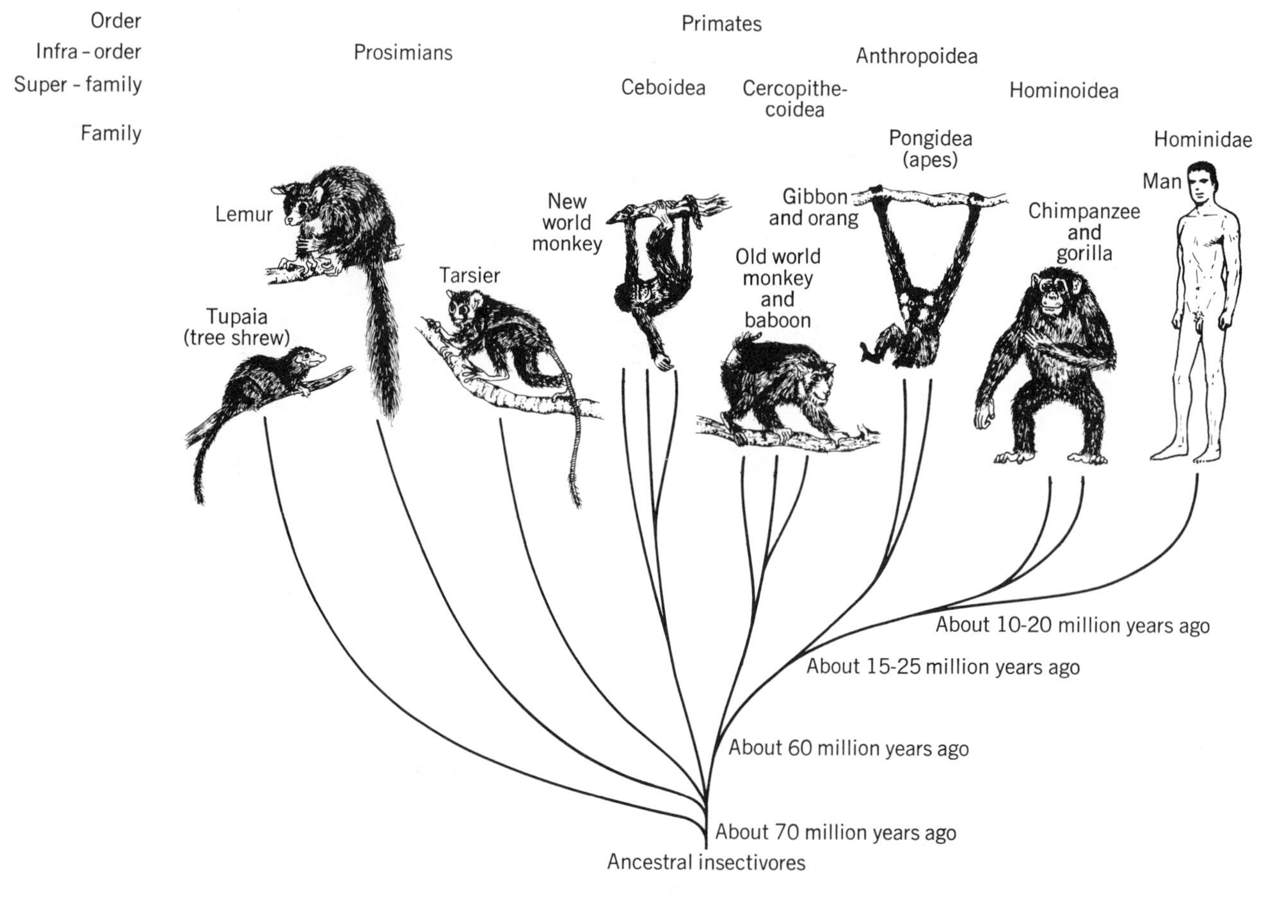

FIGURE 27-1
EVOLUTION OF THE PRIMATES

This reconstruction of the primate "family tree" contains the major taxonomic groups referred to in the text.

The New and Old World monkeys are distinguished by several anatomical differences, notably in the presence of prehensile tails in New World monkeys.

It is one of the ironies of the evolutionary process that the development of these newer forms tended to eliminate the groups that gave rise to them. There are no longer any prosimians in the Americas (outside of zoological parks), and Old World prosimians, such as the lemurs of Madagascar, are restricted to islands or other isolated habitats where geography has protected them from direct competition with the more highly evolved monkeys.

Branching of the Primate Family Tree

The branch of the evolutionary tree giving rise to man and his relatives, the apes, split from the main stem of the Old World monkeys some sixty million years ago. The time scale now grows more controversial, but it appears that five to twenty million years after the development of our apelike ancestors, several other branchings occurred. The first of these gave rise to the line that resulted in the gibbon and the orangutan. At a somewhat later date, a critical divergence produced two separate groups; one resulting in the chimpanzee and gorilla, the other in the emergence of man. Recent chemical analyses of blood proteins suggest a very close linkage between man, chimpanzee, and gorilla (Sarich & Wilson, 1967), and the point of this divergence is now placed as recently as ten million years ago.

The initial primate adaptation involved an ascent into the trees; later adaptations were required to permit the more recent descent to the ground. Among the contemporary primates there is great variation in the extent to which daily life is distributed among arboreal and terrestrial modes. Some monkeys (e.g., the langurs) spend virtually all of their days in the trees, while others (the baboons) forage for food entirely on the ground but ascend to tree limbs or cliffs for the night. Among the apes, the orangutan and gibbon are almost entirely arboreal; the chimpanzee and gorilla basically terrestrial. These latter apes have specially adapted knuckles for locomotion on the ground. The ground-dwelling patterns of life probably also entailed selection for characteristics which enabled defense against potential predators, including greater size and strength, weaponry (teeth), and social organization.

Both modern man (*Homo sapiens*) and his extinct relatives (such as *Australopithecus africanus*) are classified in the taxonomic family Hominidae. The most striking characteristics of the early Hominids were the structural changes which permitted upright posture and bipedal locomotion; these developments freed the hands for carrying and manipulating objects. About two million years ago, members of the genus Australopithecus lived in the African savannah, where the fossil record suggests that they fashioned primitive stone

Primate evolution favored good grasp and depth perception.
(Phyllis Dolinhow)

tools and hunted small game. However, their brains were relatively small and their hands not so well adapted for delicate manipulation as those of modern man. The unique characteristics of the genus Homo, including the dextrous hand, the large brain, and, finally, truly human language, appear to be very recent events on the scale of evolutionary time. Fossil records do not allow precise estimates of the beginnings of language, but the dextrous hand and large brain have changed dramatically in the last million years. As Washburn (1970) has emphasized, these changes must have occurred as the result of a complex feedback process, involving characteristics of man's life as a social hunter. For example, there must have been pressure favoring the survival of those individuals who could produce better tools for hunting. These individuals had brains capable of producing new tools and the hands to fashion them. Then, as tool-making became ever-more complex, there would be selection for individuals who could best communicate tool-making to the next generation; this meant selection for those individuals with the most effective language.

Perhaps the most important conclusions to be observed in this short discourse on evolution are those dealing with similarities and differences: Man has certain behavioral characteristics that he shares with all of the mammals (e.g., a postnatal period involving close mother-infant relations), others that mark him distinctively as a primate (a highly visual and socially oriented life), and still others that are uniquely human (including complex grammatical language, rich cultural transmission of information, and the ability to shape his own environment).

Does intelligence vary systematically among animal species?

Research on animal behavior began soon after Darwin's theories were published, and the first important investigator was the Englishman George Romanes. He published a series of books with evidence for the hypothesis of **continuity** of behavioral characteristics among animal species (e.g., Romanes, 1883). He said that one can observe gradual quantitative increments in mental capacity as one moves up a hypothetical "**phylogenetic scale**" of complexity from one-celled organisms through the invertebrates to the vertebrate classes, but at no point is there a sudden change in the quality of mental capacity. To support this concept of continuity of mental capacity, Romanes offered a variety of anecdotal and observational data.

The American psychologist Edward Thorndike invented an experimental tool with which to attack the problem of mental continuity. This was a set of puzzle boxes (Figure 27-2). He placed an animal in a box with food visible but out of reach outside the box. In

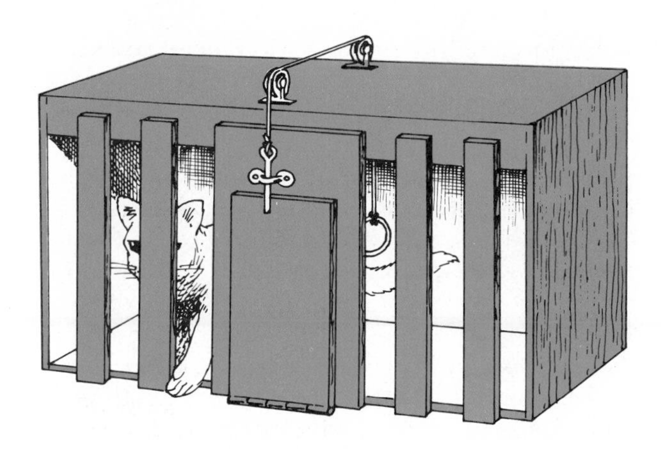

FIGURE 27-2 THORNDIKE PUZZLE BOX

Pulling the loop releases the door allowing the animal inside to emerge and obtain food.

order to obtain the food, the animal had to emit an appropriate response, for example, pulling a string, which released him from the box. Thorndike recorded the time to escape on successive trials and thus generated the first learning curves ever obtained for animals. In his doctoral dissertation published in 1898, he included performance data for chicks, cats, and dogs. His data were on the side of continuity; that is, the general form of the learning curves was the same in each species tested.

Thorndike initiated an experimental tradition that has persisted in American animal psychology. Reinforced in the 1910's by Watson's systematic formulation of behaviorism, the emphasis in the United States to date has been on laboratory studies of animal learning, often completely divorced from the *comparative* issues and primarily using animals as substitute humans, that is, as (hopefully) simple, unresisting "models" of human behavior. A further part of the tradition was the attempt to construct a general scale of animal intelligence. This attempt was typically based on a problem-solving task of some sort (puzzle boxes were among the first), in which the solution-learning of various species could be measured over trials. Lower animals would be expected to solve the problem slowly, if at all, and animals higher on the assumed "phylogenetic scale" would learn more rapidly, with man of course performing best of all.

Hints of Discontinuity

Thorndike's research suggested continuity because learning curves for different species were very similar. The typical gradual rise in speed of puzzle-solving over trials suggested to Thorndike that if animals learn, they do so by a relatively slow trial and error process. He found no evidence of "brilliant reasoning" on the part of his animals, such as might be indicated by never making errors, or by never behaving ineffectively after the first correct response. This conclusion was challenged by studies of chimpanzees by Köhler (discussed in more detail on pp. 395–96). Köhler's chimps appeared to show "insight." When food was placed outside their cage so they could not reach it by hand or with the use of a small stick, they quickly solved the problem by using the small stick to pull in a long stick that they then used to pull in the food.

Köhler was suggesting a discontinuity, saying that some animals learn in ways different from others. He accused Thorndike of using tasks in which insightful solutions were impossible or, more figuratively, of asking stupid questions and getting stupid answers.

In some ways, this chimp work foreshadowed (not always intentionally) current research in which investigators are more careful to choose tasks and problems corresponding to those the animal faces in his natural habitat. An interesting illustration is the problem Köhler set for his chimps in order to get a banana. He hung a bunch of the tasty fruit high out of reach, but he left in the cage a long stick with which, Köhler expected, the chimp would knock down a reward or two. This is undoubtedly what Köhler would have done, being a man. Chimps, being chimps, placed the stick vertically and climbed it quickly before it could fall. At the top they simply reached out and picked off a banana (see Figure 27-3).

If continuity theorists are to discount the findings of insight research, they must demonstrate that "apparent" insight depends on *prior* trial and error learning. This is in fact the direction research on these topics took after Köhler, as we will see. But first let us continue with the search for a general animal intelligence test, the *direct* line of the continuity approach, which was proceeding concurrently with these hints of discontinuity.

The Delayed-Response Test

W. S. Hunter, in 1913, published a report comparing "ideational processes" in various species. The problem he set for his animals called for a **delayed response.** The animals were kept from responding directly to a stimulus and had to wait. This ingenious procedure was designed to see how various animals "bridged the gap" between stimulus and response by means, presumably, of memory and cognition, that is, ideational processes.

Let us consider a concrete case. In one situation (see Figure 27-4), the animal faces three panels and with practice learns that the illuminated side contains food and the others do not. (Which side is lighted on a particular trial is, of course, determined randomly so that the animal cannot solve the problem by learning a spatial sequence.) When the animal has *demonstrably* learned that light means food, he is placed in a holding compartment where he can see the light but is not allowed to react promptly to it. The light in one of the three sides is turned on, then off. After a variable time interval—seconds, minutes, or hours—the subject is released from the compartment. Does he go to the correct side after this delay?

Various species were tested in situations such as this, and raccoons, monkeys, and human children did well; they could

FIGURE 27-3 PROBLEM SOLVING BY A CHIMP

The chimp's method of getting the banana was not what Köhler expected.
(Drawn from a photo in Köhler, 1925)

tolerate fairly long delays. Other species, such as the rat, failed at delays of more than a few seconds unless they were allowed to maintain a postural set; rats (and some other species) could bridge longer delays by seeing the light, pointing their body in that direction, then running straight ahead (following their noses) when released. Raccoons, on the other hand, could move around or could be moved by

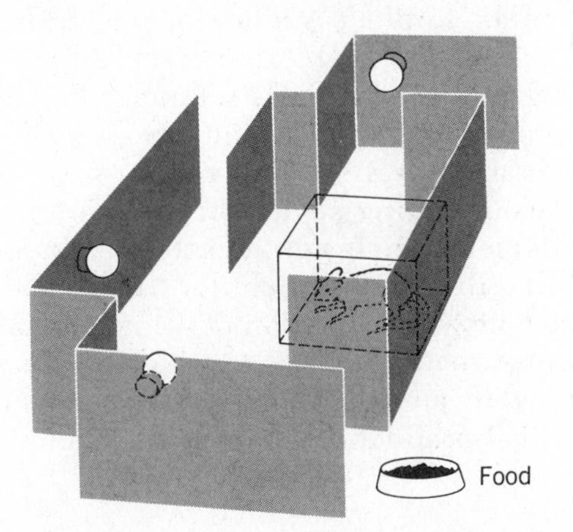

FIGURE 27-4 A DELAYED-RESPONSE APPARATUS

The animal is retained in a box while a light is briefly turned on and then off. The door is then raised and the subject is allowed to attempt entry to one of the compartments. If he chooses the compartment just illuminated, he is rewarded; if not he is returned to the start compartment for another trial.

the experimenter and still respond correctly after lengthy delays. Dogs showed still a different pattern of behavior; they often lost interest in the task altogether and tried to gain the reward by whining and otherwise eliciting sympathy from the experimenter!

In the succeeding twenty years or so, Hunter's delayed-response test proved an inspiration for many researchers interested in making a scale of animal mental abilities. By 1935, however, it had become apparent that the scaling approach based on this test was in serious difficulty. The results obtained, in terms of maximal possible delay, were found to vary more as a function of the particular conditions of testing than of the phylogenetic status of the species. In a comprehensive review of the available studies, Maier and Schneirla (1935) noted that, with appropriate test procedures, rats and cats seemed capable of delays similar to those obtained by Köhler with chimpanzees.

Attacks came from other sides, too, most notably from European investigators. Tinbergen (1951) pointed out that if delayed response was used as the measure of ideational or intellectual ability, the digger wasp would be considered among the most intelligent of animals. It can "remember" exactly how much food to bring to each of many larva nests (of varying population) even if delayed by as much as twenty-four hours; this is a delay longer than most demonstrated by mammals in situations like Hunter's. This criticism, while telling, is not completely fair. The digger wasp can delay only in a very specific task, one on which the survival of its species depends. Animals who can delay in a *variety* of situations may be demonstrating a capacity for flexibility—which is certainly part of intellectual ability—that far exceeds that of the wasp. Still, the search for a scale of animal intelligence by means of delayed-response tests came to a not undeserved end.

Attacks on Discontinuity

While continuity theory was being questioned, continuity theorists were simultaneously doing some questioning themselves. In particular, Köhler's studies of insight-learning in higher animals, mentioned above, were a potential threat to the continuity position, so American psychologists set out to provide an alternative explanation in proper scientific fashion—empirically.

Several studies showed that primates deprived of the opportunity of manipulating sticks during infancy and adolescence were unable to demonstrate insightful solutions to stick-manipulation problems as adults (Birch, 1945; Schiller, 1957). The implication was that apparent insight was a function of prior trial and error learning. Thorndike, too, had made this point, criticizing anecdotal reports of brilliant reasoning in animals by saying that those observers were seeing only the final product of a long and arduous chain of trial and error bumbling.

The study of **learning sets** (Harlow, 1949) is simultaneously an attack on discontinuity and another attempt to find a general-purpose intelligence test for animals. Essentially, learning sets are formed when an animal, say a monkey, is given a number of problems, as many as three hundred, one after the other, all based on the same principle. For example, in a series of object-discrimination problems, the monkey is rewarded on the first problem if he chooses the one of a pair of objects (circle vs. triangle) that the experimenter has arbitrarily designated as correct. After a number of trials the monkey masters that problem, and then he is given another pair of objects and again has to learn which is correct. After hundreds of successive problems of this type, each with a different pair of objects, the monkey can solve a new problem very quickly. If his choice on the first trial is rewarded, he stays with that choice and makes no errors at all; if not rewarded, he switches to the other object and thereafter never errs. If one were to observe these monkeys after three hundred prior problems, one might see their brilliance as insight; but *we* know he would be mistaken.

After being presented with many problems, a monkey becomes adept at discriminating objects.
(Courtesy H. F. Harlow)

The degree to which different species improve in their performance from the first to the tenth, to the fiftieth, to the one hundredth problem, and so on, has been used to scale species on "intelligence" (Hodos, 1970). This learning-set measure (see Figure 27-5) has many of the difficulties of the other measures that have been tried, but it at least involves an ability—discrimination—that is common

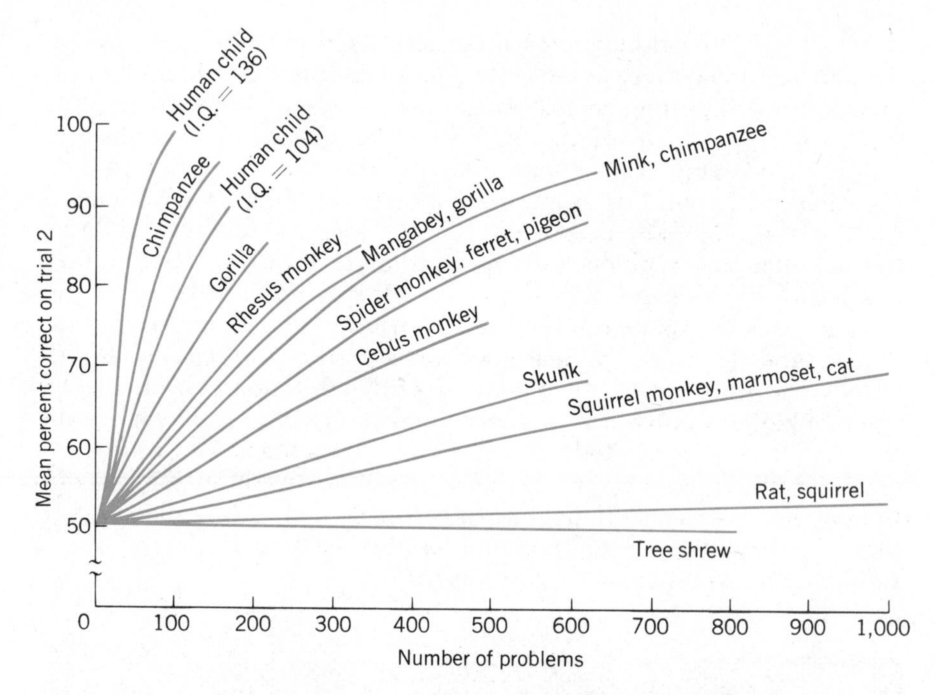

FIGURE 27-5 LEARNING-SET FORMATION IN SPECIES OF MAMMALS

This family of curves depicts the improvement in performance demonstrated by various species when subjects were given hundreds of problems with a common principle underlying their solution. The curves for humans, gorillas, and chimpanzees are based upon individual subjects, while the remaining curves represent "grouped" data.
(From Hodos, 1970)

and useful in a wide variety of species. By measuring *improvement* rather than absolute level of performance, the learning-set measures avoid some difficulties. If an animal is poorly motivated or less able to perform during the first problem, he will perform poorly, and a highly motivated, capable animal will perform well; by the fiftieth problem, the first animal may still be performing more poorly than the second, but their *rates* of improvement may be similar.

Continuity as an Assumption

During the three decades from 1930 to 1960, theories of learning were heavily influenced by two Americans, Clark Hull and B. F. Skinner. Their theories assumed continuity among species. Skinner was fond of presenting three learning or response curves—one from a rat, one from a pigeon, and one from a monkey, for example—without telling his audience which was which. The three curves looked nearly identical, as you can see in Figure 27-6. After asking which curve belonged to which species, Skinner answered his rhetorical question: "It doesn't matter. . . . Once you have allowed for differences in the ways in which [these species] . . . make contact with the environment, and in the ways in which they act upon the environment, what remains of their behavior shows astonishingly similar properties. Mice, cats, dogs, and human children could have added other curves to this figure." (Skinner, 1956, p. 230)

In other words, these theorists assumed that the basic principles of learning (classical conditioning, operant conditioning, and so forth; see Chapter 18) *do not vary among species.* Animals learn at different rates—there is an interspecies scale of intelligence—

but they all learn the same way. Thus, if one is interested in basic principles, he need not study all species. He can build his psychology on empirical data gathered from one species, and he can generalize the conclusions from research on the rat or the pigeon to all other species capable of learning, including man.

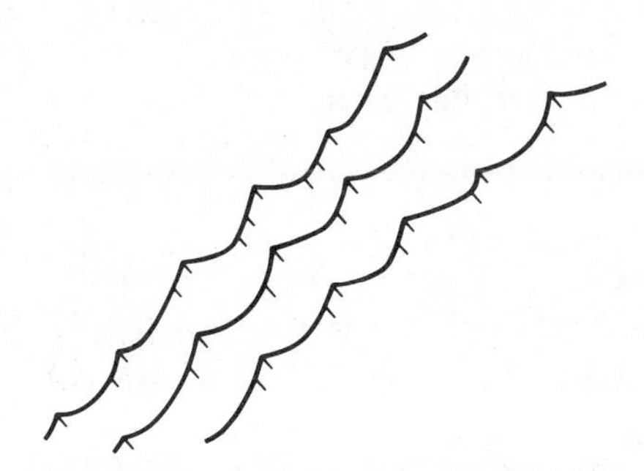

FIGURE 27-6 LEARNING CURVES OF THREE SPECIES

The curves show responses of a pigeon, rat, and monkey when taught to press a lever to gain a food reward. The "blips" represent reinforcements.
(From Skinner, 1956)

Hull wrote a book in 1943 entitled *Principles of Behavior*. He described it—literally—as a general introduction to the theory of *all* social science, despite the fact that the principles were derived almost exclusively from data on rats. This book became one of the most frequently cited books in the history of psychology. In 1971, B. F. Skinner wrote a popular nonacademic book entitled *Beyond Freedom and Dignity*. In it he extended his principles of learning, based mostly on rat and pigeon experiments, to a full-scale discussion of the notions of human freedom and responsibility. Such wide-ranging extrapolations are the natural by-products of the continuity hypothesis taken as an assumption.

There are several difficulties inherent in the assumption of continuity among species. If one gives the same task to a number of species without regard to their sensory-motor capabilities or of their motivational characteristics, one might indeed generate a scale; but is it an intelligence scale? Certainly we would find that different species would perform differently on any given task; but is better performance an indication of higher intelligence? We have noted that on a delayed-response test, the digger wasp scores as one of the most intelligent of creatures. The ability of rats to learn mazes (which are similar to their natural burrows) is probably equal to that of man. In a ping-pong test, blindness and ignorance would become equivalent. In testing human intelligence we have devised different tests for people who cannot read or write, for the blind and deaf, and for numerous other categories of people who vary in one capacity or another; we worry a lot about "culture-fair" tests (p. 362). But when comparing our intellectual abilities with those of subhuman animals, we have been rather inconsiderate of simple differences in capacity, and it has not been uncommon to find animals with sensory-motor and motivational systems quite different from ours being required to perform tasks best suited to human or primate abilities.

It is worth mentioning, too, that many psychologists act as if the sequence from rat to cat to monkey to man is an evolutionary sequence. This assumption is patently false (Hodos & Campbell, 1969). In no way is man descended from the monkeys of today; they may have common ancestors who lived millions of years ago, just as branches of a tree have a common trunk. But one branch—though it may be considered higher in some sense—does not grow from another. Thus we can recognize that even if it were possible to construct a scale of animal performance, that scale would not reflect an evolutionary sequence.

Are principles of learning really the same in earthworm, fish, rat, and man?

The current research of M. E. Bitterman and his associates clearly bears on the issue of continuity (see Bitterman, 1960, 1965). What is unusual about this research, however, is that these investigators do not take the assumptions of Hull, Skinner, and others for granted. It might or it might *not* be true that different species learn by the same principles, differing only in rates—quantitatively; little had been done to test the presumed generality among species. By 1930, about 60 percent of all studies reported in the major American journals covering animal research dealt with the behavior of the rat; the remainder investigated mostly primates like monkeys and chimps (Beach, 1950; Bitterman, 1965). This is hardly a good sample from the phylogenetic scale, but the pattern established in 1930 continued at least up to 1960; it is breaking down somewhat today.

Cross-Species Studies

Bitterman developed a quite different research strategy. In the spirit of a true *comparative* psychology, he called for study of many species, including those rarely investigated, like the earthworm. In essence, the question he sought to answer was, Can we really say the principles of learning in the earthworm are the same as in the rat or in man? He and his associates set out to answer the question by research means.

Now, asking such questions presents difficulties, some of which we have described previously (p. 769). One of the most important is the difficulty in equating motivational states and sensory-motor capabilities across species. For example, a crab can go for months without food, but a rat cannot survive more than a few days without food. Therefore twenty-four hours without food results in quite different motivational states in a crab and in a rat. Bitterman recognized this difficulty and proposed to handle it by *systematic variation* rather than by fruitless attempts at *equation*.

For example, suppose one presents various species with the following **habit-reversal** problem. Two stimuli are presented and a response to one brings a reward; the other brings nothing. After solving this simple problem in a number of trials, the animal gets a new task, one that requires reversal of the habit. The same two stimuli are presented, but the one that was previously neutral now brings the reward and the one that was previously rewarded is now neutral. When the animal solves this second problem, the value of the two stimuli is again reversed. This procedure is continued through a series of reversals. The question is, Does the animal improve over problems? Does it learn successive reversals faster and faster? Rats do, fish don't. Now, maybe fish could improve if properly motivated. To test this possibility, you might present a set of problems to several groups of fish, systematically varying the level of motivation in each group. If within this wide range of fish motivational states, no group shows progressive improvement, the possibility that motivational differences accounted for the original observation is surely decreased. The burden of proof now lies on the critic who still wishes to explain the difference between rat and fish performance as "merely motivational."

Learning Tasks

Bitterman and others working with this approach have tested a number of animals in simple tasks like habit reversal and probability matching. In the probability-matching test, the choice between two stimuli is rewarded on the basis of a certain probability less than 1.00; for example, the right-side stimulus is rewarded on 70 percent of the trials and the left-side on 30 percent. In such situations, animals either make responses that correspond to these probabilities (the fish responds to the right-side stimulus about 70 percent of the time) or they attempt to maximize their rewards by some response pattern such as *always* responding to the stimulus that is more frequently associated with reward (the rat does this). Results on species ranging from the earthworm to the monkey are shown in Table 27-1.

Note that in the table there is an entry for the decorticated rat. What this represents is a series of tests on rats who have had most of their cerebral cortex removed shortly after birth; it was an attempt to define the role of cortex in these changes in learning processes, and we see that the decorticated rat behaves rather like a turtle, a reptile with a very rudimentary cortex. For the spatial problems the responses of the turtle and the decorticated rat are the same as those of a normal rat, but they respond more like a fish on the visual problems. In general, the scale from bottom to top of the table reflects quite neatly the differences in cortical development.

Note too the emphasis on *different* categories of performance (fishlike or ratlike) in different species, rather than on quantitative differences in behavioral scores. This is a result of taking the continuity hypothesis seriously—as an untested prediction—rather than accepting it without proof as an article of faith.

TABLE 27-1
BEHAVIOR OF A VARIETY OF ANIMALS IN FOUR CLASSES OF PROBLEMS WHICH DIFFERENTIATE RAT AND FISH

Animal	Spatial Problems		Visual Problems	
	Reversal	Probability	Reversal	Probability
Monkey	R	R	R	R
Rat	R	R	R	R
Pigeon	R	R	R	F
Turtle	R	R	F	F
Decorticated rat	R	R	F	F
Fish	F	F	F	F
Cockroach	F	F	—	—
Earthworm	F	—	—	—

Note—F means behavior like that of the fish (random probability matching and failure of progressive improvement in habit reversal). R means behavior like that of the rat (maximizing or nonrandom probability matching and progressive improvement in habit reversal). Transitional regions are connected by the stepped line. The brackets group animals which have not yet been differentiated by these problems.

Bitterman, 1965.

Neither the approach nor the data, however, has been free of controversy. Ethologists have criticized Bitterman for not knowing his animals, for asking them to learn behaviors that are not particularly useful in their natural habitat. He is also criticized for saying "fish" when he means one particular fish (the African mouthbreeder) and "rat" when he uses only one variety (the common docile Norwegian rat). This second criticism Bitterman himself accepts wholeheartedly as valid, and he calls for work on other classes and phyla. Other researchers (e.g., Mackintosh, 1969) have claimed his data are misleading, that with appropriate manipulation of the stimulus situation, even fish can show improvement in habit reversals. Still, Bitterman can justly assert that he has started research on a rather wide range of species and that he has changed the continuity issue from a matter of speculative theorizing into a hot topic in empirical research. And that, certainly, is as it should be.

By using the habit-reversal task as one of his common tests, Bitterman reminds us of a very similar controversy about the learning in rats and very young children compared to learning in older children and adults. The reversal-shift studies show essentially that older children can more easily learn a new habit if the correct response changes from one value of a stimulus dimension (e.g., black) to another (white) than if they have to start responding to a previously irrelevant dimension (e.g., size)—see p. 384 for details. Young children and most animals, however, find it easier to shift to another dimension, and the difference has been interpreted as reflecting different principles of learning. Presumably, some kind of mediation is required for shifting from one value to another within the same stimulus dimension, and the development of language abilities might well be involved, at least in part.

It is appropriate, therefore, that we consider language learning in the context of the continuity tradition. It has been suggested, for example, that man operates on no new principles of learning but rather that his ideational capacity has been vastly increased by the ability to use words as reinforcers, as substitutes for "real" stimuli and responses, and as mediating bridges between response and reinforcement. Thus, studies of language learning in nonhuman animals, mostly primates, tend to look for the human language capacities in these species (see Spotlight 27-2).

Does behavior consist of fixed patterns of action, characteristic for each species?

Individual Adaptation of Species

As we have seen, American experimental comparative psychology has traditionally assumed that general principles of learning apply to all species. This accounts for the search for a test that would be suitable to assess the relative learning ability—intelligence?—of a wide range of animals. This approach was based on Darwin's notion of a basic continuity between the behavior of lower and higher animals, in behavior patterns as well as in bodily structure.

Another of Darwin's notions, commonly phrased as "the survival of the fittest," stressed the adaptation of an animal to his habitat. The emphasis was not on similar means of adaptation among species, but on decidedly different ways of adjusting, where the important stimuli, the adaptive responses, and the most effective rewards were all seen in terms of the essential survival capabilities of the organism. In Europe, studies based on this notion became the empirical support for classical ethology. Before considering the learned aspects of adaptive behavior, we shall first consider the general outline of classical ethology.

Classical Ethology

Classical ethology developed from a naturalistic field-oriented biological tradition dating back to Darwin. However, its emergence as a coherent discipline with established terminology, attitudes, and theory must be credited to the German zoologist Konrad Lorenz (1950). At the heart of this system is a basic division of behavior into two broad categories: a variable, relatively unpredictable *appetitive* phase and a stereotyped, highly predictable *consummatory* phase. For example, in a hungry animal the search for

SPOTLIGHT 27-2
Can Chimpanzees Learn Our Language?

That animals communicate with members of their own species and even with animals of other species is clear. But can a subhuman animal learn the highly complex language systems of humans? Possibly because the high phylogenetic status of humans is often ascribed in large part to language capacities, psychologists have long been interested in attempts to teach that language to other animals. Mostly these attempts have involved the "highly intelligent" primate, the chimpanzee. Early attempts were notably unsuccessful. In one study, a chimp was raised as a member of the family (Kellogg & Kellogg, 1933). The chimp learned to follow directions to some extent, but she never learned to speak. In a second attempt by another couple, the chimp was given special speech training but managed, finally, to produce only three recognizable human words—"Mama," "Papa," and "cup" (Hayes & Hayes, 1952). These studies were often used as evidence supporting the notion that only humans could learn a true language.

More recent research shows this conclusion to be at least misleading. One couple (Gardner & Gardner, 1969) suggested that chimps should not be expected to learn vocal language because they lack the vocal apparatus necessary for such speech. But they are capable of fine motor coordination, and can use their hands and arms in intricate motions. Therefore, the Gardners reasoned, if one tried to teach a chimp to use the language of human mutes—sign language—the results might be quite different. They obtained a female chimp whom they named Washoe and built her a home consisting of a house trailer with a yard and an enclosing fence. Washoe lived a pleasant life with one abnormality: no human spoke in her presence; all human-to-human, human-to-chimp, and (eventually) chimp-to-human communication was carried out using sign language.

Washoe was actively trained to use sign language. She was deliberately watched and rewarded for the proper motions, which of course occurred infrequently at first. The proper signs were usually taught directly, either by the method of **shaping** using successive approximations (see p. 464) or by actively moving her hands. She also learned by observation. Washoe learned the "language" more rapidly than previous research had suggested was possible. In three years, Washoe learned close to a hundred word-phrases, quite an increase over "Mama, Papa, cup."

One of the most interesting features of subhuman language learning demonstrated in Washoe's case was the ability to generalize "words" learned in a specific context. Signs for "more," "please," and "come" or "give me," originally learned in conjunction with a particular desired object, food, or activity were soon seen in conjunction with other desirables. "More"

food is appetitive behavior, whereas eating is the consummatory behavior. The consummatory phase has been most frequently studied and is inferred from the appearance of a set of invariant responses known as **fixed action patterns (FAP's)**. Examples include feeding patterns, mating patterns, retrieval of the young, and grooming pat-

Washoe first sees the picture of a cat.

Washoe then learns sign language for "cat."

Washoe makes the sign with both hands when shown the cat.
(Courtesy of the Gardners)

tickling was generalized to "more" food, for example, without training. Washoe was also able to combine words into simple sentences. After committing some action that she perceived as offensive to her keepers, she would signal, "Come – hug – love – sorry."

Sarah is another chimp trained by a psychologist interested in language learning (Premack, 1970). Like Washoe, Sarah was not asked to speak in human tongue and, like Washoe, she was asked to learn a language in signs. In Sarah's case, however, the "words" were pieces of colored plastic in different shapes. Each different piece, she was taught, referred to a different object; for example, a blue triangle meant "apple." Sarah quickly learned a vocabulary of close to a hundred words. This means that she was able to put a blue triangle (which was plastic but had a metal back) on a magnetized "language board" when shown an apple; if she did so, she got the apple.

Now, suppose Sarah has a blue triangle and a red square (banana) before her, and an apple is presented. Can she match the correct word with the object? Will she place the blue triangle on the language board? Yes, most of the time. Her errors were not so much mistakes, the experimenters perceived, as requests for a more preferred food. Thus, if shown apple and banana and given the blue triangle and red square, she would almost invariably place the red square on the

(*Continued*)

terns, as illustrated in Figure 27-7. According to the ethologists, the FAP is the basic behavioral unit with functional adaptive significance. An FAP, like a bodily structure, exists because it confers on the animal a selective advantage in survival and reproduction. Thus, a particular FAP will generally be found in all members of the species, although it language board; she much preferred bananas.

Another phase of training was more complex: Could Sarah understand sentences? For example, if given the instruction (in signs on the language board) "Sarah – insert – banana – pail – apple – dish," would she put the banana in the pail and the apple in the dish, as requested? The answer is Yes.

Sarah also learned to answer questions, the meaning of relational terms (e.g., "same" and "different"), and quite complicated linguistic categories. A good general illustration is this question: "What is the relation between 'red' and 'apple'?" Her answer was a choice of four possibilities: red is the "color of" apple, the "size of" apple, the "name of" apple, or the "shape of" apple. Sarah said that red is the "color of" apple over 80 percent of the time.

Perhaps the most intriguing bit of language behavior Sarah exhibited was in response to the blue plastic sign for apple. Shown this, she was asked if this *blue triangle* was a match for a round or a square object. She chose the round one. Similarly, her choices showed that she understood the apple symbol to be red and to have a stem!

Although these chimps certainly show more ability to communicate than had previously been thought possible, some psycholinguists feel that their accomplishment still falls short of genuine language behavior. These psycholinguists hold that the free use of syntactic structure is the basic characteristic of human language and that this is still to be demonstrated in an infrahuman organism. In addition, the artificial systems were devised by human beings and taught by human tutors to the chimpanzees. Chimpanzees' "language" in their natural habitat is very different indeed. But at the very least, the current research and debate over "chimp language" is helping to sharpen our thinking about what should and what should not be included in the concept "language."

Although these studies were undertaken as basic research on relations between human and animal communication, recently some of the techniques have been applied to help people suffering from aphasia (loss of speech because of damage to the brain). If an adult sustains severe damage to his cortical speech areas, which in most individuals are located in the left cerebral hemisphere, he usually cannot regain speech even though the other hemisphere is intact. But recently Premack and other psychologists (Gazzaniga, 1972) have reported encouraging progress in teaching aphasic patients to communicate again; they use the colored symbols that were designed for the research on communication with chimpanzees.

might vary between sexes, it is assumed to be genetically determined, and it will generally appear when the right stimulus configuration is present in the environment.

These assumptions of "innateness" and "invariance" were vigorously challenged by other workers as ethological studies progressed. However, it was a fundamental contribution of this approach to focus on the stereotyped, species-characteristic patterns of behavior exhibited by many animal species and to inquire about the evolutionary function of these behavioral units.

FIGURE 27-7 FIXED ACTION PATTERNS IN MICE

These drawings depict species-characteristic behavior patterns. (*A*) Rearing: an investigatory posture; (*B*) eating; (*C*) and (*D*) two forms of grooming; (*E*) social investigation; (*F*) wrestling; (*G*) copulation; and (*H*) "submissive" upright posture.
(Adapted from Van Abeelen, 1963)

The environmental stimulus releasing a fixed action pattern was called a **sign stimulus** or a **releaser.** In the classic example cited by Lorenz, a graylag goose is sitting on its nest with a clutch of eggs. An egg is removed and placed several inches away. The goose then extends its neck and rolls the egg back into the nest with the underside of the bill. The egg in this case constitutes the sign stimulus, and the retrieval response (extension and retraction of the neck) is the FAP. If one removes the egg while the retrieval response is under way, the goose will still continue the FAP all the way back to its nest, as if it still had an egg to push. For reasons not entirely clear, the definition of an FAP came to include this triggered quality—the response pattern released by a sign stimulus and, once begun, inexorable. If one looks closely at animal behavior, it is surely difficult to defend the notion that each FAP, when triggered, goes automatically and uniformly to completion, and it is not intuitively obvious why selective advantage would be conferred on animals unresponsive to environmental shifts such as the disappearance of the sign stimulus.

Behind the FAP and the sign stimulus—behind the theory of consummatory responses—were Lorenz's views of appetitive or motivational states. Lorenz had to account for the fact that a given sign stimulus would not always evoke an FAP of equal intensity; the response was sometimes vigorous, sometimes weak, and sometimes it did not occur at all. These variations were explained by hypothesizing varying internal states—appetites and motives. In human terms, a hamburger might elicit vigorous eating in a starving man, indifferent eating in a reasonably well-fed citizen, and no eating at all in someone who has just finished a large plate of spaghetti.

Lorenz saw certain behaviors—feeding, sex, aggression—as biologically necessary for the survival of the animal or his species. As a motivational explanation of such behaviors, he adopted a hydraulic model, illustrated by Figure 27-8. Lorenz saw the effects of motivation as analogous to the effects of fluids under pressure. As appetite grows, like the water level rising in a vat, pressure to respond builds up; a sign stimulus is considered to open a valve; this *releases* the pressure and triggers an FAP. Repeated FAP's result in lowered "fluid" pressure, thus accounting for decreasing intensity of response in such cases.

The hydraulic model can also account for **vacuum activities.** These are FAP's emitted in the *absence* of obvious triggering stimuli, as when a kitten might stalk or attack nonexistent objects in the environment. To explain such anomalous behaviors, it is assumed that the energy reservoirs have become so full that the valve mechanism can no longer function; the energy bursts through the checking mechanism and triggers the patterns despite the absence of an appropriate sign stimulus.

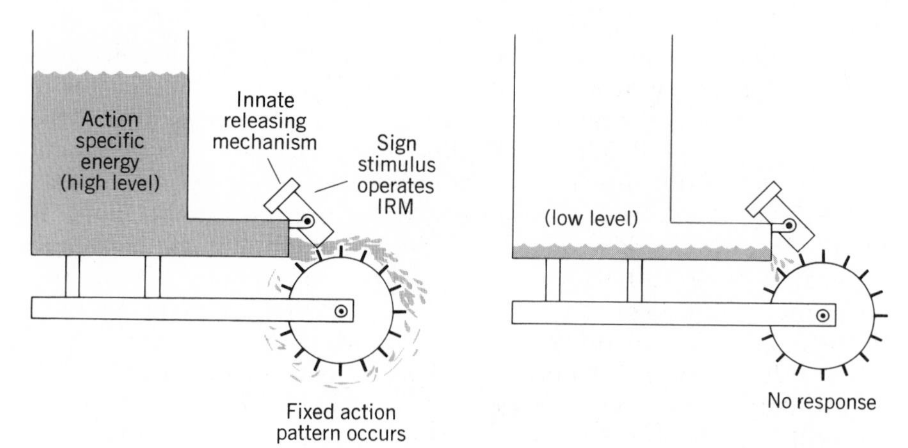

FIGURE 27-8
HYDRAULIC MODEL OF MOTIVATION

In this system, the valve mechanism (IRM) is operated by a "sign stimulus." The vigor of the resulting fixed action pattern is dependent upon the fluid level in the vat, i.e., upon the accumulation of action specific energy.

If one operates on the assumptions inherent in a hydraulic theory of motivation, he is likely to see certain behaviors as inevitable. If aggression, for example, is not released by a sign stimulus, the pressure to aggress builds and eventually the behaviors will occur spontaneously (vacuum activity). However, these possibilities are not the only ones; motive energies can also be *redirected* or *displaced.* A rooster is confronted by another rooster; instead of pecking his rival, he pecks at the ground. This is labeled **redirection**—the aggressive energy comes out, but the motor act has been channeled toward a new object. Two cats face each other in a hostile encounter;

one suddenly begins to groom himself. This is labeled **displacement**—two drive systems, aggression and fear, are in conflict; they cancel each other out, and an irrelevant activity occurs. There is a rather striking similarity between the concepts of redirection and displacement in ethology and many concepts in Freudian personality theory (p. 224). Freud, who also used a hydraulic model of drives, saw the pressure of psychic energy finding an outlet, if not in direct behavior, in redirections or compromises as exhibited in defense mechanisms or neurotic symptoms.

The motivational theory of Lorenz (and of Freud, for that matter) has often been criticized. One criticism is that, if one allows for direct and indirect manifestations of a drive and also for compromises and displacements, there is very little possibility of testing the theory; one can maintain his belief in an underlying sex or aggression drive no matter what behaviors are exhibited. Many psychologists prefer to concentrate their energies on the clarification of the actual neural and hormonal mechanisms rather than to rely on an imprecise hypothetical theory based on an analogy with plumbing systems. A second criticism—with important societal implications—is that these largely unverifiable theories assume that "outlets" for such drives as aggression must be found because these behaviors are inevitable. Accepting hostile and destructive behavior as inevitable in man leads one to propose quite different social policies from those that would be suggested by a theorist who views aggressive behaviors as learned or capable of significant modification through experience.

Nevertheless, classical ethology has been extremely valuable in identifying the relatively stereotyped action patterns in various species and the stimuli that are functionally related to these behaviors. Similarly, it may be that Freud's greatest contribution came in identifying relatively universal behavior patterns in man. The concepts of fixed action patterns and sign stimuli have done much to organize the observations of animal psychologists; the accumulation of systematic data in a specialty once characterized by anecdotal evidence of little scientific value is the true heritage of the ethological approach.

What factors limit animals' adaptive behavior?

Reading American statements about animal learning, one often gets the impression that "stimulus," "response," and "reinforcement" are such general terms that an investigator can teach any animal to make any response to any stimulus using any reinforcer he desires. Today, however, psychologists in every country are becoming aware of constraints on learning imposed by an animal's nervous system; these constraints can often be viewed in terms of the animal's life in his natural habitat. These limitations to learning in any species can be seen to involve several factors—the age at which certain kinds of learning can occur (critical periods), the types of stimulus-response linkages that can be learned readily, the sorts of responses that can be learned, the kinds of reinforcement that are effective, and the types of stimuli that are appropriate. We will discuss and give examples of each of these factors that serve to make the learning of one species different from that of another.

Critical Periods of Learning

In 1873 an Englishman named Spalding published reports of learning in chickens and ducks. He noted some unexpected findings: First, newborn chicks separated from their mother for eight to ten days after birth would not later respond to the retrieval calls of the hen. Second, newborn ducklings kept from water for several days would refuse to enter the pond when brought to it. Spalding speculated that there was an "established course" of learning in these birds and that artificial rearrangement of this course might result in behavioral abnormalities persisting for life. In other words, he was suggesting that for some behaviors there are **critical periods** in life during which the responses are apparently easily learned, but if the behavior is *not* learned *then*, it may never be learned.

This intriguing hypothesis received no research attention in animal psychology for over fifty years, as psychologists turned to puzzle boxes and mazes in their efforts to substantiate continuity. In 1935 the European ethologist Konrad Lorenz performed a simple experiment. He divided the eggs laid by a graylag goose into two groups, one group hatched by the mother and the other by him (in an incubator). The first thing the goslings in one group saw upon hatching was their mother; they became very attached to her, following her around, running to her when frightened, and generally behaving like loyal and normal offspring. The first thing goslings in the incubated group saw upon hatching was a European ethologist—Konrad Lorenz! They followed *him*, and when frightened, they ran to "Mother" Lorenz for comfort, even if their real mother was also present (see Figure 27-9). Lorenz called this phenomenon **imprinting,** and postulated that it was a result of learning during a critical period immediately after birth. At this time the bird learned which stimuli it "should" make its social responses to. These early effects are sometimes long-lasting, as Lorenz discovered when a female turtle dove that had imprinted on him came to him in mating season and fully expected him to do his duty as a male of her species!

Imprinting does not mean the same thing for all species nor is it governed by the same mechanisms in all animals. Often the obvious requirements of nature can be used to predict whether or not, or how, a bird will imprint. Some birds like the cuckoo lay their eggs in the nests of birds of other species (from which we get the word

FIGURE 27-9 IMPRINTING

Konrad Lorenz leads the goslings who have been "imprinted" upon the ethologist.

(Thomas Mc Avoy, *Life* magazine © 1972 Time Inc.)

"cuckold"). If the newborn cuckoo was hatched in the nest of birds of another species and imprinted on the first adult he saw, he would not mate with one of his own species as an adult. Therefore it is not surprising to find that cuckoos do not demonstrate this type of imprinting.

Imprinting is found not only in birds. It has been observed in insects, fish, and mammals. There are also a number of theories of human behavior (e.g., Freud's and Erikson's; see Chapter 9) that postulate critical periods for learning certain social behavior. In particular, Freud's theory of psychosexual stages in development postulates periods of changing sensitivity in various regions of the body—oral, anal, and phallic. As each of these bodily regions becomes relatively sensitive in turn, learning is more likely to occur in relation to this region. This line of reasoning is strikingly similar to that used in animal research.

In the laboratory, psychologists have investigated the exact timing of imprinting—when the critical period begins, when (and why) it ends, and when the strongest imprinting occurs. A typical study used mallard ducklings as subjects; after hatching, the ducklings were exposed to a model of a male mallard much like the duck decoys used by hunters, and later they were tested for imprinting by exposure to both a male and a female model. Response (usually "following") to the male model was considered imprinting (Hess, 1958). (See Figure 27-10.)

FIGURE 27-10 IMPRINTING IN A DUCKLING

The duckling is imprinted by placing it in the runway behind a model of a male duck which is wired for sound. Near the duckling is a trap door through which it is removed. The duckling is tested for imprinting by placing it between the male model and the female model which emits a different sound. If it follows the male, response is scored as positive.

(From "Imprinting in Animals," by Eckhard H. Hess. Copyright © 1958 by Scientific American, Inc. All rights reserved.

In some of the earliest studies (Hess, 1958), various groups of ducklings were first exposed to the male model at different times after birth. As you can see in Figure 27-11, some imprinting occurs within the first four hours after hatching, and imprinting normally terminates within 29-32 hours after hatching. Maximal imprinting was found between 13 and 16 hours.

Some more recent research has focused on factors related to the end of the critical period. Why, for example, will ducklings, whose first exposure to a male model occurs after age 32 hours, show no evidence of imprinting? Many observers noted that simultaneously with the end of imprinting periods, the infants in many species also become fearful of novel stimuli. Perhaps the development of the fear response, which is incompatible with approach and attachment behavior, is the primary factor in the decrease in imprinting; a duckling obviously cannot follow an object if he is fleeing from it in terror.

To test whether fear could be reduced and the critical period modified, Moltz and Stettner (1961) used the technique of depriving newborn ducklings of patterned visual stimulation by attaching translucent hoods to their heads; the ducklings could see light but no patterns. This procedure has the effect of markedly re-

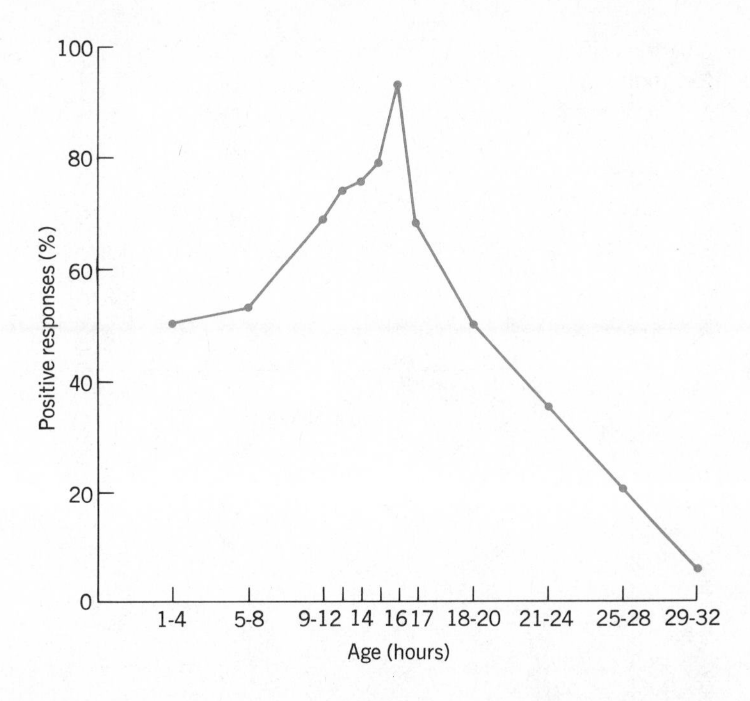

FIGURE 27-11 CRITICAL AGE FOR IMPRINTING IN MALLARD DUCKLINGS

It can be seen that the probability of obtaining successful imprinting first increases following hatching and then declines.

(Adapted from "Imprinting in Animals," by Eckhard H. Hess.)

ducing emotionality and fear, especially in reaction to novel stimuli (see Figure 27-12A). Deprived ducklings showed significantly more imprinting than did the normally raised control subjects if their first exposure was delayed until 24 or 48 hours after hatching (see Figure 27-12B). These ages are beyond the normal critical period. The fact that when fear did not occur imprinting could take place beyond the normal critical period supports the hypothesis that fear is a conflicting drive. However, other results suggest that additional factors are also implicated in the termination of the critical period; perhaps some sort of neural and hormonal maturation is involved.

There has also been research related to the beginning of critical periods. Some studies (Gottlieb, 1971) have shown that certain social responses in birds develop even before birth. The vocal response of the offspring to the calls of the mother, for example, can be detected from inside the egg, a few days before hatching. If eggs are artificially incubated away from the mother (and her vocalizations), the ducklings born from these eggs do not respond as quickly or as effectively to maternal calls. The vocal response to the mother's calls does not seem to be learned in the same sense that following behavior is, but even if they are innate stimulus-response connections, such abilities seem to lose in effectiveness if not exercised during critical periods.

Although we have been focusing on imprinting, the acquisition of many behaviors other than infant-mother attachments shows critical periods, and these periods are not necessarily restricted

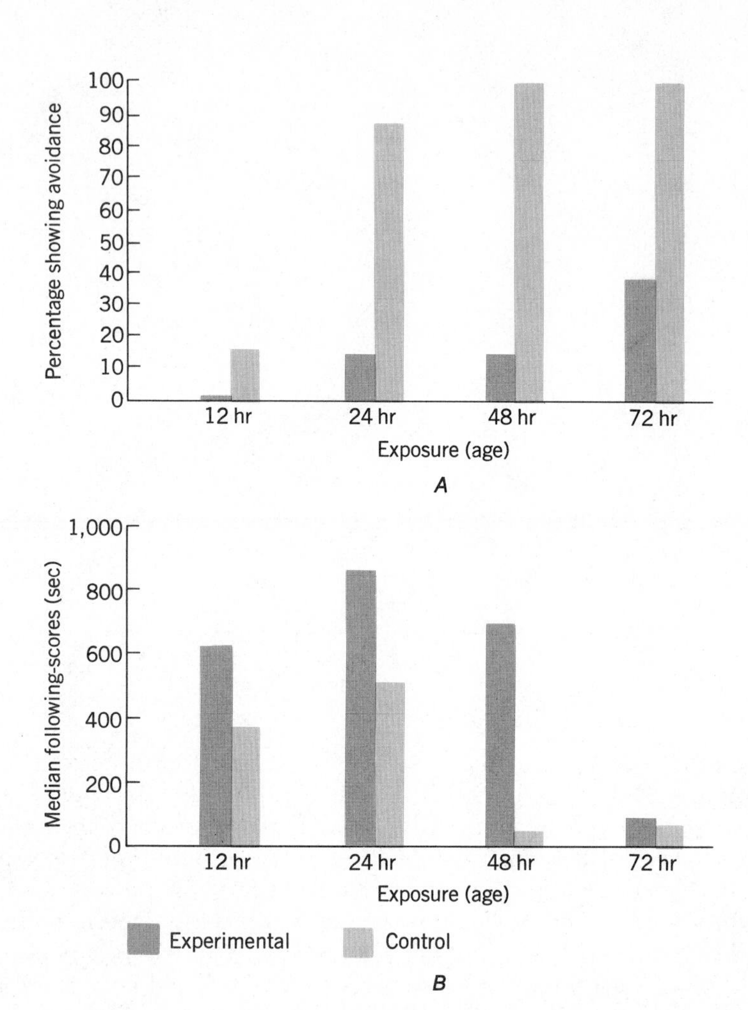

FIGURE 27-12 EFFECT OF AGE AND PRIOR VISUAL EXPERIENCE ON IMPRINTING
Domesticated mallard ducklings reared under normal conditions of illumination show an increment in avoidance (*A*) and a decrement in following (*B*) beginning at 24 hours post-hatching. Similar ducklings, reared with translucent hoods restricting patterned visual stimulation, continue vigorous following until 48 hours post-hatching and delay the appearance of avoidance responses still further.
(Moltz & Stettner, 1961)

to a few days after birth. The development of normal sexual or aggressive behavior in the adult rhesus monkey, the appearance of normal adult patterns of social interactions between dogs, and the development of language ability in man are behaviors dependent upon learning during a circumscribed period early in the life of the organism (Scott, 1962). Similarly, formation of social bonds may come early in birds (shortly after birth) while in other animals they might come much later. In dogs, there appears to be a critical period between six and eight weeks of age, such that if they are deprived of contact with humans during this time, they will never form the strong social bonds to people that are characteristic of the species. Critical bonding periods also appear in many birds and some mammals around mating time. These periods are probably dependent upon hormonal and neurological effects (like arousal) that occur at that time, and the result is a bond between mates that lasts for many years, even for life.

Critical periods for adult learning often occur around the

time of giving birth. Just as infants of many species imprint on their mothers, it is also true in some cases that the mother imprints on her offspring. It has been shown that if a mother goat is not allowed to lick and smell her kid within an hour after birth, she will reject him (Klopfer, Adams, & Klopfer, 1964). This period is probably related to the smell and taste of the mother's afterbirth. These sensory cues decrease rapidly in the first hour. An orphan goat kid will be accepted by an adoptive mother if he has been rubbed with the afterbirth of that mother (Hersher, Richmond, & Moore, 1963).

Finally, it can be pointed out that there may be a critical period for the distinctively human ability of language learning. If a child suffers injury to the left or "speech" hemisphere of the brain before the age of ten or so, recovery of language function is generally possible; the other hemisphere can acquire language in this case. However, similar injuries after puberty are followed by only minimal recovery (Lennenberg, 1967). This suggests that the plasticity of the brain necessary for basic language learning is at its maximum during the early years of life.

The Nature of the Stimulus-Response Linkage

There has been a growing awareness in recent years that different animals have evolved, through natural selection, to the point where they learn some stimulus-response relationships more quickly or better than they learn others. Imprinting may be one example, a very rapid association between a stimulus (sensory cues from the mother or Konrad Lorenz) and a response (following the mother) that occurs with no obvious reinforcement. We will consider some examples that stress the role of the stimulus in learning, some examples that stress the role of the response, and some that focus on the importance of the type of reinforcement.

One of the most interesting and most thoroughly studied phenomena of this type has been called by several names—the Garcia effect (after the man who has done most of the research), the bait-shyness effect, or simply poison-avoidance learning (Garcia & Ervin, 1968). By any name, the effect is this: if a rat eats something and then gets sick, he will avoid that food in the future. The strange thing about **bait shyness** is not so much that learning occurs so rapidly—in one trial or in no more than two or three—but that learning occurs in spite of the fact that the (negative) reinforcement—feeling sick—comes *hours* after the response is made to the stimulus. General principles of learning typically include assumptions, based on much evidence, that a delay of even one second between response and reinforcement or between a conditioned stimulus (CS) and an unconditioned stimulus (US) results in significantly decreased learning.

Whatever the biological mechanisms that underlie this curious learning ability in the rat, it is clearly to his advantage in terms of survival, as anybody who has tried to exterminate rats with poison can tell you. The advantage is compounded by other features of rat behavior. When a rat encounters a novel food in his habitat, he will take only a small portion and then wait a long time before taking more. If the novel food is a poison, the rat is therefore unlikely to die from the small portion; he will become ill—and thereafter he will avoid the bait. Thus, it is possible to see this learning ability as one that evolved through processes of natural selection. Those rats capable of becoming bait-shy were more likely to survive and reproduce, while their brother rats without the ability died.

There are additional features of bait shyness that are equally curious. The sickness, for example, can be unrelated to the food; if the rat eats something and then, later, is injected with a chemical that makes him sick—the food was pure—he will still avoid that food. And what he avoids is the taste of the food; he will eat food with different tastes even if identical in appearance to the "poisoned" food. Similarly, he will not avoid food of like temperature or texture, nor will he avoid the dish from which the poisoned food was eaten (Rozin & Kalat, 1971). In short, the rat avoids only food that tastes similar to that which made him sick.

Taste avoidance is not characteristic of all rat food avoidance, however. If, for example, a rat is shocked immediately after eating, he will reject food similar in appearance or those accompanied by the same distinctive sounds; he will not, in this case, avoid foods of similar taste.

Suppose a rat eats from several dishes, only one of which contains an unfamiliar food, and he then becomes ill. Under these conditions, he will subsequently reject only the novel food among the many eaten before becoming ill. Again the advantage to rat survival is obvious. An atypical, significant effect (an annoying or a satisfying state of affairs) is likely to be related to a new and unusual stimulus, at least in most natural habitats (Shettleworth, in press).

Bait shyness is not unique to rats, although they have been the most thoroughly studied. It has also been demonstrated in bobwhite quail (Wilcoxon, Dragoin, & Kral, 1969). In this experiment, quail and rats were given a sour dark-blue liquid to drink; thirty minutes later they were injected with a sickness-inducing chemical. Both species were later tested with liquids that were sour or blue or both. Rats avoided the taste—they rejected sour drinks but not blue liquids. Quail, however, avoided both the sour and the blue solutions. Considering that birds are highly visual animals and that food selection for them is based more on visual cues than for rats, these results make sense. Because of bait shyness, organisms that are toxic or have an unpleasant taste to other animals are thereby protected from predation. Certain other organisms gain protection by evolving to resemble those with an unpleasant taste; see Spotlight 27-3 on *mimicry*.

FIGURE 27-13
COURTSHIP AND MATING IN THE STICKLEBACK

In the first stage of courtship the male (left) zigzags toward the female. She swims toward him with her head up; her abdomen bulges with 50–100 eggs. The second and third stages are both seen from above. The male swims toward the nest he has built and makes a series of thrusts into it with his snout. He turns on his side and raises his dorsal spines toward the female, who swims into the nest. The male then prods the base of her tail and causes her to lay her eggs. When the female leaves the nest, the male enters and fertilizes the eggs. In the fourth stage the male "fans" water over the eggs to enrich their oxygen supply.

(Redrawn from "The Curious Behavior of the Stickleback," by N. Tinbergen. Copyright © 1952 by Scientific American, Inc. All rights reserved.

The bait-shyness phenomenon describes a specific stimulus-response association that is rapidly instituted, given a certain kind of reinforcement. Now consider a case where the reinforcement appears to be related to the *response* in such a way that some responses are harder to learn than others. This research was done with stickleback fish (see Figure 27-13). An investigator trained male sticklebacks to (1) bite a rod or (2) swim through a ring in an operant-conditioning procedure (Sevenster, 1968). The reinforcement was the opportunity to display to a sexually ripe female. The fish learned both responses, but his performance rate for rod-biting was considerably lower than for ring-swimming. Moreover, when reinforcement was discontinued (extinction), the rate of rod-biting actually *rose* for a time before the behavior eventually extinguished.

How is one to understand these facts? A probable answer is that rod-biting, an *aggressive* response, is basically incompatible with the sexually motivating nature of the reward. Thus, during acquisition, the fish would often swim to the rod, but instead of biting it, he would perform the zigzag dance that is typical of courtship in the stickleback (shown in Figure 27-13). Performing this dance in front of the rod indicated conflict between sex and aggression. Finally, the fish would bite the rod. Apparently courtship behavior

SPOTLIGHT 27-3
Mimicry of Bodily Appearance

The monarch butterfly (*Danaus plexippus*) and the viceroy butterfly (*Limenitis archippus*) are beautiful familiar visitors to gardens in the eastern United States. Both are orange in color with black and white markings, and to the casual observer could easily be mistaken for one another. However, they are in fact from different families of butterflies, and close examination would reveal differences in the arrangement of wing veins, leg structure, and the like, which clearly show their disparate ancestry. In addition, the majority of the "relatives" of the viceroy within the genus Limenitis are blue-black in color, and it is commonly believed that the blue-black color is the ancestral form from which the orange-based species evolved. Why, then, do the two butterflies look so much alike?

The commonly accepted answer relies on the fact that the taste of the monarch butterfly is aversive to some species of birds (such as the Florida scrub jay), which are potential predators. We have mentioned (p. 786) that quail can learn to associate the appearance of a liquid with its aftereffects. No doubt, visually oriented birds can also learn to associate characteristic patterns of color and form with bad tastes. Thus, they learn to avoid preying upon the bad-tasting monarch butterflies. In the meantime, they do continue to prey upon the blue-black viceroys. However, in an area where both genera of butterflies and their common potential predators dwell, some viceroys are born with an orange cast. These "new" variants are avoided by bird predators because of their resemblance to the bad-tasting monarchs. Selective pressures favoring the variants develop as a result of reduced predation and therefore greater chances of reproduction among the orange viceroys. The more closely the viceroy comes to resemble the monarch, that is, the more successful the mimicry, the greater is the likelihood of survival. These evolutionary pressures continue until differences in color and form between the monarch and viceroy are almost undetectable by predatory birds. There are many other examples of this kind of evolutionary mimicry.

Brower and Brower (1962) have carried out several experiments in the laboratory designed to investigate the mechanisms underlying the evolutionary advantages of mimicry. In one study they employed toads as predators and bumblebees, dragonflies, and robberflies as prey. After receiving several painful stings, all toads avoided eating bumblebees, but they continued to feed upon dragonflies, which do not look like bees. The robberfly has no capacity for stinging, but it is strikingly similar in appearance to the bumblebee, with a dark and light color pattern and a plump hairy body. Toads that had been stung by bumblebees would

activated a sexual motivational system that was incompatible with the aggressive rod-biting. When the presence of the female as reinforcement was discontinued, the conflict disappeared, so the rate of rod-biting dramatically increased for a time.

If this reasoning is accurate, then we should expect to

also avoid robberflies; control toads that had not been stung by bumblebees accepted robberflies as food 67 percent of the time. The only toad that consistently rejected robberflies without having been stung by a bumblebee happened to get hit on the nose by the robberfly the first time he tried to eat one and apparently developed a selective avoidance response on this basis. It is therefore plausible that the robberfly evolved toward its present coloration and configuration because of its evolution in an area where both bumblebees and potential predators resided. In this kind of environment, its ability to mimic the appearance of the bumblebee would protect it from experienced (but not inexperienced) predators, and selective pressure would operate to produce an ever-more realistic replica of the bee.

Predators on the other hand, can also mimic to the detriment of prey. This mimicry often involves specialized body structures that lure the prey to capture. For example, the alligator snapping turtle has a special wormlike projection from its tongue. Lying in wait with its mouth agape, the turtle wiggles this projection in enticing fashion until an unwary fish approaches too closely and becomes the victim instead of predator of the "worm." The angler fish has evolved a similar wormlike projection from the top of its head, again luring other fish to their demise. (See color Figures 5 and 6 on comparative psychology.)

The alligator snapping turtle (left) uses its tongue as a lure to entrap unwary fish, while the angler fish (right) attracts its prey by wiggling a wormlike projection from its snout.

find a very high rate of rod-biting if the reward is an opportunity to display aggressively to another male. The limited data that we possess on this question suggest that our expectation would be realized.

It is often assumed that a reinforcer is a reinforcer is a reinforcer, and that rewards that increase the probability of one response will work with equal effectiveness on other behaviors. From evidence like that just reported, such assumptions do not seem tenable.

The Role of the Response

As we have just seen, if one wants to train an animal to perform a response at a consistently high rate, he has to take care in the choice of the response to be taught. The response should be compatible with the motivational state arranged by the experimenter, and frequently a "good" response for a particular animal is one that has meaning in his daily activities in his natural habitat. The maze was first chosen as a good test of rat learning because it involved the kind of behavior—running about and exploring—that is common to the wild rat (Small, 1900). Similarly, using the pecking response of pigeons in a Skinner box utilizes a behavior that is natural and has survival advantages. The pigeon peck is also remarkably suitable for a range of motivational situations—feeding, attacking, and others.

What can happen when the choice of response is not so wise or fortunate was told by two psychologists who were engaged in training animals for zoo shows, television commercials, and the like (Breland & Breland, 1961, 1966). Using operant-conditioning techniques, they trained over five thousand animals from a wide range of species. Generally they were quite successful, but there were failures, and they began to notice a pattern in their unsuccessful training attempts. A sample failure is the case of a raccoon the psychologists wanted to teach to put coins into a metal container. After some difficulty, they got the raccoon to put a single coin into the container, but when they tried to train him to deposit two coins at once, they were totally unsuccessful. The raccoon picked up the two coins and brought them to the container, but he would not let go. Instead he stood by the container and rubbed (and rubbed and rubbed) the coins together, occasionally dipping (but not dropping) them into the container. In spite of nonreinforcement, the rubbing behavior came more and more to dominate the performance, and this trick had to be abandoned.

Another "piggy bank" trick was planned for—appropriately enough—a pig. The "coins" were large wooden disks that the pig was required to carry several feet and deposit in a large container in order to obtain a food reward. A number of pigs were successfully trained to do this, but in every case, their performance soon began to deteriorate. Instead of trotting rapidly from the coin pile to the piggy bank, the pigs began to drop the coin on their way to the container—repeatedly, deliberately. Then they would root it along for a while—push it along with their snout—and then pick it up and toss it in the air. All this fancy behavior was hardly to their advantage; the wasted time increased so that the pigs were not receiving enough nourishment to survive.

Thus, in both examples, there is a failure of the general

FIGURE 27-14
FOOD-WASHING IN THE RACCOON

This species-characteristic pattern of behavior interfered with attempts to train raccoons to pick up and release coinlike objects. (Alfred Francesconi, National Audubon Society)

procedures of conditioning. In the case of the pigs, the response is learned and then deteriorates. The "interfering behaviors" in both cases are those the animal typically displays when hungry in a food-gathering situation: "washing" in the raccoon (Figure 27-14) and rooting in the pig. The authors of this report call this interference **instinctive drift,** meaning that the response wanted was often replaced by behaviors that the animals instinctively perform in the wild.

Deliberate choice of a response pattern natural to the animal may result in evidence of considerable learning in tasks where the animal had been previously thought incompetent. Spotlight 27-2 described research on language learning in chimps. Before this recent work, it was thought nearly impossible to teach a chimp to talk. This is true if by "talk" one means communicating by the pattern of vocal sounds humans use, but if by "talk" one means the use of hand and arm motions (sign language) or manipulation of objects that correspond to words, chimps can achieve a significant level of animal–human communication.

In a delayed-response test (see p. 765), the domestic cat does quite poorly, unable to find the reward after more than a minute. To cat owners, this result does not quite jibe with their observations of their pet waiting patiently—for hours—outside a mouse hole. One psychologist set up a delayed-response test to be more like what a cat experiences in his natural hunting behavior. The cat faced two openings in a wall and observed a stimulus appear and disappear in one. After various delays, the cat was allowed to swat at the opening where the stimulus had appeared. Under these conditions the cat showed itself capable of delays much longer than had been considered possible.

Effective Rewards

The view that all rewards have the same effect on all responses should by now be thoroughly discredited. Still, there remains the problem of specifying the biological or theoretical nature of reinforcement, an issue that has a long history in psychology. As one of the earliest positions, Thorndike's (p. 763) can be considered. He claimed that the bond between a stimulus and a response will be strengthened—that is, learning will occur—if the response leads to a "satisfying state of affairs." There was not much discussion of why an effective reward was satisfying.

After Thorndike, views on reinforcement developed in two directions nearly opposite. On the one hand, Skinner defined a reinforcer as any stimulus event contingent upon a response that increases the probability of occurrence of that response. This is a purely empirical approach: *what* is reinforcing is determined by observing changes in frequency of behaviors that are followed by various events. In this tradition, there is a very active avoidance of questions concerning the underlying biological or functional nature of the reward; for example, *why* is food reinforcing for a hungry animal?

The second approach was led by Hull (1943), who was influenced by the biological concept of **homeostasis**—the tendency of many biological systems to achieve a relatively stable state with component elements in equilibrium. The model for this view was probably the biological feeding system. If the body lacks food, it somehow sets up a state of tension (**drive**) that leads to behaviors designed to reduce the tension (**drive reduction**) and restore the original equilibrium. Events that are *drive reducing*, therefore, are reinforcing. For a hungry rat, food is reinforcement because food reduces the hunger drive. (For current views of the biological nature of such systems, see Chapter 25.)

For hunger, thirst, and the avoidance of pain, the drive-reduction hypothesis functioned reasonably well. Some intractable phenomena, however, soon began appearing in scientific reports. Most of these involved sensory stimulation that was "satisfying" and increased the probability of a response without obviously reducing biological tension. A hungry rat would work to obtain saccharin solutions, which are sweet but have no nutritive value, and therefore they do not reduce the biological need for food. A male rat would work for the privilege of copulating with a female, even if no ejaculation (tension reduction) was permitted. A wide range of species would work for nothing more than the opportunity to explore the environment. For example, monkeys will quickly solve a discrimination problem for the privilege of being able to look out of his cage at the goings-on in the laboratory (Butler, 1954). In fact, he will solve complex puzzles for nothing (Harlow, 1953). See Spotlight 27-4 on curiosity in animals.

A number of animals will work very hard to get electrical stimulation to certain areas of their brain (the "pleasure centers"; see p. 717), and it is difficult to see how this stimulation relates to any kind of tension reduction. Finally, many studies indicate that a change of stimulation may be rewarding in itself. For example, if a monkey is in darkness, he will work to have the light turned on. If he is in the light, he will work to have the light turned off.

Advocates of tension-reduction theories of reinforcement came up with an ingenious set of explanations for sensory rewards and other anomalies. For example, to explain exploratory behavior, they cited studies showing that novel stimuli arouse fear and suggested that exploration reduces anxiety tension. There is probably some truth in these patchwork explanations, but with all the loopholes and qualifications, the drive-reduction theories were becoming simply too cumbersome to be useful. Many psychologists, perhaps most, turned to other approaches, and learning psychologists (p. 469) have more or less abandoned the issue of reinforcement altogether.

Current Research on Reinforcement

In comparative psychology, however, the reinforcement issue remains vital. The questions of *why* an organism does something, or why he does this and not that, or why he does this at age *X* and that at age *Y* are all being investigated. Psychologists in many areas (comparative, but also personality and social psychology) find that answers to these questions permit a more complete understanding of their subject matter.

Within comparative psychology, two approaches to the question of reinforcement have received particular attention and, as usual, they can be characterized as the American view and the European, ethological view. One of the most influential American comparative psychologists in this century has been T. C. Schneirla, and we can present his views on the nature of reinforcement without fear that they are atypical.

An American View

Schneirla (1959) proposed that the only objective descriptions of motivated behavior *across species* were in terms of *approach* and *withdrawal*. Therefore, he suggested, rewards are best characterized as the introduction of events that typically induce approach or as the removal of events that typically induce withdrawal. This view is similar to that of Thorndike in some ways. Events that are "satisfying" and hence reinforcing were defined by Thorndike as those which the animal will approach and not withdraw from.

Schneirla also proposed that approach behavior is instituted by mild stimulation and withdrawal by intense stimulation. This theory explained the rewarding effects of sensory stimulation without requiring the concept of homeostasis, but it elicited other

SPOTLIGHT 27-4
Curiosity

One of the major adaptations of many species is their plasticity, their flexibility in learning about the world in which they live. Psychologists have frequently acted as if laboratory animals would work only if rewarded with food, water, or avoidance of pain. However, it is apparent that many species will emit responses and learn about their environment without such externally supplied rewards; as is evident in the case of latent learning (p. 471). The motivational basis of such learning is generally considered to be curiosity, and the behavior patterns are commonly classified as investigatory or exploratory behavior. Learning about new sources of food, locating potential mates, and forming the "map" of one's territory that permits security of movement and rapid escape to burrows or other places of safety, are all potential benefits to the curious animal.

This chimpanzee is using a stick as a "tool" to remove edible termites from a mound. The development of such tool-using behavior requires a very high level of manipulatory curiosity.
(Phyllis Dolinhow)

However, curiosity is not without its dangers. While engaged in inspection of some novel feature of the environment, an animal may be particularly vulnerable to predation.

Some years ago, we examined the responses of several hundred mammals and a smaller group of reptiles to novel objects introduced to their cages at various zoological parks (Glickman & Sroges, 1966). As can be seen in the graph, all of the mammalian orders which we studied reacted to the novel objects and displayed habituation. That is, as they grew familiar with the objects during a single six-minute test session they showed a decline in response to the simple wooden, metal, and rubber objects that were supplied for their investigation. There were differences among the orders of mammals in terms of the average time spent investigating the objects, with the primates and carnivores in our sample exhibiting considerably more total reactivity than the rodents, insectivores, edentates and marsupials (although there were wide individual and species differences, with some marsupials being more reactive than some primates). Equally striking was the range of investigatory patterns that each species showed. These patterns were obviously limited by the sensory-motor equipment of the animal and tended to approximate the kinds of responses observed during food-gathering behavior. Confronted by a novel object, most rodents would smell it and possibly bite it; the majority of primates would emphasize visual inspection and would use their dextrous manipulatory capacity to examine it. The greatest variety and amount of investigatory activity was observed in those animals possessing (1) a

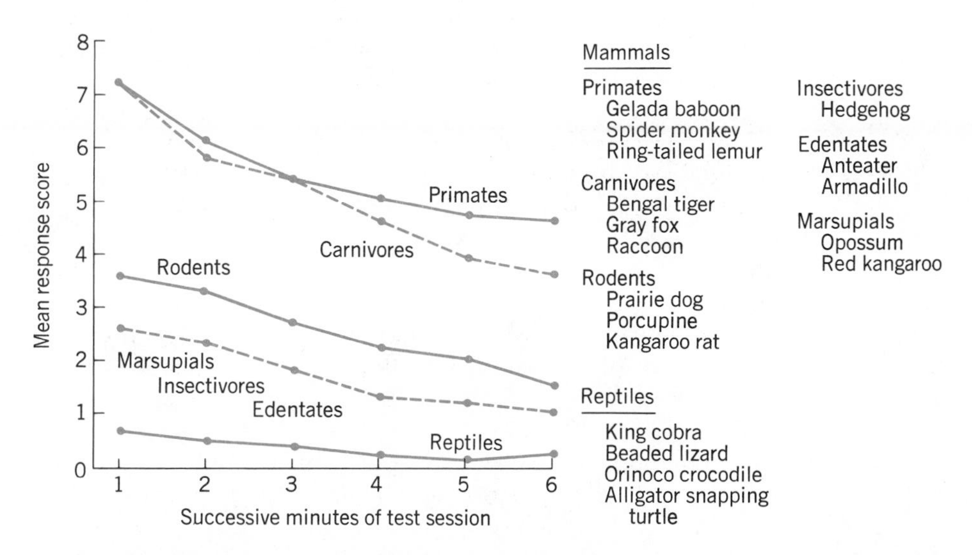

The various species showed clear differences in reactivity to novel stimulus objects. Note the decline in response during the course of the test session.
(From Glickman & Sroges, 1966)

relatively large, well-developed brain, (2) good manipulatory ability, (3) a varied diet under natural habitat conditions, and (4) relative security from predators in the natural habitat. These conditions are met by a variety of primates including the baboons, chimpanzees, and, most notably, by man.

In the laboratory, a variety of different tasks and measures have been employed to assess curiosity, including (1) the orientation of the sense receptors to a novel source of stimulation (Pavlov's "what is it?" reflex); (2) the reactions of caged animals to a novel object placed in their environment (as we did at the zoo); (3) the locomotor responses of animals placed in an unfamiliar environment; and (4) the emission of some arbitrary behavior such as lever-pressing or running a maze, in order to gain access to a source of novel stimulation.

Some additional generalizations emerge from the myriad studies carried out in this area. Stimuli likely to evoke the most direct investigation are those which are moderately novel, but not so unusual as to evoke fear, or so familiar as to be dismissed without further concern. In addition, there is apparently an optimal age for each species during which curiosity is at its maximum. Most research places this somewhere between childhood and early adult stages, with both young infants and mature experienced members of the species showing relatively less direct investigatory behavior. This almost surely correlates with the importance of early life as an optimal time for learning within the mammalian orders.

criticisms. In particular, the theory defined a reinforcement as an event producing mild arousal. What is "mild arousal"? How is it to be measured? Sexual arousal may be sought although it is very intense, while even mildly bitter drinks will be avoided; how can the theory account for these qualitative differences?

One aspect of Schneirla's position proved very fruitful, his *developmental* perspective on the reinforcement process. He argued that adult behavior and the stimuli that control it could only be understood in terms of the history of the organism. The proper study of reinforcement then begins with observation of the basic approach-withdrawal tendencies of the infant subject. An example is a recent study of how nursing behavior develops in the kitten beginning with the "neonate's basic capacity of approaching low intensity tactile, thermal and olfactory stimuli" (Rosenblatt, in press). As the kitten matures, these primitive approach tendencies become integrated into conditioned-response sequences involving preference for a specific nipple position. Development of responses to new sensory cues (from the visual system) and more complex orienting behavior then ensue as the kitten takes an ever-more active role in nursing (see Chapter 28, p. 823). In part, this emphasis on developmental processes involved a reaction against the classical ethological focus on "instinctive" behavior patterns and is representative of a continued search for indications of learning and flexibility in behavior.

A European View

In contrast to Schneirla's stimulus-intensity theory of reinforcement, the European ethologists (notably Niko Tinbergen) have seen the consummatory response as the basis for reinforcement. In broad terms, this view holds that animals will learn responses that result in the activation of species-characteristic behavior patterns necessary for the preservation of the species. In more common terminology, food is not the reinforcement; eating is!

Ethologists have a traditional interest in the description of fixed action patterns in lower animals like birds and fish; thus, it comes as no surprise to find them very conscious of the role of responses in reinforcement. However, several psychologists working in the American behaviorist tradition have also noted the response as the critical element in what is normally called reward or reinforcement. Premack (1965) has proposed that if one of two different responses is preferred at a given time, the preferred one can be used to reinforce the less preferred one. He formulated this hypothesis after observing his wife induce eating behavior in his children by offering permission to play when the dinner was finished. This reverses the typical sequence of events in a psychological laboratory, where the experimenter usually "rewards" other behavior by giving the animal the opportunity to eat or drink. In subsequent laboratory research, Premack did indeed show that if a rat was not thirsty, nevertheless it would lick at the tube of a water bottle when it learned that licking behavior led to the privilege of running in an activity wheel.

The consummatory-response view of reinforcement has been strengthened by a number of recent studies on a variety of species, all suggesting that the opportunity to engage in a species-specific behavior can be used to increase the probability of a preceding response. For example, a deer mouse will press a lever if he is then allowed to burrow in sand (King & Weisman, 1964). In several bird and fish species that exhibit species-characteristic aggressive or sexual displays (e.g., the peacock spreads his beautiful tail feathers in sexual display), it has been shown that they can be trained to perform a different response for the opportunity to display (p. 787).

It would be nice to end our review of ideas about the nature of reinforcement by pointing to one view as correct. Alas, such certitude is rare in science. All of the views we have described have some merits and some demerits, and each has a particular body of research to which it is best suited. Certainly this history is replete with examples of the dangers of taking one extreme view in exclusion of others. Perhaps the answer lies in some synthesis of all the valid important points from the various approaches. If you care to try your hand, I can assure you that success would bring great rewards—even if we do not fully understand the nature of those rewards!

Stimulus Specificity

We have discussed the response and the reinforcement, and perhaps we should conclude with a few words on the role of the stimulus in learning. At the outset, we can say without fear of contradiction that an animal cannot learn a response to a stimulus it cannot detect. For example, most mammals do not discriminate colors very well, and therefore it is difficult to train them to respond one way to one color and another way to a different hue. Only the primates, including man, respond well to color cues. This fact is rather interesting in light of the excellent color vision in many submammalian vertebrates. Many birds and fish rely on color patterns for species recognition, and many reptiles are capable of fine color discriminations.

The stimuli to which an animal is sensitive often correspond to his survival needs. An underground, burrowing rodent like the mole has little use for visual abilities and it has few, whereas high-flying predator birds must be able to see extremely well. Thus, smell and taste are highly developed senses in many rodents, while most birds exhibit exceptional visual acuity.

Young sea turtles require a special sensory capacity in order to survive. Eggs are laid in the sand on a beach, and they hatch by the warmth of the sun. The young turtles then emerge and scramble down to the sea. For many years, this behavior was a puzzle to animal psychologists; there were no parents around; what was the sensory cue to which the little turtle was responding, directing him to the sea?

Early hypotheses included a variety of nonvisual cues, but sight was implicated by the fact that blindfolded turtles wandered aimlessly. Solar navigation, common in many species (e.g., bees), was ruled out by a series of tests. Finally it was discovered that the important cue was equal brightness in both eyes—the typical seaward view in both day and night.

But brightness in a turtle's vision is primarily in the shorter wavelengths; red lights must be much more intense to elicit the same response as a low-intensity blue light. Through processes of natural selection the baby turtle has evolved to respond to the blue brightness of the sea and the sky, to which he must run to survive (Mrosovsky, 1967). If the sea turtle were set to work in a comparative psychologist's laboratory, learning should proceed with greater ease if the stimuli were colored lights with short wavelengths—blue. The greater sensitivity to these wavelengths, born of survival needs, becomes a fact experimenters must take into account, even in laboratory tasks with no life-or-death implications.

The cat is not very sensitive to sweet tastes, and it is extremely difficult to use sugar as either a reinforcer or as a discriminative stimulus in cat learning. On the other hand, the rat and the hamster are highly sensitive to sweet tastes, and in these animals sugar is a highly effective reward.

If this chapter has led you to the conclusions that each stimulus, each response, each reward—each instance of learning—must be evaluated for each species in each specific situation, then we have done our job successfully. It is perhaps unfortunate that nature is not simpler. It should not be assumed that generalizations are impossible—we have reached the generalization that the effectiveness of stimuli, responses, and rewards for any animal depends upon survival requirements in its natural habitat. But generalizations based on limited information, obtained from observation of only a few species, were bound to come into conflict with facts. In science, this is healthy and productive. In comparative psychology, we are only now experiencing the excitement and the increased knowledge that result from the conflicts between hypotheses and observations.

SUMMARY

This chapter has focused on the similarities and differences among various animal species in their ability to learn and/or to adapt to their environments. The search for continuity—the search for similarities and general principles across species—has been largely an American tradition. The emphasis has been on abilities that result in flexibility and modifiability in response, i.e., learning abilities. In Europe, more attention has been paid to the species-characteristic behavior patterns through which insects, fish, and birds adapt to their environments.

Because of their fascination with problems of learning, American psychologists generally emphasized the use of mammals in laboratory settings and assumed that general principles of learning would emerge, applicable even to man. A review of the evolution of man indicates that we share some traits with all of the mammals (nursing of the young), other traits with just the primates (emphasis on vision), and possess still a third set of characteristics that are unique to the human species (language). We might therefore expect that both general principles and specific differences will emerge when learning is viewed in comparative perspective.

Thorndike's puzzle-box experiments were among the first comparative studies of animal learning in the United States. One of the goals of the continuity approach was to develop a kind of "general intelligence test" appropriate for all species. The puzzle boxes represent an early attempt, the delayed-response test was another example, and more recently, the learning-set procedures of Harlow have been used. It was expected that most animals would perform in similar fashion but at different levels of competence. Generally speaking, this expectation was not realized; unavoidable differences in perceptual and motor abilities and in motivation made differences in performance somewhat suspect as a pure measure of intellectual or learning ability. Bitterman has proposed that systematic variation of motivational states, rather than futile attempts to equate motivational levels across species, can resolve at least some of the classic issues.

Within the continuity tradition, there were several hints of discontinuity. Köhler presented evidence for a "different type" of learning called insight. Continuity theorists, however, countered with data suggesting that insight required prior trial and error learning. For example, for a chimpanzee to show insightful solutions to stick-manipulation problems, he must have had the opportunity to play with sticks during infancy and adolescence. Also, in learning-set studies, monkeys could "insightfully" solve simple discrimination problems in a trial or two, but only after a long series of tasks incorporating the same general rule.

In the learning theories of Hull and Skinner the continuity hypothesis became almost an axiom, and researchers used rats and pigeons to examine *general* principles of learning. Recently the assertions of ethologists and some American scientists (e.g., Bitterman) that *differences* (even in general principles) should be considered along with the similarities have led comparative psychologists interested in learning back to the study of animals across a wider phylogenetic range.

In Europe all this time, the ethologists were studying the fixed action patterns (FAP's) that promoted adaptation and survival in lower animals. These patterns of behavior, which are not dependent on specific learning, were viewed as released by sign stimuli, i.e., particular stimulus configurations that trigger the FAP's. An example is the retrieval behaviors of birds to eggs placed outside the nest.

Each animal species is adapted for life in a particular habitat. To the extent that the ability to learn new responses is part of that adaptation, we would expect such learning propensities to have evolved through the same basic process of natural selection. Any given species might be expected to learn responses crucial to survival with great ease, while responses that are irrelevant or detrimental to survival would be less easily acquired or performed. These constraints on learning were first discussed in terms of critical periods, those developmental stages in which certain learning proceeds quickly and outside of which the same learning seems difficult or impossible. Many animals, for example, learn to make social responses to their parents (or, in unusual circumstances, to ethologists) in a short, critical period after birth; this has been called "imprinting."

The bait-shyness effect describes another constraint on learning. If a rat eats something (e.g., poison bait) and later becomes ill, he will avoid (shy away from) that food in the future. The stimulus avoided is often quite specific; in the rat, it is the taste of the food. Also, the rapid learning of bait-shyness occurs even though the negative reinforcement comes hours after taking the bait; the effectiveness of this reinforcement in spite of its long delay poses problems for learning theories in general.

Just which response is reinforced also makes a difference in learning. Behaviors that are characteristic of the animal in his natural habitat seem easier to train, and if one reinforces a response different from that which is "instinctive" for a given motivational state, there may be "instinctive drift" back to the typical response. Thus a raccoon trained to drop a "coin" in a box to get food will often try to "clean and wash" the coin before dropping it.

There has been considerable controversy in this century over what constitutes an effective reward. Some prominent notions included the "satisfying state of affairs" (Thorndike), "drive reduction" (Hull), and the "consummatory response" (Tinbergen). Skinnerian psychologists have defined reinforcement empirically, asserting that an event that follows a response and leads to the increased probability of occurrence of that response is a positive reinforcer. Recently it has been found that a preferred or prepotent response will reinforce a less preferred response, so that a child will eat in order to play, and a rat may be trained to drink in order to get the opportunity to run in an activity wheel.

Finally, the stimulus imposes certain constraints on learning. It is hard to train a cat to associate sweet tastes with a particular behavior, while the same association is made with relative ease by rats.

Investigators are beginning to synthesize two disparate traditions of comparative psychology—one concerned with general principles of learning, the other with adaptation to the environment. Although we can develop experimental procedures for studying learning, the ability to acquire particular kinds of habits will ultimately be related to the repertoire of adaptive behavior that each species brings to the test situation.

28
A Social Existence

What functions does social cohesion serve?
When does social dispersal occur?
What mechanisms contribute to cohesive behavior?
What mechanisms underlie dispersal behavior?
What can we learn about human social behavior from comparative psychology?

Shortly after sunrise, the hamadryas baboons of the Ethiopian lowlands leave their sleeping rocks and ascend to the "waiting" areas which lie above. The more than one hundred animals which comprise a hamadryas troop have spent the night lodged against the face of a cliff, secure from predators. But now it is time to forage for food; the troop members will leave their sanctuary and venture into the surrounding savannah or plain in search of food and water. The troop leaves en masse, but as the march proceeds, parties of animals depart from the main group and begin to feed. This process continues until the members of the troop are scattered across an area of one mile or more.

An experienced observer can see that the parties that break off from the main group are all similar in composition; in fact, these subgroups represent the fundamental social unit of the hamadryas baboon society, the **one-male group,** usually composed of one adult male, one to five females, and their offspring. Shortly after midday, the first of these units will begin the return journey, and by midafternoon the majority of the troop members will once again be in place in the waiting areas atop their cliffside retreat. Each day begins and ends with a prolonged period of social interaction among all members of the troop. The most common adult interaction involves one baboon carefully grooming the fur of another, although sex, aggression, and the vigorous play of the young are also in evidence. Finally, as dusk approaches, the animals return to their sleeping rocks on the cliff face, each one-male group remaining closely clustered together. (See Figure 28-1.)

FIGURE 28-1
ONE-MALE BABOON GROUP
A one-male unit of hamadryas baboons sleeps on the ledge of a cliff.

In the savannah and fields to the south and west some closely related baboons (*Papio anubis*) live a rather different existence. Here the nights are generally spent in trees and the troops move as a group in their feeding activities throughout the day. The one-male unit is not to be found. In its place, we have a complex system of troop organization that is better described in terms of roles, with key positions occupied by one or more adult males who control much of the troop's activities, interpose themselves when danger threatens the troop, and engage in the majority of the mating activity. In these *Papio anubis* baboons, the dominant males occupy a position near the center of the troop, surrounded by females in estrus and females with infants. The peripheral positions are taken by other adult males (where they can act as "sentries"), and the remaining females and juveniles are located between the core and the periphery (Hall & DeVore, 1965). (See color Figure 1.) Finally, in the Ethiopian highlands, a third species of baboon (*Theropithecus gelada*) exhibits either the troop or the one-male group form of social organization, depending on various ecological factors (Crook, 1967).

Within the contrasting life-styles just described are contained virtually all of the puzzles about social behavior. How are these contrasting social systems adaptive for survival in different habitats? What are the ties that bind members of these groups to one another, and what factors ultimately promote their dispersal?

The analysis of social behavior takes place at several levels. In the sections that follow, we shall first consider the presumed evolutionary-adaptive advantages of social grouping and dispersal. Grouping is advantageous for some purposes, but dispersal is advantageous for others, as we shall see. Then we will turn to the mechanisms that produce such behavior patterns.

What functions does social cohesion serve?

Protection

One of the primary advantages of a cohesive social group is the protection it affords the individual member against harm and injury. In the case of the savannah baboons, the females and young are protected by the adult males who are physically powerful, possess impressive canine teeth (see Figure 28-2), and can band together to defeat powerful foes. In the one-male groups of the hamadryas baboon, the one male must, of course, face the predator alone, but even so the females and young are considerably better off than if they were by themselves.

In the patas monkeys (*Erythrocebus patas*) we also find the one-male group as a basic unit of social interaction (Hall, 1965). Evasion of predators, however, takes a completely different form from that of the hamadryas baboon. The single male strays much farther from his party of females, infants, and juveniles; he acts as sentry. Should a predator appear, the patas male informs his party, and they all take rapid flight across the plains in which they live. The male does not confront the predator, and the females determine the direction of movement—behavior that is the opposite of the one-male groups of baboons in the Ethiopian lowlands, even though in other respects the social organization is strikingly similar.

The hamadryas baboon is a powerful animal, while the patas monkey is tall, slender, and exceptionally fast (see Figure 28-3). Each seems to have achieved a means of predator evasion that accentuates its particular talents, which are largely determined by bodily structure. Although both species live in environments that promote a social organization we call one-male groups, the means of group protection is quite different. We can begin to see the complex interrelations among heredity, habitat, and social organization.

Cohesion for protection in other species is organized in quite different ways. The grouping-together or schooling of fish, for example, has been viewed as a protective maneuver in two senses (Shaw, 1960). First, schooling tends to confuse the predator by presenting a welter of attractive stimuli. Second, if the predator does strike a peripheral fish, the remainder are "warned" and have time to swim away. Presumably if the school members were widely dispersed, the predator could actually consume more, picking them off one at a time. Human duck hunters (predators) will tell you that they would much prefer to shoot at a lone duck and that it is difficult to bag even one of a large flock. Perhaps similar principles are operating here.

Among small birds who are potential victims of larger hawks and owls, the bonding-together or mobbing technique of defense is common (Hinde, 1954). The smaller birds literally mob the potential predator; they use their greater speed and agility and fly

FIGURE 28-2
AN ADULT MALE BABOON

The canine teeth are formidable weapons against potential predators.

FIGURE 28-3
PATAS MONKEYS DRINKING AT A WATERHOLE

The females, juveniles, and infants cluster around the water's edge while the lone adult male remains at the periphery of the group out of camera range.
(J. S. Gartlan)

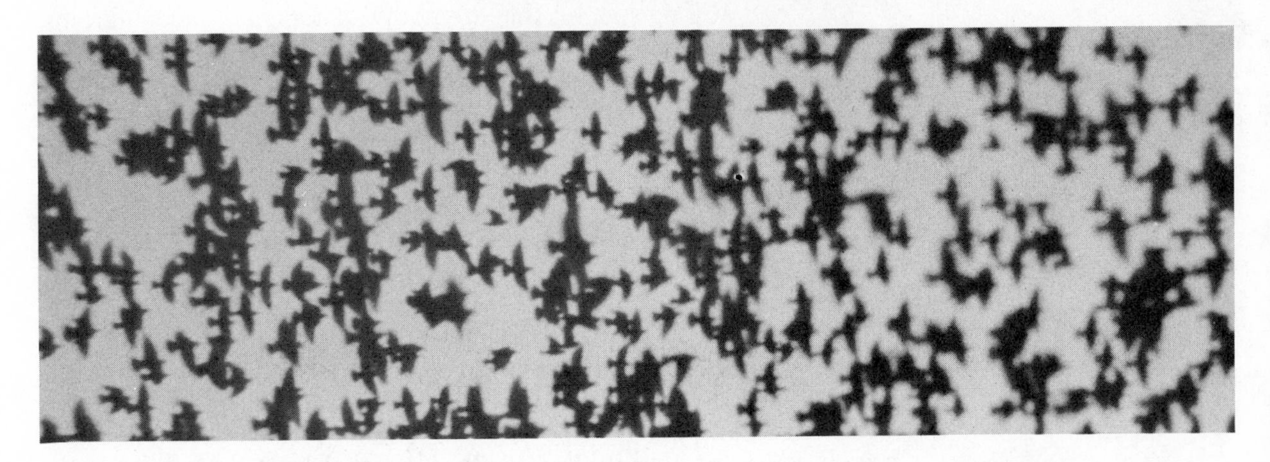

FIGURE 28-4
MOBBING BEHAVIOR

Birds that would be powerless alone band together for defense.
(Eric J. Hosking, National Audubon Society)

at him in great numbers, harassing him relentlessly until he leaves the vicinity (see Figure 28-4).

Why don't these fast birds simply flee from the slower predator, as the patas monkeys do? They must protect their nests, the eggs, and their young who cannot yet fly. Their response, of course, is not born of a conscious decision to be a good parent, but it does promote the survival of the species; the behavior pattern has evolutionary advantage. Many fish show a similar pattern of fighting ferociously in their own territory, even against great odds. But these same fish will flee an opponent when they are *away* from their home grounds. In some species, this pattern of fighting at home and fleeing when away from home is so precise that an experienced observer can predict almost to the inch (away from home territory) which of two fish will "win" the confrontation.

In some social groups members will display apparently **altruistic** or sacrificial behavior in order to protect others. Perhaps the best-known example is the "broken-wing" display of some bird species such as ducks or partridges. Threatened by a predator, the female bird protects her young (or her nest) by feigning injury and suggesting easy capture. She flutters helplessly an attractive (but safe) distance away to draw the predator from the nest. She stumbles and flutters again and again, always farther from the nest. Finally, when the predator is safely distant from the nest, she flies away with two obviously healthy wings.

Predation and Food-Gathering

Just as social structure can benefit the **prey,** so can it benefit the **predator.** Among the mammals, this is most easily seen in wolves and wild dogs. Through cooperative hunting, these animals can capture much larger prey (e.g., deer) than would be possible for any one individual (Allen & Mech, 1963). Predation in the "natural habitat" is a food-gathering behavior, not a hostile act.

Among species that are not predators, most social groups also use their cohesion in some way to increase their "take" over what it would be if all functioned as individuals. Bees, for example, have an elaborate social system which includes widely dispersed "scouts." If a scout detects a good food source, he flies back to the hive and "communicates" the location to other members of the hive. The food source is then visited by large numbers of bees.

How does the scout transmit this information on direction and distance of the food source? Karl von Frisch, an Austrian zoologist, spent most of his life investigating the intriguing communication system of bees. To study the process, von Frisch (1950) constructed special hives with glass plates so that he could observe the social interaction. One of his earliest observations was that scouts, upon returning to the hive, do a kind of dance and that the other bees are obviously excited by the dance. The other bees then fly from the hive, usually directly to the food source from which the scout has come. So the dance must communicate something. Von Frisch began translating.

Bee dances can be classified into two main types: circling and wagging (see Figure 28-5). Von Frisch surmised at first that the circling dance meant "nectar" and the wagging dance meant "pollen,"

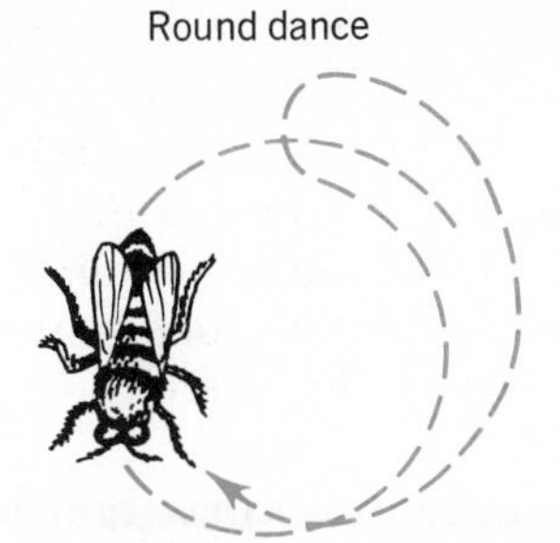

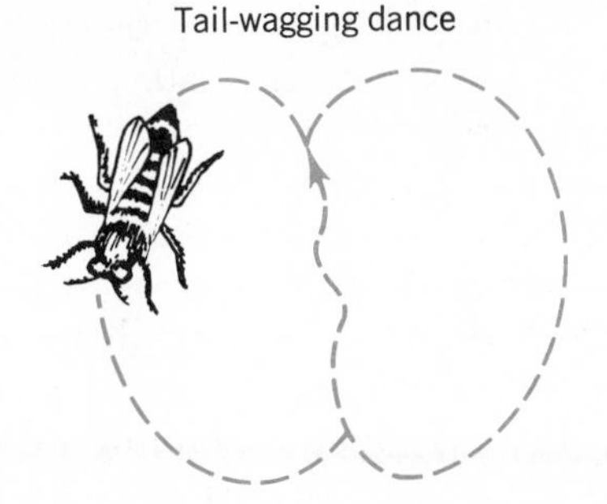

FIGURE 28-5
HONEYBEE "DANCES"

Information about the richness of the food source and its location is conveyed by the dancing patterns given by "scout" bees.
(After M. Lindauer, 1961)

but later observations showed this to be an inaccurate translation; the communication patterns were found to be much more complex than he supposed, and cues other than the dance were involved. The type of food tends to be communicated by odors on the scout, who of course has consumed a bit before telling his friends. The vigor of the dance seems to be related to the quantity of the food source; when the nectar starts running low, the dance is slower.

But what of the two different kinds of dances? What do they indicate? By setting up food sources at various distances, von Frisch discovered that with sources more than one hundred meters away, bees did only the wagging dance, and with sources less than fifty meters away bees did only the circling dance. He also concluded that the vertical direction of the dance is related to the direction (in relation to the sun) of the food source. (See Krogh, 1948.)

The language of bees is even more complex than this. The number of turns per second conveys information about distance, and the number of waggles per second is probably also important. Some bees do not perform the short-distance round dance at all; instead they dance in a kind of semi-circle that has been called the "sickle dance" (Lindauer, 1961). Although recent research (Wenner, 1967) has raised questions as to whether bees always use the information contained in their dances, the intricate communication patterns represent a remarkable aspect of food-gathering behavior in a social insect.

In higher animals such as the baboons, past experience and learning play a role in determining food-gathering patterns. Dominant males often decide the direction of troop travel in search of food. They are, of course, adults, and before assuming leadership have probably spent a decade or so as followers. No doubt they learn much about terrain and safety in this early period. In some chimpanzee troops, the dominant males sometimes defer to old (wise?) males for leadership in food-gathering situations.

In predatory animals, the period of infancy is a time to learn appropriate hunting techniques. Learning may occur in play with peers and inanimate objects or in specific maternal tutelage. It has been demonstrated that polecats need this early training period if they are to exhibit the intricate killing behavior of adults. Polecats raised in isolation have all the proper actions but the sequence is often incorrect; for example, these cats "worry" their prey (shake it back and forth to break its neck) before making the proper bite. Often individual acts such as biting are directed to an improper target area (Eibl-Eibesfeldt, 1961). It is still not clear in the social situation whether the young animal learns by itself or whether the parent guides this learning.

A clearer example of maternal tutelage may be seen in Indian tigers (Schaller, 1967). The cubs remain with the mother for a year or more, sharing the fruits of her predation and sometimes joining in the kill itself. It is difficult, however, in field studies to distinguish observational learning on the part of the cubs from learning by direct experience, when the mother slows down the prey and allows the young to make the kill. Possibly both types of learning take place.

In species where past experience is a factor in adult food-gathering, the period of infancy and adolescence is obviously important. But the young of a species sometimes make their own original contributions. In the Japanese macaque monkeys, juveniles frequently try food sources neglected by the adults, and if the food source is a good one, the adults proceed to try it themselves (Itani, 1959).

Mating

Sex, of course, is one of the most important reasons why members of a species have to meet now and then, even if they are dispersed for most of each year. The simultaneous physical presence of two partners is not required in all species—for example, in salmon the female lays eggs and the male swims by some time later and fertilizes them. Nevertheless, the evolutionary trend seems to be in the direction of both partners coming together for mating. Similar evolutionary trends are toward internal fertilization, live birth, and the prolonged presence of one or both parents after birth. These trends enhance the chances of any particular infant for survival; large numbers of offspring, necessary in the lower species where only a minute percentage will survive, give way in higher species to small brood sizes. This generally results in a more elaborate and flexible social structure.

For the vast majority of mammals, sex is a periodic activity dependent on hormonal cycles in the male and female. In the hamadryas baboon one-male group, each adult male builds his "harem" slowly, apparently by literally kidnapping juvenile females and retaining them through maturity. Mating occurs when the female goes into **estrus** (her period of sexual receptivity) and only during those times of the day when the animals are not searching for food. Either the male or the female can initiate the mounting. Males are either gentle—lightly touching the female's genital swelling—or

FIGURE 28-6
BABOON MATING BEHAVIOR
This is a typical copulatory posture for a pair of baboons. (Phyllis Dolinhow, taken at the Gombe Stream Reserve)

rough—grabbing her by the hair on her head, jerking her into position. Females initiate copulation by presenting their rear end to the male, and copulation is from the rear, as shown in Figure 28-6.

In hamadryas baboons, the male is completely loyal to the females of his group, and the females are reasonably loyal to the male. Generally it is only the youngest females, those in estrus for the first time, that will mate with males outside the group, and this promiscuity is facilitated by the fact that the dominant male is apt to be occupied with the older, experienced females whom he prefers as sexual partners. If females are caught in infidelity, however, they can expect a painful neck bite from the leader, even if their lover is a juvenile male from their own group.

In the elk of the western United States, a social organization similar to the one-male groups of the baboon can be observed (Altmann, 1956), but only during the mating (or "rutting") season. In the late summer, the antlers of the adult males develop, and these are used in aggressive encounters with other adult males. Victory in these encounters ensures exclusive mating rights with a larger harem of cows. Once the mating season is over, however, the males and females go their separate ways, the female as part of a herd composed exclusively of females and juveniles. Next fall, the process will repeat itself, and males must fight again for mates. So in this case the annual hormonal cycles affect not only the cohesion of the species, but also the nature of the social organization at various seasons of the year.

In the troop-organized savannah baboon, dominant males do not have the monopoly that exists in one-male groups. A number of adult and subadult males may be witnessed mounting a sexually receptive female. However, during the peak of estrus when the chances of successful impregnation are highest, the dominant males are the ones doing most of the copulating.

In all of these social systems, despite variation in organization, the net effect is to promote the genetic transmission of traits desirable from the standpoint of survival; the biggest, strongest, and most aggressive males do most of the copulating, and hence account for most of the offspring. On the other hand, it should not be assumed that the male always determines whose genetic characteristics get transmitted. We know that female beagles are extremely selective in their acceptance of sexual partners (Beach & Le Boeuf, 1967). In wolves observed in a zoo setting (Ginsburg, 1965), the dominant female prevented the other females from mating with the resident males.

Division of Responsibility

In many cases, membership in a social group involves a specific social role determined by sex. This fact binds the animals together in the sense that the survival of the group depends on several behaviors, some of which are provided by each sex; either sex alone would have a difficult time of it.

Sex roles tend to be different whenever there is sexual **dimorphism** in a species; that is, if the male and female exhibit prominent physical differences, the likelihood is also great that the sexes provide different behavioral contributions to group survival. Among the baboons, the much larger males with their powerful canine teeth are well adapted to their role as protector. The smaller females are more involved in the nurturance of infants.

In certain monkeys, however, the two sexes both look and act much more alike. There are also many birds (e.g., the penguin) that divide responsibility for incubation, nest defense, and feeding in an essentially equal fashion between sexes. One partner stays at home caring for the eggs or the young while the other searches for food; then they reverse these roles. Typically, in birds, the exchange between the roles of hunter and baby-sitter is accompanied by a ceremony of some type. The male (or the female) who is about to take over the incubation of the eggs bows and nods in an elaborate behavior sequence; the female (or male) then relinquishes its place atop the eggs (see Figures 28-7 and 28-8).

In many species, hunting is a male activity. But again no universal generalizations can be made, for in some animal groups the female does most or all of the hunting. The female African lion does most of the hunting, to such an extent that several observers began wondering if the King of the Jungle had any social role beyond occasional copulation. Recent studies (Schaller, 1972) indicate that the male lion is primarily concerned with the protection of the territory from intruding lions.

FIGURE 28-7
NEST-BUILDING

Adelie penguins (left) build nests for their eggs of stones with both the male and the female participating in nest construction. Subsequent incubation of the eggs is also shared.

FIGURE 28-8
MUTUAL DISPLAYS

When one parent leaves the eggs and the other takes over the responsibilities of incubation, there is often a ceremony of mutual display. (Both photos by Michael C. T. Smith, National Audubon Society)

When does social dispersal occur?

We have indicated some of the advantages of a social existence in animals, but there are also disadvantages. If the aggregation of an animal species leads to the starvation of some—because the food supply is limited—the effects on the species and on its chances for survival are complex. One might assume that in times of overpopulation or limited food resources, only the weaker would die, and the population would simply be reduced to some manageable size. But there are cases of overpopulation leading to virtual extinction of an entire species. Let us now look more closely at some of the problems of a social existence that may make **dispersal** an adaptive response.

Food Scarcity

The availability of food in any given habitat is one of the factors limiting population density and influencing social organization. In the baboons discussed previously, one typically finds either the one-male group or the troop organization. The type of social organization is related to the food availability in the area; one-male units are more frequently found in places where food is scarce. A large and tightly organized baboon troop would have to cover enormous distances each day to feed all members; troop organization requires a rather lush environment. Even among baboons organized into troops, it has been noted that the size of the troop is correlated with food supply, with smaller sizes found in less favorable habitats (DeVore & Hall, 1965). Where food is most scarce we find an almost solitary existence, with social interaction limited to brief periods of sexual activity and infant care, as in the case of the kangaroo rats of the western American deserts.

Predatory animals need prey to survive. Among the most social carnivores such as wolves, wild dogs, and hyenas, the maintenance of the group social structure requires a reasonable population of large prey (e.g., deer) or an enormous population of smaller animals (e.g., rodents). Many hunting cats, like the American cougar, live rather solitary lives in order to survive. The African lion, which is a relatively social hunting cat, is extraordinarily defensive of its group territory; it is one of the few animals that will literally kill an intruder of its own species (Schenkel, 1966; Schaller, 1972).

Increased Population

When population of a species increases, the usual social interactions become more difficult and complex. The result is often social dispersal and/or social disorganization. Such effects probably occur because social interactions are largely dependent on the ability to recognize the members of one's social group, and the mechanisms of control are based on such recognition; in groups too large, recognition of individuals is more difficult, and the likelihood of social disorganization is thereby increased.

In the troop-organized savannah baboons, it has been suggested that new troops are formed whenever the size of an existing troop exceeds certain limits (DeVore & Hall, 1965). It seems unlikely that dispersal in this case is exclusively a function of food scarcity. More probably, the population density affects social organization, causing a decrease in social cohesion. One might speculate that only a certain degree of social disorganization can be tolerated by a troop in their collective efforts to eat, mate, rear their young, and evade predators; when those limits are exceeded, the troop splits into two.

Some investigators have carried such reasoning further and asked, What happens if the population density is artificially controlled, so that natural limits are exceeded? Several such studies have been done with animals in large outdoor plots (e.g., Calhoun, 1962). If rat populations are allowed to exceed natural limits, social disorganization follows. Dominance hierarchies collapse, aggressive behaviors increase, and maternal behaviors become inefficient. In mice, such extreme crowding has been found to affect physiology (Christian, 1956). The adrenal glands become enlarged, and the hormonal balance in females is upset, producing numerous miscarriages in pregnant mice.

We must be cautious in generalizing such artificial, laboratory-based conclusions to the effects of crowding in a natural environment. In some species like the lemming (see Spotlight 28-1), the proposed mechanisms might well operate to control population size, but in most species, adaptive corrections (like splitting into two groups) occur before the unusual densities observed in the laboratory are reached. In the most adaptable of species—man—it seems that crowding can be tolerated to a much greater extent than in less flexible animals, largely by making accommodations in the social structure (Freedman, 1971).

What mechanisms contribute to cohesive behavior?

In the social existence of an animal, there are a great number of activities that we have classified as cohesive – they bring the animals together (sex), they make life more secure (evading predation, locating food), or they make specialized individual behaviors more effective (division of responsibility). Such activities have been described in general for various species; more detailed studies of the underlying mechanisms of such activities can increase our understanding of these behaviors, and it is to these mechanisms we now turn. We will focus on courtship and mating and the bonds between parents and offspring, with briefer mention of other cohesive mechanisms.

Courtship and Mating

The courtship **displays** of animals are certainly among the most beautiful behaviors that can be observed in nature (see Figure 28-9). Bird displays are always striking: males strut and dance in colorful plumage, sing intricate and compelling songs, or demonstrate their attractiveness in sweeping and acrobatic flight, and these displays may go on for extended periods before a relatively brief instance of actual copulation. Fish and even lowly spiders engage in similar displays.

The function of such displays is not entirely clear. In hunting spiders, the male displays apparently to identify himself as a member of the species—a potential lover and not a potential meal.

SPOTLIGHT 28-1
Population Cycles

Many animal populations undergo drastic cyclic fluctuations in number and density. Probably the best-known example involves the small arctic rodents popularly known as lemmings. According to a widely held belief, the density of their population swells to a point at which social disorganization occurs and a mass migration ensues. At the end of this wild march, hordes of lemmings supposedly hurl themselves into the water and drown in a kind of "ritual" suicide. Such behavior would obviously have the effect of drastically reducing population density and, presumably, a few survivors would be left to begin the population expansion anew. Recent careful observations (reported in Brown, 1966) suggest that this account of lemming death through drowning is greatly exaggerated. Lemmings sometimes show seasonal migration in search of food, mates, or better dwelling areas. However, much of this migration is carried out by solitary animals. Even when in groups, lemmings carefully follow pathways with a protective cover from predators. Arriving at a body of water, they avoid entry unless land can be seen at the other side, and they normally swim for the far shore with heads held high and nostrils kept well out of the water. Some lemmings do miscalculate and drown during windy conditions when they are not up to the task of combating waves, but that is surely not the major cause of large population decreases in the lemming.

Rapid growth of populations within an area must be associated with a high birth rate, good survival in the resident population, and/or low rates of migration or dispersal. Alternately, rapid decline in population density would be accompanied by high rates of mortality of animals residing in the affected area, extensive migration, and/or low rates of successful reproduction. Although many factors have been suggested as being responsible for population cycling, and much research has been done, we are still far from an understanding of this complex phenomenon. Scarcity of critical foods (Lack, 1954), predator pressure (Pearson, 1964), hormonal changes (Christian, 1956) and selective survival of high-aggressive, but poor-reproductive individuals (Chitty, 1957; Krebs, 1972) have all been suggested as mechanisms that could produce the rapid decline of very dense animal populations. These mechanisms are not mutually exclusive, and we might well find two or more factors interacting in a particular case of regulation of population cycling.

The female of such species is typically larger, with strong predatory instincts, so the display triggers innate mechanisms which allow the smaller male to approach and fertilize her eggs. The famous black widow is named in recognition of the fact that the male's identification behaviors are not always as successful as he would hope.

A second function of courtship display is simply to release stereotyped mating behavior (fixed action patterns) in the female. Some students of animal behavior (Armstrong, 1947) liken the

FIGURE 28-9
PAIR-BOND DISPLAYS
In both the gannet (left) and the king penguin, mutual or reciprocal displays characterize interactions between the male and female. The gannets, with necks extended, engage in a "billing" display. The king penguin extends his beak toward the sky in the beginning of an "ecstatic" display, while his partner bends her beak forward to preen the abdominal feathers. (Left, Grant Haist, and above, Arthur W. Ambler; both from National Audubon Society)

function of courtship displays to that of traffic lights at an intersection: Motorists are rather finely tuned to colors in a vertical stand at the street corner; if the color is red, they uniformly stop; if green, they go. Similarly in many animal species, certain specific colors or odors or touches or other stimuli trigger mating behavior that would not otherwise occur. In some species, such as the graylag goose, these stimuli seem to be associated with identification of an individual animal that serves as a basis for pair-bonding that continues beyond mating, even for life.

Among fish, the courtship and mating behavior of the stickleback has been extensively studied (Tinbergen, 1952). (See Figure 27-13.) First the male sets up a territory in which he builds a nest; he defends his territory against intrusion by other males. If a female with a swollen belly (full of eggs) approaches his territory, his protective-hostile behavior is inhibited; his behavior changes radically. He approaches *as if* to attack, but at the last moment, he turns and retreats toward the nest. He repeats this pattern that has been termed a "zigzag dance" several times. With each zigzag the female moves closer and closer to the nest. When she is finally over the nest, the male swims above her and nudges her back with his nose, inducing her to release her eggs; the female then swims away. The male swims over the nest and fertilizes the eggs. He now has full responsibility for the eggs; he defends the nest from predators, and he will provide oxygen for the eggs by rapid fin movements, which keep the water circulating through the nest (Tinbergen, 1952).

The courtship display of the male peacock is legendary. The peacock in full display is a popular sight at zoos, but there often only an individual bird is in action. In their natural habitat, the peacocks' display is a kind of festive contest held in a large "arena," with several males showing their colors at once in order to win the attentions of the peahens. If a peahen is aroused by one of the cocks, she indicates her choice by running to him and pecking the ground in front of him. With his colorful train raised, he turns his back to her. She runs around to his front. He rattles his plumes. After a few repetitions of this behavior sequence, the hen squats and copulation ensues (Armstrong, 1947).

Varieties of Reproductive Behavior

In animals lowest on the phylogenetic scale, asexual reproduction is common. There is no combination of male and female sex cells; a single organism, like an amoeba, simply splits in half, forming two organisms. But in the higher animals, sexual reproduction is more common, and the participation of two individuals has distinct evolutionary advantages for a species. Perhaps most important is the increase in genetic variability produced by the combination of two different sets of chromosomes; genetic variability in offspring is the basis upon which natural selection operates. If it were not for genetic variability, many species would become extinct if their habitat or living conditions changed only slightly.

In some common land snails, each snail is a true hermaphrodite, because each possesses both male and female reproductive organs. Even though the capacity for self-fertilization exists, these snails reproduce by pairing. In fact, they engage in a stimulating though primitive courtship behavior; on approach, the partners stimulate each other by driving hard darts into the other's soft parts. Soon thereafter, the male part of each snail copulates with the female organs of the other.

One of the major developments in the evolution of reproductive behavior has been the shift from external to internal fertilization. Many fish, like the salmon, rely on external fertilization. Salmon females migrate upstream and release their eggs; the males, following behind, discharge their sperm over the eggs. Such procedures are obviously inefficient. An egg becomes an adult salmon if and only if (1) the egg is alive when the sperm comes, (2) the sperm fertilizes the egg, (3) the fertilized egg hatches, and (4) the infant salmon survives dangers such as pollution and predators. Needless to say, millions of eggs will produce only a relatively small number of adult salmon.

Even with external fertilization, some fish have developed more efficient means of protecting eggs from potential destruction. The stickleback male protects the eggs. In another kind of fish, the bitterling, the female deposits the eggs inside a live clam and the male fertilizes them there; the clam provides unknowing protection (see Figure 28-10). Fish called "grunions" reproduce outside the water, on beaches, and the eggs hatch almost immediately when the next high tide hits and carries the infants out to sea. Their parents, in the meantime, might have become a meal for enterprising humans who respond to the call, "The grunions are running," and scoop the grunions off the beach before the next large wave can carry them to safety.

In the guppy (*Lebistes reticulatus*), a popular fish in home aquariums, internal fertilization is followed by live birth of the offspring. The male guppy, smaller and more brightly colored than the female, courts his mate when her belly is swollen with eggs. He swims in front of her while bending his body into an S-shape and "quivers" in this position, checking the female's forward motion. He then swims alongside the female and swings a specialized portion of his ventral fin away from his body and inserts it into the abdomen of the female. This ventral "fin" is known as the gonopodium, which has developed as a specialized appendage for the delivery of sperm.

FIGURE 28-10
BITTERLING LAYING EGGS IN CLAM
The clam shell provides a secure repository for the developing eggs.

Internal fertilization is necessary for live births, but many species that have internal fertilization do not have live births. The eggs of most birds are fertilized internally, but the eggs are laid—as eggs—and must be incubated before birth. The parents are the ones to incubate the eggs, of course, and they protect the eggs at the same time. The trend we are describing is essentially toward greater protection of the eggs and the infants, and internal fertilization provides greater protection during a critical period, even if the births are not live. In some fish, a new twist is added; infants (or eggs) live in the mouth of the parent until viable (or born), increasing the likelihood of survival (see Figure 28-11).

Among marsupials like the kangaroo and the opossum, there is similar protection of the infants after birth. The females of these mammals have pouches containing nipples. The young are born alive through the birth canal and must travel to the pouch to survive. If they reach the pouch in time, they are fed and protected until they are large enough to fend for themselves. A dramatic example of this life-or-death behavior sequence has been described in the American opossum (Hartmann, 1962). The young are born alive but, at birth, they measure no more than a quarter of an inch in length. More babies are born than there are nipples in the opossum pouch, so there then occurs a wild race from the birth canal, across the mother's abdomen, to the pouch; these tiny opossums are literally running for their lives, for the last-place finishers are doomed to starvation and death.

In the primates, including man, the reproductive pattern includes internal fertilization, live births, and usually extended care of infants by the mother, at least, and often by the father and other adults as well. These evolutionary developments not only increase the probability that any given egg will develop into a mature adult but also provide a social environment in which learning can replace the less flexible instinctive behaviors of lower animals. The period of extended care for infants favors survival, and it provides the infant with experiences that shape his adult behavior patterns in a highly adaptive fashion. Man is the most flexible of animals, capable of living in almost any habitat, and this extreme adaptability would not be possible if it were not for reproductive and child-care patterns characteristic of the more highly evolved animals.

Mating Patterns

In the laboratory rat the adult female has a period of sexual attractiveness and receptivity that occurs about six hours after ovulation; this period of receptivity is called "estrus." Most mating occurs at this time, and it is an especially favorable time for fertilization to take place. When an adult male rat is placed with a female rat in estrus, he will approach her, sniffing at her genital region. The female locomotes in short darting movements as the male approaches. The male mounts the female, touching her flanks with his forepaws. At this point, the female stops and assumes a posture known as **lordosis**—her rump is elevated and her tail is moved to the side, permitting insertion of the penis (**intromission**). After intromission, the male dismounts quickly and vigorously, and proceeds to groom his genital region. There are several options now open to the female: she may simply wait until the male's next approach, or she may go to the male and groom or sniff him. After a period of perhaps 30 seconds, the intromission sequence is repeated; after a dozen or so of these intromissions, ejaculation occurs. The period of contact between the animals during ejaculation is perhaps 1.5 seconds and, if this is the first ejaculation, there will be a quiet post-ejaculatory period lasting approximately five minutes before the mating sequence is resumed.

The reasons for this multiple intromission pattern in rats is not completely understood. It has been shown that repeated intromissions are necessary to stimulate the flow of progesterone in the female and that this hormone is necessary for successful implantation of the fertilized egg in the uterine wall (Adler, 1969). Female rats who receive an ejaculation after few intromissions are less likely to become pregnant (Wilson, Adler, & Le Boeuf, 1965). But why some rodent species exhibit this repeated intromission pattern, while others (e.g., the guinea pig) do not, remains a puzzle.

In contrast to the multiple intromission pattern, there is the single intromission pattern, characterized by a prolonged period of repetitive thrusting by the male, usually leading to ejaculation. This pattern can be observed in dogs, monkeys, and, of course, humans. In all three species the females take an active role in the coital process; they frequently solicit the attention of a male by sniffing or grooming or by assuming a provocative posture. Often the female of these species will not allow an "unacceptable" male to mate with her—a fact that owners of a prize-winning male dog have often discovered, to their dismay, when trying to breed him with an attractive bitch.

Role of Experience

A number of recent studies (e.g., Harlow, 1962) lead one to the conclusion that if mammals (rats, monkeys) are deprived of social contact with their peers during infancy, there is some impairment of their adult sexual behavior. This suggests that experience is important in these species. Males who lack the usual early social experience often make inappropriate responses to a sexually receptive female; in the rhesus monkey, the lack of early social contact seems to prevent successful adult performance (see p. 712).

Sexual responses are generally less dependent upon specific experience in mammals with limited cortical development (the rat, as compared to the monkey); thus the impairment of sexual performance is generally less in socially deprived rats than in deprived monkeys. Also, the passive sexual responses required of the female of most species are governed more by innate neurological and hormonal systems than are the more active "initiating" responses required of the male, and thus in both rats and monkeys the lack of early social contacts affects male performance more than female sexual behavior. However, these latter conclusions are based primarily on the data gathered by psychologists studying the passive components of the female sex role (for example, lordosis in the rat). Some more recent work (Bermant, 1961; Peirce & Nuttall, 1961) stresses the potentially important role that the female rat can play in initiating copulatory activity. Further study of these more active components of sex behavior of the female rat may show that social experience is more important for female mating behavior than had been thought previously.

Sensory Cues in Mating Behavior

In a sexually experienced mammal, information about the receptivity of a partner can arrive through a variety of sense modalities, and the loss of any single modality is not apt to eliminate the behavior. However, recent evidence tends to place particular weight on olfactory stimulation as a prime determinant of the attractiveness of females in the rat, dog, and monkey. In all these species, experienced males have been shown to approach selectively the odors emitted in the urine or the vaginal secretions of females in estrus. If the vaginal secretions of a female rhesus monkey in estrus are smeared on an out-of-estrus female, the male will attempt copulation. The male will persist in his copulatory behavior despite the absence of encouragement from the nonreceptive female (Michael, 1971).

Other sense **modalities** are involved in mating behavior, despite the relative importance of odors for many species. The degree of participation of any modality depends on the species and the stage of the mating process. Auditory cues are often important in early stages; we are all familiar with the yowls of courting domestic cats. The synchronization of auditory and tactile cues can be seen in frogs who aggregate in the spring amid a chorus of vigorous vocalization. The male frogs have grown expanded "thumbs" during the preceding months, and these "nuptial pads" are used to clasp the female's sides, stimulating her to release a group of eggs, which will then be externally fertilized by the male. However, male frogs make mistakes during this process and frequently mount and clasp other males. Under these conditions, the clasped male emits a "release call," and hopefully the offending male, now informed of his error, will move on.

Vision is an important sense in primates, and we might expect visual cues to be important in primate mating behaviors. In many primate species, estrous females develop prominent reddish swellings of the skin in the vaginal region. Such swellings can be used by potential mates (and by human primatologists) as indices of sexual receptivity. These swellings are, however, not characteristic of all primates; in some forest-dwelling African monkeys of the genus *Myopithecus*, the sexual skin is much reduced in size. It has been suggested that in the dense forests where line-of-sight is limited, the adaptive advantages of visual signaling of sexual state may be somewhat reduced (Rowell, 1971).

Hormonal Mechanisms

It is clear that the development of normal sexuality in the vertebrates is dependent upon the presence of appropriate hormones. Hormones affect almost every aspect of anatomy and physiology underlying sexual differences of a species, and they play a significant role in the specific mating behaviors. Estrus, for example, is dependent upon hormonal cycles in the female. (See pp. 706 ff. for a more complete discussion of the biology of sexual behavior.)

Sex hormones are produced mostly in the gonads of the male and in the ovaries of the female. If the gonads or ovaries are removed from a vertebrate, effects on sexual behavior can usually be observed, but the extent of the effect varies greatly among species, between the sexes within species, and among animals of different ages. Early removal of the gonads generally has more profound effects on adult structure and behavior than adult gonadectomies. Among species, the effects of surgery in adult mammals are greater the lower in the phylogenetic scale; rats are affected much more than humans. Indeed, in humans, it is often difficult to observe any effect whatsoever if the testes or ovaries of an experienced adult are removed. Such findings have led many investigators (e.g., Beach, 1948) to hypothesize an evolutionary trend toward decreasing hormonal control of mating, with a correlated increase in the importance of experience.

Some theorists carry this speculation even farther, suggesting that the relatively permanent pair-bonding found in man is an indirect result of freedom from the hormonal control of sex. In rats and other infraprimate mammals, mating activity in females is tightly bound to hormonal cycles. However, the human female is physiologically capable of attracting and accepting a male at any time in the hormonal cycle. Thus, sexual behavior can act as a reinforcement and help to maintain the pair bond at all times (Eibl-Eibesfeldt, 1970). This theory of the roots of human socialization is certainly an interesting variant on the theme that sex serves a purely reproductive function, but it is difficult to imagine how one could actually test the theory.

Homo sapiens is not the only primate species whose mating is not strictly bound to the ovulatory cycle of the female. Young and Orbison (1944) found that mating in chimpanzees was frequently more dependent upon the details of the general social relationship between the male and the female than the specific stage of the female's ovulatory cycle. Such freedom from the hormonal bond has also been observed in many African monkeys (Rowell, 1971), but there is also a clear tendency for the majority of copulatory activity to take place during a particular phase of the ovulatory cycle.

Parent-Offspring Bonds

In some fish the care of the fertilized eggs is the sole responsibility of the male. We have discussed one such pattern in the stickleback. In the beautiful Siamese fighting fish, the male builds a bubble nest at the water surface with mucuslike secretions from his mouth. Once the nest is constructed, he induces the female to lay her eggs in the nest. After she does so, he drives her away and will not tolerate her presence in the vicinity of the nest (see Figure 28-11).

It is interesting to note a difference in nest-building behavior between the stickleback and the Siamese fighting fish. The stickleback builds the nest at the bottom of the stream, while the bubble nest is constructed at the surface. To get oxygen to the eggs, the stickleback must "fan" them with his fins. This would not be possible for the Siamese fighting fish, for he lives in streams that do not have adequate oxygen; he himself must surface at regular intervals to gulp air. If he built his nest at the bottom, even assuming the eggs could survive, he would have to leave them unguarded during his trips to the surface. Thus his surface nest is a necessary adaptation to the environment, providing oxygen for both father and eggs and permitting continued protection for the eggs.

FIGURE 28-11
PARENTAL CARE IN FISH
The male Siamese fighting fish (left) catches some eggs which have been displaced in order to return them to his bubble nest. The mouthbreeder releases a swarm of young that have been protected within his mouth.

Males and females in many birds share the responsibility of caring for the eggs and the young. We have discussed this in the case of the penguin (p. 810). However, in mammals, where there are live births and extended periods of infant care, the primary responsibility for the offspring always falls to the female. The general relation between mother and infant can be seen as going through three stages (Schneirla & Rosenblatt, 1961): in the first, contact is initiated primarily by the mother; in the second, there is mutual approach behavior; in the third, the infant approaches but the mother "rejects," leading to eventual independence of the offspring. The timing of this process in the cat is shown in Figure 28-12.

In primates, unrelated adults often exhibit an interest in infants. If the unrelated adult is a female, this is called **aunt behavior.**

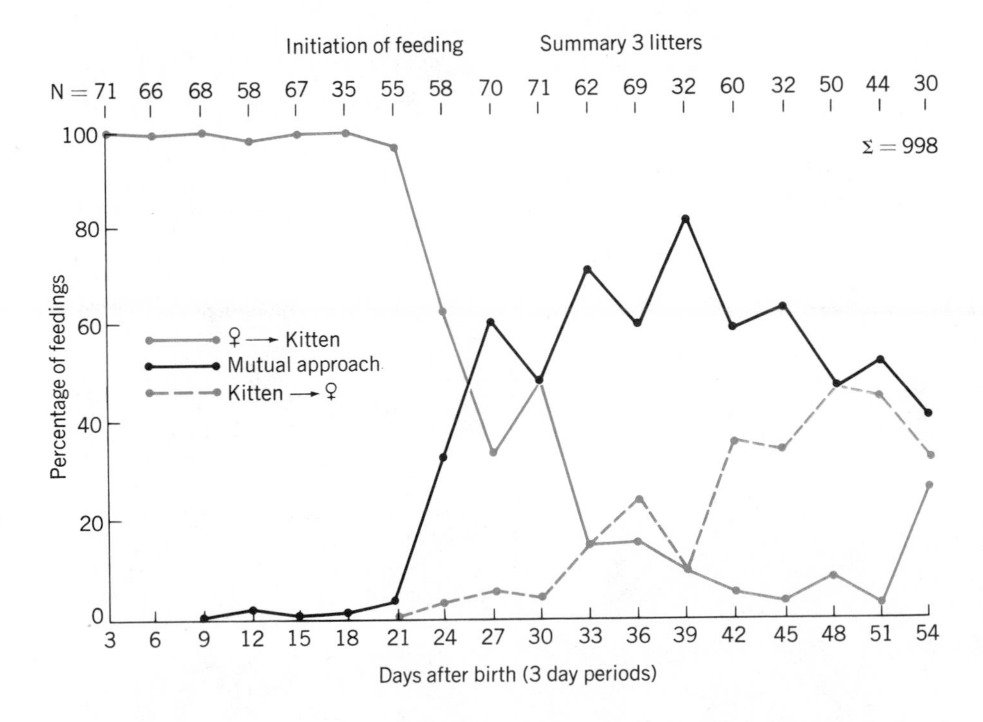

FIGURE 28-12 STAGES OF MOTHER-INFANT INTERACTION IN CATS

The initiation of feeding is first characterized by maternal approach, then by mutual approach, and finally reaches a stage where the kitten's attempts to initiate feeding are as frequent as any mutual approach.
(From Schneirla & Rosenblatt, 1961)

The aunt is typically a childless female in the mother's group. At first her interest in the infant is resented by the mother, but gradually the two cooperate in child care—interactions that have obvious survival value for the infant. Should the mother die, for example, the aunt usually "adopts" the infant as her own. It has also been observed that the presence of an aunt affects the interaction of mother and infant; with aunts present, mothers are less likely to reject their infants, probably because the infants are less dependent on the mother for all their needs (Hinde & Spencer-Booth, 1967).

Uncle behavior has been observed in Japanese macaques (Itani, 1959). Adult males become interested in infants who are more than a year old; the adult male will hug the infant, sit with him, and protect him from danger. The females at this time have entered a new birth season and cease protecting last year's baby, so the infant with no uncle would probably not survive. But, as is typical in primate interactions, uncle behavior has other functions as well. Just to name one, an uncle who protects an infant of parents in a higher caste—these primates have a strict caste system—is tolerated by the leaders of the higher caste; he may therefore rise in social status. Another interesting fact is that uncle behavior is observed in only some macaque troops; it was common in only 3 of the 18 troops studied, and not observed at all in 8. It therefore appears to be a local cultural tradition, learned and passed on generation to generation, although this conclusion remains highly speculative. What does seem clear,

Parent-young interactions are shown in several species. Under appropriate living conditions, adult rhesus monkey males are protective of infants, as seen above. The mother lion keeps her infant separate from the pride for a few months after birth, and there is intensive mother-infant interaction. At the lower right, the infant langur grasps the mother's fur actively and strongly in order to travel with her. (Left, H. F. Harlow; top & bottom, Phyllis Dolinhow)

however, is that monkey troops with uncles have an adaptive advantage; their "protected" infants have a much greater chance of survival.

Nest-Building

Thus far we have been discussing mother-infant and adult-infant bonds in broad terms. It is now appropriate to consider some of the more important specific response patterns involved. For example, the construction of nests for sleeping is a year-round activity for many mammals, but in the hours preceding the delivery of young, there is frequently an intensification of this activity.

In the interaction of inherited and learned components of nest-building in the female rat we see another demonstration of the fact that strict nativist or empiricist positions are inadequate to deal with observed behavior (see pp. 618–26, 677). Some years ago a psychologist reported that, while female rats typically build nests for their young on their very first exposure to a nest-building situation, this behavior is strongly influenced by prior experience (Riess, 1950). In rats deprived of opportunity to manipulate objects (food, other rats) before giving birth, nest-building in a test cage was severely impaired. This study, however, was criticized on several counts (Eibl-Eibesfeldt, 1961). First, by moving the mother rat to a test cage for observation of nest-building, the investigator introduced the possibility that strong competing responses, such as exploration, would interfere with building. Moreover, rats would be unlikely to build nests in an open wire-mesh cage under any circumstances; in natural settings, they build nests only in enclosed protected areas.

When the experiment was replicated with a more naturalistic nesting environment, rats that had been deprived of manipulative experience built nests on their first opportunity. Still, some obvious deficits remained in the nest-building behavior. The inexperienced mothers made many more trips than were necessary to get building materials, they performed acts out of sequence, and they would sometimes carry strips of paper to the nest, yet fail to release them from their mouths. So again, we have a demonstration, in a rather primitive mammal engaged in a complex activity, that instinctive *and* learned components interact to produce the response pattern observed in the usual situation. Neither a strict nativist nor a strict empiricist position can explain the behavior.

Retrieval Behavior

If an infant mammal strays from the mother or nest area, generally he is quickly retrieved to more secure grounds. The cues eliciting retrieval behavior have been most closely analyzed in the common laboratory rodents: mice, rats, and hamsters. Originally the attempts at analysis involved surgical interference with one sense or another; the animals were blinded or deafened or they were prevented from tasting or smelling. A systematic set of such studies led to the conclusion that deficits in retrieval behavior were proportional to the number of sense modalities eliminated (Beach & Jaynes, 1956). All senses seem to play some role.

More recently, investigators have begun exploring the role of sensory cues that previous work had completely overlooked. It has been shown that one of the primary cues eliciting retrieval in many rodents is an ultrasonic cry emitted by the errant pup (Noirot, 1966). These cries went unnoticed for many years for a very good reason: human experimenters could not hear them. The frequency range was far above the upper threshold for human hearing, and electronic instruments were necessary for humans to detect these sounds.

Retrieval behavior in rats and mice is most frequently observed in the first two weeks or so after birth, after which it decreases rapidly. This behavior change is highly (but not perfectly) correlated with the decrease in ultrasonic signaling from the pup. The decrease in responsiveness in the mother to her litter is caused by a change in the stimuli coming to her from the pups. This interpretation fits not only retrieval but can be applied to other behaviors—licking, nursing, and nest-building—as well.

Other Cohesive Relations

INFANT-INFANT Cohesion in complex social groups involves many relations besides those in mating or parental behavior. Among the most important are the interactions of infants and juveniles that we call "play." In primates the young spend much of their day in play groups, play-fighting, jumping, running, threatening, chasing, exploring strange objects, and "practicing" sex (see Figure 28-13). No doubt these interactions lead to certain cohesive bonds between playmates, but the biological significance of play remains somewhat of a mystery. An investigator of the nineteenth century (Groos, 1898) hypothesized that the function of play in mammals was to prepare the infant for adult behavior; play was seen as practice for activities that would eventually occur in a more serious context. This is an appealing argument—it *sounds* so obviously correct—but there is not a lot of empirical evidence to support it. For some unknown reason, there is very little systematic data on play in mammals (including humans), so speculation proceeds without the benefit of limitation by facts.

Assuming that the play-as-practice hypothesis is at least partly accurate, one can cite several observations that fit. We have already mentioned evidence that an infant mammal deprived of the opportunity to play will likely become an adult deficient in sexual behavior (p. 819) or predatory behavior (p. 808). These data fit, but social isolation during infancy is a rather complex and severe intervention; one cannot be sure that the lack of play is the only, or even the most important, factor. Another fact compatible with the play-as-practice hypothesis is the difference between the play of the two sexes, which often foreshadows differences in the behavior of male and female adults. The play of young males, for example, is often more rough and tumble and aggressive, at least in primates, and this is in keeping with their more aggressive role as adults.

Play is also, very simply, good exercise, and the absence of playful behavior is often a sign of illness or retardation. Another function of play is exploration. It is known that many primate juveniles

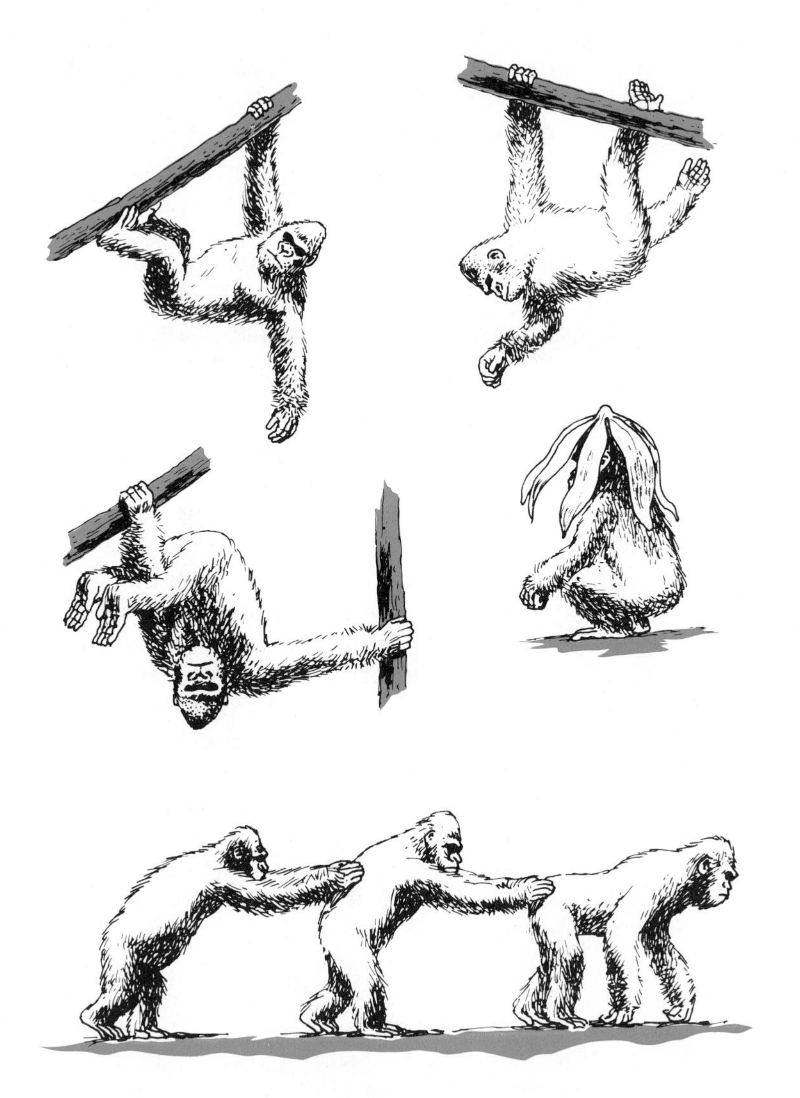

FIGURE 28-13 PLAY IN YOUNG GORILLAS
Some gorilla play takes place while the juveniles are alone and in the trees. Other play patterns are of a more social nature, as in the bottom drawing, which Schaller (1967) describes as a "snake dance."

will choose to play with moderately unfamiliar objects, animate and inanimate, and the experience with a variety of environmental events results in learning that is useful in later life. (It should be noted, however, that extremely novel objects will typically elicit fear and withdrawal rather than interest and approach. But this too can be seen in terms of survival advantage.)

Finally, many have noted that in playing, the young are receiving practice in the communication patterns they will have to know as adults (Mason, 1960). In other words, juveniles in play groups often have occasion to try out or respond to alarm calls, sexual invitations, threat gestures, and all the other myriad signals that do so much to bond group members together. They can do this in relative safety; while at play they are not usually allowed to stray into real danger, and their calls are often false alarms. The alarm call of a juvenile produces only mild interest in adults, who are content merely to satisfy themselves that no real danger exists and that the cry has been elicited, as is typical, by an unexpected but harmless object.

ADULT-ADULT If play is the major interaction of infants with infants, **grooming** is probably the most time-consuming activity observed in relations between adult primates (see Figure 28-14). This behavior has an immediately apparent goal – cleanliness; the various bugs, parasites, burrs, and clots of dirt picked up in a day's march with a primate group are cleared away. An animal with a wound presents himself more often for grooming, and many observers have noted a relationship between the seriousness of the wound and the amount of grooming received (Simonds, 1965).

But grooming is also clearly much more than a cleaning behavior; it is a friendly social interaction, and both the opportunity to be groomed *and* to groom can be used as an effective reinforcer for laboratory chimpanzees. One psychologist was able to train a chimp to press a lever for nothing more than the privilege of grooming *the psychologist's arm* (Falk, 1958). Grooming is also related to sexual relations. One male baboon with a large secure harem was never observed grooming the females, but when he grew older and lost most of his females, he conscientiously groomed the two he was able to retain (Kummer & Kurt, 1965).

In the wild hamadryas baboon described at the beginning of this chapter, grooming accounts for a major portion of the social interactions (Kummer, 1968). About 20 percent of the time that these animals were observed above the sleeping rock, they were either grooming or being groomed, far larger percentages than for all sexual and aggressive behaviors combined (around 1 percent). Grooming was also prominent in the wild chimpanzees studied by Jane Goodall (1965). Other kinds of tactile contacts observed in chimpanzees ranged from simply putting an arm on another chimp to those that could be called "kissing." The contact seemed to indicate interest and friendly intent, and it also appeared to allay anxiety.

In mammals like cats and rodents, licking and grooming with the teeth are common. Such behaviors are observed in periods of social grooming. They are seen in maternal behavior toward babies after birth, before copulation, and even preceding aggression. It appears that one class of behavior can serve many different functions.

SENSORY CUES Auditory signals and olfactory cues must also play a significant role in group cohesion, although the precise function of these cues has been studied little. In several species of monkeys, there are regular periods of very loud calling that

FIGURE 28-14 PRIMATE GROOMING BEHAVIOR

Grooming is a fundamental cohesion-promoting behavior in primates. These photos show grooming in three very different social contexts. The langur (top) carefully grooms the back of her partner. The male baboon (left) grooms a female carrying an infant, and in the family group of bonnet macaques, the female grooms the adult male.
(All photos, Phyllis Dolinhow)

occur every day. Howler monkeys, who of course get their name from such behavior, have a specially developed vocal apparatus, and they use their howls for aggressive encounters, for indicating troop movement, and apparently to show clan identity. When two groups of males meet in the jungle, they have what some have described as a "shouting contest"; the losers shut up and move on (Carpenter, 1965). They also have a regular morning howling period, in which one member starts to howl and others join—almost as if the urge were **contagious**—until the hills are alive with the sound of raucous barks and shrieks. The periodic howling probably serves to maintain a kind of auditory territory for the clan, trumpeting security for the clan member and warning to potential intruders.

Calling also serves similar functions in some wild rodents. Prairie dog social organizations consist of small groups that combine to form "towns" of several thousand animals (King, 1955). (See Figure 28-15.) There is a great deal of calling within the smaller familial units and also between groups in the town. These cohesion calls are replaced by alarm calls if an airborne predator appears, and the "news" is spread rapidly on the prairie dog "grapevine." When the predator disappears, an "all-clear" call communicates this fact, and social calling resumes.

FIGURE 28-15
PRAIRIE DOG "COTERIE"
King (1955) identifies the "coterie" as the basic social unit of the prairie dog society. Evident here is both the cohesion of this kind of group and the upright attentive posture so characteristic of this species.
(Alfred W. Bailey, National Audubon Society)

In mammals like the rodents where olfaction is a dominant sense, it is to be expected that olfactory cues could be used to promote cohesion. Many rodents have specialized glands for **scent-marking**; the rabbit has one on the underside of his chin, hamsters on their flanks, and gerbils on the abdominal surface. When these body areas are rubbed against objects in the environment, an oily substance is deposited on the objects. In many mammals, urine and feces are also used to mark a territory, as any of you who regularly walk your dog can attest.

If one considers the amount of potential information in scents, he can understand why most psychologists attribute multiple functions to scent-marking. The sex of the animal, the age, the health, and in females, the stage of the estrous cycle can be determined from the smell. One theorist proposes that scents serve to describe a population; a male can determine the number of estrous females and the number (and health) of rivals in the vicinity (Wynne-Edwards, 1962). Another suggests that, in wolves at least, scents define territory and "legitimize" the leader; in many species, dominant males do most of the marking (Schenkel, 1947).

Sexual communication through scent-marking is observed in many species. A female dog in estrus increases her urination rate markedly and thus leaves little advertisements for herself throughout her home range. All of us with male cats are aware of their "spraying" behavior; this seems to serve a dual function, to warn other males and to attract females in estrus.

Finally, there is the possibility that scent deposits function as landmarks or "memory devices." Rats will follow an odor trail, for example, in a maze. Urination and defecation in a strange place serve to make it more familiar upon return. Fear-induced urination and defecation, of course, are autonomic responses to extremely novel environments, and many psychologists have suggested that these involuntary responses were the original source of scent-marking. The evolution of the behavior toward more deliberate and voluntary control allows for more diversified use in social organization. Nevertheless, novel stimuli remain one of the primary releasers to deliberate scent-marking in many species (Kleiman, 1966).

AGGRESSION AND DOMINANCE We usually think of aggression and threats as behaviors that lead to dispersion, but within groups these behaviors are often used to promote cohesion. The male leader of a hamadryas baboon group enforces close following in his females by means of a graduated series of aggressive signals ranging from a discouraging stare to a vicious neck bite for recalcitrant offenders (Kummer, 1968).

Dominance hierarchies, found in many species, promote cohesion and efficiency by providing established answers to such questions as: Who goes first? Who leads? and Who gets the female? Military ranks serve a somewhat similar function in the armed forces.

Some of the first work on social hierarchies was done on domestic chickens who set up a rather clear "pecking order" (Schjelderup-Ebbe, 1935). On first acquaintance, chickens fight frequently, but soon the winners are recognized, and a simple threat is enough to chase a bird of lower status away. A dominant animal can even peck another without being pecked in return. The chicken hierarchy is linear, that is, if *A* is dominant over *B*, and *B* is dominant over *C*, *A* is dominant over *C*. This is not always the case in other species.

Discovering a dominance hierarchy in wild animals is not so easy to observe, because the existence of the hierarchy tends to prevent the appearance of precisely those behaviors, such as aggression, that provide the clearest measures of dominance. Since dominance is difficult to determine under natural conditions, many studies of dominance hierarchies have been carried out with animals in captivity, where small enclosures, moderately high population densities, and manipulation of the food supply can promote the frequent social interactions from which we can infer the dominance hierarchy. However, even in situations where dominance hierarchies exist, different measures of "dominance" may yield a variable picture of social interactions within the group. In a caged group of baboons, there was a significant difference between dominance orders determined on the basis of "who-threatened-whom" and dominance orders characterized by "who-was-friendly-with-whom" (Rowell, 1966). So, even under conditions where close observation is possible, what behavior one observes influences his estimate of the dominance hierarchy.

In wild animals whose social organization includes dominance hierarchies, these status arrangements probably serve a number of functions. Recall the elephant seals described in Chapter 1 (p. 13); the dominance hierarchy reduces intragroup aggression—after the hierarchy is established—and it promotes the survival of the species by the fact that dominant males—the strongest, healthiest, and most courageous—do most of the copulating when the cows arrive. In the savannah baboon described at the beginning of this chapter, nondominant males are not allowed to copulate frequently, but they nevertheless play a vital social role as food-gatherers and sentries from their positions at the periphery of the troop.

What mechanisms underlie dispersal behavior?

Within a species, the degree of dispersion or spacing is often dependent upon food resources. This is one explanation of why some baboons are found in large troops and others forage in smaller, one-male groups. Many animals will also defend territory against other members of the species; lions will literally kill intruders, while howler monkeys take the more civilized approach of just out-shouting their rivals.

In considering dispersion more broadly, relations between species must also be considered. Two concepts are paramount: avoidance and aggression. The nature of aggression will be our central concern here, but it should be recognized that avoidance behaviors are crucial too—especially for animals that are the natural prey. Many animals will allow the approach of a predator or a strange object (such as the ethologist's truck) up to a rather closely defined distance, then they flee. These flight distances have been studied extensively by the Swiss zoologist H. Hediger (1955). He notes that, in general, smaller species of animals have shorter flight distances than larger species. A small wall lizard will tolerate closer approach by man than a large crocodile. In addition, where animals have been protected from predation by man, as in national parks, their flight distance is gradually reduced. Flight distances may also be correlated with the relative speeds of the two animals; thus the antelope will let a tiger approach only to a certain distance—less than the distance the tiger can leap—for in open chase, the antelope has a great advantage (Schaller, 1967).

Types of Aggression

In Chapter 1, we discussed some of the problems in defining aggression. This term is one of the most diversely defined in all of psychology, including everything from ambition to "cold-blooded murder." At the least, we must describe three classifications: competitive, protective, and predatory aggression. These are the most common types of aggressive behaviors in the world of animals.

COMPETITIVE AGGRESSION One can commonly observe aggression, usually within a given species, that results from competition for food resources, mates, or land. In the classic case, the fight is over all three simultaneously. The male robin establishes a territory within which he will mate and rear his offspring. He will attack any intruding object with a red breast, which in nature is usually another male robin—although in the yard of a comparative psychologist may be an inanimate object designed to study the sign stimuli eliciting aggression in the robin.

The concept of **territory** in which the animal feeds and breeds has an interesting history. That animals seem to "carve out" home grounds and defend them against intruders has been noticed for centuries, even idealized in poems, plays, and novels; Aristotle made mention of the phenomenon. The scientific concept is usually credited to Howard (1920), who discussed the evolutionary advantages, especially those to newborn birds. Since then territorial defense has been observed in ants, bees, fish, lizards, seals, deer, monkeys and apes, just to name a few (Armstrong, 1947). Some writers have extended the concept to man, suggesting that phrases like "home turf" (as used by juvenile gangs) and "a man's home is his castle" reflect human territoriality. Some have even suggested the need for territorial possession as the root of all aggression, including human aggression (Ardrey, 1966).

The problem with the concept in its more extravagant forms is that it has become so broad as to be virtually incapable of disproof. There is, first of all, a trend toward defining territory even in cases where the territory *moves*. The anemone fish is so named because he adopts a living sea-anemone as his territory; immune to the poisonous darts of the anemone, he lives, breeds, and feeds in the tangle of anemone tentacles; he vigorously defends his home turf against intruders. But his territory, being alive, floats and swims around, so his home is here one day, there the next (Eibl-Eibesfeldt, 1970).

While the behavior of the anemone fish may reasonably be described by extending the concept of territoriality, the concept has been invoked to explain quite unterritorial-like behaviors. The elephant seal described in Chapter 1 does not have a home turf; he fights only to establish a dominance hierarchy. This is true of many other animals, too, for example, the elk (p. 809). The true believer in the territory-and-aggression hypothesis, when faced with such facts, resorts to the "mobile territory" explanations supported by studies like those of the anemone fish; one's "personal space"—apparently the air surrounding his body—is his territory. In these extreme formulations, territorial defense does not differ from individual defense.

PROTECTIVE AGGRESSION If a predator enters the vicinity of an animal or his group, the prey will often resort to aggression for protection. He might flee, if possible, fight if not—the "cornered rat" phenomenon. We have discussed some cases of protective aggression already, for example, the mobbing reactions of smaller birds. As I write this, two male bluejays are dive-bombing an intruding cat outside my window; jays are well known for their **sympathetic reactions** to the scolding shrieks of other jays (Armstrong, 1947). They fly over to help and then quickly leave, for the resident jay might well turn on them after the predator is banished.

Competitive and protective aggression often take different forms in the same species. The American elk uses his antlers in combat with other males during the mating season, but to attack a predator he will most likely rely on his sharp hooves. The odoriferous defense of the skunk (see Figure 28-16) and the prickly defense of the porcupine are common examples of specialized protective defense mechanisms. In primates, protective aggression often takes the form of throwing or dropping branches or even feces at the intruder, something rarely witnessed in competitive aggression.

FIGURE 28-16 AGGRESSIVE "DISPLAY" IN THE STRIPED SKUNK

The Eastern striped skunk has a highly stereotyped set of threat responses, which are generally given prior to expulsion of its infamous odor. In this photo all three animals show the tail erection and "fluffing" of the hair that characterizes the basic pattern. In addition, the animal on the left is "thumping" forward with his forepaws, while the skunk in the middle has pulled back from this position drawing some straw under his body.
(Stephen E. Glickman)

PREDATORY AGGRESSION Predatory aggression is more properly classified as feeding behavior, but since many insist on viewing predation as aggressive we will briefly mention this category of behaviors. Again, the behaviors in this class are generally quite different from those in other categories. Cats provide a good example. The predatory pattern of most cats includes crouching, stalking, and pouncing, with an absolute minimum of sounds. In contrast, when fighting another cat or when facing a belligerent member of another species, we see the classic "Halloween" cat: spitting and hissing, with arched back, and clawing with extended claws at the opponent.

Research on Aggression

We will not delve too deeply into the various theories of animal aggression except to note that there are two primary approaches to the understanding of these behaviors. The first approach is that of Lorenz, whose hydraulic model of motivation was discussed in the previous chapter, p. 778. From this vantage point, aggression is seen as resulting from an innate drive; its manifestation is therefore inevitable and will occur either directly or will find expression in some apparently nonaggressive activity. At the other extreme, there is the perspective that aggressive behaviors are like any others, learned on the basis of rewards and extinguished by nonreinforcement. Within this latter view, animals (or people) will only be aggressive when such behavior enables them to gain access to some desired reward (e.g., food or a mate), or removes a source of discomfort. These two "theories" of aggression lead to very different conclusions about how to control violence in human society. Adherents of the instinctive "energy-reservoir" view would argue that since the behavior is inevitable, the best tactic is to redirect the energy into some socially acceptable activity—such as competitive sports. Alternatively, the learning model suggests that aggressive behavior patterns will not be acquired or performed if we (1) minimize the competitive, frustrating circumstances which produce it, and (2) arrange that aggression is not rewarded. In actual fact, very few psychologists today hold strictly to one extreme view over the other, but an understanding of the two approaches can sometimes help us to understand the behavior of human researchers in studying aggression.

Shock-Elicited Aggression

If you deliver an electric shock to the feet of a pair of rats, they will attack each other. Perhaps this behavior can be classified under the heading of defensive aggression. This fact was discovered in the 1930's (O'Kelly & Steckle, 1939). In the 1940's psychologists used the fact to investigate the psychoanalytic proposition of displacement—for example, if the true target of aggression is unavailable, the aggressor will turn on an innocent target (see p. 113). Investigators rewarded rats (by turning off the shock) if they attacked each other. After such training, if another rat was not present the trained rat would attack "innocent" objects like rubber dolls (Miller, 1948b). These data were then presumed to support a redirection-of-aggression hypothesis derived from Freudian theory, but the conclusion now seems dubious. The most telling criticism is perhaps that one need not *train* an animal to be aggressive in these shocking circumstances. As both the original discovery and more recent studies show, shock elicits aggression automatically; a shocked animal will attack anything around—another animal, an iron bar, anything—even if the shock remains on. So it is hardly surprising to find the rat attacking a rubber doll if the doll is the only object around; in fact, the more interesting question, never systematically studied, is why the rat, when given a choice, chose to fight with a member of his own species rather than with an inanimate object.

In the 1960's, shock-elicited aggression was rediscovered by experimental personality theorists of a behavioristic, Skinnerian bent (Ulrich & Azrin, 1962). They demonstrated anew that pain is typically followed by aggression in many species, automatically, without learning. In later studies, it was shown that laboratory monkeys in pain will quickly learn to pull a chain that delivers an object suitable for attack, and thus the opportunity to show aggression came to be viewed as a reinforcement (Azrin, Hutchinson, & McLaughlin, 1965).

Although the precise laboratory controls characteristic of the Skinnerian researchers will doubtless add much to our understanding of aggressive behavior, the comparative psychologist does not find shock-elicited aggression to be very representative of aggression in the natural world. In natural settings, animals subjected to pain will sometimes aggress, but often they will not; a dominant animal attacking one lower in status typically does so with impunity, and dominant primates who aggress to keep their females in tow do not expect and do not receive a neck bite in return. Laboratory shock is extremely artificial and nonsocial. On the other hand, one could imagine evolutionary advantages accruing to animals who respond aggressively to nonsocial pain. If the pain were being caused by another animal, the aggressive response *might* result in the elimination of the pain and decrease the possibility of death.

Effects of Isolation

If you assume that aggression is an innate drive that must be periodically satisfied, then you would expect social isolation to result in increased aggression when two animals are put together after weeks without opportunity to aggress. This is indeed what happens. In fact, investigators with no interest in the hydraulic theories of aggression commonly use isolation to produce aggressive interactions so they can study, say, the effect of various tranquilizing drugs.

However, it is by no means clear that isolation-induced aggression supports the hydraulic theories of motivation. Isolation is a severe treatment and involves much more than the lack of opportunity to aggress. For example, if isolation starts early in life, it also means the animal has not had opportunity to learn the complex interpersonal communications that in many species are designed to avoid overt aggression, and he has not learned his place in a dominance hierarchy. An even simpler explanation is based on skin sensitivity. Animals in isolation, because of the lack of normal contacts with the animate and inanimate environment, might become quite sensitive to even affectionate grooming when later paired with another animal. If the grooming is now painful, the previously isolated animal would thus respond with pain-induced aggression much like the shock-induced attacks described above. Many humans have noted that skin deprived of normal contact with the environment—after wearing a cast some weeks, for example—becomes unusually sensitive, and a normally pleasant experience like a massage may be painful for a time following the removal of the cast.

Another fact creates problems for hydraulic theorists (and for others as well): if isolation is followed by *repeated* pairing—that is, if the isolated animal is tested in a social situation every day for several successive days—aggression does not always decrease. In some cases, especially if the animal wins in combat, aggression may even increase. If you hold to the hypothesis that isolation-induced aggression stems from building up pressure to aggress caused by lack of opportunity, then it is hard to explain why aggression does not decrease when the opportunity is presented frequently.

Hormonal Control

In the vast majority of animals that have been studied, the male hormone testosterone has been linked to aggressiveness. Animals deprived of this hormone, especially early in life, tend to place low in adult dominance hierarchies. But the overall picture is quite a bit more complicated. Most females become aggressive if their young are threatened, and these behaviors seem to result from a complex mix of changes in hormonal balance—in particular an increase in the female hormones, estrogen and progesterone—coupled with environmental stimuli such as the presence of the young.

To complicate matters further, there are species in which the female is typically the more aggressive; in mammals, hamsters are an example. The female hamster will ordinarily drive the male from her presence. She is the larger of the pair and quite capable of imposing her wishes in the interaction. During estrus, however, she becomes relatively docile and receptive. After estrus, she drives the male away again.

Sensory Cues

Adult aggression is very often triggered by specific sensory cues. In rodents, olfactory cues play an important role, and the elimination of the ability to detect odors may also eliminate aggressive behavior. In birds, visual cues are frequently sign stimuli releasing attack patterns, as we mentioned in the case of the robin and the "red breast" stimulus.

The red-winged blackbird uses the red bars on his wings to threaten and hopefully intimidate other males (see Figure 28-17). If they are deprived of their red bars of courage (by some dispassionate human experimenter with a can of black paint), they cannot hold their territory against intruders. Thus, in this case, the sensory cue is not so much an elicitor of aggression in other birds as it is a component of the total picture that enables the resident bird to maintain his territory—often without requiring actual combat.

In monkeys there is a complex set of visual and auditory cues related to aggression. These range from facial expressions that can communicate anything from "be careful" to "be ready for immediate attack" and even "I submit," to a series of auditory calls of similar flexibility.

How do adult animals come to "understand" and utilize these cues? Are there inborn reactions to specific stimuli, or do they have to learn the language during early experiences? Certainly the answers vary among species, but rarely do they support exclusively the nativist or empiricist position; typically some components of the complex behavior patterns are instinctive and some are dependent on experience, and interactions are everywhere. Monkeys raised in isolation get into more fights than do normally raised monkeys. The isolation-raised animals recognize aggression situations, but they fail to respond properly to the signals that normal monkeys use to reduce the incidence of overt aggressive behaviors (Mason, 1960). (See Figure 28-18.)

Aggression as Reward

In the discussion of shock-induced aggression, we noted that the opportunity to aggress after shock can be used as a reinforcement; that is, the shocked animals will work in order to obtain an object they can attack. This phenomenon can also be demonstrated in more nearly natural circumstances. Certain fish, for example, the Siamese fighting fish which is characterized by its general aggressiveness and fighting displays, can be trained to do tricks if his response is followed by exposure to an intruding male. (The "intruding male" can even be himself. Siamese fighting fish have been trained using the reward of a mirror placed against the tank, in which the fish sees himself and displays in a threatening fashion; his "opponent," of course, does so simultaneously.) Similarly, roosters can be trained to peck at a target if that pecking is followed by the sight of another rooster toward whom the training rooster can perform his aggressive display (Thompson, 1964).

What is one to make of these findings? Those theorists who claim that aggression is an innate drive see these results as sup-

FIGURE 28-17 STRUCTURAL CORRELATES OF "THREAT"
The red breast feathers of the robin (left) and the red wing markings of the blackbird serve a communicatory function, warning potential rivals to avoid the resident's territory.

port for their hypothesis, and the facts do fit with such assumptions. Opponents of such views, however, point out that aggressive interactions will retain their reinforcing effect only if the animal does not *lose* in the encounter. Some have suggested that aggressive behaviors

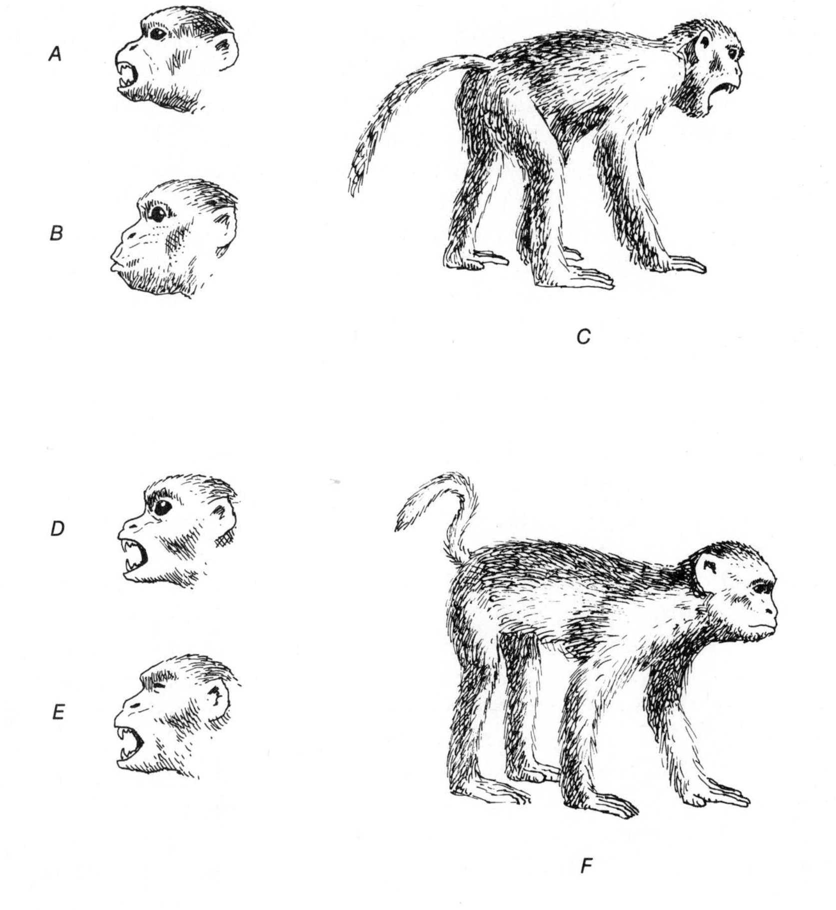

FIGURE 28-18 COMMUNICATION IN PRIMATES
Primates can communicate through facial expression and posture. *A, B,* and *C* portray facial expressions and posture characteristic of "fear" or "submission"; while *D, E,* and *F* show expressions and posture indicative of threat or high dominance status in rhesus monkeys.

are only secondarily reinforcing, they may be learned at a very early age. For example, in mammals with multiple births—like rats and dogs—the young compete for access to the nipples. Aggression often allows a newborn to pursue such truly innate goals as sucking at mother's nipple from which he has just banished his infant rival.

What can we learn about human social behavior from comparative psychology?

Man is an animal, occupying a unique branch on the evolutionary tree, but an animal nevertheless. At many points in this book we have seen that the study of animal behavior has been helpful in increasing the understanding of human behavior. Many techniques now employed in research with people were first employed with animals. For example, both classical and operant conditioning were initially studied with animals, and such research continues today. But conditioning is also employed in a variety of contexts with human subjects; recall, for example, its use in the study of infant perception (pp. 298–99) and its use in human biofeedback research (pp. 490–91).

In other cases, findings obtained with animal subjects have provided hypotheses and models for research with human beings. One example of this is the understanding of the mechanisms regulating feeding that have come from animal studies, and especially the new facts about human obesity that were discovered by seeking parallels with the behavior of animals made obese by hypothalamic lesions (see Spotlight 25-2, p. 697). Another example is the knowledge of the causes and ways of controlling some cases of pathological violence, knowledge derived originally from study of effects of experimental lesions in animal brains.

A salient question that remains is the extent to which findings and concepts derived from animal social behavior are directly applicable to the analysis of human social interactions. We have witnessed in the past few decades an almost total lack of caution among many comparative psychologists and ethologists in extrapolating their conclusions from research on lower animals to the social existence of humans. You should realize that these treatises are almost pure speculation, however fascinating they may be. They include works by Lorenz (e.g., *On Aggression*), Ardrey (*The Territorial Imperative*), and Morris (*The Naked Ape*). From the vantage point of classical ethology, the writings of Lorenz and his student and colleague Eibl-Eibesfeldt are probably the most worthy of our consideration.

In all such research we can recognize the traditional conceptual tools of the classical ethologist. Investigators seek to find fixed action patterns and attempt to identify more-or-less innate releasers or sign stimuli; social organization is seen in terms of adaptation to a particular habitat and its evolutionary advantages. Whether or not these concepts contribute much to the understanding of human behavior is an issue of controversy, but, as we have noted earlier, Freud's theory of personality is largely devoted to the description of relatively universal behavior patterns in man.

Fixed Action Patterns

To begin our discussion, we can note that there exists almost universal agreement on certain response patterns. No matter whether one calls them simple reflexes or instinctive behavior, the human baby is known to respond, without learning, to the nipple by sucking and to touches of the palm by clasping. Serious controversy begins at the level of more complex behaviors; smiling is a good example. Children, even blind children, smile when satisfied, and this behavior appears to please mothers and tighten the mother-child bond. According to Eibl-Eibesfeldt, even when the smile comes under partial voluntary control, it is used as an effective signal of appeasement in every known human culture. In the context of a threat, it is supposed to "turn off" aggressive behavior from another human.

The opponents of such a view, however, are not without empirical support. One investigator has shown that smiling behavior not only varies between countries but also that, within the United States, the smiles in one subculture are apt to be misinterpreted by people residing in different cultural habitats (Birdwhistell, 1963, 1966). One can hold a compromise position by saying that smiling may be a universal signal of appeasement—*within* a culture or subculture—but also that the behavior in its specific form adapts to the particular social environment in which it must be integrated, so that the signal from one culture could be misinterpreted in another. In other words, both instinct and the effects of experience in a culture affect the precise form of the response.

There is even more controversy about complex behavior patterns. Eibl-Eibesfeldt claims that rapid raising and lowering of the eyebrows is another human fixed action pattern, which characterizes friendly greetings between people. He presents some intriguing evidence, much of it in the form of motion pictures taken in a variety of world cultures by his unique research tool, a camera that shoots to the side—to depict "natural" rather than "posed" reactions. However, there are other patterns of social interaction that Eibl-Eibesfeldt believes to be species-characteristic, but which may not actually appear in all human cultures. "Flirting" would be one of these behavior sequences. The absence of such behavior may be attributed to **cultural overlay,** when learning overcomes instinctive reactions. This ploy makes the original hypothesis virtually incapable of empirical test, since both the presence and the absence of the FAP are readily explained.

Roots of Human Aggression

Many popular books have focused on the roots of human aggression, most specifically those of Ardrey (1966) and Lorenz (1966). Ardrey focuses on the concept of territoriality and its relation to aggression. Man, like many other animals, tries to establish a "home ground" and defends it aggressively against potential intruders. He fights for his castle, his mate, and his source of food. These propositions are not unreasonable in the light of human history. But they are not based on systematic data gathered in observations of human interactions; they remain speculative, and there is plenty of evidence from subhuman animal studies from which one could speculate in quite different directions.

Lorenz focuses on the inevitability of aggression, as encompassed in his hydraulic theory of motivation. According to Lorenz, if man is to live in peace with other members of the species, he must have outlets for his aggression—sport hunting or ritualized contests like football games. And he must broaden his view of "his clan" and territory to include more people. Most important, he must recognize the sign stimuli that release aggression in man, in order to more consciously control them. These stimuli include a threatened in-group, a hated out-group, an inspirational leader, and a number of people acting aggressively in concert (contagion).

Lorenz also speculates on answers to why man is one of the few animals that will kill members of his own species. He declares that weapons, tools that make man capable of swift and efficient elimination, produce the killing. If all wars were fought without weapons, few would die, mainly because man lacks the sharp claws and powerful teeth of other predators; it is quite difficult to kill someone with your bare hands. In mammals who possess claws and teeth, Lorenz points out, there have evolved strong inhibitions against killing a member of one's own species. When a wolf loses in combat, he will exhibit a submissive gesture such as exposing his neck, and the victorious wolf—who could kill with a single bite—turns away. In man, no such inhibitions developed, for, with his puny natural weapons, they were unnecessary. But with artificial weapons, man has the power without the usual controls—and this is a deadly combination. Lorenz likens man's predicament to that of a hypothetical dove who, by some cruel and unnatural trick of nature, suddenly acquired the powerful beak of a raven.

So, in man we have an aggressive animal with powerful weapons and few inhibitions. Lorenz is optimistic about the chances of reducing or eliminating war. Recognition of the nature of the beast, he argues, will permit man to establish artificial controls to go with his artificial weapons. Space flight may be helpful because it promotes the view of the whole earth as one's territory. He also commends the advantages of humor and satire in subtly identifying the unreasoning biological nature of human aggression. The final pages of

On Aggression are excellent illustrations of a human imagination in full flight, far above the mundane world of empirical facts. What Lorenz says might be true or it might not; there does not seem to be any objective way of testing his statements.

Criticisms of Lorenz and Ardrey are many-faceted; without an empirical base, it is as easy to criticize as it is to state. Lorenz has often been accused of "begging the question" in that he starts with a controversial position on the nature of aggression: that it is innate and will inevitably be exhibited. This proposition is unproven or unprovable (p. 779). In other cases, some of Lorenz's generalizations are seriously overstated. For example, it is claimed that animals with powerful natural weapons develop displays which inhibit an animal from killing another animal of its own species. However, lions have such "weaponry," but have not developed a display that prevents them from killing one another.

Many criticisms, especially from Americans, are based on a fear of the social implications of Lorenz's position. Acceptance of his theory, critics suggest, would blind investigators to elements in the social structure that have the effect of teaching aggression and rewarding it. They also point out, from numerous human studies, that the response to particular sign stimuli, such as frustrating situations, is extremely varied in humans. If the Lorenzian counters with the "cultural overlay argument," we are again faced with the virtual impossibility of testing the assertions.

Many students of human behavior are not convinced of the correctness of Lorenz's argument that outlets for aggression must be provided. Some maintain, in fact, that providing "outlets" may actually increase aggression by providing situations in which aggression can be practiced and learned. Therefore, to theorists who do not accept the aggressive drive as innate and as inevitably occurring when the hydraulic mechanism spills over, the plea for outlets for aggression is frightening. In their view, such efforts to release aggression safely will end up by increasing it. The controversy over the effects of TV violence (see p. 221) is caught up in this debate over catharsis versus modeling.

Finally, as was mentioned in Chapter 25, the neural circuits that mediate aggression may become abnormally active, so that an individual is pathologically violent. In these cases, neither the learning-based nor the nativistic accounts of aggression need be invoked; rather, the violent behavior is the direct result of malfunctioning brain mechanisms.

Caution in Generalizing

Scientists who study human behavior directly—psychologists, sociologists, and anthropologists—are often critical of the use or the understanding of their data by the ethological speculators. Eibl-Eibesfeldt, Ardrey, Lorenz, and Morris have a greater grasp—

in breadth—of the ethological literature, but when they turn to human social behavior, their knowledge is limited, and they tend to select experiments that fit with their preconceived notions. Let us note three examples of such selective arguments by ethologists:

1. Many social scientists, perhaps the majority, do not consider war a function of aggression, at least not of the "militant enthusiasm" Lorenz describes. At the front lines, soldiers can hardly be termed aggressive; most are deathly afraid, and if they fight at all—which is unlikely—they do so in order to avoid embarrassment among their peers (Marshall, 1947).

2. Ardrey claims that without territory men are not aggressive. In support he cites the Jews who were passive until they gained their own state, Israel. He neglects the many warlike nomads and roving pirates who were aggressive but had no territory to protect.

3. Morris (1967) claims that human females have big breasts because breasts are sign stimuli releasing sexual behavior and, when man started copulating front-to-front, sign stimuli moved from the rear (the buttocks) to the front. He overlooks the fact that in the majority of human societies, the preferred copulatory position is still from the back (Ford & Beach, 1952).

The discussion could be carried much farther, for it is easy to make statements, criticisms, and counterarguments. We can agree with Eibl-Eibesfeldt that there is a great need for more data from ethological observation of man. But perhaps a fit conclusion is a word of caution about generalizing conclusions from animal observations. Hopefully this chapter has shown that individual behaviors and social organizations are remarkably varied in both structure and function among the many animal species. One cannot even generalize safely from observations of one baboon group to another neighboring group. There are often similarities, but equally often the differences are striking. The research that we have cited on the social existence of various species indicates that each species must be studied on its own terms, without preconceptions. And this includes man!

SUMMARY

The social existence of animals may be viewed in terms of the selective advantages and the mechanisms of social cohesion and dispersal. One of the primary advantages of cohesion is protection against potential predators. Many animals band together to detect or fight off a predator that could easily surprise and overpower any isolated individual of the threatened group.

Many predators, on the other hand, band together to hunt and kill prey that would be too large and swift for an individual, as African hunting dogs subdue the antelope on which they feed. Food-gathering is a social activity in many insect species (e.g., bees). In primates, the social interactions and communication necessary for food-gathering appear to require a period of learning. Learning promotes flexibility of response to the environment, and in some macaque monkeys, juveniles have been known to introduce their elders to new sources of food.

Mating in most vertebrate species requires cohesion for at least a brief period of time. In some of these species, dominant males typically do most of the copulating, which provides for the selective genetic transmission of traits such as strength and size.

The division of responsibility for various tasks between the sexes varies considerably among animal species; very few universal generalizations can be made. One can find groups in which the female does the hunting (lions), the male tends the nest (many fish, including the Siamese fighting fish and the stickleback), and the female exercises considerable control in choice of a sexual partner (beagles). There is a tendency for the sexes to look alike in species that have no clear division of responsibility.

Social dispersion also has advantages. If food is in short supply, dispersal of the species over a wider area is desirable, sometimes necessary. Even without food scarcity, dispersal often occurs when the group population exceeds a certain size; this may result from a breakdown of the social organization caused by the large number of animals—communication is more difficult, for example, and dominance hierarchies are less easily instituted and maintained.

Reproductive behavior, in an evolutionary sense, shows a trend from asexual reproduction (e.g., the splitting of an amoeba) to sexual interactions that result in greater genetic variability. Similar trends include those toward internal rather than external fertilization of the eggs, toward live births, and toward greater periods of maternal care after birth. Because of these trends, the number of fertilized eggs per female varies from millions in lower species to one in many primate species; the chances of survival of the one fertilized egg in the latter species are relatively high. Learning (experience) is also more important in the sexual behavior of higher animals.

The sensory cues most closely related to sexual behavior are typically those important for the species in general, although olfaction seems to be of particular importance both for rodents and some presumably vision-dominated primates. Appropriate gonadal hormones are crucial for the appearance of mating behavior. However, removal of the hormone-producing glands will have varying effects depending upon the species, sex, age, and individual experience of the animal prior to loss of hormonal support. It is not rare to find the male as nest builder and protector of the eggs and young in lower species, but in mammals the female inevitably carries certain responsibilities by virtue of relatively prolonged periods of pregnancy and nursing. After birth, adults other than the mother can take an interest in the infant; fathers, "aunts," and "uncles" often do so.

Nest-building behavior in rats is a good example of the interaction of innate and learned factors; experience-deprived rats do build nests, but relatively slowly and inefficiently. Retrieval of the young and sensory cues (e.g., ultrasonic cries from rat pups) have been a major focus of recent research.

Cohesive relationships other than parent-infant include infant-infant and adult-adult. The most prominent interaction between infants is play. We have often assumed that the function of play is to practice adult behaviors, but there is surprisingly little relevant data. Grooming is a widely observed adult-adult interaction and appears to have many functions (e.g., maintenance of a social bond or dominance relation) beyond the obvious hygienic one.

Sensory cues play a significant role in group cohesion, as demonstrated by the calling of howler monkeys and prairie dogs. Scent-marking can function as a means of defining territory, indicating sexual readiness, or tracing a path.

The mechanisms underlying dispersal have been studied most extensively in terms of aggression (although aggression is often a cohesion-promoting behavior as well, within a group). Interspecies or intergroup aggression may be divided into three categories: competitive, protective, and predatory—although comparative psychologists typically consider predatory aggression as feeding behavior. In competitive aggression, defense of "territory" is a prominent concept. Within a species, the behavior patterns exhibited during protective aggression may be different from those in competitive aggression (e.g., the elk uses antlers in the latter, hooves in the former).

Research on aggression also falls into several categories. Shock-elicited aggression occurs following a painful stimulus. A period of isolation also appears to make many animals more aggressive. Hormonal factors, such as the amount of the male hormone testosterone, are clearly related to aggressive behaviors within the vertebrates. The sensory stimuli eliciting aggression have been studied in many species (e.g., the red bars on the "shoulders" of an intruding male red-winged blackbird), although the particular cues that are effective vary from one species to the next. Finally, the opportunity to aggress (or to display aggressively) is, for some species, a reward for which they will emit a learned response.

The text concludes with a discussion of the social psychology of men, the topic with which this book began. From a comparative perspective, man is indeed an animal, but the generalizations contained in recent popular books, although very thought-provoking, must be recognized as highly speculative and sometimes inaccurate.

Nevertheless, the understanding of man will benefit greatly by the consideration of his similarities with and differences from the other species with which he shares this planet.

RECOMMENDED READING

Dethier, V. *To Know a Fly.* San Francisco: Holden-Day, Inc., 1962.
A light and witty description of how one can learn about the behavior of flies, using simple techniques and creative common sense. As they say in the ads: recommended from ages 8 to 80.

Eibl-Eibesfeldt, I. *Ethology: The Biology of Behavior.* New York: Holt, Rinehart and Winston, 1970.
A textbook that presents a traditional ethological viewpoint with great vigor and fine illustrations.

Goodall, J. "My Life Among Wild Chimpanzees." *Natl. Geogr. Mag.*, 1963, *125*, 272–308.
The classic account of chimpanzees in their natural habitat.

Hinde, R. *Animal Behaviour.* New York: McGraw-Hill, 1970.
The most thorough contemporary attempt to synthesize current knowledge and concepts in ethology with those of modern comparative psychology. A very thoughtful, if somewhat difficult book.

Kummer, H. *Primate Societies.* Chicago: Aldine-Atherton, Inc., 1971.
A description of the varieties of social organization to be found among primate species; coordinated with an attempt to relate social organization to ecological factors.

Lorenz, K. *King Solomon's Ring.* New York: Thomas Y. Crowell Co., 1952.
An entertaining description of some animals that Lorenz has known, what he learned about them, and how he studied their habits. Along with the Tinbergen books listed below, this must be considered one of the best popular accounts of animal behavior study by a major scientist.

Marler, P., & Hamilton, W., III. *Mechanisms of Animal Behavior.* New York: John Wiley & Sons, Inc., 1967.
A comprehensive textbook of animal behavior that is particularly useful for the student wishing to obtain an introduction to a particular research area, e.g., migration.

Schaller, G. *The Year of the Gorilla.* Chicago: The University of Chicago Press, 1964.
A detailed account of the ecology and living habits of the mountain gorilla, as observed by Dr. Schaller in its natural habitat in the eastern Congo and western Uganda.

Tinbergen, N. *Curious Naturalists.* Garden City, N.Y.: Anchor Books (Doubleday & Company), 1968.
An account of ethologists engaged in problem-solving behavior; learning about the habits of a varied assortment of insects and birds. Written in a delightful style that conveys both the beauty of nature-watching and the excitement of scientific discovery.

——— *The Herring Gull's World.* New York: Basic Books, 1961.
A description of the life-style of a predatory bird, based primarily on field and laboratory studies carried out by Tinbergen and his colleagues.

APPENDIX: Statistics

In Chapter 2 we gave a brief introduction to psychological statistics without showing how the computations are performed. In this appendix you can carry your knowledge of statistics somewhat farther, although entire books and courses are required for detailed considerations of this subject. Here we will simply go over the statistical topics mentioned in Chapter 2 and will note some of the main symbols, formulas, and calculations. It will be helpful to review the examples in Chapter 2 as you read this appendix.

Table 1 lists some basic terms and concepts that we will be considering. Look through it now, and refer back to it later if necessary.

Description of a Frequency Distribution

In the text we pointed out that a distribution of scores or measures can be described in terms of its mean and standard deviation.[1] The mean can be found by adding all the scores and dividing by the number of scores:

$$\bar{X} = \frac{\Sigma X}{N}$$

For the standard deviation, there are two equivalent formulas, one in terms of raw scores (X) and the other in terms of deviation scores (x). The deviation-score formula looks simpler, but it requires first finding the deviation value for each item.

$$\sigma = \sqrt{\frac{\Sigma x^2}{N}}$$

That is, find the deviation (x) of each score from the mean, square these and sum them (Σx^2), divide by N, and take the square root.

The raw score formula for the standard deviation is more frequently used, especially when a calculating machine is available:

$$\sigma = \sqrt{\frac{\Sigma X^2}{N} - \bar{X}^2}$$

[1] In this appendix we are assuming that the data are distributed approximately according to the normal curve (see Figure 2-3) and that all samples are at least moderately large (consisting of thirty or more cases). Special statistics are needed for non-normal distributions and small samples.

TABLE 1
SOME BASIC STATISTICAL TERMS AND SYMBOLS

X	An individual item or measure.
N	The number of cases or items in a sample.
$\bar{X}$ or M	The mean of a distribution.
Σ	The sum of a number of items. (Σ is the capitalized form of the Greek letter sigma.) ΣX means the sum of all items or scores in the distribution.
σ or S.D.	The standard deviation of a distribution. (σ is the lowercase form of the Greek letter sigma.)
x	The deviation of an item or measure from the mean; $x = X - \bar{X}$. For a measure smaller than the mean, x is negative.
z	A way of expressing a score or measure in which its deviation from the mean is divided by the standard deviation; thus the deviation score is given in units of the standard deviation.
$\sigma_{\bar{X}}$ or SE_M	The sampling error of a mean.
r	Coefficient of correlation. Also written $r_{X,Y}$ to show that it is the correlation of two sets of measures, the X distribution and the Y distribution.
p	Probability of occurrence. If $p < .05$, the result is likely to occur less than 5 times in 100.

z-Score or Standard Score

Once you know the mean and standard deviation of a distribution, then you can express any score by taking its deviation from the mean and dividing this by the standard deviation. This is called a z-score. Thus, if $\bar{X} = 20$ and $\sigma = 10$, then a raw score of 25 can be expressed as a z-score of $\frac{25 - 20}{10} = 0.5$; a raw score of 12 can be expressed as a z-score of $\frac{12 - 20}{10} = -0.8$.

$$z = \frac{X - \bar{X}}{\sigma}$$

Many scales commonly used in psychological and educational measurement are based on z-scores. In such scales the z-score is typically multiplied by a constant (such as 100) to eliminate decimals; to the product a constant (such as 500) is added to eliminate negative values. Such transformed z-scores are called standard scores. Table 2 gives two such scales. The Stanford-Binet intelligence test is arranged to have the mean of a representative sample fall at about 100, and the standard deviation is about 15 points. The Graduate Record Examination scores are set to have the mean at 500 and each standard deviation equal 100.

TABLE 2
TWO SCALES DERIVED FROM STANDARD SCORES

Standard Score	I.Q. Score	Graduate Record Examination
$+3\sigma$	145	800
$+2\sigma$	130	700
$+1\sigma$	115	600
0σ	100	500
-1σ	85	400
-2σ	70	300
-3σ	55	200
$\bar{X}$ 0	100	500
σ 1.0	15	100

Sampling

We saw on p. 36 and in Table 2-2 that different random samples drawn from the same population will usually vary somewhat from each other. We noted there that the differences among means of such samples would be expected to be larger as the variability of the population increased; also, the differences among sample means would be expected to be larger if the sample sizes were smaller. Now we can state these relations quantitatively. If we know the standard deviation of a sample and its N, then we can estimate the standard deviation of a population of means (i.e., means of samples of the same size drawn from the same population); this sampling distribution of the mean is often called the standard error of the mean ($\sigma_{\bar{X}}$ or SE_M). Here is the formula:

$$\sigma_{\bar{X}} = \frac{\sigma}{\sqrt{N-1}} \quad \text{or} \quad SE_M = \frac{\text{S.D.}}{\sqrt{N-1}}$$

The size of $\sigma_{\bar{X}}$ varies inversely, not with N, but with the square root of N (actually of $N - 1$). This means that to cut the standard error of the mean in half, you must increase your sample size fourfold $\left(\frac{1}{\sqrt{4}} = \frac{1}{2}\right)$.

Significance of a Difference Between Sample Means

When we run an experiment with an experimental group and a control group, how can we interpret the trustworthiness or repeatability of a difference between the mean scores of the two groups? Repeating the experiment is a good way, but how can we reach the most reliable conclusion after having completed a single comparison?

Just as we can calculate the standard error of a mean, so we can calculate the sampling distribution of the differences between means of the X distribution and the Y distribution $(\bar{X} - \bar{Y})$. If we know the standard deviation of this distribution, we can compute a z-score for our obtained difference:

$$z_{\bar{X}-\bar{Y}} = \frac{\bar{X} - \bar{Y}}{\sigma_{\bar{X}-\bar{Y}}}$$

where $\sigma_{\bar{X}-\bar{Y}}$ is computed from the formula

$$\sigma_{\bar{X}-\bar{Y}} = \sqrt{(\sigma_{\bar{X}})^2 + (\sigma_{\bar{Y}})^2}$$

Just as a z-score for other data (e.g., exam scores) is considered very high or very low if it exceeds ± 2.0, a z-score for a difference between two means is considered to be large if it exceeds 2.0. If the means of the two groups represent nothing more than two estimates of the same "true" mean—if the difference, that is, represents merely random, chance fluctuations and there is no "real" difference between groups—then a z-score of 2.0 would occur less than 5 times in 100. With a z-score of 2.0 or more, we would feel fairly confident that the difference is not due to chance but rather indicates a true difference between the two groups. We express this confidence by saying the obtained difference is "significant at the .05 level" $(p < .05)$.

A z-score for a difference between means (sometimes called a "critical ratio") as large as 2.6 would occur only once in 100 if there were no real difference, so we can feel even more confident about these results $(p < .01)$.

If an experimental group has these statistics—$\bar{X} = 25$, $\sigma = 4$—and the control group has these—$\bar{X} = 19$, $\sigma = 3$—would you conclude that the difference is statistically significant?

$$\frac{25 - 19}{\sqrt{4^2 + 3^2}} = \frac{6}{5} = 1.2$$

What if the means were 25 and 19 but the standard deviations were 1 and 2?

$$\frac{25 - 19}{\sqrt{1^2 + 2^2}} = \frac{6}{2.3} = 2.6$$

Correlation

When each item has measures on two different scales, X and Y, we may want to find how closely the measures go together, as we discussed on pp. 37–41. For example, over a group of students, how closely are conformity and intelligence related; or, how closely are children's intelligence scores related to those of their mothers?

The formula for the product-moment coefficient of correlation can be written in several different ways. This is one way:

$$r_{X,Y} = \frac{\Sigma z_X z_Y}{N} = \frac{\Sigma xy}{\sqrt{\Sigma x^2 y^2}}$$

That is, for each individual, find the product of his z-scores in the two distributions, sum these products, and divide by N.

This way of expressing the formula shows that the correlation can be thought of as the average of the products of z-scores. If the two measures are positively related, then an individual who has a score above the mean in one distribution will tend to have a score above the mean in the other, so the product of his z-scores will be positive; a person below the mean in both distributions will also have a positive product (since two minus terms have a positive product). If the two measures are unrelated, then some individuals will have positive products, some will be negative, and the mean product will be zero. If the relation between the two is negative (being high on one distribution means that you are likely to be low on the other), then the mean of the products will be negative.

For computation with a calculating machine, this formula using raw scores is practical:

$$r_{X,Y} = \frac{N\Sigma XY - (\Sigma X)(\Sigma Y)}{\sqrt{[N\Sigma X^2 - (\Sigma X)^2][N\Sigma Y^2 - (\Sigma Y)^2]}}$$

In interpreting correlation coefficients, be careful not to think of them as percentages, even though correlations vary from 0 to ± 1.00. Actually, the *square* of the coefficient (r^2), multiplied by 100, indicates how much of the variation in predicting Y you can account for if you know X. If the correlation is .80, then knowledge of the X scores would allow you to account for 64 percent ($.80^2 \times 100$) of the variation in Y scores. This is a high correlation, as psychological measurements go, but it still leaves quite a bit of variance unaccounted for. As another way of picturing how tight (or how loose) such a relationship is, look back at Figure 2-6B, p. 41. And look again at the other scatterplots in Chapter 2.

Some Founders and Molders of Psychology

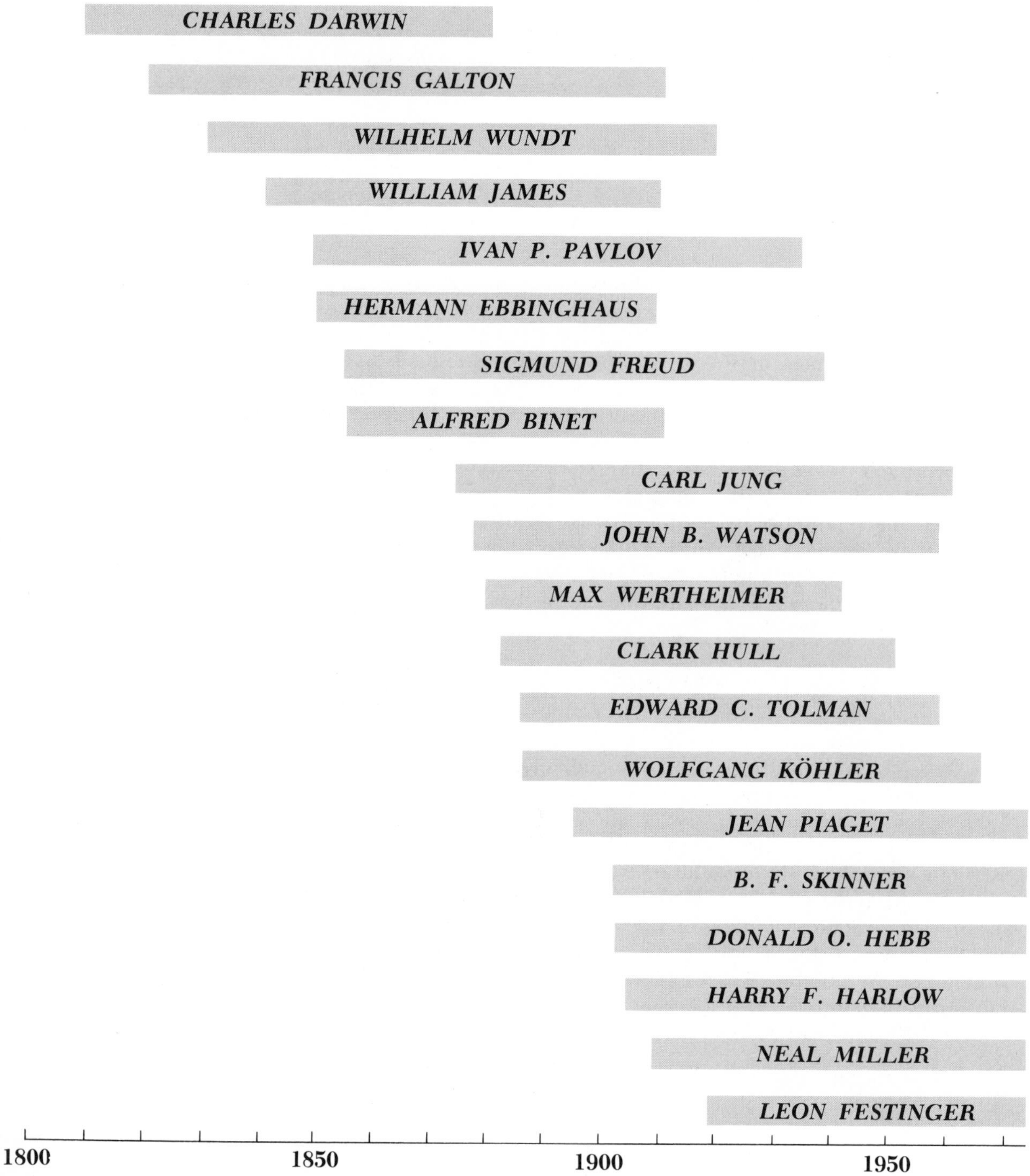

CHARLES DARWIN

FRANCIS GALTON

WILHELM WUNDT

WILLIAM JAMES

IVAN P. PAVLOV

HERMANN EBBINGHAUS

SIGMUND FREUD

ALFRED BINET

CARL JUNG

JOHN B. WATSON

MAX WERTHEIMER

CLARK HULL

EDWARD C. TOLMAN

WOLFGANG KÖHLER

JEAN PIAGET

B. F. SKINNER

DONALD O. HEBB

HARRY F. HARLOW

NEAL MILLER

LEON FESTINGER

1800 1850 1900 1950

Contributions and Influences

Origin of Species, 1859; impetus for study of comparative and developmental psychology.

Study of individual differences, Nature and Nurture; correlation technique; mental tests.

Founded first formal laboratory of psychology, 1879, University of Leipzig.

First major American text, *Principles of Psychology*, 1890.

Experiments on conditioned reflexes, 1900– , *Lectures on Conditioned Reflexes*, 1928.

First experiments on learning and memory; *Memory*, 1885.

Founder of psychoanalysis; *Interpretation of Dreams*, 1900.

First general intelligence test, 1904.

Analytical psychology; *Psychology of the Unconscious*, 1925.

Pioneer behaviorist, 1913– ; *Psychology from the Standpoint of a Behaviorist*, 1919.

Founder of Gestalt psychology, 1912; *Productive Thinking*, 1945.

Early mathematical, stimulus-response learning theorist; *Principles of Behavior*, 1943.

Cognitive neobehaviorist; *Purposive Behavior in Animals and Men*, 1932.

Gestalt psychologist; insightful behavior; *The Mentality of Apes*, 1925.

Theories of cognitive development, 1920's– ; *The Psychology of Intelligence*, 1947.

Control of behavior by reinforcement and operant conditioning; *The Behavior of Organisms*, 1938; *Walden Two*, 1948.

Neurophysiology of complex behavior; *The Organization of Behavior*, 1949.

Learning sets; affectional systems in primates.

Physiological processes in motivation and learning.

Experimental social psychology; *A Theory of Cognitive Dissonance*, 1957.

GLOSSARY

Absolute threshold Minimum physical intensity required for a stimulus to be detected.

Accessibility Characteristic possessed by mnemonic information that can be retrieved at time of test. Cf. **Availability.**

Acetylcholine A chemical that acts as transmitter agent at many synapses and at neuromuscular junctions. See Figure 23-4.

Achievement motivation The desire to succeed or do well; to accomplish something excellent, valuable, or important.

Achievement tests Standardized group tests designed to evaluate academic skills such as reading, arithmetic, and English.

Acquisition A procedure or a process resulting in the formation of an association; e.g., classical conditioning.

Action potential (also called nerve impulse) A wave of electrochemical activity that can propagate along a neuron. Most neurons are specialized to conduct such activity. See Figure 23-2.

Activity groups Groups involving people interested in common activities such as handicrafts; designed to be therapeutic.

Acuity The resolving power of the eye for spatial detail. See Figures 20-10 and 20-11.

Adaptation Process of adjusting to an environment. This may occur through learning or through evolution of instinctive behavior patterns.

Additive color mixture Adding lights of various wavelengths to produce a mixing of colors; see perception color Figure 1.

Adjective checklist Long list of trait adjectives used by rater to indicate which traits are characteristic of the subject.

Adolescence Period from puberty to maturity, the early teens to the early twenties.

Adrenal cortex Outer section of adrenal gland. The adrenal cortex is an endocrine gland; see Figure 23-9.

Adrenal medulla The inner part of the adrenal gland. The adrenal medulla secretes the hormone adrenalin; see Figure 23-9.

Afterimage Visual sensation that persists after the stimulus producing it has terminated.

Age-graded test items Test items that differentiate between children at successive age levels, young children finding an item difficult and older children finding it easier.

Agents of socialization Individuals and institutions that participate in socialization. Parents, teachers, neighbors, ministers, friends, characters in stories, movies, and television are all agents of socialization.

Aggression Behavior that results in the destruction or injury of some person or object.

Albedo Percentage of incident light that a surface reflects.

Altruistic behavior Behavior that benefits someone other than the actor, with little or no apparent benefit for the actor.

Amnesia Loss of memory for past experiences. Amnesia may occur because of everyday events or because of experimental treatments.

Amplitude See **Intensity.**

Amygdala Nuclei buried in the anterior temporal lobe; they modulate aggressive and other motivated behaviors.

Analysis-by-synthesis Theory of pattern recognition that maintains that the perceiver recognizes an object by actively synthesizing his percept of it from a portion of the available sensory information.

Androgens So-called male hormones; actually secreted by both sexes, although in greater amounts in males.

Antisocial (sociopathic) personality Character disorder showing pervasive moral deviation.

Association Term referring to unknown processes that link a stimulus to a response.

Association value Degree of meaning that an item has for a person.

Attachment Attraction to a person and dependence on that person for emotional satisfaction; the affectional bond that the infant forms to its mother.

Attitude A judgment about a person, group, or thing. It consists of a cognitive component (opinion), an emotional component, and a disposition toward action.

Aunt behavior Maternal behavior toward infant manifested by female adult animal other than the mother.

Authoritarian personality A set of attitudes and

personality characteristics that seem to occur together in prejudiced individuals. That is, a person who exhibits one of these characteristics (e.g., ethnic prejudice) is also likely to exhibit the other characteristics (e.g., latent hostility, deference to authority figures).

Autism Severe mental illness of early childhood; characterized by extreme withdrawal and isolation, absorption in fantasy, and profound defects in thinking and language.

Autokinesis Apparent motion of an actually stationary pinpoint of light in a completely dark room.

Autonomic nervous system Part of the nervous system that controls the heart, smooth muscles, and certain glands. See Figure 23-12, Table 23-1, and biological color Figure 6.

Availability Characteristic possessed by mnemonic information that is in existence regardless of whether it can be retrieved at a particular moment. Cf. **Accessibility.**

Axon Part of a neuron; specialized for propagation of action potentials. See Figure 23-1.

Bait shyness Literally, avoidance of poisoned bait. If an animal like the rat eats some food and then, an hour or so later, becomes ill, he will avoid the food on future encounters. This learning is surprising because (1) it is very rapid—one "trial" is often sufficient—and (2) the negative reinforcement is so far removed in time from the stimulus and response.

Basal age The age at which and below which the subject passes all the test items.

Basal ganglion One of a collection of motor centers lying deep within the cerebral hemispheres. See Figure 23-7.

Behavioral samples Part of an objective approach to personality assessment; an observer notes and records actual behaviors rather than judgments or inferences as is the case with rating scales.

Behavior modification Psychotherapeutic technique that applies the principles of learning in order to modify disturbed behavior, generally focusing on specific behavioral disturbances.

Behavior therapy See **Behavior modification.**

Binaural cues Cues to the location of a sound source dependent on the fact that two ears, being in slightly different locations, receive slightly different stimuli from the same sound source.

Binocular disparity The difference in the images cast on the two retinas by an object.

Biological psychology The branch of psychology that studies relations between behavior and biological processes within the organism. It draws on findings and methods of related disciplines such as endocrinology, genetics, neuroanatomy, neurochemistry, and neurophysiology. The conventional name for this branch has been physiological psychology, but the term biological psychology is a better indication of its scope.

Bipolar cell A retinal neuron whose input is from the visual receptors (rods or cones) and whose output is to retinal ganglion cells.

Brightness Psychological dimension referring to the perceived intensity of a light.

Buffer model A theory of memory proposed by Atkinson and Shiffrin that emphasizes the role of the short-term store in processing information.

Castration anxiety According to Freud, the young boy's fear that his father will retaliate for the boy's attraction to his mother and resentment of the father by castrating him.

Catharsis Reduction of an impulse through direct or indirect expression, particularly verbal and fantasy expression.

Central sulcus Groove or fissure in human cerebral cortex that separates frontal lobe from parietal lobe. See Figure 23-7.

Cephalocaudal direction The progressive development of the parts of the body and motor abilities, in a direction from head to tail.

Cerebellum Part of the hindbrain concerned especially with integration of bodily movements. See Figures 23-5 and 23-6.

Cerebral cortex The outer layers of the cerebral hemispheres, consisting of neurons and their connections; also called gray matter. The cerebral cortex is deeply folded in man and in higher mammals but is smooth in rodents and other lower mammals. See Figures 23-5 and 23-7, and biological color Figure 5.

Cerebral hemispheres The largest part of mammalian brains, including everything above the brain stem; it includes the cerebral cortex, the underlying tracts of white matter, and deeper structures such as the thalamus and basal ganglia. See Figures 23-5 and 23-6, and biological color Figure 1.

Cerebrum All of the brain above the hindbrain.

The cerebrum includes the forebrain and the midbrain. Roughly, the cerebrum is the cerebral hemispheres plus the midbrain.

Clairvoyance The state of sensing something when the object in question cannot affect a sense organ.

Classical conditioning A procedure, originally developed by Pavlov, to establish an association between a stimulus and a response. The conditioned stimulus (CS) is that stimulus to which the response is established; the unconditioned response (UR) is the original response similar to the to-be-established conditioned response (CR); and the unconditioned stimulus (US) is that stimulus that initially produces the UR. See Figure 18-2.

Client-centered nondirective therapy Psychotherapeutic technique introduced by Rogers in which the therapist follows the lead of the client in encouraging him to explore and accept his feelings and thoughts. This is accomplished through reflection of client's expressions and the conveying of acceptance and understanding of the client.

Closure One of the principles of perceptual organization: parts of the stimulus field that produce a closed unit tend to be perceived as belonging to the same unit.

Cochlea The inner ear. See Figure 24-8.

Coefficient of correlation A numerical value that indicates the degree of correspondence between two sets of paired measures; it ranges from +1.00 to −1.00. See Appendix on statistics.

Cognition Knowledge, interpretations, understandings, thoughts, and/or ideas that an individual has about himself and the environment.

Cognitive dissonance See **Dissonance.**

Cognitive map A subject's concept of his environment (Tolman).

Cognitive styles Stable, characteristic ways of approaching and handling cognitive tasks (see also **Reflectivity-impulsivity; Leveling-sharpening**).

Cohesion The condition of coming together and staying together. Used as distinct from **Dispersal,** splitting apart or separating.

Collective unconscious Consists of what Jung termed "archetypes"—the attitudes and feelings that are the residue of man's ancestral past.

Color circle Two-dimensional diagram that summarizes a variety of phenomena of color sensation and color mixture. See Figure 20-13 and perception color Figure 3.

Color solid Three-dimensional representation of all of the discriminable colors, with brightness represented on the vertical dimension, saturation in terms of distances from the central axis, and hue represented around the circumference of a double cone. See Figure 20-14 and perception color Figure 4.

Common fate One of the principles of perceptual organization: parts of the stimulus field that have a common fate, such as moving together, tend to be perceived as belonging to the same unit. See Figure 21-13.

Comparative psychology The branch of psychology that studies and compares the behavior of different species of animals, including man.

Complementaries, law of Every color has a complementary color such that if the two are mixed in appropriate proportions, the resulting mixture is achromatic (gray).

Compliance The least permanent level of social influence; a person complies (carries out an action) in order to obtain a reward or in order to avoid punishment.

Computer-assisted instruction (CAI) The use of computers to administer, score, and record a subject's progress on programmed materials.

Computer simulation The endeavor to write computer programs that will solve problems using procedures similar to those employed by humans.

Concept The common properties or relationships of objects or events, usually represented by a word or label.

Concept formation Discovering and defining the common properties or meanings of objects or events.

Concrete operations The third stage in Piaget's theory of intellectual development, in which the child reasons in a systematic and logical way. He is able to use rules based on concrete instances, but is still unable to deal with abstract qualities; the period from approximately 7 to 11 years of age.

Conditioned response (CR) The learned or acquired response to a conditioned stimulus. See **Classical conditioning.**

Conditioned stimulus (CS) A stimulus that is originally ineffective but that, through conditioning, comes to evoke a conditioned response. See **Classical conditioning.**

Conditioning The process by which conditioned responses are acquired. See **Classical conditioning, Operant conditioning.**

Cone A type of retinal receptor cell used in daylight vision. Three kinds of cones are maximally sensitive to three different regions of the visual spectrum.

Conformity A change in a person's opinions or behavior as a result of social influence. This influence usually takes the form of real or imagined pressure from another person or group of people.

Conjunctive concept A concept defined by the joint presence of several attributes, for instance, "large blue squares."

Conservation Piaget's term for the ability of the child to recognize that certain properties of an object do not change despite transformations in the appearance of the object.

Consistency theory The theory that a person strives to keep his attitudes, behavior, and cognitions consistent. If he finds them inconsistent, he attempts to reduce the discrepancies by altering beliefs or changing behavior, or both.

Constancy, perceptual The tendency for characteristics of objects in the environment to be perceived as constant even with important changes in the proximal stimulus.

Construct validity Relationship of a measure of a personality dimension to a particular theoretical formulation of that dimension.

Contagious behavior The spreading of a particular response from one animal to a group. For example, if one howler monkey starts howling, soon the entire troop is howling.

Content (or **Face**) **Validity** Extent to which the content of test items represents the behavior that the test is intended to measure.

Continuity In learning, theoretical issue concerned with question of whether learning is a gradual (continuous) strengthening of associations or a stepwise (all-or-none) process. In comparative psychology, *continuity* refers to the similarities among species: that is, whether there are general principles of learning that apply to all animals that can learn.

Contrast, perceptual Perceived enhancement of physical differences between stimuli.

Control group A group of subjects sharing all characteristics with the experimental group but not given the treatment whose effect is under study.

Convergent thinking Thinking that moves in the direction of conventional and socially accepted paths. Dictionary definitions of familiar words are distillations of convergent thinking.

Corpus callosum Large band of axons crossing from one cerebral hemisphere to the other. See position in Figures 23-7 and 23-8. The corpus callosum is cut to produce "split-brain" preparations.

Cortex Outer bark or rind. See **Cerebral cortex, Adrenal cortex.**

CR See **Conditional response, Classical conditioning.**

Creativity Ability to achieve a new, original, and imaginative solution to a problem that may be cognitive, philosophical, or aesthetic.

Credibility A characteristic of a communicator that partly determines his effectiveness in changing another person's attitude. A communicator's credibility depends on the extent to which his audience perceives him as having expert knowledge and/or attitudes and values similar to their own.

Criterion In perception, a cutoff point between two different responses, measured by β; cf. **Signal detection measures.**

Criterion validity Degree to which scores on a test are related to an agreed-upon reference point for the behavior being assessed.

Critical (sensitive) periods Periods of time that are particularly important in the development of body organs, physical attributes, cognitive functions, acquisition of new responses, and personality and social characteristics. Interruption of normal development during these periods may lead to deficiencies or malfunctions in the organism.

Cross-sectional study A study in which groups of individuals of different ages are observed and tested at a single point in time. Data are collected only once.

CS See **Conditioned stimulus, Classical conditioning.**

Cultural overlay Term meant to imply that learning based on cultural traditions and needs overlies or hides more basic or instinctive behavior patterns.

Culture-fair test An intelligence test constructed to minimize bias due to different cultural experiences, that is, biases related to social or ethnic group membership.

Cumulative recorder An instrument that records each response of a subject and makes a graph of the total number of responses over time. See Figure 18-5.

Decibel A ratio measurement of physical sound intensity; the number of decibels is one-tenth the logarithm of the ratio of the intensity in question to a reference intensity. See Figure 20-18 for intensities of some common sounds in decibels.

Deep structure Generally refers to the underlying or meaning level of language.

Defense mechanisms Modes of coping with anxiety-arousing situations and of resolving conflicts; examples are repression, denial, projection, reaction formation, rationalization, and sublimation.

Delayed-response test Situation in which a delay is imposed between the presentation of stimuli and the opportunity to respond; the accuracy of performance tests memory and mental ability.

Dendrite A specialized part of a neuron. Many kinds of neurons have numerous dendrites branching from the cell body and increasing its receptive surface. See Figure 23-1 and biological color Figure 7.

Denial A defense mechanism that permits awareness of unacceptable impulses and associated ideas but frees them of their threatening implications.

Dependent variable The observed variable which, according to the hypothesis, will change as a result of changes in the independent variable.

Derived concept A concept such as "speed" that can be derived from combining more "fundamental" concepts, such as time and distance.

Dichotic stimulation Stimulation that differs at the two ears. From the Greek roots *dicho-*, meaning "in two," or "separate," and *ot-*, meaning "ear."

Diencephalon In the fetus, the second of the five early divisions of the brain; in the adult it includes the thalamus and the hypothalamus. See Figures 23-5 and 23-6.

Difference threshold Minimum change in physical stimulus required for subject to detect a change.

Dimorphism Differences in body structure. Sexual dimorphism refers to the condition in which the male and the female of a species have different body structures.

Discriminative stimulus Signal that indicates that reinforcement is or is not currently available.

Disjunctive concepts Concepts derived by combining concepts that do not overlap (for example, *children*, derived from *boys* and *girls*).

Dispersal A splitting apart or separating. Used in contrast to **Cohesion,** coming together and staying together.

Displacement (1) In Freudian personality theory, a defense mechanism indicated by behaviors toward a person or object other than the "true" person; e.g., I am angry at my boss, but I yell at my wife. (2) In ethology, an unusual act that occurs in the midst of directed behavior, e.g., grooming in the middle of a fight. These behaviors are believed to represent a conflict, as between fear and aggression.

Display Behaviors that humans might call "showing off." In sexual display, the animals "show off" before mating; the male peacock, for example, spreads his tail plumes. In aggressive display, teeth may be bared, fur or feathers raised, or growls and hisses emitted; the Siamese fighting fish becomes more brilliantly colored in confrontation with another male.

Dissonance A state of tension generated when a person holds two cognitions that are inconsistent with one another. In dissonance theory this inconsistency refers to cognitions that carry contradictory implications for behavior.

Distal stimulus Object at a distance from the sensory surface, the energy from which produces a proximal stimulus that affects the sensory surface.

Distractor technique Method of studying short-term memory in which a few items are briefly presented to the subject, followed by some task designed to distract his attention temporarily from the to-be-remembered material.

Distribution Variation in some particular characteristic.

Distribution of practice Temporal spacing of material during the course of learning. One extreme is massed practice with no rest periods; the other extreme is spaced practice with many rest periods.

Divergent thinking Thinking that moves away from the conventional and socially acceptable. The term *divergent thinking* is often used as a synonym for *creative thinking*.

Doll Play Technique in which a child reveals his aggressions, conflicts, and emotional feelings about himself and his parents through his play with dolls.

Dominance hierarchy A social organization found in many animals in which the members of the species order themselves in terms of who dominates whom in terms of such activities as sex, aggression, and feeding. For example, a dominant male eats first, does most of the copulating, and "wins" a "threat contest" with a nondominant male.

Down's syndrome The technical term for mongolism, mental retardation associated with a genetic abnormality and manifested in such features as thick tongue, extra eyelid folds, and heart deformities, as well as deficient intelligence.

Dream Vivid experience during sleep that usually occurs during "paradoxical" or "rapid eye movement" sleep.

Drive A motive force for behavior, often seen as resulting from a biological need. If an animal has been without food for a time, he has a biological need that is typically translated into a drive—hunger.

Drive reduction The reduction of a motive force. Drive-reduction theories of reinforcement suggest that substances that reduce drives can be used to increase habit strength; e.g., food can be used to teach a hungry animal.

ECS See **Electroconvulsive shock therapy.**

Educational psychology The branch of applied psychology that uses the theories, findings, methods, and instruments of psychological science for educational purposes.

EEG See **Electroencephalogram.**

Ego Freud's term for that part of the personality that compromises between the impulsive demands of the id and the constraints of the superego and reality; it is responsible for effective adjustment.

Egocentric thought Thought process characteristic of children, when they view themselves as the reference point in their dealings with events in the external world and the perception thereof. Inability to take account of another's point of view.

Ego diffusion The inability of an individual to integrate his various part identities into a coherent sense of self.

Ego identity The individual's awareness of himself as a distinct and integrated person; the integration of his previous identifications, his traits, and abilities.

Electroconvulsive shock therapy A treatment most often used for severely depressed and some schizophrenic patients; it consists of inducing convulsions via the administration of electric shock to the brain.

Electroencephalogram (EEG) Record of the electrical activity of the brain made from the outside of the head. For EEG patterns in sleep and wakefulness, see Figure 25-6.

Emmert's law The apparent size of an afterimage varies directly with the apparent distance of the surface upon which it is projected. See Figure 20-15.

Empiricism The position that various skills or processes, like the organization of perception or space perception, are dependent on learning and past experience.

Encoding The accurate representation of one thing by another, which may be a symbol, memory trace, or nerve impulses; cf. **Memory storage, Retrieval.**

Encounter groups Groups involving people who wish to engage in "meaningful, open, and honest" interactions with others.

Endocrine gland Gland that pours its secretion (which is called a hormone) directly into the bloodstream; this provides a system for integrating many body processes. The chief endocrine glands and their locations and functions are shown in Figure 23-9.

Engram The underlying neural basis of the memory trace.

Estrogens So-called female hormones; actually secreted by both sexes, although in greater amounts in females. Both estrogens and androgens ("male" hormones) play roles in the female's estrous cycle.

Estrus The sexually receptive state in female mammals. (The related adjective is *estrous.*)

Ethology The study of animal behavior, usually in the animal's natural habitat; the focus is on those behaviors characteristic of a particular species, e.g., instinctive, species-specific behavior patterns like the sexual display of the peacock.

Experimental group The group of subjects for

whom the experimenter changes the independent variable, or variables, whose effects are being studied.

Extinction Procedure or process in which an established association is undone; see **Classical conditioning.**

Extrasensory perception Perception or knowledge of events when there is no known sensory mediation of such perception.

Extroversion Jung's term for the tendency to focus on the outside world.

Factor analysis Statistical method used to identify basic dimensions or traits that account for the relationships between different tests and other behavioral indices.

FAP See **Fixed action pattern.**

Feature analysis Theory of pattern recognition that implies the extraction of parts of patterns, such as horizontal strokes, vertical strokes, or arcs of circles, to discover which combination of features is characteristic of any particular pattern.

Fechner's law Psychophysical law stating that perceptual magnitude increases in proportion to the logarithm of the physical intensity of the stimulus: $\psi = k \log \phi$.

Feedback Return of part of the output of a system to the input, especially for purposes of correction and control of ongoing activity. Feedback occurs both in the endocrine system and in the nervous system.

Field independence and dependence The cognitive-style dimension that arranges individuals according to the extent to which they rely on external or internal cues in orienting themselves in physical and social space.

Figural aftereffect Distortion of the perception of the size, shape, distance, and so on, of a figure produced by prior stimulation with another figure.

Filter theory Theory of memory and performance proposed by D. E. Broadbent that stresses our limited capacity to process information.

Fitts' law A principle of skill learning that states that the relationship between performance and practice is a power function.

Fixation Psychoanalytic term referring to the attachment of libidinal energy to a particular psychosexual stage of development.

Fixed action pattern A species-characteristic response pattern that is presumed to have survival value for the organism.

Forebrain Part of brain that develops from forward end of neural tube. It includes the telencephalon and the diencephalon. See Figures 23-5 and 23-6.

Formal operations The fourth stage of Piaget's theory of intellectual development, in which the child becomes able to use abstract rules; the stage of adult logic; begins around 11 years of age and continues through adulthood.

Fovea Central area of the retina, that part in which vision is most acute.

Free association Psychoanalytic technique of recovering unconscious material by having the patient tell *everything* that occurs to him.

Free-recall learning Rote-learning or short-term memory procedure in which the subject attempts to report back all items presented to him, in any order that he wishes.

Frequency of a sound The physical attribute of a sound that specifies the number of cycles per second of vibration. The unit of measure is the hertz (Hz).

Frontal lobe The part of each cerebral hemisphere that lies in front of the central sulcus. The part just in front of the sulcus contains the main cortical representation of body musculature. See Figure 23-7 and color Figures 1 and 2.

Frustration Aversive emotional state resulting from interference with goal attainment.

Functional fixedness A set in which the individual is unable to see the many possible functions of an object beyond its customary function.

Gain-loss theory of attraction Proposes that *increases* in the amount of reward one individual gives another, rather than the *amount* of reward, determine how much one individual is attracted to another. Increases in reward have more impact than constant or invariant rewards; a person whose esteem for another person increases over time will be better liked than one who has always liked the other person.

Ganglion A collection or cluster of neuron cell bodies. See **Basal ganglion, Sympathetic ganglion.**

Ganglion cell Neurons whose cell bodies are in the retina and whose axons form the optic nerve and optic tract.

Generalization In stimulus generalization, any of similar stimuli evoke a particular response; in response generalization, a particular stimulus evokes a variety of similar responses, as in conditioning.

Gestalt A German word meaning form or whole. It is used to designate an approach to psychology that stressed organization and configuration in perception and insight in learning.

g factor (general intelligence factor) The most general factor common to all measures of mental ability, present to some extent on all tests of intelligence.

Goodness of a figure A measure of the perceptual organization or salience of a stimulus pattern. See Spotlight 21-5.

Grade-level index The mean grade level of all children in a norm (standardization) group who attain a particular score on an academic achievement test.

Gray matter Collections of cell bodies in the nervous system, such as the cerebral cortex and basal ganglia; so-called because they appear darker than the fiber tracts or white matter. See Figure 23-7 and biological color Figure 5.

Grooming Making neat and clean. Many animals wash themselves or others and pick off bugs and dirt. Apart from hygienic considerations, interpersonal grooming has a social side, that is, one grooms one's infant, friends, and lovers.

Group therapy Psychotherapy in which a number of patients participate together in a therapy session.

Habitat Environment in which an animal is commonly found (in the wild).

Habit reversal Learning the opposite of what has just been learned; e.g., if the white (and not the black) door has been associated with food reward, now the black (and not the white) door leads to food.

Halo effect Reduction in rater's objectivity as a result of the influence of one personality characteristic of the subject on ratings of other personality characteristics.

Hebb repetition effect The fact that the recall of a repeated list embedded in other nonrepeated lists improves with repetition in a memory-span task.

Heritability The amount or extent to which a particular trait can be attributed to genetic factors.

Hertz (Hz) The frequency of sound, in terms of cycles per second.

Hindbrain Part of the brain that develops from the third of the subdivisions of the tubular brain in the young embryo. Includes the metencephalon and myelencephalon. See Figures 23-5 and 23-6.

Hippocampus Region of evolutionarily old cortex, thought to be involved in memory and attention. Its position in human brain is shown in Figure 26-3 and biological color Figure 3; in rat brain, in Figure 25-3.

Homeostasis Tendency for a biological system to return to one particular state or level of functioning, which presumably is optimal in some sense. For example, the human body regulates temperature; body mechanisms work to increase temperature if it falls below 98.6° and to decrease it above 98.6°.

Home visit A naturalistic method sometimes used to assess parent-child interactions. A specially trained observer goes to the child's home and observes and records the way family members interact.

Hormone The secretion of an endocrine gland. See Figure 23-9.

Hue The dimension of visual perception that is largely determined by wavelength of the stimulus; red, yellow, green, and blue are hues. See perception color Figure 4.

Hunter-McCreary law A principle of serial-order learning; namely, that the proportion of errors at each serial position will be the same despite variations in the level of an independent variable.

Hypothalamus A part of the diencephalon; contains specialized centers related to motivation and drives. See Figures 23-5, 23-6, and biological color Figure 4.

Hypothesis Tentative explanatory statement or best guess about the relationship between two variables. Hypotheses are tested by experimental or observational studies.

Icon Literal reproduction of a stimulus array in memory for about a second's duration after the stimulus has ceased to affect the receptor.

Id Freud's term for that part of the personality that consists of unconscious sexual and aggressive impulses seeking immediate expression and gratification.

Identificand The person or group with whom the child identifies.

Identification The process of internalization of the characteristics of another person or group; modeling behavior after that of the other.

Identity crisis The struggle that takes place within an individual when he seeks to answer questions such as, Who am I? and arrive at a definition of his identity.

Idiot savant Mentally retarded individual who shows a specialized talent such as the ability for lightning calculation or an extraordinary memory for dates and facts.

Illumination stage That stage in creative thinking when the solution to the problem "pops into mind" quite unexpectedly.

Illusion Lack of correspondence between a percept and a physical stimulus object that gives rise to it.

Imagery Term used by Piaget to refer to the ability of the child to form primitive mental representations of objects or events; the development of imagery occurs at the end of the sensorimotor period.

Imprinting A species-specific learning that typically occurs within a limited period of time after birth; most psychologists limit the term to the learning of social responses ("following," "running to" in case of threat) to the natural mother. See **Critical periods.**

Inaccessibility See **Accessibility.**

Incubation stage That stage in creative thinking when the creative thinker leaves the problem and does something else like going to the movies.

Independent variable The variable selected or altered by the investigator to determine its effects on the dependent variable(s).

Inferotemporal cortex Cerebral cortex at the base of the temporal lobe; involved in visual form perception. See Figure 24-7.

Inoculation effect Achievement of attitudes resistant to change by "inoculating" the person first with a weakened form of the counterattitudinal arguments he will encounter later. When he eventually encounters these arguments he is able to resist them.

Insight The relatively sudden solution of a problem.

Instinct In psychology, instinct typically refers to needs or behavior patterns that are innate, or built in, and do not require learning.

Instinctive drift Tendency of an animal to drift toward species-characteristic behavior despite learned behavior.

Intellectualization The use of intellectual sophistication to avoid arousing aversive feelings while dealing with potentially threatening content.

Intelligence The ability to think and act in adaptive ways; also encompasses complex mental abilities, such as thinking, reasoning, and problem solving.

Intelligence quotient (I.Q.) The subject's mental age divided by his chronological age and multiplied by one hundred: $I.Q. = M.A./C.A. \times 100$.

Intensity, or amplitude Pertaining to sound, the physical strength of an auditory stimulus.

Internalization Process by which individual accepts influence because the induced behavior fits in with his existing value system or with what he thinks is "right."

Intromission Insertion of the penis into the vagina.

Introversion Jungian term for a person's tendency to focus on his inner world of subjective experience.

Inventory Personality measurement device in the form of a questionnaire that usually calls for simple *yes* or *no* answers.

Isolation Defense mechanism that facilitates the separation of anxiety-arousing ideas from related thoughts and attitudes.

Just noticeable difference (jnd) Minimum change in the physical stimulus required to yield the impression that the stimulus has changed.

Latent learning Learning that becomes evident only when the response is rewarded.

Lateral geniculate body (or nucleus) Visual center in the thalamus. See Figures 24-1 and 24-7.

Lateral inhibition Inhibition that a stimulated cell exerts on neighboring cells at the same level in the system. This process sharpens contours in vision and sharpens frequency discrimination in audition.

Lateral nucleus of hypothalamus Brain region involved in controlling food intake. See Figure 25-3.

Learning A relatively permanent change in the organism that results from practice and that leads to changes in behavior.
Learning curve Curve that shows functional relationship between some measure of amount of practice (independent variable) and some measure of performance (dependent variable).
Learning set Condition of being prepared to learn in a particular way. After solving several problems of the same general type, many animals behave in a way that suggests they have learned the general, underlying principle; they are prepared to learn new solutions to problems of the "old type" more rapidly.
Leveling-sharpening Cognitive-style dimension that arranges subjects according to whether they tend to recall the "big picture" and forget details or the reverse.
Level of aspiration A person's subjective goals and expectations about his performance on tests or standardized tasks.
Libido A Freudian concept referring to a basic pleasure-seeking drive of erotic nature.

Longitudinal study A study in which the same individuals are observed and tested repeatedly over an extended period of time, often a decade or longer.

Long-term memory Relatively permanent memory storage; differentiated from short-term memory.
Lordosis An elevation of the hindquarters, accompanied by temporary immobility. This posture characterizes the response of some female mammals to tactile stimulation of the back or flanks during the estrous state.
Loudness Psychological dimension referring to the experienced strength of a sound. (See Figure 20-18 for loudness of certain common sounds in **decibels.**)

Mach bands Perception of distinct lines or bands at places in a stimulus array where there are abrupt changes in the intensity gradient.
Mammal Member of the subphylum of vertebrates characterized by maternal suckling of the young, ability to internally regulate body temperature, and a hair-covered skin.
Mands Verbal responses to situations of a kind that have been positively reinforced in the past.
Manic-depressive psychosis A mental illness characterized by abrupt changes in mood from extreme excitement and euphoria to deep depression, and vice versa.
Maturation The physical, neural, physiological, and biochemical changes that take place within the organism over a period of time.
Mean A measure of central tendency of scores in a distribution. The arithmetic mean is the sum of all the scores divided by the number of scores.
Median A measure of central tendency of scores in a distribution. The median is the middle score, when the scores have been arranged from largest to smallest.
Medulla Lowest part of brain stem; above spinal cord and below pons. Contains specialized centers and fiber tracts. See Figures 23-5 and 23-6.
Memory span The number of items an individual can reproduce in order after a single presentation, typically 7 ± 2.
Memory storage The persistence of information over time; cf. **Encoding, Retrieval.**
Mental age A person's score on an intelligence test, expressed in years and months; based on age at which average children make a given score.
Mental retardation Mental subnormality, generally an I.Q. of 70 or less.
Midbrain (mesencephalon) Part of brain that develops from the second of the three subdivisions of the tubular brain in the young embryo. Includes the visual and auditory colliculi. See Figures 23-5 and 23-6.
Millisecond One thousandth of a second. Neural action potentials and synaptic events are measured in milliseconds. See Figure 23-2.
Millivolt One thousandth of a volt. Neural impulses are measured in millivolts. See Figure 23-2.
Modality A particular means or channel of accepting information, e.g., the auditory mode (for sounds), the visual mode (for sights).
Modality effects Effects in memory that differ according to the sensory modality in which the material was presented.
Modified method of free recall (MMFR) Procedure used in rote learning designed to eliminate competition of responses in a paradigm such as *A-B, A-C*.
Mongolism See **Down's syndrome.**
Monism In regard to learning, the position that there is fundamentally only one kind of learning

and that all examples of learning follow the same basic principles. Opposite of **Pluralism.**

Morpheme The smallest meaningful sound in a language. Morphemes involve some combination of phonemes.

Motion parallax Differential change of retinal images of different parts of the visual field as observer moves about in the field.

Motivation Generic term referring to activating states of the individual directing his behavior toward the fulfillment of specific needs.

Multi-factor theory of intelligence The theory that intelligence test performance is a product of several separate factors.

Nanometer A billionth of a meter; 10^{-9} meters. Wavelengths of light are measured in nanometers.

Nativism Position that various skills or processes are independent of learning, that is, are built into the basic functions of the nervous system.

Naturalistic observation Observation of events in real-life settings, such as in nursery school, on the playground, or at home, without experimental manipulation of the variables involved.

Negative afterimage Afterimage whose colors are complementary to those in the inducing stimulus. See perception color Figure 6.

Neonate The newborn; used to describe the developing individual during the first few days after birth.

Nerve fiber A branch of a nerve cell. It most often refers to an axon but can also refer to a dendrite. See Figure 23-1. Most nerve fibers conduct nerve impulses.

Nerve impulse (also called **action potential**) A wave of electrochemical activity that can propagate along a neuron. Most neurons are specialized to conduct such activity. See Figure 23-2.

Nervous system The brain, spinal cord, autonomic system, and peripheral nerves running to all parts of the body. For the main subdivisions of the nervous system, see Figure 23-5.

Neuron Single nerve cell. See Figure 23-1.

Neurosis Diagnostic term referring to emotional and behavioral disturbances that disrupt adequate adjustment but are not intense or comprehensive enough to severely diminish contact with reality; examples are irrational fears, anxiety reactions, compulsions, and sexual impotence and frigidity.

Nightmare Disturbed state that occurs either during deep nondreaming sleep or during a rapid transition between this stage and waking. A nightmare is not a dream.

Nonsense syllable A nonsensical collection of letters, such as *qbw* or *zeb*.

Normal curve The bell-shaped frequency distribution that describes many measures in psychology and other sciences. Its properties are used in making statistical inferences from measures based on samples. See Figure 2-3.

Nucleus From the Latin word for "kernel"; has several different meanings. Anatomically, (1) the central part of a cell containing the chromosomes, or (2) a cluster of neuron cell bodies, such as the lateral geniculate nucleus.

Nurturance Gratification of needs and the care, warmth, and attention given to the infant.

Object permanence Term used by Piaget to refer to the individual's realization that objects continue to exist even though they are not visible to him.

Occipital lobe The part of the cerebrum at the back of the head. It contains the primary cortical representation for vision. See Figure 24-7 and color Figures 1 and 2.

Oedipal conflict Freud's term for the boy's sexual attraction to his mother and resentment toward his father.

Olfactory bulb The sensory nucleus and tract just above the olfactory receptors. See Figure 23-8.

One-male group Type of social organization in which the basic unit consists of one male, several females, and several infants and adolescents.

Operant-conditioning techniques Procedures for producing behavior change based on Skinner's applications of principles of reinforcement; these techniques have recently gained wide application in therapy of behavior disorders.

Operant (or instrumental) response Response that produces reward.

Optic chiasm The crossing of the optic nerve fibers (so named because its form resembles that of the Greek letter chi χ). See Figures 24-1, 24-7.

Optic nerve Nerve formed by axons of the ganglion cells in the retina. It leaves the eye at the blind spot and runs to the optic chiasm; from the chiasm to the thalamus, the fibers are called the optic tract. See Figures 24-1 and 24-7.

Optic tract Made up of axons running from the optic chiasm to the lateral geniculate body in the thalamus. The optic tract fibers are continuations of the optic nerve fibers. See Figure 24-1.

Overprotection Providing more care for a child than is necessary. Overprotecting mothers tend to discourage their child's independent behavior and continue to treat him as though he were still an infant.

Paired-associate learning Rote-learning procedure in which a number of paired items are presented and the subject must learn to produce one member of the pair when probed with the other.

Paradoxical sleep Phase of sleep in which electrical activity of the brain resembles the waking pattern, although the person or animal remains asleep. Movements of the closed eyes appear in this phase, so it is sometimes called rapid eye movement (REM) sleep. Dreams usually occur during this phase of sleep.

Paranoid reaction A psychosis in which the patient entertains an elaborate scheme of false thoughts and claims; these are often delusions of persecution or of grandeur.

Parasympathetic system A division of the autonomic nervous system. For its functions, see Table 23-1. See biological color Figure 6.

Parietal lobe Lobe of cerebrum that lies back of central sulcus and extends to occipital lobe. It contains the cortical projection of the body surface. See Figure 23-7 and color Figures 1 and 2.

Partial reinforcement Schedule of reinforcement in which only some fraction of the responses that occur are reinforced.

Peers Agemates.

Percept That which is perceived; the result of the active processes of perception.

Perception Awareness by the organism of its environment.

Personality dynamics Function of behavior; explaining the *why, where,* and *when* of the workings of personality.

Peterson paradox The fact that memory for a repeated item improves as a function of the separation between presentations.

Phobia Neurosis characterized by irrational intense anxiety reactions to specific objects and situations.

Phonemes The most basic distinctive sounds in any given language.

Photopigments Special chemicals located in the visual receptor cells (rods and cones). When light strikes these pigments, they undergo a change that sets up an electrical potential. This is the first stage in the process of seeing.

Phylogenetic scale An arbitrary ranking of a group of existent animals according to some conceptual scheme. For example, we might attempt to "scale" animals according to neural complexity, but this would not represent a true evolutionary sequence.

Pitch Psychological dimension referring to how high or low a tone appears to be.

Pituitary gland Important endocrine gland, located below the hypothalamus. For its function, see Figure 23-9; for its location, see Figures 23-6 and 23-8.

Play therapy Psychotherapeutic technique based on assumption that a child's unconscious wishes, conflicts, and fears will often be revealed in his play activities.

Pluralism In learning, a theoretical issue concerned with the question of whether there is one kind of learning or many kinds; opposite of **Monism.**

Pons Part of brain stem lying above the medulla and below the midbrain. Contains specialized centers, tracts running up and down the brain stem and tracts bridging from one side of the cerebellum to the other. (These last are responsible for the name *pons,* Latin for "bridge.") See Figures 23-6 and 23-7.

Power law Psychophysical law stating that perceptual magnitude increases in proportion to the physical intensity of the stimulus raised to a given power: $\psi = k\phi^n$; also known as Stevens' law.

Prägnanz, law of Gestalt law that states that the organization of any whole will be as good as the prevailing conditions allow.

Precognition The perceiving of some event of the future, when there is no way to know about such event beforehand.

Predator The attacking animal in a food-gathering situation, e.g., the wolf in pursuit of a deer.

Prejudice A set of hostile attitudes based on and supported by generalizations derived from faulty or incomplete information.

Preoperational period Second stage in Piaget's theory of intellectual development, in which representational thought begins; the first time that the child's reactions are based on the meaning of the object rather than on its physical nature; the period from approximately 2 to 7 years.

Prestige In communication research, a communicator is said to have high prestige when he has credibility—that is, expertise and trustworthiness.

Prey Animal being pursued in a food-gathering situation, e.g., a deer being chased by wolves.

Primacy effect The stronger influence of early information over late information on cognitions, impressions, and attitudes.

Primary drives Innate motivational states reflecting physiological changes; examples are hunger, thirst, and sexual arousal.

Primary mental abilities The many independent abilities, discovered by factor analysis, that underlie performance on intelligence tests (verbal, mathematical, spatial abilities, for example).

Primate A mammal belonging to the order of primates, generally characterized by a highly developed visual system, forepaws suitably developed for grasping, and a relatively complex brain.

Proactive inhibition Interference with the memory for certain associations produced by other associations that were learned earlier in time; cf. **Retroactive interference.**

Proactive interference See **Proactive inhibition.**

Probability The relative frequency of occurrence of an event over a long run of trials; the relative frequency may be expected, observed, or calculated from a sample.

Probability matching A problem-solving task in which two or more stimuli are associated with reward with a certain probability less than 1.00. For example, white might lead to food on 70% of the trials and black on 30%, in a random sequence. Some animals "match" these probabilities with their responses, responding 70% of the time to white; others—after several trials—come to respond 100% of the time to the stimulus with the higher probability of reinforcement.

Probe technique Method of studying short-term memory in which a list of items is presented to the subject and followed by a memory test on some subset of the items.

Programmed instruction Instructional materials and procedures arranged in a linear order that the student can follow at his own pace.

Progressive retardation Among low-income and disadvantaged children, intelligence and academic achievement advance at a slower rate than is true for advantaged children. Hence the gap between the groups widens as they grow older and is reflected in the "progressive retardation" of the low-income and disadvantaged children.

Projection A defensive reaction that attributes to others one's own unacceptable repressed feelings and ideas.

Projective tests Tests using ambiguous stimuli such as inkblots and pictures for the purpose of revealing aspects of the personality of which the subject is usually unaware.

Proximal stimulus Pattern of physical energy affecting the receptor surface.

Proximity One of the principles of perceptual organization: parts of the stimulus field near each other tend to be perceived as belonging to the same unit.

Proximodistal direction The characteristic direction of progressive development of parts of the body and motor abilities, from the central part out to the peripheral or terminal segments.

Pseudoretardation Situation existing when intelligence test performance of an individual is much lower than his actual potential level of ability or functioning.

Psychoanalysis Psychotherapeutic procedures developed by Freud to uncover and resolve unconscious emotional conflicts that underlie neurotic symptoms; examples of procedures are free associations and dream interpretation.

Psychoanalyst A psychotherapist (psychologist or psychiatrist) whose therapeutic techniques and theories are derived from psychoanalysis.

Psychoanalytic theory A theory of personality and psychotherapy developed by Freud, emphasizing unconscious motivation and the importance of the early psychosexual development of the child in subsequent adult behavior.

Psychodrama A spontaneous role-playing technique used in psychotherapy.

Psychokinesis Effect of mental events on physical ones when there is no possible physical mediation, as when concentrating on a particular number on a pair of dice makes the appropriate faces come up when the dice are thrown.

Psycholinguistics Study of the psychological aspects of language and its acquisition.

Psychophysics Study of the relation between physical dimensions of a stimulus and psychological dimensions of the corresponding sensation.

Psychosexual stages According to psychoanalytic theory, there are the oral, anal, phallic, and latency stages through which human development progresses; each stage is characterized by a specific locus and mode of gratification of sexual impulses.

Psychosis A diagnostic term referring to a group of important mental disorders in which the patient has lost contact with reality; examples are schizophrenia and manic-depressive psychosis.

Psychosomatic reaction A physical disorder caused by emotional difficulties; examples are neurodermatitis and asthma.

Psychotherapy Systematic psychological (rather than physiological or chemical) intervention aimed at ameliorating psychological maladjustment.

Punishment A negative reinforcement; the production of unpleasant stimulation or removal of a positive reinforcement. See **Reinforcement.**

Q sort A technique of personality description in which the rater sorts a variety of statements according to their relevance to the subject.

Random assignment Assignment of individuals or measurements to groups solely by chance, without regard to their characteristics.

Rapid eye movement (REM) **sleep** Phase of sleep in which the closed eyes show rapid movements. The electrical activity of the brain resembles waking activity although the person or animal remains asleep. This phase is also called "paradoxical sleep," and dreams usually occur at this time.

Rating scale A continuum ranging from low to high; used to quantify interview impressions of personality characteristics or observations of behavior in natural settings.

Rationalization Defense mechanism using the rules of reason to provide acceptable explanations of otherwise unacceptable and painful ideas and actions.

Reaction formation Defense mechanism that produces behavior directly opposite to unconscious feelings and attitudes.

Reasoning Process of solving a problem by integrating two separate behaviors or bits of information.

Recall Method of testing memory in which the subject generates the response; cf. **Recognition.**

Recency effect The stronger influence of later information over earlier information on cognitions, impressions, and attitudes.

Receptive field For a given receptor cell or central cell, the receptive field is the part of the sensory surface or the part of the stimulus range that excites or inhibits the cell. For visual receptive fields, see Figure 24-6; for auditory receptive fields, see Figure 24-9.

Recognition Method of testing memory in which the subject merely identifies the correct response when it occurs with alternative possibilities; cf. **Recall.**

Redirection Behavior directed toward object or animal other than usual target, e.g., a bird pecks aggressively at the ground instead of at his foe.

Reflectivity-impulsivity Cognitive-style dimension referring to the extent to which the subject hesitates or reflects before taking action.

Reflexes Specific automatic responses to a stimulus that are not subject to voluntary control, for example, constriction of the pupil when light is bright.

Regression Defensive way of coping with a problem, by adopting an earlier, immature mode of functioning.

Regression to the mean The statistical finding that on the average parents at either extreme of a distribution (e.g., intelligence) tend to have children who are closer to the mean.

Reinforcement Stimulation following occurrence of a response that increases the probability that the response will be made again when the same situation recurs. For reinforcement in operant conditioning, see Chapter 18; for biological processes in reinforcement, see Chapter 25.

Reinforcement schedules Patterns for the administration of reinforcement, e.g., operant conditioning.

Relational concepts Those concepts that refer to relations between attributes such as *right, left.*

Releaser Stimulus that triggers fixed action pattern.

Reliability Extent to which a test yields similar scores each time it is used.

REM See **Rapid eye movement.**

Repression Unconscious exclusion from awareness of unacceptable impulses and ideas; considered by Freud to be the primary defense mechanism.

Retrieval Utilization of stored information at time of testing; cf. **Encoding, Memory storage.**

Retrieval cues Those aspects of a question or probe that point to the correct answer.

Retroactive inhibition Interference with the memory for certain associations produced by other associations that were learned later in time; cf. **Proactive interference.**

Retroactive interference. See **Retroactive inhibition.**

Retrograde amnesia Amnesia for events that occurred shortly before an accident (such as a blow to the head) or an experimental treatment (such as electroconvulsive shock).

Reversal shift Experimental procedure in which subject must make a response opposite to the one he has previously learned in order to receive a reward. For example, in discrimination learning, he must select a white stimulus on an occasion for which he previously would have chosen a black one.

Reward theory of attraction Proposes that we like people whose behavior is rewarding and dislike those whose behavior is punishing.

Rod Type of retinal receptor cell used in dim illumination.

Role Pattern of behavior typical of given social status or occupational position.

Role reversal Generally, taking the role of the "other" in a disturbing situation (see **Psychodrama**); e.g., a college radical plays policeman in a "demonstration."

Rote learning Verbatim learning; learning without regard to meaningful relations in the material.

Sample A set of scores or individuals selected from a population. If the sampling is done randomly (without regard to characteristics of the individuals chosen) the sample may be considered to be an unbiased representation of the population.

Saturation Dimension of color that refers to richness of hue; it runs from a full hue to a gray of the same brightness; pink is a weakly saturated red.

Scapegoat theory Prejudiced behavior is the result of the displacement of aggression from a vague or dangerous source onto a safe, easily identifiable target.

Scatterplot A graph showing scores made by the same individual or by defined pairs of individuals on two different variables. Figure 2-6B shows a scatterplot of I.Q. scores of pairs of identical twins.

Scent-marking Marking an object or area by leaving deposits with a characteristic smell—urine, feces, and specialized chemicals (e.g., the "spray" of a male domestic cat). Scent-marking has several functions, including establishing a territory, reducing fear (by giving a strange environment a familiar smell), and marking a trail.

Schizophrenia Severe and complex psychosis characterized primarily by withdrawal from reality and social relationships, perception and thought disturbances (hallucinations, delusions), and emotional and behavioral peculiarities.

School phobia Syndrome of disturbed behavior involving overt fear of school.

Secondary (or conditioned) drives Motivating states acquired mainly through a conditioning process through which they become associated with primary drives; examples are fear, hostility, affiliation, and approval.

Secondary reinforcement Reinforcement by a stimulus that has gained reinforcing value by having been associated with a primary reinforcement.

Selective advantage That quality possessed by a particular physical feature or behavior that is in the interests of promoting survival. The particular physical feature or behavioral trait having this advantage is therefore "selected" to be the one passed on genetically or through culture; the alternatives "die out."

Self-actualization Fundamental human tendency toward maximal realization of one's potentialities; a basic concept in humanistic theories of personality such as those developed by Rogers and Maslow.

Self-concept Term denoting the composite of ideas, attitudes, and feelings that the individual has toward himself.

Self-discovery groups See **Sensitivity groups, Encounter groups.**

Self-esteem The individual's evaluation of his own competence, ability, and personality.

Self-fulfilling prophecy A prediction that leads to changes in behavior that are likely to produce the predicted outcome.

Semantic differential Psychological rating scale used for measuring meaning of words.

Semantic similarity Similarity in terms of meaningful relationships, as differentiated from similarity of form.

Sensation Conscious awareness of a sensory quality, mediated by stimulation of a receptor.

Sense of identity Individual's recognition of himself as a self-consistent, integrated, unique individual.

Sensitivity group Group sessions conducted for the purpose of developing personal and interpersonal sensitivity to feelings and needs; the leader encourages free and honest expression of feelings among group members to enhance their own self-acceptance and growth.

Sensorimotor period First stage in Piaget's theory of intellectual development, in which the child learns to deal with objects; the period from birth to 2 years of age.

Separation anxiety Infant's fear of losing his mother. The infant views his mother as so important that he becomes upset when she is absent.

Septal area (or septum) In the brain, a region of the forebrain that forms a partition between the lateral ventricles. This was the first discovered "reward" area in the brain of the rat. See Figure 25-10.

Serialization Ordering of objects along a specified dimension such as age, height, or weight.

Serial ordering Rote-learning procedure in which a list of items is presented and the subject attempts to reproduce them in the correct order.

Serial-position effect Functional relationship, graphically represented by curve, between ordinal position of item in list and some measure of performance (number of errors in serial-order learning; probability of recall in studies of short-term memory). See **Primacy effect, Recency effect.**

Set Orientation, as in intentionally preparing oneself for certain perceptual inputs.

Sex hormones Hormones secreted chiefly by the gonads and the adrenal cortex. They are involved in reproductive behavior and in the development of secondary sexual characteristics, such as the male's beard and the female's breasts. Both males and females secrete both androgens (so-called male hormones) and estrogens (so-called female hormones), but the relative amounts of androgen and estrogen secretion differ between the sexes.

Sex-linked behaviors Behavior that differs characteristically for the sexes but that is not involved in reproduction; for example, different taste thresholds in men and women.

Sex typing Adoption of personality traits, beliefs, attitudes, and behaviors that the culture defines as appropriate for an individual's sex.

Shaping Method of successive approximations in which responses must become more and more similar to the desired response in order to be reinforced.

Shared coping Working together to solve a problem of mutual concern.

Short-term memory Relatively brief memory storage (often lasting only for seconds); differentiated from long-term memory.

Signal detection measures Signal detection measure of strength or sensitivity is d' (d prime), and the signal detection measure of the cutoff or criterion is β. See **Signal detection theory** and Figure 19-3.

Signal detection theory Theory of sensory and decision processes involved in perceptual judgments; it distinguishes between observer's sensitivity and criterion he employs. Also applied to memory tasks.

Significance In statistics, the trustworthiness of a conclusion about whether an obtained result is likely to be found upon repetition of a set of observations.

Sign stimulus Stimulus that releases or triggers a fixed action pattern.

Similarity, law of One of the principles of perceptual organization: similar elements tend to be perceived as belonging to the same unit.

Socialization Process by which an individual learns to behave in a manner approved by his culture and society; the result of all of the individual's social experiences that affect his personality, motives, values, attitudes, and behavior.

Spatially opponent cells In the visual system, cells with concentric fields where either (1) stimulation of the center is excitatory and stimulation of the periphery inhibitory or (2) the center is inhibitory and the periphery is excitatory. See Figure 24-2.

Spectrally opponent cells In the visual system, cells that are excited by stimulation in one part of the spectrum and inhibited by stimulation in another part of the spectrum; e.g., Yellow Plus–Blue Minus or Green Plus–Red Minus. See Figure 24-2.

Split brain A brain in which the corpus callosum has been cut, thus removing most of the connections between the two cerebral hemispheres.

Spontaneous recovery Process whereby a response that had been extinguished regains some of its original strength.

Stability of the I.Q. The stability of the I.Q. refers to the fact that after the age of four, individuals who grow up in an environment without significant perturbations do not show significant changes in their I.Q. scores.

Standard deviation A measure of variability of scores around the central tendency of a distribution; specifically, it is the square root of the mean of the squared deviations of each score from the mean.

Stereotype A class of objects is said to be stereotyped when identical characteristics are attributed to any object of that class, regardless of the actual degree of variation within the class. Familiar stereotypes are those sets of characteristics attributed to ethnic and racial groups.

Stevens' law See **Power law.**

Stimulation-bound behavior Behavior, such as eating, that is elicited by electrical stimulation of brain regions and that in many ways resembles normally motivated behavior.

Stroboscopic motion Apparent motion produced by the successive presentation of slightly different stationary stimuli, such as in moving pictures.

Structured observation Observation of a subject, alone or interacting, in a standard setting while he is performing tasks or solving problems given by the researcher.

Sublimation Form of displacement in which unacceptable or unsatisfied impulse is expressed in socially acceptable form.

Subtractive color mixture Mixing colors by subtracting various wavelengths, as in mixing pigments. See perception color Figure 2.

Superego Freud's term for that part of the personality that contains internalized prohibitions and imposes on the individual the restraints and moral edicts of society.

Superior colliculi Visual centers of the midbrain. See Figures 24-1 and 24-7.

Surface structure The overt or sound level of language.

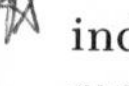

Surrogate Substitute, as in mother surrogate; an individual or object that takes the place of the mother.

Sympathetic ganglia Clusters of autonomic neural cell bodies in two chains on either side of the spinal cord. See Figure 23-12 and biological color Figure 6.

Sympathetic reaction Behavior that is "in support of" the behavior of another animal of the species, e.g., other jays come to the aid of one defending his territory against a predator.

Sympathetic system Division of the autonomic nervous system. For its functions, see Table 23-1.

Synapse A functional junction from one neuron to another. See Figures 23-3 and 23-4.

Synaptic vesicle A small globule inside an axon terminal; the vesicles contain synaptic transmitter chemicals. See Figures 23-3 and 23-4.

Systematic desensitization Behavior therapy technique developed by Wolpe based on principles of classical conditioning; most successful in the treatment of specific nonadaptive anxieties.

Systemogenesis Anokhin's principle that sensory and motor capacities of different species vary in their early development according to the requirements of the life of the animal under consideration.

Tabula rasa A blank wax tablet, used to symbolize the mind at birth in an analogy, by extreme empiricists, who hold that perception is completely unorganized at birth and that the mind is originally like a blank wax tablet upon which experience writes.

Tachistoscope Device for presenting visual stimuli of very short durations.

Tacts Verbal responses elicited by nonhuman stimuli in the environment.

Telencephalon In the fetus, the farthest forward of the five early divisions of the brain; in the adult, that part of the brain including cerebral hemispheres and corpus callosum. See Figures 23-5 and 23-6.

Telepathy Mind reading, or one person "reading" another person's thoughts.

Template-matching Theory of pattern recognition that implies comparison of a visual stimulus with a fixed standard form.

Temporal lobe The part of the cerebral hemisphere lying at the side of the head below the lateral fissure. On its upper surface is the primary auditory cortex, and on its lower surface is the visual inferotemporal region. See Figures 23-7 and biological color Figures 1 and 2.

Territory "Home turf"; usually an area of land in which an animal mates and raises his young, one that he defends against the intrusion of competitors.

Test profile Pattern of subtest scores obtained by a given individual on a test such as the WISC.

Test-taking attitudes Subject's feelings and understandings about participating in psychological testing. Positive test-taking attitudes enhance test performance whereas negative test-taking attitudes depress it.

T-groups Groups involving people desiring to learn more effective (group) problem-solving techniques.

Thalamus A part of the diencephalon; largely concerned with relaying sensory impulses to the cerebral cortex and with integration of cortical activity. See Figures 23-5 and 23-6.

Theory An integrated set of principles or hypotheses that explain a wide array of phenomena and findings and that predict new events and experimental outcomes.

Timbre The distinctive quality of sound, such as the difference between a flute and a violin playing the same note.

Total-time hypothesis A principle of rote learning; the amount of time required to learn a list depends upon the total amount of time spent studying, regardless of how this time is distributed.

Trait Any relatively stable characteristic of a person; its measurement is useful in describing and quantifying individual differences.

Transfer of training Procedure used to study effect of previously learned associations on formation of new associations. In positive transfer the old associations help and in negative transfer they hinder the formation of new associations.

Transmitter agent Chemical substance released at a neuronal terminal that diffuses across the synaptic gap and excites or inhibits the postsynaptic neuron. Acetylcholine is the transmitter agent at certain synapses. See Figures 23-3, 23-4.

Unavailability See **Availability.**

Uncle behavior In primates, care and attention received by infants from male adults other than the father.

Unconditional positive regard According to Rogers, the experience of personal acceptance needed by the individual for him to develop and maintain a healthful psychological adjustment.

Unconditioned response (UR) Response given originally to the unconditioned stimulus and similar to response to be acquired during conditioning. See **Classical conditioning.**

Unconditioned stimulus (US) Stimulus that evokes the unconditioned response during acquisition of conditioning. See **Classical conditioning.**

Underachievement Academic performance falling below that to be expected from performance on intelligence tests.

UR See **Classical conditioning.**

US See **Classical conditioning.**

Vacuum activity Instinctive behavior that occurs without its usual trigger or releaser.

Validity Extent to which a test measures what it is supposed to measure.

Variability The spread of scores around the central tendency in a frequency distribution; the standard deviation is a measure of variability.

Ventromedial nucleus of hypothalamus Brain region involved in controlling food intake. See Figures 25-1 and 25-3.

Vertebrates Animals possessing a spinal cord encased in a bony vertebral column.

Visual cliff Device for the study of space perception in very young organisms: subject is placed on a plate of glass, underneath one-half of which the surface below is several feet down, and under the other half of which a surface is visible immediately beneath the glass. See Figure 22-9.

Vocational aptitude and interest tests Assessment of patterns of individual's interests so that these can be compared with known interests of those who are successful in various vocational fields; used in vocational guidance and placement.

Weber's law Psychophysical law stating that the smallest detectable increment in the intensity of a stimulus is a constant proportion of the intensity of the stimulus already present, or $\Delta I/I = k$.

White matter Fiber tracts in the nervous system. The fatty coating of axons gives them a white appearance that contrasts with the collection of cell bodies called gray matter. See Figure 23-7 and biological color Figure 5.

REFERENCES

Abeelen, J. H. F. van. Mouse mutants studied by means of ethological methods. I. Ethogram. *Genetica,* 1963, *34,* 79–94. **777**

Adair, L. B., Wilson, J. E., & Glassman, E. Brain function and macromolecules, IV. Uridine incorporation into polysomes of mouse brain during different behavioral experiences. *Proceedings of the National Academy of Sciences U.S.,* 1968, *61,* 917–922. **737**

Adler, A. Individual psychology. In C. Murchison (Ed.), *Psychologies of 1930.* Worcester, Mass.: Clark University Press, 1930. **191**

Adler, N. T. Effects of the male's copulatory behavior on successful pregnancy of the female rat. *Journal of Comparative and Physiological Psychology,* 1969, *69,* 613–622. **819**

Adorno, T. W., Frenkel-Brunswik, E., Levinson, D. J., & Sanford, R. N. *The authoritarian personality.* New York: Harper, 1950. **114**

Agranoff, B. W. Memory and protein synthesis. *Scientific American,* 1967, *216,* 115–122. **731**

Ainsworth, M. D. S. *Infancy in Uganda.* Baltimore: Johns Hopkins Press, 1967. **316**

Albert, R. The role of mass media and the effect of aggressive film content upon children's aggressive responses and identification choices. *Genetic Psychology Monographs,* 1957, *55,* 221–285. **221**

Allen, D. L., & Mech, L. D. Wolves versus moose on Isle Royale. *National Geographic Magazine,* 1963, 200–219. **806**

Allen, G. B., & Masling, J. M. An evaluation of the effects of nursery school training on children in kindergarten, first and second grades. *Journal of Educational Research,* 1957, *51,* 285–296. **421**

Allport, G. W. *Personality: A psychological interpretation.* New York: Holt, Rinehart and Winston, 1937. **216**

Allport, G. W. *Patterns and growth in personality.* New York: Holt, Rinehart and Winston, 1961. **157**

Allport, G. W., & Vernon, P. E. *Studies in expressive movement.* New York: Macmillan, 1933. **211**

Altmann, M. Patterns of herd behavior in free-ranging elk of Wyoming, *Cervus canadensis nelsoni. Zoologica,* 1956, *41,* 65–71. **809**

American Psychiatric Association. *Diagnostic and statistical manual of mental disorders.* Washington, D.C., 1968. **238**

Anastasi, A., & D'Angelo, R. A comparison of negro and white preschool children in language development and Goodenough Draw-a-Man I.Q. *Journal of Genetic Psychology,* 1952, *81,* 147–165. **209**

Ardrey, R. *The territorial imperative: A personal inquiry into the animal origins of property and nations.* New York: Atheneum, 1966. **833, 840, 842**

Argyle, M. *The psychology of interpersonal behavior.* Baltimore: Penguin, 1967. **131**

Aristotle. *Rhetoric and poetics.* New York: Random House, 1954. **80**

Armstrong, E. A. *Bird display and behaviour.* (2nd ed.) New York: Dover Publications, 1965. **814, 816, 833, 834**

Aronson, E. Some antecedents of interpersonal attraction. In W. J. Arnold, & D. Levine (Eds.), *Nebraska Symposium on Motivation 1969.* Lincoln: University of Nebraska Press, 1969. **141, 143**

Aronson, E., & Carlsmith, J. M. Effect of the severity of threat on the devaluation of forbidden behavior. *Journal of Abnormal and Social Psychology,* 1963, *66,* 584–588. **103**

Aronson, E., & Carlsmith, J. M. Experimentation in social psychology. In G. Lindzey & E. Aronson (Eds.), *Handbook of social psychology* (2nd ed.) Vol. 2. Reading, Mass.: Addison-Wesley, 1969. **65**

Aronson, E., & Cope, V. My enemy's enemy is my friend. *Journal of Personality and Social Psychology,* 1968, *8,* 8–12. **127**

Aronson, E., & Linder, D. Gain and loss of esteem as determinants of interpersonal attractiveness. *Journal of Experimental Social Psychology,* 1965, *1,* 156–171. **143**

Aronson, E., Turner, J., & Carlsmith, J. M. Communicator credibility and communication discrepancy as determinants of opinion change. *Journal of Abnormal and Social Psychology,* 1963, *67,* 31–36. **87, 88**

Aronson, E., Willerman, B., & Floyd, J. The effect of a pratfall on increasing interpersonal attractiveness. *Psychonomic Science,* 1966, *4,* 227–228. **138, 139**

Aronson, E., & Worchel, P. Similarity versus liking as determinants of interpersonal attractiveness. *Psychonomic Science,* 1966, *5,* 157–158. **134**

Asch, S. Effects of group pressure upon the modification and distortion of judgment. In H. Guetzkow (Ed.), *Groups, leadership, and men.* Pittsburgh: Carnegie Press, 1951. **62**

Atkinson, J. W. (Ed.) *Motives in fantasy, action and society.* Princeton, N.J.: Van Nostrand, 1958. **174**

Atkinson, R. C. A stochastic model for rote serial learning. *Psychometrika,* 1957, *22,* 87–95. **475**

Atkinson, R. C., Bower, G. H., & Crothers, E. J. *An introduction to mathematical learning theory.* New York: Wiley, 1965. **494**

Atkinson, R. C., & Shiffrin, R. M. Human memory: A proposed system and its control processes. In K. W. Spence and J. T. Spence (Eds.), *The psychology of*

Text references are indicated by the boldface folios.

learning and motivation: Advances in research and theory. Vol. 2. New York: Academic Press, 1968. **524**

Atkinson, R. C., & Shiffrin, R. M. The control of short-term memory. *Scientific American,* 1971, *224,* 82–90. **524, 723**

Atkinson, R. C., & Wilson, H. A. (Eds.) *Computer-assisted instruction.* New York: Academic Press, 1969. **437**

Attneave, F. Some informational aspects of visual perception. *Psychological Review,* 1954, *61,* 183–193. **591**

Attneave, F., & Frost, R. The determination of perceived tridimensional orientation by minimum criteria. *Perception and Psychophysics,* 1969, *6,* 391–396. **589**

Ayllon, T., & Azrin, N. H. The measurement and reinforcement of behavior of psychotics. *Journal of the Experimental Analysis of Behavior,* 1965, *8,* 357–383. **244**

Ayllon, T., & Azrin, N. *The token economy: A motivational system for therapy and rehabilitation.* New York: Appleton-Century-Crofts, 1968. **231**

Azrin, N. H., Hutchinson, R. R., & McLaughlin, R. The opportunity for aggression as an operant reinforcer during aversive stimulation. *Journal of the Experimental Analysis of Behavior,* 1965, *8,* 171–180. **836**

Backman, C. W., & Secord, P. F. The effect of perceived liking on interpersonal attraction. *Human Relations,* 1959, *12,* 379–384. **132**

Baldwin, A. L. The effect of home environment on nursery school behavior. *Child Development,* 1949, *20,* 49–62. **285, 324**

Baldwin, A. L., Kalhorn, J., & Breese, F. H. Patterns of parent behavior. *Psychological Monographs,* 1945, *58,* No. 3. **324**

Bales. A theoretical framework for interaction process analysis. In D. Cartwright & A. Zander (Eds.), *Group dynamics: Research and theory.* New York: Harper & Row, 1953. **136**

Bandura, A., Grusec, J. E., & Menlove, F. L. Vicarious extinction of avoidance behavior. *Journal of Personality and Social Psychology,* 1967, *5,* 16–23. **334**

Bandura, A., & Huston, Aletha C. Identification as a process of incidental learning. *Journal of Abnormal and Social Psychology,* 1961, *63,* 311–318. **282**

Bandura, A., Ross, D., & Ross, S. A. Transmission of aggression through imitation of aggressive models. *Journal of Abnormal and Social Psychology,* 1961, *63,* 575–582. **220, 333**

Bandura, A., Ross, D., & Ross, S. A. Imitation of film-mediated aggressive models. *Journal of Abnormal and Social Psychology,* 1963, *66,* 3–11, *67,* 527–534. **12, 220, 221**

Bandura, A., & Walters, R. H. *Social learning and personality development.* New York: Holt, Rinehart and Winston, 1963. **199**

Banta, T. J., & Hetherington, M. Relations between needs of friends and fiancées. *Journal of Abnormal and Social Psychology,* 1963, *66,* 401–404. **134**

Barnes, J. M., & Underwood, B. J. "Fate" of first-list associations in transfer theory. *Journal of Experimental Psychology,* 1959, *58,* 97–105. **483**

Barron, F. Originality in relation to personality and to intellect. *Journal of Personality,* 1957, *25,* 730–742. **401, 402**

Barry, H. B., III, Bacon, M. K., & Child, I. L. A cross-cultural survey of some sex differences in socialization. *Journal of Abnormal and Social Psychology,* 1957, *55,* 327–332. **209**

Bartlett, Sir F. C. *Remembering.* Cambridge: Cambridge University Press, 1932. **406**

Baumrind, D. Child care practices anteceding three patterns of preschool behavior. *Genetic Psychology Monographs,* 1967, *75,* 43–88. **325**

Bayley, N. *Bayley scales of infant development.* New York: The Psychological Corporation, 1969. **295, 360**

Beach, F. A. *Hormones and behavior.* New York: Harper and Brothers, 1948. **821**

Beach, F. A. The snark was a boojum. *The American Psychologist,* 1950, *5,* 115–124. **770**

Beach, F. A. Coital behavior in dogs: III. Effects of early isolation on mating in males. *Behaviour,* 1968, *30,* 218–238. **712**

Beach, F. A. Hormonal factors controlling the differentiation, development, and display of copulatory behavior in the Ramstergig and related species. In E. Tobach, L. R. Aronson, & E. Shaw (Eds.), *The biopsychology of development.* New York: Academic Press, 1971. **708**

Beach, F. A., & Fowler, H. Individual differences in the response of male rats to androgen. *Journal of Comparative and Physiological Psychology,* 1959, *52,* 50–52. **711**

Beach, F. A., & Jaynes, J. Studies of maternal retrieving in rats: III. Sensory cues involved in the lactating female's response to her young. *Behaviour,* 1956, *10,* 104–125. **825**

Beach, F. A., & Le Boeuf, B. J. Coital behaviour in dogs. I. Preferential mating in the bitch. *Animal Behavior,* 1967, *15,* 546–558. **810**

Beach, G., Emmens, M., Kimble, D., & Lickey, M. Autoradiographic demonstration of biochemical changes in the limbic system during avoidance training. *Proceedings of the National Academy of Sciences U.S.,* 1969, *62,* 692–696. **738**

Beach, L. R., & Wertheimer, M. A free response approach to the study of person cognition. *Journal of Abnormal and Social Psychology,* 1961, *62,* 367–374. **616**

Beers, L. *The mind that found itself.* London: Longmans, Green and Co., 1908. **230–231**

Békésy, G. von. Variation of phase along basilar membrane with sinusoidal vibrations. *Journal of the Acoustical Society of America,* 1947, *19,* 452–460. **683**

Békésy, G. von. Auditory backward inhibition in concert

halls. *Science,* 1971, *171,* 529–536. **598**

Benary, W. Beobachtungen zu einem Experiment über Helligkeitskontrast. *Psychologische Forschung,* 1924, *5,* 131–142. **572**

Bennett, E. L., Diamond, M. C., Krech, D., & Rosenzweig, M. R. Chemical and anatomical plasticity of brain. *Science,* 1964, *146,* 610–619. **732–733**

Bennett, E. M., & Cohen, Z. R. Men and personality patterns and contrasts. *Genetic Psychology Monographs,* 1951, *59,* 101–155. **209**

Bermant, G. Response latencies of female rats during sexual intercourse. *Science,* 1961, *133,* 1771–1773. **819**

Binet, A., & Simon, T. Le dévelopment de intelligence des enfants. *L'Année psychologique,* 1908, *14,* 1–94. **352**

Birch, H. G. The relation of previous experience to insightful problem-solving. *Journal of Comparative and Physiological Psychology,* 1945, 367. **766**

Birdwhistell, R. L. The kinesis level in the investigation of the emotions. In P. H. Knapp (Ed.), *Expressions of the emotions in man.* New York: International University Press, 1963. **841**

Birdwhistell, R. L. Communication without words. In P. Alexandre (Ed.), *L'Aventure humaine.* Paris, 1966. **841**

Bishop, M. P., Elder, S. T., & Heath, R. G. Intracranial self-stimulation in man. *Science,* 1963, *140,* 394–396. **718**

Bishop, P. O., & Henry, C. H. Spatial vision. *Annual Review of Psychology,* 1971, *22.* **596**

Bitterman, M. E. Toward a comparative psychology of learning. *The American Psychologist,* 1960, *15,* 704–712. **770**

Bitterman, M. E. Phyletic differences in learning. *The American Psychologist,* 1965, *20,* 396–410. **770, 772**

Block, J. *The Q-sort method in personality assessment and psychiatric research.* Springfield, Ill.: Charles C. Thomas, 1961. **167**

Block, J. *The challenge of response sets.* New York: Appleton-Century-Crofts, 1965. **170**

Bogardus, E. S. Measuring social distance. *Journal of Applied Sociology,* 1925, *9,* 299–308. **78**

Bonney, M. E., & Nicholson, E. L. Comparative social adjustments of elementary school pupils with and without preschool training. *Child Development,* 1958, *29,* 125–133. **421**

Boring, E. G. A new ambiguous figure. *American Journal of Psychology,* 1930, *42,* 444–445. **614**

Bower, G. H. A descriptive theory of memory. In D. P. Kimble (Ed.), Learning, remembering, and forgetting. Vol. 2. New York: New York Academy of Science, 1966. **575**

Brackbill, Y. Extinction of the smiling response in infants as a function of reinforcement schedule. *Child Development,* 1958, *29,* 114–124. **298**

Brehm, J. W. Increasing cognitive dissonance by a fait accompli. *Journal of Abnormal and Social Psychology,* 1959, *58,* 379–382. **104**

Brehm, J. W., & Cole, Ann H. Effect of a favor which reduces freedom. *Journal of Personality and Social Psychology,* 1966, *3,* 420–426. **140**

Breland, K., & Breland, M. The misbehavior of organisms. *The American Psychologist,* 1961, *16,* 681–684. **790**

Breland, K., & Breland, M. *Animal behavior.* New York: Macmillan, 1966. **790**

Brindley, G. S., & Lewin, W. S. The sensations produced by electrical stimulation of the visual cortex. *Journal of Physiology,* 1968, *196,* 479–493. **673**

Broadbent, D. E. *Perception and Communication.* New York: Pergamon, 1958. **519**

Broughton, R. J. Sleep disorders. Disorders of arousal? *Science,* 1968, *159,* 1070–1078. **705**

Brower, L. P., & Brower, J. V. Z. Investigations into mimicry. *Natural History,* 1962, *71,* 8–19. **788**

Brown, A. W., & Hunt, R. Relations between nursery attendance and teachers' ratings of some aspects of children's adjustment in kindergarten. *Child Development,* 1961, *32,* 585–596. **421**

Brown, J. F. Über gesehene Geschwindigkeiten. *Psychologische Forschung,* 1928, *10,* 84–101. **581**

Brown, L. E. Home range and movement of small mammals. *Symposia of the Zoological Society of London,* 1966, *18,* 111–142. **814**

Brown, R. *Social psychology.* New York: Free Press of Glencoe, 1965. **312**

Bruner, J. S. On perceptual readiness. *Psychological Review,* 1957, *64,* 123–152. **604**

Bruner, J. S., & Goodman, C. C. Value and need as organizing factors in perception. *Journal of Abnormal and Social Psychology,* 1947, *42,* 33–44. **614**

Bruner, J. S., Goodnow, J. J., & Austin, G. A. *A study of thinking.* New York: Wiley, 1956. **386, 387, 389**

Bruner, J. S., & Potter, M. C. Interference in visual recognition. *Science,* 1964, *144,* 424–425. **607**

Bureš, J., & Burešová, O. The reunified split brain. In R. E. Whalen, R. F. Thompson, M. Verzeano, & N. J. Weinberger (Eds.), *The neural control of behavior.* New York: Academic Press, 1970. **741**

Burt, C. The structure of the mind; a review of the results of factor analyses. *British Journal of Educational Psychology,* 1949, *19,* 110–111, 176–199. **378**

Buss, A. H. Physical aggression in relation to different frustrations. *Journal of Abnormal and Social Psychology,* 1963, *67,* 1–7. **218**

Buss, A. H. Instrumentality of aggression, feedback and frustration as determinants of physical aggression. *Journal of Personality and Social Psychology,* 1966, *3,* 153–162. **218**

Butler, R. A. Curiosity in monkeys. *Scientific American,* 1954, *190,* 70–75. **792**

Byrne, D. Repression-sensitization as a dimension of

personality. In B. A. Maher (Ed.), *Progress in experimental personality research.* Vol. *1.* New York: Academic Press, 1964. **226**

Byrne, D. Attitudes and attraction. In L. Berkowitz (Ed.), *Advances in experimental social psychology.* Vol. *4.* New York: Academic Press, 1969. **128**

Byrne, W. L. (Ed.) *Molecular approaches to learning and memory.* New York: Academic Press, 1970. **739**

Byrne, W. L., Samuel, D., Bennett, E. L., Rosenzweig, M. R., Wasserman, E., Wagner, A. R., Gardner, F., Galambos, R., Berger, B. D., Margules, D. L., Fenichel, R. L., Stein, L., Corson, J. A., Enesco, H. E., Chorover, S. L., Holt, C. E., III, Schiller, P. H., Chiappetta, L., Jarvik, M. E., Leaf, R. C., Dutcher, J. D., Horovitz, Z. P., & Carlton, P. L. Memory transfer. *Science,* 1966, *153,* 658–659. **739**

Cabanac, M. Physiological role of pleasure. *Science,* 1971, *173,* 1103–1107. **698**

Calhoun, J. B. Induced mass movements of small mammals. *Public Health Monographs,* 1962, *59,* 1–33. **813**

Carew, T. J. Do passive-avoidance tasks permit assessment of retrograde amnesia in rats? *Journal of Comparative and Physiological Psychology,* 1970, *72,* 267–271. **726**

Carey, J. J. *The college drug scene.* Englewood Cliffs, N.J.: Prentice–Hall, 1968. **254, 255**

Carmichael, L., Hogan, H. P., & Walter, A. A. An experimental study of the effect of language on the reproduction of visually perceived form. *Journal of Experimental Psychology,* 1932, *15,* 73–86. **417**

Carnegie, D. *How to win friends and influence people.* New York: Simon and Schuster, 1937. **129, 132**

Carpenter, C. R. The howlers of Barro Colorado Island. In I. DeVore (Ed.), *Primate behavior: Field studies of monkeys and apes.* New York: Holt, Rinehart and Winston, 1965. **829**

Carroll, J. B., & Casagrande, J. B. In E. E. Maccoby *et al.* (Eds.), *Readings in social psychology.* (3rd ed.) New York: Holt, Rinehart and Winston, 1958. **410**

Carterette, E. C., Friedman, M. P., & Lovell, J. D. Mach bands in hearing. *Journal of the Acoustical Society of America,* 1969, *45,* 986–998. **573**

Cates, J. Psychology's manpower: Report on the 1968 national register of scientific and technical personnel. *American Psychologist,* 1970, *25,* 254–263. **22**

Cattell, R. B. *Description and measurement of personality.* New York: Harcourt, Brace and World, 1946. **171**

Cattell, R. B. *The scientific analysis of personality.* Baltimore: Penguin Books, 1965. **157**

Chapanis, A., Garner, W. R., & Morgan, C. T. *Applied experimental psychology.* New York: Wiley, 1949. **554**

Cherry, E. C. Some experiments on the recognition of speech, with one and with two ears. *Journal of the Acoustical Society of America,* 1953, *25,* 975–979. **612**

Chitty, D. Self-regulation of members through changes in viability. *Cold Spring Harbor Symposia on Quantitative Biology,* 1957, *22,* 277–280. **814**

Chomsky, N. *Aspects of a theory of syntax.* Cambridge: M.I.T. Press, 1965. **414**

Chomsky, N. The formal nature of language. In E. Lenneberg (Ed.), *Biological foundations of language.* New York: Wiley, 1967. **312**

Chorover, S. L., & Schiller, P. H. Reexamination of prolonged retrograde amnesia in one-trial learning. *Journal of Comparative and Physiological Psychology,* 1966, *61,* 34–41. **726**

Chow, K. L., Riesen, A. H., & Newell, F. W. Degeneration of retinal ganglion cells in infant chimpanzees reared in darkness. *Journal of Comparative Neurology,* 1957, *107,* 27–42. **619**

Christian, J. J. Adrenal and reproductive response to population sizes in mice from freely growing populations. *Ecology,* 1956, *37,* 258–273. **813, 814**

Clark, K. B. Desegregation: An appraisal of the evidence. *Journal of Social Issues,* 1953, *9,* 2–76. **122**

Cofer, C. N., & Appley, M. H. *Motivation: Theory and research.* New York: Wiley, 1964. **477**

Cohen, A. R. Social norms, arbitrariness of frustration, and status of the agent of frustration in the frustration-aggression hypothesis. *Journal of Abnormal and Social Psychology,* 1955, *51,* 222–226. **219**

Colbert, E. H. *Evolution of the vertebrates. A history of the backboned animals through time.* New York: Science Editions, 1961. **756**

Collins, B. E. *Social psychology.* Reading, Mass.: Addison–Wesley, 1970. **117**

Conger, J. J. A world they never knew: The family and social change. *Daedalus,* 1971, *100,* 1105–1138. **339**

Conners, K., & Eisenberg, L. *The effect of teacher behavior on verbal intelligence in Operation Head Start children.* Baltimore: Johns Hopkins School of Medicine, 1966. **440**

Cooper, E., & Dinerman, H. Analysis of the film "Don't be a Sucker": A study in communication. *Public Opinion Quarterly,* 1951, *15,* 243–264. **117**

Coopersmith, S. *The antecedents of self-esteem.* San Francisco: W. H. Freeman, 1967. **332**

Cornsweet, T. N. Information processing in visual systems. *Stanford Research Institute Journal, Feature Issue* No. 5, 1969, 16–27. **539**

Couch, A. S., & Keniston, K. Yeasayers and naysayers: Agreeing response set as a personality variable. *Journal of Abnormal and Social Psychology,* 1960, *60,* 151–174. **163**

Crandall, V., Preston, A., & Rabson, A. Maternal reactions and the development of independence and achievement behavior in young children. *Child Development,* 1960, *31,* 243–251. **322**

Crook, J. H. Evolutionary change in primate societies. *Science Journal*, 1967, 1–7. **802, 803**

Cushing, H. M. A tentative report of the influence of nursery school training upon kindergarten adjustment as reported by kindergarten teachers. *Child Development*, 1934, *5*, 304–314. **421**

Darley, J. M., & Berscheid, E. Increased liking as a result of the anticipation of personal contact. *Human Relations*, 1967, *20*, 29–40. **105**

Davis, K. E., & Jones, E. E. Changes in interpersonal perception as a means of reducing cognitive dissonance. *Journal of Abnormal and Social Psychology*, 1960, *61*, 402–410. **106**

Davitz, J. The effects of previous training on postfrustration behavior. *Journal of Abnormal and Social Psychology*, 1952, *47*, 309–315. **220**

Delgado, J. M. R. *Evolution of physical control of the brain*. James Arthur Lecture on the Evolution of the Human Brain, 1965. New York: The American Museum of Natural History, 1965. **631**

Delgado, J. M. R., Roberts, W. W., & Miller, N. E. Learning motivated by electrical stimulation of the brain. *American Journal of Physiology*, 1954, *179*, 587–593. **716**

Dement, W. The effect of dream deprivation. *Science*, 1960, *131*, 1705–1707. **176**

Dement, W., & Kleitman, N. Cyclic variations in EEG during sleep and their relation to eye movements, body motility, and dreaming. *Electroencephalography and Clinical Neurophysiology*, 1957, *9*, 673–690. **702**

Deutsch, M., & Collins, M. E. *Interracial housing: A psychological evaluation of a social experiment*. Minneapolis: University of Minnesota Press, 1951. **119**

Deutsch, M., & Gerard, H. B. A study of normative and informational social influence upon individual judgment. *Journal of Abnormal and Social Psychology*, 1955, *51*, 629–636. **68**

Deutsch, M., & Solomon, L. Reactions to evaluations by others as influenced by self-evaluation. *Sociometry*, 1959, *22*, 93–112. **140**

De Valois, R. L. Physiological basis of color vision. In Tagungsbericht Internationale Farbtagung Color 69. Stockholm, 1969, 29–47. **665**

Devor, M. G., Wise, R. A., Milgram, N. W., & Hoebel, B. G. Physiological control of hypothalamically elicited feeding and drinking. *Journal of Comparative and Physiological Psychology*, 1970, *73*, 226–232. **719**

DeVore, I., & Hall, K. R. L. Baboon ecology. In I. DeVore (Ed.), *Primate behavior. Field studies of monkeys and apes*. New York: Holt, Rinehart and Winston, 1965. **812**

Dicara, L. V. Learning in the autonomic nervous system. *Scientific American*, 1970, *222*, 30-39. **249**

Dickoff, H. Reactions to evaluations by another person as a function of self-evaluation and the interaction context. (Doctoral dissertation, Duke University), 1961. **140**

Dix, D. L. *Memorial in behalf of the pauper insane and idiots in jails and poorhouses throughout the Commonwealth*. Boston: Monroe and Francis, 1843. **230**

Dohrenwend, B. P., & Dohrenwend, B. S. Field studies of social factors in relation to three types of psychological disorders. *Journal of Abnormal Psychology*, 1967, *72*, 369–378. **229**

Dollard, J., Doob, J. W., Miller, N. E., Lowrer, G. H., & Sears, R. R. *Frustrational aggression*. New Haven: Yale University Press, 1939. **218**

Dollard, J., & Miller, N. E. *Personality and psychotherapy*. New York: McGraw–Hill, 1950. **199**

Donaldson, M. A. *A study of children's thinking*. London: Tavistock, 1963. **393**

Downer, J. L. deC. Interhemispheric integration in the visual system. In V. B. Mountcastle (Ed.), *Conference on interhemispheric relations and cerebral dominance*. Baltimore: Johns Hopkins Press, 1962. **715**

Duncker, K. Über induzierte Bewegung. *Psychologische Forschung*, 1929, *12*, 180–259. **583**

Duncker, K. On problem solving. *Psychological Monographs*, 1945, No. 270. **393, 394**

Dundsdon, M. I., & Fraser-Roberts, J. A. A study of the performance of 2,000 children on four vocabulary tests. *British Journal of Statistical Psychology*, 1957, *10*, 1–16. **209**

Dunham, H. W. Epidemiology of psychiatric disorders as a contribution to medical ecology. *Archives of General Psychiatry*, 1966, *14*, 1–19. **229**

Dunn, L. M. *Peabody Picture Vocabulary Test*. (Rev. ed.) Circle Pines, Minn.: American Guidance Service, Inc., 1965. **363**

Ehrlich, Danuta, Guttman, J., Schonbach, P., & Mills, J. Postdecision exposure to relevant information. *Journal of Abnormal and Social Psychology*, 1957, *54*, 98–102. **96**

Eibl-Eibesfeldt, I. The interactions of unlearned behavior patterns and learning in mammals. In J. F. Delafresnaye (Ed.), *Brain mechanisms and learning*. Oxford: Blackwell, 1961. **808, 825, 833**

Eibl-Eibesfeldt, I. *Ethology*. New York: Holt, Rinehart and Winston, 1970. **821**

Elkind, D., Deblinger, J., & Adler, D. Motivation and creativity: The context effect. *American Educational Research Association Journal*, 1970, *7*, 351–357. **442**

Emery, F. E. Psychological effects of the western film: A study in television viewing: II, The experimental study. *Human Relations*, 1959, *12*, 215–232. **221**

Engel, B. T., & Chism, L. A. Operant conditioning of heart rate speeding. *Psychophysiology*, 1967, *3*,

418–426. **249**

Epstein, A. N., Fitzsimons, J. T., & Simons, B. Drinking caused by the intracranial injection of angiotensin into the rat. *Journal of Physiology* (London), 1969, *200*, 98–100. **699**

Erikson, E. H. *Childhood and society*. New York: Norton, 1950. **188, 287**

Erikson, E. H. A health personality for every child: A fact finding report: A digest. Midcentury White House Conference on Children and Youth. In J. Seidman (Ed.), *The adolescent: A book of readings*. New York: Dryden (Holt, Rinehart and Winston), 1953. **318, 338**

Erikson, E. H. Identity and the life cycle. *Psychological Issues*, 1959, *1*, 1–165. **338**

Erikson, E. H. *Insight and responsibility*. New York: Norton, 1964. **191**

Erlenmeyer-Kimling, L., & Jarvik, L. F. Genetics and intelligence: A review. *Science*, 1963, *142*, 1477–1479. **367**

Ervin, S. M. Imitation and structural changes in children's language. In E. H. Lenneberg (Ed.), *New directions in the study of language*. Cambridge: M.I.T. Press, 1964. **312**

Escher, M. C. *The graphic work of M. C. Escher*. New York: Duell, Sloan and Pearce, 1961. **539**

Eysenck, H. J. *Dimensions of personality*. London: Routledge & Kegan Paul, 1947. **171**

Falk, J. L. The grooming behavior of the chimpanzee as a reinforcer. *Journal of the Experimental Analysis of Behavior*, 1958, *1*, 83–85. **828**

Fantz, R. L. Pattern vision in newborn infants. *Science*, 1963, *140*, 296–297. **625**

Fast, J. *Body language*. New York: M. Evans and Lippincott, 1970. **165**

Feshbach, N. Sex differences in children's modes of aggressive responses toward outsiders. *Merrill Palmer Quarterly*, 1969, *15*, 249–258. **209**

Feshbach, S. Aggression. In P. H. Mussen (Ed.), *Carmichael's manual of child psychology*, Vol. II. (Rev. ed.) New York: Wiley, 1970. **175, 209, 218**

Feshbach, S., & Feshbach, N. The influence of the stimulus object upon the complementary and supplementary projection of fear. *Journal of Abnormal and Social Psychology*, 1963, *66*, 498–502. **223**

Feshbach, S., & Loeb, A. A further experimental study of a response-interference versus a drive-facilitation theory of the effect of anxiety upon learning. *Journal of Personality*, 1959, *27*, 497–506. **164**

Feshbach, S., & Singer, R. *Television and aggression*. San Francisco: Jossey-Bass, 1971. **221**

Feshbach, N., & Sones, G. Sex differences in adolescent reactions toward newcomers. *Developmental Psychology*, 1971, *4*, 381–386. **209**

Feshbach, S., Stiles, W. B., & Bitter, E. The reinforcing effect of witnessing aggression. *Journal of Experimental Personality*, 1967, *2*, 133–139. **187**

Festinger, L. *A theory of cognitive dissonance*. Evanston, Ill.: Row, Peterson, 1957. **93**

Festinger, L., & Carlsmith, J. M. Cognitive consequences of forced compliance. *Journal of Abnormal and Social Psychology*, 1959, *58*, 203–211. **101**

Floyd, Joanne M. K. Effects of amount of reward and friendship status of the other on the frequency of sharing in children. Unpublished doctoral dissertation, University of Minnesota, 1964. **145**

Flynn, J. P., Edwards, S. B., & Bandler, R. J. Changes in sensory and motor systems during centrally elicited attack. *Behavioral Science*, 1971, *16*, 1–19. **715**

Ford, C. S., & Beach, F. A. *Patterns of sexual behavior*. London: Eyre & Spotteswoode, 1952. **844**

Frank, C. M. Behavior modification and the treatment of the alcoholic. In R. Fox (Ed.), *Alcoholism: Behavioral research*. New York: Springs, 1967. **253**

Freedman, J. L. Long-term behavioral effects of cognitive dissonance. *Journal of Experimental Social Psychology*, 1965, *1*, 145–155. **103**

Freedman, J. The crowd—maybe not so madding after all. *Psychology Today*, 1971, *5*, 58–61. **813**

Freud, A. *The ego and the mechanisms of defense*. New York: International Universities Press, 1946. **188**

Frisch, K. von. *Bees, their vision, chemical senses and language*. Ithaca, N.Y.: Cornell University Press, 1950. **806**

Fromm, E. *Escape from freedom*. New York: Holt, Rinehart and Winston, 1941. **191**

Gagné, R. M. *The condition of learning*. New York: Holt, Rinehart and Winston, 1965. **489**

Galanter, E. Contemporary psychophysics. In R. Brown, E. Galanter, E. H. Hess, & G. Mandler (Eds.), *New directions in psychology*. New York: Holt, Rinehart and Winston, 1962. **548**

Garcia, J., & Ervin, F. R. Gustatory-visual and telereceptor-cutaneous conditioning—adaptation in internal and external milieus. *Communications in Behavioral Biology*, 1968, *1*, 389–415. **785**

Gardner, R. A., & Gardner, B. T. Teaching sign language to a chimpanzee. *Science*, 1969, *165*, 664–672. **774**

Garner, W. R. Good patterns have few alternatives. *American Scientist*, 1970, *58*, 34–42. **589**

Garner, W. R., & Clement, D. E. Goodness of pattern and pattern uncertainty. *Journal of Verbal Learning and Verbal Behavior*, 1963, *2*, 446–452. **591, 592**

Garrett, M., Bever, T., & Fodor, J. The active use of grammar in speech perception. *Perception and Psychophysics*, 1966, *1*, 30–32. **608**

Gazzaniga, M. S. *The bisected brain*. New York: Appleton-Century-Crofts, 1970. **742**

Gazzaniga, M. S. One brain—two minds? *American Scientist,* 1972, *60,* 311–317. **776**

Gelb, A. Die Farbenkonstanz der Sehdinge. In H. von Bethe (Ed.), *Handbuch der normalen und pathologischen Physiologie,* 1929, *12,* 594–678. **578**

Geller, A., & Jarvik, M. E. The time relations of ECS-induced amnesia. *Psychonomic Science,* 1968, *12,* 169–170. **731**

Gerall, H. D., Ward, I. L., & Gerall, A. A. Disruption of the male rat's sexual behaviour induced by social isolation. *Animal Behaviour,* 1967, *15,* 54–58. **712**

Geschwind, N., & Levitsky, W. Human brain: left-right asymmetries in temporal speech region. *Science,* 1968, *161,* 186–187. **686**

Gesell, Arnold. *Infancy and human growth.* New York: Macmillan, 1928. **360**

Gibson, E. J., & Walk, R. D. The "visual cliff." *Scientific American,* 1960, *202,* 64–71. **621**

Gibson, J. J. *The perception of the visual world.* Boston: Houghton Mifflin, 1950. **575, 577**

Gibson, J. J. *The senses considered as perceptual systems.* Boston: Houghton Mifflin, 1966. **580**

Ginsburg, B. E. Coaction of genetical and nongenetical factors influencing sexual behavior. In F. A. Beach (Ed.), *Sex and behavior.* New York: Wiley, 1965. **810**

Ginsburg, H., & Opper, S. *Piaget's theory of intellectual development.* Englewood Cliffs, N.J.: Prentice-Hall, 1969. **302**

Girden, E. A review of psychokinesis. *Psychological Bulletin,* 1962, *59,* 353–388. **603**

Glanzer, M. Storage mechanisms in recall. In G. H. Bower (Ed.), *The psychology of learning and motivation: Advances in research and theory.* Vol. 5. New York: Academic Press, 1972. **526**

Glassman, E., Machlus, B., & Wilson, J. E. The effect of short experiences on the incorporation of radioactive phosphate into acid-extractable nuclear proteins of rat brain. In J. L. McGaugh (Ed.), *The chemistry of mood, motivation and memory.* New York: Plenum Press, 1972. **743**

Glickman, S. E., & Sroges, R. W. Curiosity in zoo animals. *Behaviour,* 1966, *26,* 151–188. **794**

Goldfarb, W. Infant rearing and problem behavior. *American Journal of Orthopsychiatry,* 1943, *13,* 249–266. (a) **319**

Goldfarb, W. The effects of early institutional care on adolescent personality. *Journal of Experimental Education,* 1943, *12,* 107–129. (b) **319**

Goldfarb, W. Infant rearing as a factor in foster home placement. *American Journal of Orthopsychiatry,* 1944, *14,* 162–167. **319**

Goldfarb, W. Effects of psychological deprivation in infancy and subsequent stimulation. *American Journal of Psychiatry,* 1945, *102,* 18–33. (a). **319**

Goldfarb, W. Psychological privation in infancy and subsequent adjustment. *American Journal of Orthopsychiatry,* 1945, *15,* 247–255. (b) **319**

Goldhamer, H., & Marshall, A. *Psychoses and civilizations.* Glencoe, Ill.: Free Press, 1949. **229**

Goldstein, K. *The organism.* New York: American Book Co., 1939. **195**

Goldstein, K., & Scheerer, M. Abstract and concrete behavior; an experimental study with special tests. *Psychological Monographs,* 1941, No. 239. **385**

Goodall, J. Chimpanzees of the Gombe Stream Reserve. In I. DeVore (Ed.), *Primate behavior.* New York: Holt, Rinehart and Winston, 1965. **828**

Gore, P. M., & Rotter, J. B. A personality correlate of social action. *Journal of Personality,* 1963, *31,* 58–64. **212**

Gottesman, I. I. Heritability of personality. *Psychological Monographs,* 1963, *77,* 1–21. **207**

Gottesman, I. I., & Shields, J. Contributions of twin studies of perspectives on schizophrenia. In B. A. Maher (Ed.), *Progress in experimental personality research.* Vol. 3. New York: Academic Press, 1966. **243**

Gottlieb, G. *Development of species identification in birds: An inquiry into the prenatal determinants of perception.* Chicago: University of Chicago Press, 1971. **783**

Gough, H. The adjective check list as a personality assessment research technique. *Psychological Reports,* 1960, *6,* 107–122. **166**

Gray, S. W., & Klaus, R. A. An experimental preschool program for culturally deprived children. *Child Development,* 1965, *36,* 887–898. **424**

Green, D. M., & Swets, J. A. *Signal detection theory and psychophysics.* New York: Wiley, 1966. **550**

Greene, W. A. Operant conditioning of the GSR using partial reinforcement. *Psychological Reports,* 1966, *19,* 571–578. **249**

Greenspoon, J. The reinforcing effects of two spoken sounds on the frequency of two responses. *American Journal of Psychology,* 1955, *68,* 409–416. **187**

Gregory, R. L. *The eye and brain: The psychology of seeing.* New York: McGraw-Hill, 1966. **604**

Gregory, R. L. *The intelligent eye.* New York: McGraw-Hill, 1970. **604**

Groos, K. *The play of animals* (tr. by Elizabeth L. Baldwin). New York: Appleton, 1898. **826**

Gross, C. G., Bender, D. B., & Rocha-Miranda, C. E. Visual receptive fields of neurons in inferotemporal cortex of the monkey. *Science,* 1969, *166,* 1303–1306. **674**

Grunt, J. A., & Young, W. C. Differential reactivity of individuals and the response of the male guinea pig to testosterone propionate. *Endocrinology,* 1952, *51,* 237–248. **710–711**

Guilford, J. P. *The nature of human intelligence.* New York: McGraw-Hill, 1967. **379–380, 400–401**

Guttman, L. A basis for scaling qualitative data. *American Sociological Review,* 1944, *9,* 139–150. **79**

Haber, R. N. (Ed.) *Current research in motivation.* New York: Holt, Rinehart and Winston, 1966. **477**

Hailman, J. P. *The ontogeny of an instinct: The pecking response in chicks of the laughing gull (Larus atricilla L.) and related species. Behavioral Supplement* 15. Leiden, Netherlands: E. J. Brill, 1967. **623**

Halas, E. S., Beardsley, J. V., & Sandlie, M. E. Conditioned neuronal responses at various levels in conditioning paradigms. *Electroencephalography and Clinical Neurophysiology,* 1970, *28,* 468–477. **737**

Hall, K. R. L. Behavior and ecology of the wild patas monkey. *Erythrocebus patas,* in Uganda. *Journal of Zoology,* 1965, *148,* 15–87. **804**

Hall, K. R. L., & DeVore, I. Baboon social behavior. In I. DeVore (Ed.), *Primate behavior.* New York: Holt, Rinehart and Winston, 1965. **804**

Harlow, H. F. The formation of learning sets. *Psychological Review,* 1949, *56,* 51–65. **396, 397, 480**

Harlow, H. F. Mice, monkeys, men and motives. *Psychological Review,* 1953, *60,* 23–32. **792**

Harlow, H. F. The heterosexual affectional system in monkeys. *American Psychologist,* 1962, 1–9. **819**

Harlow, H. F. Antecedent affectional control over the ontogeny of aggression. Paper presented at the 80th Annual Convention of the American Psychological Association. September 1972, Honolulu. **11**

Harlow, H. F., & Harlow, M. K. Learning to love. *American Scientist,* 1966, *54* (3), 244–272. **317**

Harlow, H. F., Harlow, M. K., & Suomi, S. J. From thought to therapy: Lessons from a primate laboratory. *American Scientist,* 1971, *59,* 538–549, **710**

Harlow, H. F., & Suomi, S. J. Social recovery by isolation-reared monkeys. *Proceedings National Academy of Sciences,* 1971, *68,* 1534–1538. **710**

Harlow, H. F., & Zimmermann, R. R. Affectional responses in the infant monkey. *Science,* 1959, *130,* No. 3373, 421–432. **317**

Harris, C. S. Perceptual adaptation to inverted, reversed, and displaced vision. *Psychological Review,* 1965, *72,* 419–444. **619**

Hartman, D. P. Influence of symbolically modeled instrumental aggression and pain cues on aggressive behavior. *Journal of Personality and Social Psychology,* 1969, *11,* 380–388. **221**

Hartmann, C. G., *Possums.* Austin: University of Texas Press, 1962. **818**

Hartmann, H. *Ego psychology and the problem of adaptation* (tr. by David Rapaport). New York: International Universities Press, 1958 (1939). **188**

Hartup, W. W. Peer interactions in childhood. In P. Mussen (Ed.), *Carmichael's manual of child psychology.* Vol. 2. New York: Wiley, 1970. **332, 333**

Hastorf, A., & Cantril, H. They saw a game: A case study. *Journal of Abnormal and Social Psychology,* 1954, *49,* 129–134. **92**

Hathaway, S. R., & McKinley, J. C. *The Minnesota multiphasic personality inventory.* (Rev. ed.) Minneapolis: University of Minnesota Press, 1943. **168**

Hayes, K. J., & Hayes, C. Imitation in a home raised chimpanzee. *Journal of Comparative and Physiological Psychology,* 1952, *45,* 450–459. **774**

Hebb, D. O. The innate organization of visual activity, I. Perception of figure by rats raised in total darkness. *Journal of Genetic Psychology,* 1937, *51,* 101–126. **618**

Hebb, D. O. *The organization of behavior.* New York: Wiley, 1949. **724**

Hediger, H. *Studies of the psychology and behavior of captive animals in zoos and circuses.* London: Butterworths, 1955. **832**

Heidbreder, E. The attainment of concepts: Terminology and methodology. *Journal of General Psychology,* 1946, *35,* 173–189. **384**

Hein, A., Held, R., & Gower, E. C. Development and segmentation of visually controlled movement by selective exposure during rearing. *Journal of Comparative and Physiological Psychology,* 1970, *73,* 181–187. **622**

Held, R., & Hein, A. Movement-produced stimulation in the development of visually guided behavior. *Journal of Comparative and Physiological Psychology,* 1963, *56,* 872–876. **621**

Herbert, J. Hormones and reproductive behavior in rhesus and talapoin monkeys. *Journal of Reproduction and Fertility,* 1970, *11,* 119–140. **709**

Hernández-Peón, R., Scherrer, H., & Jouvet, M. Modification of electric activity in cochlear nucleus during "attention" in unanesthetized cats. *Science,* 1956, *123,* 331–332. **611**

Hersher, L., Richmond, J. B., & Moore, A. U. Modifiability of the critical period for the development of maternal behavior in sheep and goats. *Behaviour,* 1963, *20,* 311–320. **785**

Hess, E. H. Space perception in the chick. *Scientific American,* 1956, *195,* 71–80. **620**

Hess, E. H. "Imprinting" in animals. *Scientific American,* 1958. **782**

Hess, E. H. Imprinting. *Science,* 1959, *130,* 133–141. **782**

Heston, L. L., & Denny, D. Interaction between early life experience and biological factors in schizophrenia. In D. Rosenthal & S. S. Katz (Eds.), *The transmission of schizophrenia.* New York: Pergamon Press, 1968. **242**

Hildreth, G. H., Bixler, H. H., *et al. Metropolitan achievement tests: manual for interpreting.* Yonkers-on-

Hudson, New York: World Book Co., 1953. **426**
Hilgard, E. R. Pain as a puzzle for psychology and physiology. *American Psychologist,* 1969, *24,* 103–113. **568**
Hill, L. M., Powell, M., & Feifer, I. *Characteristics of teacher behavior and competency related to the achievement of different kinds of children in several elementary grades.* New York: Office of Testing and Research, Brooklyn College, 1960 (mimeo). **441**
Hind, J. E., Rose, J. E., Davies, P. W., Woolsey, C. N., Benjamin, R. M., Welker, W. S., & Thompson, R. F. Unit activity in the auditory cortex. In G. L. Rasmussen & W. F. Windle (Eds.), *Neural mechanisms of the auditory and vestibular systems.* Springfield, Ill.: Charles C Thomas, 1961. **683**
Hinde, R. A. Factors governing the changes in strength of a partially inborn response, as shown by the mobbing behavior of the chaffinch (*Fringilla coelebs*), I. The nature of the response, and an examination of its course. *Proceedings Royal Society, London, Serial B.,* 1954, *142,* 306–331. **804**
Hinde, R. A., & Spencer-Booth, Y. The behavior of socially living rhesus monkeys in their first two and a half years. *Animal Behaviour,* 1967, *15,* 169–196. **823**
Hochberg, J. *Perception.* Englewood Cliffs, N.J.: Prentice-Hall, 1964. **582**
Hochberg, J. E. Nativism and empiricism in perception. In L. Postman (Ed.), *Psychology in the making: Histories of selected research problems.* New York: Knopf, 1962. **618**
Hochberg, J. E., & McAlister, E. A quantitative approach to figural "goodness." *Journal of Experimental Psychology,* 1953, *46,* 361–364. **589**
Hodos, W. Evolutionary interpretation of neural and behavioral studies of living vertebrates. In F. O. Schmitt (Ed.), *The neurosciences: Second study program.* New York: Rockefeller University Press, 1970. **767**
Hodos, W., & Campbell, C. B. G. Scala naturae: Why there is no theory in comparative psychology. *Psychological Review,* 1969, *76,* 337–350. **770**
Hoebel, B. G., & Teitelbaum, P. Weight regulation in normal and hypothalamic hyperphagic rats. *Journal of Comparative and Physiological Psychology,* 1966, *61,* 189–193. **695**
Holland, J. G., & Skinner, B. F. *The analysis of behavior: A program for self-instruction.* New York: McGraw-Hill, 1961. **436**
Hollander, E. P., & Webb, W. B. Leadership, followership, and friendship: An analysis of peer nominations. *Journal of Abnormal and Social Psychology,* 1955, *50,* 163–167. **136**
Holzman, P. S., & Gardner, R. W. Leveling, sharpening and memory organization. *Journal of Abnormal and Social Psychology,* 1960, *61,* 176–180. **406**
Holzman, P. S., & Klein, G. S. Cognitive system principles of leveling and sharpening: Individual differences in assimilation effects in visual time error. *Journal of Psychology,* 1954, *37,* 105–122. **406**
Homans, G. C. *Social behavior: Its elementary forms.* New York: Harcourt, Brace and World, 1961. **127**
Honzik, M. P., Macfarlane, J. W., & Allen, L. The stability of mental test performance between 2 and 18 years. *Journal of Experimental Education,* 1948, *17,* 309–324. **364**
Horney, K. *Neurotic personality of our times.* New York: Norton, 1937. **191**
Houston, S. A reexamination of some assumptions about the language of the disadvantaged child. *Child Development,* 1970, *41,* 947–964. **411**
Hovland, C. I., Harvey, O. J., & Sherif, M. Assimilation and contrast effects in reaction to communication and attitude change. *Journal of Abnormal and Social Psychology,* 1957, *55,* 244–252. **87**
Hovland, C. I., & Pritzker, H. A. Extent of opinion change as a function of amount of change advocated. *Journal of Abnormal and Social Psychology,* 1957, *54,* 257–261. **87**
Hovland, C. I., & Sears, R. R. Minor studies of aggression. VI. Correlation of lynchings with economic indices. *Journal of Psychology,* 1940, *9,* 301–310. **9**
Hovland, C. I., & Weiss, W. The influence of source credibility on communication effectiveness. *Public Opinion Quarterly,* 1951, *15,* 635–650. **80**
Howard, H. E. *Territory in bird life.* London: Murray, 1920. **833**
Hubel, D. H. Effects of distortion of sensory input on the visual system of kittens. *The Physiologist,* 1967, *10,* 17–45. **677**
Hull, C. L. *Principles of behavior.* New York: Appleton-Century-Crofts, 1943. **769**
Hull, C. L. Quantitative aspects of the evolution of concepts. *Psychological Monographs,* 1920, No. 123. **383**
Hunt, G. H., & Odoroff, M. E. *Follow-up study of narcotic drug addicts after hospitalization.* (U. S. Public Health Service Report No. 77) Washington, D.C.: U.S. Government Printing Office, 1963. **259**
Hunter, W. S. The delayed reaction in animals and children. *Behavior Monographs,* 1913, *2.* **764**

Inhelder, B., & Piaget, J. *The growth of logical thinking from childhood through adolescence.* New York: Basic Books, 1958. **305**
Inhelder, B., & Piaget, J. *The early growth of logic in the child.* New York: Harper, 1959. **305, 306**
Irwin, O. C. Infant speech. *Journal of Speech and Hearing Disorders,* 1948, *13,* 320–323. **311**
Iscoe, I., Williams, M., & Harvey, J. Age, intelligence, and sex as variables in the conformity behavior of negro and white children. *Child Development,* 1964, *35,* 451–460. **209**
Itani, J. Paternal care in the wild Japanese monkey,

Macaca fuscata. Journal of Primates, 1959, 2, 61–93. **808**

Jackson, D. W., & Messick, S. Content and style in personality assessment. *Psychological Bulletin,* 1958, *55,* 243–252. **163**

James, W. H., Woodruff, A. B., & Werner, W. Effect of internal and external control upon smoking behavior. *Journal of Consulting Psychology,* 1965, *29,* 184–186. **212**

Janis, I. L., & Field, P. B. Sex differences and personality factors related to persuasibility. In C. I. Hovland & I. L. Janis (Eds.), *Personality and persuasibility.* New Haven: Yale University Press, 1959. **88**

Jecker, J., & Landy, D. Liking a person as a function of doing him a favor. *Human Relations,* 1969, *22,* 371–378. **141**

John, E. R. *Mechanisms of memory.* New York: Academic Press, 1967. **736**

John, E. R., & Killam, K. F. Electrophysiological correlates of avoidance conditioning in the cat. *Journal of Pharmacology and Experimental Therapeutics,* 1959, *125,* 252–274. **736**

Jones, E. *The life and work of Sigmund Freud.* 3 vols. New York: 1953–57. **179**

Jones, E. E. Flattery will get you somewhere. *Trans-Action,* May/June 1965, 20–23. **139**

Jones, E. E., Bell, L., & Aronson, E. The reciprocation of attraction from similar and dissimilar others: A study in person perception and evaluation. In C. G. McClintock (Ed.), *Experimental social psychology.* New York: Holt, Rinehart and Winston, 1971. **134**

Jones, E. E., & Kohler, R. The effects of plausibility on the learning of controversial statements. *Journal of Abnormal and Social Psychology,* 1958, *57,* 315–320. **97, 98**

Jouvet, M. The states of sleep. *Scientific American,* 1967, *216,* 62–72. **704**

Julesz, B. Binocular depth perception without familiarity cues. *Science,* 1964, *145,* 356–362. **594, 595**

Jung, C. G. *The basic writings of C. G. Jung* (ed. by V. de Laszlo). New York: Random House, 1959. **191**

Kagan, J. Reflection-impulsivity: The generality and dynamics of conceptual tempo. *Journal of Abnormal Psychology,* 1966, *71,* 17–24. **406**

Kagan, J. Attention and psychological change in the young child. *Science,* 1970, *170,* 826–832. **294**

Kagan, J., & Moss, H. A. *Birth to maturity.* New York: Wiley, 1962. **336, 337**

Kahan, B. E., Kriginan, M. R., Wilson, J. E., & Glassman, E. Brain function and macromolecules, VI. Autoradiographic analysis of the effect of a brief training experience on the incorporation of uridine into mouse brain, *Proceedings of the National Academy of Sciences, U.S.,* 1970, *65,* 300–304. **737**

Kelley, T. L., Madden, R., Gardner, E. F., Tesman, L. M., & Ruch, G. M. *Stanford achievement test: manuals for primary, elementary, intermediate, and advanced batteries.* Yonkers-on-Hudson, New York: World Book Co., 1953. **426**

Kellogg, W. N., & Kellogg, L. A. *The ape and the child.* New York: McGraw-Hill, 1933. **774**

Kelly, G. A. *The psychology of personal constructs.* New York: Norton, 1955. **212**

Kelman, H. C. Processes of opinion change. *Public Opinion Quarterly,* 1961, *25,* 57–78. **69**

Kendler, H. H., & Kendler, T. S. Vertical and horizontal processes in problem solving. *Psychological Review,* 1962, *69,* 1–16. **385**

Kendler, H. H., Kendler, T. S., Pliskoff, S. S., & D'Amato, M. F. Inferential behavior in children, I. The influence of reinforcement and incentive motivation. *Journal of Experimental Psychology,* 1958, *55,* 207–212.

Kendler, T. S., & Kendler, H. H. Inferential behavior in children as a function of age and subgoal constancy. *Journal of Experimental Psychology,* 1962, *64,* 460–466. **391**

Kendler, T. S., & Kendler, H. H. Experimental analysis of inferential behavior in children. In L. P. Lipsitt & C. C. Spiker (Eds.), *Advances in child development and behavior.* Vol. 3. New York: Academic Press, 1967. **384**

King, J. A. Social behavior, social organization, and population dynamics in a black-tailed prairie dog town in the Black Hills of South Dakota. *Contributions from the Laboratory of Vertebrate Biology,* 1955, No. 67. **830**

King, J. A., & Weisman, R. G. Sand digging contingent upon bar pressing in deermice (*peromyscus*). *Animal Behaviour,* 1964, *12,* 446–450. **797**

Kinsey, A. C., Pomeroy, W. B., & Martin, C. E. *Sexual behavior in the human male.* Philadelphia: Saunders, 1948. **252**

Kissileff, H. R., & Epstein, A. N. Exaggerated prandial drinking in the "recovered lateral" rat without saliva. *Journal of Comparative and Physiological Psychology,* 1969, *67,* 301–308. **700**

Klaus, R., & Gray, S. The early training project for disadvantaged children. *Monographs of the Society for Research in Child Development,* 1968, *33,* No. 4. **424, 425**

Kleiman, D. Scent marking in the canidae. In P. A. Jewell & C. Loizos (Eds.), *Play, exploration and territory in mammals.* London: Academic Press, 1966. **831**

Klopfer, B. (Ed.) *Developments in the Rorschach technique.* Yonkers-on-Hudson, N.Y.: World Book Co., 1954–70. **173**

Klopfer, P. H., Adams, D. K., & Klopfer, M. S. Maternal imprinting in goats. *Proceedings National Academy of Sciences,* 1964, *52,* 911–914. **785**

Kohlberg, L. The development of children's orientations toward a moral order: 1. Sequence in the development of moral thought. *Vita Humana*, 1963, *6*, 11–33. **306**

Kohlberg, L. Stage and sequence: The cognitive-developmental approach to socialization. In D. A. Goslin (Ed.), *Handbook of socialization theory and research*. Chicago: Rand-McNally, 1969. **306, 307**

Kohler, I. Experiments with goggles. *Scientific American*, 1962, *206*, 62–72. **575**

Kohler, I. The formation and transformation of the perceptual world. *Psychological Issues*, 1964, 3, Monograph 12. **619**

Köhler, W. *The mentality of apes*. New York: Harcourt, 1925. **395**

Köhler, W., & Wallach, H. Figural aftereffects: An investigation of visual processes. *Proceedings of the American Philosophical Society*, 1944, *88*, 269–357. **574**

Kopp, R., Bohdanecký, Z., & Jarvik, M. E. Long temporal gradient of retrograde amnesia for a well-discriminated stimulus. *Science*, 1966, *153*, 1547–1549. **725, 726**

Koukkou, M., & Lehmann, D. EEG and memory storage in sleep experiments with humans. *Electroencephalography and Clinical Neurophysiology*, 1968, *25*, 455–462. **744**

Kramer, B. M. Dimensions of prejudice. *Journal of Psychology*, 1949, *27*, 389–451. **120**

Krasner, L. Studies of the conditioning of verbal behavior. *Psychological Bulletin*, 1958, *55*, 148–170. **187**

Krebs, C. J. *Ecology: The experimental analysis of distribution and abundance*. New York: Harper & Row, 1972. **814**

Krivanek, J., & McGaugh, J. L. Effects of pentylenetetrazol on memory storage in mice. *Psychopharmacologia*, 1968, *12*, 303–321. **730**

Krogh, A. The language of the bees. *Scientific American*, 1948. **807**

Kummer, H. *Social organization of hamadryas baboons*. Chicago: University of Chicago Press, 1968. **828, 831**

Kummer, H., & Kurt, F. A comparison of social behavior in captive and wild hamadryas baboons. In H. Vagtborg (Ed.), *The baboon in medical research*. Houston: University of Texas Press, 1965. **828**

Ladefoged, P. The perception of speech. In *The mechanization of thought processes*. London: H. M. Stationery Office, 1959. **607**

Ladefoged, P., & Broadbent, D. E. Perception of sequence in auditory events. *Quarterly Journal of Experimental Psychology*, 1960, *12*, 162–170. **607**

Lambert, W. E., Hodgson, R. C., Gardner, R. C., & Fillenbaum, S. Evaluational reactions to spoken languages. *Journal of Abnormal and Social Psychology*, 1960, *60*, 44–51. **615**

Lambert, W. W., Solomon, R. L., & Watson, P. D. Reinforcement and extinction as factors in size estimation. *Journal of Experimental Psychology*, 1949, *39*, 637–641. **614**

Langer, J. *Theories of development*. New York: Holt, Rinehart and Winston, 1969. **300**

Larsson, K. Individual differences in reactivity to androgen in male rats. *Physiology and Behavior*, 1966, *1*, 255–258. **711**

Lazarsfeld, P. F. (Ed.) *Radio and the printed page*. New York: Duell, Sloan, Pearce, 1944. **116**

Lazarus, A. A. The elimination of children's phobias by deconditioning. In H. J. Eysenck (Ed.), *Behavior therapy and the neuroses*. New York: Macmillan, 1960. **263**

Lea, H. C. *Materials toward a history of witchcraft* (ed. by A. C. Hawland). 3 vols. Philadelphia: University of Pennsylvania Press, 1939. **229**

Le Boeuf, B. J. Social status and mating activity in elephant seals. *Science*, 1969, *163*, 91–93. **14**

Leeper, R. A study of a neglected portion of the field of learning—the development of sensory organization. *Journal of Genetic Psychology*, 1935, *46*, 41–75. **613**

Leiter, R. G. Manual for the 1948 revision of the Leiter International Performance Scale. *Psychological Service Center Journal*, 1950, *2*, 259–343. **363**

Lenneberg, E. H. *Biological foundations of language*. New York: Wiley, 1967. **785**

Lerner, I. M. *Heredity, evolution and society*. San Francisco: W. H. Freeman, 1968. **759**

Levine, S. Sex differences in the brain. *Scientific American*, 1966, *214*, 84–90. **707**

Levitas, M. *America in crisis*. New York: Holt, Rinehart and Winston, 1969. **111**

Levy, D. M. *Maternal overprotection*. New York: Columbia University Press, 1943. **320, 322–323**

Lewin, K. *A dynamic theory of personality*. New York: McGraw-Hill, 1935. **195**

Liberman, A. M., Cooper, F. S., Shankweiler, D. P., & Studdert-Kennedy, M. Perception of the speech code. *Psychological Review*, 1967, *74*, 431–461. **609**

Lidz, T. The influence of family studies on the treatment of schizophrenia. *Psychiatry*, 1967, *32*, 235–251. **243**

Likert, R. A technique for the measurement of attitudes. *Archives of Psychology*, 1932, *140*, 44–53. **78**

Lindauer, M. Communication by dancing in swarm bees. In M. Lindauer, *Communication among social bees*. Cambridge: Harvard University Press, 1961. **807**

Livant, W. P. Grammar in the story reproductions of levelers and sharpeners. *Bulletin of the Menninger Clinic*, 1962, *26*, 283–287. **406**

Lorenz, K. Der Kumpan in der Unwelt des Vogels. *Journal für Ornithologie*, 1935, *83*, 137–213, 289–413. **780**

Lorenz, K. The comparative method of studying innate behaviour patterns. *Society for Experimental Biology, Symposia*, 1950, *4*, 221–268. **773**

Lorenz, K. *Evolution and modification of behavior*.

Chicago: University of Chicago Press, 1965. **776**
Lorenz, K. *On aggression.* New York: Harcourt, Brace and World, 1966. **750, 840, 842**
Lott, B. E., & Lott, A. J. The formation of positive attitudes toward group members. *Journal of Abnormal and Social Psychology,* 1960, *61,* 297–300. **127**
Lovaas, O. I. Effect of exposure to symbolic aggression on aggressive behavior. *Child Development,* 1961, *32,* 37–44. **221**
Lovaas, O. I., Freitag, G., Gold, V. J., & Kassorla, I. C. Experimental studies in childhood schizophrenia: 1. Analysis of self-destructive behavior. *Journal of Experimental Child Psychology,* 1965, *2,* 67–84. **175**
Luchins, A. S. Mechanization in problem solving: The effect of Einstellung. *Psychological Monographs,* 1942, No. 248. **398**

Maccoby, E. E. (Ed.) *The development of sex differences.* Stanford: Stanford University Press, 1966. **209**
MacCrone, I. D. *Race attitudes in South Africa.* London: Oxford University Press, 1957. **116**
Mackintosh, N. J. Comparative studies of reversal and probability learning: Rats, birds and fish. In R. M. Gilbert & N. S. Sutherland (Eds.), *Animal discrimination learning.* London: Academic Press, 1969. **772**
Maier, N. R. F., & Schneirla, T. C. *Principles of animal psychology.* New York: McGraw-Hill, 1935. **766**
Maier, R. A., & Maier, B. M. *Comparative animal behavior.* Belmont, Calif.: Brooks-Cole, 1970. **817**
Mark, V. H., & Ervin, F. R. *Violence and the brain.* New York: Harper, 1970. **714, 715**
Marshall, S. L. A. *Men against fire.* New York: Morrow, 1947. **844**
Maslow, A. H. Deprivation, threat and frustration. *Psychological Review,* 1941, *48,* 364–366. **218**
Maslow, A. H. *Motivation and personality.* New York: Harper, 1954. **196**
Maslow, A. H. Self-actualizing people. In G. B. Levitas (Ed.), *The world of psychology.* Vol. 2. New York: George Braziller, 1963. **197**
Mason, W. A. The effects of social restriction on the behavior of rhesus monkeys: I. Free social behavior. *Journal of Comparative and Physiological Psychology,* 1960, *53,* 582–589. **827, 838**
Mayer, J., Marshall, N. B., Vitale, J. J., Cristensen, J. H., Mashayekhi, M. B., & Stare, F. J. Exercise, food intake and body weight in normal rats and genetically obese adult mice. *American Journal of Physiology,* 1954, *177,* 544–548. **692**
Mayer, J., Roy, P., & Mitra, K. P. Relation between caloric intake, body weight, and physical work: Studies in an industrial male population in West Bengal. *American Journal of Clinical Nutrition,* 1956, *4,* 169–175. **689**
McBrearty, J. F., Garfield, Z., Dichten, M., & Heath, G. A behaviorally oriented treatment program for alcoholism. *Psychological Reports,* 1968, *22,* 287–298. **253**
McClelland, D. C. *The achieving society.* Princeton, N.J.: Van Nostrand, 1961.
McClelland, D. C., & Apicella, F. S. A functional classification of verbal reactions to experimentally induced failure. *Journal of Abnormal and Social Psychology,* 1945, *40,* 376–390. **219–220**
McClelland, D. C., Atkinson, J. W., Clark, R. A., & Lowell, E. L. *The achievement motive.* New York: Appleton-Century-Crofts, 1953. **174**
McCreary, J. W., & Hunter, W. S. Serial position curves in verbal learning. *Science,* 1953, *117,* 131–134. **475**
McGaugh, J. L. Time-dependent processes in memory storage. *Science,* 1966, *153,* 1351–1358. **726**
McGaugh, J. L., & Krivanek, J. Strychnine effects on discrimination learning in mice: Effects of dose and time of administration. *Physiology and Behavior,* 1970, *5,* 1437–1442. **727**
McGinnies, E. Emotionality and perceptual defense. *Psychological Review,* 1949, *56,* 244–251. **614**
McGuire, W. J., & Papageorgis, D. The relative efficacy of various types of prior belief-defense in producing immunity against persuasion. *Journal of Abnormal and Social Psychology,* 1961, *62,* 327–337. **89–90**
Mead, M. *Sex and temperament in three primitive societies.* New York: Morrow, 1935. **209**
Mednick, S. A. A learning theory approach to research in schizophrenia. *Psychological Bulletin,* 1958, *55,* 316–327. **242**
Mednick, S. A. The associative basis of the creative process. *Psychological Review,* 1962, *69,* 220–232. **401**
Meehl, P. E. Schizotaxia, schizotypy, schizophrenia. *American Psychologist,* 1962, *17,* 827–838. **242**
Mehrabian, A. Significance of posture and position in the communication of attitude and status relationships. *Psychological Bulletin,* 1969, *71,* 359–372. **165**
Melton, A. W. Implications of short-term memory for a general theory of memory. *Journal of Verbal Learning and Verbal Behavior,* 1963, *2,* 1–21. **511**
Melton, A. W. The situation with respect to the spacing of repetitions and memory. *Journal of Verbal Learning and Verbal Behavior,* 1970, *9,* 596–606. **514**
Meltzoff, J., & Kornreich, M. *Research in psychotherapy.* New York: Atherton Press, 1970. **266**
Melzack, R., & Wall, P. D. Pain mechanisms: A new theory. *Science,* 1965, *150,* 971–979. **684**
Mendelson, J. Role of hunger in T-maze learning for food by rats. *Journal of Comparative and Physiological Psychology,* 1966, *62,* 341–349. **719**
Michael, R. P. Neuroendocrine factors regulating primate behavior. In L. Martini & W. F. Ganong (Eds.), *Frontiers in neuroendocrinology, 1971.* New York: Oxford University Press, 1971. **820**
Michotte, A. *The perception of causality* (tr. by T. R. Miles

and E. Miles). London: Methuen, 1963. **584**

Miller, N. E. Studies of fear as an acquirable drive: 1. Fear as motivation and fear-reduction as reinforcement in the learning of new responses. *Journal of Experimental Psychology,* 1948, *38,* 89–101. (a) **215**

Miller, N. E. Theory and experiment relating psychoanalytic displacement to stimulus-response generalization. *Journal of Abnormal and Social Psychology,* 1948, *43,* 155–178. (b) **836**

Miller, N. E. Learning of visceral and glandular responses. *Science,* 1969, *163,* 434–445. **249**

Miller, N. E., & Banuazizi, A. Instrumental learning by curarized rats of a specific visceral response, intestinal or cardiac. *Journal of Comparative and Physiological Psychology,* 1968, *65,* 1–7. **490**

Miller, N., & Campbell, D. T. Recency and primacy in persuasion as a function of the timing of speeches and measurements. *Journal of Abnormal and Social Psychology,* 1959, *59,* 1–9. **86**

Miller, N. E., & Dollard, J. *Social learning and imitation.* New Haven: Yale University Press, 1941. **199**

Mills, J., & Aronson, E. Opinion change as a function of the communicator's attractiveness and desire to influence. *Journal of Personality and Social Psychology,* 1965, *1,* 173–177. **83**

Milner, B. Amnesia following operation on the temporal lobes. In C. W. M. Whitty & O. L. Zangwill (Eds.), *Amnesia.* London: Butterworths, 1966. **731**

Minard, J. G., Bailey, D. E., & Wertheimer, M. Measurement and conditioning of perceptual defense, response bias, and emotionally based recognition. *Journal of Personality and Social Psychology,* 1966, *2,* 661–668. **615**

Mischel, W. *Personality and assessment.* New York: Wiley, 1968. **157**

Mischel, W., & Grusec, J. Determinants of the rehearsal and transmission of neutral and aversive behaviors. *Journal of Personality and Social Psychology,* 1966, *2,* 197–205. **282**

Missakian, E. A. Reproductive behavior of socially deprived male rhesus monkeys (*Macaca mulatta*). *Journal of Comparative and Physiological Psychology,* 1969, *69,* 403–407. **712**

Møllgaard, K., Diamond, M. C., Bennett, E. L., Rosenzweig, M. R., & Lindner, B. Quantitative synaptic changes with differential experience in rat brain. *International Journal of Neuroscience,* 1971, *2,* 113–128. **736**

Moltz, H., & Stettner, L. J. The influence of patterned-light deprivation on the critical period for imprinting. *Journal of Comparative and Physiological Psychology,* 1961, *54,* 279–283. **782**

Montague, E. K. The role of anxiety in serial rote learning. *Journal of Experimental Psychology,* 1953, *45,* 91–96. **164**

Moray, N. Attention in dichotic listening: Affective cues and the influence of instructions. *Quarterly Journal of Experimental Psychology,* 1959, *11,* 56–60. **612**

Moreno, J. L. *Psychodrama.* Beacon, N.Y.: Beacon House, 1946. **265**

Morris, D. *The naked ape.* New York: McGraw-Hill, 1967. **750, 840, 844**

Mrosovsky, N. How turtles find the sea. *Science Journal,* 1967, *1,* 2–7. **798**

Murdock, B. B., Jr. The serial position effect of free recall. *Journal of Experimental Psychology,* 1962, *64,* 482–488. **511**

Murdock, B. B., Jr., & Walker, K. D. Modality effects in free recall. *Journal of Verbal Learning and Verbal Behavior,* 1969, *8,* 665–676. **517**

Murphy, G., & Murphy, L. B. *Asian Psychology.* New York: Basic Books, 1968. **200**

Murray, H. A. The effect of fear upon estimates of the maliciousness of other personalities. *Journal of Social Psychology,* 1933, *4,* 310–329. **223**

Murray, H. A. *Thematic Apperception Test.* Cambridge, Mass.: Harvard University Press, 1943. **173**

Murray, H. A., *et al. Assessment of men.* New York: Rinehart and Company, 1948. **175**

Murstein, B. I. *Theory and research in projective techniques.* New York: Wiley, 1963. **175**

Mussen, P. Early socialization, learning and identification. In G. Mandler (Ed.), *New directions in psychology III.* New York: Holt, Rinehart and Winston, 1967. **315, 326**

Mussen, P. Early sex-role development. In D. A. Goslin (Ed.), *Handbook of socialization theory and research.* Chicago: Rand-McNally, 1969. **328**

Mussen, P., & Distler, L. Masculinity, identification, and father-son relationships. *Journal of Abnormal and Social Psychology,* 1959, *59,* 350–356. **328, 330**

Mussen, P., & Distler, L. Child rearing antecedents of masculine identification in kindergarten boys. *Child Development,* 1960, *31,* 89–100. **328, 330**

Mussen, P., & Jones, M. C. Self conceptions, motivations, and interpersonal attitudes of late and early maturing boys. *Child Development,* 1957, *28,* 243–256. **285**

Mussen, P., & Parker, Ann. Mother nurturance and girls' incidental imitative learning. *Journal of Personality and Social Psychology,* 1965, *2,* 94–97. **328**

Mussen, P. H., & Rutherford, E. Effects of aggressive cartoons in children's aggressive play. *Journal of Abnormal and Social Psychology,* 1961, *62,* 461–464. **221**

Mussen, P., & Rutherford, E. Parent-child relations and parental personality in relation to young children's sex-role preferences. *Child Development,* 1963, *34,* 589–607. **329**

Neisser, U. *Cognitive psychology.* New York: Appleton-Century-Crofts, 1967. **492, 602, 605, 606**

Newell, A., & Simon, A. A. GPS, a program that simulates

human thought. In E. A. Fergenbaum & J. Feldman (Eds.) *Computers and thought.* New York: McGraw-Hill, 1963. **400**

Nicholson, W. M. The influence of anxiety upon learning: Interference or drive increment? *Journal of Personality,* 1958, *25,* 303–319. **164**

Nizer, L. *My life in court.* New York: Pyramid, 1961. **85**

Noirot, E. Ultra-sounds in young rodents. I. Changes with age in albino mice. *Animal Behavior,* 1966, *14,* 459–462. **825**

O'Kelly, L. E., & Steckle, L. C. A note on long enduring emotional responses in the rat. *Journal of Psychology,* 1939, *8,* 125–131. **835**

Olds, J. Self-stimulation experiments and differentiated reward systems. In H. H. Jasper, L. D. Proctor, R. S. Knighton, W. C. Noshay, & R. T. Costello (Eds.), *Reticular formation of the brain.* Boston: Little, Brown, 1958. **717**

Olds, J., & Milner, P. Positive reinforcement produced by electrical stimulation of septal area and other regions of rat brain. *Journal of Comparative and Physiological Psychology,* 1954, *47,* 419–427. **716**

Osborn, A. G., Bunker, J. P., Cooper, L. M., Frank, G. S., & Hilgard, E. R. Effects of thiopental sedation on learning and memory. *Science,* 1967, *157,* 574–576. **729**

Osgood, C. E., Suci, G. J., & Tannenbaum. *The measurement of meaning.* Urbana: University of Illinois Press, 1957. **413**

Oswald, I., Taylor, A. M., & Treisman, A. M. Discrimination responses to stimulation during human sleep. *Brain,* 1960, *83,* 440–453. **612**

Paolino, R. M., & Levy, H. M. Amnesia produced by spreading depression and ECS: Evidence for time-dependent memory trace localization. *Science,* 1971, *172,* 746–749. **742**

Papousek, H. Experimental studies of appetitional behavior in human newborns and infants. In H. W. Stevenson, E. H. Hess, & H. L. Rheingold (Eds.), *Early behavior.* New York: Wiley, 1967. **297**

Pastore, N. The role of arbitrariness in the frustration-aggression hypothesis. *Journal of Abnormal and Social Psychology,* 1952, *47,* 728–731. **219**

Patterson, G. R. An application of conditioning techniques to the control of a hyperactive child. In L. P. Ullmann & L. Krasner (Eds.), *Case Studies in Behavior Modification.* New York: Holt, Rinehart and Winston, 1965. **434**

Patterson, G. R., Littman, R. A., & Bricker, W. Assertive behavior in children: A step toward a theory of aggression. *Monographs of the Society for Research in Child Development,* 1967, *32,* No. 5. 1–43. **333**

Pearson, O. P. Carnivore-mouse predation: An example of its intensity and bioenergetics. *Journal of Mammalogy,* 1964, *45,* 177–188. **814**

Peirce, J. T., & Nuttall, R. L. Self-paced sexual behavior in the female rat. *Journal of Comparative and Physiological Psychology,* 1961, *54,* 310–313. **819**

Penfield, W., & Jasper, H. *Epilepsy and the functional anatomy of the human brain.* Boston: Little, Brown, 1954. **655**

Peterson, L. R., & Peterson, M. J. Short-term retention of individual verbal items. *Journal of Experimental Psychology,* 1959, *58,* 193–198. **514**

Peterson, L. R., Wampler, R., Kirkpatrick, M., & Saltzman, D. Effect of spacing presentations on retention of a paired associate over short intervals. *Journal of Experimental Psychology,* 1963, *66,* 206–209. **514**

Pettigrew, T. F. Personality and socio-cultural factors in intergroup attitudes: A cross-national comparison. *Journal of Conflict Resolution,* 1958, *2,* 29–42. **115**

Pettigrew, T. F. Social psychology and desegregation research. *American Psychologist,* 1961, *16,* 105–112. **116**

Pettigrew, T. F., & Cramer, M. R. Demography of desegregation. *Journal of Social Issues,* 1959, *15,* 61–71. **122**

Pfaff, D. W. Morphological changes in the brains of adult male rats after neonatal castration. *Journal of Endocrinology,* 1966, *36,* 415–416. **708**

Phoenix, C. H., Goy, R. W., & Resko, J. A. Psychosexual differentiation as a function of androgenic stimulation. In M. Diamond (Ed.), *Perspectives in reproduction and sexual behavior.* Bloomington, Ind.: Indiana University Press, 1968. **710**

Piaget, J. *The psychology of intelligence.* New York: Norton, 1951 (original French ed., 1945). **300, 301**

Piaget, J. *The origins of intelligence in children.* New York: International Universities Press, 1952, **301, 414**; Norton, 1963. **302, 303**

Pirenne, M. H. *Optics, painting and photography.* New York: Cambridge University Press, 1970. **597**

Powley, T. L., & Keesey, R. E. Relationship of body weight to the lateral hypothalamic feeding syndrome. *Journal of Comparative and Physiological Psychology,* 1969, *70,* 25–36. **695**

Premack, D. Reinforcement theory. In D. Levine (Ed.), *Nebraska symposium on motivation.* Lincoln: University of Nebraska Press, 1965. **796**

Premack, D. A functional analysis of language. *Journal of the Experimental Analysis of Behavior,* 1970, *14,* 107–125. **775**

Prescott, E., & Jones, E. Patterns of teacher behavior in preschool programs. Paper presented at the biennial meeting of the Society for Research in Child Development, Santa Monica, Calif., 1969. **441**

Raisman, G., & Field, P. M. Sexual dimorphism in the preoptic area of the rat. *Science,* 1971, *173,* 731–733. **708**

Rank, O. *The trauma of birth.* New York: Harcourt Brace, 1929. **192**

Rank, O. *Will therapy and truth and reality.* New York: Knopf, 1945. **191, 192**

Ratliff, F. *Mach bands: Quantitative studies on neural networks in the retina.* San Francisco: Holden-Day, 1965. **573**

Ratliff, F., & Hartline, H. K. The responses of Limulus optic nerve fibers to patterns of illumination on the receptor mosaic. *Journal of General Physiology,* 1959, *42,* 1241–1255. **671**

Reeves, A. G., & Plum, F. Hyperphagia, rage and dementia accompanying a ventromedial hypothalamic neoplasm. *Archives of Neurology,* 1969, *20,* 616–624. **690**

Rheingold, H., Gewirtz, J. L., & Ross, H. Social conditioning of vocalizations in the infant. *Journal of Comparative and Physiological Psychology,* 1959, *52,* 68–73. **298**

Rheingold, H. L. The modification of social responsiveness in institutional babies. *Monographs of the Society for Research in Child Development,* 1956, *21,* No. 2 (Whole No. 63). **318**

Rhine, J. B., & Pratt, J. G. *Parapsychology: Frontier science of the mind.* Springfield, Ill.: Charles C Thomas, 1957. **603**

Riesen, A. H. Stimulation as a requirement for growth and function in behavioral development. In D. W. Fiske, & S. R. Maddi (Eds.), *Functions of varied experience.* Homewood, Ill.: Dorsey, 1961. **619**

Riess, B. F. The isolation of factors of learning and native behavior in field and laboratory studies. *Annals of the N.Y. Academy of Science,* 1950, *51,* 1093–1102. **825**

Rivers, W. H. R. Introduction and vision. In A. C. Haddon (Ed.), *Reports of the Cambridge Anthropological Expedition to the Torres Straits,* Vol. *2,* Part 1. Cambridge, Eng.: The University Press, 1901. **617**

Rock, I., & Harris, C. S. Vision and touch. *Scientific American,* 1967, *216,* 96–104. **619**

Rodgers, W. L. Specificity of specific hungers. *Journal of Comparative and Physiological Psychology,* 1967, *64,* 49–58. **699**

Rodnick, E. H., & Garmezy, N. An experimental approach to the study of motivation in schizophrenia. In M. R. Jones (Ed.), *Nebraska symposium on motivation.* Lincoln: University of Nebraska Press, 1957. **242**

Rogers, C. R. *Counseling and psychotherapy: Newer concepts in practice.* Boston: Houghton Mifflin, 1942. **261**

Rogers, C. R. *Client-centered therapy: Its current practice, implications and theory.* Boston: Houghton Mifflin, 1951. **261**

Rogers, C. R. A theory of therapy, personality and interpersonal relationships, as developed in the client-centered framework. In S. Koch (Ed.), *Psychology: A study of a science.* Vol. *3.* New York: McGraw-Hill, 1959. **195, 196**

Romanes, G. J. *Animal intelligence.* New York: Appleton, 1883. **762**

Rorschach, H. *Psychodiagnostics.* Berne: Hans Huber, 1942. **172**

Rosenblatt, J. S. Suckling and home orientation in the kitten: A comparative developmental study. In E. Toback (Ed.), *Biopsychology of development.* New York: Academic Press, in press. **796**

Rosenhan, D., & White, G. M. Observation and rehearsal as determinants of prosocial behavior. *Journal of Personality and Social Psychology,* 1967, *5,* 424–431. **334**

Rosenthal, D. *Genetic theory and abnormal behavior.* New York: McGraw-Hill, 1970. **242, 245**

Rosenzweig, M. R. Salivary conditioning before Pavlov. *American Journal of Psychology,* 1959, *72,* 628–633. **457**

Rosenzweig, M. R., Bennett, E. L., & Diamond, M. C. Brain changes in response to experience. *Scientific American,* 1972, *226,* 22–29. **733**

Rosenzweig, M. R., Bennett, E. L., & Diamond, M. C. Chemical and anatomical plasticity of brain: Replications and extensions, 1970. In J. Gaito (Ed.), *Macromolecules and behavior.* (2nd ed.). New York: Appleton-Century-Crofts, 1972. **738**

Rotter, J. B. Generalized expectancies for internal versus external control of reinforcement. *Psychological Monographs,* 1966, 80 (Whole No. 609). **211**

Rowell, T. E. Hierarchy in the organization of a captive baboon group. *Animal Behavior,* 1966, *14,* 430–443. **832**

Rowell, T. E. Organization of caged groups of cercopithecus monkeys. *Animal Behavior,* 1971, *19,* 625–645. **821**

Rozin, P. & Kalat, J. W. Specific hungers and poisoning as adaptive specializations of learning. *Psychological Review,* 1971, *78,* 459–486. **786**

Russell, W. R., & Nathan, P. W. Traumatic amnesia. *Brain,* 1946, *69,* 280–300. **724**

Rutherford, E., & Mussen, P. Generosity in nursery school boys. *Child Development,* 1968, *39,* 755–765. **330**

Sameroff, A. J. The components of sucking in the human newborn. *Journal of Experimental Child Psychology,* 1968, *6,* 607–623. **698**

Sanders, M., Smith, R. S., & Weinmon, B. S. *Chronic psychosis and recovery.* San Francisco: Jossey-Bass, 1967. **231**

Sarich, V. M., & Wilson, A. C. Immunological time scale for hominid evolution. *Science,* 1967, *158,* 1200–1203. **761**

Satir, V. M. *Conjoint family therapy.* Palo Alto, Calif.: Science Behavior Books, 1964. **265**

Schachter, S. Deviation, rejection, and communication.

Journal of Abnormal and Social Psychology, 1951, *46,* 190–207. **128**

Schachter, S. Some extraordinary facts about obese humans and rats. *American Psychologist,* 1971, *26,* 129–144. **697**

Schachter, S. S., & Singer, J. E. Cognitive social and physiological determinants of emotional states. *Psychological Review,* 1962, *69,* 379–399. **220**

Schaefer, H. H., & Martin, P. L. Behavioral therapy for "apathy" of hospitalized schizophrenics. *Psychological Reports,* 1966, *19,* 1147–1158. **244**

Schaffer, H. R., & Emerson, P. E. Patterns of response to physical contact in early human development. *Journal of Child Psychology and Psychiatry,* 1964, *5,* 1–13. **316, 318**

Schaller, C. B. *The mountain gorilla.* Chicago: University of Chicago Press, 1963. **827**

Schaller, G. B. *The deer and the tiger: A study of wildlife in India.* Chicago: University of Chicago Press, 1967. **808, 833**

Schaller, G. B. Predators of the Serengeti: Part I. The social carnivore. *Natural History,* 1972, *81,* 38–49. **811**

Schenkel, R. Ausdruck-studien an Wolfen. *Behaviour,* 1947, *1,* 81–129. **831**

Schenkel, R. Play, exploration and territoriality in the wild lion. In P. A. Jewell & C. Loizos (Eds.), *Play exploration and territory in mammals.* London: Academic Press, 1966. **812**

Schiller, P. H. Innate motor action as a basis of learning manipulative patterns in the chimpanzee. In C. H. Schiller (Ed.), *Instinctive behaviour.* New York: International Universities Press, 1957. **766**

Schjelderup-Ebbe, T. Social behavior in birds. In C. Murchison (Ed.), *A handbook of social psychology.* Worcester, Mass.: Clark University Press, 1935. **831**

Schneider, G. E. Two visual systems: Brain mechanisms for localization and discrimination are dissociated by tectal and cortical lesions. *Science,* 1969, *163,* 895–902. **678**

Schneirla, T. C. An evolutionary and developmental theory of biphasic processes underlying approach and withdrawal. In M. R. Jones (Ed.), *Nebraska symposium on motivation.* Lincoln: University of Nebraska Press, 1959. **793**

Schneirla, T. C., & Rosenblatt, J. S. Behavioural organisation and genesis of the social bond in insects and mammals. *American Journal of Orthopsychiatry,* 1961, *31,* 223–253. **822**

Schreiner, L., & Kling, A. Rhinencephalon and behavior. *American Journal of Physiology,* 1956, 486–490. **12, 714**

Scott, J. P. Critical periods in behavioral development. *Science,* 1962, *138,* 949–958. **784**

Sears, R. R., Maccoby, E. E., & Levin, H. *Patterns of child rearing.* New York: Harper, 1957. **330**

Sears, R. R., Whiting, J., Nowlis, V., & Sears, P. Some child rearing antecedents of aggression and dependency in young children. *Genetic Psychology Monographs,* 1953, *47,* 135, 234. **104**

Segall, M. H., Campbell, D. T., & Herskovits, M. J. Cultural differences in the perception of geometric illusions. *Science,* 1963, *139,* 769–771. **617**

Sells, S. B. The atmosphere effect; an experimental study of reasoning. *Archives of Psychology,* 1936, No. 200. **390**

Sem-Jacobsen, C. W., & Torkildsen, A. Depth recording and electrical stimulation in the human brain. In E. R. Ramey & D. S. O'Doherty (Eds.), *Electrical studies on the unanesthetized brain.* New York: Hoeber, 1960. **718**

Shaw, E. The development of schooling behavior in fishes. *Physiological Zoology,* 1960, *33,* 79–86. **804**

Sheldon, W. H. *The varieties of temperament.* New York: Harper, 1942. **205**

Sherif, M., Harvey, O. J., White, B. J., Hood, W. R., & Sherif, C. W. *Intergroup conflict and cooperation: The robbers cave experiment.* Norman, Okla.: University of Oklahoma Book Exchange, 1961. **112**

Shettleworth, S. J. Constraints on learning. In D. S. Lehrman, R. A. Hinde, & E. Shaw (Eds.), *Advances in the study of behavior,* 4. New York: Academic Press, in press. **786**

Silverman, J. Scanning-control mechanism and "cognitive filtering" in paranoid and non-paranoid schizophrenia. *Journal of Consulting Psychology,* 1964, *28,* 385–393. **240**

Simonds, P. E. The bonnet macaque in south India. In I. DeVore (Ed.), *Primate behavior.* New York: Holt, Rinehart and Winston, 1965. **828**

Sinclair-deZwart, Hermina. Developmental psycholinguistics. In D. Elkind & J. H. Flavell (Eds.), *Studies in Cognitive Development: Essays in honor of Jean Piaget.* New York: Oxford University Press, 1969. **415**

Skeels, H. M. Adult status of children with contrasting early life experiences. *Monographs of the Society for Research in Child Development,* 1966, *31,* No. 3. **318, 365**

Skinner, B. F. How to teach animals. *Scientific American,* December, 1951. **465**

Skinner, B. F. *Science and human behavior.* New York: Macmillan, 1953. **198**

Skinner, B. F. A case history in scientific method. *The American Psychologist,* 1956, *11,* 221–233. **768**

Skinner, B. F. *Verbal behavior.* New York: Appleton-Century-Crofts, 1957. **412, 413**

Skinner, B. F. *Beyond freedom and dignity.* New York: Knopf, 1971. **751, 769**

Slater, E. A review of earlier evidence on genetic factors in schizophrenia. In D. Rosenthal & S. S. Katz (Eds.),

The transmission of schizophrenia. New York: Pergamon Press, 1968. **236**

Slavson, S. R. *An introduction to group therapy.* New York: The Commonwealth Fund, 1943. **265**

Small, W. S. An experimental study of the mental processes of the rat. *American Journal of Psychology,* 1900, *11,* 133–165. **790**

Smith, M. E. An investigation of the development of the sentence and the extent of vocabulary in young children. *University of Iowa Studies in Child Welfare,* 1926, *3,* No. 5. **311**

Snyder, F. The physiology of dreaming. *Behavioral Science,* 1971, *16,* 31–44. **703**

Solley, C. M., & Murphy, G. *The development of the perceptual world.* New York: Basic Books, 1960. **604**

Sontag, L., Baker, C., & Nelson, V. Mental growth and personality development: A longitudinal study. *Monographs of the Society for Research in Child Development,* 1958, *23,* No. 2. **365**

Spearman, C. *The abilities of man.* New York: Macmillan, 1927. **377**

Sperling, G. The information available in brief visual presentations. *Psychological Monographs,* 1960, *74* (Whole no. 498). **522, 523**

Sperry, R. W., Stamm, J. S., & Miner, N. Relearning tests for interocular transfer following division of optic chiasma and corpus callosum in cats. *Journal of Comparative and Physiological Psychology,* 1956, *49,* 529–533. **741**

Stephenson, W. *The study of behavior.* Chicago: University of Chicago Press, 1953. **167**

Sternberg, S. Memory-scanning: Mental processes revealed by reaction-time experiments. *American Scientist,* 1969, *57,* 421–457. **502**

Stevens, S. S. The surprising simplicity of sensory metrics. *American Psychologist,* 1962, *17,* 29–39. **547**

Stevens, S. S., Volkmann, J., & Newman, E. B. A scale for the measurement of the psychological magnitude pitch. *Journal of the Acoustical Society of America,* 1937, *8,* 185–190. **566**

Stouffer, S. A., Suchman, E. A., De Vinney, L. C., Star, S. A., & Williams, R. M., Jr. *The American soldier: Adjustments during army life.* Vol. *1 Studies in social psychology in World War II.* Princeton, N.J.: Princeton University Press, 1949. **122**

Straits, B. C., & Sechrest, L. Further support of some findings about the characteristics of smokers and nonsmokers. *Journal of Consulting Psychology,* 1963, 27, 282. **212**

Sullivan, H. S. *The interpersonal theory of psychiatry.* New York: Norton, 1953. **191**

Suppes, P., & Hull, S. Set theory in the primary grades. *N.Y. State Math Teachers Journal,* 1963, 46. **393**

Tanzi, E. I fatti e le induzioni nell'odierna isologia del sistema nervoso. *Rivista Sperimentale di Freniatria e di Medicina Legale.* Vol. 19, 1893. **724**

Taylor, J. A. The relationship of anxiety to the conditioned eyelid response. *Journal of Experimental Psychology,* 1951, *41,* 81–92. **164**

Terman, L. M., & Merrill, M. *Measuring intelligence: A guide to the administration of the new revised Stanford-Binet tests of intelligence.* (Rev. ed.) Boston: Houghton Mifflin, 1960. **353, 355**

Thigpen, C. H., & Cleckly, H. M. *The three faces of Eve.* New York: McGraw-Hill, 1957. **248**

Thomas, A., Birch, H. G., Chess, S., Hertzig, M. E., & Korn, S. *Behavioral individuality in early childhood.* New York: New York University Press, 1963. **315**

Thompson, C. M. *Interpersonal psychoanalysis.* New York: Basic Books, 1964. **184**

Thompson, T. I. Visual reinforcement in fighting cocks. *Journal of the Experimental Analysis of Behavior,* 1964, *7,* 45–49. **838**

Thorndike, E. L. Animal intelligence: An experimental study of the associative processes in animals. *Psychological Review, Monograph Supplement,* 1898, *2,* 8. **395**

Thurstone, L. L. Primary mental abilities. *Psychometric Monographs,* 1938, No. 1. **377**

Time, "Rusty Calley: Unlikely villain," April 12, 1971. **56**

Tinbergen, N. *The study of instinct.* Oxford: Clarendon Press, 1951. **766**

Tinbergen, N. The curious behavior of the stickleback. *Scientific American,* 1952, *187,* 22–26, **815, 816**

Tolman, E. C., & Honzik, C. M. Introduction and removal of reward and maze performance in rats. *University of California Publications in Psychology,* 1930, *4,* 257–275. **471**

Treisman, A. M. Contextual cues in selective listening. *Quarterly Journal of Experimental Psychology,* 1960, *12,* 242–248. **612**

Treisman, A. M. Strategies and models of selective attention. *Psychological Review,* 1969, *76,* 282–299. **613**

Turner, C. D. *General endocrinology.* (4th ed.) Philadelphia: Saunders, 1971. **706**

Tyler, F. T. A factorial analysis of fifteen MMPI scales. *Journal of Consulting Psychology,* 1951, *15,* 541–546. **170**

Ulrich, R. F., & Azrin, N. H. Reflexive fighting in response to aversive stimulation. *Journal of the Experimental Analysis of Behavior,* 1962, *5,* 511–520. **836**

Valenstein, E. S., Cox, V. C., & Kakolewski, J. W. Reexamination of the role of the hypothalamus in motivation. *Psychological Review,* 1970, *77,* 16–31. **718, 719**

Venables, P. Psychophysiological aspects of schizophrenia. *British Journal of Medical Psychology,* 1966, *39,* 289–297. **242**

Vernon, P. E. *The structure of human abilities.* New York: Wiley, 1950. **378–379**

Vygotsky, L. S. *Thought and language.* Cambridge: M.I.T. Press, 1962. **411, 412**

Wade, G. N., & Zucker, I. Development of hormonal control over food intake and body weight in female rats. *Journal of Comparative and Physiological Psychology,* 1970, *70,* 213–220. **698**

Wallach, H. Über visuell wahrgenommene Bewegungs richtung. *Psychologische Forschung,* 1935, *20,* 325–380. **582**

Wallach, H., & O'Connell, D. N. The kinetic depth effect. *Journal of Experimental Psychology,* 1953, *45,* 205–217. **582**

Wallach, M. A., & Kogan, N. *Modes of thinking in young children: A study of the creativity-intelligence distinction.* New York: Holt, Rinehart and Winston, 1965. **403, 404**

Wallach, M. A., & Wing, C. W. *The talented student: A validation of the creativity-intelligence distinction.* New York: Holt, Rinehart and Winston, 1969. **401**

Walster, E. The effect of self-esteem on romantic liking. *Journal of Experimental Social Psychology,* 1965, *1,* 184–197. **133**

Walster, E., Aronson, E., & Abrahams, D. On increasing the persuasiveness of a low-prestige communicator. *Journal of Experimental Social Psychology,* 1966, *2,* 325–342. **81**

Washburn, S. L. Behavior and the origin of man. *Rockefeller University Review,* 1968, 10–19. **756, 762**

Washburn, S. L. Primate studies and human evolution. In G. Bourne (Ed.), *Primates in biomedical research.* New York: Academic Press, 1972. **762**

Watson, J. Some social and psychological situations related to change in attitude. *Human Relations,* 1950, *3,* 15–56. **115**

Watson, J. D. *The double helix.* New York: Atheneum, 1968. **404**

Weatherley, D. Anti-Semitism and the expression of fantasy aggression. *Journal of Abnormal and Social Psychology,* 1961, 62, 454–457. **114**

Wechsler, D. *The Wechsler intelligence scale for children.* (Rev. ed.) New York: The Psychological Corporation, 1958. **357**

Wechsler, D. *The measurement of adult intelligence.* (Rev. ed.) Baltimore: Williams & Wilkens, 1960. **356, 357**

Wechsler, D. *The Wechsler preschool and primary scale of intelligence.* (Rev. ed.) New York: The Psychological Corporation, 1967. **357**

Weil, A. T., *et al.,* Clinical and psychological effects of marijuana in man. *Science,* 1968, *162,* 1235–1238. **256**

Weiner, B., & Kukla, A. An attributional analysis of achievement motivation. *Journal of Personality and Social Psychology,* 1970, *15,* 1–20. **212**

Welsh, G. S. Factor dimensions A and R. In G. S. Welsh & W. G. Dahlstrom (Eds.), *Basic readings on the MMPI in psychology and medicine.* Minneapolis: University of Minnesota Press, 1956. **170**

Wertheimer, M. Experimentelle Untersuchungen über das Sehen von Bewegung. *Zeitschrift für Psychologie,* 1912, *61,* 161–265. **585**

Wertheimer, M. Untersuchungen zur Lehre von der Gestalt, II. *Psychologische Forschung,* 1923, *4,* 301–350. **586**

Wertheimer, M. Psychomotor coordination of auditory and visual space at birth. *Science,* 1961, *134,* 1692. **625**

West, R. W., & Greenough, W. T. Effect of environmental complexity on cortical synapses of rats: Preliminary results. *Behavioral Biology,* 1972, *7,* 279–284. **736**

White, R. K., & Lippitt, R. *Autocracy and democracy: An experimental inquiry.* New York: Harper, 1960. **218**

Whitehorn, J. L., & Betz, B. J. Further studies of the doctor as crucial variable in the outcome of treatment with schizophrenic patients. *American Journal of Psychiatry,* 1960, *117,* 215–223. **243**

Whorf, B. L. *Language, thought and reality.* Cambridge, Mass.: Technology Press, and New York: Wiley, 1956. **383, 410**

Wilcoxon, H. C., Dragoin, W. B., & Kral, P. A. Differential conditioning to visual and gustatory cues in quail and rat; illness-induced aversions. Paper presented at meetings of the Psychonomic Society, St. Louis, Mo., 1969. **786**

Wilkins, M. C. The effect of changed material on ability to do formal syllogistic reasoning. *Archives of Psychology,* 1928, No. 102. **390**

Williams, R. J. *You are extraordinary.* New York: Random House, 1967. **208**

Wilson, J. R., Adler, N., & Le Boeuf, B. The effects of intromission frequency on successful pregnancy in the female rat. *Proceedings National Academy of Sciences,* 1965, 53, 1392–1395. **819**

Wilson, P. R. Perceptual distortion of height as a function of ascribed academic status. *Journal of Social Psychology,* 1968, *74,* 97–102. **614**

Wilson, W. C. Development of ethnic attitudes in adolescence. *Child Development,* 1963, *34,* 247–256. **115**

Winch, R. F. *Mate-selection: A study of complementary*

needs. New York: Harper, 1958. **134**

Winterbottom, M. R. The relation of need for achievement to learning experiences in independence and mastery. In J. W. Atkinson (Ed.), *Motives in fantasy, action and society*. Princeton, N.J.: Van Nostrand, 1958. **323**

Witkin, H. A., Dyk, R. B., Faterson, H. F., Goodenough, D. R., & Karp, S. A. *Psychological differentiation*. New York: Wiley, 1962. **209, 407**

Woodworth, R. S. *Personal data sheet* (psychoneurotic inventory). Chicago: C. H. Stoelting La., 1919. **168**

Worchel, P. Hostility theory and experimental investigation. In D. Willner (Ed.) *Decisions, values, and groups*. Vol. *1*. New York: Pergamon Press, 1960. **218**

Wynne-Edwards, V. C. *Animal dispersion in relation to social behaviour*. Edinburgh: Oliver & Boyd, 1962. **830**

Yerkes, R. M. (Ed.) Psychological examining in the U.S. Army. *Memoirs National Academy of Science*, 1921, *15*, 890. **359**

Yerkes, R. M., & Morgulis, S. *Psychological Bulletin*, 1909, *6*, 257. **457**

Young, W. C., & Orbison, W. D. Changes in selected features of behavior in pairs of oppositely sexed chimpanzees during the sexual cycle and after ovariectomy. *Journal of Comparative Psychology*, 1944, *37*, 107–143. **821**

Zeigler, H. P., & Leibowitz, H. Apparent visual size as a function of distance for children and adults. *American Journal of Psychology*, 1957, *70*, 106–109. **575**

Zigler, E., & Butterfield, E. C. Motivational aspects of changes in IQ test performance of culturally deprived nursery school children. *Child Development*, 1968, *39*, 1–14. **422, 423**

Zilboorg, G., & Henry, G. W. *A history of medical psychology*. New York: Norton, 1941. **230**

Zubin, J., Eron, L. D., & Schumer, F. *An experimental approach to projective techniques*. New York: Wiley, 1965. **173, 175**

INDEX

2 3 4 5 6 7 8 9 10